ENCYCLOPEDIA OF
HEALT H
&AGING

ENCYCLOPEDIA OF HEALTH & AGING

Editor

KYRIAKOS S. MARKIDES

University of Texas Medical Branch at Galveston

Associate Editors

DAN G. BLAZER

Duke University

LAURENCE G. BRANCH

University of South Florida

STEPHANIE STUDENSKI

University of Pittsburgh

Managing Editors

SARAH TOOMBS SMITH
TRACY B. WELBORN

University of Texas Medical Branch at Galveston

A SAGE Reference Publication

SAGE Publications

Los Angeles • London • New Delhi • Singapore

For information:

SAGE Publications, Inc.
2455 Teller Road
Thousand Oaks, California 91320
E-mail: order@sagepub.com

SAGE Publications Ltd.
1 Oliver's Yard
55 City Road
London EC1Y 1SP
United Kingdom

SAGE Publications India Pvt. Ltd.
B 1/I 1 Mohan Cooperative Industrial Area
Mathura Road, New Delhi 110 044
India

SAGE Publications Asia-Pacific Pvt. Ltd.
33 Pekin Street #02-01
Far East Square
Singapore 048763

Printed in the United States of America.

Library of Congress Cataloging-in-Publication Data

Encyclopedia of health and aging / editor, Kyriakos S. Markides.
    p. ; cm.
Includes bibliographical references and index.
ISBN-13: 978-1-4129-0949-5 (cloth : alk. paper)
    1. Older people—Health and hygiene—Encyclopedias. 2. Aging—Encyclopedias. I. Markides, Kyriakos S.
[DNLM: 1. Aging—Encyclopedias—English. 2. Geriatrics—Encyclopedias—English. WT 13 E564 2007]

RA777.6.E534 2007
613'.043803—dc22

                                      2006030621

This book is printed on acid-free paper.

07 08 09 10 11 10 9 8 7 6 5 4 3 2

Publisher:	Rolf Janke
Acquisitions Editor:	Jim Brace-Thompson
Developmental Editor:	Paul Reis
Project Editor:	Tracy Alpern
Reference Systems Coordinator:	Leticia Gutierrez
Copy Editor:	D. J. Peck
Typesetter:	C&M Digitals (P) Ltd.
Proofreader:	Anne Rogers
Indexer:	Molly Hall
Cover Designer:	Michelle Kenny
Marketing Manager:	Carmel Withers

Contents

Editorial Board

Jean-Marie Robine
National Institute of Health and Medical Research, France

William A. Satariano
University of California, Berkeley

Robert B. Wallace
University of Iowa

Terrie Wetle
Brown University

Steven H. Zarit
Pennsylvania State University

Managing Editors

Sarah Toombs Smith
University of Texas Medical Branch at Galveston

Tracy B. Welborn
University of Texas Medical Branch at Galveston

List of Entries

Reader's Guide

The Reader's Guide groups the entries into 11 themes or content areas. It helps the reader locate related entries in the encyclopedia. For example, under Aging and the Brain, you will find entries on Alzheimer's Disease, Imaging of the Brain, Mental Status Assessment, Neurological Disorders, and Vascular Dementia. Alternatively, if you are interested in the entry on Ethnicity and Race, you will find it under Sociodemographic and Cultural Factors along with related entries on Africa, African Americans, Asian and Pacific Islander Americans, Hispanics, Latin America and the Caribbean, Mexico, Migration, and Native Americans and Alaska Natives. The Reader's Guide also gives an overview of all the encyclopedia entries. It facilitates finding information in a specific theme or content area of interest. You can look through all of the entries in a given category and pick one or more to read.

Aging and the Brain

Alzheimer's Disease
Apolipoprotein E
Consortium to Establish a Registry for
    Alzheimer's Disease
Creutzfeldt–Jakob Disease
Delirium and Confusional States
Imaging of the Brain
Lewy Body Dementia
Mental Status Assessment
Mild Cognitive Impairment
Neurobiology of Aging
Neurological Disorders
Pick's Disease
Stroke
Syncope
Vascular Dementia
Vascular Depression

Diseases and Medical Conditions

Accelerated Aging Syndromes
Anemia
Aneurysms
Arrhythmias
Arthritis and Other Rheumatic Diseases
Calcium Disorders of Aging
Cancer
Cancer, Common Types of
Cancer Prevention and Screening
Cataracts
Cellulitis
Congestive Heart Failure
Diabetes
Ear Diseases
Eye Diseases
Foot Problems
Fractures in Older Adults
Gastrointestinal Aging
HIV and AIDS
Hypertension
Iatrogenic Disease
Immune Function
Incontinence
Infections, Bladder and Kidney
Infectious Diseases
Kidney Aging and Diseases
Menopause and Hormone Therapy

Complementary and Alternative Medicine
Dietary Variety
Gastrointestinal Aging
Nutrition and Public Health
Nutrition, Malnutrition, and Feeding Issues
Obesity
Oral Health
Vitamins, Minerals, and
    Dietary Supplements

Physical Status

Allostatic Load and Homeostasis
Biological Theories of Aging
Biomarkers of Aging
Body Composition
Body Mass Index
Cardiovascular System
Compression of Morbidity
Fluid and Electrolytes
Hearing
Men's Health
Multiple Morbidity and Comorbidity
Normal Physical Aging
Perioperative Issues
Pulmonary Aging
Skin Changes
Skin Neoplasms, Benign and Malignant
Sleep
Surgery
Temperature Regulation
Therapeutic Failure
Vision and Low Vision
Women's Health

Prevention

Anti-Aging Interventions
Exercise and Physical Activity
Fractures in Older Adults
Health Promotion and Disease Prevention
Injury Prevention
Nutrition, Malnutrition, and Feeding Issues
Obesity
Smoking
Vitamins, Minerals, and Dietary Supplements

Sociodemographic and Cultural Factors

Active Life Expectancy
Africa
African Americans
Age–Period–Cohort Distinctions
Asia
Asian and Pacific Islander Americans
Australia and New Zealand
Canada
Caregiving
Centenarians
Compression of Morbidity
Critical Perspectives in Gerontology
Demography of Aging
Disasters and Terrorism
Disclosure
Early Adversity and Late-Life Health
Economics of Aging
Education and Health
Elder Abuse and Neglect
Environmental Health
Epidemiology of Aging
Ethical Issues and Aging
Ethnicity and Race
Europe
Expectations Regarding Aging
Global Aging
Health Communication
Hispanics
Homelessness and Health in the United States
Latin America and the Caribbean
Life Course Perspective on Adult Development
Living Arrangements
Loneliness
Longevity
Marital Status
Mexico
Midlife
Migration
Multiple Morbidity and Comorbidity
Native Americans and Alaska Natives
Negative Interaction and Health
Oldest Old
Quality of Life

About the Editor

Kyriakos S. Markides, Ph.D., is the Annie and John Gnitzinger Professor of Aging Studies at the University of Texas Medical Branch at Galveston. He is also Professor and Director of the Division of Sociomedical Sciences, Department of Preventive Medicine and Community Health, at the same institution. He is the founding and current editor of the *Journal of Aging and Health*, published by Sage Publications since 1989. His research has focused on the health of older Mexican Americans, with his first study being conducted in 1976. He is currently Principal Investigator of the Hispanic Established Population for Epidemiologic Studies of the Elderly (EPESE), a longitudinal community-based study of older Mexican Americans residing in the southwestern United States. His writings have also been influential in the fields of Hispanic health and minority aging. In 1986, he coined the term *Hispanic epidemiologic paradox* (with Jeanine Coreil), currently the leading theme in the field of Hispanic health. His book *Aging and Ethnicity* (with Charles Mindel, Sage Publications, 1986) was the first major work in the field. He is the author or coauthor of more than 260 publications. The Institute for Scientific Information recently listed him among the most cited scientists in the world. He is the 2006 recipient of the Mentoring Award of the Behavioral and Social Sciences Section of the Gerontological Society of America.

Contributors

Marc E. Agronin
University of Miami

Soham Al Snih
University of Texas Medical Branch

Dawn Alley
University of Pennsylvania

Richard M. Allman
*Birmingham/Atlanta Geriatric Research,
    Education, and Clinical Center*

Luis Felipe Amador
University of Texas Medical Branch

Ross Andel
University of South Florida

Gary R. Andrews
Flinders University, Australia

Jacqueline L. Angel
University of Texas at Austin

Ronald J. Angel
University of Texas at Austin

Toni C. Antonucci
University of Michigan

Jeanne E. Bader
California State University, Long Beach

Tamara A. Baker
University of South Florida

Adam L. Bank
University of Miami

Barbara M. Bates-Jensen
University of California, Los Angeles

Marion A. Becker
University of Florida

Claudia Beghé
James A. Haley Veterans Hospital

C. S. Bergeman
University of Notre Dame

Ivonne M. Berges
University of Texas Medical Branch

John L. Beyer
Duke University Medical Center

Rajib K. Bhattacharya
University of Kansas Medical Center

Shelley B. Bhattacharya
University of Kansas Medical Center

Ellen Binder
*Washington University
    School of Medicine*

Dan G. Blazer
Duke University

Astrid Block
University of California, San Francisco

Donald Bodenner
University of Arkansas for Medical Sciences

Wanda Bonnel
University of Kansas

Sally Bould
University of Delaware

Laurence G. Branch
University of South Florida

Gloria Brandburg
University of Texas Medical Branch

Diane R. Brown
University of Medicine and Dentistry of New Jersey

J. Scott Brown
Miami University of Ohio

Lisa M. Brown
University of South Florida

Maria T. Brown
Syracuse University

Tatjana Bulat
Veterans Integrated Services Network 8
   Patient Safety Center

Jerson Cadenas
University of Texas Medical Branch

Bruce A. Carnes
University of Oklahoma Health Sciences Center

Molly Carnes
University of Wisconsin–Madison

Laura L. Carstensen
Stanford University

Chiung-Chih Chang
Kaohsiung Chang Gung Memorial Hospital, Taiwan

Neena L. Chappell
University of Victoria

Gurkamal Chatta
University of Pittsburgh

Linda M. Chatters
University of Michigan

Gary Chiodo
Oregon Health and Science University

David Chiriboga
University of South Florida

C. Edward Coffey
Henry Ford Health System

Donna Cohen
University of South Florida

Antonia K. Coppin
National Institute on Aging

David S. Craig
H. Lee Moffitt Cancer Center
   and Research Institute

Eileen M. Crimmins
University of Southern California

Ronita L. Cromwell
University of Texas Medical Branch

Judith H. W. Crossett
University of Iowa Carver College of Medicine

Leslie Curry
University of Connecticut Health Center

Jonathan R. T. Davidson
Duke University Medical Center

Dorly J. H. Deeg
*Vrije Universiteit Medical Centre/Longitudinal
    Aging Study Amsterdam*

John DeLamater
University of Wisconsin–Madison

Robert Denshaw
University of Pittsburgh

Colin Depp
University of California, San Diego

Cheryl A. Der Ananian
University of Illinois at Chicago

Abhilash K. Desai
Saint Louis University School of Medicine

P. Murali Doraiswamy
Duke University School of Medicine

Hans C. Dreyer
University of Texas Medical Branch

Larry W. Dupree
*University of South Florida/Florida Mental
    Health Institute*

Carl Eisdorfer
University of Miami Miller School of Medicine

David J. Ekerdt
University of Kansas

E. Wesley Ely
Vanderbilt University Medical Center

Charles F. Emery
Ohio State University

Karl Eschbach
University of Texas Medical Branch

David V. Espino
*University of Texas Health Science Center at
    San Antonio*

Carroll L. Estes
University of California, San Francisco

Connie J. Evashwick
California State University, Long Beach

Martine Extermann
*H. Lee Moffitt Cancer Center/University of
    South Florida*

Gerda G. Fillenbaum
Duke University Medical Center

M. Rosina Finley
*University of Texas Health Science Center at
    San Antonio*

Daniel J. Foley
*Substance Abuse and Mental Health
    Services Administration*

Sonia M. Frias
University of Texas at Austin

Robert B. Friedland
Georgetown University

Brant E. Fries
University of Michigan

Heather Fuller Iglesias
University of Michigan

Dolores Gallagher-Thompson
*Stanford University
    School of Medicine*

Vipul Ganatra
Wake Forest University Health Sciences

Jane F. Gentleman
National Center for Health Statistics

Michael D. Geschwind
University of California, San Francisco

Timothy D. Girard
Vanderbilt University School of Medicine

Harold W. Goforth
Duke University Medical Center

Deborah T. Gold
Duke University Medical Center

Heather L. Gray
*Stanford University and Veterans
  Administration Medical Center*

Shelly L. Gray
*University of Washington Geriatric
  Pharmacy Program*

George T. Grossberg
*Saint Louis University Health
  Sciences Center*

Brian R. Grossman
University of California, San Francisco

Marylou Guihan
*Institute for Health Services
  Research and Policy Studies,
  Northwestern University*

Amber M. Gum
University of South Florida

Jack M. Guralnik
National Institute on Aging

David Haber
Ball State University

William J. Hall
University of Rochester School of Medicine

Kenneth R. Hallows
University of Pittsburgh

Roberto Ham-Chande
El Colegio de la Frontera Norte, Tijuana

Steven M. Handler
University of Pittsburgh

Joseph T. Hanlon
University of Pittsburgh

Matthew T. Haren
Saint Louis University School of Medicine

Ebrahim Haroon
*University of California, Los Angeles,
  School of Medicine*

Laura M. Hawkes
University of Illinois at Chicago

Judith C. Hays
Duke University

Susan C. Hedrick
*Veterans Administration
  Puget Sound Health Care System*

Kevin P. High
Wake Forest University School of Medicine

Helen Hoenig
Duke University Medical Center

Amy Horowitz
Lighthouse International

Susan L. Hughes
University of Illinois at Chicago

Robert A. Hummer
University of Texas at Austin

Celia F. Hybels
Duke University Medical Center

Kathryn Hyer
University of South Florida

Susan S. Jack
National Center for Health Statistics

Jamie L. Jackson
Ohio State University

Yuri Jang
University of South Florida

Gordon L. Jensen
Vanderbilt University

Rita D. Jepsen
University of Connecticut Health Center

Dilip V. Jeste
University of California, San Diego

Alan M. Jette
Boston University

Daniel E. Jimenez
*Stanford University and Veterans Administration
    Medical Center*

Robert John
University of Oklahoma Health Sciences Center

Mary Ann Johnson
University of Georgia

Robert Johnson
Oregon Health and Science University

Robert M. Kaiser
University of Miami School of Medicine

Lynne Kallenbach
University of Kansas Medical Center

Robert Kane
University of Minnesota School of Public Health

Mary Kaplan
University of South Florida

Arun S. Karlamangla
University of California, Los Angeles

Ira R. Katz
University of Pennsylvania

Jason S. Katz
*University of Pennsylvania
    School of Medicine*

William Kearns
University of South Florida

Jessica A. Kelley-Moore
University of Maryland Baltimore County

Gary J. Kennedy
Montefiore Medical Center

Hyoung Soo Kim
*Louis de la Parte Florida Mental Health Institute,
    University of South Florida*

Moon Jong Kim
Pochon CHA Medical University, Korea

Amy Jo Haavisto Kind
*University of Wisconsin–Madison and Middleton
    Veterans Administration Hospital*

Eric R. Kingson
Syracuse University

Michael D. Knox
University of South Florida

Paul Kowal
World Health Organization

Andrew M. Kramer
*University of Colorado
    Health Sciences Center*

Andrew D. Krystal
Duke University School of Medicine

Anand Kumar
University of California, Los Angeles

Nagi B. Kumar
University of South Florida

Laurie Lavery
University of Pittsburgh

Helen Lavretsky
University of California, Los Angeles

David J. Lee
University of Miami School of Medicine

Heidi M. Lee
Miami–Dade County (Florida) Public Schools

Lené Levy-Storms
University of California, Los Angeles

Elena Lewis
University of Texas at Austin

Jersey Liang
University of Michigan

Casey M. Lindberg
Stanford University

Catherine I. Lindblad
*University of Minnesota
    College of Pharmacy*

Nicole Lindsey
University of Texas at Austin

Jose A. Loera
University of Texas Medical Branch

William C. Logan, Jr.
Duke University

Vera Luther
Wake Forest University Health Sciences

Scott M. Lynch
Princeton University

Lisa MacLean
Henry Ford Health System

David J. Madden
Duke University Medical Center

George L. Maddox
Duke University

Robert L. Maher, Jr.
Duquesne University

Kenneth G. Manton
Duke University

Marjorie Marenberg
Jefferson Medical College

Kyriakos S. Markides
University of Texas Medical Branch

Alayne Markland
University of Alabama at Birmingham

Meredith Masel
University of Texas Medical Branch

Todd J. McCallum
Case Western Reserve University

Megan A. McCrory
Bastyr University

Leslie McDonald-Miszczak
Western Washington University

Janet E. McElhaney
*University of Connecticut
    School of Medicine*

Ann E. McQueen
Portland State University

Mark R. Meiners
George Mason University

Carlos F. Mendes de Leon
Rush University Medical Center

Hylton B. Menz
La Trobe University

Anita C. Mercado
University of Texas Medical Branch

Toni D. Miles
University of Louisville

Deepti Mishra
University of Texas Medical Branch

Sara M. Moorman
University of Wisconsin–Madison

John E. Morley
Saint Louis University Health Sciences Center

John N. Morris
Institute for Aging Research

Nancy Morrow-Howell
Washington University

Cynthia D. Myers
H. Lee Moffitt Cancer Center

Nirmal Naidoo
World Health Organization

Yuri R. Nakasato
Oklahoma University Health Sciences Center

Paul A. Nakonezny
*University of Texas Southwestern
    Medical Center*

Audrey Nelson
James A. Haley Veterans Hospital

Jason T. Newsom
Portland State University

S. Liliana Oakes
*University of Texas
    Health Science Center*

Ezra Ochshorn
University of South Florida

Morris A. Okun
Arizona State University

S. Jay Olshansky
University of Illinois at Chicago

Anthony D. Ong
University of Notre Dame

Martin Orrell
University College of London

Hana Osman
University of South Florida

Glenn V. Ostir
University of Texas Medical Branch

Janine Overcash
University of South Florida

Erdman B. Palmore
Duke University

John Papaconstantinou
University of Texas Medical Branch

Kushang V. Patel
National Institute on Aging

Barbara J. Payne
University of Manitoba

M. Kristen Peek
University of Texas Medical Branch

Brenda L. Plassman
Duke University Medical Center

Leonard W. Poon
University of Georgia

Mihaela A. Popa
University of South Florida

Thomas R. Prohaska
University of Illinois at Chicago

Elizabeth J. Protas
University of Texas Medical Branch

Jama L. Purser
Duke University Medical Center

Mukaila A. Raji
University of Texas Medical Branch

Geetha Rao
*University of California, Los Angeles,
    School of Medicine*

Blake B. Rasmussen
University of Texas Medical Branch

Laura Ray
University of Texas Medical Branch

John Reich
Arizona State University

Carlos A. Reyes-Ortiz
University of Texas Medical Branch

Sandra L. Reynolds
University of South Florida

Joan Rittgers
Hackensack University Medical Center

Susan B. Roberts
Tufts University

Suzanne Robertson
Pennsylvania State University

Jean-Marie Robine
French National Institute of Health and Medical Research

David Rosenstein
Oregon Health and Science University

Christine M. Ruby
Duke University

Laura Rudkin
University of Texas Medical Branch

Catherine A. Sarkisian
University of California, Los Angeles

William A. Satariano
University of California, Berkeley

John A. Schinka
University of South Florida

Robert E. Schlenker
University of Colorado, Denver

Kenneth E. Schmader
Duke/Durham Veterans Administration Medical Center

Lawrence Schonfeld
University of South Florida

Richard Schulz
University of Pittsburgh

Teresa E. Seeman
University of California, Los Angeles

Besangie Sellars
University of Michigan

Amber Selwood
*University College London and North East London
    Mental Health Trust, Essex*

Joseph R. Sharkey
*Texas A&M University, School
of Rural Public Health*

Ilene C. Siegler
Duke University

Roxane Cohen Silver
University of California, Irvine

Jeff Silverstein
Mount Sinai School of Medicine

Philip D. Sloane
University of North Carolina

Nancy H. Smith
Nancy H. Smith Consulting

Julia Spaniol
Rotman Research Institute

Avron Spiro, III
Veterans Administration Boston Healthcare System

Knight Steel
Hackensack University Medical Center

Cynthia L. Stone
University of Texas Health Science Center

Lorraine M. Stone
Duke University Medical Center

Anne Strozier
University of South Florida

Cynthia Stuen
Lighthouse International

Cynthia A. Stuenkel
University of California, San Diego

Kathy Ellen Sykes
U.S. Environmental Protection Agency

Stasa Tadic
University of Pittsburgh

George E. Taffet
Baylor College of Medicine

Robert Joseph Taylor
University of Michigan

Warren D. Taylor
Duke University Medical Center

Mugdha Ekanath Thakur
Duke University Medical Center

Allison R. Thompson
*Vanderbilt Center for
Human Nutrition*

Martin J. Toohill
Utah State University

Robin Trotman
Wake Forest University Health Sciences

Mark Unruh
University of Pittsburgh

Pantel S. Vokonas
Boston University School of Medicine

Elena Volpi
University of Texas Medical Branch

Robert B. Wallace
University of Iowa

Kathleen A. Welsh-Bohmer
Duke University Medical Center

Terrie Wetle
Brown University

Lon R. White
Department of Veterans Affairs, Honolulu

Peter J. Whitehouse
Case Western Reserve University

K. A. S. Wickrama
Iowa State University

Kristine Williams
University of Kansas

Jay Wolfson
University of South Florida

Rebeca Wong
University of Maryland

Linda Ann Wray
Pennsylvania State University

Rollin M. Wright
University of Pittsburgh

Glen Xiong
University of California, Davis

Yang Yang
University of Chicago

Barbara W. K. Yee
University of Hawaii at Manoa

Steven H. Zarit
Pennsylvania State University

Wei Zhang
Duke University Medical Center

Jessica Ziembroski
University of Missouri

Introduction

There are at least three major encyclopedias in the field of aging, all of them general and comprehensive. This new encyclopedia is focused more on health and, as such, is aimed at assisting researchers, students, and practitioners working in the fields of medicine, nursing, epidemiology, public health, health services, and related areas. The topic areas reflect the range covered in the *Journal of Aging and Health,* which I founded in 1989. There is also a heavy dose of geriatrics with respect to geriatric syndromes and common diseases of aging. The field of health and aging has grown nearly exponentially during recent decades, and I hope this encyclopedia captures some of the excitement of the research enterprise in terms of new findings as well as conceptual developments guiding research, practice, and policy.

The editorial process began with appointing three associate editors with special expertise in mental health (Dan Blazer), health services and public health (Larry Branch), and geriatrics (Stephanie Studenski) to complement my expertise in epidemiology and social science. A preliminary list supplied to the editors was reviewed and revised during several face-to-face meetings. Lists of entries were reviewed by the 24 members of our advisory board and were revised accordingly.

The *Encyclopedia of Health and Aging* is organized in an A-to-Z (alphabetical) format rather than by specific themes. However, a Reader's Guide groups the entries into 11 themes or content areas: Aging and the Brain, Diseases and Medical Conditions, Drug-Related Issues, Function and Syndromes, Mental Health and Psychology, Nutritional Issues, Physical Status, Prevention, Sociodemographic and Cultural Factors, Studies of Aging, and Systems of Care.

It was decided that the encyclopedia would also include entries on health and aging in specific important countries and world regions: Mexico, Canada, Latin America, Europe, Asia, Africa, and Australia and New Zealand, with the latter being prepared by Gary Andrews just weeks before his death. As can be seen in the Reader's Guide, we give coverage to landmark studies of aging such as the Duke Longitudinal Studies, the Established Populations for Epidemiologic Studies of the Elderly, the Health and Retirement Study, and the National Long Term Care Survey. An appendix provides a list of 45 online resources on health and aging aimed at researchers, practitioners, and the lay public.

Acknowledgments

The idea for this volume came from Jim Brace-Thompson of Sage Publications. He assembled an initial list of potential entries and convinced me that the field had room for another encyclopedia if it focused on health and aging. His support and advice over the past couple of years have helped to make working on this volume easier and more fun. Others at Sage have been helpful throughout and include Rolf Janke, Steve Martin, Karen Ehrmann, Leticia Gutierrez, Paul Reis, D. J. Peck, and Tracy Alpern.

It has been a joy working with my three associate editors: Dan Blazer, Larry Branch, and Stephanie Studenski. All three are distinguished leaders in the field. I believe that, together, we made a pretty good team. Our distinguished advisory board gave us invaluable advice throughout the past couple of years. My first managing editor, Sarah Toombs Smith, played a key role in the conceptualization of the encyclopedia. Tracy Welborn, my second managing editor, was invaluable in preparing the Appendix and helping bring this project to an end. Rachel Little, my editing assistant, was an essential asset during the copyediting review process. Finally, I am especially indebted to our numerous authors who produced highly readable state-of-the-art summaries of the respective areas.

—Kyriakos S. Markides

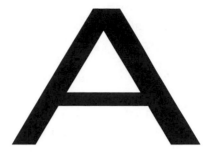

ACCELERATED AGING SYNDROMES

Approximately 35% of the factors that influence life expectancy are inherited. Accelerated aging is therefore usually associated with genetic abnormalities. None of the accelerated aging syndromes, however, leads to a uniform, systematic "speeding up" of the aging process. A number of genetic disorders can lead to premature or accelerated aging (also referred to as *progerias*), including Down syndrome, Hutchinson–Gilford syndrome, and Werner's syndrome. Down syndrome, by far the most common, is caused by three copies of chromosome 21. Yet we usually do not consider this genetic disorder to be a disorder of accelerated aging because the focus is on the mild mental retardation, characteristic physical features, and "pleasant personality" associated with the syndrome. Nevertheless, people who experience Down syndrome demonstrate a number of findings associated with premature aging such as the early appearance of changes in the brain (specifically the accumulation of senile plaques and neurofibrillary tangles) that we find in the brains of nearly all very old people and more frequently (and in a somewhat different distribution) in Alzheimer's disease. The life expectancy of Down syndrome patients is significantly shortened as well.

Hutchinson–Gilford syndrome, a very rare condition, is the earliest onset accelerated aging syndrome. It is associated with dwarfism, physical immaturity, and pseudosenility. People who are affected look like very old, wizened, and diminutive adults with distorted features (due to bone abnormalities that include diminished growth of the lower jaw and generalized osteoporosis). Their heads are large when compared with their faces, whereas the ears and noses are small. Intense progressive atherosclerosis occurs during childhood and is the primary cause of death. The syndrome appears to be a rare autosomal recessive condition but also may be autosomal dominant with incomplete penetrance (an inherited trait that does not manifest itself universally). Death usually occurs during the teens.

Werner's syndrome, which is also very rare but has typically been considered the prototypical accelerated aging syndrome, usually appears later than the previous conditions. Once the condition manifests itself, however, those affected look 20 to 30 years older than their actual ages and their life spans are shortened. The disease usually has its onset before the affected people reach full maturity, usually during or after puberty, so those affected have thin limbs and are smaller in stature and less developed in other adult characteristics than would be expected. Their appearance is striking. Werner's patients have tightly drawn faces, pinched expressions, and protruding eyes. They exhibit beaked noses, protuberant teeth, and recessive chins. Many age-related characteristics appear early, including cataracts, hypogonadism (with lowering of testosterone in males), atherosclerosis, and early onset of diabetes. Cancers frequently appear before death. As would be expected, the life spans of Werner's patients are shortened significantly. A specific genetic mutation has been associated with Werner's syndrome, namely the *WRN* on chromosome 8. When the protein encoded by this gene loses function, the result is a genomic instability that appears to hasten the aging process.

—*Dan G. Blazer*

See also Active Life Expectancy; Biological Theories of Aging

Further Readings and References

Finch CE. *Longevity, Senescence, and the Genome.* Chicago: University of Chicago Press; 1990.

Turner MS, Martin GM. Genetics of human disease, longevity, and aging. In: Hazzard WR, Blass JP, Ettinger WH, eds. *Principles of Geriatric Medicine and Gerontology.* 4th ed. New York: McGraw-Hill; 1999:21–44.

ACTIVE LIFE EXPECTANCY

Active life expectancy (ALE), part of the family of health expectancies, is a summary measure of population health (SMPH) that combines mortality and morbidity in a single metric. ALE, sometimes called healthy active life expectancy (HALE, e.g., in the United Kingdom), combines mortality data with data on the performance of activities of daily living (ADLs) and instrumental activities of daily living (IADLs) in a single metric.

Because it aims to measure how long people live or can live independently, ALE should be computed with data on the receipt of help and the need for help to perform ADLs and IADLs, respectively. When difficulty to perform ADLs and IADLs is used instead, the corresponding health expectancy belongs to the neighboring class of life expectancy without disability and, more precisely, without activity restriction. However, the terminology related to the summary measure of population health has still not been agreed on internationally.

Background

Summary measures of population health, such as ALE, answer whether overall life expectancy is increasing faster or slower than life expectancy spent in good health. This question led to the development of a new family of indicators, namely health expectancies. The general model of health transition proposed by the World Health Organization (WHO) in 1984 distinguished overall life expectancy, disability-free life expectancy, and morbidity-free life expectancy (Figure 1). Its strength lies in its ability to assess the likelihood of different health scenarios expressed as interrelationships among these three measures: a pandemic of chronic diseases and disabilities, a compression of morbidity, and contradictory evolutions that include the scenario of dynamic equilibrium.

Research on such measures, combining mortality and morbidity data at the population level, dates back to the 1960s. The first method of calculation was proposed by H. F. Sullivan in 1971. Soon research took two directions. One, following the work of Sullivan,

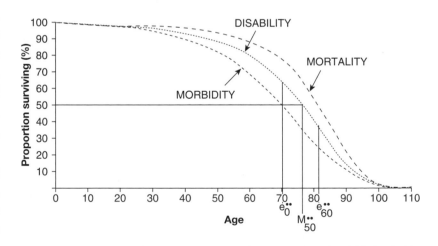

Figure 1   General Model of Health Transition

Source: World Health Organization. *The uses of epidemiology in the study of the elderly: Report of a WHO Scientific Group on the Epidemiology of Aging.* Geneva: WHO (Technical Report Series 706), 1984. Reprinted with permission.

Note: e_0** and e_{60}** are the numbers of years of autonomous life expected at birth and at 60 years of age, respectively. M_{50}** is the age to which 50% of females could expect to survive without loss of autonomy.

gave priority to data availability and calculation simplicity. The other, following the work of J. W. Bush and his collaborators, focused on several methodological refinements, including the multistate approach and weighting combinations. Health expectancies have been increasingly used in industrialized countries to assess the evolution of the populations' health status, in particular that of older people. Being independent of the size of populations and of their age structure, health expectancies allow direct comparisons of the different groups that make up populations (e.g., sexes, socioprofessional categories, regions). Since 1989, an international research network, REVES (Réseau Espérance de Vie en Santé [Network on Health Expectancy]), has coordinated research on summary measures, the need for which has been voiced by a number of international agencies such as WHO and the Organization for Economic Cooperation and Development (OECD). Indeed, in the final communiqué of its 1997 summit in Denver, Colorado, the Group of 8 (G8) encouraged collaborative biomedical and behavioral research to improve ALE and reduce disability.

The health expectancy approach has now been extended to incorporate the modern concepts of the disablement process: chronic morbidity, functional limitation, activity restriction, and physical dependency, with progressively more attention being devoted to mental health expectancy.

Calculation and Main Characteristics

The principle of any health expectancy calculation is to separate the years lived by the population of a life table between two ages into the years lived in good health and the years lived in bad health. There are basically two methods for this. The prevalence life table method (Sullivan) uses observed cross-sectional prevalence to estimate the period prevalence of health problems introduced in the summary indicator. The multistate life table method, on the other hand, uses the observed transitions between health states and death to compute the period prevalence of the health problem.

From a mathematical point of view, the multistate life table method is preferred because it is homogeneous with the period life table used to compute yearly life expectancy. However, only longitudinal surveys with at least two waves or panel surveys can provide the needed transitions. From a practical point of view, the prevalence life table method is popular due to the greater availability of cross-sectional surveys. For health monitoring, the key issue is the repetition of the same survey over time. Chronological series of cross-sectional surveys such as the National Health Interview Survey (NHIS) are available in a number of countries, but repeated comparable longitudinal surveys over time are rare and the U.S. Longitudinal Study of Aging (LSOA 1 and LSOA 2) is unique. These advantages and disadvantages explain why both methods are currently used.

In both cases, the sum of complementary health expectancies is always equal to life expectancy (LE). For example, ALE plus dependent life expectancy (DLE, i.e., life expectancy with the need of help to perform ADLs) is equal to total life expectancy (ALE + DLE = LE). LE can be decomposed into as many states as desired; for example, three states (LE with disability + LE with mild disability + LE with severe disability = LE). Health expectancies can also be divided; the ratio of ALE to total life expectancy indicates the part of life expectancy lived independently (generally expressed as a percentage).

A Minimum Set of Health Expectancies and Future Harmonization

ALE is one of several possible health expectancies, and health authorities in North America and Europe currently recommend a small set of health expectancies to better cover the different health dimensions. For example, in the United States, the set of summary measures recommended for monitoring progress toward the first goal of Healthy People 2010 includes years of healthy life defined as life without disability (YHL), years of healthy life (as used for Healthy People 2000), years of healthy life without functioning problems, years of healthy life without specific diseases, years of healthy life in excellent or very good health, and years of healthy life lived with good health behavior.

In 2005, the European Union (EU) selected healthy life years (HLY), defined as disability-free life expectancy, as one of the structural indicators to be examined every year during the European Spring Council. Using data from the European Community Household Panel (ECHP), trends in disability-free life expectancy for the EU-15 are available from 1995. Its successor, the EU Survey on Income and Living Conditions (EU–SILC), will be used from 2005 onward for the current EU-25 member states. HLY is completed by a set of summary measures computed by the European Health Expectancy Monitoring Unit (EHEMU), including activity limitation-free life expectancy, chronic condition-free life expectancy, self-perceived health expectancy, and life expectancy in good health combining the three previous indicators (no activities limitation, no chronic condition, and being in very good or good perceived health). However, some European countries, such as the United Kingdom and Denmark, have their own national series of summary indicators.

The two indicators, years of healthy life defined as life without disability used in the United States for Healthy People 2010 and healthy life years (defined as disability-free life expectancy) used in the EU as a structural indicator, are very similar in their method of computation (the Sullivan method) and data used (observed cross-sectional prevalence) but are not identical. Similar indicators are also used in other OECD countries (e.g., Australia, Canada, Japan). As for life expectancy at birth, the main (potential) interest of a summary measure of population health such as ALE is to be comparable between countries. Therefore, the next step will be harmonization of the health data, including ADL and IADL data, from cross-sectional or longitudinal health surveys.

Between 2000 and 2003, the WHO already attempted to use a single summary measure of population health, called "healthy life expectancy," to assess overall population health and judge how well the objective of good health was being achieved by countries. The indicator developed by the WHO for this purpose was a health-adjusted life expectancy (HALE) based on life expectancy at birth but including an adjustment (weights) for time spent in different health states. It is most easily understood as the equivalent

number of years in full health that a newborn can expect to live based on current rates of ill health and mortality. For the 2000 report, a great deal of simulated data was used, but during the subsequent years more empirical data were collected through population surveys such as the World Health Survey. Thus, the healthy life expectancy estimates published for nearly 200 countries by the WHO are not directly comparable from year to year because of changes in methodology and because the last set of estimates relates to 2002.

Although there has been an initial failure to develop an international SMPH, existing sets of indicators, such as those in the United States and EU, point the way toward a common effort with strong involvement from countries prioritizing simple methodology and well-accepted health concepts. All of this suggests that ALE is a good candidate for such harmonization.

—Jean-Marie Robine

See also Compression of Morbidity; Disability and the Disablement Process; Longevity; Longitudinal Study of Aging; Multiple Morbidity and Comorbidity

Further Readings and References

Jagger C. *Health Expectancy by the Sullivan Method: A Practical Guide.* Tokyo: Nihon University; 1999. NUPRI Research Paper Series, No. 68.

Jagger C, Reyes-Frausto S. *Monitoring Health by Healthy Active Life Expectancy: A User's Guide.* Leicester, England: University of Leicester and Trent Public Health Observatory; 2003.

Robine J-M, Jagger C, Mathers CD, Crimmins EM, Suzman RM, eds. *Determining Health Expectancies.* Chichester, England: Wiley; 2003.

ACTIVITIES OF DAILY LIVING AND INSTRUMENTAL ACTIVITIES OF DAILY LIVING

During the middle of the 20th century, as the scope and effectiveness of rehabilitation began to expand, standardized measurement of activities of daily living (ADLs) became more commonplace. The term *activities of daily living* was first used to refer to the basic tasks of everyday life such as eating, bathing, dressing, toileting, and transferring—the basic functions needed to maintain independent living within the community. When people are unable to perform these activities, they need help to function from other humans, mechanical devices, or both. As such, measuring ADL disability has become a standard way to describe the functional status of a person within his or her daily life and represents a tool for describing an individual's care needs.

There are no definitive or strict rules as to what constitutes an ADL disability and/or what are the component items or activities. Most researchers, however, refer to two main types of ADL disability: basic ADLs and instrumental ADLs.

Basic ADLs

There are numerous basic ADL instruments that seek to quantify basic physical functions and obtain a numerical value. These systems are useful for prioritizing care needs, estimating resource demands, and tracking progress of individuals. Most basic ADL instruments can be traced back to the Katz ADL Index or the Barthel Index.

Katz ADL Index

Sidney Katz and his colleagues coined the term *activities of daily living* and created an ADL index that encompassed six basic activities of daily life: feeding, continence, transfers, toileting, dressing, and bathing (e.g., sponge, shower, tub). The Katz ADL Index, first developed to study the effects of treatment on the elderly and the chronically ill, is frequently used in geriatrics as a very practical measure of disability related to many disorders or health conditions. Through observation and interview, the clinician rates each activity on a 3-point scale of independence/ dependence. The final stage in scoring involves summarizing the item-specific dependent/independent classification on a 7-point Guttman scale that reflects the number of ADL areas of dependency. The Guttman scaling (or hierarchical) properties of the Katz ADL scale have made it easier to track the functional progress of disabled persons.

Barthel Index of ADL

Within the rehabilitation field, the Barthel Index of ADL was one of the first methods developed to assess and communicate to other rehabilitation professionals the degree of disability of a particular individual. In essence, the Barthel index records indicators of independence in 10 different ADLs that cover personal care and mobility: bowel status, bladder status, grooming, toilet use, feeding, transfer, mobility, dressing, stairs, and bathing. The Barthel index yields an overall score that is formed by adding scores on ratings of each individual item and reflects the amount of time and assistance an individual requires. Scores range from 0 to 100 in steps of 5, with higher scores indicating greater functional independence. The Barthel index is completed by a health professional from medical records or from direct observation.

Most basic ADL questions/items reflect relatively severe levels of disability and thus are most useful with individuals who are in institutions. They are less sensitive to variations in disability at the upper levels of functioning.

Instrumental Activities of Daily Living

During the 1970s, the basic ADL concept was expanded to consider problems more typically encountered by individuals functioning in the community— activities such as getting around in the community, cooking, housekeeping, and managing money. This area of disability assessment has become known as *instrumental activities of daily living* (IADLs).

IADL assessment is typically done with less severely disabled individuals, often with people living in the community. Most of these assessments were designed to improve on the sensitivity of basic ADL scales that were found not to identify higher levels of functioning or minor changes in functioning.

Research Evidence

Measurement of the ADLs and IADLs is critical because they have been found to be significant predictors of admission to a nursing home, use of paid home care, use of hospital services, living arrangements, use of physician services, insurance coverage, and mortality. For research on the elderly, the ability to perform the ADLs has become a standard variable to include in analyses just like age, sex, marital status, and income. Estimates of the number and characteristics of people with problems performing ADLs are also important because of the increasing number of private long-term care insurance policies and proposed public long-term care insurance programs that rely on ADL measures to determine whether an individual qualifies for benefits.

In part because of their predictive value and widespread use in clinical settings, basic ADL disability assessment has also come to play a major role in large national surveys covering the long-term care population. They serve as an indicator of the number of elderly persons who are functionally disabled, identify the types and severity of those disabilities, and assess the adequacy of long-term care settings and services. A number of national surveys that measure the ability of elderly people to perform basic ADLs have been conducted. Although persons of all ages may have problems performing the ADLs, prevalence rates are much higher for the elderly than for the nonelderly. Within the elderly population, ADL prevalence rates rise steeply with advancing age and are especially high for people age 85 years and older. The general pattern of an increase in ADL disability with advancing age is fairly similar across industrialized societies, even though there may be significant differences in the prevalence of particular disabilities. Differences in health policies and health care systems mean that differing emphases are placed on interventions aimed at ADL disability.

Numerous studies exploring late-life ADL disability trends in the United States have been published over the past decade, frequently with conflicting results. In large part, discrepancies across studies are related to different methods that are used across studies to assess ADL disability. Overall, much of the research on late-life ADL disability suggests that some improvements in late-life functioning in ADLs have occurred during the past few decades within the United States. Declines have been seen primarily in the IADLs—activities such as shopping, managing money, and doing laundry. Much smaller declines in difficulty performing basic ADLs have been observed.

The research evidence further suggests that gaps in improvements across racial groups have remained steady and that gaps in improvement across socioeconomic groups have widened.

—*Alan M. Jette*

See also Disability and the Disablement Process; Driving; Exercise and Physical Activity; Mobility; Mobility Assessment; Performance Measures of Physical Function; Rehabilitation Therapies

Further Readings and References

Katz S, Akpom CA. Index of ADL. In: Murnaghan JH, ed. *Long Term Care Data: Report of a Conference on Long-Term Health Care Data Sponsored by National Center for Health Statistics and Johns Hopkins University.* Philadelphia: J. B. Lippincott; 1976.

Katz S, Downs TD, Cash HR, Grotz RC. Progress in development of the Index of ADL. *Gerontologist.* 1970;1:20–30.

Katz S, Ford AB, Moskowicz RW, et al. Studies of illness in the aged: The index of ADL—A standardized measure of biological and physiological function. *JAMA.* 1963;185:914.

Mahoney F, Wood O, Barthel D. Rehabilitation of chronically ill patients: The influence of complications on the final goal. *South Med J.* 1958;51:605–609.

ADVANCE DIRECTIVES

Advance directives are legally recognized expressions by people about how they want certain aspects of medical care to be done for or about them in the event of disability or incompetence. Advance directives are usually written documents that may need to conform to specific state laws. Verbal expressions of intent may be permitted in some states, but they may create ambiguity, leading to conflicts between parties and to costly litigation. The purpose of advance directive documents is to provide a legal enforceable basis for exercising the specific intentions of people, while they are still alive, about the medical care services they wish to receive. Specifically, they provide instructions about whether heroic measures should be taken to keep them alive in the event of a heart attack or life-threatening accident; whether they wish to have artificial life support devices such as respirators and nutrition/hydration tubes; whether they want antibiotics; the conditions for which they may want treatment; and who is delegated, in the event of incompetence, to make medical care decisions on their behalf. Advance directives also may specify people's wishes regarding participation in medical research such as who may make research decisions for them or the types of research in which they are willing to participate.

Advance directives involve specific documents, including living wills, health care surrogates/durable powers of attorney for health care, and "do not resuscitate" orders. In discussing executed legal documents, we refer to the person signing the documents as "Party A" and to persons who may have authority delegated under these documents as "Party B," "Party C," and so on. These documents should be discussed among adult family members, and persons should consider executing them as soon as they are legally competent, usually 18 years of age. The documents can always be changed. But if they are not in place, controversy and even litigation can erupt to destroy the fabric of families and loved ones. Each type of advance directive document carries a different kind of legal weight and purpose. Many states require separate documents to accomplish each task.

Health Care Surrogate/Durable Power of Attorney for Health Care

The most important document is the health care surrogate, which may also be called a durable power of attorney for health care. This document delegates legal power from Party A to Party B to make medical care decisions for Party A. A health care surrogate document is not intended for use in terminal cases exclusively but rather is used in the event that Party A is not in a position to make decisions. This may occur, for example, as a consequence of an accident, following exploratory surgery and the need to obtain authorization to perform additional procedures, or dementia.

The surrogate document can be generic or very specific. A generic surrogate document would state that Part A delegates all medical care decision making

to Party B in the event that Party A is not able to make decisions. The surrogate can transfer this authority even if Party A is not completely incapacitated, or it can specify that Party B's powers come into effect only if Party A is deemed to be legally incapacitated. If Party A is deemed to be incompetent, a legal guardian might need to be appointed by the court.

Following the more than decade-long dispute between the parents and husband of Theresa Marie (Terry) Schiavo and the international drama surrounding her death in 2005, many attorneys recommend that advance directive documents be specific and inclusive rather than general and vague. For example, a surrogate document that merely transfers general authority for making medical decisions might be subject to challenge by a family member, a liability-sensitive hospital, or even the state if there are any questions about the "real" intentions of Party A. Therefore, Party A may wish to clearly articulate particular scenarios and scopes of authority for which Party B is expressly authorized to make decisions. These could include decisions to perform surgeries; reference to specific surgeries (e.g., exploratory, diagnostic) as opposed to, or including, therapeutic surgeries or amputations; and decisions to withdraw or withhold certain medical treatments, including (but not limited to) antibiotic therapy and therapies using experimental techniques. Party A will usually designate a Party B as the primary surrogate and a Party C in the event that Party B is unwilling or unable to serve.

Some people want to have more than one person serve as their surrogates. In such instances, they may state that they want both Party B and Party C to make decisions regarding medical care. But Party A should try to avoid circumstances of disagreement between parties and a deadlock or impasse. Decisions to appoint a surrogate should always be made based on Party A's desire to have her or his intentions carried out by somebody Party A trusts to represent those intentions. The surrogate can be a relative, a loved one, or a friend.

Living Wills

Living wills are advance directives in which Party A clearly indicates how she or he wants to be treated in the event that Party A has a diagnosed terminal condition, is in a persistent vegetative state, or is in another legally defined "end of life" circumstance from which no reasonable medical recovery is likely. Depending on state laws, this may also include dementia. The general presumption in medical care is that physicians and health care organizations will seek to keep people alive as long as possible. Party A may expressly want to be kept alive under any and all circumstances or may wish to avoid the pain, expense, and humiliation associated with what might be a lengthy, but certain, dying process. Some living wills expressly delegate the responsibility for carrying out Party A's intention to a specific Party B, but this is not the rule.

Each state defines "terminal" differently and provides different guidelines for allowing Party A to state that she or he wants any and all medical interventions, wants to be allowed to die without any medical intervention, or wants to die as a consequence of removing an existing intervention.

The living will should be used in conjunction with the health care surrogate, but it is distinguished as an expression of intent about the heroic measures to keep Party A alive, whether Party A wants to be kept alive regardless of the condition or the cost of maintenance, whether Party A wants to be attached to a respirator or a nutrition/hydration tube or to receive antibiotic therapy, or whether Party A wants to be treated for a newly identified illness or condition once a terminal condition has been diagnosed. The living will is intended to serve as a guide to the care Party A wishes to have, but the surrogate is a delegation of trust and expectation. In the event that Party B disagrees with the express intentions in the living will, the surrogate's judgment likely will prevail; unless effectively challenged by an outside party, using the living will alone will serve as evidence of Party A's intentions. A scenario such as this underscores the importance of choosing a health care surrogate whom Party A knows and believes will fulfill her or his expectations about medical and end of life decisions. The formal delegation of surrogacy creates the presumption that the surrogate will be acting on behalf of Party A.

Again, specificity is important to avoid ambiguity and controversy. The particular form of the living will document is also important. In most jurisdictions, it must be signed, witnessed, and notarized. In some jurisdictions, it must follow a particular format and reference state law. Not all jurisdictions will honor the living will of another state. Persons who travel frequently, or who have residences in more than one state, should determine how each state requires living will documents to be created.

In the case of both health care surrogates and living wills, Party A should make certain that the executed documents are in a place where they can easily be accessed; a copy should be given to Party A's attorney and to the person in each document who is authorized to make decisions for and on behalf of Party A. Providing a copy to Party A's physician is also prudent. Many hospitals now formally ask patients about advance directives on admission and may even offer documents for them to sign. No legal document regarding a person's life or health should be signed without carefully considering the implications of that document and without consulting family members and loved ones. Executing a health care surrogate and/or a living will without telling anybody about them is likely to create controversy and chaos.

Some jurisdictions will accept video statements of intent regarding health care surrogates and living wills. Some jurisdictions will accept verbal nonwritten evidence of a person's intent, usually subject to a hearing and the presentation of evidence. But to avoid confusion and ambiguity, written, signed, witnessed, and notarized documents are the only reasonable assurance that a person's intentions will be carried out.

"Do Not Resuscitate" Orders

"Do not resuscitate" orders (DNRs) orders are arrangements made between Party A and her or his physician regarding resuscitation in the event of an accident such as a heart attack, a stroke, or another sudden threat to life. DNRs are most often executed by persons who have chronic, terminal, and life-threatening conditions and who do not want to take the chance of awakening in a coma, in a vegetative state, or in profound disability. A DNR is agreed to between the physician and the patient and is signed by the physician. The order is then placed in Party A's medical record. It may also be posted on Party A's refrigerator at home or worn on a medical bracelet to alert emergency medical technicians.

Even with an advance directive, some hospitals or physicians might not wish to agree to abide by the terms of a living will. In such instances, it may be necessary to transfer the person out of that institution and into the care of another physician and hospital. To avoid this controversy, people should know in advance the advance directive policies of their local hospitals and treating physicians. Copies of advance directives should be given to physicians, treating hospitals, attorneys, spouses, family members, and loved ones—and especially to those persons designated to make decisions. Advance directive documents should be revisited periodically to make certain that the intentions of the parties remain the same. Guidelines for advance directives are often available on the websites of state departments of health and state medical and bar associations.

—*Jay Wolfson and Amber M. Gum*

See also Death, Dying, and Hospice Care; Elder Abuse and Neglect; Legal Issues

Further Readings and References

American Bar Association. Estate planning FAQs. Available at: www.abanet.org/rppt/public/home.html. Accessed September 5, 2006.

ADVERSE DRUG REACTIONS

Adverse drug reactions (ADRs) are common in older adults and can result in significant health care costs, reduced quality of life, and death. Many ADRs are preventable. Because one of the most important risk factors is the use of multiple medications, health care providers should ensure that patients are maintained on the fewest number of necessary medications to manage their health conditions.

Definitions

Several well-accepted definitions of ADRs exist. The World Health Organization defines an ADR as a noxious or unintended response to a drug occurring in prophylaxis, diagnosis, and therapy, apart from failure to accomplish the intended purpose. This ADR definition refers to injuries that occur at usual medication doses. A source of confusion in the literature is the interchangeable use of the terms *adverse drug reactions* and *adverse drug events* (ADEs). The Institute of Medicine defines an ADE as injury consequential to drug use. Under this definition, an ADE not only includes an ADR, or an injury that occurs at usual doses, but also an injury that occurs with inappropriate use or overdose.

Epidemiology

Complications of ADEs may include hospitalization, increased hospital stays and health care expenditures, morbidity, and death. The incidence of ADEs varies by type of health care setting (e.g., ambulatory clinic, hospital, nursing home). In a cohort of older Medicare enrollees, the rate of ADEs was 50.1 per 1,000 person-years. In long-term care facilities, the rates of ADEs were reported as 1.9 to 9.8 per 100 resident-months. ADEs are a common cause of hospital admission of older adults and were responsible for 6% to 24% of all hospital admissions. Of all ADEs, 23% to 28% were categorized as serious.

Approximately one quarter to one half of ADEs are considered to be preventable. Errors are most likely to occur at the time of prescribing a medication or during monitoring of therapy. Prescribing errors include choosing an inappropriate medication, prescribing a medication that interacts with another medication in the individual's regimen, and prescribing a drug in the face of an established drug allergy. Errors in monitoring of therapy may include failing to obtain necessary laboratory values to monitor drug therapy and not responding promptly to signs, symptoms, or laboratory evidence of drug toxicity.

Many researchers have attempted to identify risk factors for ADEs, an endeavor that has been disappointing. The most persistent risk factor for ADEs is use of multiple medications; thus, it is important that patients be maintained on the fewest number of medications needed to manage their health conditions. Researchers have not found ADEs to vary substantially according to age or sex. Several factors are important to keep in consideration to minimize ADEs, even though they have not been identified as independent risk factors. Prescribers should keep in mind the age-related changes in kidney and liver function that may cause the body to be less efficient in eliminating medications and should adjust medication doses appropriately in older adults. Although specific medication types have not consistently been identified as independent risk factors for ADEs, certain medications may be more likely to cause ADEs if they have a narrow therapeutic window; for example, a blood level that causes the desired pharmacological effect may be similar to the blood level that causes ADEs.

Identifying ADEs in older adults may be challenging, especially in frail older adults. In some cases, ADE symptoms may present nonspecifically or be attributed to other causes. For example, a drug may be overlooked as the cause of cognitive impairment or of an increase in falls. Older individuals often have multiple chronic health conditions and take several medications, making it difficult to determine whether a new symptom is related to a new health condition, is related to an existing health condition, or is an ADE. Thus, medication use should be routinely considered as a possible explanation for any new symptom that occurs in older adults.

Prevention

A major challenge facing health care providers is preventing ADEs. Several approaches to preventing ADEs have been suggested, but little has been done in terms of systematically evaluating whether these approaches are effective. Most likely, preventing ADEs will rely on a multifaceted approach targeting health care systems, prescribers, and patients. Ideally, the efficient identification of potentially preventable ADEs would allow prevention of ADEs prior to the prescribing of a new medication through widespread use of computerized order entry with clinical decision support within health care systems. This type of intervention might

improve drug allergy identification, avoidance of serious drug–drug interactions, choice of appropriate medications, and ordering of appropriate lab monitoring parameters. Improved patient education to prompt the early recognition and detection of ADEs may reduce severity of potential ADEs. Strategies to improve patient–prescriber communication may reduce ADEs by encouraging individuals to report new symptoms as promptly as they occur. Lastly, systematic review of medications by pharmacists or other health care providers is necessary to ensure appropriate use of medications.

—*Shelly L. Gray*

See also Adverse Drug Withdrawal Events; Age-Related Changes in Pharmacokinetics and Pharmacodynamics; Drug–Disease Interactions; Drug–Drug Interactions; Inappropriate Prescribing; Kidney Aging and Diseases; Polypharmacy

Further Readings and References

Agency for Healthcare Research and Quality. Reducing and preventing adverse drug events to decrease hospital costs. Available at: www.ahrq.gov/qual/aderia/aderia.htm. Accessed September 5, 2006. AHRQ Publication No. 01–0020.

Food and Drug Administration/Center for Drug Evaluation and Research. Preventable adverse drug reactions: A focus on drug interactions. Available at: www.fda .gov/cder/drug/drugreactions/default.htm. Accessed September 5, 2006.

Institute of Medicine. *To Err Is Human: Building a Safer Health System.* Kohn LT, Corrigan JM, Donaldson MS, eds. Washington, DC: National Academy Press; 2000.

Riedl MA, Casillas AM. Adverse drug reactions: Types and treatment options. *Am Fam Physician.* 2003;68: 1781–1790. Available at: www.aafp.org/afp/20031101/ 1781.html. Accessed September 5, 2006.

ADVERSE DRUG WITHDRAWAL EVENTS

Adverse drug withdrawal events (ADWEs) are a clinical set of symptoms or signs related to the cessation of a drug. Clinical manifestation of an ADWE may be either physiological withdrawal reaction of the drug (e.g., β-blocker withdrawal syndrome) or an exacerbation of the underlying disease itself. Adverse drug withdrawal symptoms can be as benign as nausea or as severe as vomiting, seizures, and even hypertensive crisis. Information on adverse drug withdrawal symptoms sometimes can be found in the package insert of the medication, although most of our information comes from epidemiological studies.

Epidemiology

Clinicians and investigators have reported numerous cases of ADWEs, but there have been few studies of this phenomenon in the elderly. M. B. Gerety and colleagues in 1993 investigated ADWEs in a single nursing home in Texas over an 18-month period and found that 62 nursing home patients experienced a total of 94 ADWEs (mean = 0.54 per patient), corresponding to an incidence of 0.32 reactions per patient-month. Cardiovascular, central nervous system, and gastrointestinal drug classes were most frequently associated with ADWEs. More than 27% of ADWEs were rated as severe. A 1997 study of U.S. ambulatory elderly patients by Taylor Graves and colleagues investigated ADWEs in 124 patients and discovered that of the 238 drugs stopped, 62 (26%) resulted in 72 ADWEs in 38 patients. Cardiovascular (42%) and central nervous system (18%) drug classes were most frequently associated with ADWEs. In 26 (36%) of the ADWEs, patients required hospitalization or emergency room or urgent care clinic visits. Most of the ADWEs were exacerbations of underlying diseases, and some withdrawal events occurred up to 4 months after the medications were discontinued. Finally, a more recent study by J. M. Kennedy and colleagues examined ADWEs during the postoperative period in a single hospital. Of 1,025 patients studied, 50% were over 60 years of age and 34 patients suffered postsurgical complications due to drug therapy withdrawal.

Risk Factors for ADWEs

In the study by Gerety and colleagues, ADWEs were associated with multiple diagnoses, multiple medications, longer nursing home stays, and hospitalizations.

Graves and colleagues found that the number of medications stopped was a significant predictor of ADWEs. The analyses by Kennedy and colleagues revealed that the risk of an ADWE increased as the length of time off medication increased. Specific drug classes that have shown significant ADWEs in studies include antihypertensives (especially angiotensin-converting enzyme inhibitors), anti-Parkinson's medications (especially levodopa and carbidopa), benzodiazepines, and antidepressants.

Recommendations and Precautions to Prevent ADWEs

Recommendations to avoid withdrawal events involve following the same recommendations when starting a medication in the elderly ("go slow"); in other words, taper a drug over several days. One way to determine how many days one should taper a medication to avoid an ADWE would be to look at the pharmacokinetic half-life of a medication. The pharmacokinetic parameter half-life is the time taken for the plasma concentration of a drug to fall to half of its original value. It is suggested that it takes approximately five half-lives for a medication to leave the body completely. For example, if a medication has a half-life of 24 hours, it would take approximately 5 days to eliminate that drug completely from the body. When tapering a medication, to prevent an ADWE, one should reduce the dose by approximately 10% to 20% of the total daily dose every five half-lives until the medication is completely gone. Of course, vigilant monitoring of signs and symptoms of withdrawal is always recommended when taking somebody off a medication.

—*Robert L. Maher, Jr.*

See also Adverse Drug Reactions; Age-Related Changes in Pharmacokinetics and Pharmacodynamics; Drug–Disease Interactions; Drug–Drug Interactions; Inappropriate Prescribing; Polypharmacy

Further Readings and References

Gerety MB, Cornell JE, Plichta D. Adverse events related to drugs and drug withdrawal in nursing home residents. *J Am Geriatr Soc.* 1993;41:1326–1332.

Graves T, Hanlon JT, Schmader KE. Adverse events after discontinuing medications in elderly outpatients. *Arch Int Med.* 1997;157:2205–2210.

Kennedy JM, van Rij AM, Spears RA, et al. Polypharmacy in a general surgical unit and consequences of drug withdrawal. *Br J Clin Pharmacol.* 2000;49:353–362.

Advocacy Organizations

Organizations historically have helped to shape public policy in health and aging by raising awareness of issues; by educating stakeholders, decision makers, and the public; and by taking action to advance, block or otherwise shape change.

Some of the United States' most significant public programs and policies are the outcomes of widespread advocacy. The politics leading to the enactment of Medicare was driven in large part by more than a decade of advocacy by labor and aging organizations and was shaped significantly by the positions of trade organizations representing insurers and providers. The contemporary national debate over the future of the Social Security program engages thousands of national, state, and local aging organizations, mostly giving expression to near-universal opposition to privatizing or radically altering program protections for current and future generations. At the state level, the enactment of New York State's Elderly Pharmaceutical Insurance Coverage (EPIC) program was largely the outcome of pressure from grassroots senior membership organizations.

Over the years, thousands of national, state, and local advocacy organizations have formed as the result of real or perceived needs for organized support around issues. These organizations function at multiple levels within local service delivery organizations and systems as well as at local, state, and national policy levels.

At the local level, for example, nursing home ombudsman programs advocate on behalf of the rights of vulnerable elders. Area agencies on aging seek to identify and address service needs, and public health agencies work to protect the public's health interests. Often, issues emerge in the context of local experiences that become defined as systemic problems requiring policy change.

State and national organizations use multiple advocacy tools and approaches. These include producing research and policy information to help define and resolve issues, educating the public on the dimensions of issues, working directly with decision makers and stakeholders to build cases around issues, and overseeing the implementation of policy change. The structure and missions of such advocacy organizations vary widely from individual membership organizations (e.g., American Association of Retired Persons [AARP], Committee to Preserve Social Security and Medicare, Alliance for Retired Americans), to social justice organizations (e.g., National Hispanic Council on Aging, Older Women's League, Gray Panthers, Families USA), to organizational membership organizations (e.g., National Association of Area Agencies on Aging, American Association of Homes and Services for the Aged, National Council on Aging), to professional/research associations (e.g., American Public Health Association, Gerontological Society of America, National Academy of Social Insurance), to political action committees within advocacy organizations. National organizations often have state-based offices and chapters, allowing them to advocate at the grassroots level as well as at the national level. Most states also have independent advocacy groups that play significant roles in state and local policy (e.g., Coalition of Wisconsin Aging Groups, Oklahoma Alliance on Aging).

As in the past, organized advocacy will both shape and be shaped by socioeconomic trends and emerging policy issues. The growing need for income and health security currently, and presumably for the foreseeable future, under current health care policies interacts with the rising cost of health care and tax and military policies that are growing the federal debt, providing fertile ground for aging-related advocacy during the decades to come. Population aging, especially anticipated increases in the 85-years-and-older population, will propel long-term care and support of caregivers onto the agenda of advocacy organizations. The improved health of many people among today's elderly populations provides a new opportunity to use the social capital of the aging—yet another emerging area waiting for advocacy organizations to champion change. In short, aging advocacy organizations will have much reason to be centrally involved in identifying and giving direction to future health and aging agendas, policies, and programs.

—Nancy H. Smith and Eric R. Kingson

See also Aging Network; Assisted Living; Health and Public Policy; Health Care System for Older Adults; Long-Term Care; Medicaid; Medicare; National Institute on Aging

Further Readings and References

Hudson RB. *The New Politics of Old Age Policy.* Baltimore, Md: Johns Hopkins University Press; 2005.

Jansson B. *Becoming an Effective Policy Advocate: From Policy Practice to Social Justice.* Pacific Grove, Calif: Brooks/Cole; 2003.

Koff TH, Park RW. *Aging Public Policy: Bonding the Generations.* Amityville, NY: Baywood; 2001.

AFFECT AND MOOD

See DEPRESSION AND OTHER MOOD DISORDERS

AFRICA

Africa is a beautiful and aging continent. It currently has similar numbers of persons age 60 years and older as do Latin America and the Caribbean, but Africa has the lowest percentage of this population group when compared with the other major regions. Yet over the next 25 years, the percentage increase of older persons in Africa will be greater than that in Europe, North America, and Oceania. By 2050, close to 200 million older persons will live in Africa and life expectancies at birth will exceed 65 years on average (Table 1). Unlike the other continents and major regions, the male/female sex ratio will increase and dependency ratios will decrease over the next

45 years. Total fertility rates will continue to drop in countries across the continent—with northern and southern Africa having lower rates (the current average is fewer than three children per woman) than middle, eastern, and western Africa (the current average is more than five children per woman)—and by 2050 the continent will remain the only major region with an average total fertility rate above the replacement level. Combined with Africa being the only major area with an average crude death rate that will decrease over the next 40 years, the demography of the continent will certainly change.

Public health successes during the past century have contributed to global population aging, and in Africa this has occurred despite devastating epidemics, poverty, natural and manmade disasters, the residual impacts of colonization, and violent conflict. This is also despite 26 African countries having total health expenditures of less than 5% of gross domestic product (GDP) to deal with a huge portion of the world's burden of disease. Africa includes 25 of the world's 26 countries with life expectancies of less than 50 years and includes all 3 countries with life expectancies of less than 40 years. The average life expectancy for both sexes combined in sub-Saharan Africa will increase from approximately 45 years currently to 63 years by 2050, resulting in the median age increasing from 18 to 26 years during this same period. For northern Africa, the average life

Table 1   Population Age 60 Years and Older and Life Expectancies in Africa: 1950 to 2050

Year	Population Age 60 Years and Older (Thousands)	Percentage Age 60 Years and Older	Life Expectancy at Birth (Years)	Life Expectancy at 60 Years of Age (Years)
1950	11,832	5.3	38.0	n/a
1980	23,835	5.0	48.7	n/a
2005	47,416	5.2	49.9	16.1
2030	98,430	6.7	55.9	18.1
2050	192,884	10.0	65.4	19.5

Source: Adapted from United Nations Population Division, Department of Economic and Social Affairs. *World Population Prospects: The 2004 Revision* (medium variant). New York: United Nations; 2005.

Note: n/a = not available.

expectancy will increase 10 years, from 67 to nearly 77 years, with the median age increasing from 23 to 36 years. The rate of increase in older persons in Africa over the next 25 years will be more rapid than during the past five decades—and will exceed that of many other regions.

The large number of older persons, pace of aging, and factors related to growing old in Africa bolster a case for greater attention to be given to the situation of this population group, especially when one considers that the triumph of economic well-being preceding aging in the more developed world will not be accompanying aging populations in Africa.

Health Transitions Following Demographic Transitions?

Considering the environmental, financial, and occupational burdens on physical bodies in many countries in Africa—including access to sufficient water, food, and income; proper shelter; and basic services such as sanitation and health care—"old age" in Africa may start at a younger chronological age than in other regions of the world. In many countries and cultures, physical appearance is used as the gauge, especially where vital events records are nonexistent. Many countries would use the retirement age, but "retirement" usually benefits a limited proportion of the population, with a few exceptions such as South Africa. So although age 60 years and older may be a generally accepted chronological definition, when looking at life expectancies and health transitions, it is prudent to look at those age 50 years and older in Africa. For this entry, we focus on those age 60 years and older to make comparisons across regions easier.

A particularly devastating scourge in sub-Saharan Africa, HIV/AIDS, has also taken a toll on both the demographic structure and the health status of entire populations and generations. In many cases, particularly in HIV/AIDS-affected households, older persons do not have retirement options and need to continue in the formal or informal work force. Caregiving has both direct and indirect impacts on the health and well-being of older persons.

Comparing a general measure of population health status, life expectancies, indicates that Africa has lower life expectancies for both sexes at birth and at 60 years of age (Table 2). In addition, the number of years of life lived in good health is lower. A major concern for countries faced with aging populations is the compression or expansion of morbidity (as measured by healthy active life expectancy [HALE] and lost healthy years as a percentage of total life expectancy [LE]) with population aging. A public health goal would be to minimize the difference between HALE and LE, thereby maximizing the years of "healthy" life lived.

Demographic and epidemiological transitions have major implications for policy, planning, and research. Each country's transition patterns are different based on the infrastructure and social protection systems, economics, health care provision, and health risk factors and behaviors. Yet with the increasingly urbanized populations and increased numbers of older persons, the population health profiles in Africa should increasingly reflect disease, disability, and causes of death similar to those of more developed countries.

But Africa may have its own unique epidemiological transition occurring. Instead of rising noncommunicable disease rates replacing mortality from infectious diseases, the trends are for older persons to have increasing mortality from infectious diseases with relatively no change in noncommunicable disease and decreasing deaths due to injuries as a percentage of deaths (Table 3). The relative increase in mortality from all causes will see an increasing percentage of deaths in the older population groups, from approximately 19% to 24% by 2030. Older adults are faced with higher levels of morbidity and death from chronic diseases, violence, and injury—a double burden of disease.

The general understanding of the trends and changes in disease and mortality patterns is improving, yet basic data needed to assess population health status, including valid and reliable fertility and mortality rates plus improved morbidity rates, are still largely unavailable in many countries. Births and deaths are more easily identifiable states than nonfatal health conditions contributing to the epidemiological transition, yet even registration of vital events and

Table 2 Healthy Active Life Expectancy, Life Expectancy, and Lost Healthy Years as a Percentage of Total Life Expectancy, at Birth and 60 Years of Age, by Sex and Major World Region: 2002

	Females			*Males*		
	HALE (Years)	*LE* (Years)	*LHE%*	*HALE* (Years)	*LE* (Years)	*LHE%*
At Birth						
Low-mortality countries	72.0	81.2	11.4	68.0	75.1	9.5
Eastern Europe	61.0	72.2	15.5	54.0	62.9	14.2
Latin America	61.8	73.7	16.1	58.0	67.0	13.4
Eastern Mediterranean	55.9	69.4	19.5	56.4	66.1	14.7
Asia/Pacific	57.5	67.6	15.0	56.2	63.9	12.2
Africa	38.9	48.8	20.3	39.5	47.0	15.9
World	57.0	67.2	15.1	54.9	62.7	12.5
At 60 Years of Age						
Low-mortality countries	18.8	24.2	22.4	15.9	19.9	19.8
Eastern Europe	13.0	18.9	31.5	9.6	14.6	34.2
Latin America	14.1	20.8	32.2	12.3	17.5	29.9
Eastern Mediterranean	10.3	18.0	42.4	10.4	16.1	35.5
Asia/Pacific	12.9	19.0	32.2	11.1	15.9	29.8
Africa	8.3	15.8	47.3	8.3	13.9	40.2
World	14.1	20.2	30.3	11.9	16.7	28.3

Source: Adapted from World Health Organization. *World Health Report 2003.* Geneva, Switzerland: WHO; 2003.

Note: HALE = healthy active life expectancy; LE = life expectancy; LHE% = lost healthy years as a percentage of total life expectancy.

national coverage of the few existing vital registration systems on the continent are limited. Especially when it comes to older adults, with a shorter "healthy" life expectancy and increasing burdens of disease, an improved understanding of the health and well-being of this population is needed.

Recommendations and Research

A primary task must be the identification and production of information to improve our understanding of the health and well-being of older persons and the aging process. In addition to data from ministries, surveys, and surveillance sites, the World Health Organization (WHO) has undertaken primary data collection in many countries in Africa through the World Health Survey (WHS) and the Study on Global Aging and Adult Health (SAGE). Working with the countries,

these surveys will yield a rich data set on the older population. Using the WHS as a baseline, the longitudinal SAGE, which focuses on older persons, will provide follow-up health and well-being data in a number of countries in Africa as well as methodologies to improve the measurement and assessment of health status and health care use indicators. The SAGE program will also make links with existing survey and surveillance activities in other countries in Africa as well as in Asia and Europe.

Political Will

Strong political support is needed to prepare for an aging world, especially when considering the GDP and wealth of individuals and nations. Improved public awareness will be necessary to attract the political will.

Table 3   Burden of Disease by Broad Cause (Disability-Adjusted Life Years), by Sex and Year, for Population Age 60 Years and Older

		Male	Female	Total
2005	Type I	1.57	1.26	2.84
	Type II	16.88	20.86	37.74
	Type III	1.79	2.46	4.25
2015	Type I	1.69	1.44	3.13
	Type II	16.73	21.06	37.79
	Type III	1.66	2.50	4.16
2030	Type I	1.80	1.87	3.66
	Type II	16.04	21.19	37.23
	Type III	1.57	2.71	4.29

Source: Adapted from World Health Organization. *World Health Report 2006.* Geneva, Switzerland: WHO; 2006.

Note: Type I = communicable, maternal, perinatal, and nutritional conditions; Type II = noncommunicable diseases; Type III = injuries and violence.

Public Health and Health Systems Issues

A thorough appraisal of the situation of older persons is needed. Where data in countries are lacking, existing information, including the burden of disease information from the WHO, must be used. Improved health care coverage is needed for older persons along with improved training for health care professionals to deal with conditions more commonly seen in older adults. A health information system that monitors health changes and trends, plus the impact of policies and intervention, will be essential to prepare for and address the needs of an aging population.

Legal and Policy Frameworks

The existence of a comprehensive and up-to-date aging policy or framework is the fundamental basis for establishing and addressing the needs of aging and older populations. It can be a stand-alone policy or integrated into other policy documents such as the case in Tanzania, where aging is explicitly included in the country's economic growth and poverty reduction policy. Countries can use and apply indicators from the African Union Policy Framework and Plan of Action on Aging, United Nations Madrid International Plan of Action on Aging, and United Nations Millennium Development Goals.

—*Paul Kowal and Nirmal Naidoo*

See also African Americans; Ethnicity and Race; Global Aging; HIV and AIDS

Further Readings and References

Ferreira M, Kowal P. A minimum data set on ageing and older persons in sub-Saharan Africa: Process and outcome. *Afr Pop Stud J.* 2006;21(2).

Kowal PR. *SAGE: WHO Study on Global Ageing and Adult Health.* Geneva, Switzerland: World Health Organization; 2006. Available at: www.who.int/healthinfo/systems/sage/en/index.html. Accessed September 5, 2006.

Kowal PR, Wolfson LJ, Dowd JE. Creating a minimum data set on ageing in sub-Saharan Africa. *South Afr J Gerontol.* 2000;9(2):18–23.

United Nations Department of Economic and Social Affairs. *Guidelines for Review and Appraisal of the Madrid International Plan of Action on Ageing: Bottom-Up Participatory Approach.* New York: United Nations; 2006.

United Nations Population Division/Department of Economic and Social Affairs. *World Population Prospects: The 2004 Revision* (medium variant). New York: United Nations; 2005.

World Health Organization. *Mortality and Burden of Disease Statistics.* Geneva, Switzerland: WHO; 2006a.

World Health Organization. *World Health Report 2003.* Geneva, Switzerland: WHO; 2003.

World Health Organization. *World Health Report 2006.* Geneva, Switzerland: WHO; 2006b.

AFRICAN AMERICANS

African Americans constitute roughly 12.9% (36.4 million) of the U.S. population. More than half of African Americans reside in the South (55%), equal percentages reside in the Northeast (18.0%) and Midwest (18.8%), and close to a tenth reside in the West. Although New York City and Chicago have the largest Black populations overall, 5 of the 10 cities with the largest Black populations are located in the South: Baltimore, Maryland; Houston, Texas; Memphis, Tennessee; Washington, D.C.; and New Orleans, Louisiana. Blacks are more likely than non-Hispanic Whites to reside in metropolitan areas/central cities and are less likely to reside in nonmetropolitan areas. Compared with the general population, the Black population is younger and has fewer persons age 65 years and older. Overall, Black women outnumber Black men, and this is especially true among persons age 65 years and older. Roughly a tenth of the overall Black female population is age 65 years and older, compared with 7% of Black males. For Blacks over 65 years of age, roughly 62% are women and 38% are men. As a group, Blacks are less likely to be married and more likely to be never married than are non-Hispanic Whites.

Epidemiology

As of 2002 in the United States, more than one half of the Black population age 65 years and older was either poor or near poor, with an overall poverty rate of 22%, compared with 8% among non-Hispanic Whites. Differences by gender underscore the poorer status of older Black women, who had a poverty rate of 26%, whereas older Black men had a rate of 20% (vs. 10% for non-Hispanic White women and 7% for non-Hispanic White men). By and large, African Americans are more likely than the general population to be native born. Of those who are foreign born, the vast majority come from either the Caribbean region or Africa and tend to reside on the East Coast.

Marital status and living arrangements have an important impact on the health and social status of older African Americans. Older Blacks are less likely to be married than are older persons generally. Overall, African Americans maintain larger families, particularly families with four or more members. In 2002, more than half of coresident Black grandparents (persons age 30 years and older) were also fully responsible for their grandchildren (i.e., were grandparent caregivers). Roughly 45% of Black grandparent caregivers had been in that role for 5 years or more, the highest number for any racial/ethnic group. Black grandparents were nearly twice as likely as

White grandparents to have full responsibility as caregivers to their grandchildren. Grandparent caregiving was associated with higher poverty rates, particularly for those residing in the South (21%) and in specific states (30% in both Louisiana and Mississippi).

Morbidity and Mortality

Mortality, morbidity, and chronic disease profiles for contemporary African American elderly persons are shaped by their life course experiences. Today's older Blacks (age 65 years and older) were born and grew up during a time (1940 and earlier) when all major societal institutions in the United States practiced racial segregation either officially (de jure) or in practice (de facto). As a consequence, African Americans were severely restricted in their access to basic health care as well as routine health screenings and focused health promotion/disease prevention efforts. In addition to inferior (and often nonexistent) health care and services, Blacks were exposed to life conditions and circumstances that compromised their health status—in housing, education, employment, and working conditions. These myriad factors had both direct effects (e.g., occupational hazards and exposures) and indirect effects (e.g., limited education) on health that severely restricted their opportunities for healthful living. Early (including prenatal) and continued exposures to deleterious conditions such as these, across the life span, have a lasting impact on the development and health of populations well into adulthood and old age. These lifelong adverse exposures and circumstances have been implicated as an important factor in the poorer mortality, morbidity, and chronic disease profiles found among older Black adults. Nonetheless, questions remain regarding the overall relationships among aging, race, and health and whether cumulative disadvantage experienced earlier in life results in the selective survival of relatively healthier individuals among the oldest cohorts of African Americans (i.e., the "crossover" effect for mortality and health).

Despite major increases in average life expectancy for African Americans, race disparities still exist. In 2002, the average life expectancies for African Americans born in 1940 (today's 67-year-olds) were

51.5 years for men and 54.9 years for women, compared with 62.1 and 66.6 years for their White counterparts. (Information on race prior to 1970 used the category "non-White.") Life expectancies (additional years of life) for 65-year-olds were 14.6 years for Black men and 18 years for Black women—2 and 1½ years less than the comparable life expectancies at 65 years of age for White men and White women, respectively. Life expectancies at 75 years of age were 9.5 years for Black men (vs. 10.3 years for White men) and 11.7 years for Black women (vs. 12.3 years for White women).

Leading causes of death for older African Americans include heart disease, cancer, cerebrovascular disease, chronic obstructive pulmonary disease (COPD), and kidney disease. Rates of diabetes, pneumonia/influenza, kidney diseases, septicemia, and hypertension are approximately 2 to 2½ times higher among Blacks than among Whites. Heart disease death rates for Black women are higher than those for women of any other racial/ethnic group. Approximately 60% of heart disease deaths for Black men occur after 65 years of age. Although this is the lowest rate of heart disease death for this age group across several racial/ethnic groups, it obscures the fact that a full 40% of heart disease deaths for Black men occur *before* 65 years of age (classified as premature preventable deaths). Prostate cancer is a disease that is detected primarily among older men (age 65 years and older). Compared with other racial/ethnic groups, African American men have the highest incidence rate (roughly 1½ times that of White men and 2½ to 6 times that of other racial/ethnic groups) and the highest mortality rate from prostate cancer. Similarly, more than 75% of cases of breast cancer are detected in women age 50 years and older. Black women are second to White women in overall incidence of breast cancer but have lower 5-year survival rates.

Cancer surveillance data from 1975 to 2000 indicate that although colorectal cancer mortality rates decreased among the general population, they increased slightly among Blacks during this period and remained considerably higher than the rates for Whites. The incidence of colorectal cancer for both sexes, but especially for Black men, increased over this period of time and exceeded the rate among Whites. Black men have the highest incidence of colorectal cancer, followed by White men, Black women, and White women. The mortality rate for colorectal cancer among Black men similarly demonstrated an increase since 1975, whereas the mortality rate for Black women during that same period of time was largely flat. Black men have the highest colorectal mortality rate, followed by White men and Black women (tied) and White women. Gender comparisons of homicide mortality rates indicate that Black men age 65 years and older are more than 3½ times more likely than older Black women to die due to homicide. Among older persons, older Black men have the highest mortality rate due to homicide (5 times the rate for older White men), whereas the rate for older Black women is 3 times that of older White women. Deaths due to firearm-related injuries indicate that older Black women have the lowest rates, followed by older White women, Black men, and White men.

Illness and chronic disease processes in African Americans begin earlier in the life span and are well established by middle age. For example, the Black population overall has the highest percentage of hypertension as compared with other racial/ethnic groups (39% of Black women and 37% of Black men are hypertensive). Because rates of hypertension are associated with increased age, greater numbers of older persons report being hypertensive. However, Black women between 45 and 64 years of age have twice the rate of diagnosed hypertension (57%) than do White women of the same age group (28%). Roughly 50% of older Blacks suffer from arthritis and hypertension, a quarter report heart disease, and close to 20% indicate having diabetes. Roughly 27.1% of older Blacks 65 to 74 years of age have diabetes, as do 20.4% of those age 75 years and older. Black men, in particular, are especially affected, with 28% of Black men 65 to 74 years of age having diabetes, compared with 25.4% of older Black women. Older African Americans report nearly twice the rate of limitations in activities of daily living (ADLs) due to chronic conditions than do Whites. Although rates for limitations in instrumental activities of daily living (IADLs) are more comparable, older Blacks (18.4%) still report higher rates than do older Whites (11.5%). Older

Blacks are less likely to die of Alzheimer's disease than are older Whites (this disease ranks 11th among the leading causes of death for older Blacks) and have the lowest rates of suicide (per 100,000) of all racial/ethnic groupings; among older persons, Black women (1.1) have the lowest rate of suicide, followed by White women (4.3), Black men (11.7), and White men (34.2).

Health Behaviors

Older Black adults engage in a number of behaviors that are risk factors for poor health. Less than a fifth of Black men and a third of Black women between 65 and 74 years of age report eating five servings of fruits or vegetables daily; men and women age 75 years and older are comparable in their rates of consumption (approximately 20%). Roughly half of Black persons 65 to 74 years of age are physically inactive, whereas 60% of persons age 75 years and older are physically inactive. Older Blacks are more likely than both older Whites and Hispanics to be current smokers. Older Black men are 2 to 3 times more likely than older Black women to be both current and former smokers; rates of current smoking for older Black and White women are roughly comparable.

Overweight and obesity among older adults are risk factors for a number of chronic diseases (e.g., diabetes, hypertension) and contribute to overall morbidity and limitations on activity. Fully 70% of older Blacks (65 to 74 years of age) and approximately 50% of those age 75 years and older are overweight (body mass index [BMI] $\geq$ 25 kilograms per meter squared [kg/m^2]). However, rates are elevated for older Black women, who are more likely than White women to be overweight; older Black and White men are comparable in their rates of overweight. Roughly a quarter of people in the general population age 60 years and older are obese (BMI $\geq$ 30 kg/m^2). However, across all racial/gender groups, Black women have the highest prevalence rates of obesity (age adjusted).

Health Care

Access to and use of formal services has an important bearing on the health of older adults. Older Black women are more likely than older Black men and older Whites of either gender to report problems in receiving medical care and prescribed medications and are more likely to report dissatisfaction with ease in seeing a doctor. Overall, older Blacks (especially males) are more likely than older Whites of either gender to indicate no specific source of care and no specific doctor whom they see. Roughly 45% of Blacks age 65 years and older indicate that they have received a flu vaccination, compared with 67% of older Whites in this age group. Data from 2002 indicate that African Americans are the least likely of all persons age 65 years and older to report a dental visit within the past year (33%). As might be expected, this rate is even lower for older Blacks who are poor (24%) and near poor (26%). Comparisons of older persons who are nonpoor indicate that Blacks are less likely than Whites to report a dental visit within the past year (45% vs. 66%).

Future Research

In sum, the health of today's older African Americans is the result of a variety of factors associated with the social, economic, and political circumstances of their prior life histories. These adverse life conditions—experienced across the life span—may accelerate the development of illness and chronic diseases among African Americans. However, current status positions (i.e., poverty) and experiences with the health care system also have powerful influences on health. Older African Americans' current economic status indicates that poverty is a major determinant of health and bears important relationships to pivotal health behaviors and indicators (e.g., dietary choices, nutritional status). Extant mortality, morbidity, and disability profiles for older Blacks reflect significant disparities in overall health (vs. other racial/ethnic groups) as well as disparities in access to and satisfaction with appropriate care. The participation of older African Americans (particularly women) as grandparent caregivers deserves further study with regard to the economic and health consequences of these family household arrangements. Research needs to examine the health benefits and costs of involvement in these family relationships and commitments, the impact of neighborhood and community characteristics on health, and the specific contributions of and pathways through which race, socioeconomic status position, and poverty affect the health of older African Americans.

—Linda M. Chatters and
Robert Joseph Taylor

See also Africa; Ethnicity and Race; Migration

Further Readings and References

Gillum RF. Epidemiology of hypertension in African American women. *Am Heart J.* 1996;131:385–395.

Johnson NE. The racial crossover in comorbidity, disability, and mortality. *Demography.* 2000;37:267–283.

Kelley-Moore JA, Ferraro KF. The Black/White disability gap: Persistent inequality in later life? *J Gerontol B Psychol Sci Social Sci.* 2004;56:S365–S373.

Mendes de Leon CF, Barnes LL, Bienias JL, Skarupski KA, Evans DA. Racial disparities in disability: Recent evidence from self-reported and performance-based disability measures in a population-based study of older adults. *J Gerontol B Psychol Sci Social Sci.* 2005;60:S263–S271.

Smedley BD, Stith AY, Nelson AR. *Unequal Treatment: Confronting Racial and Ethnic Disparities in Health Care.* Washington, DC: National Academy Press; 2003.

AGE–PERIOD–COHORT DISTINCTIONS

Age–period–cohort (APC) analysis has played a critical role in studying time-specific phenomena in demography, sociology, and epidemiology for the past 80 years. Broadly defined, APC analysis distinguishes three types of time-related variation in the phenomena of interest: age effects (variation associated with different age groups), period effects (variation over time periods that affect all age groups simultaneously), and cohort effects (changes across groups of individuals who experience an initial event such as birth during the same year or years).

The distinctions of age, period, and cohort effects are especially important in the context of health and aging. Age is associated with the biological process of

aging internal to individuals and plays a role in the etiology of most diseases. In general, the incidence and prevalence of disease as well as mortality rates increase systematically with age. The considerable regularity of age variations across time and place reflects the developmental nature of true age changes. In contrast, period and cohort effects reflect the influences of external forces that operate in different ways. The distinction between these two components of temporal changes is often the focus of APC analysis.

Period effects may be due to major historical events such as world wars, economic crises, famine, and pandemics of infectious diseases that elevate the death rates across all ages. They may also arise with public health efforts and diffusion of medical technology innovations that reduce mortality rates for all ages. In addition, a unique period event (e.g., 1991 Kuwait oilfield fires, 2004 Christmas tidal wave, 1986 Chernobyl nuclear disaster) may induce a similar change in disease risk for all individuals alive at a point in time regardless of age. Cohort effects have been conceived as the essence of social change and are evident in many chronic diseases, cancer cites, and human mortality. A birth cohort moves through life together and encounters the same historical and social events at the same ages. Cohorts that experience different historical and social conditions differ in their exposure to socioeconomic, behavioral, and environmental risk factors. Cohort effects represent the effects of these factors that embark at the moment of exposure early in life and act persistently over time to produce health and mortality risk differences in specific cohorts.

In spite of its theoretical merits and conceptual relevance, APC analysis suffers from technical problems that restrict its widespread application in research. Limited analytic approaches produce ambiguous results, and researchers do not agree on methodological solutions to these problems. The fundamental question of determining whether the process under study is some combination of age, period, and cohort phenomena points to the necessity of statistically estimating and delineating the age, period, and cohort effects. Most current statistical APC analyses focus on aggregate population-level data. The data structure is usually in the form of rectangular age by period tables of occurrence/exposure rates of diseases or deaths. Table 1 illustrates this structure using mortality data for older U.S. males. In this table, age–year-specific death rates are tabulated in Age × Period arrays, with eight 5-year age groupings defining the rows and four 5-year periods defining the columns. There are 11 successive 10-year birth cohorts whose death rates fall in diagonal cells of the matrix. The oldest cohort, individuals age 95 years and older during the 1980–1984 period (born before 1885), is at the bottom left cell, the youngest cohort is at the top right cell, and cohorts born in between form the diagonals. The death rates of one such birth cohort are shown by the shaded cells.

The conventional statistical method for modeling the tabular data shown in Table 1 uses the APC accounting/multiple classification model. The major challenge of estimating separate age, period, and cohort effects in these data is the "identification problem"; that is, the regression coefficient estimates are not unique. This is induced by the exact linear dependency among age, period, and cohort: Period − Age = Cohort; that is, given the calendar year and age, one can determine the birth year (e.g., 1980 − 65 = 1915 in Table 1). An extensive literature in demography and social research discusses how to identify and estimate age, period, and cohort effects. (In biostatistics and epidemiology, a number of solutions to the problem have also been proposed. For reviews and comparisons of extant methodologies, see further readings and references.) The most widely used strategy is the constraints approach; that is, placing at least one additional identifying constraint on the parameter vector (e.g., constrain the effect coefficients of the first two periods to be equal, $\beta1 = \beta2$, where $\beta1$ and $\beta2$ are the coefficients of periods 1980 and 1985, respectively). The main criticism of this approach is that model estimates are sensitive to the choice of the identifying constraints. A new approach to modifying the coefficient constraints is the intrinsic estimator. This method of estimation, by using the Moore–Penrose generalized inverse, removes the arbitrariness of equality constraints on model parameters.

Table 1 Death Rates (per 100,000 Population) for Older U.S. Males: 1980 to 1999

Age (Years)	1980–1984	1985–1989	1990–1994	1995–1999
65–69	3,252.6	3,012.2	2,786.7	2,551.8
70–74	4,909.3	4,657.5	4,163.6	3,923.1
75–79	7,246.1	6,939.0	6,283.0	5,839.2
80–84	11,060.1	10,649.5	9,887.1	9,332.8 ← Cohort 1911–1919
85–89	16,407.6	16,185.5	15,092.0	14,867.6
90–94	23,628.2	24,011.4	23,007.2	22,245.9
95+	34,292.9	35,281.7	35,199.0	34,406.2

Sources: Adapted from Centers for Disease Control and Prevention, National Center for Health Statistics, and the U.S. Census.

Debate continues regarding the legitimacy of modeling assumptions of various statistical methods for APC analysis. Several themes that stand out may help shed new light on the debate, integrate extant approaches, and extend the reach of APC analysis to research on health and aging. First, from the point of view of conventional linear models, the identification problem cannot be avoided and is viewed as a necessary problem under the assumption of additive ("conventional linear") models. But these models are only one approximation of how social and demographic change occurs; nonadditive APC models must also be developed. Second, most previous studies have focused on fixed effects linear APC models of aggregate population data. Appropriate modeling techniques are needed to conduct APC analyses of micro data sets such as sample surveys that are especially useful for testing explanatory hypotheses. Third, many studies of life course and aging involve longitudinal panel designs that provide true cohort data. Estimating full APC models in these data remains a challenge.

—*Yang Yang*

See also Demography of Aging; Epidemiology of Aging; Longevity; Longitudinal Research

Further Readings and References

Fienberg SE, Mason WM. Specification and implementation of age, period, and cohort models. In: Mason WM, Fienberg SE, eds. *Cohort Analysis in Social Research.* New York: Springer-Verlag; 1985:45–88.

Robertson C, Gandini S, Boyle P. Age–period–cohort models: A comparative study of available methodologies. *J Clin Epidemiol.* 1999;52:569–583.

Ryder NB. The cohort as a concept in the study of social change. *Am Sociol Rev.* 1965;30:843–861.

Yang Y, Fu WJ, Land KC. A methodological comparison of age–period–cohort models: Intrinsic estimator and conventional generalized linear models, with response of H. L. Smith. In: Stolzenberg RM, ed. *Sociological Methodology.* Vol. 34. Boston: Blackwell; 2004:75–110.

Age-Related Changes in Pharmacokinetics and Pharmacodynamics

Pharmacokinetics represents an array of processes by which drugs are liberated, absorbed, distributed, metabolized, and eliminated from the organism. The major pharmacokinetic processes investigated in older adults are distribution and renal elimination despite extensive knowledge of global physiological age-related changes and impaired homeostatic capacity that would plausibly alter other pharmacokinetic parameters and processes. In addition, most pharmacokinetics studies on older adults have been done on single-dose administration, which does not resonate with elders' higher likelihood of chronic multiple morbidity and consequent need for chronic dosing and steady-state examinations.

Absorption involves three main processes—diffusion, penetration, and permeation—that take place through active or passive mechanisms. According to the place of administration, the sites of absorption include the oral/ocular/nasal/rectal mucosa, the gastrointestinal (GI) tract, the respiratory tract, and the skin and subcutaneous tissue. Absorption in the GI tract may be affected by age-related changes such as reduced GI motility and gastric evacuation, reduced regional blood supply, and higher likelihood of duodenal and small intestine diverticula. Even though the main form of transport through the GI tract, passive diffusion, is not affected by normal age changes, active transport through intestinal mucosa is reduced due to age-related declines such as atrophy of the intestinal mucosa that reduces the typical absorptive area, changes in the shape of the villus, lengthening of the crypts, prolonged replication time of the crypt stem cells, limited villus motility, and impaired water barrier. Many studies have reported significant age-related reductions in glucose, galactose, calcium, and iron absorption that can have clinical implications for elders. Absorption rates can also be affected by concurrent drug administration and drug interactions. Although not studied sufficiently and without major clinical implications, intramuscular and subcutaneous absorption may be affected by reduced peripheral blood flow, increased connective tissue in the muscles, and altered permeability of the capillary walls; whereas percutaneous absorption may be reduced due to decreased skin hydration and surface lipid content, increased keratinization, decreased peripheral blood supply, and impaired microcirculation.

Distribution represents the passage of the drug through the organism toward its specific place of action. Changes in the volume of distribution have been examined extensively in older adults and have been shown to affect significantly and differently hydrophilic or lipophilic drugs. Due to age-related decreases in the lean body mass and total body water, the volume of distribution for hydrophilic drugs diminishes; whereas the volume of distribution for lipophilic drugs increases due to increases in the fat tissue. These changes in the body composition may result in increased accumulation, delayed peak concentration and elimination, and increased half-life of lipophilic drugs (benzodiazepines). Drugs circulate bound to various extents to plasma proteins, but only the free fraction of the absorbed drug can operate at the place of action. Therefore, hypoproteinemia, especially hypoalbuminemia, may result in higher concentrations of free drug fractions and consequent overdose effects, especially for highly albumin-bound drugs. This aspect is additive to reductions in the volume of distribution, resulting in augmented rates of drug clearance. Another factor potentially affecting the volume of distribution for drugs is the reduced cardiac output that may occur with aging and that results in reduced splanchnic, renal, and peripheral blood supply.

Metabolism includes a wide range of enzymatic biochemical reactions that break down complex structures into simpler, more hydrophilic, and ionized chemical structures to facilitate their elimination. The majority of drugs are metabolized primarily in the liver, but some organs, such as the lungs, kidneys, GI tract, and placenta, are enzymatically equipped for drug metabolism. The first set of biotransformations, called the first pass metabolism, can occur in the intestine and the liver and may reduce the systemic bioavailability of the drugs. Some age-related changes may alter the efficacy of the first pass metabolism, resulting in an increased bioavailability for some drugs. Hepatic metabolism includes two phases of biotransformation. Through reactions of oxidation, reduction, and hydrolysis mostly mediated by cytochrome P450 monooxygenase enzymes during Phase 1, the drugs are transformed into simpler metabolites. Due to changes in the liver microsomal enzyme activity and reduced liver mass and liver blood flow, these reactions decrease slightly with aging (more so in men). During Phase 2, the drugs or their metabolites are coupled to an endogenous structure through reactions of conjugation to prepare them for elimination. Phase 2 reactions undergo only minor age-related changes but are greatly altered by concurrent drugs competing for similar metabolic pathways and enzyme inducers such as smoking and alcohol. The reduced liver blood flow may result in a decreased clearance of high-hepatic extraction ratio drugs such as tricyclic antidepressant, lidocaine, propranolol, and some opioids. The decreased Phase 1 metabolism may lead to a reduced total body clearance and increased half-life for drugs metabolized mainly via this pathway such as diazepam, chlordiazepoxide, piroxicam, theophylline, and quinidine.

Elimination of the drug from the organism takes place mainly through the kidneys and to a smaller extent through the bile, lungs, sweat, and/or skin. Only a few drugs undergo one clearance avenue, and each metabolite of a drug has its own excretion pathways. Due to significant and progressive reductions in renal volume and blood flow starting as early as middle age, renal excretion has been found to be the most impaired pharmacokinetic component among elders.

These changes are reflected in reduced glomerular filtration and tubular secretion, leading to an increased half-life of the drugs that can become expressed clinically. The age-related increased muscle mass breakdown results in elevated serum creatinine levels, making this blood marker an inadequate indicator of renal function in elders. A more accurate estimation of the creatinine clearance in older men can be obtained using the Cockcroft and Gault equation:

$$CrCl = [(140 - \text{Age [in years]}) \times (\text{Body Weight [in kilograms]})] / 72 \times \text{Serum Creatinine (in milligrams/deciliter)}$$

For older women, the equation is multiplied by 0.85.

Among the drugs with impaired renal elimination in older age, several studies have identified the following: amantadine, aminoglycosides, chlorpropamide, cimetidine, digoxin, furosemide, lithium, metformin, procainamide, ranitidine, and vancomycin.

Another elimination component with clinical implications in elders is reduced lung elimination that influences inhalation anesthetics.

Age-Related Changes in Pharmacodynamics

Pharmacodynamics describes the course of action of a drug at the effector organ level, in terms of duration and magnitude of action, and amplitude of and time to reach the peak action, for both therapeutic and adverse actions. Alterations in the number and affinity of drug receptors, postreceptor signaling processes, biochemical responses, homeostatic mechanisms, and body composition, in addition to higher likelihood of polypharmacy and concurrent pathological processes in older age, make elders more susceptible to adverse drug reactions, drug–drug interactions, or decreased/increased sensitivity to some drug action. Among the drugs reported to have increased sensitivity in older age are benzodiazepines, dopaminergic agents, H1-antihistamines, metoclopramide, neuroleptics, opioids, and warfarin. The drugs found to have decreased sensitivity in older age include β-agonists, β-blockers, furosemide, and vaccines.

Nonetheless, inconsistent definitions and screening approaches for adverse drug reactions, and methodology for data collection, sampling, and evaluation, yield controversial reports with regard to elders' higher vulnerability to adverse drug reactions. Proper knowledge about the pharmacodynamics of a drug, in addition to its pharmacokinetic age-related characteristics, should establish the foundation for medication choice and dose adjustment in geriatric patients.

—*Mihaela A. Popa*

See also Adverse Drug Withdrawal Events; Drug–Disease Interactions; Drug–Drug Interactions; Inappropriate Prescribing; Kidney Aging and Diseases; Polypharmacy

Further Readings and References

Cusack BJ. Pharmacokinetics in older persons. *Am J Geriatr Pharmacol.* 2004;2:274–302.

Guay DRP, Artz M, Hanlos JT, Schmader KE. The pharmacology of aging. In: Tallis R, Fillit H, eds. *Brocklehurst's Textbook of Geriatric Medicine.* 6th ed. London: Churchill Livingstone; 2003:155–161.

Hollenberg PF. Absorption, distribution, metabolism, and elimination. In: Minneman KP, Wecker L, eds. *Brody's Human Pharmacology.* 4th ed. Philadelphia: Elsevier Mosby; 2005:27–41.

Ritschel WA. Pharmacokinetics in the aged. In: Pagliaro LA, Pagliaro AM, eds. *Pharmacologic Aspects of Aging.* St. Louis, Mo: C. V. Mosby; 1983:219–257.

Somogyi AA. Clinical pharmacokinetics and issues in therapeutics. In: Minneman KP, Wecker L, eds. *Brody's Human Pharmacology.* 4th ed. Philadelphia: Elsevier Mosby; 2005:41–57.

Timiras PS. The gastrointestinal tract and the liver. In: Timiras PS, ed. *Physiological Basis of Aging and Geriatrics.* 3rd ed. Boca Raton, Fla: CRC Press; 2003:359–375.

AGING IN MANITOBA LONGITUDINAL STUDY

The Aging in Manitoba Longitudinal Study (AIM) is currently the most comprehensive data resource in Canada for understanding the relationship between health and aging. Begun in 1971 by the late Betty Havens, the AIM database is unique in two ways. First, it is one of the largest and most extensive population-based longitudinal studies of aging in existence. Second, it is the only population-based longitudinal study of aging that combines complete health services utilization data with interview data.

Beginning in 1971, AIM conducted in-person interviews with 4,803 randomly selected Manitobans age 65 years and older living in the community or in nursing homes. A second cross section of 1,302 seniors was surveyed in 1976, and a third cross section of 2,877 seniors was surveyed in 1983. Also in 1983, the 2,401 who were still available from the 1971 and 1976 cross sections were reinterviewed as the first panel. In 1990, a total of 3,228 survivors from all three cross sections were reinterviewed. AIM again surveyed the remaining 1,868 survivors from all previous cross sections in 1996 and surveyed the remaining 1,012 in 2001. The shortest panel is four waves over 18 years, and the longest panel is five waves over 30 years. The database contains more than 2,000 interview items and 400,000 service encounters per participant.

Interviews in 1971, 1976, 1983, 1990, and 1996 collected information on sociodemographics; social psychological, physical, and mental health status and functioning; economics; health practices; leisure activities; care and support networks; perceptions; and consumption of services. The interview data have been linked to the full spectrum of health services utilization data kept by the provincial Ministry of Health. This includes medical hospital, nursing home, and home care data from 1970, pharmacare data from 1994, and immunization data from 2003. In addition, vital statistics on date, place, and cause of death from the Canada Mortality Data Base (Statistics Canada) can also be linked to the interview data.

Research using AIM data has addressed diverse questions such as income and expenditures, self-perceived financial security, unpaid work, health status, use of physician services, home care and nursing homes, successful aging, social isolation, compression of morbidity versus expansion of disability, self-perceived health status, health locus of control, formal and informal social support, informal care, ethnic diversity, perceived respect, characteristics of the oldest old, health of aging women, sample attrition and sample mortality, influenza immunization, and persistent good health. Policies that have been implemented as a result of AIM analyses include the removal of health insurance premiums for seniors, the addition of nursing homes to universal insured services, the initiation of public home care delivery, increased awareness of older women in women's health, increased sensitivity to isolation and loneliness among older women and men, and increased sensitivity to seniors in natural disasters.

The AIM database is a valuable resource for purposes of continuing gerontological research, education, and policy development. The inclusion of both interview and utilization information makes AIM well-suited to analyses of health and social policy issues relative to seniors in general and to questions that are best answered by studying changes over time in particular.

—*Barbara J. Payne*

See also Canada

Further Readings and References

Aging in Manitoba Longitudinal Study. Available at: www.aginginmanitoba.ca. Accessed September 5, 2006.

AGING NETWORK

To promote long-term social, physical, and financial well-being for the nearly 50 million U.S. adults age 60 years and older, the Aging Network was formalized and expanded by the 1972 amendments to the Older Americans Act of 1965 (OAA). The Aging Network is a nationwide system composed of a central Administration on Aging (AoA) and its regional offices, 55 State Units on Aging (SUAs, including states, trusts, and territories), approximately 665 Area Agencies on Aging (AAAs), 235 tribal and native organizations, and thousands of service providers funded by contract with network agencies. The services funded by the network and its partner agencies and organizations comprise the essential midrange component of the continuum of long-term care.

To ensure that older adults' most pressing needs are met, the Aging Network aims to deliver supportive home- and community-based services for the elderly (and their caregivers) as well as policy development and other such planning. Older adult input into decision making is required at every level, and multiyear service plans must be approved by each higher level of the network before being implemented.

With rare exceptions, Aging Network agencies contract for services rather than provide them directly. In addition to contracting for services, network agencies are responsible for ensuring that the services they support are "comprehensive and coordinated" as well as accessible, appropriate, adequate, and accountable. In keeping with the priorities of filling service gaps and coordinating services, network agencies are mandated to act as "lead advocate" among the government agencies in their areas. In addition, federal, SUA, and AAA staff members frequently interact with one another, with foundations, with members of professional organizations; and with representatives of membership organizations such as the American Association of Retired Persons (AARP). Network staff members also interact with college and university faculty and students in the process of hiring staff; recruiting interns; and teaching gerontology, health professions, and other types of classes.

Aging Network services are diverse (e.g., care management, adult day health care, congregate meals and meals-on-wheels, transportation vouchers, ombudsmen, transition services to higher levels of care, chore exchanges and home safety checks, elder abuse and self-neglect prevention, intervention activities). Recently added priorities include reducing the prevalence of obesity, falling, and hoarding; caregiver support services; and faith-based initiatives. Although not all OAA services contribute directly to physical or mental health, all contribute substantially to the well-being of older persons and to the goals of maintaining elders' independence and autonomy and helping them to delay or avoid institutionalization, promoting family well-being and integrity, and strengthening community-based resources. Many are designed as "safety net" programs to prevent near-poor older adults (mostly women) from needing to "spend down" to become eligible for Medicaid and other means-tested programs.

OAA-supported services initially were designed to be free of charge to anyone age 60 years or older. However, donations ("suggested contributions") have been encouraged all along, and the 2000 reauthorization of the OAA permits SUAs to establish sliding fee scales based on income for certain services.

History

Each successive cohort of older Americans has been assumed to need and deserve services tailored to that cohort's particular needs, strengths, and resources. For 30 years, Social Security was the only government-supported "service." Then, in 1965, Medicare, Medicaid, and the Older Americans Act were enacted. From the beginning of the Aging Network, congregate meals and Information and Assistance (formerly Information and Referral) were universally required services. By the mid-1980s, specific services (e.g., legal services) were briefly given priority. Today, programs benefiting family caregivers and grandparents raising grandchildren also receive AoA support. In addition, the private sector now is eligible to compete for OAA funds if it accepts the legal requirement for sustainability of services created with public support.

Aging Network Successes

First and foremost, many of the services supported by the Aging Network would not exist without network funding and advocacy. Without network services, an essential tier of the continuum of long-term care would be lost—the one that bridges total independence in one's own home and institutionalization.

Another success is the extent to which Aging Network agencies have partnered with agencies and systems that traditionally did not include older adults among their targeted constituencies (e.g., mental health agencies, the independent living movement). The number of dollars appropriated to the network

under the OAA is modest in comparison with the extent and significance of network activities in most states. Because the rate of growth in traditional OAA funding has not kept pace with population aging, network successes in tapping revenue sources beyond OAA monies merit commendation. For example, even before the 1999 Supreme Court decision on *Olmstead v. L.C.*, many SUAs administered Medicaid home- and community-based waiver programs in support of adults of all ages with physical disabilities. Many SUAs also run Medicare counseling programs, and some SUAs and AAAs have taken the lead in developing educational media productions.

A third Aging Network success is the extent to which network agencies and service providers have engaged tremendous numbers of volunteers in helping to achieve OAA, SUA, and AAA goals. The number of hours contributed by volunteers often exceeds staff hours! Furthermore, older adult volunteers sometimes can gain greater access to seniors' homes and trust than can professional staff.

Aging Network Challenges

In some states, the Aging Network and the services it supports remain invisible or are low priority in the eyes of legislators and non-network agencies and organizations. A related challenge is that even though waiting lists for some OAA services are long, a majority of older adults appear to be unaware of existing services or are unwilling or unable to access them.

Not one of the five largest states, as measured by the *number* of its older citizens, is among the five largest states in its *proportion* of older citizens. This distinction becomes especially problematic each time the OAA is reauthorized and funds are appropriated for network-supported services.

Rationales for prioritized services differ widely by geography. For example, improving transportation may be a priority for numerous Aging Network agencies, but the rationales and objectives for that priority are nearly certain to differ dramatically across network and non-network federal, state, and local agencies. For example, rural AAAs, mixed urban–rural AAAs, and densely populated urban AAAs differ in their transportation priorities and challenges. Increasing the availability of affordable housing and expanding outreach are equally problematic challenges.

Funding formulas specifically favor low-income, isolated, frail, and ethnic minority elders. By itself, however, the Aging Network often is unable to fund appropriate services directly or to sustain funding when government dollars are withdrawn. Furthermore, although cultural and linguistic competence remains a network priority, that goal remains elusive.

Emerging Expectations

The oldest U.S. baby boomers became eligible for Aging Network services in 2006. As a group, their need for home- and community-based services will be greatest during the 2020–2050 period. In ongoing research exploring the pertinent expectations of approximately 300 respondents 29 to 89 years of age, respondents expect that baby boomers *could* have a much more positive aging experience than their forebears. Respondents also expect the following:

- Social services will be better integrated with health services, and in the process privacy can be protected.
- In addition to more traditional modes of physical and mental health "care," health promotion, illness prevention, and disability postponement strategies will become more available and better supported (e.g., by insurance and health maintenance organizations [HMOs]).
- Information will be disseminated electronically and via community-based opinion leaders rather than by more costly, less time-sensitive, and less culturally relevant means.
- Older adults increasingly will be respected as full partners in decision making rather than as token spokespersons or as a category of "consumers" of prepackaged plans of service.

Politics and Policies

Aging Network activities increasingly include visible efforts to promote home-based services over institutionalization, collaborations with a large and growing number of government- and community-based partners, specific activities to delay or prevent disability and dependence among U.S. elders, and greater accountability and reporting requirements (e.g., documentation of cost-effectiveness and "outcomes"). Ending services fragmentation continues to be a challenging objective, especially because many services have multiple funding sources with differing objectives, some services are funded by non-network monies, and politics is nearly certain to influence both funding and service delivery decisions. Nevertheless, it is the availability and integration of multiple services that defines the midrange of the continuum of care for which the network has substantial responsibility.

More than any other Aging Network service, the key to network success is Information and Assistance (formerly "Information and Referral"). Telephoning 800-677-1116 connects the caller with the national Eldercare Locator, a network access point. Some states also sponsor free hotlines that automatically connect callers to the AAA for the area from which they are calling. For long-distance caregivers, online directories of network components are essential.

—Jeanne E. Bader

See also Continuum of Care; Demography of Aging; Health Communication; Health Promotion and Disease Prevention; Long-Term Care

Further Readings and References

Federal Interagency Forum on Aging-Related Statistics. Available at: www.agingstats.gov. Accessed September 5, 2006.

Grantmakers in Aging. Available at: www.giaging.org. Accessed September 5, 2006.

National Association of Area Agencies on Aging. Available at: www.n4a.org. Accessed September 5, 2006.

National Association of State Units on Aging. Available at: www.nasua.org. Accessed September 5, 2006.

U.S. Administration on Aging. Available at: www.aoa.gov. Accessed September 5, 2006.

AGITATION

According to the American Psychiatric Association's *Diagnostic and Statistical Manual of Mental Disorders, Fourth Edition, Text Revision* (DSM-IV-TR), agitation is excessive, nonproductive, and repetitive motor activity associated with inner tension, marked by behavior such as pacing, fidgeting, and hand wringing. Jiska Cohen-Mansfield and her colleagues based an alternative definition on their observations of patients with dementia: improper spoken or motor activity that an outside observer judges to not result directly from the agitated individual's needs or confusion. Although the definitions differ on whether inner experience is a defining characteristic, both consider agitation to be an observable state of increased activity that is not goal directed.

Conceptual Models

The DSM-IV-TR definition is applicable to agitation as it occurs as a symptom of depression and other psychiatric disorders and possibly for describing hyperactive behavior in people with severe pain. It may be difficult to apply this definition to people with severe dementia. However, the definition can serve as a reminder that agitation may be a reflection of inner suffering, even in people who may be too impaired to report their inner experience.

Another model of agitation focuses on observable behaviors, stressing the principle that cognitive impairment, brain disease, or psychiatric illness may predispose patients to agitation but that episodes of agitation generally are precipitated by stressful social or environmental events. Early descriptions of this model were based on observations that patients suffering from war-related traumatic brain injuries became agitated and aggressive as catastrophic reactions to feeling overwhelmed (e.g., when presented with problems that were too demanding for them). Moreover, these patients were often unaware of why they became agitated. The catastrophic reactions resulted from interaction between the predisposition (the brain injuries) and the precipitants (the situations that overwhelmed the patients).

Based on this model, Geri Hall and Kathleen Buckwalter suggested that agitation may occur when people with dementia are in environments that, given their cognitive impairments, are overstimulating for them; Hall and Buckwalter's model guides care by minimizing stressors. Earlier, M. Powell Lawton and his colleagues developed an ecological aging and adaptation theory based on observations that agitation can result from either overstimulation or understimulation as well as from environments that are either overwhelming or not challenging enough. This theory holds that when people are more capable, they are able to adapt to a wider range of environmental stimuli or challenges. However, when people are more impaired, they are less able to adapt and caregivers must match characteristics of the environment to people's abilities and needs.

Epidemiology

Epidemiological research by Constantine Lyketsos and colleagues found that observable agitation or aggression was present in approximately 24% of people with dementia but in only 2.8% of other older people in the community, consistent with a role of dementia as a predisposing factor. Among those with dementia, agitation was more common in the mid- and later stages of the disease. There were no significant differences between rates of agitation in people with Alzheimer's disease and those with vascular dementia.

In patients with dementia, agitation occurs more frequently in those with greater functional deficits in the frontal lobes of the brain and in those who also exhibit other neuropsychiatric symptoms, including delusions, depression, anxiety, irritability, and apathy. Thus, specific neuropsychological deficits and neuropsychiatric symptoms can be additional predisposing factors that increase the risk of agitation or aggression for those with dementia.

Agitation and aggression in patients with dementia predict more rapid increases in disability and nursing home placement. Rates of agitation are higher for patients with dementia in nursing homes than for those in the community. However, there are questions about how much of this increase can be attributed to the greater likelihood that patients with agitation will be admitted to nursing homes and how much may be related to the difficulties in caring for patients with dementia in nursing homes.

Descriptions of Agitation

Agitation can include behaviors that are aggressive toward others or abusive to the patients themselves (e.g., hitting), appropriate behaviors that are performed with inappropriate frequency (e.g., repetitive and intrusive questions), and behaviors that are socially inappropriate in specific situations (e.g., undressing in public). Not only are aggressive behaviors intrinsically dangerous and harmful, but also their specific manifestations or symptoms can be highly stressful and burdensome to caregivers and others who interact with the patient. Observable symptoms of agitation are characterized as physically aggressive, physically nonaggressive, or verbal behaviors. Physically aggressive behaviors are directed toward other people and include hitting, pushing, scratching, kicking, and grabbing. Physically nonaggressive behaviors include general restlessness, repetitious mannerisms, pacing, trying to get to a different place, handling things inappropriately, and inappropriate dressing or undressing. Verbal behaviors include screaming, cursing, constant requests for attention, frequent complaining, and negativism.

Little research has been conducted to evaluate how frequently agitated behaviors occur in response to specific stressors, possibly because untrained caregivers frequently fail to recognize precipitants. However, researchers who have directly observed the behaviors of nursing home residents have found that most episodes of aggression occur in response to social or environmental precipitants.

Clinical Evaluation and Treatment

The initial stages of clinical evaluation of an older person with agitation must include evaluating the extent to which the behaviors represent a source of danger and doing as much as possible to ensure safety. Subsequent evaluations should be directed toward identifying predisposing conditions such as depression, anxiety disorders, and dementia. When depression or anxiety is present, treatment should be directed at the underlying condition. When dementia is present, the evaluation should look for other neuropsychiatric symptoms that may be additional predisposing factors and for stressors that may be precipitants. When depression or delusions are present, these symptoms may be appropriate targets for

psychiatric or psychological treatment, including behavioral therapy or antidepressant medications for depression and antipsychotic medications for delusions.

Precipitating factors can include medical, physical, social, or environmental stressors. Medical symptoms that can precipitate agitation include pain, constipation, and fecal impaction. Related physical stressors that can cause agitation in patients who cannot meet their own needs or describe them to others can include thirst, hunger, being too hot or cold, and needing to go to the bathroom. Thus, an initial step in addressing agitation should be to evaluate unmet needs. One way to accomplish this may be through direct inquiry; patients who cannot spontaneously describe symptoms such as pain might be able to respond to simple direct inquiries about pain and other sources of discomfort. Alternatively, the evaluation could include a process of trial and error, offering a drink of water, a sweater or blanket, or other accommodations. In fact, a goal of providing care to patients with dementia must be for caregivers to learn, over time, how to understand each patient's unique expression of unmet needs.

Other elements of evaluation and intervention should focus on reducing environmental stressors, including making caregiving as consistent as possible, ensuring that caregivers communicate with patients in simple direct language, making the physical environment as home-like as possible, and minimizing noise. Because people with dementia generally have difficulty in organizing their time and planning activities, it is also important to ensure that they have opportunities to participate in structured activities. In general, part of evaluating and managing agitation should include formulating an individualized care plan designed to improve the match between patient and environment. The care plan should strive to provide sufficient choice and challenge (without being overwhelming) so as to help the patient maintain a sense of autonomy, to structure time so as to avoid boredom, and to design the physical environment so as to avoid both understimulation (sensory deprivation) and overstimulation.

A body of research on pharmacological approaches to managing agitation in patients with dementia provides evidence that antipsychotic medications can be effective, even in patients without delusions or hallucinations. However, questions remain as to whether the potential benefits of these medications outweigh the potential side effects and risks. Other medications, including serotonin uptake inhibitors and cholinesterase inhibitors, may have some benefits in decreasing or preventing agitation.

—*Ira R. Katz and Jason S. Katz*

See also Alzheimer's Disease; Anxiety Disorders; Behavioral Disorders in Dementia; Delirium and Confusional States; Depression and Other Mood Disorders; Long-Term Care; Pain; Vascular Dementia

Further Readings and References

Camp CJ, Cohen-Mansfield J, Capezuti EA. Use of nonpharmacologic interventions among nursing home residents with dementia. *Psychiatric Serv.* 2002;53: 1397–1401.

Cohen-Mansfield J. Assessment of disruptive behavior/agitation in the elderly: Function, methods, and difficulties. *J Geriatr Psychiatry Neurol.* 1965;8:52–60.

Lawton MP. The physical environment of the person with Alzheimer's disease. *Aging Mental Health.* 2001;5 (Suppl.):S56–S64.

Lyketsos CG, Steinberg M, Tschanz JT, Norton MC, Steffens DC, Breitner JC. Mental and behavioral disturbances in dementia: Findings from the Cache County Study on Memory in Aging. *Am J Psychiatry.* 2000;157:708–714.

Mace NL, Rabins PV. *Thirty-Six Hour Day: A Family Guide to Caring for Persons with Alzheimer's Disease, Related Dementing Illnesses, and Memory Loss in Later Life.* 3rd ed. Baltimore, Md: Johns Hopkins University Press; 2001.

Sink KM, Holden KF, Yaffe K. Pharmacological treatment of neuropsychiatric symptoms of dementia: A review of the evidence. *JAMA.* 2005;293:596–608.

Smith M, Gerdner LA, Hall GR, Buckwalter KC. History, development, and future of the progressively lowered stress threshold: A conceptual model for dementia care. *J Am Geriatr Soc.* 2004;52:1755–1760.

ALASKA NATIVES

See NATIVE AMERICANS AND ALASKA NATIVES

ALCOHOL USE AND ABUSE

Alcohol abuse is a difficult disorder to identify among older adults. The *Diagnostic and Statistical Manual of Mental Disorders, Fourth Edition* (DSM-IV) refers to a maladaptive or destructive pattern of alcohol use measured over a 1-year period, leading to significant social, occupational, and/or medical impairment. Alcohol abuse is characterized by symptoms of dependence such as increased tolerance; diminished effect; withdrawal; consuming larger amounts; unsuccessful efforts to cut down; substantial activity involved in obtaining, using, or recovering from its effects; giving up on activities; and continued use despite knowledge of having persistent problems.

The Treatment Improvement Protocol (TIP) expert panel convened by the Substance Abuse and Mental Health Services Administration stated that the DSM-IV classification of alcohol problems is largely irrelevant for older adults given changes in physiology, roles and responsibilities, and activities. The TIP panel recommended two terms to categorize older alcohol users: "problem drinkers" and "at-risk drinkers." *Problem drinkers* refers to heavy drinkers as well as those who meet the DSM-IV criteria for abuse and dependence. *At-risk drinkers* refers to those exceeding recommended drinking limits, in recognition of the fact that the threshold decreases with advancing age. The TIP consensus panel recommended no more than one drink per day, a maximum of two drinks on special occasions (e.g., weddings, New Year's parties), and somewhat lower limits for women. A standard drink (standard ethanol unit) is defined as a 12-ounce can or bottle of beer or ale; a 1.5-ounce shot of spirits; a 5-ounce glass of wine; or a 4-ounce glass of sherry, liqueur, or aperitif.

Older adults are especially vulnerable to the deleterious effects of alcohol. Decreased muscle mass and increased body fat, changes in metabolism, medical comorbidities, and decreased body water all affect older adults' metabolism of alcohol. Higher blood alcohol concentrations can be observed in older adults in comparison with younger adults.

Social indicators, such as arrests for driving under the influence (DUIs), absences from work, and family or marital problems, are common indicators of problems in younger people. In contrast, older adults are less likely to demonstrate these indicators; instead, they are more likely to drink in response to losses such as death of a spouse, divorce, retirement, infrequent driving, and diminished social support networks. Research indicates that older adults more often abuse alcohol at home and alone in response to negative emotional states and loneliness.

Epidemiology

Estimates of alcohol abuse among elders vary according to survey methodology and age criteria used. Among community-based adults age 60 years and older, it has been estimated that 2% to 10% are problem drinkers. According to the National Household Survey on Drug Abuse, 9.4% of adults age 55 years and older are heavy drinkers and 2.3% are binge drinkers. Higher percentages have been noted among medical patients (e.g., 4% to 10% of older primary care patients, up to 14% of emergency room patients, and 23% of patients with substance abuse diagnoses at veterans hospitals). However, not included in these numbers are the many elders experiencing problems as a result of alcohol use but not meeting formal diagnostic criteria or those not identified and often referred to as "hidden abusers."

In the United States, few people in the older age groups receive treatment for alcohol abuse. The Drug and Alcohol Services Information System (DASIS) report noted that only 66,500 older adults were admitted to treatment in 2002. This suggests that approximately 0.1% of the more than 62 million people age 55 years and older receive substance abuse treatment. In Florida, the state with the highest median age where those age 60 years and older represent nearly 23% of the population, only 2% of older adults are in substance abuse treatment.

Two major categories of older alcohol abusers are typically described. Approximately two thirds of older alcohol abusers are believed to be "early-onset abusers" who have alcohol-related problems carried over from earlier years. They often exhibit well-developed psychological problems, as well as more recent reactions to age-related stresses. The other third are believed to be "late-onset alcohol abusers" whose alcohol problems began later in life (e.g., in their 50s), often in response to recent losses or life changes. For this group, alcohol is used to soften the impact of negative emotions such as depression, grief, sadness, loneliness, and anxiety.

Screening and Case Finding

Identifying older alcohol abusers is a challenge. In 1989, L. W. Dupree compared different strategies for identifying and referring clients to an elder-specific treatment program. A community agency referral network strategy involved treatment program staff educating community agencies about the program's services and admission criteria. That strategy produced nearly twice as many referrals, more referrals meeting admission criteria, and at less cost when compared with either a public awareness/media campaign or treatment staff visiting health clinics to seek potential clients in need of treatment. "Gatekeeper" models, in which nontraditional referral sources (e.g., meter readers, mail carriers, phone company employees) are involved in case finding, have also been successful.

Once referrals are made, age-appropriate screening tools such as the Short Michigan Alcoholism Screening Test–Geriatric Version can be helpful during the initial interview with the client. Screening for depression should be conducted given the relationship of depression and alcohol use in this age group.

Motivating Older Alcohol Abusers to Enter Treatment

Once they are identified, motivating elders to consider treatment can be difficult. Strategies based both on the transtheoretical model or stages of change model and on the motivational interviewing approach are recommended. These approaches recognize that some people are unaware of their problem and react poorly to direct attempts to convince them of treatment needs (precontemplators). Those in later stages of readiness to change (e.g., contemplation and preparation stages) may be thinking about, or already taking first steps toward, change. Through motivational interviewing approaches, counselors recognize how to judge each client's readiness and learn how to help their clients move toward changing drinking behaviors and accepting professional help.

Treatment Recommendations

The TIP panel recommended that older adults be treated in elder-specific group treatment programs; that is, those that admit only older adults. Programs should employ individuals trained to work with older adults, provide treatment at a slower pace, attend to negative affect and social support, and avoid confrontation. Programs must attend to medical conditions and recognize elders' greater sensitivity to alcohol's effects.

Elder-specific treatment approaches recommended by the TIP panel included brief intervention (BI) and brief therapies using cognitive–behavioral interventions. Because many older adults are resistant to visiting outpatient treatment centers, BI is a viable alternative. It can be delivered in a physician's office, an older adult's home, a senior center, or other nontraditional sites where substance abuse treatment is less likely to be offered. BI ranges from one to five sessions, with the counselor guiding the client through the contents of a health promotion workbook. The workbook provides general education about older adults' health, information on the use of alcohol and medications, feedback about the client's personal risk, identification of triggers for drinking and suggestions for coping strategies relative to those triggers, and behavioral "prescriptions" to help the client define and decide on an immediate goal. Early studies of BI with older adults involved primary care physicians and their patients. Subsequent applications have extended BI for use by nonmedical service providers such as psychologists, social workers, and aging services providers trained to use the workbook.

Brief therapies may consist of more sessions and aim for greater change in drinking behavior. Cognitive–behavioral therapy (CBT) along with self-management approaches focuses on teaching skills necessary for rebuilding the social support network, self-management approaches for managing negative affect (e.g., depression, grief, loneliness, anxiety), and general problem solving. Older adults identify their personal drinking behavior chain and high-risk situations for drinking, and counselors teach clients the skills necessary to prevent lapses or relapses from occurring.

—Larry W. Dupree and Lawrence Schonfeld

See also Age-Related Changes in Pharmacokinetics and Pharmacodynamics; Bereavement and Grief; Complementary and Alternative Medicine; Depression and Other Mood Disorders

Further Readings and References

Center for Substance Abuse Treatment. *Substance Abuse Relapse Prevention for Older Adults: A Group Treatment Approach.* Rockville, Md: Substance Abuse and Mental Health Services Administration; 2005. DHHS Publication No. (SMA) 05–4053.

Dupree, LW. Comparison of three case finding strategies relative to elderly alcohol abusers. *J Appl Gerontol.* 1989;8:502–511.

Office of Applied Studies. *The DASIS Report: Older Adults in Substance Abuse Treatment—Update.* Rockville, Md: Substance Abuse and Mental Health Services Administration; 2005. Available at: www.samhsa.gov. Accessed September 6, 2006.

Office of Applied Studies. *The NHSDA Report: Substance Abuse Among Older Adults.* Rockville, Md: Substance Abuse and Mental Health Services Administration; 2001. Available at: www.samhsa.gov. Accessed September 6, 2006.

Schonfeld L, Dupree LW. Age-specific cognitive–behavioral and self-management treatment approaches. In: Gurnack AM, Atkinson RM, Osgood N, eds. *Treating Alcohol and Drug Abuse in the Elderly.* New York: Springer; 2001:109–130.

ALLOSTATIC LOAD AND HOMEOSTASIS

As the human life expectancy continues to expand, there has been increasing emphasis on understanding the cumulative effect of everyday experiences on physical health during older adulthood. The wear-and-tear theory, although overly general and unable to account for the "preprogrammed" nature of biological aging, offers a useful view of the aging process. According to this theory, the human body succumbs to the accumulation of wear and tear associated with injuries and physical damage sustained in everyday life. The accumulation of biological damage over time increases the possibility that the stability of physiological functioning within various body systems, including systems essential for survival such as the nervous and cardiovascular systems, may be disrupted.

The stability of body systems, or homeostasis, appears to be particularly challenged during elevated stress. The causes of stress can be physical (e.g., hunger, cold), social (e.g., poor social network, lack of adequate financial resources), or psychological (e.g., perceived threat, negative social interaction). The body adjusts to each episode of stress by initiating a response designed to reestablish homeostasis. For example, shivering when cold is an attempt to achieve homeostasis by warming tissues, and increased heart rate is an attempt to achieve homeostasis by increasing the readiness of cells as the body expects a fight-or-flight response.

The process of reestablishing homeostasis in response to stress has been described more recently as *allostasis*; that is, maintaining stability through change. Through allostasis, the body systems attempt to match physiological function to the current environmental demands so as to maintain homeostasis. Therefore, allostasis is an essential component in maintaining homeostasis.

Stress, such as physical exertion, a lack of social support, and public speaking, increases environmental demands and challenges the body's systems to respond adequately. Each physiological response to stress (e.g., elevated blood pressure to increase alertness) causes physiological systems (e.g., the cardiovascular system) to use up resources, making them more susceptible to damage. Although a single response to stress is often adaptive, such as when people become more alert during public speaking, accumulation of stress responses over time can lead to exacerbated wear and tear and can increase the chance of system dysregulation

(i.e., exaggerated or inadequate physiological response), accelerating physical aging.

The nervous and cardiovascular systems are essential for achieving stability through change (allostasis) during stress. As the brain detects a threat or a stressful event, it signals a cascade of physiological reactions that, in turn, stimulate the brain, the cardiovascular system, and skeletal muscles, increasing the body's readiness for physical response. This physiological cascade occurs within the hypothalamic–pituitary–adrenal (HPA) axis and the sympathetic nervous system. In response to stress, the HPA axis activates the release of glucocorticoids, a type of stress hormone, into the bloodstream, mobilizing energy and increasing physiological readiness of the body for a fight-or-flight action. Although such adaptive responses are essential during a stressful situation, repeated physiological overstimulation of a body system due to stress can bring about dysregulation.

The cumulative impact of responses to daily stress has been referred to as *allostatic load*; that is, the "price of adaptation." The physiological response to stress helps people adapt to everyday experiences and stressful situations by mobilizing the resources within body systems, such as the nervous and cardiovascular systems, but it also causes wear and tear in these same body systems as responses accumulate over time. Long-term exposure to stress has been associated with hypertension, increased susceptibility to type 2 diabetes, impaired immune function, and accelerated brain aging, particularly in the hippocampal region. Similarly, higher levels of allostatic load have been associated with an increased risk of heart disease, a faster rate of cognitive and functional decline, and a higher risk of death among older persons.

Four basic indicators of allostatic load have been identified. The first indicator is frequent exposure to stress, which tends to lead to overactivation of the stress response cascade and increased physical wear and tear. The second indicator is lack of adaptation to a stressful event of the same type (e.g., public speaking), where repeated encounters with the same event lead to the same (rather than gradually decreasing) physiological arousal. The third indicator pertains to a reduced ability to shut off the response to stress once the stressful event has passed, leading to prolonged physiological activation. The final indicator is overactivation of one type of response to stress due to an inadequate response from another source. For example, repeated exposure to stress reduces the efficiency of the insulin response and increases blood levels of glucose, resulting in greater risk of type 2 diabetes. This problem increases the susceptibility of the body to other stress-related conditions such as cardiovascular disease.

The concept of allostatic load illustrates cumulative biological risk. It is derived from the underlying physiological mechanisms through which body systems (mainly the nervous and cardiovascular systems) initiate and sustain response to stress. Therefore, physiological measures affected by stress response best represent allostatic load. These measures have been categorized as the metabolic syndrome group and the neuroendocrine group. The *metabolic syndrome* group includes risk factors for poor late-life outcomes related to elevated allostatic load such as cardiovascular disease, type 2 diabetes, and cognitive dysfunction. They include systolic and diastolic blood pressure, resting heart rate, hip–waist ratio (thought to be influenced by glucocorticoid activity), blood plasma levels of glycosylated hemoglobin (an indicator of glucose metabolism), and ratio of total cholesterol to high-density lipoprotein (HDL) serum cholesterol. The *neuroendocrine* group reflects general regulatory processes and includes urinary cortisol excretion (an indicator of HPA axis activity), serum dihydroepiandrosterone sulfate (DHEA-S, a functional HPA axis antagonist), urinary norepinephrine and epinephrine excretion levels (indicators of sympathetic nervous system activity), and cytokine interleukin-6 (an indicator of inflammation and immune system function).

The predictors of allostatic load tested in research so far include socioeconomic status, social relationships, and age. Allostatic load may contribute to socioeconomic differentials in health. Individuals from low (vs. middle or upper) socioeconomic backgrounds are more likely to experience high levels of stress and to have fewer resources with which to cope, leading to more physiological wear and tear and to poorer health outcomes. Research suggests that allostatic load is higher among those with fewer years of education and that this difference may contribute to higher mortality among this group.

Social relationships also seem to play an important role in allostatic load and its outcomes, although the influence of social factors varies by age and sex. Younger men and women with positive relationship experiences appear to have lower average levels of allostatic load. High levels of social integration and frequent emotional support are associated with lower levels of allostatic load among older men, and the quality of social contact has not been found to affect allostatic load among older women. Finally, allostatic load has been found to increase with age between 20 and 60 years of age. It seems to level off during older adulthood, possibly due to selective mortality in those with already high levels of allostatic load.

Genes and early development, as well as lifestyle choices such as diet, exercise, smoking, and excessive alcohol consumption, may contribute to allostatic load. So far, however, empirical substantiation that these factors predict physiological outcomes associated with allostatic load is not available.

Finally, individual-level factors, such as coping skills and cognitive interpretation of stressful events, await empirical exploration as predictors of allostatic load. Individual differences in the pattern of stress response appear to be relatively stable, and this may lead to substantial variations in stress-related wear and tear within body systems over time. Future research should examine whether individual differences in response to stress may alter the association between established risk factors for allostatic load such as socioeconomic status and negative social relationships.

—*Ross Andel and Dawn Alley*

See also Biological Theories of Aging; MacArthur Study of
    Successful Aging

Further Readings and References

Crimmins E, Johnston M, Hayward M. Age differences in
    allostatic load: An index of physiological dysregulation.
    Exp Gerontol. 2003;38:731–734.

Glazer R. Stress-associated immune dysregulation and its importance for human health: A personal history of psychoneuroimmunology. *Brain Behav Immunity.* 2005;19:3–11.

Seeman TE, Crimmins E, Huang M-H. Cumulative biological risk and socio-economic differences in mortality: MacArthur Studies of Successful Aging. *Social Sci Med.* 2004;58:1986–1997.

Seeman TE, Singer BH, Rowe JW. Price of adaptation: Allostatic load and its health consequences. *Arch Int Med.* 1997;157:2259–2268.

ALTERNATIVE MEDICINE

See COMPLEMENTARY AND ALTERNATIVE MEDICINE

ALZHEIMER'S DISEASE

Alzheimer's disease (AD) is a concept in evolution; it is considered by most to be a degenerative brain disease that was first described in 1906 and is the most common cause of dementia. Over the past 100 years, we have learned that many biological and clinical phenomena are included under the rubric of Alzheimer's disease and that perhaps the term can best be considered a two-word eponym that reveals as much about our ignorance as about our knowledge.

AD is characterized clinically by the insidious onset of cognitive difficulties, most commonly in memory and attention, that subsequently progress to involve language, perception, praxis, and (frequently) behavioral and psychological symptoms. Neuropathologically, the condition is characterized by progressive loss of neurons in association with neurofibrillary tangles and senile plaques. The cause of AD is unknown, although a variety of genetic mutations can cause early onset of AD and genetic susceptibility factors that modify late-onset disease have been identified. Much attention has focused on early recognition of AD, and a variety of labels, such as the controversial concept of mild cognitive impairment (MCI), have been used to label people who have mild intellectual difficulty. However, these terms are used primarily in research and should not be used clinically.

AD is said to be the most common dementia worldwide, followed by vascular dementia and a variety of other neurodegenerative diseases such as Lewy body dementia and frontal lobe dementia. However, precise figures for incidence and prevalence are difficult to determine globally because of the differences in diagnostic criteria and assessment methodologies used in different countries.

Pathology

Alois Alzheimer described the combination of neurofibrillary tangles and senile plaques that are still used today to diagnose AD. Neuritic plaques are accumulations of proteins, including amyloid and others, surrounded by damaged nerve cell processes. Whereas the plaque is located extracellularly, the neurofibrillary tangle is found inside cells and is composed of tau protein as well as other associated proteins. The precise mechanisms whereby these pathological features and others cause cell death are unclear. Cell death occurs in the cortex, hippocampus, and a variety of subcortical structures such as the cholinergic basal forebrain, noradrenergic locus ceruleus, and serotonergic raphe nuclei etiology.

Genetics and Causes of Dementia

Familial AD has been described for more than 50 years. The association of plaques and tangles developing late in life in individuals with trisomy 21 or Down syndrome implicated this chromosome in the genetics of early-onset autosomal dominant disease. Numerous mutations have been described in chromosome 21 as well as in chromosomes 1 and 14, all of which appear to alter amyloid processing. Although a variety of claims have been made for other susceptibility loci, the only well-confirmed risk factor for late-onset disease is apolipoprotein ε4, produced by a gene on chromosome 19. Apolipoprotein ε is a cholesterol transport protein that exists in three forms: 2, 3, and 4. Individuals who have one or two copies of the apolipoprotein ε4 form are more at risk for AD and some other diseases. The relationships between these genetic abnormalities and other pathological processes in AD are unclear. Most of the focus has been on the potential damaging role of amyloid. However, cells may die because of inflammatory processes or other mechanisms such as excess excitation due to neurotransmitters (e.g., glutamate). The major risk factor for AD is age, and the relationship between normal aging changes in the brain and AD is controversial. Despite decades of intensive research, there are no biological markers that can clearly differentiate AD from normal aging.

Diagnosis

AD is a diagnosis of exclusion. In other words, when the typical pattern of insidious onset and slow progression of intellectual difficulties is identified, the clinician should try to determine a specific cause of this deterioration. A combination of blood tests to identify potentially reversible metabolic forms of dementia, such as hypothyroidism, should be conducted. Moreover, a CAT scan or some other brain imaging technology should be performed at least once during the course of the illness to make sure that structural lesions, such as tumors, blood clots, and/or strokes, are not the cause of the dementia. The most difficult differential diagnostic issues are associated with those conditions that do not have clear biological footprints. Hence, the differential diagnosis to separate normal aging, AD, and depression is often challenging. Acute confusional states or delirium can occur in AD but also need to be differentiated from chronic progressive dementias as a cause of cognitive impairment.

Treatment

Dementias such as AD should be treated with a combination of pharmacological and nonpharmacological approaches with the overarching goals of improving the quality of life for both the patient and the caregiver.

Pharmacological Treatments

Five drugs have been approved in the United States for the treatment of AD. All but one of these are cholinesterase inhibitors that address the deficiency in acetylcholine associated with the loss of cells in the cholinergic basal forebrain. Donepezil is the most commonly used cholinesterase inhibitor, followed by galantamine and rivastigmine. All of these drugs can affect other cholinergic systems in the body, causing gastrointestinal upset, such as nausea and diarrhea, or muscle cramps. Rivastigmine has more side effects than do the other two drugs. The cognitive benefits of these drugs are minimal, and little data support their effectiveness (e.g., impact on quality of life) in clinical practice. The last drug approved for the treatment of AD is memantine, a glutamate receptor antagonist. This different mechanism of action creates a different side effect profile, including relatively infrequent constipation, dizziness, and confusion. This drug has efficacy similar to that of the cholinesterase inhibitors.

A variety of approaches have been used to develop treatments to actually slow the biological progression of the disease. Basic biological research and epidemiological studies suggest that antioxidants, anti-inflammatory agents, or estrogen replacement therapy might be expected to work to slow progression, but randomized controls have not supported this.

It is important to recognize that behavioral symptoms such as depression, agitation, and psychosis can occur and that commonly used antidepressants and antipsychotics may be helpful. However, the evidence for their effectiveness is not great, and there are potential side effects, including death.

Psychosocial Treatments

Patient and caregiver education is essential, and referral to the Alzheimer's Association is often helpful. Patients should be encouraged to keep physically and mentally active. Early financial and legal planning should be recommended. Community resources should be explored prior to being needed. Hospice services are often helpful at end of life. Developing a life plan that incorporates realistic goals and purposes in life will likely help maintain, if not improve, quality of life.

Future Directions

AD is a heterogeneous concept with many poorly understood biological, clinical, and cultural aspects. Despite much recent work on the genetics and neuroimaging, our understanding of considerable variability of AD is rudimentary. Also, it is becoming increasingly difficult to clearly differentiate AD from other conditions such as Parkinson's disease and vascular and frontal dementias. This is likely due to the fact that aging affects many biological systems and that patients actually suffer many overlapping age-related pathologies. Despite the efforts to develop more precise diagnostic tests, AD will likely remain a social marker, which is a label that is applied clinically. Unrealistic enthusiasm for finding cures for AD leads to excessive expectations from approaches such as vaccines and stem cells. This hype runs the risk of creating false hopes based on a faith in science that borders on scientism.

AD raises a variety of ethical issues, including those relating to participation in research such as appropriate mechanisms for informed consent and the use of placebo in drug trials. Moreover, end of life care for people with dementia needs considerable improvement. The medical profession needs to be cautious about conflicts of interest in its relationship with the pharmaceutical industry.

There is no doubt that age-related cognitive impairment can create tremendous suffering and that the number of affected people will grow as the world ages. We need to evaluate more carefully how we can improve quality of life of elders with dementia in the context of the many other problems that the world is facing, including the health challenges of children.

—*Peter J. Whitehouse*

See also Consortium to Establish a Registry for Alzheimer's Disease; Delirium and Confusional States; Lewy Body Dementia; Memory; Mental Status Assessment; Mild Cognitive Impairment; Pseudodementia

Further Readings and References

Clark CM, Karlawish JH. Alzheimer disease: Current concepts and emerging diagnostic and therapeutic strategies. *Ann Intern Med.* 2004;140:71.

Cummings JL. Alzheimer's disease. *N Engl J Med.* 2004;351:56–67.

Whitehouse PJ, Juengst ET. Anti-aging medicine and mild cognitive impairment: Practice and policy issues for geriatrics. *J Am Geriatr Soc.* 2005;53:1417–1422.

Whitehouse PJ, Maurer K, Ballenger J, eds. *Concepts of Alzheimer Disease: Biological, Clinical, and Cultural Perspectives.* Baltimore, Md: Johns Hopkins University Press; 2000.

AMBULATION

See MOBILITY

ANABOLIC THERAPIES

Involuntary weight loss is the result of many chronic progressive diseases, often leading to diminished lean body mass, frailty, susceptibility to illness, and increased mortality. Various anabolic agents have been used to combat weight loss with mixed results. Similar to the frustration experienced by advocates of weight loss in the obese, none of the pharmacological appetite stimulants available at the current time have been uniformly successful in combating involuntary weight loss in the elderly population. Some of these agents have been U.S. Food and Drug Administration (FDA) approved to combat weight loss, and others are used off-label for this purpose.

Androgens

Serum testosterone levels decline with advancing age; however, the benefits of increasing serum levels by androgen supplementation are controversial. Testosterone has been shown to increase muscle mass in older men, but adverse effects on the prostate are greater and hematocrit levels are higher than in younger individuals. Oxandrolone is a chemical derivative of testosterone that increases muscle mass but has decreased toxicity. In the elderly, oxandrolone administered daily for 3-month intervals over a year resulted in improved appetite and mental improvement. More recently, the metabolic effects of oxandrolone were thoroughly evaluated in healthy, overweight elderly men. Highly significant reductions in abdominal fat were noted, and insulin sensitivity was improved. Positive effects were most pronounced in men with low testosterone levels, and the benefits were sustained for at least 12 weeks after discontinuation of therapy. Taken together, these preliminary studies suggest that oxandrolone significantly increases lean body mass and reduces body fat in healthy elderly men.

Dronabinol (tetrahydrocannabinol)

Dronabinol, the active ingredient in marijuana, has been used as an antiemetic and appetite stimulant primarily in cancer and AIDS patients with mixed results. Little is known about the use of dronabinol in the elderly. Dronabinol, megestrol acetate (MA), and a combination of the two were compared in a randomized study of 469 cancer patients with a mean age of approximately 65 years. MA was superior to dronabinol in terms of appetite (75% vs. 49%) and in the number of participants who gained more than 10% of their body weight (11% vs. 3%). Combination therapy showed no advantage over MA alone. However, in one intriguing study of 15 Alzheimer's disease patients hospitalized on a dementia study unit, dronabinol increased body weight and improved resident behavior. No serious adverse reactions were noted. Taken together, these studies indicate that dronabinol is a weak orexigenic (appetite-stimulating) agent and is less potent than MA. There may be a role for its use in treating patients with dementia, but convincing evidence is lacking at the current time.

Megestrol acetate

A review of 26 studies involving MA was published recently. The vast majority of these studies involved cancer (86%) and AIDS (11%) patients. MA increased appetite, led to weight gain, and improved quality of life. In the elderly, MA also has been shown to increase appetite and well-being. MA is well tolerated, although it is associated with an increased incidence of blood clots in the legs. MA also has been shown to cause muscle wasting and suppression of the adrenal glands.

Mirtazapine

Mirtazapine is a noradrenergic and specific serotonergic antidepressant that has been shown to be as effective as trazadone and tricyclics and to be more effective than fluoxetine and paroxetine in moderate to severe depression. A randomized study of 297 severely depressed middle-aged adults showed an increase of 0.8 kilograms with mirtazapine, compared with a loss of 0.4 kilograms in the placebo group. In a study of 25 nursing home residents with major depression treated with mirtazapine, the mean gain in weight was 2.5 pounds, but 25% gained more than 5 pounds. Interestingly, in the same study, 25 residents treated with sertraline showed nearly identical results, suggesting that the weight gain with mirtazapine may be either secondary to treating the underlying depression or (less likely) a generalized attribute of several of the newer antidepressants.

Growth hormone

Growth hormone (GH) has been proposed as a treatment of healthy elderly individuals with the hope of "reversing" the aging process. Virtually 100% of older people have reduced levels of GH in their blood, but whether it is beneficial to reverse this decline in healthy elderly by GH administration is highly controversial. In 1990, GH was given three times weekly for 6 months and produced a highly significant 8.8% increase in lean body mass and a 14.4% decrease in fat mass compared with controls. However, it was noted soon thereafter that a 6-month treatment course using similar doses of GH was associated with a high rate of side effects and that 18 of 62 participants withdrew because of swollen breasts, elevated sugar levels, or carpal tunnel syndrome (numb fingers due to pinched nerve at the wrist). Lean body mass increased and fat mass decreased; however, there was no difference in strength or functional ability between the groups. Side effects were very common in the GH group, and dose reduction was required in nearly one fourth of the treated group. A recent study of healthy elderly men showed that resistance training, but not GH, resulted in increased muscle strength and power.

These studies indicate that 6 months of GH therapy for healthy elderly individuals results in improved lean body mass and decreased fat free mass; however, functional ability does not appear to be improved, and GH treatment is associated with an unacceptably high side effect profile.

Discussion

It is difficult to make recommendations for the proper use of appetite stimulants in the elderly given the paucity of data available for most orexigenic agents. However, the use of any appetite stimulant should be looked on as a trial, and if there is no response within 4 to 6 weeks, the agent should be discontinued. In terms of specific recommendations, with the high prevalence of depression in nursing home residents, mirtazapine should be used as a first-line agent for weight loss. Other antidepressants may have equal efficacy, but what little data are available involve primarily mirtazapine. A reasonable second-line agent would be MA. It is the most studied of any of the appetite stimulants and is safe for the most part. There are little data to support the use of oxandrolone and dronabinol in nursing home residents. However, recent positive data concerning the metabolic effects of oxandrolone in healthy elderly men are intriguing, and a trial in male residents who fail mirtazapine and MA may be warranted. Dronabinol is expensive and is the least studied of the appetite stimulants. It may be useful for agitated patients with dementia, but there are other less expensive agents available with similar efficacy.

In summary, despite intense efforts to combat cachexia and weight loss in the elderly, there is no evidence that pharmacological intervention has had a significant impact on mortality. Most orexigenic agents are modestly effective in preventing or reversing weight loss, and the response is not universal, being restricted to subpopulations of patients. Clearly, more research needs to be done to better evaluate appetite stimulants in this patient population.

—Donald Bodenner

See also Body Composition; Body Mass Index; Sarcopenia

Further Readings and References

Goldberg RJ. Weight change in depressed nursing home patients on mirtazapine. *J Am Geriatr Soc.* 2002;50:1461.

Jatoi A, Windschitl HE, Loprinzi CL, et al. Dronabinol versus megestrol acetate versus combination therapy for cancer-associated anorexia: A North Central Cancer Treatment Group study. *J Clin Oncol.* 2002;20:567–573.

Pascual Lopez A, Roque I, Figuls M, et al. Systematic review of megestrol acetate in the treatment of anorexia-cachexia syndrome. *J Pain Symptom Mgmt.* 2004;27:360–369.

Rudman D, Feller AG, Nagraj HS, et al. Effects of human growth hormone in men over 60 years old. *N Engl J Med.* 1990;323:1–6.

Schroeder ET, Zheng L, Ong MD, et al. Effects of androgen therapy on adipose tissue and metabolism in older men. *J Clin Endocrinol Metab.* 2004;89:4863–4872.

Versiani M, Moreno R, Ramakers-van Moorsel CJ, et al. Comparison of the effects of mirtazapine and fluoxetine in severely depressed patients. *CNS Drugs.* 2005;19:137–146.

Volicer L, Stelly M, Morris J, et al. Effects of dronabinol on anorexia and disturbed behavior in patients with Alzheimer's disease. *Intl J Geriatr Psychiatry.* 1997;12:913–919.

ANEMIA

Anemia is the most frequently encountered hematological problem in geriatric practice and is associated with increased risk of functional decline, cognitive impairment, and death. Anemia is defined as a suboptimal concentration of red cells (erythrocytes) in the blood, usually measured by a decrease in the amount of hemoglobin. Hemoglobin forms the red pigment in red blood cells (RBCs) that transport oxygen from the lungs to different tissues and organs of the body. The RBCs are produced by stem cells in the bone marrow under the influence of erythropoietin (EPO), a hormone secreted by the kidneys. The World Health Organization (WHO) defines anemia as a hemoglobin concentration lower than 13 grams per deciliter in men and lower than 12 grams per deciliter in women.

According to the WHO criteria, the prevalence of anemia in the general population is approximately 1% to 2%; it is estimated to be four to six times higher among men and women over 65 years of age, and it is approximately 20% among people over 85 years of age. Incidence of anemia appears to be higher among men than among women in every age group over 65 years. Potential causes for anemia include blood loss, nutritional deficiency (Vitamin B12, iron, and folate deficiencies), and inflammation secondary to disease processes (e.g., cancer, renal failure, chronic infections) and concomitant medications. However, despite an exhaustive workup, the etiology of anemia remains unclear in approximately 25% of elderly patients. In this group, it is postulated that anemia may be a consequence of a stem cell defect, possibly related to the aging process.

Anemia is more prevalent among those of lower socioeconomic status where nutritional deficiencies are a factor, implying that nutritional supplements may reverse anemia in elderly populations. Unfortunately, this is not always the case; one study that provided dietary supplements to achieve weight gain among underweight elderly found that despite a positive impact on nutritional status and desired weight gain, anemia was not improved.

In the absence of iron, folate, or Vitamin B12 deficiency, it is reasonable to pursue the hypothesis that hemoglobin production is compromised by molecular mechanisms secondary to chronic disease and/or inflammation. New insights into the mechanisms of iron metabolism and hemoglobin production suggest that anemia of chronic inflammation (ACI) and anemia of chronic disease (ACD) have the same pathophysiology. Thus, the peptide hormone hepcidin, the dominant inhibitor of dietary iron absorption, is decreased by anemia and hypoxia to promote hemoglobin production. However, infection and inflammatory cytokines such as interleukin 6 (IL-6) up-regulate hepcidin, decreasing circulating iron. Thus, treating the underlying disease may reverse ACD.

The use of recombinant erythropoietic agents (i.e., EPO) is now routine in cancer patients on myelosuppressive chemotherapy as well as in patients with renal failure. The role of EPO is also being investigated in ACD. EPO is a peptide hormone produced by the kidneys via an oxygen sensor to stimulate red blood cell production. There may also be a role for EPO in the clinical treatment of unexplained anemia among the elderly, but currently there are no data to support this practice.

—*Gurkamal Chatta*

See also Cardiovascular System; Kidney Aging and Diseases

Further Readings and References

Ania BJ, Suman VJ, Faribanks VF, et al. Incidence of anemia in older people: An epidemiologic study in a well defined population. *J Am Geriatr Soc.* 1997; 45:825–831.

Carmel R. Anemia and aging: An overview of clinical, diagnostic, and biological issues. *Blood Rev.* 2001;15: 9–18.

Chatta GS, Lipschitz DA. Aging and hematopoiesis. In: Hazzard WR, Blass JP, Ettinger WH Jr, Halter JB, Ouslander JG, eds. *Principles of Geriatric Medicine and Gerontology.* 5th ed. New York: McGraw-Hill; 2003: 763–770.

Clark R, Grimley Evans J, Schneede J, et al. Vitamin B12 and folate deficiency in later life. *Age Ageing.* 2004;33: 34–41.

ANEURYSMS

An aneurysm is a weakened area of a blood vessel that results in a ballooning or bulging outward of the vessel wall. Aneurysms occur primarily in arteries and can be found anywhere in the body. Common sites for aneurysm formation include the brain (cerebral aneurysm) and the main blood vessel supplying the body (thoracic aortic aneurysm in the chest and abdominal aortic aneurysm below the stomach). Aneurysms can be fusiform or saccular in shape. Although some are asymptomatic, rupture of an aneurysm can be a life-threatening emergency. Approximately 200,000 abdominal aortic aneurysms are diagnosed in the United States each year. The prevalence of cerebral aneurysms is approximately 5% in the U.S. population. Both cerebral and aortic aneurysms are more common in older adults.

Aneurysms are caused by weakening of the wall of the blood vessel. Risk factors include atherosclerosis (a buildup of plaque within walls of blood vessels), high blood pressure, smoking, and infection of the blood vessel. Aneurysms may also be congenital or related to an inheritable disease such as Marfan's syndrome, fibromuscular dysplasia, or polycystic kidney disease. Symptoms vary according to the location of the aneurysm and whether the aneurysm is growing in size. Small stable aneurysms might not cause any symptoms. Back pain between the shoulder blades is the most common symptom of a thoracic aneurysm. The pain can be quite severe and sudden in onset when associated with rupture or dissection of the aneurysm. Abdominal aortic aneurysms may cause abdominal pain or early satiety (a sensation of fullness after eating only a small amount of food). Cerebral aneurysms may cause localized headaches, double vision, or pain in the face or neck. Light sensitivity, stiff neck, and nausea can occur when a cerebral aneurysm ruptures. A ruptured cerebral aneurysm results in a subarachnoid hemorrhage (bleeding inside the lining of the brain), which has a very high 1-month mortality rate of approximately 50%.

Many aneurysms are discovered during the workup of another problem. Aneurysms may also be detected on physical examination. For example, an abdominal aortic aneurysm may present as a midline pulsatile mass or as a bruit (turbulent blood flow within the aneurysm). Imaging tests such as ultrasounds, computed tomography scans, angiography, and magnetic resonance imaging can be employed to detect the location of an aneurysm and determine its size. Treatment depends on size and location. Thoracic aortic aneurysms are usually surgically repaired when detected. However, small abdominal aortic aneurysms (< 5 centimeters) may be managed with serial imaging tests to monitor for growth because there is a low incidence of rupture. Rapidly growing aneurysms (those > 5 centimeters in diameter) are treated either with an endovascular stent or by open surgical repair. In the endovascular stent procedure, a catheter is inserted into the blood vessel to deploy a wire sheath or stent within the walls of the aneurysm to relieve stress and decrease risk of rupture. Open surgical repair of an aortic aneurysm is usually performed by bypassing the aneurysm with a synthetic tube graft. Cerebral aneurysms, particularly those larger than 10 millimeters, are treated either by clipping the aneurysm or by inserting a coil into the aneurysm (coil embolization), promoting eventual obliteration of the aneurysm. This is less invasive, and initial studies suggest fewer adverse outcomes during the first year compared with surgery. Medications to lower blood pressure are also commonly used for all types of aneurysms.

—*Laurie Lavery*

See also Cardiovascular System; Smoking; Stroke

Further Readings and References

Ailawadi G, Eliason JL, Upchurch GR, Jr. Current concepts in the pathogenesis of abdominal aortic aneurysm. *J Vasc Surg.* 2003;38:584–588.

Brown PM, Pattenden R, Vernooy C. Selective management of abdominal aortic aneurysms in a prospective measurement program. *J Vasc Surg.* 1996;23:213–220.

Molyneux A, Kerr R, Stratton I, et al. International Subarachnoid Aneurysm Trial (ISAT) of neurosurgical clipping versus endovascular coiling in 2,143 patients with ruptured intracranial aneurysms: A randomised trial. *Lancet.* 2002;360:1267–1274.

ANTI-AGING INTERVENTIONS

What is an anti-aging intervention? This is a particularly important question today given the presence of a large and growing industry of entrepreneurs who are selling to the public the age-old idea that anti-aging interventions already exist and that much longer lives can be achieved by people who are currently alive. The idea that the aging of people is subject to modification, dramatic life extension is possible, and physical immortality is within our grasp dates back thousands of years. The ancient Hindus sought immortality, Alexander the Great roamed the world searching for it, the Greek physician Galen (2nd century AD) and the Arabic philosopher/physician Avicenna (11th century AD) believed in it, alchemists achieved positions of prominence pursuing it, Ponce de Leon discovered Florida in his quest for the "fountain of youth," and countless stories of immortality have permeated the literature. Is there truth to any of the claims that anti-aging interventions exist today? It all depends on how one defines an anti-aging intervention.

Anti-Aging: The Practitioner's View

For trained physicians, aging is often defined by the age-related diseases and disorders people experience as they grow older. In fact, aging is often portrayed as a disease that is amenable to treatment, just like any other disease that physicians are trained to diagnose and treat. This is not an unexpected view of aging given the Western disease-oriented model of medical education. Examples of the conditions that anti-aging practitioners endeavor to treat or postpone include cardiovascular disease, cancer, sensory impairments, muscle and bone loss, loss of skin elasticity, and decline in sexual function. By postponing or reducing the onset, risk, or severity of these diseases and disorders through a combination of diet, exercise, nutritional supplements, and hormone replacement, some clinicians in the anti-aging industry claim that they have stopped and even reversed aging in their patients. The treatments for these conditions, which are often preceded by a battery of tests intended to measure biological age, are then referred to as anti-aging medicine.

At one level, it is difficult to argue with the belief that aging has been modulated through this combination of tests and interventions given that many of the

patients who make these changes in their lives often claim that they feel better. Indeed, reducing the risk of death—through early detection, careful monitoring through annual physicals, and behavior modification—has been possible for centuries. Ironically, science in a way supports the view that aging is a disease and that anti-aging interventions exist by suggesting that because an aging or death program cannot be built into our genes as a product of evolution, a biological loophole allows what we see and feel as "aging" to be inherently modifiable by our own actions. Thus, by lowering the risk of cardiovascular disease through preventive maintenance or by using pharmaceuticals, it may seem like aging has been delayed; the use of facial creams that reduce the appearance of wrinkled skin would appear to reverse aging; and interventions that increase muscle mass, reduce body fat, improve or restore sexual function, and increase bone density might appear to some as if the proverbial fountain of youth had been discovered.

The patients undergoing these anti-aging treatments may ask what difference it makes whether they are actually growing younger, reversing the biological process of aging, or living longer? If they feel better, what else matters? This may very well be the rationale that underlies much of the anti-aging industry today. Indeed, the difference between feeling better and modulating the biological process of aging accompanied by documented life extension is the foundational difference between the scientist's and practitioner's views of an anti-aging intervention.

Anti-Aging: The Scientist's View

Scientists who study the biology of aging view it as a process of accumulated damage to the building blocks of life (e.g., proteins, fats, carbohydrates, DNA) that begins early in life, eventually leading to the malfunction and/or dysregulation of the components of cells and the tissues and organs they form, and ultimately leading to the death of the whole animal. From this perspective, aging makes humans and other animals more susceptible to disease, but aging itself is not a disease. Indeed, the diseases and disorders that appear throughout life are thought of by scientists as by-products of aging but not as aging itself.

To the scientist who studies aging, referring to aging as a disease is akin to claiming that a fever resulting from an infection is a disease. Treating a fever may make a patient feel better, but its underlying cause remains both present and unchanged. Therefore, reductions in the risk of death from fatal and nonfatal age-related conditions, improvements in muscle mass and bone density, and other measurable improvements in the human body (now possible through behavior modification and medical intervention) do not represent modifications of the underlying aging processes that give rise to these diseases and disorders.

Subjective statements that a patient feels better following an anti-aging intervention are insufficient proof that aging has been altered. The battery of tests portrayed as biomarkers of aging may be reliable measures of change in specific physiological attributes of an individual, but there is no scientific support for the claim that aging itself is being measured. In fact, efforts to measure these time-dependent changes in a way that enables one to assess biological age or the effect of an intervention reliably have failed. Improving biomarkers in an individual, such as increased glucose tolerance and reductions in cholesterol. may reduce the risk of certain diseases, but this is insufficient proof that aging has been altered. Postponing heart disease and cancer through careful monitoring may reduce the risk of death and extend life, but even this is insufficient proof that aging has been altered. Science requires empirical evidence that aging can be measured and modified, and this can occur only if the biological process of aging itself is operationally defined and subject to measurement. Currently, neither has been accomplished.

From a scientific perspective, a genuine anti-aging intervention would need to reduce the rate and/or amount of accumulated damage that contributes to aging and to extend life. To date, no intervention has been scientifically demonstrated to have both of these properties. This is the case not because it has not necessarily been accomplished but rather because it is not currently possible to measure aging so that scientists know with certainty that experimentally induced life extension is occurring because of changes in disease pathology or because of a modification to aging itself. Distinguishing between the biological factors that contribute to aging and those that contribute to pathology and disease is critical to understanding why some proponents of anti-aging medicine mistake preventive medicine for delayed aging.

The Future

Whether it is possible to develop interventions that can be proven to influence the biological process of aging in humans or other animals has yet to be determined. What is known with certainty is that scientists can demonstrate and empirically verify that the duration of life of a number of species can be extended experimentally in the laboratory. Although some think that such life extension is a result of decelerated aging, this claim cannot as yet be verified because of the difficulty in distinguishing between effects on disease pathology and effects on biological aging.

The future of biogerontology and the scientific pursuit of interventions that may decelerate the process of aging are both promising and exciting. Various summaries of the literature in this area have documented significant progress in identifying some of the genetic and physiological pathways that influence duration of life. There is reason to be optimistic that research advances in this area will continue, and there is ample justification for continuing the pursuit of interventions that will decelerate the process of aging in humans and other species.

—*S. Jay Olshansky*

See also Biological Theories of Aging; Biomarkers of Aging

Further Readings and References

Butler RN, Sprott R, Warner H, et al. Biomarkers of aging: From primitive organisms to humans. *J Gerontol A Biol Sci Med Sci.* 2004;59:560–567.

General Accounting Office. *Anti-Aging Products Pose Potential for Physical and Economic Harm.* Washington, DC: GAO. Available at: www.gao.gov/new.items/d011129.pdf. Accessed September 6, 2006. Special Committee on Aging, Publication No. GAO-01–1129.

Olshansky SJ, Carnes BA. *The Quest for Immortality: Science at the Frontiers of Aging.* New York: Norton; 2001.

Olshansky SJ, Hayflick L, Carnes BA, et al. The truth about human aging. *Sci Am.* 2002;(June). Available at: www.sciam.com/agingstatement.cfm. Accessed September 6, 2006. Also published in *J Gerontol A Biol Sci Med Sci.* 2002;57:B1–B6.

ANXIETY DISORDERS

Anxiety is an emotional and physiological reaction to distress—either real, imagined, or unknown. It is a "normal" emotion; having some anxiety allows people to prioritize needs, develop ambition, improve focus, and seek social interactions. But when anxiety is excessive, it can become distracting or overwhelming. When anxiety causes a sustained impairment, it is called an anxiety disorder.

Epidemiology

The most extensive estimate of anxiety disorders in the elderly is from the Epidemiologic Catchment Area (ECA) studies conducted during the early 1980s. The combined prevalence of phobia, panic disorder, and obsessive–compulsive disorder (the only anxiety disorders measured at all five sites) in people over 65 years of age was 5.5%. Although anxiety disorders were the most common psychiatric condition in the elderly (a finding consistent with that of all age populations sampled), the prevalence was much less than that experienced by the middle-aged group. Still, the numbers of elderly with anxiety disorders are significant, especially for women over 65 years of age, for whom the prevalence of any anxiety disorder (6.8%) was higher than that for men at any age.

Types of Anxiety Disorders

Currently, there are 12 different anxiety disorders identified, and they are explored in the following subsections.

Specific Phobia

Specific phobias are excessive and persistent fears toward an object or a situation. Although these are the most common anxiety disorder, they are the least likely to be treated because people with a specific phobia simply tend to avoid situations that activate that specific fear. Specific phobias fall into four categories: fear of animals (e.g., dogs, snakes), fear of natural events (e.g., storms, heights, water), fear of blood–injection–injury (e.g., seeing blood, experiencing an injury, receiving medication by injection), and fear of situations (e.g., driving, flying, bridges, enclosed spaces). Fears of animals and natural events are common during childhood and usually diminish with age. Fears of blood or injections are frequently found clustered in families. Persons with these fears may get lightheaded or dizzy at the sight of blood or at a doctor's office or hospital. Situational phobias are closely related to panic disorder and often persist into old age.

Generalized Anxiety Disorder

Generalized anxiety disorder (GAD) is excessive anxiety or worry that continues for at least 6 months. In the elderly, GAD is the second most common anxiety disorder (after phobias) with a prevalence of approximately 2% to 3%. Common themes of anxiety include worry over one's job, finances, health, or injury to loved ones. Associated symptoms include restlessness, poor energy, difficulty in concentrating, irritability, muscle tension, and disturbed sleep. A person with GAD recognizes that his or her anxiety is excessive but has difficulty in controlling worry. In fact, the anxiety may actually exceed the impact that the feared event might have.

Panic Disorder

A panic attack is an episode of intense anxiety accompanied by physical symptoms. These symptoms may include palpitations, pounding heart, sweating, tremors, shortness of breath, choking sensations, chest pain, nausea, lightheadedness, chills, and numbness and tingling in the hands and feet. The attack usually intensifies over a 5- to 10-minute period and may last anywhere from 5 to 30 minutes.

During an attack, elderly individuals may complain that they feel as if they are having a heart attack or stroke, that they are "going crazy," or that they are going to die. When panic attacks recur and become the focus of an individual's fear, the condition is called a panic disorder.

Panic attacks can be caused by many different things. Certain medications (e.g., caffeine, some cold medications) and medical conditions (e.g., hyperthyroidism) may cause panic attacks. Panic attacks may also be associated with many of the other anxiety disorders. Development of panic disorder in late life is relatively uncommon. Most typical is for patients to develop panic disorders earlier in life with waxing and waning symptoms over time. The prevalence of panic disorder in the elderly is relatively low at 0.3% to 0.4%.

Often, persons with panic attacks develop a strong desire to flee (the fight-or-flight response). When this leads to a pattern of avoiding places where the attacks have occurred or might occur, it is called agoraphobia. Thus, patients may be diagnosed as having panic disorder *with* or *without* agoraphobia.

Agoraphobia Without History of Panic Disorder

Some patients may become anxious or fear being embarrassed and begin to avoid places from which escape may be difficult, even though the anxiety does not lead to recurrent panic attacks. This is called agoraphobia without a history of panic disorder. For the elderly, anxiety symptoms may include fear of losing bladder or bowel control or fear of fainting/falling and being unable to get up. The result is that an individual will avoid leaving home so as to escape potential embarrassment. Some elderly do indeed have legitimate concerns that their physical problems have the potential for embarrassment or need for assistance. Thus, the diagnosis of agoraphobia should be made only when the fear or avoidance is clearly in excess of what is usually associated with that medical condition.

Social Phobia

Social phobia is excessive anxiety in social or performance situations. Examples include public speaking, eating in public, using public restrooms, going to parties, and talking with authority figures. In the elderly, this may be seen in avoidance of eating, drinking, or writing in public because of fears that others will notice their hands shaking due to tremor. Social phobia tends be lifelong, but the severity may fluctuate.

Obsessive–Compulsive Disorder

Obsessions are persistent thoughts or impulses that a person experiences as intrusive. The person feels unable to stop the thought from recurring. The most common obsessions are about contamination, doubting, ordering, aggression, and sexual imagery. Attempting to ignore or suppress the obsession leads to an increase in the anxiety. Compulsions are repetitive behaviors done to reduce or prevent the obsessional anxiety. Common compulsive activities include hand washing, checking behaviors, ordering, praying, counting, and repeating words or phrases.

Obsessive–compulsive disorder (OCD) usually begins during adolescence or early adulthood with a gradual onset and then develops a waxing and waning course. The kinds of obsessions or compulsions may change over time. Approximately 15% of persons affected with OCD show a progressive worsening, whereas approximately 5% may have episodic presentations with minimal symptoms between episodes. In the elderly, reports of the prevalence of OCD have varied from 0% to 1.5%; however, a review of specialty OCD clinic populations has shown that patients over 60 years of age are not uncommon.

Posttraumatic Stress Disorder

In posttraumatic stress disorder (PTSD), an individual develops characteristic clusters of symptoms following an exposure to a traumatic event. That event may be experienced either directly (e.g., being a victim of an assault or a crime, being involved in a motor vehicle accident, being diagnosed with a life-threatening illness) or indirectly (e.g., witnessing a violent event, learning about the unexpected death of a loved one). The symptoms cluster around three types of response: reexperiencing, avoidance, and arousal. In *reexperiencing,* the person feels as if he or she is reliving the event. This may occur as recurrent and intrusive memories or dreams or as marked physical or mental distress when exposed to reminders of the trauma. In *avoidance,* the person tries to stay away from things that are associated with the trauma. This may include physical reminders (e.g., persons or places associated with the trauma), mental items (e.g., thoughts, feelings), and interactions (e.g., conversations about the trauma). The avoidance of thoughts and emotions may progress so that the person has a decreased interest in activities, feelings of being detached or numb, or a sense of a foreshortened future. In *arousal,* the patient feels "activated" so that he or she is hypervigilant or has difficulty in falling asleep, decreased concentration, exaggerated startled response, or episodes of irritability or anger outbursts.

PTSD may occur at any age. Symptoms usually develop soon after the event (within the first 3 months); however, they may also be delayed months or years (usually diagnosed when the onset of symptoms begins more than 6 months after the trauma occurred), showing up at a later time. For 50% of people with PTSD, the symptoms usually resolve within the first 3 months, but in others, the symptoms may become chronic. The intensity and length of the symptoms is directly related to the severity of the trauma. There are no reliable data on the prevalence of PTSD in the elderly.

Acute Stress Disorder

Acute stress disorder has symptoms similar to those of PTSD except that this diagnosis is used when symptoms of anxiety, reexperiencing, avoidance, and hyperarousal occur for at least 2 days during the first month after the trauma. However, if symptoms are still significant after 4 weeks, the diagnosis of PTSD is made.

Anxiety Disorder Due to a General Medical Condition or Substance

Anxiety may also be caused by physical diseases, certain medications, or drugs. In fact, most late-onset panic attacks are actually associated with cardiovascular, gastrointestinal, or chronic pulmonary diseases. Common physical problems that may cause anxiety are cardiac arrhythmias, mitral valve prolapse, asthma, chronic obstructive pulmonary disease, hypoglycemia, and hyperthyroidism. Common medications that can cause anxiety include anticholinergic medications and steroids. Other drugs, such as caffeine, alcohol, and cocaine, may also cause anxiety.

Treatment

Effective treatments have been found for all anxiety disorders. A physician should be consulted to evaluate possible physical causes of anxiety. Treatment alternatives include medications and psychological therapies.

—*John L. Beyer*

See also Control; Disasters and Terrorism; Posttraumatic Stress Disorder; Stress

Further Readings and References

American Psychiatric Association. *Diagnostic and Statistical Manual of Mental Disorders.* 4th ed. Washington, DC: APA; 2000.

Flint AJ. Generalised anxiety disorder in elderly patients: Epidemiology, diagnosis, and treatment options. *Drugs Aging.* 2005;22:101–114.

Lang AJ, Stein MB. Anxiety disorders: How to recognize and treat the medical symptoms of emotional illness. *Geriatrics.* 2001;56(5):24–34.

Lauderdale SA, Sheikh JI. Anxiety disorders in older adults. *Clin Geriatr Med.* 2003;19:721–741.

Lenze EJ, Pollock BG, Shear MK, Mulsant BH, Bharucha A, Reynolds CF III. Treatment considerations for anxiety in the elderly. *CNS Spectr.* 2003;8(Suppl.):6–13.

Robins LN, Regier DA, eds. *Psychiatric Disorders in America: The Epidemiologic Catchment Area Study.* New York: Free Press; 1991.

Sheikh JI, Cassidy EL. Treatment of anxiety disorders in the elderly: Issues and strategies. *J Anxiety Disord.* 2000;14: 173–190.

Wetherell JL, Sorrell JT, Thorp SR, Patterson TL. Psychological interventions for late-life anxiety: A review and early lessons from the CALM study. *J Geriatr Psychiatry Neurol.* 2005;18(2):72–82.

APOLIPOPROTEIN E

Apolipoprotein E (APOE) is a plasma protein whose main functions are neuronal repair and lipid transport and metabolism. This protein is encoded by the apolipoprotein E gene (APOE), which is located on chromosome 19 and has three common alleles: ε2, ε3, and ε4. The ε3 allele is the most prevalent, with a frequency of approximately 78%, whereas the e4 allele has a frequency of 14% and the ε2 allele has a frequency of 8%. Individuals inherit one allele from each parent, so there are six possible APOE genotypes: ε2/ε2, ε2/ε3, ε2/ε4, ε3/ε3, ε3/ε4, and ε4/ε4. APOE appears to have a complex role in a number of medical conditions that increase in prevalence with age. In most of these conditions, the APOE ε4 allele appears to be associated with a poorer outcome.

Given the main function of APOE, early work on the APOE gene focused on its role in coronary heart disease. Compared with individuals with the APOE ε3/ε3 genotype, the ε4 allele is generally associated with increased risk of coronary heart disease and risk factors for the disease. In addition, using the ε3/ε3 genotype as the reference group, individuals with an ε4 allele typically have higher levels of cholesterol, whereas those with the ε2 allele have lower cholesterol levels. Furthermore, the ε4 allele is reportedly a significant risk factor for coronary atherosclerosis during early middle age, but its effect may decline during later years. Finally, long-term survival after myocardial infarction may be inversely associated with the APOE ε4 allele.

Recent interest in this gene has focused on its association with Alzheimer's disease (AD). In 1993, investigators reported an association between the APOE ε4 allele and increased risk of AD. Hundreds of studies have since confirmed and further defined this association. Findings from a meta-analysis showed that, when compared with individuals with an ε3/ε3 genotype, Caucasians homozygous for ε4 (i.e., ε4/ε4) have a 12 to 15 times higher risk of developing AD, whereas those with the ε3/ε4 genotype are roughly 3 times more likely to develop AD. Among African Americans and Hispanics, the association was still present, albeit somewhat weaker. The ε4 allele also appears to accelerate the age of onset of dementia by 5 to 15 years in a dose-dependent manner. This means that individuals with two ε4 alleles have the earliest age of onset, followed in order by those with one ε4 allele and those with no ε4 alleles. The APOE ε4 allele accounts for an estimated 50% of nonfamilial AD. However, not all individuals with an ε4 allele get AD, and many of those without an ε4 allele do get the disease. Therefore, APOE ε4 is considered a "risk gene" for AD; that is, it increases the risk of developing the disease but cannot be used to determine who will get the disease. Further complicating the picture are findings suggesting that the APOE gene may interact with environmental factors to alter risk of AD. For example, individuals with an ε4 allele and a history of head injury may be particularly vulnerable to develop AD later in life, compared with those with either the ε4 allele or head injury alone. Some findings indicate that the ε4 allele as a risk factor for AD may lose its potency by the time an individual reaches 90 years of age. These findings have led some to propose that APOE ε4 may control *when,* not *if,* an individual gets AD.

The destructive neuropathological process of AD begins decades prior to the overt cognitive impairment that is the hallmark of the disease. Given the long insidious course of the disease, researchers have attempted to identify APOE ε4–related characteristics of the preclinical stage of the disease, when intervention and treatment may be most effective. Toward this goal, they have investigated potential differences in cognition, brain morphology, and brain physiology among cognitively normal and mildly impaired individuals. A recent meta-analysis reported that cognitively intact older individuals with two ε4 alleles performed more poorly than individuals with either one ε4 allele or no ε4 alleles on measures of global cognitive functioning, episodic memory, and executive function. The effects were small and limited to a few cognitive domains. Group differences became smaller with age, again supporting the notion that the deleterious ε4 effect decreases very late in life. The longitudinal data, although more limited, suggest that older adults with one or more ε4 alleles show greater decline across multiple cognitive domains over several years when compared with those with no ε4 allele.

Several studies of brain morphology and function in middle-aged and older cognitively normal individuals also show small differences between ε4 and non-ε4 carriers. Findings from volumetric magnetic resonance imaging (MRI) studies indicate that, among cognitively intact older individuals, hippocampal size and asymmetry differ in relation to ε4 status, with the ε4 carriers exhibiting a pattern similar to that observed in AD patients. Similarly, cognitively healthy ε4 carriers were shown to have lower rates of cerebral glucose metabolism on positron emission tomography (PET) in the same brain regions as patients with AD, but the same pattern was not observed in those with no ε4 allele. Lastly, in middle-aged and older adults with mild memory complaints (but normal memory performance), functional MRI has shown that individuals with APOE ε4 alleles show a pattern of brain activation during a memory performance more similar to AD patients as compared with those with no ε4 allele. Longitudinal assessment after 2 years showed that greater baseline brain activation correlated with verbal memory decline. These results indicate that brain volume and activation patterns differ according to APOE status. This finding may eventually allow us to predict future cognitive decline and progression to dementia.

In light of the health conditions linked to APOE ε4, it is probably not surprising that this allele has also been associated with earlier mortality that may be partially explained by its association with both AD and coronary heart disease. However, regardless of the numerous medical conditions associated with APOE ε4, the presence of the e4 allele alone is not sufficient to predict who will get any given disease.

—*Brenda L. Plassman*

See also Alzheimer's Disease; Creutzfeldt–Jakob Disease; Neurobiology of Aging

Further Readings and References

Eichner JE, Dunn ST, Pereen G, Thompson DM, Stewart KE, Stroehla BC. Apolipoprotein E polymorphism and cardiovascular disease: A HuGE review. *Am J Epidemiol.* 2002;155:487–495.

Farrer LA, Cupples LA, Haines JL, et al. Effects of age, sex, and ethnicity on the association between apolipoprotein E genotype and Alzheimer disease: A meta-analysis. *JAMA.* 1997;278:1349–1356.

Lehtovirta M, Laakso MP, Frisoni GB, Soininen H. How does the apolipoprotein E genotype modulate the brain in aging and in Alzheimer's disease? A review of neuroimaging studies. *Neurobiol Aging.* 2000; 21:293–300.

Small BJ, Rosnick CB, Fratiglioni L, Backman L. Apolipoprotein E and cognitive performance: A meta-analysis. *Psychol Aging.* 2004;19:592–600.

APOPTOSIS

See BIOLOGICAL THEORIES OF AGING

ARRHYTHMIAS

Arrhythmia or dysrhythmia is an abnormal beating of the heart resulting from a disturbance in the electrical impulses controlling heart muscle contractions. Approximately 4 million Americans, most over 60 years of age, experience arrhythmias. Although there are many causes, heart disease is by far the most common. Arrhythmias can range from minimally important to life threatening; they can be asymptomatic or cause severe symptoms. Arrhythmias are characterized by the rate of heart muscle contractions (heartbeats per minute), pattern of contractions, and location of initiation of the electrical impulse for contractions. Specific arrhythmias have varying combinations of these characteristics.

Tachycardia is defined as a rapid heart rate (> 100 beats per minute [bpm]), whereas bradycardia occurs when the heart beat is too slow (< 50 bpm). The pattern of heart contractions may be regular (equal intervals between beats), irregular (variable intervals), or a combination thereof. The contraction of the upper (atria) and lower (ventricles) chambers of the heart is initiated by an electrical signal arising from the sinoatrial node, the normal pacemaker of the heart, located in the right atrium. A change in location of initiation of this signal is a cause of arrhythmia. Arrhythmias arising from a signal in the ventricle (ventricular arrhythmias) are more immediately life threatening than arrhythmias arising from a signal in the atria (atrial arrhythmias).

Causes

Smoking, emotions/stress, alcohol use, and caffeine use can cause arrhythmias by affecting the hormones and nerve impulses that regulate the sinoatrial node. In general, these arrhythmias tend not to be serious. Electrolyte imbalances, such as low levels of magnesium or potassium in the blood, can also increase the risk of an arrhythmia. Thyroid disease and certain medications, including specific antidepressants, also contribute to the occurrence of arrhythmias. However, heart disease, which includes coronary artery disease, heart attack, congestive heart failure, and heart valve disease, is the most common cause of arrhythmias. For some arrhythmias, a cause cannot be ascertained, even after extensive investigation.

Symptoms

Arrhythmias may be silent and not cause any symptoms. When symptoms do occur, the most common one is palpitations. Palpitations are described as a feeling of "skipped beats," fluttering in the chest, or the heart "flipping over." Chest pain or discomfort, dizziness, fainting, shortness of breath, and fatigue can also occur. Arrhythmias can lead to congestive heart failure, stroke, and sudden death. Approximately 15% of strokes in the United States are attributable to one type of arrhythmia, namely atrial fibrillation. Approximately 500,000 deaths per year are due to arrhythmias.

Diagnosis

Many arrhythmias are first detected by a physician during a physical exam. An electrocardiogram (ECG) provides a tracing of the electrical signal of the heart and can be used to confirm or diagnose an arrhythmia. However, arrhythmias may be intermittent or paroxysmal and not captured on an ECG. A Holter monitor records the electrical signal over a 24- to 48-hour time period, and an event monitor can be used to capture the heart rhythm over a period of days or weeks. Electrophysiology studies can help detect symptomatic but transient arrhythmias not captured by less invasive means. Diagnosis is important because untreated arrhythmias can cause ongoing damage to the heart and further increase the risk of arrhythmias, setting up a vicious downward spiral in heart function.

Specific Types of Arrhythmias

- Premature atrial contractions (PACs) are early extra beats arising in the atria. No treatment is necessary for PACs.
- Premature ventricular contractions (PVCs) are early extra beats arising from the ventricles. PVCs are very common in older adults and account for the sensation of "skipped beats." They rarely require treatment unless they are frequent and symptomatic.
- Atrial fibrillation (AF) is a common arrhythmia in older adults, especially in those with heart disease and following surgical procedures. AF has an irregular pattern and can be constant or intermittent. It is characterized by disorganized atrial signaling of the contraction, causing the atria to fibrillate or "quiver." This results in the loss of atrial contraction. Loss of atrial contraction increases the risk of clot (thrombus) formation within the atria due to blood stasis. These thrombi can then travel to the blood vessels in the brain and cause strokes. Although AF can have a normal rate, it frequently results in tachycardia. The rapid rate and loss of atrial contraction decreases the effectiveness of the heart to pump blood and can contribute to the syndrome of congestive heart failure. AF usually requires treatment to prevent symptoms, either correction of the arrhythmia or (if this is not possible) control of the heart rate. Medication to prevent thrombi is also often prescribed.
- Paroxysmal supraventricular tachycardia (PSVT) is a rapid heart rate initiated in the atrium and is caused by an abnormal pathway for electrical signals to pass from the atria to the ventricles. It frequently results in symptoms and requires treatment.
- Heart block occurs when the electrical signal is slowed or blocked from traveling to the ventricles. This tends to cause a slow and irregular rhythm. Complete heart block results in dissociation between the contractions of the atria and those of the ventricles. A pacemaker is the usual treatment for this arrhythmia.
- Ventricular tachycardia (VT) is a rapid heart rate originating from the ventricles, resulting in decreased

effectiveness of the heart to pump blood. VT may be life threatening and requires treatment.

- Ventricular fibrillation (VF) also originates from the ventricles, but the signal is so disorganized that the ventricles are unable to contract and therefore are unable to pump blood to the body. This is a medical emergency requiring immediate cardiopulmonary resuscitation and defibrillation (shocking the heart).

Treatment

Treatment depends on the type and severity of the arrhythmia. Some arrhythmias require no treatment. Specific lifestyle changes that can decrease the risk of certain arrhythmias include quitting smoking, limiting alcohol and caffeine intake, and avoiding medications that can promote arrhythmias. Medications are commonly used to treat arrhythmias by controlling the heart rate and by maintaining a normal rhythm after electrical cardioversion. Electrical cardioversion, where an electrical shock is delivered, can be used to resynchronize the heart rhythm.

Several mechanical devices are also used to treat arrhythmias, especially the more dangerous ones. An artificial pacemaker is a device that sends electrical signals to the heart muscles to initiate contraction and control the rhythm of the heart. It is useful to control arrhythmias that are too fast or too slow and in heart block. An implanted cardioverter–defibrillator (ICD) is a mechanical device used primarily to treat VT and VF. It monitors the heart rhythm and delivers an electrical shock when the rhythm is too fast or irregular to resynchronize or defibrillate the heart. ICDs have improved survival in patients with life-threatening ventricular arrhythmias. Catheter ablation is a procedure in which a high-frequency electrical signal is delivered through a catheter to the area of the heart initiating or conducting the abnormal rhythm to destroy this area and prevent its deleterious effect on heart rhythm. Ablation procedures are used for an increasing array of arrhythmias, including PSVT and AF.

—*Laurie Lavery*

See also Cardiovascular System; Congestive Heart Failure; Thyroid Disease; Valvular Heart Disease

Further Readings and References

Campbell RW. *International Handbook of Arrhythmias.* New York: Marcel Dekker; 1997.

Cannom DS. Matching cardiac rhythm management technology to patient needs: Pacing/Ablation/Implantable cardioverter defibrillators. *Am J Cardiol.* 2000;86: 58K–70K.

Goldberger Z, Lampert R. Implantable cardioverter–defibrillators: Expanding indications and technologies. *JAMA.* 2006;295:809–818.

Guerra PG, Talajic M, Roy D, Dubuc M, Thibault B, Nattel S. Is there a future for antiarrhythmic drug therapy? *Drugs.* 1998;56:767–781.

Nattel S, Opie LH. Controversies in atrial fibrillation. *Lancet.* 2006;367:262–272.

Roberts-Thomas KC, Kistler PM, Kalman JM. Atrial tachycardia: Mechanisms, diagnosis, and management. *Curr Problems Cardiol.* 2005;30:529–573.

ARTHRITIS AND OTHER RHEUMATIC DISEASES

Arthritis and other rheumatic diseases are the most prevalent chronic conditions in the United States and are a leading cause of disability. These conditions are characterized by chronic pain and progressive physical impairment of joints and soft tissues. They encompass more than 100 diseases and conditions, including osteoarthritis (OA), rheumatoid arthritis (RA), fibromyalgia, systemic lupus (SLE), gout, and bursitis. The most common forms of arthritis in the elderly are described in this entry.

Osteoarthritis

OA, the most common form of arthritis in the elderly, is characterized by focal degeneration of joint cartilage and new bone formation at the base of cartilage lesion (subchondral bone) and at the joint margins (osteophytes). OA can be defined as the result of both mechanical and biological events that destabilize the normal coupling of degeneration and synthesis of articular cartilage and subchondral bone and may be initiated by multiple factors, including genetic, developmental, metabolic, and traumatic causes. OA involves all tissues of the diarthrodial joint and is manifested by morphological, biochemical, molecular, and biomechanical changes of both cells and matrix that lead to a softening, fibrillation, ulceration, and loss of articular cartilage; sclerosis and eburnation of subchondral bone; and formation of osteophytes and subchondral cysts. OA is clinically characterized by joint pain, tenderness, limitation of movement, crepitus, occasional effusion, and variable degrees of local inflammation. The natural history of the disease takes approximately 20 years to be expressed, and most patients are age 60 years and older. Radiographic surveys reveal that the majority of respondents over 55 years of age have radiographically confirmed disease. It is estimated that 90% of people over 70 years of age have radiographic evidence of OA in at least one joint. Over 55 years of age, women are affected more than men. Between 40 and 50 years of age, there is little difference in male versus female prevalence.

Rheumatoid Arthritis

RA affects approximately 1% of the world's population. RA is a chronic, multisystem, autoimmune, and inflammatory disorder that involves peripheral joints in a symmetric distribution. The potential of the synovial inflammation to cause cartilage damage and bone erosions and subsequent changes in joint integrity is the feature of the disease. Symptoms include pain, stiffness, swelling of multiple joints, tenosynovitis, and bursitis. Inflammation may extend to other joint tissues and cause bone and cartilage erosion, joint deformities, movement problems, and activity limitations. RA can also affect connective tissue and blood vessels throughout the body, triggering inflammation in a variety of organs, including the lungs and heart, and increasing a person's risk of dying of respiratory and infectious disease. RA is a chronic disease that leads to joint damage within the first 2 years; is a cause of marked functional limitation; causes a 30% loss of work within the first 5 years, and shortens life by 5 to 7 years.

Chondrocalcinosis

Chondrocalcinosis (CC) or calcification within cartilage is usually due to deposits of calcium pyrophosphate dihydrate (CPPD) crystals. These deposits may be sporadic, familial, or secondary to a variety of metabolic abnormalities. The sites most commonly affected are the knee, wrist, and symphysis pubis. CC is readily visualized on plain radiographs, although sensitivity varies according to film and radiographic technique. Sporadic CC is seen most commonly and is age related.

Epidemiology of Arthritis

A number of population-based national health surveys conducted during the past 40 years have told us much of the prevalence and consequences of arthritis. Those surveys estimate the prevalence of self-reported arthritis at 5% for the adult population, increasing to 60% for those age 65 years and older. The prevalence is higher among women than among men, and evidence suggests a temporal trend toward increased prevalence. Based on data from the Hispanic Health and Nutrition Examination Survey, the prevalence of arthritis in Hispanics is lower than that reported in other ethnicities. Marked differences in incidence, severity, process of care, and outcome in a number of arthritis and musculoskeletal conditions exist among different racial/ethnic groups. For example, African American women are 2 to 3 times more likely than Caucasian women, and more likely than Mexican American women, to have radiographic knee OA. Severe and bilateral radiographic knee OA is more likely to be seen in African American women and men than in Caucasians. African Americans, Hispanics, and Asians appear to be 3 to 15 times less likely than Caucasians to undergo total joint replacement for OA of the hip and are also less likely to have primary OA as the reason for the hip replacement. Said Ibrahim and colleagues, in a 2002 study of total joint replacement for knee and hip OA in African American and Caucasian male veterans, found significant ethnic differences in their awareness and understanding of total joint replacement, as well as in their perceptions of the risks and benefits thereof. Higher rates of RA have been found in certain groups; for example, 5.3% in certain Native American tribes. Women are affected 2 to 3 times more often than men, but in persons over 50 years of age the disease frequency becomes more equal. RA can occur at any age; however, the onset of disease is most common between 40 and 60 years of age and one third of patients can develop RA after 60 years of age.

Risk Factors for Arthritis

Several factors are known to be associated with a greater risk of arthritis. Females age 15 years and older account for 60% of arthritis cases. An estimated 22.8 million females self-reported arthritis from 1981 to 1991, and prevalence increases with age. From 1989–1991 to 2020, the prevalence of self-reported arthritis among females age 15 years and older is projected to increase from 22.8 million to 35.9 million. Moreover, approximately 4.6 million females report arthritis as a major or contributing cause of activity limitation. Half of the elderly population is affected by arthritis, and the risk increases with age. Certain genes are known to be associated with a higher risk of some types of arthritis. For example, family studies have demonstrated an increased risk of RA in siblings of persons affected with RA; concordance has been found to be 12% to 15% in monozygotic twins and 4% in dizygotic twins. Also, factors such as the collagen content of cartilage and the ability of chondrocytes to synthesize proteoglycan are genetically determined. Primary OA in the form of Heberden's nodes also points to the importance of a genetic factor in pathogenesis. Polymorphisms of the type 2 collagen gene have also been identified in a family with premature OA. Socioeconomic status (SES) has also been associated with arthritis. For instance, a lower level of formal education has been suggested as a risk factor in the development or progression of RA. Low SES in patients with RA has been associated with worse disease activity, physical health, mental health, and quality of life when compared with high-SES patients. Similarly, OA patients who had not completed high school showed poorer clinical status than did patients who had completed high school.

Overweight and obesity have been found in population-based studies as a risk factor for developing knee OA. Obese women are four to five times more likely to have knee OA than are persons of average weight. The relationship of increased body weight with hip OA is weaker than that with knee OA. Unilateral disease in the hip is not clearly associated with being overweight, whereas bilateral disease is associated. Also, there is a positive association between obesity and hand OA, suggesting that obesity is a systemic risk factor for OA. Injury to joints has been associated with arthritis, specifically OA. Major acute knee injuries, including cruciate ligament and meniscal tears, are common risk factors for knee OA. Osteoarthritic changes have been reported in up to 89% of people after meniscectomy. Most people who have experienced complete anterior cruciate ligament rupture will develop knee OA. Similarly, OA has been associated with a variety of sport activities, including marathon running (hip OA), soccer playing (knee and hip OA), and American football playing (knee OA). Standing, bending, walking long distances over rough ground, lifting, and moving heavy objects appear to increase the risk of hip OA. Occupations are also associated with arthritis. For example, high rates of OA have been found in farmers (hip OA), jackhammer operators (elbow OA), miners (knee and spine OA), and cotton mill workers (hand OA).

Treatment

The ultimate goals of arthritis treatment are to reduce pain and discomfort; prevent deformities and loss of normal joint function; and maintain normal physical, social, and emotional function. Management begins with effective communication between physician and patient. The most effective symptomatic therapy combines several approaches and may be more effective if a multidisciplinary team—including a rheumatologist, physiatrist, orthopedist, physical therapist, occupational therapist, psychologist, psychiatrist, nurse/nurse coordinator, dietitian, and social worker—is involved. The therapeutic program should include a combination of patient education, physical measures, psychosocial interventions, drugs, and surgical interventions.

—Soham Al Snih

See also Disability and the Disablement Process; Immune Function; Multiple Morbidity and Comorbidity; Musculoskeletal Aging: Osteoarthritis

Further Readings and References

American College of Rheumatology. Classification criteria for rheumatic diseases. Available at: www.rheumatology.org/publications/classification. Accessed September 6, 2006.

American College of Rheumatology. Management guidelines for rheumatic diseases. Available at: www.rheumatology.org/publications/guidelines. Accessed September 6, 2006.

Centers for Disease Control and Prevention. Prevalence and impact of arthritis by race and ethnicity—United States, 1989–1991. *Morbidity Mortality Weekly Rep.* 1996; 45:373–378.

Centers for Disease Control and Prevention. Public health and aging: Projected prevalence of self-report arthritis or chronic joint symptoms among persons aged ≥ 65 years—United States, 2005–2030. *Morbidity Mortality Weekly Rep.* 2003;52:489–491.

Ibrahim SA, Siminoff LA, Burant CJ, Kwoh CK. Differences in expectations on outcome mediate African American/White differences in "willingness" to consider joint replacement. *Arthritis Rheum.* 2002;46:2429–2435.

Reginster JY. The prevalence and burden of arthritis. *Rheumatology.* 2002;41:3–6.

ASIA

Asia is a vast region encompassing 50 nations of different social, economic, and cultural backgrounds. According to the United Nations Population Division, it is subdivided into (a) Eastern Asia (e.g., China, Hong Kong, Japan, Korea), (b) Southeastern Asia (e.g., Indonesia, Malaysia, the Philippines, Thailand), (c) South Central Asia (e.g., Bangladesh, India, Iran, Pakistan), and (d) Western Asia (e.g., Cyprus, Georgia, Iraq, Syria, Turkey).

Population Aging

A major demographic phenomenon of the 21st century is world population aging. Projections estimate more than 825 million people age 65 years and older in the world by 2025, and this figure will increase to nearly 1.5 billion by 2050. According to United Nations projections, Asia will become home to the largest proportion of older persons during the next 30 years, with 478 million people age 65 years and older by 2025 and more than 900 million by 2050.

Population aging in Asia is the result of demographic transition involving low fertility combined with declining old age mortality. By 2000, the total fertility rate (TFR) in Asia declined by two thirds to 2.5 births per woman from its 1950 level of 5.9. A modest reduction to 2.1 births per woman over the next 50 years is projected. On the other hand, life expectancy at 65 years of age is expected to increase by 22%, from 14.6 years to 17.9 years, between 2000 and 2050. The result of this lower fertility rate and increased life expectancy in Asia has been an increased proportion of the total population age 65 years and older, from 4.1% in 1950 to 5.9% in 2000. The aging population of Asia is expected to expand to 10% by 2025 and to 16.7% by 2050. Consequently, population aging is going to be a major demographic preoccupation in Asia during the 21st century.

As observed by John Knodel, Asian aging differs from aging in the Western nations in several respects. First, the West has grown significantly older during the past 50 years, whereas for Asia population aging lays nearly entirely ahead. Second, the aging of Asia is more accelerated in that the annual rate of growth of the population age 65 years and older was 2.1% in 1950–1955 and will increase to 3.5% in 2025–2030. In contrast, in Europe the growth rate was 1.8% in 1950–1955, rose to 2.0% in 1975–1980, and is projected to decline to 1.5% in 2025–2030. Indeed, in only 26 years, from 1970 to 1996, the population age 65 years and older in Japan grew from 7% to 14%. Similarly swift increases are expected in China and elsewhere in Eastern and Southeastern Asia (e.g., South Korea, Taiwan, Thailand), fueled by dramatic drops in fertility. This stands in sharp contrast to

European nations, where the same process would take 45 to 115 years to complete.

On the other hand, the aging and feminization of the older population are less striking in Asia than in the West. Although the elderly population in Asia is aging, the extent of the process will remain well below that for the West. Specifically, in Europe people age 80 years and older are expected to constitute 5.2% of the population in 2025 and 10% in 2050. In Asia, the proportions of the population age 80 years and older will be only 1.7% and 4.2% in 2025 and 2050, respectively. In addition, compared with the West, women represent a smaller proportion of the population age 65 years and older in Asia. For example, sex ratios (number of men per 100 women) in the population age 65 years and older in Asia were between 79 and 85 from 1950 and 2000 and are projected to remain at a similar level by 2050. In Europe, sex ratios among older adults fluctuated between 60 and 66 during the past half century. These ratios are projected to increase to 69 and 73 by 2025 and 2050, respectively.

The timing and eventual levels of population aging differ substantially across regions and individual countries in Asia. On a regional level, population aging is most advanced in Eastern Asia and is least advanced in Western Asia. In 2000, people age 65 years and older accounted for 7.7% of the total population in Eastern Asia, whereas they constituted only 4.7% in Western Asia. Such differences will become even more pronounced during the next 50 years. By 2050, 23.6% of people in Eastern Asia will be age 65 years and older. The elderly will make up only 11.6% of the total population in Western Asia.

Even greater variations exist across countries. By the middle of the 2000s, countries such as China, Japan, South Korea, and Singapore are anticipated to have 20% to 36% of their populations age 65 years and older. Because of their below-replacement fertilities, Japan, South Korea, and China are likely to experience a decline in total population sometime during this century. At the same time, in Cambodia, Lao People's Democratic Republic, and Pakistan, the elderly will account for less than 9% of their total populations.

Important differences may play out within nations as well. In many countries, older people are becoming concentrated in rural areas as young adults leave rural areas for the cities and some older urban migrants return to rural communities as they reach old age. In Japan and Korea, overall population aging coincides with rural depopulation and population stagnation in small and medium-sized towns, suggesting that this pattern will increasingly be seen throughout Asia during the first half of this century.

Health Transitions

Largely consistent with its tempo of economic development and epidemiological transition, health in old age in Asia appears to be below the average for the world. On the basis of recent estimates by C. D. Mathers and colleagues, life expectancies at 60 years of age in 2000 in Asia and Pacific nations, including China, India, and other Asian countries and islands, were 15.9 years for men and 19 years for women. These were significantly lower than those for the low-mortality countries, including Western Europe, North America, Japan, Australia, and New Zealand (19.9 years for men and 24.2 years for women), and those for Latin America (17.5 years for men and 20.8 years for women). On the other hand, life expectancies at 60 years of age in Asia and Pacific nations are similar to those in the Eastern Mediterranean (16.1 years for men and 18 years for women) and in Eastern Europe (14.6 years for men and 18.9 years for women) but are significantly higher than those in sub-Saharan Africa (13.9 years for men and 15.8 years for women).

At these older ages, regional differences in expected life span lived in full health or healthy active life expectancy (HALE) at 60 years of age strongly parallel those in life expectancy. For instance, in 2000, HALEs in the low-mortality nations were 15.9 years for men and 18.8 years for women, substantially higher than those in Asia and Pacific nations (11.1 years for men and 12.9 years for women). Whereas lost healthy years represented only some 20% of life expectancy in low-mortality countries, they accounted for approximately 30% in Asia and Pacific nations. In Africa, HALE was 8.3 years for both men and women at 60 years of age in 2000, constituting 40 to 47% of life expectancy at this age.

There is some evidence that disability rates have been falling over time in a number of developed countries, including the United States, Canada, France, and Japan. However, in developing nations, population aging appears to be associated with increasing disability. According to a recent study, Taiwan does not appear to be experiencing any improvement in functioning given that the prevalence of functional limitations increased from 1993 and 1999. This assessment should nevertheless be qualified in view of the limited amount of such research across the world.

Key Issues for Further Research

A significant amount of work on the basic demography of aging has already been done and is well disseminated in Eastern and Southeastern Asia. However, there is less such research, particularly of a national scope, on South Central Asia (e.g., Bangladesh, India, Pakistan) and Western Asia (e.g., Iraq, Syria, Turkey), perhaps because of the timing of their demographic transitions. Nevertheless, both regions are expected to age significantly during the next 50 years, with the proportions of the population age 65 years and older reaching 13.2% in South Central Asia and 11.3% in Western Asia. Because these regions vary substantially from the rest of the world in demographic and epidemiological transitions, economic and social development, core cultural values, and public policies, their experience with population aging is likely to be quite different.

On the other hand, much work remains to be done with reference to the interface between population aging and health. In particular, estimates of basic population health indicators and summary population health measures (e.g., health expectancy) could be improved. Current estimates are relatively few and are based primarily on cross-sectional data derived from Eastern Asia. Research focusing on health changes in old age and involving testing of causal hypotheses is extremely rare. Recent studies of health expectancies and trajectories using repeated observations at the individual level in Japan have become available and represent a step in the right direction.

Population aging takes place within the context of various core cultural values and religions as well as profound social changes (e.g., social and economic transformations, urbanization, changes in family structure). A key issue for research on aging in Asia to address is how social and economic development influences the well-being of the elderly. A common view is that, with declining family support, the welfare of many elders will be threatened unless there is greater government intervention. However, the evidence so far provides no clear confirmation of this view. Although development may intensify some of the potential adverse consequences of population aging, at the same time it may enable societies to better cope with these challenges. Advantages include better health and long-term care, more efficient applications of savings and capital to provide financial security, and new goods and services for older people.

Despite the common impression that older women suffer social and economic disadvantages disproportionately in comparison with older men, there is little systematic research of this issue in the Asian context. Women's experience throughout their life course is conditioned by social institutions and cultural values that differ substantially across societies. For instance, in the Asia–Pacific region, countries have been shaped by several civilizations, including Confucian culture in China, Korea, Japan, and parts of the Indo-China peninsula; Buddhism in Burma, Thailand, Cambodia, and Eastern Asian nations; Islam in Malaysia, Brunei, Indonesia, and parts of the southern Philippines; and Christianity in the Philippines and Korea. These may lead to considerable variations in the way in which gender influences well-being. Further research is clearly needed if sound policies incorporating a gender dimension are to be developed.

The AIDS pandemic has emerged as one of the foremost health challenges globally during the 21st century. Although AIDS is most commonly associated with Africa, Asia has not been spared. To this point, however, the spread has been very uneven among different regions and countries. As of 2003, only Cambodia, Myanmar, and Thailand had estimated adult HIV prevalence levels ranging from 1.2% to 2.6%. India and China, despite quite low levels of infection (still < 1%), still have the largest number of HIV-infected persons in the world by virtue of their large populations. There is already a noticeable impact of AIDS on these nations. In Cambodia, life expectancy is 4 years lower than it would have been in the absence of AIDS. In China, the impact of AIDS on life expectancy relative to the non-AIDS scenario is projected to rise from a gap of 0.3 year in 2000–2005 to 1.2 years in 2015–2020.

With AIDS generally viewed as a disease affecting adults of reproductive age and their infant children, the impact of this disease on older persons has received little attention. Even when it does, the focus is often on those infected. A far greater number of older persons, however, are affected as parents of AIDS victims. Impacts of AIDS on parents can occur through the strain of giving care and associated opportunity costs, providing financial and material support, raising surviving grandchildren, suffering emotional stress, and losing old-age support that children would have provided. The impact of AIDS can be particularly severe given the extended period of illness and disability, the untimely death, and possible social stigma. Much research concerning how AIDS affects the experience of individual and population aging remains to be undertaken.

Finally, a comparative perspective would be most useful in advancing our knowledge of aging and health in Asia. Cross-cultural comparison is a powerful way to evaluate the external validity of a given observation within a given nation and hence is an important step in understanding underlying causal mechanisms. Cross-cultural differences in a given observed linkage, on the other hand, motivate investigators to account for such variations and to evaluate specific hypotheses underlying these differences. Currently, single-nation studies still dominate. In these studies, cross-cultural comparisons are at best implicit or indirect. This reflects two major barriers to the implementation of comparative research. First, there is still very limited contextual understanding of aging and human development in many countries. Second, there is a lack of comparable data necessary for estimating parallel models involving more than a small number of covariates.

Although gerontological research in Eastern and Southeastern Asia has been increasing during the past two decades, there is still an extremely limited understanding of aging in other Asian nations. Therefore, a major research priority is to extend the scope of cross-cultural comparisons by including these nations. Ideally, this will be undertaken by using a multilevel strategy that involves data at the levels of nations, subregions within nations, households, and individuals. Because an in-depth understanding of the sociocultural contexts of the nations under study is required for interpreting observed similarities and differences, integrating macro and micro research, on the one hand, and quantitative and qualitative research, on the other, will greatly enhance our understanding of cross-cultural differences in aging.

—*Jersey Liang*

See also Active Life Expectancy; Africa; Australia and New Zealand; Canada; Demography of Aging; Europe; Latin America and the Caribbean; Mexico

Further Readings and References

Kinsella K, Phillips DR. Global aging: The challenge of success. *Pop Bull.* 2005;60(1):3–40.

Knodel J. The demography of Asian ageing: Past accomplishments and future challenges. *Asia–Pacific Pop J.* 1999;14(4):39–56.

Liang J. Cross-cultural comparative social gerontology. *Contemp Gerontol.* 2003;10(2):59–64.

Liang J, Shaw BA, Krause N, et al. Changes in functional status among older adults in Japan: Successful and usual aging. *Psychol Aging.* 2003;18:684–695.

Mathers CD, Murray CJL, Lopez AD, Salomon JA, Sadana R. Global patterns of health expectancy in the year of 2000. In: Robine JM, Jagger C, Mathers CD, Crimmins EM, Suzman RM, eds. *Determining Health Expectancies.* New York: John Wiley; 2003:359–376.

United Nations. *World Population Ageing, 1950–2050.* New York: United Nations; 2002.

United Nations. *World Population Prospects: The 2002 Revision,* Vol. 3: *Analytical Report.* New York: United Nations; 2003.

United Nations. *World Population Prospects: The 2004 Revision, Highlights.* New York: United Nations; 2005.

ASIAN AND PACIFIC ISLANDER AMERICANS

The Asian and Pacific Islander (API) elderly population is diverse. These people or their ancestors came from nearly 50 countries with distinct cultures, traditions, and histories, and they speak more than 100 languages and dialects. The API elderly population is considered as a "model minority" because, as a group, these people are physically healthy. This healthy portrait may be misleading because although it is true for a subset of the Asian immigrant elderly (e.g., Chinese, Japanese), it is not true for others (e.g., Hmong, Native Hawaiians, acculturated Asian Americans). A unique study compiled 1990 age-adjusted death rates by API ethnic groups (i.e., seven states with 73% of the API population). In terms of death rates per 100,000 population, Pacific Islanders (Hawaiian at 901.4 and Samoan at 907.7) had rates comparable to the rate for Blacks (816.8) and much higher than the rates for Whites (527.4), API aggregated (350.5), other Asian ethnic groups (Asian Indian at 275.2, Korean at 292.3, Japanese at 298.8, Chinese at 304.0, Filipino at 329.4, and Vietnamese at 415.9), and Guamanian (444.3). This study illustrates the great health diversity across API ethnic groups, from the best of health to the poorest of health.

A healthy API elders profile may be produced falsely by selective migration that brings healthier immigrants to Western countries, return migration by sick elders to their homeland, select samples of healthy API respondents, accumulation of mortality and health status data errors, or scarcity of good-quality data on API populations. Acculturation and modernity lessen acute health conditions or diseases and increase chronic and disabling health conditions among API elders of longer residence in Western societies or among API American-born elders. Discrimination history and its legacy have a negative impact on socioeconomic status, educational and employment opportunities, and access to health care and also increase stressors, producing a poorer quality of life during the twilight years.

Asian Americans

According to the 2000 U.S. census, there were 1,143,590 Asian American elders age 60 years and older, with the fastest rate of growth being fueled by immigration and the "graying" of API baby boomers (born between 1946 and 1964). API elders (age 65 years and older) are roughly 34.6% native born, 23.3% foreign born living in the United States less than 10 years, and 42.1% foreign born living in the Unites States 10 years or more in 1989–1994. In 2002, Asian American elders were composed of 29% Chinese, 21% Filipino, 20% Japanese, 9% Korean, 8% Vietnamese/Cambodian, 1% Hmong, and 12% from other Asian ethnicities. A large majority of Asian elders are foreign born (78.6%) and have limited English proficiency (41%). Limited English proficiency, cultural differences, immigration with lack of citizenship (25.7% for the API population vs. 2.9% for the U.S. population), and lack of insurance coverage are significant barriers to health care access by the Asian elderly. Underuse of health services is exacerbated by lack of regular physicians and significant access barriers to a complex health care system.

In 2000, heart disease was the leading cause of death among Asian men, and cancer was the leading cause of death among Asian women. The lower incidence of heart disease among Asian Americans, especially women, contributed to better health outcomes for the Asian elderly group. There are high rates of certain cancers (e.g., lung cancer among Vietnamese, Cambodian, and Hmong males; colorectal and liver cancers; cervical cancer among Vietnamese women) and an alarming growth in the rates of breast cancer among Japanese and Chinese American women who are native born or long-term residents. The rate of dementia among Asian American elders appears to be comparable to that among Caucasian elders; however, the Asian American elderly had a higher rate of vascular dementia and a lower rate of Alzheimer's dementia, although this ratio may be changing. Another health disparity for the Asian elderly is the lower rates of health screening and disease prevention. For instance, immigrant Vietnamese, Cambodian, and Hmong women have low breast and cervical cancer screening rates as compared with those of Caucasian and African American women.

Several studies indicate comparable depression, somatic psychiatric distress, and dementia rates between Caucasians and the Asian American elderly. Mental health conditions, such as Alzheimer's disease and other dementias, are stigmatized and Asian families may conceal these family secrets by taking sole responsibility for their demented relatives until family resources are exhausted. Chinese caregivers have lacked information about Alzheimer's disease, said that culturally and linguistically appropriate services were not available, and had negative interactions with health care providers. Suicide, depression, and post-traumatic stress syndrome are significant mental health disparities for the Asian elderly, who may also be coping with acculturation shifts in intergenerational relationships, loss of homeland, and culture. The Asian elderly live with their spouses and other relatives in higher proportions than do members of the general population or other ethnic groups. This high level of Asian intergenerational living arrangements can be a source of social support or an enormous family burden that creates family tensions. Although the national aggregated statistics indicate a physically healthy API elderly population, including lower mortality, self-reported disability, and activity limitation, there is an underuse of preventive health and mental services by the Asian elderly, perhaps due to a lack of satisfaction with the quality of health care. Future generations of API elders may experience greater health disparities and a worsening of health profiles, as seen among American-born, acculturated, and multiracial elders.

Native Hawaiian and Pacific Islanders

According to the 2000 U.S. census, there were 43,802 Native Hawaiian and Pacific Islander elders. Native Hawaiians and Pacific Islanders are a relatively young population, with only 5% of the population age 65 years and older. Pacific Islanders are composed of 45.9% Native Hawaiians, 15.2% Samoans, 10.6% Guamanians, 4.2% Tongans, 1.6% Fujians, and 20% other Pacific Islanders. Life expectancies for

Hawaiian, Samoan, and Guamanian males were 71.5, 71.0, and 72.4 years, respectively, as compared with 73.2 years for Caucasians. Heart disease is a major cause of death and disability among Native Hawaiians. Data from Hawaii indicated that Native Hawaiian, Samoan, and Chamorro had significantly higher mortality rates for most causes of death. Investigators have attributed this health disparity to advanced disease diagnosis and high rates of hypertension and obesity, heart disease, cancers, stroke, and diabetes; cultural and socioeconomic barriers such as poverty that result in poorer health access; and health behaviors such as higher smoking rates, lower physical activity, and poor nutrition. For example, Native Hawaiian women have the second highest incidence of breast cancer and the highest cancer death rate of any ethnic group in Hawaii.

The prevalence of psychiatric mental health disorders of Pacific Islander elders is currently unknown, but indicators suggest that greater mental health disparities are associated with lower educational attainment, poverty, and poorer health behaviors such as smoking, as compared with other ethnic groups in Hawaii. Native Hawaiian adolescents and elderly have the highest rate of suicide in Hawaii. Discrimination, negative stereotyping, breakdown of family and social support systems, and poorer educational outcomes contribute to a higher level of depression and negative health and mental health outcomes for Native Hawaiian elders. Native Hawaiian and Pacific Islander elders suffer from health and mental health disparities comparable to those found among African American elders.

—*Barbara W. K. Yee*

See also African Americans; Asia; Ethnicity and Race; Hispanics; Latin America and the Caribbean; Mexico; Native Americans and Alaska Natives

Further Readings and References

Anderson NB, Bulatao RA, Cohen B, eds. *Critical Perspectives on Racial and Ethnic Differences in Health in Late Life*. Washington, DC: National Academy Press; 2004.

Braun K, Yee BWK, Brown CV, Mokuau N. Native Hawaiian and Pacific Islander elders. In: Whitfield KE, ed. *Closing the Gap: Improving the Health of Minority Elders in the New Millennium.* Washington, DC: Gerontological Society of America; 2004:55–67.

Hoyert DL, Kung HC. Asian or Pacific Islander mortality, selected states, 1992. *Monthly Vital Statist Rep.* 1997:46(1). DHHS Publication No. (PHS) 97–1120.

Miller BA, Kolonel LN, Berstein L, et al., eds. *Racial/Ethnic Patterns of Cancer in the United States 1988–1992.* Bethesda, Md: National Cancer Institute; 1996. NIH Publication No. 96–4104.

Yee BWK, Yeo G. *Asian and Pacific Islander Elders* (brief bibliography CD-ROM ed.). Washington, DC: Association for Gerontology in Higher Education; 2004.

Zhan L. Caring for family members with Alzheimer's disease: Perspectives from Chinese caregivers. *J Gerontol Nurs.* 2004;30:19–29.

ASSISTED LIVING

Assisted living has emerged as an important type of residential care outside of nursing homes. Assisted living can be broadly defined as a group residential program that provides personal care and supportive services and can respond to unscheduled needs for assistance. These programs have a stated philosophy of care that respects individual choice, privacy, and autonomy. In practice, the term *assisted living* is used to describe a very wide variety of settings, and in spite of major efforts such as those by the Assisted Living Workgroup, a consensus definition remains elusive.

The number of residents in these programs, their disability levels, and the level of services available have increased nationally. A 2002 survey of state assisted-living programs estimated that 1 million adults were being served in more than 36,000 facilities. This report also described the wide variety of regulatory structures that states have adopted in the absence of federal regulation. Assisted living serves primarily a private pay market. Most states do now have programs that can fund assisted living in part through Medicaid. Typically, the state's Medicaid funds are used for personal care services for low- to moderate-income individuals, and residents pay for their own room and board. These programs can be quite small, and the characteristics of programs and their regulatory environments vary greatly across states.

Assisted living is receiving increased attention because of its potential for providing cost-effective services while preserving resident autonomy. Questions remain about how to achieve the best match among care needs and services, provider qualifications and training, certification/inspection standards, quality assurance, and payment systems as well as, more generally, how to balance access, cost, and quality of care.

Assisted living has only recently been a topic for serious research. A recently published study collected longitudinal data on 2,078 residents in 193 facilities across four states to assess the relationship between facilities and resident outcomes to guide policy and practice, especially state regulations. Designed to assess the components of care and relate them to resident outcomes, the study found a large number of significant predictors, but the pattern of results was inconsistent and effect sizes were small. The researchers could find no single component that defines "good" assisted-living care. Therefore, they recommended that policy and practice not focus narrowly on any one area or restrict the type of care that supports diversity to accommodate individual care needs and preferences.

—Susan C. Hedrick and Marylou Guihan

See also Assistive Devices; Caregiving; Home Care; Institutional Care; Mobility; National Long Term Care Survey

Further Readings and References

Assisted Living Workgroup Steering Committee. *Assuring Quality in Assisted Living: Guidelines for Federal and State Policy, State Regulations, and Operations.* Washington, DC: American Association of Homes and Services for the Aging; 2003.

Hedrick SC, Guihan M, Chapko M, et al. Outcomes of the VA assisted living pilot program. Paper presented at: AcademyHealth annual research meeting; 2005; Boston.

Zimmerman S, Sloane PD, Eckert JK, et al. How good is assisted living? Findings and implications from an outcomes study. *J Gerontol B Psychol Sci Social Sci.* 2005;60:S195–S204.

Assistive Devices

Assistive devices are used to compensate for (i.e., function in spite of) physical limitations. They can provide differing levels and types of mechanical assistance, and they fit into two broad categories: mobility aids and self-care aids. *Mobility aids* are devices external to the body that provide support during locomotion. They include single-point canes (used for balance and minor support) and wheelchairs or electronic mobility (providing total support). *Self-care aids* are devices external to the body that enhance the performance of self-care activities. These devices range from can openers, used by people with and without disability, to bath benches, used only in the face of disability. Self-care aids can be quite sophisticated and limitation specific; for example, environmental control units for individuals with deficient immune systems and electronic speech synthesizers for those lacking the ability to phonate.

Orthoses and prosthetics are often identified as assistive devices. An orthosis is a mechanical support that fits to the limb itself, supporting a joint or limb segment affected by muscular or structural weakness or injury. Braces and splints are static orthoses, providing support only. Dynamic orthoses add hinges and springs to allow for movement. Often an attachment is added to the orthosis to allow the performance of special tasks; for example, page turners or pencil holders on wrist or hand splints.

Prosthetics replace missing body parts. They include simple cosmetic additions that make disfigurement less noticeable (e.g., breast prostheses, prosthetic eyes) as well as prosthetics that functionally replace missing limbs. Prosthetic technology is advancing rapidly, now allowing replacement limbs to be controlled by the patient's own nerves and muscles.

The goal for each assistive device will vary by patient situation. For best results, the right device needs to be selected, fitted well, and maintained in good condition. The most common reasons for dissatisfaction with a device are inadequate or improper original information, improper choice of device, and improper fit. Much unsatisfactory equipment is obtained by the patient without professional counsel or prescription. Broken, poorly fitted, or poorly maintained equipment obtained from yard sales, online sources, or community or family members can produce harm rather than improve function. Many physicians are trained to prescribe or recommend assistive devices, as are physical or occupational therapists and specialists in prosthetics. Third-party payers usually require a professional prescription before they pay for an assistive device.

After receiving a new device (especially a mobility aid or prosthetic), training from a licensed therapist ensures safe and efficient use. A device (especially a prosthetic) may be used for the rest of the patient's life. Ongoing monitoring for fit and repair are particularly important. Often, as rehabilitation (or limitation) progresses, a new device or another fit will be necessary to continue maximum functional support.

As older adults are living longer, maintaining independence has become a common goal. Assistive devices can provide cost-effective alternatives to institutional care. Most older adults would rather use an assistive device for self-care and mobility than need to rely on the assistance of other persons.

—*William C. Logan, Jr., and Helen Hoenig*

See also Activities of Daily Living and Instrumental Activities of Daily Living; Assisted Living; Disability and the Disablement Process; Frailty; Hearing; Injury Prevention; Mobility; Vision and Low Vision

Further Readings and References

Lansley P, McCreadie C, Tinker A. Can adapting the homes of older people and providing assistive technology pay its way? *Age Ageing.* 2004;33:571–576.

Taylor DH, Hoenig H. The effect of equipment usage and residual task difficulty on use of personal assistance, days in bed, and nursing home placement. *J Am Geriatr Soc.* 2004;52:72–79.

Warner M, Cohen D, Elderly people's services: Home truths. *Health Serv J.* 2004;114:28–29.

Australia and New Zealand

Australia and New Zealand are the two largest countries of the Oceania region in the Southern Pacific. With many similarities between them, they also differ in a number of ways. Both countries were settled as British colonies during the 18th and 19th centuries, displacing long established indigenous populations.

Aboriginal settlers arrived on the continent that is now Australia from Southeast Asia approximately 40,000 years before the first Europeans began exploration during the 17th century. No formal territorial claims were made until 1770, when Captain James Cook took possession in the name of Great Britain. Six colonies were created during the late 18th and 19th centuries; they federated and became the Commonwealth of Australia in 1901.

The Polynesian Maori reached New Zealand in approximately 800 A.D. In 1840, their chieftains entered into a compact with Britain, the Treaty of Waitangi, in which they ceded sovereignty to Queen Victoria while retaining territorial rights. In that same year, the British began the first organized colonial settlement. A series of land wars between 1843 and 1872 ended with the defeat of the native peoples.

The now predominantly Anglo-Saxon origin Caucasian populations in both countries have become increasingly multicultural with continuing migration from across the globe and (more recently) Asia. The indigenous people of Australia and New Zealand are a relatively small group within each country's population. In 2001, Australia's Aboriginal and Torres Strait Islander population numbered 458,500 persons, whereas New Zealand's Maori population was 526,281 persons.

Australia and New Zealand are among the world's more developed nations, and their aging populations reflect this. In 2005, the estimated median age for Australia was 36.5 years and for New Zealand was 33.5 years. Life expectancy at birth is among the world's highest, being 80 years for Australia (males 78 years, females 83 years) and 79 years for New Zealand (males 76 years, females 81 years). Fertility rates of both countries are low at 1.76 children born per woman in Australia and 1.79 in New Zealand. Currently, the proportion of population age 65 years and older in Australia is 12.9% (males 1,145,274, females 1,452,002) and in New Zealand is 11.7% (males 206,650, females 266,087). Indigenous populations in both countries have significantly shorter life expectancies. The gap in life expectancy at birth

between indigenous and nonindigenous people is 20 years in Australia, whereas it is 5 to 7 years in New Zealand.

In common with other developed countries, fertility has fallen below the replacement level (the number of babies a woman would need to bear to replace herself and her partner; i.e., 2.1 on average) in both countries. This occurred in 1976 in Australia and in 1980 in New Zealand. Despite this, in 2000 the number of births exceeded the number of deaths in both countries because the age structure of each population was still relatively young. Natural increase will continue to contribute to population growth for the first 30 to 40 years of this century in each country. However, in the longer term, as the population ages and deaths eventually outnumber births, any population growth in either country will stem from net overseas migration gains.

The Australian Bureau of Statistics suggests that in 30 years, persons age 65 years and older will represent 21.3% of the population, and by 2051 they could represent a quarter of the population or between 6.4 million and 6.8 million people. The New Zealand population is relatively young as a result of higher birth rates and significant periods of net migration in the past, but like the rest of the world, New Zealand's population is aging, with the proportion of people age 65 years and older projected to increase from 11.9% to 13.6% by 2011. From 2011, the proportion of older people will increase to 17.6% by 2021, to 24.8% by 2041, and to approximately 25.3% by 2051 (1.18 million people).

Morbidity and Mortality

Diseases of the circulatory system, cancers, and diseases of the respiratory system account for more than three quarters of the main causes of death among people age 65 years and older in both countries.

The Australian Burden of Disease Study, using disability-adjusted life years (DALYs), reported that the leading causes of total burden of disease were ischemic heart disease and stroke, which together accounted for 18% of the burden. Chronic obstructive pulmonary disease (COPD) ranked third, and lung cancer and dementia ranked fifth and sixth, respectively. Osteoarthritis was ranked 10th, after colorectal cancer and asthma. For persons age 65 years and older, the top causes of healthy years lost as a result of disability (in rank order) were dementia, adult-onset hearing loss, stroke, visual disorders, osteoarthritis, heart disease, Parkinson's disease, diabetes, benign prostatic hypertrophy, and COPD.

The rankings for the burden of disease in New Zealand, based on 1996 data, are also dominated by chronic conditions. Cardiovascular disease accounted for 24% of DALYs lost by the whole population in 1996 and is the leading cause of death and disability in New Zealand: Fully 44% of all deaths are due to cardiovascular disease, and 87% of these deaths occur in persons over 65 years of age. The rates differ by gender, with men having a significantly higher rate than women (31 per 1000 men vs. 19 per 1000 women).

National Policies

Growing awareness of the impact of population aging on social, health, and economic arenas emerged in both Australia and New Zealand during the 1990s. By the beginning of the new century, the need for proactive policies and policy and program action was apparent, and in 2001 the New Zealand minister for senior citizens launched the New Zealand Positive Aging Strategy, whereas in 2001–2002 the minister for aging in Australia announced the Australian National Strategy for an Aging Population. Both of these initiatives were driven by the general concepts of active or positive aging and a desire to present aging issues in a broader economic and developmental context away from the prevalent focus on disability and dependence of older persons.

The main themes of the Australian National Strategy for an Aging Population are as follows:

- *Retirement income:* pensions and superannuation
- *A changing workforce:* employment for mature-age workers
- *Attitude, lifestyle, and community support issues:* housing, transport, lifelong learning, and volunteering
- *Healthy aging:* health promotion and maintaining health and well-being through physical, mental, and social activities
- *World-class care issues:* health and aged care

The New Zealand Positive Aging Strategy set the following 10 goals for achievement:

- Secure and adequate income for older people
- Equitable, timely, affordable, and accessible health services for older people
- Affordable and appropriate housing options for older people
- Affordable and accessible transport options for older people
- Ensuring that older people feel safe and secure and can "age in place"
- A range of culturally appropriate services that allow choices for older people
- Ensuring that older people living in rural communities are not disadvantaged when accessing services
- Ensuring that people of all ages have positive attitudes toward aging and older people
- Eliminating ageism and promoting flexible work options
- Increasing opportunities for personal growth and community participation

Health and Aged Care in New Zealand

New Zealand also initiated an Older Peoples Health Strategy with the following eight objectives:

- Older people, their families, and *whanau* (Maori expression for extended family) are able to make well-informed choices about options for healthy living, health care, and/or disability support needs.
- Policy and service planning will support quality health and disability support programs integrated around the needs of older people.
- Funding and service delivery will promote timely access to quality integrated health and disability support services for older people, family, *whanau*, and carers.
- The health and disability support needs of older Maori and their *whanau* will be met by appropriate integrated health care and disability support services.
- Population-based health initiatives and programs will promote health and well-being in older age.
- Older people will have timely access to primary and community health services that proactively improve and maintain their health and functioning.
- Admission to general hospital services will be integrated with any community-based care and support that an older person requires.

- Older people with high and complex health and disability support needs will have access to flexible, timely, and coordinated services and living options that take account of family and *whanau* carer needs.

In New Zealand since 2004, funding for disability support services for older people has been devolved to 21 district health boards, which are largely elected community health boards charged with the responsibility of maintaining and improving the health of the populations in their districts. These responsibilities include funding primary health care, community health services, hospital-based services, and long-term support for older people; that is, all people age 65 years and older and those 50 to 64 years of age with complex health needs more commonly associated with older age.

This approach is linked to the establishment of primary health organizations in New Zealand. The concept behind these is for groups of primary health professionals to work together to provide more accessible and affordable primary health care funded by the government.

Needs assessment and service coordination agencies were established to undertake holistic assessments of individual needs and to work with these individuals to develop a support package to meet their needs. These agencies are responsible for managing the transition to residential care and have succeeded in reducing entry rates to residential care to below those of population growth in older age groups. At the same time, the number of people receiving community support services has increased.

The bulk of disability support services funding (approximately 63%) for older people still goes to residential care, compared with approximately 14% that goes to support people at home. Approximately 20% of funding is for assessment, treatment, and rehabilitation services.

However, most people entering residential care are highly dependent, and many have only a short time to live. For example, 22% of people entering residential care in 2000 died within 3 months and 40% died within a year.

Initially, most community and residential care was provided by either public or not-for-profit (usually religious and welfare) organizations. During the 1990s, demand for residential care in New Zealand increased significantly and private for-profit organizations entered the market, building larger facilities with modern amenities. They also diversified into retirement villages that provide a range of accommodations, from independent units to full hospital care, on the same site.

Health and Aged Care in Australia

Australia's health policy is funded and delivered by several levels of government and is supported by private health insurance arrangements. In place are systems for the delivery of health, income support, and housing and community services to support aging people. Medicare, the national health insurance scheme, is funded and administered by the Australian (commonwealth) government and provides coverage for a range of primary care services, including visits to medical practitioners. This is supported by optional private health insurance for ancillary services and private hospital treatments. The public hospital system is funded jointly by the Australian, state, and territory governments and is administered at the state/territory level.

Most nonhospital medical services, pharmaceuticals, and health research receive funding directly or indirectly from the Australian government. Public hospital services and home and community care for aged and disabled persons are funded jointly by the Australian, state, and territory governments. Residential facilities for aged persons are funded by a number of sources, including the Australian government.

The states and territories are primarily responsible for the delivery and management of public health services and the regulation of health care providers and private health facilities. They deliver public hospital services and a wide range of community and public health services. Public hospitals, which provide the majority of acute care beds, are funded by the Australian, state, and territory governments.

The private sector, operating in the delivery of, and insurance for, health services, receives both direct and indirect government subsidies. Within this sector, organizations operating for-profit and not-for-profit play a significant role in providing health services, public health, and health insurance. For example, privately owned nursing homes provide the majority of long-term aged care beds.

Aged care services in Australia have been significantly restructured since 1985, when the Home and Community Care Act was introduced. During the late 1990s and the beginning years of the new century, a series of inquiries and national reviews have been undertaken. Government attention to the implications of population aging was sharpened with the release of the first Intergenerational Report by the Australian Government Treasurer in 2002. A succession of government inquiries and reports have had an impact on health and aged care services in terms of policy, funding, and programs, with the most recent being Economic Implications of an Aging Australia from the Productivity Commission in 2005, a report prepared at the request of the Council of Australian Governments.

Nationally, there are two main forms of care delivery: residential care and community care. *Community care* includes the Home and Community Care Program (HACC), Community Aged Care Packages (CACP; i.e., low-level care in patients' homes), and Extended Aged Care at Home (EACH, high-level care in patients' homes). Aged Care Assessment Teams assess people's eligibility for residential care, CACP, and EACH.

There are also other flexible related aged care programs. Multipurpose Services provides services to people in rural and remote regions, and the Aged Care Innovative Pool, which provides flexible care places, aims to develop innovative services for health care delivery such as rehab and support services for older people after hospital discharge or people with dementia. Other aged care services programs include a commonwealth hearing services program, respite services, and day therapy centers.

Depending on individuals' circumstances and needs, there are other services available outside the health care system, including income support (e.g., Carers Allowance), community services, and housing. Specialist health and hospital services for older people, including rehabilitation, geriatric evaluation

and management, psychogeriatric and mental health, and respite and palliative care, are available.

Conclusion

In broad terms, Australia and New Zealand are relatively wealthy democratic societies with strong traditions of providing comprehensive public health and social services to their populations. The prospect of significant population aging, and especially the emergence of an aging baby boomer generation, has drawn greater public and government attention to the issues of providing more effective, better quality, and more responsive and efficient health and care services to meet the needs of older persons, their families, and their carers. In both countries, the past decade in particular has seen a series of reviews and reforms in health and aged care arrangements at the national, state, and local levels in response. The aged health and care sectors cover a broad spectrum that has been effectively integrated in part but that still has serious disjunctions in many areas such as the transition from acute to long-term care or from hospital to community. In both countries, more investment is being made in research, evaluation, and innovation in an attempt to ensure the achievement of "healthy aging" of the growing older population. The challenges are posed not only by the demographic pressures per se but also by the prospects of associated burgeoning health problems such as diabetes, obesity, and rapidly increasing numbers of persons with dementia. Much has been achieved, but much remains to be done if the health and other goals of the national strategies of both countries are to be achieved.

—*Gary R. Andrews*

See also Active Life Expectancy; Africa; Asian and Pacific Islander Americans; Canada; Demography of Aging; Europe; Latin America and the Caribbean; Mexico

Further Readings and References

Australian Institute of Health and Welfare. *Residential Aged Care in Australia 2003–04: A Statistical Overview.* Canberra, Australia: AIHW; 2005. AIHW Cat. No. AGE 43.

Bennett S, Magnus P, Gibson D. *Obesity Trends in Older Australians.* Canberra: Australian Institute of Health and Welfare; 2004. Bulletin 12.

Cornwall J, Davey J. *Impact of Population Ageing in New Zealand on the Demand for Health and Disability Support Services, and Workforce Implications.* Wellington, New Zealand: Ministry of Health; 2004.

Costello P. *2002–03 Budget Paper No. 5: Intergenerational Report 2002–03.* Canberra: Commonwealth of Australia; 2002.

Mathers CD, Vos T, Stevenson CE, Begg SJ. The Australian Burden of Disease Study: Measuring the loss of health from diseases, injuries, and risk factors. *Med J Austral.* 2000;172:592–596.

Ministry of Health. *Health of Older People in New Zealand: A Statistical Reference.* Wellington, New Zealand: Ministry of Health; 2002.

Ministry of Health. *Health of Older People Information Strategic Plan: Directions to 2010 and Beyond.* Wellington, New Zealand: Ministry of Health; 2006.

Productivity Commission. *Economic Implications of an Ageing Australia: Research Report.* Canberra, Australia: Productivity Commission; 2005.

World Health Organization. *Active Ageing: A Policy Framework.* Geneva, Switzerland: WHO; 2002.

B

BALANCE

Falls continue to be a major health problem for older adults. Falls can be serious, resulting in major injuries or even death. Age-related declines in balance contribute to falls, and many falls can occur as people are moving. Therefore, the ability to remain balanced while the body is in motion is a specialized type of balance known as *dynamic balance*. Walking is one activity that requires dynamic balance. As the legs move, the upper body must move to accommodate the ever-changing base of support. With age, this task becomes more difficult due to physiological changes that result from the natural aging process. This entry focuses on the adaptations that older adults make during walking to compensate for declines in balance and suggests types of exercise for improving dynamic balance in older adults.

Changes That Affect the Older Adult Walking Pattern

Lower Extremity Spatial and Temporal Measures

Walking is an activity that involves phases of instability. The transition into swing phase is inherently unstable as one foot is lifted off of the floor and a single limb now supports the weight of the person. Furthermore, the swinging foot pushes against the floor to move the body forward, creating a situation that is dynamically unstable. These phases are necessary to produce the forward motion desired when walking.

Older adults modify their walking pattern to reduce these unstable phases as instability poses a challenge to age-related declines in dynamic balance. One of the most obvious changes is that older adults slow down; their walking velocity decreases. But cadence, or the number of steps taken in one second, usually remains the same with age. Therefore, if stepping frequency remains the same yet older adults are slowing down, the observed decrease in walking velocity is due primarily to reduced step length. A measure that accounts for changes in walking velocity and reflects changes in step length is the gait stability ratio (GSR). GSR is the ratio of cadence (steps per second) to velocity (meters per second) and is expressed in units of steps per meter. GSR is used to assess stability of the walking pattern as GSR is inversely related to balance. Therefore, as the value of GSR increases, balance ability decreases. Increases in GSR indicate that older adults take more steps per unit of distance. Thus, a greater portion of the gait cycle is spent in double-limb support, thereby reducing the unstable phases of walking. Table 1 provides an illustration of age-related increases in walking stability for healthy older adults. A significant decrease in older adults' walking velocity was accompanied by similar cadence. GSR was significantly greater, indicating an increased number of steps per meter and greater stability of walking.

Table 1   Age-Related Changes in Walking Velocity, Cadence, and Gait Stability Ratio

	Velocity (meters/second)	Cadence (steps/second)	Gait Stability Ratio (steps/meter)
Older adults	1.22 ± 0.22*	1.78 ± 0.16	1.48 ± 0.19*
Young adults	1.38 ± 0.21	1.85 ± 0.11	1.36 ± 0.17

*Significant difference between age groups ($p < .05$).

Upper Body Movements

Increased stability of lower extremity spatial and temporal characteristics is also reflected in head and trunk movements of older adults. During walking, angular velocities that produce head flexion and extension motion are reduced. Similarly, angular velocities that produce trunk flexion and extension movements are also decreased. Reductions in head and trunk velocities indicate that older adults increase upper body stability during walking.

Coordination between head and trunk movements during walking also demonstrates increased stability. Head-on-trunk movements must compensate for trunk motion to achieve dynamic balance of the upper body during walking. Optimal dynamic balance of the upper body occurs when head-on-trunk motion is equal in amplitude, but opposite in direction, to trunk movement. This type of coordination ensures that the head remains stable and balanced over the trunk during dynamic activities such as walking. For young adults during walking, the amplitude of head-on-trunk motion is greater than that of trunk movement but opposite in direction. In contrast, for older adults the amplitude of head-on-trunk motion is equal and opposite to trunk motion. Therefore, older adults reduce head-on-trunk movement to achieve greater stability and maintain dynamic balance during walking.

Older Adult Walking Strategy

The walking strategy adopted by older adults is one that promotes stability. This strategy encompasses movements of the whole body as stability is increased for both the lower extremity and upper body motion. Although this strategy may be effective for preventing falls, it diminishes forward motion, negating the effectiveness of walking. This might not be a problem for older adults as they move through their homes. However, use of a stabilized walking pattern becomes a disadvantage when ambulating in the community. This is especially true for situations that are constrained by time. For example, greater stability of the walking pattern can impede older adults from crossing the street safely before the traffic light changes. Also, hurrying to catch the bus can place them at risk for falling because they are unaccustomed to walking speeds that increase the unstable phases of gait.

Suggested Exercises

Suggested exercises to improve dynamic balance in older adults must incorporate activities that focus on the dynamic elements that are reduced in the older adult walking pattern. Exercises that emphasize controlled periods of single limb support while the body continues to move would help enhance the transition into swing phase during walking. Furthermore, exercises that promote step lengthening would help increase swing time during walking. The martial arts, when modified to suit the needs of older adults, can prove to be effective for enhancing dynamic balance. Tae Kwon Do is a martial art that combines kicking, blocking, and striking techniques, requiring participants to actively shift their weight between the lower extremities while the upper extremities are moving. Tae Kwon Do also requires coordination of upper extremity movement while stepping between positions of long wide stances. This type of movement necessitates stabilization of the body for efficient movement of the extremities to maintain balance during these dynamic activities. Thus, Tae Kwon Do is an excellent exercise for increasing dynamic balance in older adults.

—*Ronita L. Cromwell*

See also Exercise and Physical Activity; Frailty; Gait Disorders; Mobility; Mobility Assessment

Further Readings and References

Cromwell RL, Newton RA. Relationship between balance and gait stability in healthy older adults. *J Aging Phys Activ.* 2004;11:90–100.

Cromwell RL, Newton RA, Forrest G. Influence of vision on head stabilization strategies in older adults during walking. *J Gerontol A Biol Sci Med Sci.* 2002;57:M442–M448.

National Institute on Aging. *Exercise: A Guide From the National Institute on Aging.* Gaithersburg, Md: NIA Information Center; 2001. NIH Publication No. 98–4258.

BEHAVIORAL DISORDERS IN DEMENTIA

Known only as senility for thousands of years or hardening of the arteries for the past several decades, dementia has become a major health problem for older adults in the developed world and increasingly in the developing world. Behavioral symptoms have been observed in 60% to 98% of patients with dementia. Many individuals with dementia and their families find behavioral disorders to be the most challenging and distressing effects of dementia. These symptoms are often a determining factor in a family's decision to place a loved one in an institution.

Dementia is a decline in mental functions that generally include short- and long-term memory and is often associated with changes in language, logical thinking, and personality. Most dementias are incurable. The term *behavioral disorders* describes a large group of symptoms that occur to at least some degree in all individuals with dementia, including delusions (present in 20% to 40% of dementia patients), hallucinations (10% to 20%), agitation (60% to 80%), aggression (30%), depression (40%), anxiety (15%), elation/euphoria (5%), apathy/indifference (40% to 60%), disinhibition (10%), aberrant motor behavior such as pacing (40%), insomnia (50%), and appetite/eating change (35%).

Living with dementia is emotionally painful and financially draining not only for the person who suffers from dementia but also for his or her family. Cost of caring for behavioral disorders in people with dementia accounts for more than 30% of total cost of caring for people with dementia. Although behavioral disorders can be life threatening, there is reason to be optimistic. The person suffering from dementia and his or her family can learn about ways to prevent or reduce agitation and other behavioral symptoms with simple, low-tech, nondrug interventions. There are also medicines that can help. Early diagnosis and treatment are keys to successful outcomes of behavioral disorders in dementia.

Early in the course of dementia, people often recognizes their shortcomings and may feel embarrassed about them. Due to inability to remember simple words during an everyday conversation, they may get frustrated and irate at themselves as well their loved ones. People in this stage also often get depressed and worry about the future. People may experience personality changes such as apathy (lack of motivation for daily activities and self-care but without any emotional discomfort). Some may develop severe depression and even contemplate suicide. However, many people with mild dementia attribute declining memory and other abilities to natural consequences of aging and do not seem to be terribly upset.

In advanced stages, more severe memory problems predominate. People with dementia in moderate to severe stages forget easily and entirely and often become disoriented even in their own homes. Eventually, people with dementia can no longer understand what they read and are unable to follow conversations. People often react to these losses with several daily periods of confusion and fear for no obvious reason. Insomnia is a common source of distress in this stage. *Sundowning* consists of agitation, confusion, and disorientation that often starts in late afternoon and becomes especially severe at night. Delusions (fixed false beliefs) are often prominent in this stage. People with dementia often become paranoid about money and may fear that their caregivers want to harm them. Hallucinations (seeing nonexistent people or animals) are not uncommon in these stages and may cause anxiety and agitation. People with dementia in the advanced stages may begin to wander around while dressed inappropriately in the middle of the night. People with dementia often get frightened by their loved ones, whom they can no longer recognize. They often respond to this fear with anger and aggression. On the other hand, some may experience long periods of silence. It is common for people with dementia to show significant changes in expression and in general appearance from one hour to the next. Aggressive behavior (e.g., screaming, throwing objects, attempting to hit others) is one of the most frightening behaviors in someone who has dementia. Verbal assaults are more common than physical ones. Fortunately, such hostile behaviors are usually temporary.

In the end stages of dementia, people become incoherent, do not recognize their family, can comprehend only their names and a few other words, and are totally dependent on caregivers for all of their personal activities such as toileting, bathing, grooming, and (ultimately) eating. They often resist care, and agitation is the only way to show their discomfort or express their needs.

Treatment

The basic principle in helping people with dementia experiencing behavioral disorders is to adopt a philosophy of care that emphasizes quality of life. Personalized care plans build on the strengths of a person with dementia, enhance positive self-image, and promote autonomy.

The first step in treating behavioral disorders in dementia is to find and treat the cause. Behavioral disorders are often manifestations of unmet needs (e.g., food, hunger, thirst, toileting, discomfort, loneliness, boredom) of the person with dementia. Behavior disorders may in part be reactions to the actions of people around the person with dementia. For example, talking too loudly or too fast or contradicting the afflicted person's perceived reality might cause agitation. Misinterpretation of the person's behavior as intentionally malicious rather than as manifestations of a diseased brain not only may cause the caregiver distress but also may generate inappropriate reactions to behavioral problems further, thereby exacerbating them. Changes in routine, changes in environment, and adverse effects of a newly prescribed medication are other easily correctable

causes of behavioral disorders in dementia. A person exhibiting severe behavioral disorders should receive a thorough medical evaluation, especially when symptoms come on suddenly. Sometimes, symptoms reflect an underlying infection or medical illness. For example, the pain or discomfort caused by pneumonia or a bladder infection can result in agitation. Many behavioral disorders (e.g., severe depression, psychotic symptoms, wandering) are a direct expression of damage to parts of the brain influencing emotions, perceptions, and personality. Some behavioral disorders (e.g., wandering, pacing) are often disturbing to others but not to the person with dementia. In such cases, after ensuring safety, it is best not to try to "fix" the behavioral problem but rather to tolerate it.

Behavioral disorders in people with dementia are managed primarily by individualized nondrug interventions. Medications can be effective in the management of severe psychosis, depression, or agitation, but they must be used carefully and are most effective when combined with behavioral interventions (Table 1).

Nondrug Interventions

By helping people in the early stages of dementia to prepare themselves emotionally for the slow but relentless decline with the help of emotional support from

Table 1   Medications Recommended for Behavioral Disorders

Problem	Medications That Might Help
Depression	Antidepressants (especially an SSRI) Anti-dementia drugs
Anxiety	Antidepressants (especially an SSRI) Buspirone Anti-dementia drugs
Psychosis	Atypical antipsychotics
Aggression	Atypical antipsychotics Anticonvulsants/mood stabilizers
Mixed (depression and psychosis)	Antidepressants plus atypical antipsychotics
Mixed (depression and aggression)	Antidepressants plus atypical antipsychotics

Note: SSRI = selective serotonin reuptake inhibitors.

health care professionals, family members and early stage support groups may prevent severe depression and reduce the risk of suicide. Improving physical functioning and maintaining current functioning reduce the risk of frustration and feelings of inadequacy and helplessness with which people with dementia often struggle. Assessing retained abilities of people with dementia and instituting specific programs to maintain these abilities for as long a time as possible may also help improve these persons' sense of self-worth and well-being. Environmental modifications can help compensate for the effects of dementia and can also decrease agitation experienced by people with dementia. By helping people with dementia reminisce, remember past joyful memories, and relive those memories, caregivers can brighten their present. Appropriate communication involves interacting with the afflicted persons within their own frame of reference for the world, even if it has little to do with reality, and validating their feelings. In the advanced stages, gentle silent contact is often all that people with dementia need to feel less lonely and to feel that they are still living human individuals. Despite the serious health problems people with dementia experience, they are able to share moments of tenderness and love for their families and caregivers through all stages of the disease. It is important to realize that there are things that can be done to allow people with dementia to remain "alive"—not just living with the disease.

Ensuring the long-term well-being of caregivers through support, education, and training is crucial to successful management of behavioral disorders. Caring for behavioral disorders in dementia needs to be approached with a new vision, focusing on life-enhancing care with experienced caregivers. Such an environment includes respect, choices, love, spirituality, and music. Care providers need to offer hope and stories of inspiration to people with dementia and their loved ones. Ongoing stimulation of the mind, body, and soul of a person with dementia at home, as well as in an institutional setting, can sustain older adults with dementia at a far higher level than is generally believed.

—*George T. Grossberg and Abhilash K. Desai*

See also Agitation; Alzheimer's Disease; Anxiety Disorders; Emotions and Emotional Stability; Mental Status Assessment; Pseudodementia; Vascular Dementia

Further Readings and References

Mahoney EK, Volicer L, Hurley AC. *Management of Challenging Behaviors in Dementia.* Baltimore, Md: Health Professions Press; 2000.

Szwabo PA, Grossberg GT, eds. *Problem Behaviors in Long-Term Care: Recognition, Diagnosis, and Treatment.* New York: Springer; 1993.

Treatment of dementia and its behavioral disturbances: The Expert Consensus Guideline Series. *Postgrad Med Spec Rep.* 2005;(January):1–107.

BEREAVEMENT AND GRIEF

Death is a common and natural part of life. Despite its commonality, the death of a loved one can often be an extremely painful and stressful experience. In the United States, the *Diagnostic and Statistical Manual of Mental Disorders, Fourth Edition, Text Revision* (DSM-IV-TR) describes bereavement as a "normal" reaction to the death of a loved one, with expressions of grief such as feelings of sadness, insomnia, poor appetite, and weight loss lasting no longer than 2 months. Grief and bereavement are not universal concepts. How individuals cope with loss and how long they mourn vary from culture to culture and from person to person, and people's reactions to a loss run the spectrum from returning to baseline levels of emotional well-being shortly after the death of a loved one to experiencing emotional disturbance many years later. Although there are substantial individual differences, the bereavement pattern theory notes five distinct bereavement patterns: chronic depression, chronic grief, depressed improved, common grief, and resilience.

Bereavement Patterns

According to this bereavement pattern theory, those identified as having a *chronic depression* pattern were depressed prior to bereavement and had high levels of depression after the loss. These individuals were experiencing emotional distress that was exacerbated by the loss of their loved one. In contrast, in the *chronic grief* pattern, distress was due to the cognitive and emotional trauma of losing a beloved friend or relative. These individuals became depressed following the loss and remained depressed 18 months later.

The *depressed improved* pattern showed high levels of depression pre-loss with subsequent low levels of depression post-loss. Death was seen as the end of a struggle. The person who died had a chronic illness that required a lot of attention and care and subsequently strained relationships.

The *common grief* pattern is perhaps the most well-known and easily identifiable pattern, falling in line with the DSM-IV-TR. Individuals going through common grief had low pre-loss levels of depression, exhibit short-lived grief reactions, and return to pre-loss levels of functioning relatively quickly.

The *resilience* pattern, once thought to be rare, unhealthy, and indicative of psychopathology, has proven to be an adaptive way to cope with loss. Those thought of as resilient do not exhibit any pre-loss distress; they are absent of any grief symptoms and continue to function adequately following the loss.

Protective Factors

If resilience is a protective factor against grief and bereavement, the dimensions that promote resilience should be explored. As the first dimension, hardiness (a personality trait) consists of three factors: a commitment to discovering meaning to one's own life, the belief that the outcome of events is shaped by one's environment over which one has control, and the belief that positive and negative life experiences have the ability to teach and allow one to grow. Hardy individuals tend to be more confident, use active coping and social support, and appraise potentially stressful situations as less threatening, thereby reducing their levels of distress.

Self-enhancement is another dimension associated with resilience. It has been argued that to be mentally healthy, one does not need to accept one's own physical limitations and negative characteristics; rather, one should have biases that are unrealistic and overly positive in favor of the self. There are some negatives to

high self-esteem. Those who tend to self-enhance also tend to score high on narcissism scales and tend to elicit negative and unfavorable impressions from others. This is a trade-off that self-enhancers seem willing to make.

Perhaps the most unlikely dimension of resilience is repressive coping. Repressive copers tend to avoid unpleasant thoughts, emotions, and memories using emotion-focused mechanisms such as emotional dissociation. Although emotional dissociation has long been believed to be maladaptive and associated with long-term health risks, it has been shown to foster adaptation to extreme adversity and not cause somatic or other health problems.

Until recently, the utility and power of positive emotion and laughter had been ignored. Recent research has shown that positive emotions can undo the damage of negative emotions and thereby reduce the levels of emotional distress caused by an aversive event. One study has suggested that bereaved individuals who genuinely laughed and smiled when speaking about their recent losses had better adjustment over several years of bereavement than did those who did not, and such behavior also increased the level of support that the bereaved received from those they considered to be important members of their social environment.

Risk Factors

As noted when describing hardiness and positive emotion, *social support* plays an important role in protecting one from experiencing high levels of grief. The lack of social support has been identified as a risk factor in bereavement. Those who are socially isolated, lack support from close friends or relatives, or perceive the support as unsupportive run the risk of chronic depression or chronic grief if not already depressed.

The *manner in which a loved one dies* is another risk factor in bereavement. The sudden unexpected losses for which people are unprepared are more difficult to deal with than natural causes of death. The greater the number of deaths an individual needs to deal with at a time can significantly alter the manner in which he or she copes with the loss. A violent or horrific death not only can affect the grief trajectory an individual follows but also makes him or her more susceptible to posttraumatic stress disorder. When the person feels responsible for the loved one's death, guilt may follow and therefore complicate the bereavement. When others are seen as responsible for a loved one's death, the surviving family member or friend may feel a loss of control over life and fall into a state of depression. The loss of a loved one should be acknowledged and mourned appropriately. There are times when grief is discouraged and the loved one is allowed to pass without the proper farewell or acknowledgment. This can put the survivor at risk in bereavement.

Personal vulnerability is the third and final risk factor in bereavement. The more dependent the deceased was on the survivor, or the more dependent the survivor was on the deceased, the more complicated the bereavement. If the deceased depended heavily on the survivor, death forces the surviving individual to fill that void and perhaps create a new identity independent of the role the individual filled while the deceased was alive. If the survivor depended on the deceased, the individual must now learn to be assertive and do things on his or her own. If high self-esteem can protect an individual from experiencing high levels of distress, the opposite—low self-esteem—could lead to high levels of grief. Those who have histories of mental illness are also more susceptible to exhibiting higher levels of grief than are those who have no psychological vulnerability.

One study by Dolores Gallagher-Thompson and colleagues highlighted the damaging effects that these risk factors can have. Fully 16% of participants died 18 months after their spouses had died, compared with only 2% in the control group. All of those who died had characteristics in common; they were older men in poor health, they had little social support, and their wives were their main confidantes. All of them were highly dependent on their wives and could not adapt after their losses.

Treatment for Grief and Bereavement

Most bereaved individuals cope effectively with the loss of their loved ones, but many experience moderate to severe physical and emotional distress.

Psychologists need to be aware of the impact that bereavement can have on individuals' lives and the factors that put these individuals at risk. Individual and group psychotherapy of various orientations has been used to treat those suffering from complicated bereavement, but results of studies analyzing the effectiveness of these various interventions have been mixed. Cognitive–behavioral therapy has proven to be effective in treating those with complex grief reactions. In some studies, cognitive techniques (e.g., thought challenges) were combined with behavioral techniques (e.g., learning to talk about upsetting emotions) to reduce the symptoms of grief.

Cultural Considerations

Mental health professionals should be keenly aware of the culture of the bereaved, just as they would pay attention to treatment modality, risk, and protective factors. The meaning of death is likely to differ between ethnic and cultural groups; normative ways of expressing grief, mourning practices, and rituals will vary. For example, in the Jewish faith, *shiva* consists of the 7 days of mourning when most family members remain at home and do not go on with their normal everyday lives. A *shiva* candle is lit and remains burning for the entire 7 days. The practice of covering mirrors may be symbolic; people should not look at their reflections because they do not want to reflect on themselves. In Mexico, the dead have their own day, *Dia de los Muertos* (Day of the Dead), a festive holiday that allows families to remember their dead and celebrate the continuity of life. Grief and bereavement are complex constructs that are not always easily defined. Culture can provide insight as to what is a normal reaction for someone who has lost a loved one, but the psychologist must look beyond the culture of origin, analyze the risk and protective factors of the individual, and formulate a treatment plan based on empirically supported principles.

—*Dolores Gallagher-Thompson,*
Daniel E. Jimenez, and Heather L. Gray

See also Caregiving; Death, Dying, and Hospice Care; Emotions and Emotional Stability; Posttraumatic Stress Disorder; Stress; Suicide and the Elderly

Further Readings and References

Bonanno GA, Moskowitz JT, Papa A, Folkman S. Resilience to loss in bereaved spouses, bereaved parents, and bereaved gay men. *J Personal Social Psychol.* 2005;88:827–843.

Florsheim M, Gallagher-Thompson D. Cognitive/behavioral treatment of atypical bereavement: A case study. *Clin Gerontol.* 1990;10:73–76.

Gallagher D, Thompson LW, Peterson J. Psychosocial factors affecting adaptation to bereavement in the elderly. *Intl J Aging Hum Dev.* 1981–1982;14:81–97.

Gantz F, Gallagher-Thompson D, Rodman J. Cognitive/behavioral facilitation of inhibited grief. In: Freeman A, Dattilio FM, eds. *Comprehensive Casebook of Cognitive Therapy.* New York: Plenum; 1992:201–207.

Niemeyer RA. Psychological research on death attitudes: An overview and evaluation. *Death Stud.* 2004;28:309–340.

Niemeyer RA. Research on grief and bereavement: Evolution and revolution. *Death Stud.* 2004;28:489–490.

Thompson LW, Kaye J, Tang PCY, Gallagher-Thompson D. Bereavement and adjustment disorders. In: Blazer D, Steffens DC, Busse EW, eds. *Textbook of Geriatric Psychiatry.* 3rd ed. Washington, DC: American Psychiatric Press; 2004:319–338.

BIOLOGICAL THEORIES OF AGING

Aging is a complex natural process that involves a gradual progressive decline in tissue and organ function. These biological processes of aging result in increasing susceptibility to environmental challenges and an increasing risk of disease and death. Aging processes encompass molecular, physiological, and genetic processes that in combination contribute to the progressive declines in tissue functions that affect the mind and body. The complexity of aging processes is further indicated by their differential effects on the tissues and organs of complex organisms. Thus, the aging phenotype is the consequence of homeostatic changes in natural intrinsic biological processes and the increased susceptibility to environmental extrinsic factors that accelerate the development of the aging phenotype. In general, these characteristics suggest that aging is associated with major losses of fitness, as indicated by the failure of specific tissue and organ functions. Current physiological, genetic, and biochemical studies indicate that aging, longevity, and the retardation or slowing down of aging processes can be achieved in animal models. These studies demonstrate that life extension can be attained by slowing down aging, combating age-associated diseases, or decreasing causes of death among the young. These relatively recent developments of our understanding of some of the biological mechanisms of aging clearly suggest that the underlying mechanisms of aging involve molecular, genetic, physiological, and metabolic processes. The ability to "manipulate" these processes that either retard or accelerate the aging phenotype are basic experimental approaches toward understanding the complex biological mechanisms of aging and longevity.

What Are the Underlying Causes of Aging?

Aging is a complex of biological processes involving mechanisms of regulation of altered gene expression, protein synthesis and degradation (protein turnover), and processes associated with oxidative metabolism and biological processes of detoxification. Furthermore, a major causative factor that has the potential to alter regulatory processes involves products of oxidative metabolism; that is, the metabolic production of oxygen-free radicals or reactive oxygen species (ROS) that damage macromolecules such as deoxyribonucleic acid (DNA) and proteins. Current theories on the molecular mechanisms of aging and longevity assurance propose that aging results from the accumulation of various intrinsic endobiotic toxins, also referred to as "metabolic rubbish," whose production is due to the failure of metabolic detoxification processes. These natural biological processes are the body's mechanisms for protection against intrinsic (endobiotic) and environmental toxins.

There are a variety of theories of age-associated molecular interactions that focus on the development of cellular and organ dysfunction and deterioration. Many of these theories address the mechanisms of molecular, genetic, physiological, and environmental factors that affect cell and tissue homeostasis in aging.

Most recently, theories of molecular mechanisms of aging have focused on evidence that aging involves the metabolic generation of oxygen-free radicals (ROS) that damage macromolecules and the consequences of the failure to remove or repair these macromolecules. In aging tissues, these oxidatively damaged macromolecules affect the efficiency of tissue and organ function. Thus, the processes of aging and development of age-associated diseases has been attributed to the deleterious effects of oxygen-free radicals (ROS) that cause oxidative damage to macromolecules. Furthermore, because critical metabolic functions are localized within intracellular "factories" called organelles (metabolic power houses), oxidative damage to these structures may affect their efficiency of biological function. This is a major cause of the age-associated progressive decline in tissue function. This entry summarizes selected current theories of the molecular mechanisms of aging:

Somatic Mutation Theory

The somatic mutation theory proposes that the capacity of cells to repair oxidatively damaged DNA is an important determinant of the rate of aging. Studies showing a general relationship between longevity and efficiency of DNA repair support this hypothesis. For example, increased activity of certain enzymes associated with DNA repair that are responsive to stress-induced DNA damage is also associated with increased life span. Mitochondria are the major intracellular organelles that house the metabolic machinery for respiration and energy production (adenosine triphosphate [ATP] synthesis), fatty acid, and steroid metabolism. Mitochondria convert oxygen and food to energy in the form of ATP. This biological energy (ATP) is needed for most cellular processes. The importance of efficient mitochondrial function in longevity determination is well established experimentally. Furthermore, stress-induced damage to mitochondrial DNA (mtDNA) and its ability to efficiently repair the damaged DNA contributes to the age-associated development of oxygen-free radicals that result in the oxidative damage to macromolecules, including DNA and proteins, that in turn affects life span.

Mitochondrial Theory

Mitochondrial theory proposes a connection between molecular stress and aging due to the accumulation of mtDNA damage. It is well established that there is an age-related increase in mitochondrial dysfunction that involves the release of electrons, resulting in an increase in production of oxygen-free radicals (ROS). The ROS are harmful by-products of mitochondrial oxidative metabolism and are produced by dysfunction of the mitochondrial electron transport machinery. The mitochondrial electron transport chain carries out the basic functions of respiration and ATP synthesis. The failure of this electron transport chain results in the release of ROS that are normally required for energy production (ATP). These radicals result in oxidative damage of mitochondrial proteins. These damaged proteins accumulate in aged tissues, resulting in the dysfunction of the cells' major source of energy. Therefore, the occurrence of mitochondrial dysfunction results in impaired ATP production and decline in tissue bioenergetics. The overall result is a decrease or decline in the ability of tissues and organs to carry out energy requiring metabolic processes.

Theories of Protein Modification and Waste Accumulation

For proteins to carry out their functions, they must first be properly folded. When intrinsic (metabolic) and extrinsic (environmental) toxins generate ROS, proteins that are damaged by the ROS are often misfolded. Oxygen-free radicals are notorious for their ability to cause the misfolded protein syndromes that include neurodegenerative and other diseases of aging. If these proteins are not replaced, their functions are altered, thereby affecting the efficiency of organellar, cellular, and organ function. Protein damage due to oxidative radicals cannot be repaired. These damaged proteins must be replaced through the process of protein turnover. The significant accumulation of damaged proteins in aged tissues suggests that protein turnover, which is essential for removal and replacement of damaged proteins, is slowed down in aged tissues. Thus, the accumulation of these proteins is a basic factor in the gradual decline in tissue function associated with the development of physiological characteristics of aging, including age-related diseases. Protein turnover involves the functions of specific proteins called chaperones, which play a key role in the regulation of proper protein folding, and *proteasomes*, which play a role in the degradation of misfolded proteins. The activities of both proteasomes and chaperones have been reported as decreased in aged tissues. The decline in function of these proteins results in decreased efficiency of the protein turnover machinery, thereby causing an accumulation of damaged proteins that results in progressive decline in cell and tissue function.

Network Theories of Aging

Because of the complexity of the aging processes, it is evident that multiple types of damage to macromolecules (e.g., DNA, protein) could accumulate. The "network" theory proposes that the factors associated with the various processes of aging emphasize the importance of interactions and synergism among these different processes. Furthermore, the complexity of multicellular organisms due to particular cell- or tissue-specific phenotypes and their functions suggests that some organs may be more susceptible to aging because of their "cell types." For example, although the gradual accumulation of mtDNA mutations occurring over years may determine the level of accumulation of oxidatively damaged mitochondrial proteins, the level of damaging ROS production may be greater in tissues that require more energy metabolism such as the heart and brain. This results in a gradual decline in energy production in these tissues, ultimately resulting in a collapse of their function. Understanding the levels of metabolic interactions and interconnections of the various aging processes is, therefore, basic to understanding the rates of development of aging characteristics in specific tissues and organs of complex organisms. This would explain the higher level of susceptibility of various organs to age-associated dysfunction and disease and may further provide basic information for the development of pharmaceutical interventions against age-associated cellular deterioration.

Aging of Specific Cell Types

Complex organ functions are accomplished by highly specialized cell types whose abundance and localization are specific for each organ. Thus, cells damaged because of their particular metabolic functions could coexist alongside relatively undamaged cells. This raises the question of the frequency and rate of replacement of seriously damaged cells that might account for the age-associated accumulation of these cells and the significant impairment of tissue function. For example, the architecture of the liver places the liver cells or hepatocytes in a specific cord array where the potential stem cells that replace damaged hepatocytes are closest to the portal vein, whereas the hepatocytes aligned along the cord and away from the vein carry out various specific liver functions. Thus, the level of damage of the stem cells and the cells along the cord affects the ability of the damaged liver both to regenerate and to conduct its metabolic functions. Similarly, the architecture of the brain facilitates the complex neuronal functions and immunoinflammatory processes that are carried out by highly specialized cells. These cells exhibit different rates of aging, depending on their metabolic functions. Those cells that are highly susceptible to oxidative damage and accumulation of damaged proteins may account for various neurodegenerative diseases. The kidney consists of a unique architecture that facilitates its specific functions. Thus, the medulla is of particular interest because it mediates ionic exchange in an environment of increased ionic strength (due to high urea levels), favoring oxidative damage and misfolding of proteins. Therefore, it is important to understand the specific functions of highly specialized differentiated cells, their architectural positions within the organ, and how susceptible these functions are to aging mechanisms such as oxidative stress and detoxification.

Summary and Concluding Remarks

The optimal allocation of metabolic resources, mainly energy, between cellular maintenance and repair and cellular growth and reproduction is an important factor for the maintenance of a healthy and sound physiological condition. This allocation of metabolic resources involves the ability to maintain and repair macromolecules that have been damaged by either intrinsic challenges (metabolic factors such as oxidative metabolism) and extrinsic challenges (environmental toxicants). Intrinsic challenges include dysfunctional processes that produce damaging agents such as oxidative-free radicals and failure to properly detoxify both intrinsic and extrinsic toxicants.

Aging results from the accumulation of cellular and molecular damage due to increasing limitations in these maintenance and repair functions. Such damage accumulates throughout life and, importantly, accumulation of damaged proteins is indicative of failure of the machinery that regulates removal of damaged proteins.

Longevity is controlled primarily through genes that regulate the levels of tissue and organ maintenance and repair functions. The activities of specific gene clusters that determine the rate at which damage accumulates (maintenance and repair) may be altered early in the life cycle such that their activities would favor longevity, for example, decreased oxygen-free radical production and levels of oxidatively damaged macromolecules.

The mechanisms of cellular and molecular aging are strongly influenced by environmental factors that affect the rates of intrinsic aging.

—*John Papaconstantinou*

See also Neurobiology of Aging; Normal Physical Aging

Further Readings and References

Burkel A. Physiology and pathophysiology of poly(ADP-ribose)ylation. *Bioessays.* 2001;23:795–806.

Carrard G, Bulteau AL, Petropooulos I, Friguet B. Impairment of proteasome structure and function in aging. *Intl J Biochem Cell Biol.* 2002;34:1461–1474.

Gems D, McElwee JJ. Broad spectrum detoxification: The major longevity assurance process regulated by insulin/IGF-1 signaling. *Mech Ageing Dev.* 2005;126:381–387.

Grube K, Burkle A. Poly(ADP-ribose) polymerase activity in mononuclear leukocytes of 13 mammalian species correlates with species-specific life span. *Proc Natl Acad Sci USA.* 1992;89:11759–11763.

Kipling D, Davis T, Ostler EL, Faragher RG. What can progeroid syndromes tell us about human aging? *Science.* 2004;305:1426–1431.

Kirkwood TB. Understanding the odd science of aging. *Cell.* 2005;120:437–447.

Murias M-L, Muller M, Schachter F, Burkle A. Increased poly(ADP-ribose) polymerase activity in lymphoblastoid cell lines from centenarians. *J Mol Med.* 1998;76:346–354.

National Institute on Aging. *Aging Under the Microscope: A Biological Quest.* Bethesda, Md: Department of Health and Human Services, National Institutes of Health; 2002. Available at: www.niapublications.org/pubs/microscope/index.asp. Accessed September 8, 2006. NIH Publication No. 02–2756.

Papaconstantinou J. Unifying model of the programmed (intrinsic) and stochastic (extrinsic) theories of aging: The stress response genes, signal transduction–redox pathways of aging. *Ann NY Acad Sci.* 1994;719:195–211.

Promislow DE. DNA repair and the evolution of longevity: A critical analysis. *J Theor Biol.* 1994;170:291–300.

Wallace DC. Mitochondrial diseases in man and mouse. *Science.* 1999;283:1482–1488.

Soti C, Csermely P. Aging and molecular chaperones. *Exp Gerontol.* 2003;38:1037–1040.

Biomarkers of Aging

Biomarkers are biological characteristics that can be used as "markers," or measurable indicators, of underlying biological processes or traits that are difficult to observe directly. In aging research, biomarkers have generally been used to study three types of processes: disease processes associated with age, physiological processes that change with age, and aging itself.

Biomarkers of Disease

The use of biomarkers to diagnose and monitor disease is the model for biomarker research. A useful example of biomarkers in medicine comes from endocrinology, where glycated hemoglobin is used as an indicator of long-term blood glucose. A biomarker is useful in this case because long-term blood glucose levels are difficult to measure accurately and oral glucose tolerance tests for diabetes require patients to fast, making the tests somewhat difficult to administer. However, tests of the level of glycated hemoglobin (Hba1c) do not require fasting, are simple to perform, and can be interpreted as the average level of circulating glucose over the previous 60 to 90 days. Although tests of glycated hemoglobin cannot take the place of more complex measures in a complete diagnosis of diabetes, they can provide a useful initial indicator of the interaction between diet and metabolism and thus be a useful biomarker of long-term blood glucose.

A variety of biomarkers have been used to study other age-related diseases, including cancer, Alzheimer's disease, and cardiovascular disease. Biomarkers are used in a variety of ways: to assess exposure to risk factors (e.g., exposure to carcinogens), to gain insight into disease mechanisms (e.g., the role of inflammation in Alzheimer's disease), to understand susceptibility to a disease (e.g., genetic risk), to diagnose diseases (e.g., the use of blood pressure to diagnose hypertension), and to make treatment decisions and assess risk of disease outcomes among those who already have a disease (e.g., monitoring lipid levels in patients with atherosclerosis). The use of biomarkers in clinical practice is rapidly expanding as new and better markers of disease risk are being developed.

Biomarkers of Physiological Processes

Just as biomarkers can be used to study disease processes, biomarkers can shed light on normal physiological changes with age. For instance, the stress response in the hypothalamic–pituitary–adrenal (HPA) axis becomes increasingly dysregulated and inefficient with age. HPA axis activity is complex, involving a range of stress hormones and responses. Cortisol is a stress hormone that is highly responsive to changes in environmental stressors and can be easily collected in saliva or urine, making cortisol a useful biomarker of the stress response. Using cortisol as a biomarker of stress allows one to make comparisons of the stress responses across individuals and to look for factors that moderate this response. However, there are limitations to this approach. Cortisol is simply a marker of a much more complex stress process, and levels of cortisol can be affected by other factors, such as genetics and metabolism, in addition to stress. For this reason, it is sometimes helpful to use multiple markers of a complex process.

A great deal of what is known about age-related changes in the immune system comes from research using multiple biomarkers to understand different dimensions of the immune system. One important biomarker of immune function is T-cell count. T-cells attack infected or damaged cells and mobilize other parts of the immune system. Although the total number of T-cells remains fairly stable with age, the number of functioning T-cells declines and T-cells in older people take longer to renew than they do in younger people. These findings offer potential explanations for reduced immunity among older adults. In addition, increases in inflammatory proteins, such as interleukin 6 (IL-6) and C-reactive protein (CRP), have been observed with age. These proteins are part of the acute phase response to injury or infection but appear to be chronically elevated among older people and may contribute to the development of chronic disease.

Multiple biomarkers are also used to create summary measures of physiological function. Measures of allostatic load or cumulative biological risk add risk across a range of biomarkers to create an indicator of overall functional capacity or frailty. In clinical practice, the metabolic syndrome is used to identify individuals at high risk for poor metabolic and cardiovascular outcomes, including heart disease, stroke, and diabetes. Patients are classified as having metabolic syndrome if they exhibit clinical risk on three or more of a set of five biomarkers of metabolic function: waist circumference, blood pressure, triglycerides, fasting blood glucose, and high-density lipoprotein (HDL) cholesterol.

Biomarkers provide an important tool for the study of age-related physiological changes. Although it is difficult to measure the stress response, immune function, or metabolic dysregulation directly, biomarkers associated with each of these processes, such as cortisol, CRP, and indicators of metabolic syndrome, are measured more easily. Use of these biomarkers provides a relatively noninvasive way to monitor physiological changes with age.

Biomarkers of Aging

An important area of biomarker research in aging has been the search for biomarkers of the aging process, that is, markers of "biological age" that predict age-related outcomes better than chronological age. This line of research reflects an underlying premise that the rate of aging varies in systemic ways across individuals and populations. Normal aging appears to be quite variable, as evidenced by differences in the age at onset of disease and disability. A biomarker of aging would allow researchers to identify individuals aging at different rates and to directly test potential anti-aging therapies. Although some interventions, such as caloric restriction and the use of antioxidants, alter mortality patterns and extend the life span of laboratory animal models, it is unclear whether these interventions actually delay or slow aging itself.

A trait would need to meet at least three criteria to be considered a biomarker of aging. First, it should predict physiological function across multiple domains in an age-coherent way and do so better than chronological age. Second, it should predict remaining longevity from an early age. Third, its measurement should not alter other age-sensitive traits such as life expectancy and disease state. Although no biomarker that satisfies all of these criteria has yet been identified, several promising biomarkers may prove to be useful as biomarkers of aging. One such marker is CD4 memory T-cells. This type of T-cell is predictive of remaining life span in mice and increases with age, but it decreases in mice exposed to caloric restriction. Another potential biomarker of aging is telomere length. Each time a vertebrate cell divides, the chromosomes get shorter as their ends, or telomeres, are removed and not replaced. Although telomere length is an indicator of cell division history rather than a direct indicator of aging, it might be informative as an indicator of aging in cells where replicative potential is crucial to function.

The difficulties inherent in identifying biomarkers of aging include lack of a common definition of aging or an agreement about the role of biomarkers, extensive biological variation in aging between individuals that makes generalizations difficult, and overlapping aging and disease processes and accompanying difficulty in identifying benign versus pathogenic age-related change. Demonstrating that a given characteristic changes with age is not sufficient to call it a biomarker of aging. A biomarker must divide individuals of a given chronological age into groups that vary in a range of other age-sensitive traits such as mortality risk and functional capacity. Despite these difficulties, the potential of biomarkers to provide insights into the fundamental causes of aging drives the search for biomarkers of the aging process.

Conclusion

Biomarkers today are used by health practitioners and researchers in a variety of settings, including clinical settings, laboratories, and community-based surveys. Epidemiological studies using biomarkers (e.g., MacArthur Study of Successful Aging, Baltimore Longitudinal Study of Aging, Women's Health and Aging Study, National Health and Nutrition Examination Survey) have expanded our knowledge base about aging in the community, population differences in health, and the clinical significance of many biomarkers. Some of the most commonly used biomarkers include blood pressure as a marker of cardiovascular health and cholesterol levels and glycated hemoglobin as markers of metabolic health. However, biomarker technology is rapidly evolving, and biomarkers are being used in population surveys to assess nutritional status, genetic background, and function in many organs and systems (e.g., immune system, lung function, kidney function, liver function, reproductive function).

Fundamentally, biomarkers provide a measurement tool for observing physiological processes, including disease processes, physiological changes related to aging, and the aging process. Although biomarker research is advancing rapidly, in many ways it is still in its early stages. Many biomarkers of disease are commonly used in clinical practice, and population-based research on biomarkers of age-related processes is leading to the discovery of additional clinically relevant biomarkers. However, consensus has yet to emerge about reliable biomarkers of the aging process that could be used to test anti-aging interventions. The great advantage of biomarkers is that they represent a window to physical processes that are difficult to observe and quantify directly, providing tools for aging researchers and health practitioners in a variety of disciplines to better understand changes in health with age.

—Dawn Alley

See also Allostatic Load and Homeostasis; Biological Theories of Aging; Metabolic Syndrome; Normal Physical Aging

Further Readings and References

Butler RN, Sprott R, Warner H, et al. Biomarkers of aging: From primitive organisms to humans. *J Gerontol A Biol Sci Med Sci.* 2004;59:560–567.

Crimmins EM, Seeman TE. Integrating biology into demographic research on health and aging (with a focus on the MacArthur Study of Successful Aging). In: Finch CE, Vaupel JW, Kinsella K, eds. *Cells and Surveys: Should Biological Measures Be Included in Survey Research?* Washington, DC: National Academy Press; 2001:9–41.

Miller RA. Biomarkers of aging: Prediction of longevity by using age-sensitive T-cell subset determinations in a middle-aged, genetically heterogeneous mouse population. *J Gerontol A Biol Sci Med Sci.* 2001;56: B180–B186.

Rothman N, Steward WF, Schulte PA. Incorporating biomarkers into cancer epidemiology: A matrix of biomarker and study design categories. *Cancer Epidemiol Biomarkers Prev.* 1995;4:301–311.

BODY COMPOSITION

Aging is associated with significant changes in body composition, including a decrease in bone and lean mass and an increase and redistribution of fat mass. Theses changes have important implications for the health and functioning of older adults because of their associations with chronic diseases and geriatric syndromes, including mobility impairment, falls, and functional decline. There is evidence to suggest that at least a portion of what has been attributed to age-related changes in body composition is due to factors such as decreased physical activity, excess energy consumption, decreased consumption of particular macro- or micronutrients, hormonal changes, or a combination of these factors. Many of these factors may be reversible, although more research is needed to elucidate the role of exercise, nutrition, and hormone replacement in various patient populations.

Measurement

The body cell mass is generally composed of skeletal components (e.g., muscle, bone), interstitial fluids, and adipose tissue. Several methods based on different models are available to measure body composition in older adults. Each method has different strengths and weaknesses that are beyond the scope of this entry. Methods for measuring body compartments derive from their chemical components; potassium is the dominant intracellular element, sodium is the dominant extracellular/interstitial element, calcium is the dominant element in bone, and fat is the defining component of adipose tissue. Anthropomorphic measurements, hydrodensitometry/air plesmography, and bioelectrical impedance all provide information about a two-compartment model composed only of fat mass and fat-free mass. Anthropometric methods use skinfold thickness, arm or waist circumference, and other somatic measurements. Bioelectric impedance systems use electrical current to detect a voltage drop across the measured tissue. Hydrodensitometry and air plesmography measure the displacement of water and air, respectively. Dual-energy X-ray absorptiometry (DXA) adds a third component, bone mineral content, to the body composition model. Other imaging methods can measure body subcompartments and therefore can use a four-component model. Computed tomography (CT) and magnetic resonance imaging (MRI) can differentiate between subcutaneous adipose tissue (SAT) and visceral adipose tissue (VAT). Magnetic resonance spectroscopy (MRS) can provide further information about the location and amount of fat within muscle or organs such as the liver. These methods have been particularly valuable for studies that evaluate risk factors for chronic disease.

Changes in Lean Mass

Lean mass peaks during the third to fourth decades of life, followed by a steady decline with advancing age, particularly after 65 years. A loss in body potassium with age has been well documented. Skeletal muscle is the predominant component of lean mass. *Sarcopenia* is a commonly used term for the loss of muscle mass that occurs with aging. Skeletal muscle mass and/or size remains relatively constant during the third and fourth decades of life and begins to decline noticeably at approximately 45 years of age. A progressive decline occurs in the cross-sectional area of whole muscle and muscle fibers. The age- and sex-adjusted prevalence of sarcopenia varies between 6% and 27%, depending on the definition and measure of muscle mass used. In one study of older adults, the prevalence of sarcopenia increased to more than 50% in men over 80 years of age. There are some data to suggest that sarcopenia occurs to a greater extent in the lower extremities than in the upper extremities, although this may be related to changes in physical activity. Sarcopenia has been identified in both lean and obese (body mass index [BMI] > 27 kilograms per meter squared [kg/m²]) individuals. Other important changes in muscle with aging include a decrease in muscle strength, a decrease in muscle efficiency (muscle strength per unit of muscle mass), and a decrease in muscle protein synthesis. Peak muscle strength declines 8% to 10% per decade starting at approximately 40 years of age.

Sarcopenia is due to a number of underlying mechanisms, including intrinsic changes in the muscle and the central nervous system, changes in hormonal stimuli, and lifestyle factors. Intrinsic changes in muscle include a reduction in the specific type of muscle proteins (fast myosin heavy-chain isoforms) and Type II muscle fibers as well as damage to muscle mitochondrial DNA. Central nervous system changes include loss of alpha motor units from the spinal cord with selective denervation of muscle fibers. Because neural innervation is critical for muscle fiber maintenance, the loss of functioning motor units results in a decrease in the number of muscle fibers, with eventual skeletal muscle wasting. A number of hormones and cytokines affect muscle mass. Age-associated declines in testosterone and estrogen appear to accelerate loss of muscle mass, although the effect of estrogen may be mediated through its conversion to testosterone. Age-associated reductions in growth hormone, dehydroepiandrosterone (DHEA), and insulin sensitivity are postulated to contribute to sarcopenia, although confounding factors necessitate that more studies be done to clarify their relationship to muscle wasting. Activation of proinflammatory cytokines (e.g., interleukin 1, tumor necrosis factor, interleukin 6) that commonly occurs in older adults with acute and chronic illnesses causes accelerated protein breakdown in muscle and contributes to sarcopenia. Alterations in nutritional requirements and intake in older adults contribute to sarcopenia. Older adults require greater relative protein intake than do younger adults and often do not meet such requirements. Inadequate protein and/or caloric intake contributes to the development of sarcopenia. Vitamin D deficiency is also associated with muscle atrophy and impaired contractility, and there is a high prevalence of this deficiency in older adults. Deficiencies of Vitamin B6, magnesium, and potassium may also contribute to muscle loss. Lastly, decreases in physical activity that are common in older adults contribute to accelerated muscle loss. Exercise can increase muscle mass, even in very old or frail populations. Generalized weight gain from increased energy and protein intake in individuals with undernutrition can also increase muscle mass. The effects of other interventions for reversing sarcopenia, such as anabolic hormone therapy, have shown mixed results and require further study.

Changes in Fat Mass

Cross-sectional studies have shown that body weight and BMI increase with age in both men and women. The increase in fat mass appears to level off between 65 and 75 years of age. Fat redistributes centrally, with increases in waist circumference thought to reflect abdominal adiposity. The increase in abdominal adiposity occurs in both men and women but appears to accelerate after menopause in women. Visceral adipose tissue (VAT), muscle adipose tissue, and liver fat increase with age. Visceral and muscle adipose tissue have been shown to be important risk factors for insulin resistance, diabetes, and mortality from cardiovascular disease. It is unclear whether these regional increases in fat are only markers for more complex metabolic processes or have a more direct causative role in the pathogenesis of insulin resistance and related morbidity. Age-associated changes in fat mass are related to changes in physical activity and hormonal factors, including sex steroids. In addition to age-associated changes in fat mass, there has been an increase in the prevalence of obesity in older adults. It is now estimated that approximately 20% of the population age 65 years and older is obese.

Relationships With Functional Outcomes

Cross-sectional and longitudinal studies have shown that low muscle mass is associated with poor functional performance, self-reported disability, and increased fracture risk. In one study, the likelihood of functional disability was twofold greater in older men and threefold greater in older women with severe sarcopenia, compared with those with normal muscle mass. The effects of low muscle mass on function are probably mediated in large part by declines in muscle strength, although there may be a threshold below which muscle mass is independently associated with physical function. The combination of low muscle mass and obesity, or "sarcopenic obesity," may confer higher risk for self-reported disability than does either body composition type alone. High BMI is associated with impairment in performance of daily activities, mobility impairments, and increased risk for functional decline.

—*Ellen Binder*

See also Body Mass Index; Normal Physical Aging; Obesity; Osteoporosis; Sarcopenia

Further Readings and References

Fiatarone Singh MA. Benefits of exercise and dietary measures to optimize shifts in body composition with age. *Asia Pac J Clin Nutr.* 2002;11:S642–S652.

Janssen I, Ross R. Linking age-related changes in skeletal muscle mass and composition with metabolism and disease. *J Nutr Health Aging.* 2005;9:408–419.

St-Onge M. Relationship between body composition changes and changes in physical function and metabolic risk factors in aging. *Curr Opin Clin Nutr Metab Care.* 2005;8:523–528.

Body Mass Index

For adults age 18 years and older, the body mass index (BMI), or Quetelet index, is one of the best indirect indicators of degree of obesity. Calculated as weight (in kilograms) divided by height (in meters) squared (kg/m^2), adults are typically classified into one of four categories based on criteria established by the World Health Organization (WHO): underweight (BMI < 18.5 kg/m^2), normal weight (BMI 18.5 to 24.9 kg/m^2), overweight (BMI 25 to 29.9 kg/m^2), or obese (BMI ≥ 30 kg/m^2). An additional category, clinically severe or morbid obesity, corresponds to a BMI of 40 kg/m^2 or more and represents adults who are at least 100 pounds over their ideal body weight. Current estimates place approximately 22.3% of U.S. adults as obese (19.5% of men and 24.5% of women), with 2% being underweight. The optimal BMI for longevity appears to fall between 20.5 and 24.9 kg/m^2 for men and women of all ages, although recent evidence suggests that the longevity advantage may extend to those who are moderately overweight.

Under some conditions, the BMI may underestimate or overestimate degree of obesity. Underestimation may occur in adults who have lost muscle mass such as older adults, whereas overestimation may occur in those who are muscular. Underestimation or overestimation may also occur because the BMI calculation often relies on self-reported height and weight, which can change with age and with an individual's willingness to report this information correctly; for example, adults typically overestimate height and underestimate weight. The BMI also does not consider body fat distribution. For adults with an excess of body fat around the abdominal region (android or central obesity), other indirect measures may be more appropriate, including waist-to-hip ratio and waist circumference. For example, as adults age, body fat tends to shift from peripheral to central sites, causing an associated increase in waist-to-hip ratio with little or no increase in BMI.

Despite these potential limitations, the literature indicates good agreement between BMI and indexes of health such as mortality. The BMI–mortality relationship, often reported as U-shaped or J-shaped, shows mortality risk to increase in underweight (BMI < 18.5) and obese

(BMI ≥ 30) adults. Adjusting for factors that can potentially confound this relationship, such as smoking status and underlying disease, reduces the strength of the BMI–mortality relationship but does not eliminate it. Epidemiological data further show a consistent relationship between increasing BMI and a variety of chronic illnesses, including type 2 diabetes, hypertension, coronary artery disease (e.g., heart attack), high cholesterol, sleep apnea, degenerative joint disease, and certain cancers. Increasing BMI has also been associated with depression, low self-esteem, physical disability, social discrimination, and unemployment.

In summary, the BMI has proven to be an important tool in clinical and epidemiological studies. Because its calculation is simple and inexpensive and can be applied generally to all adults, the BMI has been used successfully to estimate body composition, develop reference standards, establish baseline data for longitudinal studies, monitor trends in specific populations, and assess risks for adverse health outcomes in all age groups.

—*Glenn V. Ostir*

See also Metabolic Syndrome; Multiple Morbidity and Comorbidity; Nutrition and Public Health; Obesity

Further Readings and References

Flegal KM, Graubard BI, Williamson DF, Gail MH. Excess deaths associated with underweight, overweight, and obesity. *JAMA.* 2005;293:1861–1867.

National Heart, Lung, and Blood Institute. *Clinical Guidelines on the Identification, Evaluation, and Treatment of Overweight and Obesity in Adults.* Washington, DC: Department of Health and Human Services, National Institutes of Health; 1998. NIH Publication No. 98–4083.

Schoenborn CA, Adams PF, Barnes PM. *Body Weight Status of Adults: United States, 1997–98.* Hyattsville, Md: National Center for Health Statistics; 2002. Advance Data From Vital and Health Statistics, No. 330.

BONE MASS

See OSTEOPOROSIS

Calcium Disorders of Aging

It is important to recognize calcium disorders when they present in older patients. Hypercalcemia, or elevated calcium levels, is seen more commonly than hypocalcemia, or low calcium levels. The most common symptoms of individuals with hypercalcemia include drowsiness, fatigue, muscle weakness, high blood pressure, constipation, and dehydration. Sometimes, individuals can present to the hospital in a coma. The most common cause of elevated calcium levels in people who present in an outpatient clinic is primary hyperparathyroidism, a condition where the hormone that regulates the body's calcium level, the parathyroid hormone, is overproduced. This overproduction leads to high levels of calcium. Long-term complications include kidney stones, osteoporosis, high blood pressure, and (with very elevated calcium levels) life-threatening illness. This disorder can be corrected with the surgical removal of the parathyroid gland.

A serious form of hypercalcemia is seen in patients who have a history of cancer. When cancer spreads to the bones, this alters the body's regulation of calcium. More than 95% of the calcium in our body is stored in our bones and can be released in excess when metastasis from certain cancers occurs.

A less common form of hypercalcemia is due to excess consumption of calcium, Vitamin A, or Vitamin D in the diet. In the past, many patients used antacids and baking soda to relieve heartburn. Most older antacids contain high levels of calcium. Consuming very large amounts of these antacids can lead to hypercalcemia. Newer medications for heartburn and stomach ulcers do not contain large amounts of calcium.

The most common symptoms of hypocalcemia are mental confusion, muscle spasms, tingling, and seizures. Some of the causes of low calcium include prior surgical removal of the parathyroid glands, renal failure, and poor dietary intake of calcium and Vitamin D. Vitamin D deficiency is a very common and treatable cause of hypocalcemia. Vitamin D is derived from the diet and is converted to the active form by several organ systems. The first step in this transformation is initiated in the skin. In older adults, the skin becomes less efficient in converting the substrates of Vitamin D to its active form. As individuals live farther away from the equator and have limited sunlight exposure, their bodies do not produce adequate amounts of Vitamin D. These persons also tend to wear more clothing in cooler climates, blocking the effects of sunlight in converting Vitamin D to its active form. Vitamin D is further modified by the liver and kidney, so diseases of these organs can contribute to Vitamin D deficiency. Individuals who have liver failure, difficulty in absorbing fats, and/or chronic kidney disease are at risk for Vitamin D deficiency. Not only will Vitamin D deficiency cause low calcium levels, but also long-term deficiency leads to loss of bone or osteoporosis. Patients with osteoporosis should take in approximately 800 international units of Vitamin D per day. This will not only maintain calcium levels and but also prevent fractures.

—*Rajib K. Bhattacharya*

See also Fluids and Electrolytes; Fractures in Older Adults; Kidney Aging and Diseases; Osteoporosis

Further Readings and References

Carroll MF, Schade DS. A practical approach to hypercalcemia. *Am Fam Physic.* 2003;67:1959–1966.
Rural Nurse Organization Digital Library. Hypocalcemia clinical resources. Available at: http://ruralnurseor ganization-dl.slis.ua.edu/clinical/nephrology/electrolyte/ calcium/hypocalcemia.html. Accessed September 8, 2006.
Taniegra ED. Hyperparathyroidism. *Am Fam Physic.* 2004;69:333–339.

CANADA

Canada's aging population reflects the country's status as a more developed country, with just over 12% of its people age 65 years and older, projected to rise to more than 15% in 2011 when the baby boom generation begins to reach that age and to a high of more than 24% around 2036. The oldest old, or those age 80 years and older, are proportionately the fastest-growing segment of the population. Life expectancy at birth for men is the mid-70s and for women is the early 80s; at 65 years of age, life expectancy for men is the early 80s and for women is the mid-80s. The major causes of death are circulatory diseases (including heart disease and stroke), cancers, and respiratory diseases (including chronic degenerative diseases such as emphysema and chronic bronchitis). Women outnumber men in old age, increasingly so as they age. That is, women comprise approximately 60% of the elderly population but nearly 70% among those age 85 years and older.

Canada's population is multicultural; this is especially true among its seniors, more of whom are foreign born than among younger age groups. The ethnic composition of seniors reflects immigration policies of an earlier period, so that the majority are currently from other Western countries speaking one of Canada's two official languages: English and French. Visible minorities from Asia, Africa, and the Caribbean, currently a small but important proportion of Canada's senior population, will constitute growing proportions of its elderly population in future cohorts given that more recent immigration has been from these countries. First Nation people also constitute a small proportion of the Canadian senior population because of higher fertility and higher mortality rates than is evident in the general population. However, a rapid aging of their population is expected, with a doubling of their percentage age 65 years and older projected by 2016.

Canada consists of 10 provinces and 3 northern territories within political federalism. Not surprisingly, its elderly population is unevenly distributed geographically, with major concentrations in the south. The less economically prosperous provinces of Manitoba and Saskatchewan have the highest percentages of elderly people (15%) because young persons leave for jobs elsewhere, and the economically prosperous province of Alberta has the lowest percentage of elderly people (10%) because the young migrate for jobs there. Cities also vary considerably, with Canada's "oldest" city being Victoria, where more than 19% of the population is age 65 years and older.

In Canada, the physical health of seniors declines as they age. Seniors are more likely to suffer from chronic conditions than from acute illnesses; more than three quarters of all seniors living at home report being diagnosed with at least one chronic health condition. The most common is arthritis and rheumatism, followed by high blood pressure, food or other allergies, cataracts, back problems, and heart problems. Fewer seniors (approximately one third) suffer from any functional health problems; that is, functional disability or difficulties with basic or instrumental activities of daily living. Diseases that impair cognition also increase with age, specifically dementia (from less than 10% for those age 65 years and older to more than 20% for those age 80 years and older). Still, Canadians are becoming healthier longer; that is, overall levels of disability and disease are being postponed to later in life.

However, mental well-being, the subjective evaluation of one's overall quality of life that includes concepts such as happiness, life satisfaction, morale, trait affect, and domain-specific subjective physical health, do *not* decline as Canadians age. More than three quarters of seniors rate their health as *good, very good,* or *excellent.* In terms of sense of coherence (a view of the world that life is meaningful, events are comprehensible, and challenges are manageable), those age 75 years and older are three times more likely than 18- and 19-year-olds to score high on this measure.

When needed, it is the informal network of family and friends (primarily family) who provide care in Canada. Caregiving, not the formal health care system, provides the vast majority of care to seniors. It is usually provided by a woman—a wife if there is one, otherwise a daughter. Women, furthermore, are more likely to provide personal care and emotional support, whereas men are more likely to provide instrumental assistance with activities such as home maintenance and repair. Canadians regularly interact with and assist others; this is not usually referred to as *caregiving* unless the recipients are unable to perform the activities themselves.

Much of the research in Canada, as elsewhere in the West, focuses on one primary caregiver. Despite the popularity of terms such as the *sandwich generation,* the *generation in the middle,* and *hidden victims* to describe middle-aged family members providing care to seniors while simultaneously raising their children and working for pay, statistically few caregivers are in this situation. Rather, serial caregiving is a more accurate descriptor given that most persons finish child rearing prior to becoming caregivers to their parents. This task tends to be completed before they become caregivers to their spouses. In addition, despite the emphasis within much research on caregiver burden, and despite the fact that most caregivers experience some burden, heavy or extreme burden is sporadic and not continuous for most. Furthermore, despite the burden, nearly all caregivers wish to, and intend to, remain in this role and report that they are coping with its demands.

Canada's formal health care system is not one of socialized medicine. Rather, physician and hospital services are universally accessible through the provision of publicly insured services. Physicians are guaranteed remuneration for their work but operate mainly as private entrepreneurs, billing governments for their services. Medicare rests on five principles: universality, portability, accessibility, comprehensiveness, and nonprofit administration by a public agency. It is often referred to as defining the Canadian identity, distinct from the country's powerful southern neighbor, the United States, where no universal health care system exists. Nevertheless, Medicare in Canada has been criticized because of its medical focus and exclusion of nonmedical services, especially for an aging society. Notably, nursing home and home care are not included within the Canada Health Act. Given that delivery of health services falls within provincial jurisdiction and not federal jurisdiction, this results in varying levels and types of services in continuing care outside of the acute care sector (physicians and hospitals).

Much research focuses on the social determinants of health and a population health model of care, reflecting the influence of health economist Bob Evans. The importance of this perspective is evident in several national and provincial reports examining Canada's health care system since 1990. All of the reports call for a definition of health that is broader than a biomedical definition, recognition of informal caregivers, more health promotion and disease prevention from the health care system, and a shift from institution-based care to more community-based care. Despite the consensus within these reports (with the 2002 Romanow Report being the most recent), health reform since the early 1990s has seen a retrenchment of vested medical interests rather than a broadening from medical care to health care.

The current global neoliberal agenda has seen the rhetoric of health reform used to close hospital beds (and even entire hospitals), drastically increase outpatient surgeries, and turn home care from a community support system for those with chronic illness (primarily seniors) to a postacute care hospital support system with little (if any) attention to health promotion and the broader social determinants of health. There is major concern at the current time that Canada's signature on numerous international trade agreements will seriously affect its provision of health care to its citizens because those agreements contain provisions that would see Canada needing to reimburse private companies for lost future earnings if it decided to convert any of those services to public ones. The Romanow Report argues that Canada must, at every opportunity, explicitly state that its health care is not subject to these provisions.

In sum, the health status of Canadian seniors reflects their lives in a more developed nation. They live relatively long lives; their physical health declines as they age, but this decline is occurring later and later. Interestingly and contrary to their physical health, Canadian senior' psychological well-being or overall quality of life is excellent and often better than that reflected for younger adults. When their health does fail, family members are the most likely to provide assistance, doing so willingly. When seniors require formal services, they access Canada's universal Medicare system of physicians and hospitals. Long-term home care, so important for the chronic health problems experienced during old age, is currently in jeopardy as health reform retrenches back to a medical focus.

—*Neena L. Chappell*

See also Aging in Manitoba Longitudinal Study

Further Readings and References

Chappell NL, Penning MJ. Family caregivers in the context of health reform. In: Johnson D, ed. in chief. *The Cambridge Handbook of Age and Ageing.* Cambridge, England: Cambridge University Press; 2005:455–462.

Coburn D. Beyond the income inequality hypothesis: Class, neo-liberalism, and health inequalities. *Social Sci Med.* 2004;58:41–56.

Penning MJ. In the middle: Parental caregiving in the context of other roles. *J Gerontol B Psychol Sci Social Sci.* 1998;53:S188–S197.

Williams AP, Deber R, Barenek P, Gildiner A. From Medicare to home care: Globalization, state retrenchment, and the profitization of Canada's health-care system. In: Armstrong P, Armstrong H, Coburn D, eds. *Unhealthy Times: Political Economy Perspectives on Health and Care in Canada.* Don Mills, Ontario: Oxford University Press; 2001:7–30.

CANCER

Of all risk factors for cancer, aging is the most important. Between birth and 39 years of age, males have a 1-in-71 risk of having a cancer, whereas females have a 1-in-51 risk. Between 40 and 59 years of age, this risk is 1 in 12 for males and 1 in 11 for females, and between 60 and 79 years of age, it is 1 in 3 in males and 1 in 4 in females. What are the reasons for this dramatic increase?

Many explanations are proposed. The first one is a pure cumulative effect. One generally needs several mutations before a cancer emerges, and that takes time to happen. Mutations can happen for several reasons. One is direct injury to the genes such as sun exposure or radioactive products. Another is simply copying errors during cell divisions. Just like copying a long text on a word processor is nearly impossible to do without at least a few mistakes, so is DNA copying. Our cells come with very elaborate "spell check" mechanisms, but a few errors may persist. Some are lethal for the cell and some are meaningless, but others can push a cell down the path to cancer, especially those that disturb the "spell check" and cell cycle control mechanisms. Mutations that lead to an impairment of natural cell death are also frequently involved in cancer in that they allow damaged cells to survive. Another mechanism is that some people inherit more fragile chromosomes that tend to break down more easily than normal ones, explaining some familial cancers. Another mechanism could be the activation of an enzyme called telomerase that allows cells to multiply by avoiding a shortening of the caps at the ends of chromosomes. Another hypothesis is that, with age, cells become less resistant to oxidative damage. In addition, errors accumulate in the mechanisms that render a gene active or inactive. These are called epigenetic mechanisms. Also, the immune system may become less effective in eliminating cancer cells, and the ability to recognize new antigens decreases with age. Also, complex interactions that happen at the level of the tumor are not yet fully clarified. The immunological differences between a cancer cell and a normal cell are very subtle; after all, the substrate is one's own cells.

Other aspects of aging affect cancer treatment. For example, kidneys lose efficiency. The body contains less water and more fat. The bowel absorbs certain nutrients less effectively. These changes may affect the distribution of medications in the body. Many systems become more sensitive to stressors. For example, in the presence of diarrhea, dehydration develops more quickly and the compensatory thirst reflex is diminished. On the other hand, older persons are less sensitive to acute nausea after chemotherapy, although delayed nausea can remain a problem.

New cancer treatments during the past 50 years have had a greater impact on the young than on the old. Between 1950 and 2002, the U.S. death rate from cancer decreased by more than 60% in children and by 10% to 50% in young adults, but it increased by 10% to 20% in adults over 65 years of age. The causes of this discrepancy are multiple. First, cancer treatments have long been developed primarily for younger patients. The toxicity of these treatments was judged to be too high for older patients. Also, as competing causes of mortality are better treated, older patients are more likely to die from their cancers than they were before. Clearly, much effort still remains to improve the care of older cancer patients.

How does age objectively affect the ability to receive various cancer treatments? Several series show that elective surgery in older adults presents little more risk than in younger adults. Good preparation is the key. On the other hand, emergency surgery is accompanied by higher complication rates because the emergency condition itself stretches the stress reserves of the organism. With modern techniques, radiation therapy in older adults is as well tolerated as it is in younger adults. Daily transportation to the radiation center for up to 5 to 6 weeks can, however, be quite burdensome for older adults and those around them. Chemotherapy can be offered without too many restrictions to seniors in good health or with minor to moderate health problems. A study conducted at the Moffitt Cancer Center demonstrated that although half of the patients in their 70s or 80s experienced some significant side effects from their chemotherapy, as a group they were still able to maintain most normal activities throughout the treatment (but were more tired and needed occasional help

for more burdensome tasks). Such tolerance may be in part due to the many treatment consequences that do not have symptoms. For example, very low white blood counts, if not accompanied by infection, have little impact on the functioning of the patients. A key to good tolerance of chemotherapy is excellent supportive care. Ideally, and especially in patients with comorbidities, comprehensive care should be provided by a specialized geriatric oncology multidisciplinary team. Fortunately, the overall toxicity of chemotherapy regimens has decreased markedly over the past 15 years, and an increasing array of well-tolerated treatments is now available.

—*Martine Extermann*

See also Age-Related Changes in Pharmacokinetics and Pharmacodynamics; Biological Theories of Aging; Cancer, Common Types of; Multiple Morbidity and Comorbidity; Normal Physical Aging; Surgery

Further Readings and References

American Cancer Society. Statistics for 2006. Available at: www.cancer.org/docroot/STT/stt_0.asp. Accessed September 9, 2006.
National Cancer Institute. Surveillance, epidemiology, and end results. Available at: http://seer.cancer.gov. Accessed September 9, 2006.

CANCER, COMMON TYPES OF

Based on 2005 estimates from the Surveillance, Epidemiology, and End Results (SEER) registry of the National Cancer Institute and American Cancer Society, the most frequent types of cancer in men are (in descending order) prostate, lung, colorectal, bladder, melanoma, lymphoma, kidney, leukemia, mouth and pharynx, and pancreas. In woman, they are breast, lung, colorectal, uterine corpus, lymphoma, melanoma, ovary, thyroid, bladder, and pancreas. For all cancers, including the most common types (colon, breast, prostate, lung, and non-Hodgkin's lymphoma), most cases occur in those who are age 65 years and older.

Bladder Cancer

Bladder cancer is a disease that presents mostly in elderly people and in men more often than women. When bladder cancers are superficial, they can be surgically removed using a special instrument (cystoscope) that provides access to the bladder through the normal urinary drainage system rather than through an operation that requires opening the abdomen. A cotreatment (called an adjuvant treatment) with BCG (Bacillus Calmette–Guérin) vaccine instillations into the bladder is often added. When the tumor penetrates into the bladder muscle, the bladder must be resected or, if resection is not possible, treated with combined chemotherapy and radiation therapy. If bladder cancer is metastatic (spread to other distant sites), chemotherapy is the treatment of choice.

Breast Cancer

Breast cancer is the most frequent cancer among women. Most breast cancers will be sporadic (not related to inheritance), and approximately 5% to 10% are familial breast cancers. Familial breast cancers usually occur at an earlier age than do sporadic ones.

Although any type of breast cancer can happen at any age, some characteristics become more frequent with age. For example, a higher proportion of breast cancers will be hormone receptor positive. Normal breast cells have receptors for female hormones, estrogens and progesterone, which help breasts to develop during adolescence and pregnancy. When a breast cancer develops, its cells can either keep or lose these receptors. Hormone receptor-positive breast cancers tend to have a more indolent (slowly progressing) behavior. Receptor-positive breast cancer can also be treated more effectively with current cancer treatments. Another receptor, Her2, has become important in breast cancer care recently. A smaller proportion of breast cancer cases in older women overexpress the Her2 receptor. The Her2 receptor is a receptor for a molecule called the epidermal growth factor. Many normal body cells express some Her2, but cancer cells can sometimes have more receptors than normal cells. When Her2 is overexpressed, the breast cancer is more aggressive but is also more responsive to a specific cancer therapy.

The standard approach to breast cancer treatment involves multiple strategies. Surgical removal can require either lumpectomy (removal of the cancer and a margin of normal tissue) or mastectomy (removal of the entire breast). Radiation therapy and/or chemotherapy are offered to those with a large tumor or lymph node involvement. If Her2 is overexpressed, special antibody treatment is offered. If the tumor is hormone receptor positive, antiestrogen therapy is started. Survival, even if the breast cancer has become metastatic, can extend for several years, especially if the spread is limited to the bone or the soft tissues.

Colorectal Cancer

For treatment purposes, colorectal cancers are divided into colon cancers and rectal cancers because the approach is different for each location. There is little change in the behavior of colon cancer as age advances. There is a trend toward having more cancers on the right side of the colon versus the left side in older patients. The primary treatment of a localized colorectal cancer is surgery. This can be done at any age provided that the general condition of the person permits safe anesthesia. If the surgery is elective, there is very little increased risk in older patients compared with younger patients. In emergency situations, however, older patients experience more complications and deaths than do younger patients. Therefore, efforts are made to prevent emergency surgery or, if the patient presents with an acute situation, to try to stabilize the situation with rapid treatments to improve the ability of the person to withstand the stress of surgery. After surgery, if the tumor invades the lymph nodes around the colon, adjuvant (cancer medications even if the tumor appears to be removed so as to prevent recurrence) chemotherapy should be given. Rectal cancers arise in an area of the colon that is not wrapped in peritoneum; that is, the special lining of the abdominal organs. Therefore, the risk of local invasion and recurrence is higher. For this reason, combined radiation and chemotherapy are frequently provided before or after surgery.

Metastatic disease is usually treated with chemotherapy and targeted therapies (molecules or antibodies that act against specific proteins believed to promote cancer growth). If there are only a small number of tumors that have spread, they may be removed surgically, sometimes leading to prevention of recurrence.

Head and Neck Cancers

The vast majority of head and neck cancers are linked to tobacco and alcohol. However, some other risk factors, such as dust from exotic woods or viruses (e.g., the Epstein–Barr virus), have been identified. In general, treatment consists of surgery with or without radiation and/or chemotherapy. In certain cases, where preservation of an important body part such as the larynx (voicebox) is a priority, treatment with radiation and chemotherapy is provided first and surgery is reserved in case of relapse.

Kidney Cancer

Kidney cancer is quite resistant to standard chemotherapy and radiation therapy. Therefore, the treatment focuses heavily on surgery. If the cancer is only in the kidney, surgery can often provide a cure. When the disease has spread to a few places, surgery can be done to resect these additional tumors (which frequently develop in the lung) and improve survival. It has been shown that even when the additional tumor areas cannot be removed, surgically removing the involved kidney improves prognosis. New therapies that target specific proteins of the kidney cancer, such as sunitinib, sorafenib, and temsirolimus, are beginning to improve the prognosis of metastatic renal cancer.

Leukemia

Leukemia means "white cells in the blood." The name comes from the fact that many (but not all) leukemias, or blood cancers, present with a high white blood cell count. There are four major types of leukemias and some rarer ones. The major types are acute myelogenous leukemia (AML), acute lymphoblastic leukemia (ALL), chronic myelogenous leukemia (CML), and chronic lymphocytic leukemia (CLL). Acute leukemias (AML and ALL) are defined by the proportion of very immature cells, called "blasts," in the bone marrow. When the proportion of blasts is 20% or more, acute leukemia is considered to be present. Normal bone marrow has less than 5% blasts. An ALL is a leukemia made of precursors of lymphocytes. An AML is a leukemia made of precursors for all other blood cell types and their various subtypes. Although ALL is 10 times more frequent than AML in children, AML is 10 times more frequent than ALL in the elderly. The prognosis of ALL worsens sharply with age. Although the age effect in ALL is not entirely understood, one contributing factor is that ALL in older people is more likely to have unfavorable chromosome mutations associated with resistance to treatment. Treatment of leukemia is a lengthy chemotherapy regimen combining multiple agents, usually composed of three phases: (a) an induction chemotherapy using intensive treatments with substantial side effects, usually lasting 2 to 3 months, with the goal of inducing a remission (i.e., no visible leukemia cells); (b) a few months of consolidation therapy, usually still with an intensive treatment program, with the goal of reinforcing the remission; and (c) a period of approximately 2 years with a low-dose maintenance therapy, usually with pills. This combination treatment approach has produced the best results in children, although bone marrow transplantation can sometimes produce even higher rates of remission. The data are less extensive in older adults, but the same strategy is applied by analogy.

The treatment of AML is structured similarly to that of ALL. Although modern consolidation regimens usually relieve the need for a maintenance therapy, there is still some debate on the topic. All subtypes of AML respond to fairly similar treatments with one exception. The AML M3, or promyelocytic leukemia, has a chromosome mutation, [t:15;17], that makes it very sensitive to all-*trans*-retinoic acid (a drug of the same family as Accutane). When this drug is added to chemotherapy, this leukemia has a much better rate of cure than do the other AMLs.

CML is characterized by a very specific mutation, namely the Philadelphia chromosome. This is an exchange of a piece of an arm between chromosome 9 and chromosome 22 (called a *translocation,* written [t:9;22]). This joins two genes called bcr and abl. CML goes through three phases over time: the *chronic* phase, where the marrow blast count is normal; the *accelerated* phase, where the blast count is increased but does not reach 20%; and the *blastic* phase, where the blast count transforms into an acute leukemia (either AML or ALL). Bone marrow transplantation is still the only treatment proven to bring a cure for CML. However, bone marrow transplantation is not an option for most older patients because it is a very aggressive form of treatment with a high risk of serious complications. The rate of complications increases, and the ability to withstand them decreases with age. Research protocols are exploring less toxic regimens. The treatment strategy is changing rapidly as a new family of medications targeting the protein made by the bcr/abl mutation emerges. The paramount drug in this family is imatinib (Gleevec), which produces a high percentage of complete remissions. People with chronic phase CML who experience a complete remission with this drug have very few progressions over 5 years. However, it is not yet known what happens beyond that period of time. Responses are also seen in accelerated and blastic phases, but their duration is short, and combinations with chemotherapy are being explored.

CLL is the most frequent leukemia among older adults. Rather than an excessive production of cells, it is caused by a failure of old lymphocytes to die when their time comes. These lymphocytes keep circulating in the blood, and the white blood cell count rises slowly. The behavior of CLL is variable. Many patients live several years or even decades with it, but it can sometimes have a more aggressive behavior. Unfortunately, no treatment to date has changed the survival rate of patients with CLL. Because the condition often is not lethal and aggressive treatment has not changed life expectancy, the goal of treatment is primarily to relieve symptoms rather than to attempt a cure. Many fairly tolerable drugs are available: chemotherapy drugs (e.g., chlorambucil, fludarabine) and antibodies (e.g., rituximab, alemtuzumab). There is considerable debate as to the order and combinations in which to use these drugs, and treatment needs to be tailored individually.

Lung Cancer

The vast majority of lung cancers are related to smoking. The effect of smoking is cumulative; therefore, lung cancers tend to occur at over 50 years of age. Many elderly are affected by lung cancer. There are several types of lung cancer based on the appearance of the cells under the microscope (called the histology): squamous cell carcinoma, adenocarcinoma, large cell carcinoma, bronchio–alveolar carcinoma, and small cell lung cancer. These histological types can sometimes coexist. For the purpose of treatment, they are divided into small cell lung cancer (SCLC, approximately 20% of patients), which is very sensitive to chemotherapy, and non–small cell lung cancer (NSCLC, approximately 80% of patients), which is less sensitive. The treatment of NSCLC, whenever possible, includes surgery. Surgery can be less invasive, such as taking a wedge out of the lung with a special instrument without opening the chest surgically, or can be aggressive, such as surgically removing an entire lung. Thoracic surgery is feasible until an advanced age, but the morbidity and mortality of the largest resections rise with age and their use should be considered carefully. More and more, other treatment modalities (most frequently chemotherapy and radiation therapy) are added to surgery. Radiation therapy can also be used instead of surgery in patients who cannot tolerate surgery. If the NSCLC is more advanced, chemotherapy, with or without radiation therapy, can be given. In NSCLC, as in other cancers, many therapies targeting specific proteins are being tested. This is a rapidly evolving field. The prognosis of lung cancer might be better in older patients, according to certain series of patients followed to date. This is especially true for a subgroup of lung cancers occurring in older women who never smoked.

The treatment of choice for SCLC is chemotherapy with radiation therapy added if the disease is limited in size. Surgery is rarely used. Although SCLC is very sensitive to chemotherapy, it has a strong tendency to relapse.

Melanoma

The primary treatment for melanoma is surgery. If the melanoma does not penetrate deeply into the skin, it is curative most of the time. If the melanoma infiltrates deeply or has spread to the regional lymph nodes, interferon therapy can be given to decrease the risk of relapse. The doses required for optimal benefit are quite high, however, and this treatment is often tolerated poorly by older people. Metastatic melanoma is very difficult to treat because it does not respond well to currently available agents.

Non-Hodgkin's Lymphoma

Hodgkin's lymphoma (Hodgkin's disease) is mostly a disease of young adults and is rare in the elderly. Non-Hodgkin's lymphomas, on the other hand, are quite frequent. There are multiple subtypes, but they fall into two major categories: high-grade lymphomas and low-grade lymphomas. High-grade lymphomas grow fast. The vast majority respond well to chemotherapy and go into remission. Roughly half of high-grade lymphomas never relapse and are cured. The standard treatment for these lymphomas is a combination chemotherapy called CHOP with an anti-lymphoma antibody called rituximab. This chemotherapy has a significant risk of infectious complications due to low blood counts. Older persons are more sensitive to low blood counts, so growth factors to stimulate white blood cell production are usually given along with the lymphoma treatment. Low-grade lymphomas behave more like chronic diseases. They are also sensitive to chemotherapy, but nearly all relapse after a variable interval. To this point, no treatment has been shown to prolong the survival of these patients (counted in years). Therefore, it is not rare to simply monitor these lymphomas and not begin treatment until they begin to cause bothersome symptoms.

Ovarian Cancer

Outside of familial syndromes, the risk of ovarian cancer rises after menopause up to approximately 80 years of age and then declines. Ovarian cancer has a relatively stealthy behavior at the early and most curable stages. If it is found at those stages, surgery followed by chemotherapy offers a good chance for a cure. Most of the time, however, the disease is found at a more advanced stage, when it has spread throughout the abdomen. The best prognosis is achieved with an aggressive surgery that tries to take out as much tumor as possible, followed by chemotherapy. A specialized surgeon is preferred for this complex procedure. Although ovarian cancer is very sensitive to chemotherapy, it has a high tendency to relapse at advanced stages.

Pancreatic Cancer

The behavior of pancreatic cancer is essentially the same in younger and older adults. The vast majority of pancreatic cancers are called adenocarcinomas. However, sometimes the cancer cell type is different, and the cancer is called a lymphoma, a neuroendocrine tumor, or a small cell cancer. Only the adenocarcinomas are discussed here. When discovered early enough, a pancreatic cancer can be surgically resected. Most tumors arise in the head of the pancreas. The operation used most often is a pancreatico–duodenectomy (also known as Whipple surgery), which removes the head of the pancreas, the duodenum (a part of the small intestine), and sometimes part of the stomach. It leaves in place the tail of the pancreas, which contains most of the insulin-secreting cells, and thereby reduces the risk of inducing diabetes. Some older adults in otherwise good health, even up to the ninth decade of life, have tolerated this surgery well. After surgery, additional treatment, either chemotherapy alone or a combination of chemotherapy and radiation therapy, is provided to further prevent relapse. Unfortunately, 80% of pancreatic cancers present at a stage where they cannot be removed. At this point, chemotherapy, with or without targeted therapies, can decrease symptoms and prolong survival to some extent.

Prostate Cancer

Nearly every man who lives into his 80s will have prostate cancer. However, this cancer is often very small and slow growing and might never cause problems. It is often found in older people who have died of entirely unrelated causes. A major challenge today is to determine when a "significant" prostate cancer is present. The treatment of prostate cancer is guided by two major features: its stage (as in other cancers) and the degree of maturity of its cells (called differentiation). The degree of differentiation is expressed by the Gleason score, derived from observation of prostate tissue under a microscope. The higher the score, the less differentiated the cells and the more aggressive the tumor. Localized prostate cancers are treated first with surgery or radiation therapy. The two treatment approaches yield equivalent results, and each has its own set of side effects. An alternative way of delivering radiation therapy is through seed implants. Short-term results are equivalent for low-risk prostate cancer, but long-term results are not yet known. Seed implants can be combined with standard radiation therapy. Poorly differentiated tumors always need additional treatment, whereas the use of additional treatment in well-differentiated tumors is more dependent on factors such as the life expectancy of the patient, other medical problems, and patient preference. Androgen (male hormone) suppression is the cornerstone of additional treatment of prostate cancer. Androgen suppression can be achieved through either surgical castration or (more frequently) by injections or pills. Studies are under way to assess whether the addition of chemotherapy and targeted therapies would improve survival and reduce rates of tumor progression. When prostate cancer spreads (metastasizes), it is most likely to be found in the bone; only 5% of prostate cancers spread to other organs. Metastatic prostate cancer is treated with additional antiandrogen therapies, chemotherapy, localized radiation therapy, or radioactive materials that fix to the bone such as radioactive strontium and samarium. Again, prognosis is very variable. Older people with metastatic prostate cancer can live for years in reasonably good health. For example, President François Mitterand governed France for 14 years with a metastatic prostate cancer.

Thyroid Cancer

The most frequent types of thyroid cancer are based on the type of cancer cell and are called papillary, follicular, medullary, and anaplastic. Thyroid cancer has highly variable behavior. The key prognostic factor is the level of tumor cell differentiation. A well-differentiated tumor, even if metastatic, can grow very slowly over many years, whereas a poorly differentiated cancer has an aggressive behavior. The thyroid often develops nodules (lumps). Most nodules are not cancer and are considered to be benign; many of these contain fluid. Solid nodules that are "cold" on a thyroid scan because they do not take up labeled iodine as normal thyroid cells do are suspicious and should always be biopsied. If the stage (extent of spread) is limited, surgery is the cornerstone of treatment. In case of relapse or metastatic disease, radioactive iodine can often be used. Thyroid cancers as a group are poorly responsive to radiation and chemotherapy.

Cancer of the Uterus

Although cervical cancer has become rare in developed countries, endometrial cancer (cancer of the lining of the uterus) is still relatively frequent. The maximum risk of endometrial cancer is after menopause. With annual pelvic examinations and attention to unusual vaginal bleeding, most endometrial cancers can be detected at an early stage and are curable by hysterectomy (surgical removal of the uterus). However, if the cancer penetrates deeply into the uterine muscle or invades the lymph nodes, adjuvant chemotherapy, with or without radiation therapy, is needed. Metastatic endometrial cancer has some degree of response to chemotherapy.

—*Martine Extermann*

See also Cancer; Cancer Prevention and Screening; Multiple Morbidity and Comorbidity; Surgery

Further Readings and References

American Society of Clinical Oncology. People living with cancer. Available at: www.plwc.org. Accessed September 9, 2006.

National Cancer Institute. Cancer topics. Available at: http://cancernet.nci.nih.gov/cancertopics. Accessed September 9, 2006.

UpToDate Patient Information. Health topics A to Z: Information written for patients. Available at: http://patients.uptodate.com/atoz.asp. Accessed September 9, 2006.

CANCER PREVENTION AND SCREENING

The best way to control cancer is to prevent it. The most effective cancer prevention measure is smoking cessation. According to the National Cancer Institute, cigarette smoking causes 87% of lung cancer deaths and is responsible for most cancers of the larynx, oral cavity and pharynx, esophagus, and bladder. The risk of cancer with smoking is cumulative. Stopping at any age is beneficial; at first the risk plateaus, and then it may even decrease over time.

A sedentary lifestyle and obesity increase the risk of many cancers such as breast, colon, endometrial, and prostate cancers. Exercise might decrease the risk of breast cancer. One study, the Iowa Women's Health Study, suggests that intentionally losing weight might reduce the risk of obesity-related cancers.

There is an increasing interest in using medications to prevent cancer. Studies have examined the use of aspirin to decrease the risk of colon cancer in patients with colon adenomas (benign noncancerous growths) with promising short-term results. However, at least one randomized prevention study using very low-dose aspirin did not show a preventive effect. Some epidemiological cohorts suggest that participants taking statins (drugs that lower cholesterol levels) might also have a reduced risk of cancer.

Another effective method of decreasing cancer mortality is to use screening tests to detect cancers at early stages, when they have the highest chances of cure. The best-established screening test is the Papanicolaou test, familiarly known as Pap smear. This test scrapes a few cells from the cervix of the uterus and analyzes them for signs of malignant transformation (change in cellular appearance suggestive of the development of cancer tendency). This test has dramatically reduced the mortality from cervical cancer in developed countries. In developing countries, cervical cancer is still very much a concern, and large efforts to screen these women are being undertaken. The risk of cervical cancer is highest in younger women. It is associated with infections with human papilloma virus. Women age 70 years and older in good health who have had three normal Pap smears in a row can stop getting Pap smears. However, postmenopausal women are also at risk for endometrial cancer, so regular gynecological visits should be continued.

A simple but effective cancer screening test is an annual skin examination by a dermatologist. This allows the removal of common skin cancers such as basal cell carcinoma and squamous cell carcinoma. These very frequent cancers are due to sun damage, rarely metastasize, and are usually cured by simple surgical resection. If ignored, however, they can be locally invasive, causing local damage, pain and dysfunction. More critically, a yearly skin examination allows the early detection of melanoma. Melanoma is a tumor in which stage makes a dramatic difference in prognosis. A melanoma less than 1 millimeter thick at the time of surgery has very little chance of having spread and will most likely be cured. A thicker melanoma that has spread to the lymph nodes has a much worse prognosis. There is some evidence that melanomas have a worse prognosis in older people. It is unclear whether this is because they are thicker or ulcerated when detected or is due to another reason.

Sigmoidoscopy and colonoscopy are less comfortable than a skin examination. However, they are also very effective cancer screening tests. In a Norwegian series, participants in their 50s who were screened had five times fewer colon cancers 13 years later than did participants who were not screened (0.5% vs. 2.5%). No specific data are available in the elderly, but as the baseline risk of colon cancer increases, the absolute benefit of screening might also increase with age. Most guidelines recommend getting at least one colonoscopy or sigmoidoscopy and fecal occult blood test (FOB) at 50 years of age. Several recommendations advise getting an FOB every year, a sigmoidoscopy every 5 years, and a colonoscopy every 10 years. If polyps are found, repeat colonoscopies should be done. It is unclear whether and how frequently people without polyps need to be retested.

Patients with a family history of colon cancer should have a colonoscopy 10 years prior to the age of the earliest colon cancer in the family.

Mammography is a widely used screening examination that has markedly reduced the average size at which breast cancers are detected. It also improves survival from breast cancer. Currently, the age at which mammography is no longer appropriate is not known. Studies have included patients up to 75 years of age. In a large Swedish trial, the benefit to overall survival started to be seen after 5 years and kept increasing. Therefore, it is reasonable to suggest that every woman who would be expected to live at least another 5 to 10 years could benefit from a mammogram.

The role of prostate-specific antigen (PSA) screening for prostate cancer is more debated. PSA screening has been proven to detect more prostate cancers than have other methods. However, improved survival among men who have been screened with PSA has not been shown. The difficulty comes from several aspects of prostate cancers. Some are aggressive in their behavior, whereas others are very indolent (slow growing) and will never trouble the patient in his lifetime. In fact, most men in their 80s have a few areas of cancer within the prostate that will never affect their health. Furthermore, the PSA test does not detect all prostate cancers; patients with a normal PSA level can have prostate cancer. Large studies are ongoing to clarify the role of PSA prostate cancer screening.

—*Martine Extermann*

See also Cancer; Health and Public Policy; Health Promotion and Disease Prevention; Motivation; Multiple Morbidity and Comorbidity

Further Readings and References

American Cancer Society. Prevention and early detection. Available at: www.cancer.org/docroot/PED/ped_0.asp. Accessed September 9, 2006.

American Society of Clinical Oncology. People living with cancer. Available at: www.plwc.org. Accessed September 9, 2006.

National Cancer Institute. Screening and testing to detect cancer. Available at: www.cancer.gov/cancertopics/screening. Accessed September 9, 2006.

UpToDate Patient Information. Health topics A to Z: Information written for patients. Available at: http://patients.uptodate.com/atoz.asp. Accessed September 9, 2006.

CARDIOVASCULAR HEALTH STUDY

The Cardiovascular Health Study (CHS) is a population-based longitudinal study of coronary heart disease and stroke in adults age 65 years and older funded by the National Heart, Lung, and Blood Institute of the National Institutes of Health. A total of 5,201 men and women were recruited from four communities: Forsyth County, North Carolina; Sacramento County, California; Washington County, Maryland; and Pittsburgh, Pennsylvania. An additional 687 African Americans were recruited after the initial baseline survey. The population from the Pittsburgh Field Center was entirely urban, whereas the other three field centers recruited a mixture of urban and rural populations.

Eligible participants were sampled from Medicare eligibility lists in each area. Those eligible included all persons living in the household of each individual sampled from the Health Care Financing Administration (HCFA) sampling frame who were age 65 years and older at the time of examination, were noninstitutionalized, were expected to remain in the area for the next 3 years, and were able to give informed consent and did not require a proxy respondent at baseline. Potentially eligible individuals who were wheelchair bound in the home at baseline, or who were receiving hospice treatment, radiation therapy, or chemotherapy for cancer, were excluded.

Extensive physical and laboratory evaluations were performed at baseline to identify the presence and severity of cardiovascular disease (CVD) risk factors such as hypertension, hypercholesterolemia, and glucose intolerance; subclinical disease such as carotid artery atherosclerosis, left ventricular enlargement, and transient ischemia; and clinically overt CVD. These examinations in the CHS permit evaluation of CVD risk factors in older adults, particularly in groups previously underrepresented in epidemiological studies such as women and the very old. The first of two examination cycles began in June 1989.

Periodic interim contacts are schedules to ascertain and verify the incidence of CVD events, the frequency of recurrent events, and the sequellae of CVD.

Rationale

Risk factors for coronary heart disease (CHD) and stroke, and for other CVDs, have been determined in middle-aged population groups, but the strength and importance of these factors in older individuals have not been clearly defined. Some studies have found conventional risk factors, such as cholesterol and smoking, to weaken with advancing age. Other studies have found that in the elderly there might even be a protective effect of risk factors that have been found to be important in younger populations. Conflicting findings raise the possibility that selective survival may significantly alter the importance of CVD risk factors in predicting the outcome, or even the incidence, of disease.

Objectives

The main objective of the CHS is to identify factors related to the onset of CHD and stroke. The CHS is designed to determine the importance of conventional CVD risk factors in older adults and to identify new risk factors in this age group, especially those that may be protective and modifiable. Other objectives are the following:

- To quantify associations of conventional and hypothesized risk factors with CHD and stroke
- To assess the association of indicators of subclinical disease, identified by noninvasive measures such as carotid ultrasonography and echocardiography, with incidence of CHD and stroke
- To quantify the association of conventional and hypothesized risk factors with subclinical disease
- To characterize the natural history of CHD and stroke and to identify factors associated with clinical course
- To describe the prevalence and distributions of risk factors, subclinical disease, and clinically diagnosed CHD and stroke

—*Richard Schulz*

See also Cardiovascular System

Further Readings and References

Cardiovascular Health Study. Available at: www.chs-nhlbi .org. Accessed September 9, 2006.

CARDIOVASCULAR SYSTEM

Aging is the sum of the deteriorative and compensatory changes during postmaturational life, resulting in increased vulnerability. Aging does not produce disease but rather increases susceptibility to disease. The delineation between disease and normal appears to be artificial because diseases of the cardiovascular system (CVS) are nearly ubiquitous in older people. The prevalence of coronary artery disease in the United States reaches 75% in older individuals after the sixth decade in men and two decades later in women. Although these autopsy data are more than four decades old, they are still relevant today. Similarly, depending on the definition, the prevalence of arterial hypertension reaches the same level in Western cultures. In early aging studies, because of these diseases, increases in diastolic blood pressure and decreases in cardiac output were thought to be due to age.

Since then, longitudinal studies of highly screened older individuals show reduced *apparent* impact of aging on resting cardiovascular function. The lack of change at rest in screened older individuals is evidence of the adequacy of the compensatory strategies used by the old heart and vascular system. However, using compensatory mechanisms to maintain homeostasis leaves older persons more vulnerable to subsequent challenges.

In addition to the effects of subclinical disease, there are protean effects of physical inactivity. Humans become increasingly sedentary as they age. For typical age changes, one third is due to age itself, one third is due to lifestyle choices such as inactivity, and one third is due to subclinical disease. The relative magnitudes of the three factors are really uncertain, but the disease-related third is the best understood and may be decreasing in magnitude. The others are still somewhat less clearly defined.

Aging and Disease-Mediated Changes in the Vascular Tree

The large conduit arteries display the ravages of age, leading to increased stiffness. Elastin becomes fragmented in the internal elastic lamina and media of the aorta, perhaps because of inappropriate activation of proteolytic enzymes called matrix metalloproteinases. The media may calcify and collagen molecules increasingly become crosslinked, thereby stiffening the matrix. The aortic lumen diameter increases, as does the vessel length and wall thickness. Because the aorta is fixed proximally and distally, the increase in length results in the tortuous ectatic aorta seen "uncoiling" on chest X-rays of older persons.

Endothelial cells at areas of turbulence have high cellular turnover and become irregular in size and shape, suggesting that cellular senescence may be occurring at those sites. In engineered endothelial cells with persistently long telomeres, age-associated abnormalities are reduced.

Functional Changes in the Aging Arteries

Old aortas relax normally when exposed to direct nitric oxide (NO) donors, such as nitroprusside, but are less responsive to agents whose effects are mediated by NO, such as acetylcholine. Aortas from older animals have high NO synthase activity but produce less NO. Because NO contributes to resting arterial tone, old arteries are tonically contracted. Forearm arterial blood flow increases less in older individuals in response to acetylcholine than in younger individuals, but it is relatively preserved in athletically active older people. As expected, the response to direct NO donors is the same for all groups.

The measures of arterial wall stiffness include pulse wave velocity (PWV, how fast the pressure pulse is propagated in the arterial wall) and systolic and pulse blood pressures (BPs). PWV doubles from 20 to 80 years of age, independent of BP. The stiff artery wall allows pressure waves reflect from the periphery rapidly so that the aortic valve is still open when they return, thereby increasing the load on the heart. For men, systolic BP increases 5 millimeters of mercury (mm Hg) per decade until 60 years of age, and then the slope shifts to 10 mm Hg per decade. For women, systolic BP starts lower but shifts to the high slope earlier. In contrast, diastolic BP increases a little and then decreases so that overall it remains unaltered with age (80 in men, 70 to 80 in women). Older athletes have lower systolic BP and PWV than do sedentary old people, but young people are still better than older athletes. At least one mechanism for arterial stiffening involves nonenzymatic glucose crosslinks between collagen molecules. ALT-711 is a crosslink breaker and transiently decreases vessel stiffness.

Aging and Atherosclerosis

As shown in Table 1, there are significant differences between the age-related changes and atherosclerosis, but aging increases the risk of atherosclerosis unequivocally. Smooth muscle cells from old arteries are less differentiated, more likely to proliferate, and frequently polyploid (another marker of dedifferentiation). The higher propensity to proliferate increases the probability of developing atherosclerosis. When older rabbits are put on atherogenic diets, the resulting lesions are more severe than those in young rabbits fed for a similar duration.

The impact of aortic stiffening and its manifestations, increased systolic BP and widened pulse pressure, are risk factors for stroke, renal failure, and heart disease, and the rapid propagation of pressure waves by the stiff aorta may induce cardiac hypertrophy. In young people, the pressure waves return after the

Table 1   Age-Related Changes in Larger Arteries Versus Atherosclerosis

Atherosclerosis	Age-Related Changes
Western man	Occur in most species
Heterogeneous	Uniform in large arteries
Compromises lumen	Lumen enlarges
Inflammation	No white cells participate
Cholesterol is cofactor	Cholesterol independent
Related to turbulence	Not localized to stress sites and shear stresses

aortic valve is closed, and coronary artery perfusion improves by increasing the pressure in the proximal aorta during diastole. This is lost when the reflections are early. Additive forces at reflection sites, such as above the aortic bifurcation, may traumatize vessel walls, resulting in abdominal aortic aneurysms.

Changes With Aging in Cardiac Anatomy

Only the most modest changes in the right side of the heart occur with age. In contrast, the left atrium and ventricle undergo extensive changes that appear to be adaptive with aging. The left atrial size increases and the left atrial wall thickens in response to pumping into a stiffer left ventricle (LV). The LV also hypertrophies with increases in LV wall thickness, LV mass, and heart weight with age—all considered to be "normal." Unfortunately, although normal, changes in the dynamics of filling still result. LV cavity size may be reduced modestly at rest, especially when the measurements are made in the recumbent position. Because LV filling occurs at low pressures, differences in position can make significant differences in the age-related effects on filling dynamics. Both the aortic valve and the mitral annulus develop calcific deposits. The deposits in the mitral annulus may predispose to problems in cardiac conduction. Aortic valve calcification is associated with coronary artery atherosclerosis; however, it is uncertain whether both just covary with age. The leaflets of both valves thicken, but this is greatest in the aortic valve.

Cardiomyocyte hypertrophy is part of the response to increased loading described previously. The heart is renewing, continually repopulated from stem cell populations (resident and/or bone marrow derived), so this may need reinterpretation. The newest cardiomyocytes, those most recently differentiated, are thought to be the smallest. If aging of the heart continually calls on the precursor reserves, myocyte hypertrophy may reflect depletion of the process. The loss of cardiomyocytes is by both apoptosis and necrosis; the number of cardiomyocytes may be reduced by 50% with age in healthy human and animal hearts.

Nowhere is cellular dropout more impressive than in the sinoatrial (SA) node. The volume of the SA node decreases with age. The number of pacemaker cells is reduced (90% gone by 70 years of age), with replacement by fat. More modest losses occur at the atrioventricular (AV) node, and minimal changes are present in the distal conduction system.

At the microscopic level, lipofuscin, a lipid waste produce, accumulates within the cells. The functional impact of lipofuscin is unknown. Surrounding the cells is fibrous tissue in a delicate pattern, not similar to the dense patches of fibrosis seen after myocardial infarction. Overall, total collagen doubles in the old rat heart.

An insoluble product of the protein transthyretin may deposit in the heart, resulting in senile cardiac amyloid. The deposition can be massive, profoundly altering cardiac function and leading to heart failure. A polymorphism in the transthyretin gene is very common in African Americans, making this cause of heart failure surprisingly common in Blacks over 80 years of age. On an echocardiogram, it has a characteristic speckled pattern that is more likely to be recognized if it is suspected. These transthyretin-based amyloids are essentially unique to the elderly.

Changes in Cardiac Function With Age

Resting heart rate does not change with adult aging, but there is a marked decrease in maximum heart rate in response to exercise or stress. When propranolol and atropine are given to block both sympathetic and parasympathetic input to the heart, the intrinsic heart rate decreases 5 or 6 beats per minute (bpm) each decade. The resting heart rate in an 80-year-old is roughly equal to the intrinsic heart rate. At rest in the 80-year-old, parasympathetic tone is minimal, so the effect of atropine is reduced greatly.

Maximum heart rate, reflecting sympathetic and parasympathetic influences, decreases 10 bpm per decade. For men, (220 – age) predicts the target maximum for exercise testing. Women have a lower peak heart rate during youth and a more gradual fall in maximum; thus, a correction factor of 0.85 is used. Exercise training cannot modify the age-associated decline in maximum heart rate. Sympathetic stimulation appears to be adequate as serum norepinephrine and epinephrine are elevated at rest in normal elderly.

With exertion, the catecholamines increase further (even higher than those of the young under the same stress). Clinicians use heart rate to assess severity of illness and are likely to underestimate the severity in the elderly if the clinicians do not consider the decrease in maximum heart rate.

Nearly all healthy older people have atrial premature beats (APBs) on 24-hour ambulatory monitoring. The APBs are not associated with increased cardiac disease risk and are considered to be normal. Isolated ventricular ectopic beats occur during exercise testing in more than half of highly screened elders over 80 years of age.

The age-related decrease in maximum oxygen use on exercise testing (VO$_2$ max) is highly significant. With age, maximum work and VO$_2$ max decrease due to a combination of cardiac and muscle changes. The relationship between cardiac output and VO$_2$ max remains unchanged with age as all activities become a larger percentage of the VO$_2$ max in the old and are perceived as more difficult to do. Sedentary older individuals gain greatly from exercise training, which can extend their lives by up to 30 years. Even in highly trained individuals, VO$_2$ max decreases despite continued training.

Resting LV ejection fraction (EF), the fraction of blood ejected from the ventricle with each systole, is approximately 65% at all ages, but there are smaller increases in LVEF in response to exercise with age. At maximum effort, left ventricle ejection fraction (LVEF) in the young is 80%, and by 80 years of age it is only 70%. The absence of age-related change in resting LVEF is the result of successful adaptations. In isolated heart muscle from old rats, patterns of contraction and relaxation are changed—slower force generation and much slower relaxation but no change in peak force. The inotropic and lusitropic (improving relaxation) responses to sympathetic drugs decrease with age.

Aging impairs resting diastolic function in animals and humans. Left atrial contraction becomes vital to LV filling. In young people, left atrial systole contributes 15% of LV filling ("topping off the ventricle"). In the elderly, left atrial systole can provide up to 50% of LV filling. An atrial gallop (S4) is a normal finding on physical examination in those over 75 years of age, a manifestation of this increased contribution of left atrial systole to ventricular filling. This also explains, in part, why atrial fibrillation (where a function atrial contraction is lost) may precipitate heart failure in the elderly.

LV filling pressures may increase when old people do a bout of exercise. There is no increase in LV end diastolic filling pressure in younger people. That is, older people use Starling's law to increase cardiac output with exercise, likely because the other responses, including the muted increase in heart rate and the inability to augment cardiac ejection, relaxation, and filling, are inadequate. The responsiveness is also decreased to some cardioactive drugs, including atropine and β-adrenergic agonists. These agents may require higher doses to reach a desired effect in the elderly.

The actual determinants of the age-related decrease in VO$_2$ max are debated. VO$_2$ max depends on cardiac output, muscle mass, and oxygen extraction. Diastolic function is a key contributor to determining VO$_2$ max in the elderly. Age, systolic function, peak heart rate, left ventricular mass, and gender are also important. In a cross-sectional study, one measure of diastolic function determined more than 60% of VO$_2$ max that the screened population of men attained. As would be expected, lifelong athletes have better resting diastolic function than do their sedentary counterparts.

Cardiac contraction and relaxation are dictated by calcium fluxes. For contraction, a small amount of calcium enters the cells via the slow L-type calcium channels and stimulates the release of ten- to twenty-fold more calcium from the sarcoplasmic reticulum (SR), which then allows actin and myosin to interact. Active relaxation includes the calcium reuptake by the cardiac SR, extrusion from the cell by the sodium–calcium (Na–Ca) exchanger, and the sarcolemmal calcium pump. Fully 90% of calcium cycles in and out of SR in young hearts. Calcium reuptake into the SR is decreased by 50% in old hearts, and the content of the key SR pump is decreased in old human hearts as well. This slows cardiac relaxation and results in smaller SR stores for release in the next contraction. Gene therapy, or increasing the content of the SR pump, dramatically improves old rat heart function. The only other intervention available is endurance exercise training.

Older cardiomyocytes are intrinsically stiffer. This is due to active stiffness, increased calcium leak from the SR, and passive stiffness resulting from viscoelastic changes within the cell. In addition, collagen increases outside the cells. Thus, the stiffness of the old ventricle is increased, and this impairs filling.

The contraction and relaxation of the old LV might not be uniform. Segments of the old heart start to relax while others are still contracting. Because LV pressure must be low before filling can start, this prolonged contraction shortens the time for filling to occur. Therefore, all of the determinants of diastolic function are modified by age.

Each mitochondrion has its own genome with relatively poor ability to correct mutations. A number of investigators report that mitochondrial DNA deletions increase with age. The implications of this finding remain uncertain because each myocyte has roughly 1,000 mitochondria.

Clinical Implications of Age-Related Cardiac Changes

Aging decreases one's ability to tolerate challenges to homeostasis, especially in the cardiovascular system. The mortality after myocardial infarction increases dramatically with age, as does the probability of developing heart failure. Although aging increases the risk of atherosclerosis, including coronary atherosclerosis, the pathogenesis of myocardial infarction and the myocardial infarction itself are not normal aging. The response to the systemic challenges produced by the infarction (e.g., low cardiac output, need for replacement cells, cytokine release) may well be impaired because of the aging process. Consistent with this, there is an age-related increase in mortality after experimental infarction in mice and rats. We suggest that homeostenosis, the depletion of reserves, may be the cost of invoking compensatory mechanisms just to maintain homeostasis. The increased reliance on atrial systole is such an example. As noted previously, atrial systole contributes up to 50% of left

ventricular filling at rest in the elderly, compared with 15% in youth; there is little further reserve to invoke.

B-type natriuretic peptide (BNP) elaboration and release by the left ventricle also increase with age. Although clinically an age correction for the upper limit of normal for serum BNP concentrations, this may reflect the impaired renal clearance of the peptide as much as it reflects changes in cardiac function.

Congestive heart failure (CHF) has become increasingly common, reaching a prevalence of more than 10% and becoming the most common reason for hospitalization of the elderly. CHF is frequently primarily diastolic dysfunction because the age-related diastolic dysfunction is additive to that caused by hypertension or other disease.

—George E. Taffet

See also Aneurysms; Arrhythmias; Cardiovascular Health Study; Congestive Heart Failure; Valvular Heart Disease

Further Readings and References

Avolio AP, Chen SG, Wang RP, Zhang CL, Li MF, O'Rourke MF. Effects of aging on changing arterial compliance and left ventricular load in a northern Chinese urban community. *Circulation.* 1983;68:50–58.

Cain B, Meldrum DR, Joo KS, et al. Human SERCA2a levels correlate inversely with age in senescent human myocardium. *J Am Coll Cardiol.* 1998;32:458–467.

Kitzman DW. Normal age-related changes in the heart: Relevance to echocardiography in the elderly. *Am J Geriatr Cardiol.* 2000;9:311–320.

Lakatta EG. Cardiovascular system. In: Masoro EJ, ed. *Aging: Handbook of Physiology.* New York: American Physiological Society; 1995:413–474.

Lakatta EG, Sollott SJ. Perspectives on mammalian cardiovascular aging: Humans to molecules. *Comp Biochem Physiol.* 2002;132:699–721.

Matsushita H, Chang E, Glassford AJ, Cooke JP, Chiu CP, Tsao PS. eNOS activity is reduced in senescent human endothelial cells: Preservation by hTERT immortalization. *Circ Res.* 2001;89:793–798.

Olivetti G, Melissari M, Capasso JM, Anversa P. Cardiomyopathy of the aging human heart, myocyte loss, and reactive cellular hypertrophy. *Circ Res.* 1991;68:1560–1568.

Schmidt U, del Monte F, Miyamoto MI, et al. Restoration of diastolic function in senescent rat hearts through adenoviral gene transfer of sarcoplasmic reticulum Ca^{2+}-ATPase. *Circulation.* 2000;101:790–796.

Tanaka H, Monahan KD, Seals DR. Age-predicted maximal heart rate revisited. *J Am Coll Cardiol.* 2001;37:153–156.

Vaitkevicius PV, Lane M, Spurgeon H, et al. A cross-link breaker has sustained effects on arterial and ventricular properties in older rhesus monkeys. *Proc Natl Acad Sci USA.* 2001;98:1171–1175.

Vanoeverschelde J-L, Essamri B, Vanbutsele R, et al. Contribution of left ventricular diastolic function to exercise capacity in normal subjects. *J Appl Physiol.* 1993;74:2225–2233.

Wang M, Takagi G, Asai K, et al. Aging increases aortic MMP-2 activity and angiotensin II in nonhuman primates. *Hypertension.* 2003;41:1308–1316.

CAREGIVING

Caregiving can be defined as providing assistance and support to family members in need. The type and amount of assistance and support required fluctuates throughout the life span. In the context of aging, caregiving commonly refers to caring for an older adult with a chronic illness or a functional disability. It is estimated that between 45 million and 52 million adults in the United States engage in unpaid family caregiving for older relatives.

During the past century, medical advances greatly reduced the incidence of deaths related to acute causes. As the number of older adults surviving formerly fatal conditions (and thereby living with disabilities) increases, so too does the number of family caregivers. In fact, rather than dying more rapidly from acute causes, the pathway to the end of life now more commonly begins with a chronic disease leading to one or more functional disabilities and *eventually* to death. This shift has meant that currently older adults live longer and with more functional disabilities than at any time in recorded history. The number of family caregivers is expected to continue to rise in accordance with this shift.

Most researchers define caregiving as providing assistance with activities of daily living (ADLs) and assistance with instrumental activities of daily living (IADLs). ADLs involve personal care such as getting in and out of bed or a chair, dressing, toileting, bathing, and feeding oneself. IADLs are tasks common in everyday life such as paying bills, grocery shopping, and preparing meals. The majority of caregivers assist the care recipient with more than one activity. Although most caregiving research is based on function, there is also disease-based research that focuses on health- and quality of life-related issues specific to the care recipient's disease. Regardless of whether the focus of care is on a functional disability or a disease state, there appears to be great variability in the type of assistance provided by caregivers.

Although the caregiving literature has devoted considerable attention to caregivers for Alzheimer's disease patients, older care recipients also commonly suffer from cancer, diabetes, mental illness, heart disease, and stroke. Many elders are affected by multiple ailments simultaneously, serving to complicate care regimens and magnify the burden on caregivers.

Models of Caregiving Stress

Caregivers are at increased risk for mental and physical health problems. Conceptually, much of the literature on family caregiving applies stress and coping models to identify factors associated with caregivers' well-being. Most models indicate that individual characteristics (e.g., gender, age, ethnicity, relationship to the care recipient), stressors (e.g., care recipient factors, role strain), stress appraisal (e.g., caregiver competence), and resources (e.g., social support, access to community resources) influence caregivers' health outcomes, particularly for dementia-related care. More recent models highlight the role of culture in determining caregiver well-being and seek to uncover caregiver resources and health behaviors that differentiate physical health outcomes. Based on these models, researchers have conducted studies highlighting a number of factors associated with health outcomes among caregivers. Several of these factors are discussed in this entry.

Care Recipient and Disease/ Disability Factors

Although all types of caregiving are associated with emotional strain, those individuals caring for dementia patients report more difficulties than do caregivers for physically impaired but cognitively intact individuals. Caregivers for Alzheimer's patients consistently report more symptoms of depression than do caregivers for cancer and Parkinson's patients, resulting in higher rates of clinical depression in the former subpopulation.

Not only does the presence of dementia place a larger burden on the caregiver, but also the severity of the dementia affects the caregiver. More frequent behavior disturbances, most common in care recipients with moderate dementia, are associated with increased caregiver depression. Disruptive behavior, particularly violence on the part of care recipients, is also a predictor of caregiver violence.

Caregiver Demographics

Female spouses, daughters, and daughters-in-law constitute the majority of caregivers, although the numbers of male spousal and male adult–child caregivers continue to rise. Estimates of the overall percentage of female caregivers in the United States range from 70% to 80%, and female caregivers consistently report higher rates of depression than do male caregivers.

Patient–Caregiver Relationship

At least half of all caregivers are spouses. Spouses, most often wives, commonly report receiving insufficient support from other family members and consequently provide care with fewer social supports than do other family caregivers. Factors shown to adversely affect the patient–caregiver relationship include being a spouse as opposed to an adult child caregiver, spending more than 40 hours per week caregiving, and role strain due to competing demands.

Caregiving and Culture

Research on caregiving and ethnicity indicates that there are cross-cultural differences in the nature and effects of caregiving. Although a number of ethnic differences in caregiver health have been reported, the origins of these differences are unclear because most research fails to identify specific cultural factors.

In studies examining caregiving among European Americans, Latinos, Asian Americans, and African Americans, ethnic minority caregivers are often of lower socioeconomic status, younger, less likely to be a spouse, and more likely to receive informal support. They provide more care and possess stronger filial obligation beliefs than do European American caregivers. African American caregivers generally report lower levels of caregiver burden and depression than do European American caregivers, whereas Latino and Asian American caregivers are often more depressed than their European American caregiver peers. All ethnic minority caregivers report poorer physical health than do their European American caregiver counterparts.

Longitudinal research involving African Americans suggests that cultural beliefs about caregiving exert a direct influence on health outcomes. This stands in contrast to findings for European American caregivers, in whom higher levels of mastery and identification with cultural values for care are associated with poorer health outcomes. African Americans appraise aspects of caregiving as less stressful than do European Americans, and the former tend to derive more benefit and meaning from the experience through a greater reliance on religious coping mechanisms. Latino caregivers share similar cross-cultural patterns with respect to cultural factors, expressing higher religiosity and stronger views on filial support when compared with European Americans. There is little published research about caregiving in the American Indian and Alaska Native populations. The work that has been done suggests that native caregivers draw on cultural resources such as beliefs about aging and disease and reliance on extended families.

Caregiving and Health

Caregiving is emotionally stressful for the vast majority of caregivers. Higher rates of depressive symptomatology have been found consistently among caregivers. The related concept of *burden* has also been used in describing the mental health of caregivers. Burden encompasses feelings of embarrassment, overload, resentment, and isolation commonly reported by caregivers.

Research on physical health shows that caregiving is associated with low self-rated health and poor health behaviors. Longitudinal studies indicate that caregivers also show declining physical health over time and are at higher risk for mortality compared with noncaregivers. Caregivers are also more likely to show poor immune system functioning through stress hormone dysregulation and insufficient antibody response than are noncaregivers.

Positive Aspects of Caregiving

The act of caregiving clearly has a negative impact on health for most people, but many others also report receiving benefits while engaged in caregiving. In fact, positive aspects of caregiving, such as companionship and perceived rewards, may reduce stress and improve health outcomes for some caregivers. Caregivers scoring high on religiosity measures and those deriving meaning from caregiving show fewer mental health problems and are more likely to report interpersonal growth compared with caregivers scoring low on religiosity. Satisfaction with social support also differentiates those reporting greater benefits.

Caregiving and Social Support

Social support, defined as interpersonal transactions involving aid, affect, and/or affirmation, has been examined extensively in the context of caregiving over the past two decades. It is clear that close personal relationships have mental health benefits for everyone, including caregivers. Studies also indicate that social support has a positive impact on the immune system and may help caregivers to remain healthier and live longer. Researchers have examined numerous aspects of social support and found that perceived support relates most strongly to lower rates of health problems associated with caregiving.

Interventions for Caregivers

Programs designed to reduce caregiver burden include not only support groups but also educational and clinical interventions. Despite examining a broad range of health outcomes, very few interventions have shown significant effects. Although the interventions examined in most studies do not prove to be effective quantitatively, a majority of caregivers report interventions designed to assist them as beneficial and valuable. Furthermore, there is evidence that interventions can improve health outcomes by enhancing service use and also can delay institutionalization.

Conclusion

The number of older adults requiring care is increasing so rapidly that most Americans will care for an older adult at some point in their lives. Because it is clear that caregiving is stressful, researchers have outlined many of the variables that influence caregiver stress such as care recipient factors, demographic factors, and patient–caregiver relationship issues. The relationship between cultural context and caregiver mental and physical health is being explored to a greater extent today, as are the positive aspects of caregiving. The main goal of this research is to create a knowledge base from which to design interventions for decreasing burden and increasing competence to provide the best care for caregivers.

—*Todd J. McCallum*

See also Activities of Daily Living and Instrumental Activities of Daily Living; Advocacy Organizations; Assisted Living; Continuum of Care; Home Care; Social Networks and Social Support

Further Readings and References

Aneshensel CS, Pearlin LI, Mullan JT, Zarit SH, Whitlach CJ. *Profiles in Caregiving: The Unexpected Career.* San Diego, Calif: Academic Press; 1995.

Castleman M, Gallagher-Thompson D, Naythons M. *There's Still a Person in There: The Complete Guide to Treating and Coping With Alzheimer's Disease.* New York: J. P. Putnam; 1999.

Kahana E, Biegel D, Wykle M. *Family Caregiving Across the Lifespan.* Thousand Oaks, Calif: Sage; 1994.

Schulz R. *Handbook on Dementia Caregiving.* New York: Springer; 2000.

Yeo G, Gallagher-Thompson D. *Ethnicity and the Dementias.* Washington, DC: Taylor & Francis; 1996.

Caribbean

See Latin America and the Caribbean

Cataracts

Cataracts are the leading cause of reversible visual loss among adults age 55 years and older. Cataracts result from the clouding of the natural lens, the part of the eye responsible for focusing light and producing clear sharp images. The lens is contained in a sealed bag or capsule. As old cells die, they become trapped within the capsule. Over time, the cells accumulate and cause the lens to cloud, making images look blurred or fuzzy.

Cataracts can occur in one or both eyes and can be related to one of the following categories: age related (> 50% of all American over 65 years of age have cataracts), congenital, secondary (from steroid use or health conditions such as diabetes), or traumatic (eye injuries can lead to cataracts either directly or many years later).

There are three types of cataracts: nuclear, cortical, and subcapsular. *Nuclear* cataracts are located in the central area of the lens and are usually a result of advancing age. *Cortical* cataracts are located in the periphery of the lens and grow inward; they are associated with patients who suffer from diabetes. The *subcapsular* type of cataract develops at the back of the lens and is more common in patients who take steroids or have diabetes.

A cataract usually develops slowly and causes no pain. At first, the cloudiness affects only part of the lens and patients may be unaware of symptoms. Symptoms of advancing cataracts include cloudy or foggy vision, blurry vision, and changes in color vision. There may also be frequent changes in eyeglass/contact prescription strength. Patients may also notice halos/glare, poor night vision, double vision, and/or progressive loss of vision.

Risk factors for cataracts include family history, ultraviolet exposure, free radicals, medications, smoking, excessive alcohol use, and medical problems such as diabetes. Cataracts are diagnosed by a complete ophthalmological exam, including a visual acuity test, a slit lamp examination, and a retinal exam.

The only effective cataract treatment involves surgery to remove the cloudy natural lens and replace it with a clear artificial lens. There are several variations in both the removal and replacement portions of the surgery. *Extracapsular surgery* removes the lens of the eye but leaves the capsule intact. *Intracapsular surgery* removes the entire lens and capsule. The lens is replaced with either an intraocular lens implant (IOL), contact lens, or glasses. The type of procedure performed is decided by the physician and the patient.

Most cataracts occur with age and cannot be avoided. For early detection, people older than 60 years of age should get their eyes examined every other year. Stopping smoking, eating a balanced diet, and protecting oneself from ultraviolet exposure with sunglasses may help.

—*Deepti Mishra*

See also Diabetes; Driving; Eye Diseases; Normal Physical Aging; Vision and Low Vision

Further Readings and References

Abrams WB, Berkow R, eds. *The Merck Manual of Geriatrics.* Whitehouse Station, NJ: Merck; 1995.

Barker LR, Burton JR, Zieve PD. *Principles of Ambulatory Medicine.* Baltimore, Md: Wilkins & Wilkins; 2001.

American Academy of Ophthalmology. Cataract. Available at: www.medem.com/MedLB/article_detaillb.cfm?article_ID=ZZZSXEVUF4C&sub_cat=119. Accessed September 9, 2006.

MayoClinic.com. Cataracts. Available at: www.mayoclinic.com/health/cataracts/DS00050. Accessed September 9, 2006.

Cellulitis

Cellulitis is a form of skin and soft tissue infection that frequently affects the elderly. These types of infections have varied presentations and can encompass a variety of common and uncommon etiologies. Due to impaired host defenses and multiple comorbidities, infections such as cellulites not only are more common than in the general population but also can confer increased morbidity and mortality to older adults.

Cellulitis is an acute and spreading infection of the skin with some extension into the subcutaneous tissues. The most commonly involved locations are the extremities; however, factors such as decreased skin turgor and inactivity can predispose the elderly to skin infections in a variety of other locations such as the presacral area between the buttocks and the genitalia. There are several important predisposing factors. Edema (fluid buildup) can be due to removal of veins from the leg for use in coronary artery bypass grafts, mastectomy, venous insufficiency, or heart failure. Cracks, sores, and other openings in the skin predispose to cellulites. These skin problems can be due to pressure ulcers, athlete's foot (tinea pedis), chronic nail infections (onychomycoses), venous insufficiency, leg edema, and overweight. In cellulites, the skin typically is red, hot, swollen, and/or edematous and is painful to the touch. It is often accompanied by fever, malaise, and swollen lymph nodes (lymphadenitis). Erysipelas is a more superficial form of cellulitis that is associated with marked swelling of the skin and inflammation of the cutaneous lymphatic vessels but does not involve subcutaneous tissues. The margins of the involved tissues are raised and sharply demarcated (the "wall" of erysipelas). This is in contrast to cellulitis, where the margins may be distinct with regard to erythema (redness) but there is no palpable sharp demarcation of swelling or induration (firmness).

Older adults are susceptible to infections by a variety of unusual organisms. In general, streptococci and staphylococci are the most common causative agents of cellulitis in the elderly. With a relatively immunosuppressed state and a less than optimal protective epidermal (skin) barrier, the elderly are also susceptible to less commonly isolated or opportunistic pathogens. Potential portals of entry of infection in elderly patients may include body areas susceptible to chronic moisture, including the intertriginous areas (skin folds), gastrostomy tube sites, surgical sites, fissured toe webs, gluteal folds, perineum, and scrotum.

A recent development is the emergence of community-acquired methicillin-resistant *Staphylococcus aureus* (CA-MRSA). This organism has a predilection for skin and soft tissue infections, including recurrent furunculosis (boils) and soft tissue abscesses. In serious cases, this organism can spread to other organ systems, including the lung. A highly destructive form of pneumonia can result. Outbreaks within institutionalized settings and persons with close contact are often reported.

Treatment of cellulitis is centered on predicting the most likely causative organism and then using directed antibiotic therapy, either intravenously or orally, based on the severity of illness and the antibiotic chosen. Needle aspiration for microbiological culture is not indicated in routine care. When fever or other signs of systemic inflammatory response syndrome (SIRS) are present, a blood culture should be obtained, and parenteral (nonoral [either intravenous or intramuscular] injection) antibiotics are recommended. In the elderly, signs of SIRS such as fever might not be present, and one should pay careful attention to subtle signs of more severe infection. In the case of infected ulcers, soft tissue abscess, furunculosis, and (often) hidradenitis suppurativa (draining infected sweat glands), adequate removal of infected tissue and restoration of adequate blood supply are of paramount importance and often are more effective than systemic antibiotics. As an adjunct to treatment of extremity cellulitis, one must include local toenail and fingernail care, treatment of onychomycosis, prevention of pressure ulcers, treatment of tinea pedis, improvement in venous return to decrease lymphedema, and prevention of fissures and cracking. In rare instances, long-term suppressive antibiotic therapy can be used to prevent recurrences of cellulitis, such as in elderly patients with predisposing conditions (e.g., severe lymphedema, chronic fissures), but concern for resistance warrants careful patient selection.

—*Robin Trotman and Kevin P. High*

See also Biological Theories of Aging; Infectious Diseases; Normal Physical Aging; Pressure Ulcers; Skin Changes

Further Readings and References

National Institute of Allergy and Infectious Diseases. Group A streptococcal infections. Available at: www.niaid.nih.gov/factsheets/strep.htm. Accessed September 9, 2006.

Swartz MN. Cellulitis. *N Engl J Med.* 2004;350:904–912.

University of Maryland Medical Center. Cellulitis. Available at: www.umm.edu/altmed/ConsConditions/Cellulitiscc.html. Accessed September 9, 2006.

Yoshikawa TT, Norman DC. *Infectious Disease in the Aging: A Clinical Handbook.* Totowa, NJ: Humana; 2001.

Yoshikawa TT, Ouslander JG. *Infection Management for Geriatrics in Long-Term Facilities.* New York: Marcel Dekker; 2002.

CENTENARIANS

One of the most fascinating phenomena of population aging is the exponential growth in the number of centenarians. As of 2000, the count of remarkable individuals who have lived to be 100 years of age and older tallied more than 50,000 in the United States, a number projected to reach 214,000 in 2020 and 834,000 in 2050. Even though demographic statistics on centenarians are often challenged by the inaccuracy of the data, the growth of centenarians is evident in all industrialized countries. Owing to the dramatic increase in the number of persons over 100 years of age, studies are focusing on the longevity characteristics of super-centenarians (those who are over 110 years of age) and semi-super-centenarians (those who are over 105 years of age). The increase of centenarians has important social and economic implications for our society, including reconceptualization of age and aging and modification of social policies and services. Also, centenarians—the survivors of the human species—provide a unique opportunity to explore human aging and longevity from the perspective of the relative contributions of nature (genetics) and nurture (environment, nutrition, activities, psychosocial, and behavioral aspects) as well as their interactions. From this perspective, cross-cultural comparisons of factors contributing to longevity are especially important.

Centenarians today were born at the turn of the 20th century, experienced numerous historical events (e.g., World Wars I and II, the Great Depression, President John F. Kennedy's assassination, the first moon landing) in their younger years, and celebrated their 10th decade of life at the new millennium. Given that the life expectancy at birth in 1900 was 48 years, today's surviving centenarians are extraordinary individuals who have lived twice their expected time. Globally, the official human longevity record is held by the French woman Jeanne Calment, who died in 1997 at 122 years of age. With increased average life expectancy and medical advancement, survival curves of populations have become rectangularized and more individuals are approaching the potential human life span.

Most studies of centenarians can be characterized as descriptive prior to the 1980s. Systematic studies of genetic, biological, and behavioral influences have increased exponentially during the past two decades. Recent studies have reported on centenarians in the United States (Georgia and New England), Sweden, Denmark, France, Germany, Italy, Sardinia, Japan (Tokyo and Okinawa), Korea, and other countries.

One of the most striking characteristics of centenarians is the disproportionate gender ratio. The general tendency of female longevity becomes more pronounced during extreme old age. This ratio varies from four to six females to one male. A majority of centenarians (> 80%) are also non-Hispanic Whites. During the next few decades, however, the racial/ethnic composition of centenarian populations will change profoundly. J. C. Day's study of U.S. population projections in 1996 indicated that the number of centenarians of color will grow faster than that of non-Hispanic Whites. This projection suggests the importance of understanding cultural and ethnic characteristics of older minorities to properly respond to their needs. Centenarians are more likely to have lower educational attainment and unmarried status and are more likely to live alone compared with other cohorts of older populations. Approximately half of centenarians are reported to live in nursing homes.

Leonard W. Poon and colleagues showed with their 2000 study that the survival patterns of four groups of centenarians by gender (male or female) and race (African American or non-Hispanic White American).

They charted the number of days of survival after reaching 100 years of age among 137 centenarians who were part of the Georgia Centenarian Study. The champion survivors were the African American females, followed by non-Hispanic White American females and African American males. The gender difference in survival during the first 2 years was not significantly different; however, the difference was significantly pronounced after 3 years in favor of females. Both gender and race were associated with survivorship, with African Americans showing longer survival times than White Americans. Racial mortality crossover effects were shown to be clear at the extreme old age. This crossover effect is an important and worthwhile research question for future explorations.

A wide range of individual difference in physical function and disease profile is apparent in centenarians. Some centenarians are extremely mobile and functionally independent, whereas others suffer comorbidity resulting in frailty and dependency. In the New England Centenarian Study, approximately 35% of the sample of centenarians were free from functional disability and a majority (close to 90%) had been functionally independent up to 90 years of age. The prevalence of age-related diseases, such as cancer, heart disease, and diabetes, was significantly lower among centenarians than among younger older adults. In the centenarian data from Japan, Sweden, and the United States, the prevalence rates of dementia range from 40% to 63%. Findings from various studies clearly indicate that decline in physical and cognitive function is not inevitable with aging.

The Georgia Centenarian Study showed age differences in intelligence among nondemented adults in their 60s, 80s, and 100s. Centenarians performed significantly worse on average than did octogenarians and sexagenarians in learning new information and retrieving familiar information as well as on tests of intelligence such as vocabulary, block design, arithmetic, and picture arrangement. The exception was in everyday problem solving, where cognitively intact and community-dwelling centenarians performed as well as the younger groups. In general, the magnitudes of age differences were smaller in crystallized intelligence (e.g., information contained in the lexicon such as vocabulary) than in fluid intelligence (e.g., learning new information such as paired associate learning). Education was found to have a profound positive effect in mitigating the level of performance differences between individuals, especially among centenarians.

Research on personality characteristics of older populations shows that centenarians are less likely to be energetic and open but are more likely to be introverted, easygoing, and relaxed. When dealing with stressful life situations, centenarians are known to use cognitive coping strategies rather than active behavioral coping. A study using the Georgia Centenarian data showed an interesting age variation in mental health consequences of physical health problems. Although centenarians had greater levels of disability and disease, their subjective perception of health and mental health status were less likely undermined by their health problems when compared with the younger old in their 60s and 80s. Given that individuals evaluate self and situations through social comparisons, the adverse effects of health problems may be lessened for centenarians, whose age peers have a higher prevalence of health problems and mortality rates. It is also suggested that centenarians have differential expectations and perspectives of life as well as lowered reference points based on realities of advanced old age. Centenarians are more likely to consider disability and disease as changes that occur with aging rather than as health problems; thus, these conditions are more acceptable to them. Also, due to their lifetime experiences, centenarians may have advantages in dealing with life stresses. They may have developed efficient personal coping strategies and so may be more adapted to their adverse health conditions than are their younger counterparts. Finally, centenarians may be benefiting from selective survivorships. Their special status as survivors beyond the expected life span may bolster the psychological state of centenarians and help them to make positive evaluations of themselves. These psychological assets and coping strategies may be sources of emotional strength and resilience for centenarians.

Increasing research on centenarians is promising because the traditional categorization of older adults (integrating those age 60 or 65 years and older into a single group) has concealed the diversity within older populations that span more than 40 years of life. As the literature indicates, individual variation or diversity is the key characteristic of centenarians, and this feature will become more pronounced in the future. Diversities indicate that people with various backgrounds become centenarians and that there are multiple paths to living beyond the average life span. With their growth in numbers and diversified characteristics, centenarians have yet to be explored. From this perspective, studies of similarities and differences in longevity predictors from different cultures, as well as contributors to genetic and environment interactions for longevity, will be important next generations of centenarian research. The search for answers to human longevity and survival will continue.

—*Leonard W. Poon and Yuri Jang*

See also Demography of Aging; Longevity; Oldest Old; Twin Studies

Further Readings and References

Day JC. *Population Projections of the United States by Age, Sex, Race, and Hispanic Origin.* Washington, DC: Government Printing Office; 1996. Current Population Reports, Publication No. P25-1130.

Hagberg B, Alfredson BB, Poon LW, Homma A. Cognitive functioning in centenarians: A coordinated analysis of results from three countries. *J Gerontol B Psychol Sci Social Sci.* 2001;56:141–151.

Jang Y, Poon LW, Martin P. Individual differences in the effects of disease and disability on depressive symptoms: The role of age and subjective health. *Intl J Aging Hum Dev.* 2004;59:125–137.

Martin P, Rott C, Hagberg B, Morgan K, eds. *Centenarians: Autonomy Versus Dependence in the Oldest Old.* New York: Springer; 2000.

Poon LW, Johnson M, Davey A, Dawson D, Siegler I, Martin P. Psychosocial predictors of survival among centenarians. In: Martin P, Rott C, Hagberg B, Morgan K, eds. *Autonomy Versus Dependence in the Oldest Old.* New York: Springer; 2000.

Poon LW, Sweaney AL, Clayton GM, et al. The Georgia Centenarian Study. *Intl J Aging Hum Dev.* 1992;34:1–17.

CEREBROVASCULAR DISEASE

See STROKE

CLINICAL TRIALS

Clinical trials and health research represent important scientific endeavors designed to provide bases for understanding human biology and health, for preventing disease, for testing new medical technologies and treatments, and for enhancing quality of life. Despite the potential benefits of clinical trials and health-related research, rates of participation are generally low, hovering around 3%. Participation is especially low among racial/ethnic minorities, medically underserved populations, and older persons. Increasing the participation of racial/ethnic minorities in health research has emerged as a major issue for scientists over the past two decades given the National Institutes of Health (NIH) Revitalization Act of 1993. Accordingly, it is the policy of the NIH that women and members of minority groups and their subpopulations must be included in all NIH-supported biomedical and behavioral research projects involving human participants unless a clear and compelling rationale is presented. Additional impetus is given to the need to have minorities participate in health research because of their higher morbidity and mortality across many diseases and conditions. For example, the health disparities between African Americans and Whites are well documented with regard to higher rates of diabetes, hypertension, cardiovascular disease, stroke, and other conditions for African Americans. Similarly, health disparities are documented for Hispanic subpopulations and some Asian groups. To eliminate these disparities and to develop appropriate interventions and treatments that will work best for minorities, it is essential that they be participants in clinical trials and health-related research. Moreover, they need to participate in sufficient numbers for meaningful analyses.

In addressing the need to understand how to increase the participation of minorities, a growing body of literature has examined recruitment barriers and strategies and also has refined concepts and approaches to the issue. For example, it is important to consider how the different types of studies, from behavioral to clinical, affect the willingness of minorities to participate in health-related studies. Research on recruitment has distinguished between clinical treatment trials that are offered to individuals with illness symptomatology as opposed to prevention, behavioral and nontherapeutic kinds of studies often conducted on healthy populations. Clearly, willingness to participate in health-related research such as clinical treatment trials may be motivated by the presence or absence of illness or disease. In addition, participation may be affected by the degree of participant burden as well as by the incentives that are offered.

Among the barriers to minority participation in health research are experiences of past discrimination that are associated with lower levels of trust in the health care system and scientific research. Prior studies indicate that African Americans are more likely than Whites to be concerned about being exploited, being treated as a "guinea pig," and being treated dishonestly regarding the risks of research participation. Studies also show that minorities are less likely to be aware of clinical trials and may also be less likely to be offered clinical trials by their physicians. In addition, socioeconomic factors may impede participation in health research because significant numbers of minorities have low incomes and lack access to consistent primary care and, accordingly, to clinical trials. Other barriers include cultural factors related to language and health beliefs as well as low literacy that can impede communication between research staff and prospective participants. Additional barriers stem from medical ineligibility to participate and instrumental concerns such as lack of child care, lack of access to transportation, lack of release time from work, and lack of geographic proximity to research sites.

Several studies have attempted to understand rates of research participation by race and age. With regard to older persons, previous research indicates that their enrollment in health research tends to be less than that of younger persons across all racial/ethnic minority groups, with older minorities participating at a lower

rate than older Caucasians. One study of participation by age and race found that persons age 65 years and older were significantly underrepresented in cancer clinical trials, with persons 65 to 74 years of age participating at 1.3% compared with 3.0% for persons 30 to 64 years of age. This finding was consistent across African American and Hispanic subgroups. Although the elderly accounted for two thirds of persons with breast, lung, colorectal, or prostate cancer, they represented only one third of participants in clinical trials from 1992 to 2000.

Overall, numerous studies tend to indicate that minority individuals are less willing to participate in clinical trials and health research, as evidenced by the documented lower rates of minority participation. However, some researchers have produced contradictory findings suggesting that minorities are *not* less willing than Whites to participate in health research. These findings indicate that there are few differences between Whites and minorities in their willingness to participate in clinical studies when minorities are made aware of the studies and meet the medical requirements. The differences appear to occur with regard to access, with fewer minorities than Whites being asked to participate.

In addition to the literature on factors influencing minority participation in health research, a number of studies have examined strategies for recruitment. The necessity of building trusting relationships in minority communities is a major theme. In emphasizing the importance of developing relationships with trusted members of the community, some studies suggest incorporating a community participatory approach to research, using appropriate language, and addressing prevailing beliefs that discourage community members from participation. It is also suggested that these strategies are needed prior to the recruitment of minority elders into health-related research. Findings from other studies contend that it is essential to understand the culture of each ethnic minority group as well as to understand their attitudes and experiences toward health research. Garnering the participation and support of minority elders may also necessitate a process of negotiating through the different layers of trust and approval that require research staff to devote significant amounts of time and resources. However, it is suggested that these steps are essential to successful recruitment and retention of elderly minority individuals in health-related research.

Other studies have examined the effectiveness of recruitment techniques with minority populations. In one study, researchers conducted a randomized trial to test the effectiveness of mailing an advanced notification letter as a recruitment technique for encouraging the participation of older African Americans and Whites in a mailed survey. Based on their findings, the researchers concluded that although Whites would respond to a recruitment letter, additional strategic efforts were needed to recruit African Americans. For working with rural older African Americans and their female caregivers, another study indicates that face-to-face in-person strategies are most effective for these target populations. The literature also indicates that having a doctor's recommendation can be a major motivating factor for recruitment of minorities into clinical studies, although using the media proved to be more effective than using a clinic registry to recruit Latina women into a cancer-prevention trial. Similarly, other researchers have used social marketing principles for working with community partners and organizing recruitment activities.

The issue of retention of minorities is addressed much less in the literature. From among the few studies on this issue, research indicates that factors promoting retention are mutual support, the opportunity to engage in meaningful social activity, feeling cared for, and cultural sensitivity. It is less clear how factors such as remuneration, ethnicity of the group leader, and religious factors influence retention in health-related studies. In another retention focus study, researchers examined the efficacy of employing a case management strategy to keep older African American men in a cancer screening intervention. These findings indicated that case managers appear to be particularly useful in enhancing retention in research because they not only connect persons with services they might need, such as transportation and health care, but also serve as an additional resource and source of social support.

In summary, involving minorities as participants in health research remains an important goal for biomedical and behavioral researchers if gains are to be made in reducing the disparities in morbidity and mortality that exist in minority populations. In particular, minority elders are needed as research participants given their higher prevalence of illness and medical conditions in comparison with younger age groups. Although knowledge and expertise around strategies for recruitment and retention of minorities in health research have increased and been documented in the literature, it appears that strategies vary by research issues, minority populations, geography, type of research, and other factors. Much still remains to be understood and tested in advancing a science of minority recruitment and retention.

—*Diane R. Brown*

See also Health Promotion and Disease Prevention

Further Readings and References

Brown DR, Alexander M, eds. Increasing the participation of older minorities in health research. *J Aging Health.* 2004;16(Suppl.):1S–176S.

Brown DR, Topcu MG. Willingness to participate in clinical treatment research among older African Americans and Whites. *Gerontologist.* 2003;43:62–72.

Hall WD. Representation of Blacks, women, and the very elderly (aged > or = 80) in 28 major randomized clinical trials. *Ethnic Disease.* 1999;9:333–340.

Hutchins LF, Unger JM, Crowley JJ, Coltman CA, Albain KS. Underrepresentation of patients 65 years of age and older in cancer-treatment trials. *N Engl J Med.* 1999;341:2061–2067.

COMORBIDITY

See MULTIPLE MORBIDITY AND COMORBIDITY

COMPLEMENTARY AND ALTERNATIVE MEDICINE

Complementary and alternative medicine, commonly referred to as CAM, is a group of unconventional medical systems, practices, and products not currently considered to be part of the conventional biomedical care provided by medical doctors and other conventional health professionals. A nationwide government health survey released in May 2004 indicated that 36% of U.S. adults used some form of CAM, as noted by Patricia M. Barnes and colleagues in 2004. When prayer for health reasons specifically was included, the number of U.S. adults using CAM in the past year rose to 62%. Back pain topped the list of conditions for which CAM was used, confirming prior studies finding musculoskeletal pain linked to CAM use.

The survey found that if the use of prayer for health reasons is included, CAM use is more likely among older adults than among younger adults. In contrast, excluding prayer for health reasons yields a U-shaped relationship between CAM use and age, with the youngest and oldest groups of adults reporting the least use of CAM. Other predictors of CAM use include female gender, education, hospitalization during the past year, and having been a smoker in the past but not currently. Earlier surveys, including one by David M. Eisenberg and colleagues in 1998, found that most CAM users also see medical doctors for conventional medical care but usually do not disclose CAM use to their medical doctors. The same study found that consumers spent an estimated $27 billion out of pocket on CAM in 1997.

Despite their popularity, for most CAM therapies there are unanswered key questions regarding safety, cost-effectiveness, efficacy, and mechanisms. Facilitating the scientific evaluation of CAM is a key objective of the National Center for Complementary and Alternative Medicine (NCCAM) at the National Institutes of Health (NIH). NCCAM's predecessor, the Office of Alternative Medicine (OAM), opened at the NIH in 1992 in the Office of the Director with the mission of providing the American public with reliable information about the safety and effectiveness of CAM practices. A 1998 congressional mandate expanded the OAM into NCCAM. The OAM's 1993 budget of $2 million grew to NCCAM's 2005 budget of more than $123 million. NCCAM's programs include funding research, developing scientific databases, providing a public information clearinghouse, and facilitating national and international cooperative efforts in CAM research and education. (Additional information may be found at http://nccam.nih.gov.)

The National Cancer Institute (NCI) established the Office of Cancer Complementary and Alternative Medicine (OCCAM) in 1998 to coordinate and enhance the activities of the NCI in the CAM arena. Several surveys have indicated that many, if not most, cancer patients use complementary therapies during or after treatment for cancer. Patients' motivations for using CAM include improving quality of life, boosting immunity, prolonging life, and curing disease. Few patients reject conventional treatment entirely and use only alternative therapies. (Additional information may be found at www3.cancer.gov/occam.)

At the request of the NIH and the Agency for Healthcare Research and Quality, the Institute of Medicine (IOM) produced a comprehensive report on CAM in 2005 to discuss what is known about Americans' reliance on CAM and to help set guidelines for research. The IOM concluded that CAM is being integrated into medical practice in hospitals and physicians' offices, some health maintenance organizations (HMOs) are covering selected CAM therapies, and insurance coverage for CAM is increasing, and it suggested that health care should strive to be comprehensive and evidence based, with conventional medical treatments and CAM held to the same standards for demonstrating clinical effectiveness. (The full report is available at www.iom.edu.)

NCCAM groups CAM into five domains. Examples of published and ongoing research in each domain are presented next. Additional information on NIH-funded studies is located in the Computer Retrieval of Information on Scientific Projects (CRISP) database (http://crisp.cit.nih.gov).

Alternative medical systems are built on complete systems of theory and practice, often predating modern Western biomedicine. Homeopathy and naturopathy are examples of alternative medical systems arising in Western culture. Homeopaths intend to stimulate the body's healing through providing minute doses of natural products. Naturopaths work to prevent illness or restore health using nutritional modifications, dietary supplements, herbals, homeopathic remedies, hydrotherapy, massage, and counseling. Traditional Chinese medicine exemplifies an alternative medical system from Eastern culture, employing mind–body therapies, natural products, massage, acupuncture, and the concept of energy flow as central to healing. Acupuncture has been the subject of several studies for osteoarthritis of the knee, for which it is currently being studied in a clinical trial supported by NCCAM.

Mind–body interventions (e.g., meditation, prayer, Tai Chi, yoga) aim to increase the mind's capacity to enhance bodily function and reduce symptoms. Recognizing the importance of prayer to older adults, the National Institute on Aging (NIA) at the NIH is funding secondary analyses of large existing data sets on health and behavior to answer questions about the correlates of religiosity and spirituality to health in elderly African Americans and other racial/ethnic groups of elderly Americans. The NIH has supported research on yoga for hyperkyphosis of the spine and has supported Tai Chi, a meditative movement therapy, for promotion of psychosocial and physical benefits.

Biologically based therapies include foods, vitamins, and other dietary supplements. Products made from botanicals that are used to maintain or improve health have been called herbal supplements, botanicals, or phytomedicines. Elderly adults are at particular risk for marginal to significant deficiency of vitamins and trace minerals, and their diets may require supplementation. In addition to using multivitamin and mineral supplementation, it is estimated that as many as 65% to 88% of elderly adults are using dietary supplements that are nonmineral natural products, primarily botanical supplements. Despite a lack of evidence on safety or efficacy, several studies have reported that many elderly adults use supplements for disease prevention, treatment or symptom management for conditions such as cancer (saw palmetto); osteoarthritis, rheumatoid arthritis, and fibromyalgia (mainly glucosamine and chondroitin); depression; and dementia. Many of these supplements are used concurrently with multiple prescription medications.

Increased understanding of the composition and function of herbal supplements raises serious concerns about their widespread use by elderly individuals due to adverse effects and drug–supplement interactions. Herbal and nutritional supplements have been demonstrated to possess steroid hormone modulatory effects (isoflavones), antiplatelet activity (garlic, ginger, ginko, and ginseng), gastrointestinal manifestations (essiac), hepatotoxicity (kava), and nephrotoxicity; adverse interactions with corticosteroids (echinacea and ephedra) and central nervous system depressant drugs; and additive effects when used with opioid analgesics (St. John's wort).

Adulteration and product quality issues are of particular concern. As a result of current standards for packaging and processing, the contents of supplements vary significantly from batch to batch as well as from the claims on the labels. Products have been found to have less than half the potency listed on the labels, to contain unsafe levels of toxic metals, and to include prescription drug compounds. Dietary supplements result in increased health-related out-of-pocket expense, which is of importance to adults living on fixed incomes. Several NIH-funded studies on biological therapies in older adults are under way.

Manipulative and body-based methods are physical modalities such as massage, chiropractic adjustments, and osteopathic manipulations. Results of a study on persistent low back pain indicated that massage was superior to self-care on symptoms and was superior to self-care and acupuncture on disability. The massage group used the least medications and had the lowest costs of subsequent care, suggesting that massage might be an effective alternative to conventional medical care for persistent back pain, as noted by Daniel C. Cherkin and colleagues in 2001.

Energy therapies are of two types. The first is exemplified by therapeutic touch, Reiki, and other therapies intending to manipulate biofields claimed to be within and around the body. NCCAM is funding research on the effects of Reiki on anxiety and cancer activity in patients with newly diagnosed prostate cancer. The second type is bioelectromagnetic-based therapies involving the unconventional use of electromagnetic fields for therapeutic purposes. A survey of patients who had rheumatoid arthritis, osteoarthritis, or fibromyalgia found that 18% reported using magnets or copper bracelets, as noted by Jaya K. Rao and colleagues in 1999. NCCAM has funded studies on the effects of magnets for fibromyalgia pain and quality of life, migraine headache pain, and osteoarthritis of the knee. Results have been conflicting.

Rigorous research is needed to further evaluate CAM therapies and their integration into conventional medical care.

—*Cynthia D. Myers, Nagi B. Kumar, David S. Craig, and Anne Strozier*

See also Anti-Aging Interventions; Dietary Variety; Health Promotion and Disease Prevention; Vitamins, Minerals, and Dietary Supplements

Further Readings and References

Barnes PM, Powell-Griner E, McFann K, Nahin RL. *Complementary and Alternative Medicine Use Among Adults: United States, 2002.* Hyattsville, Md: National Center for Health Statistics; 2004. Advance Data From Vital and Health Statistics, No. 343.

Cherkin DC, Eisenberg D, Sherman KJ, et al. Randomized trial comparing traditional Chinese medical acupuncture, therapeutic massage, and self-care education for chronic low back pain. *Arch Int Med.* 2001;161:1081–1088.

Eisenberg DM, Davis RB, Ettner SL, et al. Trends in alternative medicine use in the United States, 1990–1997. *JAMA.* 1998;280:1569–1575.

Kumar NB, Allen K, Bell H. Perioperative herbal supplement use in cancer patients: Potential implications and recommendations for presurgical screening. *Cancer Control.* 2005;12:149–157.

Rao JK, Mihaliak K, Kroenke K, Bradley J, Tierney WM, Weinberger M. Use of complementary therapies for arthritis among patients of rheumatologists. *Ann Intern Med.* 1999;131:409–416.

COMPRESSION OF MORBIDITY

The term *compression of morbidity* was introduced as a hypothesis by James F. Fries in 1980. He hypothesized that, with improved lifestyles and health care, the age of onset of morbidity could be put off longer than the age at death, resulting in a decrease in the length of time spent with morbidity. Proponents of this idea concluded that disability in the older population and health care costs would be reduced in future years. When introduced, the hypothesis countered a generally pessimistic outlook that increasing life expectancy among those with incurable chronic conditions was leading to increased morbidity and what Ernest Gruenberg termed a "failure of success." Kenneth Manton responded to Fries's suggestion with his theory of dynamic equilibrium, which posits that mortality and morbidity change would occur in equilibrium; that is, morbidity would not compress or expand.

The compression of morbidity concept has encouraged a steady stream of research over the past 25 years and has been important in changing health policy aims in many countries and international agencies. However, there is no empirical evidence that a compression of morbidity has occurred generally or is likely to be a regular pattern of health change in the foreseeable future. Whether individual empirical investigations have found morbidity to be compressing, expanding, or in equilibrium depends on the definition of *morbidity* used and the time period under study.

Part of the reason why the compression of morbidity has not occurred is that Fries based his theory on faulty assumptions about what was likely to happen to mortality and morbidity. He posited that there was an average age beyond which life expectancy would not increase and that increases in life expectancy would cease at the oldest ages. This was assumed to be 85 years, an age now exceeded by regional subpopulations in Japan. Examination of mortality change at the oldest ages over the past two decades has demonstrated that mortality decline is occurring at very old ages and that, although there may be a limit to human life expectancy, it is over 85 years and decades longer than the life expectancy now observed in even long-lived populations.

Fries also assumed that changes in lifestyle would be important in delaying the onset of chronic conditions, but research has shown that any delays in onset age have been smaller than the extension of life that has occurred among those who have chronic conditions, resulting in age-specific increases in the proportions of the population with chronic conditions. Thus, the presence of chronic conditions is expanding. On the other hand, many countries have seen recent decreases in age-specific disability and improvements in functioning, resulting in some observations of a longer life without disability and increases in nondisabled life that exceed the increases in disabled life. This provides evidence of some compression of disability. Models of healthy life expectancy have demonstrated the complex links between changes in mortality and morbidity; only under a limited set of circumstances will a compression of morbidity occur. Empirically, we should expect to observe periods of compression, expansion, and equilibrium.

—Eileen M. Crimmins

See also Active Life Expectancy; Health and Public Policy; Instruments; Longevity; Multiple Morbidity and Comorbidity

Further Readings and References

Fries JF. Aging, natural death, and the compression of morbidity. *N Engl J Med.* 1980;303:130–135.

Robine JM, Jagger C, Mathers C, Crimmins E, Suzman R, eds. *Determining Health Expectancies.* Sussex, England: Wiley; 2003.

CONFUSIONAL STATE

See DELIRIUM AND CONFUSIONAL STATES

CONGESTIVE HEART FAILURE

Congestive heart failure (CHF) is a clinical syndrome characterized by an inability of the heart to pump enough blood and oxygen to meet the energy needs of the body. Heart failure is a common and costly disease that has a great impact on quality of life, mortality, and functional status. Approximately 5 million people in the United States have CHF, which affects mainly older adults (6% to 10% of those age 65 years and older). Approximately 5% of all medical admissions to the hospital are attributable to CHF, and it is the most common reason for admission for older adults. Fully 30% to 40%

die within the first year after diagnosis, and 60% to 70% die within 5 years. CHF accounts for approximately 2% of all U.S. health care expenditures—$28 billion in direct and indirect health care costs.

Etiology

Risk factors for developing CHF in the United States include coronary artery disease, high blood pressure (hypertension), defective heart valves, diabetes mellitus, cardiac dysrhythmias, and cardiomyopathy. Cardiomyopathy can be idiopathic or caused by drugs, infection, thyroid disease, or alcohol.

The most common cause of CHF is left ventricular (LV) systolic dysfunction, resulting from damage to the heart muscle primarily from coronary artery disease. Damage to the LV decreases its strength, measured as the ejection fraction (EF) or proportion of blood that is pumped through the heart with each contraction (systole). A reduced ejection fraction results in decreased forward blood flow with each systole and, therefore, diminished perfusion of other organs. Remodeling of the undamaged heart muscle also occurs, leading to changes in the size and function of the left ventricle that can further decrease LV systolic function. Remodeling of the heart and organ hypoperfusion lead to activation of systemic neurohumoral pathways, such as the plasma rennin–angiotensin–aldosterone system, which can cause further decompensation of cardiac function, creating a vicious cycle of multisystem failure.

As LV systolic function (and therefore EF) declines, an increase in heart rate typically occurs to increase cardiac output. However, the increased rate strains an already weakened heart by increasing myocardial oxygen demand, resulting in further decompensation of function. The rapid heart rate also decreases LV filling time and can, paradoxically, decrease cardiac output.

However, not all heart failure results from LV systolic dysfunction. In community studies, approximately half of patients with symptomatic heart failure had preserved systolic function of the left ventricle. In the Cardiovascular Health Study, heart failure with preserved LV systolic function was common (55%), especially in women and older adults. Although the pathophysiology is not well understood, poor compliance is a likely mechanism. Compliance is the ability of the heart muscle to relax between contractions (diastole). Poor compliance reduces the size of the LV that can be filled with blood prior to the next contraction. Impaired diastolic filling results in decreased forward blood flow (although the EF remains normal) and decreased perfusion of organs similar to LV systolic dysfunction.

Symptoms

The cardinal symptoms of CHF include shortness of breath (dyspnea), cough, swelling of the feet and ankles (peripheral edema), and chronic fatigue. The impaired ability of the heart to pump blood results in blood "backing up" into the pulmonary veins, with leaking of fluid into the lung tissue (pulmonary edema). Pulmonary edema contributes to dyspnea and cough. Fluid leaks out from other veins, causing peripheral edema. Reduced perfusion of muscles, as the body attempts to direct impaired blood flow to more vital organs such as the brain and kidneys, contributes to fatigue. Other symptoms include nighttime urination (nocturia) and disordered breathing during sleep.

Multiple studies have also shown that CHF is a risk factor for disability, mortality, and decreased quality of life. A growing body of literature also suggests that changes in cognitive function may be associated with CHF.

Severity of clinical symptoms in CHF is rated according to the New York Heart Association classification system:

- *Class I (mild):* no symptoms
- *Class II (mild):* mild symptoms with activity but no symptoms at rest
- *Class III (moderate):* noticeable limitation in ability to exercise due to symptoms; comfortable only at rest
- *Class IV (severe):* unable to do any activity without decompensation; symptoms at rest

Diagnosis

The diagnosis of CHF is based on clinical symptoms. However, making the diagnosis can be challenging, especially in older adults. Many of the cardinal symptoms can occur in other conditions such as anemia, chronic lung disease, pneumonia, renal disease, and venous insufficiency. The presentation can be sudden, especially if related to myocardial ischemia, or can develop slowly over time. Frequently, CHF is characterized by chronic symptoms with intermittent exacerbations.

Examination of a patient with CHF may reveal labored respirations, hypoxia, distended neck veins due to increased jugular venous pressure, a rapid heart rate, and leg swelling. A chest X-ray is commonly used to identify an enlarged heart and pulmonary edema as well as to exclude other pulmonary disease. Echocardiography can be used to evaluate LV function and valve disease. An electrocardiogram (ECG) can identify cardiac ischemia, abnormal cardiac rhythms, or abnormal conduction that can contribute to CHF. Measurement of blood B-type natriuretic peptide, secreted by myocytes in response to excessive stretching, is elevated in decompensated heart failure and can aid in the diagnosis.

Treatment

Although there is no cure for CHF, several treatment modalities are available to improve symptoms, delay progression, and decrease hospital admissions.

Drugs are the primary treatment for CHF and include diuretics, angiotensin-converting enzyme inhibitors (ACE-I), angiotensin II receptor blockers (ARBs), β-blockers, digoxin, and blood thinners. *Diuretics,* or water pills, promote salt wasting and water loss. A decrease in total body fluid results in decreased ventricular filling pressures and, therefore, decreased work of the heart. Diuretics also help rid the lungs of fluid, thereby relieving dyspnea. *ACE-I and ARBs* cause dilatation of the venous system, thereby decreasing blood pressure. With a lower blood pressure, the heart needs to work less hard to maintain forward blood flow and perfusion. Treatment with ACE-I and ARBs has been shown to not only decrease symptoms but also slow progression of heart failure through cardiac remodeling. *β-Blockers* decrease the heart rate, allowing longer filling time during diastole. This greater filling of the ventricles increases cardiac output and, therefore, perfusion of the body. *Digoxin* is an inotrope that can increase the force of contractions of the heart and, therefore, increase the ejection fraction. Digoxin can also be used to control the heart rate in atrial fibrillation; that is, an irregular heart rhythm that impairs ventricular filling. Reduced EF results in stasis of blood within the heart cavities. Stasis can increase stroke risk through formation of blood clots. *Blood thinners,* such as warfarin, are commonly used in more severe stages of heart failure where the risk of stasis and clots is higher.

Treatment of the underlying causes of CHF is also essential. This includes management of hypertension and coronary artery disease to decrease the risk of ischemia and strain on the heart. Replacement of the poorly functioning heart valves may be indicated. In severe heart failure, an evaluation for cardiac transplant may be appropriate. However, transplantation is limited by the number of available organs.

Lifestyle changes may also contribute to a decreased risk of developing CHF, an improvement in symptoms, a decrease in the number of hospitalizations for CHF exacerbations, and improvement in quality of life. Low-salt diets, regular exercise, weight loss, smoking cessation, and avoidance of caffeine all have been shown to have some benefit in the management of CHF.

Cardiac resynchronization therapy has proven to be beneficial in more severe CHF, especially when medical treatment fails to control symptoms. Cardiac remodeling in CHF can cause desynchrony between contractions of the ventricles of the heart due to delayed transmission of electrical impulses. This results in impaired perfusion. A device similar to a pacemaker can be implanted to send small electrical impulses to the ventricles to synchronize contraction, leading to increased pump strength, increased perfusion, and improved symptoms.

Because of the complexity of diagnosis and management of CHF, patient education and multidisciplinary support outside of the hospital setting are also necessary to help improve understanding and adherence to treatment regimens and, subsequently, to decrease symptoms, hospital admissions, and health care costs and to improve quality of life.

—*Laurie Lavery*

See also Cardiovascular System; Diabetes; Hypertension; Valvular Heart Disease

Further Readings and References

Hogg K, Swedberg K, McMurray JJ. Heart failure with preserved left ventricular systolic function: Epidemiology, clinical characteristics, and prognosis. *J Am Coll Cardiol.* 2004;43:317–327.

Hunt SA, Abraham WT, Chin MH, et al. A report of the American College of Cardiology/American Heart Association Task Force on Practice Guidelines. *Circulation.* 2005;112:1825–1852.

Kitzman DW, Gardin JM, Gottdiener JS, et al. Importance of heart failure with preserved systolic function in patients ≥ 65 years of age: CHS Research Group—Cardiovascular Health Study. *Am J Cardiol.* 2001;87:413–419.

McMurry JJ, Pfeffer MA. Heart failure. *Lancet.* 2005;365: 1877–1889.

CONSORTIUM TO ESTABLISH A REGISTRY FOR ALZHEIMER'S DISEASE

The Consortium to Establish a Registry for Alzheimer's Disease (CERAD) was funded in 1986 by the National Institute on Aging to develop brief, standardized, valid, and reliable measures to assess severity in Alzheimer's disease (AD). Although well-accepted diagnostic criteria for Alzheimer's disease were available, approaches to measurement and the specific measures used varied from site to site. In consequence, aggregation of information across sites or studies was problematic, reducing the potential to carry out correlational studies (e.g., between clinical and neuropathological findings), studies of AD subgroups (e.g., early onset vs. late onset), or studies of special populations (e.g., AD patients of different races/ethnicities).

Working with all 23 initial Alzheimer Disease Research Centers, CERAD developed and evaluated standardized assessments for the following areas: clinical, neuropsychological, behavioral pathology, neuroimaging, and neuropathological. CERAD also developed a standardized means for determining family history and use of patient care services.

The clinical battery obtains information on demographic characteristics, clinical history (including activities of daily living [ADLs] and cognitive functioning), physical and neurological examination, clinical laboratory and neuroimaging findings, and stage of disease. It provides diagnostic criteria for determining the presence of cognitive impairment and dementia and of type of dementia.

The neuropsychological battery, which takes approximately 40 minutes to administer, assesses those areas of cognitive functioning most likely to be affected in AD. The measures currently include verbal fluency; a 15-item version of the Boston Naming Test; the Mini-Mental State Examination; word list memory, recall, and recognition tasks; and constructional praxis copy and recall. Norms and test–retest reliability are available. A 48-item Behavioral Rating Scale for Dementia (BRSD), as well as an abbreviated 17-item version, measures the presence and frequency of pathological behaviors in eight domains.

The neuroimaging assessment specifies the manner in which images should be taken and provides guidelines for reading. Intrasite agreement is good, but intersite agreement is poor. Consequently, the neuroimaging protocol is rarely used. The neuropathology protocol, with guidelines for neuropathological assessment and criteria for AD and other neuropathological disorders, including Parkinson's disease, and good interrater agreement, has been widely adopted.

The family history assessment helps to identify family members with AD, Parkinson's disease, and Down syndrome. The brief (approximately 15-minute) services assessment protocol permits identification of health and social services used by, and needed for, patients with AD and their caregivers.

The CERAD assessments have been well received in the United States and abroad. They have been translated into more than a dozen languages and used in both clinical and epidemiological studies. Publications based on CERAD data range from clinical and epidemiological studies to health economics. CERAD materials and up to 7 years of data on 204 African American AD patients, 890 White AD patients, and 463 controls, including autopsy information on 202 AD cases, are available on CD-ROM. Further information and a bibliography through 2002 are also available (http://cerad.mc.duke.edu).

—*Gerda G. Fillenbaum*

See also Alzheimer's Disease; Geriatric Assessment; Imaging of the Brain; Instruments; Mental Status Assessment; National Institute on Aging; Outcome and Assessment Information Set (OASIS); Psychiatric Rating Scales

Further Readings and References

Heyman A, Fillenbaum G, Nash F, eds. Consortium to Establish a Registry for Alzheimer's Disease: The CERAD experience. *Neurology.* 1997;49(Suppl. 3).

CONTINUUM OF CARE

The continuum of care is a framework for discussing the ideal system for those needing long-term care. In 2005, Connie J. Evashwick defined a continuum of care as a client-oriented system made up of services and integrating mechanisms that guides and monitors patients through an array of health, mental health, and social services across all levels of intensity of care. A continuum of care is a comprehensive coordinated system of care designed to meet the needs of people with complex and/or ongoing problems efficiently and effectively. A continuum is more than a collection of fragmented services; it also includes mechanisms for organizing those services and operating them as an integrated system.

A continuum of care is client oriented rather than provider or payer oriented, and it provides services according to a client's needs rather than according to a provider's convenience or a payer's rigid guidelines. Recipients may be people of any age and with any disease condition, ranging from children with congenital anomalies, to young adults with lengthy recovery periods from trauma, to frail seniors with chronic diseases and the multifaceted symptoms of aging. The ideal continuum takes a holistic approach, considering the health, mental health, social, and financial aspects of a person's situation. The dynamic interactions of these elements are considered, and services are provided in a coordinated way rather than a disjointed way. A continuum also emphasizes wellness rather than illness. Ideally, once a person engages with a continuum, the continuum guides and tracks the person over time—through spells of both illness and wellness. The continuum of care concept does not imply that a person must be sick to be part of a continuum; rather, on becoming ill, the person would have easy access to the services needed. At other times, the person may participate in wellness, health promotion, and disease management activities.

The key to the comprehensive array of health, mental health, and social services included in the continuum of care is to be able to give clients access to the services they need when they need them. The services need not be owned by a single entity for the continuum to be managed effectively. The organizational arrangements among providers may be ownership, contracts, affiliations, or even informal but strong relationships. All levels of intensity of care refer to the range from acute high-technology interventions in institutions to ongoing support services at home (e.g., homemakers). The continuum incorporates both acute and long-term services, intertwining the two with common integrating mechanisms rather than creating two separate systems of care.

The goal of a continuum of care is to facilitate the client's access to the appropriate services quickly and efficiently. Ideally, a continuum of care accomplishes the following:

- Takes a multifaceted approach to the client's and family's situation
- Matches resources to the client's condition, avoiding duplication or omission of services and use of inappropriate services
- Monitors the client's condition and changes services as needs change
- Coordinates the services of many professionals and organizations

- Integrates care provided in a range of settings
- Streamlines patient flow and facilitates easy access to needed services
- Maintains a comprehensive record incorporating clinical, financial, and utilization data across settings
- Pools and negotiates comprehensive financing

By doing these, a true continuum of care should (a) enhance quality of care and client satisfaction through appropriateness, ease of access, and ongoing continuity of care; (b) increase provider efficiency; and (c) achieve cost-effectiveness by maximizing the use of resources.

The most effective continuums are designed as service configurations appropriate for specific client groups. Several continuums of care may exist simultaneously within the same community and even within the same organization. For example, a major medical center may have a rehabilitation center, a cancer center, a pediatric program for children with special health care needs, an HIV/AIDS program, and an authorized Program of All-Inclusive Care for the Elderly (PACE). Each one may have a core set of services used by its clients, and each may be organized as its own continuum with its own case management, information system, and organizational arrangements. The continuums may overlap in their use of select services. For example, all centers might use the parent organization's home health agency or refer to the same protective housing complex. A community-based continuum for seniors built on frequent but informal relationships might include money management by an Area Agency on Aging contractor, a church-operated adult day center, respite provided by the local Alzheimer's Association, support groups sponsored by a local skilled nursing facility, and care coordination and legal services offered by the local Jewish Family Service or Catholic Charities.

The continuum of care concept implies that a person remains part of an organized continuum of care. It further implies that, rather than having the consumer decide on the provider of each separate service, the organization will suggest services based on preestablished relationships (formal or informal). A continuum may not preclude a client or family from selecting an alternative provider, but it can eliminate the necessity of doing so. The consumer's participation may be ongoing (as in a managed care arrangement) or time limited (as in a terminally chronic illness).

Each community has its own combination of available resources, funding sources, and organizations. Indeed, most communities have a vast number of organizations engaged in providing specific long-term care services. Multiple continuums of long-term care exist, sometimes in parallel and sometimes intersecting. A person with a permanent mental health condition and a person with a hip fracture may use entirely separate services, yet each could be receiving long-term care organized as a continuum of care. An older person with Parkinson's disease who falls and breaks her hip may use two continuums simultaneously: a short-term rehabilitation continuum for several months to promote recovery and a Parkinson's continuum on a longer-term basis.

Services

More than 60 distinct services can be identified in the complete continuum of care. For simplicity, the continuum of care framework groups the services and settings into seven categories: extended care, acute inpatient care, ambulatory care, home care, outreach, wellness, and housing. These seven categories represent the basic types of health and health-related assistance that a person would need over time, through periods of both wellness and illness. Table 1 lists the major services within these categories. In addressing the needs of specific target populations, additional support services, such as legal counseling, social services, retirement planning, and guardianship, could be included.

Extended inpatient care is for people who are so sick or functionally disabled that they require ongoing nursing and support services in a formal health care institution but who are not so acutely ill that they require the technological and professional intensity of inpatient hospitalization. Most extended care facilities are referred to as nursing homes, although this broad term includes many levels and types of clinical care.

Acute inpatient care is hospital care for those who have major and acute health care problems. For most people, a typical hospital stay of 5 to 8 days represents the intensive aspect of a longer spell of illness, preceded by diagnostic testing and succeeded by follow-up care.

Ambulatory care is provided in a formal outpatient health care facility, whether a physician's office or a hospital clinic. It encompasses a wide spectrum of preventive, maintenance, diagnostic, and recuperative services for people who manifest a variety of conditions, from those who are entirely healthy and simply want an annual checkup, to those with major health problems who are recuperating from hospitalization, to those who require ongoing monitoring for chronic diseases.

Home care encompasses a variety of nursing, therapy, and support services provided to people who are homebound and have some degree of illness but whose needs can be satisfied by bringing services into the home setting. Home health programs range from formal organizations providing skilled nursing care or hospice to relatively informal networks arranging housekeeping or friendly visitors for friends and family members.

Outreach programs make health services and social services readily available in the community rather than inside the formidable walls of a large institution. Health fairs in shopping centers, senior membership programs, and emergency response systems all are forms of outreach. These are often targeted at the healthy or mildly ill to keep them connected with the health care system. Those who are severely ill and homebound may also be reached by community organizations that extend their services into the home such as Meals on Wheels and telemonitoring.

Wellness programs are provided for those who are basically healthy and want to stay that way by actively engaging in health promotion or for those who have chronic diseases and want to maintain health despite their conditions. Wellness programs include health education, exercise programs, health screenings, and disease management.

Housing for frail populations recognizes that health determines housing options and that, conversely, the home setting affects health and health care. Housing incorporating or providing access to health and social support services ranges from independent apartments affiliated with a health care

Table 1 Services in the Continuum of Care

EXTENDED
___Skilled Nursing Facilities
___Step-down Units
___Swing Beds
___Nursing Home Follow-up

ACUTE
___Med/Surg Inpatient Unit
___Psychiatric Inpatient Unit
___Rehabilitation Inpatient Unit
___Interdisciplinary Assessment Team
___Consultation Service

AMBULATORY
___Physicians' Offices
___Outpatient Clinics
___Interdisciplinary Assessment Clinics
___Day Hospital
___Adult Day Care
___Mental Health Clinic
___Satellite Clinics
___Psychosocial Counseling
___Alcohol and Substance Abuse

HOME CARE
___Home Health-Medicare
___Home Health-Private
___Hospice
___High Technology
___Durable Medical Equipment
___Home Visitors
___Home-Delivered Meals
___Homemaker and Personal Care
___Caregiver

OUTREACH & LINKAGE
___Screening
___Information and Referral
___Telephone Contact
___Emergency Response
___Transportation
___Senior Membership Program
___Meals on Wheels

WELLNESS & HEALTH PROMOTION
___Educational Programs
___Exercise Programs
___Recreational and Social Groups
___Senior Volunteers
___Congregate Meals
___Support Groups

HOUSING
___Continuing Care Retirement
   Communities
___Independent Senior Housing
___Congregate Care Facilities
___Adult Family Homes
___Assisted Living

Source: Evashwick, C. (2005). Definition of the Continuum of Care. In C. Evashwick (Ed.), *The continuum of long-term care.* Albany, NY: DelMar Publishers, Inc. Reprinted with permission.

system that sends a nurse to do weekly blood pressure checks, to assisted living with on-site personal care and social services, to group homes for those with mental illness.

These categories within the continuum of care are provided for heuristic purposes only; they are not meant to be either prescriptive or inclusive. Figure 1 shows the services schematically. The order of the categories and the services they include can vary depending on the need at hand—duration of stay, intensity of care, stage of illness, disciplines of professionals, type of physical plant, and/or availability of informal support. Within each category are health, mental health, and social services, potentially provided by professional clinicians and by various provider organizations.

Rather than a list of services, a more accurate visualization would be a multidimensional matrix showing the interrelationship of all these factors in caring for a single individual and family. Such a matrix would be dynamic rather than static because the relationships would be different for each person and would change over time as the person's needs change.

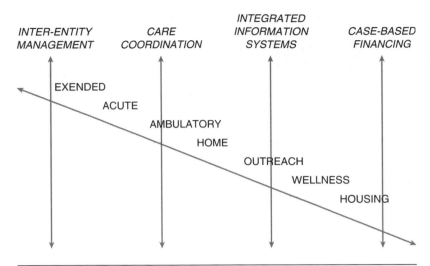

Figure 1   Services and Integrating Mechanisms of the Continuum of Care

Source: Evashwick, C. (2005). Definition of the Continuum of Care. In C. Evashwick (Ed.), *The continuum of long-term care.* Albany, NY: DelMar Publishers, Inc. Reprinted with permission.

Within the categories, as well as between them, services of the continuum are distinct, primarily because of historical development and the wide array of applicable federal, state, and local laws and regulations. Each service has different regulatory, financing, target population, staffing, and physical requirements. Each has its own admission policies, patient treatment protocols, and billing system. Each organization has its own referral and discharge networks.

Integration Mechanisms

A primary reason to organize services into a continuum is to achieve integration of care, yet the operational differences among services make unified planning and management quite difficult. To gain the system benefits of efficiencies of operation, smooth patient flow, and quality of service, structural integrating mechanisms are essential. Whether within a single large organization or across several organizations in the community, formal structures are needed to manage coordination. Four fundamental integrating management systems are identified: interentity management, care coordination, information systems, and financing.

Interentity management means that management structures and operating policies are in place to enable

services to coordinate care, facilitate smooth patient flow, and maximize use of professional staff and other resources. Examples include product line management, centers of excellence, joint planning committees, transfer arrangements, and managed-care contracts that delineate client flow procedures as well as financial arrangements.

Care coordination refers to the coordination of clinical components of care, usually by a combination of a dedicated person or team and established processes that facilitate communication among professionals of various disciplines across multiple sites and services. Case managers are common and may be based in hospitals, physician groups, health plans, home health agencies, or any other health or social service agencies. Teams that coordinate care are typical of rehabilitation settings.

Information systems refers to one client record that combines financial, clinical, and utilization information to be used by multiple providers and payers across multiple sites. Recent advances in electronic medical records (EMRs) increase opportunities to share information in real time within an organization, and regional health information organizations (RHIOs) are designed to facilitate sharing across organizations in the same community.

Financing removes barriers to continuity and appropriateness of care by having available adequate and flexible financing for long-term care, as well as acute care, that does not limit care based on externally defined eligibility criteria. Examples include health maintenance organizations (HMOs), PACE, some continuing-care retirement communities (CCRCs), and the Veterans Affairs Health System.

Evolution

During the late 1960s and the decade of the 1970s, the focus was on capacity building; that is, getting more services to be extant and accessible so that a broad continuum of care was available. Although issues of access still exist in some areas, most communities now have sufficient supplies of the major services. Case management received a major thrust during the 1980s and is now well established. During the mid-1980s through the mid-1990s, creating integrated continuums of care received attention and consideration throughout the nation and great strides were made to establish comprehensive integrated systems of care. However, by the late 1990s, managed care experienced a backlash and began to decline or stabilize, and Medicare instituted payment systems for long-term care services that forced separation rather than integration. The early years of the new millennium saw withdrawal from organizational relationships, reversion to a silo mentality, and lack of commitment to integration of care. By the middle of the first decade of the 21st century, technology and the drive for efficiency had advanced the priority of implementing electronic medical records and regional health information organizations, giving hope for the first time that the management information system integration mechanisms would become a reality and bring returned focus to the benefits of creating a continuum of care.

As the baby boomer population swells the ranks of the nation's seniors and more younger people with disabilities are living longer, the challenge to develop an approach to long-term care that is efficient, affordable, and appropriate for the individual and the family, and is simultaneously affordable and cost-effective for society, becomes more imperative. The concept of the continuum of care is a framework for thinking about how to organize health and related services to achieve these goals.

—*Connie J. Evashwick*

See also Assisted Living; Caregiving; Death, Dying, and Hospice Care; Geriatric Team Care; Health Care System for Older Adults; Home Care; Institutional Care; Legal Issues; Long-Term Care; Managed Care; Palliative Care and the End of Life; Social Networks and Social Support

Further Readings and References

Evashwick C. *The Continuum of Long-Term Care.* Albany, NY: Thomson Delmar Learning; 2005.
Pratt J. *Long-Term Care.* Sudbury, Mass: Jones & Bartlett; 2004.

CONTROL

The multifaceted concept of control is highly relevant to the lives of older adults. This entry examines three components of control: personal control beliefs, primary and secondary control strategies, and social control. For each aspect of control, we provide a conceptual overview, review age trends, and illustrate links with the mental and physical health of older adults.

Personal Control Beliefs

Based on a social learning approach to behavior that focused on perceived degree of control over reinforcements, Julian B. Rotter developed the Locus of Control Scale and published it in 1966. Rotter's scale assesses the extent to which people generally believe that they have the internal resources to control their outcomes (an "internal") or that the world exerts causal influence over their outcomes (an "external"). Similar scales soon arose assessing a wide range of concepts related to control beliefs, either generalized control beliefs or control beliefs specific to a given domain such as health. Rival constructs, such as personal mastery and self-efficacy, also were developed. Ellen F. Skinner classified control-related constructs based on having the means to achieve goals, having the ability to achieve goals, and perceiving that one's means of control will achieve goals.

Age Trends

Despite the unfavorable increase in the ratio of losses (e.g., health) to gains (e.g., emotion regulation) during later adulthood, the intuitive notion that control beliefs decline with age has not received empirical support. Possibly, older adults become more selective in the domains that they seek to control (e.g., maintaining a residence) and discount the importance of domains over which they have less control (e.g., loss of family members and friends). The presence of differential changes in control due to aging has forced a broadening of the concept of control. In addition, although the concept is traditionally thought of as a trait-like individual difference variable that is stable over time and situations, intervention studies have shown that personal control is modifiable. In field studies, it has been demonstrated that control-enhancing experimental manipulations generally have positive effects on older adults' mental health and physical functioning. Conversely, there is a body of research showing that being "in control" is not always beneficial because some aspects of life are in fact not controllable.

Personal Control Beliefs and Physical and Mental Health

Studies show that higher levels of perceived control are associated with better mental health, better physical health, and engagement in a wide array of positive health behaviors. It is not clear whether these generalizations hold up when the actual (objective) controllability of the environment is taken into account. For example, does perceived control lead to a better disease trajectory when the course of the disease is unpredictable?

Primary and Secondary Control Strategies

According to the most comprehensive life span theory of control, a key to successful aging is the use of primary control strategies. The concept of primary control strategies (changing the world to achieve goals) is complemented by the concept of secondary control strategies (changing how one views the world in support of goal pursuit or accommodation) when controllability is low. Compared with secondary control, primary control is postulated to have greater adaptive significance.

Adults coordinate the use of primary and secondary control strategies to optimize their development through the processes of selection and compensation. Selective processes can involve either primary control (focusing resources on goal pursuit) or secondary control (using cognitions that affect motivation, such as positive outcome expectancies, to pursue the goal). Similarly, compensation processes can involve either primary control (using external

resources to overcome barriers to goal attainment) or secondary control (using self-protective strategies to minimize the pernicious effects of losses).

Age Trends

The four types of strategies just noted are thought to increase nonlinearly from birth to late middle age. From late middle age to death, selective primary control is believed to decline and the other three control strategies are believed to increase. Using data from the National Survey of Midlife Development in the United States (MIDUS) study, researchers have investigated age differences in persistence (a selective primary control strategy) and positive reappraisal (a compensatory secondary control strategy). As predicted, younger adults reported lower ratings of positive reappraisal than did middle-aged and older adults. Contrary to expectations, older adults reported higher ratings of persistence than did middle-aged and younger adults.

Primary and Secondary Control and Subjective Well-Being

Consistent with theory, persistence has been shown to be a strong predictor of subjective well-being among younger adults and positive reappraisal has been shown to be a strong predictor of subjective well-being among older adults. Furthermore, the age differences in how well persistence and positive reappraisal could predict subjective well-being were more pronounced when adults were facing health or financial challenges.

Social Control

Social control theory has its roots in the sociological work of Émile Durkheim, who argued that socially integrated individuals are less likely than socially isolated individuals to engage in risky or deviant behaviors. Direct social control occurs when individuals experience attempts by members of their social networks to regulate their behavior. Indirect social control occurs when individuals are influenced to behave in certain ways by norms pertaining to a sense of obligation to other people. When an older adult's own attempts to self-regulate are perceived to have failed, direct social control strategies are most likely to be initiated by significant others. Surveys show that spouses and other family members are the network members most likely to exert social control on the health behaviors of older adults. Furthermore, cigarette smoking and exercising are the health behaviors of older adults that network members seek to change most frequently.

Age Trends

Compared with young and middle-aged adults, older adults have smaller social control networks, are urged to change fewer health behaviors, and experience health-related social control attempts less frequently. Significant others may assign a lower priority to regulating the health behaviors of older adults compared with younger adults, and older adults may be more forceful than younger adults in their rejection of attempts by significant others to influence their health behaviors.

Social Control and Physical and Mental Health

Individuals who exert social control are known as agents, and individuals who are the recipients of social control attempts are known as targets. According to the dual-effects hypothesis, social control benefits targets by fostering a healthy lifestyle, but it is also costly to targets by diminishing their sense of control and by straining their relationships with agents. Research has shown that intensity of direct social control attempts (frequency of attempts plus importance to influence agent) and positive control strategies (rewarding target for trying to change) are positively related to health behavior. However, intensity and negative control strategies (pressuring target to change) are positively related to agitation, whereas intensity, negative control strategies, and positive control strategies all are positively related to guilt.

Subsequent research has not provided support for the dual-effect hypothesis, and an alternative hypothesis called domain specificity of effects has proposed that positive social control influences positive affect (e.g., happiness), which in turn influences engaging in healthy behaviors. Similarly, negative social control influences negative affect (e.g., sadness), which in turn influences hiding of unhealthy behaviors.

Even in close relationships, there are individual differences in relationship satisfaction. Possibly, relationship satisfaction provides a backdrop or context that affects the impact of social control on older adults. Several such effects were observed in a study of older adults who varied in their relationship satisfaction. Among older adults with low relationship satisfaction, direct social control was associated with more negative affect and more hiding of unhealthy behaviors from network members. Among older adults with high relationship satisfaction, indirect social control was associated with more positive affect, more negative affect, and more hiding of unhealthy behaviors from network members.

Despite the intriguing theory, research, and interventions that have accumulated on control and aging, research questions remain open. Who benefits from control? For example, when desire for control is low among older adults, is their mental and physical health harmed by efforts to make them take control of their lives? When desire for control is high among older adults, does social control lead to psychological reactance and hiding of unhealthy behaviors? A second question has to do with why control works. For example, when older adults are confronted with a challenge that life poses, does control influence how they (a) appraise the situation (viewing the situation as a catastrophe or as a challenge), (b) cope with the situation (dampening negative emotional reactions or solving the problem), and (c) engage with their social support system (avoidance or mobilization of network members)?

—*Morris A. Okun and John Reich*

See also Depression and Other Mood Disorders; Emotions and Emotional Stability; Self-Efficacy; Social Networks and Social Support; Stress; Subjective Well-Being

Further Readings and References

Heckhausen J, Schulz R. A life-span theory of control. *Psychol Rev.* 1995;102:284–403.

Lewis MA, Rook KS. Social control in personal relationships: Impact on health behaviors and psychological distress. *Health Psychol.* 1999;18:63–71.

Rodin J. Aging and health: Effects of the sense of control. *Science.* 1986;233:1271–1276.

Zarit SH, Pearlin LI, Schaie KW, eds. *Personal Control in Social and Life Course Contexts.* New York: Springer; 2003.

CORONARY HEART DISEASE

See CARDIOVASCULAR SYSTEM

CREUTZFELDT–JAKOB DISEASE

Creutzfeldt–Jakob disease (CJD, also known as Jakob–Creutzfeldt disease) is one of a group of rare fatal brain diseases caused by proteins called prions. The term *prion* is the name coined by Stanley Prusiner, for "proteinaceous infectious particles," to describe the proteins he identified that cause transmissible spongiform encephalopathies (TSEs), or prion diseases. Prusiner was awarded the Nobel Prize for physiology and medicine in 1997 for his discovery of the prion.

The normal cellular form of prion protein (PrP^C) is a protein found on cell membranes in humans and animals. The precise role of the prion protein in normal nerve cell function has yet to be determined. In prion disease, PrP^C somehow manages to change shape from a primarily helical structure to a pleated sheet structure, becoming a misshapen prion protein called the prion or PrP^{Sc}. PrP^{Sc} becomes a template for conversion of existing normal prion proteins (PrP^C) to PrP^{Sc}, beginning a devastating chain of reactions to convert nearby PrP^C to become PrP^{Sc}. As many PrP^C are converted to PrP^{Sc}, the accumulation of PrP^{Sc} injures nerve cell function, causing disease and ultimately leading to death. The altered function of nerve cells in the brain results in the broad spectrum of symptoms seen in patients with CJD.

CJD is characterized by a rapid deterioration in mental function, behavior, and movement. CJD affects roughly 1 person per 1 million people per year worldwide. In the United States, there are approximately 250 to 400 cases per year, with variation from year to year. There are three main types of CJD: sporadic (or classical), hereditary (genetic or familial), and acquired (transmitted through eating beef contaminated with prions or iatrogenic [occurring as the result of treatment by a health provider]). The following is a brief overview of each type of human prion disease.

Human prion diseases can be divided into three types by the way in which they occur: sporadic, genetic, and acquired. *Sporadic* or *classical* Creutzfeldt–Jakob disease (sCJD) is the most common form of human prion disease, accounting for approximately 85% to 90% of cases. sCJD occurs without any known cause, without a family history of the disease, and in the absence of a mutation in the gene that codes for prion protein. The median age for onset of symptoms is roughly 68 years (average age of 60 years), with an average survival of roughly 8 months and approximately 90% of patients dying within 1 year from symptom onset. The most common first symptoms in CJD are cognitive such as confusion and memory loss. Other common first symptoms are discoordination, prominent behavioral and personality changes, and constitutional complaints (e.g., headache, malaise, fatigue).

Approximately 15% of human prion diseases are *genetic* (heritable) and are due to a mutation (a change or an error) in the gene that codes for the prion protein. Genetic human prion diseases are generally classified into three types: familial CJD (fCJD), Gerstmann–Sträussler–Scheinker syndrome (GSS), and the very rare fatal familial insomnia (FFI). Every person has two copies of every gene: one copy received from the mother and one copy received from the father. Human genetic traits are the result of having the two copies of each. A mutation is an error in a gene. For autosomal-dominant diseases, a person needs only one copy of a mutated gene to inherit the associated trait or disease; for recessive diseases (or traits), a person needs both copies of a gene to have mutations to get a disease or trait. Mutations in the prion protein gene are autosomal dominant. Thus, for a person with genetic CJD, with one normal and one mutated prion protein gene, each of the person's children has a 50% chance of receiving the bad copy. Thus, there is a 50% risk of transmitting the disease to each child regardless of the child's or parent's gender. Genetic forms of CJD often have a slower course and an earlier age of onset (typically in the 30s to 50s) compared with sCJD, with many patients living for several years after the onset of symptoms. More than 30 mutations in the prion protein gene have been identified. Patients with fCJD often present with symptoms and course similar to those for patients with sCJD. GSS usually begins with either parkinsonism (slowed movement) or ataxia (discoordination), and patients with FFI often develop intractable insomnia and/or dysautonomia; for example, problems maintaining blood pressure, body temperature, heart rate, or gut motility.

Acquired or *iatrogenic* CJD (iCJD) is a form of CJD that occurs from transmission of prions from one individual to another. Although the prion that causes CJD is referred to as an infectious protein, CJD is not considered to be contagious in the traditional sense; that is, through air or casual physical contact. Prion diseases are transmissible through direct transfer of prions (often from nervous system tissue) from a patient with prion disease to another patient by certain medical or surgical procedures. Acquired or iatrogenic CJD accounts for less than 1% of all CJD cases. iCJD has occurred through the following procedures: corneal transplants, dura mater grafts (transplantation of membrane tissues surrounding the brain), neurosurgical procedures inadvertently using prion-contaminated surgical instruments, and the use of natural pituitary-derived (not synthesized in a laboratory) human hormones such as human growth hormone (hGH). Fortunately, iCJD is extremely rare, with only some 270 cases ever identified.

Unfortunately, the usual methods of medical decontamination to remove or kill infectious agents, such as viruses and bacteria, do not destroy the prion. The use of decontamination methods that can destroy the prion, stricter infection control measures, and the development of recombinant human growth hormone (made in the laboratory) have greatly decreased the possibility of iatrogenic transmission. The newest form of an acquired CJD, variant CJD (vCJD), has been shown to be transmissible by blood transfusion.

vCJD is the newest, and perhaps the most publicized, form of iCJD. Evidence strongly suggests that it is due to the transmission of prion disease in bovine, bovine spongiform encephalopathy (BSE, also known as mad cow disease), to people through consumption of prion-contaminated beef. The BSE epidemic in the United Kingdom peaked during the mid-1980s, and the first cases of a new form of CJD (vCJD) were identified roughly a decade later in 1995 in the United Kingdom. Patients with vCJD are usually younger than sCJD patients and present predominantly with psychiatric symptoms. Complaints of pain and numbness often follow soon. Later, these symptoms are followed by rapidly progressive motor and cognitive symptoms and signs. The clinical presentation and neuropathology of vCJD are somewhat distinct from those of sCJD. vCJD usually affects young adults, with a mean age of 29 years and a range of 12 to 74 years. All but a few cases have been under 50 years of age. As of May 2006, approximately 181 cases of vCJD had been reported in the world: 161 from the United Kingdom, 14 from France, 2 from Ireland, and 1 each from Hong Kong, Saudi Arabia, Italy, and the Netherlands. One case was identified in Canada and another case was identified in the United States, but these patients resided in the United Kingdom during the BSE epidemic and are believed to have acquired the disease there. Kuru is an acquired human prion disease found only among the Fore tribe in the central highlands of New Guinea. It was caused by the practice of ritualized cannibalism of deceased relatives. The disease has essentially died out with the elimination of the practice of ritualistic cannibalism.

Prion diseases are also found in animals. BSE is a progressive, degenerative fatal disease that affects the central nervous system of adult cattle. Scrapie is a similar disease that affects sheep and goats. It is believed that the BSE epidemic occurred in the United

Kingdom through the practice of feeding scrapie-contaminated feed to cattle. Chronic wasting disease (CWD) is a brain wasting disease found in elk and deer in several geographic regions of North America. BSE is the only animal prion disease that is known to have been transmitted to people.

Diagnosis of CJD

CJD can be difficult to diagnose, particularly during the early stages, because the first symptoms may be vague and may overlap with many other neurological conditions. CJD is typically characterized by the rapid onset (over days to weeks) and progression (over weeks to months) of neurological symptoms such as impaired memory, confusion, depression, behavioral changes, and discoordination. Visual changes, such as blurred or double vision, may also occur. Other motor symptoms, such as tremors and rigidity, occur often later in the disease. All patients eventually develop dementia—the loss of intellectual functions (e.g., thinking, remembering, reasoning) severe enough to interfere with a person's daily functioning. During the terminal stage of the illness, patients develop a state of akinetic mutism (the inability to talk or carry out purposeful behavior even though the eyes may still be open). Death is usually caused by pneumonia related to the inability to swallow or complications of immobility and being bed bound.

In the absence of positive genetic testing for a prion protein gene mutation, only a brain biopsy or an autopsy can provide a definitive diagnosis of CJD. Diagnosis is suspected with the occurrence of a rapidly progressive dementia (typically occurring over less than a year) and a combination of motor, behavioral, and other symptoms. The current diagnostic criteria also use certain tests to add support to the diagnosis. Specific abnormalities can often be found on electroencephalogram (EEG, a test that measures electrical brain waves), and in some patients several cerebrospinal fluid (CSF) proteins, including tau, neuron-specific enolase (NSE), and 14-3-3, may sometimes be elevated; however, there is disagreement about how specific these tests are for prion disease. Recently, brain magnetic resonance imaging (MRI) has been shown to aid significantly in the diagnosis of many forms of human prion disease. vCJD can be differentiated from sCJD by clinical symptoms, EEG, and MRI. Initially, CJD may be confused with other treatable rapid progressive dementias such as Hashimoto encephalitis and paraneoplastic conditions (autoimmune-mediated neurological diseases occurring in the setting of cancer). Therefore, medical tests are necessary to rule out other treatable conditions.

Current Treatment

There is no known cure for CJD or any prion diseases. Treatment at the current time focuses on alleviating symptoms and making the patient feel comfortable. This means that medications may be given to relieve muscle spasms, reduce insomnia, manage aggressive behaviors, or calm anxiety. A person with CJD becomes dependent for all physiological needs (e.g., eating, toileting, bathing). Providing a safe environment to address aggressive or agitated behavior and meeting physiological needs may require monitoring and assistance beyond what a family can manage on its own. Family counseling may be necessary for coping with the rapid changes required and caring for a loved one with CJD. Legal advice may be prudent early in the disease process to help form an advance directive; that is, a legal document that outlines what type of care the affected individual would like at the end of life. Researchers around the world are actively searching for potential treatments for prion disease. Treatment studies for CJD are currently under way in several countries.

—Michael D. Geschwind,
Chiung-Chi Chang, and Astrid Block

See also Alzheimer's Disease; Delirium and Confusional States; Imaging of the Brain; Mental Status Assessment; Neurological Disorders

Further Readings and References

Belay ED, Holman RC, Schonberger LB. Creutzfeldt–Jakob disease surveillance and diagnosis. *Clin Infect Dis.* 2005; 41:834–836.

Gambetti P, Kong Q, Zou W, et al. Sporadic and familial CJD: Classification and characterisation. *Br Med Bull.* 2003;66:213–239.

Korth C, Peters PJ. Emerging pharmacotherapies for Creutzfeldt–Jakob disease. *Arch Neurol.* 2006; 63:497–501.

Prusiner SB. Detecting mad cow disease. *Sci Am.* 2004; (July):86–93.

Will RG. Acquired prion disease: Iatrogenic CJD, variant CJD, kuru. *Br Med Bull.* 2003;66:255–265.

CRITICAL PERSPECTIVES IN GERONTOLOGY

Critical perspectives in gerontology emerged during the late 1970s and early 1980s in the United States (Carroll Estes, Laura Katz Olson, and Jill Quadagno), Canada (John Myles and Victor Marshall), and Europe (Peter Townsend, Alan Walker, Chris Phillipson, and Anne Marie Guillemard) in response to limited (micro)social gerontology perspectives on the aging process, individual life course development, disengagement, life satisfaction, and dependency. Work in critical gerontology has developed under the rubrics of radical gerontology, political gerontology, the moral economy of aging, cultural and humanistic gerontology, and the political economy of aging, with the latter being perhaps the most well recognized.

Scholars in the political economy of aging argue that broad social, economic, and political factors and structural arrangements (e.g., social stratification) are integral to understanding the aging process and the "life chances" of older persons both as individuals and as groups. Race, ethnicity, class, and gender are highlighted as crucial dimensions of old age and aging, but not just as individual characteristics or attributes. More specifically, race, ethnicity, class, and gender are to be understood at the macro level as systemic features of our society as expressed in subtle and not so subtle ways (e.g., institutional racism, patriarchy) and with significant effects on all aspects of aging, including health and illness. Other key elements in the political economy of aging are the role and effects of systems of governance and power struggles therein

(e.g., the state), economic production (e.g., capitalism), and the production of ideas (e.g., ideology, systems of communication and cultural production) on old age and the aging. Peter L. Berger and Thomas Luckmann's early work on the social construction of reality has been developed and incorporated as integral to understanding old age and the political economy of aging, advancing the points that old age and aging are socially produced through processes not only at the micro level but also at the meso (organizational and institutional) and macro (social system) levels. All levels of analysis are deemed to be essential to understanding the meaning and lived experience of old age and an aging society, including the dynamics and consequences of inequality within the nation and the world.

From its inception, critical gerontology has been a multidisciplinary project influenced by diverse theoretical and philosophical traditions and drawing deeply from critical theory—the role of intellectuals in shaping social thought (Antonio Gramsci), the connection between a critical consciousness and social action (Frankfurt School), the concepts of dominance and power in relation to the state and individual agency (neo-Marxists and neo-Weberians), the struggles for legitimacy and crises faced by the state (Jurgen Habermas, Claus Offe, and James O'Connor), the role of patriarchy in structuring the experiences of women and feminist theories of the state (Joan Acker, Catherine MacKinnon, and Gayle Rubin); the importance of feminist epistemology and the recognition of intersectionality (Sandra Harding, Dorothy Smith, and Patricia Hill Collins), the influence of institutional racism (Gary King, Michael Omi, Henry Winant, and [in gerontology] James Jackson), and the connections between inequality and health throughout the life course (David Williams, Chiquita Collins, Nancy Krieger, Stephanie Robert, and [in gerontology] Kokos Markides). Other theoretical influences include cultural studies, social constructionism, psychoanalytic perspectives (Simon Biggs), the sociology of knowledge, and (increasingly) work on globalization and risk.

The are five elements key to understanding the influence of critical gerontology perspectives on health and aging: (1) criticism of the biomedical model of aging within the field of gerontology and the larger society; (2) attention to the larger economic, political, and sociocultural factors and forces that shape health, health care, and health policy in old age; (3) incorporation of the multiple levels of analysis (micro, meso, and macro) through which experiences of health and health care in old age are negotiated and structured, including race, class, ethnicity, and gender; (4) recognition of the importance of social constructions of old age and aging that are marshaled and deployed within the family, in the media, and in policy arenas; and (5) a commitment to the links among the development of social theory, research, and the organization of social and political action.

As a social institution, biomedicine has come under fire for its atomized view of health and inattention to both the social conditions that influence well-being and the human actions through which these conditions arise. Critical gerontology has offered its own critique of biomedicine, namely the biomedical model of aging. Emphasizing the etiology, clinical treatment, and management of diseases of the elderly as defined and treated by medical practitioners, the biomedical model of aging accords limited attention to the social and behavioral processes and problems of aging.

The biomedicalization of aging is attributed to two interrelated phenomena: (a) the defining of aging as a medical problem and (b) the practice of aging as a medical problem in the realms of scientific knowledge, professional status and training, policy formation, and public understanding. The practice of aging as a medical problem in each of these realms acts to influence and reinforce these ideas and practices in the other realms. Just as important, biomedical definitions, practice, and policy represent an individualizing model of aging that is consistent with the current political and economic struggles designed to transform much of what has been seen as public responsibility, such as health and health care, into matters of private individual responsibility.

A related component of biomedicalization is the commodification of aging. Commodification is the process of taking a good or service that has been produced and used (but not bought or sold) and turning it into an item that is exchanged for money. The continuing and growing influence of the medical engineering model of health has contributed to the commodification of old age and aging over the past half century. This is reflected in the shift in the mode of production of medical goods and services from an orientation of fulfilling human needs, such as food, shelter, or functional assistance for those with impairments, to a mode of medical production oriented toward monetary exchange for the creation of private profit and increasingly enormous private wealth. Biomedicalization is involved because these new goods and services have been defined as biomedically related and appropriated by the medical profession with the legitimation and support of state policy, with medical providers serving as gatekeepers to the certification of illness and access to the benefits of health care according to health policy.

The transformation of the health needs of the aging into commodities for specific economic markets has helped to produce the *aging enterprise,* a term coined by Carroll Estes to describe the set of interests that benefit from a definition of aging as a problem to be dealt with by experts. It has supported a high-technology, pharmaceutically intensive, and specialized expert-led approach to treating parts of the problem presented by older "consumers" (more recently called customers) who seek goods and services to address health and illness. Due to its dominant position in gerontology and geriatrics, the biomedical model of aging has exerted a strong influence over the development of social policy and the distribution of research and medical care funding—indeed, over the organization, financing, and delivery of medical care in the United States.

Critical gerontologists have argued that the dominance of the biomedical model of aging obscures the extent to which illness and other problems of the elderly are influenced and shaped by potentially modifiable social factors such as (a) income and education, (b) safe and supportive housing environments that promote health and well-being, (c) opportunities for meaningful human connection, and (d) public financing for needed rehabilitation and nonmedical supports and health-promoting services and activities. As a dissenting voice, critical gerontologists suggest alternate sets of definitions of the problem(s) and policy solutions to address complex social and environmental factors and forces that significantly shape, structure, and modify the basic processes of old age and aging on multiple levels.

Insofar as the biomedicalization of aging fosters the tendency to equate old age with disease and dependency, old age is seen as pathological, abnormal, and undesirable. This contributes to the stigmatization of the old and, in turn, to potentially negative attitudes of members of society toward older persons and of older persons toward themselves. One consequence may be a diminishing sense of personal control and self-efficacy, both of which are vital to self-esteem and positive functioning in old age. Critical gerontologists have documented the ways in which the portrayals of older people as useless, burdensome, and unable to think shape action within families, within the media, and by the state in the form of policy. Critical scholars have reframed questions of the association between age and illness as a social process rather than a biological process, insisting on the examination of health and illness in the context of inequalities produced by race, class, and gender as they are experienced (and accumulate) over the life course.

Critical gerontologists have contended that the biomedical model erroneously equates (and conflates) the needs and definitions of physicians, the medical profession, and a vast medical industrial complex with the health and health care needs of the aging and the larger society. The multilevel approach attends to the structural interests of multiple stakeholders (the state and policymakers; transnational corporations and the medical, insurance, and pharmaceutical industries; nonprofit organizations; and the elderly themselves) and how their actions affect the health and health care of older persons. A critique of the biomedical model of aging suggests the need for changes in how (a) public policy is framed and resources are allocated (or not) to research, services, and human needs; (b) the media reports on health and aging; (c) ideologies of productivity and independence devalue older people; (d) care work is distributed primarily (and

inequitably) to women as formal and informal care providers between public and private social worlds; and (e) the lives of older people are valued (and devalued) within their families, in the workplace, and by the state and the market. Critical gerontologists examine the institutional roles and powerful structural interests both within and between the state and different corporate sectors as well as the larger economic system of national and global capitalism. In so doing, a relevant topic of inquiry is the privatization of public services and health policy such as Medicare. More recently, the attention of critical gerontologists has turned toward globalization and its effects on health and aging.

In committing to critical analysis of health and aging, a major goal of critical gerontology is praxis— the linkage of theory and research to action and social change in the service of reducing social inequalities in health and aging, dismantling the pernicious effects of ageism, and combating social injustice. Aspiring to such goals requires an openly critical, reflexive, and interdisciplinary approach—one that may be unflinchingly critical of current organizational and societal arrangements and institutions (the status quo). Currently, critical gerontologists are responding to the enlarged scope of work required to address complex and interconnected societal and global problems arising from the rapidity and magnitude of change, technology, and modernity, much of which is expressed in the processes of globalization and the near-hegemonic ideology of the market as well as the growing awareness of the interconnectedness of the different spheres of society. Scholars in critical gerontology are pressing forward with critiques and debates on postmodernism and antimodernism (Jan Baars, Dale Dannefer, Chris Phillipson, Simon Biggs, Alan Walker, Carroll Estes, and Joe Hendricks) that have significant relevance for critical gerontology of health and aging.

A critical gerontology perspective on social policy of health and aging seeks to provide alternatives in conceptual and paradigmatic thinking that locates some of the key factors of "healthy aging" in the larger society, economy, and body politic and that prioritizes the production of health care as a social good for all individuals rather than as an economic good for individuals who can afford to purchase it privately. Future critical gerontology in health and aging will be driven by a number of issues such as the following:

- The dramatic rise in social inequality (gap between the rich and the poor) in society between Americans of all ages and its rise within the older generation; the consequences of the high social inequality for the health and quality of lives of older women, minorities, people with disabilities, and poor and middle-class people; and the effects of social inequality on both health care access and health outcomes across the older generation and amplified by institutionalized sexism, racism, classism, and ableism

- The effects of privatization and corporate rationalization on the elderly; how the (enacted and threatened) changes in social policy that trade off federal universal social provision for decentralized state, locally determined, and/or individually elected provision affect the health and health care of the aging, particularly for those who are most vulnerable; and whether devolution, deregulation, and globalization are fostering a "race to the bottom" that affects the health of the elderly

- The critiques of the biomedicalization of disability and the commodification, privatization, and rationalization of rehabilitation and personal assistance services offered by the independent living movement and other social movements for the civil rights of people with disabilities; the consideration of disability as an axis of oppression and inequality on par with, and continually intersecting with, race, class, gender, sexuality, and age, the effects of which accumulate across the life course; the social construction of people with disabilities as a demographic, financial, and social problem; and the questions about both citizenship and risk (individual and societal) introduced by impaired/disabled bodies and aging bodies

- Where the welfare state is going, what this means for the economic and health security of the elderly, and what the effects are for the health and health care of older persons and inequalities and inequities within (more specific concerns are the future of Social Security, Medicare, and Medicaid in the short and long term and their consequences for older Americans by race, ethnicity, class, gender, and [dis]ability)

- The effects of globalization and the rise of multinational institutions of financial capital for the health, health care, and health policy for the elderly in the United States and around the world

- Developments of the resistance to the encroachment of global capital on the lives of the elderly and others in society and the relative success of competing social movements in health and aging; for example, those organizing for entitlement versus privatization, universal health care, and long-term care

In each of these areas, a major task for critical gerontologists is to illuminate alternative understandings and visions of what is possible in health, health care, and health policy in and for later life. The critical lens is intended to open up a distance between what people are told are the "choices" available to them and their own views on personal and collective needs. The critical lens is intended to facilitate our ability to discriminate between what we are taught to believe and the opportunities to build alternative possibilities for us and for our aging society. This represents an emancipatory project built on both critique and reflexivity designed to encourage our abilities and perceptions of the aging self as a conscious agent in spite of the circumstances in which social actors find themselves. For many critical scholars, it is essential that common causes be discovered and built on rather than disempowering differences between social groups.

—*Carroll L. Estes and Brian R. Grossman*

See also Epidemiology of Aging; Life Course Perspective on Adult Development

Further Readings and References

Baars J, Dannefer D, Phillipson C, Walker A, eds. *Aging, Globalization, and Inequality: The New Critical Gerontology.* Amityville, NY: Baywood; 2006.

Bengtson VL, Schaie W, eds. *Handbook of Theories of Aging.* New York: Springer; 1999.

Berger P, Luckmann T. *The Social Construction of Reality.* Garden City, NY: Anchor; 1967.

Biggs S, Lowenstein L, Hendricks J, eds. *The Need for Theory: Critical Approaches to Social Gerontology.* Amityville, NY: Baywood; 2003.

Dannefer D. Cumulative advantage/disadvantage and the life course: Cross-fertilizing age and social science theory. *J Gerontol B Psychol Sci Social Sci.* 2003;58:S327–S337.

Estes C. *The Aging Enterprise.* San Francisco: Jossey-Bass; 1979.

Estes CL, et al. *Social Policy and Aging: A Critical Perspective.* Thousand Oaks, Calif: Sage; 2001.

Estes CL, Biggs S, Phillipson C. *Social Theory, Social Policy, and Ageing: A Critical Introduction.* London: Open University Press; 2003.

Minkler M, Estes C, eds. *Critical Gerontology: Perspectives From Political and Moral Economy.* Amityville, NY: Baywood; 1999.

Phillipson C. *Capitalism and the Construction of Old Age.* London: Macmillan; 1982.

Walker A. Towards a political economy of old age. *Ageing Society.* 1981;1:73–94.

Death, Dying, and Hospice Care

The experience of death and dying has changed in the United States since the 19th century. Back then, most people died in their homes surrounded by family and friends. Rituals included adults as well as children, especially in keeping vigil as the dying person slowly drifted into death. Beginning in the 20th century, the rate of infant mortality dropped sharply. Life expectancy increased by approximately 30 years during the 20th century, and now a newborn is expected to live well into the seventh or eighth decade of life. The causes of death have also shifted from infectious diseases, such as diarrheal diseases, respiratory infections, and parasitic diseases (including typhoid fever, diphtheria, and tuberculosis) that preyed on the very young, to chronic diseases (including cancer, stroke, and cardiovascular diseases) that affect mostly the elderly. This epidemiological shift in the patterns of disease is attributed to better hygiene and housing, improved diet, safer roads and work conditions, safer transportation vehicles, and the unprecedented development of medical technology starting with the advent of antibiotics during the mid-20th century.

During the early 1900s, approximately 80% of deaths occurred at home; only 20% occurred in institutional settings (hospitals and nursing homes). By the early 21st century, this trend was reversed, and now nearly 80% of deaths occur in hospitals and nursing homes surrounded by advanced medical technology, including ventilators, dialysis machines, and artificial feeding tubes. The availability of technologically sophisticated medical interventions has resulted in the extension of life in debilitated conditions that prolong the natural process of dying, leading to the development of hospice care.

The hospice movement was born out of the philosophy that it is possible to maintain a high quality of life for as long as possible but to give priority to the *quality* of life rather than the *quantity* of life. This is achieved through surrounding the person experiencing a life-limiting illness with loved ones and through focusing on palliative and spiritual care rather than on medical interventions that prolong the dying process. Hospice is not necessarily a place; it is a program of medical, social, and spiritual services provided to the dying individual and his or her family. Hospice services can be provided in the person's home, a hospital, a nursing home, an assisted-living facility, or a free-standing hospice center. In the United States, anyone facing a life-limiting illness can qualify for hospice services regardless of age, sex, religion, race, or medical diagnosis and also regardless of ability to pay. Services are funded by all traditional medical funding sources such as Medicare, Medicaid, health maintenance organizations, private insurance companies, and private funding.

St. Christopher's Hospice, the first-ever hospice, was founded in 1967 in London by Dame Cicely Saunders. The concept of hospice care was later brought to the United States by Florence Wald, dean of the Yale School of Nursing, who invited Saunders to become a faculty member at Yale. The Connecticut Hospice, the first hospice in the United States, was then opened in 1974 in Branford, Connecticut. Hospice services have become increasingly accepted over the years, and in 2001 approximately 3,200 hospice programs provided care to 775,000 patients in the United States alone. One fourth of all those who died in 2001 did so while receiving hospice services. Hospice services are provided by a multidisciplinary team that includes physicians; nurses; home health aides; social workers; spiritual counselors; volunteers; and speech, physical, and occupational therapists.

During the 19th century, high infant mortality and the involvement of the extended family made death a familiar and accepted part of life. With the advent of antibiotics, vaccines, and other life extensions, people's attitude changed to one where death was treated as a taboo topic. Cultural attitudes about death have since progressed from death denying to death recognizing, thanks to the efforts of Elisabeth Kübler-Ross, the Swiss psychiatrist who published the landmark book *On Death and Dying* in 1969. This book of interviews with dying cancer patients identified the stages of grief that have become the gold standard: denial, anger, bargaining, depression, and (finally) acceptance. Critics later discounted Kübler-Ross's writings because of the implication that all humans react similarly and that emotions occur in a linear fashion, charges that Kübler-Ross denied. Some people clearly experience death in the way Kübler-Ross described, but others may skip one or more of the stages or may vacillate repeatedly between the stages. In spite of the controversial aspects of her writings, Kübler-Ross is indisputably credited with breaking down the barriers surrounding discussions of death and dying and spearheading many of the now familiar interdisciplinary interventions.

One of the most valued services provided by hospice programs is helping family members and other caregivers with their grief, mourning, and bereavement following the death of the hospice patient. Whereas bereavement refers to the specific death event and the feeling of deprivation of a valuable part of life, grieving over the loss of life, physical and

social functions, and/or companionship may start at any time—even before death occurs. This is referred to as *anticipatory grief.* Grief can be triggered when social isolation becomes the norm after serious life-limiting illness develops. Frequently, caregivers are so involved in the care of the terminally ill person that social contacts diminish incrementally, resulting in devastating social isolation. Social isolation affects the terminally ill person as well as the caregivers, and social death, or the gradual withdrawal from all social contacts and responsibilities, becomes the norm. Anticipatory grief can affect all members of the terminally ill person's milieu, even when death does not actually occur (i.e., during a relapse or remission of the disease). The fact that death is yet to occur delays the normal processes of grief and presents a complicated course of coping with the loss. Grief is exhibited in physical, emotional, and behavioral reactions. Physical reactions consist of loss of sleep and/or appetite and/or a heavy feeling on the chest. Emotional reactions of anxiety, sadness, anger, and depression are common. Behavioral reactions are expressed by hitting one's chest, crying, and/or even exhibiting extreme stoicism.

Eventually, healing starts through the process of mourning, a time that allows for integrating the loss in everyday activities. People exhibit to the world that they are in a period of mourning by wearing a black armband or clothing of certain colors (e.g., white in some Asian and north African countries, black in Europe and the United States), avoiding appearances of enjoyment (by withdrawing from activities such as going to the theater and even watching television or listening to the radio), or by not wearing makeup or cutting one's hair (common in some Native American tribes). Mourning rituals may be culture specific, but the experience of grieving the loss of a loved one is general and universal. Social norms dictate when the mourning period ends. When the mourning period is officially over, a return to normalcy and to routine life experiences, such as working and resuming social connections, is expected. An assessment may be needed to determine whether the bereaved is progressing effectively in the mourning process or whether the grief is complicated and unresolved. This condition can develop if the death of the loved one occurred unexpectedly (as in case of the death of a child), if there are unresolved conflicts between the deceased and the person experiencing the grief, or if the caregiver was immersed in caregiving duties and responsibilities immediately preceding the death.

Complicated and unresolved grief resulting from the loss of a loved one must be distinguished from major depression, which is a psychiatric diagnosis. Complicated grief is characterized by an inability to cope for more than 6 months after the occurrence of death. Feelings of disbelief, anger and bitterness, yearning and longing for the deceased person, and feeling preoccupied by the death are examples of this experience. Complicated grief can be diagnosed by administering assessment tools such as the Inventory of Complicated Grief. Hospice professionals are trained to recognize the variety of grief symptoms at very early stages and can either provide appropriate counseling themselves or make referrals to other specialists who routinely deal with grief counseling.

—*Hana Osman*

See also Bereavement and Grief; Palliative Care and the End of Life

Further Readings and References

DeSpelder LA, Trickland AL. *The Last Dance: Encountering Death and Dying.* 7th ed. Boston: McGraw-Hill; 2005.

Doka KJ, ed. *Disenfranchised Grief: New Directions, Challenges, and Strategies for Practice.* Champaign, IL: Research Press; 2002.

Kübler-Ross E. *On Death and Dying.* New York: Macmillan; 1969.

National Hospice and Palliative Care Organization. Caring connections. Available at: www.caringinfo.org/i4a/pages/index.cfm?pageid=3281. Accessed October 1, 2005.

Prigerson HG, Maciejewski PK, Reynolds CF, et al. Inventory of Complicated Grief: A scale to measure maladaptive symptoms of loss. *Psychiatric Res.* 1995;59:65–79.

Shear K, Frank E, Houck PR, Reynolds CF III. Treatment of complicated grief: A randomized controlled trial. *JAMA.* 2005;293:2601–2608.

DELIRIUM AND CONFUSIONAL STATES

Delirium, sometimes referred to as an *acute confusional state,* is a disturbance of consciousness and cognition that develops and fluctuates over a short period of time. This syndrome often occurs in response to a medical condition, but it may also be the result of the administration or withdrawal of drugs. Delirium can occur in patients of any age, but it is distinctly common among older patients and is associated with prolonged hospital stays, increased health care costs, and an increased likelihood of dementia and death.

The specific diagnostic criteria for delirium, as outlined by the American Psychiatric Association in the *Diagnostic and Statistical Manual of Mental Disorders, Fourth Edition, Text Revision* (DSM-IV-TR), are (a) disturbance of consciousness (i.e., reduced clarity of awareness of the environment) with reduced ability to focus, sustain, or shift attention; (b) change in cognition (e.g., memory deficit, disorientation, language disturbance) or the development of a perceptual disturbance that is not better accounted for by a preexisting, established, or evolving dementia; and (c) development of the disturbance over a short period of time (usually hours to days) and a tendency to fluctuate during the course of the day. Delirium may be associated with a disruption of the sleep–wake cycle, and deterioration often occurs in the evening (a condition known as *sundowning*). In addition to impaired awareness of the environment (i.e., inattention), the delirious patient demonstrates increased or lowered alertness (restlessness and hyperactivity or sluggishness and lethargy). Other symptoms associated with delirium include hallucinations and/or delusions and emotional disturbances, with fear, anger, and depression being common.

Although delirium is typically attributed to a general medical condition, substance intoxication, or substance withdrawal, numerous factors play a role in the development of delirium. These factors include infection (especially urinary tract infection and pneumonia), heart disease, neurological disease (e.g., stroke, meningitis, seizure), respiratory failure or illness, abnormal sodium levels, urinary retention, constipation, surgery, pain, and treatment with prescription medications. Although these conditions may lead to delirium in any patient, risk factors make some persons more predisposed to delirium (e.g., older age, dementia, hearing or vision impairment, depression, immobility, alcohol abuse). In fact, multiple factors commonly result in delirium, especially in older hospitalized patients.

Drugs are frequently implicated in the development of delirium in older patients because most of these patients are exposed to multiple medications. Older patients are particularly vulnerable to adverse drug reactions, including delirium, due to a reduced ability to metabolize and excrete the drugs via liver and kidney function. Many of the medications regularly prescribed to older patients are likely to cause delirium. These include, but are not limited to, sedatives, analgesics, antihypertensives, antiarrhythmics, and antibiotics. The deliriogenic effect (promoting delirium) of these medications often compounds the confusion brought on by an acute medical illness such as those described previously.

Estimates of frequency of delirium depend on the environment and population studied. The 1981 East Baltimore Mental Health Survey studied the prevalence of psychiatric disease in 810 adults in a community setting. The study estimated that delirium was present in 0.4% of persons over 18 years of age, 1.1% of those over 55 years of age, and 13.6% of those over 85 years of age. Most research evaluating older patients hospitalized with acute medical illnesses (e.g., pneumonia, heart failure) has found that 10% to 20% of these patients are delirious at the time of their admission to the hospital and that an additional 10% to 20% of them become delirious during their hospital stay. For example, Timo Erkinjuntti and colleagues evaluated 2,000 consecutive medical admissions of patients age 55 years and older and reported that delirium was present in 15.1% of patients at admission. A higher percentage of patients undergoing surgery will develop delirium. L. W. Smith and J. E. Dimsdale analyzed 44 studies of delirium in patients undergoing cardiac surgery from 1963 to 1989 and reported that 32% of these patients developed delirium. When including emergent as well as elective surgery, most studies have found that 35% to 65% of patients will develop delirium after emergency procedures. Perhaps the highest number of delirious patients can be found in the intensive care unit (ICU). In 2004, E. Wesley Ely and colleagues reported that 82% of 224 mechanically ventilated patients in medical and coronary intensive care units experienced delirium.

The number of patients found to be delirious in research studies is typically higher than that recognized by health care professionals in routine clinical practice. The signs and symptoms of delirium often go unappreciated in the course of routine medical care. In addition, delirium may be mistaken for another neurological disease. For example, differentiating delirium from dementia poses particular challenges, especially given that a patient with dementia is predisposed to developing delirium in the setting of an acute illness. However, although dementia is associated with abnormalities of cognitive function, it does not result in an impaired awareness of the environment, inattention, or an abnormal level of consciousness—all defining characteristics of delirium. In addition, dementia typically has an insidious onset, whereas an acute onset is a diagnostic requirement of delirium.

Delirium is associated with multiple adverse effects that have been well documented. Hospitalized patients with delirium are up to 10 times more likely to experience medical complications. For example, delirious ICU patients are more likely than nondelirious patients to pull out catheters and remove themselves from mechanical ventilators. Numerous studies have documented that delirium results in prolonged hospital stays, increased hospital costs, and an increased need for discharge to a long-term care facility (nursing home) after hospital treatment. In 1990, Joseph Francis and colleagues studied 229 inpatients age 70 years and older and reported that the 50 patients who developed delirium had longer hospital stays (12.1 days vs. 7.2 days), were more likely to be institutionalized (16% vs. 3%), and were more likely to die (8% vs. 1%) compared with patients without delirium. Similar outcomes have been noted in ICU patients who develop delirium. Ely and colleagues, in a study of 275 mechanically ventilated ICU patients, reported that delirium was associated with a threefold increase in the risk of death during the 6 months after hospitalization. In addition to this increased risk of death, delirium is associated with an increased risk of developing long-term cognitive impairment during the years following hospitalization. In 2004, J. C. Jackson and colleagues analyzed nine studies that included 1,885 hospitalized medical and surgical patients and reported that delirium was associated with the development of dementia during the 1 to 3 years after hospitalization.

Despite the frequent occurrence of delirium in older hospitalized patients, the currently recommended strategies of prevention and treatment are relatively ineffective or of unproven benefit. Therefore, the mainstay of delirium management is the treatment of its underlying cause(s). That is, attention must be directed toward the resolution of the medical illness leading to delirium and/or the exposure to mind-altering drugs or medications. At the same time, clinicians must also work to prevent complications that may arise from the disruption of consciousness and cognition.

In high-risk patients, such as older patients with dementia who are hospitalized with acute medical illnesses, efforts to prevent delirium are warranted. Recommended approaches include repeatedly reorienting patients with calendars, information boards, and communication from health care workers and family; stimulating patients cognitively and physically with activities and exercise several times each day; promoting good sleep patterns via a sleep protocol and a sleep-friendly environment; minimizing visual and auditory difficulties with glasses and hearing aids; and attending to nutrition so as to prevent dehydration and metabolic abnormalities. In 1999, S. K. Inouye and colleagues reported that these strategies resulted in a significant reduction in the occurrence and duration of delirium in a randomized controlled trial of 852 older patients hospitalized with a variety of medical illnesses.

Antipsychotics remain the mainstay of pharmacological therapy for delirium. For example, haloperidol (a "typical" antipsychotic) is reported to improve most symptoms of delirium, especially in the treatment of hyperactive aggressive patients. Newer "atypical" antipsychotics have been used successfully to treat delirium as well. In specific cases of substance withdrawal delirium, other pharmacological therapies may be indicated (e.g., benzodiazepines in the treatment of alcohol withdrawal). It is important to note,

however, that clinical research studies supporting the use of medications to treat delirium are scarce and that each of the recommended medications carries the risk of adverse side effects. In fact, no large, placebo-controlled, randomized controlled trials have been conducted to evaluate the efficacy or safety of haloperidol—a drug recommended by the American Psychiatric Association—for the treatment of delirium. Therefore, the possible benefits of treatment must be weighed against the associated risks when considering pharmacological therapy for delirious patients. Older patients are especially susceptible to the adverse effects of drugs, and treatment should be initiated with low doses.

—Timothy D. Girard and E. Wesley Ely

See also Adverse Drug Reactions; Adverse Drug Withdrawal Events; Age-Related Changes in Pharmacokinetics and Pharmacodynamics; Agitation; Alzheimer's Disease; Behavioral Disorders in Dementia; Mild Cognitive Impairment; Neurological Disorders

Further Readings and References

American Psychiatric Association. Practice guidelines for the treatment of patients with delirium. *Am J Psychiatry.* 1999;156:1–20.

American Psychiatric Association. *Diagnostic and statistical manual of mental disorders.* 4th ed. Washington, DC: APA; 2000.

Ely EW, Shintani A, Truman B, et al. Delirium as a predictor of mortality in mechanically ventilated patients in the intensive care unit. *JAMA.* 2004;291:1753–1762.

Erkinjuntti T, Wikstrom J, Palo J, et al. Dementia among medical inpatients. Evaluation of 2000 consecutive admissions. *Arch Intern Med.* 1986;146:1923–1926.

Francis J, Martin D, Kapoor WN. A prospective study of delirium in hospitalized elderly. *JAMA.* 1990;263:1097–1101.

Inouye SK, Bogardus ST Jr, Charpentier PA, et al. A multicomponent intervention to prevent delirium in hospitalized older patients. *N Engl J Med.* 1999;340:669–676.

Jackson JC, Gordon SM, Hart RP, et al. The association between delirium and cognitive decline: A review of the empirical literature. *Neuropsychol Rev.* 2004;14:87–98.

Smith LW, Dimsdale JE. Postcardiotomy delirium: Conclusions after 25 years? *Am J Psychiatry.* 1989;146:452–458.

DELUSIONAL DISORDERS

See SCHIZOPHRENIA, PARANOIA, AND DELUSIONAL DISORDERS

DEMENTING ILLNESS

See ALZHEIMER'S DISEASE

DEMOGRAPHY OF AGING

Whereas demography is the study of the size, composition, and territorial distribution of the population, demography of aging refers to the changing proportion of older adults in the population. In the United States, fertility trends during the 20th century declined steadily, with the notable exception of the post–World War II baby boom from 1946 to 1964. Mortality rates also declined throughout the century, but in a very different way. During the first half of the century, mortality declined fastest among the very young as improved sanitation and hygiene decreased the rates of infectious disease. During the second half of the century, mortality declined fastest among middle-aged and older adults with improvements in surgical techniques and treatments for a variety of diseases, most notably cardiovascular disease. Both the fertility and mortality trends resulted in an older population as more people survived infancy and childhood during the early part of the century and aged longer due to decreased old age mortality. During the 21st century, the U.S. population will continue to age as the baby boomers begin to reach 65 years of age in 2011 and survive to mid-century.

Size and Location of the U.S. Population

In the United States in 2000, persons age 65 years and older made up approximately 13% of the population. The age of 65 years is important because that is the time when people traditionally retire from paid employment to receive income through the Social Security program. By 2100, the population age 65 years and older will constitute approximately 23% of the population (Figure 1). Of particular concern is the potential growth in the population age 85 years and older because they are the most likely to require medical and social services. In 2000, those age 85 years and older represented approximately 2% of the population; by 2100, this proportion will more than triple to approximately 7%.

Older adults live in all 50 states and constitute approximately 13% of the U.S. population, but they are concentrated in certain areas. Table 1 shows the 10 states with the highest percentages of persons age 65 years and older in 2000 and those projected for 2030. Not surprisingly, Florida is the oldest state, with

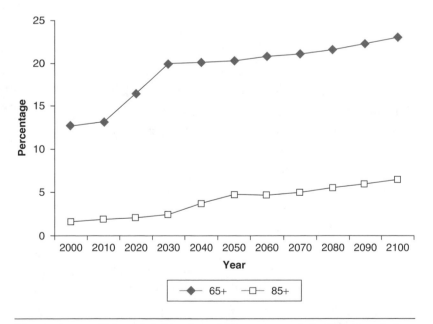

Figure 1   Older Adults' Projected Proportions of the U.S. Population, 2000 to 2100: Ages 65 Years and Older and 85 Years and Older

Source: U.S. Census Bureau, 2005.

17.6% of its residents age 65 years and older. Other states in the top 10 are diverse states such as West Virginia, Iowa, North Dakota, South Dakota, and Maine. By 2030, Florida will still be the oldest state, with 27.1% of its population age 65 years and older. New to the top 10 will be Wyoming, New Mexico, Montana, Vermont, and Delaware. States no longer in the top 10 will include Pennsylvania, Iowa, Rhode Island, Arkansas, and Connecticut. The age structure of these states can change due to both in-migration of retirees, as in Florida's case, and out-migration of young adults to urban areas for economic opportunity, as is probably the case with Iowa.

Life Expectancy

One of the major reasons for the explosive growth of the older population during the 20th century was the increase in the average life expectancy, which is the average number of years a person can expect to live from a specified age (usually birth). During the last half of the 20th century, life expectancy increased for both men and women, although women's life

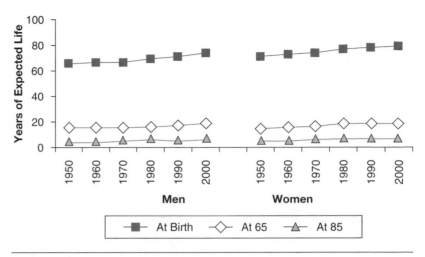

Figure 2   Changes in Life Expectancy in the United States by Gender: 1950, 1960, 1970, 1980, 1990, and 2000

Source: U.S. Census Bureau, 2005.

expectancy was longer than men's at every period. At birth, men and women in 1950 could expect to live 65.6 and 71.1 years, respectively. By 2000, they could expect to live 74.1 and 79.5 years, respectively (Figure 2). Life expectancy also differs by race/ethnicity (Figure 3). Average life expectancy for Whites at birth was 69.1 years in 1950. By 2000, it had grown to 77.4 years. Average life expectancy for African Americans at birth grew from 63.9 years in 1960 (1950 data not available) to 71.7 years in 2000; African Americans have participated in improvements in life expectancy, but not relative to Whites.

Compositional Characteristics

Age

The age structure within the older population also will change during the 21st century (Table 2). Between 2000 and 2100, the general population is projected to grow by a factor of 1.1 times. At the same time, the population age 65 years and older will grow by a factor of 0.8 times, reflecting the deaths of the baby boomers around mid-century. However, those who are age 85 years and older during the same time will increase by a factor of 3.1 times. Centenarians will increase dramatically, by a factor of 45.5 times, although their numbers will remain relatively small.

Table 1   Changes in the Top 10 Oldest States (by Percentage Aged 65 Years and Older) Between 2000 and 2030 in Rank Order

2000		2030	
Florida	17.6	Florida	27.1
Pennsylvania	15.6	Maine	26.5
West Virginia	15.3	Wyoming	26.5
Iowa	14.9	New Mexico	26.4
North Dakota	14.7	Montana	25.8
Rhode Island	14.5	North Dakota	25.1
Maine	14.4	West Virginia	24.8
South Dakota	14.3	Vermont	24.4
Arkansas	14.0	Delaware	23.5
Connecticut	13.8	South Dakota	23.1

Source: U.S. Census Bureau, 2005.

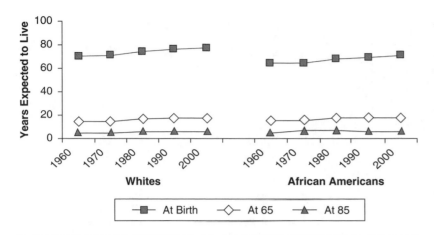

Figure 3   Changes in Life Expectancy in the United States by Race: 1960, 1970, 1980, 1990, and 2000

Source: U.S. Census Bureau, 2005.

Gender

At age 65 years and older, females predominate, but this varies by age. For example, in 2000, the ratio of females to males in the population age 65 years and older was 1.4 to 1. However, the ratio of females to males in the population age 85 years and older was 2.4 to 1. By 2050, the ratio of females to males in the population age 65 years and older is projected to be 1.3 to 1, whereas the ratio for the population age 85 years and older is projected to be 1.7 to 1. The implication is that men's life expectancy relative to women's life expectancy will increase during the 21st century.

Differences in marital status and life expectancy between the genders also suggest differences in how older adults live. Whereas 75% of men age 65 years and older are married, only 44% of women that age are married. In contrast, 45% of older women are widowed, whereas only 15% of older men are widowed. One way marital status differences manifest themselves is in the living arrangements of older adults (Figure 4). Whereas 73% of older men live with a spouse and only 19% live alone, 41% of older women live with a spouse and 40% live alone. In addition, older women are more likely to be living with other family members, potentially affecting women's labor force participation by increasing the need for providing care to an older parent.

Racial and Ethnic Differences

The older population is predominantly White due to differences in life expectancy between Whites and other racial/ethnic groups. Figure 5 shows the proportions of the older population by race and ethnicity in 2000 and projections for 2100. In 2000, non-Hispanic Whites constituted 84% of the population age 85 years and older. The next two largest groups were non-Hispanic African Americans (8%) and Hispanics (6%). Due largely to increased immigration among Hispanics and Asians, as well as higher birth rates in non-White communities, by 2100 non-Hispanic Whites will represent less than half of the older population (48%). At the same time, older African Americans will increase from 8% to 13% of the older population, older Hispanics will increase from 6% to 28%, and older Asians will increase from 2% to 10%.

Table 2   Increase in Centenarians, Persons Age 85 Years and Older, and Persons Age 65 Years and Older: 2000 to 2100

	Number	Percentage	Change in Percentage
Centenarians			
2000	65,000	0.02	45.5
2100	5,323,000	0.93	
85 years and older			
2000	4,312,000	1.6	3.1
2100	37,030,000	6.5	
65 years and older			
2000	34,835,000	12.7	0.8
2100	131,163,000	23.0	
Total population			
2000	275,306,000	100.0	
2100	570,954,000	100.0	1.1

Source: U.S. Census Bureau, 2005.

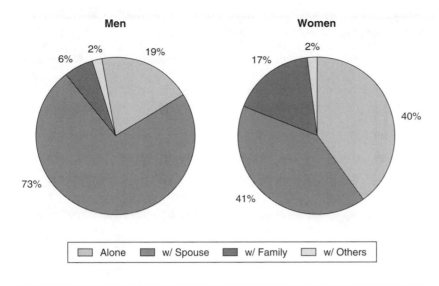

Men   Women

Alone   w/ Spouse   w/ Family   w/ Others

Figure 4   Living Arrangements for U.S. Population Age 65 Years and Older by Gender

Source: Adapted from Health and Retirement Study. (1998). Ann Arbor: University of Michigan (with funding from the National Institute on Aging, grant number NIA U01AG009740).

Differences in Socioeconomic Status

There are also differences in socioeconomic status (SES) in the older population. Most researchers examine SES using two standard measures: income and education. Table 3 presents differences in educational attainment for Whites and African Americans in 1950, 1975, and 2000. At all three periods, Whites have higher educational attainment than African Americans, and although both races experience higher educational attainment during the later years, African Americans do not catch up to Whites because they started out so disadvantaged relative to Whites. The result of this education differential is seen in Figure 6, showing the proportions of the older population living at or near the poverty level, which in 2004 was $9,060 for an older individual and $11,418 for an older couple. Clearly, both African American and Hispanic elders are more likely than Whites to be poor or near poor.

International Perspectives

Although the aging of the population is a major concern for the United States, the country is not alone; in fact, the United States is not even among the oldest nations in the world. The oldest country in 2000 was Japan, as defined by the median age of all its citizens. According to statistics published by the United Nations, of the 10 oldest nations in 2000, 5 were in Western Europe, 2 were in Scandinavia, 2 were former Soviet bloc countries (Bulgaria and Croatia), and Japan rounded out the list. It is interesting to speculate on the reasons why this mix of countries may be the oldest; for example, one would think that life expectancy in Bulgaria would not be as long as that in Switzerland, so it might come as a surprise that the median age in Bulgaria is 39.1 years compared with 40.2 years in Switzerland, as noted in the United Nations publication, *World Population Prospects: The 2002 Revision.*

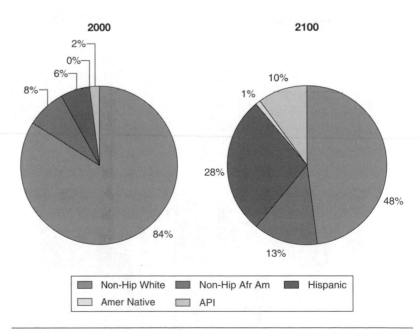

2000   2100

Non-Hip White   Non-Hip Afr Am   Hispanic
Amer Native   API

Figure 5   Proportions of Older Americans by Race and Ethnicity: 2000 and 2100

Source: U.S. Census Bureau, 2005.

Note: API = Asians and Pacific Islanders.

Table 3   Trends in Educational Attainment by Gender, Race, and Ethnicity: 1950, 1975, and 2000

Grade Level	1950	1975	2000	Percentage Change 1975–1950	Percentage Change 2000–1975	Percentage Change 2000–1950
Whites						
9 to 11	9.3	14.9	12.9	60.2	–13.4	38.7
High school graduate	10.0	20.1	36.9	101.0	83.6	269.0
Some college	4.1	8.2	18.8	100.0	129.3	358.5
4+ years college	3.5	7.9	16.1	125.7	103.8	360.0
African Americans						
Up to 8	87.0	78.1	30.8	–10.2	–60.6	–64.6
9 to 11	4.1	9.2	23.6	124.4	156.5	475.6
High school graduate	2.8	7.7	26.9	175.0	249.4	860.7
Some college	1.3	2.4	11.0	84.6	358.3	746.2
4+ years college	0.9	2.3	7.6	155.6	230.4	744.4

Source: Adapted from National Center for Health Statistics. *Data Warehouse: Educational Attainment by Age, Sex, and Race-Hispanic Origin. United States, 1940–2004. CPS (CPE04a)*; 2005. Available at: http://209.217.72.34/aging/TableViewer/tableView.aspx? ReportId=319. Accessed June 13, 2005.

In contrast, the same United Nations report stated that the 10 countries of the world that have the highest life expectancies are composed of 2 countries from Western Europe, 2 from Scandinavia, 2 from Asia, and 4 others from various parts of the world. Switzerland's average life expectancy was 79.1 years in 2000, but Bulgaria, although nearly as "old" as Switzerland, is not among the top 10. The reason for this most likely is that Switzerland is an "old" country due to better health and greater longevity of the Swiss, whereas Bulgaria is "old" due to the out-migration of its youth toward economic opportunities elsewhere.

By 2050, Japan is projected to still lead the world in being the oldest country, but by that time five of the oldest countries will be from the former Soviet bloc, three from Western Europe, and two from Asia. Again we find that none of the former Soviet Union republics is on the list of the top 10 countries in average life expectancy in 2050, according to United Nations figures. These projections are based on the best current knowledge, however, and one might expect that economic opportunities in the former Soviet Union republics would improve in the

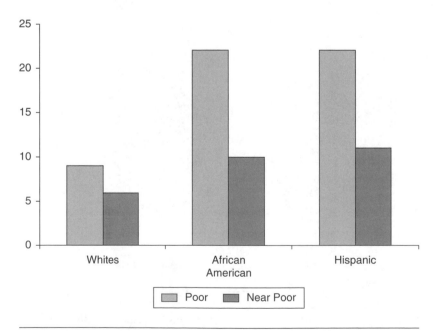

Figure 6   Percentages Living in Poverty and Near Poverty Among U.S. Older Adults by Race/Ethnicity: 2001

Source: U.S. Census Bureau, 2005.

future. Still, they might not improve relative to the rest of the world.

The demography of aging is an important topic considering the resources that most societies devote to health and social welfare systems for older adults. It is critically important to understand the impact that aging societies will have on funding for acute and long-term health care services for older adults. At the same time, and particularly for countries with few resources to devote to the well-being of their older adults, it is also important to understand the impact that the aging of the population will have on informal systems of care for older adults, primarily their families.

—Sandra L. Reynolds

See also Active Life Expectancy; Age–Period–Cohort Distinctions; Longevity

Further Readings and References

Health and Retirement Study. Ann Arbor: University of Michigan (with funding from National Institute on Aging); 1998.

Himes CL. *Elderly Americans.* Washington, DC: Population Reference Bureau; 2001. Population Bulletin, Vol. 56, No. 4.

National Center for Health Statistics. Trends in health and aging. Available at: www.cdc.gov/nchs/agingact.htm. Accessed September 11, 2006.

Perls TJ. The Living to 100 Healthspan Calculator. Available at: www.agingresearch.org/calculator. Accessed September 11, 2006.

United Nations. *World population prospects: The 2002 revision—Highlights.* New York: United Nations; 2003.

U.S. Census Bureau. U.S. interim projections by age, sex, race, and Hispanic origin. Washington, DC: U.S. Census Bureau, Population Division, Population Projections Branch; 2005. Available at: www.census.gov/ipc/www/usinterimproj. Accessed September 11, 2006.

DEPRESSION AND OTHER MOOD DISORDERS

Depression is one of the most disabling of health conditions worldwide and is expected to become more so within a generation. However, studies of community residents demonstrate a surprisingly low prevalence of major depression among those age 65 years and older. From 1% to 2% of women and less than 1% of men meet diagnostic criteria for major depression. Both current and lifetime prevalence rates are lower among older persons than among the middle-aged. These relatively low rates persist after accounting for suicide and institutionalization, both of which are associated with depression.

However, the prevalence of depressive symptoms that do not meet the threshold for a clinical diagnosis is considerable for seniors, with most studies reporting rates of 15% or more. These subsyndromal states are not benign. Minor depression is associated with excess disability, increased use of health services, and poor health outcomes, including higher mortality. Although rates of dysthymia (2%), a minor depression lasting 2 or more years, and of adjustment disorder with depressed mood (4%) are higher than those for major depression, the prevalence of these states is also lower in older adults than in younger adults. Similarly, the prevalence of bipolar disorder decreases across the age spectrum, from a prevalence of approximating 1.5% during young adulthood to 0.1% among persons age 65 years and older.

The prevalence rates of both major and minor depression relate to the setting and methods used to identify cases. Major depression is found in 6% to 10% of older patients in primary care clinics and in 12% to 20% of nursing home residents. Rates varying from 11% to 45% have been reported among elderly patients requiring inpatient medical care. The prevalence of minor depression in outpatient medical clinics varies from 8% to more than 40%. Major depression is the most common disorder among elderly patients seen in psychiatric settings and accounts for at least 40% of outpatient and inpatient admissions. Similarly, bipolar disorder is common among older psychiatric patients, representing between 3% and 10% of admissions of older adults.

Although aging does not markedly affect the presentation of major depression, differences between younger and older depressed patients are apparent. Older patients more often express somatic concerns and less frequently report depressed mood or guilty preoccupations. Among patients who deny sadness, a persistent loss of pleasure and interest in previously enjoyable activities (anhedonia) is necessary for a diagnosis of major depression. Thus, a person need not exhibit a depressed mood to meet criteria for major depressive disorder.

Diagnosis is complicated by symptoms of major depression overlapping with those of physical illness. Older patients with serious medical illness may be preoccupied with thoughts of death because of associated disability or pain. The *Diagnostic and Statistical Manual of Mental Disorders, Fourth Edition* (DSM-IV) criteria for major depression require that the depressive symptoms not be a direct effect of a general medical condition or medication used to treat it, but this distinction based on cause may be difficult to make reliably. The alternative diagnosis, mood disorder due to a general medical condition, should be used when depression appears to be a direct result of a medical condition such as hypothyroidism. Patients with psychotic depression have sustained irrational beliefs and, like those with thoughts of suicide, are more prone to recurrent episodes.

A diagnosis of mania requires a period of elevated mood lasting for at least a week plus three additional symptoms such as inflated self-esteem, grandiosity, hypersexuality, increased activity, decreased need for sleep, pressured speech, racing thoughts, flight of ideas, and distractibility. Paranoid or grandiose ideas may be present but are implausible rather than bizarre. Older patients with bipolar disorder are more likely than younger persons to exhibit a mix of depression and irritability. Pressured tangential speech is common, although the severity of thinking disturbance is less pronounced than it is in young adults. Flight of ideas, hypersexuality, and grandiosity may be present but are typically less prominent. Late-onset mania is often associated with stroke.

Medical disorders that imitate depression are particularly important to consider in older patients because of the increased prevalence of physical illnesses during late life. For example, older hyperthyroid patients may present with apathy and diminished energy that may be mistaken for the anhedonia of depression. The distinction of apathy from true depression becomes particularly important among patients with Parkinson's disease, carcinoma of the pancreas, or dementia because depressive syndromes that occur commonly in these disorders are responsive to antidepressant medications.

Major depression may be a prodrome of dementia or may develop after the onset of cognitive decline. Differentiation may be difficult because depression is commonly accompanied by symptoms of impaired concentration, indecisiveness, and apathy (also associated with dementia). An older person with depression but not dementia may complain of memory loss and poor concentration and may be unable to perform simple cognitive tests. Distinguishing depression from dementia requires evidence that the cognitive impairment is not consistently present, appeared with the onset of depression, and reverses with improvement in mood. Conversely, patients with genuine dementia may have symptoms that imitate depression, including apathy, psychomotor retardation, and sleep disturbance. Approximately 20% of patients with early Alzheimer's disease meet criteria for major depression.

The syndrome of vascular depression is associated with anhedonia and the absence of guilty preoccupations. Patients with vascular depression have a late age of onset, risk factors for vascular disease, and prefrontal subcortical white matter hyperintensities on T2-weighted magnetic resonance imaging. There is also evidence of nonamnestic cognitive deficits in tasks requiring initiation, persistence, and self-monitoring. Depressed patients with such defects in executive function may experience a remission of disturbed mood in response to antidepressants but may remain substantially disabled.

Feelings of sadness, disturbed sleep, and loss of appetite are common among bereaved seniors but usually resolve within 2 months. However, more than 1 in 10 bereaved adults develops major depression within 2 years of the loss. In contrast, bereaved seniors seem less likely to develop a depressive disorder. Bereavement complicated by major depression is characterized by guilt and morbid preoccupations with the deceased or suicidal ideas beyond the transient thoughts of joining the deceased that would be expected in association with the loss. Also, uncomplicated bereavement is not associated with marked functional impairment.

Major depression is often a recurrent disorder in both youth and old age. Observational studies in which treatment was not provided indicate that up to one third of depressive episodes run a chronic course and that another third exhibit partial remission with residual disability. For patients who suffer their first episode during late life, the period between initiation of treatment and recovery may be prolonged. Depressed persons use disproportionately more health services, including outpatient visits, specialist consultations, and laboratory assessments. Comorbid medical illness predicts less favorable outcome of late-life depression, and depression predicts greater than expected mortality from cardiovascular events among primary care patients.

As many as 75% of older adults who commit suicide are depressed, and the majority will have seen their primary care physicians within a month of death. Persons age 65 years and older represent less than 13% of the population but account for 25% of suicides, predominantly among White males. Firearms and hanging are the methods most commonly employed. Beyond depression and the White male demographic, risk factors for late-life suicide include advanced age, comorbid physical illness, living alone, and alcoholism.

The treatment of major depression entails three phases: acute treatment to achieve a remission of symptoms, continuation to prevent relapse, and maintenance to prevent recurrence. Continuation treatment seeks to sustain recovery for a minimum of 6 months following remission of symptoms. Maintenance treatment is provided to patients with recurrent depression and spans at least 3 years. Recurrent episodes complicated by suicidality or psychosis may warrant lifelong treatment. Psychotherapy, antidepressants, and electroconvulsive therapy (ECT) have proven to be effective for both younger and older patients.

Although most patients prefer treatment for depression by a primary care provider, depression most often goes unrecognized or undertreated in this setting. Although the frequency with which primary care physicians prescribe antidepressants has risen sharply, a near majority of patients do not obtain refills after their initial prescriptions. Integration of mental health specialists into primary care settings achieves outcomes superior to those of antidepressant therapy prescribed by primary care providers. Nonetheless, full recovery rates in integrated clinics are rarely better than 50%.

The recommendation of ECT is made when the risk of waiting for an antidepressant to reverse suicidal intent or the refusal of food and fluids outweighs the inconvenience of hospital treatment and fears of "shock therapy." Although maintenance ECT is sometimes used to prevent relapse, the burden that maintenance ECT places on patients and their families limits its usefulness for the long-term management of late-life major depression.

Advances in recognition, characterization, and treatment of depression have been substantial, but the desired impact on associated morbidity and mortality of the illness during late life remains far from ideal.

—*Gary J. Kennedy*

See also Alzheimer's Disease; Anxiety Disorders; Bereavement and Grief; Emotions and Emotional Stability; Posttraumatic Stress Disorder; Psychiatric Rating Scales; Stress; Suicide and the Elderly; Vascular Depression

Further Readings and References

Alexopoulos GS, Meyers BS, Young RC, et al. Executive dysfunction and long-term outcomes of geriatric depression. *Arch Gen Psychiatry.* 2000;57:285–290.

Bruce ML, Ten Have TR, Reynolds CF III, et al. Reducing suicidal ideation and depressive symptoms in depressed older primary care patients: A randomized controlled trial. *JAMA.* 2004;291:1081–1091.

Gallo JJ, Bogner HR, Morales KH, et al. Depression, cardiovascular disease, diabetes, and 2-year mortality among older primary care patients. *Am J Geriatr Psychiatry.* (in press).

Kennedy GJ, Marcus P. Use of antidepressants in older patients with co-morbid medical conditions: Guidance from studies of depression in somatic illness. *Drugs Aging.* 2005;22:273–287.

Kessler R, Berglund P, Borges G, et al. Trends in suicide ideation, plans, gestures, and attempts in the United States, 1990–1992 to 2001–2003. *JAMA.* 2005; 293:2487–2495.

Krishnan KRR, Hays JC, Blazer DG. MRI-defined vascular depression. *Am J Psychiatry.* 1997;154:497–501.

DIABETES

Diabetes is a group of chronic metabolic diseases characterized by hyperglycemia due to a defect in insulin secretion, insulin action, or both. Diabetes mellitus increases morbidity, mortality, and health care costs through acute and chronic complications, including ketoacidosis, hyperosmolarity, cardiovascular disease, kidney disease, retinopathy, neuropathy, and limb amputations.

The prevalence of diabetes increases with age. Approximately 8.7% of American adults are affected by diabetes mellitus, and most develop type 2 diabetes mellitus (T2DM). The incidence of T2DM increased by 61% in the United States between 1990 and 2002. Population estimates from the Centers for Disease Control and Prevention (CDC) indicate that approximately 19 million persons have diabetes mellitus. In addition, estimates of the prevalence of prediabetes (impaired fasting glucose [IFG] or impaired glucose tolerance [IGT]) indicate that approximately 35 million persons 40 to 74 years of age have IFG and that 16 million have IGT, totaling 51 million adults with prediabetes using the new American Diabetes Association (ADA) diagnostic criteria. Furthermore, Third National Health and Nutrition Examination Survey (NHANES III) data show that at least 47 million individuals in the United States have metabolic syndrome, a combination of conditions and diseases (obesity, hypertension, dyslipidemia, and T2DM) tightly linked by increased insulin resistance, dramatically increasing the risk of cardiovascular events.

Classification, Etiology, and Pathogenesis

In addition to the two major types of diabetes (type 1 diabetes mellitus [T1DM] and T2DM), rarer types of diabetes include gestational diabetes, diabetes due to medications (e.g., glucocorticoids), and secondary diabetes due to diseases of the exocrine pancreas (e.g., infections, cancer). T1DM, formerly termed insulin-dependent diabetes mellitus or juvenile diabetes, is caused by the autoimmune destruction of the pancreatic β-cells, leading to absolute insulin deficiency. Both genetic predisposition and environmental factors such as infections are important in the pathogenesis of T1DM. In fact, concordance rates for T1DM are only approximately 50% in monozygotic (identical) twins. T1DM most commonly develops during childhood or adolescence and is the prevalent type of diabetes mellitus diagnosed before 30 years of age. T1DM accounts for 5% to 10% of diabetes and is clinically distinguished by sudden onset, severe hyperglycemia, and a susceptibility to develop diabetic ketoacidosis (DKA).

T2DM, formerly called non-insulin-dependent diabetes mellitus or adult diabetes, usually develops over a prolonged period in stages, beginning with insulin resistance that requires an increase in insulin secretion to maintain normoglycemia. Over time, progressive β-cell dysfunction in predisposed individuals occurs, leading to impaired glucose tolerance. Progressive pancreatic β-cell failure and increased insulin resistance ultimately lead to T2DM. Genetic predisposition is very important for the development of T2DM because the concordance between identical twins is approximately 80%. Nonetheless, lifestyle is also an important player in the development and severity of T2DM. It is well known that the recent increase in the prevalence of T2DM is tightly correlated with increased prevalence of obesity and decreased physical activity levels. T2DM is more common in adults; however, over the past decade, its prevalence in children and adolescents has been increasing dramatically, linked mainly to childhood obesity.

Criteria for Diagnosis and Screening

Screening for diabetes is recommended for all individuals with known risk factors and for those over 45 years of age. If normal, screening should be repeated every 3 years. The ADA has issued the following criteria for diagnosis of diabetes:

1. Symptoms of diabetes and a casual plasma glucose ≥ 200 milligrams per deciliter (mg/dl) (≥ 11.1 millimoles per liter [mmol/L]). *Casual* is defined as any time of day without regard to time since the last

meal. The classic symptoms of diabetes include polyuria, polydipsia, and unexplained weight loss.

or

2. Fasting plasma glucose (FPG) ≥ 126 mg/dl (≥ 7.0 mmol/L). Fasting is defined as no caloric intake for at least 8 hours.

3. Two-hour plasma glucose level ≥ 200 mg/dl (≥ 11.1 mmol/L) during an oral glucose tolerance test using a glucose load containing the equivalent of 75 grams of anhydrous glucose dissolved in water.

In the absence of unequivocal hyperglycemia with acute metabolic decompensation, these criteria should be confirmed by repeat testing on a different day. The oral glucose tolerance test (OGTT) is not routinely recommended, however, if the fasting glucose level is normal.

Hyperglycemia not sufficient to meet the diagnostic criteria for diabetes would be categorized as either IFG or IGT, which are now officially termed *prediabetes*:

IFG = FPG 100 mg/dl (5.6 mmol/L) to 125 mg/dl (6.9 mmol/L)

IGT = 2-hour plasma glucose 140 mg/dl (7.8 mmol/L) to 199 mg/dl (11.0 mmol/L)

Signs, Symptoms, and Chronic Complications

T2DM is often diagnosed during a routine medical examination or as an incidental finding, so patients may have had the disease asymptomatically for years before diagnosis, although they may already have active long-term complications. When blood glucose rises too high (usually > 180 mg/dl), it is detected in the urine because it overcomes the ability of the kidneys to reabsorb it. As a consequence, large volumes of urine (polyuria) are produced by the increased osmolar load in the renal tubules. This eventually leads to abnormal thirst (polydipsia) secondary to dehydration. In older people, this latter mechanism of compensation may be impaired due to reduced thirst sensation and may lead to one of the most dangerous acute complications of T2DM, hyperosmolarity, which has a high mortality rate. Patients may also

experience excessive hunger because their bodies cannot use glucose as a source of energy due to the lack of insulin and/or reduced insulin action; thus, patients eat more (polyphagia) but nevertheless lose weight. Extreme hyperglycemia may lead to confusion, drowsiness, seizures, and nonketotic hyperosmolar hyperglycemic coma. Recently, there has also been an increase in the incidence of diabetic ketoacidosis and ketotic hyperglycemic coma in T2DM with severe β-cell impairment.

After years of poorly controlled hyperglycemia, late complications will occur, including eye (retinopathy), renal (nephropathy), cardiovascular (myocardial infarction, stroke, and peripheral vascular disease), and nerve (neuropathy) complications. Diabetic retinopathy can progress to retinal detachment or hemorrhage, which can cause blindness. Diabetic nephropathy develops in a smaller percentage of T2DM patients. Microalbuminuria, a sign of progressive decrease in glomerular filtration rate, can progress to end-stage renal disease requiring hemodialysis and kidney transplant. Diabetic retinopathy and nephropathy can be prevented by tight glycemic control, reflected by near-normal glycosylated hemoglobin A_{1C} (HbA_{1C}) levels. Macrovascular complications are responsible for cardiovascular disease, the major cause of death among patients with T2DM. Coronary artery disease, stroke, and claudication are other results of macrovascular complications. Diabetic neuropathy is related mainly to hyperglycemia, which increases the formation of polyols and nerve damage, particularly of the small peripheral nerves, and is also compounded by microangiopathy due to reduced vascularization of the nerves. Diabetic neuropathy commonly occurs as distal, symmetric sensory deficits with numbness, tingling, and paresthesias in a stocking–glove distribution. Autonomic neuropathy occurs primarily in diabetics with polyneuropathy and can cause postural hypotension, disordered sweating, impotence and retrograde ejaculation (in men), impaired bladder function, delayed gastric emptying, esophageal dysfunction, constipation, and diarrhea. Sensory denervation in the lower extremities impairs the perception of trauma, predisposing to foot ulcers and gangrene (diabetic foot), ultimately leading to amputation of the extremity involved. Finally, in uncontrolled diabetes cellular immunity is decreased, putting patients at higher risk for infection from fungi and bacteria. Skin infections and oral and vaginal thrush are very common.

Assessment, Management, and Treatment

Evaluation of the older diabetic patient can be time-consuming. A thorough medical history and physical examination is an important part of management. If the patient is unable to understand or communicate, information should be taken from members of the family or caregivers. The history should also include a review of medications (with particular attention to polypharmacy), alcohol ingestion, dietary quantity and pattern, level of physical activity, falls, incontinence, sexual dysfunction, depression, and anxiety. The physical exam should include assessment for complications, including blood pressure as well as a complete eye, vascular, cardiac, abdominal, skin, and neurological exam. Particular attention should be paid to a thorough foot exam. Lab tests should include measurement of fasting glucose and HbA_{1C}, a urine test for ketones and microalbuminuria if the patient has no evidence of overt proteinuria, a lipid profile, blood urea nitrogen (BUN) and serum creatinine levels, liver enzymes if thiazolidindiones are considered for treatment, and electrocardiogram (ECG). Retina angiography requiring contrast dyes should be performed only when necessary because of risk of acute renal failure.

The mainstays of diabetes management are education, diet, and exercise. Thus, consultations should include diabetes educators, dieticians, and (for older patients) physical therapists to determine the type and intensity of exercise regimen. Exercise and lifestyle changes have been shown to be superior to early drug treatment in delaying the onset of T2DM in prediabetic patients. Also, self-monitoring of blood glucose (SMBG) is essential for successful control of diabetes and its complications; the patient and/or caregivers should be deeply involved in the care and management of diabetes. In T2DM, weight loss is usually desirable unless the patient is very old and/or frail, in which case dietary management should focus more on distributing the caloric intake adequately throughout the day, also considering the drug regimen.

Diabetes treatment is monitored by reviewing the SMBG log and following the HbA_{1C} levels over time (Table 1). HbA_{1C} represents the integrated blood glucose control over the past 2 to 3 months. The Diabetes Control and Complications Trial (DCCT) and the United Kingdom Prospective Diabetes Study (UKPDS) have shown that the lower the HbA_{1C}, the fewer the chances of developing diabetes complications. The ADA recommends that action be taken when HbA_{1C} is greater than 8% and considers diabetes to be under control when the HbA_{1C} is 7% or less. The test should be performed every 3 months for insulin-treated patients, during treatment changes, or when blood glucose is elevated. For stable patients on oral agents, the recommended frequency is at least twice per year.

If adequate control of hyperglycemia is not achieved by diet and exercise, oral antihyperglycemic drugs should be considered. The current available

Table 1   Relationship of A_{1C} to Average Plasma Glucose Levels

Hemoglobin A_{1C} (%)	APG (mg/dl)	Interpretation
4	65	Nondiabetic range
5	100	Nondiabetic range
6	135	
7	170	Target for diabetes in control
8	205	Action suggested per ADA guidelines
9	240	
10	275	
11	310	
12	345	

Source: Copyright © 2002 American Diabetes Association. From *Diabetes Care*, Vol. 25, 2002; 275–278. Reprinted with permission from The American Diabetes Association.

Note: APG = average plasma glucose.

classes of oral antidiabetic agents reduce plasma glucose levels by targeting four processes: (1) stimulation of pancreatic β-cells to produce more insulin (e.g., sulfonylureas, nonsulfonylurea secretagogues, incretins), (2) reduction of glucose output by the liver (e.g., biguanides, thiazolidinediones), (3) stimulation of glucose uptake by muscle and adipose tissues (e.g., thiazolidinediones, metformin), and (4) reduction of glucose absorption by the gut (α-glucosidase inhibitors). When the patient does not attain the glycemic goals on oral therapy (β-cell failure), insulin therapy must be started. A brief list of all these agents and their effects is presented in Table 2.

Dyslipidemia and hypertension increase the risks of late complications and thus require special attention. The lipid targets for diabetic patients are low-density lipoprotein (LDL) cholesterol less than 100 mg/dl, high-density lipoprotein (HDL) cholesterol greater than 40 mg/dl, and triglycerides less than 150 mg/dl. Statins have been shown not only to reduce cholesterol but also to have an anti-inflammatory effect that may be also responsible for reduced cardiovascular events in treated patients.

Regarding hypertension, the UKPDS has clearly shown that aggressive antihypertensive treatment is the most important intervention to reduce morbidity and mortality from cardiovascular events. Thiazide diuretics can be used safely as first-line antihypertensive drugs in diabetic patients, although some reports suggest that they may worsen glucose control. Nonetheless, thiazide diuretics should be recommended as first-line antihypertensives in African American patients due to their protective effect on cardiovascular events in this group. Angiotensin-converting enzyme (ACE) inhibitors are the other class of first-line antihypertensives for diabetes and are usually preferred over thiazide diuretics because they reduce the incidence of diabetic nephropathy and improve insulin sensitivity. Angiotensin II receptor blockers (ARBs) can be used safely in place of ACE inhibitors because ARBs share the same clinical advantages, although they are more costly. Calcium channel blockers are also effective antihypertensives but should be used with caution because, when compared with ACE inhibitors, they may increase the risk of cardiovascular events; thus, they should be used only as a second- or third-line choice and not in patients who have had recent coronary events. β-Blockers should be avoided in patients treated with insulin secretagogues or insulin with histories of hypoglycemic episodes because they can mask the symptoms of hypoglycemia, although they can be used safely in most diabetics and should be included in the regimen of patients with coronary artery disease. Nonetheless, the most important target is to achieve a blood pressure level below 130/80 millimeters of mercury (mm Hg), which in many cases can be achieved only with combination therapy. Finally, aspirin may be added to the treatment regimen of older diabetes patients given its protective effect against cardiovascular events. However, the addition of aspirin should be considered according to the degree of polypharmacy and possible negative gastrointestinal effects.

Factors Affecting Treatment in the Elderly

Elderly patients commonly have coexisting illnesses that aggravate T2DM. The elderly should be treated as aggressively, in terms of glycemic control, as their general situations allow. Treatment should be individualized in the geriatric population; thus, it is very important for physicians to evaluate for geriatric syndromes of polypharmacy, depression, cognitive decline or dementia, injurious falls, urinary incontinence, chronic pain, disability, and frailty. In addition, patients' general conditions should be examined for the presence of altered sensation, difficulties in food preparation and consumption, altered recognition of hunger and thirst, altered renal and hepatic function, presence of acute infections, decreased exercise and mobility, neuropsychiatric disorders, and social factors such as financial status and current living conditions.

—*Jerson Cadenas and Elena Volpi*

See also Cardiovascular System; Kidney Aging and Diseases; Metabolic Syndrome; Multiple Morbidity and Comorbidity

Table 2 Most Common Oral Diabetic Agents

Type	Subtype	Process Targeted	Advantages	Disadvantages
Insulin secretagogues (can be used in monotherapy or combination therapy)	Sulfonylurea secretagogues (glyburide, glipizide, glimepiride)	Lower blood glucose by stimulating the release of insulin from the pancreas, requiring functioning β-cells in the pancreatic islets	Stimulate insulin secretion effectively associated with lower incidence of adverse events (e.g., hypoglycemia, weight gain)	Half-life quite long; stimulate insulin secretion regardless of blood glucose levels, risking hypoglycemia; cost very high
	Nonsulfonylurea secretagogues (nateglinide, repaglinide)	(Same as above)	Shorter half-lives mean more physiological increase in insulin secretion only during meal; stimulatory effect is unrelated to blood glucose level, thereby exposing patients to hypoglycemia, albeit to a lesser extent than sulfanylureas; may be useful in patients who eat at irregular times such as geriatric patients	More expensive than sulfanylureas
Incretins	Exenatide; others are being developed	Resemble the enteric hormone GLP-1 or prolong the life of GLP-1 and so stimulate insulin secretion only when blood glucose increases above the normal range	Do not expose to the risk of hypoglycemia	Very expensive; only exenatide currently approved and commercially available, although other products are in last stages of approval
Biguanides	Only metformin hydrochloride available in United States	Improve glucose tolerance, lowering basal and postprandial glucose.	Decrease hepatic glucose production and intestinal absorption of glucose; also improve peripheral insulin sensitivity; unlike sulfonylureas, do not induce hypoglycemia and hyperinsulinemia because they do not increase pancreatic insulin secretion	Lactic acidosis a serious but rare metabolic adverse effect; contraindicated in patients with renal dysfunction, congestive heart failure, metabolic acidosis, and those undergoing radiological studies with contrast material

Type	Subtype	Process Targeted	Advantages	Disadvantages
Thiazolidinediones	Rosiglitazone and pioglitazone	Bind to peroxisome proliferator-activated receptor (PPAR-γ), a transcription cofactor that modifies expression of genes that encode proteins involved in glucose and lipid homeostasis	Increase glucose uptake in skeletal muscle and adipose tissue and, to a lesser extent, decrease hepatic glucose output, enhancing the effectiveness of insulin; improve glycemic control without stimulating insulin secretion, thereby preserving β-cell function and not exposing to the risk of hypoglycemia	Expensive; may rarely involve liver failure, which may require liver transplant; liver function should be checked and monitored
α-Glucosidase inhibitors	Acarbose and miglitol	Delay glucose absorption in the small intestine, thereby reducing postprandial hyperglycemia	Safe	Very common side effects of loose stools and flatulence
Insulin therapy	Rapid-acting (T_{max} = 55 minutes): lispro, glulisine, and aspart	Controls hyperglycemic surges after meals	Compared with regular insulin, short-acting insulin analogs achieve a more physiological postprandial insulin profile and a better control of postprandial hyperglycemia	Expensive
	Short-acting (T_{max} = 1.5 to 2 hours): regular insulin	Controls hyperglycemic surges after meals	Over-the-counter, inexpensive	Worse control of postprandial hyperglycemia than short-acting analogs
	Intermediate-acting (T_{max} = 4 to 12 hours): NPH, semilente, and lente	Provides baseline insulin between meals and may provide blunted insulin peak during meal (typical use: breakfast injection for lunch glucose control)	Can be used in combination (premixed) with short-acting insulin to reduce number of daily injections (e.g., 70/30, 50/50)	Hypoglycemia if peak does not correspond to a meal; meal hyperglycemia if used alone
	Long-acting (T_{max} = 14 to 24 hours): ultralente	Provides baseline insulin throughout the day	Controls morning fasting blood glucose	Hypoglycemia with prolonged fasting; meal hyperglycemia
	Very long-acting (T_{max} > 24 hours, peakless): glargine	Provides baseline insulin throughout the day	No peak; provides physiological baseline insulin level	Expensive; risk of hypoglycemia with prolonged fasting

Sources: Adapted from Burr B, Nagi D. *Exercise and Sport in Diabetes.* New York: John Wiley; 1999; Cheta DM. *Preventing Diabetes: Theory, Practice, and New Approaches.* New York: John Wiley; 1999; Goldstein BJ, Muller-Wieland D. *Textbook of Type 2 Diabetes.* London: Martin Dunitz; 2003; Hillson R. *Practical Diabetes Care.* New York: Oxford University Press; 2002; and American Diabetes Association. 2006 clinical practice recommendations: Standards of care. Available at: www.diabetes.org/for-health-professionals-and-scientists/cpr-pda.jsp.

Further Readings and References

American Diabetes Association. 2006 clinical practice recommendations: Standards of care. Available at: www.diabetes.org/for-health-professionals-and-scientists/cpr-pda.jsp. Accessed September 12, 2006.

Burr B, Nagi D. *Exercise and Sport in Diabetes.* New York: John Wiley; 1999.

Cheta DM. *Preventing Diabetes: Theory, Practice, and New Approaches.* New York: John Wiley; 1999.

Goldstein BJ, Muller-Wieland D. *Textbook of Type 2 Diabetes.* London: Martin Dunitz; 2003.

Hillson R. *Practical Diabetes Care.* New York: Oxford University Press; 2002.

DIETARY SUPPLEMENTS

See VITAMINS, MINERALS, AND DIETARY SUPPLEMENTS

DIETARY VARIETY

Dietary variety may be described in a number of ways. The most basic definition is the number of different food or beverage items consumed in a meal, a day, or over a longer period of time such as a month or a year. In the United States, the average adult consumes approximately 17 or 18 unique food or beverage items per day; however, many of these items may be repeated over time on other days. Dietary variety can be classified into different types, including total dietary variety, variety within food groups, and sources of variety that are dense or weak in vitamins and minerals or energy. Variety can also be described on a food level (food variety) or an ingredient level (ingredient variety). It should be noted that there is no consensus among researchers on a standard definition for dietary variety. Table 1 lists and defines several examples of different classifications of dietary variety that have been described to date.

Dietary variety influences nutrient intake, with the relative amounts of specific types of variety in the diet affecting overall dietary quality. Adults who consume a greater number of micronutrient-dense foods have higher vitamin and mineral intakes. In contrast, those who consume a greater number of energy-dense foods, many which tend to be "empty calorie" sources that are low in micronutrients, have lower vitamin and mineral intakes. Several studies show that selecting a diet higher in micronutrient-dense variety is associated with reduced morbidity and mortality. However, those studies do not generally take into account micronutrient-dense variety and energy-dense variety at the same time. Therefore, whether consuming a diet lower in energy-dense variety is also associated with those variables is not known.

Dietary variety also influences caloric intake and hence body weight status. People consume approximately 25% more calories in a meal when they are served a greater variety of foods that differ in sensory properties such as flavor, texture, and appearance. For example, when sandwiches with three different fillings are served, more calories are consumed than when one sandwich type is served. The same is true for different yogurt flavors or pasta shapes. The effects of dietary variety on consumption appear to extend beyond a single meal. Adults who consume a greater variety from different food groups over several days or months consume more calories from each of those groups. However, variety may have either beneficial or detrimental effects on body weight, depending on the food group. More variety from energy-dense groups, such as sweets, snacks, condiments, entrees, and carbohydrate-based foods, is consumed by people who have higher than desirable body weights, whereas more variety from energy-weak vegetables, fruits, and legumes is consumed by people who have lower healthier body weights. Reducing energy-dense variety and increasing energy-weak and micronutrient-dense variety may help reduce excess body fat. One way commercial and popular diets may work to reduce calorie intake is by limiting food variety.

The effects of variety on caloric intake and body weight are not limited to humans. Laboratory animals (e.g., rats, cats, hamsters) also consume approximately 25% more calories and gain more weight when fed different flavored chows. The fact that variety stimulates consumption in several species suggests a

Table 1 Definitions and Examples of Different Types of Dietary Variety

Dietary Variety Type	Definition and Examples
Total dietary variety	Number of unique food and beverage items; mixed dishes and recipes are considered one item
Ingredient variety	Number of ingredients; items in mixed dishes and recipes are considered individually
Food group variety	Number of unique nutritionally important food groups from which at least one item was consumed (fruit/vegetable, dairy, grain, and meat/protein)
Micronutrient-dense variety	Number of unique food and energy-containing beverage items consumed from important sources of protein or micronutrients (e.g., fruit/vegetable-based items, dairy products, grains, nuts, legumes, mixed main and side dishes)
Micronutrient-weak variety	Number of unique food and beverage items consumed from poor sources of protein or micronutrients (e.g., high-sugar beverages, noncaloric beverages with caloric condiments added, candy, cakes, other sweets, condiments)
Energy-dense variety	Number of unique food items having a high number of calories per unit weight of food (e.g., cakes, candy, other sweets, carbohydrate-based items with > 10% calories from fat, cereals, pancakes, French fries, mixed main and side dishes)

Sources: Adapted from Roberts SB, Hajduk CL, Howarth NC, Russell R, McCrory MA. Dietary variety predicts low body mass index and inadequate macronutrient and micronutrient intakes in community-dwelling older adults. *J Gerontol Biol Sci.* 2005;60:613–621; and Yao M, McCrory MA, Ma G, et al. Relative influence of diet and physical activity on body composition in urban Chinese adults. *Am J Clin Nutr.* 2003;77:1409–1416.

Note: Each type of dietary variety should be specified in terms of a certain eating occasion or time period such as variety consumed over a meal, a day, or a month. Classifications might not be mutually exclusive.

role for dietary variety in evolution; during prehistoric times, a more varied diet would have helped to maximize calorie, vitamin, and mineral consumption during times when food was plentiful, in turn helping to maintain or minimize depletion of body stores during times of starvation.

Sensory-specific satiety is thought to be the underlying reason why variety enhances food consumption. Sensory-specific satiety refers to the observation that as a food is consumed, its palatability (taste pleasantness) decreases, whereas the palatability of unconsumed foods remains high. Thus, when only one or a few foods are available, satiation sets in more quickly than when a greater variety of foods are available. Having more flavors and textures to choose from allows the palatability of the meal to be maintained at an overall high level because when sensory-specific satiety sets in for one food, another previously uneaten food that still tastes good can be selected. Overconsumption at restaurants, buffets, potlucks, and special holiday meals, as well as underconsumption of leftovers, can be explained by sensory-specific satiety and dietary variety.

Sociodemographic factors, psychological factors, and biological factors are associated with the consumption of different amounts and types of variety. For example, people with higher incomes and more education consume greater total dietary variety as well as greater energy-weak and micronutrient-dense variety. The latter two suggest that persons of higher socioeconomic status may have better nutritional status due to selection of foods varying widely in nutrients such as fiber, protein, vitamins, and minerals.

The psychological construct called dietary disinhibition, which can be defined as overeating opportunistically, is associated with greater total dietary variety consumed. Greater dietary disinhibition, independent of other factors, is associated with higher body mass index (BMI) as well as weight gain, whereas people who lose weight become less disinhibited eaters. Potentially, dietary variety may mediate relationships between disinhibition and body weight change.

Aging is another factor that may influence how much dietary variety is consumed. Weight loss during older age can lead to frailty, serious illness, and death. This age-associated weight loss, resulting primarily from a reduction in caloric intake, may be due to both psychosocial factors and physiological factors. Psychosocial factors may include social isolation and reduced or fixed income that can result in reductions in food choices and food accessibility. Physiological factors include altered hormonal signals and reduced senses of taste and smell, both of which lead to a decline in the ability to regulate food intake. Reduced sensory input may make consumption of dietary variety less appealing, which may lead to dietary monotony and therefore weight loss and reduced intake of protein, vitamins, and minerals, all of which are especially important for maintaining health, particularly during older age. However, both older and younger adults are more likely to achieve adequate intake of these nutrients when a greater variety of micronutrient-dense foods is included in their diets.

In summary, dietary variety is one of the most important dietary factors influencing overall health. Having variety available stimulates consumption. When the relative balance of food variety is energy dense, this is likely to lead to overconsumption of calories and weight gain. When the variety of food consumed is micronutrient dense and energy weak, this is beneficial because although more calories are derived from these foods, they tend not to lead to weight gain and at the same time provide important nutrients for maintaining overall health. However, energy-dense variety can also be beneficial in extreme old age, helping to prevent or slow the rapid weight loss that often precedes death.

—Megan A. McCrory and Susan B. Roberts

See also Nutrition and Public Health; Nutrition, Malnutrition, and Feeding Issues

Further Readings and References

MacIntosh CG, Morley JE, Chapman IM. The anorexia of aging. *Nutrition.* 2000;16:983–995.

McCrory MA, Fuss PJ, McCallum JE, et al. Dietary variety within food groups: Association with energy intake and body fatness in men and women. *Am J Clin Nutr.* 1999;69:440–447.

Roberts SB, Hajduk CL, Howarth NC, Russell R, McCrory MA. Dietary variety predicts low body mass index and inadequate macronutrient and micronutrient intakes in community-dwelling older adults. *J Gerontol A Biol Sci Med Sci.* 2005;60:613–621.

Rolls BJ, Dimeo KA, Shide DJ. Age-related impairments in the regulation of food intake. *Am J Clin Nutr.* 1995;62:923–931.

Rolls BJ, Rowe EA, Rolls ET. How sensory properties of food affect human feeding behavior. *Physiol Behav.* 1982;29:409–417.

Yao M, McCrory MA, Ma G, et al. Relative influence of diet and physical activity on body composition in urban Chinese adults. *Am J Clin Nutr.* 2003;77:1409–1416.

DISABILITY AND THE DISABLEMENT PROCESS

The disablement model, a continuum leading from active pathology to impairments, to functional limitations, and ultimately to disability, is a sociomedical model designed by a sociologist for use in epidemiological and clinical research. Saad Nagi's disablement model describes how chronic and acute conditions affect functioning in specific body systems, generic physical and mental actions, and activities of daily life. The disablement model can help inform research (epidemiology of disability) and public health (prevention of disability) activities.

In the disablement model, active pathology involves the interruption of normal cellular processes and the simultaneous homeostatic efforts of the organism to regain a normal state. Active pathology can result from infection, trauma, metabolic imbalance, degenerative disease processes, or another etiology. Examples of active pathology are the cellular disturbances consistent with the onset of disease processes such as osteoarthritis, cardiomyopathy, and cerebrovascular accidents.

Impairment refers to a loss or abnormality at the tissue, organ, and body system level. Active pathology usually results in some type of impairment, but not all impairments are associated with active pathology (e.g., congenital loss or residual impairments resulting from trauma). Impairments can occur in the primary locale of the underlying pathology (e.g., muscle weakness around an osteoarthritic knee joint), but they may also occur in secondary locales (e.g., cardiopulmonary deconditioning secondary to inactivity).

Functional limitations, the distinct consequences of pathology at the level of the individual, represent restrictions in the basic performance of specific tasks and actions (e.g., walking, transfers).

Disability is defined as difficulty or limitation in performing activities in one or more domains of daily life (from personal care to hobbies) due to a health or physical problem. Disability is not a personal characteristic; instead, it is the expression of a physical or mental limitation in a social context.

Not all impairments or functional limitations precipitate disability, and similar patterns of disability may result from different types of impairments and limitations in function. Furthermore, identical types of impairments and similar functional limitations may result in different patterns of disability.

The disablement model can be illustrated with a clinical example. Two patients with rheumatoid arthritis may present with a very similar clinical profiles with moderately severe impairments such as restricted range of motion and muscle weakness. Their patterns of function may also be similar with a slow painful gait and difficulty in grasping objects. Their disability profiles, however, may be radically different. One individual may restrict or eliminate his or her outside activities, require help with all self-care activities, spend most of the time indoors watching television, and be unemployed and depressed. The other individual may fully engage in his or her social life, receive some assistance from a spouse in performing daily activities when needed, be driven to work, and be able to maintain full-time employment through workplace modification.

The Disablement Process

In their work on the disablement process, Lois M. Verbrugge and Alan M. Jette maintained Nagi's

original concepts but extended his model by specifying specific dimensions of disability and included in the model relationships among sociocultural factors (e.g., physical and social environments) and personal factors (e.g., lifestyle behaviors and attitudes) with the core disablement concepts.

Verbrugge and Jette defined disability as a broad range of role behaviors that are relevant in most people's daily lives. Five commonly applied dimensions of disability evolved from this line of scientific inquiry:

- *Basic activities of daily living (ADLs):* including behaviors such as basic personal care
- *Instrumental activities of daily living (IADLs):* including activities such as preparing meals, doing housework, managing finances, using the telephone, and shopping
- *Paid and unpaid role activities:* including occupation, parenting, grandparenting, and student roles
- *Social activities:* including attending church and other group activities and socializing with friends and relatives
- *Leisure activities:* including sport and physical recreation, reading, and distinct trips

The subdomains of disability behavior highlight the varied nature of role task behavior, from fairly basic self-care activities to advanced and complex social, work, and leisure activities.

Verbrugge and Jette's work was an attempt to attain a full sociomedical framework of disablement that they defined as the impact that chronic and acute conditions have on functioning of specific body systems and on people's abilities to act in necessary, usual, expected, and personally desired ways in their society. They coined the term *disablement process* and defined it as the dynamics of disablement; that is, the trajectory of functional consequences over time and the factors that affect their direction, pace, and pattern of change. Feedback effects are included in the disablement process to cover dysfunction spirals and secondary conditions; that is, new conditions launched by a given disablement process.

Verbrugge and Jette argued that one might analyze and explain disablement relative to three sets of variables: predisposing risk factors, intra-individual factors, and extra-individual factors. These categories of variables, which are external to the main disablement pathway, are defined as follows:

- *Risk factors* are predisposing phenomena that are present prior to the onset of the disabling event and that can affect the presence and/or severity of the disablement process. Examples include sociodemographic background, lifestyle, and biological factors.
- *Intra-individual factors* include lifestyle and behavioral changes, psychosocial attributes and coping skills, and activity accommodations made by the individual following the onset of a disabling condition.
- *Extra-individual factors* pertain to the physical context, as well as the social context, in which the disablement process occurs. Environmental factors relate to the social factors, as well as the physical environmental factors, that bear on the disablement process. These can include medical and rehabilitation services, medications and other therapeutic regimens such as exercise and physical activity, external supports available in the person's social network, and the physical environment.

The ICF Model of Disability

One of the more recent developments related to models of disability is the development of the International Classification of Functioning, Disability, and Health (ICF) by the World Health Organization in 2001. The ICF is meant to codify a classification of functioning, disability, and health to provide a unified standard international language and framework for the description of health and health-related state. In contrast to the disablement process, the ICF views the concept of disability as an umbrella term and does not provide a single way to determine disability status.

As in the disablement process, the ICF identifies three levels of human function: functioning at the level of body or body parts, the whole person, and the whole person in his or her complete environment. These levels, in turn, contain three aspects of human function: body functions and structures, activities, and participation. The term *disability* is used to denote a decrement at each level (i.e., impairment), an activity limitation, and a participation restriction.

The first component of the ICF model is *body functions and structures,* which are defined as the body's physiological functions. Body structures are organs, limbs, and their components. Impairments are body function or structure difficulties that cause significant deviation or loss.

The ICF defines the *activities* and *participation* concepts as follows: In the context of health experience, activity is an individual executing a task or an action, and activity limitations are difficulties an individual has in executing activities. Participation is participating in a life situation, and participation restrictions are difficulties an individual experiences with life situations.

The ICF framework includes two contextual factors: environmental and personal. *Environmental factors* are defined as a person's physical, social, and attitudinal environment, including subdomains of products and technology, natural environment/human-made environmental changes, support and relationships, attitudes, services, systems, and policies. *Personal factors* are the specific background of an individual's life and are composed of the individual's features that are not a part of a health condition or a health state. Personal factors include gender, race, age, other health conditions, fitness, lifestyle, habits, upbringing, coping styles, social background, past and current experience, character style, and other psychological assets.

Epidemiological Evidence

Much research has been done to identify risk factors for the onset of disability by applying the disablement model. In systematic literature reviews, the greatest strength of evidence for an increased risk of disability or functional limitation has been reported for cognitive impairment, depression, disease burden, increased or decreased body mass index, lower extremity functional limitation, low frequency of social contacts, low level of physical activity, no alcohol use compared with moderate use, poor self-perceived health, smoking, and vision impairment.

Other risk factors, usually related to different chronic diseases, include hypertension, elevated blood lipids and glucose, low bone density, and alcohol and drug misuse. Research has also shown that certain psychological and psychosocial characteristics, such as poor self-efficacy, coping strategies, depression, and social integration, predict the development of disability.

—*Alan M. Jette*

See also Activities of Daily Living and Instrumental Activities of Daily Living; Assistive Devices; Balance; Mobility; Mobility Assessment

Further Readings and References

Nagi SZ. Some conceptual issues in disability and rehabilitation. In: Sussman MB, ed. *Sociology and Rehabilitation.* Washington, DC: American Sociological Association; 1965:100–113.

Nagi SZ. Disability concepts revisited: Implications for prevention. In: Pope AM, Tarlov AR, eds. *Disability in America: Toward a National Agenda for Prevention.* Washington, DC: National Academy Press; 1991:309–327.

Verbrugge LM, Jette AM. The disablement process. *J Social Sci Med.* 1994;38:1–14.

World Health Organization. *International Classification of Functioning, Disability, and Health (ICF).* Geneva, Switzerland: WHO; 2001.

DISABILITY-FREE LIFE

See ACTIVE LIFE EXPECTANCY

DISASTERS AND TERRORISM

Natural and human-made disasters often strike with overwhelming force and little warning. In addition to occurring randomly and unpredictably, terrorist activities have a faceless enemy with malevolent intent and are usually tinged with political ramifications. Importantly, terrorism and natural disasters are ongoing threats to individuals and their communities, adding to the stress of their everyday lives. When a large-scale disaster or terrorist event occurs, every aspect of community life can be disrupted, and these experiences can affect an individual's emotional, social, physical, and environmental support system.

In the immediate aftermath of a disaster, it is normal for adults of all ages to experience myriad powerful emotional reactions, including shock, disbelief and numbness, fear and anxiety, anger and sadness, and unfamiliar feelings such as survivor guilt. Somatic symptoms (e.g., nausea, loss of appetite, headaches) are also common, as are ongoing memories and mental pictures of the disaster, sleep disturbances or nightmares, and difficulties in concentrating. Because survivors often accurately recognize the grave danger to which they were exposed during the disaster, mild to moderate acute or posttraumatic stress reactions are not uncommon.

Disasters also have immediate social consequences in that many seek to be close to friends, family, neighbors, or similarly affected others; have a desire to talk about their experiences; and want to try to help those in need. Whereas most healthy older persons will be able to prepare for, respond to, and recover from a disaster with minimal assistance, vulnerable populations of older adults may be at risk for short- and long-term negative psychological consequences. Assistance and support may be particularly important for older adults who are socially isolated, frail, physically ill, disabled, or cognitively impaired or who have histories of exposure to extreme and prolonged traumatic stressors.

Informal caregivers, such as family, neighbors, and close friends, are often first on the scene following a disaster and can be instrumental in providing emotional support and securing shelter, medical care, food, and water. During times of crisis, social support systems are critical to the well-being of older adults. Several studies have found that anticipated or perceived support (the belief that significant others care and will provide assistance if required), rather than the actual receipt of assistance, following a disaster is associated with better psychological outcomes. In addition, the degree of social embeddedness (the size, closeness, and activity level of the person's social network) is also directly related to mental health functioning. Unfortunately, these socially protective resources are particularly vulnerable to disruption and decline following a disaster. Although social support is often mobilized when an older person's life or health is threatened by a natural disaster, assistance is less available when property is damaged or destroyed, electricity and/or telephone communication is lost, and daily routines are disrupted. Members of an older adult's social support network may themselves be survivors of the same disaster. Social network members may be relocated, injured, or unable to assist because their immediate needs exceed their current resources. Compounding the situation, disruption and destruction of community services can diminish the availability of formal sources of social support such as senior center activities and meals on wheels. As a result of the need for support and services by the population at large, demand may surpass existing resources, leaving traditional networks unable to provide much needed support to older adults.

Significant deterioration of the social support system has the potential to result in adverse short- and long-term psychological consequences. To offset potential mental health problems, provisions for disaster preparation, response, and recovery need to be adequate. Social support can come from various sources, but not every type of support may be available or appropriate. For example, it is not unusual for dysfunctional family interactions to worsen during stressful circumstances. This can be particularly problematic after a disaster given research suggesting that the detrimental effects of negative social exchanges on older adults' well-being exceed the beneficial effects of positive social exchanges. Although family members are more likely than friends to provide instrumental support to older adults, in some instances family relational behaviors can have a negative impact on perceived social support. Sometimes, members of an older adult's family may feel obliged to assume a supportive role because of relational ties as opposed to a true desire to provide care. Because friendships tend to be formed voluntarily, they are not influenced by feelings of familial obligation; therefore, friends and close neighbors can be a source of assistance to older adults who need help in accomplishing disaster-related tasks. For older adults, deeper and broader social support networks play a significant role in ameliorating the negative impact of traumatic life events.

During periods when social networks are depleted or disrupted, crisis intervention workers can provide temporary support and assistance in rebuilding support systems. Steps to reestablish and strengthen support networks can include educating family members about the range of normal psychological reactions to disaster. Survivors can also be provided with the opportunity to talk about their feelings and experiences if they so desire. Offering contact with others who have experienced the same trauma can buffer the negative effects of disaster. Setting realistic expectations about the quantity and quality of family interpersonal support to be provided in the disaster's aftermath may decrease the potential for interpersonal conflict and minimize negative interactions. To the extent possible, resuming normal daily activities and maintaining social connectedness can help preserve social embeddedness and foster recovery.

Older adults typically have an extensive and varied accumulation of life experiences that affect short- and long-term vulnerability or resilience after a disaster. In addition, the nature and severity of the traumatic event, personal history and experiences, and pre-event psychological characteristics influence individuals' psychological outcomes. Age is one of many pre-disaster, within-disaster, and post-disaster risk factors that mediate the severity of adverse consequences. Although some elderly persons may be at increased risk for psychological distress after a disaster, overall older age may be protective. In comparison with younger adults, elderly persons generally assume fewer responsibilities in caring for children, parents, and employers and thus report feeling less burden after a disaster. Other factors that may account for this age group's ability to manage disaster-related stress include earlier experiences with coping and managing other similar stressful events and elderly persons' lifetimes of evaluating the effectiveness of different coping strategies. In addition, older adults appear to be less emotionally reactive to, and have fewer memories of, negative events and are more likely to focus on adaptive processes such as minimizing the threat of a stressor, strongly suggesting that individuals have a greater investment in emotion regulation as they age.

Although a body of research indicates that older adults tend to be more resilient than younger adults, persons exposed to interpersonal violence or abuse (as children or adults), Holocaust survivors, and former prisoners of war may be more vulnerable to psychological distress following a disaster. A significant trauma history can sensitize an individual to new stressors, thereby potentiating its effect. Exposure to extreme prolonged stress is believed to result in permanent developmental effects that can increase vulnerability to future traumatic events throughout the life span. In addition, encountering new negative events can reactivate distress surrounding prior life traumas.

In addition to providing survivors with water, food, shelter, and medical care, triage for mental health problems should be included in the hierarchy of basic disaster response. Early disaster mental health assessment should identify those persons at greater risk for developing acute stress disorder, posttraumatic stress disorder (PTSD), depression, and complicated bereavement and should refer them for future evaluation. However, for the majority of older adults, most disaster-related psychological distress will resolve in time without formal intervention. For those who need more than psychological first aid following a disaster, special effort may be required to overcome personal and system barriers to treatment. For example, some community-dwelling older adults may be reluctant to admit they feel overwhelmed, confused, or distressed because they fear that such an admission may lead to loss of freedom and institutionalization. Others may refuse to ask for help because of the stigma associated with mental health treatment. Some may believe that only seriously mentally ill people receive mental health services, fear that their reaction to the event is evidence of becoming demented, or perceive acceptance of psychological treatment as a sign of personal weakness.

Overcoming these barriers involves educating those at risk for adverse psychological outcomes about typical reactions to disaster and providing information about the nature of mental health intervention. However, some older adults may still be reluctant to accept assistance from government agencies or may be daunted by the amount of paperwork required to receive disaster aid. Older adults may turn to religious leaders, family members, informal social networks, and/or their personal physicians for relief from their distress. Although older persons are at low risk for mental health problems, those who do develop serious psychiatric distress may go unrecognized, remain untreated, or receive inadequate treatment following a disaster.

Crisis intervention services are now widely recognized as an effective treatment modality for emergency mental health care to individuals and groups. Guidelines published by the Centers for Disease Control and Prevention recommend that, following a traumatic event, clinicians allow persons to talk only when they are ready, validate their emotional reactions, avoid diagnostic and pathological language, and communicate "person to person" rather than "expert to victim." The challenge to mental health professionals and trained volunteers is to balance the special needs of vulnerable populations with those of others in the disaster-affected community. After a disaster, intervention should be focused on building a recovery environment that restores normalcy, returning people to their usual sources of social support.

—Lisa M. Brown, John A. Schinka,
and Roxane Cohen Silver

See also Posttraumatic Stress Disorder; Social Networks and Social Support; Stress

Further Readings and References

Brown LM, Cohen D, Kohlmaier J. Older adults: Issues in assessment and treatment. In: Bongar B, Brown LM, Beutler L, Zimbardo P, Breckenridge J, eds. *Psychology and Terrorism.* New York: Oxford University Press; in press.

Folkman S, Lazarus RS, Pimley S, Novacek J. Age differences in stress and coping processes. *Psychol Aging.* 1987;2:171–184.

Huerta F, Horton R. Coping behavior of elderly flood victims. *Gerontologist.* 1978;18:541–546.

Norris FH, Friedman MJ, Watson PJ, Byrne CM, Diaz E, Kaniasty K. 60,000 disaster victims speak: I. An empirical review of the empirical literature, 1981–2001. *Psychiatry.* 2002:65:207–239.

Phifer JF. Psychological distress and somatic symptoms after natural disaster: Differential vulnerability among older adults. *Psychol Aging.* 1990;5:412–420.

Verger P, Dab W, Lamping DL, et al. The psychological impact of terrorism: An epidemiologic study of posttraumatic stress disorder and associated factors in victims of the 1995–1996 bombings in France. *Am J Psychiatry.* 2004;161:1384–1389.

DISCLOSURE

Medical disclosure encompasses all communication that passes between patient and physician during the course of medical treatment. It begins not with what the physician discloses to the patient (diagnosis and treatment options) but rather with the medical interview in which the patient discloses the symptoms and concerns that led to the office visit. The medical interview consists of active listening to discover the reason for the patient's visit, probing for symptoms and concerns, and uncovering the meaning of these details to the patient. The medical interview begins with verbally examining the patient, continues during the physical examination, and concludes after the doctor discusses the medical condition and explains treatment options to the patient before both agree on a treatment plan.

The medical interview is the most common and best method of information gathering. Doctors have been found to make 60% to 80% of medical diagnoses based solely on the information gathered during the medical interview. Doctors with the most effective communication skills listen carefully, do not badger the patient with questions, do not interrupt, make eye contact, and indicate that they care. The patient–doctor interaction has been shown to influence several important outcome measures, including patient satisfaction, health status and well-being, treatment compliance and therapeutic interventions.

The patient–doctor encounter is a dynamic and complex process because patients and doctors talk to each other with different terms. The doctor attempts to be objective and uses medical terminology, whereas the patient uses nontechnical words to describe the subjective experience of the medical condition. As a consequence, the patient–doctor encounter may breed misunderstandings and unfulfilled agendas. On the one hand, the doctor needs to invest the time needed to establish the patient's problems; on the other hand, the patient needs to be open and honest with the doctor, providing all related information and actively seeking to understand the medical condition, tests and diagnostic procedures, and treatment options. Seeing a doctor of the same race has been considered to be a factor that may improve patient–doctor relationships, and research has found improved patient satisfaction when the patient and the doctor shared the same race; however, the level of patient-centered communication did not differ with the race of the doctor (same as or different from that of the patient).

Although little is known about the development of the doctor–patient relationship, common sense would support the notion that a long-standing relationship between the doctor and the patient offers greater value than multiple visits to many different doctors. However, in today's managed health care environment, a long patient–doctor relationship might not be possible. Past efforts to improve patient–doctor communication skills have generally focused on doctors' ability to communicate well, but recent research has examined the effect of a good patient–doctor relationship on doctors' professional and personal lives. One recent study found positive work feelings to be associated with openness with patients and attentiveness to the psychosocial aspects of care.

The likelihood of developing a good patient–doctor relationship will remain weak if the patient is passive or uninvolved. Research has shown that very few patients fully understand what their doctors have told them and that roughly half of patients leave their doctors' offices uncertain of what they are to do specifically about their health. Patients need to develop the skills to question their doctors, communicate openly and honestly about their health and well-being, and participate in the selection of treatment options presented to them.

A good patient–doctor relationship becomes crucial for the elderly because they have more contacts with doctors than do younger adults (a mean of 10 encounters per year among those 65 to 74 years of age and a mean of 15 encounters per year among those age 85 years and older). In 2003, people age 65 years and older accounted for 12% of the total U.S. population, and this age group is projected to represent nearly 20% of the total U.S. population by 2030. As America's older population grows larger, it also becomes more diverse. For example, the Latino population is growing rapidly and is projected to grow from 37 million in 2002 to 100 million by 2050. Latinos age 65 years and older are projected to be the largest ethnic minority in this age group, with the largest segment being of Mexican origin (67%). Minority patients (in particular African American, Latino, and American Indian older adults) mistrust medical research and institutions and are therefore underrepresented in clinical research studies. Cultural attitudes about one's proper attitude toward authority figures (e.g., respectful listening, pretending to understand) can also impede clear communication.

A fundamental concern of older patients is how practice requirements of short visits might negatively affect their relationship with a doctor. The elderly, with multiple chronic and acute medical conditions, cognitive deterioration, sensory impairments, reduced socialization, and financial strain, are asked to decide on complex treatment choices and make end of life planning. In 2000, 20.7% of Latinos age 65 years and older reported that they were not satisfied with the quality of the health care they received (vs. 15.6% of the U.S. population age 65 years and older who reported they were not satisfied). Relationships and the nature of communications between the patient and the doctor are likely affected by the social, cultural, economic, and educational backgrounds of those involved, resulting in a more dependent or passive role by patients who defer to doctors in medical decision making.

In general, elderly patients tend to defer to physicians; however, research has shown that the elderly with greater experience with the health care system and knowledge of health care costs related to their chronic conditions are more likely to question

doctors' treatment decisions than are younger inexperienced patients. Research through the 1980s and 1990s showed that older patients received more information, questions, and communication time concerning drugs than did younger patients, whereas younger patients received more information on treatment and preventive options. Nevertheless, older patients are less likely to inform their doctors of drug compliance issues, use of over-the-counter medications, or use of herbal remedies (complementary and alternative medicine [CAM]). This lack of disclosure puts them at higher risk for drug interactions because older patients are on more medications. The more medications they take, the more likely they are to have compliance problems and the greater potential for adverse drug interactions.

The goal of improving the older patient–doctor relationship is to promote a holistic encounter that addresses the medical and psychosocial needs and healing pathways of the patient. Older patients typically have three or more chronic medical conditions that mask one another and make treatment for any one disease more difficult. It may take two or more visits to assess the geriatric patient adequately. Setting treatment and care goals for elderly patients may be more complex because many medical problems in the elderly cannot be solved. Therefore, a good relationship between the elderly patient and the doctor is needed for balanced and realistic goal setting. The doctor must be able to recognize when treatment may no longer be justified and must assist the patient and the patient's family or designated health proxy with end of life decisions.

Cultural competence training is becoming an integral part of the training of doctors. Cultural beliefs about how "bad news" should be delivered is especially important. In some cultures, the expectation is that a family member or close friend should be given the information, which they then disclose to the patient at a culturally appropriate time and place. In a medical community that stresses confidentiality of patient information, such expectations can be difficult to meet. Other factors, such as stress associated with immigrant or refugee experience, may change perceptions of health or health behavior. In one study,

Ethiopian refugees who fled to the United Kingdom because of war found that their health worsened because of housing problems, racial strife, and other new social challenges. Unfamiliarity with medical terminology or nuances of English can also impede communication.

Doctors need to be taught effective communication skills such as not badgering patients with questions, interrupting patients as infrequently as possible, looking patients in the eyes, and encouraging patients to participate in decision making. Minority patients should be encouraged to bring advocates or family members to their doctors' offices to be translators or advocates for the patients during treatment planning, which may improve their quality of care. Doctors must not forget the effective strategies to enhance communication during the patient–doctor encounter—using a well-lit room, minimizing noise and interruptions, carefully introduce oneself to establish a friendly relationship, facing the patient directly, sitting at eye level, addressing the patient by his or her last name, speaking slowly in a deep tone, inquiring about hearing deficits (and adjusting the volume of one's voice accordingly), writing questions in large print if necessary, allowing sufficient time for the patient to answer, and touching the patient gently on the hand, arm, or shoulder during conversation.

—*Jose A. Loera*

See also Geriatric Assessment; Instruments; Multiple Morbidity and Comorbidity; Polypharmacy

Further Readings and References

Cooper LA, Roter DL, Johnson RL, Ford DE, Steinwachs DM, Powe NR. Patient-centered communication ratings of care, and concordance of patient and physician race. *Ann Intern Med.* 2003;139:907–915.

Kaplan SH, Gandek B, Greenfield S, Rogers W, Ware JE. Patient and visit characteristics related to physicians' participatory decision-making style: Results from the Medical Outcome Study. *Med Care.* 1995;33:1176–1187.

Williams ES, Skinner AC. Outcomes of physician job satisfaction: A narrative review, implications, and directions for future research. *Health Care Manage Rev.* 2003;28:119–139.

DISEASE PREVENTION

See HEALTH PROMOTION AND DISEASE PREVENTION

DIVORCE

See MARITAL STATUS

DRIVING

Driving a motor vehicle is one of the most powerful statements of independence in Western societies. This is especially the case in the United States, where even urban distances may be great and public transportation may be scarce. On the other side, statistics pertinent to older drivers have been heavily publicized, showing that drivers age 65 years and older have a higher fatality rate per mile driven than does any other age group except drivers under 25 years of age. Consequently, the topic of retiring from driving is a source of considerable apprehension for elders, their families, health care providers, and society at large.

Age-related disabilities most likely to affect driving skills involve eyesight, cognition, and neuromuscular coordination and strength. In addition, a variety of medications commonly used by older individuals may jeopardize safe driving.

Most elderly drivers are aware of their limitations and progressively restrict their driving to daylight conditions and familiar surroundings while avoiding rush hours and high-traffic roads. Older drivers are also more likely to wear safety belts and less likely to speed, tailgate, or consume alcohol prior to driving. When fatalities do occur, they are the most likely victims. Motor vehicle accidents are the leading cause of accidental death for individuals 65 to 74 years of age and are the second most common cause of accidental death (after falls) for individuals age 75 years and older. The fatality rate for drivers age 85 years and older is nine times higher than that for drivers 25 to 69 years of age.

With the aging of the population, it is projected that older drivers will represent 20% of the driving population by 2020, so that both consumers (American Association of Retired Persons [AARP]) and government organizations are joining forces to try to limit the risks posed by older drivers without unnecessarily constricting their privileges.

The American Medical Association (AMA) and the National Highway Traffic Safety Administration (NHTSA) recently conducted an extensive review of the issue of older drivers' safety and suggested an office procedure to identify individuals at risk that can be performed in any primary care setting, namely the Assessment of Driving-Related Skills (ADReS), as noted in the *Physician's Guide to Assessing and Counseling Older Drivers.*

Visual acuity is measured with a Snellen chart, and visual fields are measured by confrontation. Relevant cognitive skills are measured by trail making and clock drawing. Motor function is measured by a rapid-pace walk and determination of range of motion of the neck, shoulders, elbows, fingers, and ankle.

The clinical assessment should also address conditions that predispose to altered mental status, near syncope, or syncope before an accident actually occurs. These include seizures, transient ischemic attacks, strokes, cardiac arrhythmias, diabetes, sleep apnea, use of certain psychotropic medications, opioid analgesics, sedating antihistamines, and muscle relaxants.

The first purpose in assessing driving safety is identification of conditions amenable to treatment and rehabilitation. In addition, vehicles can be modified to accommodate the disabilities of the individual. Retiring from driving should be recommended only for conditions that are not amenable to restorative interventions. Alternative modes of transportation should be available.

When unsafe older drivers resist the recommendation to undergo rehabilitation or to retire from driving, it is important to identify the specific reasons and to try to compensate with individualized interventions. If this also fails, reporting to state authorities becomes a consideration

Most, but not all, states encourage reporting of unsafe drivers by physicians and offer immunity for this breach of confidentiality. Also, physicians have been named in lawsuits about accidents involving drivers considered to be unsafe because of health reasons. Ethical principles, however, suggest that no report be done before the unsafe older driver has been counseled and warned adequately. Family involvement is obviously desirable if the patient's consent to elicit it can be obtained. If decision-making capacity is in question and no family members are available to deal with the situation, a court decision may be necessary.

The occurrence of an accident is frequently what prompts patients, families, and public officials to consider driving restrictions, but aging individuals themselves may wonder whether they are still fit to drive. A self-assessment tool is included in the AMA/NHTSA guide. The AARP and the American Automobile Association (AAA) offer refresher courses on traffic regulations. Psychologists and rehabilitation specialists can offer paper-and-pencil tests, but probably the most predictable test of driving fitness is road testing.

Unfortunately, self-rated performance does not appear to be a good predictor of actual driving skills.

—*Claudia Beghé*

See also Activities of Daily Living and Instrumental Activities of Daily Living; Geriatric Assessment; Mental Status Assessment; Mobility; Mobility Assessment

Further Reading and Reference

Wang CC, Kosinski CJ, Schwartzberg JG, Shanklin AV. *Physician's Guide to Assessing and Counseling Older Drivers.* Washington, DC: National Highway Traffic Safety Administration; 2003.

DRUG–DISEASE INTERACTIONS

A drug–disease interaction occurs when an administered drug exacerbates an underlying disease in a patient. Drug–disease interactions are one type of inappropriate prescribing. However, drug–disease interactions can be a potential result of both inappropriate and appropriate medication use. Table 1 provides an abbreviated list of potential drug–disease interactions.

Table 1   Examples of Potential Drug–Disease Interactions

Congestive heart failure (systolic dysfunction)
- First-generation calcium channel blockers
  Type 1A antiarrhythmics

Chronic obstructive pulmonary disease
- Noncardioselective β-blockers
  Sedative hypnotics

Arrhythmias
- Tricyclic antidepressants

Chronic renal failure
- Non-aspirin, nonsteroidal anti-inflammatory drugs

Parkinson's disease
- Acetylcholinesterase inhibitors
- Antipsychotics (except clozapine and quetiapine)
- Metoclopramide

Diabetes
- Atypical antipsychotics
- β-Blockers
- Corticosteroids
- Thiazide diuretics

Depression
- α-Blockers
- Barbiturates
- Corticosteroids
- Digoxin
- Lipophilic β-blocker benzodiazepines
- Water-soluble β-blockers

Benign prostatic hyperplasia
- Anticholinergics
- Bethanechol
- Opioid analgesics
- Pseudoephedrine
- Skeletal muscle relaxants
- Tricyclic antidepressants

Hypertension
- Central nervous system stimulants
- Non-aspirin, nonsteroidal anti-inflammatory drugs
- Pseudoephedrine

Falls
- Conventional antipsychotic benzodiazepines
- Sedative hypnotics
- Selective serotonin reuptake inhibitors
- Tricyclic antidepressants

Constipation
- Anticholinergics
- Calcium channel blockers
- Iron supplements
- Opioid analgesics
- Tricyclic antidepressants

Heart block
- Digoxin
- Tricyclic antidepressants

Peptic ulcer disease
- Aspirin
- Corticosteroids
- Non-aspirin, nonsteroidal anti-inflammatory drugs
- Potassium supplements

Peripheral vascular disease/Raynaud's
- β-Blockers

Urge incontinence
- Acetylcholinesterase inhibitors
- β-Blockers
- Bethanechol
- Diuretics
- Lithium
- Selective serotonin reuptake inhibitors

Stress incontinence
- α-Blockers
- Anticholinergics
- Conventional antipsychotics
- Long $t_{1/2}$ benzodiazepines
- Tricyclic antidepressants

Source: Lindblad CI, Hanlon JT, Gross CR, et al. Clinically serious drug–disease interactions in the elderly: Opinion of a consensus panel. Unpublished poster, 2005.

Epidemiology

The elderly are well known to be a small section of the population, yet they consume at least one third of prescription medications in the United States. The elderly also often have multiple comorbidities that lead to their increased drug use. An increase in the number of medications increases the risk of a drug–disease interaction in the elderly. Furthermore, as people age, physiological changes in their bodies decrease their ability to compensate for drug-related injury. The combination of increased medications and decreased homeostatic reserve is magnified in those patients considered to be frail or at increased risk (e.g., low body weight, age 85 years and older, decreased renal function, use of narrow therapeutic range drugs, history of prior adverse drug reaction).

Research on drug–disease interactions is just beginning to commence. Multiple studies have documented that approximately 6% to 30% of elderly patients have evidence of one or more drug–disease interactions. The prevalence of drug–disease interactions has been difficult to measure because we do not have a single source of information about drugs that may exacerbate diseases. The most commonly used list of inappropriate medications is Beer's criteria. Beer's criteria contain only a subset of all possible drug–disease interactions. A thorough review of the literature recently identified more than 60 possible drug–disease interactions. Furthermore, little overlap exists between studies examining drug–disease interactions, and guidelines differ on severity and prevalence. Despite the relatively high prevalence of drug–disease interactions, there is a paucity of information on their association with health outcomes. Inappropriate prescribing, which includes drug–disease interactions, may increase hospitalizations and mortality. Risk factors for drug–disease interactions include, but are not limited to, advanced age, being married, multiple medication use, and comorbidities. Finally, poorer health has been associated with increased use of inappropriate medications that may include medications with the potential to cause a drug–disease interaction.

Interventions

Pharmacists can play a major role in identifying potential drug–disease interactions in the elderly. Our lack of a single source to identify common drug–disease interactions (only drug–drug interactions) underscores the need to examine each patient closely and determine any risks associated with his or her medications. Also, the importance of asking about which nonprescription medications are used cannot be overstressed. One third of all medications used by the ambulatory elderly are sold without prescriptions. Health care professionals should also inquire about the use of dietary supplements, including vitamins and herbal agents. Furthermore, the appropriateness of each prescribed medication should be assessed using a variety of methods. If the patient's medical history and medication list are not screened, a drug–disease interaction may be more likely to occur. Interventions could be targeted for community-dwelling elderly because they often do not have the benefits of regular medication reviews, as do patients in nursing home or hospital settings.

Recommendations

Ethics plays a major role in drug–disease interactions. Some patients may require a medication with the potential to exacerbate an underlying disease, but the morbidity- or mortality-reducing benefits of the medication might well outweigh the risk of the drug–disease interaction. The patient needs to be informed of the concerns and involved in the decisions if possible. The patient may just require closer monitoring. Another possible way to prevent drug–disease interactions involves technology. Once a list of drug–disease interactions has been defined, each can be programmed in and evaluated at the time of prescribing using automated alerts and other warning systems. A solution may also lie in comprehensive geriatric assessment that involves a multidisciplinary team providing care for an elderly patient. The team approach can help increase awareness with the patient and other health care professionals. Finally, clinicians need to decide on reasonable endpoints for each patient after comorbidities, functional status, and life expectancy are taken into consideration.

—Catherine I. Lindblad

See also Adverse Drug Reactions; Age-Related Changes in Pharmacokinetics and Pharmacodynamics; Drug–Drug Interactions; Inappropriate Prescribing; Medication Adherence; Medication Errors; Polypharmacy

Further Readings and References

Food and Drug Administration/Center for Drug Evaluation and Research. Preventable adverse drug reactions: A focus on drug interactions. Available at: www.fda.gov/cder/drug/drugReactions. Accessed September 12, 2006.

Lindblad CI, Artz MB, Pieper CF, et al. Potential drug–disease interactions in frail, hospitalized elderly veterans. *Ann Pharmacother.* 2005;39:412–417.

Merck. Disease interactions. Available at: www.merck.com/mmhe/sec02/ch013/ch013f.html. Accessed September 12, 2006.

DRUG–DRUG INTERACTIONS

Drug–drug interactions can be defined as the effect that the administration of one medication has on another drug. The two major types of drug–drug interactions are *pharmacokinetic interactions,* where drug absorption, distribution, metabolism, and excretion are affected, and *pharmacodynamic interactions,* where pharmacological effect is altered.

Epidemiology

Drug–drug pharmacokinetic interactions most likely to be clinically significant are those that involve (a) inhibition or induction of metabolism of narrow therapeutic range drugs or (b) inhibition of their renal clearance. Drug–drug pharmacodynamic interactions can also be clinically important in older adults, but they are understudied. Especially understudied is the overall burden of taking multiple different drugs that share similar pharmacological effects and their impact on geriatric syndromes.

The incidence of potential drug–drug interactions ranges from 2% to 17% of all prescriptions. These drug–drug interactions occur in 6% to 42% of elderly patients. Fortunately, the incidence of clinically significant drug–drug interactions that result in adverse health outcomes is low in the elderly.

Interventions to Prevent or Manage Drug–Drug Interactions

A number of different approaches can be taken to prevent or manage drug–drug interactions. Software programs available to prescribers and dispensers of medications help screen for potential drug interactions. However, there is little agreement across sources, and there are many false-positive alerts. Also, complete and accurate lists of medications taken by older patients are difficult to keep up to date. Therefore, health professionals should encourage patients to bring all prescription, over-the-counter, and dietary supplements to every health care encounter so that a complete listing of drugs can be established. Clinicians should consider avoiding the new prescribing of narrow therapeutic range drugs when equally effective alternatives are available. For those patients already taking a narrow therapeutic range drug, providers should screen for drug–drug interactions when adding a new drug to the regimen. For those few instances when a drug–drug interaction cannot be avoided, providers should adjust doses and/or dosage intervals for affected medication and monitor the patients closely.

Recommendations

Consensus lists of clinically important drug–drug interactions for older adults should be established. Once they are established, drug interaction software programs must use these consensus lists so that there can be concordance between screening by electronic prescribing software and screening by pharmacy software.

—Joseph T. Hanlon

See also Adverse Drug Reactions; Age-Related Changes in Pharmacokinetics and Pharmacodynamics; Drug–Disease Interactions; Inappropriate Prescribing; Medication Adherence; Medication Errors; Polypharmacy

Further Readings and References

Indiana University Department of Medicine. Drug interactions. Available at: www.drug-interactions.com. Accessed September 12, 2006.

Malone DC, Abarca J, Hansten PD, et al. Identification of serious drug–drug interactions: Results of the partnership to prevent drug–drug interactions. *J Am Pharm Assoc.* 2004;44:142–151.

Seymour RM, Routledge PA. Important drug–drug interactions in the elderly. *Drugs Aging.* 1998;12: 485–494.

DRUG UNDERUSE

Drug underuse, or undermedication, is defined as the omission of drug therapy that is indicated for the treatment or prevention of a disease or condition. The consequence of drug underuse in the care of an older adult may include uncontrolled symptoms, such as pain and dyspnea, which decrease the quality of life. Underuse may also have a significant relationship with negative health outcomes in the elderly, including functional disability, increased health services use, and death.

Measurement

The Assessment of Underutilization of Medication (AOU) instrument is a systematic method to measure drug underuse. The AOU includes a screening question and a 3-point rating system of no omission, marginal admission, or omission based on a modification of the work developed by Helene L. Lipton and colleagues. To perform the assessment, two clinical evaluators independently review pertinent clinical information, including the relevant problem list of active disease states and symptoms, and the active list of prescribed medications at a particular time point. The evaluators then determine whether an omission of a drug treatment for a condition or symptom from the patient's problem list exists. This instrument has demonstrated good interrater reliability.

Epidemiology

A number of studies have documented drug underuse in older adults. Some studies have evaluated the complete medication regimen, whereas other investigators have studied specific diseases or conditions such as hypertension and depression. One study found that lack of physician prescribing accounted for one or more necessary drugs being omitted from 55% of 236 ambulatory elders. The underuse of aspirin, angiotensin-converting enzyme (ACE) inhibitors, β-blockers, 3-hydroxy-3-methyl-glutaryl-coenzyme A reductase (HMG-CoA reductase) inhibitors, and warfarin in older adults has been well recognized. Unfortunately, between 1990 and 2002, the rate of use of ACE inhibitors for congestive heart failure, β-blockers and aspirin for coronary artery disease, and warfarin for atrial fibrillation remained consistently below 60%. An investigation showed that for patients age 65 years and older, 21% received a β-blocker after hospital discharge for an acute myocardial infarction (MI). Patients 75 to 84 years of age and those age 85 years and older were 14% and 44% less likely, respectively, than those 65 to 74 years of age to receive a β-blocker post-MI. Underuse of cardiac drugs with proven benefits may worsen outcomes and increase morbidity and mortality among the elderly. Moreover, a study conducted in community-dwelling elders found that for patients age 65 years and older, certain chronic medical diseases (e.g., hyperlipidemia, arthritis) were undertreated in the presence of concurrent diabetes mellitus, pulmonary emphysema, or psychotic syndromes.

Interventions to Reduce Drug Underuse

Medications may be withheld from older adults for different reasons such as concern for increased risk of adverse effects, invalid contraindications, and lack of literature supporting optimal dosing in the elderly population. A number of approaches to improve medication prescribing, including drug underuse, have been examined. These approaches include health services intervention trials involving clinical pharmacy activities and multidisciplinary geriatric team care approaches.

Recommendations

At every medical encounter, it is necessary to review and evaluate an older adult's medication regimen. The clinician should determine the appropriateness of each and every medication and should also determine whether there is an omission of a needed drug for an established disease or condition. Further research is needed to develop better measures and predictors for drug underuse. In the future, computer systems with decision support informatics may improve medication prescribing and reduce drug underuse.

—Christine M. Ruby

See also Adverse Drug Reactions; Age-Related Changes in Pharmacokinetics and Pharmacodynamics; Drug–Drug Interactions; Inappropriate Prescribing; Polypharmacy

Further Readings and References

Fulda TR, Soumerai SB, Lipton HL. Computer-based drug-utilization review. *N Engl J Med.* 1995;333:1290–1291.

Malone DC, Hutchins DS, Haupert H, et al. Assessment of potential drug–drug interactions with a prescription claims database. *Am J Health Syst Pharm.* 2005;62:1983–1991.

Soumerai SB. Benefits and risks of increasing restrictions on access to costly drugs in Medicaid. *Health Aff.* 2004;23:135–146.

DUKE LONGITUDINAL STUDIES

The Duke Longitudinal Studies of Aging, initiated in 1955, consist of two separate studies. The first longitudinal study began in 1955 with 271 persons 60 to 90 years of age. The participants were not a probability sample but rather were selected from a pool of volunteers who lived in Durham, North Carolina. Each panelist came to the Duke Medical Center for a 2-day series of medical, psychiatric, psychological, and social examinations. The examinations were repeated periodically until 1996.

The second longitudinal study, also known as the Adaptation Study, began in 1968 with 502 persons 46 to 70 years of age. These panelists were a probability sample of members of the local health insurance association stratified by age and sex. The study was designed so that at the end of 5 years, there would remain approximately 40 persons in each of 10 5-year age–sex cohorts. This design makes possible various kinds of cross-sequential analyses to separate the effects of age, period, and cohort.

Purposes

The studies focused on "normal aging" in two senses: healthy aging and typical aging. Those persons studied were relatively healthy in that most were ambulatory community residents who were willing and able to come to the Duke Medical Center for tests and examination. The studies focused on more common or typical patterns and problems of aging rather than on abnormalities. The goal was to help distinguish between normal processes of aging and those that may accompany aging because of accident, stress, maladjustment, or disuse.

A second purpose was to use the longitudinal method of repeated observations over time—the best way to measure changes accurately—and the effect of one kind of change on another kind of change. The third purpose was to do as much interdisciplinary analysis as possible.

Themes

The five volumes reporting the results of these studies contain more than 100 specific findings. However, four general themes tie together the findings from several substantive areas.

1. *Declining health and physical function.* This is the typical pattern of normal aging in most areas.

2. *Exceptions to physical decline.* Substantial minorities show no decline and may even have improvement in sexual activity, cardiovascular function, hypertension, depression, health ratings, and so on.

3. *Little or no decline in social and psychological function.* Intelligence, as measured by the usual tests, shows much less decline over time than cross-sectional studies imply. Older adults also maintain their social contacts and do not disengage from their social networks.

4. *Wide variations in aging patterns.* Individual variation tends to persist or increase with aging.

In summary, the Duke Longitudinal Studies found that normal aging includes many patterns of change, including stability and even improvement.

—*Erdman B. Palmore*

See also Longitudinal Research; Longitudinal Study of Aging

Further Readings and References

Busse EW, Maddox GL. *The Duke Longitudinal Studies of Normal Aging, 1955–1980.* New York: Springer; 1985.

Palmore E, Nowlin J, Wang H. Predictors of function among the old-old. *J Gerontol.* 1985;40:244–250.

EAR DISEASES

Hearing loss, a major functional disability for many in the geriatric cohort, is associated with increased social isolation, embarrassment, and depression. It is well known that communication is vital for maintenance of personal relationships, physical mobility, and quality of life. For the elderly, hearing loss may present a significant barrier to initiating and maintaining communication. In addition to the loss of loved ones and gradual physical impairments, sensory loss may encourage an elderly individual to withdraw from societal involvement. Prompt identification of hearing loss, accurate testing, and appropriate treatment are essential in optimizing appropriate medical care.

Prevalence

The definition of hearing impairment varies within the otolaryngology community. Some sources consider an elevation of 20 decibels above the hearing threshold to define hearing loss, whereas others use 26 decibels as the criterion. The current average is 25 decibels above the hearing threshold in the poorer ear. For noninstitutionalized elderly, the prevalence of hearing impairment varies from 30% to 83%. In 1986, the National Center for Health Statistics stated that hearing impairment was the fourth most prevalent condition in the elderly. In 2003, it was the most prevalent chronic condition among males over 65 years of age and was the third most prevalent condition for males and females combined. Current estimates of hearing impairment among the geriatric cohort are 56% of persons 65 to 69 years of age and 89% of persons older than 85 years of age.

In 2003, of 28 million hearing-impaired individuals, 75% were over 55 years of age. It is well accepted that men experience a higher rate of hearing impairment than do women, especially in higher frequencies. In 1990, George Gates and colleagues described three factors in addition to genetic predisposition associated with presbycusis (age-related hearing loss): (1) intrinsic damage and age-related degeneration, (2) lifetime occupational and recreational noise exposure, and (3) chronic diseases, ototoxic medications, and diet. With age, the accumulation of these factors is likely to result in progressive hearing loss.

Age-Related Changes

The outer ear includes the pinna and external canal. Earlobes and creases grow with age. The pinna and external meatus lose elasticity and muscle tonicity, leading to thinning and fragility. The pinna is often a site for squamous and basal cell carcinomas. In fact, 90% of squamous cell carcinomas in older adults occur on the face or ears. Cerumen production decreases from diminished gland activity.

The middle ear is a mediator to the inner ear. It extends from the tympanic membrane to the cochlea, including the epitympanic recess and bony structures such as the stapes, malleus, and incus. It linearly transmits signals up to 130 decibels to the cochlea and raises the pressure by 25 to 30 decibels to amplify sound for adequate interpretation by the cochlea. With age, the tympanic membrane stiffens and the tensor tympani and stapedius muscles lose their elasticity. Arthritis appears to result in degeneration of the incudomalleal and incudostapedial ossicle joints. Despite these middle-ear changes, audiologic studies have shown minimal effect on hearing. The middle ear's amplification and transmittal functions appear not to be affected by age.

Most hearing loss with age occurs in the inner ear. The inner ear includes the cochlea and organ of Corti. The auditory nerve has approximately 30,000 neurons connecting the sensory cells to the cochlear nucleus. In 1954, H. F. Schuknecht found a decrease in the number of auditory neurons and degeneration with age that he termed *presbycusis*. He defined four types of presbycusis that are still used today in audiology terminology: sensory, neural, strial, and cochlear.

Sensory presbycusis is characterized by degeneration of the organ of Corti. The cochlea experiences loss of outer and inner hair cells in the organ of Corti and neural degeneration. Cell loss begins at the cochlear base and proceeds to the outer hair cells, resulting in high-frequency hearing loss. In 1993, Schuknecht reviewed hundreds of human temporal bones and concluded that, among the four types of presbycusis, sensory cell loss is the least significant type of loss. There has been evidence in animal models that reactive oxygen metabolites (ROMs) contribute to sensory presbycusis. Physiologically, ROMs can damage mitochondrial DNA (mtDNA), resulting in mtDNA deletions. Research studies have shown that rats fed with Vitamins E and C had better hearing and fewer mtDNA deletions than did controls. Therefore, nutritional intake may prove to be therapeutic in sensory presbycusis.

Neural presbycusis occurs when cochlear neurons degenerate, a process that begins before 20 years of age. Spiral ganglion cell loss occurs in all cochlear regions. At least 20% to 30% of spiral ganglion loss is needed for audiometrically detectable hearing loss.

Strial presbycusis is the most common form of presbycusis. It occurs with atrophy of the stria vascularis, resulting in diminished vascular supply to the cochlea. The atrophy begins in the base of the cochlea and extends to the mid-cochlea with progression of age. The stria vascularis functions as the power source of the cochlea. It generates electrochemical gradients and regulates ion homeostasis. The atrophy results in diminished adenosine triphosphatase (ATPase) function and reduced endocochlear potential (EP). For example, a 25% to 50% viability of the stria in rats reduced the EP from the normal 80 to 90 mV to 60 mV. Auditory nerve function also diminishes with age. Hair cell loss is mild with strial presbycusis.

Cochlear presbycusis is characterized by spiral ligament atrophy and basilar membrane stiffening. Spiral ligament atrophy begins during childhood but is noticed during adulthood when hearing loss becomes apparent. The atrophy begins in the cochlear apex, where fibrocytes lose attachment to the basilar membrane. As the ligament shrinks, the cochlear duct configuration may be altered and ultimately the basilar membrane may separate from the lateral wall.

There are several age-related changes to the central nervous system from the cochlear nucleus to the auditory cortex. Diffuse neuronal degeneration with neuronal and dendrite loss is seen with increasing age. Due to the wide interindividual variation, it is difficult to localize specific changes correlating with clinical hearing loss. It is postulated that the majority of age-related changes occur in the superior temporal gyrus of the auditory cortex. Speech discrimination also diminishes with age. The integration of several environmental and cognitive factors for proper speech discrimination, including background noise, degree of cognitive impairment, and tone variations, vary substantially from the quiet testing conditions of a laboratory or an audiogram clinic. Therefore, using an audiogram as the sole measure of hearing competency is often inadequate.

Diagnosis of Presbycusis

Symptomatically, patients often complain of a bilateral, symmetric, high-frequency hearing loss. It usually is a gradual loss with accelerating progression as one ages. When seeing a patient with a complaint of presbycusis, it is essential to perform a thorough history. Functional assessments, including functional limitations, affect activities of daily living (ADLs) and instrumental activities of daily living (IADLs), and physical impairments should be addressed. A thorough drug history, including the use of prescription, over-the-counter, and herbal medications, should be performed with an emphasis on ototoxic medications. Self-assessment scales, such as the Hearing Handicap Inventory in the Elderly (HHIE) scale, can also be used. The HHIE uses a self-report methodology with a series of statements probing social and emotional responses to hearing impairment using a yes/no/sometimes format.

On physical exam, an otoscopic exam should be performed to assess for cerumen impaction or collapsed tympanic membrane. In the office, tuning forks can be used when the deficit is at least 25 decibels to roughly gauge whether presbycusis is a conduction or sensorineural deficit. Clinically, it is optimal to use the 512-hertz tuning fork because forks of lower frequencies may produce a tactile vibration as opposed to a heard vibration. A fork can be used to distinguish between conductive and sensorineural hearing loss. The tuning fork should be activated by tapping on the elbow or the knuckle. Tables and chairs should not be used because they can produce a higher overtone that will interfere with the results.

Air conduction measures the ability of airborne sound waves to be transmitted along the external canal to the tympanic membrane and the middle ear. Air conduction is tested by placing the fork close to the external canal with the broad side of one of the prongs facing the ear. One should avoid placing the prongs parallel to the side of the ear because this may produce an auditory "dead spot" where the tones are not heard.

Bone conduction measures the ability of the inner ear and auditory nerve to receive and process sound. The handle of the fork is placed directly on the skull for the fork vibrations to be placed directly to the inner ear. The handle may also be placed on the mastoid bone, forehead, or closed mandible. It is important to mask the input from the opposite ear because this can falsely elevate the frequency heard and skew the diagnosis. The patient can distract the opposite ear by rubbing paper over it while the examiner is using the fork on the other ear.

When a fork is placed outside of the ears and a hearing loss is appreciated, the Rinne and Weber tests need to be performed. They are done to differentiate between conduction and sensorineural deficits. For the Rinne test, after the fork is struck, the patient is asked whether the fork seems to be louder when held behind the ear, directly on the mastoid, or directly next to the ear. Each location should be held for about 1 second. The fork should be moved back and forth and should be struck again if needed until the patient can differentiate a difference. If the fork vibrations are louder behind the ear (bone conduction) than next to the ear (air conduction), there is a conductive hearing loss. This results from an obstruction of the sound waves reaching the inner ear such as cerumen or otosclerosis.

To confirm the Rinne test findings, a Weber test is done. After striking the fork, it is placed on the forehead and the patient is asked in which ear the sound is louder. With conductive hearing loss, it will sound louder in the poorer ear. This is in contrast to sensorineural loss, which will sound louder in the better ear. Tuning forks have their limitations, and audiometric tests have gradually replaced the forks. Audiometric tests are readily available and are usually done by consultants.

Management

Hearing loss management has changed remarkably during recent decades. One study during the 1960s found that few nursing homes could accommodate aging deaf residents. Often, residents were left struggling in nursing homes after leaving their deaf communities. There was little federal advocacy and a need for improved awareness and education about hearing impairments in the elderly.

Today, much research is being conducted to maximize functional ability among the hearing impaired. The field of audiology is growing, and more nursing homes offer audiology services. Rehabilitation programs are being created to assist the hearing impaired. It is found that a patient's response to a rehabilitation program depends on several factors, including personality, age, gender, personal health, and perception of the hearing impairment. Participation with a spouse or peer significantly reduces the self-perception of hearing loss. This reinforces the need for family and peer involvement to maximize therapy effectiveness.

Hearing devices are available in varying sizes and prices. An audiologist can assist in recommending the appropriate device, depending on the degree of impairment. Medicare benefits do not cover the cost of hearing aids. The Veterans Administration does cover the cost of the initial set of hearing aids. Health providers should routinely screen for hearing impairment and provide adequate treatment to optimize patients' quality of life.

—*Shelley B. Bhattacharya*

See also Hearing; Quality of Life

Further Readings and References

Gates G, Cooper J, Kannel W, Miller N. Hearing in the elderly: The Framingham cohort, 1983–1985: I. Basic audiometric test results. *Ear Hear.* 1990;11:247–256.

Hazzard W, Blass J, Halter J, Ouslander J, Tinetti M. *Principles of Geriatric Medicine and Gerontology.* 5th ed. New York: McGraw-Hill; 2003.

Kricos P, Lesner S, eds. *Hearing Care for the Older Adult: Audiologic Rehabilitation.* Boston: Butterworth–Heinemann; 1995.

Maurer JF, Rupp RR. *Hearing and Aging: Tactics for Intervention.* New York: Grune & Stratton; 1979.

Sataloff RT, Sataloff J. *Occupational Hearing Loss.* 2nd ed. New York: Marcel Dekker; 1993.

Schuknecht HF. Ear, nose, and throat emergencies. *Med Clin N Am.* 1954;1:241–263.

Schuknecht HF, Gacek MR. Cochlear pathology in presbycusis. *Ann Otol Rhinol Laryngol.* 1993;102:1–16.

Schulte BA, Schmiedt RA. Lateral wall Na,K-ATPase and endocochlear potentials decline with age in quiet-reared gerbils. *Hearing Res.* 1992;61:35–46.

Taylor KS. Effects of group composition in audiologic rehabilitation programs for hearing impaired elderly. *Audiology Online* [serial online]. October 2003. Available at: www.audiologyonline.com/articles/arc_disp.asp?article_id=498. Accessed September 13, 2006.

Weinstein, B. *Geriatric Audiology.* New York: Thieme Medical; 2000.

EARLY ADVERSITY AND LATE-LIFE HEALTH

There is growing recognition that early socioeconomic adversity can have long-term consequences for mental and physical health. Adverse life circumstances during childhood may initiate and shape problematic trajectories of poor mental and physical health. However, the health consequences of childhood adversity tend to emerge during later years. Although youths have lower rates of serious illnesses than do adults, an emerging pattern of socioeconomic health inequalities becomes evident by late adolescence and continues into adulthood. Some youths are capable of avoiding the influence of early adversities, thereby redirecting adverse health trajectories. For others, however, adverse mental and physical health trajectories continue and potentially disrupt the successful transition to adulthood as youths become more vulnerable to adult health problems by their selection into adverse life circumstances. That is, early adversities appear to compound across the life course to produce cumulative consequences from one stage of life to another. Recent research suggests that the effects of early adversity on health persist across the life span, with diminished strength of the association between early adversity and health evident only during later old age.

Early Adversity

The socioeconomic characteristics of one's family of origin share strong links with the early adverse circumstances of an individual. Social stress research clearly documents that people of lower socioeconomic status (SES) experience more stressful events and circumstances than do people of higher social status. This is particularly evident among lower SES parents when considering family stressful events. Lower SES parents are also disadvantaged in the quality and quantity of psychological and social resources they can rely on to cope with family adversity. Thus, for lower SES parents, the opportunity to control family stressful events and circumstances or to protect children from the influence of such circumstances is limited.

Lower family income often serves as a marker for early family adversity. Research shows that parents who work in low-paid employment are the most materially disadvantaged in terms of income. They also experience risk of exposure to an array of related stresses such as higher job and financial insecurity and more work instability. Thus, children from low-income families may face reduced access to housing, proper sanitation, vehicles, household equipment, food, and health insurance. In addition, these children often live in disadvantaged communities that offer poor health, educational, recreational, and social services.

Poor parental education also serves as an important marker of early adverse circumstances of an individual that shapes family income and, in turn, family economic hardship. Research shows that families with poorly educated parents experience greater family adversity than do families with comparatively better educated parents even when the families possess identical levels of income. For example, studies reveal that parental education is associated not only with poorer pulmonary function of adults but also with declines in pulmonary function over time. This may be attributed to the fact that higher levels of education among parents offer greater access to social–psychological resources, skills, and information that helps to protect children from adverse influences stemming from stressful family circumstances.

Family structure also serves as an important marker of early family adversity. Research shows that consistent single motherhood contributes to persistent family financial difficulties, scarce job prospects, and employment limited to marginal occupations. In addition to risks linked with low income, female-headed families often lose the "safety net" that exists when part of a two-parent family. Female-headed single-parent families often face reduced access to housing, vehicles, household equipment, food, health insurance, and other important services. Thus, children from single-parent families typically experience greater early adverse circumstances than do children from intact families.

In addition, cohort studies have shown that early experiences in historical adverse circumstances, such as the Great Depression, World War II, and natural and human-made disasters, are important determinants of health of adults regardless of their early family socioeconomic conditions. These cohorts have lived their formative years under extreme socioeconomic deprivation, resulting in long-term health consequences. Studies have also revealed that ascribed adverse social status, such as racial/ethnic minority status, exerts persistent detrimental influences on mental and physical health across the life course that begin at early ages and operate independently of income and education. Social scientists argue that the health disadvantages faced by minorities are associated with systematic racial/ethnic discrimination related to health services as well as day-to-day social discrimination experienced by minority individuals.

Influence of Social Adversity on Physical Illness

The social epidemiological studies elucidate physiological, psychosocial, and behavioral mechanisms by which early socioeconomic adversities initiate and shape long-term physical health trajectories through various mechanisms. First, early adversity exerts a latency effect on individual physical health by contributing to damages and behavioral risks that persist across the life course. Children from socioeconomically disadvantaged families are more likely to be born with permanent damage or chronic physical health problems, such as small brain size, low birth weight, asphyxia, birth defects, and disabilities, than are comparatively advantaged children. Second, lack of proper nutrition, lack of timely immunization, and inadequate access to health care for children place disadvantaged youths at increased risk for long-term health problems. Poor parenting, inadequate health behavior training, and risky parental lifestyles associated with family adversity may amplify the detrimental influence of socioeconomic disadvantage on the physical health trajectories beginning during the early years.

Family adversity during childhood also imposes structural constraints on choices regarding health-related behaviors of youths, potentially contributing to the development of unhealthy behavioral trajectories. Economically disadvantaged youths may have less access to health information and less control over sleeping hours or food choices. Moreover, intergenerational research documents direct transmission of specific health risk behaviors and risky lifestyles from parents to children. Economically disadvantaged families are also more likely to live in social environments where unhealthy eating, smoking, and heavy drinking occur than are comparatively advantaged families. Numerous community studies document the contextual influence of adverse social environments on the development of unhealthy adult lifestyles. Finally, developmental research shows that those who adopt risky behaviors early in life face the highest risk of continuing such behaviors across the life span.

Influence of Early Social Adversity on Mental Disorders

Numerous studies demonstrate evidence of an association between early family adversity and mental health problems during later life. These studies document associations between childhood family adversities and multiple mental health problems, such as cynical hostility, hopelessness, and depressive symptoms, with such associations even appearing beyond the middle years. Mental disorders that occur during one's early years confer strong risks of recurrent disorders during adulthood and continuation of recurrence through later life. Existing research suggests that early social adversity contributes to early mental disorders in several ways. First, developmental research shows that various stressors indicative of adversity may contribute directly to diminished psychological resources, a sense of continuing entrapment, anger, hopelessness, frustration, and other negative emotions among youths. Second, stressful daily experiences have psychological consequences for parents. Psychological problems such as depression and irritability can contribute to low parenting commitment, rejection of and hostility toward children by parents, and other ineffective parental practices. These psychological and behavioral problems among parents increase the risk of psychiatric difficulties among youths. Third, poor families tend to live in disadvantaged neighborhoods. Community

studies show that youths living in deprived neighborhoods face increased risk for the development of emotional and behavioral problems over and above individual and family risk factors. Recent neighborhood studies show that neighborhood adversity during childhood exerts a lagged effect on adult mental health through chronic stress in the neighborhood. Potential mental health problems that develop during adolescence can disrupt adult status attainment, and this in turn further erodes individual mental health during the adult years.

Poor mental health contributes to physical health problems directly and indirectly. Psychiatric and medical research documents that chronically internalizing problems associated with stressful life experiences during the early years may exert direct deleterious influences on physiological processes, including activation of the hypothalamic–pituitary–adrenocortical axis as well as the neuroendocrine, autonomic, and metabolic functioning of individuals. Negative emotions are associated with increases in blood lipids, free fatty acids, blood pressure, and heart rate as well as suppressed immune system functioning. Such physiological malfunctioning can contribute to the development and/or progression of a wide range of chronic medical conditions over time, including obesity, diabetes, diminished metabolic control, hypertension, infectious disease, cancer, and other cardiovascular, respiratory, and gastrointestinal illnesses. Internalized depressed feelings and hostility may also contribute to poor physical health indirectly by influencing health-related behaviors such as physical inactivity, smoking, and alcohol consumption.

Mental and physical health difficulties stemming from early adversity are mutually influential across the life course. Sensory and neurobiological disorders have the strongest relationship with psychological disorders. However, the association or comorbidity between mental health and physical health is not purely spurious due to the common influence of early adversity. This suggests that early adversity initiates several etiological processes that lead to a variety of problematic health outcomes during later years.

—*K. A. S. Wickrama*

See also Demography of Aging; Life Course Perspective on Adult Development; Successful Aging

Further Readings and References

Miech RA, Caspi A, Moffitt TE, Wright BRE, Silva, PA. Low socioeconomic status and mental disorders: A longitudinal study of selection and causation during young adulthood. *Am J Sociol.* 1999;104:1096–1131.

O'Rand AM, Hamil-Lucker J. Processes of cumulative adversity: Childhood disadvantage and increased risk of heart attack across the life course. *J Gerontol B Psychol Sci Social Sci.* 2005;60:117–124.

Wickrama KAS, Conger RD, Abraham WT. Early adversity risks and later health: The intergenerational transmission of adversity through mental disorder and physical illness. *J Gerontol B Psychol Sci Social Sci.* 2005;60:125–129.

Eating Disorders

See Nutrition, Malnutrition, and Feeding Issues

Economics of Aging

The improved economic status of America's elderly populations is a 20th-century success story. Today, the economic status of older Americans closely resembles that of other adult populations; some are very well off, many are comfortable, many live modestly, and some have very low incomes.

This entry begins by discussing the evolution of the nation's retirement income security system. The economic status of today's older Americans is then described, paying special attention to the diversity of circumstances among today's elders. The likely contours of the economic status of tomorrow's elderly populations are the discussed briefly, and it is concluded that, as in the past, diversity of circumstances will characterize the income position of tomorrow's older populations. It is suggested that, as is the case today, the economic well-being of the vast majority of older Americans—especially the most vulnerable—will depend especially on maintaining sound universal social insurance protections. While mindful that health insurance protections have critical implications for the economic well-being of older Americans, this entry focuses primarily on sources of cash income and their impact on economic status.

The Evolution of the Old-Age Retirement Income Support System

Retirement and retirement income systems are relatively new and evolving institutions. Paradoxically, industrialization created both the need and the opportunity for the nation's "old-age retirement income support system." Improvements in nutrition, sanitation, and public health led to more people reaching old age and living longer once they were there. A growing economy raised living standards, providing new opportunities for leisure as well as for the expansion of public and private income and health protections for older Americans. Movement from agricultural and small-scale production to manufacturing production raised wages even as it increased insecurity. Workers became subject to the vagaries of economic cycles. Employers, often interested in workers who could keep up with the speed and dexterity demands of new technologies, required orderly means of turning over their workforces. Unions wanted employment opportunities in the growing manufacturing economy for younger members.

American workers and their families needed protection against many identifiable risks—risks related to disabling industrial accidents, deaths of workers, and old age as well as risks related to outliving one's savings or seeing retirement incomes eroded by inflation. Then, as is the case now, pensions—both public and private—provided a partial solution to the needs of working persons while simultaneously addressing the interests of employers and unions. By the mid-1950s, "retirement" had emerged as a new institution and as a normative expectation of older Americans.

Although income from employer pensions, employment, assets, and welfare is important, Social Security—the Old-Age, Survivors, and Disability

Insurance (OASDI) program—is the heart and soul of the nation's retirement income system. Based on the social insurance approach to economic security, the program is designed to provide universal protections for the American public against selected risks. In exchange for making modest payments through regular employer and employee payroll tax contributions over the course of their work lives, working Americans earn for themselves and their families the right to benefits when earnings are lost as a result of retirement, long-term severe disability, or death. Because social insurance, unlike private insurance or private pensions, is designed to provide widespread basic protection, the system provides proportionally larger benefits to low-wage workers, even though high-wage workers generally receive larger monthly benefit amounts. Social Security was intended as a supplement to personal savings, employer-provided pensions, and (for some) earnings from continued work during their old-age years—not as the sole source of income that it often is.

The Social Security Act of 1935 established Social Security, which was then known as old-age insurance or old-age benefits, as well as means-tested protections for the needy, aged, and blind. During its first 40 years, the act was amended many times, generally adding and strengthening its social insurance provisions and, at times, its public assistance (welfare) provisions. For instance, protections were added in 1939 for aged wives and dependent children of retired workers and for surviving wives and dependent children of workers and retirees. The 1950 amendments established Social Security as the dominant source of protection for the old. Also, needs-based welfare protections were added for needy disabled individuals in 1950, as noted in 2006 by the Social Security Administration.

This was followed by the creation of the Disability Insurance (DI) program in 1956 and then Medicare and Medicaid in 1965. Initially, disability insurance provided cash benefits for long-term severely disabled workers 50 to 64 years of age and disabled adult children of workers. Medicare was intended primarily to provide hospital and medical insurance to workers over 65 years of age and was later expanded to provide benefits to disabled workers, whereas Medicaid was intended to provide medical coverage primarily to the needy aged, disabled, and families caring for children. In 1972, the Social Security Act was amended to place all categories of needy adults—elderly, blind, and disabled—into one federal program for needy adults, namely Supplemental Security Income (SSI). The 1972 amendments also created the cost-of-living adjustments (COLAs), which were implemented to ensure that retiree benefits kept pace with inflation, according to the Social Security Administration in 2006.

Beginning in the mid-1970s, legislative attention focused primarily on emerging financing problems. In 1977, and again in 1983, amendments were implemented to address short-term problems resulting from poor economic performance (e.g., high inflation, lower than expected wage growth) and long-term problems resulting from project demographic change (e.g., fertility declines, improved mortality, projected aging of the baby boom cohorts) and economic change (e.g., slower growth of wages and the economy) and (in 1977) a flawed benefit formula.

Today, although its short- and mid-term finances are very secure, the program faces another long-term shortfall, again a result of demographic change and of anticipated changes in the economy. Under the most commonly accepted set of assumptions, the program has sufficient funds to meet all payments through 2041, after which there will be a roughly 26% shortfall. In the unlikely event that future congresses and presidents put off Social Security reform, beginning around 2041, the anticipated revenue stream would cover only 74% of promised benefits.

Economic Status of Today's Elderly Populations

The economic status of older adults in the United States today is greatly improved, and there is much diversity of circumstances among different elder populations. In 2004 inflation-adjusted dollars, the median income of elderly households had increased from $13,228 in 1960 to $24,509 in 2004. Since the mid-1950s, poverty, as measured in 2005 by the U.S. Census Bureau's poverty thresholds, has decreased for all age groups but most noticeably for adults age 65 years and older. Among persons in this age group, poverty rates declined precipitously from 35.2% in

1959 to 14.6% in 1974 and continued to decline more slowly to 9.8% in 2004. To put this in context, in 2004 the poverty threshold was $9,060 for unrelated persons age 65 years and older and was $11,418 for couples with one person in that age group. But these data and trends provide only part of the income story.

For instance, a significant portion of today's retirees live in near poverty with incomes between 100% and 125% of the poverty threshold. According to the Census Bureau, an additional 6.7% of persons over 65 years of age lived in near poverty in 2004. These near-poor elderly are very vulnerable to any measure of income loss or increase in expenses, and they are offered little economic protection from these unexpected losses outside of Social Security and Medicare.

Disaggregating the elderly further by race/ethnicity, gender, marital status, and advanced age provides greater insight into their economic well-being. In terms of absolute poverty rates, Black and Hispanic elders are more likely to be poor or near poor than are their White counterparts, nonmarried elders of all races and ethnicities are more likely to be poor or near poor than are married elderly couples, and nonmarried women of all races and ethnicities are more likely to be poor or near poor than are nonmarried men. For example, only 7.5% of White non-Hispanics had below poverty-level incomes in 2004, compared with 13.6% of non-Hispanic Asians, 23.9% of non-Hispanic Blacks, and 18.7% of similarly aged Hispanics of all races. Similarly, among White non-Hispanics age 85 years

and older, 7.5% of men and 15.3% of women have below poverty-level incomes, compared with 15.1% of similarly aged non-Hispanic Black men and an astounding 31.7% of non-Hispanic Black women, as noted by the Census Bureau in 2005.

Similarly, whereas the median household income of persons 65 to 74 years of age was $30,854 in 2004, it was only $20,467 for those age 75 years and older. These racial, ethnic, age, and gender differences in poverty after retirement are tied specifically to the differences these groups experience in terms of earnings (linked to Social Security benefit amounts) during their working years and in terms of their likelihood to be employed in labor sectors that do not provide private pensions.

Social Security is, as the data in Table 1 highlight, the most important source of cash income for the vast majority of older households, providing nearly 40% of elder household incomes, followed by income from earnings, accounting for one fourth of the income going to elder units (see "all units" column in Table 1).

But more significantly, the second, third, fourth, fifth, and sixth columns in Table 1 show that the contributions of these income sources vary substantially by income quintile. More than 70% of the income going to the bottom 60% of the elder income distribution comes from Social Security. In turn, the impact of income from earnings, employer pension, and assets is greatest on the 20% of elder units that received more than $40,928 in 2004.

Table 1 Relative Importance of Selected Sources of Income to Elderly (Age 55 Years and Older) Households by Quintiles: 2002

Percentage of Total Income From:	All Units	Under $9,721 (Q1)	$9,721–$15,180 (Q2)	$15,181–$23,880 (Q3)	$23,881–$40,981 (Q4)	$40,982 and Over (Q5)
Social Security	39.4	82.6	84.0	67.0	47.0	19.8
Government pension	8.8	0.7	2.2	5.3	11.1	10.4
Private pension/annuity	9.9	2.5	4.1	9.2	13.8	10.0
Income from assets	13.6	2.4	3.6	7.4	9.8	18.9
Earnings	24.9	1.1	2.3	7.0	14.7	38.4
Public cash assistance	0.7	8.9	1.6	1.0	0.2	0.1

Source: Adapted from Social Security Administration. Income of the population 55 or older, 2002. Available at: www.ssa.gov/policy/docs/statcomps/income_pop55/2002/sect7.html#table7.5.

Similarly, when examining the different age groups in the over 65 years category, we discover that not all persons over 65 years of age receive their income from the same sources or receive the same amounts of income from those sources. For example, among those age 80 years and older, only 6% receive some income from earnings, employer pension, and assets compared with 45% of persons 65 to 69 years of age.

When breaking down the population over 65 years of age by gender or race/ethnicity, we discover similar discrepancies in economic reliance on public programs as income. As we see in Figure 1, minority elderly are less likely than White elderly to receive income from public or private pensions or from assets and are more likely to receive income from Social Security and public assistance programs such as SSI. Hispanic elderly rely more on earnings from work and less on benefits other than Social Security than do their White and Black counterparts. These differences are also visible between the genders, with women relying more on income from Social Security, assets, and public assistance, whereas men have access to more income from earnings and retirement benefits other than Social Security (i.e., private, public, or government employee pensions).

As we can see in Figure 1, although older Americans in general enjoy higher median incomes and lower poverty rates than ever before, there are marked differences among subgroups of this population. These differences leave unmarried women, minorities, and lower income workers much more vulnerable to poverty during their later years and much more vulnerable to detrimental effects of decreases in public protections such as Social Security, SSI, Medicare, and Medicaid. These differences pose challenges for current and future cohorts of the old.

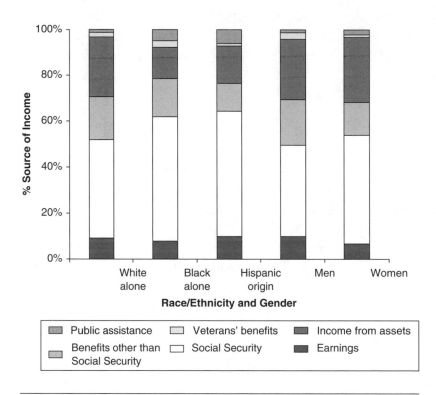

Figure 1   Percentages of Persons Age 65 Years and Older With Income From Specified Sources by Race, Hispanic Origin, and Gender: 2002

Source: Adapted from Social Security Administration. Income of the population 55 or older, 2002. Available at: www.ssa.gov/policy/docs/statcomps/income_pop55/2002/sect7.html.

Notes: Beginning with data for 2002, respondents may identify themselves in more than one racial group. The categories "White alone" and "Black alone" reflect respondents who reported only one race. Less than 1% of persons age 55 years and older reported more than one race. The Social Security category includes retired worker benefits, dependents' or survivors' benefits, disability benefits, transitionally insured benefits, or special benefits for those age 72 years and older. The measure of receipt of dividend income (included in income from assets) is being changed to correct an error. The previous measure included all persons owning stocks or mutual funds, which may or may not have issued dividends. The new measure includes only those receiving income from dividends. For example, 18% of persons age 65 years and older received dividend income in 2002 under the new methodology, compared with 23% under the old methodology. This change has only a small effect on the percentage of persons age 65 years and older receiving income from assets (55% under the new methodology vs. 56% under the old methodology). Persons of Hispanic origin may be of any race.

The Future

What of the future? As baby boomers (the nearly 78 million American residents born from 1946 through 1964) approach their retirement years, new questions are being raised about how well they will fare and what challenges they face for their economic well-being.

Some seem likely to fare even better than today's retirees. The poverty rate for persons over 65 years of age in this country has declined over time and will continue to decline over the coming decades. The Urban Institute maintains that because poverty thresholds do not reflect real-wage increases, relative poverty rates will exceed absolute poverty rates.

There are two common relative poverty measures. One relative measure among retired adults is the replacement rate; that is, the percentage of preretirement income that has been replaced by postretirement income sources such as Social Security, private pensions, and income from assets. Another relative measure of economic status among retired adults is a comparison of retirees' incomes with workers' incomes or the national average wage. Retirees with a per capita income falling below 75% of the median replacement rate, or below 45% of the national average wage, can be considered as living in poverty. For persons retiring in the immediate future, relative poverty rates will be similar to the rate for today's retirees. However, for future retirees born between 1956 and 1965, also known as late boomers, relative poverty may climb as high as 46%. As a group, baby boomers have historically earned higher real (inflation-adjusted) incomes than did their parents at similar points in their life course. In general, baby boomers are accumulating wealth at the same pace as, or faster than, their parents and are likely to have higher living standards during their retirement when measured in terms of poverty rates and absolute dollars. However, it is likely that many—perhaps one half according to a 2003 congressional budget analysis—will not be able to maintain a standard of living that compares as favorably with their working years. For those able to extend their working lives, the cost of living longer can be offset by more employment income. In general, the Congressional Budget Office (CBO) also found that baby boomers in lower income brackets will be much more dependent on future governmental benefits than recent studies indicate and that future reductions in these benefits will have a direct detrimental impact on their retirement finances.

For the individual retirees of the future, economic status during old age will depend on demographic and economic developments that are difficult to predict, including changes to the availability and size of government benefits, unplanned changes in marital or health status, their savings and returns on assets, how long they will live, the security of private or government pension incomes, health insurance protections, and potential future earnings.

Most fundamentally, the aggregate economic well-being of baby boomers and other elders of the future will depend on how the nation addresses challenges of Social Security financing, employment opportunities for older persons, financial instabilities in the private and public employee pension systems, health insurance financing problems, and risks related to long-term care.

Although the politics of privatization has driven the Social Security debate for the past few years, it has become increasingly clear that from an analytical perspective, the projected Social Security financing problem presents a relatively easy problem to address. Some combination of moderate changes can address the problem, including perhaps raising the cap on taxable wages, extending coverage to new state and local government employees, diversifying trust fund investments to include investing a small portion of the trust funds in the private sector, slightly increasing the payroll tax for both employees and employers, and further raising the age of eligibility for full benefits. A moderate approach to Social Security reform can preserve the bulk of currently promised benefits to future retirees.

The private pension system presents less tractable problems. The Pension Benefit Guarantee Corporation (PBGC), which provides pension insurance for single- and multiple-employer pension plans, functions as a useful indicator of the state of defined benefit pensions in today's economy. From 2001 to 2004, the federal government assumed responsibility, through the PBGC, for a number of large and significantly underfunded pension plans from the steel and airline industries. These underfunded pension plans have effectively doubled the numbers of participants and beneficiaries receiving payments from the PBGC single-employer program.

In addition to increased federal assumption of payments for defined benefit pensions, a growing number of employers have implemented defined contribution or cash balance or hybrid plans to replace traditional defined benefit plans, thereby shifting greater risk onto employees. Among the many reasons for these shifts is that as retirees live longer, the costs of financing their future benefits increase.

Of even greater concern are the rising costs of health care, reductions in occupationally based employee and retiree health insurance protections, and the increasing costs of Medicare and Medicaid.

The Centers for Disease Control and Prevention (CDC), in its 2005 chart book on American health trends, reported that the United States spent approximately $1.7 trillion on health care, or 15% of the gross domestic product (GDP), compared with approximately 13.5% of the GDP in 1995. At the same time, private health insurance coverage and employer-provided health insurance coverage for Americans under 65 years of age have declined since 1999, while the proportions of uninsured adults and Medicaid enrollees have increased, as noted by the Census Bureau in 2005.

In 2006, the board of trustees for the Centers for Medicare and Medicaid projected rapid increases in combined Medicare expenditures over the next 10 years. These projected increases are consistent with historical data from 1970 to 2004 and result from increased health care costs, increased numbers of beneficiaries, and increased use and intensity of medical services per beneficiary. According to these projections, Medicare expenditures will begin exceeding contributions in 2013, and the Medicare trust funds, under intermediate estimates, are expected to be depleted by 2020. Similar cost increases and future financing problems also exist for the Medicaid program. The Urban Institute reported that between 2000 and 2004, Medicaid expenditures grew by 50%. Like Medicare increases, these rising Medicaid costs are rooted in increased enrollment and increased health care costs.

Long-term care costs also represent a substantial risk to the economic well-being of middle-class elderly today and in the future. As the numbers of older adults increase with the retirement of the baby boomers, the number of persons with physical and cognitive impairments will also increase, as will the demand for long-term care services. This will increase the drain on what the CBO has indicated are already substantial resources devoted to financing long-term care services (> $200 billion in 2004 or approximately $24,000 per impaired older adult). These estimates include the value of unpaid care, an integral part of long-term care provided by families and friends of impaired older adults.

Financing sources for long-term care include (in order of size) donated care, Medicaid, Medicare, out-of-pocket expenditures, and long-term care insurance. Table 2 details the sources of payment for institutional, home-based, and total long-term care costs in 2004.

The rules that govern public long term-care programs heavily influence the financing patterns of long-term care by discouraging middle- and upper-class families from making financial preparation for future long-term care needs and instead encouraging them to rely on governmental assistance. The financial demands on governmental

Table 2   Long-Term Care Expenditures for the Elderly by Source of Payment: 2004 (billions of dollars)

	Institutional Care	Home-Based Care	Total
Public programs			
Medicaid	36.5	10.8	47.3
Medicare	15.9	17.7	33.6
Private resources			
Donated care	0	76.5	76.5
Out-of-pocket payments	35.7	8.3	44.0
Private insurance	2.4	3.3	5.6
Other[a]	2.0	2.5	4.4
Total	92.4	119.0	211.4

Source: Data compiled from Congressional Budget Office. *Financing Long-Term Care for the Elderly.* Washington, DC: Government Printing Office; 2004.

Notes: Donated care is measured as the cost of replacing that care with professional services. Numbers might not add up to totals due to rounding.

a. Includes local public programs, minor federal spending, charity care, and so on.

programs for retirees will continue to increase as the number of retirees depending on governmental financing of long-term care increases and as health care costs continue to rise.

Conclusion

This entry has documented the evolution of the retirement income security system in the United States, consequent improvements in the economic well-being of older populations, and the diversity of economic circumstances existing across today's elder populations. In discussing the likely economic circumstance of future elderly populations, it is clear that the diversity of economic circumstances will persist and that there is much uncertainty about the implications of future trends. Given this uncertainty, it will be important—especially to those at greatest risk—to maintain and finance the floor of protection provided under the nation's universal income and health protections for elderly populations.

—*Maria T. Brown*

See also Health and Public Policy; Homelessness and Health in the United States; Long-Term Care; Medicaid; Medicare; Work, Health, and Retirement

Further Readings and References

Diamond PA, Orszag PR. *Saving Social Security: A Balanced Approach.* Washington, DC: Brookings Institution; 2004.

Holtz-Eakin D. Baby boomers' retirement prospects: An overview. Presented at congress of the U.S. Congressional Budget Office, November 2003.

Holtz-Eakin D. The cost and financing of long-term care services. Congressional Budget Office testimony before the Subcommittee on Health Committee on Energy and Commerce, U.S. House of Representatives, April 2005.

Kingson ER. Demographic trends and the future of older workers. In: Crown WH, ed. *Handbook on Employment and the Elderly.* Westport, Conn: Greenwood; 1996:57–80.

Kingson ER, Berkowitz ED. *Social Security and Medicare: A Policy Primer.* Westport, Conn: Auburn House; 1993.

Kingson ER, Williamson JB. Economic security policies. In: Binstock RH, George LK, eds. *Handbook on Aging and the Social Sciences.* San Diego, Calif: Academic Press; 2001:369–386.

Reno V, Lavery J. *Options to Balance Social Security Funds Over the Next 75 Years.* Washington, DC: National Academy of Social Insurance; 2005. Social Security Brief No. 18.

EDUCATION AND HEALTH

Education is one of the most commonly used measures of socioeconomic position in population-based studies of health. In a life course perspective, educational attainment indicates one's point of entry into the social stratification system when transitioning from adolescence to adulthood. It structures both employment opportunity and earnings and thereby shapes the probability of exposure to health-damaging or health-enhancing agents. In addition to these substantive reasons, there are two key analytic advantages to using education over other socioeconomic indicators. First, education can be ascertained for all adults, whereas income and occupation might not be available for everyone, especially for women and older adults. Excluding persons who are unemployed or who do not have incomes (i.e., more disadvantaged individuals) would reduce variation in socioeconomic position and attenuate associations with health. Second, educational attainment is typically completed by early adulthood, prior to the onset of age-associated medical conditions, and so studies that link education to health are less susceptible to "reverse causation." In contrast, interpreting the causal order of studies that use income or occupation is more tenuous because poor health can have an adverse impact on employment status, income, and occupation.

Numerous studies have shown a positive association between education and health. One major study showed that despite overall decline in U.S. mortality rates between 1960 and 1986, the disparity in mortality grew between poorly and highly educated people 25 to 64 years of age. For instance, the age-adjusted mortality rate declined by 50% among White men with high educational attainment, whereas only a 15% decline was observed in men with low education. Educational differences in mortality patterns over the same time period were less dramatic in women. This work was expanded by I. T. Elo and S. H. Preston using data from the National Longitudinal Mortality Survey (1979–1985) that included information on older adults. The largest disparity in mortality by level of education was observed in working-age men (25 to 64 years). Although disparities in mortality rates continued into older ages (65 to 89 years), they were less severe in older adults than in younger adults, perhaps reflecting selective survival effects. Nonetheless, the association of education with mortality in older adults suggests that old-age mortality will continue to decline in the future as successive cohorts with higher levels of education enter older ages.

In addition to premature mortality, a lower level of education increases the risk of age-associated medical conditions and disability. One notable study examined education in relation to disability-free or active life expectancy, an important outcome among older adults that captures disease burden, quality of life, and mortality. Using data on a representative sample of older Blacks and Whites in North Carolina in 1986–1987, J. M. Guralnik and colleagues reported that older Black women who graduated from high school had an active life expectancy 3.9 years longer than those who did not graduate from high school. Education disparities in active life expectancy for older Black men, White women, and White men were 2.9, 2.8, and 2.4 years, respectively. Interestingly, racial differences in active life expectancy, when stratified by sex and education level, were substantially smaller than education differences. As with mortality, increasing educational attainment among older adults over time will contribute to declining prevalence of disability in the population, but the contribution will likely diminish over time. Although it is unclear whether educational disparities in disability will narrow or widen, a recent study showed that racial disparities remain unchanged while educational disparities grew among older adults between 1982 and 2000.

Three aspects of education that are relevant to health research are quantity, credentials, and quality. The first is simply the total amount of education received, which is commonly measured by years of formal education completed. In a human capital perspective, schooling provides cognitive, social, and technical skills needed for work as well as continued learning throughout life. Schooling also helps to shape behaviors and personality traits such as self-motivation, goal-directedness, and work ethic. Higher levels of education therefore lead to greater stock of human capital that can positively shape health over the life course. Indeed, pathways through which higher quantity of education might relate to health indirectly include a higher sense of personal control or mastery over the environment (i.e., the belief that one's actions—not luck or outside forces—lead to desirable outcomes), more supportive and equitable social relationships, and positive health-related behaviors (e.g., healthy diet, physical activity, not smoking). Furthermore, reading and communication skills gained through education contribute to better health literacy, which can help avoid disease risks as well as improve management of chronic diseases. In addition to building human capital, quantity of education might affect health directly by promoting development of a brain reserve capacity early in life (as measured by greater dendritic branching and/or larger brain size) that delays manifestation of age-associated neuropathology later in life (e.g., Alzheimer's disease).

Credentials are another aspect of education with health implications. In contrast to quantity of education, the credential approach does not value each year of education attained the same but rather assigns benefit only when additional education confers a degree. For example, the 1-year difference between completing 10th grade and completing 11th grade is not the same as that between completing 11th grade and completing 12th grade when a high school diploma is awarded. Credentials provide access to jobs that pay better, provide benefits (e.g., health insurance, retirement plans), and reduce risk of occupational exposure to health-damaging agents. Although several studies have demonstrated health benefits associated with higher degree credentials (e.g., high school graduate, college graduate), few health studies have examined the added benefit of credentials beyond total years of education. Catherine Ross and John Mirowsky, in their cross-sectional analysis of persons 18 to 95 years of age, did not find that a college degree provided any additional health benefit after adjusting for total years of education. One consideration that needs to be made when examining credentials is generational effects. The social and economic value of a credential certainly varies by birth cohort. For instance, a high school diploma earned in 1940 was viewed as a greater achievement than one conferred in 1980. As the distribution of educational attainment in the population shifts, the health salience of a higher degree could decline over time. Similar to generational effects, geography should also be taken into account when examining education disparities in health across different areas (e.g., secondary education in a developing country would likely confer relatively greater health benefit than secondary education in a developed country), and country of origin should be considered when investigating disparities in immigrant populations.

Less attention has been devoted to the quality or selectivity aspect of education. It is widely recognized that quality of education varies geographically and by institution. Public school budgets for primary and secondary levels are determined in part by local taxes, which can leave inner-city and rural schools at a disadvantage and compromise quality of education. Graduates from resource-deprived schools will likely not have gained the same skills, behavior, and knowledge as graduates from well-funded schools. Therefore, variation in the quality of education can attenuate associations with health when using either a quantity or credential approach to education assessment. Selectivity of a school can be a marker of educational quality, although this is more relevant for colleges and universities. The selectivity of the institution where a person attained a degree could reflect not only his or her stock of human capital but also the types of social networks and contacts made through schooling that could help a person obtain higher paying jobs. Ross and Mirowsky, in their study sample, applied standard criteria for ranking the selectivity of universities for college graduates but found only marginal benefits of college selectivity associated with health after accounting for quantity of education.

A major limitation that should be noted when assessing the relationship between education and health is that the economic returns on education are not uniform. For example, racial/ethnic minorities typically have lower earnings than do non-Hispanic Whites with the same level of education, and women experience lower returns than do men. These inequalities exist across all levels of education and become more pronounced when stratifying by race and gender. Therefore, it is important to consider multiple indicators of socioeconomic position—not education alone—when investigating racial/ethnic differences in health and to examine, within racial/ethnic groups, variation in health as a function of education.

In summary, education is a powerful predictor of health in older adults. There are multiple pathways through which education relates to health, including work and economic conditions, social and psychological resources, and health-related behaviors. Education can also relate to health directly through neurodevelopment. Measurement of education is practical and accessible across populations, although the benefits of education might not remit uniformly across age, gender, and racial/ethnic subgroups.

—*Kushang V. Patel and Jack M. Guralnik*

See also Demography of Aging; Economics of Aging; Ethnicity and Race; Socioeconomic Status

Further Readings and References

Bennett DA, Wilson RS, Schneider JA, et al. Education modifies the relation of AD pathology to level of cognitive function in older persons. *Neurology.* 2003;60:1909–1915.

Elo IT, Preston SH. Educational differentials in mortality: United States, 1979–85. *Social Sci Med.* 1996;42:47–57.

Guralnik JM, Land KC, Blazer D, Fillenbaum GG, Branch LG. Educational status and active life expectancy among older Blacks and Whites. *N Engl J Med.* 1993;329:110–116.

Ross CE, Mirowsky J. Refining the association between education and health: The effects of quantity, credential, and selectivity. *Demography.* 1999;36:445–460.

Ross CE, Wu C. The links between education and health. *Am Sociol Rev.* 1995;60:719–745.

Schoeni RF, Martin LG, Andreski PM, Freedman VA. Persistent and growing socioeconomic disparities in disability among the elderly: 1982–2002. *Am J Public Health.* 2005;95:2065–2070.

ELDER ABUSE AND NEGLECT

Elder abuse and *neglect* are general terms that refer to the mistreatment of older adults, typically those who are vulnerable due to physical or mental disorders. Mistreatment can occur in community or institutional settings and may be perpetrated by formal and informal caregivers or unscrupulous individuals who attempt to gain elders' confidence only to take advantage of them.

The National Center for Elder Abuse (NCEA), a consortium of protective services and aging services administered by the National Association of State Units on Aging, considers three basic categories of elder abuse:

- Domestic elder abuse: *acts committed by spouses, siblings, adult children, friends, or caregivers within older adults' or caregivers' homes*
- Institutional abuse: *acts committed by caregivers in residential facilities, such as nursing homes, assisted-living facilities, and foster homes, who have legal or contractual obligations to provide care and protection*
- Self-neglect or self-abuse: *neglect or acts committed by older adults themselves*

The NCEA describes more specific forms of mistreatment that are also identified within state statutes across the United States:

- Physical abuse: *inflicting or threatening to inflict physical pain or injury; depriving one of basic needs*
- Emotional abuse: *inflicting mental pain, anguish, or distress through verbal or nonverbal acts*
- Sexual abuse: *nonconsensual sexual contact of any kind*
- Exploitation: *illegal taking, misuse, or concealment of funds, property, or assets*
- Neglect: *refusal or failure to provide food, shelter, health care, or protection*
- Abandonment: *desertion by the responsible caregiver*

The first three types of abuse in the preceding list involve intentional acts by caregivers or other perpetrators. Exploitation implies gaining or being in a position of trust so as to misuse the elder's assets. Perpetrators may include formal and informal caregivers as well as deceitful strangers. Neglect and abandonment both involve caregivers' failure to provide care or protection.

Self-neglect is often included under the rubric of elder abuse even though it does not involve a perpetrator. Elders who live alone and who fail to maintain activities of daily living (ADLs) are at high risk for loss of independence.

Explanation

More than one explanatory model may apply to any case of mistreatment. Most models focus on the relationship between the caregiver and the care recipient.

The caregiver stress model postulates that family members mistreat elders in reaction to the strain and frustration of caring for persons with declining physical or cognitive function.

Several models attempt to explain acts of violence. Among spouse caregivers, domestic violence that began earlier in the marriage may continue when the spouse's role shifts to caregiving. Among adult children who become caregivers for a parent, violence toward the parent may be related to growing up in an abusive household, either as retaliation or as learned behavior. Caregivers with serious substance abuse problems or personality disorders are at greater risk for committing acts of mistreatment.

Exploitation is related to personal gain. The more dependent a family caregiver is on an older adult's income, property, house, or assets, the greater the likelihood that financial exploitation will occur. Strangers or con artists who prey on older adults are likely to gain the confidence of the older adults over a short period of time so as to profit and leave to avoid being caught.

Institutional abuse and neglect are related to staffing issues. Inadequate staffing, poorly trained staff, or a high rate of turnover among nursing assistants and aides may result in a lack of attentiveness and failure to meet the individualized service needs of residents. Even with mandated training on Alzheimer's disease and related disorders, nursing home staff often do not know how to manage behavior problems and even discourage adaptive behaviors. In most cases, abuse in long-term care facilities is related to neglect. Physical or sexual abuse by nursing home staff suggests inadequate screening and criminal background checks. In the United States, all states have ombudsman programs that advocate for nursing home residents' concerns and work toward resolving complaints.

Epidemiology

Elder abuse is largely an underidentified problem. A widely cited epidemiological study, the National Elder Abuse Incidence Study (NEAIS), relied on a nationally representative sample of 20 counties in 15 states to collect national incidence data of domestic elder abuse, neglect, and self-neglect among persons age 60 years and older in 1996. For each county, data were derived from reports submitted to and substantiated by Adult Protective Services (APS) agencies and reports made by "sentinels," that is, specially trained individuals from community agencies having frequent contact with older adults. The NEAIS results indicated that an estimated 450,000 community-based (noninstitutionalized) elders had been abused and/or neglected during that year and that an additional 101,000 exhibited self-neglect.

Other studies suggest that an estimated 1 million to 2 million Americans age 65 years and older have been victims of mistreatment during any given year. Although prevalence rates vary considerably within the published literature, some indicate that an average of 3% to 5% of the older population experience some form of elder abuse. Some studies suggest that women are more likely than men to be victims of abuse, neglect, and exploitation, whereas others suggest little difference due to sex, race, or ethnicity.

Investigation of Suspected Cases

Most cases of mistreatment and self-neglect go unreported. Suspected cases that are investigated fail to be confirmed through investigation unless the signs and symptoms are easily observed by someone else or by self-report of the older adult. Physical abuse, sexual abuse, and neglect by a caregiver are likely to be documented and may be confirmed by physicians. Exploitation may be documented through bank withdrawals, abuse of power of attorney or guardianship, or misuse of assets or property without the elder's permission or knowledge. Verbal abuse and threats of abuse may be overlooked unless observed directly.

Older victims are reluctant to report their caregivers as perpetrators. Cases of abuse or neglect are often reported by family members, hospital or other medical professionals, law enforcement officers, in-home service providers, friends or neighbors, or the older victims themselves.

Self-neglect may be reported only when the situations become serious enough to warrant attention such as emergency room or hospital visits, signs of deteriorating homes as noted by friends or neighbors, or when law enforcement officers respond to calls from concerned individuals. The challenge to APS and others is that many older adults viewed as victims of self-neglect may be unwilling to accept help and, if their cases are serious enough, may require legal actions such as appointing guardians if they are assessed as incompetent or otherwise lacking capacity.

In the United States, reports are made to a central hotline system in each state. If this preliminary contact indicates signs of mistreatment, the investigation process is conducted by the local APS. The NEAIS and other studies indicate that the APS investigation process substantiates far fewer cases of abuse than would trained sentinels or service providers who have more contact with older adults. In the United States, abuse in institutional settings such as nursing homes may be addressed through reports to the respective state ombudsman program.

The Federal Nursing Home Reform Act or Omnibus Budget Reconciliation Act of 1987 provided standards for improving quality of care within the nation's nursing homes, reducing physical and chemical restraint, and maintaining the safety of these residents. Although no such federal legislation exists for the assisted-living industry, all such facilities licensed by each state require that residents be provided with a list of their rights as residents and procedures by which they or their guardians can file complaints concerning possible violations.

Risk Factors

Risk factors are usually categorized by the victim's characteristics, the perpetrator's characteristics, or the interaction of the two. Risk factors for older adults likely to become victims include depression, social isolation, Alzheimer's disease and other forms of memory impairment, and reliance on others to meet ADLs, including financial dependence. For caregivers, possible risk factors that may lead to abusing a vulnerable older adult include an increase in caregiver burden or stress, psychological disorders, substance abuse, and dependence on the older adult's property or income. In caregiver–care recipient interactions, family dynamics and prior relationships may increase the risk of abuse and neglect.

Self-neglect constitutes a large portion of the cases investigated by APS. Individuals often live alone with significant health, cognitive, or other problems. Their symptoms may be the result of physical, mental, or cognitive disorders or some combination of the three. Such an individual is at increased risk for loss of independence.

Consequences of Abuse and Neglect

Obvious short-term consequences of elder abuse and neglect include death, physical injuries, pressure ulcers (bed sores), emotional trauma, and depleted bank accounts. Longer-term consequences include increased use and costs of health services, including outpatient and inpatient visits, admission to nursing homes, and increased risk of mental health problems.

All forms of elder mistreatment and self-neglect serve to lower a person's quality of life and increase the risk of loss of independence. Further research on the epidemiology and identification of these problems remains a priority.

—*Lawrence Schonfeld*

See also Advocacy Organizations; Ethical Issues and Aging; Health Care System for Older Adults; Legal Issues

Further Readings and References

Bonnie RJ, Wallace RB. Elder Mistreatment: Abuse, Neglect, and Exploitation in an Aging America—Panel to Review Risk and Prevalence of Elder Abuse and Neglect. Washington, DC: National Academy Press; 2002.

Fulmer T, Street S, Carr K. Abuse of the elderly: Screening and detection. *J Emerg Nurs.* 1984;10:131–140.

National Center on Elder Abuse. *National Elder Abuse Incidence Study: Final Report, September 1998.* Washington, DC: Department of Health and Human Services, Administration on Aging. Available at: www.aoa.gov/eldfam/Elder_Rights/Elder_Abuse/ABuseReport_Full.pdf. Accessed July 1, 2005.

National Center on Elder Abuse. NCEA website. Available at: www.elderabusecenter.org. Accessed September 13, 2006.

Pillemer K, Finkelhor D. The prevalence of elder abuse: A random sample survey. *Gerontologist.* 1988;28:51–57.

ELECTROLYTES

See FLUID AND ELECTROLYTES

EMOTIONS AND EMOTIONAL STABILITY

Historically, aging has been characterized by loss and deterioration; indeed, in many domains loss is ubiquitous. However, the domain of emotion, including experience and regulation, appears to be an exception. A large amount of research conducted over the past two decades has illustrated that in areas such as mental health and disorders, the story is more complicated, and that in normal aging, emotional regulation and experience appear to improve.

Originally, theories surrounding the theme of loss as it applied to the aging process were based on observations about social and personality changes. It was clear that the elderly engaged in fewer social interactions than did their younger counterparts, including within the small circles in which they had previously participated. This withdrawal was seen as an emotional disinvestment and, importantly, was theorized as an essential part not only of the aging process but also of the dying process. It was hypothesized in disengagement theory that this withdrawal reflected emotional preparation for death. A related hypothesis was that aging was accompanied by a dampening of emotional responses or, as Karl Jung suggested, a tendency to turn inward. Although it is true that older adults are not as socially active as they once were, more recent research suggests that this decrease results not from a desire to become emotionally unattached but rather from a desire to become selectively attached. A social "pruning" process occurs, with emotionally meaningful partners being retained and less meaningful partners being excluded. This selection process appears to aid the regulation of emotion.

Research has shown that day in and day out, the emotional lives of older adults are more stable than those of younger people. The reduction in variability is associated with emotional maturity and stability. Although studies have shown that the emotional response levels of the autonomic nervous system are reduced with age, older adults still experience emotions subjectively as intensely as do their younger counterparts; and the pattern of autonomic responses in older adults is similar to that in younger adults. In other words, although older adults tend to have a smaller magnitude of autonomic response, they show the same patterns of physiological differentiation.

There is a growing body of evidence that older adults experience the same emotional intensity as do younger adults but regulate or manage these emotions better. Based on real-time sampling in everyday life, older adults experience negative emotions less frequently than do younger adults, and when older adults do experience them, the negative emotions last for a shorter amount of time. Positive emotions are experienced with comparable intensity and frequency between younger and older adults. Thus, the overall ratio of positive to negative becomes increasingly favorable.

Researchers have puzzled over the positive trajectory of emotional development given such a different storyline from overall cognitive performance or physical health; some refer to it as the *paradox of aging.* How can it be that older people experience significant loss but retain emotional well-being? Socioemotional

selectivity theory offers an explanation based on life span changes in motivation. The theory is premised on the contention that humans monitor their place in the life cycle and with age gradually perceive future horizons as more constrained. In contrast, younger people perceive the future as vast and open-ended. The more expansive one's time perspective, the more goals will be directed toward acquiring information and expanding horizons. In other words, under conditions where the future looms large, people are motivated to gather information and expand their horizons. In contrast, when time is perceived as constrained, emotionally meaningful goals are pursued because they can be realized in the moment. Because of the constraints mortality imposes, older adults on average have a shorter time horizon than do younger adults and thus are more likely to pursue emotionally meaningful goals.

Recent findings suggest that motivational changes also affect cognitive processing and that these changes appear to operate in the service of emotion regulation. There are reliable age differences in memory and attention where younger people disproportionately attend to negative information and older people disproportionately focus on the positive, a developmental pattern referred to as the *positivity effect.* Interestingly, some research suggests that these observed age differences in emotional experience not only are tied to broad categories such as "positive" and "negative" but also apply to specific emotional states and other dimensions.

One of the specific emotions that may differ with age is sadness. Potentially because they place a greater emphasis on emotionally meaningful goals, older adults may be more willing to experience the emotion of sadness than are younger adults. This counterintuitive finding suggests that an emotional richness or maturity, rather than a superficial pleasantness, is pursued with age. After all, life offers many lessons and experiences as people learn to cope with loss and deal with life's many challenges. In addition, older adults score higher on overall mood stability ratings, and also score lower on the dimension of sensation seeking (items such as excitement), than do younger adults. This evidence for older adults' ability to regulate their emotions better than younger adults was further supported in a study where younger adults experienced more arousing states than did older adults. But how does all of this apply to mental health and the aging process? If people become better regulators over the years and are more satisfied with their lives, shouldn't their mental health improve as well? Unfortunately, the story is a bit more complicated when considering mental health and disorders.

Depression research in the aging population is one area of study that can help us to understand some of the complications involved with analyzing mental health. Research on the prevalence of major depression shows that it is less common in older adults than in middle-aged and younger adults. At the same time, depressive symptoms increase in very old adults. Specifically, *diagnosed* mood disorders have been found to be at their lowest prevalence rates among older adults and younger adults and at their highest rates among middle-aged adults. Self-reported symptoms also tend to be highest among middle-aged adults, but some research suggests that there may be a slight upward trend in prevalence at the very end of the life span. Some argue that depression rates are low because mood disorders manifest themselves differently in different age groups and thus may be overlooked. In general, however, there still remains a positive picture regarding mental health and the aging process; although there may be an increase in dysphoria during very old age, most adults over 65 years of age are at a lower risk for experiencing mood disorders and related symptoms than they were 20 years earlier.

Of course, well-documented changes in the brain decrease a person's cognitive resources, but the degree to which this decline affects emotional factors is largely unknown. In other words, it is unclear how much emotion and cognition are functionally connected. Some researchers argue that cognitive decline affects the complexity of emotional states and experiences. Based on self-reports of emotional descriptions, middle-aged adults may achieve higher levels of emotional complexity than do older adults. Therefore, for tasks that include both emotional and cognitive components, older adults may perform increasingly worse as the cognitive element is emphasized or stressed. What remains unclear, then, in light of research suggesting that older adults have a richer and more mature emotional experience, is just how necessary or important the cognitive component is to emotional experience.

Research over the past few decades has provided some basic answers to questions surrounding emotional well-being and health with respect to the aging process. Understandably, there have been a number of assumptions surrounding many areas of the aging process. Fortunately, however, this research has prospered, and with the aid of longitudinal studies and research devoted to understanding cultural and demographic differences, it will continue to provide enormously important insights into a population that will grow to unprecedented levels over the next generation.

—*Casey M. Lindberg and Laura L. Carstensen*

See also Agitation; Anxiety Disorders; Behavioral Disorders in Dementia; Depression and Other Mood Disorders; Mental Status Assessment; Positive Attitudes and Health

Further Readings and References

Blanchard-Fields F. The role of emotion in social cognition across the adult life span. In: Schaie K, Lawton M, eds. *Annual Review of Gerontology and Geriatrics,* Vol. 17: *Focus on Emotion and Adult Development.* New York: Springer; 1998:238–265.

Carstensen LL, Fung H, Charles S. Socioemotional selectivity theory and the regulation of emotion in the second half of life. *Motivat Emot.* 2003;27:103–123.

Carstensen LL, Isaacowitz D, Charles ST. Taking time seriously: A theory of socioemotional selectivity. *Am Psychol.* 1999;54:165–181.

Levenson RW. Expressive, physiological, and subjective changes in emotion across adulthood. In: Qualls S, Abeles N, eds. *Psychology and the Aging Revolution: How We Adapt to Longer Life.* Washington, DC: American Psychological Association; 2000:123–140.

END OF LIFE ISSUES

See PALLIATIVE CARE AND THE END OF LIFE

ENVIRONMENTAL HEALTH

Older adults are more susceptible than others to exposures from environmental hazards, in part because they have a reduced reserve capacity to respond to these hazards. Also, many suffer from chronic diseases such as heart disease that require taking numerous medications. They also have accumulated in their bodies toxicants from exposures in the workplace and community, and some of these toxicants remain in the body for long periods of time, including lead, mercury, and polychlorinated biphenyls (PCBs). All of these factors contribute to increased risks for older adults. Air pollution, extreme temperatures, secondhand smoke, heavy metals, waterborne disease outbreaks, and pesticides can pose health problems for all people but disproportionately affect the health of both the very young and older adults. Breathing unhealthy air exacerbates chronic conditions such as asthma, chronic obstructive pulmonary disease (COPD), heart disease, and diabetes. Drinking water containing microbial contaminants can cause gastrointestinal disease, hypertension, and diabetes. Extreme temperatures for extended periods of time also threaten the health and well-being of older adults.

Air Pollution

Environmental factors contribute to heart disease, the leading cause of death in the United States, and other chronic conditions, including stroke, COPD, asthma, and diabetes. Older adults are more susceptible to air pollution than is the general population. Studies have shown a direct relationship between rising levels of particle pollution and increases in medication use, hospitalizations, and premature deaths. Particle pollution (particulate matter) and ozone are responsible for loss of lung function and heart arrhythmias. (One can learn more about the air quality in a community by visiting the Environmental Protection Agency website at www.epa.gov/airnow.)

Secondhand Smoke

Secondhand smoke is one of the most life-threatening indoor air pollutants. It is as detrimental to inhale the same dose of secondhand smoke as it is to smoke a cigarette. Each year, secondhand smoke is associated with more than 38,000 deaths from heart disease and lung cancer.

Extreme Heat

Excessive heat events (EHEs) take a disproportionate toll on the health and lives of older adults. More people die from EHEs than from hurricanes, lightning, tornadoes, floods, and earthquakes combined. EHEs are prolonged periods with temperatures 10 degrees Fahrenheit (5.5 degrees Celcius) above the average high temperature for a region. These events are life threatening; the longer the event and the higher the relative temperature, the greater the risk. Approximately 80% of heat stroke deaths occur in individuals age 50 years and older. Older adults are at high risk for EHEs because the body's cooling mechanism becomes impaired with age and older adults often take medications further stressing the body. Other factors that increase the risk include living alone, a trend that has been increasing over the past decades for older adults, and being confined to one's bed. Communities are encouraged to establish Heat/Health Watch Warning Systems to identify when a heat-related public health threat is likely and communicate needed steps to protect public health.

Heavy Metals

Lead is a neurotoxicant that accumulates in the body. The health effects from lead include high blood pressure, digestive problems, nerve disorders, memory and concentration problems, and muscle and joint pain. Some research has shown that even very low levels of lead exposure in older women are associated with decreased neurological performance. As bones start to break down during menopause, high levels of lead may be released into the blood. Lead can enter the drinking water through leaded pipes. Unsafe lead levels can occur due to corrosion within household plumbing systems or due to lead being present in community water service lines. Because lead was phased out of gasoline during the 1970s, the major remaining source of lead exposure is found in leaded paints used on houses built before 1978. Home renovation in older homes can pose a health risk to older adults, and safe paint removal techniques are recommended to limit exposure.

Organophosphate Pesticides

Pesticides are used in approximately 90% of all U.S. households to prevent or control pests or weeds. People are exposed to pesticides by eating foods contaminated by pesticides. They can be exposed to chemicals in their homes and can also be exposed outdoors due to exposure to spray or drift or by contact with treated foliage or other treated surfaces. Exposure to high levels of pesticides can cause headaches, nausea, dizziness, and muscle twitching. Long-term exposure or excessive exposure to some pesticides can lead to cancer or effects on the nervous system. To minimize health risks, one can use a pest management system that combines nonchemical control strategies with reduced toxic pesticide use. It is important to read the labels to ensure safe use of pesticides around the home and garden.

Water Quality

Chemical and microbial contaminants can enter the drinking water from natural sources or as a result of human activity. If consumed, these contaminants can cause minor health problems or result in serious health outcomes, including death. Most exposure to drinking water contaminants occur in the home or in other buildings. Recreational activities, such as swimming and fishing, can also expose people to water pollution. Contact with water pollution can also occur when sewers overflow. Older adults face a greater risk from water contaminants because of changes in their physiology and health status. Microbial contaminants, including parasites (e.g., *Cryptosporidium, Giardia*), bacteria (*Escherichia coli, Clostridium difficile*), and viruses, cause gastrointestinal infections and illnesses.

—*Kathy Ellen Sykes*

See also Allostatic Load and Homeostasis; Disasters and Terrorism; Injury Prevention

Further Readings and References

Cascio WE, Hazucha M, Bromberg PA, Devlin RB. Environmental factors. In: Runge M, Ohman M, eds. *Netter's Cardiology.* Teterboro, NJ: Icon Learning Systems; 2004:627–631.

Klinenberg E. *Heat Wave: A Social Autopsy of Disaster in Chicago.* Chicago: University of Chicago Press; 2002.

Peterson CA, Calderon RL. Trends in enteric disease as a cause of death in the United States, 1989–1996. *Am J Epidemiol.* 2003;157:58–65.

U.S. Environmental Protection Agency. Aging Initiative. Available at: www.epa.gov/aging. Accessed September 13, 2006.

EPIDEMIOLOGY OF AGING

One of the major findings from the epidemiology of aging (indeed, from aging research in general) is that the aging process and the disease process are strongly related but also different. Although aging is associated with an increasing risk of disease, disability, and death, there is considerable variability *within* age groups. Indeed, this variability increases with age. For example, if we examined 500 people 20 to 25 years of age, we would find that their mean value of overall health would be relatively high and that the standard deviation would be relatively small; most of these young people are in good health. In contrast, if we examined 500 people 70 to 75 years of age, we would find that their mean value of overall health would be considerably lower and that the standard deviation would be much greater; some older people are doing much better than others. This finding leads to one of the critical questions in the study of aging and health: Why does the health of some people decline more slowly than the health of other people of the same age?

Epidemiology, both as a perspective and as a set of analytic methods, is especially well suited to examining patterns of health in aging populations. Epidemiology is based on the premise that health outcomes are not distributed randomly in the population. Rather, the incidence and prevalence of health outcomes follow specific patterns. The purpose of epidemiology is first to describe and then to explain those patterns in the population. This information, in turn, will establish the foundation for future public health interventions.

Aging and Health Outcomes

Standard categorical diseases represent the most common health outcomes in epidemiological research. Definitions of categorical diagnosed conditions, such as breast cancer and coronary heart disease, are based on the proposition that a standard set of presenting symptoms and signs reflect a single pathological condition. In general, aging is associated with an increase in the incidence and prevalence of categorical diseases. Incidence is defined as the number of new conditions diagnosed in a given population over a given period of time. An incidence rate is the number of new cases of a condition found in a given population over a specific period of time (e.g., calendar year) divided by the number of people in the population at risk for the condition during that time and then multiplied by a standard number, in most cases from 1,000 to 100,000. Prevalence refers to the number of people in a given population alive with the condition over a specific time period. The longer people survive after being diagnosed with a condition, the greater the prevalence and the higher the prevalence rate. Although age-specific incidence and prevalence rates increase for most health conditions, the increase is most pronounced for chronic conditions such as coronary heart disease, stroke, and most forms of cancer.

Research to understand the reasons for the association between aging and disease incidence and prevalence is very important, but aging and disease involves much more. For example, older people are at elevated risk not only for single conditions but also for multiple conditions. Multiple morbidity is defined as the presence of two or more health conditions diagnosed in the same older person. Comorbidity, a related term, is defined as the presence of one or more conditions among people diagnosed with an "index" condition. Results from the National Health Interview Survey indicated that the percentage of people age 60 years and older who reported having two or more of the nine most common conditions increased steadily with age. Specifically, the percentage of women who reported two or more conditions increased from 45% among those 60 to 69 years of age, to 61% among those 70 to 79 years of age, to 70% among those age 80 years and

older. Among men, these percentages were 35%, 47%, and 53%, respectively. The presence of, and treatment for, multiple conditions may affect the risk of subsequent diseases as well as the presentation of the symptoms of those diseases. The presence of previously diagnosed conditions, including their past and current treatments and monitoring, may affect the nature and interpretation of symptoms for current conditions. It has been observed that conditions such as falls, confusion and urinary incontinence may be the presenting symptoms for a variety of treatable diseases. It has also been reported that a myocardial infarction or a perforated ulcer may occur without pain and that pneumonia and infections may occur without fever.

Functioning, disability, and quality of life also represent important health outcomes. Physical functioning is defined as the relative ease in performing tasks that are necessary for independence and mobility in everyday life. Functioning ranges from specific generic tasks, such as ease in lifting, to more complicated tasks associated with the performance of social roles. Unlike other public health statistics, such as the incidences of disease and mortality, the measurement of functioning is not limited to dichotomous classification. Instead, measures of functioning are more likely to be based on an ordinal, interval, or continuous scale, typically expressed as the level of difficulty in particular tasks. Moreover, the level of functioning is generally variable and can decline or improve at different points in the life course. This has implications for the timing of assessment as well as the establishment of criteria for judging functional change. Disability, a social variable, is defined as the inability or difficulty in performing a social role, such as volunteer activities, because of a functional impairment or limitation.

Research Agenda

Research in the epidemiology of aging addresses a number of fundamental questions:

1. What is the overall distribution of health outcomes in the population? How do health outcomes vary among age groups? How do they change as people age? To

what extent do health outcomes vary within age groups?

2. To what extent do differences among and within age groups vary by gender, race, ethnicity, socioeconomic status, and geographic region?

3. To what extent do differences among and within age groups vary by the independent and joint effects of biological, behavioral, social, and environmental factors?

4. To what extent are differences among and within age groups associated with age differences in the following:
   a. The prevalence of the same risk factors?
   b. The salience or strength of the same risk factors?
   c. The frequency and timing of exposure over the life course to the same risk factors?
   d. Exposure to a different set of risk factors? How does the timing of these factors across the life course, coupled with developmental physiological factors, affect the subsequent risk of disease, disability, and death during the middle and senior years?

Research Design

Human aging represents a complex blend of physiological, behavioral, social, and environmental changes that occur in both the individual and the wider community. The epidemiology of aging employs three basic research designs to understand this complex blend: the cross-sectional design, the case–control design, and the longitudinal design. In the *cross-sectional* study, participants are assessed at one point in time. The purpose is to examine associations among specific variables (demographic, biological, behavioral, social, and environmental) and health outcomes of interest. Research on age-associated patterns of health and functioning are based on cross-sectional examinations from large population-based studies. The age differences found in cross-sectional studies reflect a variety of factors that include age, cohort, and period effects. It is not possible with this design to conclude that the age differences, in fact, reflect the results of aging. The *case–control* design is perhaps the most common design in epidemiology and is especially well suited to studying relatively rare conditions. Cases represent those people with the disease or health outcome under study. Controls, in turn, are people without the condition. By means of either participant selection or statistical adjustment, the objective is to ensure that the

controls are like the cases with the exception of health outcome status. Cases and controls are then compared to identify ways in which the two groups are different. This information, in turn, may suggest clues as to why the cases developed the disease and the controls did not. Often, clues are sought by interviewing cases and controls about past behaviors and circumstances. Retrospective bias is always a danger with this design because being either a case or a control may color a person's remembrances of things past. The likelihood of this bias may be affected by age-associated reductions in cognitive function. This design is also subject to a survivor bias. The longer the time that elapses between diagnosis and the time the case is interviewed, the greater the likelihood the case series includes just the survivors and not a representative group of cases. Thus, the information about the possible causes of the condition may be confounded by causes associated with survival. *Longitudinal* design is perhaps the strongest for examining aging in the population. This design involves selecting a sample of participants and then following them over time to examine changes in health outcomes as well as changes in the factors that could affect those health outcomes. This design is especially well suited to examining changes in overall health and functioning. The Institute of Medicine has recommended that cohort studies of older populations include not only people age 65 years and older but also those 55 to 64 years of age. This will allow research into the transition into the senior years. The efficiency of longitudinal design is sometimes enhanced by including historical records. Depending on how complete and how accurate those records are, a historical cohort or historical longitudinal study enables researchers to follow the sample from the past to the present and beyond.

Types of Epidemiological Studies of Aging

Of the various types of studies in the epidemiology of aging, the following represent some of the most common ones.

1. *Clinic/Laboratory-based populations for epidemiological studies of the elderly.* These are early

studies based on relatively homogeneous populations that include detailed assessments of physiological markers of aging as well as behavioral and social factors. The Baltimore Longitudinal Study of Aging (BLSA) represents an exemplar for this type of study.

2. *Adapted populations for epidemiological studies of the elderly.* These are population-based studies that developed into epidemiological studies on aging as the original cohorts of those projects aged. Exemplars for this type of study include the Framingham Heart Study, the Honolulu Heart Study, and the Alameda County Study.

3. *Established populations for epidemiological studies of the elderly.* The most recent epidemiological studies have been based on longitudinal studies that were designed specifically for the purpose of research on aging. In 1984, the National Institute on Aging (NIA) initiated a collaborative study that serves as an exemplar for many studies of this kind. The project, the Established Populations for Epidemiologic Studies of the Elderly (EPESE), was the first collaborative study in the epidemiology of aging, health, and functioning.

4. *Special populations of epidemiological studies of the elderly.* Some longitudinal studies focus on important subgroups of older populations. For example, the MacArthur Study of Successful Aging was designed to examine older persons who perform at the highest levels and are most able to preserve their health and functioning. On the other hand, the Women's Health and Aging Study consisted of female residents of Baltimore, Maryland, age 65 years and older who scored in the lowest one third on a number of selected items.

5. *Special populations of epidemiological studies of elderly with selected chronic conditions.* These longitudinal studies consist of older people diagnosed with specific chronic conditions. Their purpose is to examine the causes and consequences of older people diagnosed with specific conditions. Examples include the Cardiovascular Health Study and the National Cancer Institute (NCI)/NIA Comorbidity and Cancer Study.

Challenges

There are a number of challenges associated with the conduct of research in this area. With all the talk about the aging of the population, it is sometimes hard to fully appreciate how difficult it is to actually locate older people for research studies. Even people age 55 years and older still represent a minority in most populations. Special effort is required to recruit participants who are representative of the population of interest. Although this is an important challenge for all studies in epidemiology, it is especially important here because of the wide variations in health and functioning that characterize older populations. This challenge is compounded by new studies that require more time and effort on the part of participants. Study protocols often involve direct measures of physical performance (e.g., tests of upper and lower body strength), biological specimens, and detailed assessments of the household and neighborhood environments. Longitudinal studies, the best design to study the aging process (as noted previously), typically require repeated assessments over time. Another challenge is determining the timing of assessments in longitudinal studies, especially in studies of functional status. Unlike the discrete occurrence of many health outcomes (e.g., presence or absence of a diagnosis), level of functioning can vary over time. Identifying and examining functional transitions represent one of the major topics in the epidemiology of aging. Finally, increased attention is being given to a life course perspective to better understand the likelihood of health outcomes during the middle and senior years. Accordingly, epidemiologists of aging must consider the implications of looking across the life course— from childhood to the present—to better understand the patterns of health, functioning, and longevity during the senior years.

—*William A. Satariano*

See also Age–Period–Cohort Distinctions; Established Populations for Epidemiologic Studies of the Elderly; Honolulu–Asia Aging Study, Honolulu Heart Program; Longitudinal Research; Multiple Morbidity and Comorbidity

Further Readings and References

Gilford DM, ed. *The Aging Population in the Twenty-First Century: Statistics for Health Policy.* Washington, DC: National Academy Press; 1988. Institute of Medicine

Commission on Behavioral and Social Sciences and Education.

Guralnik JM, LaCroix AZ, Everett DF, Kovar MG. *Aging in the Eighties: The Prevalence of Comorbidity and Its Association With Disability.* Hyattsville, Md: National Center for Health Statistics; 1989. Advance Data From Vital and Health Statistics, No. 170.

Ostfeld A, Gibson DC, eds. Epidemiology of Aging: Summary Report and Selected Papers From a Research Conference on Epidemiology of Aging, June 11–13, 1972, Elkridge, Maryland. Bethesda, Md: National Institutes of Health; 1975.

Ouslander JG, Beck JC. Defining the health problems of the elderly. *Annu Rev Public Health.* 1982;3:55–83.

Satariano WA. *Epidemiology of Aging: An Ecological Approach.* Sudbury, Mass: Jones & Bartlett; 2006.

ESTABLISHED POPULATIONS FOR EPIDEMIOLOGIC STUDIES OF THE ELDERLY

In recognition of the rapidly growing size of the elderly population, the National Institute on Aging initiated a project in 1980 to investigate health risks that affect adults as they age. This initiative led to the Established Populations for Epidemiologic Studies of the Elderly (EPESE) project. The specific goals of the EPESE project were to provide estimates of the magnitude of health problems of community-dwelling older adults, to examine risk factors for these health problems for the purpose of informing appropriate interventions to prevent disability and postpone mortality, and to provide basic information on the social, mental, behavioral, and economic conditions of older adults and the relation of these conditions to health and health changes over time. Initially, three studies were funded: the East Boston Senior Health Project, the Iowa 65+ Rural Health Study, and the Yale Health and Aging Project. In 1985, the Piedmont Health Survey of the Elderly was added as a fourth study.

The EPESE studies were planned to have a number of important design features in common to facilitate cross-study comparisons and analyses. These design features served two overriding goals: (1) to obtain reliable prevalence estimates of important health problems and (2) to provide unbiased estimates of the associations between risk factors and major health outcomes. To achieve these goals, each of the four studies was designed as a population-based longitudinal study with standardized assessment of major risk factors and outcomes, relying on well-established and previously validated measures wherever possible. The cohorts in each study were selected to be representative of the target population, defined on the basis of being age 65 years and older, with sufficient heterogeneity in target populations across the projects to achieve a reasonably adequate representation of the entire elderly population in the United States during the early 1980s. It should be recognized that certain subpopulations that have grown substantially in size and proportion over the past 20 years, such as older Latinos and Asian Americans, were not represented in the EPESE studies.

The East Boston Senior Health Project focused on a working-class population of predominantly Italian American background who lived in the geographically defined community of East Boston, an island located in Boston Harbor. All residents age 65 years and older were eligible for the study. The Iowa 65+ Rural Health Study targeted all noninstitutionalized older adults living in two rural counties in east-central Iowa (Iowa and Washington counties). The Yale Health and Aging Project conducted a random sample of all older adults living in the city of New Haven, Connecticut. The random sample was stratified by sex and housing type (public housing, age-restricted housing, or community). The Piedmont Health Survey of the Elderly conducted a stratified random sample of the older population of five counties in the north-central Piedmont area of North Carolina, employing a sampling design to obtain a cohort that would contain approximately 55% African Americans.

The longitudinal design of each of the projects was the second common design feature. This feature served to provide optimal information on risk factors that are prospectively linked to age-related changes in health. Each study conducted a total of seven interviews at yearly intervals. Face-to-face interviews were conducted at baseline and repeated at the third and sixth anniversaries of the baseline interviews.

Telephone interviews were conducted during intervening years, corresponding with the first, second, fourth and fifth anniversaries of baseline. Uniformly high participation rates were achieved at all sites, with baseline participation rates ranging from 80% to 85% and follow-up participation rates generally exceeding 95% of survivors.

A third design feature was the inclusion of a common core set of instruments used across all four studies for the ascertainment of health-related risk factors and outcomes. Core assessments focused on prevalence of major chronic conditions, basic sociodemographic characteristics, and well-established medical and lifestyle risk factors for chronic disease such as blood pressure, smoking, alcohol consumption, and physical inactivity. There was a growing recognition, however, that there were health outcomes other than the traditional measures of incident disease and cause-specific mortality that were thought to have particular relevance to an aging population. Important examples of such outcomes include functional status and disability, cognitive impairment, and hearing and vision problems. Assessment of these outcomes was incorporated into the EPESE interviews. The EPESE studies also recognized the need to examine a broader spectrum of risk factors for poor health and function during older age, leading to the inclusion of brief measures of social networks, mental health, and personality features in the core assessment instruments. Another important area of common interest was the use of health care services, with a particular emphasis on hospitalizations, nursing home care, and home health services.

In addition to the core elements of assessment, each EPESE study was designed to develop one or more themes that were of specific interest to that site. This was achieved by adding more detailed questions to some of the measures that were part of the common core interview or by adding new questions or instruments to the interview. The East Boston Senior Health Project developed a special focus on cognitive impairment and added more detailed testing of cognitive function to its core instrument. Another area of interest was health care use, with additional questions on the use of, and satisfaction with, various forms of health care services that were available to seniors in East Boston. Topical areas of specific interest in the Iowa 65+ Rural Health Study were related to rural health issues, retirement, and oral health. The main interview instrument was expanded with sections on farm work experiences, musculoskeletal problems (e.g., aches, pains, stiffness), dental health history and service use, hearing loss, and quality of sleep. The Yale Health and Aging Project had a primary interest in psychosocial risk factors for health in older adults and included more detailed assessment of the structure and function of social support networks, neighborhood perceptions, social activity, and religious beliefs and practices. The Piedmont Health Survey of the Elderly was designed to answer basic questions related to racial differences and urban–rural differences in health. The questionnaire added special sections on medication use, functional status, mental health, and social support.

The EPESE studies have led to a number of ancillary studies that have made important contributions to our understanding of specific health issues during older age. For example, investigators of the East Boston Senior Health Project conducted one of the first systematic studies of the prevalence and incidence of Alzheimer's disease. The Iowa site used the EPESE framework to conduct a more detailed clinical study of oral health. Another ancillary study examined driving history and antecedents and consequences of driving cessation using participants from the Iowa and New Haven EPESE sites. In the Yale Health and Aging Project, a separate substudy was designed to examine recovery patterns and predictors of recovery after hospitalization for major acute medical conditions, including myocardial infarction, stroke, and hip fracture. Ancillary studies at the North Carolina site focused on Black–White differences in dementia and the use of antidepressants in older adults. The EPESE studies also formed the basis for another influential epidemiological study of aging health, namely the MacArthur Foundation Research Network on Successful Aging. This study was designed to investigate characteristics of older adults who were thought to be aging successfully. Participants were selected from the EPESE studies in East Boston, New Haven, and North Carolina based on the absence of disability in basic self-care tasks and higher than average performance on both physical and cognitive performance tests. A unique feature of the MacArthur study was the collection of blood and urine specimens in this selective cohort to identify biomarkers of changes in health over time.

In sum, the EPESE studies have provided a wealth of new information on a range of health issues that affect older populations. The overall health picture is characterized by a high prevalence of common age-related chronic conditions such as cardiovascular diseases, cancers, diabetes, hip fractures, and neurological disorders (e.g., Alzheimer's disease). Other conditions, such as arthritis and depression, show a less consistent increase during older age. The overall health of older adults is further characterized by the functional consequences of these health conditions that also show a pronounced increase with age. At the same time, the findings show a considerable degree of resilience in that many older adults are able to minimize the functional consequences of chronic health problems that affect them. Other EPESE findings have established that many risk factors for common chronic conditions are similar to those identified in middle-aged populations, although some risk factors clearly appear to lose some of their potency. They also underscore the importance of a constellation of psychosocial characteristics for the overall health and well-being of older adults and recovery from acute disease episodes. Psychosocial characteristics have also been found to be a major determinant of the use of health care services, especially those related to chronic disease and disability such as nursing home care. Finally, the EPESE studies have been instrumental in beginning to chart the extent and nature of racial disparities in health and to quantify the duration of life without major disability or active life expectancy.

—*Carlos F. Mendes de Leon*

See also Active Life Expectancy; Epidemiology of Aging; Government Health Surveys; Hispanic Established Population for Epidemiologic Studies of the Elderly; Longitudinal Research; MacArthur Study of Successful Aging; National Institute on Aging

Further Readings and References

Berkman LF, Seeman TE, Albert M, et al. High, usual, and impaired functioning in community-dwelling older men and women: Findings from the MacArthur Foundation Research Network on Successful Aging. *J Clin Epidemiol.* 1993;46:1129–1140.

Cornoni-Huntley J, Ostfeld AM, Taylor JO, et al. Established Populations for Epidemiologic Studies of the Elderly: Study design and methodology. *Aging Clin Exp Res.* 1993;5:27–37.

Evans DA, Funkenstein HH, Albert MS, et al. Prevalence of Alzheimer's disease in a community population of older persons: Higher than previously reported. *JAMA.* 1989;262:2551–2556.

Hunt RJ, Beck JD, Lemke JH, Kohout FJ, Wallace RB. Edentulism and oral health problems among elderly rural Iowans: The Iowa 65+ Rural Health Study. *Am J Public Health.* 1985;75:1177–1181.

Marottoli RA, Mendes de Leon CF, Glass TA, et al. Driving cessation and increased depressive symptoms: Prospective evidence from the New Haven EPESE—Established Populations for Epidemiologic Studies of the Elderly. *J Am Geriatr Soc.* 1997;45:202–206.

Mendes de Leon CF, Beckett LA, Fillenbaum GG, et al. Black–White differences in risk of becoming disabled and recovering from disability in old age: A longitudinal analysis of two EPESE populations. *Am J Epidemiol.* 1997;145:488–497.

Seeman TE, Singer BH, Rowe JW, Horwitz RI, McEwen BS. Price of adaptation: Allostatic load and its health consequences—MacArthur Studies of Successful Aging. *Arch Intern Med.* 1997;157:2259–2268.

ETHICAL ISSUES AND AGING

The organization, financing, and delivery of health care for older adults raise ethical issues for health care practitioners, researchers, and policymakers. During recent years, attention has focused on encouraging informed consumer choice and meaningful participation in health care decisions. Continued advances in medical technology and science present an ever-changing array of ethical concerns and dilemmas in areas of application such as genetic enhancement and end of life care. Broad societal concerns regarding privacy have resulted in vigorous policymaking to protect individual rights to privacy of medical information. The increasing ethnic diversity among older adults requires an informed appreciation of varied preferences and values regarding health care. Finally, the evolution of managed care and privatized financing models has raised questions regarding access, quality, and equitable distribution of resources. After briefly summarizing guiding principles central to biomedical ethics, this entry reviews ethical issues particularly relevant to the care of older adults and their families.

Guiding Ethical Principles

Drawn from the field of biomedical ethics and generally applied to the care of older adults, central ethical principles include autonomy, beneficence, paternalism, and distributive justice. *Autonomy* concerns the right of an individual to make choices free from undue interference unless such actions are likely to harm others. Individual values regarding expression of autonomy are varied and range from the desire for direct involvement in decisions to preferences for delegating decision-making authority to a family member or health care professional.

Beneficence, a construct underlying the Hippocratic oath and other professional ethics codes, requires that health care providers promote the patient's welfare and avoid doing harm (nonmaleficence). In care of frail older adults where questions of risk to health and safety are common, the principle of nonmaleficence may impose a further affirmative duty to proactively minimize such risk.

Paternalism refers to actions in which one individual makes decisions on behalf of another. In bioethics, moral distinctions have been drawn between two forms of paternalism. In cases where an individual is unable to execute a decision, paternalistic intervention in the patient's best interest is morally justified. Conversely, health care professionals are not morally justified to make decisions for someone who is fully capable of doing so.

Finally, the concept of *distributive justice* guides decisions on resource allocation and involves equitable distribution of costs and benefits as well as balancing of individual rights and collective rights.

Application to Older Adults

The care of older adults presents ethical challenges as a consequence of factors unique to this group. Older adults are at increased risk for chronic illness and cognitive losses, leading to more frequent encounters with the health care system and possibly calling into question their ability to participate fully in health decisions. Decisions regarding life-sustaining medical interventions may pose extraordinary ethical dilemmas as older adults near the end of life. Age-based stereotypes among health care professionals and even well-intentioned family members may cause exclusion from discussions and decisions as well as failure to provide the full array of options for consideration. Finally, older adults may lack knowledge of available resources and delivery systems, limiting their ability to make fully informed choices, or may lack the resources to implement preferred options.

Balancing Safety and Autonomy

Models of consumer-directed care for older adults and persons with disabilities emphasize the right of clients to make autonomous decisions about the care and support they receive. Challenges for health care providers include balancing individual rights to self-determination with a duty to protect patients from harm, defining acceptable risks and associated responsibilities, and determining the respective roles of government, providers, and consumers. These issues are especially common in community-based care, where case managers and home health care providers frequently negotiate complex care decisions with clients and families, balancing elder preferences with risk of harm. Case managers and other care providers must be mindful of the delicate line between convincing and coercing a client to accept unwanted services or placement. Feminist ethics theory, which has been applied to marginalized or vulnerable populations and emphasizes the important dynamics of family and caregiver relationships, may be useful in guiding such negotiations. Considerations of autonomy also arise in communal living settings such as nursing homes and assisted living, where rights of individuals must be continuously balanced with the safety, comfort, and well-being of other residents.

Supporting Informed Decisions

Meaningful involvement of an individual in health care decisions requires a determination of his or her ability to make an informed choice. Such ability, often referred to as decisional capacity, is generally considered to be intact when the individual can consistently communicate a preference or choice, understand relevant information, appreciate the decision and its consequences, and manipulate relevant information rationally. Despite this guidance, assessment of capacity may be difficult because capacity may fluctuate over time (e.g., with a change in medical condition or delirium), may be decision specific in nature (based on the complexity or urgency of a given situation), and may be contextual (made in a particular moment in a specific set of circumstances). For example, an individual with mild cognitive impairment may be capable of clearly expressing wishes regarding assignment of a particular home health aide yet be incapable of understanding a full range of treatment options for midstage breast cancer. Furthermore, although ethically appropriate approaches for involving persons with cognitive impairment in research have received recent attention, guidelines have not been fully developed.

Honoring Preferences for End of Life Care

Care at the end of life presents a host of ethical challenges such as the nature of information provided to the patient and family, decisions regarding life prolongation, honoring patient preferences, and rights to assisted suicide. Substantial effort has been directed toward advance care planning as a means to guide such decisions. Advance care planning involves ongoing discussions—prior to a medical crisis—among patients, their health care providers, and family members regarding preferences for health care treatment in the event of future incapacity. Approaches to establish advance care planning by proxy for residents who lack decision-making capacity are also being

explored. Potential benefits of advance directives include ensuring that patient wishes are clearly articulated and honored, decreasing emotional burden on family members required to make difficult end of life decisions for their loved one, and minimizing the possibility that surrogate decision makers will make a decision that is inconsistent with the individual's values. However, despite years of effort in education and promotion, the prevalence of advance directives among the U.S. population is quite low and practical problems persist. Advance directives might not provide clear guidance to clinicians and families, and evidence suggests a poor correlation between surrogate decisions and patient wishes regarding treatment decisions. In addition, current approaches are culturally insensitive and documents are not always readily accessible. Moreover, several studies have indicated that the presence of advance directives might not alter delivery of care at the end of life.

Another important ethical consideration for patients at the end of life is the provision of appropriate care and services in keeping with patient preferences. For example, although hospice services and other palliative care strategies have been shown to improve symptom control and satisfaction with care, referrals to hospice are often made so late in the course of the illness that few, if any, of these potential benefits are experienced. Contributing factors include both financial and administrative barriers, as well as ethical concerns of beneficence, autonomy regarding clear communication, and justice.

Biotechnology

Rapid advances in biotechnology pose many ethical challenges, particularly in the use of interventions that may extend survival of those with serious illness but do not cure the underlying disease. The most obvious example of this is the use of ventilators or feeding tubes, which may in some circumstances be viewed as extending the process of dying. Ethically appropriate approaches to care under these circumstances include consideration of the patient's preferences and directives, a clear understanding and articulation of the objectives of such interventions, agreement on measures to determine whether objectives are being met, and a willingness to terminate ineffective treatments in keeping with patient preferences.

Life extension, in contrast, refers to strategies for increasing the maximum life span and is one of the most scientifically and ethically complex uses of biotechnology. There is contentious debate as to whether such interventions should be defined as medical treatment or enhancement technology, with significant implications for federal and state regulation. Currently, federal policy is unclear, and the states focus little attention on life extension, anti-aging, and alternative medicine products.

Another area in which emerging science is raising ethical questions is genetic testing for Alzheimer's disease. Ethical concerns include the impact of knowing one's susceptibility to an incurable disease; the potential for discrimination in access to insurance, health care, and long-term care; data confidentiality; disclosure of information to employers, insurers, and relatives; justice in access to testing; and the relative cost, reliability, and benefit of such tests.

Honoring Privacy

Privacy of personal information has been the focus of substantial federal policy development. One component of the Health Insurance Portability and Accountability Act of 1996 (HIPAA) addressed privacy and security of health information. The intent of the HIPAA privacy rules is to protect individuals from unnecessary disclosure of their personal health information and to give each person control over how such health information is disclosed. The HIPAA statute, although critical in protecting privacy of individuals, also presents significant challenges for health care systems in terms of information sharing, provision of patient care, and research involving health records.

Respecting Cultural Diversity

Increasing ethnic and cultural diversity among older adults requires an informed appreciation of diverse views on health care. For example, expectations about the duties and responsibilities among generations in a family vary substantially between cultures. Whereas some may value formal health care providers in caring for a dependent family member, others believe that relatives should be exclusive caregivers. Expectations of how and to whom health information is provided, and how health decisions are made, also vary widely by cultural group. Cultural expectations may also vary widely within an ethnic/racial group depending on generation, educational level, or length of residence in the country. Considering an individual's cultural context is critical, as is recognizing the values that most cultures share such as a respect for dignity among older adults.

Allocating Resources

The need to set priorities for allocating limited health care resources is fraught with ethical dilemmas and should be guided by the principle of distributive justice. Concepts such as age-based rationing and quality-adjusted life years have been debated as frameworks for determining access to resources. Examples of allocation challenges include developing equitable policies regarding access to emerging biotechnology, defining societal expectations regarding the role of family caregivers, and achieving consensus on public and private responsibilities in the financing of long-term care.

To summarize, the care of older adults raises many ethical concerns. The principles of bioethics may be used to guide actions of health care professionals as they navigate among long-standing dilemmas (e.g., patient involvement in decisions and access to care) and modern challenges that accompany technological developments (e.g., life extension, genetic screening).

—*Leslie Curry and Terrie Wetle*

See also Advance Directives; Advocacy Organizations; Caregiving; Continuum of Care; Death, Dying, and Hospice Care; Elder Abuse and Neglect; Legal Issues; Palliative Care and the End of Life; Patient Safety

Further Readings and References

Beauchamp T, Childress J. *Principles of Biomedical Ethics.* New York: Oxford University Press; 1989.

Collopy BJ. Autonomy in long term care: Some crucial distinctions. *Gerontologist.* 1988;28(Suppl.):10–17.

Gostin LO. National health information privacy: Regulations under the Health Insurance Portability and Accountability Act. *JAMA.* 2001;285:3015–3021.

Jeckler N. *Aging and Ethics.* Totowa, NJ: Humana; 1991.

McCullough LB, Wilson NL. *Long-Term Care Decisions: Ethical and Conceptual Dimensions.* Baltimore, Md: Johns Hopkins University Press; 1995.

Moody HR. Cross-cultural geriatric ethics: Negotiating our differences. *Generations.* 1998;22(3):32–39.

Post SG. Establishing an appropriate ethical framework: The moral conversation around the goal of prolongevity. *J Gerontol A Biol Sci Med Sci.* 2004;59:B534–B539.

ETHNICITY AND RACE

American society is aging rapidly. Coupled with fertility decline across the past several decades and rapid and large increases in life expectancy during late adulthood, the fastest-growing segments of the population are now over 65 years of age. For example, the population over 65 years of age is growing at a rate slightly exceeding 1% per year, whereas the population over 85 years of age is growing at a rate approaching 10% per year. In contrast, the population under 65 years of age is growing at a rate of just less than 1% per year. The older population is a heterogeneous mixture of races and ethnicities, and describing the growth in this population as a whole belies the considerable change in the nature of this population over time.

To be sure, death rates are higher for most racial/ethnic minority groups, making the older population more homogeneously non-Hispanic White than the younger population. However, birth rates have historically been higher for many minority groups, migration rates (especially for Hispanic populations) have been increasing, and death rates have fallen at roughly equivalent rates across races. The net result is an aged population that, although largely non-Hispanic White, is becoming increasingly heterogeneous over time. For example, as recently as 1970, non-Whites (including Hispanic Whites) comprised roughly 5% of the total population over 75 years of age, but just three decades later (by 2000) they comprised approximately 10% of the same population. Furthermore, given that non-Hispanic Whites are projected to constitute less than 50% of the total population within a few decades, the proportion of the older population that is non-White (including Hispanic Whites) will certainly increase, providing greater impetus for focusing on racial/ethnic health disparities in aging research.

Over the past several decades, increasing attention has been paid to racial/ethnic diversity in the older population. The most obvious examples of such increases in attention are the changes in the measurement of race and ethnicity in the U.S. Census. These include (a) the beginning of self-identification of race in 1960, (b) the addition of the indicator for Hispanic ethnicity (in the census short form for all members of the population) in 1980, and (c) the addition of multiple-race categories in 2000. These changes highlight the growing recognition of the complexity of studying the racial/ethnic composition of the population. At the same time, these measurement changes have made it difficult, if not impossible, to determine the exact extent of change in racial/ethnic composition of the population. For the sake of brevity and to prevent tedious language, throughout this entry the term *White* is used to represent non-Hispanic Whites, the term *Black* is used to represent Hispanic and non-Hispanic Blacks, and the term *Hispanic* is used to represent Hispanics of any race. Certainly, this is not an entirely satisfactory racial categorization, but most research in gerontology and other fields tends to simply use White and non-White—with non-White including Hispanics—as the measure of race. Furthermore, we use the term *minority group* in a literal sense to represent Hispanics as well as non-White races.

In gerontology and its contributing disciplines (e.g., sociology, psychology), considerable work has been done investigating racial/ethnic differences in aging and health. Most research has focused on differences among Whites (roughly 85% of the population over 65 years of age), Blacks (roughly 8%), and Hispanics (roughly 5%, but may be any race). This focus is not surprising given that these three groups constitute the vast majority of elders in the United States. Less work has been done investigating Native Americans and

Asians (including Pacific Islanders). The former group constitutes less than 1% of the older population, and most surveys—even large major national surveys—fail to obtain sufficient numbers of Native Americans to allow for adequate comparisons between Native Americans and other racial/ethnic groups. The latter group constitutes just under 3% of the older population. However, the rate of increase in the Asian population is greater than the rates for most other racial groups, so it is surprising that relatively little health research in the United States has examined this group. What is known about these two subpopulations is that (a) Native American elders tend to be less healthy and have a drastically shorter life expectancy than do Whites and even other minority groups, and (b) Asian American elders tend to be healthier than Whites. In fact, the longest lived group in the United States today are Asian American females, whose life expectancy at birth is well beyond 80 years.

Most research investigating the health of minority aged populations has been conducted within the past three decades and has focused on the health of non-Hispanic Whites versus Blacks versus Hispanics. Despite more than a decade of calls for examination of within-minority group heterogeneity in health (e.g., Mexican Americans vs. Puerto Ricans vs. Cubans), virtually no research has investigated such heterogeneity. Similarly, virtually no research has investigated heterogeneity within the "White" majority elder population despite the fact that similar heterogeneity exists within this population as within minority populations. These research deficits are likely the result of having inadequate sample sizes to consider more refined racial/ethnic heritage categories adequately as well as limited measurement of heritage in most surveys.

Little research considers Black, White, and Hispanic differences in health simultaneously; instead, most research either compares Blacks with Whites, compares non-Hispanic Whites with Hispanics, or compares non-Hispanic Whites with all other racial/ethnic groups. Current key areas of investigation in racial/ethnic disparities in health include (a) the comparison of health and mortality rates for Whites versus Blacks and (b) the comparison of health and mortality rates for Hispanics versus non-Hispanic Whites. It is well known that

Blacks have poorer health and higher mortality rates than do Whites for most of the life course. However, research since the 1970s has discovered that Black mortality rates beyond 75 years of age fall below mortality rates for Whites, producing a "crossover." Two explanations for this crossover have been advanced: a data quality explanation and a heterogeneity explanation. The former explanation claims that the crossover is not real; instead, it is the result of age misreporting by Black elders. The latter explanation claims that the crossover results because of sizable heterogeneity within the Black population. Highly frail Blacks are "selected" out of the population via mortality prior to old age, leaving a small but highly robust subset of Blacks at older ages who, in fact, have better health than do Whites. Crossovers have been found between Blacks and Whites not only in mortality rates but also in health.

In research focusing on health, a competing hypothesis, the double jeopardy hypothesis, proposes that aging and the cumulative disadvantage of minority status combine to produce an increasing Black–White health differential during later life. Research is inconclusive regarding this hypothesis, with many arguing that selective mortality and the choice of health measure examined determine whether support is found for the hypothesis.

Other key health disparities between Whites and Blacks have been found as well. Blacks have higher rates of stroke death at advanced ages than do Whites, in part stemming from having higher rates of hypertension at all ages. Blacks also have higher rates of obesity (especially Black women), as well as higher rates of type 2 diabetes, across the life course. In terms of subjective measures, Blacks tend to rate their health worse than do Whites, although some research has found the opposite, especially when respondents are asked to compare their health with that of their peers, something elders of all races and ethnicities tend to do. Finally, in terms of mental health, Blacks tend to have more depressive symptoms, but have lower levels of diagnosable depressive disorder, during later life than do Whites, yielding an incomplete picture of Black–White differences in mental health.

In terms of Hispanic versus White health, research has consistently found that Hispanics at younger ages have better health than do Whites and that the disparity is more pronounced between non-Hispanic Whites and recent immigrants than between Whites and second-generation or higher generation Hispanics. This finding has been termed the *Hispanic paradox* because the expectation is that minority groups uniformly have worse health than the non-Hispanic White majority, which tends to have higher levels of socioeconomic status and does not face discrimination in the labor force and other aspects of social life. Research has been less consistent, however, regarding White and Hispanic health differences during later life. Some research shows an advantage to Hispanics in some dimensions of health, but other research shows a disadvantage.

Explanations of the Hispanic paradox generally fall into two categories: the healthy migrant hypothesis (a selection argument) and the cultural differences hypothesis. The former hypothesis is a selection-based argument positing that Hispanic health superiority is an artifact of selective migration: Only healthy Hispanics immigrate to the United States. This hypothesis has yet to receive much support for explaining the health advantage of young Hispanics and has even less support for explaining any health advantage for Hispanic elders. This hypothesis has little hope for understanding Hispanic health advantages at old age, in part because most Hispanic migrants are young, and good health during youth does not necessarily translate into good health during later adulthood. The latter hypothesis— the cultural differences hypothesis—posits that Hispanic health advantages, at least during youth, are attributable to the existence of better health behaviors among Hispanic immigrant populations (e.g., lower smoking rates, better diets). Research in this vein has shown that part of the Hispanic health advantage is, in fact, attributable to better health behaviors among recent immigrants. A key approach to testing this hypothesis has been to consider "assimilation" to American culture to be detrimental by eroding traditional preimmigration cultural practices, so a key measure has been immigrant generation and language spoken in the home. This approach has little potential to explain Hispanic health advantages, where they exist, among elders because most immigrants are young and thus older immigrants—even first-generation immigrants—have extensive exposure to American culture by old age and have likely adopted the relatively poorer health behaviors of the culture.

General Well-Being and Aging

In addition to direct examination of health, research has considered mediators of the race/ethnicity–health relationship. We call these mediators measures of general well-being because they are not simply mediators; to some extent, they are also measures of health.

Research on general well-being and aging includes research on quality of life, stress, and social support. A considerable body of research has emerged investigating racial disparities in these domains, but such research has not produced results consistent enough to paint a clear picture. Some research suggests that social support networks, especially kinship support networks, are larger and support is more available for minority elders (especially Blacks) than for White elders. At the same time, however, research on general quality of life suggests that, despite this apparent support advantage, minority elders have lower levels of life quality than do Whites. This result may reflect issues concerning the measurement of support (e.g., perceived availability vs. actual receipt of instrumental support), or it may reflect that available support is inadequate to meet the needs of minority elders. Research has not shown consistently that life events stress during later life is more prevalent for minorities than for Whites, but some evidence suggests that chronic stress (e.g., financial stress) is more prevalent. Although stress exposure differences may or may not exist, research has begun to show that minority elders, or at least Blacks, may be more vulnerable to the effects of stress. Such research is consistent with the view presented previously that minority elders, although perhaps having more extensive support networks, might not have adequate instrumental support.

New Research Areas and Suggestions

Research on racial/ethnic differentials and aging continues to increase in volume, yet there are numerous areas that remain relatively unexplored. Here we discuss two interesting avenues of research: (a) early-life events and their impacts on later life health and economic conditions and (b) skin color, discrimination, and their consequences. The former line of research—on early-life events—to date has focused on the later life consequences of early-life events without regard to race. The consistent finding is that early-life conditions play a strong role in affecting later life health and mortality risk. Extending the focus of this research to racial/ethnic health disparities during later life should be an important contribution given the considerable changes in racial/ethnic relations within the United States over the course of the past century. For example, although racial/ethnic equality in socioeconomic status does not exist today, some minority group members have attained higher levels of education and income than were possible in generations whose members were of working age prior to the civil rights movement. Thus, early-life socioeconomic conditions may help explain a considerable amount of racial/ethnic inequality in health between majority and minority group members of comparable current socioeconomic status.

The second area of research—skin color and discrimination—is another promising avenue for future research. Recent research has shown that skin color may be more important to health than self-defined race. The assumption behind this research is that the real non-socioeconomically driven consequences of race are produced by discrimination and that discrimination results from the majority's recognition of skin color and not self-identified race. In brief, the lighter the skin, the less discrimination is experienced; the darker the skin, the more discrimination is experienced. If the chronic experience of discrimination is a driving force in the production of hypertension differentials by race; for example, skin color may be a fundamental predictor of racially based health inequality.

A key difficulty that remains in exploring especially these but also other avenues of research on racial/ethnic health disparities is the limitation of data. To be sure, there are a number of repeated cross-sectional and panel data sets that facilitate the study of aging and health, and all of them have data on race. However, the measurement of race in these surveys is (a) limited to very few categories and/or (b) variable from wave to wave. For example, some key data sets include the Established Populations for Epidemiologic Studies of the Elderly (EPESE), the Hispanic EPESE, the National Health and Nutrition Examination Survey (NHANES) and NHANES I Epidemiologic Follow-up Study (NHEFS), the Health and Retirement Study/Asset and Health Dynamics Among the Oldest Old (HRS/AHEAD), the National Long Term Care Survey (NLTCS), and the National Health Interview Survey (NHIS). The EPESE, especially the Duke University sample (Piedmont Health Survey), contains a large oversample of Blacks but has measurement neither of Hispanic ethnicity nor of other races. The NHANES (and NHEFS) measures race as White, Black, and other, with no Hispanics (or indicator thereof) and no other racial detail. The HRS/AHEAD measures race similarly. The NLTCS provides more racial detail, measuring race in five categories: White; Black; Asian or Pacific Islander; American Indian, Eskimo, or Aleut; and other. Finally, the NHIS changed measurement of race across waves and consistently measures race only as White, Black, and other. These measurement limitations in extant major surveys make it impossible to fully consider racial disparities in health across the life course and especially during later life, particularly with regard to early-life events and skin color. Instead, future research attempting to further explore racial disparities in health in-depth will require the collection of new data, which by design will be limited in their usefulness in addressing racial disparities using a life course perspective.

—Scott M. Lynch
and J. Scott Brown

See also African Americans; Asian and Pacific Islander Americans; Hispanics; Native Americans and Alaska Natives

Further Readings and References

Brown JS, Lynch SM. Race, aging, and health: The history and future of the double jeopardy hypothesis. *Contemp Gerontol.* 2004;10:105–109.

Lynch SM, Brown JS, Harmsen KG. Black–White differences in mortality deceleration and compression and the mortality crossover reconsidered. *Res Aging.* 2003;25:456–483.

Markides KS, Black SA. Race, ethnicity, and aging: The impact of inequality. In: Binstock RH, George LK, eds. *Handbook of Aging and the Social Sciences.* 4th ed. San Diego, Calif: Academic Press; 1996:153–170.

Martin LG, Soldo BJ, eds. *Racial and Ethnic Differences in the Health of Older Americans.* Washington, DC: National Academy Press; 1997.

Williams DR, Collins C. U.S. socioeconomic and racial differences in health: Patterns and explanations. *Annu Rev Sociol.* 1995;21:349–386.

EUROPE

Europe consists of countries that differ in history, geography, climate, political system, and health care system. Since the falling apart of the former Soviet Union and the former Yugoslavia, the number of countries has increased. Since May 2004, the European Union (EU) numbers 25 countries. In that year, the total population of the EU amounted to 457 million inhabitants. The EU does not include several countries—some in Western Europe (e.g., Norway, Switzerland), some in Eastern Europe (e.g., Rumania, Bulgaria), and many of the newly formed countries (e.g., Croatia, Belarus). The share of older persons (age 65 years and older) in the EU population is 16.4% on average. This share is expected to nearly double to 29.9% by 2050.

The heterogeneity across European countries manifests itself in the widely different shares of the population age 65 years and older as well as in the widely different rates of increase in this share (Figure 1). In 2004, the proportions of older persons ranged from 11.1% in Ireland to 19.2% in Italy. The expected increases by 2050 range from a modest 7.1 percentage points in Sweden to a spectacular 18.7 percentage points in Spain, resulting in a range from 22.1% in Luxembourg to 35.6% in Spain as the lowest and highest expected proportions, respectively, of the population age 65 years and older. Moreover, the share of the oldest-old population (age 80 years and older) is expected to nearly triple by 2050, with the highest proportion expected in Italy (14.1%).

The variety in these demographic projections stems from differences in fertility, mortality, and migration. Among these, fertility has the most impact. First, the post–World War II baby boom differed across countries in intensity and duration. For instance, in the Netherlands the baby boom lasted until 1970, whereas in other countries it was over before 1960. Second, the countries differ in their rates of decline in fertility since the 1960s. For instance, in the Netherlands the fertility rate dropped from 2.8% to 1.6%. This drop has been steepest in the Mediterranean countries. Migration is expected to have the greatest impact in the new EU member states, resulting in a decline of the total population and a relatively large increase in the proportion age 65 years and older. Although mortality at older ages shows consistent declines, the rate of decline is again different across countries and even shows increases in Denmark, the Netherlands, Norway, and several Eastern European countries. France shows the most consistent declines.

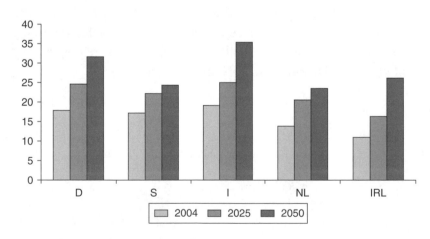

Figure 1   Populations Age 65 Years and Older in 2004 and Projections for 2025 and 2050 for Selected Countries

Source: Eurostat. Population Projections 2004–2050. Eurostat News Release 48/2005. © European Communities, 2005.

Note: D = Germany; S = Sweden; I = Italy; NL = the Netherlands; IRL = Ireland.

Morbidity and Disability

Availability of Data

Comparison of morbidity and disability across European countries is more difficult than comparison of mortality because each country shapes its health policy using its own concepts and measurement of health indicators. A few early international studies included European countries but were limited in scope or included only a selection of the older population. Only in the 1990s did a number of cross-national surveys that used common instruments and sampling methods become available. The best known is the European Community Household Panel survey, conducted in the noninstitutionalized population in 13 countries. For the assessment of health during older age, however, this survey is less suitable because in many countries a sizable proportion of older persons live in institutions.

Through the impetus of the EU Fifth Framework Program, in which the study of aging populations was a key action, a number of new cross-European studies were initiated, with several of them including new member states. The data from these studies are now becoming available. In one Fifth Framework project, the Comparison of Longitudinal European Studies of Aging (CLESA), data from six ongoing longitudinal population studies were harmonized, so that comparable data on health became available.

Morbidity

Morbidity refers to the prevalence of chronic conditions. Among the five most prevalent chronic conditions, musculoskeletal diseases, including arthritis and osteoporosis, rank on top. In the age group 65 to 84 years, their combined prevalence ranges from nearly 40% to more than 70%, depending on the country. Among the CLESA countries, older persons in Spain have the highest prevalence (approximately 70%), whereas the prevalence is lowest (approximately 40%) in the Netherlands. Heart diseases, including myocardial infarction, angina pectoris, heart failure, and peripheral artery disease, rank second among chronic

conditions. Also for this category of diseases, prevalence differs widely across countries. In particular, heart diseases show a north–south gradient. The prevalence is highest in Finland (46% in the age group 75 to 84 years) and lowest in Italy (18%). Respiratory diseases, including chronic bronchitis, emphysema, and asthma, rank next, with particularly high prevalence in Spain and Italy (approximately 34%) and lower prevalence in the Netherlands and Sweden (approximately 15%). Diabetes ranks fourth, again with different prevalence rates across countries. In contrast to the distribution of heart disease, diabetes is more prevalent in Mediterranean countries (15% to 20%) and less prevalent in the north of Europe (approximately 11%). Stroke and cancer share the fifth rank in prevalence. Their prevalence ranges from 5% to 11%, again with significant differences across Europe. As with diabetes, the prevalence of stroke is relatively high in Mediterranean countries and lower in Scandinavian countries. Cancer has the highest prevalence in the Netherlands and the lowest in Scandinavian countries.

The observed differences in the various prevalence rates across Europe can be explained, at least in part, by differences in lifestyle. On the one hand, smoking is still more common among southern European and Dutch adults, whereas among Scandinavians smoking rates have been declining. This is reflected in higher rates of cancer and stroke in southern Europe and of cancer in the Netherlands. On the other hand, the Mediterranean diet has been shown to be protective against heart disease, which is reflected in a clear north–south gradient in heart disease prevalence.

Despite their different prevalence rates, all of the chronic conditions just discussed have similar associations with mortality across countries. Cancer has the highest risk of mortality (hazard ratio of 1.9), followed by diabetes (1.5), heart diseases (1.3), and respiratory diseases (1.2).

Disability

Disability is the inability to perform usual daily activities. More complex activities, such as shopping, preparing a meal, and doing housework, are termed instrumental activities of daily living (IADLs). More basic and obligatory activities, such as bathing, dressing, and toileting, are termed activities of daily living (ADLs). The former are more likely to be affected by sociocultural factors than are the latter. Nevertheless, a surprising variety in prevalence of ADL disability is observed across European countries, ranging from 6% to 35%. Although the few available studies show different patterns, ADL disability turns out to be highest in Italy and Spain and lowest in Finland. Again, a north–south gradient is observed and may be explained by socioeconomic and cultural differences. There is ample evidence for socioeconomic differences in morbidity and disability across Europe. Among older persons in Mediterranean countries, only a small minority have completed elementary education, whereas the majority of older persons in northern countries have done so. Differences in ADL prevalence may also stem from differences in the meaning of dependence and the availability of family help. Self-reported disability may be greater when help is available within the family, as is the norm in Mediterranean countries, unlike in northern countries.

The north–south gradient in ADL disability is reflected in disability-free life expectancy; whereas life expectancy from 65 years of age is shorter in northern countries, the number of years spent without disability is greater than in Mediterranean countries. This gradient is most visible for men.

As is the case with chronic conditions, despite the diversity in prevalence across countries, the predictive abilities of ADL disability for mortality are very similar across countries (hazard ratio of 2.9). Also, the associations between disability and a more objective performance-based disability score are similar across countries.

IADL disability shows a different pattern from that of ADL disability, with Italy and Finland ranking among the lowest prevalence rates (approximately 25% in the age group 75 to 84 years) and Spain, the Netherlands, and Sweden ranking among the highest (nearly 50%). IADLs are particularly sensitive to cultural biases, and this is shown when the separate activities are compared across countries for older men and women separately. The prevalence rates appear to vary with norms about the gender division of household work. Women are more independent in cooking, and men are more independent in shopping. Housework is least affected by gender biases. Cultural biases related to family norms and living arrangements are demonstrated in preparing meals, where older women show more disability in countries where households are usually shared with children and less disability in countries where older unmarried women generally live alone.

Self-Rated Health

Older people's own evaluations of their health are known to be sensitive to sociocultural factors. Thus, it is not surprising that self-rated health differs across European older populations. However, there is not a clear gradient. Older persons in both Finland and Spain rate their health as worst, and older persons in Sweden and the Netherlands report the best health. Older persons in Eastern Europe also rate their health as worse than those in Western Europe. Although specific data on the older population are still lacking, for the middle-aged population it has been calculated that material deprivation, economic satisfaction, perceived control, and participation in civic activities account for up to 30% of the east–west differences.

In most countries, women rate their health as somewhat worse than do men. There are, moreover, clear gender differences in the predictive ability of self-rated health for mortality. In most countries, older men's self-perceptions of health are more predictive of mortality than are older women's self-perceptions. The gender differences can be explained, to a large extent, by differences in health profiles and lifestyle. In addition, differences in standards of health may play a role. Women generally know more about their health than do men and are more willing to act on perceived health declines. These behavioral differences may bring older women more years of life, albeit often in less than ideal health.

Mental Health

Common mental health conditions during older age are depression, anxiety, and dementia. In all three conditions, the psychiatric diagnosis can be distinguished from the milder, but still clinically relevant, syndromal or "subthreshold" condition. For the affective disorders, the psychiatric diagnosis does not increase—or even decreases—with age. The diagnosis of depression has a prevalence of approximately 2%. The diagnosis of dementia is not very prevalent at 65 years of age (1%), but it increases steeply with age, especially after 80 years of age. At age 90 years and older, 30% of the population has dementia.

Among the subthreshold conditions, depression has the greatest prevalence among people age 65 years and older. It is for this condition that most data are available across Europe. On a harmonized scale score with a range of 0 to 12, the country mean scores range from 1.6 in Ireland to 3.2 in Germany. A systematic analysis of national context variables shows that higher gross national product and health expenditures and more extensive mental health care are associated with higher levels of depressive symptoms.

A widely reported phenomenon in depression is that women have higher levels than do men. The gender differential is consistent across countries but varies in size. Among the countries of the CLESA project, women had significantly more subthreshold depression than did men except in Sweden. The prevalence rates ranged from 13% in Dutch men to 39% in Italian women. The higher symptom load of women can be attributed partly to a greater burden of physical health problems and partly to more disadvantaged social and economic conditions. However, these factors explain only up to 50% of the gender differential, so that other yet undiscovered pathways exist.

An association between subthreshold depression and disability is observed at older ages. Again, there are variations in the strength of this association across European countries. As with levels of subthreshold depression, in strength of association between depression and disability, national context plays a role. In particular, in countries with a high gross national product, high health expenditures, and extensive mental health care, this association is attenuated. Moreover, in countries with high orthodox religious beliefs and a high adherence to the Roman Catholic Church, this association is exacerbated.

Use of Services

The use of services is related directly to the concept of welfare state and the prevailing norms about the role of the family in a country. The causal relation of public service provision with cultural norms and orientations is ambiguous given that availability of services may conform to family orientations or, vice versa, family orientations may reflect availability of services. Support for family solidarity shows a north–south gradient, being highest in Mediterranean countries and lowest in Scandinavian countries. This is exemplified by the proportions of the older population living alone and being institutionalized, both of which show a decreasing north–south gradient. Nevertheless, of all support provided to frail older persons, informal support from family members and others is greater than support from services in all countries except Denmark, which has the most extensive home care services.

Cross-country variety in the provision of informal support also stems from demographic and socioeconomic differences. In particular, percentages of never-married and divorced persons, fertility rates, percentages of women in the labor force, and life expectancies of male and female spouses determine availability of informal support. In addition, religious orientation is a contributing factor. All of these factors, moreover, show differential trends and fluctuations over time. When European countries are clustered according to their values on this variety of factors in 2000, Scandinavian countries and the Netherlands are characterized by a higher level of provision of formal care, a lower level of family care, fewer contacts between family members, lower fertility, and a higher proportion of women living alone. Germany, Ireland, Italy, and Spain are characterized by a lower proportion of older people receiving formal care, more contacts between family members, and a lower proportion of divorced women. Greece and Portugal have similar characteristics but are distinguished by a high level of religiousness and lower economic welfare. Several countries in the middle of Europe—Austria, Belgium, France, and the United Kingdom—show an average position on the basis of these characteristics.

It can be concluded that in terms of use of services and care provision, the north–south gradient is not clear-cut. Moreover, the amount of difference is likely to change as demographic and economic factors are changing. Whether there will be convergence between national systems depends on the influence of these objective factors as weighed against cultural and attitudinal factors.

Conclusion

There is not one way of aging in Europe. The data available show cross-European differences in virtually all indicators of health among the various older populations. And these differences do not appear to be very systematic. However, this heterogeneity should be seen not as an obstacle but rather as an advantage for further exploration of critical factors that influence health as people age.

—*Dorly J. H. Deeg*

Further Readings and References

Bobak M, Pikhart H, Rose R, Hertzman C, Marmot M. Socioeconomic factors, material inequalities, and perceived control in self-rated health: Cross-sectional data from seven post-communist countries. *Social Sci Med.* 2000;51:1343–1350.

Daatland SO, Herlofson K. "Lost solidarity" or "changed solidarity": A comparative European view of normative family solidarity. *Ageing Soc.* 2003;23:537–560.

Deeg DJH, Wahl H-W. The potential of cross-European studies of ageing [special issue]. *Eur J Ageing.* 2004; 1:1–108.

Janssen F, Mackenbach JP, Kunst AE, for the Netherlands Epidemiology and Demography Compression (NEDCOM). Trends in old-age mortality in seven European countries, 1950–1999. *J Clin Epidemiol.* 2004;57:203–216.

Jylhä M, Guralnik JM, Ferrucci L, Jokela J, Heikkinen E. Is self-rated health comparable across cultures and genders? *J Gerontol B Psychol Sci Social Sci.* 1998;53:S144–S152.

Knoops KTB, De Groot LCPGM, Kormhout D, et al. Mediterranean diet, lifestyle factors, and 10-year mortality in elderly European men and women: The HALE project. *JAMA.* 2004;292:1433–1439.

Minicuci N, Noale M, Bardage C, et al., for the Comparison of Longitudinal European Studies of Aging (CLESA) Working Group. Cross-national determinants of quality of life from six longitudinal studies on aging: The CLESA project. *Aging Clin Exp Res.* 2003;15:187–202.

Nikula S, Jylhä M, Bardage C, et al., for the Comparison of Longitudinal European Studies of Aging (CLESA) Working Group. Are IADLs comparable across countries? Sociodemographic associates of harmonized IADL measures. *Aging Clin Exp Res.* 2003;15:451–459.

Walker A, Maltby T. *Ageing in Europe.* Buckingham, England: Open University Press; 1997.

Exercise and Physical Activity

The literature on exercise and physical activity in older adults has exploded over the past two decades as the field of health and aging has come to realize the significance of regular physical activity as a means of promoting health in older adults as well as the difficulty in promoting regular physical activity in this predominantly sedentary population. The focus of this entry is on physical activity in older populations. It provides a brief summary of the status of research in several key areas, including the types and levels of physical activity among older populations, the factors and antecedents associated with physical activity, the health benefits of physical activity among diverse groups, and the current evidence on programs and interventions promoting regular physical activity among older adults. The entry concludes with recommendations on needed research and promising directions in physical activity.

Several interrelated terms are used to describe physical activity in the literature, including exercise, regular physical activity, specific activities such as walking, and leisure time physical activity. *Physical activity* is defined as engaging in a body of movements produced by skeletal muscles that result in energy expenditure above the basal level. *Leisure time physical activity* is defined as participating in physically active hobbies or sports or exercising within a 2-week period. These measures are typically based on self-reports and are used in national surveys and ongoing surveillance. The types of exercises used to qualify the types of movement can be classified as aerobic, strength and resistance training, range of motion, or balance. Regular physical activity is a lifestyle, exercise is a behavior, and the terms are not interchangeable.

Findings from the *Surgeon General's Report on Physical Activity* conclude that older adults exercise less than, and are more sedentary than, other adult age groups. More than 60% of older adults do not participate in regular physical activity, and 31% are sedentary. There are demographic differences in the levels and types of physical activity within the older population. Within the older population, those age 75 years and older, females, and non-Whites are more physically inactive.

In terms of specific types of activity, older adults are more likely to participate in aerobic exercise than in strength training. Walking is the most popular form of aerobic activity among older adults. In fact, one quarter of those age 65 years and older meet current public health recommendations of walking five or more times per week for 30 minutes per time. Data from the 2001 National Health Interview Survey show that 11% of respondents age 65 years and older report engaging in strength training 2 or more days per week. Smaller percentages of those age 75 years and older, females, Blacks, and Hispanics report participating in recommended levels of strength training. Finally, the percentage of older adults who engage in regular physical activity is improving. Based on the Behavioral Risk Factor Surveillance Survey, older adults reporting no leisure time physical activity decreased from 30.5% in 1988 to 25.1% in 2002.

Benefits of Physical Activity

Research on the health benefit of exercise and physical activity in older adults is extensive and is based on epidemiological studies, observational studies, and intervention trials. A broad spectrum of health benefits have been observed, ranging from pathology, biomarkers of chronic disease, and health risk factors to disability, functional status, mental health, and quality of life. Health benefits have been observed among healthy older adults as well as among those with specific chronic illnesses, impaired mobility, and other disabilities. Benefits have been demonstrated among older adults in the community, home-bound older adults with limited mobility, and nursing home residents. Meta-analyses and evidence-based reviews summarizing outcomes of physical activity have been reported for several measures, including improved bone mass and bone mineral density, reduction in blood pressure and hypertension, improved insulin resistance, and improved mental health outcomes. Some researchers have even concluded that there is sufficient evidence that activity in older adults improves outcome measures across all domains of the disablement process except disability (on which findings are inconsistent).

Correlates of Physical Activity and Exercise Participation

Information concerning the correlates of participation in physical activity can be examined at two broad levels: attrition during recruitment and attrition during regular physical activity or relapse once regular physical activity has been initiated. These correlates can be further divided into modifiable correlates (e.g., attitudes, perceptions) and nonmodifiable correlates (e.g., demographic characteristics). Demographic characteristics among older adults associated with nonparticipation in regular physical activity include being female, older, and non-White; living in a rural residence; and living alone. Elderly who are current smokers, are in poor health, and have lower educational attainment are also less likely to be physically active. Reviews on self-reported barriers to physical activity in older adults identify poor health, lack of motivation, time constraints, fatigue, and environmental factors (e.g., bad weather, neighborhood safety concerns, lack of sidewalks). Perceived self-efficacy for physical activity, social support, and perceived benefits of regular physical activity are associated with increased activity. Finally, advice and brief behavioral counseling given by health care professionals to older patients appear to be associated with increased physical activity.

Correlates associated with successful adherence to physical activity programs for older adults are informed by the research on correlates of physical activity. Intervention components are often designed from behavior change theories reflecting these correlates. Recent reviews of physical activity interventions with older adults show considerable agreement in terms of psychosocial and motivational factors associated with exercise adherence and the theoretical models that guide the interventions. Interventions based on social–cognitive theory generally and on self-efficacy specifically are effective in promoting physical activity. Interventions that include motivational tools, such as goal setting, self-monitoring, gradual progression, performance feedback, and social support, are also effective.

Program characteristics are also related to participation in physical activity. Older adults tend to prefer individual-based exercise programs over group-based ones and are more likely to participate in programs that provide choices among activities. Programs that include telephone supervision and motivational interviewing have been shown to be effective with older adults. Although not fully explored in older populations, exercise programs that typically include gradual progression, include nonvigorous activities, and address concerns for safety may contribute to the success of exercise programs. Examples of programs that have incorporated many of these individual and program characteristics include Strong for Life, Community Health Advice by Telephone (CHAT), and the Community Healthy Activities Model Program for Seniors (CHAMPS II).

Innovations and Future Directions

Recently, there have been innovative programs designed for older adults that increase physical functioning. These programs focus on strength, resistance, and balance exercises and may include Tai Chi, cobblestone walking, and the use of therabands. Tai Chi exercises improve physical functioning, improve balance, and reduce falls in older adults as well as improve quality and duration of sleep. Cobblestone walking is a method by which older adults walk on a mat that is embedded with smooth stones. There is some evidence that cobblestone walking, as compared with flat surface walking, improves balance, blood pressure, and walking speed in older adults. Another new and inexpensive tool for resistance training is the use of therabands, which have proven to be effective with persons with osteoarthritis and older persons with functional limitations. These innovations should

be explored more fully in terms of health benefits and wide-scale dissemination.

Another advancement in promoting physical activity among older adults is the application of broader ecological models that recognize not only the interactions between the person-based factors influencing physical activity (e.g., biological, motivational) but also the social environmental and policy factors that influence performance of regular physical activity. For example, it has been found that older adults in neighborhoods with heavy traffic, trash, and litter were less likely to be physically active than were older adults free of such neighborhood problems. These environmental factors should be explored in terms of health disparities among ethnically diverse older populations.

Changes in physical activity have been linked to life transitions. For example, it has been found that assuming a caregiver role contributes to attrition in group-based exercise programs among older minority adults. It has been demonstrated that a moderate-intensity exercise program for older caregivers increases the level of exercise and improves blood pressure, sleep quality, and psychological distress. Other life transitions, such as loss of spouse and retirement, may also be promising areas for exploration of sedentary risk and physical activity interventions.

Finally, as physical activity programs with proven efficacy and effectiveness emerge, efforts should be directed at translating research into community practice and dissemination. For this to occur, cost and cost-effectiveness need to be established and research on effective models of dissemination should be conducted. Successful translation of research to practice should contribute to increasing regular physical activity among older adults.

—*Thomas R. Prohaska and Laura M. Hawkes*

See also Control; Health Promotion and Disease Prevention; Self-Efficacy

Further Readings and References

Balfour J, Kaplan G. Neighborhood environment and loss of physical function in older adults: Evidence from the Alameda County Study. *Am J Epidemiol.* 2002;155:507–515.

Brosse A, Sheets E, Lett H, Blumenthal J. Exercise and the treatment of clinical depression in adults: Recent findings and future directions. *Sports Med.* 2002;32:741–760.

Conn V, Minor M, Burks K, Rantz M, Pomeroy S. Integrative review of physical activity intervention research with aging adults. *J Am Geriatr Soc.* 2003;51:1159–1168.

King A, Rejeski W, Buchner D. Physical activity interventions targeting older adults: A critical review and recommendations. *Am J Prev Med.* 1998;15:316–333.

Kokkinos P, Narayan P, Papademetrious V. Exercise as hypertension therapy. *Cardiol Clin.* 2001;19:507–516.

Li F, Fisher J, Harmer P. Improving physical function and blood pressure in older adults through cobblestone mat walking: A randomized trial. *J Am Geriatr Soc.* 2005;53:1305–1312.

Wilcox S, Tutor-Locke C, Ainsworth B. Physical activity patterns, assessment, and motivation in older adults. In: Shepard RJ, ed. *Gender, Physical Activity, and Aging.* Boca Raton, Fla: CRC Press; 2002:13–39.

EXPECTATIONS REGARDING AGING

Attributing health problems and disability to "old age" is a widespread phenomenon among older adults that is especially pronounced among adults in their 70s and older. For many older adults, attributing health problems to old age may serve as a successful coping mechanism in the face of age-associated changes. For others, attributing health problems to old age per se may be dangerous. For example, older adults who attribute health problems to old age are at increased risk for mortality. Examining whether or how attributing health problems to old age actually causes older adults to experience worse health outcomes has been an active area of research for more than 10 years.

The term *expectations regarding aging* (also referred to as *expectations for aging* or *age expectations*) refers to one's beliefs about his or her own aging across multiple domains as well as beliefs about what is an expected part of aging for older adults in general. Older adults with low expectations regarding aging expect declines in physical and mental health-related quality of life with aging and believe that many age-associated problems are attributable to old age itself. Older adults with high expectations regarding aging, on the other hand, expect to attain and maintain high levels of health-related quality of life into old age and believe that many

age-associated problems are not actually caused by aging itself. Older adults with higher expectations regarding aging are more likely to be younger and to have better physical and mental health-related quality of life. Depressive symptoms are strongly associated with lower expectations regarding aging.

The Expectations Regarding Aging (ERA-38) Survey is a 38-item instrument with acceptable reliability and validity in English and Spanish that can be used to measure age expectations across 10 domains: general health, cognitive function, mental health, functional independence, sexual function, pain, urinary incontinence, sleep, fatigue, and appearance. Unlike many instruments that measure attitudes toward aging or beliefs about aging, scores on the ERA-38 are not "positive" versus "negative" or "right" versus "wrong." Instead, higher scores on the ERA-38 are indicative of expecting achievement and maintenance of high physical and mental functioning with aging (for self and others), and low scores are indicative of expecting decline with aging. Although there are no cutpoints for what is optimal, having lower expectations for aging is associated with health behaviors that may put older persons at risk for bad outcomes. For example, older adults with lower expectations regarding aging are more likely to feel that it is not important to seek health care for age-associated problems or depression. In addition, older persons with low expectations regarding aging are less likely to participate in regular physical activity.

Another way to measure individual expectations regarding aging is by asking older persons to estimate their future health-related quality of life using traditional or utility-based health-related quality of life surveys; interestingly, although most older adults tend to overestimate their actuarial life expectancy, most older adults underestimate their future health-related quality of life after 70 years of age. In other words, most older adults expect to live longer but in poorer health than they actually experience. Despite the fact that disability rates among older adults in the United States continue to decline, widely pervasive negative stereotypes about older adults may contribute to the commonly held misconceptions that quality of life is poor for most older adults.

—Catherine A. Sarkisian

See also Active Life Expectancy; Successful Aging

Further Readings and References

Brouwer WB, van Exel NJ. Expectations regarding length and health related quality of life: Some empirical findings. *Social Sci Med.* 2005;61:1083–1094.

Sarkisian CA, Hays RD, Berry SH, Mangione CM. Expectations regarding aging among older adults and physicians who care for older adults. *Med Care.* 2001;39:1025–1036.

Sarkisian CA, Hays RD, Mangione CM. Do older adults expect to age successfully? The association between expectations regarding aging and beliefs regarding healthcare seeking among older adults. *J Am Geriatr Soc.* 2002;50:1837–1843.

Eye Diseases

Visual problems are among the most feared disabilities in the elderly. According to the World Health Organization, more than 161 million people globally were afflicted with visual impairments in 2002. Of these, approximately 37 million were blind. These numbers are expected to grow as the geriatric cohort rises. Visual impairments significantly affect physical well-being and psychosocial quality of life. Studies have found increasing evidence that visual loss increases the risk of depression in community-dwelling older adults. It is a common risk factor for falls and hip fractures.

Epidemiologically, the prevalence of low vision is higher among Hispanics than among African Americans or Caucasians. Significant risk factors for developing visual impairments include being female and over 50 years of age.

Pathophysiological Visual Changes With Age

The human eye undergoes significant changes with time, resulting in progressive visual loss. The vitreous gel slowly loses its attachment to the retina, leading to periodic "floaters." The lens hardens, becomes sclerotic, and progresses to impairment in near-vision accommodation, resulting in presbyopia. The lens also clouds with time, leading to cataracts.

The eyelids lose elasticity and become loosely adherent to the orbit. Fascial plane atrophy may lead to fat herniation into the lid tissue, leading to the common phenomenon of "bags" under the eyes. As people age, lacrimal gland secretion declines, resulting in dry eyes. Saline drops are usually effective for symptomatic treatment. Ectropion is seen when the lower lid has laxity and rotates away from the orbit. This can interfere with the transport of tears into the lacrimal sac, resulting in epiphora (persistent tearing). Entropion can be more concerning. Here, tissue planes within the bottom eyelid lose adhesion, allowing the eyelid margin to rotate medially. Lashes often rub directly against the conjunctiva and cornea, resulting in irritation and scarring. Ectropion and entropion can be treated with excision of redundant tissue if symptomatic therapy is unsuccessful.

Eyelid tumors usually result from chronic sun exposure. They are typically basal cell carcinomas and are treated with local excision. Metastasis is rare.

Subconjunctival hemorrhage is frequently noted in the elderly population. It usually occurs spontaneously or secondary to trauma and usually does not require treatment, resolving without complications. Chronic sunlight may cause a connective tissue degeneration between the eyelids, leading to conjunctival thickening (pingueculum). If the thickening progresses over the cornea and medially to the pupil, pterygium results. These conditions most commonly occur in dry, dusty, or smoky environments. Surgical intervention is needed only if the visual axis is obstructed.

Because the cornea is inherently required to be transparent for sharp vision, it must nourish itself without the use of cell-containing fluids such as blood vessels to maintain its transparency. To eliminate any cloudy residue accumulation over the cornea, a metabolic pump in corneal endothelial cells is present to dehydrate the cornea. From adulthood, the corneal endothelial cells cease to divide and cell density begins to decline. As a result, the cornea may become cloudy and fluid may collect. Hypertonic saline drops can be used to manage mild cases; corneal grafts may be needed to replace the endothelial cells for severe cases. Bacterial corneal ulcers are common in the elderly, due primarily to impaired tear secretion, diminished epithelial structure, and immunity. Antibiotic therapy is usually indicated.

Cataracts

Cataracts remain the leading cause of low vision and blindness worldwide, with more than twice the proportion of any other ocular disorder. In addition, cataracts have been found to be the leading cause of blindness in nursing homes. A cataract is defined as the opacification of the lens of the eye. Approximately 95% of persons over 65 years of age have some degree of lens opacification. The progression of cataracts is slow and may vary between eyes. The lens is located behind the iris and is suspended by ciliary body fibers. It is a biconvex transparent structure with an elastic capsule whose shape changes with ciliary contraction. The ciliary body contracts to allow sharper resolution of the image against the retina. The lens is avascular and acellular without any innervation. The lens is bathed by the aqueous and vitreous humor. With age, the lenticular fibers increase in density, reducing the lens transparency and ultimately leading to cataract formation. Risk factors for cataract formation are ultraviolet B (UVB) exposure, prolonged corticosteroid use, diabetes, prior intraocular surgery, hypertension, smoking, and ionizing radiation.

The prime symptoms of cataracts include poor night vision, difficulties with glare, and seeing halos around light. Objects may appear blue or yellow in color. In early cataract formation, distance vision is more commonly affected than near vision. The cataract location often determines the extent of visual loss. A centrally located cataract will give visual symptoms in areas of bright light. Bright light will constrict the pupil and occlude the dense central portion of the lens, thereby diffusing the incoming light. The patient may have improved vision with low light compared to ambient light because the pupil is fully dilated in low light and not impinging on the cataract-affected lens.

On examination, cataracts can be visualized with an ophthalmoscope (at +2 or +3 lens on the dial) or by slit lamp. The lens will appear cloudy. If cataracts are suspected, it is imperative that visual acuity in both eyes be checked using a Snellen chart with the patient using his or her corrective lenses. When cataracts are seen or suspected, the patient should be referred to an ophthalmologist for a dilated examination and assistance with treatment.

Surgery is the treatment of choice for cataracts. Cataract surgery is the most common procedure performed in adults over 65 years of age. There are approximately 1.3 million procedures performed annually at an expense of $3.4 billion. The surgery involves removal of the opacified lens. It may be intracapsular with complete lens removal or extracapsular with retention of the posterior capsule. Surgery is indicated when visual function is reduced to a level that interferes with daily activities. The interference can range from glare disability and reduced capability to perform recreational activities to difficulty in reading, driving, and performing one's job duties. Surgery should not be performed if the patient is unwilling, is physically unfit, or wears glasses or corrective lenses that provide proper functional vision.

Demographically, unoperated cataracts are four times more common among African Americans than among Caucasians. Complications occur in approximately 5% of patients with cataract extraction. Inflammation, infection, bleeding, retinal detachment, and glaucoma are potential risks.

Macular Degeneration

The prevalence of age-related macular degeneration (AMD) increases with age. The Beaver Dam Eye Study found that approximately 30% of patients age 75 years and older had early AMD. Risk factors include far-vision ability, decreased hand grip strength, light iris color, family history, short height, nicotine use, sunlight exposure, and systemic hypertension.

AMD is characterized by the formation of drusen along Bruch's membrane, which lies between the retina and the choroid. There are two forms of AMD.

The more common (or atrophic) form is nonvascular and characterized by drusen formation with atrophic retinal pigment epithelial changes. The second form is neovascular or exudative. There is subretinal choroidal neovascularization, leading to hemorrhage and ultimately to retinal scarring. Although less common, it accounts for the majority of vision loss attributable to AMD.

On ophthalmologic examination, drusen appears as small white or yellow deposits on the retina. During visualization, one should look for atrophy, fluid accumulation, or scarring. Atrophy may be noted to the macular region that is temporal to and slightly below the optic disc. If macular atrophy is present, visual acuity is usually compromised. Neovascular AMD is accompanied by hemorrhage, fluid accumulation, or lipid accumulation beneath or within the retina.

Central vision is often compromised in patients with advanced AMD. With severe macular damage, their visual image will have a central obliteration. Moving their heads laterally can help patients to fill the empty void.

Glaucoma is divided into primary and secondary groups. Approximately 95% of patients have primary glaucoma. Primary glaucoma is divided into open, closed, and congenital. Secondary glaucoma is divided into open and closed. Secondary open angle glaucoma is caused by external causes such as steroids, inflammation, and obstructed venous return. Closed angle secondary glaucoma results from trauma, neoplasia, surgery, and iris degeneration. Primary open glaucoma and closed angle glaucoma are the most frequently encountered cases in clinical geriatric practice.

Primary open angle glaucoma is the most common glaucoma in the United States. The prevalence is approximately 3% after 75 years of age; however, it causes 15% to 20% of the cases of blindness annually. Glaucoma affects both genders equally, but it afflicts more African Americans and begins at a younger age in that cohort. It is often asymptomatic until the stage is severe, and at that point neural damage may be irreversible. For this reason, annual glaucoma screening is crucial because visual acuity alone might not detect early glaucoma changes.

Open angle glaucoma renders elevated intraocular pressure due to increased resistance to aqueous outflow within the trabecular meshwork. Glaucoma causes visual loss from the death of retinal ganglion cells in the optic nerve. Despite the association with elevated intraocular pressure, some patients may have normal pressures. Symptomatically, patients may notice halos around lights and sudden blurring with increases in intraocular pressure.

Diagnosis is made by seeing cupping of the optic disc on ophthalmologic examination. The red filter on the direct ophthalmoscope may aid in visualization. With age, the disc color fades from pink to pale. A cup-to-disc ratio of 0.7 or higher is usually seen. Scotomas are also present on visual field examination.

Treatment of glaucoma is based on the degree of intraocular pressure, visual field loss, and optic nerve damage. Miotics are used to increase the outflow of the aqueous humor. β-Blockers and carbonic anhydrase inhibitors are used to reduce the production of aqueous fluid. The goal of therapy is to maintain the intraocular pressure at 20 millimeters of mercury (mm Hg). Initially, patients are placed on miotic and topical β-blocker drops. Timolol is often used because it has little effect on pupillary size and, therefore, will result in minimal night vision impairment. Systemic effects, including congestive heart failure (CHF) exacerbations, can occur with timolol. Levobunolol (Betagan) is a newer agent with fewer systemic side effects. As symptoms worsen, stronger miotics and carbonic anhydrase inhibitors (Diamox) can be used. Once goal intraocular pressure is attained, the ophthalmologist should examine the patient three times per year for routine follow-up. Surgery is reserved for cases where medical management fails.

Closed angle glaucoma is less common, but early detection is necessary to avoid blindness. As the intraocular pressure rises, the aqueous humor fluid is unable to leave the anterior chamber due to bowing of the iris. The point of iris–lens contact is the most common source of fluid obstruction. Symptoms often occur when the eye is dilated because iris bowing occurs maximally during dilation. Therefore, the use of mydriatic agents may spur a sudden blurriness of vision instigated by the closed angle.

Women are affected more than men, and a family history is usually present.

Symptoms are usually unilateral. Ocular pain, blurred vision, and halos around bright light are often reported. Most of these symptoms are attributed to corneal epithelial edema that has developed from the increased intraocular pressure. Symptoms are often alleviated with well-lit rooms and daylight exposure.

On examination, intraocular pressures are often 60 to 90 mm Hg. A shallow anterior chamber may be noted by shining a light to the lateral side of the eye and noticing a shadow from the bowed iris on the nasal portion of the eye. During an acute attack, corneal edema and clouding of the anterior chamber may be noted.

If acute closed angle glaucoma is suspected, an immediate referral to an ophthalmologist is necessary. Ophthalmology treatment is usually begun by carbonic anhydrase inhibitors and miotics. If untreated, severe open angle glaucoma can result in blindness within 2 to 3 days. All patients with a prior history of acute glaucoma need to be seen promptly by an ophthalmologist. Iridectomy is the treatment of choice. This can be done surgically or by laser therapy.

Diabetic Retinopathy

Type 1 diabetics have a higher predilection for retinopathy. After 15 to 20 years of type 1 diabetes, one third of patients have severe diabetic retinopathy and one half have progressive retinal disease. Diabetic retinopathy is less prevalent in type 2 patients; however, once it is present in type 2 patients, it progresses more quickly than in type 1 patients.

Diabetic retinal disease is divided into two categories: nonproliferative and proliferative. Nonproliferative lesions are in the macula and can present as retinal hemorrhages, hard and soft exudates, or intraretinal microvascular anomalies (IRMAs). Hemorrhages can manifest as microaneurysms or dot–blot hemorrhages. Both present as red dots on macular examination. Hard exudates are lipid deposits that may be yellow or white on ophthalmoscopic examination. IRMAs are dilated vessels that may represent vascular proliferation or dilated capillaries.

Proliferative retinopathy occurs at a later stage than does nonproliferative retinopathy and can progress to blindness. New vessels and fibrous tissue grow along the inner retinal surface and the vitreous gel. The growth causes vitreous gel contraction, resulting in vessel and retina traction. This cycle ultimately progresses to retinal detachment and vitreous gel hemorrhage.

The National Diabetic Retinopathy Study (DRS) identified risk factors correlated with progression of diabetic retinopathy to blindness. High-risk factors include (a) the presence of new vessel growth on the disc occupying 25% of the optic disc area, (b) any new vessel growth on the disc with hemorrhage, and (c) new vessel growth occupying more than 50% of the disc area. The DRS determined that the presence of these characteristics increases the likelihood of blindness by 30% to 50% within 3 to 5 years if not given appropriate photocoagulation therapy. Two treatment forms for diabetic retinopathy exist. Photocoagulation therapy is used in patients with proliferative retinopathy and can reduce visual loss by nearly 60% over 5 years. The DRS showed that photocoagulation resulted in some loss of visual acuity in patients with preexisting macular edema. Therefore, reduction of macular edema is recommended prior to therapy. Vitrectomy is indicated when the hemorrhage infiltrates the vitreous fluid or when retinal detachment with formation of traction bands occurs. The procedure removes the old blood and the opaque vitreous fluid. It is usually reserved for advanced cases because it does not restore maximal vision consistently.

Blindness

In Western countries, blindness is caused by AMD (26%), glaucoma (20.5%), cataract (11.2%), diabetic retinopathy (8.9%), or ischemic optic neuropathy (4%). In 2004, the Eye Diseases Prevalence Research Group published an epidemiological study on the prevalence of low vision and blindness. The group found that, among African Americans, cataracts and glaucoma accounted for more than 60% (36.8% and 26.0%, respectively) of the cases of blindness, whereas among Caucasians, AMD was the leading cause (54.4%) of blindness. The prevalence of age-specific blindness was higher for African Americans than for Caucasians and Hispanics. The group's data had limited information on persons over 85 years of age, but from observations and analysis of historical trends, the group found that the prevalence of blindness rises rapidly in that cohort, which had 69% of the observed blindness.

Because the latter group—the oldest old—is the fastest-growing segment of the population, it is imperative to practice preventive techniques such as annual ophthalmic screenings, smoking cessation, blood pressure control, and appropriate vitamin supplementation.

Management

Physicians should develop a screening system to diagnose and treat the elderly with visual impairments regardless of their degree of functional independence. The Department of Veterans Affairs provides routine low-vision care to older veterans as part of their health benefits package. In the Blind Rehabilitation Centers, veterans who are legally blind are seen for up to 16 weeks in low-vision rehabilitation programs.

Most frail older individuals live at home and not in long-term care facilities. A functional assessment should be done in a patient's daily environment whenever possible. It is important to assess the patient's visual goals and prioritize his or her goals around the treatment. Rehabilitation professionals can conduct low-vision assessments. A rehabilitation plan will outline the results of the assessment and provide a treatment plan to be shared among the patient, family, and health care professional. Such a plan would typically include the use of low-vision devices, rehabilitation therapy, and instructions to maximize remaining vision.

To optimize the visual environment of an impaired individual, several noninvasive simple tools can be recommended:

1. *Improve the lighting.* Most elderly persons require two to three times more light than do younger persons. Fluorescent light spreads evenly, and such lights are cost-effective. Halogen light is bluer and may require filtering.

2. *Increase contrast.* Providing areas of dark and light backgrounds in the bathroom, kitchen, and bedroom can help visual ability.

3. *Use color.* Bright clear colors are often seen better than are darks and pastels. Yellow against navy is an effective color scheme because it combines color and contrast.

4. *Use organization strategies.* A system where doors are never left partially open and chairs are always placed under the table when not in use should be developed. Clothing should be organized by color, and the kitchen should be organized with colored rubber bands.

Screening for visual impairment is essential for a complete geriatric assessment, whether as an outpatient or in a nursing facility. Deprivation of the sense of vision is a risk factor for several comorbidities and can often be treated.

—*Shelley B. Bhattacharya*

See also Geriatric Assessment; Vision and Low Vision

Further Readings and References

Congdon N, O'Colmain B, Klaver CC, et al. Causes and prevalence of visual impairment among adults in the United States. *Arch Ophthalmol.* 2004;122:477–485.

Horowitz A. Prevalence and consequences of vision impairment in later life. *Topics Geriatr Rehab.* 2004;20:185–195.

Olson RJ. Visual results after penetrating keratoplasty for aphakic bullous keratoplasty and Fuchs' dystrophy. *Am J Ophthalmol.* 1979;88:1000–1004.

Resnikoff S, Pascolini D, Etya'ale D, et al. Global data on visual impairment in the year 2002. *Bull World Health Org.* 2004;82:844–851.

U.S. National Library of Medicine. Interactive health tutorials (diabetes: eye complications; glaucoma; and macular degeneration). Available at: www.nlm.nih .gov/medlineplus/tutorial.html. Accessed September 14, 2006.

FEEDING ISSUES

See NUTRITION, MALNUTRITION, AND
FEEDING ISSUES

FLUID AND ELECTROLYTES

With aging, the kidney is usually able to maintain a balance of fluid and electrolytes under normal conditions. However, the aging kidney is unable to compensate for extremes in fluid and electrolytes. In addition, older patients are more likely to have diminished kidney function and are more likely to be taking multiple medications, both of which may interact with the kidney to alter fluid and electrolyte balance.

The regulation of specific solutes is affected by the progressive nephron loss seen in older adults. There have been attempts to dissociate the effects of aging per se from those of the decreased kidney function seen in older individuals, but this has proven to be difficult. In general, with a decline in kidney function, the regulation and excretion of urea nitrogen, creatinine, other nitrogenous wastes, and perhaps uremic toxins are compromised. However, this loss of regulation may be offset by the decline in muscle mass and decreased protein intake that is generally seen in the aged. Partial regulation of bicarbonate, calcium, and organic phosphate is maintained until there is significant nephron loss. Although balances of water, potassium, and sodium are generally well maintained until approximately 90% of nephrons are lost, older adults have a marked decrease in the functional reserve to respond to variability in these critical parameters. In each case, this decreased functional reserve is likely due to a combination of renal and extrarenal factors, including medications, which can lead to pathological disorders of water and electrolytes in the aged.

Volume overload, pulmonary edema, and congestive heart failure are common problems for older patients. The presence of volume overload can be troubling due to excessive leg swelling and shortness of breath due to fluid filling up the airspaces in the lung. The aged kidney is less able to respond to sodium loading or volume expansion. In addition, aging is associated with a reduction in kidney function that also leads to volume overload. Aging is also thought to explain the changes in circadian variation in sodium excretion that lead to nocturia (urination during the night). Nocturia may disturb sleep if it is excessive.

In older adults, sodium reabsorption in the kidney may be affected because of changes in the response of the kidney to atrial naturietic peptide (ANP). ANP is released by the atria when the atrial myocytes are stretched due to volume overload. ANP acts to vasodilate the renal arterioles and inhibit sodium reabsorption. Studies suggest that the release of ANP is preserved but that there is a renal defect in response to ANP, leading to relative volume expansion after a volume challenge.

In the aged population, the incidence of chronic kidney disease, chronic liver disease, and congestive heart failure contributes to the high rate of clinically important volume overload. Diuretics, or medications that increase the excretion of salt and water, are the mainstay of medical therapy for volume overload. However, diuretics have substantial untoward effects on electrolytes, lipid profiles, and nocturia, especially among older patients. The role of nutrition (e.g., high salt intake) is an exacerbating factor that is often overlooked. Health care providers should focus on a diet history and work closely with geriatric nutritionists to counsel patients with volume overload.

Although fluid losses can cause the depletion of extracellular fluid volume, the development of volume depletion in the healthy population is unusual due to dietary intake and the recovery of salt and water by the kidney in response to volume depletion. Although fluid losses in the younger population present with tachycardia, thirst, and lightheadedness, fluid loss in older individuals presents with nonspecific signs and symptoms. The most accurate measure of acute fluid loss in older adults is a change in weight.

Common causes of fluid loss include the gastrointestinal tract (e.g., diarrhea) and the kidney (e.g., following overly aggressive diuresis). In addition to the frequent use of diuretics, there are multiple reasons why the aging kidney works less efficiently at conserving sodium under conditions of sodium deprivation. These reasons include a reduction in renal mass, a loss of nephrons, interstitial scarring, and changes in hormones that regulate sodium excretion. Indeed, it has been shown that it takes older individuals twice as long for their kidneys to conserve sodium adequately.

The prompt diagnosis and treatment of volume depletion prevent complications such as acute renal failure and shock. First-line therapy includes volume expanding the patient so that there is adequate tissue perfusion. Recent studies have examined the use of oral, subcutaneous, and intravenous volume expansion. The severity of the clinical situation and the ability of the patient to cooperate with prescribed therapy should guide the mode of volume expansion. The second goal of therapy is to stem the losses of fluid. In some cases, this may be as simple as reducing the dose of the diuretic.

Impaired urinary concentration, diminished thirst, and the potential for deterioration of fluid intake due to decreased consciousness or decline in functional status all coexist in older adults. Due to this combination of renal and extrarenal factors, hypernatremia is relatively common. In a recent national cohort study of community-dwelling persons, mild hypertonicity and overt hypertonicity were observed in 40% and 20% of the sample, respectively. Hypertonicity was positively associated with older age, Hispanic or African American race, impaired glucose tolerance, and diabetes. In general, older patients with infections and decreased access to free water should be monitored closely.

An acute increase in plasma sodium concentration causes the movement of water out of cells. This decrease in cell volume can lead to a decrease in brain volume that, in turn, can cause cerebral hemorrhage. The symptoms of hypernatremia include fatigue, lethargy, seizures, and coma. More severe neurological symptoms often occur at plasma sodium concentrations of greater than 160 to 170 milliequivalents per liter (meq/L).

There is a decreased urinary concentration in older adults that reflects threats to the water conservation system. Renal water conservation depends on three interrelated processes: (a) generation (salt reabsorption and countercurrent multiplication by the loop of Henle) and (b) maintenance (countercurrent exchange by the vasa recta) of the corticopapillary osmotic gradient, followed by (c) antidiuretic hormone (ADH)-dependent water reabsorption along the length of the collecting duct. The anatomic integrity and physiological integrity of all these processes are threatened in the aging kidney. Primary or secondary tubulointerstitial injury disturbs the function of the loop of Henle, vasa recta, and collecting duct. Loss of solute reabsorptive capability (sodium in the ascending limb of Henle's loop and urea in the medullary collecting duct) and solute trapping capability (vasa recta) impairs the accumulation of salt and urea in the medullary interstitium. Enhanced solute excretion (osmotic diuresis) by itself impairs sodium reabsorption in the thick ascending limb of Henle's loop and urea and water reabsorption in the collecting duct, and it may also disrupt vasa recta function.

Impaired urinary concentrating ability is a nearly invariable finding in the aging kidney irrespective of the degree of renal insufficiency. Of note, the ADH responses to both osmotic stimulation and volume pressure stimulation seem to be intact. However, there may be a decreased renal tubular response to ADH. Thus, diminished maximal urinary concentrating ability, often initially recognized by patients as nocturia, can be an early sign of underlying kidney disease. Frank polyuria (increased urine output) may occur later in life, especially if dietary solute intake is not restricted.

Hyponatremia is the most common electrolyte disorder observed in the older population and also is the most common disorder found in hospitalized patients. The increased prevalence of hyponatremia in this population can be largely attributed to compromised urinary-diluting ability in the aging kidney. Thus, mild hyponatremia is common in older patients because the aged kidney has a limited capacity to handle the osmotic stress produced by wide variations in water intake. More severe hyponatremia may occur in those patients who are concomitantly on certain medications and in those who have heart or liver failure.

Older adults are often subject to polypharmacy, and certain medications induce mild to moderate hyponatremia. In particular, the selective serotonin reuptake inhibitors widely used for depression have been associated with hyponatremia. Hydrochlorothiazide, a mild diuretic used for hypertension, may cause hyponatremia. Another medication that is becoming more widely used for nocturia, desmopressin, may lead to hyponatremia. Desmopressin should be initiated with caution because reports have shown that hyponatremia may develop during the first few weeks of therapy.

Hyponatremia can lead to fatigue, weakness, poor memory, stupor, coma, seizures, and (potentially) death. The symptom severity of hyponatremia results from both the duration of hyponatremia and the sodium concentration. Elderly patients with chronically low serum sodium concentrations can have no symptoms or few symptoms. On the other hand, hospitalized patients who develop the same degree of hyponatremia acutely may have severe neurological sequelae. The sodium concentration, chronicity of hyponatremia, and severity of symptoms all are used to guide the therapy of hyponatremia. Often, if medications are involved in the development of hyponatremia, the only intervention is to discontinue the offending agent. In most cases, restricting the intake of free water will lead to improvement of the sodium concentrations. In addition, loop diuretics can be added to dilute the medullary interstitium of the kidneys and thus decrease the gradient for renal water reabsorption. Less commonly, adding solute (e.g., salt) to the diet to increase the daily solute load, or adding medications that antagonize the cellular effects of ADH in the distal nephron (e.g., demeclocycline), becomes necessary.

Older persons are more likely than younger persons to develop hyperkalemia despite lower total body potassium levels. A decrease in the activity of the renin–angiotensin system leads to effective hypoaldosteronism. A low aldosterone level decreases the secretion of potassium by the kidney. Older patients are less able to respond appropriately to potassium loading and demonstrate defects in both renal and extrarenal adaptation.

A number of medications can exacerbate the tendency to develop hyperkalemia. Angiotensin-converting enzyme inhibitors (ACE-Is) and angiotensin-II receptor blockers (ARBs) block the renin–angiotensin system and thereby decrease renal secretion of potassium. The use of nonsteroidal anti-inflammatory drugs (NSAIDs) decreases the distal fluid delivery that is necessary for potassium secretion. The use of spironolactone for congestive heart failure, alone or in combination with an ACE-I, has led to fatal hyperkalemia.

The homeostasis of divalent cations, such as calcium and magnesium, appears to be preserved with normal aging. However, in a substantial proportion of older adults who develop chronic kidney disease, as well as in postmenopausal women, calcium homeostasis is only moderately well preserved. The regulation of calcium metabolism becomes disordered in chronic kidney disease due to an increase in serum phosphate and a decrease in Vitamin D3 production. In addition, a number of medications may affect calcium balance. Hypercalcemia may also result from iatrogenic causes. To treat osteoporosis aggressively, older patients may be given Vitamin D supplements and elemental calcium. Cases of hypercalcemia due to the ingestion of toxic levels of Vitamin D have been reported. Both calcium homeostasis and magnesium homeostasis are affected by the use of diuretics.

Diuretics are commonly used to improve blood pressure control, treat heart failure, and control lower extremity edema. When an older patient receives a loop diuretic such as furosemide, the development of hypocalcemia and hypomagnesemia is common. Conversely, thiazide diuretics enhance calcium retention in the kidneys, potentially contributing to hypercalcemia.

The finding of a low serum phosphate concentration is not unusual, particularly in persons hospitalized with an acute illness. Phosphate is found in many foods, so hypophosphatemia usually indicates severe malnutrition. However, there is decreased gut absorption of phosphate and an impairment in renal tubular reabsorption of phosphate. Phosphate reabsorption in the kidney is linked to the expression of specific sodium phosphate channels in the proximal tubule that decreases with aging.

In summary, older adults are generally able to maintain fluid and electrolyte balance under normal conditions but have a limited ability to adapt to highly variable intake or loss of water or electrolytes. An upper limit or a lower limit for excretion of solutes and water can be demonstrated, and the two tend to converge with advancing age. It is critical that those who care for older patients are vigilant to the effects of medication, illness, and nutrition on water and electrolytes.

—*Mark Unruh and Kenneth R. Hallows*

See also Calcium Disorders of Aging; Kidney Aging and Diseases

Further Readings and References

Beck LH. Changes in renal function with aging. *Clin Geriatr Med.* 1998;14:199–209

Callreus T, Ekman E, Andersen M. Hyponatremia in elderly patients treated with desmopressin for nocturia: A review of a case series. *Eur J Clin Pharmacol.* 2005;61:281–284.

Choudhury D, Raj DSC, Levi M. Effect of aging on renal function and disease. In: Brenner B, ed. *Brenner and Rector's The Kidney.* 7th ed. St. Louis, Mo: W. B. Saunders; 2004:2305–2342.

Dick IM, Devine A, Beilby J, Prince RL. Effects of endogenous estrogen on renal calcium and phosphate handling in elderly women. *Am J Physiol Endocrinol Metab.* 2005;288:e430–e435.

Sands JM. Urine-concentrating ability in the aging kidney. *Sci Aging Knowl Environ.* 2003;24(June18):pe15.

Weir MR. Non-diuretic-based antihypertensive therapy and potassium homeostasis in elderly patients. *Coron Artery Dis.* 1997;8:499–504.

FOOT PROBLEMS

Foot problems are one of the most important, yet most often overlooked, contributors to impaired mobility in older people. Maintaining good foot health will ensure good mobility and consequently maintain an older person's independence and quality of life.

Prevalence of Foot Problems

It has long been recognized that foot problems are highly prevalent in older people and have a significant detrimental impact on older people's independence and quality of life. Population-based studies indicate that at least one in three older people report painful feet, and studies involving clinical assessments indicate that at least one in two older people present with some type of foot abnormality. The most common foot problems are chronic in nature and reflect the long-term physiological changes that occur to the sensory, muscular, articular, neurological, and vascular systems with advancing age. By far the most common problems are hyperkeratotic lesions (corns and calluses), followed closely by nail disorders and structural deformities such as hallux valgus (bunions) and lesser toe deformities (hammertoes and clawtoes). Factors associated with foot problems include female gender, obesity, and comorbidities such as diabetes mellitus and osteoarthritis. The prevalence of foot problems appears to have a nonlinear relationship with age in that prevalence rates increase until 65 to 75 years of age and then decline thereafter. This is probably because the development of foot symptoms requires some degree of weight-bearing activity, so even older people with severely deformed feet might not develop symptoms if those individuals are sedentary.

Impact of Foot Problems

As with most musculoskeletal ailments, the primary impact of foot problems in older people is pain and discomfort. However, even in the absence of symptoms, foot problems can contribute to impaired physical functioning when performing basic activities of daily living (ADLs) such as housework, gardening, shopping, cooking, and cleaning. Up to 20% of housebound older people attribute their limited mobility to the condition of their feet. Older people with foot problems walk more slowly than those without foot problems, and it was reported recently that older people with foot problems perform poorly in balance and functional tests and are more likely to suffer from falls.

Management of Common Foot Problems in Older People

Hyperkeratosis (Corns and Calluses)

Hyperkeratosis is a normal physiological response to friction applied to the skin and develops as a protective mechanism to prevent damage to deeper tissues. Hyperkeratosis can occur on any bony prominence in the body; however, the foot is a common site both due to its weight-bearing function and because the skin on the foot is subjected to friction from footwear. When the friction applied to the skin becomes excessive, the resultant thickening can become painful, increasing the pressure on the underlying dermis and predisposing to skin breakdown and ulceration. Broadly speaking, there are two types of hyperkeratosis: calluses (also called keratomas or tylomas), which develop on the plantar surface of the foot and appear as a diffuse thickening, and corns (also called heloma dura), which are more common on the toes and can be differentiated from calluses due to the presence of a sharply demarcated central core. Corns can also develop in between the toes (heloma molle) and are often macerated due to the associated moisture.

Calluses and corns are caused by a range of factors, including ill-fitting footwear, bony prominences, malunited fractures, short or long metatarsals, and faulty foot biomechanics resulting in abnormal plantar pressure distribution. Probably the most common cause of calluses and corns in older people, however, is the wearing of inappropriate shoes such as those with an elevated heel and/or inadequate room in the forefoot. In addition to the selection of more appropriate footwear, calluses and corns should be debrided using a scalpel, resulting in immediate relief of pain and decreasing the pressures borne by the metatarsal heads when walking. Longer-term management includes (a) using foot orthoses to distribute pressures over the plantar surface more evenly and (b) having surgery to realign prominent metatarsal heads. However, metatarsal osteotomy is often associated with transfer lesions; that is, the development of new lesions at previously lesion-free sites due to postoperative changes in foot function.

Nail Disorders

Onychomycosis is a highly prevalent fungal nail infection caused by dermatophyte, saprophyte, and yeast organisms. The infection results in yellow–brown discoloration, thickening, crumbling, and offensive odor. Conscientious management of foot hygiene, including washing the feet with soap and water and remembering to dry thoroughly, can prevent many fungal nail infections. Shoes, socks, and/or hosiery should be changed daily to prevent excess moisture buildup. A wide range of treatments have been used to treat the condition; however, the "gold standard" treatment is terbinafine, an oral medication that has been shown to cure the condition in 6 to 12 months. In the presence of contraindications to oral medication, topical treatments may be used; however, this takes a much longer time, it requires considerable compliance, and complete cure rates are significantly lower.

Onychauxis refers to abnormal thickening of the nail that may result from a wide range of causes, including injury, trauma from ill-fitting shoes, infection, peripheral vascular disease, diabetes, and nutritional deficiency. In some cases, pressure from bedclothes or tight hosiery can lead to quite severe pain. If left untreated, subungual hematomas (blood blisters under the nail) may form, creating a potential site for infection and ulceration, particularly in older people confined to bed. Regular maintenance of basic foot hygiene, including regular filing of nails, will prevent excessive buildup. However, more severe cases may require the use of a special drill to reduce the thickness of the nail or removal of the whole nail under local anesthetic.

Onychocryptosis refers to "ingrown" toenails, where a spicule of nail penetrates the skin, leading to inflammation, pain, and increased risk of secondary infection. People with abnormally curved nails are more likely to develop onychocryptosis; however, in many cases the condition is simply caused by inappropriate nail cutting and/or ill-fitting footwear. Toenails should be cut straight across, and shoes should have sufficient room in the toe box to prevent constriction. Although some cases can be managed successfully by applying topical antiseptics and allowing the nails to grow out normally, recurrent cases often require a minor surgical procedure that involves removing the offending portion of nail under local anesthetic.

Toe Deformities

More commonly referred to as bunions, hallux valgus is the most common deformity of the foot in older people and refers to the abnormal medial prominence of the first metatarsal head resulting from a lateral deviation of the first metatarsal. Hallux valgus is a multifactorial condition caused by muscle imbalance, structural deformity of the metatarsals (sometimes an inherited trait), faulty foot mechanics, and the detrimental effects of ill-fitting footwear. The enlarged first metatarsal head creates problems with finding suitable footwear, and the friction created by the shoe may lead to the formation of a bursa over the site. This can be very painful, and in older people with frail skin it can lead to ulceration. Treatment of hallux valgus includes changing footwear to that with a broader forefoot, applying foam or silicon pads over the joint, using foot orthoses, and having surgery. Surgery would appear to provide better long-term results than would orthoses; however, there is a wide range of surgical techniques, and not all may provide similar results.

Hallux limitus is a condition in which there is limited range of motion at the first metatarsophalangeal joint. If this progresses to complete fusion of the joint, it is termed hallux rigidus. For hallux limitus, treatment involves using foot orthoses to facilitate propulsion or manipulation and injection with corticosteroid. For hallux rigidus, surgery might be necessary to reinstate adequate range of motion at the first metatarsophalangeal joint. The use of nonsteroidal anti-inflammatory drugs may also provide pain relief.

Long-term wearing of ill-fitting footwear, in association with faulty foot mechanics and muscle weakness, can lead to the development of clawing, hammering, and retraction of the lesser toes. Hammertoes and clawtoes are two of the most common foot complaints in older people and can lead to the development of corns on the dorsum of the interphalangeal joints and calluses under the metatarsal heads. Treatment involves modifying footwear, using various splinting devices, and managing the secondary lesions. Recurrent cases often require surgery to realign and stabilize the affected metatarsophalangeal or interphalangeal joints. In severe cases involving recurrent infection and ulceration, amputation of the toe may be indicated.

Footwear Considerations

Footwear advice and modification play an important role in the management of foot problems in older people. Up to 80% of older people wear ill-fitting shoes that have been shown to predispose to the development of toe deformities and associated hyperkeratotic skin lesions. Furthermore, many older people wear shoes with potentially hazardous features such as high heels, inadequate fixation, and poor grip that may predispose to falls and fractures. Pedorthics, the modification of footwear characteristics to reduce shock and shear, relieve excessive pressure from sensitive or painful areas, and accommodate and support deformities, is a useful conservative management strategy for older people with foot problems and can have beneficial effects on balance and functional ability.

—*Hylton B. Menz*

See also Arthritis and Other Rheumatic Diseases; Activities of Daily Living and Instrumental Activities of Daily Living; Diabetes; Gait Disorders; Pain; Skin Changes; Venous Stasis Ulcers; Wound Healing

Further Readings and References

Benvenuti F, Ferrucci L, Guralnik JM, Gangemia S, Baroni A. Foot pain and disability in older persons: An epidemiologic survey. *J Am Geriatr Soc.* 1995; 43:479–484.

Dunn JE, Link CL, Felson DT, Crincoli MG, Keysor JJ, McKinlay JB. Prevalence of foot and ankle conditions in a multiethnic community sample of older adults. *Am J Epidemiol.* 2004;159:491–498.

Menz HB. Foot care. In: Carmody S, Forster S, eds. *Aged Care Nursing: A Guide to Practice.* Melbourne, Australia: AusMed Publications; 2003:51–61.

Menz HB, Morris ME. Footwear characteristics and foot problems in older people. *Gerontology.* 2005;51:346–351.

Formal Caregiving

See Caregiving

Fractures in Older Adults

After 50 years of age, approximately 40 in 100 women will sustain one or more fractures. Low bone mass or osteoporosis is an important determinant of bone fracture. Bone mass can be reduced to the point where a bone can fracture without trauma. Architectural dimensions such as bone length can increase the risk of fracture. A longer bone inherently confers a less strong structure. An individual's susceptibility to trauma (or falls) and ability to protect against injury are also predictors of fracture. The greatest fracture predictor, however, is prior fracture history. The major types of fractures in older adults are hip, vertebral, and wrist.

Hip Fractures

Hip fractures occur commonly, cause considerable impairment, and are associated with a high risk of death in older adults. Fully 80% of hip fractures occur in individuals over 60 years of age. More specifically, 10 in 1,000 women at 65 years of age and 125 in 1,000 women over 85 years of age are affected. There are approximately 250,000 hip fractures annually in the United States, a number projected to increase substantially during the coming decades because of the aging population. Hip fracture mortality is high, approaching 25% during 1 year. Of those elders who survive, only 60% recover their prefracture walking ability. The lifetime risk of hip fracture is 18% in women and 6% in men. Risk factors for hip fracture are advanced age, low bone mass, a maternal history of hip fracture, impaired neuromuscular function, arthritis, peripheral neuropathies, impaired cognitive function, poor vision, sedating medications, environmental hazards, and other medical problems such as Parkinson's disease. An older adult with a hip fracture will often present with a recent history of a fall and complain of pain in the hip and groin. The individual will often have an inability to ambulate and noticeable shortening and external rotation of the affected leg. Surgery is usually performed to prevent shortening of the leg, reduce the hospital stay, and facilitate rehabilitation. Relieving pain and preventing physical deterioration are vital following surgery. Blood clots in the leg and lungs are complications of hip fracture associated with a high mortality. Other postoperative complications include delirium, postoperative pneumonia, infection, and muscular atrophy. Although the majority of patients return to their previous activities, some increase in disability is the rule rather than the exception. Up to 20% require an increased level of residential or hospital care.

Vertebral Fractures

Vertebral fracture is the most common type of osteoporotic fracture. European studies show that before 65 years of age, these fractures are more common in men and are associated with trauma. Between 65 and 69 years of age, they are equally common in men and women (12% to 13%). After 70 years of age, they are more common in women. At 50 years of age, a woman's lifetime risk of a vertebral fracture is 16%. Geographic and ethnic differences in vertebral fracture prevalence exist in individual populations. Two thirds of vertebral fractures occur without symptoms. When symptoms are present, they are often described as a radiating pain from the back encircling the patient. In frail older adults, sudden bending, moderate lifting, or a cough can result in fracture. Although pain will usually resolve in 4 to 6 weeks, pain medication is often necessary. Regular exercise helps to prevent further weakness and bone loss. Many times, a patient with a vertebral fracture presents with only a hump on his or her back (commonly referred to as a dowager's hump) and loss of height. Dowager's hump is caused by multiple compression fractures, causing the thoracic spine to appear outwardly curved. Treatments involve preventing further bone loss, increasing bone mass, and (sometimes) restoring the height of the vertebra through vertebroplasty or kyphoplasty. Both of these latter procedures involve injecting cement percutaneously into the individual vertebra. Vertebral fractures are an important predictor of future fractures (vertebral and hip), can lead to problems with chronic pain, and are associated with increased mortality.

Wrist Fractures

Fractures of the wrist, mainly the distal radius, are a common clinical problem, particularly in older White women with osteoporosis. The prevalence of these fractures does not show the same increase with age as do the other types of fractures. Distal radius fractures increase in frequency before 50 years of age, plateau by 60 years of age, and show a modest increase thereafter. They are associated with low bone density and subsequent hip fracture (especially in elderly men). Colles's fracture is the most common type of distal radius fracture. Older adults usually present with pain, swelling, and bruising of the wrist. Injury occurs with a fall onto an outstretched hand that affects the distal radius. Differential diagnoses include soft tissue injuries, neuropathies, and wrist ganglia. The goal of treatment is to correct and maintain anatomical alignment. Most radius fractures can be managed in a short arm immobilization cast. It has been reported that patients who had Colles's fractures with as little as a 10° dorsal tilt were much more likely to have pain, stiffness, weakness, and poor function. Following prolonged immobilization, physical therapy will help regain motion and strength.

Minimal Trauma Long-Bone Fractures

Minimal trauma long-bone fractures have been characterized only recently and are thought to be a variant of osteoporotic low-trauma, low-impact, or minimal-trauma fractures. In the past, many patients suffering from minimal trauma long-bone fractures were erroneously thought to be suffering from institutional elder abuse, sometimes resulting in litigation. The majority of patients suffering from minimal trauma long-bone fractures are frail nursing home patients. Minimal trauma long-bone fracture incidence has been found to be 84 per 1,000 nursing home residents per year. The elders are typically frail, bedbound, and immobile. Osteoporosis is thought to be a predominant risk factor leading to minimal trauma long-bone fractures. Most of them occur in the lower extremities below the hip, although the location can be in any long bone. Femoral shaft fractures seem to carry the highest mortality risk. Diagnostic evaluation is the same as that for other suspected long bone fractures. The clinician should have a high index of suspicion for possible pathological mechanisms, especially in men, when osteoporosis is not suspected. Treatment would include primary repair and a focus on decreasing bone fragility, with the latter perhaps including pharmacological therapies and therapies to enhance mobility.

Fracture Prevention

Fracture prevention must address different risk factors. Diets that include adequate calcium and Vitamin D and that maintain weight within normal limits are necessary to maintain bone mass. Physical activity that encourages walking and weight-bearing activities is associated with a reduced hip fracture risk. Medications that can reduce alertness, such as long-acting hypnotics and sedating antihistamines, should be avoided. Limiting alcohol intake is important because excess alcohol intake increases the risk of falls. Excess alcohol also has a direct toxic effect on the bone, predisposing to an increased risk of osteoporosis. Walking aids, stair and bath rails, ramps, and stair lifts should be used for patients at risk for falls. Homes should be evaluated for fall risks such as loose carpeting and irregular flooring surfaces. Prevention and early identification of osteoporosis should be conducted. Biphosphonate medications are beneficial in reducing the risk of nonvertebral fracture in post-menopausal women. There is some evidence for a reduction in risk of hip fracture with hip protectors in patients at risk for fracture. It is unclear whether exercise results in the reduction of hip fracture risk. Reduction in the rate of hip fractures in post-menopausal women treated with hormone replacement therapy needs to be balanced with potential harm.

—*David V. Espino*

See also Calcium Disorders of Aging; Foot Problems; Frailty; Mobility; Mobility Assessment; Osteoporosis

Further Readings and References

Haentjens P, Autier P. Colles fracture, spine fracture, and subsequent risk of hip fracture in men and women: A meta-analysis. *J Bone Joint Surg (Am)*. 2003;85: 1936–1943.

Handoll HH, Madhok R. Rehabilitation for distal radial fractures in adults. *Cochrane Database Syst Rev*. 2002;(2):CD003324.

Lips P. Epidemiology and predictors of fractures associated with osteoporosis. *Am J Med*. 1997;103:3S–11S.

Martin-Hunyadi C. Clinical and prognostic aspects of spontaneous fractures in long term care units: A thirty-month prospective study. *Revue de Medecine Interne*. 2000;21(9).

Papaioannou A. Diagnosis and management of vertebral fractures in elderly adults. *Am J Med*. 2002;113:220–228.

Parmelee-Peters K, Eathorne S. The wrist: Common injuries and management. *Prim Care Clin Office Pract*. 2005; 32:35–70.

FRAILTY

The U.S. health care system is faced with the challenge of maintaining or improving the health of its aging population. In geriatric medicine, resources have been allocated to better understand factors associated with the onset and progression of frailty. Although a great majority of older adults consider themselves to be in good health and lead independent lives, a significant proportion (an estimated 25%) of the population age 65 years and older are considered to be frail, with the proportion increasing with increasing age. The 1990 *American Medical Association White Paper on Elderly Health,* for example, estimated that approximately 46% of the population age 85 years and older are frail. The report went on to discuss the need to prepare for a growing frail population.

The recommendation made by the AMA has proven to be difficult given that, more than a decade after the report, no clear consensus or general agreement on how best to define or operationalize frailty has been reached. Further complicating matters is that the term *frailty* has been, and continues to be, used interchangeably with *disability* and *comorbidity* and shares common characteristics with the term *failure to thrive*. Because no clear and precise definition of frailty exists, any estimate of prevalence is uncertain. More important, however, is that without a clear idea of what frailty means, there can be only a limited clinical response in terms of prevention and treatment.

Frailty has been described in a variety of ways such as a global condition of impaired strength, endurance, and balance as well as vulnerability to trauma and other stressors. Others have restricted the term to those at risk for requiring, or already requiring, assistance to perform basic activities of daily living (ADLs). Still others have defined frailty as a combination of inactivity with low energy intake, weight loss, or low body mass index; a reduced ability to perform important practical and social activities of day-to-day living; an excess demand placed on reduced capacity; or, more generally, a state that puts the person at risk for adverse health outcomes. Frailty has also been described in biological terms, where the body's ability to cope with stressors decreases with age, resulting in declines in multiple physiological domains.

L. P. Fried and colleagues argued in 2001 that frailty is a syndrome with well-defined physiological, biological, and environmental markers. An older adult, under this definition, is classified as frail if he or she exhibits three of the following five criteria: (a) unintentional weight loss (of 10 pounds or more during a year), (b) general feelings of exhaustion, (c) weakness (as measured by grip strength), (d) slow walking speed, and (e) low levels of physical activity. On the other hand, Marybeth Brown and colleagues indicated in 2000 that frailty would best be assessed by four objective functional tests: an obstacle performance test, a test of hip abduction strength, the semitandem portion of the Romberg test, and the pegboard test. Other simple tests of frailty assessment include a timed one-leg standing balance test and the Timed Up and Go test, the latter of which involves rising from a chair, walking 3 meters, turning around, and sitting down. Although each of these tests has certain advantages as well as certain disadvantages, the tests share a common goal to improve the diagnostic accuracy of frailty from a physical or functional point of view. This view of frailty has been criticized by some as not being more inclusive to other markers of health and well-being. Under an alternative definition, frailty would also include (in addition to physical and functional parameters) indicators of cognitive and psychological well-being and social support.

Although a consensus definition of frailty is lacking, most agree that frailty is not an all-or-none phenomenon but rather follows a trajectory or gradient of risk and that the trajectory need not be one-way. Acknowledging that frailty is reversible and not an inevitable product of aging is important because it brings optimism to primary and secondary intervention efforts. Emerging research now shows that the major causes of frailty, although age related, are not due to aging itself. For example, sarcopenia or loss of muscle, atherosclerosis, cognitive impairment, and malnutrition can be prevented or reversed to some degree by active intervention strategies. At the population level, increasing evidence shows that education and the promotion of healthy lifestyles (e.g., nutrition, exercise, social/intellectual activity), starting from an early age and continuing throughout the life course, may promote the development of healthy aging and reduce the incidence of frailty and dependency. Secondary prevention efforts, including earlier screening for and treatment of illnesses such as hypertension, diabetes, heart disease, and osteoporosis, are likely to play an important role. Social services

interventions or the introduction of new technologies to assist physically or cognitively impaired older adults may also play a role in slowing or reversing the development of frailty.

Without active primary or secondary prevention, however, there is little doubt about the impact of frailty on older adults, their families (particularly those involved in caregiving), and society as a whole. Older frail adults are at considerable risk for a range of adverse health outcomes (e.g., acute and chronic illness, falls, disability, mortality) and for increased use of community and hospital resources and long-term care facilities. Quality and meaning of life are also likely to suffer, increasing the possibility of psychological health problems. These poor outcomes contribute not only to the burden of medical care but also to an economical and social burden.

The study of frailty as a syndrome of illness faces a number of obstacles. Perhaps the most critical challenge is to construct a clear and precise definition that meets with the general approval of the research community as well as older adults. If no consensus can be achieved, the value of future frailty research may be limited. If, however, a consensus definition of frailty can be reached, this would have considerable impact on the development of a standardized measurement tool. In turn, this measurement tool would be potentially useful from clinical, social, and research perspectives. From a clinical viewpoint, this measure could help facilitate timely prevention programs among those who are considered at risk (i.e., pre-frail) or intervention programs among those who are already classified as frail. From a social viewpoint, older adults and their families may better understand available treatment choices and the effect these choices would have on their longevity and quality of life. From a research viewpoint, a measure of frailty would have the potential to serve as an outcome, as an indicator of health status, and as a predictor of future events where comparisons could be made across studies. The wide range of uses would likely improve our understanding of frailty in older adults and better identify areas where prevention efforts or intervention programs may be targeted. The discovery of effective programs to prevent or delay frailty in older adults is a public health priority, with the benefits to be shared by all of society.

—Ivonne M. Berges and Glenn V. Ostir

See also Activities of Daily Living and Instrumental Activities of Daily Living; Gait Disorders; Geriatric Assessment; Mobility; Mobility Assessment

Further Readings and References

Brown M, Sinacore DR, Binder EF, Kohrt WM. Physical performance measures for the identification of mild to moderate frailty. *J Gerontol A Biol Sci Med Sci.* 2000; 55:M350–M355.

Council on Scientific Affairs. American Medical Association white paper on elderly health: Report of the Council on Scientific Affairs. *Arch Intern Med.* 1990;150:2459–2472.

Fried LP, Tangen CM, Walston J, et al. Frailty in older adults: Evidence for a phenotype. *J Gerontol A Biol Sci Med Sci.* 2001;65:M146–M156.

FUNCTIONAL STATUS ASSESSMENT

See ACTIVITIES OF DAILY LIVING AND INSTRUMENTAL ACTIVITIES OF DAILY LIVING

GAIT DISORDERS

Walking is often referred to as a series of controlled falls because walking requires the ability to shift weight and balance on one limb, take a step, and catch the body mass with the stepping limb. The ability to walk is a fundamental requirement for independence in mobility; however, the changes that occur with aging can limit mobility and potentially affect independence. An estimated 13% to 15% of older adults experience gait disorders even with "normal aging." The gait changes associated with aging are slowed speed, decreased step and stride lengths, and a compensatory increase in the number of steps per second or cadence.

Other biomechanical changes occur in the stance and swing phase of gait. During stance, older adults display a wider base of support, greater hip abduction, more "toe out," and greater amount of time in double support than do younger individuals. During the swing phase of gait, less dorsiflexion is compensated for by greater hip and knee flexion and results in great toe clearance. There is reduced trunk and pelvic rotation and less vertical movement compared with that in younger people. All of these create a more stable but less fluid gait. These changes are gradual and progressive, and they tend to be more noticeable in individuals who are age 70 years and older. Both internal and behavioral issues are implicated. Internal alterations in musculoskeletal, neuromuscular, and physiological systems contribute to the changes observed in gait, whereas behavioral factors such as reduced physical activity, perceptions of reduced health status, and fear of falling are also cited. Finally, increasing comorbidities of aging—arthritis, joint replacements, and strokes—interfere with lower extremity function and gait.

Musculoskeletal changes are both subtle and profound. Reduced range of motion in the trunk, hips, knees, and ankles can have a direct impact on walking. Kyphotic postures with increased thoracic flexion and forward head move the center of mass anteriorly and limit step initiation during early swing. Reduced strength in the hip and knee extensors and ankle plantar flexors decrease the vertical force production needed to take a step. Decreased gait speed may result from a reduction in muscle mass, increased fatty content in the muscle, and a shift in fiber composition, especially a decrease in the number of Type II muscle fibers.

Nervous system changes parallel those in the musculoskeletal system. Reduced visual, vestibular, and proprioceptive sensations affect gait. The peripheral nervous system has reduced nerve conduction velocities, longer latencies, and higher thresholds that influence the ability to respond quickly to sudden changes. In addition to loss of muscle fibers, there is a loss of motor units and reduced myoneural excitability. All of these together result in poorer ability to stand on one leg, a critical component of walking. There are also increasing problems integrating sensory and motor information.

Physiological changes encompass reduced cardiovascular and pulmonary capacity. Although the energy expenditures during walking are similar for younger and older adults, reduced walking speeds will compensate for any increase in energy expenditure with aging. Older adults often complain that they have limited endurance when walking and may require more frequent rests. Reduced cardiopulmonary capacity may result in a decreased exercise tolerance for any activity, often manifest during stair climbing when energy demands can stress an individual's capacity. Poor autonomic vascular responses may put an older person at risk for postural hypotension when moving from lying or sitting to standing. When pathology is added, cardiopulmonary capacity could limit the functional goals for a particular patient. For example, an older person with an amputation is often not a candidate for ambulation training with a prosthesis because the energy demands exceed the individual's capacity.

Other requirements for gait are the ability to change speeds, stop and start quickly, navigate obstacles or ramps, walk with a narrow base, walk sideways or backward, or walk on surfaces that are uneven or of different textures. The ability to perform these tasks is often impaired with increasing age. Older adults commonly have greater difficulty in recovering from a sudden perturbation, and this in turn may result in a tendency to fall. Likewise, attending to multiple tasks at the same time, such as carry something while walking, is also compromised with age.

Common pathologies associated with aging further exacerbate gait disorders. Arthritic pain influences walking by slowing velocity, introducing asymmetries, and limiting the range of movement responses. Frailty in older adults, especially the oldest old, often produces very slow and unsteady gaits. Although individuals with severe cognitive impairment can still walk, problems related to executive function and decision making can compromise walking. Multiple medications can produce dizziness and staggering when walking. Diabetes can result in peripheral neuropathies in the lower extremities that limit sensation and motor control. Individuals who are stroke survivors experience hemiparesis and spasticity that further reduce muscle strength, joint movement, and motor control. Individuals with Parkinson's disease

have problems with gait and postural control over and above the gait disorders associated with aging. Older adults who are frail, have cognitive impairment, have suffered strokes, or have Parkinson's disease are at higher risk for falls and fall-related injuries than are older adults who are healthy.

Older adults may also use various assistive devices, such as canes and walkers, as aids during walking. These devices limit gait speed and stride length and also enhance the demands of multitasking. Although assistive devices are intended to reduce the risk of falls in older adults, there is some evidence that simply using the device increases the risk of falls.

Some factors contributing to gait disorders with aging can be changed with appropriate interventions. Muscle weakness, reduced range of motion, and loss of motor control can improve with exercise, training interventions, and physical therapy. Individuals can increase safety awareness and eliminate environmental hazards such as household clutter to reduce the risk of falls. Careful assessment of individual problems can prevent or reverse gait disorders in elders. Because mobility is strongly linked to quality of life in older adults, reducing the sequelae that lead to gait disorders can have an enormous impact.

—*Elizabeth J. Protas*

See also Assistive Devices; Disability and the Disablement Process; Frailty; Injury Prevention; Mobility; Mobility Assessment

Further Readings and References

Bloem BR, Gussekloo J, Lagaay AM, Remarque EJ, Haan J, Westendorp RG. Idiopathic senile gait disorders are signs of subclinical disease. *J Am Geriatr Soc.* 2000;48: 1098–1101.

Bootsma-van der Wiel A, Gussekloo J, de Craen AJM, van Exel E, Bloem BR, Westendorp RGJ. Common chronic diseases and general impairments as determinants of walking disability in the oldest-old population. *J Am Geriatr Soc.* 2002;50:1405–1410.

Schaap LA, Pluijm SMF, Smit JH. The association of sex hormone levels with poor mobility, low muscle strength, and incidence of falls among older men and women. Clin Endocrinol. 2005;63:152–160.

GASTROINTESTINAL AGING

Many age-related changes in gastrointestinal (GI) function are not due to aging alone. The presence of concurrent diseases (e.g., diabetes and atherosclerotic disease) may have more impact on GI tract function in older adults. Given the large functional reserve capacity of the GI tract, older adults can retain normal physiological function during aging. However, aging is associated with an increased prevalence of several GI disorders, so clinically significant abnormalities in GI function, including reduced food intake and constipation, should be evaluated and not attributed to aging.

Oral Cavity and Esophagus

Taste sensation and saliva production decrease with aging. A number of drugs and diseases can also affect taste, and reversible causes of taste impairment must be considered. Drugs can also affect saliva production and may contribute to the severity of acid reflux in the elderly. Although dentition may be well preserved, the presence of dental decay and tooth loss can lead to problems with mastication and reduced caloric intake. Poor dentition (often from ill-fitting dentures) is common, and in some populations more than 60% of the elderly are edentulous (toothless).

In healthy people, aging has only minor effects on esophageal motility. Upper esophageal sphincter pressure gradually decreases with age and is associated with a delay in swallow-induced relaxation. Lower esophageal sphincter pressure does not seem to change unless other disease processes are present. Secondary peristalsis (waves of muscle contraction anywhere in the GI tract that move contents along) is elicited less consistently by esophageal distention, which may impair the clearance of refluxed acid and bile. Presbyesophagus (a condition associated with marked abnormalities in esophageal peristalsis) is attributable to neurological or vascular disorders that affect esophageal function more often than it is to age-related changes.

Gastroesophageal reflux disease (GERD) describes a backflow of acid from the stomach into the swallowing tube or esophagus. It appears to be as prevalent in elderly people as in young people, and although it causes milder symptoms, it tends to be associated with more severe disease, possibly because of impaired acid clearance. Body weight and an increased incidence of hiatus hernia may also be important factors for development of GERD. Esophagitis is the inflammation and ulceration that forms from irritation of the esophagus. The elderly are at higher risk for drug-induced esophagitis and its complications because of high prescription rates. Often, over-the-counter drugs, such as nonsteroidal anti-inflammatory drugs (NSAIDs), may contribute to esophageal injury.

Stomach

Aging has no significant effect on stomach secretion of acid and pepsin. However, conditions that reduce acid production are common. Hypochlorhydria is a reduction in basal and stimulated gastric acid secretion that does occur with aging and can be related to atrophic gastritis. Atrophic gastritis is a histopathologic finding characterized by chronic inflammation of the gastric mucosa with loss of gastric glandular cells and replacement by intestinal-type epithelium and fibrous tissue. Atrophic changes are increased by *Helicobacter pylori* infection. Appropriate treatment early in life may prevent some of these changes that occur gradually over time.

Evidence indicates that aging diminishes the barrier function of the gastric mucosa to protect against insult. Factors involved with mucosal protection that decrease with aging include gastric mucosal blood flow and secretion of prostaglandin, glutathione, bicarbonate, and mucus production. These changes may account for the increased risk of gastric and duodenal ulcers in the elderly, particularly those caused by NSAIDs and *H. pylori*. Aging is associated with slowing of gastric emptying that may prolong gastric distention. In older adults, this effect would contribute to early satiety and lead to decreased food intake.

Small Intestine

Aging has only minor effects on the small intestine. Some alterations exist in the structure of the villi (small finger projections into the lumen of the gut). Although decreases in the neuronal content of the myenteric plexus (nerve network throughout the intestines) and in small intestinal immune function occur, the clinical significance is not yet known. Aging does not result in major changes in small intestinal motility, transit, permeability, or absorption. Bacterial overgrowth in the small intestine may occur more readily among older adults and is commonly seen among those with coexisting illnesses such as hypochlorhydria, small intestinal diverticula, and diabetes mellitus. Bacterial overgrowth may be asymptomatic or cause relatively nonspecific symptoms (e.g., anorexia, weight loss). Bacterial overgrowth is a common cause of diarrhea. With aging, Vitamin D absorption and sensitivity are impaired, and even calcium absorption diminishes in older adults with normal Vitamin D levels. Vitamin D deficiency also contributes to lower calcium levels. Decreased calcium absorption is a major factor in age-related bone loss in men and women; thus, dietary calcium requirement is higher in the elderly.

Large Intestine

Aging does not appear to cause major changes in colonic or anorectal motility. Despite a reduced perception of anorectal distention and increased collagen deposition in the colon, rectal compliance and tone are normal with aging. This reduced rectal wall sensitivity, together with a modest delay in colonic transit, may play a role in constipation.

The definition of constipation includes the following: infrequent bowel movements (typically fewer than three times per week), difficulty during defecation (straining during more than 25% of bowel movements or a subjective sensation of hard stools), or the sensation of incomplete bowel evacuation. Individual variation in stool frequency and defecation patterns are normal. A frequent cause of constipation is related to drug use and side effects. It may also be a related to underlying metabolic or neurological disease. Obstruction and fecal impaction (partial or total blockage by compressed or hardened feces) as a cause for constipation is important to exclude in all older adults.

Fecal incontinence is the recurrent uncontrolled passage of fecal material for at least 1 month. It often affects not only quality of life but also social interactions. Fecal incontinence occurs in up to 50% of nursing home residents. Common causes are constipation with fecal impaction, excessive laxative use, neurological disorders (e.g., autonomic neuropathy), anorectal surgery or previous obstetric injury, and colorectal disorders (e.g., rectal prolapse, radiation injury). Fecal incontinence can often occur with diarrheal illness, but the two may occur separately.

A gut diverticulum (singular) is an outpouching of the wall of the gut to form a sac. Diverticula (plural) may occur at any level from esophagus to colon. For unknown reasons, a diverticulum (usually in the left colon) can burst, leaking bacteria-rich feces into the abdominal cavity. The resulting diverticulitis is usually confined to the surface of the adjacent colon, producing an acute, and sometimes devastating, illness characterized by severe abdominal pain in the left lower part of the abdomen and fever. The prevalence of diverticular disease is age dependent, increasing to 30% by 60 years of age and to 65% by 85 years of age. Most patients remain asymptomatic, 20% may develop diverticulitis, and 10% may develop bleeding associated with the diverticula. A high-fiber diet may be associated with reduced risk of developing diverticular disease and may also reduce subsequent complications once disease exists.

Pancreas

Pancreatic structure changes with aging, resulting in decreases in overall weight, duct hyperplasia, and lobular fibrosis. Overall, these changes do not affect pancreatic exocrine function significantly. As a result of decreased sensitivity of the pancreatic β-cell to glucose, insulin secretion decreases and insulin resistance increases with aging, thereby contributing to higher risks of glucose intolerance and type 2 diabetes mellitus.

Liver and Biliary Disease

Some age-related changes in liver enzymes (e.g., aminotransferases, hepatic alkaline phosphatase, bilirubin) may be clinically significant, but other tests of liver function do alter with aging. These alterations may include liver size, blood flow, and perfusion, all of which affect drug metabolism in the liver. Hepatic volume decreases by approximately 17% to 28% between 40 and 65 years of age; weight decreases by approximately 25% between 20 and 70 years of age. Phase 1 enzymatic reactions (oxidation, reduction, and hydrolysis), which take place in hepatocytes and which metabolize drugs, decrease linearly with aging. Phase 2 reactions (conjugation) remain essentially unchanged. Decreased hepatic blood flow, together with decreased hepatic weight, accounts for decreases in some hepatic drug elimination in the elderly. Hepatic regeneration is delayed but not impaired greatly. The overall survival rates of transplanted livers are not substantially different in older and younger patients. Evidence suggests that livers from donors age 65 years and older may be viable for transplantation. Cholelithiasis (gallstones) prevalence increases in older adults. Both stimulated and fasting concentrations of cholecystokinin (a peptide hormone released from duodenal mucosa that contracts the gallbladder and relaxes the biliary sphincter) are higher in elderly people. However, gallbladder emptying rates and gallbladder volumes do not change with aging, suggesting diminished sensitivity to the effects of cholecystokinin.

—*Alayne Markland*

See also Cancer; Cancer, Common Types of; Diabetes; Incontinence; Oral Health

Further Readings and References

Camilleri M, Lee JS, Viramontes B, Bharucha AE, Tangalos EG. Insights into the pathophysiology and mechanisms of constipation, irritable bowel syndrome, and diverticulosis in older people. *J Am Geriatr Soc.* 2000;48:1142–1150.

Hall KE. Effect of aging on gastrointestinal function. In: Hazzard WR, Blass JP, Halter JB, Ouslander JG, Tinetti M, eds. *Principles of Geriatric Medicine and Gerontology.* 5th ed. New York: McGraw-Hill; 2003:593–600.

National Diabetes Information Clearinghouse. Introduction to diabetes. Available at: http://diabetes.niddk.nih.gov/intro/index.htm. Accessed September 16, 2006.

National Digestive Diseases Information Clearinghouse. Digestive diseases. Available at: http://digestive.niddk.nih.gov/ddiseases/a-z.asp. Accessed September 16, 2006.

GERIATRIC ASSESSMENT

People age 65 years and older are a fast-growing segment of the world population. Most remain healthy even to their later years; for others, old age means living with multiple comorbidities, limited social and economic resources, and physical and mental disabilities. Preserving current functions in healthier seniors and identifying those at high risk for disability are major goals of comprehensive geriatric assessment (CGA). To achieve these goals, the geriatric assessment team collects information on the mental, functional, social, and biological status of older persons. The team then uses the information to plan and implement evidence-based interventions to promote healthy aging and independent living. CGA requires specialists in several disciplines. The CGA team members include (at a minimum) nurses, physicians, social workers, physical and occupational therapists, pharmacists, and dietitians. Members of the CGA team collect information in four major domains of healthy living: mental, functional, social, and biological. These domains have the most impact on function and quality of life for old people. CGA findings guide decisions on need for rehabilitation, nursing home and hospice care, and ambulatory and inpatient services. Research shows that CGA-based evaluation and management of the elderly is associated with decreased functional decline in hospitalized elders, increased psychological well-being, and better pain management in outpatient settings.

Geriatric Assessment of Mental Health Status

Cognitive Domains

Folstein's Mini-Mental State Examination (MMSE) and Clock Drawing Test (CDT) are among the most widely used tools to screen for impairment in global and executive cognition. The MMSE tests orientation, attention and calculation, registration and recall, language, and visual construction. MMSE scores range from 0 to 30, with higher scores indicating better cognitive function. A cutpoint of 23 or less is considered a positive screen for possible cognitive impairment. Low MMSE scores should trigger a more in-depth search for potentially treatable causes of cognitive impairment (e.g., depression, hypothyroidism) and adaptation of patients' care regimen to their level of cognitive handicap.

The CDT assesses aspects of cortical and subcortical substrate of executive function. Executive function refers to cognitive domains of abstract thinking, impulse control, planning, tasks sequencing, and visuospatial organization. Patients are instructed to draw the face of a clock with all of the numbers in their correct positions and to then put the clock's hands at a specific time (e.g., 20 minutes after 8 o'clock). A common scoring method allocates 1 point for each of the following: a complete circle, complete numbers, correct positions of numbers, and correct positions of the clock's hands. The CDT is a quick, easy-to-administer screening test for early and middle dementia. Similar to the MMSE, the inability to do the CDT predicts subsequent decline in ability to live independently in the elderly.

Affective Domains

Depressive symptoms are the most commonly assessed aspect of affective domain during CGA. Untreated depression is associated with increased disability, poor adherence to needed care, poor recovery after illness (e.g., cancer, heart attack), and premature death. A widely used tool is the Yesavage Geriatric Depression Scale (GDS), a 5- to 10-minute interviewer-administered scale that comes in short and long versions. A score of at least 6 in the short version (0 to 15 scoring range) or at least 11 in the long version (0 to 30 scoring range) suggests possible depression and indicates the need for more in-depth clinical evaluation and possibly treatment. The GDS has good sensitivity, validity, and reliability comparable to lengthier scales such as the Hamilton Depression Rating Scale and the Zung Self-Rating Depression Scale.

Geriatric Assessment of Functional Status

A decline in functional status is a major presentation of acute and chronic ailments in the elderly. Early recognition of such decline may lead to early treatment for the underlying cause and interventions (e.g., physical therapy, speech therapy) to slow or prevent the onset of permanent disability. The most widely used functional assessment tool is the six-item Katz Index of Activities of Daily Living (ADL) scale. The Katz ADL scale assesses dependency in bathing, dressing, eating, transferring from a bed to a chair, using the toilet, and continence. ADL disability is defined as needing help with, or inability to perform, one or more of these ADLs.

Other functional assessment tools include the seven-item Lawton Instrumental Activities of Daily Living (IADL) scale. The Lawton IADL scale captures the ability to manage money, prepare meals, use the telephone, take medications, do housework, shop, and travel. A decline in either ADLs or IADLs predicts premature death, a poor outcome postsurgery, and nursing home placement. Among the performance-based assessment tools of mobility, gait, and balance are the Tinetti gait and balance test and Podsiadlo and Richardson's timed Up and Go test.

The Tinetti balance and gait scale assesses people's difficulty in getting up from a chair, whether they sway (with or without nudging), their unsteadiness while standing still or turning around, their height of step, their symmetry of step length, their clearance of feet from the floor, and their staggering motion. In the timed Up and Go test, the inability to rise from a chair, walk 3 meters forward, turn around, walk back to the chair, and sit down in 10 seconds or less indicates a high risk of falls and is a signal that more in-depth evaluation of risk factors for falls is needed. Impairments on these scales strongly predict subsequent falls. Finding such impairments should trigger an in-depth multicomponent clinical assessment, followed by interventions for identified risk factors for falls. These interventions are designed to reduce hazards from environmental and in-home obstacles, medication inappropriateness, vision, balance, gait and orthostatic blood pressure impairments, and cognition and muscle-related dysfunctions.

Geriatric Assessment of Social and Family Status

Socioeconomic resources assume a greater influence on function and overall health in older persons. Unfortunately, with aging comes a diminution of these resources, potentially leading to decreased capacity to cope with adverse change in health. In this context, the CGA team evaluates current health-related socioeconomic circumstances of an older person and designs interventions for alternative community-based resources and other social support that may lessen the adverse impact of social deprivation.

Areas of evaluation and possible actions include the following:

- Advance directives to health care staff and family about preferences for care in the face of terminal illnesses, unsound mind, and other specified health situations
- Access to insurance and funds to purchase timely and high-quality health care
- Adequacy and safety of housing, water, heat and cooling, and access to transportation
- Inquiry about elder abuse, self-neglect, intemperate use of alcohol, and abuse of tobacco and other drugs
- Caregiver assessment for coping resources and stress

A widely used global measure of socioeconomic and functional status in seniors is the Older Americans Resources and Services (OARS) Multidimensional Functional Assessment Questionnaire. The OARS tool assesses the status of health-relevant social and economic resources, mental and physical health, and ADLs. The OARS tool is also used to predict the need for health care services relevant to maintaining independent living in seniors.

Geriatric Assessment of Biological Status

Prevention of comorbidities through early recognition and timely management of common geriatric syndromes starts with a thorough history and physical examination. In CGA, particular attention is paid to preventive actions and clinical examination of the skin, ears, eyes, teeth, dentures, and rectum as well as the person's mobility. Preventive actions include the following:

- Immunizations for influenza and pneumonia
- Screening for breast cancer and colon cancer
- Nutritional status assessment for weight loss, adequacy of food intake, and oral health as well as blood test for albumin, total lymphocyte count, and cholesterol

Geriatric syndrome assessments include the following:

- *Dementia.* This is a syndrome of acquired memory and other cognitive deficits such as disorientation and language difficulties chronic and severe enough to impair leisure, self-care, and other vital ADLs. Positive screening on the MMSE or the CDT should trigger a more detailed evaluation for potentially treatable contributors to the cognitive deficits and interventions to palliate cognitive, functional, and behavioral symptoms.
- *Delirium.* This is an acute mental status change in attention, alertness, perception, and other cognitive domains. Delirium is linked to longer hospital stays, institutionalization, and premature death. The goal of evaluation is to identify and manage the underling precipitants of the acute mental status decline while keeping the patient safe and comfortable.
- *Falls and fractures.* This evaluation should include a bone scan for bone density in those at risk and an assessment of gait and balance problems, injuries, and potentially reversible contributors to falls such as sedative medications.
- *Sensory impairment evaluation.* This includes testing for adequacy of hearing, vision, and gustatory functions.
- *Pain.* This assessment should occur at every contact with a senior, followed by monitored plans to treat pain if present.
- *Bladder and bowel functions.* Assessment and evidence-based interventions (e.g., medications, surgery, behavioral therapy) should be used to reduce incontinence-related morbidity.

Conclusion

CGA is the key to measuring multiple dimensions of older persons' well-being and ability to live independently. The assessments provide the framework for interventions to enhance the quality and quantity of life of seniors and to slow transitioning into functional dependency. With concerted public health initiatives to bring the comprehensive geriatric assessment closer to more elders worldwide, old age can begin to be viewed not as a burden but rather as a privilege to be savored and lived fully.

—*Mukaila A. Raji*

See also Activities of Daily Living; Continuum of Care; Disability and the Disablement Process; Frailty; Gait Disorders; Geriatric Team Care; Instruments; Mental Status Assessment; Mobility Assessment; Outcome and Assessment Information Set (OASIS); Psychiatric Rating Scales; Socioeconomic Status

Further Readings and References

Burns A, Lawlor B, Craig S, eds. *Assessment Scales in Old Age Psychiatry.* 2nd ed. London: Martin Dunitz; 2004.

Cohen HJ, Feussner JR, Weinberger M, et al. A controlled trial of inpatient and outpatient geriatric evaluation and management. *N Engl J Med.* 2002;346:905–912.

Folstein MF, Folstein SE, McHugh PR. Mini-Mental State: A practical method for grading the cognitive state of patients for the clinician. *J Psychiatric Res.* 1975;12:189–198.

George LK, Fillenbaum GG. OARS methodology: A decade of experience in geriatric assessment. *J Am Geriatr Soc.* 1985;33:607–615.

Haywood KL, Garratt AM, Fitzpatrick R. Older people specific health status and quality of life: A structured review of self-assessed instruments. *J Eval Clin Pract.* 2005;11:315–327.

Pham HH, Schrag D, Hargraves JL, et al. Delivery of preventive services to older adults by primary care physicians. *JAMA.* 2005;294:473–481.

Tinetti ME. Clinical practice: Preventing falls in elderly persons. *N Engl J Med.* 2003;348:42–49.

Yesavage JA, Brink TL. Development and validation of a geriatric depression screening scale: A preliminary report. *J Psychiatric Res.* 1983;17:37–49.

GERIATRIC PROFESSION

Geriatrics is a branch of medicine that deals with the problems and diseases of old age and aging people. Geriatric medicine allows the optimal treatment of the older patient. Geriatric medicine allows health care professionals to maximize function and quality of life for the longest period of time. It requires treating much more than the affected organ system associated with the disease; socioeconomic and family issues need to be addressed as well.

During the 13th century, Roger Bacon wrote about how eating in moderation could ward off aging. During the 19th century, George Day wrote about the little interest, or lack of interest, that other doctors showed in caring for the elderly. Then in 1909, the term *geriatrics* was first used by Ignatz L. Nascher, an Austrian immigrant to the Unites States, who promoted social and biological research in aging and senility as a distinctive stage of life. Marjory Warren from Britain was the first physician to create special geriatric units in general hospitals and taught medical students about the care of elderly people. Geriatric medicine originally fought for a less discriminative society for elderly people, who were then experiencing discrimination, as they still are today.

In the United States, life expectancy has experienced impressive increases since the Great Depression after the passage of the Social Security Act in 1935, the establishment of the Senate Special Committee on Aging in 1961, and the introduction of Medicare and Medicaid during the 1960s and 1970s. Two landmark events that helped promote geriatrics in the United States were the founding of American Geriatrics Society in 1942 and the founding of the Gerontological Society of America in 1945. In the United States, geriatrics became established in the Veterans Administration service because of the marked increase in aging of its large patient population. It was during the 1970s that education and research in geriatrics began to develop, with Congress authorizing the creation of the Geriatric Research, Education, and Clinical Centers (GRECCs) that helped develop geriatric faculty, establish the first fellowship programs, and implement the interdisciplinary team training programs in geriatrics. This led to the establishment of the gerontological nurse practice group in 1968.

The major advances credited to geriatric medicine are the many screening tools used in geriatric assessment, including Dorothea Barthel's functional evaluation of patients undergoing rehabilitation, special hospital acute care units, day hospitals, home visit programs to assess and treat the elderly, and recognition of the importance of resistance exercising. Geriatric medicine has been responsible for great advances in the care of the elderly, with the vast majority of medical schools now having programs in geriatrics and training in the care of older patients having become a standard component of medical students and residency training programs. However, geriatric medicine has struggled with its identity. Is it a specialty in its own right, with its clinical interdisciplinary and multidisciplinary research team approach to patient care and investigation, or is it a subspecialty of internal medicine?

Fellowship in Geriatrics for Physicians

The field of geriatrics was determined to be neither a subspecialty nor fully within the domain of general medicine. It was judged to be an area of added competence, and in 1988 the first geriatric examination was administered jointly by the American Board of Internal Medicine and the American Board of Family Medicine, followed by recognition from the Accreditation Council for Graduate Medical Education (ACGME).

In 1995, the 2-year geriatrics fellowship requirement was lowered to 1 year, and there are now approximately 122 accredited fellowship programs. Applicants must be physicians or have an equivalent degree; must have completed an ACGME-accredited residency specialty in internal medicine, geriatric psychiatry, or family practice; and must be a U.S. or Canadian citizen or have permanent resident status. Graduates of medical schools outside the United States and Canada require certification by the U.S. Medical Licensing Exam (USMLE) or the Federal Licensing Exam (FLEX).

Geriatrics–Gerontological Nursing Certification

Eligibility requirements for gerontological certification in nursing are to hold a currently active registered nurse license in the United States or its territories, to have practiced the equivalent of 2 years full time as a registered nurse in the United States or its territories, to have a minimum of 2,000 hours of clinical practice within the past 3 years in the area of gerontological nursing, and to have 30 continuing education contact hours in the area of gerontological nursing within the past 3 years.

Doctor in Pharmacy

The doctor of pharmacy (Pharm.D.) degree requires 4 academic years, and in 1997 the American Council on Pharmaceutical Education (ACPE) adopted national standards, setting the stage for the final steps of a 10-year accreditation revision process that resulted in the implementation of the doctor of pharmacy as the sole professional degree. The Council on Credentialing in Pharmacy (CCP) was formed in 1998 by a consortium of organizations dedicated to providing leadership, standards, public information, and coordination of voluntary pharmacy credentialing programs. The CCP was established by 11 founding member organizations to ensure credentialing requirements and courses for doctors in pharmacy in specialized areas such as geriatrics; that is, council geriatrics certification (CGC). There are several combined programs offered in pharmacy, with aging and social studies designed to integrate gerontology into the pharmacy doctor program.

Gerontological Social Worker

Requirements for the master of social work degree from an accredited school of social work must comply with requirements and guidelines for academic course work and field practicum established in 1994 by the Council for Social Work Education (CSWE). It is a 2-year degree, with required courses the first year and elective courses the second year. Students must complete 900 hours in field practice or approximately 40% of students' time overall. The Council on Social Work Education Gero-Ed Center (National Center for Gerontological Social Work Education) is a reliable source for information on training requirements.

—*Jose A. Loera*

See also Geriatric Team Care; Gerontological Nursing; Social Work Roles in Health and Long-Term Care

Further Readings and References

Evans JG. Geriatric medicine: A brief history. *Br Med J.* 1997;315:1075–1077.

Morley JE. Geriatric medicine: A true subspecialty. *J Am Geriatr Soc.* 1993;41:1150–1154.

Nascher IL. Geriatrics. *NY Med J.* 1909;90:358.

GERIATRIC TEAM CARE

Increased longevity has resulted in great numbers of individuals living well into their 80s and 90s; however, longevity also means that most older adults live with multiple chronic illnesses. Chronic illness shifts the focus of care from curing the illness to controlling symptoms, maximizing the patient's function, and helping the patient and family manage the illness. Chronic care usually requires multiple medications, frequently necessitates ongoing lab work or other medical tests, and generally requires the physician to spend more time and effort helping to managing the elder's health. The elder's health care needs can also be complicated by illness-related declines in cognitive function, smaller social networks, and decreased financial assets. No one clinician can be expected to be an expert in all of these areas. The need for multiple clinicians to communicate with each other regularly to coordinate services and manage the health and health-related needs of a defined group of elders has resulted in the growth of geriatric interdisciplinary teams.

Team care is characterized by good communication, coordination of service so that duplication of services is minimized, a patient focus, common goals around care, respect for other team members and a recognition of the team members' ability to contribute to patient care, flexibility in roles, mechanisms for resolving conflicts, shared responsibility for team actions, and evaluation and feedback of team performance. A geriatric health care team can deliver either multidisciplinary or interdisciplinary care. In multidisciplinary care, various disciplines meet and discuss care, but the treatments are generally independent of each other, with each discipline addressing a specific issue or concern. In contrast, the interdisciplinary care team aspires to a far more collaborative model; members from disciplines agree to bring individual expertise together to create an overall care plan, prioritize interventions, jointly coordinate the delivery of care, and evaluate the outcomes against jointly agreed-on goals. A second important distinction is the role of the patient on the team. In multidisciplinary care the patient is considered the recipient of care, whereas in interdisciplinary care the patient is a fully participating team member with responsibility to help implement the agreed-on plan.

Benefits of Geriatric Team Care

Despite elders' need for coordinated services, few financial incentives exist in traditional fee-for-service Medicare for providers to work together to integrate care across settings. Although quality might improve, without financial integration, providers do not realize savings from reducing unnecessary hospitalizations or duplicative services. Consequently, the likelihood of geriatric team care is highest in the settings where the provider of care is also financially responsible for all of the elder's health care costs (inpatient, outpatient, or nursing home placement). Thus, interdisciplinary geriatric teams are most common in programs for the all-inclusive care for elderly (PACE), where the provider is financially accountable for all Medicaid and Medicare costs and reimbursement is paid monthly as a fixed amount regardless of the use of services. PACE elders are generally very frail and have multiple medical, psychological, social, and financial needs that require ongoing review and careful monitoring. Because the needs are extensive with multiple professionals and paraprofessionals working together, these health care teams can be large. These teams meet regularly to review care plans and maximize elder function, seeking to avoid hospitalizations and nursing home placement. Similarly, hospice care, or care at the end of life, usually delivers care as a team because the multiple needs of the dying patient and family require knowledge and skills that are beyond the capacity of one clinician. Again, for elders receiving the Medicare hospice benefit, the hospice is reimbursed through an all-inclusive rate that pays the costs for coordinated care.

Geriatric teams working around common goals are also common when assessing elders in inpatient or outpatient settings. Multidimensional interdisciplinary assessment of elders, generally called comprehensive geriatric assessment (CGA), is targeted at frail elders who have multiple chronic conditions, many prescribed medications, and functional deficits. CGA assesses older adults in four domains: physical health, functional status, psychological health, and socioenvironmental parameters. A controlled trial of inpatient CGA and outpatient geriatric evaluation and management by Cohen and colleagues demonstrated that specialized geriatric team care, as compared with usual care, resulted in significant reductions in functional decline, improvement in mental health outcomes, and reduction in nursing home placement for no increase in costs.

Studies within hospitals have demonstrated repeatedly that good communication skills and close collaboration between nurses and physicians results in superior patient outcomes. Eric Coleman's work recognized that transitions between levels of care also require good coordination, require understanding of the patient and family about the needs of the patient, and are another point where health care teams can avoid errors, reduce health care costs, and improve patient outcomes. A skilled clinician following the patient home or to a skilled nursing home can help prepare the elder and caregiver for issues facing the elder at discharge, answer questions that arise, offer technical knowledge, and provide emotional support if the patient returns home.

Team Composition

Geriatric teams vary in size, composition of members, and locus of care. The core professional members of geriatric teams are typically the patient, family, physician, nurse, social worker, psychologist, and pharmacist. As needs change, the team composition changes and reflects additional services providing care. As noted earlier, PACE teams are much larger than teams in other settings. Team size averages 10 members, with some teams having up to 50 members; paraprofessional aides and drivers are accepted team members in PACE but are rarely members in other settings.

Membership from multiple disciplines creates challenges for the team. Although professionals may be acquainted with the range of services that elders need, they do not usually know the education or roles of other professionals with whom they work on the geriatric care team. Because professionals are generally trained in their own discipline and learn their own terminology, problem-solving approach, and professional behaviors, the skills, language, and socialization of other disciplines are not understood. The unique set of skills that each discipline brings is further augmented by the personal and professional experience of team members. Many tasks on teams can overlap, and multiple clinicians may assume that the task is "their" domain. It is important that team members recognize overlapping skills and understand whether the domain and tasks are redundant or complementary. For example, nurses, physicians, or pharmacists may help a patient to "manage" medications by explaining the side effects of a medication, what time of day to take the medication, and whether the medication should be taken with other medications, food, or water. A social worker may also believe that he or she helps to manage medications by teaching a patient how to fill a pill dispenser or how to obtain financial assistance to ensure an ongoing supply of the medications. The tasks are different, but unless teams take the time to clarify the language, the nuances of tasks performed by a different discipline will not be recognized.

Conflict is an inevitable part of teams. Members are trained in distinct disciplines and have diverse perspectives and expertise. Effective communication requires acknowledging and discussing the differences with constant recognition of the shared team goals and an acknowledgment that the way to achieve the goal is through important team discussion. Defining language and terminology can reduce misunderstandings. Respect for team members and trust in skills must be modeled and become part of the team's culture. Teams should establish decision-making and negotiation processes that recognize the skills of each discipline but acknowledge the diverse approaches to achieving the goal.

Team Meetings

Because so much work must be accomplished by the group in meetings, it is imperative that the team use its meeting time well. Team members must agree to create the structure for meetings. Effective and efficient team meetings do the following:

- Use an agenda that specifies the purpose or expected outcome of the meeting.
- Establish time frames to accomplish the tasks.
- Create a meeting record to summarize the group's decisions.
- Identify measurable goals. (Specify which team member is responsible for what activities by a designated date.)
- Evaluate the meeting so that members can express concerns about the process and the team can improve over time.
- Establish meeting roles for members, including the leader or facilitator, the timekeeper, and the recorder. (Ideally, leadership roles rotate so that all members get experience.)

The John A. Hartford Foundation invested $13 million to create geriatric interdisciplinary team training (GITT) programs so as to encourage the development of educational materials for student trainees and preceptors. The results of the 4-year, nine-site trainings revealed the need for training in knowledge of team members' education and skills and for honing of communication and conflict management skills. Evaluation revealed the effectiveness of the program.

—Kathryn Hyer

See also Geriatric Assessment; Geriatric Profession; Gerontological Nursing; Social Work Roles in Health and Long-Term Care

Further Readings and References

Cohen HJ, Feussner JR, Weinberger M, et al. A controlled trial of inpatient and outpatient geriatric evaluation and management. *N Engl J Med.* 2002;346:905–912.

Coleman EA, Berenson RA. Lost in translation: Challenges and opportunities for improving the quality of transitional care. *Ann Intern Med.* 2004;140:533–536.

Fulmer T, Hyer K, Flaherty, E. Geriatric interdisciplinary team training program: Evaluation results. *J Aging Health.* 2005;17:443–470.

Mukamel D, Temkin-Greener H, Delavan R, et al. Team performance and risk-adjusted health outcomes in the Program of All-Inclusive Care for the Elderly (PACE). *J Am Geriatr Soc.* 2006;46:227–237.

Naylor M, Brooten D, Campbell RL, Maislin GM, McCauley KM, Schwartz JS. Transitional care of older adults hospitalized with heart failure: A randomized clinical trial. *J Am Geriatr Soc.* 2004;52:675–684.

Rubenstein L. Comprehensive geriatric assessment: From miracle to reality. *J Gerontol A Biol Sci Med Sci.* 2004; 59:473–477.

GERONTOLOGICAL NURSING

Gerontological nurses (GNs) are those nurses who specialize in care of both aging adults and the older adult population. These nurses provide care based on a specific skill set that includes knowledge of the normal aging process, common disorders of older adults, and unusual presentation of common illnesses. GNs assist patients and their families to promote health and optimal function, often while patients are dealing with one or more chronic diseases. Nurses use a comprehensive approach to patient care that focuses on the interplay of physical, psychological, and social factors.

The overwhelming majority of persons receiving health care in the United States are older adults, including an estimated 48% of hospital patients, 80% of home care patients, and 85% of all nursing home residents. Disability can result from diseases such as Alzheimer's disease, depression, arthritis, osteoporosis, vision, and hearing impairments. Although the health status of older adults is quite variable, an "average" older adult is estimated to have multiple chronic illnesses and take multiple medications. Heart disease, cancer, and cerebrovascular accident are leading causes of disease in older adults. The often complex interplay of physical aging changes, chronic illness, psychosocial losses of aging, multiple medications, and acute illness that can affect patient health indicates a need for knowledgeable GNs.

Gerontological Nursing Roles

There are diverse entry points to nursing, including licensed practical nurse, registered nurse, advanced practice nurse, and doctorally prepared nurse. Nurses can specialize in gerontology at any of the various levels of nursing practice. Roles vary, with licensed practical nurses providing basic clinical care, registered nurses and advanced practice nurses assisting patients with chronic disease management, and nurse researchers studying clinical problems such as pain management for patients with dementia. Sometimes referred to as "geriatric" nursing (a more focused term specific to illnesses of the older adult), the term *gerontological nursing* is considered more encompassing of the broader psychosocial realms and is commonly used.

GNs help prevent, identify, and manage common problems of more frail older adults such as confusion, falls, and skin breakdown; they are guided by standards of care or best practice resources. Resources for best practice protocols (guidelines for care), such as those developed by the Hartford Geriatric Nursing Initiative and the Nurse Competence in Aging Initiative, include topics ranging from management of pain, delirium, dementia, and depression to social issues such as advance directives, discharge planning, and supporting family caregivers.

Sample GN activities include preventing illness and disability in older adults by administering influenza vaccine or performing blood pressure screenings, teaching an elder or a family caregiver at a clinic about medication management or healthy diet and exercise, helping an older adult to cope with a mobility disorder such as arthritis in the home setting using appropriate pain management and adaptive equipment, and managing acute injury (e.g., hip fracture) in the hospital setting in relation to physical aging changes, multiple diagnoses, and often complex medication regimens.

GNs have broad functional roles as well. In an educator role, GNs can help families to better understand the physical or emotional issues that a loved one may be experiencing and why particular treatments are important. Knowing common stages and changes across the course of a chronic disease such as Parkinson's disease, nurses help patients and families to prepare and cope with disease progression. GNs who specialize in dementia care, in addition to working with patients, may work with community groups to provide caregiver education and to assist in leading support groups.

GNs often have leadership roles in long-term care and hospital settings. Their work involves supervising a team of nursing staff and helping to coordinate a team of health care providers. They often play important roles in facilitating communication for the health care team and families. Using quality improvement approaches that include technology and standardized assessments, GNs work within health care systems to promote safe and efficient care in venues such as safe medication administration systems. When working collaboratively as part of larger interdisciplinary teams, GNs may engage in practice, case management, education, research, administration, and advocacy for older adults.

Curriculum Standards and Certifications

In preparing nurses to care for the growing population of older adults, collaborative initiatives by a number of gerontological nursing organizations have resulted in resources to support nursing education. To promote competency in gerontological nursing, the American Association of Colleges of Nursing has developed curriculum standards in gerontological care for both basic and advanced nursing education programs, recommending 30 competencies for undergraduates and 47 competencies for advanced practice. The American Nurses Association (ANA) responded to the aging of the population and workforce trends by making gerontological nursing a priority focus for the profession. The ANA Nursing Standards of Care have been expanded to include age-appropriate and culturally sensitive care. Specific criteria for providing competent care for older adults across health care settings have been published, and certification for basic and advanced practice nurses has been developed.

Basic certification is available for registered nurses who work primarily with older adults and who have developed competence in assessing, managing, implementing, and evaluating health care to meet specialized needs of older adults. Primary challenges include identifying and using the strengths of older adults and assisting to maximize independence, minimize disability, and (when appropriate) achieve a peaceful death. Advanced certification is available for nurse practitioners and clinical nurse specialists who provide advanced nursing care to older adults. These practitioners have expertise in providing, directing, and influencing the care of older adults and their families and significant others in a variety of settings. These nurses have developed in-depth understanding of the dynamics of aging and of the intervention skills necessary for health promotion and management of health problems.

Practice Settings

In addition to clinics and hospital settings, GNs provide care in settings such as assisted living, long-term care, and patients' homes. In assisted-living facilities, nurses work with older adults with various frailties who need some assistance in caring for themselves; they monitor and screen for problems with a focus on maintaining function. In long-term care settings, specific tools guide nurses in assessing older adult clients and preventing common problems such as falls, skin breakdown, and restraint use. GNs working with patients at the end of life focus on promoting comfort and pain relief and on assisting patients and families with nutrition and hydration concerns. In the home setting, GNs may advise family caregivers of available home-based support services such as home-delivered meals, bathing assistance, adult day care, and caregiver training and support groups. In understanding diverse practice settings, GNs can use best practices in patient care to promote quality of life and often prevent patients from transferring to more costly, medically focused care settings. The Hartford Geriatric Nursing Initiative has developed resources for nurses working in each of the various practice settings.

A continued and increased demand for qualified GNs and nursing faculty is anticipated. With the general aging of the population and the rapid growth of the population age 85 years and over, it is expected that the number of older adults receiving health care will require additional qualified nurses to meet the needs for care. With an aging nursing workforce, faculty roles for those prepared to teach gerontological nursing will increase as well. More nurses specializing in gerontological nursing are needed now and will continue to be needed in the future.

—*Wanda Bonnel and Kristine Williams*

See also Assisted Living; Geriatric Assessment; Geriatric Profession; Geriatric Team Care

Further Readings and References

Alliance for Aging Research. *Medical Never-Never Land: Ten Reasons Why America Is Not Ready for the Coming Age Boom.* Washington, DC: Alliance for Aging Research. Available at: www.agingresearch.org/brochures/nevernever/nevernever.pdf. Accessed September 16, 2006.

Beers MH, Berkow MD, eds. *The Merck Manual of Geriatrics.* 3rd ed. Whitehouse Station, NJ: Merck; 2005. Available at: www.merck.com/mrkshared/mmg/sec1/ch2/ch2b.jsp. Accessed September 16, 2006.

Mezey M. Challenges in providing care for persons with complex chronic illness. In: Binstock RH, Cluff LE, Von Merix O, eds. *The Future of Long-Term Care.* Baltimore, Md: Johns Hopkins University Press; 1996:119–142.

Stotts NA, Deitrich CE. The challenge to come: The care of older adults. *Am J Nurs.* 2004;104(8):40–47.

Global Aging

The population of the world is aging, a result of the fact that most societies have undergone or are experiencing fertility declines and falls in mortality. The median age of people in the world was 23.6 years in 1950, increased to 26.5 years in 2000, and is projected to reach 36.2 years in 2050. This global trend is perceived as the result of a human demographic success because societies have achieved sustained drops in adult mortality and low fertility levels close to those desired by the individuals. However, the speed of aging and the conditions under which such aging is occurring are widely variable across countries and groups, such that the likely consequences of the population aging phenomenon will vary as well.

The fraction of the total population that is age 65 years and older across the globe provides a first picture of this diversity in aging. Europe has been, and is projected to continue as, the oldest continent, with close to 16% of its population age 65 years and older in 2000. By 2030, this figure is expected to reach 24%. At the other extreme is sub-Saharan Africa, with only 2.9% of its population age 65 years and older in 2000 and 3.6% projected in 2030. Between these two extremes, North America follows Europe with 12.6% of the older population (those age 65 years and older) in 2000 and 20.3% expected in 2030, followed by Oceania (10.2% and 16.3%, respectively), Asia (6% and 12%), Latin America and the Caribbean (5.5% and 11.6%), and Near East/North Africa (4.3% and 8.1%). Regional averages cover the vast range among countries; those with the highest proportions in 2000 were Italy, Japan, Greece, Germany, and Spain.

The speed of growth of the fraction of the population age 65 years and older among rich and poor nations provides another view of the aging phenomenon. Although the proportion of the older population is higher in developed countries than in developing nations, the speed of aging is currently faster among developing countries. This is because increasingly through time, the later the mortality and fertility declines are achieved in a country, the faster the changes seem to occur and the speed of aging accelerates. For example, in developed countries such as France and Sweden, it took approximately 100 years through the 19th and 20th centuries for the fraction of the population age 65 years and older to get from 7% to 14% of the population. In contrast, it took Spain and the United Kingdom 45 years during the second half of the 20th century to experience this change, and it should take only 27 years for China (in 2027) and 21 years for Brazil (in 2032) to attain similar percentages.

In many developed countries, the people who are age 80 years and older (often labeled the *oldest old*) are currently the fastest-growing group. This is an important phenomenon that is receiving attention because in the past the population projections have underestimated the survival gains among the oldest-old population and because health care and long-term care for this age group represent a major social and economic concern in all countries. In Japan, for example, the oldest old corresponded to 21.7% of the population age 65 years and older in 2000, but this fraction is projected to increase to 39.3% by 2030.

Women represent another group within older adults who receive particular attention. This is because women are overrepresented both among the population age 65 years and older and among the oldest old given that women have higher life expectancies than men in most of the world. In addition, women are more likely than men to be poor in most countries of the world. In 2000, women outnumbered men four to three in the population age 65 years and older and nearly two to one in the population age 80 years and older. In many countries in Europe, this is a result of the higher mortality experienced by cohorts of men during World War II. This phenomenon is less evident in developing countries because men outnumber women at older ages in some countries of Western Asia. For every 100 women in the population age 65 years and older, there are approximately 50 men in Russia and Ukraine and approximately 70 men in the United States, United Kingdom, Italy, Bulgaria, and Australia, in contrast to 103 men in India and 117 in Bangladesh. Scholars estimate that gains in life expectancy will be such that the gender gap in developed countries will close, whereas the gap in developing countries will widen. Overall, it is expected that women will continue to outnumber men among older adults in the foreseeable future.

These trends in world population aging are without precedent in human history and convey an image of changing the prevalent economic and social balance among age groups. The new demographic regime implies that in relative terms, the world is moving toward having more people of older ages, fewer young people, and older workers, thereby transforming epidemiological patterns and health care demands. The challenge for the world is to accommodate the needs of the growing number of older adults while investing heavily in the young and securing a productive labor base for the economic systems. For developed countries, the pressure of the relative number of old people and a labor shortage is already evident or imminent in the short run; for developing countries, these will be issues for the medium run. This differential in volume and timing of the population aging across rich and poor nations is viewed as representing several opportunities to meet the global challenge.

First, labor-scarce aging countries are looking for services to meet the health care demands of their population and for mid-level labor force to meet the desired growth in information technology and other markets. These countries will turn to service-oriented labor-surplus countries to meet some of the care demands of older adults; having cheaper health care will be seen as an advantage for developed countries and as a source of labor for developing countries. At the same time, the information era provides opportunities to meet demands for labor without necessarily relocating the labor force from one place to another, thereby mitigating the thorny issues of immigration for some countries.

Second, the aging phenomenon is foreseeable and quite certain; developing countries know that they have a window of time before their population starts aging in earnest, and this period can be used to invest in desirable infrastructures, particularly those that refer to sustainable financial markets and health care and social protection systems. This is not an issue of allocating resources to the older population, although given their relative numbers, the older population will increasingly gain political power to allocate such resources in societies. Rather, the issue requires allocating resources to all age groups because the young generations are the backbone of the productive labor force and should be receiving the investments necessary to make them highly productive during working ages and as healthy as possible over their life cycle to minimize the cost of health care and maximize their well-being during their future old age.

Globally, new economic modes of production are expected to emerge, with experience being valued and put to use as much as, or more than, youthful energy in the labor market. Health research and human resources will continue to be in high demand because countries will need to develop their own resources and adopt the technologies that work in their own context.

Inequality across countries and within societies is likely to carry over during the new aging process, but the information era is facilitating the collaboration across nations to combat diseases and to disseminate scientific findings, and this could potentially assist in closing the knowledge gap across the globe. For the health sciences, the challenge continues to be one of identifying the vulnerable groups—those more likely to be disabled and/or ill—and helping to minimize the impact of individuals' lifelong behaviors and constraints on old-age disability and illness.

Just as economic markets have long started to develop with an understanding of the advantages of acting globally, the demographic phenomenon of aging brings to the forefront the interdependence of societies and the need to act globally also in terms of people. Increasingly, it will be important for the health and economic well-being of the Japanese old population, for example, not only that the Brazil financial markets work effectively but also that the young people of Sri Lanka receive the best education and health care possible. In the past, every major change in the world demographic regime has been accompanied by a transformation in the economic and social systems, including the provision of health care. As a global phenomenon, the world is now just beginning to experience the consequences of population aging. The new systems of relations that will develop, and that in turn will undoubtedly shape a new demographic regime in the long run, are highly unknown.

—*Rebeca Wong*

See also Africa; Asia; Australia and New Zealand; Europe; Latin America and the Caribbean

Further Readings and References

Kinsella K, Phillips DR. *Global Aging: The Challenge of Success.* Washington, DC: Population Reference Bureau; 2005. Population Bulletin, Vol. 60, No. 1.

National Research Council. *Preparing for an Aging World: The Case for Cross-National Research.* Washington, DC: National Academy Press; 2001.

United Nations. *Population Challenges and Development Goals.* New York: United Nations; 2005.

GOVERNMENT HEALTH SURVEYS

Health surveys conducted by the federal government play an extremely important role in understanding the nation's health progress, problems, and disparities. The National Center for Health Statistics (NCHS) has been, and continues to be, the key producer of such surveys. The NCHS also produces numerous publications that summarize the data, which are extremely useful for researchers, students, and policymakers.

The National Health Interview Survey (NHIS), conducted by the NCHS, is the leading source of annual health information for the civilian, noninstitutionalized resident population of the United States. Ongoing since 1957, the NHIS is used by governmental, academic, and private researchers to monitor health and illness trends in the United States, understand health and health care disparities across groups, determine barriers to health care, and inform health policy. The annual survey, cross sectional and nationally representative in design, includes oversamples of minority group subpopulations and usually includes approximately 100,000 individuals per year. The extremely large size of the NHIS is very important for obtaining health and health care estimates for relatively small population subgroups. Analysts often combine NHIS data across several years to even further elevate sample size. Because the NHIS is household based, all individuals in selected households are included. Furthermore, both adults and children are included. Key sets of measures available in the survey include information on health, health care use, health insurance, health behavior, household composition, and socioeconomic and demographic characteristics. The NHIS design and content are updated roughly every 10 years.

Over the past decade, data from the NHIS have become even more useful because individuals age 18 years and older at the time of the survey have been linked statistically with the National Death Index (NDI) during subsequent years. The NCHS, through computer matching, checks each survey respondent with the annual NDI to best determine whether the sampled person died during the year of the survey or during subsequent follow-up years. For example, the 1990 NHIS has now been linked with the NDI through December 2002. If a match to the NDI is identified, the timing and cause of death information for that person is linked to the corresponding NHIS data. This linkage permits the use of NHIS data as a rich baseline sample for the analysis of mortality and mortality differentials for the noninstitutionalized adult population of the nation. The data set, called the NHIS–NDI, is even more powerful when multiple years of the NHIS are combined to yield an even larger baseline sample. The data have been a very important resource for better understanding U.S. adult mortality patterns by race/ethnicity, nativity, gender, socioeconomic status, cigarette smoking, weight status, religious involvement, and more over the past decade.

A similar data linkage has been undertaken through a joint effort of the National Heart, Lung, and Blood Institute and the National Institute on Aging. In this case, multiple years of the Current Population Survey (CPS) have been linked to the NDI to create the National Longitudinal Mortality Study (NLMS) database. Although the baseline data set used in this effort, the CPS, is not a health survey and is focused on employment and other socioeconomic characteristics of the U.S. population, the linkage to the NDI has effectively created a very large database that supports comprehensive studies of demographic and socioeconomic differentials in U.S. adult mortality. Together, the NHIS–NDI and the NLMS have had a major influence on the mortality literature in public health, demography, and gerontology over the past decade.

Elderly individuals surveyed in the NHIS in 1984 and 1994 were also resurveyed during subsequent years for longitudinal research purposes. These two efforts comprised the Longitudinal Study of Aging I and Longitudinal Study of Aging II, respectively, collaborative efforts between the NCHS and the National Institute on Aging aimed at measuring changes in health status, functional status, living arrangements, and health services use of these two cohorts as they moved into the oldest ages. These data sets are useful not only for measuring changes in elderly health but also for understanding how such changes differ during the later period (1990s) compared with the earlier period (1980s). The data are also linked to the NDI for mortality research purposes.

Another major and very important survey program run by the NCHS is the National Health and Nutrition Examination Survey (NHANES). The NHANES is a unique, nationally representative, cross-sectional database of adults and children in the United States that combines survey interviews with physical examinations to provide a more comprehensive picture of health than either method can do alone. Although ongoing since the early 1960s, the survey changed in 1999 to become a continuous program that now includes a nationally representative set of approximately 5,000 individuals per year. Like the NHIS, the NHANES can be pooled across years to increase sample size; furthermore, individuals who have been surveyed in the NHANES have also been linked to the NDI so that subsequent mortality among survey participants can be analyzed. During recent years, the NHANES has oversampled African Americans, Mexican Americans, adolescents, and persons age 60 years and older to provide more accurate health estimates for those subgroups. In the home interview portion, participants answer questions about health status, disease history, diet, health behavior, and sociodemographic characteristics. The health examination portion is performed in a mobile exam center, where many tests are performed, with some of them depending on respondents' age and gender. The examination portion of the NHANES, in combination with its very large sample size and high-quality survey data, makes this a truly unique federal resource.

The NCHS also conducts large, nationally representative surveys focusing on health care and expenditures. The National Health Care Survey (NHCS) is in reality a family of surveys that gather information about health care services, health care availability, and the health problems of individuals who receive care. This set of surveys, instead of being household based, is most often health provider based, with data coming from both provider and patient records. As with most federal surveys, demographic and socioeconomic data are also collected to best examine health care differences across groups. This family of surveys includes the National Ambulatory Medical Care Survey, the National Hospital Ambulatory Medical Care Survey, the National Survey of Ambulatory Surgery, the National Hospital Discharge Survey, the National Nursing Home Survey, the National Home and Hospice Care Survey, the National Employer Health Insurance Survey, and the National Health Provider Inventory.

A second very important survey program on U.S. health care is the Medical Expenditure Panel Survey (MEPS) collected by the Agency for Healthcare Research and Quality working together with the NCHS. The MEPS contains several survey components: households, nursing homes, medical providers, and insurance providers. Key features of the MEPS include its longitudinal design, large sample size, coverage of the nation as a whole, and link to the NHIS. Indeed, the MEPS collects its household data from a sample of individuals who were participants during the previous year of the NHIS, thereby making the design less costly and linking data back to NHIS responses from the previous year.

The NCHS also compiles and collects other health and vital records data that are extremely useful to researchers. These include, for example, the huge national files of birth and death records, the National Survey of Family Growth, and the National Immunization Survey. As just one example of the importance of such data, the NCHS annual mortality data file, compiled from death certificates from around the country, has been an extremely important resource in monitoring age, sex, racial/ethnic, and cause of death mortality patterns in the U.S. population since the early portion of the 20th century. For health, demographic, and aging students and researchers, such data are an invaluable benchmark for conducting more in-depth studies.

The NCHS website (www.cdc.gov/nchs) includes a wealth of information on each of the data sets discussed here as well as reports summarizing the data, methodological tips for using and understanding the data, and key links to related sites. A number of other important health and aging surveys are sponsored by federal government grants but are carried out by university researchers, medical school faculty, and private firms. Among the most prominent are the Health and Retirement Study, the Established Populations for

Epidemiologic Studies of the Elderly (EPESE), and the National Long Term Care Survey.

—Robert A. Hummer
and Nicole Lindsey

See also Duke Longitudinal Studies; Established Populations for Epidemiologic Studies of the Elderly; Ethnicity and Race; Health and Retirement Study; Longitudinal Study of Aging; MacArthur Study of Successful Aging; National Health Interview Survey; National Long Term Care Survey

Further Readings and References

National Center for Health Statistics. NCHS website. Available at: www.cdc.gov/nchs. Accessed September 16, 2006.

National Research Council. Critical perspectives on racial and ethnic differences in health in late life. In: Anderson NB, Bulatao RA, Cohen B, eds. *Panel on Race, Ethnicity, and Health in Late Life: Committee on Population, Division of Behavioral and Social Sciences and Education.* Washington, DC: National Academy Press; 2004.

Rogers R, Hummer R, Nam C. *Living and Dying in the USA: Behavioral, Health, and Social Differences of Adult Mortality.* San Diego, Calif: Academic Press; 2000.

U.S. Department of Health and Human Services. *Healthy People 2010.* 2nd ed. Washington, DC: Government Printing Office; 2000.

GRIEF

See BEREAVEMENT AND GRIEF

HEALTH AND RETIREMENT STUDY

The Health and Retirement Study (HRS), founded in 1990, is an ongoing panel (cohort) population study of older Americans supported by the U.S. National Institute on Aging (NIA) with additional support from other U.S. federal agencies. Design details, documentation, questionnaires, and the historical and scientific evolution of the HRS can be found on the HRS website (http://hrsonline.isr.umich.edu). As originally conceived, the HRS was designed to follow a representative sample of age-eligible individuals and their spouses as they made the transition from active work to retirement so as to determine the health, social, economic, and family factors that predict the timing and nature of the retirement process as well as postretirement health, social, and economic outcomes. The core data collection activity has been a biennial survey conducted either in-person or by telephone. The first HRS survey was performed in 1992 with a target population of noninstitutionalized persons 51 to 61 years of age. Subsequent HRS surveys have been conducted biennially during even years; surveys are currently scheduled to be conducted in 2006, 2008, and 2010.

After establishing the first HRS cohort, the need for companion information across the age spectrum of older adults was recognized. Thus, HRS investigators created the Assets and Health Dynamics Among the Oldest Old (AHEAD) study as a separate but similar population investigation. The AHEAD cohort was first surveyed in 1993 and consisted of persons born before 1924 who were age 70 years and older at the time. The AHEAD study was designed to examine the dynamic interactions among health, family, and economic forces during the postretirement period. The AHEAD study included two survey waves in 1993 and 1995, at which time it was amalgamated into the HRS even-year cycle, beginning in 1998, with greater harmonization of aims and content. Since that time, additional birth cohorts have been added to the study (for details, see the HRS website), so that the HRS/AHEAD provides substantial information on all older American age groups. In addition to the core surveys, the HRS/AHEAD routinely conducts mortality surveillance and performs "exit interviews" with surviving spouses, children, or other informants concerning medical expenditures and family interactions with the deceased participants during the final stages of life. Exit interviews were also designed to provide information about the disposition of economic assets following death.

One of the important strengths of the HRS is to provide a broad range of health, social, and economic information on the same individuals and families in a comprehensive fashion that is responsive to multidisciplinary health, social, behavioral, economic, and policy research on older Americans. The HRS provides detailed information on a number of important domains: demographics, health status, housing, family structure, work history and current employment, disability, retirement plans, net worth, income, and health and life insurance. In addition, HRS data are enriched by several important links with information from employers and from administrative data. HRS supplementary information includes administrative data from Social Security earnings and benefits records, the National Death Index, Medicare claims records, and employer pension programs. Also, each biennial HRS survey contains several "experimental modules"; that is, short studies intended to (a) explore the quality consistency of survey data, (b) explore new types of items or item domains, (c) collect more detailed information on selected areas of inquiry, and (d) provide conceptual and partial content linkage to other similar national surveys in the United States and elsewhere. In addition, several ancillary studies conducted on the HRS cohort provide new information in areas such as household economic consumption, the costs and challenges of diabetes mellitus, and the occurrence and natural history of dementia and Alzheimer's disease. The HRS website provides further details on all of these activities.

Special Features of HRS/AHEAD

Sample Design and Sample Characteristics

The comprehensive goals of the HRS were limited by trade-offs between survey length (driven by the data requirements of the various retirement and aging models) and budget constraints. The original sample size was based on the amount of statistical power needed for various types of analyses. Sample composition was based mainly on scientific goals and considerations. For example, the oversample of Black and Hispanic census tracts was deemed to be crucial to success in studying the process of retirement. Many of the factors that influence retirement decisions for minorities were thought to be quite different from those for Whites. The influences of family structure and various medical conditions among minority populations was thought to differ because of more extensive family relationships, divergent economic status, and different use of medical care. Minorities were also thought to be less likely to have jobs with private pensions as well as fewer economic resources generally

as they approached retirement age. Both Blacks and Hispanics were oversampled at the rate of two to one relative to Whites. HRS investigators also oversampled residents of the state of Florida because of U.S. congressional support and the high densities and numbers of older persons.

Previous retirement studies also paid relatively little attention to work and retirement among women, with the consequent inability to analyze retirement as a joint decision for couples where women or both spouses were working. The economy had changed drastically since the last major retirement study during the 1970s, and the prevalence of two-earner families was substantially higher. Thus, despite the baseline target population of persons 51 to 61 years of age, spouses were included regardless of age. Thus, the index unit of observation became the age-eligible spouse in the sample, whereas the characteristics of the spouse of an age-eligible person were regarded as an important source of variation that would influence the retirement decisions of both family members.

The decision concerning the original target age range was difficult. On the one hand, it was desirable to begin collecting data for a retirement study before retirement decisions had been made because recreating retirement decisions ex post facto is not analytically satisfactory. But the cost of adding a younger cohort, where few had retired, was substantial. It was decided to set the age range for the HRS at 51 to 61 years partly on the grounds that a common age at which private pension plans provided strong retirement incentive was around the mid-50s and it would be well to collect several years of data prior to that decision point.

Study Content

Study content in the HRS was and is developed by four working groups: Labor Force Participation and Pensions, Health Conditions and Health Status, Family Structure and Mobility, and Economic Status. Content decisions are proposed by these committees, made up of HRS investigators and invited consultants, supplemented by selected workshops and symposia sponsored by the HRS to make sure that topics and study content are relevant. Final content is modified by the steering committee and approved by the monitoring committee, with the latter being assembled by NIA. The following briefly summarizes some of the more important elements and innovations of study content.

Labor Force Participation and Pensions

The HRS built on the designs of prior national labor surveys that extensively measured work and job characteristics relevant to retirement decisions, including job demands and characteristics, the features of individual employer pension plans, and the assessment of work time flexibility, with special attention paid to an accurate longitudinal work history. During the course of the HRS, the types of pensions offered to American workers have changed substantially.

Health Conditions and Health Status

One frequent criticism of past surveys of retirement decisions was the lack of health information and inability of the data to establish causality in the relation of health problems, work activities, and retirement. Although causality cannot be guaranteed from any cohort survey design, health and functional status items and health transitions are prominently represented in the HRS so as to understand their roles in work maintenance and retirement as well as health status after retirement. Functional status receives equal weight as disease epidemiology because it is the former that translated more directly into work capacity. As a new feature, the 2006 HRS survey contains, and subsequent surveys will continue to contain, measures of physical performance in a large cohort subsample. However, important chronic conditions of older people are well characterized, and ancillary detailed disease information is available from the linked Medicare data set. Direct measurements of cognitive function and preventive behaviors are present for all participants, and both are extremely important health domains when attempting to understand health trajectories among older people.

Family Structure and Mobility

One of the distinctive and innovative design features of the HRS is the attention paid to extended family structure. This allows assessment of intergenerational activities such as providing care for frail parents (tending to push people out of the workforce) and needing to provide financial support for either children or parents (tending to keep people in the workforce). The HRS includes economic and demographic information about respondents' children, including their geographic proximity, the health and economic status of respondents' (and spouses') living parents, and the economic status, family structure, and proximity of respondents' (and spouses') siblings.

Economic Status

As was the case with job characteristics and pensions, the HRS has the benefit of a number of surveys in which both income and assets were measured with a high degree of success. The HRS pays considerable attention to family income, wealth, and assets. Additional data collection activities are in place to determine household expenditures for important purchases such as food, housing, utilities, and various types of insurance necessary for certain economic models.

Summary

The HRS continues to be an important multidisciplinary study of the health, social, and economic status of older Americans. At the time of this writing, more than 900 peer-reviewed publications, working papers, dissertations, and book chapters have appeared using HRS findings. Study data from a given wave are made available online to all investigators, usually within 6 to 9 months after completion. The HRS is able to provide data to address important technical, theoretical, and national policy matters in many domains of aging. It has been emulated in several other countries, offering the possibility of critical cross-national research.

—*Robert B. Wallace*

See also Aging in Manitoba Longitudinal Study; Duke
Longitudinal Studies; Longitudinal Research;
Longitudinal Study of Aging; Oldest Old

Further Readings and References

Juster FT, Suzman R. An overview of the Health and
Retirement Study. *J Hum Resources.* 1995;30(Suppl.):
S7–S56.
Soldo BJ, Hurd MD, Rodgers WL, Wallace RB. Asset and
health dynamics among the oldest old: An overview of
the AHEAD study. *J Gerontol B Psychol Sci Social Sci.*
1997;52:1–20.

Health and Public Policy

The question is not so much how health influences
public policy as how public policy influences health.
The answer is that public policy has a great influence
on health but that there are many important factors
leading to this conclusion. The first issue is to agree
on a definition of health. We use the World Health
Organization (WHO) definition provided many years
ago, namely that health is the absence of physical,
mental, or social infirmity or disease. The public
policy influence on health affects whole populations
and not just individuals; therefore, it is measured, for
example, in terms of rates with which diseases occur
in whole populations, mortality rates, and rates of
physical function, emotional function, and mental
function (not simply dysfunction) in the population.

National Health Insurance

The United States is very different from the rest of the
developed world in terms of health and public policy.
By the end of the 20th century, all but a few developed
countries—the United States and South Africa are the
two most often cited—had adopted public policies
that health care is a right of citizenship and that, therefore, the government accepts a responsibility to pay
for the health care of its citizens. In general, the government payment for the health care of its citizens
is accomplished through a national health insurance
(NHI) plan. However, there are wide variations in the
amounts or percentages that NHI pays, from 100% to
well under half.

Some countries even go so far as to supplement their
NHI with a national health service (NHS) through
which the health care of their citizens is in fact provided
by health care providers working for the government.
The United Kingdom's NHS is an example of this and
has been described as one of the greatest social achieve-
ments of the 20th century, with its promise to provide
free health care for the British people from cradle to
grave. But times have changed since that NHS was set
up in 1948. Today, the United Kingdom, other countries
with an NHS, and most of the countries with NHI are
constantly looking for ways to improve the efficiency
and effectiveness of their health care services. The perception of longer waiting times to see providers and
even copayments in some situations are part of the NHI
and NHS in many countries.

The United States does not have NHI. The country
operates under a public policy that payment for health
care is not the government's responsibility in the main
but rather a private responsibility in which health care
services are purchased like other goods and services
in the economy.

It is of some interest to understand how the United
States got to this policy while the rest of the world
migrated to a different policy. Historians suggest that
Germany was the first country to implement industrialization successfully on a large scale toward the end
of the 19th century. Germany's successes with industrialization created another new public policy—the
retirement with pensions of able-bodied workers to
make room for younger employees. Until that time,
the retirement of able-bodied workers with lifelong
pension was virtually unheard of as a national policy.
During the first half of the 20th century, the United
States provided international leadership in counterbal-
ancing the rights of labor with the power of management. The issues of child labor, workplace safety, and
wages had dominated labor's agenda during that era.
But with the advent of World War II and the U.S.
policy of wage and price control, organized labor
focused its emphasis on benefits such as health care,
an emphasis that far outlived the armistice. Over time,

health care insurance became a fringe benefit of labor force participation for both workers and their families.

With the rise of socialism around the world after the end of World War II, national governments in both the developed and developing countries raised the issue of whether health care should be a right of citizenship. Over time, the vast majority of developed countries, as well as many developing countries, adopted public policies of NHI under the premise that health care is a right of citizenship.

Many times, the United States has also considered—but never adopted—a public policy of NHI. During the 1950s, the American Medical Association campaigned aggressively against the proposal for NHI under the slogan that NHI was "socialized medicine." The implication, of course, was that the United States should not have anything to do with anything related to socialism, the first cousin of communism.

A decade later, NHI was again on the U.S. national agenda, and again it was destined to fail. This time, however, two very important public health policies, Medicare and Medicaid, were passed by Congress in 1965 (Some say that these were passed as a compromise to stop the national campaign for NHI.) In simplest terms, Medicare provided national *hospital* insurance for older people, whereas Medicaid provided national *health* insurance for poor people. Both of these groups—those age 65 years and older and the poor—are typically people out of the workforce and therefore usually not eligible for employment-related health care benefits.

The most recent attempt to change the United States' health policy in the direction of NHI was undertaken by President Bill Clinton at the beginning of his first term in 1993. This initiative of health care reform met the same fate as all its predecessors; it was not passed.

International Comparisons of Spending

One indicator of the public policy toward health is the percentage of a country's resources spent on maintaining the health of the population. Table 1 presents the recent rates of gross domestic product (GDP) and

the rates of per capita health expenditures spent on health from 1960 through 2002, the last year available at the time of this writing.

In 1960, Canada spent the largest percentage of its GDP on health at 5.4%, the United States was second at 5.1%, and all countries were clustered between 2.9% and 5.4% except Spain at 1.5%. By 1970, the United States and Canada were equal at 7.0% of GDP, and the United States has remained as the country spending the largest percentage of GDP on health. It was the first country to spend more than 10% of GDP on health (12.0% in 1990) and in 2002 was one of three countries that spent more than 10%: the United States at 14.9%, Switzerland at 11.2%, and Germany at 10.9% in 2002.

Table 1 also presents the per capita expenditures on health. Every 10 years since 1960, the United States has more than doubled its per capita expenditures on health. In 2002, the United States spent $5,317 per person on health ($26,585 per family of five). The next closest countries were Switzerland at a distant $3,446 and Norway at $3,065. Three in four developed countries listed in the table did not even spend half the amount on health that the United States did in 2002.

International Comparisons of Health

The criteria that the WHO uses to assess the health status of populations are indicative of the world consensus on what the important outcomes of successful national health policy are and include the following:

- *Mortality:* life expectancy at birth; healthy life expectancy; probability of premature mortality (dying between 15 and 60 years of age); probability of dying under 5 years of age; neonatal mortality rate; maternal mortality ratio
- *Morbidity:* HIV prevalence among the population 15 to 49 years of age; tuberculosis (TB) prevalence; TB incidence; number of poliomyelitis cases
- *Health services coverage statistics:* percentage of 1-year-olds immunized with one dose of measles; percentage of 1-year-olds immunized with three doses of diphtheria, tetanus, and pertussis (DPT3); percentage of 1-year-olds immunized with three doses of Hepatitis B; antenatal care coverage; births attended by skilled health personnel; contraceptive prevalence rate; children under 5 years of age sleeping under

Table 1 Total Health Expenditures as Percentages of Gross Domestic Product and per Capita Health Expenditures (in Dollars): Selected Countries and Years, 1960 to 2002

Country	1960	1970	1980	1990	1995	1998	1999	2000	2001	2002
Health expenditures as percentages of gross domestic product										
Australia	4.1	NA	7.0	7.8	8.2	8.6	8.8	9.0	9.1	NA
Austria	4.3	5.3	7.6	7.1	8.2	7.7	7.8	7.7	7.6	7.7
Belgium	NA	4.0	6.4	7.4	8.7	8.6	8.7	8.8	9.0	9.1
Canada	5.4	7.0	7.1	9.0	9.2	9.2	9.0	8.9	9.4	9.6
Czech Republic	NA	NA	NA	5.0	7.3	7.1	7.1	7.1	7.3	7.4
Denmark	NA	NA	9.1	8.5	8.2	8.4	8.5	8.4	8.6	8.8
Finland	3.8	5.6	6.4	7.8	7.5	6.9	6.9	6.7	7.0	7.3
France	3.8	5.4	7.1	8.6	9.5	9.3	9.3	9.3	9.4	9.7
Germany	NA	6.2	8.7	8.5	10.6	10.6	10.6	10.6	10.8	10.9
Greece	NA	6.1	6.6	7.4	9.6	9.4	9.6	9.7	9.4	9.5
Hungary	NA	NA	NA	NA	7.5	7.3	7.4	7.1	7.4	7.8
Iceland	3.0	4.7	6.2	8.0	8.4	8.6	9.4	9.2	9.2	9.9
Ireland	3.7	5.1	8.4	6.1	6.8	6.2	6.3	6.4	6.9	7.3
Italy	NA	NA	NA	8.0	7.4	7.7	7.8	8.1	8.3	8.5
Japan	3.0	4.5	6.5	5.9	6.8	7.2	7.4	7.6	7.8	NA
Korea	NA	NA	NA	4.2	4.1	4.4	4.7	4.6	5.3	5.1
Luxembourg	NA	3.6	5.9	6.1	6.4	5.8	6.2	5.5	5.9	6.2
Mexico	NA	NA	NA	4.8	5.6	5.4	5.6	5.6	6.0	6.1
The Netherlands	NA	NA	7.5	8.0	8.4	8.1	8.2	8.2	8.5	9.1
New Zealand	NA	5.1	5.9	6.9	7.2	7.9	7.8	7.9	8.0	8.5
Norway	2.9	4.4	7.0	7.7	7.9	8.5	8.5	7.7	8.9	9.6
Poland	NA	NA	NA	4.9	5.6	6.0	5.9	5.7	6.0	6.1
Portugal	NA	2.6	5.6	6.2	8.2	8.4	8.7	9.2	9.3	9.3
Slovak Republic	NA	NA	NA	NA	NA	5.7	5.8	5.5	5.6	5.7
Spain	1.5	3.6	5.4	6.7	7.6	7.5	7.5	7.5	7.5	7.6
Sweden	NA	6.9	9.1	8.4	8.1	8.3	8.4	8.4	8.8	9.2
Switzerland	4.9	5.4	7.3	8.3	9.7	10.3	10.5	10.4	10.9	11.2
Turkey	NA	2.4	3.3	3.6	3.4	4.8	6.4	6.6	NA	NA
United Kingdom	3.9	4.5	5.6	6.0	7.0	6.9	7.2	7.3	7.5	7.7
United States	5.1	7.0	8.8	12.0	13.4	13.2	13.2	13.3	14.1	14.9

Per capita health expenditures (in dollars)

Country	1960	1970	1980	1990	1995	1998	1999	2000	2001	2002
Australia	93	NA	684	1,300	1,737	2,077	2,231	2,379	2,504	NA
Austria	77	190	762	1,344	1,865	1,953	2,069	2,147	2,174	2,220
Belgium	NA	147	627	1,340	1,882	2,041	2,139	2,288	2,441	2,515
Canada	121	289	770	1,714	2,044	2,291	2,400	2,541	2,743	2,931
Czech Republic	NA	NA	NA	553	876	918	932	977	1,083	1,118
Denmark	NA	NA	943	1,554	1,843	2,141	2,297	2,353	2,520	2,583
Finland	62	190	584	1,414	1,428	1,607	1,641	1,698	1,841	1,943
France	69	206	699	1,555	2,025	2,231	2,306	2,416	2,588	2,736
Germany	NA	266	955	1,729	2,263	2,470	2,563	2,640	2,735	2,817
Greece	NA	171	464	838	1,269	1,428	1,517	1,617	1,670	1,814
Hungary	NA	NA	NA	NA	674	775	820	847	961	1,079
Iceland	57	163	698	1,598	1,853	2,252	2,540	2,559	2,680	2,807
Ireland	42	117	511	791	1,208	1,487	1,623	1,774	2,059	2,367
Italy	NA	NA	NA	1,397	1,524	1,800	1,853	2,001	2,107	2,166
Japan	29	144	559	1,105	1,530	1,742	1,829	1,958	2,077	NA
Korea	NA	NA	NA	329	491	589	714	777	943	996
Luxembourg	NA	161	637	1,533	2,053	2,291	2,734	2,682	2,900	3,065
Mexico	NA	NA	NA	290	380	427	463	494	536	553
The Netherlands	NA	NA	750	1,419	1,827	2,016	2,098	2,196	2,455	2,643
New Zealand	NA	205	488	987	1,238	1,441	1,527	1,611	1,710	1,857
Norway	49	140	659	1,385	1,892	2,314	2,561	2,747	3,258	3,409
Poland	NA	NA	NA	298	423	563	571	578	629	654
Portugal	NA	54	283	661	1,080	1,290	1,424	1,570	1,662	1,702
Slovak Republic	NA	NA	NA	NA	NA	559	578	591	633	698
Spain	16	97	363	865	1,195	1,371	1,467	1,493	1,567	1,646
Sweden	NA	305	924	1,566	1,733	1,961	2,119	2,243	2,370	2,517
Switzerland	166	350	1,031	2,040	2,555	2,967	2,985	3,111	3,288	3,446
Turkey	NA	24	76	165	184	312	392	446	NA	NA
United Kingdom	84	160	472	977	1,393	1,607	1,725	1,839	2,012	2,160
United States	143	348	1,067	2,738	3,698	4,098	4,302	4,560	4,914	5,317

Sources: Table reprinted from National Center for Health Statistics. *Health, United States, 2005: With Chartbook on Trends in the Health of Americans.* Washington, DC: Government Printing Office; 2005. The data from all countries except the United States are from Organization for Economic Cooperation and Development. Health policy and data. Available at: www.oecd.org/els/health. U.S. data are from Centers for Medicare and Medicaid Services. National health expenditure data. Available at: www.cms.hhs.gov/statistics/nhe.

Notes: These data include revisions in health expenditures and may differ from previous editions of *Health, United States.* Per capita health expenditures for each country have been adjusted to U.S. dollars using gross domestic product purchasing power parities for each year. NA = data not available.

insecticide-treated nets; antiretroviral therapy coverage; TB detection rate; TB treatment success; children under 5 years of age with acute respiratory infection symptoms taken to facility; children under 5 years of age with diarrhea receiving oral rehydration therapy; children under 5 years of age with fever receiving treatment with any antimalarial; children 6 to 59 months of age receiving Vitamin A supplementation; births by caesarian section

- *Environmental and behavioral risk factors:* regarding *individual-level risk factors*—prevalence of current tobacco use; percentage of condom use by young people (15 to 24 years of age); newborns with low birth weights; children under 5 years of age stunted for age; children under 5 years of age underweight for age; prevalence of obesity among population age 15 years and older; regarding *community-level and environmental factors*—access to improved water sources; access to improved sanitation; percentage of population using solid fuels

Notice that in addition to the indicators of the rates of diseases (most of them preventable), the WHO criteria also include indicators of longevity (life expectancy), physical vigor (healthy active life expectancy [HALE]), access to health care, and other nondisease factors.

The performance of health systems can be assessed and ranked congruently across countries using the functions and goals developed by the WHO. The functions include financing (collecting, pooling, and purchasing), provision (service delivery), stewardship (oversight), and resources development. The WHO goals include responsiveness (i.e., the health system needs to be client oriented and to treat clients with respect), health (i.e., average level of population health and distribution of health within the population), and fairness in financial contribution (i.e., fairness in financing and financial risk protection for households). The achievement of the goals is evaluated from the perspective of the resources available in each country.

Analyses done using this assessment system led to the conclusion that there is not always a linear relationship between the efficiency of the health system and the level of health. Efficiency is directly related to expenditure per capita and to allocation of resources to

cost-effective interventions. Based on the criterion of the level of health of the population, the WHO's *World Health Report 2000* reported that the 10 highest-performing health systems are those in Oman, Malta, Italy, France, San Marino, Spain, Andorra, Jamaica, Japan, and Saudi Arabia, whereas the 10 lowest performers are those in South Africa, Sierra Leone, Swaziland, Democratic Republic of Congo, Lesotho, Malawi, Botswana, Namibia, Zambia, and Zimbabwe. According to the criterion of the overall health care system performance, the 10 highest-performing health systems are those in France, Italy, San Marino, Andorra, Malta, Singapore, Spain, Oman, Australia, and Japan, whereas the 10 lowest performers are those in Zambia, Lesotho, Mozambique, Malawi, Liberia, Nigeria, Democratic Republic of Congo, Central Africa Republic, Myanmar, and Sierra Leone.

One would expect to see some indicators of better health status in the United States as a result of its greatly increased expenditures on health. However, the United States is not ranked that well in international comparisons. In the WHO's *World Health Report 2000,* the United States was ranked 37th in the world based on the criterion of the overall health care system performance and 72nd in the world based on the criterion of the health of the population. Interestingly, Cuba was ranked essentially the same at 39th based on the criterion of the overall health care system performance but was ranked much better at 36th based on the criterion of the health of the population. In terms of infant mortality, a 2005 article by Ruth E. K. Stein and colleagues stated that 40 countries had infant and child morality rates equal to or lower than the rate in the United States.

—*Laurence G. Branch*

See also Aging Network; Managed Care; National Institute on Aging

Further Readings and References

Evans DB, Tandon A, Murray CJL, Lauer JA. Comparative efficiency on national health systems: Cross national econometric analysis. *Br Med J.* 2001;323:307–310.

Gakidou E, Murray CJL, Frenk J. Measuring preferences on health system performance assessment. Available at: www.who.int/health-systems-performance/docs/articles/paper20.pdf. Accessed June 20, 2006. World Health Organization, GPE Discussion Paper Series, No. 20.

Stein REK, Stanton B, Starfield B. How healthy are U.S. children? *JAMA*. 2005;293:1781–1783.

U.S. Department of Health and Human Services. Health, United States, 2005. Available at: www.cdc.gov/nchs/data/hus/hus05.pdf. Accessed April 20, 2006.

World Health Organization. Men ageing and health: Achieving health across the life span. Available at: http://whqlibdoc.who.int/hq/2001/WHO_NMH_NPH_01.2.pdf. Accessed June 20, 2006.

World Health Organization. *The World Health Report 2000*. Geneva, Switzerland: WHO; 2000. Available at: www.who.int/whr/2000/en/whr00_en.pdf. Accessed June 20, 2006.

HEALTH CARE SYSTEM FOR OLDER ADULTS

During 2006, most health policy experts would categorically deny that there is a health care system for older adults in the United States. Health services researchers have frequently used the term "the health care nonsystem" to describe what is available to the older population.

A health care system is commonly defined as the practice of health and medical professionals preventing and treating illness as well as maintenance of mental and physical well-being. The system aspect refers to the structures that facilitate the organization, delivery, and financing of the health care services as well as the structures that monitor the access, quality, and cost of these health care services. Putting all of this together, a health care system is defined as the structures that facilitate the organization, delivery, and financing, as well as monitor the access, quality, and cost, of health care services designed to prevent, treat, and manage illnesses and to preserve the mental and physical well-being of patients through an array of inpatient, outpatient, institutional or community long-term care, rehabilitation, pharmaceutical, and community services provided by trained medical and allied health professionals.

From the perspective of this definition of a health care system, one can understand the skepticism of the many researchers who refer to the U.S. health care system for older adults as a nonsystem. In all but one or two of the other countries of the developed world, and increasingly in many developing countries, the cornerstone of the health care system is national health insurance (NHI). NHI is typically a formal public policy recognizing that health care is a right of citizenship and that the central government has a responsibility to its citizens to provide access to quality health care services and finance them. Under NHI, the central government then has the designated responsibility to establish the health care delivery system for its citizens. The central government has the responsibility to facilitate the organization, delivery, and financing, as well as to monitor the access, quality, and cost, of health care services designed to prevent, treat, and manage illnesses and to preserve the mental and physical well-being of patients through an array of inpatient, outpatient, institutional or community long-term care, rehabilitation, pharmaceutical, and community services provided by trained medical and allied health professionals.

But the United States does not have NHI. Can Medicare be considered as NHI for those age 65 years and older? Many would like to think so, and many others would like to hope so, but unfortunately that is not the case. At the time of this writing in 2006, Medicare does not facilitate the organization, delivery, and financing, as well as the monitor the access, quality, and cost, of health care services designed to prevent, treat, and manage illnesses and to preserve the mental and physical well-being of patients through an array of inpatient, outpatient, institutional, or community long-term care, rehabilitation, pharmaceutical, and community services provided by trained medical and allied health professionals.

The charter of Medicare, as enacted into legislation in 1965, was to provide comprehensive and complete hospital (not for all health care organizations or facilities) insurance (under Medicare Part A, with no additional premiums to enrollees) to those age 65 years and older who enroll. Therefore, the federal government has responsibilities for financing inpatient care, monitoring its quality, and controlling its costs. Some copayments and deductibles are incurred by patients even for inpatient episodes. Thus, it is accurate to infer that the federal government has responsibility for a hospital care system for the elderly, but hospital care should never be confused with health care.

Medicare Part B (outpatient care) was also enacted in 1965 and financed by enrollee premiums and additional funding by the federal government. Some, but not all, outpatient care is provided to elders who enroll in Part B. Some copayments and deductibles are also incurred by patients for outpatient care. Outpatient care under Part B has always been limited; it was not until more than 30 years later that an act of Congress allowed some, but not all, evidence-based preventive services to be covered under Part B.

In 1997, the federal government allowed those eligible for Medicare Part A (inpatient care) and enrolled in Medicare Part B (outpatient care) to enroll in managed care organizations (MCOs). For those who enrolled in Medicare Part C, the MCO does indeed have all of the responsibilities of a health care system to coordinate the health care of the enrollees. Interestingly, however, even the MCOs do not have responsibility for providing institutional long-term care to enrollees unless it is for rehabilitation and usually following an inpatient episode.

In 2006, Medicare Part D, the pharmacy benefit, was implemented under a structure similar to Medicare Part B, relying on a combination of premiums, deductibles, and copayments for financing. Therefore, only older people in Medicare Part C, and not the other Medicare enrollees, are really under a health care system by the usual definition.

In 1965, Medicaid was also enacted by Congress to provide health care—not just hospital care—to poor people. The mechanism of implementation was a federal–state partnership, with financing based on funding from both the federal government and the state governments. Within certain parameters dictated by the federal government, the participating states have leeway in defining who is eligible for Medicaid in their states (based on the federal poverty level) and what services can be provided (based on minimum core services and additional discretionary services).

Institutional long-term care is one of the core services; most states also have community-based alternatives to long-term care programs. Under the Medicaid model, each state has the responsibility for managing the health care system based on the usual definition for its poor enrollees.

Other citizens who opt to receive their health care through an MCO also have a true health care system by our definition. But what about the rest of the U.S. population? They do not receive health care under a health care system.

The basic reason that the United States does not have a health care system is that during the second quarter of the 20th century, health care evolved as a fringe benefit of employment in the country. President Franklin D. Roosevelt imposed wage and price controls on the U.S. economy, and so companies began to offer expanded benefits—including health benefits—to attract employees, and the labor unions quickly followed suit by bargaining for similar benefits for their members. A few years prior to Roosevelt's wage and price controls, a new concept in health insurance was pioneered in Texas and evolved into the Blue Cross and Blue Shield health insurance organizations. From that point until the current time, the United States has developed an enormous health care insurance industry and a cultural ethic that health care is a fringe benefit of labor force participation. In 1954, Congress blessed the alliance between work and health coverage by establishing tax subsidies for employer-financed health care insurance. As the rest of the world moved away from this model during the latter half of the 20th century and began adopting the model of NHI that encourages a bona fide health care system, the United States has stayed its course of health care as an insurance benefit of labor force participation subsidized by federal tax benefits to employers.

But perhaps things will change in the United States. In June 2006, Ronald Brownstein, a national political correspondent for the *Los Angeles Times*, wrote an editorial indicating that organized labor and a conservative Republican, who is in line to chair the House Ways and Means Committee, finally agree that it is time to reconsider the model of employment-based health care insurance. This means that it may once again be time for the United States to consider some form of NHI that brings with it incentives to develop a true health care system.

—*Laurence G. Branch*

See also Aging Network; Geriatric Team Care; Institutional Care; Long-Term Care; Managed Care; National Institute on Aging

Further Readings and References

Branch LG, Jette AM. A prospective study of long-term care institution among the aged. *Am J Public Health.* 1982;72:1373–1379.

Evashwick C, ed. *The Continuum of Long-Term Care: An Integrated Systems Approach.* 2nd ed. Albany, NY: Thomson Delmar Learning; 2001.

Guralnik JM, Alecxih L, Branch LG, Wiener JM. Medical and long-term care costs when older persons become more dependent. *Am J Public Health.* 2002;92: 1244–1245.

Jette AM, Tennstedt S, Branch L. Stability of informal long term care. *J Aging Health.* 1992;4:193–211.

Pratt JR. *Long-Term Care: Managing Across the Continuum.* New York: Aspen; 1999.

HEALTH COMMUNICATION

The concept of health communication among and with older adults represents an interface of two complex phenomena. Health is more than the absence of disease; it is a state of optimal physical, mental, emotional, and spiritual well-being. Communication is more then merely sending a message; it is bidirectional and entails an exchange of mutual understanding between a sender and a receiver. With increasing age, both health and communication abilities may be compromised. Thus, effective health communication with the aging population requires sensitivity as to how these two phenomena may change with age. Understanding the way health affects communication among older adults will enhance the effectiveness of strategies for communicating with them.

When individuals attain an optimal state of health, their physical, mental, emotional, and social needs are met. These needs exist on a hierarchy, with the most basic being the need for food and shelter followed by higher level emotional and social needs. Lack of having any of these needs met, including mental stimulation, may cause a failure to thrive. Health needs and risks increase with age, although aging and disease are not synonymous. Over the past century, health risks have shifted from primarily acute infectious diseases to chronic noninfectious diseases. Thus, maintaining met needs and, therefore, optimal health requires ongoing efforts by individuals interacting with their environment to get their needs met. A key mechanism for getting one's needs met is interpersonal communication or face-to-face interactions with a multitude of health care providers, some of whom are family caregivers. Another mechanism includes mass communication (e.g., commercials, newsprint, magazines, brochures) with which society communicates with older adults about their health risks. The success of an elder's interpersonal communication with another person or vice versa and/or mass communication messages depends on an understanding of how elders "decode," or receive and understand, messages as they age.

The human body has five senses with which to decode or receive interpersonal and mass communication messages, but the acuity of these senses diminish with increasing age and the presence of one or more diseases. These five senses are vision, hearing, touch, smell, and taste. Vision, hearing, and touch are the primary modalities for sensory reception in relation to verbal and nonverbal communication messages. Individuals use their eyes and ears to understand spoken messages (i.e., verbal communication) and body language (i.e., nonverbal communication, including vocal nonverbal communication). Spoken messages also have nonverbal vocal components, including speech rate, tone, and loudness, that can be heard. In fact, more than 80% of what one understands about a message comes from nonverbal communication. Thus, the importance of the five human senses in allowing one to understand nonverbal communication cannot be understated.

Although many sensory deficits could be corrected or improved with aids, many older adults refuse to use them properly or even at all. Thus, achieving effective health communication with older adults who resist using corrective aids to improve their sensory deficits will at most require substantial effort by health care providers and caregivers to compensate for their deficits. Achieving effective health communication with those older adults who do not resist using corrective aids to improve their sensory deficits will at least require a basic understanding of the ever-changing interface of health and communication issues with increasing age.

"Encoding," or individuals' ability to express themselves via communication channels, also can diminish with age. Expressing oneself requires both verbal and nonverbal communication channels; although one can gesture without speaking, rarely does one speak without some form of gesturing (e.g., eye contact). The ability of elders to express themselves may decrease with age in two ways, one of which is normal and the other of which is not. For example, with normal aging, elders may take longer to produce a verbal and/or non-verbal response by speaking slowly and/or pausing in between statements or phrases. Another way is not normal; instead, it is pathological. The pathology can occur on biological and social levels. On a biological level, Alzheimer's and other chronic diseases, not limited to but including medications, heart conditions, depression, stroke, nutrition deficiencies, and Parkinson's disease, can severely affect elders' ability to both express themselves and understand others. The variety of impairment levels from these diseases and their inherent chronic nature add to the complexity of how health can affect communication among elders.

The complexity is no less so on a social level. Ageism can be a powerful barrier to effective communication with elders. Ageism can occur within and/or between individuals. That is, individuals can have ageist attitudes about themselves or a tendency to attribute communication deficits to aging when, in fact, the deficits are not caused by age at all. For example, accepting that hearing loss is just something one must live with because he or she is "old" is potentially an example of an intraindividual ageist attitude and/or knowledge deficit. Interindividual ageist attitudes could arise in intergenerational interactions. Persons in their 20s may presume to have difficulty in communicating with persons in their 80s just because the latter are "old" and not because the younger persons have any

evidence that communication will be difficult. Such persons may speak in a patronizing way (e.g., too loud, using terms of endearment) to elders that inadvertently conveys disrespect. Another example could be when elders presume that they will not have anything in common with persons from a much younger generation, so they do not try very hard to understand the younger persons or engage them in conversation.

Social communication barriers from ageism and generation gaps can be ameliorated in several ways. Education for everyone, including older adults, aimed at increasing knowledge about what is and is not normal aging is one promising avenue. Numerous efforts are currently under way to educate all levels of health professionals about the specific needs of older adults. Even universities have begun to offer gerontology majors and/or minors with the aim of increasing interest in an aging-related occupation. Attitudes may be more difficult to improve because they may or may not be based on correct knowledge about health communication and aging. That is, attitudes—including ageist attitudes—may be based on opinions regardless of one's knowledge about the truths on aging. One potential remedy is to expose all ages of the human population to the diverse ways in which humans age. Some age well and others less so, and the best way to see this is in face-to-face interactions among individuals of all different ages. Inevitably in such interactions, some encounters would reinforce negative stereotypes about older adults and the communication abilities, whereas others would negate them. The net result would make it difficult for someone to have "one" universal negative attitude toward older adults because the person should have at least one interaction that would counter his or her negative stereotype. A major rationale for why real face-to-face interactions with a variety of older adults would improve younger persons' (and maybe even older persons') attitudes toward older adults is that most ageist attitudes derive from myth and not fact and/or actual experiences.

With education and more opportunities for inter-generational communication exchanges mentioned as two broad strategies, there are more specific interpersonal strategies for achieving effective health communication with older adults:

1. Get their attention by using and maintaining eye contact, speaking slowly, reducing background noises, positioning yourself in front of them, taking your time and being patient with their slow processing, and directing and redirecting their attention often.

2. Speak in a calm tone of voice by being close enough to them and/or directing your voice in their "good" ears and speaking slowly with an overall "cool" body language.

3. Watch your language by using simple and highly familiar words, keeping messages short and sweet.

4. Use yes/no questions in a few different ways to determine specific needs.

5. Repeat, rephrase, and repair to correct their responses without pointing out mistakes.

6. Use touch on approach to signal persons who might not be able to see or hear you, to sustain attention, to calm and reassure, to get attention, to communicate nonverbally, and to say "I love you."

7. Learn to be a good listener by listening and watching for verbal and nonverbal cues and by being patient and not interrupting.

Although the concept of health communication may be complex, the strategies for health communication with older adults are not. Still, the strategies represent behavioral techniques that will take practice and should improve as one develops a relationship with an older person. In fact, one will know that he or she has developed a relationship with someone when one feels emotionally connected with an older adult in the moment. The quality of the communication has implications not only for the quality of care but also for the older adult's quality of life. The strategies described here are a means to that end.

—*Lené Levy-Storms*

See also Positive Attitudes and Health; Quality of Life; Self-Care; Self-Rated Health

Further Readings and References

Kohler S. *How to Communicate With Alzheimer's: A Practical Guide and Workbook for Families.* Los Angeles: Granny's Rocker; 2004.

National Institute on Aging. Working with your older patient: A clinician's handbook. Available at: www.niapublications.org/pubs/clinicians2004/index.asp.Accessed September 17, 2006.

Quadagno J. *An Introduction to Social Gerontology: Aging and the Life Course.* 2nd ed. New York: McGraw-Hill; 2002.

van Servellen G. *Communication Skills for the Health Care Professional: Concepts and Techniques.* Gaithersburg, Md: Aspen; 1997.

HEALTH EXPECTANCY

See ACTIVE LIFE EXPECTANCY

HEALTH PROMOTION AND DISEASE PREVENTION

Health promotion and disease prevention for older adults are two very different enterprises in contemporary America. Health promotion takes place primarily on one's own or is conducted in the community under the guidance of a wide variety of practitioners who may or may not be licensed or certified. Disease prevention takes place primarily in medical clinics, is increasingly covered by Medicare, and is conducted by licensed medical personnel.

The effectiveness of health-promoting activities for older adults has been consistently supported by research studies, although lingering questions remain. Can the benefits achieved in short-term research projects be sustained over the long term? Can health promotion interventions be initiated successfully by busy clinicians in medical settings? Do the benefits of insurance coverage for health promotion interventions outweigh the costs of implementing them?

In contrast, similar questions are not asked about disease prevention and detection for older adults (in the form of medical screenings and immunizations). Over the past 15 years, coverage by Medicare has expanded rapidly for these services. In addition to pneumococcal and influenza immunizations, medical screenings now covered under Medicare include tests or exams for the following conditions: cardiovascular disease, diabetes, breast cancer, osteoporosis, cervical cancer, colorectal cancer, and prostate cancer.

The expansion of Medicare services to include medical screenings over the past decade has been a boon to the health of older Americans. But more than research results have contributed to this expansion. Some 7,000 lobbyists in Washington, D.C., promote medical priorities exclusively, and in 2000 two organizations alone—the American Medical Association and the American Hospital Association—spent $28.5 million lobbying Congress.

There are few lobbyists and not much money, however, spent to persuade Congress to include health promotion in Medicare or other insurance coverage. Consequently, health-promoting activities are infrequently covered by insurance, are not linked to medical care, and are practiced by only a minority of older adults. For instance, approximately one in four older adults gets adequate exercise or practices good nutritional habits consistently.

This entry briefly summarizes three health-promoting strategies for older adults and four prevention interventions.

Health Promotion: Exercise

Exercise and physical activity reduce morbidity and mortality related to coronary heart disease, hypertension, obesity, diabetes, osteoporosis, certain cancers, and mental health disorders. Although most studies have been observational and cannot prove causal association, the strength, consistency, and number of studies, combined with controls for confounding variables, leave little doubt of a causal relationship. Most of the 200 randomized clinical trials published in peer-reviewed journals between 1980 and 2000, and identified by a Centers for Disease Control and Prevention–funded project at the University of Illinois at Chicago, supported the positive impact of exercise on older adults.

Although the benefit of exercise programs on older adults is consistently well established, the applicability of these studies to Medicare-approved clinical sites is lacking. Few studies have involved risk reduction counseling in busy primary care clinical settings. In addition, most studies are completed in 4 months or less, and the limited findings on long-term exercise compliance have been discouraging.

Nutrition

The research evidence on the benefits of good nutrition on morbidity and mortality is equally persuasive. Older adults receive health benefits from a limited dietary intake of saturated fat, trans fat acid, and sodium as well as from an emphasis on nutrient-dense, high-fibrous foods such as fruits, vegetables, and whole grain products. There is also little dispute about the importance of caloric balance; that is, the relationship between caloric input and expenditure. Older persons with poor nutritional habits are at increased risk for obesity, glucose intolerance, hypertension, high blood cholesterol, cancer (e.g., colon, rectum, prostate, gallbladder, breast), sleep apnea, and osteoarthritis.

Again, the positive impact of nutritional programs on older adults in the community is consistently well established, but few studies have taken place in coordination with primary care settings and the supervision of clinicians. The data on long-term nutritional compliance is discouraging because fat, sugar, and salt-containing diets are popular components of the American diet and good nutrition is often perceived as unappealing or inconvenient.

Mental Health

Approximately 85% of older adults are satisfied with their lives, comparable to attitudes of middle-aged and younger adults. The National Institute of Mental Health estimates that 15% of Americans age 65 years and older suffer from persistent symptoms of depression. The majority of older patients with clinical depression or persistent depressive symptoms go untreated or receive inadequate treatment.

Effective pharmaceutical interventions for moderate and severe depression in older adults exist, and the new Medicare prescription benefit may help some older adults to access them more easily. Also available are effective nonpharmaceutical interventions for persistent depressive symptoms in older persons, including cognitive–behavioral therapy, exercise, pet support, peer support groups, life review interventions, and stress management.

Medicare coverage for mental illness does not equal that for physical illness. Medicare patients pay 50% of Medicare-approved amounts for most outpatient mental health care, compared with only 20% for other medical services. Medicare also imposes a 190-day lifetime limit on inpatient psychiatric hospital care, compared with no cap on care in a general hospital.

Prevention: Immunizations

More than 90% of deaths from flu and pneumonia occur in people age 65 years and older. Researchers report that vaccinations can prevent up to 60% of these deaths among older adults. An older person's chances of being hospitalized for heart disease or stroke are reduced sharply during the flu season following a vaccination.

A gradual increase in immunizations has been due in large part to Medicare reimbursement and an increased awareness of the importance of vaccination. In 1999, the percentage of older adults vaccinated for influenza was 68%, and the percentage vaccinated for pneumonia was 55%. However, vaccination rates vary by ethnicity. In 1999, approximately 70% of Whites received flu shots, whereas only 49% of Blacks were immunized.

Smoking Cessation

Between the first U.S. Surgeon General's report on tobacco in 1964 and the one issued in 2004, the number of evidence-based adverse health effects associated with smoking increased. In addition to the 10 cancers for which smoking is identified as a cause, other conditions include cardiovascular diseases, respiratory diseases, low bone density and hip fractures, cataracts, and gastric ulcer. In general, the percentage of older adults who smoke is roughly half that of younger adults, but this may be more attributable to a higher mortality rate than quit rate. Smokers who survive into old age are not resistant to the health hazards; in fact, smoking continues to increase their morbidity and mortality risks. Smokers who quit after

70 years of age not only reduce their risks but also improve their physical function and overall health.

In 2005, Medicare approved smoking cessation counseling for approximately 4 million older smokers who have tobacco-related diseases or are on drug regimens adversely affected by smoking. Eligible beneficiaries are covered for two quit attempts per year, each consisting of up to four counseling sessions.

Alcohol Moderation

There is no consensus among alcohol researchers about what constitutes acceptable drinking and what constitutes problem drinking. Given the substantial increase in the proportion of body fat with aging and the concomitant decrease in volume of total body water, however, an increasing number of experts are recommending a maximum of one drink per day; that is, 12 ounces of beer, 5 ounces of wine, or 1.5 ounces of spirits.

Estimates of the percentage of older Americans who are problem drinkers vary widely, from 2% to more than 10%. Estimates are complicated by the fact that problem drinking among older adults takes place outside the glare of work and community life and that most problem drinkers are not identified by primary care physicians.

Approximately one third of elderly alcoholics are late-onset reactive problem drinkers who are easier to treat than chronic lifelong problem drinkers. Approximately one third of persons who attend Alcoholics Anonymous (AA) meetings are age 50 years and older, and an increasing number of communities operate AA programs specifically for older adults who share common problems such as widowhood and retirement. Professionally run treatments programs are costly and not accessible to many older problem drinkers.

Injury

Approximately 60% of persons who die from falls are age 65 years and older. Falls can be reduced by lower body strength building, proper monitoring of medications, and removal of environmental hazards. Other influential factors, such as balance abnormalities, visual disorders, and cognitive or physical impairment, require a multidisciplinary geriatric assessment for identifying those at risk for falls and to help prevent serious injury.

Motor vehicle safety is an important issue for older adults as well. A number of physiological changes, such as arthritis, slower reflexes, visual impairment, and cognitive impairment, affect the driving of older adults. The American Association of Retired Persons' (AARP) 55-Alive Mature Driving Program and other driver safety classes may be helpful in keeping some older drivers safe. There is little guidance for older adults on when to stop driving. State bills to require drivers age 75 years and older to take road tests have consistently failed. Five states require physicians to report motorists who have health problems that could affect their driving ability.

Traffic impediments are likely to be more hazardous to older drivers, and some states are improving road sign lettering, broadening highway lanes, and increasing road illumination. Older pedestrians can be protected by lengthier crossing periods at signalized intersections. Removal of crosswalk markings at sites with no traffic signals or stop signs also helps to protect the safety of older pedestrians.

Much attention has been paid to life expectancy and the impact that diseases such as heart disease, cancer, stroke, and chronic obstructive pulmonary disease have on it. More attention, however, needs to be paid to health expectancy; that is, the number of healthy years a person can expect to have left. To improve health expectancy, older adults will need to increase exercise and physical activity, improve eating habits, reduce or eliminate smoking, increase immunizations, prevent injury, and strengthen their connections to the people and activities they love.

—*David Haber*

See also Exercise and Physical Activity; Injury Prevention; Smoking; Vitamins, Minerals, and Dietary Supplements

Further Readings and References

Haber D. *Health Aspects of Aging: A Selective Annotated Bibliography for Gerontology Instruction.* Washington, DC: Association for Gerontology in Higher Education; 2004.

Haber D. *Health Promotion and Aging.* New York: Springer; 2003.

McGinnis J, Foege W. Actual causes of death in the United States. *JAMA.* 1993;270:2207–2212.

HEARING

Hearing impairment is the third and fourth most common chronic condition reported by White and Black adults, respectively, in the United States. Approximately 28 million Americans have hearing impairment, with more than 500,000 of these having severe to profound hearing impairment. There are numerous age-associated changes to the auditory system that can lead to the development of hearing loss. Progressive age-associated sensorineural hearing loss, referred to as presbyacusis, is caused primarily by structural changes and damage to the cochlea and in its most common form results in symmetrical high-frequency hearing loss. Genetic variations are thought to influence the intraindividual progression of hearing loss in older adults.

Age-associated changes in the processing of sounds in the brain have also been documented but are less well understood. Part of this decline is thought to be due the loss of neurons and changes in neuronal functioning in the auditory cortex. These changes may be at least partly responsible for poorer test performance on word recognition and other auditory processing tests, although declining hearing acuity is responsible for a large part of this reduced performance. Nevertheless, some research has documented that the age-associated decline in speech processing is present even after controlling for hearing acuity. This age-associated decline in speech processing is particularly evident in the context of background noise.

Currently, age is by far the most important and well-documented risk factor for developing hearing impairment in adults. Because there is no universally accepted definition of hearing impairment, prevalence rates can vary considerably depending on the definition and the assessment methodology (e.g., self-report vs. clinical assessment). Self-reported and clinically confirmed rates of hearing impairment in Whites under

Table 1 Ten Ways to Recognize Hearing Loss

The following questions will help you to determine whether you need to have your hearing evaluated by a medical professional. Three or more "yes" answers indicate that a hearing evaluation by an otolaryngologist (an ear, nose, and throat specialist) or an audiologist may be indicated.

1. Do you have a problem hearing over the telephone?

2. Do you have trouble following the conversation when two or more people are talking at the same time?

3. Do people complain that you turn the TV volume up too high?

4. Do you have to strain to understand conversation?

5. Do you have trouble hearing in a noisy background?

6. Do you find yourself asking people to repeat themselves?

7. Do many people you talk to seem to mumble (or not speak clearly)?

8. Do you misunderstand what others are saying and respond inappropriately?

9. Do you have trouble understanding the speech of women and children?

10. Do people get annoyed because you misunderstand what they say?

Source: National Institute on Deafness and Other Communication Disorders. *Hearing Loss and Older Adults.* Bethesda, Md: National Institutes of Health; 2001. NIH Publication No. 01-4913.

50 years of age are generally less than 10%, whereas rates of 40% to 50% or more are common in Whites age 80 years and older; the corresponding self-reported rates for Blacks are lower (< 5% and > 30%). Clinical definitions of hearing impairment that incorporate losses in the higher frequencies (e.g., 4,000 hertz) result in much higher prevalence estimates in the elderly (e.g., approximately 90% in persons age 80 years and older). Adult-onset hearing impairment occurs earlier in males than in females, and the differences in rates as a function of gender increase with age. Although age-specific trends in hearing impairment rates appear stable during recent years, the aging of the U.S. population will result in large increases in the number of Americans with this sensory impairment.

Hearing Impairment Risk Factors

Both chronic noise exposures (e.g., occupational exposure to noisy machinery) and brief but intense exposures (e.g., firearm discharges) are thought to be the most important preventable causes of adult-onset hearing loss. All structures of the ear can be damaged by severe acoustic trauma. Excessive noise exposure results in both mechanical and metabolic damage to the cochlea. However, there appears to be significant intraindividual variation regarding the damaging effects of noise. Blacks may be less susceptible to noise-related hearing loss than are Whites.

Smoking has been shown to be associated with an increased risk of hearing impairment in case–control studies (pooled risk ratio [RR] = 2.89, 95% confidence interval [CI] = 2.26 to 3.70) and cohort studies (RR = 1.97, 95% CI = 1.44 to 2.70). Possible mechanisms by which smoking increases the risk of hearing impairment include nicotine-induced vasoconstriction and increased blood viscosity resulting in reduced blood flow to the cochlea. There is also limited evidence to suggest that noise exposure and smoking combined may lead to greater hearing loss than does either of these risk factors without the other.

A variety of other modifiable risk factors for hearing loss have also been studied, although the strength and consistency of these associations are not well documented. Selected medical conditions, including hypertension, heart disease, and diabetes, may increase the risk of adult-acquired hearing impairment. Other cardiovascular risk factors, such as lipid abnormalities (e.g., elevated serum cholesterol and triglycerides), excessive alcohol intake, and high-fat diets, have been shown to be associated with hearing loss in some, but not all, studies. Recent studies suggest that moderate alcohol consumption may lead to a lower risk of hearing impairment.

Psychosocial and Health Correlates of Hearing Impairment

Hearing impairment is associated with wide-ranging psychosocial consequences, including increased risk of depression, social isolation, loneliness, low morale, impaired activities of daily living (ADLs) and functional status, poor self-rated health, and impaired cognitive function. With few exceptions, little is known about the psychosocial functioning of hearing-impaired adults from minority ethnic/racial groups other than White non-Hispanics. It is unclear whether hearing loss is related to an increased risk of mortality. The psychosocial impact of hearing impairment appears to be magnified by the presence of other comorbid conditions such as visual impairment. Mortality risk is greater in adults with both sensory impairments than in those with hearing impairment only or visual impairment only.

Prevention and Management of Hearing Impairment

Primary prevention strategies for hearing impairment are largely unproven; however, smoking prevention and cessation, as well as continued efforts to limit worker exposure to excessive occupational noise, will likely lower the risk of developing hearing impairment or reducing its severity as adults age. Despite the efforts of the Occupational Safety and Health Administration (OSHA), which regulates workplace noise exposure in the mining and manufacturing industries, excessive occupational noise remains a pervasive problem affecting up to 30 million working age adults. An estimated 10 million adults currently have noise-induced hearing loss due to occupational exposures. Early hearing damage is often not detectable by workers because it occurs first in the higher frequencies that are less essential for speech understanding (e.g., > 4,000 hertz). However, continued exposures eventually involve the lower frequencies, yet these damaging effects might not become apparent until after retirement as a result of the presbyacusic process described previously. Finally, population-level improvements in the prevention and treatment of cardiovascular risk factors may also lower the risk and severity of progressive hearing loss given that hypertension, smoking, elevated serum cholesterol, and diabetes have been shown to be associated with hearing loss in some studies.

Secondary-level prevention strategies center on effective screening for hearing impairment, including the identification of underlying, but readily treatable, otological conditions (e.g., excessive ear wax, otitis media). Routine hearing screening for persons age 65 years and older has been recommended by the U.S. Preventive Services Task Force, yet only a small percentage of adults (< 30%) with undetected hearing impairment report that they have ever had their hearing tested. Rapid-onset hearing loss, although infrequent, requires immediate assessment and possible treatment with glucocorticoid to reduce the likelihood of permanent damage. Finally, there are numerous medications with known ototoxic properties (e.g., cisplatinum). Patients taking these drugs need close monitoring to detect any adverse effects on hearing acuity.

Tertiary-level prevention strategies include treating underlying disease affecting the auditory systems as well as providing hearing aids, assistive devices (e.g., listening devices), and rehabilitative services. There is evidence that the provision of such devices and services improves quality of life and helps to mitigate some of the psychosocial consequences of hearing impairment. Access and use of tertiary-level strategies in older populations is far from optimal. For example, population-based surveys have documented that the prevalence of hearing aid use among adults with clinically confirmed hearing loss is no better than 25%. The cost of hearing aids is cited as one factor for these low rates of use. Routine coverage for acquisition of hearing aids is not available through Medicare despite the Centers for Disease Control and Prevention's *Healthy People 2010* guidelines for the U.S. population that seek to increase access to hearing rehabilitation services and adaptive devices, including hearing aids, cochlear implants, and tactile or other assistive or augmentative devices. Finally, additional research is needed to determine why up to 30% of adults who obtain hearing aids stop wearing them. Randomized trials are also needed to determine whether assistive listening devices (e.g., telephone amplifiers) and the provision of rehabilitative services lead to cost-effective improvement in outcomes.

—David J. Lee and Heidi M. Lee

See also Demography of Aging; Ear Diseases; Multiple Morbidity and Comorbidity; Vision and Low Vision

Further Readings and References

Center for Communication and Consumer Services. Hearing loss and older adults. Available at: www.aoa.gov/prof/ notes/notes_hearing_loss.asp. Accessed September 17, 2006.

Consensus Conference. Noise and hearing loss. *JAMA.* 1990;263:3185–3190.

Lee DJ, Gómez-Marín O, Lam BL, Zheng DD. Trends in hearing impairment in United States adults: The National Health Interview Survey, 1986–1995. *J Gerontol A Biol Sci Med Sci.* 2004;59:1186–1190.

Nomura K, Nakao M, Morimoto T. Effect of smoking on hearing loss: Quality assessment and meta-analysis. *Prev Med.* 2005;40:138–144.

Weinstein BE. *Geriatric Audiology.* New York: Theime; 2000.

Yueh B, Shapiro N, MacLean CH, Shekelle PG. Screening and management of adult hearing loss in primary care: Scientific review. *JAMA.* 2003;289:1976–1985.

HISPANIC ESTABLISHED POPULATION FOR EPIDEMIOLOGIC STUDIES OF THE ELDERLY

In 1992, it became apparent that although important epidemiological data on elderly non-Hispanic Whites and African Americans had become available through the Established Populations for Epidemiologic Studies of the Elderly (EPESE) project begun during the 1980s in East Boston (Massachusetts), New Haven (Connecticut), North Carolina, and rural Iowa, comparable data were not available for Hispanic elderly. Much of the other existing knowledge in the area was based on data from the Hispanic Health and Nutrition Examination Survey (HHANES) conducted from 1982 to 1984. The HHANES covered Mexican Americans in the Southwest, Cuban Americans in Dade County (Florida), and Puerto Ricans in the greater New York City area. Unfortunately, the study was limited to persons under 75 years of age, and the number of elderly persons included in the study was too small to provide stable estimates of their health status. In addition, the HHANES did not include instruments measuring the physical functioning of participants.

In response to a special initiative of the National Institute on Aging, a fifth EPESE project was initiated, the Hispanic EPESE, which included elderly Mexican Americans from five southwestern states: Texas, California, New Mexico, Arizona, and Colorado. The primary purpose of the study was to provide estimates of the prevalence of key physical health conditions, mental health conditions, and functional impairments in older Mexican Americans and to compare this prevalence with that in other populations. In addition, the researchers wanted to investigate predictors and correlates of these health outcomes cross-sectionally.

The baseline data were collected in 1993 and 1994, with follow-up at 2 years in 1995 and 1996. To the extent possible, the study was modeled after the existing EPESE studies, particularly the Piedmont (North Carolina) EPESE. The Hispanic EPESE aimed at obtaining a representative sample of community-dwelling Mexican American elderly residing in the five southwestern states mentioned previously. Approximately 85% of Mexican American elderly persons reside in these states, and the researchers were able to obtain U.S. Census Bureau 1990 data that are generalizable to roughly 500,000 older people. The final sample size of 3,050 participants at baseline is comparable to that of the other EPESE studies and is sufficiently large to provide stable estimates of most health characteristics of interest.

The major goal of the Hispanic EPESE is to study the prevalence of important health problems and associated factors among older Mexican Americans. Specifically, the Hispanic EPESE is designed to estimate the prevalence and incidence of key physical health conditions, mental health conditions, cause specific mortality, impairments and disabilities, and use of hospitals and nursing homes among Mexican Americans age 65 years and older living in the southwestern United States. The study aims to evaluate associated risk factors and to quantify the changes in these related factors. A further purpose of the study is to assess changes in physical, social, and cognitive functioning as well as mental well-being.

Funding was obtained for two additional follow-ups at 5 years (1998–1999) and 7 years (2000–2001). Four important health outcomes were examined: mortality, physical function, depression, and institutionalization. Focus on the uniqueness of the Mexican American population included immigrant status, level of acculturation, strong family supports, high levels of extended living arrangements, high rates of poverty and low literacy, and poor access to health care. Also, of the medical conditions, the researchers focused primarily on diabetes, which is highly relevant in this population.

Additional follow-ups at 11 years (2004–2005) and 13 years (2006–2007) provide opportunities for examining longer-term changes. During the 11-year follow-up, an additional 902 persons age 75 years and older were added to the sample. These participants have a somewhat higher overall level of education. Diversifying the cohort of persons age 75 years and older will enable the researchers to better understand the influence of socioeconomic and cultural variation on the lives and health of a rapidly growing segment of the U.S. population, namely Mexican Americans age 75 years and older. Such understanding is critical to planning services for subsequent cohorts of older Mexican Americans whose level of education is higher than that of current older Mexican Americans. Correlates of physical, emotional, and cognitive function will be examined along with how these three areas of function are interrelated and coexist in the same individuals as well as how they influence other outcomes such as short-term mortality, institutionalization, and burden on family members.

—*Laura Ray and Kyriakos S. Markides*

See also Established Populations for Epidemiologic Studies of the Elderly; Hispanics; Latin America and the Caribbean; Longitudinal Study of Aging; Mexico; Migration

Further Readings and References

Black SA, Ray LA, Angel RJ, Espino DV, Miranda M, Markides KS, eds. *Resource Book of the Hispanic Established Population for the Epidemiological Study of the Elderly.* Ann Arbor, Mich: National Archive of Computerized Data on Aging; 2003. Available at: www.icpsr.umich.edu (search: Study No. 2851). Accessed September 17, 2006.

Markides KS, Stroup-Benham CA, Goodwin JS, Perkowski LC, Lichtenstein M, Ray LA. The effect of medical conditions on the functional limitations of Mexican American elderly. *Ann Epidemiol.* 1996;6:386–391.

HISPANICS

By 2002, the Hispanic population was estimated at more than 37.4 million, representing 13.3% of the U.S. population and becoming the largest ethnic minority population (with African Americans a close second). By far the largest segment of the Hispanic population were of Mexican origin (67%), followed by Central and South Americans (14.3%), mainland Puerto Ricans (8.6%), other Hispanics (6.5%), and Cuban Americans (3.7%). The Hispanic population is growing rapidly and is expected to reach more than 103 million by 2050. Although only 5.6% of the total Hispanic population is age 65 years and older, the numbers and proportions of this segment of the Hispanic population are expected to increase dramatically during the next several decades.

Although Hispanics are generally disadvantaged socioeconomically, they appear to have favorable mortality and health profiles, a phenomenon often referred to in the literature as the *Hispanic paradox.* With respect to mortality, there appears to be an advantage at all ages and Hispanic origins. It is greatest among persons of Cuban origin and lowest among Puerto Ricans. The advantage is evident in major causes of death, such as cardiovascular disease and cancer, and is typically attributed to a "healthy migrant" effect. Hispanic immigrants, like all immigrants to the United States, appear to be selected for good health. Any mortality advantage appears to disappear by the second generation as the children of immigrants adopt the American lifestyle.

There is some suggestion in the literature that mortality rates based on census and vital statistics data may underestimate mortality among the various Hispanic groups. A problem with the data (also found in Asian American and Native American populations) is misclassification of ethnicity. However, corrections for such biases indicate that mortality rates among

Hispanics remain relatively low. Longitudinal survey studies that establish ethnicity by self-report do not have the problem of misclassification of ethnicity on death certificates. Such studies also show a Hispanic advantage in mortality. If indeed there is substantial return migration to their country of origin by Hispanic immigrants after being included in the survey, their mortality rates could be biased downward, especially at older ages. Although this is not a concern with the Cuban American population, it is one with the Mexican-origin population. However, such biases do not appear to explain away the mortality advantages in the Mexican American population. One recent study of mortality of Medicare recipients found a lower overall mortality advantage among older Hispanics than that found in studies using other sources. Nevertheless, there was still an advantage, giving further support to the Hispanic paradox.

The favorable mortality rates of Hispanics in major causes of death (e.g., cardiovascular, cancer) cannot be explained fully by traditional risk factors. For example, there is no evidence that rates of hypertension are lower among Hispanics than among non-Hispanic Whites. Data from the Hispanic Established Population for Epidemiologic Studies of the Elderly (EPESE) that included 3,050 Mexican Americans age 65 years and older showed rates of measured hypertension comparable to those of older non-Hispanic Whites.

Another factor that might be associated with low cardiovascular and cancer mortality in Mexican Americans is their traditionally lower smoking rates. However, smoking rates of Mexican American men have been comparable to rates for the general population during the past two decades. Smoking rates are also high among Puerto Rican and Cuban American men. Men in most Hispanic populations, especially Puerto Ricans and Mexican Americans, exhibit heavy alcohol consumption patterns that may explain high mortality from cirrhosis of the liver and is also probably related to high rates of Hepatitis C.

Most Hispanic populations have high rates of diabetes, which is a risk factor for cardiovascular disease. They also have high rates of obesity and physical inactivity, both of which are factors that result in higher cardiovascular disease mortality. High rates of diabetes among Mexican Americans and Puerto Ricans have been attributed to high rates of poverty and obesity. However, even after these factors are taken into account, Mexican Americans continue to have substantially higher rates of diabetes than do non-Hispanic Whites. These high rates have been attributed partly to genetic factors related to the high degree of American Indian admixture. Puerto Ricans also have significant American Indian admixture as well as African American ancestry. On the other hand, Cuban Americans, especially the older generation, are primarily of European ancestry and have rates of diabetes that are comparable to those of non-Hispanic Whites.

Data from the Hispanic EPESE show that high rates of diabetes among Mexican Americans continue into old age. However, there is a significant drop in prevalence after 75 years of age, most likely resulting from higher mortality among diabetics. Among Mexican Americans, diabetes appears earlier in life, is more severe, and is associated with more complications. Recent data from the Hispanic EPESE show that the negative effects of diabetes in older Mexican Americans are exacerbated by high rates of depression and high depressive symptomatology. Depressed diabetics are less physically and socially active and are less likely to care for themselves adequately; thus, they are more likely to experience complications and earlier death.

Partly because of high rates of diabetes, older Mexican Americans (despite possible favorable overall mortality profiles) appear to be more disabled than older non-Hispanic Whites. This has also been found to be the case for older mainland Puerto Ricans but not older Cuban Americans, whose health profile is close to that of the non-Hispanic White population. Data from the Hispanic EPESE show higher rates of disability in each of five activities of daily living (ADLs)—eating, toileting, dressing, bathing, and transferring—among older Mexican Americans than among older non-Hispanic Whites. The same is true for instrumental activities of daily living (IADLs). There is also some evidence that older Puerto Ricans are slightly more disabled than older Mexican Americans, whereas older Cuban Americans are less disabled than older Mexican Americans.

Another reason for high disability rates among older Hispanics living in the community may be the population's low rates of institutionalization. Low institutionalization rates have been attributed to strong family supports and to discrimination against members of certain Hispanic groups. Hispanic families are more likely to view nursing homes as a last resort. Research on Mexican Americans suggests that those who are institutionalized, even though they are few in number, tend to be more physically and mentally impaired than non-Hispanic White nursing home residents. At the same time, this implies that more disabled older Mexican Americans than older non-Hispanic Whites are cared for in the community, placing additional burdens on the family. As Hispanics become more acculturated and assimilated into the larger society, and as more and more people move away from their parents' communities at a younger age, there may very well be an increased need for nursing homes and assisted-living facilities.

With respect to mental health, the evidence is less clear. The 1982–1984 Hispanic Health and Nutrition Examination Survey (H-HANES) revealed low rates of depressive symptomatology among Mexican Americans 20 to 74 years of age. The Hispanic EPESE, on the other hand, has found high rates of depressive symptomatology among older Mexican Americans. Earlier research suggested higher rates of depressive symptomatology among mainland Puerto Ricans than among residents of Puerto Rico. These rates for mainland Puerto Ricans were also higher than the rates for Mexican Americans, Cuban Americans, and African Americans. Recent data from the Hispanic EPESE suggest that older Mexican Americans living in heavily Hispanic neighborhoods are less likely to report high depressive symptomatology, suggesting a protective effect of Hispanic concentration.

It is not clear what the prevalence of Alzheimer's disease and other dementias is among older Hispanics. Recent research suggests that Caribbean-origin Hispanics (e.g., Puerto Ricans, Dominicans) are more genetically predisposed to Alzheimer's disease than are non-Hispanic Whites, possibly because of high rates of African American ancestry. Comparable data on Mexican Americans are not currently available.

Older Hispanics in all groups are less likely to have Medicare than are older non-Hispanics. In addition, most Hispanics are less likely to have supplemental private insurance, although many have Medicaid. Nevertheless, older Hispanics are considerably more likely to be insured than are middle-aged and younger Hispanics, and this may very well explain older Hispanics' relatively high rates physician use. And although older Hispanics might not underuse physician services, there is some evidence that they may delay seeking treatment for certain symptoms and that some may be unaware that they have diabetes and/or hypertension.

In sum, the health status of Hispanics and older Hispanics seems paradoxical given the population's relatively low socioeconomic status (with Cuban Americans being an exception). Mortality rates appear to be favorable in all Hispanic groups, in both genders, and at all ages. Even though there is suspicion that biases in mortality data might be responsible, the majority of the evidence points to a mortality advantage that may very well reflect a healthy migrant effect. At the same time, older Hispanics (again with Cuban Americans being the exception) appear to be more disabled than older non-Hispanic Whites, possibly because of high rates of diabetes and physical inactivity. As the various Hispanic populations continue to grow and age rapidly, more attention needs to be given to their special health problems and health care needs. Research also needs to appreciate the diversity of the Hispanic population with respect to age, country of origin, immigration history, cultural background, and socioeconomic characteristics.

—*Kyriakos S. Markides*

See also Hispanic Established Population for Epidemiologic Studies of the Elderly; Latin America and the Caribbean; Mexico; Migration

Further Readings and References

Black SA, Markides KS, Ray LA. Depression predicts increased incidence of adverse health outcomes in older Mexican Americans with type 2 diabetes. *Diabetes Care.* 2003;26:2822–2828.

Elo IT, Turra CM, Kestenbaum B, Ferguson BR. Mortality among Hispanic elderly in the United States. *Demography.* 2004;41:109–128.

Haan MN, Mungas DM, Gonzales HM, et al. Prevalence of dementia in older Latinos: The influence of type 2 diabetes. *J Am Geriatr Soc.* 2003;51:169–177.

Hummer RA, Reindl M, Rogers RG. Racial and ethnic disparities in health and mortality among the U.S. elderly population. In: Bulatao RA, Anderson NB, eds. *Understanding Racial and Ethnic Differences in Health in Later Life.* Washington, DC: National Academy Press; 2004:53–94.

Markides KS, Rudkin L, Angel RJ, et al. Health status of Hispanic elderly in the United States. In: Martin L, Soldo B, eds. *Racial and Ethnic Differences in Late Life Health in the United States.* Washington, DC: National Academy Press; 1997:285–300.

HIV AND AIDS

Approximately 5 million people are infected with the human immunodeficiency virus (HIV) every year, with hundreds of thousands being older adults. HIV damages a person's immune system so that it cannot fight off diseases. As the immune system weakens, a person faces the danger of life-threatening infections and cancers and eventually is diagnosed with acquired immunodeficiency syndrome (AIDS). At any point in the disease process, even before an HIV test is positive or symptoms develop, an HIV-infected person can infect others. Transmission usually occurs through sex, needle sharing, or use of blood products.

The number of HIV/AIDS cases among older people is growing for two major reasons. First, HIV/AIDS is popularly perceived as a young person's disease. Older persons and their health care workers often do not perceive that they are at risk. Older individuals, with little fear of unwanted pregnancies, are less likely to use condoms during sexual intercourse or to participate in routine HIV testing. They often know less about HIV than do younger people—how it is spread and the importance of using condoms, of not sharing needles, and of getting tested. The availability of drugs for erectile dysfunction have further expanded the number of elderly persons having risky sex on a regular basis.

Second, because of the availability and success of antiretroviral therapy in the developed world, most persons with HIV infection who adhere strictly to up-to-date medical regimens, will live out a normal life span. This means that individuals infected during early adulthood may now be reaching their 50s, 60s, and 70s.

Epidemiology

In the United States, 9% of new AIDS cases involve persons age 55 years and older, and 14,000 people were age 65 years and older at the time of their AIDS diagnoses. Thousands more are living with HIV infection, and thousands more do not know their HIV status. Since the beginning of the epidemic, 50,000 people age 55 years and older have been diagnosed with AIDS. Early in the epidemic, contaminated blood products were a major risk factor, and the largest percentage of these HIV infections occurred in persons over 60 years of age. Because effective treatments were not available, most of these patients died quickly. Regarding more recent epidemiology in the United States for those age 50 years and older, 84% are male, 60% are Black or Hispanic, and 57% are gay/bisexual and/or injection drug users.

Major Risk Factors

Advancing age itself is a risk factor for many infectious diseases, including HIV, due to lower immune functioning. The primary mode of transmission for older adults is having sex without the use of a latex or polyurethane condom. The virus passes from the infected person to the partner in blood, semen, and/or vaginal fluids. Condoms, if used properly, prevent an infected person from transferring HIV to another person.

Another major risk factor is sharing needles with an infected person. Injected drugs may be illegal or may be therapeutic substances. For example, patients with diabetes who inject insulin or draw blood to test glucose levels may share needles to save money. For those who receive medical care in developing countries, contact with HIV-infected blood through transfusions or other procedures is still a major risk factor.

Assessment of Risk

Older people often do not get diagnosed until later in the disease because health care workers often fail to consider an HIV diagnosis. Some are uncomfortable asking people who look like their parents or grandparents about their sex lives and whether they use drugs. Older people are less likely than younger people to talk about their sexual behavior or drug use with their doctors.

HIV infection is often initially misdiagnosed first as an age-related disease. HIV dementia may be misdiagnosed as Alzheimer's disease, HIV pain may be misdiagnosed as arthritis, and HIV wasting may be misdiagnosed as cancer. The Centers for Disease Control and Prevention (CDC) recommends that health care workers take sexual and drug histories from their older patients and discuss their HIV risk. A thorough risk assessment includes a frank discussion of sexual and drug (including alcohol) use behaviors. This provides an opportunity to discuss risky behaviors and how to modify them. HIV risk-assessment techniques have been widely published.

HIV Testing

The number of older HIV infected persons is much higher than is actually reported because health care providers do not always test this population for HIV/AIDS and older people often mistake the signs of HIV/AIDS for normal aging. Also, older people may be ashamed or afraid of being tested until they have serious symptoms. For these reasons, older people often have the virus for years before being tested. By the time of diagnosis, the virus may have affected the immune system so much that survival time is very short. Early detection of HIV leads to a longer life and reduced transmission to others.

When people become aware of their infection, they usually take steps to avoid infecting others. The CDC strongly encourages all health care providers to include HIV testing, when indicated, as part of routine medical care. Testing is becoming more available in community settings such as homeless shelters, retirement communities, low-income housing, senior centers,

and mobile testing sites. Rapid HIV antibody tests produce results in minutes, helping to ensure that patients are informed of their diagnosis and receive lifesaving treatment. A home HIV test kit is also available at drugstores. Because it can take as long as 6 months after infection for HIV antibodies to be detectable and result in a positive test, testing should be repeated frequently until 6 months after the last episode of risky behavior.

Treatment for HIV

The latest U.S. treatment guidelines are available at www.aidsinfo.nih.gov. A combination of various antiretroviral drugs is used to treat HIV, although other drugs may be needed to prevent opportunistic infections. With aging patients, those providing treatment will need to be keenly aware of underlying disorders of aging, potential drug–drug interactions, proper dosing, and overlapping toxicity of concurrent drugs.

Multiple Effects

HIV may affect older persons in many ways. Infected persons may become depressed or experience other symptoms associated with the HIV mental health spectrum. Many may be homeless or alone without a strong network of friends or family to help. They may be coping with diseases associated with aging, such as diabetes, heart problems, and high blood pressure, that further exacerbate their weakened health status.

In addition, many young people who are HIV infected turn to their parents or grandparents for support. Older people may find themselves caring for adult children who are infected or for their orphaned HIV-infected grandchildren. These older surrogate parents are at increased risk for stress-related conditions. There are many psychosocial issues associated with AIDS and older adults, and many special services are needed for this population.

Prevention

The costs of preventing HIV infections vary widely, but the cost almost always represents a small fraction of the cost of providing lifelong pharmaceutical treatment. HIV prevention activities include education, counseling, HIV testing, and prevention supplies such as condoms and sterile injection equipment. Two of the challenges of prevention among older persons are their limited HIV knowledge and their mistaken belief that they are not at risk.

Health care providers should be able to demonstrate the proper use of both the male condom and the female condom and to discuss issues such as abstinence, being faithful to one's sexual partner, personal and mutual masturbation, safe use of needles, and the need for screening for other sexually transmitted diseases. HIV testing for early detection is the key to prevention. When persons who carry the virus have been identified, education and counseling can target the behaviors that put their partners and others at risk. All older persons need to know how to take the necessary precautions to minimize the possibility of transmission of this deadly disease. There is still no cure for HIV infection, so disease prevention strategies are emphasized.

—*Michael D. Knox*

See also Health Communication; Immune Function; Infectious Diseases; Sexuality

Further Readings and References

Centers for Disease Control and Prevention. AIDS among persons aged greater than or equal to 50 years: United States, 1991–1996. *MMWR Weekly.* 1998; 47(2):21–27. Available at: www.cdc.gov/mmwr/preview/mmwrhtml/ 00050856.htm. Accessed September 17, 2006.

Centers for Disease Control and Prevention. HIV/AIDS surveillance report. Available at: www.cdc.gov/hiv/stats/hasrlink.htm. Accessed September 17, 2006.

Goodkin K, Heckman T, Siegel K, et al. "Putting a face" on HIV infection/AIDS in older adults: A psychosocial context. *J AIDS.* 2003;33:S171–S184.

Knodel J, Watkins S, VanLandingham M. AIDS and older persons: An international perspective. *J AIDS.* 2003;33: S153–S165.

Knox MD, Chenneville T. AIDS prevention: The clinician's role. In: Fernandez F, Ruiz P, eds. *Psychiatric Aspects of HIV/AIDS.* Baltimore, Md: Lippincott Williams & Wilkins; in press.

Linsk NL, Fowler JP, Klein SJ. HIV/AIDS prevention and care services and services for the aging: Bridging the gap between service systems to assist older people. *J AIDS.* 2003;33:S243–S250.

Mack KA, Ory MG. AIDS and older Americans at the end of the twentieth century. *J AIDS.* 2003;33:S68–S75.

Manfredi R. HIV infection and advanced age emerging epidemiological, clinical, and management issues. *Ageing Res Rev.* 2004;3(1):31–54.

HOME CARE

Home care is one of the fastest-growing components of the U.S. health care industry. The term *home care* encompasses three models of care: skilled home health care, home-based long-term care services, and high-tech home care. Growth in this industry has been fueled by several important trends: (a) advances in the technological capacity to provide complex care at home, (b) the search for less costly alternatives to hospital and nursing home care, (c) the emergence of third-party payment for a variety of forms of home care, and (d) the strong and consistent preferences of consumers and their families to receive care in their homes whenever possible.

Skilled Home Health Care

The first home care programs began during the 1880s and became housed in local public health departments during the Progressive Era when concerns about communicable disease stimulated the development of visiting nurse services. Between 1915 and 1960, hospitals began to provide home care posthospitalization; however, real growth in this model began in 1965 when skilled home care was included as a benefit in Medicare. The Medicare benefit, an adjunct to hospital care, was limited to persons who were homebound; certified by a physician to require skilled nursing and speech, occupational, and/or physical therapy; and in need of intermittent (vs. continuous) care.

Medicare home health care programs and users have grown substantially. From 1967 to 1997,

Medicare home care was reimbursed retrospectively based on the number of visits provided. From 1967 to 1997, the number of Medicare-certified agencies increased from 1,753 to 10,444. From 1974 to 1997, the number of clients served per year grew from 500,000 to 3.5 million, the number of visits increased from 10 million to 250 million, and reimbursements grew from $1 million to $1.7 billion. Most of this growth occurred between 1989 and 1996 after a class action lawsuit forced the Department of Health and Human Services to expand its interpretation of the Medicare eligibility criteria. Once the interpretation was expanded, reimbursements skyrocketed, growing at an annual rate of 33% between 1989 and 1997. To stem this rate of growth, the Balanced Budget Act of 1997 put in place an Interim Payment System (IPS) and mandated the development of a Prospective Payment System (PPS) for Medicare home care. Under the IPS, reimbursements declined rapidly and an estimated 1,000 agencies went out of business. The new PPS was initiated in 2000 and pays providers prospectively for care, based on a case mix adjuster that takes into account the severity of the patient's condition. Currently, little is known about the impact of the PPS for home care on client outcomes. This is an issue that urgently requires research.

Medicare home health care users are predominantly (91%) aged beneficiaries whose most common principal diagnoses are diseases of the circulatory system, injury and poisoning, and diseases of the musculoskeletal system. Skilled home health care is also reimbursed by Medicaid, by private insurance policies, and by Medicare managed care plans. In most cases, these payers model the benefit after the Medicare skilled care benefit.

Homemaker/Chore Programs

Low-tech homemaker and home health aide services are intended to help people remain in the community and forestall nursing home use. These programs provide assistance with personal and instrumental activities of daily living (IADLs) to persons of any age with disabilities who seek to remain in their homes. It is estimated that 12,000 home care providers (64% of the total supply) in the United States in 2000 were uncertified providers who may provide low-tech services.

The most rapidly growing reimbursement source for low-tech home care during recent years has been the Medicaid Section 2176 home and community-based care waiver that was created by Congress in 1981 to decrease the use of nursing homes by Medicaid-eligible aged, disabled, and developmentally disabled beneficiaries. Under this program, states apply for permission from the federal government to modify benefits otherwise required for Medicaid programs. States can expand services covered, expand income eligibility criteria, or target specific geographic areas for increased benefits. Across the states, spending for individuals with developmental disabilities has increased most rapidly, accounting for approximately 75% of total waiver expenditures in 2001 as states have moved to provide care to this population in less restricted, more integrated group and small homes outside of nursing homes and state institutions. Despite this rapid growth, it is important to note that the generosity of Medicaid waiver programs and the scope of services provided vary greatly by state. More uniformity in services provided across states may occur in the future as states comply with the Supreme Court's *Olmstead v. L.C.* decision that mandates that states strive to enable persons with disabilities to receive care in the most integrated setting possible. As a result of the *Olmstead* decision, many states are now diverting funds previously spent on nursing homes to support greater amounts of in-home services.

High-Tech Home Care

The third type of home care combines skilled home care with high-tech medical equipment and pharmaceuticals. Services provided under this model include enteral and parenteral nutrition, intravenous antibiotics, electric left ventricular assist devices, oxygen concentrators and portable ultrasonic nebulizers, and telemedicine. These programs generally involve a partnership between a home care agency and a pharmacy, and they enable persons who previously spent weeks in intensive care units to receive care in the home, at work, or overnight while sleeping. The Medicare and private home care models described previously account for approximately 75% (or $30 billion) of total home care industry expenditures, and the high-tech sector accounts for the remaining 25%.

As stated previously, home care in its various forms has grown rapidly and is expected to continue to grow rapidly as the technical boundaries of care that can be provided safely and effectively at home continue to expand, in accordance with the expressed preferences of the overwhelming majority of health care consumers.

—*Susan L. Hughes*

See also Assisted Living; Death, Dying, and Hospice Care; Long-Term Care; Palliative Care and the End of Life

Further Readings and References

Coleman B, Fox-Grage W, Folkemer D. State long-term care: Recent developments and policy directions—2003 update. Available at: www.ncsl.org/programs/health/forum/ltc/LTC_draft.htm. Accessed September 17, 2006.

Hughes S, Renehan M. Home health. In: Evashwick C, ed. *The Continuum of Long Term Care.* Albany, NY: Thomson Delmar Learning; 2005:87–112.

McCall N, Peterson A, Moore S, Korb J. Utilization of home health services before and after the Balanced Budget Act of 1997: What were the initial effects? *Health Serv Res.* 2003;38(1):85–106.

Rosenbaum S. *Olmstead vs. L.C.: Implications for Older Persons With Mental and Physical Disabilities.* Washington, DC: American Association of Retired Persons; 2003.

HOMELESSNESS AND HEALTH IN THE UNITED STATES

Homelessness, according to the Stewart B. McKinney Act of 1994, involves an individual without an immovable sufficient nighttime residence. To be homeless, however, means more than to lack a domicile; it is a symptom of personal and societal disaffiliation. It is estimated that there are between 1 million and 2 million homeless people in the United States. Homelessness affects a wide variety of people—healthy and sick; employed and unemployed; veterans of the armed forces; men, women, and children; adolescents; and older adults. Approximately 25% of the homeless population in the United States is over 50 years of age, 25% is under 31 years of age, and 50% is between 31 and 50 years of age. Ethnically, approximately 49% of the homeless population in the country is African American, 32% is Caucasian, 12% is Hispanic, 4% is Native American, and 3% is Asian.

The homeless population in the United States has a higher incidence and prevalence of both acute and chronic medical conditions compared with the general (non-homeless) population. For some homeless persons, ill health can be a precipitating factor of homelessness. For others, however, homelessness itself generates illness because of the constant exposure to the weather, crowded shelters, unsanitary living conditions, lack of sleep, poor nutrition, adverse lifestyle practices, and lack of health care. There are many medical conditions that are common among homeless individuals, including substance abuse, acute infections, upper respiratory problems, musculoskeletal problems, hypertension, mental illness, dermatologic disease, gastrointestinal ailments, ophthalmologic disease, dental disease, and trauma. However, mental illness, substance abuse, and musculoskeletal problems are among the most prevalent disease conditions found in the general homeless population in the United States. With limited access to health care services, these health problems often go untreated or treatment is delayed. Homeless individuals, therefore, are caught in a cycle that requires medical care earlier but prevents access until more costly care is required.

Access to health services by homeless individuals is limited by a few key barriers to care—financial, bureaucratic, programmatic, and personal. *Financial* barriers to care include lack of health insurance, limited health care benefits, and limited (or lack of) income. *Bureaucratic* barriers to care include restrictive eligibility criteria for health care benefits, arduous registration procedures, long waits at clinics, inflexible clinic scheduling, restricted clinic hours, and lack of transportation to clinics. *Programmatic* barriers to care include lack of outreach health services that are geared toward the special needs of homeless individuals, scarce social services, multiple providers, and disrespectful or negative attitudes of health care providers (potentially alienating homeless individuals from seeking medical care). *Personal* barriers to care include mental illness and substance abuse, lack of self-efficacy to compete for social and health services in the traditional institutional setting, and the low priority given to health care compared with the basic needs of finding food and shelter.

For many homeless individuals, the county hospital and emergency room (ER) setting has become the primary source of usual medical care. This is perhaps in part because homeless persons generally enter the health care system when treatment of an acute or chronic illness appears to be critical, ERs are open at all times, appointments are not necessary, and many county hospitals are located in areas where the homeless reside.

The hospital and ER setting, however, is not ideal for homeless individuals to receive primary health care services. The hospital and ER is also a more costly setting to deliver primary health care to homeless individuals. Moreover, continuity of care is usually limited in the ER setting, and the principal complaints or medical issues of the homeless persons are usually the only medical conditions treated. However, homeless individuals generally suffer from multiple health problems. Thus, readmission rates (and health care costs) for homeless individuals are often high after discharge from the hospital and ER setting. It is estimated that hospitalization rates of homeless persons are four times greater than the U.S. norms, and many of these hospital admissions are for preventable medical conditions. This has a direct financial impact on the U.S. health care system. It is estimated that the average cost of a hospital stay in New York, for example, is $2,400 more for a homeless patient than for a non-homeless patient.

Hospitals and ERs need to explore alternative modes of health services delivery not only to improve access to care for homeless individuals but also to reduce the high costs of hospitalization and medical care associated with the homeless population. One alternative model that is being used by a few county hospital systems in cities across the United States (e.g., Dallas, Los Angeles, San Francisco, New York) to provide primary care to homeless individuals is mobile medical unit programs and clinic-based outreach centers (i.e., homeless outreach programs). Previous research suggests that homeless individuals receiving care from accessible homeless outreach programs designed to address their special needs will indeed use the health services and return for subsequent visits. This pattern of use is perhaps a result of the mobile medical units and outpatient clinics providing services where homeless people congregate, thereby eliminating transportation and access barriers, and of the services being delivered by health care professionals who are sensitive to the special needs of homeless individuals. Also, these homeless outreach/outpatient services are generally free of charge, and patients are seen on a walk-in basis (no appointments are needed). The latter is extremely important because the need to make appointments can deter homeless persons from seeking care. Previous research has also found that, for homeless individuals, there are fewer barriers to returning for care at a familiar and accessible site already visited (e.g., a mobile medical unit, a community-based outpatient clinic) than to seeking care at a new site or at an inpatient setting.

In conclusion, homelessness affects a wide variety of people across the United States. The homeless population is a vulnerable population and one that has (and engenders) numerous and complex health problems. With limited access to health care services, the health problems associated with homeless individuals often go untreated or treatment is delayed (until more costly care is required). Communities (and county hospital systems) that make a commitment to their homeless populations by making social support services (e.g., outreach medical services) accessible to homeless individuals will, in the long run, not only mitigate many of the barriers that prevent the homeless population from obtaining primary medical care but also mitigate unnecessary and costly health care expenditures. This benefits both the community and the homeless population.

—*Paul A. Nakonezny*

See also Demography of Aging; Economics of Aging; Education and Health; Living Arrangements

Further Readings and References

Han B, Wells BL, Taylor AM. Use of the health care for the homeless program services and other health care services by homeless adults. *J Health Care Poor Underserved.* 2003;14:87–99.

Hudson CG. *An Interdependency Model of Homelessness: The Dynamics of Social Disintegration.* New York: Edwin Mellen; 1998.

Kushel MB, Vittinghoff E, Hass JS. Factors associated with the health care utilization of homeless persons. *JAMA.* 2001;285:200–206.

Nakonezny PA, Ojeda M. Health services utilization between older and younger homeless adults. *Gerontologist.* 2005; 45:249–254.

Wojtusik L, White MC. Health status, needs, and health care barriers among the homeless. *J Health Care Poor Underserved.* 1998;9:140–152.

HOMEOSTASIS

See ALLOSTATIC LOAD AND HOMEOSTASIS

HONOLULU–ASIA AGING STUDY, HONOLULU HEART PROGRAM

The Honolulu–Asia Aging Study (HAAS) is a prospective epidemiological cohort study with a conceptual focus on neurodegenerative diseases and stroke during late life. It uses the cohort and accrued data of the Honolulu Heart Program (HHP), which began in 1965 with the interview and examination of 8,006 Japanese American men who were born between 1900 and 1919 and were living on the island of Oahu.

The HAAS is a National Institute on Aging (NIA)–funded component and addition to the HHP, a prospective cohort study of heart disease, stroke, and cancer that was established by the National Heart, Lung, and Blood Institute (NHLBI). The HHP was designed to confirm reports that middle-aged men of Japanese ancestry living in the United States had a substantially higher risk of coronary heart disease than did Japanese men living in Japan. Prospective cohort studies of men born between 1900 and 1919 who were residing in Japan, Honolulu, or San Francisco comprised the larger NI–HON–SAN (Nippon–Honolulu–San Francisco) multicentered study that began in 1965. Follow-up examinations in the HHP were conducted from 1967 to 1969 and from 1971 to 1974 with the collection of extensive information related to heart disease, cancer, and stroke.

Between 1991 and 1993, the NIA, NHLBI, National Institute of Nursing Research, and Department of Veterans Affairs cosponsored and completed reexaminations of 3,734 surviving study participants (age range 71 to 93 years), the fourth examination of the full cohort since the inception of the HHP. The fourth HHP examination included measurement of cognitive function and screening for cognitive impairment, detection and differential diagnosis of cases of dementia by standardized clinical evaluation, objective and subjective assessments of physical functioning, depression screening, history of chronic diseases and other medical conditions, and other lifestyle, health, and behavioral factors. Similar to the baseline NI–HON–SAN multicentered study, the HAAS was designed in cooperation with researchers from centers in Japan, Taiwan, and the United States, and cohort studies paralleling the HAAS were conducted during this time in Seattle, Hiroshima, and Taipei.

Subsequent 2- to 3-year interval follow-up HAAS/HHP examinations were conducted as follows: 1994 to 1996 on 2,705 men in a fifth examination (age range 74 to 95 years), 1997 to 1999 on 1,991 men in a sixth examination (age range 77 to 98 years), 1999 to 2000 on 1,523 men in a seventh examination (age range 79 to 100 years), and 2001 to 2003 on 1,200 men in an eighth examination (age range 81 to 103 years). Three additional follow-up examinations are currently planned and in progress.

Methods for screening, clinical diagnosis, and classification of dementia are standardized across all HAAS examinations. Individuals judged to meet *Diagnostic and Statistical Manual of Mental Disorders, Third Edition–Revised* (DSM-III-R) criteria for dementia also have brain computed tomography (CT) or magnetic resonance imaging (MRI) scans and blood tests, including complete blood count, chemistry profile, Vitamin B12 level, red blood folate level, rapid plasma regain, and thyroid function tests.

An autopsy component of the HAAS began in 1992 to corroborate and address accuracy of clinical criteria for diagnosis of Alzheimer's disease and other neurodegenerative diseases. Autopsies are sought on all deaths within the cohort, and approximately 20% of the decedents' next of kin grant this permission. Among the cohort decedents who were diagnosed with dementia, approximately 50% of next of kin grant permission for their autopsies. Brains are fixed by immersion in 10% buffered formalin for at least 10 days, with brain weight measured before and after fixation. Extensive microscopic analyses are carried out on 42 brain regions. More than 650 brain autopsies had been completed by the end of 2005.

Another important source of information on brain structure and aging derives from an MRI study of a subsample of participants in the fifth examination ($n = 621$ scans). The subsample included approximately a 10% random sample of cognitively normal participants with oversampling of those with prevalent dementia, those who scored poorly on the Cognitive Abilities Screening Instrument but did not meet criteria for dementia, those with an apoE e4 genotype, and those with a clinically confirmed stroke. Scans were acquired with a GE Signa Advantage 1.5 Telsa machine. The acquisition protocol included a T1-weighted sagittal sequence, a three-dimensional coronal spoiled gradient echo sequence, and axial T2 and proton density-weighted fast-spin echo sequences. Number of lacunes, cortical and subcortical infarcts, and white matter lesions were graded and quantified by trained radiologists.

In the seventh examination, the NIA funded the Honolulu–Asia Aging Study of Sleep Apnea (HAASSA), in collaboration with researchers conducting the NHLBI-funded Sleep Heart Health Study (SHHS), to investigate relationships between sleep-disordered breathing and deficits in neuropsychological functioning, especially attention and concentration. Participants without an existing diagnosis of moderate or more severe dementia and those not on treatment for sleep apnea or on oxygen therapy were recruited to undergo an unattended overnight polysomnography (PSG) conducted in their homes according to criteria established previously for the SHHS. Less than half of the eligible participants at the seventh examination ($n = 718$) participated in the PSG sleep study. The PSG was conducted with a Compumedics PS-2 system with the following montage: central electroencephalogram (C_4/A_1 and C_3/A_2), right and left electrooculogram, chin electromyogram, a single bipolar electrocardiogram, finger pulse oximetry, chest and abdominal excursion by respiratory inductance plethysmography, airflow by oronasal thermocouples, body position, and ambient light. Scoring of the sleep studies for severity of sleep apnea, including an apnea–hypoxia index and percentage oxygen desaturation, were standardized and followed the criteria established by the SHHS reading center.

The HAAS provides a unique opportunity to assess previously collected clinical data in a cohort that is undergoing ongoing surveillance for the incidence of Alzheimer's disease, vascular dementia, and Parkinson's disease as well as other common conditions during late life, including stroke, cardiovascular disease, diabetes, and obstructive sleep apnea. Epidemiological research in cohorts studied longitudinally from middle to late life provides a special opportunity to examine the determinants of aging-related phenomena and aging-associated diseases. The extensive historical data gathered prospectively during middle age can provide knowledge about the importance of midlife health status and lifestyle behaviors that can contribute to healthy aging.

—*Daniel J. Foley and Lon R. White*

See also Asia; Cardiovascular Health Study; Cardiovascular System

Further Readings and References

Foley DJ, Masaki K, White LR, et al. Sleep-disordered breathing and cognitive impairment in elderly Japanese-American men. *Sleep.* 2003;26:596–599.

Kagan A, Harris BR, Winkelstein W, et al. Epidemiologic studies of coronary heart disease and stroke in Japanese men living in Japan, Hawaii, and California: Demographic, physical, dietary, and biochemical characteristics. *J Chron Dis.* 1974;27:345–364.

Korf ESC, White LR, Scheltens P, Launer LJ. Midlife blood pressure and the risk of hippocampal atrophy: The Honolulu–Asia Aging Study. *Hypertension.* 2004;44:29–34.

Petrovitch H, White LR, Ross GW, et al. Accuracy of clinical criteria for AD in the Honolulu–Asia Aging Study, a population study. *Neurology.* 2001;57:226–234.

White LR. Toward a program of cross-cultural research on the epidemiology of Alzheimer's disease. *Curr Sci.* 1992;63:456–469.

White L, Petrovitch H, Ross GW, et al. Prevalence of dementia in older Japanese-American men in Hawaii: The Honolulu–Asia Aging Study. *JAMA.* 1996;276:955–960.

HORMONE THERAPY

See MENOPAUSE AND HORMONE THERAPY

HOSPICE CARE

See PALLIATIVE CARE AND THE END OF LIFE

HYPERTENSION

Hypertension is defined as a persistent elevation of arterial blood pressure. It is one of the most common medical conditions in the Western world. Despite a growing awareness of hypertension and its complications, its treatment is still inadequate for many older adults. There can also be secondary problems with access to health care, inappropriate treatment goals by primary physicians, and individual ignorance of the seriousness of the disease. Many older adults are unaware that they have high blood pressure because they are symptom free until experiencing complications such as a stroke or myocardial infarction.

Hypertension can be described or classified in different ways. These classifications are used together to describe types of hypertension appropriately. Blood pressure has two components: systolic and diastolic. When both systolic and diastolic blood pressures are elevated, it is simply called *hypertension.* Hypertension is called *isolated systolic hypertension* when the systolic blood pressure is elevated without the diastolic blood pressure being elevated. Isolated systolic hypertension is the most common type of hypertension in older adults. *Isolated diastolic hypertension* is less common in older adults and occurs when the diastolic blood pressure is elevated without elevation of the systolic blood pressure.

Another way to describe hypertension is by the degree of elevation of blood pressure from normal to Hypertension Stage 2. Table 1 illustrates the seventh report of the Joint National Committee (JNC 7) classification. This classification is used for treatment as well as to identify individuals at risk for complications. For example, when left untreated, individuals with Hypertension Stage 2 have a higher risk of complications than do those with Hypertension Stage 1.

Table 1 Classifications of Hypertension

Classification	Systolic Blood Pressure (mm/Hg)	Diastolic Blood Pressure (mm/Hg)
Normal	< 120	< 80
Prehypertension	120–139	80–89
Hypertension Stage 1	140–159	90–99
Hypertension Stage 2	160	100

Source: Adapted from Chobanian, AV, Bakris, GL, Black, HR, Cushman, WC, Green, LA, Izzo, JL Jr, Jones, DW, Materson, BJ, Oparil S, Wright, JT Jr, & Roccella, EJ. Seventh report of the Joint National Committee on Prevention, Detection, Evaluation, and Treatment of High Blood Pressure; 2003. *Hypertension* 42(6):1206–52.

Note: These classifications apply to adults who are not taking medications for hypertension and are not acutely ill.

Therefore, one of the objectives of the hypertension treatment is to decrease the blood pressure to the appropriate level of blood pressure (target goal) to minimize future complications and prevent mortality.

Another way to describe or classify hypertension is by the cause of the hypertension as primary or secondary. *Primary hypertension* has been associated with a family history of hypertension, salt intake, obesity, and alcohol use. Primary hypertension, also called idiopathic or essential hypertension, is the most common type of hypertension. Nearly 90% of hypertensive older adults have primary hypertension. Primary hypertension is not caused by any other disease, and it tends to be more common and severe in African Americans than in non-Hispanic Whites. *Secondary hypertension* is caused by other medical conditions or drugs. Common causes of secondary hypertension are renal artery stenosis, thyroid disorder, pheochromocytoma, and drugs such as corticosteroids. Secondary hypertension is less common than primary hypertension and can even coexist with primary hypertension. For example, a person can suffer from primary hypertension and renal artery stenosis, causing secondary hypertension. Treatment for secondary hypertension is aimed at the disease that is causing the blood pressure elevation. Drugs can cause or worsen hypertension. Even over-the-counter medications, such as the pseudoephedrine frequently used in cold medications and nonsteroidal anti-inflammatory medications, can exacerbate hypertension.

Prevalence of hypertension increases with advancing age in the United States. For those over 65 years of age, the prevalence is at least 60%, depending on a person's age and ethnicity. There is a clear relationship between high blood pressure and age. This relationship is seen mainly in industrialized populations and likely is due to environmental factors.

Environmental and age-related factors predispose individuals to hypertension. Environmental factors that are associated with hypertension include diets with high salt content, obesity, and a sedentary lifestyle. Obesity increases the risk of cardiovascular mortality, diabetes, and hypertension. Active older adults have been found to have less obesity and a lower risk of cardiovascular diseases. High peripheral vascular resistance, reduced large artery compliance, increased blood pressure variability, and relatively greater systolic hypertension characterize hypertension in older adults. Age-related changes in multiple systems, including the cardiovascular systems, predispose older adults to hypertension. It is likely that age-related changes and environmental factors interplay, causing the increase in the prevalence of hypertension in older adults.

Hypertension in older adults has been associated with a number of complications such as stroke, myocardial infarction, and other cardiovascular diseases. Systolic blood pressure, more so than diastolic blood pressure, has been identified as a powerful risk factor for morbidity and mortality. Event with mild elevations of systolic blood pressure, these complications are seen more frequently than they are in normotensive adults.

Cardiovascular disease is the number-one killer in the United States for both men and women over 50 years of age. Cardiovascular diseases are strongly associated with hypertension. The incidence of cardiovascular diseases increases with age, especially in women. The female-to-male risk for cardiovascular diseases is nearly the same at 75 years of age, whereas in younger individuals the risk is more common in men. Congestive heart failure (CHF) or congestive heart disease (CHD) is one of the cardiovascular diseases and is one of the most common causes of hospitalization in older adults. It can be a debilitating disease and a major cause of morbidity and mortality in older adults. Left ventricular hypertrophy, another complication of long-standing hypertension, has been associated with heart failure, myocardial infarction, and sudden death. Complications and risks of chronic hypertension include the following:

- Chronic renal disease
- Left ventricular hypertrophy
- CHF or CHD
- Myocardial infarction
- Transient ischemic attack
- Intracerebral hemorrhage
- Stroke
- Coronary artery disease
- Peripheral vascular disease
- Hypertensive retinopathy

- Cognitive impairment
- Vascular dementia

Diagnosis

Initial diagnosis of hypertension should be based on at least two measurements of blood pressure at rest over a few weeks. Proper measuring of blood pressure is essential for accuracy. Blood pressure should be measured in a warm quiet setting after 5 minutes of rest with appropriate equipment and technique. Caffeine or drugs that can increase blood pressure should be avoided prior to the blood pressure testing. It is recommended to check the blood pressure while sitting and standing to evaluate for positional changes in blood pressure. If blood pressure drops while standing, the physician needs to be extra careful when considering the use of medication to control the blood pressure. More specifically, the physician should be cautious because medication can exacerbate the blood pressure drop and cause orthostatic hypotension.

After an older adult is diagnosed with hypertension, he or she will require evaluation for possible secondary causes of hypertension and target organ damage due to long-standing high blood pressure. Examples of medical problems that are target organ damage due to hypertension include stroke, myocardial infarction, and left ventricular hypertrophy. In addition to identifying target organ damage, the overall cardiovascular risk factors, such as smoking, dyslipidemia, and obesity, should be identified. Assessing for possible causes of hypertension, target organ damage, and other cardiovascular risk factors may trigger additional treatments to minimize future cardiovascular morbidity and mortality.

A complete history, physical exam, electrocardiogram, and laboratory testing that include hemoglobin, blood chemistries, urinalysis, and lipid profiles are required in the initial assessment of a hypertensive older adult. The history should include the duration of hypertension, prior drug treatment, family history, diet, and psychosocial factors such as work and stress. The physical examination should include a heart, lung, and extremities examination; fundoscopy evaluation; and neurological assessment.

Usually, uncomplicated primary hypertension is asymptomatic. Some symptoms that have been associated with, but are not unique to, hypertension are headaches and tinnitus. When older adults have target organ damage such as heart failure due to chronic elevation of blood pressure, symptoms can include shortness of breath, lower extremity edema, and fatigue. The signs and symptoms that an individual will experience depend on the organ system that has been affected by the long-standing hypertension.

Treatment

Appropriate control of arterial blood pressure has been shown to be beneficial for the great majority of older adults. The goal of treatment is to minimize future complications for long-standing high blood pressure. In general, the target goal is to keep the blood pressure below 140/90 millimeters of mercury (mm/Hg) if possible. If that target blood pressure cannot be reached, an intermediate target goal of blood pressure below 160/90 mm/Hg will be favorable in older adults. Older adults with diabetes mellitus or renal disease will require more aggressive treatment. The target goal of blood pressure for this group should be 130/80 mm/Hg.

For those over 85 years of age, treatment benefits of hypertension are controversial. There is not an ideal target goal for blood pressure management in this group. This is due partially to the heterogeneity of this age group and to the insufficient information about treatment benefits of hypertension in this group. Management of individuals, especially for those over 85 years of age, must take into consideration current medications and overall health status. Possible side effects of drug treatment should be weighted against the benefit of blood pressure control. In older adults with limited life expectancy, the goal of treatment should be to minimize symptoms related to elevation of the blood pressure and not to maintain blood pressure at a target number.

Hypertension treatment in older adults is multidimensional and very similar to that in younger individuals. It includes lifestyle modifications and antihypertensive medications when target goals cannot be reached with lifestyle modifications alone. Lifestyle modifications include weight loss if obese, limited alcohol and sodium intake, 30 minutes of aerobic exercise (e.g., walking) per day, and smoking cessation. Lifestyle modifications should be implemented, but not at the expense of poor nutrition or decreased quality of life, especially in the very old or those with limited life expectancy.

Antihypertensive drug therapy is usually tolerated in older adults. Medications to control blood pressure should be started at a low dose, and the dose should be increased slowly. Possible side effects should be monitored closely. Older adults are at a higher risk for drug–drug interactions and drug–disease interactions due to higher prevalence of medication use and number of diseases. Medications for high blood pressure should be evaluated against an individual's current medication regimen to prevent drug–drug interactions. Also, some medications can exacerbate a coexisting medical problem such as urinary incontinence or asthma. These require a careful understanding of the side effect profile of the medication for hypertension and individual medical problems so as to avoid a drug–disease interaction.

Therefore, the drug chosen to treat hypertension will depend on an individual's current drug therapy and medical conditions. If the older adult does not have any coexisting conditions, thiazide diuretics and β-blockers will be the drugs of choice in most cases. Both groups of drugs have been shown to reduce blood pressure and its complications.

A part of the initial evaluation of hypertensive individuals includes assessing for possible causes of hypertension, target organ damage, and other cardiovascular risk factors. Lifestyle modifications with or without drug management should be used as part of the treatment of hypertensive older adults. The goal of treatment is to minimize cardiovascular complications and avoid unwanted side effects. Older adults are more likely to experience side effects of antihypertensive medications such as orthostatic hypotension, fatigue, and headache. Therefore, in individuals with limited life expectancy who are over 85 years of age, treatment goals should be to prevent symptoms associated with hypertension and to promote quality of life.

—*Luis Felipe Amador*

See also Cardiovascular System; Congestive Heart Failure; Kidney Aging and Diseases; Stroke; Valvular Heart Disease

Further Readings and References

Chobanian AV, Bakris GL, Black HR, et al. Seventh report of the Joint National Committee on Prevention, Detection, Evaluation, and Treatment of High Blood Pressure. *Hypertension.* 2003;42:1206–1252.

MRC Working Party. Medical Research Council trial of treatment of hypertension in older adults: Principal results. *Br Med J.* 1992;304:405–412.

Prisant LM, Moser M. Hypertension in the elderly: Can we improve results of therapy? *Arch Intern Med.* 2000;160:283–289.

Rigaud AS, Forette B. Hypertension in older adults. *J Gerontol A Biol Sci Med Sci.* 2001;56:217–225.

Sowers JR, Lester M. Hypertension, hormones, and aging. *J Lab Clin Med.* 2000;135:379–388.

I

IATROGENIC DISEASE

The literature suggests that the prevalence of iatrogenic disease is extensive, and clearly those who are older are at a greater risk for acquiring such a condition. Elders access the health care system a disproportionate number of times and receive a disproportionate number of prescriptions for drugs. Unlike younger individuals, most elders have multiple chronic conditions. Therefore, any intervention directed to a single medical problem has the potential of adversely affecting any other diseases the elders might have.

Yet without a doubt, the incidence of iatrogenic disease is underestimated for a variety of reasons. First, there is no standard definition of iatrogenesis. Some authors have studied those conditions specifically caused by physicians. Others have included only those illnesses that result from accessing the health care system in general. Still others have scrutinized care in a single site, most often the hospital setting. Fewer publications are to be found addressing the hazards that follow medical prescriptions, including (but not limited to) drugs, in the outpatient and home settings. Far less has been written about illness that results from care in long-term care facilities. How many iatrogenic events are simply not reported because they seem minor to the providers or because they might result in unfavorable investigations into quality of care? How many events are not reported

because of fear of litigation? And how many negative events are attributed to the progression of illness; that is, are simply unrecognized by patients or medical providers as being consequences of the interventions?

In addition, it is impossible to know how many elders undergo medical interventions that are simply unnecessary. Even if there are no complications of the procedure, and even if the drug prescribed is taken without incident, might it be appropriate to label these interventions as iatrogenic events? For example, an elder who undergoes an unnecessary surgical procedure may be fearful both before and after the event and may have postponed a planned trip because of it. This would be true even if the procedure were judged to be a success. Similarly, an elder who spends money on an unnecessary pharmaceutical agent might then need to limit spending for a quite different necessary or simply desirable item. Is that an iatrogenic event?

In addition, there is the problem of unnecessary testing. By way of example, an older person who is suffering from mild to moderate abdominal pain may well be advised to have an abdominal computed tomography (CT) scan. Perhaps the study raises the question of an abnormality and a magnetic resonance imaging (MRI) is recommended. This might not completely clarify the situation, and so it is followed by a series of other studies, perhaps culminating in multiple endoscopic procedures and biopsies that reveal only a number of benign lesions of no clinical consequence. Perhaps bleeding follows one such biopsy and a repeat endoscopic study is needed to control it. The best course of action might have been to do nothing because the abdominal pain lasted only 24 hours and was the consequence of eating some leftovers that were left over for too long. Clearly, the individual suffered a number of undesirable consequences from accessing the medical system, but it is unlikely that the experience would be classified as iatrogenic by many authors, although some would suggest that such was in fact the case. A clinical observation, stated with only a measure of tongue in cheek, is that a test that is not indicated is always abnormal.

Lastly, there may well be procedures carried out that have no value whatsoever for the patient but are recommended because of the narrow view of a specialist. For example, a cardiac catheterization may be recommended by a cardiologist for an elder whose life expectancy and quality of life from other conditions might not reasonably warrant such an aggressive approach. Because the primary care doctor likely is hesitant to advise the patient to disregard the recommendation of the specialist, the procedure is carried out. Also, a reimbursement system that pays markedly disproportionately for procedures may increase the likelihood of this happening. Even if the procedure is carried out without a hitch, might this be viewed as an iatrogenic event?

Many of the best studies highlight the risks that elders face when hospitalized. Some sites within the hospital may pose greater risks than others. Information accompanying elders who are transferred from a long-term care facility to an emergency department may be incomplete. When elders are initially cared for in a busy and noisy emergency department by individuals who are not familiar with the elders' prior state of health, the stage may be set for many of the complications, such as delirium and falls, seen on the hospital unit. Older persons may well experience a disproportionate number of iatrogenic events in an intensive care unit. But regardless of the location within the facility, hospitals carry a substantial risk for elders. These risks include those associated with bed rest for any but the briefest period of time, exposure to any number of medications, infections from organisms that are resistant to antibiotic therapy, falls, delirium, and pressure ulcers.

It has been demonstrated that bed rest for even a few days results in rapid deconditioning. Clearly, some individuals, such as those who are hypotensive, require bed rest. But not infrequently, a physician will order bed rest on admission, and there the order stands for much of the hospitalization. That elder may require extensive rehabilitation following discharge if the prehospitalization level of function is to be achieved.

A disproportionate number of medications are prescribed for elders. Therefore, drug–drug interactions are more common than they are in younger individuals. Perhaps because of the ease with which they can be ordered in the hospital, drugs are ordered for any number of conditions that might not be deemed to require medications if the individuals were not in an acute care facility. Mark H. Beers has written extensively about the inappropriate use of medications in the elderly. The drugs may be inappropriate for this age group regardless of dose. Also because of age-related changes, especially in renal function, the dose may be excessive and therefore the drug may cause undesirable effects.

Older persons are hospitalized disproportionately, and their lengths of stay are disproportionately long. Therefore, they have an increased exposure to microorganisms found in an acute care setting. Some infections, such as those caused by *Clostridium difficile,* often follow the use of antibiotics that may have been prescribed unnecessarily. Others, such as those caused by the *Staphylococcus* organism, may be difficult to treat because the organism has become resistant to most antibiotics. These resistant organisms are especially common in institutional settings.

For a number of reasons, elders are especially likely to fall in the hospital setting. Sleeping pills and anxiolytics, which are widely prescribed, may contribute to confusion. Persons who have received large fluid challenges because of "keep open" intravenous orders require frequent toileting. But the environment is responsible for many falls as well. The bed in the hospital likely is at a height different from that of the individual's bed at home. Therefore, stepping out of it is hazardous for someone who awakes in the middle of the night to go to the bathroom and who is somewhat disoriented for reasons such as those mentioned previously. In addition, many patients are tethered to the bed because of an intravenous line, a monitor, or perhaps a Foley catheter. These pieces of equipment increase the likelihood of falling if an individual is not experienced at moving about with them. Lighting may be poor, the floor may be slippery, and of course the bathroom is in an unfamiliar location. Nurses might not respond as fast to the call button being pressed as the elder may wish, thereby requiring the individual to go to the bathroom without assistance. Understandably, it is during the first day in the hospital that the greatest number of falls occur.

Approximately 10% of all elders entering a hospital become delirious. Unlike dementia, a progressive neurological illness, delirium is characterized by confusion, transient (and often rapid) changes in levels of attention and concentration, and perhaps even hallucinations. Delirium may appear abruptly in an individual who was normal previously and may persist for some time, or it may clear just as abruptly. Delirium is associated with increased length of hospital stay, poor outcomes, and increased costs of care. Sharon Inouye has written extensively about the need to recognize the condition and prevent its appearance whenever possible through a formal program of orienting the individual.

Bed sores, known as decubitus ulcers, are especially troublesome to both elders and caregivers. There are a number of scales used to alert the nursing staff to those persons who are especially likely to develop pressure ulcers. Turning the elder every 2 hours has been recommended as a preventive measure, although evidence to support this frequency of intervention is lacking. Immobility, poor nutrition, and a lack of normal sensation increase the risk of developing a decubitus ulcer. Regrettably, even when the nursing care is exemplary, these lesions—created by pressure often over a bony prominence—may occur. Treatment has changed considerably over the past few decades. In general, it is necessary to keep pressure ulcers clean but moist, and of course all pressure should be eliminated if at all possible. Pressure ulcers are scaled depending on their depth and what tissues are damaged. Once a relatively severe (Grade 3 to 4) pressure ulcer develops, it may take a long period of time before the lesion heals or it may never do so.

A number of physiological changes associated with aging, and especially common conditions, may contribute to the disproportionate risk of iatrogenic disease faced by older persons entering a hospital. Some surgical procedures are associated with an increasing rate of complications in elders. Nutritional deficits are common in elders requiring hospitalization, and changes in the body composition, such as relatively more fat and less muscle, may make the healing process more difficult. In general, reserve capacity is lost with age. Although an 80-year-old individual may function quite well under usual circumstances, small insults may produce quite significant problems because of a further loss of reserve capacity. For example, because muscle mass, and therefore muscle strength, declines with age, any additional loss associated with bed rest is likely to be clinically more significant in older individuals than in younger ones. Similarly, changes in the lung, spine, muscle mass, and hematopoietic and cardiovascular systems that are common in elders may make older persons more likely to develop confusion, blood clots, pulmonary emboli, respiratory insufficiency, and pneumonia as well as more likely to fall. Incontinence of urine, present in large numbers of elderly women, may make it more difficult to treat decubitus ulcers. Similarly, diminished hearing likely increases the risk of delirium and may make it more difficult for elders to follow directions when testing and therapeutic interventions require their active participation.

Although hospitals have been the focus of studies about iatrogenic illness, there is reason to believe that many examples can be found in other settings as well. Clearly, large numbers of prescriptions are written for drugs that expert committees deem to be inappropriate, at any dose, for elders. Similarly, older individuals who reside in board and day care facilities are prescribed large numbers of inappropriate medications. Because the number of long-term care beds now exceeds the number of acute care beds, and because 90% of these individuals are elderly and usually are afflicted with one or more advanced chronic diseases, it is likely that the risk of iatrogenic disease in these settings is substantial.

In 2000, the Institute of Medicine brought to the attention of the medical profession and the public many of the issues related to iatrogenic disease in a volume, *To Err Is Human: Building a Safer Health System*. Recently, accrediting agencies, such as the Joint Commission for the Accreditation of Health Care Facilities, have taken considerable interest in trying to prevent iatrogenic illness. By way of example, formal procedures are required so that an elder entering the operating room for an amputation has the correct limb amputated. Similarly, the introduction of computerized medical records will in time make the issue of the illegibility of physicians' notes and orders, an inappropriate source of humor for a long time, of historical interest only.

In the near future, there may well be administrative changes within the hospital setting designed to decrease the prevalence of iatrogenic illness. These may include a larger role for pharmacists, standardized order sets, and special protocols for certain groups of patients such as elders. For example, bed rest orders may be restricted to persons with certain diseases or to those who are likely to become syncopal on assuming the standing position. Likely what is also needed is a standardized assessment tool that includes predictors of iatrogenic illness, including function prior to an acute illness, so that preventive measures can be instituted and targeted to each individual in that setting.

—*Knight Steel and Joan Rittgers*

See also Ethical Issues and Aging; Geriatric Assessment; Inappropriate Prescribing; Legal Issues; Medication Errors

Further Readings and References

Beers MH. Explicit criteria for determining potentially inappropriate medication use by the elderly. *Arch Intern Med.* 1997;157:1531–1536.

Inouye SK, Bogardus ST, Baker DI, Leo-Summers L, Cooney LM. The Hospital Elder Life Program: A model of care to prevent cognitive and functional decline in hospitalized older patients. *J Am Geriatr Soc.* 2000; 48:1–10.

Institute of Medicine. *To Err Is Human: Building a Safer Health System.* Kohn L, Corrigan J, Donaldson M, eds. Washington, DC: National Academy Press; 2000.

IMAGING OF THE BRAIN

Brain imaging is a procedure that allows physicians to examine the structure of the brain or take pictures of how it looks. This is an important tool for the evaluation of brain and neurological disorders, including stroke, seizures, some psychiatric illnesses, and head injuries. There are primarily two types of technology used to image the brain: computed tomography scans (CT or CAT scans) and magnetic resonance imaging (MRI), both of which are also used to image other parts of the body. Although they both take pictures of the brain, there are important differences regarding availability, cost, tolerability, and when one might be preferred over another for medical reasons.

Brain imaging provides important information that may be critical to the management of individuals with certain medical problems. An emergent brain scan is typically used to evaluate the development of new neurological problems such as weakness in the arm or leg, drooping of the face, sudden onset of confusion, and difficulty with speech or vision. These problems could be the result of, for example, a cerebrovascular accident or stroke. There are primarily two kinds of stroke: ischemic, where the brain is injured due to a reduction in, or a lack of blood flow to, the region; and hemorrhagic, where bleeding occurs in the brain. A brain scan, usually a CT scan, is needed to determine whether there is any bleeding visible because the presence of a hemorrhagic stroke requires treatment different from that for an ischemic stroke. Thus, the brain scan provides important information that the physician uses to guide treatment.

Imaging may also be used for some symptoms or disorders to make sure that they are not caused by another problem that should be treated in a different way. An example of this is dementia such as Alzheimer's disease. In older adults, Alzheimer's disease is the most common cause of serious memory loss as well as loss of other cognitive functions. However, less commonly, other diseases of the brain, including brain tumors, stroke, and brain infections, may cause symptoms mimicking Alzheimer's disease. Because the treatment for these disorders would be very different from that for Alzheimer's disease, it is important to evaluate whether they are present. In the case of Alzheimer's disease, brain imaging serves to rule out one of these other findings. If they are not present, the brain scan may show findings of atrophy (shrinking of brain regions) that may support a diagnosis of Alzheimer's disease but would not definitively result in a specific diagnosis. Other disorders that may be evaluated with brain imaging to exclude serious concerns would include severe headaches, particularly of a sudden onset, and new development of psychosis such as hallucinations (seeing or hearing things that are not present).

Types of Brain Imaging

Computed Tomography

CT scans were first used during the 1970s and still remain the most widely available and convenient tools for most clinical practice. Notably, they are also less expensive than the alternative, namely MRI. The CT scanner takes multiple X-ray pictures of the brain from a small device that rotates 360 degrees around the head. These multiple pictures are sent to a computer, which then reconstructs the pictures into a coherent image of the brain that can be viewed in various ways. Because these machines are widely available, CT scans are often used when brain imaging is needed in an emergency.

Like most radiographic procedures, CT scans do involve exposure to radiation. In general, these amounts are limited and the exposure falls well below government recommendations for individuals who work around radiation. In some cases, iodine-containing contrast agents or other contrast agents may be used. For brain imaging, these are administered by vein and are used so that certain regions or findings can be better seen in the pictures. Allergic reactions to these contrast agents are possible and may be more common in people with shellfish allergies.

Magnetic Resonance Imaging

MRI scans became available during the 1980s. Rather than using radiation to take pictures of the body, MRI relies on extremely strong magnetic fields that cause atoms to align themselves in certain directions. A second magnetic pulse then shifts the alignment of the atoms, and when that pulse ends the atoms return to their original alignment; this return causes them to emit a radiofrequency signal that is detected by the MRI device. The signal is different in different types of tissue and allows computers to reconstruct an image of the brain or other body regions. In general, MRI scans provide more highly detailed pictures of brain structure than do CT scans and so may be preferred over CT depending on availability, the brain region being examined, and the reason for obtaining the scan.

Although they do not use radiation, MRI scans have other concerns. The biggest concern is the presence of metal implanted in the body that could include pacemakers or other metal devices, shrapnel from combat wounds, metal near the eye as can be seen in steelworkers, and even metal-based tattoos or permanent makeup. Because MRI scans depend on magnets for their images, this can move or shift any metal present in the body, so in some cases people with metal in their bodies cannot be scanned using an MRI machine and must receive CT scans instead. Individuals should not even bring metal items into the room housing the MRI machine.

The MRI procedure is also more grueling than that for CT scans. The patient receiving an MRI scan must remain motionless for a longer period of time than for a CT scan because movement reduces the quality of the images. In addition, due to the machinery needed to create the magnetic field, individuals are slid into a small, narrow enclosed space. Although one can see out of the MRI device by mirrors, and voice contact with the technician is possible, individuals with claustrophobia may have a difficult time completing the scan. To combat this, occasionally patients with claustrophobia will be given a short-acting sedative to make the procedure more tolerable. "Open" MRI devices that reduce the feeling of claustrophobia have been developed; unfortunately, these are not widely available and might not provide brain images of the best quality.

Functional Imaging

CT and MRI scans examine brain structure but do not provide information on how the brain is functioning. Techniques that provide measures of brain function are used primarily for research, although some specific clinical uses are common.

The most widely used functional imaging methods include single photon emission computed tomography (SPECT) and positron emission tomography (PET). These methods are similar in that they involve injection of manufactured radioactive compounds that allow measures of blood flow in the brain or brain use of glucose (sugar), each of which is associated with brain region metabolism. A functional version of MRI (fMRI) also exists. fMRI does not measure brain activity directly; rather, it measures blood flow that is associated with brain activity.

Again, these tools are used primarily in research and have limited clinical use. Importantly, PET imaging may prove to have a role in diagnosing specific types of dementia and is increasingly being used in evaluating and monitoring some types of cancer.

Brain Imaging in Aging-Related Research

All of these are important tools in research examining brain changes seen with aging as well as disorders of the brain seen in older populations. Some degree of atrophy, or slight shrinking in the brain, is normal even in healthy individuals as they age. However, structural imaging studies have found differences in various brain regions in older individuals with Alzheimer's disease and depression when compared with healthy individuals. Such findings provide important information on which brain regions are involved in memory, cognition, and mood. Further knowledge in this area should lead to a better understanding of those diseases and better treatments.

Functional imaging studies not only provide important information on brain function in these and other disorders but also improve our understanding of how the brain works. The brain is quite complex; multiple different regions may interact even for simple functions. For example, in language, different brain regions are involved in the perception of speech as well as in comprehension and in whether one reacts emotionally to what is said. In addition, different types of speech, such as rhyming, may require the use of other brain regions. The structure and function of the brain is a complex field, and these tools provide a window into how it works. Other imaging methods in development, such as improvements in functional imaging and the ability to examine the chemical composition of brain regions through magnetic resonance spectroscopy (MRS), will further our understanding. This rapidly developing field will ultimately guide the development of therapeutics and so translate into better treatments for disorders affecting the brain.

—*Warren D. Taylor*

See also Alzheimer's Disease; Apolipoprotein E; Creutzfeldt–Jakob Disease; Lewy Body Dementia; Neurobiology of Aging; Stroke

Further Readings and References

DeCarli C, Massaro J, Harvey D, et al. Measures of brain morphology and infarction in the Framingham Heart Study: Establishing what is normal. *Neurobiol Aging.* 2005;26:491–510.

Knopman DS, DeKosky ST, Cummings JL, et al. Practice parameter: Diagnosis of dementia (an evidence-based review)—Report of the Quality Standards Subcommittee of the American Academy of Neurology. *Neurology.* 2001;56:1143–1153.

Silverman DH, Small GW, Chang CY, et al. Positron emission tomography in evaluation of dementia: Regional brain metabolism and long-term outcome. *JAMA.* 2001;286:2120–2127.

IMMIGRATION

See MIGRATION

IMMUNE FUNCTION

Many people in the seventh decade of life have witnessed an explosion of health care changes. Within their lifetimes, the advent of antimicrobials (antibiotics), immunizations, medications to correct underlying problems and prolong life, new technologies to diagnose and treat disease, and even economics have changed medicine nearly beyond recognition.

There are still people alive today who remember the influenza pandemic of 1918, when a particularly virulent influenza virus killed between 20 million and 40 million people worldwide over a 2-year period. An estimated 675,000 Americans died—10 times more than died in World War I, which was finally ending. Widespread vaccination has diminished the threat of this disease and other public health concerns such as polio, measles, and pneumonia. The virulence of the 1918 influenza strain has not been repeated since, although another pandemic threatens as "bird flu" makes it way into the human population.

Immunology Overview

The human organism is designed to ward off disease and is usually successful. The first form of protection is innate; skin and the mucous membranes, such as those lining the lungs, respiratory tract, and gastrointestinal system, serve as a first line of defense against invading pathogens (viruses and bacteria). Coughing, sneezing, and blinking are other mechanisms of defense as the body tries to clear pathogens. If these innate barriers are overwhelmed or fail, the pathogens enter the bloodstream. Then the components of the hematopoietic (blood) system are activated to isolate and destroy the pathogens.

The immune system is effective because immune cells are able to differentiate between "self" (cells or organs belonging to the host) and "nonself" (foreign pathogens such as bacteria, viruses, or protein structures that are not recognized by the host cells). Rapid response to invasion of the host by foreign pathogens can lead to containment of the pathogen, destruction of the foreign bodies, and cellular changes to allow

healing. We have all witnessed this in the healing of a simple flesh wound; the skin is broken, local redness and swelling occurs, and pus may be expressed. But with simple local care, the skin heals itself. The immune cells have done their job and the host is preserved. When the host fails to distinguish self from nonself, the invading pathogens present as an overwhelming burden, or the host response is insufficient even for a small infection, a person can experience an overwhelming or life-threatening infection. Because the immune system recognizes self versus nonself, it is also the first line of defense against cancers. A dysfunctional immune system is implicated in autoimmune disease (e.g., rheumatoid arthritis, lupus) and chronic inflammatory states when the body attacks its self.

All cells express self on their outer membranes that are exposed in the blood plasma and present on organ tissue. These proteins, called the major histocompatibility complex (MHC), are genetically encoded. The MHC is like a hand that can pick up foreign proteins inside the cell and express them on the cell surface. Thus, when an immune cell in the circulating blood "sees" an MHC that does not contain a foreign protein on the cell surface, it "recognizes" the cells as belonging to the host organism and no response is triggered. A failure to recognize self would result in an attack on one's own cells with devastating consequences. These proteins must be matched when organs are transplanted to avoid rejection of the transplant.

The lymphocytes (white blood cells) that circulate in the blood provide a quick response to invading bacteria or viruses and divide into many cell types according to immunological response. Neutrophils, monocytes, and macrophages, relatively nonspecific in their immunological activity, are among the first cells to respond to foreign bacteria or viruses. As they find pathogens, they engulf and destroy them, and they release biochemicals to recruit more immune cells to the area of infection. Natural killer cells are also part of this innate immune response that can kill virus-infected or cancer cells that express MHC containing foreign proteins.

Another group of cells respond with more specificity to invading pathogens and impart a "memory" to the immune response. The bone marrow derived (B-) and thymus-derived (T-) lymphocytes develop immune responses specific to the pathogen, and when this memory is restimulated, it greatly enhances the immunological defenses. In the case of vaccination, for example, viruses contained in the vaccine are phagocytosed by macrophages; proteins from the virus are picked up by the MHC "hand" inside the cell and expressed on the cell surface. T-cells "see" the MHC containing the foreign protein and are stimulated to "help"—by helping the B-cells differentiate and produce antibodies and by helping the cytotoxic T-lymphocytes to become virus-specific killer T-cells. The memory of these B- and T-cells then ensures a vigorous immune response to those pathogens when an infection occurs. This memory also develops with an infection, so that reinfection is prevented or produces a more mild disease.

The B-lymphocytes express antibodies (immunoglobulin) on their cell surface and become plasma cells that secrete antibodies to bind specific proteins (the antigen) on a foreign pathogen or cell. Of the antibodies that exist on mucous membranes and circulate in the bloodstream, approximately 80% have antitoxin, antiviral, and antibacterial functions.

Aging and Immunology

As people age, the host barriers of defense begin to weaken; skin thins and becomes more friable, blood vessels rupture more easily, and protective cell barriers (e.g., those lining the respiratory tract) become more fragile. More susceptible to infections, older people are treated for more urinary tract infections, respiratory infections, and pneumonias.

As people age, they frequently have more comorbid (coexisting) medical problems and take more medications, diminishing their ability to recuperate from severe illnesses. Prolonged periods of bed rest and inactivity due to illness may lead to deconditioning that could result in permanent disability. Thus, a disease such as influenza—self-limiting in young adults—can become disabling and even life threatening in older persons.

Cellular decline of the immune system affects both antibody-mediated (B-cell) and T-cell-mediated responses. This decline contributes to the increased frequency and severity of infectious diseases. Viral diseases are cleared more slowly, although the specific mechanism for this decline is unclear. The capacity of T-cells to respond to and mobilize immune defenses to new pathogens may be diminished. The types of cytokines that mediate the immune response shift, and cytotoxic T-cell function declines. The response of B- and T-cells to vaccines is also diminished, causing the vaccine to be less effective in persons over 65 years of age.

Influenza

Influenza is foremost among infectious diseases associated with an increased risk for serious complications and death with aging. A recent epidemiological study suggests that influenza may be the sole cause of deaths due to respiratory illness, heart diseases, strokes, and diabetes that occur in persons age 70 years and older during the winter months when influenza is circulating. Symptoms of infection with influenza range from silent disease (where the infected person does not feel ill), to a mild upper respiratory infection, to a severe illness with potentially fatal complications. The most common symptom is a dry cough. Although children often have high fevers, older people might not be able to mount fevers. Sore throat, muscle aches, runny or stuffy nose, and fatigue are also common symptoms, but gastrointestinal symptoms (e.g., nausea, vomiting, diarrhea) are not as common. Duration of the illness is typically 1 to 2 weeks but may persist for as long as three weeks in older persons.

The virus is highly contagious. An infected person can easily spread the viral particles to infect many others. Thus, within a community, there can be a sudden eruption of cases. The virus travels suspended in droplets, typically of saliva. A cough or sneeze sprays viral particles into the air where they can remain suspended for some time. An uninfected person can inhale the droplets or can contact the virus through mouth contact from hands or infected surfaces. A person is contagious 24 hours before the onset of symptoms and for up to 7 days after that. This extended period of contagion makes environments such as nursing homes a high risk of serious influenza illness in older persons; the virus may be transmitted from health care workers or other infected residents.

Once the droplets are inhaled into the respiratory tract, they come into direct contact with the respiratory epithelium (protective cell barrier). If the immune response is insufficient, the virus infects many cells lining the respiratory tract. These host cells are transformed, becoming virus factories and replicating the virus at the expense of normal cell function. The infected cell eventually dies and is sloughed off. Progressive loss of the protective cell barrier occurs as more cells of the respiratory tract and lungs become infected. Circulating lymphocytes, B-cells and T-cells, gather to destroy infected cells. Cytokines are released from the immune cells to assist in suppressing the infection. They cause local swelling and inflammation, giving rise to the troublesome symptoms of fever, cough, sore throat, malaise, and muscle aches. Loss of cells from the respiratory tract weakens the barrier and increases the risk of pneumonia, disability, and death.

Influenza also increases the risk of heart attacks, strokes, and exacerbations of congestive heart failure. Heart diseases, diabetes mellitus, and chronic obstructive pulmonary disease (COPD) are common in the older adult population and increase the risk of hospitalization or the spiral of prolonged bed rest, deconditioning, and disability. Many might not fully recover, with loss of independence at home or transfer to an assisted-living facility or nursing home, even 3 months after hospitalization.

Influenza vaccination is a cost-saving medical intervention. In spite of the decline in the immune response to influenza vaccination with aging, current vaccines are highly effective for preventing hospitalization and death from an influenza. However, significant barriers to vaccination remain. Public health efforts are needed to improve vaccine availability and to educate people about the disease and prevention programs.

—*Janet E. McElhaney and Rita D. Jepsen*

See also Biological Theories of Aging; Biomarkers of Aging; HIV and AIDS; Multiple Morbidity and Comorbidity; Pneumonia and Tuberculosis

Further Readings and References

Crosby AW. *America's Forgotten Pandemic: The Influenza of 1918.* Cambridge, England: Cambridge University Press; 1989.

Gomez CR, Boehmer ED, Kovacs EJ. The aging innate immune system. *Curr Opin Immunol.* 2005;17:457–462.

McElhaney JE. The unmet need in the elderly: Designing new influenza vaccines for older adults. *Vaccine.* 2005; 23(Suppl. 1):S10–S25.

Monto AS. Global burden of influenza: What we know and what we need to know. *Intl Congr Ser.* 2004;1263:3–11.

Pawelec G, Ouyang Q, Wagner W, Biol D, Wikby A. Pathways to a robust immune response in the elderly. *Immunol Allergy Clin N Am.* 2003;23:1–13.

World Health Organization. Immunization against diseases of public health importance. Available at: www.who.int/ vaccines-diseases. Accessed September 18, 2006.

INAPPROPRIATE PRESCRIBING

Inappropriate prescribing can be defined as prescribing of medications that have more potential risk than potential benefit or prescribing that does not agree with accepted medical standards.

Epidemiology

The prescribing of inappropriate drugs can be measured by the application of explicit criteria (e.g., "Do not use" lists [commonly referred to as "Beers criteria" in the United States], drug utilization review) or of structured implicit criteria that incorporate clinical review of medical records (e.g., Medication Appropriateness Index). Inappropriate prescribing may include problems with suboptimal choice, dosing, duration, duplication, drug–drug interactions, and drug–disease interactions. Depending on which measurement approach is used, the prevalence of inappropriate prescribing in older adults has been reported to range from 14% to 92%. The risk factors for inappropriate prescribing are not well defined but likely involve a combination of patient, provider, and system factors. Complications of inappropriate prescribing may include functional status decline, worsening of self-rated health, increased hospitalization, and mortality.

Interventions to Improve Inappropriate Prescribing

A number of different approaches to improve prescribing have been examined, including the innovation of "academic detailing" (where a health educator instructs a physician in his or her office), computer order entry and feedback, drug utilization review, formulary and other restrictions, community education, opinion leader and physician education, clinical pharmacist activities, and multidisciplinary specialized geriatric team care approaches. Evidence from randomized controlled health services intervention trials suggests that clinical pharmacy and multidisciplinary team interventions can consistently improve inappropriate prescribing for the elderly. Few trials are of sufficient size to document improvement in patient outcomes (e.g., death, disease, dollars, disability, discomfort, dissatisfaction).

Recommendations

One approach to improve inappropriate prescribing is to require geriatric pharmacotherapy training for medical, nursing, and pharmacy school students, residents, and fellows. Implementing electronic prescribing with helpful medication decision support tools and regular (at least annual) drug regimen reviews is also likely to reduce inappropriate prescribing. Future research is necessary to develop new and better measures of inappropriate prescribing that have established predictive validity. Moreover, further large-scale multicenter intervention studies are needed to determine their impact not only on process measures but also on distal health outcomes (e.g., adverse drug reactions, functional status and health services use, associated costs).

—*Joseph T. Hanlon*

See also Age-Related Changes in Pharmacokinetics and Pharmacodynamics; Drug–Disease Interactions; Drug–Drug Interactions; Drug Underuse; Iatrogenic Disease; Medication Adherence; Medication Errors; Polypharmacy

Further Readings and References

Chutka DS, Takahashi PY, Hoel RW. Inappropriate medications for elderly patients. *Mayo Clin Proc.* 2004;79:122–139.

Fick DM, Cooper JW, Wade WE, et al. Updating the Beers criteria for potentially inappropriate medication use in older adults: Results of a U.S. consensus panel of experts. *Arch Intern Med.* 2003;163:2716–2724.

Hanlon JT, Schmader KE, Ruby CM, Weinberger M. Suboptimal prescribing in elderly inpatients and outpatients. *J Am Geriatr Soc.* 2001;49:200–209.

Liu GG, Christensen DB. The continuing challenge of inappropriate prescribing in the elderly: An update of the evidence. *J Am Pharm Assoc.* 2002;42:847–857.

Zhan C, Sangl J, Bierman AS, et al. Potentially inappropriate medication use in the community-dwelling elderly: Findings from the 1996 Medical Expenditure Panel Survey. *JAMA.* 2001;286:2823–2829.

INCONTINENCE

Urinary incontinence (UI), the involuntary loss of urine, is a prominent medical condition in the elderly population affecting women more than men. It is estimated that 15% to 30% of community-dwelling elderly and as many as 50% of nursing home residents have UI. Risks of UI include skin breakdown, urinary tract infections, social isolation, and depression. It is important for individuals to understand that UI is not a normal part of the aging process. UI is undertreated due in part to both health providers and patients underdiagnosing and underreporting the problem.

Transient or Reversible Causes

The evaluation process begins with an attempt to identify the cause of incontinence. Reversible or transient causes should be identified first. A mnemonic device used to identify reversible causes is "D–I–A–P–P–E–R–S":

D   Delirium or confusional state

I   Infection—urinary (only symptomatic)

A   Atrophic urethritis or vaginitis

P   Pharmaceuticals—benzodiazepines, alcohol, diuretics, anticholinergic agents, α-adrenergic agents, calcium channel blockers

P   Psychological disorders

E   Excess urine output (endocrine disorders or excessive urine production)

R   Restricted mobility

S   Stool impaction

If reversible or transient causes for the UI are not identified, chronic causes are investigated. These chronic causes are classified based by their pathophysiology.

Chronic Causes

There are four basic types of UI. The most common type is *urge incontinence,* which affects both men and women. It is characterized by involuntary contractions of the detrusor (bladder) muscle associated with a strong urge to void. This condition is known as detrusor hyperactivity or overactivity (DO). In cases where neurogenic etiologies have been established, it is termed detrusor hyperreflexia. The condition is further classified as having "preserved" or "impaired" bladder contractility.

Another type of UI is *stress incontinence.* This is defined as an involuntary loss of urine associated with an increase in intra-abdominal pressure. It is the most common type of incontinence in younger women and is usually associated with a weakened or unstable urethral sphincter or weakness of the muscles that support the urethra. Stress incontinence is rarely seen in men; however, when diagnosed, it is usually associated with urethral weakness secondary to invasive instrumentation.

The third type of UI is called *overflow incontinence.* This is more common in men than in women and is associated with the obstruction of urinary flow out of the bladder. It can also develop as a cause of bladder distension. The obstruction may be secondary to an enlarged prostate gland, tumors, genitourinary prolapse, and urethral strictures. Bladder distention is usually related to a dysfunction in bladder contractility.

The fourth type of UI is *functional incontinence.* It is defined as the loss of urine related to external factors. These factors may stem from lack of cognition and/or neurological and musculoskeletal conditions. Usually, the individual has a normal functioning urinary system. However, individuals must be evaluated for possible underlying etiologies such as detrusor hyperactivity, which may have initially contributed to the need to urinate.

Behavioral Management Options (First-Line Therapy)

Daily routine/habit review for UI includes fluid intake (amount and timing), irritant intake (e.g., tobacco, coffee/tea), diet and weight reduction, bedside commode or urinal use, daytime elevation of legs, bladder training (cooperative ability) needed, prompted voiding regimens (in the cognitively impaired), pelvic floor muscle training (Kegel exercises), and biofeedback (used in DO).

Nonpharmacological Management

Nonpharmacological management for UI can include intravaginal devices (weighted cones and pessaries), external devices (urethral plugs and penile clamps), catheterization (indwelling or intermittent) and condom catheters, implantable devices (for electrical stimulation of muscles), caps for urethral meatus, and injectables (periurethral bulking injections such as bovine collagen, crosslinked collagen, autologous fat, and carbon bead technology).

Pharmacological Management

Managing UI via pharmacology can include detrusor overactivity with normal contractility (DO: relaxant medication such as anticholinergic, smooth muscle relaxant, combo anticholinergic/antimuscurinic, smooth muscle relaxant such as oxybutynin, muscurinic antagonist such as tolterodine, calcium channel blockers, and tricyclic antidepressants [TCAs]), detrusor hyperactivity with impaired contractility (DHIC: bladder relaxant medication in low doses, especially feasible if sphincter incompetence coexists); stress (TCAs, such as imipramine and doxepin, or α-adrenergic agonists, such as phenyl-propanolamine, pseudoephedrine, and estrogen, with progesterone if uterus present, and stopping angiotensin-converting enzyme [ACE] inhibitors if cough present), overflow/urethral obstruction (α-adrenergic antagonists, such as terazosin, prazosin, doxazosin, and 5α-reductase inhibitor, tamsulosin finasteride, antiandrogens, and/or luteinizing hormone-releasing factor [LHRH] analogues in nonsurgical candidates [in men] and estrogen [in women]), and overflow/underactive detrusor (α-adrenergic antagonist, bethanechol for side effects of certain unavoidable anticholinergic agents).

Surgical Management

Recently, there has been a shift from vaginal surgery, such as Kelly plication, anterior colporrhaphy, and needle urethropexy (Stamey, Raz, or modification of the Pereyra procedure), to suprapubic surgery (Burch colposuspension, Marshall–Marchetti–Krantz, or sling).

In men, some of the more common surgical procedures include transurethral resection of prostate (TURP) and radical prostatectomy for prostate cancer—perineal or abdominal approach; the abdominal approach includes nerve-sparing procedures that may decrease problems with erections and UI, artificial sphincters, and permanent urostomy.

A Systematic Approach to Management and Treatment

Following a detailed history and physical, including the measurement of a postvoid residual (PVR) and the collection of urine for analysis (UA with culture and sensitivity as indicated) and blood (evaluation of kidney function, hyperglycemia, and/or hypercalciuria), the following steps are recommended:

- Detrusor overactivity with normal contractility
  o Behavioral measures
  o Pharmacological measures

- Detrusor hyperactivity with impaired contractility
  o With normal bladder retention—behavioral measures with or without pharmacological therapy
  o With abnormal urinary retention—techniques to enhance urination such as the valsalva maneuver and "double voiding," pharmacological therapy, and catheterization (intermittent or permanent in treatment failure)

- Stress urinary incontinence
  o Behavioral measures
  o Pharmacological/Nonpharmacological measures
  o Surgery

- Urge/Overflow urinary incontinence
- Urethral obstruction
  o Kidney ultrasound (US)
  o Behavioral measures if hydronephrosis, abnormal urinary retention, recurrent urinary tract infections (UTIs), and gross hematuria are not present
  o Pharmacological measures
  o Surgery

- Overflow
  o Underactive detrusor
  o Catheterization (indwelling or intermittent) for several weeks followed by voiding trial
  o Pharmacological measures
  o Permanent catheterization (in the case of treatment failure)

Fecal Incontinence

Fecal incontinence (FI) is the involuntary loss of stool. It is not known exactly how many people have this condition, although one study found that 7.1% of the general population reported FI. In another study, it was found that the overall prevalence of FI was 18.4%.

In nursing homes, the incidence is estimated to be more than 50%. FI can result in social isolation and depression.

Evaluation of a patient with FI consists of a detailed medical history, physical examination that includes a digital rectal exam (DRE), and detailed questioning about the severity, duration, and frequency of the FI and whether it is associated with constipation or diarrhea. In chronic conditions, both stool samples and blood samples may be collected to evaluate infectious or endocrinological (hyperthyroid or hypercalcemic) etiologies for the diarrhea. Additional medical testing may include a flexible sigmoidoscopy or colonoscopy, anorectal manometry, assessment of rectal compliance and sensation, anorectal electromyography, anal endosonography and magnetic resonance imaging, and defecography.

Causes of FI can be categorized into three areas:

1. Anorectal disorders such as trauma, fistulas, rectal prolapse, internal hemorrhoids, neoplasms, and inflammatory and infectious disorders

2. Neurological disorders such as dementia, diabetes mellitus, stroke, neoplasms, and spinal cord injury or disease

3. Miscellaneous causes such as diarrhea, constipation, laxative abuse, and psychiatric illness

The two most common causes of FI are diarrhea and constipation with or without associated fecal impaction. It is important to clarify which of the preceding is present prior to initiating treatment so as to avoid aggravating the underlying cause. Both diarrhea and constipation can be transient or chronic. Chronic conditions must be further investigated to maximize disease stabilization and prevent disease progression.

Stopping medications that have contributed to the problem or beginning medications to alleviate the problem depends on the problems etiology. In the case of diarrhea, antidiarrheals may be initiated only after an infectious cause has been eliminated. Stool bulking agents via fiber supplements may be given, and a modified diet may be instituted.

In the extreme case of constipation with fecal impaction, a bowel regimen is initiated and the patient is strongly encouraged to develop a consistent and normal stooling pattern. A combination of stool softeners, irritant and osmotic laxatives, and a manual disimpaction of stool may be needed to initiate the process.

Individuals with neurological disorders may require toilet training. Some individuals may also benefit from biofeedback therapy. In patients with impaired cognition, prompted defecation is implemented.

Surgical options found to be beneficial include hemorrhoidectomy, repair of rectal prolapse, repair of anal sphincter defects, sphincteroplasty of native sphincter or creation of a new sphincter mechanism using graciloplasty, artificial sphincter implants, and colostomy (as a last resort).

—M. Rosina Finley, S. Liliana Oakes, Cynthia L. Stone, and David V. Espino

See also Infections, Bladder and Kidney; Kidney Aging and Diseases

Further Readings and References

Akhtar AJ, Padda M. Fecal incontinence in older patients. *J Am Med Dir Assoc.* 2005;6(1):54–60.

American Academy of Family Physicians. *Urinary Incontinence: Assessment and Management in Family Practice* [video]. Leawood, Kan: AAFP; 2002.

Jarvis GJ. Surgery for urinary incontinence. *Baillieres Clin Best Pract Res Obstet Gynaecol.* 2000;14:315–334.

Rao SS. Pathophysiology of adult fecal incontinence. *Gastroenterology.* 2004;126:S14–S22.

Resnick NM. Urinary incontinence. In: Cassel C, ed. *Geriatric Medicine: An Evidence-Based Approach.* 4th ed. New York: Springer; 2003:931–955.

Resnick NM. Urinary incontinence in the elderly. *Med Grand Rounds.* 1984;3:281–290.

INFECTIONS, BLADDER AND KIDNEY

The most common cause of bacterial infection in the elderly is urinary tract infection (UTI). However, it is important to distinguish between symptomatic infections and asymptomatic infections because the implications and treatment recommendations for these two entities are different.

Several conditions put older adults at increased risk for UTIs. First, postmenopausal women experience changes in the genitourinary mucosa due to the loss of estrogen that results in increased bacterial colonization of the vagina. Men experience prostatic hypertrophy that can cause obstruction and turbulent urine flow within the urethra. In addition, certain genitourinary abnormalities, such as prostate stones, urethral or ureteral strictures, bladder diverticula, and cystoceles, are more common in older adults. Patients with certain neurological diseases, such as Alzheimer's disease, Parkinson's disease, and cerebrovascular disease, may experience impaired bladder emptying and ureteral reflux. Furthermore, the use of both external and internal urinary catheters for the management of incontinence or obstruction in older adults increases the risk of UTI.

Patients with symptomatic UTIs may present with signs and symptoms of cystitis (urinary urgency, frequency, dysuria, suprapubic tenderness, and incontinence) or with signs and symptoms of pyelonephritis (fever and costovertebral angle tenderness, with or without signs and symptoms of cystitis). The diagnosis of symptomatic UTI in patients with functional impairment or in patients unable to communicate their symptoms is often difficult. In these patients, a diagnosis of UTI is probable if they exhibit a fever in addition to urinary retention or evidence of urinary tract obstruction. Also, a UTI should be considered in all patients with indwelling urinary catheters who develop fevers.

A urine culture is required for the definitive diagnosis of UTI. In individuals who are symptomatic, one culture with at least 10^5 colony-forming units per milliliter (CFU/ml) quantitative bacterial count (a measure of the degree of bacterial infection) is diagnostic. The diagnosis of UTI can be made by a urine culture with at least 10^4 CFU/ml quantitative bacterial count if the patient exhibits signs and symptoms of pyelonephritis (e.g., costovertebral angle tenderness). Also, a urine culture with at least 10^4 CFU/ml quantitative bacterial count in symptomatic men is considered diagnostic of a UTI. In patients who are chronically catheterized, a new catheter should be inserted prior to obtaining the urine specimen for culture because all patients with chronic urinary catheters are bacteriuric (i.e., have bacteria in the urine with or without actual infection of the person), often with more than one organism, and the urine culture will reflect the colonization of the catheter and not necessarily the causative agent of a UTI. In patients who are functionally impaired, an in-and-out catheterization might need to be obtained. A urine culture with at least 10^3 CFU/ml of a single organism on quantitative bacterial count in a patient whose urine specimen was obtained by in-and-out catheterization is diagnostic of a UTI.

Although asymptomatic bacteriuria is frequently present in elderly individuals, it has not been associated with any long-term adverse outcomes, and antimicrobial therapy is not indicated for patients with asymptomatic bacteriuria unless they are undergoing invasive genitourinary procedures. Importantly, pyuria (the presence of white blood cells in the urine) cannot differentiate asymptomatic bacteriuria from symptomatic bacteriuria. Only clinical symptoms can be used to make this distinction.

In patients with acute cystitis (acute bladder infection), trimethoprim-sulfamethoxazole and nitrofurantoin are appropriate first-line agents. Of note, ciprofloxacin is a better choice when local trimethoprim-sulfamethoxazole resistance rates in *Escherichia coli* are at least 20%. In patients with evidence of pyelonephritis, a fluoroquinolone or third-generation cephalosporin is appropriate empiric therapy. Pretreatment urine cultures are helpful in guiding antimicrobial therapy.

In women with cystitis, 3 to 7 days of antibiotic therapy is sufficient. In patients with pyelonephritis or in men with cystitis, 14 days of antimicrobial therapy is recommended. Furthermore, in men with relapsing infection (often due to prostatitis), 6 to 12 weeks of antimicrobial therapy is necessary. In patients with an indwelling catheter, 5 to 7 days of antimicrobial therapy is usually sufficient. Of note, the catheter should be replaced early in the treatment course because the biofilm (layer on the catheter with growing bacteria) that forms on urinary catheters is generally not eradicated with antimicrobial therapy. Furthermore, early catheter replacement is associated with an earlier resolution of fever and a decreased risk of relapse.

—*Vera Luther and Kevin P. High*

See also Incontinence; Institutional Care; Kidney Aging and Diseases; Long-Term Care

Further Readings and References

Hooton TM, Besser R, Foxman B, et al. Acute uncomplicated cystitis in an era of increasing antibiotic resistance: A proposed approach to empirical therapy. *Clin Infect Dis.* 2005;39:75–80.

Nicolle LE. Urinary tract infection. In: Yoshikawa TT, Ouslander JG, eds. *Infection Management for Geriatrics in Long-Term Care Facilities.* New York: Marcel Dekker; 2002:173–195.

Nicolle LE. Urinary tract infections in the elderly. In: Hazzard WR, Blass JP, Halter JB, et al., eds. *Principles of Geriatric Medicine and Gerontology.* 5th ed. New York: McGraw-Hill; 2003:1107–1116.

Nicolle LE, Bradley S, Colgan R, et al. IDSA guidelines the diagnosis and treatment of asymptomatic bacteriuria in adults. *Clin Infect Dis.* 2005;40:643–654.

INFECTIOUS DISEASES

Aged adults are more prone to infection and experience a higher rate of infection-associated morbidity and mortality than do their younger counterparts. Elderly persons have several risk factors that may predispose them to infection, including the presence of comorbid conditions, waning immunity, malnutrition, and environmental factors. In addition, aged persons may manifest illness differently from other adults, often with more subtle signs and symptoms. Therefore, the identification of illness and initiation of appropriate treatment may be delayed in these patients. Risk-factor modification should be instituted, if possible, to decrease morbidity and mortality in older adults.

The presence of comorbid medical conditions is the major risk factor that significantly predisposes elderly patients to infection. Examples of such conditions are immobility, cognitive decline, chronic obstructive pulmonary disease (COPD), diabetes mellitus, rheumatoid arthritis, and renal failure. Many of these comorbidities result in diminished innate immunity and a decrease in barriers to infection. For instance, patients with cognitive decline, patients with urinary incontinence, and immobile patients may have impaired skin integrity that increases their risk of skin and soft tissue infections. Also, patients with COPD have decreased mucociliary clearance and a suppressed cough mechanism that increases their risk of lower respiratory tract infections. Furthermore, patients with diabetes mellitus may have decreased lower extremity sensation due to a peripheral neuropathy or diminished lower extremity perfusion due to peripheral vascular disease. Thus, they are at increased risk for foot ulcers and osteomyelitis of the foot. In addition, patients with indwelling devices (e.g., prosthetic heart valves, pacemakers, prosthetic joints) are at a higher risk for infection.

In addition to specific comorbid illnesses, changes in aged adults' immune system (or immune senescence) may also predispose older adults to infection. Immune senescence is characterized by the simultaneous reduction in some aspects of innate immunity despite an up-regulation of basal levels of inflammation. For example, natural killer (NK) cell activity is reduced, but C-reactive protein and interleukin 6 (IL-6) levels are increased. In addition, there is a reduction in adaptive immune responses that is characterized by a decline in naive T-cell subsets as well as cytokine production. The clinical relevance of any of these changes in immune response with age remains uncertain.

Another risk factor for infection that affects many aging adults is malnutrition. Up to 60% of older adults admitted to the hospital suffer from protein–energy malnutrition that has been linked to delayed wound healing, decubitus ulcer formation, community-acquired pneumonia, and increased risk of nosocomial infection. In addition, older adults may have deficiencies of particular micronutrients, such as vitamins and minerals, that can affect their ability to mount vaccine responses or immune responses to infection. Although adequate nutrition should be encouraged and provided for older adults, clinical studies have not demonstrated conclusively which nutrients are most important. Overall, data support the use of protein/calorie supplementation in the hospital setting, daily trace mineral supplements (selenium and zinc) in long-term care, and perhaps a multivitamin/mineral supplement in community-dwelling older adults.

Environmental factors such as lower socioeconomic status and crowded living conditions (long-term care facilities) constitute another risk factor for infection in older adults. Residents living in close proximity to one another are at increased risk for respiratory infections such as those caused by the influenza virus. Because long-term care facilities are among the highest-use venues for antibiotics, these residents are also at risk for colonization with antibiotic-resistant organisms such as methicillin-resistant *Staphylococcus aureus* (MRSA) and vancomycin-resistant enterococci (VRE).

In addition to having multiple risk factors that increase the risk of infection-associated morbidity and mortality, it is important to note that aged persons may manifest illness differently from other adults and present with nonspecific symptoms such as mental status changes, decreased appetite, and exacerbation of underlying illnesses. Failure to recognize disease in older adults may significantly delay the initiation of appropriate therapy. Elderly persons also have lower mean baseline body temperatures than do their younger counterparts and may fail to reach body temperatures that are recognized as "fevers." For that reason, it has been suggested that fever in elderly adults be defined as (a) persistent elevation of body temperature at least 2° Fahrenheit (F) over baseline values, (b) oral temperatures of at least 99°F on repeated measures, or (c) rectal temperatures of at least 99.5°F on repeated measures.

When a disease entity is diagnosed in an older adult, appropriate antimicrobial therapy should be instituted. However, antibiotic management in the older adult deserves special attention because elderly patients are at increased risk for adverse drug reactions and metabolize drugs differently from young adults. Polypharmacy is common in elderly individuals, and care should be used when prescribing medications for older adults so that potential drug interactions can be avoided. For example, certain antibiotics may increase the toxicity of other drugs; for example, patients who are taking warfarin (a medication that prevents blood clots by "thinning the blood") will often have a supratherapeutic international normalized ratio (INR, where a test for the degree of blood thinning will show too much thinning) when antimicrobials are prescribed if there has not been a reduction in their warfarin dose). Older adults also experience physiological changes that may predispose them to adverse drug reactions. For example, elderly individuals have increased adipose tissue and decreased total body water, and these can cause an increase in the volume of distribution of certain medications. Elderly adults may also have a decreased

ability to eliminate certain drugs due to a reduction in renal function. Adjustment in medication dose is often necessary in the elderly to avoid potential drug toxicity, but this must be balanced against the need to dose concentration-dependent antibiotics (e.g., quinolones) at the upper limit of safe doses to achieve maximum efficacy and reduce the risk of resistance.

Preventive efforts to reduce the risk of infection in older adults include the administration of appropriate vaccines based on patients' ages, comorbid conditions, and risk. Specific diseases for which vaccination should be considered are influenza, pneumococcal disease, tetanus, and hepatitis. In addition, older adults who will be traveling abroad require a special evaluation for appropriate immunization.

Although the killed virus influenza vaccine is only moderately immunogenic, it has been shown to significantly reduce influenza-associated illness, secondary complications, hospitalizations, and death in older adults. The influenza vaccine is currently recommended for all patients over 50 years of age or with underlying medical illnesses. In addition, medical personnel, household contacts, and caregivers for the elderly should be immunized to prevent transmission of the virus to susceptible individuals.

The pneumococcal vaccine can help prevent fatal *Streptococcus pneumoniae* disease in the elderly. It is recommended for patients age 65 years and older as well as for patients under 65 years of age with comorbid conditions. Patients should receive a repeat vaccination if more than 5 years have elapsed since the first dose and the patients were younger than 65 years of age at the time of initial vaccination.

Aging adults are also at increased risk for tetanus, as evidenced by subprotective antibody levels in up to 60% of men and 70% of women over 50 years of age. Completion of a tetanus vaccine series should be done for patients who have uncertain histories or who have not received three doses. In addition, booster vaccines should be given to all adults at 10-year intervals or more frequently if the patients experience high-risk injuries.

The Hepatitis B vaccine should be considered in aged persons at increased risk for exposure to infected bodily fluids. For example, vaccination should be considered for those who volunteer at health care facilities where they may have contact with patients. Hepatitis A vaccination should be considered for persons who travel to areas where water or sanitary conditions are uncertain, for those with chronic Hepatitis C, and for men who have sex with men.

To increase the number of eligible patients who actually receive appropriate immunizations, the Centers for Disease Control and Prevention (CDC) and its Advisory Committee on Immunization Practices (ACIP) have outlined several strategies for improving vaccine administration:

1. *Age based:* where immunizations in all persons at 50 years of age are reviewed and those with qualifying comorbid conditions are vaccinated

2. *Organizational* (e.g., standing orders): where routine vaccinations are administered to elderly at-risk patients in office, nursing home, and hospital settings by a blanket order for all patients

3. *Community based:* public health promotions that focus on underserved populations

4. *Provider based:* physician reminder systems

Of these various strategies, standing orders have been shown to be the most effective.

Although vaccination may help reduce morbidity and mortality in aging persons, caution should be exercised in the use of the yellow fever vaccine in traveling older adults. Adults over 60 years of age are much more likely to experience serious adverse events (e.g., encephalitis, fever, hypotension, respiratory failure, lymphopenia, thrombocytopenia, renal failure) with this live virus vaccine than are their younger counterparts.

—*Vera Luther and Kevin P. High*

See also Age-Related Changes in Pharmacokinetics and Pharmacodynamics; Immune Function; Systemic Infections; Temperature Regulation; Wound Healing

Further Readings and References

Centers for Disease Control and Prevention. ACIP recommendations. Available at: www.cdc.gov/nip/publications/ACIP-list.htm. Accessed September 18, 2006.

Crossley KB, Peterson PK. Infections in the elderly. In: Mandell GL, Bennett JE, Dolin R, eds. *Principles and Practice of Infectious Diseases.* San Diego, Calif: Elsevier; 2005:3517–3524.

Faulkner CL, Cox HL, Williamson JC. Unique aspects of antimicrobial use in older adults. *Clin Infect Dis.* 2005;40:997–1004.

High KP, Loeb M. Infection in the elderly. In: Hazzard WR, Blass JP, Halter JB, et al., eds. *Principles of Geriatric Medicine and Gerontology.* 5th ed. New York: McGraw-Hill; 2003:1071–1081.

Yoshikawa TT, Ouslander JG, eds. *Infection Management for Geriatrics in Long-Term Care Facilities.* New York: Marcel Dekker; 2002.

INFORMAL CAREGIVING

See CAREGIVING

INJURY PREVENTION

Injury is classified as either unintentional or intentional. *Unintentional injury* occurs with no intentional human motivation (e.g., falls, traffic accidents), whereas *intentional injury* occurs as a result of discernible human motivation (e.g., suicide, assault). The vast majority of injury-related deaths are unintentional, but both types of deaths are preventable. In the United States, with a total of 39,311 deaths in 2001 of deaths in people age 65 years and older, those due to injury were 83.2% unintentional and 16.2% intentional (0.6% were of undetermined intention). Of unintentional injury deaths in older people, 29.6% were from falls, 18.5% from traffic-related events, 8.2% from suffocation, 2.9% from fire-related events, 1.8% from poisonings, and 1.0% from drownings. Of deaths from intentional injury, 13.7% were from suicide, 2.4% from homicide, and 0.1% from legal intervention or war.

Fall-related injuries requiring hospitalization are disproportionately high for institutionalized residents of nursing homes or other facilities when compared with those for community-dwelling older adults. Risk factors for falling may be intrinsic (characteristics of the person) or extrinsic (circumstances of the fall). Intrinsic risk factors include older age (> 80 years), female gender, sensory impairment, depressive mood, cognitive impairment, polypharmacy (five or more medications), neurological conditions (e.g., Parkinson's disease), gait disturbance, functional limitations, diabetes, urinary incontinence, and musculoskeletal problems (e.g., arthritis, foot problems). Extrinsic risk factors include environmental hazards inside or outside the home (e.g., poor lighting, floor obstacles, slippery terrain). The risk of falling increases with certain circumstances; for example, during the winter in regions where ice storms are more common.

To prevent falls, detection and modification of risk factors are essential tasks. To accomplish this, there are many potential interventions such as recommending exercise (e.g., Tai Chi, a form of Chinese martial arts that combines strength and balance training); instructing in home-based exercise focused on balance and strengthening; reducing or discontinuing psychotropic medications; modifying environmental hazards by installing handrails, grab bars, and night lights in homes or providing low-heeled shoes; correcting visual deficits; advising on the appropriate use of assistive devices; using bone-strengthening medications (e.g., calcium, Vitamin D, antiresorptive agents); and using hip protectors. An environmental assessment should review the home environment carefully given that most falls occur at home and many older adults spend most of their time at home. Small changes can go a long way toward preventing falls that could result in long hospital stays and declines in strength that eventually lead to disability.

Rates for motor vehicle-related injury are twice as high for older men than for older women. In the United States in 2001, deaths of older adults caused by motor vehicle traffic crashes were approximately three times higher for occupants (drivers or passengers) than for pedestrians. Age-related decreases in vision, hearing, and cognitive functions, as well as physical impairments, may affect not only older adults' driving ability but also older pedestrians' capacity to cross streets. Also, physical frailty increases susceptibility to injury in a crash. Thus, a crash that results in nonfatal injuries to a younger person might kill an older adult driver or passenger. Interventions could focus on improving the design of motor vehicles (making them easier to drive and providing better protection in the case of a crash), changing the environment to improve traffic

and pedestrian safety, and changing the behavior of older drivers, passengers, and pedestrians. For example, increasing the size and illumination of instrument panels and road signs would improve their nighttime readability. Intersections with timed crossings have been shown to be safer than those that do not provide cues of the length of time left to cross. Environmental alterations, such as installing median islands on wide roadways and longer walk signals, might help older pedestrians. A screening and testing program assessing drivers' functional and cognitive abilities could help older adults to gauge their own abilities and make decisions about their driving behavior. The American Automobile Association (AAA) has developed a "Lifelong Safe Mobility" campaign that includes driver screening tools as well as other safety features.

In 2001, 5,393 Americans over 65 years of age committed suicide. Of those, most (85%) were men, and most (73%) used firearms to kill themselves. Risk factors for suicide include a previous suicide attempt(s), a history of mental disorders (particularly depression), a history of alcohol and substance abuse, a family history of suicide, feelings of hopelessness, loss (relational, social, work, or financial), physical illness, isolation, a feeling of being cut off from other people, and easy access to lethal methods. Protective factors for suicide include easy access to a variety of clinical interventions and support for help seeking, family and community support, and cultural and religious beliefs that discourage suicide and support self-preservation instincts. The high rate of suicide in the elderly can be reduced through continued maintenance of emotional supports (spending time with family and friends) and seeking help when signs of depression are noted (including sadness, anxiety, guilt, anger, mood swings, lack of emotional responsiveness, helplessness, hopelessness, chronic fatigue or lack of energy, sleeping too much or too little, loss of sexual desire, and unexplained aches and pains).

Other causes of injury relevant in older adults are suffocation and fire-related events. Unintentional suffocation includes choking or respiratory blockage due to inhalation or ingestion of food or objects or mechanical air obstruction. Suffocation deaths among older adults may be due to problems in chewing and swallowing foods, or swallowing in general, possibly as a consequence of illness or disability. In addition, older people who live alone might not be able to get the help they need when they do choke. In adults, choking can often be prevented if the following precautionary measures are taken: cutting food into small pieces; chewing food slowly and thoroughly, especially if wearing dentures; avoiding laughing and talking while chewing and swallowing; and avoiding excessive intake of alcohol before and during meals.

Persons age 65 years and older are also at increased risk for fire-related injuries and deaths. They are especially vulnerable if they are poor, live alone, are currently smokers or alcohol abusers, live in manufactured homes or substandard housing or in rural areas, or live in homes without smoke alarms, fire extinguishers, or carbon monoxide detectors. Cooking is the primary cause of residential fires; most victims of fires die from inhalation of smoke or toxic gases and not from burns. To prevent injuries, detection and modification of some risk factors would help; for example, providing and checking smoke alarms and fire extinguishers at least annually. When cooking, older adults should never leave the stove unattended and should wear tight-fitting clothing. They should not wash electric blankets repeatedly because this can damage their electrical circuitry. They should never smoke in bed or near a gas stove or oxygen supply. At least 3 feet of space should be provided around space heaters, and older adults should have their home heating system checked annually. By practicing a few simple fire safety tips, older adults can reduce their chances of experiencing a fire and subsequent injury or death.

—Carlos A. Reyes-Ortiz

See also Depression and Other Mood Disorders; Disability and the Disablement Process; Fractures in Older Adults; Health Promotion and Disease Prevention; Mobility; Mobility Assessment; Obesity

Further Readings and References

AAA Foundation for Traffic Safety. Senior driver website. Available at: www.seniordrivers.org. Accessed August 18, 2005.

Anderson RN, Minino AM, Fingerhut LA, Warner M, Heinen MA. *Deaths: Injuries, 2001.* Hyattsville, Md: National Center for Health Statistics; 2001. National Vital Statistics Reports, Vol. 52, No. 21.

Centers for Disease Control and Prevention/National Center for Injury Prevention and Control. Falls and hip fractures among older adults. Available at: www.cdc.gov/ncipc/factsheets/falls.htm. Accessed August 9, 2005.

Centers for Disease Control and Prevention/National Center for Injury Prevention and Control. Suicide: Fact sheet. Available at: www.cdc.gov/ncipc/factsheets/suifacts.htm. Accessed August 18, 2005.

Federal Emergency Management Administration. Fire risks for older adults. Available at: www.usfa.fema.gov/downloads/pdf/publications/older.pdf. Accessed August 17, 2005.

INSTITUTIONAL CARE

Long-term care of older persons in the United States is provided in either institutional or community-based residential settings. Institutional long-term care settings include primarily nursing facilities. Community-based residential long-term care settings include care provided in someone's home and group shelter and care residences such as assisted-living facilities. Most long-term care now occurs in community-based residences rather than in nursing facilities.

Nursing facilities and assisted-living facilities have several similarities. Any resident of a long-term care setting has some degree of physical and/or cognitive disability that prevents the resident from attending to many of his or her own daily functions. These functions are known as activities of daily living (ADLs), including getting out of bed, bathing, dressing, toileting, walking across a small room, and eating, and instrumental activities of daily living (IADLs), including taking medicines, driving, preparing meals, doing laundry, and managing finances. Residents of both settings may receive services from multiple providers (e.g., physicians, nurses, social workers, physical therapists, nursing aides and assistants). The multidisciplinary team attempts to assist long-term care residents in reducing the impact of their functional limitations.

The distinction between the two settings lies in the amount of supportive care required by their constituents and the physical structure or environment in which that support is provided. Each setting is staffed to deliver varying aspects of care at differing levels of intensity. Nursing facilities are equipped to meet all of the functional needs of individuals who cannot live independently and who do not have the functional support they require to continue living in their own homes or with their families. Nursing facilities provide functional support while delivering a higher level of continuous nursing care 24 hours per day. The goal of nursing facility care is to restore or preserve the highest attainable level of independence for each resident. Care in nursing facilities also aims to prevent disease progression in their chronically ill populations and to treat the acute complications and illnesses that arise.

The nursing facility culture in the United States is highly institutionalized. Regulations and safety standards set by the federal and state governments, along with physicians' and nurses' orders, guarantee rigorous oversight of residents' environment, activities, and bodily functions. To comply with regulations and safety standards, nursing facilities impose rules and a certain amount of control over residents' personal space. Most residents live in rooms shared with one other person, further compromising personal space and privacy.

Although variable in the amount and intensity of nursing and supportive services they offer, assisted-living facilities generally provide less health-related services, such as meals, housekeeping, and assistance with getting dressed, to a constituency that is not as functionally impaired as are residents of nursing facilities. Assisted-living residents generally live in their own apartments, or residences, within a building that has a nurse on-site for some amount of time during the day. Regulation of assisted-living settings is less uniform and is applied with less rigor and punitive oversight than nursing facilities face. Although not as institutional as nursing facilities, assisted-living facilities usually impose some rules on the use of residential space. Also, assisted-living staff are involved with some aspects of every resident's daily routine. Albeit

less formal, observation and monitoring of residents' activities do occur. The remainder of this entry focuses on institutional care in nursing facilities.

Trends in Use of Nursing Facilities

The 1999 National Nursing Home Survey of all U.S. nursing facilities estimated that a total of 1,628,300 residents occupied 1,879,600 available beds in 18,000 existing nursing facilities in the United States for an occupancy rate of approximately 87%. The number of nursing facility beds exceeds the number of acute care beds in the United States. The survey recorded 2.5 million discharges for a rate of 134 discharges per 100 beds over a 6-month period. The average number of beds per facility was approximately 105. In 1999, 67% of nursing facilities were for-profit, whereas 27% were owned by not-for-profit organizations. Nearly 40% of nursing facilities were independently owned, whereas 60% belonged to a chain of nursing facilities. Geographically, the southern and midwest regions of the country accounted for two thirds of all nursing facilities. In 1999, 61% of nursing facilities were located in metropolitan areas.

Nearly 17,500 nursing facilities (97%) were certified by Medicare, Medicaid, or both in 1999. Facilities with Medicare and/or Medicaid certification demonstrated compliance with federal requirements to receive payment for Medicare- or Medicaid-funded care. The number of Medicare- and/or Medicaid-certified nursing facilities dropped by nearly 1,000, to a total of 16,489 facilities, from 1999 to 2004. Despite the decline in available nursing facility beds, the occupancy rate among certified beds declined from 87% in 1999 to 84% in 2004. The steepest declines occurred among for-profit facilities and facilities with fewer than 50 beds.

Characteristics of Nursing Facility Residents

More than 25% of all U.S. residents over 25 years of age will experience at least one nursing facility stay in their lifetimes. People reside in nursing facilities either on a short-term basis (< 6 months) or on a long-term basis (6 months to years). Short-stay residents are admitted to nursing facilities specifically to receive short-term rehabilitation, end of life care, or care either for a medically unstable condition or for a prolonged but subacute illness that does not warrant hospitalization. Rehabilitation stays and care for a medically unstable condition are considered as skilled levels of care. Long-stay residents are admitted to nursing facilities because they have significant cognitive and/or physical impairments and need long-term supervision or assistance with daily functions.

The overall average length of stay for current nursing facility residents in 1999 was 892 days. Most current residents were transferred to the nursing facilities after hospital stays (46%) or from private or semiprivate living situations (30%). The average length of stay for residents who were discharged in 1999 was 272 days, with 68% of those discharged staying less than 3 months. Discharged residents had recovered or were stabilized and returned to more independent settings, were transferred to other nursing facilities or to acute care or hospital settings, or were deceased.

In 2004, more than 90% (1.5 million) nursing facility residents were age 65 years and older. Of all people age 65 years and older in the United States that year, more than 7% experienced a nursing facility stay; of all people age 85 years and older, more than 25% experienced a nursing facility stay. Trend observers expect these numbers to grow. In 2004, most residents were either between 75 and 84 years of age (35.1%) or between 85 and 94 years of age (31.6%); the remainder were 65 to 74 years of age (15.1%) or age 95 years and older (5.2%). Between 1999 and 2004, the percentage of female residents declined by approximately 1.5% to 67%. Diversity of racial backgrounds increased slightly between 1999 and 2004. In the latter year, 10.9% of residents were non-Hispanic Blacks and 3.6% were Hispanics. Less than 2% were Asians/Pacific Islanders or Alaskans/ Native Americans. The remaining 83.8% of residents were non-Hispanic Whites.

Most nursing facility residents appear to have both some degree of cognitive impairment and some loss of physical function. From 2000 to 2004, the number of residents who did not require any help with their daily functions declined somewhat. Two thirds of residents required help with at least one activity of daily living, most commonly bathing, and 40% required help with most or all activities of daily living. Approximately half of residents required help with toileting. More than 50% of residents could walk, either on their own or with an assistive device, and 6% of the nursing facility population spent at least 22 hours per day in bed or in a reclining chair. Fully 70% of residents demonstrated some degree of cognitive impairment, with 26% being very mildly or mildly cognitively impaired and more than 30% demonstrating moderate or moderately severe impairment.

In 1999, the top five primary diagnoses at admission were diseases of the circulatory system (23%), mental disorders (17%), diseases of the nervous system (15%), injury and poisoning (7.3%), and endocrine diseases (7%). Approximately 46% of nursing facility residents took 6 to 10 medications on a daily basis, and nearly 25% took 11 or more, suggesting that most residents may have been treated for multiple chronic medical conditions. On average, 20% to 25% of residents received antipsychotic medications and more than 40% received antidepressants.

Increasingly, nursing facilities have become places to die, and 23% of all deaths in the United States in 2001 occurred in nursing facilities. Projections from 1997 on remaining lifetime use on admission to a nursing facility between 70 and 80 years of age reached 2.6 years. Expected remaining lifetime nursing facility use on admission at 85 years of age was 2.5 years.

Institutional Care Economics

Nursing facility expenditures topped $110 billion in 2003, up from $87 billion in 1998. The average annual cost of nursing facility care exceeded $57,000 per person. The average daily rate in 2003 amounted to $158.26 for a semiprivate room. Medicaid paid 46% and out-of-pocket payments accounted for 28% of all nursing home expenditures. Medicare contributed 12%, representing 7% of Medicare's annual budget. Private insurance and other public insurance paid for the remainder.

Nursing facility beds are generally considered either skilled or nonskilled. Residents receiving skilled care consume more services (e.g., physical therapy, occupational therapy, intravenous medication, wound care) than do residents receiving custodial nonskilled care (e.g., assistance with activities of daily living). Therefore, nursing facilities receive a higher reimbursement for occupants of skilled beds than for occupants of nonskilled beds.

Medicare pays only for the skilled and rehabilitation care of its qualifying beneficiaries; it does not pay for long-term custodial care. Medicare requires a minimum of 3 nights of hospitalization for its beneficiaries to qualify for coverage of a skilled or rehabilitation nursing facility stay. In 1997, Medicare switched to a prospective payment system. It paid, and continues to pay, a predetermined inclusive daily rate for skilled stays for up to 100 allowable days. The predetermined reimbursement rate schedule is based on the amount and duration of services that a resident with skilled needs is expected to consume. The daily rate includes room, board, staff, and skilled services. Similarly, nursing facilities charge a single but inclusive daily rate for long-term custodial care.

Medicaid, a state and federal program, traditionally has paid the bulk of nursing facility expenditures. Medicaid pays the nursing facility only costs for eligible people with limited income and assets. To become eligible for Medicaid, most long-stay nursing facility residents must pay nursing facility costs out-of-pocket until their savings and other resources are spent.

Institutional Care Staffing

The nursing home administrator, the director of nursing, and the medical director share the leadership roles of each nursing facility. The nursing home administrator oversees the daily operation of the facility. The director of nursing supervises all nursing staff and nursing activities. The medical director oversees the delivery of medical care to the nursing facility resident population by the physicians who have privileges to see patients at the facility. The director of nursing and the medical director report to the nursing home administrator. The nursing home administrator

and the director of nursing are employed full-time by the nursing facility. The medical director is not a nursing facility employee; he or she fulfills a contractual obligation and serves at the will of the board of the nursing facility.

Registered nurses (RNs), licensed practical nurses (LPNs), and nursing assistants represent the bulk of the nursing facility workforce. Staff ratios in 2002 averaged one RN per 50 beds and one LPN per 25 to 30 beds. Nurses performed duties requiring higher levels of skill and responsibility, including wound care, medication administration, and documentation. In 2002, RNs and LPNs spent an average of 1 hour per patient-day. Nursing assistants performed nearly all custodial care, spending an average of 2 hours per patient-day.

In 2003, the nursing workforce topped 1.9 million individuals across all long-term care settings. Turnover rates in nursing facilities remained high in 2002—49% among RNs and LPNs and 71% among nursing assistants. Nearly 100,000 nursing staff vacancies were reported in the nursing facility setting in 2002. Overall, nursing facility staff receive less compensation than do their hospital-based colleagues. In 2002, RNs in nursing facilities earned an average of $16.64 per hour and LPNs earned an average of $11.90 per hour. Nursing assistants, who are generally much less educated (and for whom English often is not their first language), earned an average of $7.45 per hour.

Quality of Care

Since the enactment of the Omnibus Budget Reconciliation Act of 1987, the federal government has launched a number of measures to improve the quality of care in nursing facilities. These initiatives established training requirements for staff, fortified residents' rights, implemented standards of care, and achieved major goals of limiting the use of restraints and psychoactive medications in this vulnerable population. The federal government also set standards for resident safety and quality of life. Every Medicare- and Medicaid-certified nursing facility needed to demonstrate compliance with requirements in the following areas: residents' rights, quality of life, routine resident assessments, development of care plans, dietary and nutrition services, environmental safety, infection control, pharmacy services, and medical and nursing care. Federal and state governments coordinated inspections of nursing facilities for compliance every 9 to 16 months. Nursing facility quality and performance are now publicly reported in terms of certain outcomes or measures such as the prevalence of pressure sores, weight loss, and incontinence. Information on deficiencies cited in routine surveys and inspections is publicly reported as well. Information on all Medicare- and Medicaid-certified nursing facilities is available to consumers on Medicare's website (www.medicare .gov/NHCompare).

—*Rollin M. Wright*

See also Health Care System for Older Adults; Long-Term Care; Long-Term Care Insurance; Medicaid; Medicare

Further Readings and References

Centers for Medicare and Medicaid Services. Nursing homes. Available at: www.cms.hhs.gov/Certificationand Complianc/12_NHs.asp. Accessed September 18, 2006.

Dollard KJ, for American Health Care Association. Facts and trends: The nursing facility sourcebook 2001. Available at: www.ahca.org/research/nfbook.htm. Accessed September 18, 2006.

Jones A, for National Center for Health Statistics. The National Nursing Home Survey: 1999 summary. Available at: www.cdc.gov/nchs/data/series/sr_13/sr13_152.pdf. Accessed September 18, 2006.

National Commission on Nursing Workforce for Long-Term Care. Act now for your tomorrow. Available at: www.ahca.org/research/workforce_rpt_050519.pdf. Accessed September 18, 2006.

Ouslander JG, Weinberg AD. Institutional long-term care services in the USA. In: Tallis RC, Fillit HM, eds. *Brocklehurst's Textbook of Geriatric Medicine and Gerontology.* London: Elsevier Science; 2003: 1469–1475.

Teno J, for Center for Gerontology and Health Care Research. Facts on dying: Policy relevant data on care at the end of life. Available at: www.chcr.brown.edu/dying/ 2001data.htm. Accessed September 18, 2006.

INSTRUMENTS

The average number of health conditions is 5.6 for a person age 70 years and older. With that in mind, it is important to conduct a complete clinical assessment as a guide to the care and management of senior patients. In addition to concurrent diagnoses, geriatric syndromes (conditions that are influenced by many factors) such as pain, dementia, and falls are considerations for the clinician. Issues of caregiver support, financial concerns, multiple medications, and psychosocial health all are cause for comprehensive assessment techniques. This entry discusses comprehensive geriatric assessment (CGA) techniques specific to outpatient seniors. Methods of rapid assessment in the outpatient setting, clinical intervention, and techniques to tailor the geriatric assessment to specific clinical settings are addressed.

Definition of Comprehensive Geriatric Assessment

The term *comprehensive* generally refers to looking beyond the elements assessed in a generic history and physical examination to the domains of functional, emotional, and psychosocial support. Evaluating issues that might not be readily apparent is a primary function of CGA. The CGA provides a clinician with insight into how a person exists in the community outside the walls of an examination room.

A CGA can provide health assessment data that provides a clinician with a baseline view of a patient's condition at the time of initial visit. In the area of oncology, CGA is used to understand the extent of comorbidities so as to determine how a senior patient may undergo and tolerate cancer treatment. A CGA to assess various patient demographics can be developed. For example, a CGA used in a long-term care environment may consist of more self-care activities, skin integrity, and dementia, whereas a CGA used predominantly among community-dwelling seniors may focus more on exercise tolerance and driving. A CGA can be tailored to any type of patient population depending on the general needs. When developing a CGA, it is important for a clinical site that valid and reliable clinical and research measures be used so that data can be compared with those from other sites or patient populations.

The Evolution of Geriatric Assessment

In 1973, the CGA was frequently used for determining which patients would benefit from nursing home placement. During the late 1970s, the CGA was shown to enhance diagnostic accuracy in potentially treatable conditions. This was an important finding for advancement in the care of older patients because it showed that more comprehensive assessment data were necessary to understand the heath care needs of older persons. Not long after this time, geriatric assessment instruments began to become used more readily in clinical practice. Many of the instruments were very comprehensive in that they were rather time-consuming to administer and included many domains contributing to the health and social support of older patients.

Increased emergence of inpatient geriatric assessments units during the 1980s offered care to many seniors who were hospitalized. Most geriatric assessment units were affiliated with Veterans Administration medical centers or medical schools. In 1983, two thirds of the physicians associated with the units had no formal training in geriatrics. Most of the units offered care on an outpatient basis; however, it was noted that the units consumed substantial resources both in the time required to conduct the assessments and in the health care professionals needed to offer interdisciplinary care. Interdisciplinary geriatrics care can be very expensive, and it has been shown that when facilities experience financial difficulties, geriatric assessment units are often discontinued.

Benefits of Conducting the Comprehensive Geriatric Assessment

Although it has been stated that conducting a CGA requires a great deal of time and effort, there are many benefits that have been shown in the literature. Data retrieved as part of the CGA (for both inpatient and outpatient care) have been associated with a reduction in nursing home placement, decreased number of medications, decreased hospitalization costs, and prolonged survival. CGA has been shown to detect multiple problems when used with breast cancer patients and in general practice. General geriatric outpatient seniors who underwent a CGA and related care have been shown to have less functional decline than have those who did not receive the assessment and related treatment. A CGA can be administered on a regular basis to assess treatment status, determine disease progression, and consider fluctuations in health and wellness of the older person.

One of the biggest drawbacks to conducting a CGA is the length of time required to conduct an interdisciplinary evaluation. For a busy outpatient clinic, several hours to conduct a CGA is unrealistic, especially when several disciplines may be required to evaluate the patient. Although much of the literature suggests that CGA should consider domains of functional, social, emotional, cognitive, spiritual, and physical functioning, it is very difficult to assess all of those domains effectively in one initial clinical visit. One consideration is to perform rapid assessment techniques to conduct a CGA.

Rapid Assessment Techniques in Outpatient Geriatric Assessment

Rapid assessment techniques refer to options that shorten or accelerate the evaluation process. Several of the instruments often included in the CGA, such as the Geriatric Depression Scale (GDS) and the Mini-Mental State Examination (MMSE), have been abbreviated and shown to be valid and reliable in their shortened forms. The first five items of the GDS have been shown to be predictive of the total score. This can reduce the assessment time required for the full screening information. The MMSE has also been abbreviated to several items predictive of the total score.

Another option to expedite the CGA process is to send the instrument to the patient prior to his or her initial clinic visit. Self-administered assessment instruments can be returned by the patient at the clinical visit and can be reliable. Phone administration is also an option for several of the commonly used CGA instruments. Both the activities of daily living (ADLs) and the GDS have been shown to be valid and reliable when administered via the telephone. Another prescreening measure is the abbreviated CGA (aCGA). The aCGA considers three domains: depression as measured by the GDS, cognition as measured by the MMSE, and functional status as measured by ADLs and the instrumental activities of daily living (IADLs).

Another option is to use prescreening instruments to target those seniors who may benefit from the entire CGA. Simply looking at a patient does not reveal the extent to which he or she may have limitations and require help. Some seniors may appear to be very independent, but when they are assessed, actual and potential limitations may surface. Clinical prescreening is a process in which a shortened version of an assessment is conducted to gain insight into the health status of a senior patient and to determine whether further screening is necessary. Prescreening has been used in the area of mammogram procedures and cervical cancer detection to help target more specialized screening to those with the greatest need. Prescreening techniques have also been used to target those seniors who are at risk and may require a community-based care program. Prescreening instruments allow the clinician to conduct a multifaceted assessment, as used in CGA, in a reduced amount of time. Those seniors who screen positive on the prescreening tool would then be screened with the entire CGA.

When Screening Reveals Limitations in the Senior Patient

If screening in a particular domain, such as depression or cognition, indicate deficits, it is crucial to intervene in some manner. Intervention may consider continued diagnostics, potential referrals, various medical and nursing interventions, and other elements that can enhance the quality of life and well-being of a senior patient. Despite the conduction of a CGA and development of appropriate interventions, the best efforts

are wasted if the patient does not adhere, at least to some extent, to the plan provided by the health care team.

Several factors generally increase the likelihood of adherence to recommendations prescribed by a senior health care team. First, community providers generally favor letters from the consulting institutions with specific assessment data and recommendations along with provider-to-provider communication by telephone. In addition, if patients agree and are party to the recommendations, adherence is more likely. Patients are less likely to comply with, or adhere to, the treatment plan in cases where a large number of recommendations were developed and there is inadequate caregiver support.

The Future of CGA

Although this entry has defined and operationalized CGA, a great deal of further research is needed. Questions remain as to when a CGA should be repeated in chronically ill seniors and in general assessments of community-dwelling elderly persons. Methods of CGA data collection are being used online for patients to complete prior to clinical visits. More commonly, performance test evaluations are being added to the self-report measures that often make up the CGA. The assessment instruments that encompass the CGA are dynamic in that the needs of senior populations change and perhaps alternative assessments may become necessary. Frequent CGA refinement must be completed to meet the needs of senior health care concerns.

—*Janine Overcash*

See also Geriatric Assessment; Geriatric Profession; Geriatric Team Care; Mobility Assessment; Polypharmacy

Further Readings and References

Cefalu CA, Kaslow LD, Mims B, Simpson S. Follow-up of comprehensive geriatric assessment in a family medicine residency clinic. *J Am Board Fam Med.* 1995;8:337–340.

Frank E. Enhancing patient outcomes: Treatment adherence. *J Clin Psychiatry.* 1997;58(Suppl. 1):11–14.

Fried L, Storer D, King DE, Lodder F. Diagnosis of illness presentation in the elderly. *J Am Geriatr Soc.* 1991; 39:117–123.

Maly RC, Hirsch SH, Reuben DB. The performance of simple instruments in detecting geriatric conditions and selecting community-dwelling older people for geriatric assessment. *Age Ageing.* 1997;26:223–231.

Mann E, Koller M, Mann C, van der Cammen T, Steurer J. Comprehensive geriatric assessment (CGA) in general practice: Results from a pilot study in Vorarlberg, Austria. *BMC Geriatr.* 2004;4:4.

Stuck AE, Elkuch P, Dapp U, Anders J, Iiffe S, Swift CG. Feasibility and yield of a self-administered questionnaire for health risk appraisal in older people in three European countries. *Age Ageing.* 2002;31:463–467.

KIDNEY AGING AND DISEASES

Human kidney function declines with age, reflecting both normal processes and the cumulative impact of comorbid diseases such as hypertension and diabetes. It is crucial to recognize the decline in kidney function in older adults because poor kidney function compromises drug metabolism and may lead to kidney failure. On average, a single human kidney reaches its maximum size during the fourth decade of life. Kidney mass declines by approximately 10% per decade thereafter, with the major decline in mass localized to the cortical or outer layer of the kidney. Normal aging processes play a role in diabetic and hypertensive kidney disease; however, these changes occur at a faster rate in patients with these conditions.

Progressive arteriole hyalinosis, tubulointerstitial fibrosis, and glomerulosclerosis reduce the mass of an aging kidney. Several important vascular changes occur in the aging kidney where the arterioles of the kidney undergo sclerotic changes. Although these changes are seen in individuals with normal blood pressure, they are worse in hypertensive individuals. Often, the arteriolar changes are seen in association with glomerulosclerosis in the outer part of the kidney. The aging kidney also develops evidence of injury to the tubules. The tubule is the portion of the nephron located distal to the glomerulus and proximal to the collecting ducts. Tubular damage is concentrated in the outer medulla and the medullary rays, the

part of the kidney most dependent on capillary blood flow. The interstitium or matrix portion of this region may have a high concentration of invading monocytes and macrophages, reflecting inflammatory processes and subsequent decline in kidney function. Transforming growth factor-β (TGF-B), an inflammation-activating factor, is prevalent in this area of the kidney. In addition to vascular and tubular changes, the kidney develops glomerulosclerosis, or "scarring," of the glomerular capillary bed at the beginning of the nephron. Glomerulosclerosis is a prominent anatomical change seen with the aging kidney. Although glomerulosclerosis is a rare finding in younger individuals, it becomes more common with age. Studies show that less than 5% of glomeruli are sclerotic in individuals under 40 years of age. The percentage of sclerotic glomeruli increases to between 10% and 30% by 70 years of age.

Although a number of experimental approaches have been used to study the anatomical changes associated with aging, the most valuable has been the "remnant kidney model" that involves the removal of one kidney and a large fraction of the other kidney from an animal test subject. Using this approach, the influence of reduced nephron mass has been studied. The increase in kidney intracapillary pressure seen in the remnant kidney model sets in motion a cascade of events also seen in normal bilateral aging kidneys. There is an immediate increase in RNA synthesis, followed by an increase in DNA synthesis. Mesangial cells multiply, epithelial cells hypertrophy, epithelial foot processes increase in number, and glomerular capillary length increases. Growth factors increase in activity, although the primary events and the exact cellular mechanisms are not fully understood. Growth factors such as angiotensin II (AII) and TGF-B have been proposed as primary mediators of the anatomical and cellular changes seen. As more nephrons are lost to this process, the remaining nephrons compensate. Compensation leads to hypertrophy, which in turn leads to increased damage and sclerosis.

Reactive oxygen products (ROIs), advanced glycosylated end products (AGEs), and lipids—all products of cellular metabolism—play a role in the loss of kidney function. Experiments show that rats given antioxidant substances show less glomerulosclerosis later in life. Furthermore, studies show that treatment of experimental animals with aminoguanidine, a substance known to inhibit AGE formation, decreases proteinuria, glomerulosclerosis, and age-related hardening of arteries. 3-Hydroxy-3-methylglutaryl coenzyme A (HMG-CoA) reductase inhibitors, or "statins," given to diabetically induced rats show that lowering serum cholesterol leads to reduced proteinuria and less glomerulosclerosis. Although high blood pressure, diabetes, and high cholesterol all could damage the kidneys, none of these conditions is absolutely necessary for the kidneys to show anatomical changes and functional decline associated with aging.

In clinical practice, the serum creatinine and blood urea nitrogen (BUN) concentrations are commonly used as indicators of glomerular filtration rate (GFR); that is, the filtration capacity of the kidneys. Although laboratory measurements of creatinine and urea are accurate and reliable, it is important to keep in mind certain factors when using these markers. Because creatinine is a by-product of muscle metabolism, variations in muscle mass and changes in lean body weight influence the serum creatinine level. For example, an unchanging serum creatinine concentration may reflect proportional decrements in kidney function and muscle mass. As muscle mass decreases with age, the aging kidney has less creatinine to clear and might not "appear" to be less effective. This is why serum creatinine levels remain relatively stable with advancing age; the gradual senescence of nephrons and slowly decreasing GFR are partially counterbalanced by declining muscle mass.

It is also important to keep in mind the semilogarithmic relationship between the serum creatinine concentration and kidney function. At a normal GFR, a relatively large and abrupt decrease in GFR will result in a relatively small change in the serum creatinine concentration. For example, a 50% reduction in GFR in a small older woman will increase the serum creatinine concentration from 0.5 milligrams per deciliter (mg/dl) to 1.0 mg/dl. The latter is a normal serum creatinine concentration in most labs, but it would be erroneous to interpret this value as reflecting a normal GFR. This could be especially catastrophic if therapy were delayed. If one waits until the serum creatinine is "grossly" elevated (2.0 mg/dl)—representing more than 75% reduction from the baseline GFR—irreversible changes may already have occurred.

This limitation of serum creatinine in accurately reflecting kidney function has led to a search for alternative markers. Cystatin C has been shown to be a reliable marker of diminished kidney function in older adults. Cystatin C is found in all cells and therefore is not linked to muscle mass alone. Because the role of Cystatin C measurement in clinical practice remains unclear, the National Kidney Foundation recommends using a prediction formula to screen for decreased kidney function. Prediction equations using age, sex, and race along with serum creatinine are highly practical in determining kidney function in the elderly. The use of these equations requires only the input of demographic factors and may be computed using the Internet or a personal digital assistant (PDA).

Alterations in liver function, body fluid content, multiple medications, and declining kidney function all can result in altered drug metabolism. Diminished renal function can have profound effects on the clearance of water-soluble drugs. The effect will be more dramatic if the relative water concentration of the body is reduced or if polypharmacy is involved. Both polypharmacy and reduced water concentration are common in elderly individuals. In simple terms, water-soluble drugs will reach higher peak levels and have longer half-lives in old people with diminished renal function. This can lead to an increased risk of developing unwanted drug side effects or complications.

Certain drugs may exacerbate the problems that an aging kidney is facing while trying to maintain homeostasis. Nonsteroidal anti-inflammatory drugs (NSAIDs) may increase intraglomerular pressure by blocking prostaglandin production. Prostaglandins counteract the effects of AII on the renal vasculature. Loss of prostaglandins may lead to unbalanced hemodynamics in the kidney, favoring AII-mediated vasoconstriction. Diuretics may further inhibit an aged kidney's ability to preserve water in the face of water deprivation. Angiotensin-converting enzyme (ACE) inhibitors, a common and effective blood pressure medication that is thought to be "kidney protective," may increase the risk of acute renal failure by limiting the renal system's ability to autoregulate blood pressure during periods of stress.

Several inflammatory kidney diseases and renal artery stenosis are common in older adults. Minimal change disease, usually associated with children, has a second peak in incidence during the firth and sixth decades of life. There is a second peak in incidence of poststreptococcal glomerulonephritis seen in the elderly. Pauci-immune necrotizing glomerulonephritis is also common among those individuals age 65 years and older. Renovascular disease, a term used to describe arterial sclerosis in the kidney, is common in the older population. Another common renal disorder found in the elderly is renal artery stenosis (RAS), a narrowing of the renal arteries that can lead to significant hypertension and kidney failure. To diagnose RAS, one may use magnetic resonance angiography (MRA), renal ultrasound with Doppler, or the captopril renogram. The treatment of RAS depends on the severity of the lesion and the clinical presentation. Treatment options for RAS include renal angioplasty and stenting, renal bypass surgery, and medical management. Treatment of RAS remains controversial, with some data supporting conservative medical management.

Treatment of kidney failure in the older population is similar to that available to younger patients. Options include hemodialysis, peritoneal dialysis, kidney transplantation, and symptomatic medical management. The mean age at onset of dialysis in the United States is now 63 years, and similar demographics are seen in Europe and Canada. Age alone is no longer thought to be an excluding factor in determining whether or not a person receives renal replacement therapy. Hemodialysis patients in their 80s have shown a preserved quality of life. Older patients with kidney failure seem to do equally well on either hemodialysis or peritoneal dialysis unless a comorbid condition such as cardiovascular disease is present. Recent data show that more people over 65 years of age are receiving kidney transplants. However, as compared with individuals under 65 years of age with end-stage renal disease (ESRD), older patients receive fewer transplants. This is because of the increased prevalence of comorbid conditions such as advanced cardiovascular disease and cancer—diseases that prevent eligibility for transplantation.

It is difficult to convey the changes in lifestyle and symptom severity that will be experienced by an older patient starting renal replacement therapy. There is great variability in the inconvenience, discomfort, and symptoms experienced by patients who may be influenced by coping style, mood, social support, and comorbid illness. The elective withdrawal of dialysis is common and may be a reasonable plan of care when agreed on prospectively by the patient and health care team.

—*Mark Unruh and Robert Denshaw*

See also Diabetes; Fluid and Electrolytes; Hypertension; Incontinence; Infections, Bladder and Kidney

Further Readings and References

Anderson S, Brenner BM. Effects of aging on the renal glomerulus. *Am J Med.* 1986;80:435–442.

Caballero C, Iglesias MC, Rodriguez-Puyol M, Rodriguez-Puyol D. Age-related increase in expression of TGF-β1 in the rat kidney: Relationship to morphologic changes. *J Am Soc Nephrol.* 1998;9:782–791.

Choudhury D, Raj DSC, Levi M. Effect of aging on renal function and disease. In: Brenner B, ed. *Brenner and Rector's The Kidney.* 7th ed. St. Louis, Mo: W. B. Saunders; 2004:2305–2342.

Li YM, Steffes M, Donnelly T, et al. Prevention of cardiovascular and renal pathology of aging by the advanced glycation inhibitor aminoguanidine. *Proc Natl Acad Sci USA.* 1996;93:3902–3907.

National Kidney Foundation. K/DOQI clinical practice guidelines for chronic kidney disease: Evaluation, classification, and stratification. *Am J Kidney Dis.* 2002;39:S1–S266.

Percy C, Pat B, Poronnik P, Gobe G. Role of oxidative stress in age-associated chronic kidney pathologies. *Adv Chronic Kidney Dis.* 2005;12:78–83.

Stevens LA, Levey AS. Chronic kidney disease in the elderly: How to assess risk. *N Engl J Med.* 2005;352:2122–2124.

LATIN AMERICA AND THE CARIBBEAN

Latin America and the Caribbean (LAC) refers to the region formed by all political units south of the United States. The aging of LAC will manifest in earnest and accelerate starting around 2030. The share of the total population age 65 years and older was 5% in 2000 and is projected to reach 17% in 2050. However, by 2025, Argentina, Barbados, Brazil, Chile, Cuba, Puerto Rico, Uruguay, and Trinidad already should achieve fractions of at least 15%. Aging in LAC will occur faster and prematurely compared with previous aging in developed countries, presenting special challenges for the region.

In 2000, the age composition of the populations in all countries of LAC reflected a combination of mortality declines that began mostly after World War II, but not all countries experienced similar transitions. For example, Bolivia and Haiti still lag relatively behind in the mortality gains achieved by the region. Although fertility began to drop prior to 1945 in a few countries (Argentina, Cuba, Puerto Rico, and Uruguay), most of LAC had high fertility until the late 1960s and early 1970s. Then a decline started to spread throughout the region, launching the aging process in LAC. Uruguay is the oldest country, with 13% of the population age 65 years and older in 2000, compared with 3.5% in Nicaragua and Honduras. Societies that experienced the most rapid fertility declines will also exhibit the fastest aging. Between 2000 and 2050, the fraction of the population age 65 years and older will rise from 10% to 27% in Cuba and from 5% to 18% in Brazil.

The current elderly of LAC are a particularly important group in the global aging phenomenon. Those who reach 60 years of age between 2000 and 2025 were born between 1940 and 1965 and experienced dramatic gains in survival during their childhoods. Unlike those who aged earlier in developed countries, these cohorts are survivors of a regime in which infectious diseases were still highly prevalent and grew up in relative poverty. Their childhood survival was more a result of adoption of imported medical technologies after World War II rather than an improvement in standards of living. The likely consequences of this unprecedented pattern of aging are unknown. The issue is that, compared with old individuals in developed countries, these cohorts may exhibit higher prevalence of chronic illnesses and disability during old age because of their childhood survival regime. Another peculiar feature of the LAC aging is that many countries are experiencing a mixed epidemiological pattern in which noncommunicable diseases have begun to gain importance while mortality from communicable diseases is still prevalent. Countries with relatively low incomes and education, such as Guatemala and Haiti, have especially high mortality due to diseases such as cholera, malaria, and dengue fever, particularly among the rural and indigenous populations. The consequences for the onset of chronic illness and disability during old age after surviving under such a mixed regime are also unknown.

One of the concerns for the region is that aging will occur faster than in developed countries. For example, it will take Colombia, Brazil, and Chile only 20 to 25 years to get from 7% to 14% of the population age 65 years and older as a share of the total—around 2030 to 2035—whereas the United States will take 70 years to achieve a similar percentage (in 2013). This accelerated aging means that countries must face rapid growth in their absolute numbers of older adults. The portion of the population age 65 years and older will increase by a factor of 2.5 in Costa Rica between 2000 and 2030, and doubling will occur in Brazil, Chile, Mexico, and Peru over the same period.

Another concern for LAC is that aging will be largely premature in the sense that the demographic process will accelerate while countries still have low standards of living. Furthermore, aging has started in a fragile institutional environment where the vast majority of the sources offering minimum levels of social and economic support for the elderly are being reformed with yet uncertain consequences. A well-known and widespread drive toward reform of social security systems took place in LAC over the past two decades. A similar and interrelated reform started later among many health sectors in the region, in the short run reducing rather than increasing the protection of their populations. These reforms were perceived in the international economic arena as necessary, however, and were designed to make the systems financially sustainable and beneficial for economic growth. Nevertheless, in nearly all cases, a fast aging process will take place in the midst of weak economic performance, fragile institutional relations, and perhaps decreased access to health care services.

The consequences of the aging phenomenon are likely to differ as countries face a variety of constraints and willingness to adopt reforms and make postreform adjustments. There is a large variance in the structure and achievement of the health care systems across the countries and the role played by the public health sector. The contrasts in overall health coverage are broad; Cuba has virtually universal coverage, whereas Chile reports 4% lacking access to care, compared with 13% in Uruguay and 40% in Mexico.

The geographic proximity of LAC to the United States and Canada sets the LAC aging process apart from the global picture as well. In 2000, 12.6% of the United States and Canada combined populations were age 65 years and older, compared with 5% of the LAC combined populations. For 2030, the corresponding projections are 20.3% and 11.6%. In particular, for small sending countries in Central America and the Caribbean, emigration to the United States has contributed to aging of the sending nations in a significant manner because young adults are most likely to leave seeking economic opportunities. Also, Mexico is historically tied to the United States and has the highest steady volume of economic emigrants to the United States. Although a distant second, Canada has begun to gain importance as a destination country for LAC emigrants. This flow of migrants contributes to a relatively "young" population in the receiving nations and is likely to continue to foster the north economies' competitiveness in the global markets. Sizable remittances sent back by migrants are a large means of support for several LAC countries, especially for the support of elderly relatives. In the future, it seems likely that LAC will continue to send labor, perhaps increasingly to meet the need for hands-on health care of aging societies in the north.

Because of the high migration and economic interdependence among the countries of the continent, the aging processes of north and south are highly intertwined as well. One feature of the migrant flow north is that there is circulatory or repeated migration, and most migrants intend to return to their origin eventually. Thus, in many sending countries of LAC, concerns over the well-being of their people include the migrants to the north and the possible returning flow after productive years abroad. Policies in both northern and southern countries are beginning to address the long-run consequences of such critical migration, with attention being paid to the working conditions and work benefits of cross-national migrants, aiming to minimize their old-age illness and disability and to guarantee their health care coverage and social support during old age.

Comparative studies with cross-national purposes in LAC have been undertaken during recent years. A study on the health and well-being of older adults in seven urban centers of LAC, *Salud y Bienestar en el Envejecimiento* (SABE), was fielded around 2000 among individuals age 60 years and older in Argentina, Barbados, Brazil, Cuba, Chile, Mexico, and Uruguay. Among the SABE samples, women and the very old are more likely to declare themselves in bad health and to self-report a greater number of chronic conditions. These patterns are similar to those found elsewhere. Although the prevalence varies across the region, women report especially high levels of diabetes and its main risk factor; namely, obesity. Comparing the sampled SABE cities with the United States, the most interesting result is that LAC populations display levels of self-reported diabetes and obesity that are as high as, or higher than, those found in the United States. Research expected during the coming years will shed further light on the aging processes of the LAC countries.

There is a relatively short period of time before aging accelerates in LAC. Scholars perceive that the opportunity should be taken to build up the health infrastructure and meet the needs of the growing older populations. However, providing basic services to rural communities, securing educated and healthy children and a labor force, combating historically profound inequalities, and developing stable financial markets are some of the current priorities of most countries in LAC.

—Rebeca Wong

See also Canada; Demography of Aging; Global Aging; Hispanics; Mexico; Migration

Further Readings and References

Brea J. *Population Dynamics in Latin America.* Washington, DC: Population Reference Bureau; 2003. Population Bulletin, Vol. 58, No. 1.

Interamerican Conference on Social Security. *Evaluation of the Reforms: The Americas Social Security Report 2003.* Mexico City, Mexico: CISS; 2003.

National Research Council. *Preparing for an Aging World: The Case for Cross-National Research.* Washington, DC: National Academy Press; 2001.

Palloni A, McEniry M, Wong R, Pelaez M. The tide to come: Elderly health in Latin America and the Caribbean. *J Aging Health.* 2006;18:180–206.

LEGAL ISSUES

Many legal issues during later life involve competency and guardianship, which in simple words refer to a person's ability to live independently and make decisions and to who should make such decisions if the person is not able. Competency can be diminished due to a number of factors common during late life, including diseases that impair cognitive functioning and reduce independence. Sometimes, these issues affect younger persons who have suffered disability due to acute illness or serious trauma. When a person is deemed to be incompetent, several legal options exist to designate someone else to make decisions for the individual. These include guardianship, conservatorship, power of attorney, and advance directives.

Defining Competency and Capacity

The terms *competency* and *capacity* should be distinguished. Competency is a legal term that refers to an individual's abilities to make decisions independently regarding specific criminal or civil issues. Competency is determined in legal proceedings. Capacity is a clinical determination made by health care professionals that refers to a person's ability to perform specific tasks. Capacity is not the proverbial "all or nothing"; rather, people have the capacity to make specific decisions and engage in specific behaviors.

Legal definitions of competency are predicated on four components: (a) presence of a disabling medical condition, (b) cognitive impairment, (c) functional impairment, and (d) risk. Having a disabling medical or psychiatric diagnosis (e.g., Alzheimer's disease, schizophrenia) does not automatically make someone incompetent. Rather, the disease must be judged to have caused cognitive impairment that in turn leads to functional impairment in daily living and decision making (i.e., limited capacity), thereby placing the person at an unacceptable level of risk. This risk may be defined either as physical risk to himself or herself or others or as functional risk regarding ability to manage finances and make decisions about family and assets.

Determining Competency

An individual is considered to be legally competent unless another person questions his or her competency and files a legal petition to determine the person's competency. For older adults, questions regarding competency are most common for civil matters, especially medical decision making, estate, and living arrangements. The challenging person is usually a family member, but a health care professional may file a petition. The petition leads to a court hearing or, in some instances, an administrative hearing, during which time medical evidence and other testimony are presented to a judge, who makes the final determination of legal competency.

Assessing Capacity

Medical evidence is used to document the presence of a disabling condition and the person's level of capacity. First, an appropriate medical examination should be conducted to diagnose the underlying disease or disorder. Capacity assessment is performed by a psychiatrist, a psychologist, or another health care professional with similar competence in cognitive and psychiatric assessment. It focuses on cognitive and functional impairment and risk, with a primary focus on decisional capacity. Reassessment may be needed in cases of progressive or fluctuating conditions.

Decisional Capacity and Informed Consent

The most commonly accepted definition of decisional capacity involves four components: (a) understanding (of the facts in a situation), (b) appreciation (of how the information applies to one's personal situation), (c) reasoning (rationally weighing advantages and disadvantages of options), and (d) stating a choice. For formal decisions regarding health care and research, the law requires that the professional engage in an informed consent process with the individual. The professional must inform the person about the situation, options, benefits and risks, and the individual's rights, so that the person has adequate understanding (the first criterion in decisional capacity). The professional is responsible for ensuring that the person is truly informed and has the capacity to make such decisions.

Professionals use a variety of methods to assess decisional capacity across these four domains. Most common is a nonstandardized clinical interview, although research with older adults diagnosed with mild Alzheimer's disease demonstrates significant disagreement among health care professionals regarding capacity to make health care decisions. General neuropsychological assessment can be useful, although specific functional abilities might not correlate precisely with general cognitive functioning. The Department of Veterans Affairs has developed a set of guidelines for capacity assessment. The guidelines recommend that the assessment include a general clinical interview, specific standardized tests of psychiatric and cognitive functioning, and specific assessment tools focused on decision-making capacity. They suggest that the clinical interview contain questions for financial, health care, and independent living concerns; these questions assess understanding of the situation, perceptions of any problems, and future preferences. In structured interview approaches, typically the person is presented with information about his or her situation or a vignette and then is asked specific questions regarding his or her understanding (e.g., what are the risks of this medication?), appreciation (e.g., how might this medication affect your life?), reasoning (e.g., why do you prefer one choice over the other?), and making a final choice (e.g., what do you prefer?). In general, these types of assessment tools result in better reliability and validity than do unstructured interviews.

The findings from capacity assessments make up part of the expert medical evidence presented at competency hearings. The professional who assesses capacity reports on the person's specific abilities that are intact and impaired. This professional does not make a recommendation regarding legal competency.

Legal Options for Incompetent Persons

When a person is judged to be legally incompetent, a number of options exist. Basically, other people are appointed to make decisions and manage certain affairs for the person. Most states in the United States recognize two types of formal roles: guardianship and conservatorship.

Legally Appointed Guardians or Conservators

A guardian has rights to make decisions regarding the care of the person (e.g., health care, living arrangements), whereas a conservator has rights to make decisions regarding the person's estate and assets. Designation of a guardian or conservator is based on legal proceedings, with the judge making the final determination based on medical evidence and other testimony. Some legal and medical experts have argued that the rights of guardians/conservators should be limited to the specific activities for which the individual has lost capacity; this preserves as many of the individual's rights as possible but can be difficult to implement if the individual's capacities change frequently. Most state laws require that the designated guardian/conservator make decisions in the best interest of the individual but provide little additional guidance.

Informal Proxy Decision Makers

Often, decision makers are not formally designated by judges in court proceedings. In many health care situations, when a person has been assessed as incapable of making a certain decision, health care professionals turn to the closest family members. In the United States, some states have specific laws to guide the selection of the proxy, with first choice usually being the spouse, followed by the closest next of kin (e.g., adult child, parent, sibling). Proxy decision making for research participation follows similar guidelines in most states. Conflicts among family members may be avoided through advance planning.

Advance Planning

When older adults are competent, they are able to circumvent the guardianship or conservatorship legal process through the use of two legal mechanisms: powers of attorney (POAs) and advance directives. With POAs, individuals can designate who they want to represent them in the event they lose capacity. The scope of designation can be very specific, such as authority to sign a particular document, conduct certain business, or pay bills, or it can be general, essentially affording the designee the power to conduct any and all business and decision making as if the designee were the individual. Some of these can be temporary "limited" powers of attorney for specific times or activities. Others can be "general durable" powers of attorney that remain in effect until the persons revoke them or die and can be specified as "springing" to take effect at a specified time such as when the persons lose capacity. The primary advantage to a POA is that the older person is able to choose the person he or she trusts most to make decisions and specify the types of decisions the POA is allowed to make. Thus, a POA preserves as much of the person's autonomy as possible. Some medical settings that treat high numbers of older adults, particularly those with progressive dementing illnesses, have made it standard practice to encourage and offer all of their patients POA documents while they are still competent. Another option is an advance directive, whereby the individual documents specific wishes for a later time if he or she is to become incapacitated. Any advance planning documents should be given to persons who can use them; that is, an attorney and/or the person(s) designated to serve in decision-making capacities. As long as a person remains competent, any advance planning document may be revoked in writing at any time.

—*Amber M. Gum and Jay Wolfson*

See also Advance Directives; Elder Abuse and Neglect, Geriatric Assessment; Inappropriate Prescribing; Patient Safety

Further Readings and References

Administration on Aging. Elder rights and resources: Legal assistance. Available at: www.aoa.gov/eldfam/Elder_Rights/Legal_Assistance/Legal_Assistance.asp. Accessed November 10, 2005.

American Bar Association. Estate planning FAQs. Available at: www.abanet.org/rppt/public/home.html. Accessed August 1, 2005.

Department of Veterans Affairs. *Clinical Assessment for Competency Determination: A Practice Guideline for Psychologists.* Milwaukee, Wis: National Center for Cost Containment; 1997.

Moye J. Assessment of competency and decision making capacity. In: Lichtenberg PA, ed. *Handbook of Assessment in Clinical Gerontology.* New York: John Wiley; 1999:488–528.

LEWY BODY DEMENTIA

As the population has aged over the past 20 years, recognition of dementia has improved. With increased recognition, it is clear that not all dementia is of the Alzheimer's type. The recently described Lewy body dementia, also known as dementia with Lewy bodies (DLB), is generally recognized as among the more common "new" dementias. The eponymous inclusion bodies were first reported in 1912, whereas case reports of this new type of dementia appeared during the 1980s.

Lewy bodies are spherical, eosinophilic, cytoplasmic inclusion bodies first described in subcortical nuclei in Parkinson's disease. Diffuse Lewy body disease was first described in 1984. Patients with diffuse (i.e., cortical as well as subcortical) Lewy bodies also often have plaques. The clinical history usually includes cognitive impairment, fluctuating severity, and parkinsonian movement disorder. Autopsy series find that 15% to 25% of all elderly demented patients have Lewy bodies, many with plaques, some with tangles, and many with evidence of ischemic damage as well. Lewy body disease may be the most common group of dementias after Alzheimer's-type dementia, although most cases of dementia seen clinically are mixed in symptomatology as well as pathology. Prevalence has been cited as up to 26.3% of all dementia and up to 5% of the general population, with incidence of 0.1% to 3.2% per year for all new dementia cases. Gender distribution is even, and age of onset is after 40 years but most commonly after 75 years. Survival is thought to be approximately 8 years, but more rapid (2 years) and much more indolent (20 years) courses have been described.

Consensus guidelines for clinical diagnosis of DLB were developed by Ian G. McKeith and colleagues in 1996. First, as common to dementias, there must be progressive cognitive decline that interferes with functioning. Memory impairment might not appear early but occurs during the disease course. Loss of attention, visuospatial skills, and frontal/subcortical skills all may be evident. The clinical picture must include at least one of the following: fluctuating attention and cognition, well-formed visual hallucinations, and spontaneous parkinsonism. Two of these features make probable DLB; one feature makes a possible diagnosis. Supportive features include antipsychotic sensitivity, syncope and transient loss of consciousness, delusions and other hallucinations, and depression.

The diagnosis of DLB is made clinically; neither laboratory studies nor imaging are helpful. Although there is association with the APOE4 allele, knowledge of APOE status is not helpful in the diagnosis of an individual or helpful in counseling family members about risk of this dementia. Overall, DLB appears to be no more familial than Parkinson's disease.

The clinical diagnostic signs of Lewy body dementia are hallucinations, fluctuating attention and performance, and (often subtle) parkinsonism. Hallucinations are most often visual, vivid, and (often) not threatening. They are well-formed, three-dimensional images often of people or animals, and the patient may find them more puzzling than distressing. Persecutory delusions can occur as well and are threatening to the patient. Fluctuation is much more marked than is seen in other dementias; it may occur day to day or more quickly. It may resemble delirium. Compared with patients with Alzheimer's disease, patients with DLB are much more likely to (a) have daytime lethargy, (b) sleep more than 2 hours during the daytime, (c) stare into space at length, and

(d) have episodes of disorganized speech. Attempts have been made to find neuropsychological differences between DLB and Alzheimer's dementia, particularly tests that can be used bedside. Executive functioning is more likely impaired, and memory (as measured by the Folstein Mini-Mental State) is less impaired in DLB than in Alzheimer's disease. Patients with DLB are more likely to be distracted by irrelevant visual stimuli during interview or testing and have more difficulty in set shifting. They may, for instance, be more likely to bring in material from a previous question than to address the current question.

The importance of recognizing DLB is that it responds so idiosyncratically to antipsychotic medication. Because the symptoms that bring most patients to a physician are the visual hallucinations, clinicians unaware of the diagnosis will prescribe antipsychotic medication to target the psychotic symptoms. In DLB, the response to typical or atypical antipsychotics is almost always rapid onset of extrapyramidal effects with rigidity far beyond what would usually be expected for the dose. Unfortunately, the visual hallucinations do not respond to antipsychotics, and increasing the antipsychotic dose will lead to more severe side effects with no effect on the hallucinations. Antipsychotic medication may even be dangerous to the patient with DLB; there is a case report of prolonged coma following a single dose of clozapine, with the patient recovering after 2 weeks in intensive care.

The original description of Parkinson's disease concluded that the senses and the intellect are not affected; however, it is clear that a substantial number of patients with idiopathic Parkinson's disease develop dementia as part of their illness. Similarly, patients with DLB do not develop parkinsonian symptoms until somewhat later in the disease (unless provoked by antipsychotic medication use). The distinction between DLB and dementia of Parkinson's disease, then, is one of time course; DLB is diagnosed if mental status changes occur at least a year before movement disorder. When hallucinations, confusion, and fluctuations in attention develop after motor symptoms, the diagnosis is dementia of Parkinson's disease. If all symptoms occur within a short time span, the diagnosis is Parkinson's disease. Medications specific for Parkinson's disease can, of course, produce hallucinations and delusions, generally visual hallucinations. The following experience of one patient is illustrative. At first, there were "patterns" on the blank hospital wall that the patient found attractive. Then she saw "dead dogs from the surgery lab" in the next bed. Finally, she saw the kind avuncular attending as a "White slaver," and she saw the laundry cart as coming to fetch her away for his trade.

Cholinergic deficit is found relatively early in DLB, as demonstrated by an autopsy series that correlated Alzheimer's versus Lewy body pathology with cholinergic deficit. Loss of choline acetyltransferase was significantly greater in Lewy body disease than in Alzheimer's disease until very late in the disease. The most common treatment for the visual hallucinations is the cognitive enhancers donepezil (Aricept), galantamine (Razadyne, formerly Reminyl), and rivastigmine (Exelon). Although none of these is approved for use in treating DLB, the data in published reports consistently support the use of cholinesterase inhibitors. Some clinicians, in fact, will use these medications primarily for DLB patients rather than for Alzheimer's dementia.

In most cases, a clinical diagnosis of DLB will be confirmed by the neuropathological findings at autopsy; there are few false positives using consensus criteria. Lewy bodies are eosinophilic cytoplasmic inclusion bodies found primarily in subcortical nuclei in Parkinson's disease. In DLB, there may be diffuse, brainstem, cortical, or mixed patterns. Older literature recognized the cortical form of DLB; other distributions of pathology have become evident, and there probably is a unifying disease process we do not yet understand. Lewy bodies are composed of alpha synuclein, ubiquitin, and other proteins best seen with specific immunocytological staining; there are some differences in chemical composition and morphology in the Lewy bodies depending on where they are found. Although senile plaques often coexist with DLB, neurofibrillary tangles seldom do. Some patients with clinically diagnosed Alzheimer's disease are found to have Lewy bodies as well. The taxonomy of dementias with Lewy bodies and parkinsonian features has become complicated, including dementia with Lewy bodies, Lewy body variant of Alzheimer's disease, and Parkinson's disease dementia. Other names have also been suggested.

There is no specific treatment for DLB, and other than the general acceptance of cholinesterase inhibitors and advice to avoid antipsychotics, little agreement exists. Some studies have used atypical antipsychotics with some benefit, particularly clozapine in doses as low as 6.25 milligrams and sometimes quetiapine, also in low doses. Tacrine, donepezil, rivastigmine, and galantamine all have been studied, and the currently marketed cholinesterase inhibitors seem equally likely to benefit the psychotic symptoms, some of the dementia-related behavioral features loosely referred to as "agitation," and apathy. Neither meta-analysis nor comparison of these agents has been done, and no role is suggested for memantine. As with most dementias, management of the environment and education of caregivers are most beneficial.

DLB, like some vascular dementia, frontotemporal dementia, and others, is clearly a dementia, but one that might not show memory loss early in the course. Without significant memory loss early, and with depressive symptoms and psychotic symptoms, the diagnosis can be missed. Awareness of this illness will help avoid missed diagnosis and thus avoid treatment that is of no benefit and may produce significant side effects.

—*Judith H. W. Crossett*

See also Alzheimer's Disease; Apolipoprotein E; Delirium and Confusional States

Further Readings and References

Doubleday EK, Snowden JS, Varma AR, Neary D. Qualitative performance characteristics differentiate dementia with Lewy bodies and Alzheimer's disease. *J Neurol Neurosurg Psychiatry.* 2002;72:602–607.

Ferman TJ, Smith GE, Boeve BF, et al. DLB fluctuations: Specific features that reliably differentiate DLB from AD and normal aging. *Neurology.* 2004;62:146–157.

McKeith IG, Galasko D, Kosaka K, et al. Consensus guidelines for the clinical and pathologic diagnosis of dementia with Lewy bodies. *Neurology.* 1996;47:1113–1124.

Zaccai J, McCracken C, Brayne C. Systematic review of prevalence and incidence studies of dementia with Lewy bodies. *Age Ageing.* 2005;34:561–566.

LIFE COURSE PERSPECTIVE ON ADULT DEVELOPMENT

A life course perspective on adult development is one that sees continuity between phases of adult development. In general, the relative rank order of individuals during childhood (e.g., the smartest kid in the class, the fastest runner on the track) is maintained throughout life. This generalization is modified by the area of function (e.g., intelligence, cognition, personality), the level of social class or educational attainment, and the physical health status of the individual. These three areas influence each other, making for a complex set of pathways that need to be understood.

Furthermore, there are relatively few studies that have more than 50 years of data, so that studies that started with individuals in their 20s can now speak to what happens by 70 years of age and studies that started with individuals 70 years of age can speak to what happens by 100 years of age. Studies with serial cohorts can provide some important hints about how adjacent stages of the life span are related, and studies that start during middle or later life with archival data about levels of functioning earlier in the life cycle can also add to our understanding. It is rare to have longitudinal data that follow large cohorts of persons into extreme old age when they are no longer capable of being tested in the laboratory with the same set of measures employed earlier, and those that do often employ proxy respondents. Measurement tends to shift from assessments of intellectual functioning to mental status measures and from physical performance to activities of daily living (ADLs).

First and foremost, work from longitudinal studies is preferred. Cross-sectional studies are an important first step in figuring out what is worth studying longitudinally. Indeed, when similarities in performance and behavior are seen cross-sectionally, that is the exception and worthy of comment and future study; however, that is rarely the case. Age is not an explanatory variable but rather a marker of the passage of time set within a particular sociohistorical context. The actual time of measurement of the status of the individual and the status of knowledge in medicine both contribute to an understanding of aging and health associations. The goal of adult developmental psychology is to replace age with a variable with more explanatory power. Relationships between aging and health (or, more accurately, aging within levels of physical health status) determine the experience of aging for most persons and their family members.

The content of this entry revolves around a set of important questions:

1. Where do we see continuity, and where do we see change, in psychological development? The literature would suggest that there is significantly more continuity in personality and social functioning than in cognitive and intellectual functioning. Personality is maintained even with the onset of memory disorders such as Alzheimer's disease for functions that do not depend on memory (e.g., conscientiousness), and social functioning is maintained until the final phases of impairment. Levels of cognitive and intellectual performance decline earlier if speed is involved in the function tested, such that vocabulary and crystallized intelligence are preserved even during extreme old age. Diseases such as hypertension, heart disease, and diabetes have been implicated in changes in cognitive and neuropsychological performance, and personality constructs such as hostility and anger have been related to the earlier development of hypertension, heart disease, and diabetes.

2. How predictable is the life span? Within a stage of development (young adulthood, middle age, and old age) where we have data, predictability is quite reasonable.

3. How long do variables need to predict to satisfy the criteria of a life course or life span perspective? This is really a theoretical question, and new data from infancy are challenging our notions of life span on the power of variables such as birth weight to have consequences for the rest of the life span.

4. How important is age as a variable? Age is the best summary variable that we have. It is important to know the actual time of measurement of the age because it means something different to be 40 years old in 1960 than it does to be 40 years old in 2000. Thus, understanding age by time of measurement is a powerful combination. The birth cohort of the individual also conveys important information. Those born between 1946 and 1964—the baby boom cohort—have experienced their aging differentially because they are such a large cohort that society has always adjusted to make room for them. The aging of this cohort will have a profound impact on society.

5. Is there an age where the life span no longer makes any sense? Life span developmental psychology today has less to contribute to geriatrics than it could or should in the future. Geriatric syndromes such as frailty are not really seen earlier in the life cycle.

6. What do we know about "extreme" aging and super-centenarians? Data from centenarians are being pooled on a worldwide basis. The Rule of 3 appears to apply; one third are in outstanding shape, one third are plagued by the age-related declines in sensory and motor functions assumed, and one third are moribund given the peculiar nature of our health care systems to maintain survival independent of independent functioning. Research on the genetic determinants of extreme aging with biological and psychosocial data is progressing, but no answers are yet available.

7. What is normal aging? This question is probably best answered within levels of physical disease. Those with specific diseases may well have predictable life courses that are different from those of their age peers with different diseases and combinations of diseases.

8. What role does the development of disease play? It plays a central role, but we do not yet have sufficient data to specify this.

9. What role does the socioeconomic status (SES) gradient play in aging? The SES gradient seems to suggest that those at the lower end of the economic distribution tend to accumulate diseases earlier in

their life span than do those at the upper end. Furthermore, treatments for disease may also be different for the SES groups. However, for those who survive into extreme old age, there may be a crossover effect.

10. How much can be attributed to aging and individual process, and how much is dependent on the social milieu? This may depend on the age of the person. Later in the life cycle, the social milieu may increase in importance. Thus, studying aging in couples and families may be more important during the final quarter of the life cycle than earlier. It is also important to remember that the size of a generation may be 15 to 40 years wide. Thus, a person 40 years of age may be a grandparent while having living parents and grandparents.

In sum, the life span approach to adult development has been useful in understanding development of the individual up to the time of the oldest old (approximately 85 years of age). Current work should extend our understanding of the life span for the final 30 years up to 115 years of age.

—*Ilene C. Siegler*

See also Age–Period–Cohort Distinctions; Demography of Aging; Longitudinal Research; Midlife; Normal Physical Aging; Psychosocial Theories; Socioeconomic Status; Work, Health, and Retirement

Further Readings and References

Costa P, Siegler I, eds. *Recent Advances in Psychology and Aging* (Advances in Cell Aging and Gerontology, Vol. 15, Mattson MP, series ed.). New York: Elsevier; 2004.

Mayer KU, Baltes PB, Baltes MM, et al. What do we know about old age and aging? Conclusions from the Berlin Aging Study. In: Baltes PB, Mayer KU, eds. *The Berlin Aging Study: Aging From 70–100.* New York: Cambridge University Press; 1999:475–519.

Schaie KW. *Developmental Influences on Adult Intelligence: The Seattle Longitudinal Study.* Oxford, England: Oxford University Press; 2005.

Siegler IC, Bosworth HB, Elias MF. Adult development and aging in health psychology. In: Nezu AM, Nezu CM, Geller PA, eds. *Comprehensive Handbook of Psychology,*
Vol. 9: *Health Psychology.* New York: John Wiley; 2003:487–510.

Siegler IC, Bosworth HB, Poon LW. Disease, health, and aging. In: Lerner RM, Easterbrooks MA, Mistri J, eds. *Comprehensive Handbook of Psychology,* Vol. 6: *Developmental Psychology.* New York: John Wiley; 2003:423–442.

Siegler IC, Poon LW, Madden DJ, Dilworth-Anderson P. Psychological aspects of normal aging. In: Blazer DG, Steffens DC, Busse EW, eds. *Textbook of Geriatric Psychiatry.* Washington, DC: American Psychiatric Association; 2004:121–138.

Stern PC, Carstensen LC. *The Aging Mind: Opportunities in Cognitive Research.* Washington, DC: National Academy Press; 2000.

LIVING ARRANGEMENTS

During the later years of the life course, where and with whom one lives greatly influences the quality of one's life. Yet one's living arrangements are not solely the result of individual choices. The options from which an older person can choose are determined by his or her economic and social resources as well as by his or her state of health. The living arrangements and level of independence vary greatly among the elderly. Most older couples live independently in the community, and many widowed individuals continue to live alone well into their 80s and 90s. As their capacity to live independently declines, some move in with their children and others choose to, or are forced to, move to assisted-living environments. Those with the most severe incapacities often have no choice but to enter nursing homes.

Fully 95% of the U.S. population age 65 years and older lives in the community, and three quarters of these individuals own their own homes. Among the oldest old (> 85 years of age), home ownership is less common, as it is among minorities, unmarried individuals, and those with low incomes. Elderly Hispanic and Black metropolitan residents are the least likely of all groups to own their own homes. These differences in home ownership result in large part from a lack of affordable housing, especially for individuals with low retirement incomes.

Today, approximately 54% of individuals age 65 years and older live with their spouses only, 31% live alone, 13% live with relatives, and 2% live with others to whom they are not related. However, significant gender and racial differences exist. Elderly men are more likely than elderly women to live with their spouses. In 2003, 71.2% of men age 65 years and older lived with their wives, whereas only 41.1% of women still lived with their husbands. Among the unmarried, older Black and Hispanic individuals are less likely than their non-Hispanic White peers to live alone and are more likely to live with others because of economic need as well as the cultural preference to do so. In 2003, approximately one third of Black, Asian, and Hispanic elderly individuals lived with people other than their spouses (33.5%, 35.8%, and 36%, respectively). Similarly, foreign-born elderly individuals who migrated to the United States during late adulthood are more likely to live with others than are those who migrated earlier in life or those who are native born. For elderly Mexican-origin immigrants, the propensity to move in with family often occurs in the event that they suffer a loss in their capacity to care for themselves.

When a spouse dies, most older people tend to live alone and maintain their independence as long as possible. Since 1970, the number of older single individuals has increased and the rate of growth has been particularly high for women, who tend to outlive their husbands. In 2003, 10.5 million, or one third of all elderly individuals, lived alone. In addition to being mostly female, those who live alone tend to be older and to report good health. Elderly people who live alone also have lower incomes than do married couples. As a consequence, poverty rates are high among elderly individuals who live alone. Compared with married couples, twice as many men and four times as many women who live alone had incomes below poverty in 2003. Elderly minority women living alone are particularly vulnerable to poverty. In 2003, 40.3% of Black women lived in poverty, compared with 26.4% of Black men. Among Hispanics, 40.8% of women and 14.7% of men who lived alone had incomes below poverty.

For many older people and their family members, living in the community is the best situation, but elderly persons with disabilities need special care and assistance with shopping, dressing, and transportation. Researchers show that between 70% and 80% of those elders with disabilities who do not live in institutionalized housing environments reside with their spouses, with other family members, or with caregivers who are unrelated to them. Of those who are noninstitutionalized, 13% live with relatives and only 2% live with unrelated caregivers. Many elderly individuals with severely disabling cognitive impairment live at home, and approximately 75% of these individuals receive family care.

Although older adults prefer to live independently in the community, as they grow older, they increase their risk of dependency on others who are unable or unwilling to provide care. Approximately 8% of individuals live in housing specially constructed for them, including retirement communities and assisted-living quarters.

The population of elders who are housed in these institutionalized alternatives, which encompass a variety of services and housing supports for persons unable to live independently, has grown swiftly since 1985. During the past decade, assisted-living facilities, including assisted-living quarters, board-and-care facilities, congregate housing, continuing-care communities, and adult foster care homes, grew significantly in popularity, with more than 11,000 nationwide in 1998. Although these facilities are designed to assist the frail elderly with performing activities of daily living (ADLs), the 1999 National Long Term Care Survey showed that less than one half of residents in assisted-living facilities were receiving care in such residential settings.

In most cases, a nursing home tends to be the last resort for placement of frail and disabled elderly persons. Even when nonmarried older adults, who often lack social support, suffer a decline in functional capacity, they do not change their living arrangements or enter nursing facilities. Since the mid-1970s, nursing home utilization rates have generally decreased, but for some groups—notably elderly Blacks—they have risen, doubling from 3% to 6% between 1973 and 1999. In 1999, 1.6 million elderly (roughly 5% of the elderly population) lived in nursing homes. Most nursing home residents are women, over 85 years of age, and widowed. The most common origin prior to entry into a nursing facility is a hospital. As a result, the vast majority of residents require substantial assistance with ADLs, with more than 75% of residents needing help with at least three ADLs such as bathing, showering, and dressing.

—Jacqueline L. Angel and Elena Lewis

See also Activities of Daily Living and Instrumental Activities of Daily Living; Long-Term Care; Oldest Old; Quality of Life; Social Networks and Social Support

Further Readings and References

Angel JL, Angel RJ, Markides KS. Late life immigration, changes in living arrangements, and headship status among older Mexican-origin individuals. *Social Sci Q.* 2000;81:389–403.

Hays JC. Living arrangements and health status in later life: A review of recent literature. *Public Health Nurs.* 2002; 19:136–151.

Jackson DJ, Longino CF Jr, Zimmerman RS, Bradsher JE. Environmental adjustments to declining functional ability: Residential mobility and living arrangements. *Res Aging.* 1991;13:289–300.

Pynoos J, Golant S. Housing and living arrangements for the elderly. In: Binstock RH, George LK, eds. *Handbook of Aging and the Social Sciences.* San Diego, Calif: Academic Press; 1996:303–325.

Wilmoth JM. Living arrangements among older immigrants in the United States. *Gerontologist.* 2001;41:228–238.

LONELINESS

Loneliness is a common problem among older adults. In community studies, the percentage who report feeling lonely ranges from 10% to more than 50%, and the prevalence may be higher in institutional settings. A significant proportion of older adults also report that loneliness is the main problem for their age group. Cross-cultural comparisons have reported loneliness to be experienced across cultures, although it may be expressed differently depending on the lifestyles of various populations. In some cultures social loneliness may be more prevalent, whereas in others emotional loneliness may be reported. Given societal changes over the past several decades (e.g., greater longevity, higher incidence of being divorced or widowed, fewer children, geographic separation from family members), one could expect the proportion of loneliness to be high in this age group. Yet loneliness does not appear to be universal during late life. In longitudinal studies, a small number of older adults report being lonely the entire study period, whereas others report loneliness at only some of the assessments. Some participants never report being lonely over an extended time.

Loneliness is a discrepancy between the social and emotional relationships desired and those actually experienced. This discrepancy can be either in the number of social contacts or in the quality of relationships. Loneliness is sometimes incorrectly assumed to mean being alone. But many older adults report living in solitude and never feeling lonely, whereas others are surrounded by family and friends and report intense feelings of loneliness. Loneliness is different from sadness, although persons who are lonely can feel sad. Similarly, loneliness is different from depression, although loneliness can be a symptom of depression. Although similar in concept to perceived social support, loneliness is different from social isolation, and some researchers have noted that factors such as cognitive or functional decline, often associated with social isolation in older adults, are not always associated with loneliness. Loneliness is an emotional feeling about relationships and can develop when there are changes in actual social contacts (e.g., death of a spouse or friend, changes in physical health that limit contact) or changes in the desire for relationships. Two types of loneliness have been described: social loneliness, which is more quantitative and linked to the absence of contacts, and emotional loneliness, which is more qualitative and linked to the absence of social bonds.

Several demographic factors have been linked to loneliness. Studies have shown that the prevalence of loneliness increases with age, not because of older years but rather due to factors associated with increasing age such as increasing disability, changes in social contacts, and institutionalization. Other researchers have noted increases in emotional loneliness, but not social loneliness, with age. Differences in reporting by sex have been observed, with a higher prevalence in women. Some researchers have reported that women report more loneliness if the actual *word* loneliness is used and that men report more if the *concept of* loneliness is addressed. In men, marital history and current partner status have been shown to predict loneliness; in women, marital history and the nature of friendships is associated with loneliness. These findings support the concept that men may rely on their spouses for companionship, whereas women rely on family and friends. Being married tends to protect against loneliness, so that widowhood tends to be a risk factor for loneliness. Childlessness has been related to loneliness in some, but not all, studies addressing that issue. Some life events have been shown to be risk factors for loneliness, including death of a family member or friend and changing residences. There may be urban and rural differences in factors associated with loneliness.

Loneliness in older adults is associated with poorer physical and mental health. Feeling lonely is both associated with and an outcome of depression. Deteriorating physical health, sleep problems, impairments in vision and/or hearing, impairments in mobility, and memory problems are associated with loneliness, as is poor self-rated health. Loneliness may also be associated with the type of chronic disease, with a higher risk of loneliness in those with episodic diseases, such as lung disease, peripheral vascular disease, and arthritis, than in those with chronic diseases with courses more stable or known.

Several adverse outcomes have been predicted by loneliness during late life. Feeling lonely has been shown to predict depression. Whether loneliness is a risk factor for suicide is not clear. Some researchers have found that neither depression nor loneliness alone during late life predicts suicide but that those who are both depressed *and* lonely are at a higher risk. Others have found loneliness to predict suicide indirectly through other pathways. Loneliness has been found to predict mortality generally, although it is not clear whether declining health leads to loneliness and then mortality or whether loneliness leads to declining health and then mortality. Older adults who are lonely use more health care services and prescription medications and are at a higher risk for entering nursing homes. Loneliness can lead to decreased nutritional intake and increased alcohol use.

Overall, loneliness is assumed to be a temporary condition, and older persons who feel lonely can recover. Treating loneliness could potentially reduce the risk of depressive disorders and increase the overall quality of life for older adults. Loneliness could be treated through cognitive–behavioral modifications or through increasing self-efficacy. Feeling more confident in their abilities could help elders to address the causes of loneliness and formulate solutions. These solutions can include increasing the quality of relationships, getting involved in activities where older adults can develop relationships, and increasing companionship relationships for those adults who derive most of their support from children and other relatives. Finally, cognitive processes can play an important role. Whereas outside events can affect the desire for relationships, cognitive–behavioral therapy can potentially help with older adults' perception of the discrepancy.

—*Celia F. Hybels*

See also Bereavement and Grief; Control; Depression and Other Mood Disorders; Emotions and Emotional Stability; Positive Attitudes and Health; Suicide and the Elderly

Further Readings and References

Blazer DG. Self-efficacy and depression in late life: A primary prevention proposal. *Aging Mental Health.* 2002;6:315–324.

Cacioppo JT, Hawkley LC, Crawford E, et al. Loneliness and health: Potential mechanisms. *Psychosomatic Med.* 2002;64:407–417.

Penninx BWJH, Van Tilburg T, Kriegsman DMW, Boeke AJP, Deeg DJH, Van Eijk JTM. Social network, social support, and loneliness in older persons with different chronic diseases. *J Aging Health.* 1999;11:151–168.

Perlman D. European and Canadian studies of loneliness among seniors. *Can J Aging.* 2004;23:181–188.

LONGEVITY

Longevity is the experiencing of a long life. The term is used differently by various authors, but one common way of defining longevity is with respect to having a life span near that of the observed species maximum. For humans, the longest verified life span is that of Jeanne Louise Calment, who died in 1997 at 122 years and 164 days of age.

The most common measure of longevity for a population is life expectancy; that is, the average years of life remaining after a given age or event. Life expectancy for a population is typically summarized as life expectancy at birth. This figure is most often calculated by applying a schedule of age- and sex-specific mortality rates current for that population during a given period to a hypothetical birth cohort that experiences the observed current rates. One limitation of life expectancy calculated in this way is that future longevity may depart substantially from a current calculation of life expectancy as age-specific rates change. During the 20th century, most birth cohorts in most nations substantially outlived the life expectancies calculated for their years of birth as age-specific death rates continued to fall throughout their life courses. Other useful life table-based measurements of longevity include the median age at death, the late-life modal age at death, and the distribution and dispersal of age at death.

Life expectancy at birth has not been measured with precision for any larger human population before the middle of the 18th century. Available evidence suggests that life expectancy in premodern societies was between 20 and 30 years. Because a large fraction of deaths occurred during infancy and childhood, life spans exceeding 50 years may have been common despite the low life expectancy at birth. Life expectancy at birth has been estimated to be approximately 40 years in many European nations and in the United States by the beginning of the 19th century.

Life expectancy began to increase rapidly in industrializing nations at the end of the 19th century and through the 20th century. The proximate cause of increasing life expectancy was the epidemiological transition from a situation where most deaths were attributable to communicable causes and occurred throughout the life course to a situation where most deaths are now attributable to degenerative causes and are concentrated in ages near the average life expectancy. Improvements in nutrition, sanitation, and public health practices are thought to have made the largest contribution to increases in life expectancy during the 19th and 20th centuries.

United Nations estimates of life expectancy at birth for the 2000–2005 period were 79.3 years for women and 71.9 years for men in the more developed regions of the world and were 65.2 years for women and 61.7 years for men in the less developed regions. Life expectancy at birth in the United States was estimated to be 80.1 years for women and 74.8 years for men in 2003.

Increases in life expectancy at birth slowed during the second half of the 20th century. This slowing is attributable to the progressive elimination of excess juvenile mortality. Recent and future increases in life expectancy occur primarily through lowering mortality at older ages. A life extended at these ages has a smaller effect on the calculation of life expectancy at birth because the years added are correspondingly few. It is noteworthy, however, that the deceleration of the increase in life expectancy during the latter decades of the 20th century were accompanied by an acceleration in the decline of mortality rates at older ages. Improvements in medical care may have contributed substantially to these declines.

This record of continual improvement in life expectancy raises considerable current debate about the future of longevity. Is the human life span fixed, or is it plastic to intentional genetic or environmental manipulation? Can longevity increases of the recent past be sustained, or are low mortality populations now nearing biologically imposed limits?

Recent United Nations population projections suggest that continuing mortality declines will increase life expectancy at birth for both sexes combined to approximately 88 years by the middle of the 21st century. This calculation expresses assumptions in the projection model about the future course of current trends.

That the human life span has inherent species-specific biological limits is implicit in the fact that mortality rates generally rise exponentially with age after reproductive maturity. What remains a matter of controversy is whether national populations with the highest life expectancy are currently approaching fixed limits. One school of thought suggests that further large declines in mortality rates in low-mortality populations are unrealistic as human populations reach the limits of their biological warranty periods.

It has long been known that life spans of laboratory rodents may be extended through experimental manipulation of nutrient-dense but calorie-restricted diets, compared with control populations subject to ad libitum feeding. Although these findings suggest the plasticity of life span, their generalizability outside of laboratory settings and to human populations is not known. Research with human participants on experimental manipulation of the life span faces both practical difficulties (because the experimental period would optimally include the majority of a human life span) and ethical obstacles (because the health risks of interventions are unknown).

Biodemographers suggest that there is no evidence that the pace of age-specific mortality decline is currently decreasing. One of the most telling arguments of biodemographers against the notion that current life expectancies are near fixed limits is that mortality rates continue to decline at the oldest ages in the national populations with the lowest mortality. Regarding this point of view, although there are likely biological limits to human longevity, we do not know what they are or whether we are near them.

Although life expectancy generally increased in most regions of the world during the 20th century, changes in longevity have not been positive in all national populations at all times. Life expectancy declined sharply in Russia and some components of the former Soviet Union over the period from the mid-1980s to the mid-1990s, with the changes driven largely by increases in mortality at middle ages. This pattern has more recently reversed. Countries with a high prevalence of HIV infection have also experienced sharp reductions in life expectancy. The United Nations estimated reductions in life expectancy exceeding 20 years in the sub-Saharan countries where HIV infection is most prevalent.

Pessimists about the future of life expectancy suggest that the high current prevalence of obesity and other chronic disease risks in the United States and other more developed countries portend future slowing, and perhaps even reversal, of recent gains in life expectancy as their effects play out later in the life course of current populations of children and younger adults. The conjecture is speculative and controversial.

Increases in life expectancy present profound challenges to many societies that experience them. This is particularly true in conjunction with the rapid fall in fertility to below replacement levels in many of the most long-lived populations. Many countries in more developed regions face prospects of increasing rates of old-age dependency, with resulting fiscal pressures on medical care and income support for growing older populations. In less developed regions especially, increased rates of survival to older ages have come about in part through medical interventions that have increased the longevity of populations whose members have nonetheless experienced high rates of severe deprivation at points in their life courses. There is some concern that in these settings, increased survival may be associated with increasing prevalence of morbidity in aged populations.

More broadly, continuing increases in life expectancy in more developed countries since the second half of the 20th century raise important questions about the social–cultural definition and institutional structuring of older ages. Recent and future cohorts of older adults have been, and will continue to be, in a sense pioneers given that the average life span has been pushed well past historical limits. Routine survival decades past the conclusion of active labor force participation is unprecedented in human history and may require continuing cultural and institutional innovation.

—*Karl Eschbach*

See also Centenarians; Oldest Old

Further Readings and References

Hjelmborg JB, Iachine I, Skytthe A, et al. Genetic influences on human life span and longevity. *Hum Genet.* 2006; 119:312–321.

Olshansky SJ, Passaro DJ, Hershow RC, et al. A potential decline in life expectancy in the United States in the 21st century. *N Engl J Med.* 2005;352:1138–1145.

United Nations, Department of Economic and Social Affairs. *World Population Prospects: The 2004 Revision—Highlights.* New York: United Nations; 2005.

Wachter KW, Finch CE, eds. *Between Zeus and the Salmon: The Biodemography of Longevity.* Washington, DC: National Academy of Sciences; 1997.

Wilmoth JR. Demography of longevity: Past, present, and future trends. *Exp Gerontol.* 2000;35:1111–1129.

LONGITUDINAL RESEARCH

Longitudinal studies are those in which measurement occurs at more than one point in time. These can use qualitative, quantitative, or a combination of methods. The purpose of longitudinal research is to determine the mechanisms and predictors of change or stability in phenomena over time. Most theories on aging focus on the movement of individuals or groups through time, explaining processes such as adaptation, health decline, and accumulating disparity. However, much of the existing research on health and aging has used cross-sectional study designs, where all of the data are collected at one time point. Longitudinal studies are beneficial for establishing causality; measuring change; and separating age, period, and cohort effects.

There are three main types of longitudinal study designs: repeated cross section, panel, and rotating panel. First, *repeated cross-section* studies are those with similar measurement at two or more time points on different samples drawn from the same population. This study design is most appropriate for measuring change in a population over time. Examples of this design include the National Health Interview Survey that draws a new random sample representing the United States' population each year. Because the samples represent the population at that time point, it is reasonable to expect that the demographic composition (e.g., age, race, gender) of the sample would vary over time as well. Other examples are the National Home and Hospice Surveys and the Survey of Consumer Finances.

Second, *panel* studies are those that collect data from the same respondents at two or more points in time, generally on the same or related topics. This study design is most appropriate for measuring change within individuals. Examples of panel studies include the Health and Retirement Study, the Established Populations for Epidemiologic Studies of the Elderly, and the Longitudinal Study on Aging. Panel studies typically use a prospective design where respondents are followed forward through time and asked questions about their current state of being. However, some data may be collected retrospectively by asking respondents to recall events or information in their past or between observation points. Integrating retrospective questions in a prospective panel study increases the window of observation, but these responses can be subject to recall bias. Respondents tend to be most accurate about significant events in their lives such as marriage, birth of children, and hospitalization.

The third type of longitudinal study design is a *rotating panel,* which is a combination of the previous two study designs. Like a panel study, this type of design collects a sample of respondents and follows them for a specified length of time that is generally fairly short. Then, consistent with the repeated cross-section design, a new representative sample is recruited and followed for the same length of time as the first sample. These separate samples often overlap in waves, allowing one to compare the two cohorts at the same time point. The advantage of this approach is that one is able to measure change in a population and change within individuals simultaneously. It also minimizes the impact of study attrition over time because each selected respondent is followed for a short period of time, even if the study continues for decades. An example of this design is the Consumer Expenditure Survey, which draws a new sample every quarter and follows those respondents for 15 months. After five consecutive quarters, the sample is dropped. The study continues to rotate new cohorts of respondents into the survey, and they are then followed over time.

Longitudinal research is beneficial for research in health and aging for several reasons. First, having multiple waves of data collection allows one to lag the "exposure window" prior to the "outcome window" and isolate causal mechanisms. When all data are collected at one time point, it is difficult to separate cause and effect between variables. For example, if depression and physical disability are measured at the same time point, it is impossible to determine which one occurred first and may be influencing the other one. Longitudinal research can test such a mechanism and determine whether depression leads to physical disability over time or vice versa.

A second benefit of longitudinal research is the ability to measure change over time. Many studies have two observation points, but a growing number have three or more waves. Two time points allow one to measure whether change occurred over time and the direction of change such as weight loss, incident health conditions, and satisfaction with neighborhood. With three or more time points, one can capture rate of change over time. Increasingly, researchers are estimating trajectories of change for a wide range of outcomes, including cognitive impairment and depression. These trajectories may be nonlinear (do not increase at a constant rate over time) or may be affected by intervening variables over time. Time-variable change can be accounted for in statistical techniques such as latent growth curves, event history, and hierarchical linear modeling, allowing a broader understanding of the dynamics of long-term change and stability.

Third, longitudinal research designs are beneficial for separating age, period, and cohort effects. Cross-sectional study designs allow one to observe age differences in a population, but it is impossible to conclude whether those differences are a product of the aging process, cohort membership, or period influences. Following persons or populations over time makes it possible to separate these three domains and to make more accurate conclusions about human development and change over time. For example, if one were to study the impact of early-life polio on health during older adulthood, it would be important to consider when the polio vaccine was introduced and significantly lowered the risk of contracting polio in the population (period effect), how old persons were when the vaccine was introduced given that it is related to the length of exposure (cohort effect), and how the process of aging may affect the ability to compensate for the resulting paralysis or muscle

weakening among those who had polio (age effect). If these three domains are confounded in the study, one may conclude incorrectly that the risk of polio increases as a person ages.

Despite these distinct advantages over cross-sectional study designs, longitudinal research presents a number of challenges. First, researchers must develop a research question appropriate to the time lag between observation points. Some causal relationships take years to develop (e.g., the impact of obesity on disability), whereas other relationships are more proximate (e.g., adjustment following a residential move). When using existing data sources, one might not have flexibility to select the length of observation window. Consequently, the research question must be crafted to fit the available data. If the time lag between waves is too long or too short to observe the relationship of interest, the association might appear not to exist. Similarly, the impact of one variable on another may vary over time, yielding different estimates of relationship strength between variables depending on the time lag between measurement points. Thus, the length of the observation window is critical to consider when interpreting the results.

A second potential challenge of longitudinal research is the accurate measurement of change. Questions, number of items in a scale, and answer choices must be identical across waves to measure change. This is an important issue for all of the longitudinal study designs described previously because shifts in language and vocabulary may influence how a question is asked or what it may mean over time. A researcher must determine whether two questions with altered wording are conceptually identical. Another common example is change in answer categories over time. If answer choices for a question are reduced from five categories to four categories between waves, it is difficult to assess real change because respondents' answers may vary by available response categories.

Finally, one challenge of longitudinal research is specific to panel and rotating panel studies, namely nonrandom attrition between observation points. Repeated cross-section designs avoid the pitfall of nonrandom attrition, but this design cannot measure intraindividual change. Panel studies of older adults are particularly vulnerable to bias due to selective mortality over time. Although nonresponse is also a potential source of selection bias, it tends to be less common in samples of older adults due in part to greater residential stability relative to younger adults. When the primary source of study attrition among older adults is death, the remaining sample at later waves tends to be younger, more affluent, and healthier than the population. Thus, estimates of health over time are likely to underestimate change and decline. Increasingly, researchers are employing methods to adjust model estimates for such selection bias.

—*Jessica A. Kelley-Moore*

See also Aging in Manitoba Longitudinal Study; Duke Longitudinal Studies; Established Populations for Epidemiologic Studies of the Elderly; Government Health Surveys; Longitudinal Study of Aging; National Institute on Aging

Further Readings and References

Alwin DF, Campbell RT. Quantitative approaches: Longitudinal methods in the study of human development and aging. In: Binstock RH, George LK, eds. *Handbook of Aging and the Social Sciences.* San Diego, Calif: Academic Press; 2001:22–43.

Glenn ND. *Cohort Analysis.* Beverly Hills, Calif: Sage; 1977.

Menard S. *Longitudinal Research.* Newbury Park, Calif: Sage; 1991.

Rogosa DR. Myths about longitudinal research. In: Schaie KW, Campbell RT, Meredith WM, Rawlings SC, eds. *Methodological Issues in Aging Research.* New York: Springer; 1988:171–209.

Singer JD, Willett JB. *Applied Longitudinal Data Analysis: Modeling Change and Event Occurrence.* Oxford, England: Oxford University Press; 2003.

Longitudinal Study of Aging

In 1956, Congress enacted Public Law 84-652, the National Health Survey Act (NHSA), mandating development and implementation of an annual health survey of the civilian noninstitutionalized population of the United States. The NHSA called for a program of surveys to evaluate the nation's health. One major survey in this program is the National Health Interview Survey (NHIS, originally called the Health Interview Survey), which collects epidemiological data to document the prevalence of physical disease, disability, and health behavior of a national probability sample of persons across the life span. The NHIS program is flexible enough to adapt to changing needs for data on special populations and issues. In 1980, the lack of information on the nature and extent of health and related problems of the elderly population prompted the U.S. Public Health Service (PHS), National Center for Health Statistics, and National Institute on Aging (NIA) to consider assessing the data requirements for the study of health and long-term care of the oldest old in the United States. Under cosponsorship of these agencies, the study committee recommended development of a supplemental questionnaire to address the unique health and long-term care needs of the elderly.

That decision led to the Longitudinal Study of Aging (LSOA I) in 1984 and to its expansion (LSOA II) in 1994. Today, the LSOA is the foremost survey focusing on the health dynamics and trends of elderly Americans. Its general purpose is to examine aging and mortality patterns to gain more information than can be found on death certificates. The LSOA is a particularly rich resource for information on the oldest old and for identifying potential areas of intervention regarding elder care. For example, one can assess changes (if any) in the health status, as well as care and living arrangement status, of individuals as they age. The wealth of data collected provides an opportunity to describe the continuum of long-term care from dependency in the community, to institutionalization, to death. Both the 1984 LSOA I and the 1994 LSOA II contain follow-up interviews that lasted through the end of the decade.

The universe for the LSOA I contains 7,541 community-dwelling persons age 70 years and older who were participants in the 1984 Supplement on Aging (SOA) household interview survey. Multistage probability sampling was performed to ensure representation of certain subgroups of elderly: the oldest old, ethnic minorities, and elderly family caregivers. Because of funding limitations, a subsample of 5,151 persons was selected for the first follow-up interview administered in their homes in 1986. All individuals age 70 years and older when they participated in the 1984 SOA were eligible to be interviewed in 1988 and 1990. To ensure successful relocation and response rates of the original cohort, subsequent telephone surveys were conducted with computer-assisted telephone interviews (CATIs) in 1986, 1988, and 1990. LSOA surveys were also appended to the National Death Index and to Medicare claims data files (1984–1991). The prospective research design, which tracks the same individuals over time, distinguishes the LSOA from other cross-sectional studies of aging and health.

The LSOA survey questionnaire includes measures of functional status and health care use for individuals over a 6-year period, permitting assessment of any changes over that time. Estimates of mortality rates by demographic, social, economic, and health characteristics that are not available from the vital statistics system are also possible. Data from several sources enrich the LSOA data set. Available information includes the NHIS, the 1984 Health Insurance Supplement, the 1984 baseline SOA, the follow-up LSOA interviews, Medicare records, the National Death Index, and multiple causes of death files.

Specific topics explored in the 1984 SOA include family structure and living arrangements, housing characteristics, relationships and social contacts, use of community services, occupation and retirement (income sources), health conditions and impairments, activities of daily living (ADLs), instrumental activities of daily living (IADLs), those who provided help with ADLs and IADLs, use of health services, nursing home stays, and health opinions. In the LSOA I study, follow-up interviews were conducted in 1986, 1988, and 1990 to update the baseline data for transitions in care and living arrangements, changes in occupation, changes in physical limitations, difficulties with ADLs and IADLs, impairment in physical mobility, nursing home stays since last interview, hospital stays during past year, contacts with doctors during past year, hospital and nursing home stays before death, and socioeconomic information.

The LSOA II study explored many of the same areas as the first study to document changes in the life cycle and caregiving of the aging population, as reported by the National Center for Health Statistics in 2005. Like the LSOA I survey, the LSOA II survey aimed to determine whether elderly individuals reported any changes in living arrangements and their capacity to carry out ADLs. The study includes a nationally representative cohort of 9,447 adults over 70 years of age (civilian and noninstitutionalized) at the time of the LSOA II interview. Similar to the methodology employed for the LSOA I, U.S. Census Bureau staff performed face-to-face interviews at baseline in the respondents' homes. Follow-up surveys were administered by the National Opinion Research Center at the University of Chicago using CATIs.

The LSOA II includes information from the baseline 1994 NHIS, the 1994 Family Resources Supplement (in place of the 1984 Health Insurance Supplement), and Phase I of the 1994 National Health Interview Survey on Disability as well as information on respondents who were reinterviewed in 1997–1998 and 1999–2000. One can use the data set to examine patterns in health service use, including medical insurance, family structure, housing, formal and informal sources of care, employment history, transportation, use of assistive devices and technologies, and social network. Again, the prospective research design makes it possible to examine the sequence and consequences of health events for functional independence through dependence (including death) in the community or institutionalization. Although most survey questions were identical to items in the 1984 LSOA I, new information was gathered on individual risk behaviors, including health opinions. In addition to interviews conducted with survivors, additional information was collected about decedents' hospitalization and nursing facility admissions from their named contacts of next of kin. Also, the Family Resources Supplement replaced the Health Insurance Supplement and provided in-depth information on caregiving, care receiver needs, unmet care needs, and the reasons behind unmet needs.

In summary, the LSOA is an excellent resource for examining the lives of elderly Americans as they enter the oldest age categories. The data provide much-needed information about how very old people care for themselves as a result of changes in their health and functioning.

—*Jacqueline L. Angel*

See also Continuum of Care; Duke Longitudinal Studies; Longitudinal Research; Oldest Old

Further Readings and References

Fitti JE, Kovar MG. *Supplement on Aging to the 1984 National Health Interview Survey.* Hyattsville, Md: National Center for Health Statistics; 1987. Vital and Health Statistics, Series 1, No. 21.

Kovar MG, Fitti JE, Chyba MM. *The Longitudinal Study of Aging: 1984–90.* Hyattsville, Md: National Center for Health Statistics; 1992. Vital and Health Statistics, Series 1, No. 28.

National Center for Health Statistics. The second Longitudinal Study of Aging. Available at: www.cdc.gov/nchs/about/otheract/aging/lsoa2.htm. Accessed September 20, 2006.

Wunderlich GS, ed. *A National Health Care Survey: A Data System for the 21st Century.* Washington, DC: National Academy Press; 1992.

LONG-TERM CARE

Long-term care (LTC) may well be one of the most important challenges of the 21st century. Life expectancy in the United States has been increasing ever since records have been kept. In 2000, the life expectancy for a male was 74.3 years and for a female was 79.7 years. Compared with life expectancies in 1900 of 46.3 years for men and 48.3 years for women, and in 1950 of 65.6 years for men and 71.1 years for women, the increases during the 20th century were remarkable.

But as James Fries noted in 1980 and Sidney Katz and his colleagues pointed out in 1983, adding years to life is only one part of the challenge. If humans' biological makeup were such that at 80 years of age all people would become frail, vulnerable, and

incapable of living independently, then increasing life expectancy from 80 to 85 years would simply mean adding 5 years of frailty, vulnerability, and dependence to the final years of life. Quite frankly, who would want that? If, on the other hand, humans' biological makeup were such that all people would have 1 year of frailty, vulnerability, and dependence during the final year of our life—no more and no less—then increasing life expectancy from 80 to 85 years would mean adding 5 years of independent living to the final years of life. And who would want that? Quite frankly, just about everyone.

The actual circumstances seem to be somewhere in the middle. In general terms, for every 3 years of additional life expectancy we seem to gain, 2 of those years are years of independence and the 3rd year is one of frailty, vulnerability, and dependence. From another perspective, half of all people who reach 65 years of age will spend at least some of their remaining lives in nursing homes.

As a consequence of all these factors, these final years of frailty, vulnerability, and dependence of individuals give rise to the need for efficient, effective, and humane long-term care during those final years.

Long-Term Care

What do we mean by the phrase *long-term care?* In 2001, C. J. Evashwick defined LTC as informal or formal health or health-related services provided over time to people with functional disabilities with a goal of increasing the care receivers' independence. This is a very useful definition because if provides us with answers to the following basic questions:

- *Who gets it?* People who have functional disabilities over an extended period of time
- *What do they get?* A wide range of health and health-related support services
- *Who gives it?* Informal (usually unpaid, usually female relatives) or formal (usually paid, usually trained) providers
- *For how long?* Over an extended period of time
- *To what end?* With the goal of maximizing the independence of care recipients

The only other questions of importance are the following:

- *Where is it provided?*
- *Who pays for it?*

Let us address these issues one at a time.

The Clients or Recipients of LTC

The clients of LTC can be of any age or gender, but there is a strong association with advancing age. For example, the percentage of the population under 65 years of age residing in nursing homes on any given day is extremely small, but 2% to 3% of those 65 to 74 years of age reside in nursing homes, as do 5% to 7% of those 75 to 84 years of age and 20% to 25% of those age 85 years and older.

But the need for LTC is not decided by age; rather, it is decided by function. The usual criterion for needing LTC is a limitation or lack of independence in the basic activities of daily living (ADLs), typically bathing, dressing, eating, transferring from a bed or chair, toileting (including cleaning oneself afterward), and walking across a small room.

What Do LTC Clients Get?

LTC clients in fact often will need most of the services available to anyone—both acute care services and LTC services. On a periodic basis, they need acute care services, such as hospital care, primary medical care, dental care, eye care, and foot care, because they have acute care needs just like any other person their age. But in addition, their limitations in function that preclude independent living imply that they need daily care as well. The daily care typically involves assistance with the ADLs; assistance with the tasks necessary to live in the community such as paying bills, taking medications, grocery shopping, preparing meals, and housekeeping; and (sometimes) assistance with the daily management of chronic medical problems such as dementia, pressure sores, and incontinence.

Who Provides LTC?

The vast majority of LTC, often estimated to be two thirds to three quarters, is provided by unpaid informal family members. Given the societal custom of men marrying women several years younger than themselves, and the 5- to 7-year superiority in life expectancy of wives compared with their husbands, older men needing informal LTC usually have wives as their providers. Older women needing informal LTC have typically outlived their husbands, and the caregiving role usually is assumed by daughters or daughters-in-law.

Formal LTC, or care that is paid for and typically provided by nonrelatives trained in some aspect of caregiving, traditionally has been provided by institutions such as skilled nursing homes.

How Long Is the LTC Provided?

The expectation is that the LTC would be needed for at least 90 days. In certain circumstances, other limits are expected. Hospice care (a form of LTC), for example, is expected to be needed for not more than 180 days. In any event, the general expectation is that the care will be for a long period but not necessarily indefinitely. Rehabilitation in a skilled nursing facility following a hip fracture/replacement or a stroke, for example, is expected to be long term (perhaps up to 90 days) but not indefinite. Still, such care is considered LTC.

Where Is LTC Provided?

As stated previously, LTC traditionally was provided in nursing homes, either skilled nursing facilities or intermediate care facilities. During the last quarter of the 20th century, however, the settings in which LTC is provided changed dramatically. In Massachusetts, for example, there are more frail and vulnerable older people receiving formal LTC services in their homes than there are those receiving LTC in nursing homes. And in addition to nursing homes and residences, formal LTC is provided in assisted-living facilities, continuing-care retirement communities, other residential settings, and nonresidential settings such as adult day care centers.

Who Pays for LTC?

To gain a proper perspective, the health care dollar in the United States in 2003 gave 31 cents to hospitals, 32 cents to physicians and dentists, 14 cents to pharmaceuticals, 7 cents to nursing homes, 2 cents to home care, and 14 cents to all other categories. From another perspective, the whole bill of LTC—both institutional and community—is considerably less that the interest on the national debt.

Of the money paid to nursing homes in 2003, 28% comes directly from the monthly checks and savings of the LTC clients and their families, and another 8% comes from insurance paid for by premiums from the clients. Medicaid pays for nearly half (48%), and Medicare pays for another 12%. The remaining 4% comes from a variety of other sources, like other private funds.

For home health care in 2003, 15% was paid by the clients or their families, another 14% was paid by insurance they purchased, 35% was paid by Medicaid, and 36% was paid by Medicare.

What Is the Goal of LTC?

The short answer is improved quality of life compared with what it would have been without the LTC. Whenever the person is no longer able to be independent and is expected to be dependent for an extended period of time, some LTC support will be necessary. When such support is formal (i.e., paid and specialized) and paid for from public money, there is also an expectation of effectiveness (e.g., it accomplishes the goal of meeting the dependent client's daily needs) and efficiency (e.g., it meets such needs in a cost-effective manner). Legislation during the 1980s also required that such care be provided in the least restrictive environment; the Boren amendment, which also directly linked Medicaid nursing home rates with minimum federal and state quality of care standards, was passed in 1980 but repealed in 1997. But how do we measure quality of life for those frail and vulnerable enough to need LTC? The consensus is still forming.

—Laurence G. Branch

See also Activities of Daily Living and Instrumental Activities of Daily Living; Assisted Living; Caregiving; Home Care; Long-Term Care Insurance

Further Readings and References

Arias E. United States life tables, 2002. *Natl Vital Stat Rep.* 2004;53(6).

Evashwick CJ, ed. *The Continuum of Long-Term Care.* 2nd ed. Albany, NY: Thomson Delmar Learning; 2001.

Fries JF. Aging, natural death, and the compression of morbidity. *N Engl J Med.* 1980;303:103–135.

Katz S, Branch LG, Branson MH, Papsidero JA, Beck JC, Greer DS. Active life expectancy. *N Engl J Med.* 1983;309:1218–1224.

LONG-TERM CARE INSURANCE

Long-term care (LTC) insurance is a way to pay privately for care in a nursing home, in one's own home, or in other community settings when chronic illness or disability leaves that person unable to care for himself or herself for an extended period of time. It is a relatively new product that was first seen on the market during the early 1980s. Prior to that time, LTC was viewed by the insurance industry as an uninsurable event because it involves a significant emphasis on custodial care. However, nursing home care and services designed to help people stay at home often can result in catastrophic costs that can impoverish families and leave state Medicaid programs with a difficult financial burden. Current national health account estimates from the Center for Medicare and Medicaid Services indicate that private insurance covers approximately 8% of all nursing home care and 21% of all home care. Estimates from the American Health Insurance Plans suggest that approximately 6 million of the 9 million LTC insurance policies sold are still in force.

LTC insurance is a hybrid product that merges features found in health, disability, and life insurance.

Like health insurance, it helps the policyholder to prepare for medical expenses. Unlike health insurance, the benefits are not limited to medical skilled care. Benefits can extend to a wide range of supportive services, including assisted-living arrangements, visiting nurses, home health aides, chore services, adult day care, and respite services, all of which can allow family members to continue to participate in caregiving. Like disability insurance, the policy covers payments made to entities due to an inability to do normal daily activities because of physical or cognitive impairments. Typically, benefits are triggered if the policyholder needs help in two or more activities of daily living (ADLs) such as bathing, eating, and dressing. Supervision needs secondary to Alzheimer's disease are an example of coverage for mental health.

Similar to life insurance, policy premiums are structured to be paid over a long period of time on a level schedule that builds up reserves to help cover cost of care that typically occurs in the future, usually when people are in their 70s and 80s. Because it is possible that young or middle-aged persons might need LTC due to accidents or illness, the level premium rate, set at the age of purchase, becomes larger with age. Insurers recommend that people purchase this type of coverage during their working years to make sure they will qualify for coverage and have ample time to pre-fund the necessary reserves.

Typically, the policyholder specifies a fixed dollar payment to be received when care is needed. This, combined with the choice of how long benefits will be paid, sets the maximum amount of the total benefit available from the policy. Increasingly, daily benefit amounts are integrated so that they can be paid in a flexible way that meets the specific needs of the policyholder. This relatively new approach extends the time of coverage if the cost of services is less than the maximum allowed per day, week, or month. For example, a policy that pays up to $100 per day for 3 years of nursing home care will pay out a maximum of $109,500 in benefits. If the policy also allows for flexible use of home and community services that cost less than $100 per day and are needed less often than daily (e.g., three home visits per week at $60 per visit), the time of coverage can be extended when the benefits are integrated. This approach is a good example of the product evolution that is still occurring as the LTC insurance market matures. During the early 1980s, insurers were reluctant to move much beyond nursing home-only policies.

Numerous other features that make LTC insurance a challenge to market need to be considered. For example, to help keep premiums down, it is common to offer a deductible period ranging from 20 to 100 days. During this time, the insured pays for the cost of care. Inflation protection is an option that adds significantly to the premium, helping to keep the benefit current with the cost of care—an important consideration given the long time before policyholders are likely to need benefits. A nonforfeiture benefit adds significantly to the premium because it is designed to give the policyholder money back if the policy is terminated. However, it is generally not advisable to buy a policy that might be dropped or exchanged.

Public interest in LTC prompted Congress to pass legislation in 1996 establishing policy features that qualify LTC insurance to be tax deductible under certain circumstances. Congress has not yet made LTC premiums directly deductible by individuals or deductible through retirement plans—strategies that would provide a more significant incentive to purchase this type of protection. However, as part of the 2006 Medicaid reform legislation, Congress allowed all states to replicate an LTC insurance incentive strategy that has operated in several states since 1993. These states offer asset protection under special Medicaid rules that give purchasers of private LTC insurance help in avoiding impoverishment from LTC expenses. Without the special asset protection, shorter, more affordable coverage can still leave purchasers at risk for impoverishment from catastrophic expenses. Faced with this possibility, people often go without LTC insurance even though they could afford some protection. The state programs are intended to encourage more middle-income people to buy LTC insurance.

The market for LTC insurance is still underdeveloped. An estimated 85% of Americans over 45 years of age (82 million people) have neither public nor private insurance coverage for LTC. Middle-income families represent the largest segment of this population and are most at risk for ending up impoverished and on Medicaid if they need LTC and have not prepared financially for that risk.

—*Mark R. Meiners*

See also Economics of Aging; Long-Term Care; Managed Care; Medicare; Palliative Care and the End of Life

Further Readings and References

America's Health Insurance Plans. Long-term care insurance in 2002: Research findings. Available at: www.ahip.org/content/default.aspx?bc=39|341|328|454. Accessed September 20, 2006.

Axelrod-Stone J. Medicaid's Long-Term Care Insurance Partnership Program: CRS report for Congress. Available at: www.law.umaryland.edu/marshall/crsreports/crs documents/RL3261001212005.pdf. Accessed September 20, 2006.

Lewis S, Wilken J, Merlis M. Regulation of private long-term care insurance: Implementation experience and key issues. Available at: www.kff.org/insurance/upload/Regulation-of-Private-Long-Term-Care-Insurance-Implementation-Experience-and-Key-Issues-Report.pdf. Accessed September 20, 2006.

Meiners MR, McKay HL, Mahoney KJ. Partnership insurance: An innovation to meet LTC financing needs in an era of federal minimalism. *J Aging Social Policy.* 2002;14:75–83.

MacArthur Study of Successful Aging

The MacArthur Study of Successful Aging was initiated in 1988 to study factors associated with "successful aging"; that is, living longer while avoiding major cognitive and physical disability. Participants were recruited on the basis of age (70 to 79 years only) and physical and cognitive functioning from three communities in the eastern United States: Durham, North Carolina; East Boston, Massachusetts; and New Haven, Connecticut. More than 4,000 age-eligible men and women were screened using four criteria of physical functioning and two criteria of cognitive functioning to identify those functioning in the top third of the age group. The screening criteria were as follows: (a) no self-reported disability on the Katz Activities of Daily Living (ADLs) scale, (b) no more than one disability on the Rosow–Breslau and Nagi self-reported scales of physical function and mobility, (c) ability to hold a semitandem balance for at least 10 seconds, (d) ability to stand up from a seated position five times within 20 seconds, (e) score of at least 6 on the 9-item Short Portable Mental Status Questionnaire, and (f) ability to recall at least three of six elements from a short story after delay. Of the 1,313 potential participants who met the screening criteria, 1,189 (91%) agreed to participate in the study and provided informed consent.

Baseline data were collected during 1988–1989 and included a 90-minute face-to-face interview for standard sociodemographic and socioeconomic data, health status, chronic illnesses, medications, psychosocial characteristics, and health behaviors as well as an examination for vital signs, height, weight, waist and hip circumference measurement, and detailed assessments of physical and cognitive performance. Participants were also asked to provide blood samples at the time of the face-to-face interview/examination as well as 12-hour overnight urine samples collected from 8 o'clock the evening of the interview to 8 o'clock the next morning.

Beginning in 1991, surviving cohort members were reinterviewed and all measures from the baseline interview/examination were reassessed between 24 and 32 months after the first interview. Of the 1,118 surviving members of the original cohort, 1,012 (90%) completed this second interview and examination. A majority also provided blood samples, and overnight 12-hour urines samples were collected from a randomly selected subset of 200 participants.

A third interview and examination was conducted during 1995–1997 after a mean interval of 57 months from the second interview. No blood or urine samples were collected. Of the 916 surviving cohort members, 722 (79%) completed the interview and examination.

In addition to detailed health and functioning assessments from the two face-to-face follow-up contacts, other ongoing follow-up health outcomes data are being collected from two sources: (a) Medicare Provider Analysis and Review claims records from the Centers for Medicare and Medicaid Services documenting health events serious enough to cause hospitalization and (b) causes and dates of death from the National Death Index. There were 489 deaths in the cohort through 2000.

The MacArthur Study of Successful Aging was, and continues to be, unique among large-scale prospective cohort studies because it recruited older adults who had been aging well (with respect to maintaining a high level of physical and cognitive functioning ability), collected a wealth of data on psychosocial and biological factors (including assessments of resting levels of the stress hormones epinephrine and cortisol) as well as detailed physical and cognitive performance assessments, and followed these older adults to see which of them continued to age well. There was 7.5 years of follow-up on physical and cognitive functioning and 14 years (and growing) of follow-up on total and cause-specific mortality and major morbidity (based on Medicare hospitalization claims data).

Major findings of the MacArthur Study of Successful Aging include demonstration of associations between elevated levels of resting stress hormone (specifically, cortisol and epinephrine) and declines in physical and cognitive functioning, between markers of chronic inflammation (high levels of C-reactive protein or low levels of albumin in the serum) and onset of physical disability, and between low blood vitamin levels (and high levels of homocysteine) and declines in physical and cognitive functioning. The study also demonstrated convincingly the role of psychosocial factors in maintaining health and level of functioning (and their relationship with biological parameters as well). Social integration and emotional support were shown to predict reduced risks for cognitive decline and to correlate negatively with levels of stress hormones. Stronger instrumental self-efficacy beliefs (i.e., regarding one's ability to deal with instrumental activities of daily living [IADLs]) predicted better memory performance, whereas weaker self-efficacy beliefs and depressive symptomatology were associated with greater risk of developing new physical disability. In addition, relationships seen in young adults between sociodemographic characteristics and health were confirmed. For instance, low socioeconomic status, cigarette smoking, and low levels of regular physical exercise all were found to predict declines in physical performance. Because the cohort was selected for high functioning at baseline, it is unlikely that these findings reflect the effect of poor underlying health or disability on psychosocial factors (e.g., depressive symptoms) or health behavior (e.g., reduced exercise), and it is likely that the findings from the MacArthur Study of Successful Aging indeed reflect causal roles for psychosocial factors, health behaviors, and stress hormones.

The MacArthur Study of Successful Aging was also the first to investigate the role of comprehensive biological indexes in mediating the effect of psychosocial and behavioral factors on health outcomes. Although traditional biological markers, such as blood pressure and lipids, tend to have smaller associations with health risk in older adults than in younger cohorts, risk in older adults accrues from elevations in multiple biological factors and composite risk scores constructed from multiple biological systems can provide better risk prediction. The concept of *allostatic load* has been advanced to capture the total dysregulation across multiple physiological systems, a total that is postulated to have a significant impact on health risks. This concept originates from the observation that the internal physiological milieu adapts to environmental demands (this phenomenon has been called allostasis), as in the classic "fight-or-flight" response to a physical danger and the adrenalin rush before challenging situations such as public speaking. When allostatic adaptation efforts are excessive (in terms of frequency, duration, and/or extent), it can lead to gradual loss of the body's ability to maintain system parameters within normal operating ranges. Frequent or chronic physiological arousal has been associated with ultimate dysregulation of major physiological systems (including the hypothalamic–pituitary–adrenal axis, the sympathetic nervous system, and the immune system). Allostatic load is the total accumulation of such dysregulation across physiological systems and was hypothesized to mediate the effects of psychosocial stresses on health and functioning.

A composite allostatic load score constructed from traditional biological markers (e.g., blood pressure, lipids) and stress hormones in the MacArthur Study of Successful Aging predicted a variety of health outcomes (including incident cardiovascular events, decline in physical and cognitive functioning, and total mortality), although none of the biological markers on its own had a large association with health outcomes. Consistent with its role as a mediator of psychosocial effects on health, allostatic load was found to be an important mediator of socioeconomic differences in mortality independent of differences in underlying health and health behaviors.

Ongoing work in the MacArthur Study of Successful Aging includes investigating the independent roles of perceived usefulness, positive affect, and personal mastery in older adults as well as determining the importance of sequentially monitoring biological markers as people age.

—Arun S. Karlamangla
and Teresa E. Seeman

See also Allostatic Load and Homeostasis; Biomarkers of Aging; Positive Attitudes and Health; Stress; Successful Aging

Further Readings and References

Berkman LF, Seeman TE, Albert M. High, usual, and impaired functioning in community-dwelling older men and women: Findings from the MacArthur Foundation Research Network on Successful Aging. *J Clin Epidemiol.* 1993;46:1129–1140.

Karlamangla AS, Singer B, Chodosh J, Seeman TE. Urinary cortisol excretion as a predictor of incident cognitive impairment. *Neurobiol Aging.* 2005;26:S80–S84.

Karlamangla AS, Singer B, Greendale G, Seeman, TE. Increase in urinary epinephrine excretion is positively associated with subsequent cognitive decline in elderly men: MacArthur Studies of Successful Aging. *Psychoneuroendocrinology.* 2005;30:453–460.

Seeman TE, Berkman LF, Charpentier PA. Behavioral and psychosocial predictors of physical performance: MacArthur Studies of Successful Aging. *J Gerontol A Biol Sci Med Sci.* 1995;50:M177–M183.

Seeman TE, Crimmins E, Huang MH, et al. Cumulative biological risk and socio-economic differences in mortality: MacArthur Studies of Successful Aging. *Social Sci Med.* 2004;58:1985–1997.

Seeman TE, Singer BH, Rowe JW, Horwitz RI, McEwen BS. Price of adaptation: Allostatic load and its health consequences. *Arch Intern Med.* 1997;157:2259–2268.

MALNUTRITION

See NUTRITION, MALNUTRITION, AND FEEDING ISSUES

MANAGED CARE

Managed care can be thought of as an outgrowth of health insurance. It is basically a contract to provide, or arrange to have provided, a defined set of health services for a defined population. The population may be defined in terms of a geopolitical area, a set of beneficiaries in a given program, employees of a company, or volunteers who choose to enroll. The greatest problems occur with the latter because of selection effects.

In the case of older persons, managed care has been used actively with the two programs that serve them: Medicare and Medicaid. Politicians' attraction to managed care is based on several elements:

1. It provides a way of making liabilities explicit. Medicare and Medicaid are viewed as entitlement programs, meaning that the demands and costs cannot be forecasted easily. Managed care is a prospectively paid program.

2. It distances the government from politically difficult situations. To the extent that hard rationing or denial of coverage decisions are needed, the managed care company, rather than the government, will take the heat.

3. Many believe that it will save money. In truth, managed care saves the government money only if the premiums are well negotiated. They rarely are. More often, the premiums are set to attract managed care organizations (MCOs) that are quick to depart the scene if the rates drop.

Managed care should be an ideal vehicle to achieve many of the goals of geriatrics in many ways, including the following:

- Its payment approach supports the concept of investment in comprehensive assessment with the expectation of subsequent savings through less use of expensive services.
- Its infrastructure can support geriatric assessment and consultation teams.
- It can invest in better primary care.
- It can implement information systems that provide greater continuity of care.

Nonetheless, managed care has not lived up to its potential. Given the poor systems of risk adjustment, most MCOs try to avoid developing a reputation for being good at caring for complex geriatric cases for fear of attracting more of them. MCOs have been more likely to look for financial benefits for favorable selection; that is, attracting healthy clients and getting paid at average rates.

Managed Care in Medicare

The Centers for Medicare and Medicaid Services (CMS) has been pursuing a managed care agenda for more than two decades. The original concept was to have Medicare set a capitation rate based on the prevailing fee-for-service rate. The adjusted average per capita cost (AAPCC) was set at 95% of the county level after adjusting with readily available administrative data (e.g., age, nursing home residence, Medicaid enrollment). County rates varied widely, and those with high AAPCCs were often attractive to MCOs. However, complaints from rural and more frugal areas created subsequent adjustments that tilted to payments away from the high areas and caused many MCOs to withdraw from the market. The Medicare managed care programs were initially called Medicare + Choice, and have now been rechristened Medicare Advantage. The Medicare Modernization Act included major inducement payments to attract MCOs back into the Medicare arena.

Medicare spawned two programs of special interest. The social health maintenance organization (SHMO) was patterned on a concept originated many years ago that argued that better social care could reduce demands for medical care. The SHMO expanded the purview of the health maintenance organization (HMO) to include some long-term care (LTC) coverage, which was paid for by paying 100% of the AAPCC and allowing a new category of nursing home certifiable that was paid at a higher rate. Four SHMOs were created during the first wave. One withdrew after several years of demonstration funding, and another was added during a second wave. The first wave of SHMOs offered few targeted geriatric services and added LTC as a benefit for a small minority of enrollees. An evaluation of both generations of SHMOs found that they provided few advantages over traditional Medicare HMOs, and they eventually were scheduled to be merged into the larger parent program by 2007.

Another variant of Medicare managed care was the program developed by Evercare, a health plan and service provider. It contracted to provide Medicare services to Medicare beneficiaries living long term in nursing homes. This group receives a higher Medicare capitation rate because nursing home residence is used as a marker of greater risk for medical care. Evercare made active use of nurse practitioners they hired to complement the work of primary care physicians. By shifting the location of services to rate for many problems in nursing homes, including paying the homes an added few for the extra care, Evercare was able to dramatically reduce the use of hospitals and emergency rooms without impairing quality of care. Both the SHMOs and Evercare emphasized the need to improve rate setting to recognize the varied risk among Medicare beneficiaries. Subsequent efforts developed better risk adjustment models that incorporate diagnoses.

Managed Care in Medicaid

Medicaid programs were also attracted to managed care. In essence, Medicaid is at least two different programs. It proved to be relatively simple to develop capitated rates for women and children because most beneficiaries used very few services and those who did were readily identified by diagnoses and programs. The Medicaid benefits for older persons, in contrast, are defined largely by the gaps left by Medicare. A number of states introduced capitated programs for all or part of Medicaid services. Some states elected to cover all but the nursing home costs. Arizona has probably the most developed program through its Arizona Long-Term Care System (ALTCS). It contracted initially with counties, and later with other MCOs, to provide capitated LTC services while acute care remained covered under fee-for-service Medicare. It negotiated capitated rates that assumed that a proportion of those receiving LTC would be cared for in the community and increased that forecasted proportion each renegotiation. ALTCS was evaluated as providing very good services compared with a neighboring state.

Minnesota introduced the Prepaid Medical Assistance Program (PMAP) during the 1980s. PMAP covered all Medicaid expenses except nursing home care and some waiver services, but it was recently amended (and renamed Minnesota Senior Care) to cover the first 180 days of nursing home care and waiver services. Wisconsin has created a managed care approach, Wisconsin Family Care, that contracts with counties to provide LTC services under a capitated arrangement. Texas has contracted for care in Houston, but its spread to other parts of the state has been challenged. The Visiting Nurse Service (VNS) in New York City has developed a managed care program for LTC, VNS Choice, that allows patients to retain their own doctors' services.

Managed Care and the Dually Eligibles

The subset of individuals who are jointly eligible for care under Medicare and Medicaid represents a special high-risk group. Given that most older people on Medicaid become eligible by virtue of spending down to medically needy status, these individuals are disproportionately high users of both Medicare and Medicaid services. Several managed care programs have been designed specifically to address this group. A basic rationale for such capitated care is the opportunity to coordinate funding and services better and create options beyond nursing homes for those who need LTC, but the models differ by who is targeted. The best known is the Program for All-inclusive Care of the Elderly (PACE). PACE is targeted very specifically at dually eligible persons who are deemed to be eligible

for nursing home care but are still living in the community—a small subset of the dually eligible. PACE has now achieved operational status as a recognized alternative under Medicare. The heart of PACE care is a commitment to interdisciplinary teamwork and day care. This means that an enrollee must give up his or her regular physician. These requirements have impeded enrollment. An evaluation of the PACE program while it was still a demonstration found that it did reduce hospital use but did not affect functional status.

Given the problems in attracting clients to PACE, many programs have been experimenting with variants that would allow enrollees to keep their regular doctors. One such model is the Wisconsin Partnership Program (WPP). It uses a case management team of a nurse, a nurse practitioner, and a social worker to replace the interdisciplinary care team under PACE. The nurse practitioner is responsible for liaising with the physician. An evaluation of this program found that it did not change functional levels, but it was well received by consumers and their families. Nor did it affect use. Indeed, it was less effective than comparable PACE programs. One reason may be that each participating physician had only a few patients and hence was not motivated to change his or her modus operandi.

The Minnesota Senior Health Options (MSHO) program was designed to extend the Medicaid managed care to cover duals. It contracted with health plans, which in turn subcontracted much of the care to other organizations. MSHO imposed few service demands on the plans beyond mandating case management. In contrast to WPP, MSHO served seniors in both nursing homes and the community. It used the same nursing home eligible risk adjuster capitated payment employed by PACE and WPP for those clients in that payment cell. MSHO did not affect the functional levels of its enrollees. It did show a substantial reduction in hospital use among its nursing home enrollees, but that rate was comparable to what its major provider of such care achieved on its own. There were no substantial effects on quality. Here too, each physician who served the community clientele had only a handful of MSHO clients.

Massachusetts has launched a managed care program for dual eligibles, Senior Care Options

(SCO), that is much more prescriptive. It requires evidence of active geriatric practice and a network of experienced providers for both medical and social care. This greater restriction, as expected, has reduced the number of plans that have bid to become part of the program, but its results will be worthy of tracking.

The passage of the Medicare Modernization Act, which calls for transferring coverage for drugs from Medicaid to Medicare, has created a major impetus for Medicaid beneficiaries to enroll in Medicare managed care. It seems reasonable that more dual programs will be created.

Summary

Managed care seems theoretically suited to caring for older persons, but its implementation has not lived up to that promise. Many governmental units have been attracted to the concept in the hopes of saving money, but its capacity to save money depends entirely on how the capitation rates are constructed. So far, MCOs seem ready to flee if they do not like the rates. Hence, it seems unlikely that rate setting will ever benefit the government.

—*Robert Kane*

See also Economics of Aging; Health and Public Policy; Long-Term Care; Medicaid; Medicare

Further Readings and References

Kane RL. Managed care as a vehicle for delivering more effective chronic care for older persons. *J Am Geriatr Soc.* 1998;46:1034–1039.

Leutz WN, Abrahams R, Greenlick M, Kane RA, Prottas J. Targeting expanded care to the aged: Early SHMO experience. *Gerontologist.* 1988;28:4–17.

Morris R. Welfare reform 1973: The social services dimension. *Science.* 1973;181:515–522.

MARITAL STATUS

There is a long-standing research finding that marriage is beneficial to the health of adults of all ages. During later life especially, as health declines become more common, marriage can impart important benefits such as caregiving and social support. This entry focuses on (a) explanations of why marriage is linked to good health and the evidence among older adults, (b) the impact of widowhood on health among older adults, and (c) the limited research on divorce and health among older adults.

Marriage and Health

There are two primary arguments for why marriage and health should be connected. First, the marital selection perspective posits that healthy people tend to marry other healthy people, whereas less healthy people are more likely to remain unmarried or become divorced, separated, or widowed. Second, the marriage protection perspective refers to married adults having access to beneficial social, psychological, and physical resources that influence physical and mental health positively. There appears to be more evidence for the protection argument than for the selection perspective. Among all adults, the mechanisms through which marriage is thought to be protective of health include healthy behaviors, social support, and economic resources.

Research indicates that marriage generally leads to an increase in healthy behaviors such as regular visits to the doctor, exercise, and eating well. In addition to healthy behaviors, researchers argue that marriage provides two health-enhancing resources: social and economic support. Adults who are married generally benefit from increased emotional support. Research indicates that married adults tend to feel loved, esteemed, and cherished. Clearly, social support is dependent on the quality of the marital relationship. Finally, married households typically have higher income than do single households.

Much research has focused on the connection of marriage to health, and one interesting corollary is the hypothesis that there may be age differences in the effects of marriage on health. Recent evidence suggests that marriage is associated with positive health outcomes across all age groups, with the strongest effects among those 18 to 44 years of age. However, marriage shows consistent effects on health among those age 65 years and older. For example, using National Health Interview Survey data, nationally representative data for the U.S. civilian noninstitutionalized population, C. A. Schoenborn found in 2004 that married persons age 65 years and older were less likely than their widowed, divorced, or separated counterparts, and also less likely than never-married persons and those living with partners, to be in fair or poor self-rated health. This finding is consistent across other health outcomes. For instance, widowed older adults were more than twice as likely to experience some activity limitation (45.6%) than were married older adults (28.9%). Similarly for psychological distress, older married adults were less likely to have serious psychological distress than were older adults who were not married.

Widowhood and Health

Of particular interest to researchers is the relationship of spousal loss to health. Widowhood has been shown to be significantly correlated with poor health when compared with married persons, as mentioned previously, and increased life expectancy will contribute to increasing numbers of widows in the United States over the next several decades. In addition, a continued high divorce rate coupled with the aging of the baby boom generation may also lead to increased divorce rates among older adults. It is important to explore the health effects of these life transitions separately to better understand their significance.

More than 10.5 million adults over 65 years of age are widowed. The transition to widowhood can be accompanied by myriad health issues for several reasons. The loss of a spouse, in addition to being emotionally devastating, can mean the loss of one's primary caregiver, social support, and financial resources. Widowhood can be followed by increased hospital stays or use of long-term care facilities as well as comorbidities such as depression, limitations in activities of daily living (ADLs), and fair or poor self-rated health.

Further evidence from the Changing Lives of Older Couples survey suggests that widowhood is a significant predictor of depression in both men and women

age 65 years and older. However, these researchers found that the effect of widowhood on mental health was dependent on marital quality. For individuals who reported a higher level of dependence on their spouses, anxiety levels increased over the two waves of data; for those who reported less dependence on their spouses, anxiety levels decreased. Finally, the results of this study indicated that adjustment to widowhood was most difficult for those who responded that the quality of their marital relationships was high. Respondents who reported more conflict in their relationships had less difficulty in making the adjustment to widowhood.

Divorce and Health

With the divorce rate not showing any signs of diminishing significantly, there will likely be substantially higher numbers of divorced persons over 65 years of age than there are currently. According to census numbers for 2004, of approximately 35 million American adults over 65 years of age, approximately 8% (2.7 million) were divorced. American Indian and Alaska Native persons had the largest percentage of divorced older adults at 13.7%, followed by 11.2% of non-Hispanic Blacks, 7.4% of Hispanics, 7% of Whites, and 6.3% of Asians and Pacific Islanders.

Although statistics about divorce and health exist, studies that include older adults are limited. However, the 1999–2002 National Health Interview Survey produced data about a variety of health outcomes in divorced persons age 65 years and older. The results indicate that divorced persons, as compared with those who were never married or were living with partners or married, were more likely to be in fair or poor health, have activity limitations, or have limitations in physical or social functioning. Divorced persons were also more likely than those who were never married, married, or widowed to suffer from low back pain, headaches, or serious psychological distress.

Another study that focused on divorce and health among older adults used longitudinal data from the Americans' Changing Lives survey and tested hypotheses about the relationship between divorce and self-assessed health in persons 28 to 98 years of age at baseline. These authors found striking gender differences such that the transition to divorce between Time 1 and Time 2 had different effects on self-assessed health for men and women when controlling for time elapsed, health, age, income, education, race, and employment status. For men 60 years of age, divorce was associated with a 10% to 15% decrease in the probability of reporting excellent or very good health; however, for women the same age, the transition was associated with a 20% to 25% *increase* in the probability of reporting excellent or very good health. This trend continued for those making the transition to divorce at 70 years of age. For men, that transition was associated with a 30% to 35% decrease in the probability of reporting excellent or very good health; for women, it was associated with a 25% to 30% increase.

The literature about divorce and health lacks evidence about older people who are divorced or who divorce during old age. During the coming decades, as the U.S. divorce rate rises or even stays high, greater numbers of older divorced people will be available for study about their health. More research is needed to help shed light on the reasons for divorce during old age and subsequent effects on health.

—*M. Kristen Peek and Meredith Masel*

See also Loneliness; Social Networks and Social Supports; Socioeconomic Status

Further Readings and References

Schoenborn CA. *Marital Status and Health: United States, 1999–2002.* Hyattsville, Md: National Center for Health Statistics; 2004. Advance Data From Vital and Health Statistics, No. 351.

Smith KR, Zick CD. Linked lives, dependent demise? Survival analysis of husbands and wives. *Demography.* 1994;31:81–93.

Waite LJ. Does marriage matter? *Demography.* 1995;32: 483–507.

Waldron I, Hughes ME, Brooks TL. Marriage protection and marriage selection: Prospective evidence for reciprocal effects of marital status and health. *Social Sci Med.* 1996; 43:113–123.

Williams K, Umberson D. Marital status, marital transitions, and health: A gendered life course perspective. *J Health Social Behav.* 2004;45:81–98.

MEALS ON WHEELS PROGRAM

See CONTINUUM OF CARE

MEDICAID

Medicaid was enacted in 1965, under Title 19 of the Social Security Act, to assist states in paying for the health care of the very poor. Medicaid set minimum national standards of who should be covered and what services they should receive, but it gave the states the flexibility to determine the remainder of their individual state programs. As a result of this flexibility, each state Medicaid program is unique. An individual eligible for services in one state might not be eligible in another. Moreover, the services covered in one state might not be covered in another.

Eligibility

In general, eligibility is based on fitting into a specific category of eligibility and meeting an income and resource test. These financial tests vary not only across states but also by service needs within a state. Covered categories include being aged, blind, disabled, or a member of a single-parent family with dependent children. Income tests are usually tied to specific levels related to poverty, and the resource test is based on having financial and other "countable" assets under specific thresholds. In some states, the income test can be met when needed medical care costs are sufficiently high to reduce income. Pregnant women and children whose family incomes are below 133% of the federal poverty level and recipients of adoption or foster care assistance are also eligible. In 2004, some 42.4 million people were enrolled in Medicaid. In 2003, Centers for Medicare and Medicaid reported spending $267 billion on Medicaid services. Children accounted for 46% of enrollees, adults in families accounted for 25%, nonelderly blind and disabled people accounted for 19%, and aged people accounted for 10%. Although children and nondisabled adults constitute the largest number of beneficiaries, they consume the smallest share of the expenditures. In 2003, 30% of Medicaid payments were for older people, 41% were for nonelderly people with disabilities, only 16% were for children, and only 10% were for adults in families, according to Kaiser Family Foundation figures published in 2006.

Different State, Different Program

Medicaid was established such that states have a tremendous amount of latitude in establishing an administrative structure, what services they will pay for, how much and by what method they will pay providers, how they calculate income and assets, and in which optional categories benefits will be covered. States receive federal matching funds for every dollar spent on Medicaid services, but the precise federal match, or participation rate, is inversely related to the state's fiscal capacity (measured primarily by using per capita income), ranging from no more than 83% for the poorest states to no less than 50% for the richest ones.

Consequently, each of the 50 states, the District of Columbia, and each of the 5 U.S. territories has a different Medicaid program. Someone who is eligible in one state, district, or territory might not be eligible in another. Expenditures vary greatly between states, ranging from a per capita average of $2,334 in California to $7,749 in New York, according to Centers for Medicare and Medicaid figures in 2004.

What Medicaid Covers

Mandatory health services provided under Medicaid include inpatient and outpatient hospital care, physician services, laboratory and X-ray services, primary and preventive care, nursing facility and home health care, and other medically necessary services. But Medicaid also provides coverage for some Medicare beneficiaries when Medicare does not cover their needs. In 2002, Medicaid provided supplemental health coverage for 7.2 million Medicare beneficiaries (18% of all Medicare enrollees), according to Commission on Medicare and Medicaid figures in 2002. This kind of spending constitutes 42% of all

Medicaid expenditures, according to the Kaiser Commission on Medicaid and the Uninsured in 2004. For certain low-income Medicare beneficiaries, Medicaid pays the Medicare Part B premium (which covers physician services) as well as the Medicare deductibles and copayments. Medicaid is also a major source of coverage for long-term care, financing 47% of national long-term care expenditures. In 2001, 35% of Medicaid spending went toward long-term care, as the Health Policy Institute noted in 2002.

Changes to Medicaid

Historically, Medicaid was tied to eligibility in other public assistance programs, such as Aid to Families with Dependent Children (AFDC) and Supplemental Security Insurance (SSI). However, beginning in 1984, a series of expansions in Medicaid coverage reflected a significant shift in the philosophical underpinnings of the program. First was a critical change to provide coverage of prenatal care, and in 1988 Medicaid began to assist low-income Medicare beneficiaries with their Medicare deductibles, copayments, and premiums. For persons age 65 years and older with incomes below 100% of the federal poverty level, Medicaid pays Medicare Part A and Part B premiums, deductibles, and coinsurance; for those with incomes between 100% and 120% of poverty, Medicaid pays the Medicare supplementary medical insurance Part B premium. Finally, individuals who were receiving Medicare because of disabilities but lost entitlement to Medicare benefits because they returned to work may now purchase Medicare Part A. Alternatively, individuals who have incomes below 200% of the federal poverty level and are not eligible for Medicaid benefits may qualify to have Medicaid pay their monthly Medicare Part A premiums.

Increased Coverage Through Managed Care

Increasingly, managed care is becoming the dominant form of reimbursement for Medicaid services. Managed care provides financial incentives to avoid inappropriate and marginally useful services and to focus more attention on primary care and coordination of care. Between 1991 and 1994, the number of Medicaid beneficiaries enrolled in managed care plans nearly tripled, from 2.7 million to 7.8 million, reaching 25.3 million by 2003.

Medicaid waivers states are always looking for ways to control state health care spending and expand coverage to the uninsured. States can propose to the federal government demonstration programs that are exempt from federal requirements. If approved by the Centers for Medicare and Medicaid Services, states are still able to receive federal matching funds so long as the program promotes Medicaid objectives and the effect on the federal government is budget neutral. The advantage to a state of requesting a waiver is that it can establish a program that does not necessarily serve all beneficiaries or necessarily serve a group of beneficiaries across the state. Moreover, such programs can have different eligibility requirements and waiting lists. Many waivers exist in each state. The greatest number of waivers are in the area of long-term care. Less than a handful of states have established statewide home- or community-based long-term care services, and yet every state has multiple waivers to provide some aspect of home- or community-based care. These experiments are being performed in hopes of finding better ways to offset nursing home care (which is a required statewide service).

Sometimes, waivers are so successful that they become an integral part of health care delivery. For example, the Program of All-Inclusive Care for the Elderly (PACE) began as a federal demonstration waiver and is now a unique capitated managed care benefit for the frail elderly. It features a comprehensive medical and social service delivery system financed by integrated Medicare and Medicaid dollars. The Balanced Budget Act of 1997 (BBA) established PACE as a permanent entity within the Medicare program and as a state option under the Medicaid program. As of 2003, 17 states had approved PACE providers and 2 states had pending PACE activity. The BBA also authorized the State Child Health Insurance Program (SCHIP) known as Title XXI. SCHIP enables states to initiate and expand health care to uninsured low-income children.

Tightening Coverage and Eligibility

Medicaid represents a real political conundrum for policymakers. This program covers millions of people who otherwise would not have health care coverage. As a result, access to necessary care is improved and health care providers can get paid for providing this care. Although most Medicaid beneficiaries are relatively low cost (because they are children or healthy mothers), many Medicaid beneficiaries are disabled or quite ill. Therefore, the program, which is now larger than Medicare in both numbers of people and dollars expended, is a significant part of each state budget.

This does not, however, diminish the desire of many to find ways to spend less on Medicaid. On February 8, 2006, President George W. Bush signed into law the Deficit Reduction Act of 2005. The Congressional Budget Office estimates that this legislation will reduce Medicaid expenditures by $43.2 billion over the next decade, according to the Kaiser Commission on Medicaid and the Uninsured in 2006. Approximately half of the reductions in expenditures will be through the provision of premiums and higher copayments and deductibles for beneficiaries. But states will also be able to change the benefits covered. In addition, this law dramatically changed the way in which the distribution of savings prior to Medicaid would be examined and counted. Prior to this change in the law, individuals applying for nursing home care needed to divest all but approximately $2,000 in financial and other countable assets. Those who transferred assets at below-market rates within 3 years of applying to Medicaid were subject to a delay in eligibility based on how long it has been since they transferred those assets. Under the new law, instead of 3 years, Medicaid will look back 5 years. Moreover, instead of applying the penalty to the date of the asset transfer, the penalty date will be applied to the date of application, resulting in a longer period of time during which one will be denied Medicaid. Furthermore, anyone with more than $500,000 in home equity will not be able to apply for Medicaid benefits.

—Robert B. Friedland

See also Medicare

Further Readings and References

Health Policy Institute, Georgetown University, based on data from Burwell B, Eiken S, Sredl K. Medicaid long-term care expenditures in FY2001. Memorandum, MEDSTAT Group; 2002.

Kaiser Commission on Medicaid and the Uninsured. *Deficit Reduction Act of 2005: Implications for Medicaid.* Washington, DC: Kaiser Commission on Medicaid and the Uninsured; 2006.

Sommers A, Cohen M. Medicaid's high cost enrollees: How much do they drive program spending? Issue Paper, Kaiser Commission on Medicaid and the Uninsured; 2006. Henry J. Kaiser Family Foundation.

MEDICARE

Medicare was enacted in 1965 under Title 18 of the Social Security Act to help older people obtain and pay for medical care. Prior to passage of Medicare, approximately half of Americans age 65 years and older had any health insurance (vs. 75% of those under 65 years of age who had insurance). Many who sought private coverage were denied because of their older age or because of preexisting medical conditions. Many others could not afford coverage even if they were accepted by the insurance company. Medicare's financing structure reflects political compromises at various junctures; therefore, Medicare has different parts, with each part having its own set of financing structures.

Who Is Eligible for Medicare?

In general, to be eligible for Medicare at 65 years of age, a person (or one's spouse) must have worked at least 40 quarters in Medicare-covered employment. Those who work sufficient quarters are entitled to Part A (primarily hospital coverage) of Medicare at 65 years of age. Those eligible for Part A can then choose Part B (physician coverage). They can also choose to be in a managed care plan (Part C) or remain in a fee-for-service arrangement, and they can also join a pharmaceutical plan that is governed under Part D. People age 65 years and older whose work histories are not sufficient to result in eligibility can also enroll in Part A by paying a monthly premium. Younger workers and their dependents can also qualify if they have been receiving federal disability insurance for 2 years or have end-stage renal disease. In 2005, there were approximately 42.4 million Medicare beneficiaries, including 6.7 million under 65 years of age.

Medicare Coverage and Financing

Medicare was designed to cover acute care benefits such as hospital and physician care, but over the years the benefits under Part A and Part B have changed. In particular, preventive care benefits have been added. Most recently, however, a portion of prescription drug costs was added. The following provides an overview of coverage by the Medicare Trust Fund.

Part A: Hospital Insurance Trust Fund

Medicare Part A is an earned benefit, and for most people it requires no premium on eligibility. For each episode of acute illness, inpatient hospital care is covered for the first 60 days less a deductible ($952 in 2006). For Days 61 to 90 in a hospital, a beneficiary must pay a daily copayment ($238 in 2006). Beyond 90 days, beneficiaries may elect to draw on a 60-day lifetime reserve with a daily copayment ($4,756 in 2006). Part A also covers the following:

- Inpatient psychiatric care (190-day lifetime maximum)
- Skilled nursing care or rehabilitation associated with recuperation for up to 100 days following a hospitalization (there is no cost sharing for the first 20 days, and the daily copayment for Days 21 to 100 was $119 in 2006)
- Skilled nursing or rehabilitation benefits provided in the home and prescribed by a physician
- No deductibles, no coinsurance, and no limits on the number of covered days
- Hospice care, with services ranging from a home health aide to medical supplies and limited short-term inpatient care

Coinsurance for some services, however, does apply. Note that with hospice coverage, regular Part A coverage is forgone in exchange for the hospice coverage.

The Hospital Insurance Trust Fund is financed primarily by payroll taxes (85%), taxes from Social Security (5%), and interest payments on reserves (9%). Most of the annual trust fund income is used to fund current-year benefits. The Hospital Insurance Trust Fund is essentially operating on a "pay as you go" basis.

Part B: Supplementary Medical Insurance

Part B is voluntary for those eligible for Part A and is heavily subsidized by taxpayers. In 2006 and earlier, the Part B premium was set at 25% of anticipated Part B program costs ($88.50 per month in 2006) and was the same for everyone who chose Part B coverage. Starting in 2007, however, Part B premiums will be set at 25% of expected Part B costs for everyone whose individual income is less than $80,000 but will be set at higher amounts for beneficiaries with incomes above this threshold.

Part B generally pays 80% of physician and outpatient services after an annual deductible, leaving a 20% copayment. In 2006, the deductible was $124. This deductible is now indexed (as of 2006) to the increase in the average cost of Part B services for aged beneficiaries rather than medical inflation in general. Coverage under Part B includes the following:

- Physician services
- Laboratory and other diagnostic tests
- X-ray and other radiation therapy
- Outpatient services at a hospital, rehabilitation facility, or rural health clinic
- Home dialysis supplies and equipment
- Ambulance services
- Physical and speech therapy
- Mammography screening and screening Pap smears
- Outpatient mental health services (although only 50% of the approved amount is covered)
- Initial routine physical examination, cardiovascular blood screening tests, and diabetes screening tests and services

The Supplementary Medical Insurance trust fund is financed primarily (75%) by transfers from the general fund of the U.S. Treasury and by monthly Part B and Part D premiums paid by Medicare beneficiaries. Because the Supplementary Medical Insurance trust fund is financed on a year-by-year basis, it is always "adequately financed."

Part C: Managed Care Plans

Medicare Part C was officially created by the Balanced Budget Act of 1997 to incorporate the efficiencies of managed care plans into the Medicare system. These managed care plans receive a monthly payment from Medicare and are required to cover all Medicare services. In 1997, the program was called Medicare + Choice. However, Medicare + Choice was not very successful. The number of plans fell from 346 in 1998 to 151 in 2003. In 2003, legislation changed the name of Medicare Part C from Medicare + Choice to Medicare Advantage and, more important, changed the way managed care plans were to be paid. Initially, it was assumed that managed care plans could be paid less than the average cost of care, but it was soon recognized that managed care plans needed to be paid more through 2013 to expand this market. It is expected that Medicare Advantage payments will average 8.4% more than Medicare payments made on behalf of beneficiaries not in managed care plans, as noted by Brian Biles and colleagues in 2004.

Part D: Outpatient Prescription Drug Coverage

In June 2004, Medicare began to offer a Medicare-endorsed prescription drug discount card. These discount cards expired at the end of 2005. In 2006, Medicare enabled and facilitated the creation of a private market for outpatient prescription drugs though private plans. During the first year, there were many plans to choose from in each market, and current beneficiaries had until May 15, 2006, to enroll without a financial penalty for delaying. New beneficiaries must enroll when they first join Medicare or else pay a financial penalty for joining at a later age. Beneficiaries with these prescription drug plans will remain in Medicare but also enroll in a separate private prescription drug plan. Alternatively, beneficiaries can enroll in a Medicare managed care plan (Medicare Advantage plans) for all Medicare-covered benefits, including outpatient prescription drugs. The specific drugs covered and the premiums charged for each prescription drug plan vary by plan and by region of the country. Each plan has its own scope and depth of coverage, list of drugs covered, and drug distribution method. These Part D plans are intended to provide coverage for 75% of the cost of covered prescriptions for the first $2,250 in prescription drug expenses after a $250 deducible. They will provide no coverage for drug expenses between $2,250 and $5,100 but will resume coverage at 95% of covered prescription drug expenses in excess of $5,100. (Note that all of these amounts will be indexed to the increase in drug expenditures financed through Part D.)

What Medicare Does Not Cover

Medicare does not cover the following:

- Routine physical examinations (beyond an initial examination)
- Nonsurgical dental services
- Hearing aids
- Eyeglasses
- Most long-term care in nursing facilities, in the community, or at home
- Outpatient prescription drugs (until 2006); outpatient prescription drugs not included in the formularies of prescription drug plans (after 2006)

Unlike most private insurance, Medicare does not cap a beneficiary's out-of-pocket costs (e.g., supplemental insurance, copayments, deductibles). In 2002, Medicare beneficiaries spent on average $3,757 on health care, or 22% of their average household income, as noted by Stephanie Maxwell and colleagues in 2002. This amount does not include the out-of-pocket expenditures for long-term care.

Medicare Expenditures

Medicare is a major payer in the U.S. health care system, accounting for 17% of personal health care expenditures nationwide in 2004. Medicare represents 30% of national health expenditures for hospitals and 20% of national health expenditures for physicians. From the perspective of beneficiaries, Medicare covers approximately 55% of health care spending.

In 1970, Medicare expenditures were 0.7% of gross domestic product (GDP). By 2004, Medicare expenditures had increased to 2.6% of GDP. By 2035, the projected Medicare expenditures could be 7.8% of GDP. If this projection by the trustees of the Social Security Trust Funds is correct, by 2015 the cost rate of Medicare (expenditures as a percentage of taxable payroll) is projected to reach 3.63%, whereas the income rate (program revenues as a percentage of taxable payroll) may be only 3.20%. By 2035, the gap between expenditures and revenue could be even larger, with the cost rate at 6.43% and the income rate at 3.37% of taxable payroll. At these rates of cost and income growth, the Hospital Insurance Trust Fund will be exhausted by 2019.

Supplemental Coverage

As of 2002, most Medicare beneficiaries (88%) had supplemental Medicare coverage, as noted by Maxwell and colleagues. For the most part, this coverage pays for Medicare's copayments and deductibles; only a few policies cover services not included in Medicare. Very-low-income Medicare beneficiaries, however, can get assistance with copayments and deductibles, and even Part B premiums, through their state Medicaid programs.

—*Robert B. Friedland*

See also Economics of Aging; Health and Public Policy; Long-Term Care; Managed Care; Medicaid

Further Readings and References

Biles B, Dallek G, Nicholas LH. Medicare Advantage: Déjà vu all over again? *Health Affairs* Web exclusive. 2004;(December 15):W4-586–W4-597. Available at: http://content.healthaffairs.org/cgi/content/full/hlthaff.w4.586/DC1. Accessed September 21, 2006.

Maxwell S, Storeygard M, Moon M. *Modernizing Medicare Cost-Sharing: Policy Options and Impacts on Beneficiary and Program Expenditures.* New York: Commonwealth Fund; 2002.

U.S. Department of Health and Human Services/Centers for Medicare and Medicaid Services. *2004 Annual Report of the Boards of Trustees of the Federal Hospital Insurance and Federal Supplementary Medical Insurance Trust Funds.* Washington, DC: Government Printing Office; 2004.

MEDICATION ADHERENCE

Medication adherence or compliance describes patient medication-taking behavior and is defined as the degree to which a person's taking of medication corresponds with health or medical direction, as noted by R. B. Haynes in 1979. Historically, the term *compliance* was used as a part of the traditional biomedical model of drug treatment, but it can be interpreted as being pejorative. *Adherence* is considered as a more acceptable term because it recognizes the patient's autonomy and requires patient agreement to the recommendations given by the health care professional.

Epidemiology

Medication adherence among the elderly ranges widely, from 20% to 82%, with the most frequent estimation being around 60% depending on the detection methods used. Although there are no "gold standard" measures, ways to measure patients' adherence include pill counts, patient self-report, pharmacy claims data monitoring, drug levels, and electronic medication monitoring devices such as the Medication Event Monitoring System (MEMS). Factors that affect medication adherence in the elderly are related to drugs, patients, and the medical environment. Drug-related factors include number of drugs, complexity of drug regimen, packaging, and side effects. Patient-related factors include multiple morbidities, cognitive decline, and health beliefs. Age per se is not a predictor of adherence. Factors related to the medical environment include the patient–provider relationship, patient access/barriers to medications, and social support. Patient nonadherence may result in poor clinical outcomes, leading to additional drug therapy and/or unnecessary hospitalizations, with increased overall costs of patient care.

Interventions to Improve Medication Adherence in the Elderly

Studies on interventions to improve adherence show a range of interventions that differ by complexity (from simple to complex/multifaceted), content (from educational to behavioral), and approach (from generalized to patient-tailored interventions). Simple interventions include calendar blister packs, unit-of-use packaging, and pillboxes. Educational interventions increase a patient's knowledge about the disease or medications and include providing pamphlets, brochures, or counseling. Behavioral interventions target patient medication-taking behavior by giving reminders (written or by automated telephone). The most recommended interventional approach is individualized to a particular patient using specifically tailored multifaceted interventions (e.g., automated telephone reminders with brief counseling).

Recommendations

Health care providers need more education to be better able to counsel their patients, simplify their drug regimens, and monitor patient responses to treatment strategies. Further research on which approaches best improve medication adherence and disease/health outcomes is needed. Further research is needed to be able to better define the critical concepts of "adequate adherence" or the "threshold of adherence" necessary for clinically measurable benefit. Finally, health care professionals need to allow patients a larger role in the decision-making process (a concept of concordance), and the impact of this autonomy on adherence needs to be measured.

—*Stasa Tadic*

See also Control; Drug Underuse; Self-Efficacy; Self-Rated Health

Further Readings and References

Cooper AF, Jackson G, Weinman J, Horne R. Cardiothoracic factors associated with cardiac rehabilitation attendance: A systematic review of the literature. *Clin Rehab.* 2002; 16:541–552.

Haynes RB. Determinants of compliance: The disease and the mechanics in treatment. In: Haynes RB, Taylor DW, Sackett DL, eds. *Compliance in Health Care.* Baltimore, Md: Johns Hopkins University Press; 1979:3–18.

Lane B. Improving medication adherence. *NY City Voices.* 2001;(January–March). Available at: www.newyorkcity voices.org/index.html. Accessed September 22, 2006.

Leventhal H, Nerenz DR, Steele DJ. Illness perceptions and coping with health threat. In: Baum A, Taylor SE, Singer JE, eds. *Handbook of Psychology and Health,* Vol. 4: *Social Psychological Aspects of Health.* Hillsdale, NJ: Lawrence Erlbaum; 1984:219–252.

O'Hea EL, Grothe KB, Bodenlos JS, Boudreaux ED, White MA, Brantley PJ. Predicting medical regimen adherence: The interactions of health locus of control beliefs. *J Health Psychol.* 2005;10:705–717.

Weiden PJ, Rao N. Teaching medication compliance to psychiatric residents: Placing an orphan topic into a training curriculum. *Acad Psychiatry.* 2005;29:203–210.

MEDICATION ERRORS

Medication errors are commonly defined as any preventable events that may cause or lead to inappropriate medication use or patient harm while the medications are in the control of health care professionals or consumers. Medication errors caused by consumers are usually adherence and compliance errors and are not considered in this entry. Medication errors can occur anywhere in the medication use process, including the prescribing (by physicians and physician extenders), documenting (primarily by physicians and nursing staff), dispensing (by pharmacists), administering (by nursing staff), and monitoring (collective responsibility of all members of the health care team) steps. This entry addresses only medication dispensing and administering errors.

Epidemiology of Medication Errors

Dispensing Errors

There are few studies dealing with dispensing errors. One recent study measured medication dispensing errors in 50 pharmacies located in six U.S. cities. The researchers found, by direct observation, that dispensing errors occurred on 1.7% of new and refill prescriptions. Only 6.5% of identified errors were judged to be clinically important.

Administration Errors

There are few studies of drug administration errors. One recent study investigated medication administration errors in 36 health care institutions, 12 of which were long-term care facilities in two states (Colorado and Georgia). The researchers found, by direct observation of health care providers during the administration of medications, that the mean error rate was 19% (605 of 3,216 doses administered) and that this rate did not differ across institutions. However, the percentage of errors rated as potentially harmful was only 7%. Current Centers for Medicare and Medicaid Services guidelines for long-term care facilities state that an error rate of at least 5% suggests systematic problems.

Despite the frequency of medication errors, most do not cause serious or permanent patient injury. However, medication errors are often associated with increased health care use such as the need for additional monitoring, use of antidote medications, and/or transfers to higher levels of medical care.

Interventions to Reduce Medication Errors

Reducing Administration Errors

Administration errors can occur if the following dictum is not followed: right drug, right route, right dose, right time, and right patient. Once again, the independent verification of medications by other health care workers, as well as the use of unit–dose dispensing, can reduce this type of medication error. Recently, bar code medication administration computer programs have been developed to verify the identity of the medication, patient, and nursing staff prior to drug administration. These systems have been shown to be successful at reducing medication administration errors in a variety of clinical settings.

Reducing Dispensing Errors

Common causes of dispensing errors include unsafe pharmacy work environments where the workload is too heavy, there are too many distractions, and/or the work area itself is poorly designed. The most commonly used technique is to perform an independent verification of a medication by another pharmacist prior to releasing the medication from the pharmacy. Another technique to reduce this type of error includes the use of unit–dose dispensing, where medication is dispensed in a package that is ready to administer to the patient.

Recommendations

Additional attention is needed at every step of the medication use process to develop new strategies to detect, mitigate, and eliminate medication errors. Continued research and quality-improvement efforts aimed at translating these strategies into clinical practice are necessary to ensure that medications are used in the safest way possible.

—*Steven M. Handler*

See also Age-Related Changes in Pharmacokinetics and Pharmacodynamics; Drug–Disease Interactions; Drug–Drug Interactions; Drug Underuse; Inappropriate Prescribing; Medication Adherence; Polypharmacy

Further Readings and References

Barker KN, Flynn EA, Pepper GA, Bates DW, Mikeal RL. Medication errors observed in 36 health care facilities. *Arch Intern Med.* 2002;162:1897–1903.

Cohen MR, ed. *Medication Errors: Causes, Prevention, and Risk Management.* Washington, DC: American Pharmaceutical Association; 1999.

Flynn EA, Barker KN, Carnahan BJ. National observational study of prescription dispensing accuracy and safety in 50 pharmacies. *J Am Pharm Assoc.* 2003;43:191–200.

Suggested definitions and relationships among medication misadventures, medication errors, adverse drug events, and adverse drug reactions. *Am J Health Syst Pharm.* 1998;55:165–166.

MEMORY

Despite a wealth of anecdotal evidence of age-related memory change, programmatic research on this topic is relatively recent, dating back no further than the 1970s. Most memory and aging research has relied on the laboratory methods of cognitive psychology and cognitive neuropsychology, often comparing convenience samples of healthy younger adults (18 to 30 years of age) with those of healthy older adults (age 60 years and older). Since the mid-1990s, the emergence of an interdisciplinary cognitive neuroscience of aging has caused a rapid increase in research examining the neural bases of age-related changes in memory. Findings reflect a complex mixture of age-related stability and decline across different memory functions and their neural correlates as well as a high degree of between-person variability.

Behavioral Findings

The results of experimental laboratory studies suggest that sensory memory, an initial repository for raw sensory information, remains stable with age. For example, younger and older adults' visual sensory memory stores are similar in capacity and duration. There also appears to be relatively little age-related change in short-term memory, which holds limited amounts of information in conscious awareness over brief periods of time. When younger and older adults are presented with random strings of digits or letters and asked to repeat them back in the same order after a short delay (3 to 30 seconds), older adults remember about as many items as do younger adults.

So-called "working memory" tasks, requiring the coordination of two simultaneous activities (processing new information while holding onto other information), do tend to be vulnerable to the effects of age. For example, older adults typically do worse than younger adults on tasks that require holding words in memory while answering text comprehension questions or that require remembering digits while solving mental arithmetic problems. The cause of age differences in working memory is still under debate, but there is consensus that several factors seem to be involved, including age-related cognitive slowing, age-related declines in a basic "cognitive resource" (e.g., attentional capacity), and age-related declines in the ability to inhibit processing of goal-irrelevant information.

Long-term memory, which stores information over longer periods—minutes, days, or even years—is also vulnerable to the effects of aging, although the degree of age-related change varies as a function of the type of memory task and the nature of the to-be-retrieved information. Given this diversity, it is useful to distinguish among episodic, semantic, and procedural long-term memory. In general, age differences are most pronounced in episodic memory, which involves remembering specific events ("episodes") and their context. An everyday example is trying to recall what one had for lunch yesterday. In the laboratory, older adults' episodic memory difficulties are reflected in reduced accuracy and slowed response on tests of memory for newly learned materials (e.g., words, pictures). Age-related deficits tend to be particularly pronounced when it is necessary to retrieve the contextual details of past events. For example, if statements are presented by two sources, a later recognition test may show only small age differences in memory for the statements but large age differences in memory for the source of each statement.

Although age differences in episodic memory can be attributed in part to age-related declines in processing speed, cognitive resources, and inhibition of irrelevant information, these factors cannot fully explain the decline in episodic memory. Additional causes include age-related decline in the spontaneous use of effective encoding strategies (e.g., imagery, elaborative processing), age deficits in the ability to recollect contextual details, and conservative response tendencies among older adults.

In contrast to episodic memory, semantic memory is relatively immune to age-related decline. Semantic memory includes general knowledge of facts, word meanings, and other information not associated with a specific temporal or spatial context. For example, older adults typically perform as well as, or better than, younger adults on tests of vocabulary and general knowledge. Word-finding problems and "tip of the tongue" experiences, a frequent memory complaint in older adults, appear to be caused by a mild age-related decline in the retrieval of phonological information.

A third form of long-term memory, implicit or procedural memory, is also relatively unaffected by age. Implicit memory is indicated by a change in behavior following exposure to information without intentional or conscious retrieval of that information. For example, when asked to solve anagrams, both younger and older adults are quicker to identify words to which they were recently exposed, even if they cannot consciously remember that prior exposure.

Neural Bases

Although normal aging is associated with structural and functional changes in many brain areas, medial–temporal and frontal cortical regions have been shown to play a crucial role in memory and in age-related memory change. The medial–temporal region is involved in the initial "binding" of conscious experience into coherent memories. Age-related shrinkage of the entorhinal cortex, a medial–temporal structure, has been identified as a predictor of normal age-related episodic memory decline. Neuroimaging studies have shown that parts of the hippocampus, a medial–temporal structure, are less active in older adults than in younger adults during a number of cognitive tasks, including memory encoding and working memory. However, there are also reports of age-related increases in activation in neighboring parahippocampal cortex during recognition decisions.

The prefrontal cortex is involved in coordinating and planning higher cognitive functions, including memory. Prefrontal regions are among those most affected by age-related cortical volume loss, and age-related declines in dopaminergic projections to the prefrontal cortex may also contribute to this region's role in age-related changes in memory. The prefrontal cortex shows significant changes in use with age during encoding and retrieval from working memory and long-term memory. Both decreases in activation (e.g., of left prefrontal areas during encoding) and increases in activation (e.g., of left prefrontal areas during retrieval, of bilateral dorsolateral prefrontal cortex during working memory) have been observed in older adults. In addition, older adults often activate the same frontal cortical area bilaterally during tasks for which younger adults activate either the left or right side. Although the significance of this age-related decrease in hemispheric asymmetry is still under debate, current evidence favors the view that it helps older adults to compensate for declines in overall processing efficiency.

Role of Physical and Intellectual Activity

Studies using subjective measures of physical health and fitness (e.g., health questionnaires) have not provided clear evidence for a relationship between health and memory in older adults. Objective measures have provided more conclusive, and generally positive, results. For example, in a recent longitudinal study, biological age as indexed by so-called biomarkers (e.g., visual acuity, grip strength, peak expiratory flow) was shown to be a stronger predictor of memory decline than was chronological age. Similarly, results from an ongoing large-scale study (Victoria Longitudinal Study) have indicated a positive association between intellectual activity and the degree of age-related memory decline. However, it is unclear whether this association reflects a protective effect of intellectual engagement or whether it results from self-selection (i.e., individuals with high intellectual ability and low vulnerability to cognitive decline seek out more cognitively demanding activities than do individuals with lower intellectual ability).

Intervention studies have demonstrated that older adults' memory can be boosted by physical and intellectual activity. Little is known about possible life span changes in susceptibility to such interventions because most studies have included only older participants. A recent meta-analysis of intervention studies conducted from 1966 to 2001 found that aerobic fitness training in older adults can improve executive functioning (e.g., coordination, planning) and, to a lesser extent, controlled cognitive processes (e.g., control of attention during the initial learning of a new skill). However, the extent of these improvements depended on characteristics of the training program (e.g., combined strength and aerobic training were optimal, long-term programs were more effective than short-term programs) and of the study population (e.g., mostly female samples showed greater benefits than did mostly male samples). To the extent that executive functioning and cognitive control contribute to memory performance, therefore,

the data suggest that fitness training may boost at least some forms of memory.

A recent multisite randomized controlled trial with more than 2,800 participants (Advanced Cognitive Training for Independent and Vital Elderly [ACTIVE] study) confirmed previous findings of performance improvements for both laboratory-type episodic memory tasks (e.g., word list recall) and memory for information relevant to daily activities (e.g., remembering shopping lists) after mnemonic strategy training. The training impact remained significant over a 2-year period, but participants failed to show generalization to memory tasks that were not specifically trained.

—*Julia Spaniol and David J. Madden*

See also Alzheimer's Disease; Cardiovascular System; Depression and Other Mood Disorders; Exercise and Physical Activity; Geriatric Assessment; Imaging of the Brain; Longitudinal Research; Mental Status Assessment; Mild Cognitive Impairment; Neurobiology of Aging; Normal Physical Aging; Stroke

Further Readings and References

Ball K, Berch DB, Helmers KF, et al. Effects of cognitive training interventions with older adults: A randomized controlled trial. *JAMA*. 2002;288:2271–2281.

Balota DA, Dolan PO, Duchek JM. Memory changes in healthy older adults. In: Tulving E, Craik FIM, eds. *The Oxford Handbook of Memory*. Oxford, England: Oxford University Press; 2000:395–409.

Cabeza R, Nyberg S, Park D, eds. *Cognitive Neuroscience of Aging*. Oxford, England: Oxford University Press; 2005.

Colcombe S, Kramer AF. Fitness effects on the cognitive function of older adults: A meta-analytic study. *Psychol Sci*. 2003;14:125–130.

Hultsch DF, Hertzog C, Small BJ, Dixon RA. Use it or lose it: Engaged lifestyle as a buffer of cognitive decline in aging? *Psychol Aging*. 1999;14: 245–263.

MENOPAUSE AND HORMONE THERAPY

Menopause, like puberty, is a natural event experienced by virtually every woman who lives long enough. The term *menopause* officially refers to the final menstrual period and can be identified only in retrospect in the absence of menstrual cycles for 12 months. The average age of menopause is 51 years; menopause is considered to be premature when it occurs in women under 40 years of age. The cardinal symptom of the menopausal transition, the years leading up to the last menstrual period, is a change in the menstrual cycle. For some women, the cycle length shortens; for other women, bleeding becomes heavier and periods are longer; and for yet other women, bleeding becomes irregular and unpredictable. Vasomotor symptoms ("hot flashes") also occur, but for the uninitiated they are not always recognized immediately. Most women describe episodes of intense warmth (enough to throw off the covers in bed) often starting in the chest, neck, and face, accompanied by perspiration (sometimes enough to require a change of nightgown), and subsequently a chill (enough to put covers back on). Some women have no symptoms, most women will notice some hot flashes, and a few women will experience hot flashes so severe that they must stop whatever they are doing or will experience bleeding so heavy that they are confined to home. When the menopausal transition is abrupt because of surgical removal of the ovaries or compromise of ovarian function by chemotherapy for breast or other cancers, hot flashes are often more frequent and more severe than during the natural transition.

For women who have had their uteri removed at younger ages and cannot monitor their menstrual cycles, a simple office blood test can be helpful to determine whether or not they are menopausal. Follicle-stimulating hormone (FSH) is secreted by the pituitary gland in response to a decline in ovarian hormones, so that an elevated FSH confirms the menopausal transition. Measurement of estrogen and progesterone concentrations are usually not necessary, and because ovarian hormone secretion is often erratic during the menopausal transition, results can be difficult to interpret.

In addition to the anticipated "low" levels of estrogen characteristic of postmenopausal women, estrogen concentrations intermittently surge to very high levels during the menopause transition. Over time, higher estrogen levels contribute to heavy bleeding, growth of uterine fibroid tumors, and increased risk of uterine cancer. Any departure from a woman's characteristic menstrual pattern, then, should be reviewed with her physician.

Irregular cycles and anticipation of menopause render some women less vigilant about contraception. Paradoxically, although fertility is substantially reduced at this age, unexpected pregnancies do occur. Protection against sexually transmitted diseases remains an important practice for women engaging in new sexual partners at this time of life.

The menopausal transition usually lasts several years, but for some women the process takes as long as a decade. After the menopausal transition is complete and menstruation ceases, persistent low levels of estrogen contribute to increasing symptoms of hot flashes, vaginal dryness, and painful intercourse. For the vast majority of women, hot flashes are self-limited and gradually diminish over a period of 3 to 5 years. Vaginal symptoms might respond to over-the-counter lubricants and moisturizers. Bone loss in susceptible women, if unchecked by appropriate therapy, can lead to osteoporosis and increased risk of fracture—most commonly of the wrist, spine, and hip—during the decades ahead.

The practice of prescribing estrogen for symptomatic menopausal women was popularized more than 40 years ago by Robert Wilson in his 1966 book, *Feminine Forever.* What started out as a therapy for relief of hot flashes and vaginal dryness evolved over several decades (despite an absence of clinical trial evidence of safety and efficacy) to a panacea for lifelong prevention of osteoporosis, cardiovascular disease, and dementia. The recommendation for most women to take estrogen for life was largely embraced by the medical profession and endorsed by medical groups as part of their official guidelines. Some insurance plans mandated that all postmenopausal women be prescribed hormone replacement therapy because of the perceived benefits. From 1990 to 1995, conjugated equine estrogen, known as Premarin, was the most widely dispensed prescription drug in the United States; by 2001, the market was worth more than $3.3 billion.

During the 1990s, a number of clinical trials were initiated to test the hypothesis that estrogen prevented heart disease in women. In 1998, the Heart and Estrogen/Progestin Replacement Study (HERS), the first large randomized controlled trial of hormone therapy with clinical endpoints such as heart attack and death, reported that after 4.1 years of therapy, hormone therapy did not prevent heart attacks in women with histories of heart disease as had been predicted. In fact, women on hormone therapy suffered increases in heart attacks early in the course of the study. The HERS findings, although surprising and unpopular, set the stage to challenge the dogma of "estrogen forever." Several other trials in women with heart disease were completed during the years after HERS and reported disappointing results consistent with the HERS trial.

The Women's Health Initiative (WHI) was initiated in 1992 and enrolled 27,347 women with an average age of 63 years in the largest clinical trial ever undertaken in women. Women were randomly assigned to either the most commonly used form of hormone therapy or a placebo pill (i.e., double-blind placebo-controlled trial). Women with hysterectomies ($n = 10,739$) were prescribed either estrogen alone (0.625 milligrams [mg] conjugated equine estrogen [Premarin] by mouth daily) or a look-alike placebo pill. Women with uteri ($n = 16,608$) were randomly assigned to either combined therapy with an estrogen and a progestin (0.625 mg conjugated equine estrogen with 2.5 mg medroxyprogesterone acetate [Prempro] by mouth daily) or a look-alike placebo pill. The study was designed to follow women for 8.5 years and carefully monitor their health by tracking the number of heart attacks, strokes, blood clots in the legs or lungs, cancers of the colon and breast, and fractures of the hip. Women over 65 years of age were evaluated for the onset or worsening of dementia.

In 2002, after 5.6 years of monitoring, the combined hormone study of the WHI was halted, and reports that followed indicated that the risks of hormone therapy exceeded the benefits of preventing disease in healthy women. The investigators stopped the study because the risk of breast cancer in the women assigned to hormone therapy exceeded the trial's predefined acceptable rate of new cases of breast cancer and no overall benefit for women's health was apparent. The investigators also reported that women on combined hormone therapy experienced an increase in heart attacks, especially during the first year. The risk of strokes and blood clots increased early and persisted throughout the study. The risk of dementia was increased by combined hormone therapy in women over 65 years of age. The WHI trial was the first randomized clinical trial to show that hormone therapy effectively reduced hip fractures and colon cancer and confirmed that combined therapy protected against an increase in uterine cancer that is known to occur in women with uteri taking estrogen alone.

During the months following release of the WHI results, both women and physicians were fearful about possible risks and stopped using hormone therapy. A number of women who went off hormone therapy continued to experience vasomotor symptoms (hot flashes) as well as vaginal dryness. Although other drugs have been tested for treatment of these symptoms with limited success, estrogen therapy remains the gold standard for symptom relief. In several follow-up studies from large practice groups, approximately 25% of women went back on hormone therapy for symptom relief after initially stopping. The WHI also reported that among the study participants who had hot flashes at the beginning of the trial, more than half continued to have hot flashes once they stopped hormone therapy at the end of the study. Perhaps all women initiating hormone therapy for symptom relief should be cautioned that although symptoms will be improved during therapy, there is a 50% chance that hot flashes will recur when hormone therapy is stopped.

Shortly after publication of the combined hormone therapy WHI results, the Food and Drug Administration (FDA) rewrote its guidelines to recommend that hormone therapy no longer be prescribed for long-term prevention of diseases of aging. The FDA specified three acceptable uses, or indications, for hormone therapy and stipulated that the term be changed from *hormone replacement therapy* to simply *hormone therapy*. The FDA also recommended that all manufacturers of hormone therapy include in their labeling the same risks and benefits reported by the WHI because in the absence of other information the risks and benefits of all hormone preparations are assumed to be similar.

Estrogen therapy is currently indicated by the FDA for relief of vasomotor and vaginal symptoms, but with several caveats for use. From the standpoint of hot flashes, estrogens should be prescribed in the lowest effective dose for the shortest possible time. Most manufacturers of menopausal estrogen products are now marketing them at half the dose recommended prior to the publication of the WHI, and some preparations are available in even lower doses. Clinical trials have shown that lower doses are nearly equally effective at alleviating symptoms. However, no large or long-term trials similar to the WHI have been conducted to answer the question as to whether lower doses or other preparations, such as the estrogen patch, are safer than those tested in the WHI.

Vaginal symptoms are also improved by estrogen therapy. The FDA, in the new guidelines, stipulates that if a woman's symptoms are limited to vaginal dryness or painful intercourse, she should consider using vaginal estrogens. Preparations are available as creams, tablets, or a silastic ring that slowly releases estrogen over 3 months. When used at lower doses, vaginal estrogens do not increase blood levels of estrogen substantially, so vaginal estrogen is an option for women who should not, because of history of blood clots or breast cancer, take estrogen systemically.

The third indication for estrogen therapy is prevention of osteoporosis. The FDA stipulates that other drugs are available for osteoporosis prevention and treatment, so estrogen should be used for this purpose only if the other agents have not been well tolerated and women have been counseled about their risks.

In 2004, the results of the estrogen-only arm of the WHI were published. In this study of 10,739 women without uteri who were followed for 6.8 years, the results were different from those with combined hormone therapy. Heart attack and breast cancer cases were not increased, whereas strokes and blood clots were increased to a similar extent as had been reported with combined therapy. Colon cancer was not reduced as had been shown with combined therapy. The reduction in osteoporotic fractures in women

assigned to estrogen was similar to that in women assigned to combined therapy.

Based on the results of the WHI, the current role of hormone therapy is limited to symptom relief. A number of questions, however, have been generated by careful evaluation of the WHI results: Did the particular estrogen or progestin used in the trial affect the outcomes? Would a different preparation, such as the estrogen patch, lower doses of estrogen, or micronized progesterone, have been safer? One of the most persistent questions posed is whether the WHI would have demonstrated heart benefits if the women studied had been younger and more recently menopausal. Is there a "window of opportunity" during which estrogen therapy must be started for cardiovascular benefit?

Further analysis of the WHI suggests that cardiac benefits might improve when estrogen is started in younger women. Currently, several randomized clinical trials are under way in younger women closer to the age of menopause. Although these trials are not large enough to determine differences in rates of heart attack, stroke, and death, they will determine effects of hormone therapy on the thickness of the carotid arteries and coronary artery calcium score, both measures known to correlate with heart attack risks. The results might challenge the new current dogma about the role of hormone therapy for symptom relief only in postmenopausal women as the evolution of this important story continues.

—*Cynthia A. Stuenkel*

See also Alzheimer's Disease; Health Promotion and Disease Prevention; Osteoporosis; Women's Health

Further Readings and References

NIH State-of-the-Science Panel. National Institutes of Health State-of-the-Science Conference statement: Management of menopause-related symptoms. *Ann Intern Med.* 2005; 142:1003–1013.

U.S. Preventive Services Task Force. Hormone therapy for the prevention of chronic conditions in postmenopausal women: Recommendations from the U.S. Preventive Services Task Force. *Ann Intern Med.* 2005;142:855–860.

Women's Health Initiative Steering Committee. Effects of conjugated equine estrogen in postmenopausal women with hysterectomy. *JAMA.* 2004;291:1701–1712.

Writing Group for the Women's Health Initiative. Risks and benefits of estrogen plus progestin in healthy postmenopausal women. *JAMA.* 2002;288:321–333.

MEN'S HEALTH

Men live for a shorter time than do women, although women live greater proportions of their lives with some degree of disability, on average. In addition, men have poorer health outcomes than do women. Biological differences explain some of the patterns of mortality and morbidity, but men also appear to leave medical interventions until later in the course of the disease process compared with women. Men's ideas about masculinity have a significant impact on health and illness, beliefs, and risk-taking behavior, and they play a major role in men's tendency to ignore warning signs of illness.

Certain diseases in particular differ dramatically between men and women. Men develop schizophrenia earlier and have worse outcomes than do women. Depression is up to three times more common in females than in men, but older White men are much more likely to commit suicide. The most common form of dementia, Alzheimer's disease, occurs more commonly in women, whereas vascular dementia occurs more commonly in men. Men are less often caregivers than are women, but men have a higher rate of caregiver "burnout."

The sexes also differ in their response to drugs. Men are much less responsive than women to the analgesic response of kappa opioids. Alcohol is metabolized more slowly in men than in women, and alcohol-related liver damage occurs more quickly and at lower doses of alcohol consumption in women than in men.

Sexuality

Arousal disorders in men are more likely to be inadequate genital arousal disorder (erectile dysfunction) and hypersexuality, whereas women are more likely to present with inadequate mental arousal disorder. For both sexes, arousal disorders markedly affect physical and emotional satisfaction.

Erectile dysfunction (impotence) is extremely common in older men. The most common cause is atherosclerosis, resulting in poor blood flow to the penile artery and venous leaks. Other causes include medications, endocrine conditions (e.g., prolactinoma, hypothyroidism, hyperthyroidism, diabetes mellitus), neuropathy, lumbar spinal stenosis, multiple sclerosis, and epilepsy. Cigarette smoking markedly increases the likelihood of males developing erectile dysfunction. Psychological causes of erectile dysfunction are rare in older men, although performance anxiety may worsen organic disease.

Older males with erectile dysfunction are very likely to have vascular disease in other organs. Thus, it is important to screen in these men for coronary artery disease, cerebrovascular disease, and peripheral vascular disease. Because men tend not to consult physicians as often as do women, it is important that, when men present with erectile dysfunction, these and other health issues are addressed.

Current treatment for erectile dysfunction is a phosphodiesterase-5 inhibitor such as sildenafil (Viagra), tadafil (Cialis), or vardenafil (Levitra). These drugs cannot be used in males taking nitrates, and they need to be used with caution in men taking α-adrenergic blockers. Side effects include hypotension, syncope, indigestion, headache, and blindness. The response to phosphodiesterase-5 inhibitors is poor in hypogonadal (low-testosterone level) men and can be improved with testosterone replacement. Other treatments for erectile dysfunction include intracavernosal (into the penis tissues) injections with alprostadil, papaverine, or phentolamine and insertion of a penile prosthesis. Safe sex needs to be emphasized with all men undergoing treatment for erectile dysfunction. A number of studies have shown that the most frequent use of prostitutes occurs on the days Social Security checks become available.

The health care provider needs to be aware that homosexuality occurs as commonly in older men as in younger men. Because of previous social mores, many older men have been unable to declare their sexual preference, and family conflict can erupt when an older man begins a homosexual relationship. A number of social issues, particularly the right to allow a lifelong male partner to make health decisions or issues associated with inheritance, can be obstacles to appropriate health care. The health practitioner needs to be aware of the possibility of AIDS in older gay men. In the United States, the most rapid increase in AIDS is occurring in men over 60 years of age.

Incontinence

Although incontinence generally is thought of as a female problem, it is also a serious problem in older men. By the time they reach 80 years of age, overactive bladder syndrome (urinary frequency and nocturia) is as common in men as in women. Overactive bladder can be associated with urge incontinence, one of the most common reasons for older men being placed in nursing homes.

The prevalence of lower urinary tract symptoms (LUTS)—urgency, frequency, nocturia (urinary frequency at night), incontinence, and reduced urine flow—increases with age and may significantly affect sexual functioning (LUTS is commonly associated with erectile dysfunction) and quality of life. LUTS sometimes occurs when the bladder fills and cannot empty adequately or appropriately, leading to leakage (overflow incontinence). Benign prostatic hyperplasia (BPH) also increases with age, being present in as many as 50% of men 50 years of age and in nearly 90% of autopsies of men over 80 years of age. It is usually assumed that BPH is responsible for LUTS, particularly when the urine flow rate is reduced. However, numerous cross-sectional studies have shown either no relationships or inconsistent relationships among LUTS, BPH, and urine flow. Moreover, urine flow may be low in young men without symptoms. LUTS is most often due to dysynergy (lack of coordination) in the contraction of the lower bladder musculature. In animals, testosterone has been shown to inhibit detrusor muscle contraction; therefore, low testosterone levels may promote unstable function of the detrusor (bladder) muscle and LUTS, particularly

in men with concomitant BPH. Treatment of LUTS consists of α-adrenergic blockers, 5-α reductase inhibitors, or prostatectomy. In some men, treatment with an herbal, saw palmetto, is effective.

Transient or permanent stress urinary incontinence occurs in men following prostate biopsy or prostatectomy. One third of these men are still incontinent 24 months following surgery. Incontinence due to dementia, depression, or mobility impairment (functional incontinence) is another important type of incontinence in older men.

Prostate Cancer

There are 230,000 new cases of prostate cancer diagnosed each year in the United States. Prostate cancer is more common in African Americans than in Whites and is less common in men of Chinese origin. Diagnosis is made by finding an abnormal rectal examination or an elevated prostate-specific antigen (PSA), followed by multiple prostate biopsies. The PSA is not an ideal test, but its sensitivity and specificity can be improved somewhat by getting a free PSA or measuring the different molecular forms of PSA. Treatment of early-stage prostate cancer consists of either surgery or irradiation. Treatment of metastatic prostate cancer consists of either lowering testosterone levels with gonadotropin-releasing hormone analogs or using testosterone receptor blockers. Whether prostate cancer should be treated in men over 80 years of age depends on their general health and predicted survival. Numerous new therapies for prostate cancer are under investigation. These include gene therapies, antisense therapies, apoptosis promoters, tropoisomerase inhibitors, endothelin-A inhibitors, and angiogenesis inhibitors. Bisphosphonates are considered to be the treatment of choice to prevent bone complications of prostate cancer.

In a large study of males over 55 years of age with a PSA levels less than 3 nanograms per milliliter (ng/ml), the 5-α reductase inhibitor finasteride reduced the prevalence of prostate cancer by 25% over a 7-year period. However, high-grade Gleason tumors (more aggressive types of cancer tissues) were more common in the finasteride-treated group. Although there were fewer urinary symptoms in the finasteride-treated group, there were more sexual side effects. Unfortunately, this study failed to make it easy to decide whether finasteride should be used for prostate cancer prevention.

Andropause

Andropause is defined as a low testosterone level in older men that is causing symptoms. Testosterone levels decline in males at the rate of 1% per year after 30 years of age. At the same time, sex hormone-binding globulin levels increase. This results in even lower levels of free or bioavailable (free plus albumin-bound) testosterone. Approximately 3% to 5% of men 40 to 50 years of age, and 40% to 70% of men 70 years of age, are hypogonadal. It has been estimated that there are 4 million to 5 million hypogonadal men in the United States. The symptoms of hypogonadism in older men are a decline in libido (enthusiasm for sex) and a decreased quality of erection. Testosterone stimulates nitric oxide synthase, and so as it declines, inadequate levels inhibit the ability of phosphodiesterase-5 inhibitors (e.g., Viagra) to produce adequate erections. It is important to recognize that low libido is also caused by a variety of other conditions such as depression, medical illness, and social factors.

Low testosterone levels are associated with a decline in muscle mass, strength, and function. Testosterone replacement can reverse these problems. Testosterone stimulates the production of satellite cells, inhibits the formation of preadipocytes, stimulates protein synthesis, and inhibits protein degradation through the ubiquitin–proteasome system. Testosterone administration stimulates visuospatial cognition. Low testosterone levels at middle age predict an increase in Alzheimer's disease in older persons. In animal models of Alzheimer's disease, testosterone inhibits the production of amyloid-β protein (implicated in the development of Alzheimer's disease). Low testosterone levels are associated with an increase in hip fractures. Testosterone replacement increases bone mineral density. The effects of testosterone on bone appear to be both direct and secondary through aromatization to estrogen. Testosterone increases hematrocrit, in some cases to levels greater than 55, in which case administration needs to be stopped. Testosterone appears to have no deleterious effects on the cardiovascular system. A few persons receiving testosterone have developed sleep apnea. Testosterone administration is occasionally associated with gynecomastia (breast enlargement in the male).

The role of testosterone in the pathophysiology of prostate cancer is uncertain. There is no epidemiological evidence that testosterone is associated with prostate cancer. Retrospective studies have failed to demonstrate an increase in prostate cancer with testosterone administration, but these studies have been very small. There is a need for a large men's health study to determine the effects of testosterone on the prostate.

Currently, testosterone in older men should be considered a quality of life drug. Thus, its use should be limited to symptomatic males with low testosterone levels. In general, low testosterone is defined as a level below 300 nanograms per deciliter (ng/dl). In older males whose total testosterone is between 300 and 500 ng/dl, a free or bioavailable testosterone level should be obtained to determine their gonadal status. The forms of testosterone used for treatment are injectable, patch, buccal, and gel. The gels are the most popular forms. Outside the United States, an oral form, testosterone undecanoate, is available. A nasal form of testosterone administration is under development. There is much excitement about the use of selective androgen receptor molecules (SARMs) to increase muscle mass with fewer effects on the prostate. The injectable steroid hormone nandrolone is a highly effective SARM. Other SARMs under development are nonsteroids that can be absorbed orally.

Options

Men have a number of unique health problems. Unfortunately, many men are risk takers, thereby increasing their poor health outcomes, and their perceptions of masculinity create a tendency to ignore warning signs of illness and put off seeking health care. Physicians provide more consultation time for women than for men, even after adjusting for family planning, pregnancy, childbirth, and child rearing, with primary care being considered first and foremost for women and children. Men need to be encouraged to take a more active part in their health care. Failure to present early can lead to premature death, as shown in a European health survey where it was found that although melanoma incidence is higher in women than in men, later presentation by men led to a higher death rate from melanoma. It would appear that males are doomed to die earlier than women not only by their genetics but also by their risk-taking behaviors and unwillingness to take better care of their health.

—*John E. Morley and Matthew T. Haren*

See also Age–Period–Cohort Distinctions; Cardiovascular System; Caregiving; HIV and AIDS; Sexuality; Vascular Dementia; Women's Health

Further Readings and References

Jones WK. Men's health as a public health issue. *J Men's Health Gender.* 2004;1:147–150.

Morley JE. The aging man and woman: Are the differences important? *J Men's Health Gender.* 2004;1:224–226.

Morley JE, Perry HM III. Androgen treatment of male hypogonadism in older males. *J Steroid Biochem Mol Biol.* 2003;95:367–373.

Mulcahy JJ. Erectile function: The barometer of men's health. *J Urol.* 2005;173:341.

Thompson IM, Goodman PJ, Tangen CM, et al. The influence of finasteride on the development of prostate cancer. *N Engl J Med.* 2003;349:215–224.

MENTAL STATUS ASSESSMENT

Cognitive decline in general, and memory impairment in particular, are common complaints encountered by physicians who treat older adults. Several cognitive screening tests are available to health care providers to assess their patients' cognitive functioning objectively and to monitor change in function over time.

Some decline in memory and cognitive function in older adults relative to those during early adulthood is normal. However, advancing age is the major risk factor for Alzheimer's disease (AD), a neurodegenerative disorder characterized by prominent symptoms of memory problems and cognitive decline, with the incidence or number of new cases of AD increasing significantly over 75 years of age. In addition, over the past decade, there has been increasing recognition of mild cognitive impairment (MCI) among older adults, defined as a state of cognitive and functional ability that lies along a continuum between normal aging and the milder forms of AD. MCI affects up to one third of older adults and is predictive of the subsequent development of dementia.

The problem is that many older individuals with these milder cognitive deficits often go unrecognized, presenting with socially appropriate behaviors that mask their underlying cognitive losses. General practitioners sometimes recognize only a small percentage of patients displaying signs of mild cognitive impairment and even underdetect moderate to severe dementia.

The situation is complicated even more by the fact that family members might not be aware of any significant problems during the early stages of AD. Also, informant reports sometimes are unreliable, with family members either minimizing or exaggerating actual cognitive and memory deficits. In addition, clinical depression often is thought to result in memory decline. Although the data do not support depression as a causal factor of memory problems, its presence certainly can interact with and further muddy accurate detection of an underlying organically based cognitive impairment.

Primary care physicians typically have only limited time to conduct thorough cognitive assessments. Nevertheless, with the projected accelerating growth of the older adult population in the United States over the next several decades, primary care physicians will be expected to detect and diagnose early signs of dementia and related neurological conditions so that cost-effective therapies can be initiated. It has been estimated that the prevalence of AD could be cut in half if onset were delayed by 5 years.

Although there are interventions that can treat certain reversible diseases that produce cognitive impairment, these represent only a small percentage of dementias. The vast majority of dementia cases are irreversible due to AD (50% to 85%) or vascular dementia (10% to 20%). Nevertheless, available treatments can slow the progression of AD and extend the quality of life for both patients and caregivers. The hope is that early detection of cognitive decline can forestall, or at least delay, the more profound cognitive and functional loss that occurs with the more advanced stages of AD.

Therefore, a need exists to use objective and reliable mental status screening instruments that can assess cognitive processes most effectively and efficiently and can help differentiate normal cognitive changes from potential signs of pathology.

Mental Status Assessment

Mental status screening tests are brief standardized measures of various cognitive functions such as memory, attention, orientation, and language. When used in the primary care practice or other medical settings, they provide clinicians with an objective metric of patients' cognitive functioning that can be used to help determine current diagnoses and may serve as a baseline for tracking change over time. As a screening tool, they are limited in both sensitivity (accurately identifying true cases) and specificity (accurately identifying noncases). Hence, clinicians are cautioned to use the screen as part of a broader assessment of patient functioning that includes detailed assessment of the medical history, presenting complaint, functional ability, and emotional status. Interpreted in isolation, a screening tool may give false-positive results owing to any of a number of sources of confounding (e.g., low education, sensorimotor limitations). In addition, false-negative results can result in (a) mild staged disorders where cognitive impairment is ambiguous or in (b) highly functioning individuals, commonly with many years of education, who can accommodate for some cognitive problems on standardized tests. However, with these limitations noted, the mental status examination may serve a valuable role in the evaluation of older patients and may be the only evaluation of neuropsychological functioning for those who are suffering from serious neurological,

sensory, or physical impairment as well as for those who resist more formal assessments because of concerns about being labeled.

Historically, mental status assessment has ranged from the informal and unstructured evaluation of cognitive functioning to the more formal paper-and-pencil mental status examinations. Only recently have standardized tests of cognition been used routinely within neurological examinations. There are a number of cognitive screening instruments available. Three of the more widely used instruments are described next. All three are inexpensive, require minimal training to administer, and (in most instances) include at least some reference norms.

The Mini-Mental State Examination

The Mini-Mental State Examination (MMSE) is a brief 30-point test, originally published by Marshal Folstein and his colleagues in 1975, that taps the domains of orientation, attention and concentration, language, constructional ability, and memory. The test takes approximately 5 to 10 minutes to complete and can be administered in virtually any distraction-free environment. A few of the items require paper and a pencil, with most requiring only a verbal response from the respondent. Materials required include the test form, a single stimulus sheet, blank paper, a pencil, a watch, and a pen. Scoring can be done quickly. The current version of the test contains some minor revisions from the original test as well as scoring norms for age and education. Originally, a score of less than 21 (≤ 20) of a possible 30 points was thought to be indicative of possible dementia. However, in subsequent investigations it was found that a cutoff score of 23 or 24 best discriminated those with dementia or delirium. In general, cognitive performance as measured by the MMSE varies within the population by age and education, with scores declining with advanced age. Many individuals with MCI who have high levels of education or high levels of intellectual ability still tend to do well on the test. Also, the ability of the MMSE to detect dementia is affected by ethnicity, age, and education; it is most accurate for Caucasians with at least 12 years of education. The

MMSE has been widely used in clinical practice, as well as in a wide range of clinical and epidemiological research, as a measure of cognitive functioning.

Short Portable Mental Status Questionnaire

The Short Portable Mental Status Questionnaire (SPMSQ) is a 10-item test developed by Eric Pfeiffer and his colleagues in 1975 to evaluate the cognitive functioning of older adults. It contains questions on time and place orientation, recent events, and personal history along with a serial subtraction task. The SPMSQ, a revision of the earlier Mental Status Questionnaire that had been norm referenced primarily on an institutional sample of individuals, was administered to a reference group of Caucasian and African American community-based older adults residing in the southern United States along with clinic- and hospital-based samples of older adults. Scoring is based on the number of errors, with zero to two errors considered to be indicative of normal functioning and larger numbers of errors considered to be indicative of correspondingly greater cognitive impairment. Adjustments are made for both education and ethnicity. In validation studies, scores from the SPMSQ correlated well with clinical diagnoses of organic disorder. The SPMSQ has been validated across varying educational levels and across cultures, with translations in several languages. The SPMSQ is hampered by the need for an informant to validate those questions about personal information. In addition, the areas of language, learning, and memory are not assessed, thereby reducing the instrument's efficacy to screen for dementia.

Clock Drawing Test

The Clock Drawing Test (CDT) requires examinees to draw the face of a clock and include the numbers in the correct locations along with the hour and minute hands indicating certain times; for example, "10 minutes before 2." Despite the apparent singular nature of the task, the CDT taps into a number of neurocognitive domains, including attention and organization, planning, visuospatial ability, motor skill, and

conceptualization and abstraction. The CDT can be administered in less than 5 minutes. Scoring procedures vary, from the very simple binary rating of normal or abnormal to a more sophisticated 0- to 10-point rating that takes into account the types of errors committed. The specificity and sensitivity of the CDT have been found to vary according to the type of scoring method used. Also, normative data for some scoring procedures are not available. The CDT has been demonstrated to have adequate sensitivity and specificity in detecting probable dementia. However, because there are no items that tap short-term memory processes, it is insensitive to the milder forms of dementia. This deficit has been addressed with a variation of the CDT known as the "Mini-Cog." This test consists of a three-word memory task, followed by the CDT that serves the added function of a distractor task, and then delayed recall of the three words. The Mini-Cog shows strong promise as a brief yet valid screening method for the milder forms of dementia.

General Guidelines for Cognitive Screening

It might seem that routine objective cognitive screening of all older adults for possible cognitive decline or dementia would be an obvious choice, and indeed some authors have recommended this. However, in 2001 the Quality Standards Subcommittee of the American Academy of Neurology concluded that there is insufficient evidence to recommend cognitive screening of individuals who are asymptomatic. Others have arrived at the same conclusion, emphasizing the risks involved in labeling someone as demented. At the same time, the Quality Standards Subcommittee recommended as a guideline that patients who display mild cognitive impairment should be recognized and monitored for any cognitive and functional decline given that they are at increased risk for dementia. Furthermore, it was recommended as a guideline that *general* cognitive screening instruments, such as the MMSE, should be considered for use with individuals suspected of having cognitive impairment, whereas *brief* cognitive screening instruments should be used with caution because of their limited scope.

Risks and Benefits

Routine mental status screening to detect cognitive decline and dementia does entail some risks of harm. These include the potential adverse psychological effects that can occur with both false-positive and true-positive findings, labeling effects, and the risk of not qualifying for long-term health insurance. However, the risks associated with dementia screening have not been examined systematically.

At the same time, there are clear benefits of screening for cognitive decline and dementia. As described previously, dementia and cognitive loss often go undetected. Early detection of AD provides a chance for individuals to begin medications such as cholinesterase inhibitors that may slow the progress of dementia and allow individuals to maintain independence and autonomy for some additional months. There are benefits for the caregivers as well and the potential reduction of corresponding financial expenditures. Finally, early screening for dementia provides an opportunity for individuals and their families to make advance plans for care that otherwise might not be made. It allows a discussion among family members and others of issues such as the nature of the dementia, prognosis, financial planning, and loss, and it provides an opportunity to plan for future events that might include residential placement.

—*Martin J. Toohill and*
Kathleen A. Welsh-Bohmer

See also Alzheimer's Disease; Delirium and Confusional States; Geriatric Assessment; Instruments; Mild Cognitive Impairment; Vascular Dementia

Further Readings and References

Boustani M, Peterson B, Harris R, et al. Screening for dementia. Available at: www.ahrq.gov/clinic/uspstf/uspsdeme.htm. Accessed June 22, 2005.

Cisewski D, Green RC, Welsh-Bohmer KA. Mental status evaluation in the neurologic examination of dementia. In: Rizzo M, Eslinger P, eds. *Principles and Practice of Behavioral Neurology and Neuropsychology*. Philadelphia: W. B. Saunders; 2004.

Freedman M, Kaplan E, Delis D, et al. *Clock Drawing: A Neuropsychological Analysis*. New York: Oxford University Press; 1994.

METABOLIC SYNDROME

The metabolic (or insulin resistance) syndrome was first described by J. P. Camus in 1966. Two decades later, Gerald Reaven popularized the concept of the metabolic syndrome. The components of the metabolic syndrome are diabetes (associated with hyperinsulinemia), hypertension, hyperuricemia, coagulation abnormalities, lipid abnormalities, myosteatosis (fatty muscle), and nonalcoholic steatohepatitis (NASH, fatty liver). The lipid abnormalities of the metabolic syndrome include hypertriglyceridemia, decreased high-density lipoprotein (HDL, good cholesterol), and increased low-density lipoprotein (LDL, bad cholesterol). These LDL particles are strongly related to stroke and myocardial infarction. In contrast, HDL particles are associated with increased longevity and are common in centenarians. Recently, it has been suggested that cognitive dysfunction should be added as another component of the metabolic syndrome.

The etiology of the metabolic syndrome has a clear genetic predisposition. Persons with a genetic predisposition who overeat and do not exercise develop visceral obesity, which is highly associated with insulin resistance. Insulin resistance is the most accepted underlying mechanism of the metabolic syndrome. Persons with visceral obesity have an increase in adipokines (peptide hormones derived from fat). This includes cytokines, such as tumor necrosis factor alpha, interleukin 6, leptin, adiponectin, and resistin. Increasing evidence suggests that these adipokines have a crucial role in energy homeostasis by affecting food intake, insulin sensitivity, glucose and lipid metabolism, the coagulation system, and inflammation. Leptin is a peptide hormone that decreases food intake and increases energy metabolism. Thus, its increase in the metabolic syndrome appears to be an attempt to decrease the accumulation of adiposity that occurs as a precursor to the metabolic syndrome. Leptin is under the regulation of testosterone, with higher levels occurring as testosterone levels decline with aging. Resistance to the central effects of leptin occurs in obese persons. The leptin resistance of obesity appears to be due to hypertriglyceridemia, which blocks the ability of leptin to cross the blood–brain barrier. In addition, such persons have a lower than expected level of adiponectin for their level of adiposity. Adiponectin is a hormone that enhances insulin sensitivity by modulating the same intracellular pathway as is modulated by the thiazolidinediones (one type of medication for diabetes) such as rosiglitazone and pioglitazone. In animal models, administration of adiponectin reverses insulin resistance.

Recent studies in muscle have suggested that insulin resistance occurs because of an accumulation of free fatty acids and triglycerides within the cells. This can occur either from high circulating lipid levels or from a defect in mitochondrial oxidative phosphorylation. This latter defect reduces energy metabolism and therefore intracellular use of free fatty acids in the cell. The end result of the process is that the insulin receptor substrate is phosphorylated, blocking its ability to activate the glucose receptor (GLUT-4) on the cell membrane in response to exposure to insulin.

Metabolic syndrome can be considered the classical "couch potato" syndrome. The prevalence of the metabolic syndrome in older persons has been reported to occur in 6.7% of persons 20 to 29 year of age, in 43.5% of persons 60 to 69 years of age, and in 42.0% of persons age 70 years and older. An estimated 47 million persons in the United States have metabolic syndrome. With aging, there is a tendency for muscle to develop a mild insulin resistance. This physiological insulin resistance of aging is a confounding factor in defining insulin resistance in older persons.

It is now well established that even mild degrees of hyperglycemia can increase mortality in persons with acute illness such as myocardial infarction and septicemia. This has led to aggressive treatment of hyperglycemia in patients in intensive care units. However, the United Kingdom Prospective Diabetes Study (UKPDS) showed that although lowering glucose had some mild beneficial effects on diabetic complications, treating blood pressure produced a much better risk reduction than did treating diabetes. A number of other studies have demonstrated that lowering blood pressure in persons with diabetes mellitus is more efficacious at preventing cardiovascular endpoints than it is in nondiabetics. Persons with

the metabolic syndrome have elevated levels of plasminogen-activating inhibitor 1 (PAI-I), an important modulator of the fibrinolytic syndrome. PAI-1 plays a role in enhancing thrombotic progression.

Myosteatosis (the infiltration of fat into muscle) leads to progressive muscle weakness. Persons who have lost muscle mass and are obese (the obese–sarcopenic) are at major risk for increased functional deterioration and mortality.

Recently, cognitive decline has become considered as part of the metabolic syndrome. Persons with diabetes mellitus have a higher risk of developing Alzheimer's disease. In addition, persons with poor glycemic control have poor cognitive function. The mechanisms by which metabolic syndrome may lead to impaired cognition are multifactorial. First, persons with diabetes and hypertension are at higher risk for developing vascular dementia. A number of studies have shown that both hypoglycemia and hyperglycemia produce cognitive dysfunction that improves when glucose is restored to normal levels. Hypertriglyceridemia has also been shown to lead to poor cognitive function. Leptin increases memory, and because triglycerides inhibit leptin entry into the central nervous system, this is one possible mechanism by which triglycerides produce cognitive impairment. Finally, insulin in the brain is degraded by insulin-degrading enzyme, which also degrades amyloid-β protein. Thus, hyperinsulinemia may slow the degradation of amyloid-β protein, increasing its levels so that it inhibits memory.

Clinically, the diagnosis of the metabolic syndrome is made when a person has at least three of the following:

- A waist circumference greater than 102 centimeters (cm) in a male or 89 cm in a female
- Fasting triglyceride levels greater than 150 milligrams per deciliter (mg/dl)
- An HDL cholesterol level less than 40 mg/dl in men or less than 50 mg/dl in females
- A blood pressure greater than 130/85 millimeters of mercury (mm/Hg)
- A fasting blood glucose greater than 110 mg/dl

It is reasonable to consider some changes in these criteria with aging, but this has not been explored.

An intervention program in 3,234 persons over 3 years showed that some features of the metabolic syndrome can be controlled. Administration of metformin prevented the progression of the metabolic syndrome. A lifestyle intervention of exercise and weight loss resulted in a 41% decrease in the presence of the metabolic syndrome. There are no studies showing whether intervention would improve endpoints such as function, mental status, hospitalizations, and mortality.

—John E. Morley and Moon Jong Kim

See also Alzheimer's Disease; Diabetes; Hypertension; Obesity; Vascular Dementia

Further Readings and References

Morley JE. The metabolic syndrome and aging. *J Gerontol A Biol Sci Med Sci.* 2004;59:139–142.

Orchard TJ, Temproia M, Goldberg R, et al. The effect of metformin and intensive lifestyle intervention on the metabolic syndrome: The Diabetes Prevention Program Randomized Trial. *Ann Intern Med.* 2005;142:611–619.

Ragon N, Jarvik L. Insulin resistance, affective disorders, and Alzheimer's disease: Review and hypothesis. *J Gerontol A Biol Sci Med Sci.* 2004;59:178–183.

Reaven GM. Role of insulin resistance in human disease (Syndrome X): An expanded definition. *Annu Rev Med.* 1993;44:121–131.

MEXICO

After the violence of the Mexican Revolution of 1910 to 1921, Mexico entered a long period of political stability. Peace brought social progress, economic development, and improvement in public health. In 1930, the population was 16.9 million and was growing at 1.8% annually, the total fertility rate was 6.0%, and life expectancies at birth were 35.5 years for men and 37.0 years for women. Largely due to the diffusion of antibiotics and massive vaccination programs, a remarkable decline in mortality was experienced during the 1940s, favoring all ages but particularly infants and children. As a consequence, demographic growth was rapid because lower mortality occurred while the

birth rate remained high. Under this scenario, the population in 1960 was 35.6 million, the total fertility rate reached the historical maximum of 6.1%, life expectancies were 56.3 years for men and 59.5 years for women; and the population growth rate of 3.4% was the highest the country had ever seen. Such dynamics set up a demographic pressure that jeopardized development. In response to actual and potential socioeconomic problems, official population policies of the 1970s focused on reducing demographic increases through literacy, schooling, dignifying women's roles, and modern family planning. Although the beginning of the demographic transition called attention to the consequences of a future aging population, concerns were nearly nonexistent. The only warnings, from actuarial estimates projecting financial crisis for social security, were ignored. But by the beginning the 21st century, Mexico had 99.8 million inhabitants, the total fertility rate had dropped to 2.4%, and life expectancies were 74.6 years for men and 79.0 years for women. Now the increasing presence of an aged population became obvious and startling, with its critical impact on social security and health services looming over the coming decades. During the 60-year period between 1930 and 1990, the percentage of the population age 65 years and older grew slowly from 2.6% to 3.5%, but then it jumped to 4.6% in 2000—in just one decade. For the year 2030, it is projected to be 11.7%. By 2050, it will come to 24.6%, with life expectancies of 82.1 years for men and 85.6 years for women.

The distribution of deaths by age is a striking way to show the significance of an aging population. From mortality statistics for 1930, 1960, 2000, and 2030 (projected), Table 1 shows such distributions by sex in three age groups: 0 to 9 years, 10 to 74 years, and 75 years and older. This atypical age grouping helps to compare the mortality behavior of children (from highest risks of infancy to an age where mortality is lowest) with mortality patterns of the oldest population (here characterized by people age 75 years and older). In 1930, males 0 to 9 years of age accounted for 55.9% of deaths. That figure went down to 53.7% by 1960 and decreased dramatically to 15.7% by 2000. Moreover, it is expected to be as low as 2.6% in

Table 1 Percentages of Deaths by Age Group and Sex: Mexico, 1930 to 2030

Census	Men				Women			
	0–9 Years	*10–74 Years*	*75+ Years*	*Total*	*0–9 Years*	*10–74 Years*	*75+ Years*	*Total*
1930	55.9	41.4	2.7	100	51.6	44.0	4.4	100
1960	53.7	38.4	7.9	100	48.4	34.5	17.2	100
2000	15.7	56.7	27.6	100	14.8	45.6	39.6	100
2030	2.6	49.1	48.2	100	2.1	38.8	59.1	100

Sources: Adapted from Consejo Nacional de Población (National Council of Population). Tablas de Mortalidad: México, 1930–2030 (Mortality tables: Mexico, 1930–2030). Inside report, not published; Consejo Nacional de Población. Proyecciones de la Población de México, 2000–2050 (Population Projections of Mexico, 2000–2050). Available at: www.conapo.gob.mx/00cifras/5.htm. Accessed September 22, 2006; INEGI. Censos Generales de Población y Vivienda, 1930–2000 (General Censuses of Population and Dwelling, 1930–2000). Instituto Nacional de Estadística, Geografía e Informática (National Institute of Statistics, Geography and Data Processing).

2030. The corresponding figures for females in that youngest age group are 51.6% in 1930, 48.4% in 1960, 14.8% in 2000, and 2.1% in 2030. This transformation is a major result of lower infant and child mortality rates combined with decreasing levels of fertility.

For the oldest population (age 75 years and older), figures show a reverse pattern. Men who died in 1930 after reaching 75 years of age were only 2.7% of the total, whereas the corresponding percentage for women was 4.4%. In 1960, the percentage of deaths in men age 75 years and older rose to 7.9%, whereas the corresponding percentage in women rose much higher to approximately 17.2%. Numbers indicate not only an increase in survival to advanced age for both sexes but also the typical higher survival rate of women. For the year 2000, those who had reached 75 years of age accounted for 27.6% of deaths in men and 39.6% of deaths in women. These trends of lower mortality and fertility, higher life expectancies, and changing age structures yield projections suggesting that among men dying in 2030, nearly one half (48.3%) will be at least 75 years of age. For women, the figure will be nearly three fifths (59.1%). The shift of mortality toward oldest ages will be quite significant and characteristic of an aging population.

Concentration of mortality in the oldest old has a strong link with changes in causes of death. For ages 65 years and older, during the period 1970 to 2000, the leading cause of death for both men and women was heart diseases. But other illnesses have changed in their importance as causes of mortality. In men, cancer was the third leading cause of death in 1970 but rose to second during the period 1980 to 2000. In women, there was a similar trajectory, but for them in 2000 the second leading cause of death was diabetes. Diabetes is a condition whose prevalence and impact (in terms of complications and mortality) are notably on the increase. From the eighth leading cause of death among men and the fifth leading cause of death among women in 1970, diabetes rose to third among men and to second among women by 2000. In conjunction with epidemiological transition assumptions, receding causes of death in older adults are pneumonia, influenza, and intestinal infections. This latter ailment shows a clear correlation between health and socioeconomic development.

In 1970, intestinal infections were the fourth leading cause of death among men and the fifth leading cause of death among women. Those corresponding places declined to eighth and sixth by 1980, were 11th and 8th by 1990, and went down to 12th and 13th by 2000. These trends are not just recent but also show an epidemiological transition among older adults with distinct features.

One of the health characteristics of an elderly population is frailty, shown by a higher prevalence of chronic diseases and disabilities. Thus, in addition to causes of death, one needs to consider nonlethal effects of health deterioration. Table 2 shows life expectancies for the year 2000 for men and women in selected ages between 60 and 100 years. With data from the 2000 National Health Survey, life expectancies are compared with life expectancies with probable chronic diseases (LEPDs). In a country with large socioeconomic inequality, the time between acquiring a disease and getting a diagnosis can be significant. Life expectancies with diagnosed diseases (LEDDs) are included. Finally, inactive life expectancies (ILEs, life expectancies of those unable to perform some basic activities of daily living [ADLs]) are also estimated.

Table 2 shows that, under current mortality and socioeconomic conditions, a 70-year-old man has a life expectancy of 14.5 years, of which 11.4 years on average will be spent with a chronic illness; only for approximately 7.6 years of those years will the patient's condition be diagnosed, and the patient is expected to have a disability that will prevent him from fully performing basic ADLs for approximately 5.5 years. The corresponding numbers in women of this age are 15.4 years (life expectancy), 12.9 years (LEPDs), 10.6 years (LEDDs), and 7.3 years (ILEs). These figures, and the figures for other ages in Table 2, confirm that life expectancies are higher for women but that women spend more time in poor health and dealing with disabilities.

Population aging and related changes in mortality and health are occurring in Mexico under high heterogeneity, where shifts in socioeconomic difference do not always produce favorable change. An aging population in cities and regions of northern Mexico shows patterns of morbidity and mortality that resemble those of developed countries, whereas in rural and less developed regions, such as the southeastern part of the country, intestinal infections still predominate among the leading causes of death.

At the beginning of the 21st century, Mexico and its many societies are seeking to accommodate globalization, where economic and social values follow external trends. Aging also is a global process. It is clear that aging and the changes it brings will not have a common pattern everywhere; in Mexico, the changes brought by an aging population will present particular challenges. Aging and its related pressure on health services, social security financing, family relations, and political issues will need to be addressed by a multidisciplinary approach and with a collaborative mood.

—*Roberto Ham-Chande*

See also Demography of Aging; Global Aging; Health and Public Policy; Hispanics; Latin America and the Caribbean; Longitudinal Research; Migration; Hispanic Established Population for Epidemiologic Studies of the Elderly

Table 2   Life Expectancies, Life Expectancies With Probable Chronic Diseases, Life Expectancies With Diagnosed Diseases, and Inactive Life Expectancies by Age and Sex: Mexico, 2000

Age (years)	*Men*				*Women*			
	LE	*LEPD*	*LEDD*	*ILE*	*LE*	*LEPD*	*LEDD*	*ILE*
60	21.4	15.3	9.9	6.0	22.8	18.0	14.5	8.7
70	14.5	11.4	7.6	5.5	15.4	12.9	10.6	7.3
80	8.9	7.7	5.3	4.6	9.4	8.4	6.9	5.5
90	4.8	4.6	3.2	3.2	4.9	4.6	3.9	3.6

Sources: Adapted from Consejo Nacional de Población (National Council of Population). Tablas de Mortalidad: México, 1930–2030 (Mortality tables: Mexico, 1930–2030). Inside report, not published; Consejo Nacional de Población. Proyecciones de la Población de México, 2000–2050 (Population Projections of Mexico, 2000–2050). Available at: www.conapo.gob.mx/00cifras/5.htm. Accessed September 22, 2006; SSA. Encuesta Nacional de Salud, 2000 (National Survey of Health, 2000). Secretaría de Salud (Secretary of Health).

Note: LE = life expectancies; LEPD = life expectancies with probable chronic diseases; LEDD = life expectancies with diagnosed diseases; ILE = inactive life expectancies.

Further Readings and References

Ham-Chande R. *El envejecimiento en México: El siguiente reto de la transición demográfica.* Tijuana, Mexico: El Colegio de la Frontera Norte; 2003.

Robine J-M, ed. *Determining Health Expectancies.* West Sussex, England: Wiley; 2003.

MIDLIFE

Midlife is a significant stage of adult development that, despite the population bulge resulting from the baby boomers reaching middle age, is still frequently overlooked. According to the U.S. census, by 2010, more than one fourth (26%) of the population will be between 45 and 64 years of age. *Midlife* or *middle age* is a somewhat elastic term stretching from early adulthood to old age. Societal changes, such as changes in family structure and employment histories, have led to a more varied midlife experience. This entry explores physical, social, and psychological health during midlife and considers how midlife shapes the transition to old age.

Physical Health

During midlife, the physical changes that occur affect both current perceived health and later health outcomes. These physical changes range from wrinkles and balding to increased risk of severe health conditions such as cardiovascular disease and cancer. Among women, one of the most recognized physical changes during midlife is menopause; among men, sexual dysfunction becomes increasingly common. The main areas of concern for midlife women are cardiovascular disease, breast cancer, osteoporosis, and obesity. Studies of midlife suggest that women are more likely to experience various health problems such as asthma, arthritis, thyroid disease, constipation, gum and mouth problems, and chronic sleep problems. Men, on the other hand, have more problems with drug and alcohol abuse. Men are also at risk for heart attacks, ulcers, back problems, and other conditions. Interestingly, although men are more likely to engage in vigorous activity and exercise for short periods of time, women devote more time and effort to the maintenance of their health through diet monitoring and consistent exercise.

Socioeconomic Status Differences During Midlife

Midlife has been assumed to be a period of stability for families, but in many cases it is affected by societal factors such as socioeconomic status (SES). Higher-level occupations, more hours worked, nonminority status, higher levels of education, and being married all are associated with more positive physical and mental health outcomes. Although women's labor force involvement has been increasing, middle-aged women are still less likely to be employed at the same rate as are men. When they do hold equal-level positions, women are paid lower wages. Lower incomes and education levels are associated with reduced access to resources and greater exposure to environmental risk factors. These influences are evident during middle age as lower SES individuals become increasingly vulnerable to illness and disease.

Psychological Health

Psychological well-being during midlife is a relatively new area of study. Theories of adult development, specifically Erik Erikson's psychosocial stages, have identified midlife as a stage during which adults face the challenge of generativity versus stagnation. The goal of generativity involves teaching and guiding the next generation as well as being productive in one's own career and life goals. Erikson suggested that attainment of generativity is necessary for positive psychological well-being during midlife. Midlife is a transition stage with the developmental goals of preparing children for adulthood and preparing oneself for old age. This is not to suggest that all people experience the same life transitions during midlife; for example, some will become first-time parents during midlife. In general, however, midlife consists of both continuity and discontinuity in development. Some psychological characteristics (e.g., personality, intelligence) remain relatively stable, whereas others (e.g., cognitive functioning, psychological well-being) may change greatly during this phase of life. When considering factors that predict successful aging, midlife is a especially important. Midlife is a time during which adults begin to learn to cope with, and compensate for, increasing losses that become more apparent as old age approaches.

In addressing psychological well-being during midlife, research has shown that life satisfaction is at its highest during midlife, a time when subjective well-being and happiness are rated higher than in any other age group. In this respect, midlife can be viewed as the prime of life, the time when people are at the zenith of their careers and incomes, and a time when families most often thrive. Adults in midlife report higher levels of purpose in life, autonomy, and personal growth compared with those in other age groups, another indication of positive psychological well-being. Specific areas of life experience have also been linked to psychological well-being during midlife such as satisfaction with work, parenthood, and success at balancing multiple roles. The perception of adults across the life span is that midlife is the time in life when people are expected to function best.

A considerable amount of attention has been given to the so-called midlife crisis. According to the popular media, people at midlife are troubled by middle age because they feel that they have not achieved, and will never achieve, their life goals or that their life goals were unimportant or trivial. Research indicates that although some do experience such a crisis, the incidence of the midlife crisis has been overdramatized. Midlife is generally a time of higher well-being and less depression than at all other stages of life.

In sum, midlife is a generally positive life period. Many people have achieved their personal and professional life goals. On the other hand, people who are at risk—people who are vulnerable because of lifetimes of poverty, few resources, and environmental stressors—are most likely to begin to suffer significant physical and psychological distress. During midlife, one can begin to experience the difficulties resulting from cumulative life deficits or begin to enjoy benefits

earned. Midlife is a time of accomplishment and fulfillment, but it is also a time of transition, with current and prior life circumstances fundamentally influencing the transition into later life.

—*Toni C. Antonucci, Heather Fuller Iglesias, and Besangie Sellars*

See also Active Life Expectancy; Demography of Aging; Longevity; Quality of Life

Further Readings and References

Baltes PB, Baltes MM, eds. *Successful Aging: Perspectives From the Behavioral Sciences.* Cambridge, England: Cambridge University Press; 1990.

Brim OG, Ryff CD, Kessler RC, eds. *How Healthy Are We? A National Study of Well-Being at Midlife.* Chicago: University of Chicago Press; 2004.

Lachman ME. *Handbook of Midlife Development.* New York: John Wiley; 2001.

Lachman ME, James JB, eds. *Multiple Paths of Midlife Development.* Chicago: University of Chicago Press; 1997.

Willis SL, Reid JD, eds. *Life in the Middle: Psychological and Social Development in Middle Age.* San Diego, Calif: Academic Press; 1999.

MIGRATION

Along with Asians, Hispanics make up the majority of the immigrant population of the United States. Today, approximately 40% of Hispanics are foreign born, and more than half of them arrived between 1990 and 2002. Because of high rates of immigration and high fertility, the Hispanic population remains relatively young; only 5.1% of Hispanics are age 65 years and older. Although the vast majority of immigrants are young, a growing number are arriving during mature and late adulthood, to a large extent as the result of a deliberate family reunification policy. In addition to legal immigrants, more than 6 million undocumented migrants, 79% of whom are Mexican, live and work in the United States.

Physical Health of Older Hispanics in the United States

Immigrants who arrive during adulthood, and especially those who arrive after 50 years of age, face serious difficulties in acculturation and assimilation. Although immigrants tend to be selected for better health, the stresses that older immigrants experience can potentially undermine their physical and mental health. Low levels of acculturation have serious implications for health care and the early diagnosis of diseases such as cancer and heart disease. Mexican-origin women over 65 years of age are often fearful of, and have little knowledge of, mammography and other screening tests.

Despite serious socioeconomic disadvantage, older Hispanics, and especially foreign-born Mexicans and other Hispanics, have lower mortality rates than do similarly aged non-Hispanics. This mortality advantage can be attributed to a lower prevalence of heart diseases and cancer. Morbidity rates for most major chronic diseases, except diabetes in the Mexican-origin population, remain low among older Hispanics. Evidence concerning the relative prevalence of disabilities and functional limitations among older Hispanics, including immigrants, is limited and inconclusive. Some evidence suggests that older Hispanics are at higher risk for disability than are non-Hispanics, whereas other data suggest that older Hispanics are similar to non-Hispanic Whites. Again, intragroup differences emerge. Some researchers find evidence that older Cubans experience the lowest levels of disability, whereas Puerto Ricans suffer the most.

Mental Health and Addictions

Although the data are again limited and inconclusive, some evidence indicates that the prevalence of psychiatric disorders is lower among Mexican immigrants than among their U.S.-born counterparts or non-Hispanics. Estimates of depression among older Hispanics differ greatly. Some studies report very low levels of depression, whereas others report higher rates. The data suggest that among older immigrants, women are at a higher risk for depression than are men. In general, the Hispanic-origin population tends to report lower overall lifetime use of alcohol, tobacco, and illicit drugs than does the non-Hispanic population, and older Hispanics report lower rates of alcohol consumption than do their younger counterparts. Foreign-born Hispanics report lower rates of tobacco use than does the native-born population.

Health Care Coverage and Access to Health Care

Although estimates vary widely and are no doubt subject to serious error, a small but significant proportion of older Hispanics, and especially foreign-born Mexicans, have no health insurance. As many as a quarter of older Hispanic-origin immigrants do not qualify for Social Security benefits, mostly because they did not contribute for the required 10 years. These individuals must rely on Medicaid for health care coverage. Because of generally elevated rates of poverty, the Hispanic population finds itself disproportionately dependent on Medicaid. Even those Hispanics who receive Medicare often do not get all of the care they need because Medicare requires the payment of a monthly premium and copayments and does not pay for all services. These costs can be prohibitive for Hispanics, and especially immigrants, who have low average incomes. For the middle class, Medigap policies cover many of these extra costs. A large number of retired Hispanics lack such supplementary coverage and are therefore at risk for not receiving the care they need. Data from the Hispanic Established Population for Epidemiologic Studies of the Elderly (EPESE) reveal that only a minority of older Mexican-origin individuals have supplementary coverage and that even fewer of the foreign-born Mexicans have such coverage.

Conclusion

Immigrants, including Hispanic immigrants, are generally young and in good health. During recent years, however, mature adults represent a growing fraction of the immigrant population. These individuals face serious acculturative stresses that might potentially have negative health consequences. Despite serious economic disadvantages and the stresses of migration, older Hispanics, including foreign-born Mexicans, have very favorable morbidity and mortality experiences compared with the non-Hispanic population. Although these favorable morbidity and mortality rates might be methodological artifacts, it is possible that cultural factors, such as supportive families, are health protective. A serious shortcoming in our current knowledge of immigrant health relates to the fact that most of the research on older Hispanic adults does not differentiate among different Hispanic groups. Given the huge differences in the migration histories and motivations of different Hispanic groups, understanding the health risks of this population requires more detailed research focused on specific aspects of the migration and incorporation experience.

—Ronald J. Angel and Sonia M. Frias

See also Demography of Aging; Hispanic Established Population for Epidemiologic Studies of the Elderly; Hispanics; Native Americans and Alaska Natives

Further Readings and References

Angel RJ, Angel JL. *Who Will Care for Us? Aging and Long-Term Care in Multicultural America.* New York: New York University Press; 1997.

Angel RJ, Angel JL, Markides KS. Stability and change in health insurance among older Mexican Americans: Longitudinal evidence from the Hispanic EPESE. *Am J Public Health.* 2002;92:1264–1271.

Escobar JI, Nervi CH, Gara MA. Immigration and mental health: Mexican Americans in the United States. *Harvard Rev Psychiatry.* 2000;8:64–72.

Friendland RB, Pankaj V. *Welfare Reform and Elderly Legal Immigrants.* Washington, DC: National Academy on Aging; 1997.

Markides KS, Ray LA, Stroup-Benham CA, Treviño F. Acculturation and alcohol consumption in the Mexican American population of the southwestern United States: Findings from the HHANES 1982–1984. *J Am Public Health.* 1997;80:42–46.

MILD COGNITIVE IMPAIRMENT

Whereas normal aging and dementia may appear to be somewhat distinct and at opposite ends, mild cognitive impairment (MCI) resides between the two poles within this continuum. MCI is neither normal aging nor dementia; rather, it is an intermediate state between the two. The exact boundaries between normal aging and MCI and between MCI and dementia are defined clinically. Although clinically defined terms such as MCI might initially appear to be arbitrary, MCI as a standardized entity is critical in helping patients, family members, researchers, and clinicians to predict, prevent, treat, and manage progressive cognitive decline before MCI becomes full-blown dementia such as Alzheimer's disease (AD).

Earlier renditions of MCI included generic terms such as very early Alzheimer's disease, prodromal dementia, predementia, and isolated memory impairment. Due to this confusion and poorly defined criteria for MCI, an international multidisciplinary group of clinicians and researchers convened in Stockholm, Sweden, in 2003 and attempted to arrive at a standardized consensus definition. They defined the conditions of MCI as follows:

1. The person is not normal or is demented.

2. There is cognitive deterioration as demonstrated by objective measurable decline over time with or without subjective decline as reported by the person and/or an informant.

3. Activities of daily living (ADLs) are preserved and complex instrumental functions are either intact or impaired only minimally.

It was hoped that by arriving at a more widely applicable formal definition for MCI, people from various backgrounds and different perspectives could communicate more effectively with each other.

MCI Subtypes

With Alzheimer's disease being the most common type of dementia, other dementing illnesses include vascular dementia, mixed dementia, frontotemporal dementia, and dementia with Lewy bodies. Several subtypes of MCI have also been proposed. Amnestic mild cognitive impairment (a-MCI) involves memory impairment and is the precursor to Alzheimer's disease. It is estimated that 10% to 15% of people with a-MCI progress to AD each year. Multiple-domain MCI (md-MCI) involves impairment in several cognitive domains such as language, executive function, and visuospatial skills. Combining the terms a-MCI and md-MCI, one may be classified as having multiple-domain MCI with memory impairment (md-MCI + a) or multiple-domain MCI without memory impairment (md-MCI – a). Finally, another form of MCI may involve no memory loss (– a) and only one of the nonmemory domains such as language, executive function, or visuospatial impairment. md-MCI – a and single nonmemory domain MCI may be precursors to dementia with Lewy bodies, frontotemporal dementia, and vascular dementia.

Detection and Diagnosis

Detection of MCI begins when the individual or a family member acknowledges memory dysfunction in the individual, who is given a clinical evaluation. A commonly employed screening tool for memory impairment is the Mini-Mental State Examination (MMSE). The MMSE used alone is not sufficient as a diagnostic tool. It was originally developed to help distinguish normal memory function from more advanced stages of dementia. The utility of the MMSE in the primary care setting to separate normal, MCI, mild AD, and depressed groups was examined in a pilot study with 86 persons 55 to 85 years of age. Total MMSE score was significantly lower in the early AD group than total MMSE scores in the normal, MCI, and depressed groups. MSSE score was also lower in the MCI group than in the normal controls. However, MMSE scores in the MCI and depressed groups were not significantly different. MMSE did not adequately distinguish persons with MCI from those with depression. Therefore, the more specific evaluation of depression cannot be overly emphasized in the elderly population, especially when the diagnosis of MCI is considered. Finally, more precise diagnosis of MCI requires a comprehensive clinical evaluation and multidomain neuropsychological testing such as the Clinical Dementia Rating (CDR).

Progression of MCI to Dementia

Genetic and brain imaging studies provided validity to the MCI construct as prodromal AD. In a prospective study of more than 1,000 patients who were clinically diagnosed as having MCI, researchers studied 494 patients who provided DNA samples for apolipoprotein E (APOE) genetic analyses. As in AD, APOE ε4 carriers with MCI had greater cognitive impairment, lower functional activities scores, and greater hippocampal atrophy. There was a genetic dose-dependent effect on hippocampal atrophy; that is, patients with two APOE ε4 alleles had greater hippocampal volume loss than did those with one APOE ε4 allele, who in turn had greater volume loss than did those without any APOE ε4 allele. This genetic effect of the APOE ε4 allele on the hippocampus was observed consistently in other studies. The hippocampus plays an important role in learning and memory. The exact mechanism by which the APOE gene affects neuronal function and degeneration is poorly understood. It has been hypothesized that the APOE gene is involved in cholesterol metabolism and oxidative stress.

It is hoped that treatment of MCI would prevent progression to more symptomatic dementias such as AD. Therefore, it is important to identify which patients will progress to AD and which patients are ideal treatment candidates. This task remains difficult. Cerebrospinal fluid (CSF) biomarkers, which included β-peptide-42 (Aβ42) and phosphorylated tau (P-tau), had some predictive value for AD in 78 patients with MCI. Although these tests are fairly specific as markers that would indicate progression from MCI to AD, the tests were not very sensitive and therefore would not be adequate screening tools. The population studied was derived from a memory disorders clinic and might have limited application to the general population. The search for better predictors of MCI progression to dementia via either neurocognitive instruments or biological markers (blood tests or neuroimaging findings) remains an active area of research.

Depression and MCI

Depression commonly occurs concurrently with memory impairment, and the prevalence of depression is increased in patients with memory deficits. As discussed previously, it may be difficult to differentiate depression from MCI. Individuals could have depression that mimics MCI or depression in addition to MCI. Therefore, the effective detection and treatment of depression could improve mood, memory, and overall quality of life regardless of whether memory impairment exists. To assess MCI treatment efficacy, characterization of depressive symptoms may also be important. Interestingly, depression was found to be predictive of MCI progression to AD. In a cohort of 114 patients with amnestic MCI followed for a mean period of 3 years, of the 41 patients with depression, 35 (85%) developed dementia. This conversion from MCI to dementia was much greater than that in the nondepressed patients, only 24 (32%) of whom developed dementia. Depression had a relative risk of 2.6 (95% confidence interval of 1.8 to 3.6) for MCI progression to dementia. In addition, patients with a poor response to antidepressants are at increased risk for developing dementia. Researchers found that 23 of 35 patients with depression who developed dementia did not respond to antidepressants. In contrast, all 6 depressed patients who did not convert to dementia responded to antidepressants. The reason behind these findings is unclear and awaits further research.

Treatment

There are no Federal Drug Administration (FDA)-approved treatments for MCI. The goals of treatment for MCI include reversing the relative "mild" cognitive impairment and, more important, delaying its progression to dementia. In general, approaches to discovering treatment regimens for MCI are similar to those for discovering treatment regimens for AD. To this point, published studies on MCI have tested donepezil, Vitamin E, naproxen, and rofecoxib.

Donepezil was tested in a-MCI patients in a 24-week, multicenter, randomized, double-blind, placebo-controlled study. Treatment with donepezil ($n = 133$), compared with treatment with placebo ($n = 137$), showed improvement on secondary cognitive measures (including Alzheimer's Disease Assessment Scale–cognitive [ADAS-cog] total scores), in tests of attention and psychomotor speed, and in patient global assessment (PGA) scores. This led to a larger study that compared donepezil (10 milligrams [mg] per day, $n = 253$), Vitamin E (2000 international units [IU] per day, $n = 257$), and placebo ($n = 259$) in a-MCI patients for 3 years. The primary outcome was the cumulative diagnoses of possible or probable Alzheimer's disease. At the end of the study, the donepezil group showed a lower rate of AD during the first 12 months of the study but not at the end of the 3-year study. However, among carriers of one or more APOE ε4 alleles (a risk factor for rapid progression to Alzheimer's disease), the benefit of donepezil was seen for the entire 3-year period. Vitamin E in this study, and naproxen (a traditional nonsteroidal anti-inflammatory drug [NSAID]) and rofecoxib (cycloxygenase-2 [COX-2 inhibitor]) in another study, did not show efficacy. In fact, rofecoxib showed statistically significantly increased progression to dementia. Rofecoxib was recently withdrawn from the market due to increased cardiac risks. Other acetylcholine esterase inhibitors, including galantamine and rivastigmine, have also been studied for MCI, but the results are not yet published. There is a warning label on galantamine concerning increased death rates in two studies for MCI. These two studies were presented to the public and did not show cognitive efficacy. In summary, emerging treatments options have not yet shown any clinical benefit for MCI. Nevertheless, treatment and prevention of MCI progression are still being investigated. Further examination of risk factors for MCI progression to dementia and better characterization of treatment candidates may be critical in finding specific treatment options. Defining MCI as a standardized clinical entity was a first step.

—Glen Xiong and
P. Murali Doraiswamy

See also Alzheimer's Disease; Apolipoprotein E; Behavioral Disorders in Dementia; Lewy Body Dementia; Vascular Dementia

Further Readings and References

Aisen PS, Schafer KA, Grundman M. Effects of rofecoxib or naproxen vs. placebo on Alzheimer's disease progression. *JAMA*. 2003;289:2819–2826.

Benson AD, Slavin MJ, Tran TT, Petrella JR, Doraiswamy PM. Screening for early Alzheimer's disease: Is there still a role for the Mini-Mental State Examination? *Prim Care Companion J Clin Psychiatry*. 2005;7:62–67.

Farlow MR, He Y, Tekin S. Impact of APOE in mild cognitive impairment. *Neurology*. 2004;63:1898–1901.

Herukka SK, Hallikainen M, Soininen H, Pirttila T. CSF Aβ42 and tau or phosphorylated tau and prediction of progressive mild cognitive impairment. *Neurology*. 2005;64:1294–1297.

Modrego PJ, Ferrandez J. Depression in patients with mild cognitive impairment increases the risk of developing dementia of Alzheimer's type. *Arch Neurol*. 2004; 61:1290–1293.

Petersen RC. Mild cognitive impairment as a diagnostic entity. *J Intern Med*. 2004;256:183–194.

Petersen RC, Thomas RG, Grundman M. Vitamin E and donepezil for the treatment of mild cognitive impairment. *N Engl J Med*. 2005;352:2379–2388.

Salloway S, Ferris S, Kluger A. Efficacy of donepezil in mild cognitive impairment: A randomized, placebo-controlled trial. *Neurology*. 2004;63:651–657.

Winblad B, Palmer K, Kivipelto M. Mild cognitive impairment—Beyond controversies, toward a consensus: Report of the International Working Group on Mild Cognitive Impairment. *J Intern Med*. 2004;256:240–246.

MINERALS

See VITAMINS, MINERALS, AND DIETARY SUPPLEMENTS

MINIMUM DATA SET

The term *minimum data set* (MDS) has been used in long-term care (LTC) to identify core information about individuals and, more particularly, since 1990 for the national nursing home MDS assessment instrument. In this entry, the term refers not only to the assessment instrument but also to the process of assessment.

Comprehensive Assessment and the Technology of Assessment

The roots of MDSs for LTC lie in comprehensive geriatric assessment. Such assessment is critical to ensuring health and appropriate care by focusing on the problems that persons acquire as they age and the mechanisms that drive these conditions.

Comprehensive assessment has both direct and indirect effects. Direct effects, by identifying not only diseases and conditions but also strengths, preferences, and needs, provide the clinician with information to construct an appropriate, individualized plan of care. This plan identifies appropriate services, goals, and milestones. As people age and need more or different care, information can follow them to care providers, enriching their medical histories. For example, whether a person was able to walk *prior to* breaking a hip is essential to identifying attainable goals for rehabilitation.

The indirect effects are also important. With comprehensive data in a common language, one can contrast alternative approaches, such as home care versus nursing home care, for comparable individuals and with the same outcome measures. These data support quality measures by which providers can be rated for public reporting, inspection can be targeted, or incentive systems can "pay for performance." This information can also provide benchmarks to compare programs, states, or even nations and to identify best practices that achieve superior performance.

Accomplishing these effects, however, requires an effective MDS. The technology of such systems includes four major attributes:

- *Comprehensive assessment of a broad range of characteristics in a standardized language.* There is always a critical balance between the breadth and depth of characteristics and the length of the instrument. Indeed, "minimum" data sets are often not small; nevertheless, they should have only the items truly necessary for their purposes. One gets good data when the assessment directly helps the assessor—the assessor who is caring for the individual—rather than when the assessment is paperwork, only to be shipped off elsewhere for use by others.

- *Careful design to make the assessment work properly.* An MDS needs to be specific in defining each assessment item, including time frame (e.g., "during the past 7 days"), exclusions (e.g., "do not include setup"), and examples. While making an MDS look longer, such specificity makes it simpler, ensuring consistent and usable information. Although some items may need to reflect directly the voice of the individual being assessed (e.g., whether a terminally ill patient has unfinished business), it is usually best to use multiple additional sources of information including caregivers, family members, direct observation, and the medical record—all integrated by the assessor who selects the most appropriate information.

- *Rigorous scientific testing to determine that an MDS design meets its goals.* Any MDS should be thoroughly tested on a variety of criteria, most critically reliability (i.e., two independent assessors of the same person score items the same way) and validity (i.e., it actually measures the concepts addressed).

- *Multiple uses of data to not only reduce redundancy but also create offsetting incentives for the user.* When data are collected only for payment determination or only for quality assurance, assessors might record only that which makes them look best. However, if the same data are collected for *both* purposes—and for care planning and other purposes as well—incentives to over- or underreport are neutralized.

The first implementation of this technology was the National Nursing Home Resident Assessment Instrument/Minimum Data Set (RAI/MDS). Despite concerns, its nationwide implementation has contributed to better quality of care and outcomes, intensity-based payment, quality measures used for consumer report cards, targeted quality of care surveys, and medical eligibility for government-sponsored programs. For example, six scientific articles published simultaneously by the *Journal of the American Geriatrics Society* in 1997 showed that the U.S. introduction of the RAI improved the quality of nursing home care.

Integrating Across LTC Sectors

To date, virtually all MDSs have been designed for a single LTC sector, as with the assessment systems implemented to date by the U.S. government. After adopting the RAI for nursing homes, it implemented an incompatible MDS (the Outcomes and Assessment Information Set, OASIS) for Medicare home care and then yet another (the Functional Impairment Measure) for inpatient rehabilitation. Other areas, such as assisted living and palliative care, remain without any standardized assessment system.

However, individual LTC sectors are rarely linked, making it difficult to follow persons across settings. There is no organized way to communicate important clinical information, and there is no common language. Common elements make it possible to make smooth transitions between sectors and enhance continuity of care, measure and assure quality of care as persons move among care providers, develop coordinated eligibility criteria, compare cost and quality across different mixes of settings and services, and facilitate the expansion and clinical use of an integrated information technology that spans multiple sectors.

Although each sector requires some specific assessment information (e.g., information about the home environment for a community-based elder), there is an opportunity to have critical measures of function, cognition, and so on common across all sectors.

An example of such a system is the integrated suite of MDSs by interRAI, an international research consortium. interRAI gives its assessment systems without charge to governments and caregiving organizations. The suite covers the major LTC sectors, including frail older adults in the community, home care, assisted living, nursing homes, postacute care, palliative care, acute care, and inpatient and community-based mental health. Additional systems are under way for intellectual disability and younger persons with disabilities.

These MDSs have been developed with the approaches outlined previously, including that they are rooted in care planning but also provide quality measures, case–mix systems, eligibility screeners, and a common assessment language across acute, postacute, and LTC settings.

In addition to the RAI implemented in all U.S. nursing homes, 10 states have adopted the home care system, where compatibility with the nursing home MDS has been crucial. Elsewhere in the world, these MDSs have been adopted nationwide in Iceland and Estonia (both home care and nursing homes) and in Switzerland and Hong Kong (home care), with a major pilot scheduled in China. Canada is the most advanced country in adopting these systems; seven provinces have implemented these MDSs, and the Canadian Institute for Health Information has designated three as national standards.

—Brant E. Fries and John N. Morris

See also Continuum of Care; Geriatric Assessment; Instruments; Long-Term Care; Outcome and Assessment Information Set (OASIS)

Further Readings and References

Fries BE, Fahey CJ, ed. *Implementing the Resident Assessment Instrument: Case Studies of Policymaking for Long-Term Care in Eight Countries.* New York: Milbank Memorial Fund; 2003. Available at: www.milbank.org/reports/interRAI/ResidentAssessment_Mech2.pdf. AccessedAugust 26, 2005.

Hawes C, Morris JN, Phillips CD, Fries BE, Mor V. Development of the Nursing Home Resident Assessment Instrument in the U.S. *Age Ageing.* 1997;26(Suppl. 2): 19–26.

Hirdes JP, Fries BE, Morris JN, et al. Integrated health information systems based on the RAI/MDS series of instrument. *Healthcare Mgmt Forum.* 1999;12:30–40.

interRAI. interRAI website. Available at: www.interRAI.org. Accessed August 26, 2005.

Morris JN, Fries BE, Steel K, et al. Comprehensive clinical assessment in community setting: Applicability of the MDS-HC. *J Am Geriatr Soc.* 1997;45:1017–1024.

Morris JN, Murphy K, Nonemaker S, et al. *Resident Assessment Instrument, Version 2.0.* Washington, DC: Government Printing Office; 1996.

MISTREATMENT

See ELDER ABUSE AND NEGLECT; LEGAL ISSUES

MOBILITY

Mobility, which has been operationalized as an individual's ability to move from one place to another and arrive at the desired destination, is essential for independent living among older adults. Mobility impairments and/or mobility disability among the older adult population places a tremendous burden on the public health system due to its effect on the health, physical functioning, and quality of life of older adults. Limitations in mobility are strongly predictive of disability and are usually the first type of disability experienced by older adults. Mobility is necessary for accomplishing activities of daily living (ADLs) but is particularly essential for the performance of independent activities of daily living (IADLs) due to their dependence on lower extremity functioning. Difficulties with mobility are also associated with adverse events, including falls, loss of balance, and hip fractures. In addition, there is evidence that mobility limitations in older adults precede restriction of participation in activities and can lead to social isolation, anxiety and depression, and increased risk of nursing home placement.

The research evidence indicates that individuals who develop difficulties in walking or with mobility are most likely to develop difficulty in their ability to perform ADLs and/or IADLs. For example, one study found that individuals age 80 years and older who reported difficulty in performing mobility tasks (e.g., walking one quarter mile, climbing 10 steps) were twice as likely to develop difficulty in their ability to perform IADLs (e.g., grocery shopping, preparing meals) and ADLs (e.g., dressing, bathing) or to be admitted to nursing homes. Another study found that people age 65 years and older who did poorly on objective measures of mobility were more likely to have disabilities in ADLs 4 years later than were those who did well on the objective mobility measures.

Epidemiological estimates of the prevalence of mobility impairments indicate that approximately 14 million adults over 50 years of age have limitations in mobility and that 14% to 18% of adults over 65 years of age use assistive devices to enhance mobility. Moreover, the prevalence of mobility impairment increases with age, with the oldest old (> 85 years) having the highest prevalence of mobility impairments. In fact, the oldest old are twice as likely to have impairments in mobility relative to those between 65 and 74 years of age. Likewise, the Established Populations for Epidemiologic Studies of the Elderly (EPESE) project found that among people age 65 years and older who had intact mobility, 36% lost their mobility over a 4-year period of time, and that for every 10-year increase in age after 65 years, older adults were twice as likely to report losing their mobility. Furthermore, of those who developed mobility limitations in the EPESE project, only 18% regained mobility.

Several demographic and health-related factors are associated with mobility impairment. More women than men, and more African Americans than Whites, report mobility limitations. Similarly, after adjusting for age and gender, those with mobility limitations are more likely to report having less than a high school education, living alone, having a lower income, and being underemployed. Several physiological changes associated with aging, including changes in body mass composition, weakness, gait and balance abnormalities, underlying chronic illnesses, ratings of poor health status, acute events, and periods of immobility, have negative impacts on mobility and contribute to the loss of lower limb functioning. Finally, modifiable health behaviors, such as smoking and a sedentary lifestyle, increase the risk of mobility limitations.

Changes in body mass composition, including sarcopenia and increased adiposity, are associated with functional declines and disability. Age-related sarcopenia, which is a decrease in muscle mass and muscle strength, is considered to be one of the most important components in the causal pathway leading to both frailty and disability. Sarcopenia results in the loss of both isometric muscle strength and muscle power. These muscular changes are associated with a decrease in walking speed and a decrease in the ability to walk 1 kilometer without difficulty, both of which are markers of limitations in mobility and lower extremity functioning. Epidemiological evidence indicates that older men and older women with Class II sarcopenia are two and three times more likely, respectively, to develop difficulty in walking and/or climbing stairs relative to those with a normal skeletal mass.

The association between overweight and mobility limitations is of particular concern given the rise in prevalence of obesity. Women age 70 years and older with the highest percentage of body fat and/or a body mass index of at least 30 are twice as likely to report limitations in mobility. Similarly, men age 70 years and older with the highest percentage of body fat and/or a body mass index of at least 35 are 1.5 times more likely to report limited mobility. Obesity is believed to precede functional declines for several reasons. First, obesity is associated with degenerative arthritis of the lower extremities, a known precursor to mobility limitations. Obesity increases the risk of several chronic illnesses, including heart disease, diabetes, and metabolic syndromes, all of which can contribute to functional limitations. It is also a marker for a sedentary lifestyle, which contributes to limitations in mobility. Finally, obesity is typically associated with a proinflammatory state that may contribute to muscle erosion and functional decline. Sarcopenic obesity, which is an increase in adiposity accompanied by a loss in muscle mass, is also believed to precede mobility limitations.

Many chronic and acute illnesses contribute to the development of mobility impairments. Arthritis, diabetes, heart disease (e.g., angina, myocardial infarction, congestive heart failure), stroke, peripheral vascular disease, lung disease, cancer, depression, vertigo, and balance problems all are associated with decreased mobility. Arthritis is the leading cause of disability due in part to its effects on lower extremity functioning and mobility. One study found that knee osteoarthritis, stroke, heart disease, and depressive symptoms account for the largest proportion of mobility limitations. Similarly, another study found a high prevalence rate of mobility in limitations among diabetics. More than three quarters (78.3%) of individuals age 75 years and older with diabetes report limitations in their ability to walk one quarter mile, climb 10 steps, stand for 2 hours, or stoop, bend, or kneel. There is some evidence that the effects of illnesses are task specific such that each illness has its own fingerprint on mobility. For example, knee osteoarthritis has been shown to affect tasks related to ambulation or transfers, whereas cardiovascular disease has been shown to increase the difficulty of tasks involving aerobic work capacity. People with chronic illnesses may also limit activities to reduce their symptoms, resulting in a decreased capacity and preclinical disability. Understanding the fingerprints of chronic illnesses will enhance interventions targeting a reduction in mobility limitations.

Cross-sectional studies have also demonstrated that the number of chronic illnesses that a person has is linearly associated with mobility difficulties and is predictive of future mobility limitations. Illnesses may contribute individually to the risk of developing mobility limitations, or they may work synergistically. The strongest evidence for the synergistic effects of disease on mobility comes from the arthritis literature. For example, one study found that the risks of developing difficulties with mobility were 4.4 and 2.3 times higher for individuals with knee osteoarthritis only and heart disease only, respectively, compared with individuals without heart disease or knee osteoarthritis. For individuals with both diseases, the risk was 13.6 times higher. Other studies have shown that individuals with arthritis are more likely to develop a disability only in the presence of other chronic illnesses.

It is evident that maintaining mobility is important for prolonging independent living and functioning in older adults. Successful mobility is influenced by three factors: (a) the abilities, capabilities, and health status of the person doing the walking; (b) the requirements of the task or activity at hand; and (c) the features or context of the environment in which the action is taking place. Loss of mobility is purported to be an interaction of these factors, such that a decline in a person's ability to walk or ambulate, combined with an environment that is not conducive to mobility or a difficult task, will result in mobility limitations.

Although still in its infancy, recent research has focused on the modifiable environmental factors associated with mobility limitations. Features of the physical environment are hypothesized to mediate the relationship between functional limitations and mobility disability. To capture the interaction between the individual and the environment during mobility, Anne Shumway-Cook and colleagues proposed eight environmental dimensions: the distance traveled, time constraints on locomotion, ambient conditions (i.e., weather), terrain conditions (e.g., road conditions, sidewalk conditions), physical load interaction, attention demands, postural transitions, and density of traffic (both vehicular and pedestrian). The basic premise of this model is that the characteristics of the individual and his or her environment conjointly determine disability. Hence, interventions designed to reduce mobility limitations should consider personal and contextual factors. Suggested intervention strategies for reducing mobility limitations include those to enhance the environment in which a person resides, assistive devices to facilitate mobility, balance training, fall reduction programs, interventions to reduce disease burden, and exercise or physical activity interventions to promote strength and muscular endurance.

—*Cheryl A. Der Ananian*

See also Arthritis and Other Rheumatic Diseases; Disability and the Disablement Process; Exercise and Physical Activity; Obesity; Sarcopenia

Further Readings and References

Davison KK, Ford ES, Cogswell ME, Dietz WH. Percentage of body fat and body mass index are associated with mobility limitations in people aged 70 and older from NHANES III. *J Am Geriatr Soc.* 2002;50:1802–1809.

Fried LP, Bandeen-Roche K, Chaves PH, Johnson BA. Preclinical mobility disability predicts incident mobility disability in older women. *J Gerontol A Biol Sci Med Sci.* 2000;55:M43–M52.

Fried LP, Guralnik JM. Disability in older adults: Evidence regarding significance, etiology, and risk. *J Am Geriatr Soc.* 1997;45:92–100.

Lauretani F, Russo CR, Bandinelli S, et al. Age associated changes in skeletal muscles and their effect on mobility: An operational diagnosis of sarcopenia. *J Appl Physiol.* 2003;95:1851–1860.

Shumway-Cook A, Patla A, Stewart A, Ferrucci L, Ciol MA, Guralnik JM. Environmental components of mobility disability in community-living older persons. *J Am Geriatr Soc.* 2003;51:393–398.

MOBILITY ASSESSMENT

Because most older adults are ambulatory, a major focus of mobility assessment is on assessing people who can still walk. Here, mobility is defined as the ability to safely move through the home and community environment to accomplish everyday activities. Although functional mobility problems in older adults have not received as much attention as medical diseases, the sequelae are at least equally important for ongoing independence, long-term health, and quality of life. Anyone working with older adults should be aware of simple methods for assessing mobility, and anyone can be an advocate for an older adult who needs help by documenting problems. These tests can also be used to identify mobility problems that need further attention and to determine the effects of community and public health interventions. They can help identify environmental circumstances that increase mobility difficulty, and in some cases they can elicit underlying biopsychosocial causes of mobility problems in older adults.

Independence with home and community mobility requires safe performance of many tasks that most people take for granted, including walking at slow or fast speeds on level, uneven, or graded surfaces; stepping over or around obstacles; standing in place or turning; walking up and down curbs, steps, or stairs; and standing up from, and returning to, seated surfaces. At times, one must move about safely in hurried, cluttered, or low-lit environments. The need to carry objects, talk, and/or respond to distractions while moving also places demands on individual performance. Certain simple assessment tools can be safely administered by nearly any family member, friend, or community health official to determine whether an older person is experiencing a mobility problem that will interfere with these normal daily activities.

Epidemiology

A large proportion of older adults remain independently mobile into late life, and many might not have major problems with mobility unless they experience an accumulation of physiological deficits with age or, less commonly, if they experience an overwhelming injury or an acute medical event. For example, according to the most recent data from the Medicare Expenditure Panel Survey, approximately 53% of adults age 65 years and older do not have, or do not report, limitations with mobility. Fewer than 1% are unable to walk as a primary mode of moving through the environment. Nevertheless, the number who are ambulatory but report mobility limitations is quite substantial, with 31%, 11%, and 4% of the Medicare population reporting mild limitations (difficulty not requiring assistive equipment or personal help), moderate limitations (difficulty requiring assistive devices such as canes and crutches), and severe limitations (difficulty requiring the assistance of at least one other person), respectively. So, at a minimum, approximately 14.1 million persons age 65 years and older have at least some mobility difficulty. Overall, approximately 19 million people—roughly 10.1% of all noninstitutionalized residents—have some motor difficulty.

From one third to one half of all older adults reporting mobility problems say that their limitations began before 50 years of age, suggesting a time when mobility limitations are developing but barely noticeable as a problem. This suggests a need for simple tests that can be administered to large numbers of people beginning at or before midlife, before mobility problems become severe and disabling, and perhaps even before they interfere with daily life. Early identification of mobility problems might help delay or prevent mobility problems, disability, dependency, and adverse health events.

Many old people with mobility limitations do not look sick. They may feel as if they are "slowing down," becoming more fatigued with the same level of activity, or they may feel a need to gradually alter the frequency and speed with which, or the way in which, they accomplish everyday tasks. They may begin to limit the variety and number of regular activities or the types of environments into which they willingly venture. Many may be partly or completely unaware that these complaints are closely linked with progressive mobility problems.

Many individuals with mobility limitations also do not think of themselves as having a disability. For example, community-dwelling persons age 65 years and older were asked to report whether they had any disability. When those who self-reported no problems were evaluated objectively, many mobility problems were identified, including limitations with walking and with the ability to stand up from a chair and return to the seated position. Although too subtle in some cases to be identified as troublesome by the persons with the problems, scores on some very simple performance-based tests of walking and standing (administered by trained research assistants) could predict those most likely to experience new disabilities, nursing home placement, or death during the next 10 years.

Many people with mobility problems are already seen routinely by primary care practitioners, yet functional limitations might not be detected until the disability is advanced. Several studies have documented major underdiagnosis and undertreatment of mobility problems by primary care health professionals. In fact, few primary care physicians routinely administer standardized tests of mobility performance to their older adult patients even though the consequences of poor mobility are well documented in the literature and effective treatments exist. If untreated, the sequelae of poor mobility may rival those of any other single untreated chronic medical condition in the older adult population. In addition, several recent studies report that people with mobility problems often receive substandard general health care, including less frequent receipt of other important general screenings and preventive services such as mammograms, Pap smears, and counseling about high-risk health behaviors.

Primary Causes of Mobility Problems

Recent studies have determined that major disabling medical conditions and diseases, such as stroke and Parkinson's disease, are not the most frequent causes of poor gait or instability. Far more common are general musculoskeletal complaints, especially arthritis and back problems, which are the primary cause of mobility limitations for approximately 40% of persons 50 to 69 years of age and for approximately 35% of those age 70 years and older. The next most important single causes of mobility limitations are far less prevalent than musculoskeletal complaints but include (in order of frequency) falls, heart disease, motor vehicle accidents, chronic lung disease, cerebrovascular disease, other accidents, osteoporosis/bone/cartilage disorders, and diabetes. Serious vision problems, dizziness, balance complaints, and obesity are also present more frequently in people with mobility problems.

In many cases, mobility problems will be apparent and detectable, even in the absence of any major disease diagnosis. In fact, even people with disease might not necessarily have mobility limitations. Mobility limitations seem to be more strongly related to impairments in distinct physiological systems and body regions, especially when multiple physiological impairments are present. Particularly important are impairments in the central nervous system; perceptual sensory systems; peripheral nervous system; muscles, bones, and joints; and systems that impair the ability to produce energy such as in nutritional or metabolic deficiencies. Mobility problems in older adults are more likely to occur as the number of multiple physiological impairments increases, even when the severity of each individual limitation seems mild.

Methods of Assessment

In the past, the most common method of assessing mobility in older adults was to simply ask about the presence of problems with gait or balance. This approach gives useful information about the nature and severity of limitations that exist such as where, when, and how often an individual experiences limitations or difficulty. On the other hand, isolated use of self-reports is no longer considered to be the "gold standard" for mobility assessment, primarily because performance-based tests have been shown to predict important outcomes even when the individual being tested reports no limitations. There is no substitute for direct observation of how someone moves as he or she walks into a room or how someone moves about in the environment, and this type of movement can easily be quantified in an efficient and clinically meaningful way. Current clinical guidelines suggest a combination of approaches, including self-report and direct observation of performance. Follow-up referral for specialized biomechanical, exercise physiology, or physical therapy gait assessment may be necessary if initial screening suggests that a more complex problem exists or that a more detailed assessment is warranted. For most individuals, however, simple assessments combined with a brief assessment of performance will help elicit the underlying mobility problems.

Some examples of questions to ask ambulatory older adults about the presence or absence of mobility problems include the following:

- Because of a health or physical problem, do you have any difficulty in walking?
- How much difficulty do you have in walking across a room?
- Do you need help from another person when walking?
- Do you use special equipment or aids to help you walk?
- Are you able to walk outside the home?
- How much difficulty do you have in walking one quarter of a mile (approximately two to three blocks)?
- How much difficulty do you have in climbing 10 steps without resting?
- Do you have difficulty in getting up from a chair?
- Have you experienced a recent fall?
- Are you having problems with your balance?

Simple Tests to Detect a Mobility Problem

Because walking is the most central component of most mobility tasks for people who are ambulatory, and because most older adults are ambulatory, it makes sense that walking is one of the most important mobility tasks to assess. Much work in the geriatrics literature has focused on simple measures of walking speed that can be administered by nearly anyone who can walk with an older adult safely while using a stopwatch to time speed of gait. Measurement distances usually are short—typically more than 8 feet and less than 50 feet. Speeds over different distances can be compared by converting stopwatch times to velocities (by dividing the distance walked by the amount of time needed to walk it). A simple protocol, reference values for normal walking speeds, and suggested clinical cutpoints are shown in Table 1. With careful attention to the safety of the persons being tested, most people with minimal training and a lot of common sense can safely perform these assessments, which may be useful for measuring the outcomes of community exercise interventions as well as for identifying people with mobility problems who may benefit from further clinical referral and assessment.

Walking speed is thought to be a good measure of mobility because as physiological impairments accumulate, systems of movement control for walking become less redundant and consequently walking becomes gradually less efficient. Although detailed scales for rating the quality or pattern of walking are available and can be helpful, it turns out that gait speed is a very sensitive indicator of efficiency, quality, and safety of mobility. For most individuals whose health is stable, gait speed remains remarkably consistent to the point where even transient declines as small as 0.1 meter per second (m/s) over a 6-month period are important and have recently been shown to increase 5-year mortality risks. Thus, repeated measures of gait speed are useful for monitoring status and outcome longitudinally. In addition, as compared with individuals who walk faster, speeds below 1.0 m/s are useful in identifying individuals

Table 1 Sample Protocol for a Gait Speed Test and General Suggestions for Interpreting the Results

1. Measure a 10-meter distance and mark with tape on the floor.

2. Stand with the person being measured approximately 2 to 3 meters from the starting point.

3. Give the same instructions in the same way to every person tested: "When I say 'go,' I want you to walk down the hall at your normal comfortable pace. Don't stop until I say 'stop.' This is not a race; I'm just trying to get an idea of your usual walking pace, okay? We'll begin when I say 'go.' Ready? Go."

4. Begin timing with the stopwatch when the lead foot crosses the starting line and end timing when the lead foot crosses the finish line. Do not instruct the person to stop walking until he or she is 2 to 3 meters beyond the finish. Turn around and repeat the test. Compute the average of the two walking trials.

5. Divide the distance (10 meters) by the average walking time. This gives speed in meters per second.

- Is the speed faster than 1.0 m/s?
  Yes: Individual is within *normal range* for walking speed, although he or she may be walking more slowly compared with a previous time point.
  No: Individual is a *slow walker* and should be evaluated further to determine the temporal nature of the problem and whether physical activity, exercise, assistive technology, or rehabilitation should be prescribed.

- Is the speed slower than 0.6 m/s?
  Yes: Compared with faster walkers, this person is probably at the *highest risk* for falls, new disability, institutionalization, and death. The individual has marked mobility problems and should be referred to a primary care practitioner for assessment to determine whether intervention is warranted.

- If the speed is faster than 0.6 m/s but slower than 1.0 m/s, is it faster than 0.8 m/s?
  Yes: Compared with faster walkers, this person is at *medium risk* for adverse events and is probably still ambulatory outside the home but is at risk for losing community mobility. The primary care practitioner should be made aware of the mobility problem and a decision should be made regarding primary prevention of disability and further mobility decline.
  No: Compared with faster walkers, this person is at *moderate risk* for adverse events and is likely experiencing substantial problems with mobility outside and inside the home.

Quick reference for general categories of health risk:

< 0.6 m/s	0.6 to < 0.8 m/s	0.8 to < 1.0 m/s	≥ 1.0 m/s
—High risk	—Moderate risk	—Medium risk	—Within normal range or mild limitations only
—Focus: Intervention/ compensation/prevention	—Focus: Intervention/ prevention	—Focus: Prevention/ intervention	—Focus: Prevention

- Loss of more than 0.1 m/s over a 3-month period is a warning sign of increased risk and/or declining mobility, even when follow-up shows that the decline was transient.

- Loss of more than 0.2 m/s may indicate a serious decline in mobility.

Sources: Adapted from Cesari M, Kritchevsky SB, Penninx BWHJ, et al. Prognostic value of usual gait speed in well-functioning older people: Results from the Health, Aging, and Body Composition Study. *J Am Geriatr Soc.* 2005;53:1675–1680; Perera S, Mody SH, Woodman RC, Studenski SA. Meaningful change and responsiveness in common physical performance measures in older adults. *J Am Geriatr Soc.* 2006;54:743–749; Perera S, Studenski S, Chandler JM, Guralnik JM. Magnitude and pattern of decline in health and function in 1 year affect subsequent 5-year survival. *J Gerontol Biol Sci A.* 2005;60:894–900; Purser JL, Kuchibhatla MN, Fillenbaum GG, Harding T, Peterson ED, Alexander KP. Identifying frailty among hospitalized older adults with significant coronary artery disease. *J Am Geriatr Soc.* 2006 Nov; 54(11):1674–81; Purser JL, Weinberger M, Cohen HJ, et al. Walking speed predicts health status and hospital costs for frail elderly male veterans. *J Rehab Res Dev.* 2005;42:535–546; and Studenski S, Perera S, Wallace D, et al. Physical performance measures in the clinical setting. *J Am Geriatr Soc.* 2003;51:314–322.

Note: m/s = meters per second.

with mobility problems who are at greater risk for adverse health events and conditions (Table 1). Regarding this group of slow walkers, several research groups have suggested that speeds slower than approximately 0.60 m/s indicate the highest risks of subsequent poor outcomes.

Another useful test of mobility is to observe older adults standing up from the seated position. Several versions of this test have been described, including whether an individual can stand from a chair without using arms to assist, the amount of time required to perform five chair stands, and the number of chair stands performed in 30 seconds. Of these tests, the ability to stand without using arms is a good screen to quickly identify those having the most difficulty. The number of chair stands performed in 30 seconds may be faster to administer than the five-chair stand test and allows those who cannot easily perform multiple

stands to receive meaningful scores. A sample protocol is shown in Table 2 along with suggested cutpoints for interpretation.

The timed Up and Go test (Table 3), which is recommended by the American Geriatrics Society for primary care mobility screening, combines standing from a seated position with walking a short distance (3 meters) and then turning and returning to the original seated position. If this test takes someone longer than 30 seconds to perform, there is a definite mobility problem and further assessment by a health care professional is warranted. Speeds longer than 20 seconds are also slow and may indicate developing problems. Unlike previously described walking and standing tests, the timed Up and Go test adds a turning component that may do a better job of eliciting balance problems.

Several other tests are also useful for assessing mobility problems related to balance. One is the time

Table 2 Sample Protocol for a Chair Stand Test and General Suggestions for Interpreting the Results

1. Have the person being tested sit on a standard chair, preferably one with no arm rests. The individual's feet both should be flat on the floor.

2. Stand beside or in front of the individual and give the following instructions in the same way to every person tested: "In just a moment I want you to cross your arms in front of your chest and stand completely up from the chair. Once you are fully standing, return to a seated position and repeat that same activity as many times as possible until I say 'stop.' Your arms should be crossed because I do not want you to use them to push up from the chair. I will time how many times you can stand up in 30 seconds. Begin when I say 'go.' Ready? Go."

3. With a digital stopwatch, begin timing at the word "go" and count the number of times the individual is able to complete a full stand in a 30-second period.

• Can the person stand without using arms to assist?
  Yes: Proceed with the multiple chair stand test.
  No: This individual has a severe mobility, leg strength, or balance problem and may be at risk for falls.

• Does the person stand 7 or fewer times?
  Yes: Compared with people who can stand more times, this person is at the *highest risk* for falls, new disability, institutionalization, and death.

• Individuals who have declined by 1 or 2 stands may be experiencing mobility decline and should be monitored. Those who have declined by a greater number may benefit from clinical referral for further assessment.

Quick reference for general categories of health risk:

< 7 stands	*> 7 stands*
—High risk	—Within a normal range
—Focus: Intervention/compensation/prevention	—Focus: Prevention

Source: Adapted from Purser JL, Kuchibhatla MN, Fillenbaum GG, Harding T, Peterson ED, Alexander KP. Identifying frailty among hospitalized older adults with significant coronary artery disease. *J Am Geriatr Soc.* 2006 Nov; 54(11):1674–1681.

Table 3   Suggested Protocol for the Timed Up and Go Test and General Guidelines for Interpreting the Test

1. Place a standard straight-back chair in the testing area and measure a distance 3 meters in front of the chair. Mark with a piece of tape that will be easily visible by the person being tested.

2. Have the person being tested sit in the chair with both feet flat on the floor.

3. Stand beside the individual and give the following instructions in the same way to every person tested: "In just a moment, I want you to stand up from the chair, walk to this line on the floor [point to the tape marked on the floor], turn around, and then return to sitting in the chair. Begin when I say 'go.' Ready? Go."

4. With a digital stopwatch, begin timing at the word "go" and stop timing once the individual has returned to the seated position.

Quick reference for general categories of health risk:

< 20 seconds (fast)	20 to < 30 seconds (slow)	≥ 30 seconds (very slow)
—Low risk of mobility dependence	—Gray zone —Varying levels of mobility dependence and risk	—High risk of mobility dependence
—Focus: Prevention	—Focus: Prevention/intervention	—Focus: Intervention/compensation/ prevention

Source: Adapted from Podsiadlo D, Richardson S. The timed "Up-and-Go": A test of basic functional mobility for frail elderly persons. *J Am Geriatr Soc.* 1991;39:142–148.

and number of steps necessary to turn 360 degrees in a standing position. The time needed to perform the test is probably the most useful information because it provides a nice continuous score that can be used to compare individuals and to evaluate change over time, especially in response to mobility-related interventions. The ability to bend over and pick up an object (e.g., a coin) from the floor is another especially useful test to determine whether an individual is experiencing dizziness or balance-related problems that prevent normal mobility. For individuals with a balance problem, these tests typically will elicit observable staggering, unsteadiness, or complaints of instability, lightheadedness, or dizziness that should be noted by the person administering the test. However, administration by untrained persons involves risk, so priority should be placed on ensuring that adequately trained personnel are available to prevent avoidable falls and/or injuries.

The four square test developed by Wayne Dite and Viviene A. Temple may be particularly useful in identifying older adults at risk for repeated falls. This test requires creating a "four square" box on the floor using regular walking canes. The individual is asked

to start in Box 1 and then step as quickly as possible into Boxes 2, 3, and 4 and then back into Box 1; then the individual is asked to reverse direction and step consecutively into Boxes 4, 3, 2, and 1. The older person is timed as he or she steps consecutively and through the full clockwise-followed-by-counterclockwise sequence. Individuals who take longer than 15 seconds to perform the test are at greater risk for multiple falls.

For all tests of balance, great care should be taken to ensure the safety of the person being tested. Test results will likely be highly correlated with the ability to stand and walk efficiently; thus, if necessary, the previously described gait speed and chair stand tests may suffice to capture most mobility problems, including those involving balance, especially when there is concern about safety.

Regarding balance, clinical guidelines published by the American Geriatrics Society suggest that mobility assessment should always involve questioning the older person about whether recent falls have occurred because a history of previous falls is the strongest predictor of balance problems and subsequent falls. This interview should elicit details about the environmental circumstances that surrounded each fall, with follow-up falls risk assessment by trained health care professionals.

Person–Environment Assessment

A new approach to mobility assessment views mobility problems not as static, biological, or disease-based characteristics of an individual but rather as a biopsychosocial process. From this view, mobility problems are only partly determined by biological limitations. Psychosocial and environmental causes are viewed as just as potentially detrimental to mobility as are individual biological impairments. In fact, determining that biological impairments are present might not be sufficient to delineate mobility problems, many of which will become evident only when a person interacts with his or her environment. Fears, past experiences, depression or other psychological states, mobility self-confidence, and pain all could interact with environmental conditions and biological impairments to influence mobility performance.

Recent approaches focus on how and why a person's interactions with the environment become restricted over time rather than on his or her biological impairments. Assessment tools that have been developed target the point at which an individual begins to alter the frequency of performing specific daily activities, the way in which the activities are performed, the number of different types of activities engaged in or eliminated, and the length of time needed to engage in certain tasks. This type of mobility assessment may help identify individuals who do not seem to have current limitations with simple tasks in nonchallenging environments but who may be at greater risk in more difficult environments and who are beginning to restrict their mobility.

A second new person–environment assessment approach was described by Anne Shumway-Cook and colleagues. They used an Environmental Analysis of Mobility Questionnaire (EAMQ) to assess the frequency with which different aspects of the environment are encountered as well as the frequency with which certain types of mobility tasks and environments are avoided intentionally. Questions focus on encounters with specific distances that might be necessary for independent mobility, the time needed to go places, ambient conditions that might be encountered (e.g., weather, lighting, temperature), variable terrains that one might need to walk over, weights of objects that must be carried while moving, competing attentional demands that might occur, necessary changes in posture or position, and the density of people and objects in the environment. This type of assessment shows great promise as a biopsychosocial assessment tool for several reasons. First, the theory on which the tool is based views mobility limitations not as a characteristic that defines an individual but rather as activity limitations that may be variably present depending on the environmental circumstances of the mobility activity. Second, this tool may help target intervention because limitations in certain dimensions, and not others, may give clues as to the underlying causes of impairment. This type of mobility assessment may also help identify individuals who currently are not disabled but who may be at future risk due to gradual activity restrictions. It could also help identify environmental obstacles that could be modified or circumstances in which it might be beneficial to practice mobility tasks.

Preliminary work using the EAMQ tool suggests that older adults with mobility problems tend to avoid some, but cannot avoid all, challenging environments. The more tasks and types of conditions avoided, the lower the observed mobility level. Also, speed demands and the need to carry objects are very important dimensions that make mobility more difficult. Current thinking is that the broader an individual's experience with, exposure to, and/or practice moving in different types of environmental conditions, the better prepared the individual will be to successfully negotiate a novel and challenging mobility situation. Of course, adaptation or avoidance may ultimately become necessary for certain fixed mobility problems or disabilities, but this decision should not be made without considering whether eliminating mobility tasks might also contribute to growing mobility difficulty over time. Alternatively, assistive devices may promote ongoing independent mobility while minimizing the number of tasks avoided or eliminated from a daily mobility repertoire.

—*Jama L. Purser*

See also Geriatric Assessment; Mobility; Performance Measures of Physical Function

Further Readings and References

American Geriatrics Society, British Geriatrics Society, and American Academy of Orthopedic Surgeons Panel on Falls Prevention. Guidelines for the prevention of falls in older persons. *J Am Geriatr Soc.* 2001;49:664–672.

Calkins DR, Rubenstein LV, Cleary PD, et al. Failure of physicians to recognize functional disability in ambulatory patients. *Ann Intern Med.* 1991;114:451–454.

Dite W, Temple VA. A clinical test of stepping and change of direction to identify multiple falling older adults. *Arch Phys Med Rehab.* 2002;83:1566–1571.

Iezzoni LI, McCarthy EP, Davis RB, Siebens H. Mobility difficulties are not only a problem of old age. *J Gen Intern Med.* 2001;16:235–243.

Iezzoni LI, McCarthy EP, Davis RB, Siebens H. Mobility impairments and use of screening and preventive services. *Am J Public Health.* 2000;90:955–961.

Perera S, Studenski S, Chandler JM, Guralnik JM. Magnitude and pattern of decline in health and function in 1-year affect subsequent 5-year survival. *J Gerontol A Biol Sci Med Sci.* 2005;60:894–900.

Podsiadlo D, Richardson S. The timed "Up-and-Go": A test of basic functional mobility for frail elderly persons. *J Am Geriatr Soc.* 1991;39:142–148.

Shumway-Cook A, Ciol MA, Yorkston KM, Hoffman JM, Chan L. Mobility limitations in the Medicare population: Prevalence and sociodemographic and clinical correlates. *J Am Geriatr Soc.* 2005;53:1217–1221.

Shumway-Cook A, Patla A, Stewart AL, Ferrucci L, Ciol MA, Guralnik JM. Assessing environmentally determined mobility disability: Self-reported versus observed community mobility. *J Am Geriatr Soc.* 2005;53:700–704.

Studenski SA. Mobility. In: Hazzard WR, Blass JP, Halter JB, Ouslander JG, Tinetti ME, eds. *Principles of Geriatric Medicine and Gerontology.* New York: McGraw-Hill; 2003:947–960.

MOOD DISORDERS

See DEPRESSION AND OTHER MOOD DISORDERS

MOTIVATION

Numerous scientific studies have documented a positive relationship between engagement in healthy behaviors and good physical and mental health. For example, regular physical exercise has been demonstrated to improve endurance, strength, and physical function, and to decrease feelings of sadness, in older adults. Likewise, smoking cessation may decrease the risk of a recurrent heart attack by up to 50% within 1 year in both younger and older adults. Despite the wide publicity associated with these findings, the available evidence suggests that many older adults do not engage in healthy behaviors, nor do they believe that they should make any changes to improve their health. Therefore, it is of great importance to understand the factors that enhance or reduce older adults' motivation to engage in healthy behaviors.

Health behaviors can be defined as any action, or lack thereof, that affects one's physical or psychological functioning. Examples of health behaviors include smoking, physical exercise, alcohol use, seatbelt use, regular visits to one's physician and dentist, eye exams, flu shots, sunscreen use, mammograms, breast self-exams, and Pap tests. Motivation may be defined as a need or desire to take action and includes setting goals, generating a plan of action, and performing specific behaviors to reach one's goals.

Several different theories have been proposed to understand the nature of the relationship between motivation and performance of health behaviors. These theories include (a) utility models (e.g., health belief model, protection motivation theory, theory of reasoned action, theory of planned behavior); (b) self-regulation models (e.g., self-regulation theory, cognitive–behavioral theory); (c) social–cognitive theory; and (d) the transtheoretical model of change (TTM).

Utility models state that one's motivation to act is dependent on one's beliefs in his or her personal vulnerability to a health threat and his or her beliefs about its seriousness. One's beliefs about the costs and benefits of each possible action determine motivation to perform specific protective behaviors. Self-regulation models, on the other hand, focus primarily on how specific life events are interpreted as threats to one's health and the development of skills for engaging in protective actions.

Social–cognitive theories of motivation tend to examine how self-efficacy (the belief or expectation that one can perform a specific behavior successfully and one's confidence in obtaining a desired outcome) relates to motivation to engage in healthy behaviors. Self-efficacy has been found to be related to goal setting, goal commitment, perseverance, and effort, and it has been consistently correlated with levels of physical activity. There is some evidence that older adults, as compared with younger adults, have lower levels of self-efficacy with respect to physical exercise and have lower expectations of positive benefits from exercise.

According to the TTM, individuals move through six different stages of change as they attempt to modify specific behaviors. During the first stage, *precontemplation,* the individual does not intend to modify his or her behavior in the foreseeable future, often because the individual is unaware that his or her current behavior is maladaptive. During the *contemplation* stage, one is aware that a problem exists and is considering making a change but has not yet decided to take action. During the *preparation* stage, one plans to make some behavioral change within the next month and has tried unsuccessfully to make a change within the past year. During the next stage, *action,* the individual has changed his or her behavior but has maintained the change for less than 6 months. During the *maintenance* stage, one has maintained the change for at least 6 months and the focus is on preventing relapse. During the final stage, *termination,* one has totally eliminated any desire to engage in the maladaptive behavior for at least 5 years after the initial behavioral change. Individuals usually move back and forth between stages (relapse) in a cyclical manner. With respect to physical exercise, older adults have been found to be more likely to be in either the precontemplation or maintenance stage.

Unfortunately, there have been very few large-scale empirical studies that have directly examined older adults' motivation to change health-related behaviors. One exception to this is the Canadian National Population Health Survey (NPHS), an epidemiological study of 17,354 Canadians age 60 years and older. A substantial proportion of respondents reported inadequate performance of health behaviors across a number of domains. For example, one fourth of all respondents, and 42% of those age 75 years and older, were sedentary (defined as engaging in fewer than one physical activity per month). Nearly 50% of respondents stated that they never used sunscreen, and 32% stated that they had not visited a dentist in at least 5 years. Approximately 17% of respondents were current smokers, most (75%) of whom reported no intention of smoking less or quitting. Many respondents had never had a flu shot (44%), and 27% had not had an eye exam in at least 2 years. Among women, 25% reported that they had never had a breast examination by a physician, and 27% stated that they had never performed a breast self-exam. In addition, 21% of women reported that they had never had a Pap test. On the more positive side, few older adults reported heavy alcohol use, and 95% had received a blood pressure check within the past 2 years.

Most respondents (nearly two thirds) indicated that they had not done anything during the past year to improve their health, and a similar number stated that they did not believe they should do anything to improve their health. The most frequently reported barrier to improving their health was lack of willpower, reported by 45% of those individuals who believed that they should do something to improve their health and who reported at least one barrier to doing so. Individuals with higher levels of education were generally more likely to report engaging in healthy behaviors.

In terms of practical applications, it appears to be critical for health care practitioners and public health educators to employ individualized intervention strategies to increase older adults' motivation to engage in healthy behaviors. With respect to the TTM, matching an individual's current stage of change to the appropriate intervention is essential. For example, older adults who are inactive would be more likely to benefit from interventions focused on changing their thoughts and beliefs about exercise rather than interventions focused on specific exercises or activity goals. In addition, because healthy behaviors are often only weakly related, practitioners should concentrate on helping individuals to modify one or two health behaviors at a time rather than multiple areas.

A need exists for additional research on motivation and health behaviors in older adults that uses longitudinal designs, incorporates randomized clinical trials, and includes samples of minority older adults and cognitively impaired older adults, who remain understudied in this research domain. With this knowledge, practitioners and public health educators will be better able to help older adults initiate and maintain healthy behaviors.

—*Adam L. Bank and Carl Eisdorfer*

See also Exercise and Physical Activity; Health Promotion and Disease Prevention; Quality of Life; Smoking

Further Readings and References

Leventhal H, Rabin C, Leventhal EA, Burns E. Health risk behaviors and aging. In: Birren JE, Schaie KW, eds. *Handbook of the Psychology of Aging.* 5th ed. San Diego, Calif: Academic Press; 2001:186–214.

Morely JE, Flaherty JH. It's never too late: Health promotion and illness prevention in older adults. *J Gerontol A Biol Sci Med Sci.* 2002;57:338–342.

Netz Y, Raviv S. Age differences in motivational orientation toward physical activity: An application of social–cognitive theory. *J Psychol.* 2004;138:35–48.

Newsom JT, Kaplan MS, Huguet N, McFarland BH. Health behaviors in a representative sample of older Canadians: Prevalences, reported change, motivation to change, and perceived barriers. *Gerontologist.* 2004;44:193–205.

Prochaska JO, DiClemente CC, Norcross JC. In search of how people change: Applications to addictive behaviors. *Am Psychol.* 1992;47:1102–1114.

Wallace KA, Lahti E. Motivation in later life: A psychosocial perspective. *Top Geriatr Rehab.* 2005;21:95–106.

MULTIPLE MORBIDITY AND COMORBIDITY

It is well known that aging is associated with an increase in both the incidence and prevalence of single chronic health conditions. Aging, however, is also associated with the development of multiple concurrent health conditions; older people are more likely than younger people to have more than one health problem. The concepts of *multiple morbidity* and *comorbidity* have been introduced to better characterize studies of health in older populations. Multiple morbidity is defined as the presence of multiple health conditions in the same person. Comorbidity describes the presence of multiple health conditions in people diagnosed with a specific index disease. For example, an epidemiological study of multiple morbidities might provide data on the number and types of conditions found among older community residents, whereas a study in the epidemiology of comorbidity might examine the number and types of health conditions found among older women with breast cancer.

Multiple Morbidity

Research indicates that there are patterns of multiple morbidities among people in the general population. Results from the National Health Interview Survey indicate that the percentage of people age 60 years and older who reported having two or more of the nine most common conditions increased steadily with age. The 10 conditions are arthritis, hypertension, cataracts, heart disease, varicose veins, diabetes, cancer (except nonmelanoma skin cancer), osteoporosis, hip fracture, and stroke. Specifically, the percentage of women who reported two or more conditions increased from 45% (among those 60 to 69 years of age), to 61% (among those 70 to 79 years of age), to 70% (among those age 80 years and older). Among men, the percentages were 35%, 47%, and 53%, respectively. These results provide compelling evidence that multiple morbidity is not unusual in older populations. On the contrary, for most older people, multiple morbidity provides the best characterization of general health. Moreover, as an indication of the severity of multiple morbidity, the presence of two or more health conditions is associated with an increased likelihood of functional limitations and disability. Multiple studies on non-Hispanic Whites and African Americans in the United States indicate that multiple morbidities are associated with race and ethnicity. African American men and women are more likely to exhibit multiple morbidities than are non-Hispanic White men and women. Therefore, it might be that studies that focus on a single health condition may underestimate the extent of health disparities between non-Hispanic Whites and African Americans in the United States.

Comorbidity

Most of the research on multiple health conditions has focused on comorbidity; that is, studies in which the participants consist of people with an index condition. Many studies on comorbidity have focused on heart disease and cancer in older populations. There are two consistent findings from the research in this area. First, older patients with comorbidity have shorter duration and poorer quality of life than do patients without comorbidity after taking into account other prognostic indicators. Second, patients with comorbidity are typically administered less intensive forms of therapy than are patients without comorbidity, again after taking into account relevant covariates. One common interpretation of this finding is that physicians are concerned that standard therapies for either heart disease or cancer may be too risky in the presence of other conditions. Researchers and practitioners in geriatrics have incorporated measures of comorbidity, together with other prognostics indicators (e.g., physical functioning, cognitive functioning), to better characterize the physiological age of patients. Results of such assessments are used to tailor specific treatments for older patients with multiple conditions.

Measures

The standard approach for measuring multiple health conditions is to summarize the number and severity of conditions. The Charlson Index, clearly the most commonly used measure, provides an overall score based on a composite of values weighted by level of severity and assigned for any of 19 selected conditions. The severity score for each condition is based on an early study of the 1-year, age-adjusted relative risks of death for hospitalized patients with selected conditions. The overall comorbidity score is based on the sum of the scores for the individual conditions. Like other measures of multiple health conditions, the Charlson Index assumes an additive relationship among conditions. In other words, possible multiplicative relationships are not considered in the final score. In addition, the timing of the onset of conditions (i.e., whether an individual condition preceded or followed another) is not considered and makes no difference in the overall score.

Sources of Information

Medical records, administrative databases, and personal interviews are the three major sources of information on multiple health conditions. Medical records have been the most common source of data for measures of comorbidities. Although medical records are generally considered to be the most complete source of data on multiple diagnoses, there is concern that a review of medical records may be too time-consuming and costly for large cohort studies. Electronic administrative databases have been evaluated as a more efficient source of data. Databases range in size and complexity from computerized discharge summaries of individual hospitals to computerized records of the U.S. Medicare and Medicaid populations. Although these data can be accessed more readily than can regular medical records, there is concern that administrative databases, in some cases, may be driven by specific billing practices and might not provide a completely comprehensive assessment of past diagnoses. Personal interviews also have been used as sources of information on multiple morbidities and, to a lesser extent, studies of comorbidities. There are several advantages to the personal interview. First, it is an efficient and less costly procedure than a review of medical records. Second, in case–control studies, it ensures that data on comorbidity are obtained in the same manner for both cases and controls. Third, it provides an opportunity to obtain alternative data on severity such as the respondent's reported functional limitations. Despite these strengths, there are potential weaknesses. The interview might not completely ascertain the respondent's past conditions. Furthermore, participants, especially older people, might not know or accurately recall all diagnoses.

The Future

Although this area of research has significant implications for public health and clinical medicine, there are significant challenges as well. Methodological research should include comparisons of the utility and validity of different indexes, different data sources, and different analytic techniques. Future work in this area will provide a more comprehensive and accurate assessment of health in older populations.

—*William A. Satariano*
and Mihaela Popa

See also Activities of Daily Living and Instrumental Activities of Daily Living; Arthritis and Other Rheumatic Diseases; Depression and Other Mood Disorders; Diabetes; Hypertension; Obesity

Further Readings and References

Charlson ME, Pompei P, Ales KL, MacKenzie CR. A new method of classifying prognostic comorbidity in longitudinal studies: Development and validation. *J Chron Dis.* 1987;40:373–383.

Gijsen R, Hoeymans N, Schellevis FG, Ruwaard D, Satariano WA, van den Bos GAM. Causes and consequences of comorbidity: A review. *J Clin Epidemiol.* 2001;54: 661–674.

Guralnik JM, Lacroix AZ, Everett DF, Kovar MG. *Aging in the Eighties: The Prevalence of Co-morbidity and Its Association With Disabilities.* Hyattsville, Md: National Center for Health Statistics; 1989. Advance Data From Vital and Health Statistics, No. 170.

McGee D, Cooper R, Liao Y, Durazo-Arvizu R. Patterns of comorbidity and mortality risk in Blacks and Whites. *Ann Epidemiol.* 1996;6:381–385.

Van den Akker M, Buntinx F, Metsemakers JF, Roos S, Knottnerous JA. Multimorbidity in general practice: Prevalence, incidence, and determinants of co-occurring chronic and recurrent diseases. *J Clin Epidemiol.* 1998;51:367–375.

MUSCULOSKELETAL AGING: INFLAMMATION

The major components of the integrated musculoskeletal system are the muscles, bones, and joints. Aging is defined as the progressive degradation of biological function over time that results from an accumulation of biological damage that eventually exceeds the repair capacities of the body. Clinically, inflammation refers to redness (rubor), heat (calor), swelling (tumor), and pain (dolor) that are detected locally during physical examination. Biomarkers of systemic inflammation include elevated levels of proinflammatory cells, C-reactive protein (CRP), erythrocyte sedimentation rate (ESR), and cytokines such as interleukin 1 (IL-1), tumor necrosis factor α (TNF-α), and interleukin 6 (IL-6). These biomarkers of inflammation are typically elevated in the geriatric population.

There are several degrees of inflammation. Monitoring the ESR can sometimes be misleading in the elderly population where elevated ESR levels are not uncommonly related to other factors such as infection, congestive heart failure, hypercholesterolemia, and malignancy. High-sensitivity CRP is probably the best supported inflammatory marker to assess risk of atherosclerosis. Results of less than 1.0 milligram per deciliter (mg/dl) (9.5 nanomoles per liter [nmol/L]) represent low risk, results of 1.0 to 3.0 mg/dl (9.5 to 28.6 nmol/L) represent average risk, and results greater than 3.0 mg/dl represent high risk. Results greater than 10 mg/dl (95.2 nmol/L) help distinguish clinically significant inflammatory processes from clinically noninflammatory processes. Increased levels of ultrasensitive CRP (> 1 mg/dl but < 10 mg/dl) are seen in chronic diseases associated with aging (e.g., atherosclerosis, Alzheimer's disease, diabetes, metabolic syndrome, osteoarthritis, fibromyalgia). Higher levels of ultrasensitive CRP ($\geq$ 10 mg/dl) are seen in inflammatory conditions such as rheumatoid arthritis (RA), crystal-induced arthropathies (more pseudogout than gout), polymyalgia rheumatica (PMR), giant cell arteritis (GCA), idiopathic inflammatory myopathies (IIM), Sjögren's syndrome (SS), and septic arthritis. Other less common inflammatory conditions are systemic lupus erythematosus (SLE), ankylosing spondylitis (AS), psoriatic arthritis (PsA), small vessel vasculitis, polychondritis, and reflex sympathetic dystrophy (RSD).

Immunosenescence is the age-determined decrease of the immune system capacity to mount an adequate protective response to foreign entities. The high degree of variability in immune responses among individuals of all ages increases during old age. It is paradoxical that the aging immune system is associated with a decline in immune responses and reduced antibody response to antigens, whereas the incidence of many autoantibodies (e.g., rheumatoid factor, antinuclear antibodies) is increased in the elderly population. This may imply an overactive but inefficient immune system given that the incidence of most autoimmune diseases is lower in the elderly. On the other hand, several autoimmune diseases increase with advanced age, including GCA, Hashimoto's thyroiditis, and SS.

Thus, not only does immunosenescence allow infections to take on a more atypical or severe form, but also vaccines used to prevent infections will be less effective and autoimmune diseases will have a different clinical inflammatory presentation and course. Polymyositis (PM) and scleroderma starting after 50 years of age are associated with increased mortality. SLE tends to be milder in older individuals. Two clinical presentations of RA can be defined in the elderly population: elderly-onset rheumatoid arthritis (EORA) and young-onset rheumatoid arthritis (YORA). EORA is the de novo development of RA in persons over 65 years of age. EORA has less female predominance, a more acute onset of disease, and a higher ESR than does YORA. EORA has more involvement of large joints, in particular shoulder joints. YORA encountered in elderly patients is RA that developed before 65 years of age and persisted to old age. Older patients with gout are more likely to have polyarticular involvement, to be female, to have involvement of the small joints of the fingers, and to develop tophi (buildup of gout crystals under the skin or in other places) early during the course of their

illness, often in atypical locations. There is a greater association of gout with diuretic use and renal disease in elderly populations. Sporadic inclusion body myositis (S-IBM) is the most common inflammatory myopathy in patients over 50 years of age. Incidence rates of polymyositis–dermatomyositis (PM–DM) are bimodal, peaking during childhood and then again in adults with a mean age of 45 to 64 years. The mean age is higher (60 years) for those with malignancy-associated myositis, and the elderly have a higher incidence of malignancy. The response to therapy and the outcome are poorer than in younger adults. Patients with PMR are classically older than 50 years of age (90% are older than 60 years of age), and most are White. PMR is a syndrome characterized by pain and morning stiffness in the neck, shoulder girdle, and pelvic girdle, with common constitutional symptoms such as malaise and fatigue. Typically, the ESR is higher than 50, and frequently it is higher than 80. PMR can occur as a separate entity or in association with GCA as temporal arteritis.

Inflammation is a risk factor for atherosclerosis. Endothelial cell dysfunction related to rheumatoid vasculitis could be the initiating factor in the accelerated cardiovascular mortality of RA. Chronic endothelial cell dysfunction may leave the vessels in RA with an enhanced susceptibility to both classic cardiovascular risk factors and RA-related ones that may interact in complex ways.

The management of inflammatory conditions in the elderly is complicated by their diagnostic uncertainty, comorbidity, changes in pharmacokinetics and tissue responsiveness, and increased adverse drug events. The objectives of therapy are to control pain, stop disease progression, and improve functional status. There is no cure available for the majority of these conditions. Physical therapy is important. Disease-modifying antirheumatic drugs (DMARDs), including the new biological agents (TNF and IL-1 blockers), do change the course of RA and potentially slow or prevent structural joint damage. Infection and tuberculosis are always a concern. DMARDs are used in other inflammatory conditions with unclear outcomes. Low-dose aspirin plus steroids diminishes the incidence of cranial ischemic (critical loss of circulation) complications in GCA. Steroids are still the treatment of choice for PMR, as allopurinol is for chronic gout. Exercise can be used as a complement to the overall management of inflammation.

—*Yuri R. Nakasato and Bruce A. Carnes*

See also Arthritis and Other Rheumatic Diseases; Biological Theories of Aging; Infectious Diseases; Musculoskeletal Aging: Osteoarthritis

Further Readings and References

Elosua R, Bartali B, Ordovas JM, Corsi AM, Lauretani F, Ferrucci L. Association between physical activity, physical performance, and inflammatory biomarkers in an elderly population: The InCHIANTI Study. *J Gerontol A Biol Sci Med Sci.* 2005;60:760–767.

O'Rourke KS. Myopathies in the elderly. *Rheum Dis Clin N Am.* 2000;26:647–672

Tutuncu Z, Kavanaugh A. Rheumatic disease in the elderly: Rheumatoid arthritis. *Clin Geriatr Med.* 2005;21: 513–525.

Yung RL. Changes in immune function with age. *Rheum Clin N Am.* 2000;26:455–473.

MUSCULOSKELETAL AGING: OSTEOARTHRITIS

The major components of the integrated musculoskeletal system are the muscles, bones, and joints. Aging is defined as the progressive degradation of biological function over time that results from an accumulation of biological damage that eventually exceeds the repairing capacities of the body. Age-associated changes in joint tissues include roughening of the articular cartilage surface and osteophyte formation. Chondrocytes are the main cells in charge of cartilage repair. With aging, chondrocytes experience a reduced proliferative capacity and a reduced synthetic capacity to produce matrix components. The cartilage undergoes thinning due to less hydration while the collagen network becomes stiffer. The cartilage then becomes less deformable or able to respond to compression and more prone to injury. Age-related

joint changes are usually not severe enough to cause significant cartilage erosion.

Osteoarthritis (OA) is a type of arthritis characterized by chronic low-grade inflammation based on systemic inflammatory markers such as erythrocyte sedimentation rate (ESR) and C-reactive protein (CRP). Osteoarthritis, thought to be a misnomer for a noninflammatory condition, usually presents with evidence of local inflammation early on. It is considered to be a joint failure because multiple tissues are involved, including the synovium (joint lining), the underlying bone, the periarticular tissue, and the cartilage. OA prevalence increases with age, and it is calculated that by 65 years of age two thirds of the population will have radiographic evidence of OA in at least one joint. Before 50 years of age, men have more OA than do women, but this inverts after 50 years of age except for hip OA (always more prevalent in men). OA affects the hands, spine, hips, and knees, and it usually spares the ankles, wrists, and shoulders. African American men are 35% more likely than White men to have hip OA. Evidence also suggests an inverse relationship between OA and osteoporosis, both of which are frequent conditions in the elderly. Radiography remains the standard for diagnosing this condition. Magnetic resonance imaging (MRI) is more specific, but its cost precludes its pervasive use. Eburnation (indicative of full-thickness cartilage loss), osteophytes (bone buildup around the edge of the joint), and joint space narrowing (JSN) are the main radiographic and anatomical findings.

OA includes structural changes different from aging such as progressive cartilage loss, remarkable osteophyte formation, thickening of the joint capsule, and sclerosis of subchondral bone. OA morphological changes have been noted to begin during the fourth decade of life and become increasingly prevalent up to the eighth decade, a suggested upper limit after which the incidence of the disease appears to level off or possibly decline. In centenarians, the prevalence of symptomatic OA of the hip, knee, shoulder, or spine is only 54%. OA is not necessarily a consequence of aging, and factors associated with longevity may also protect individuals from developing OA.

Meniscal tears (damage to the special pads inside the knee joint) are highly prevalent in both asymptomatic and clinically osteoarthritic knees of older individuals. However, osteoarthritic knees with meniscal tears are not more painful than those without tears, and meniscal tears do not affect functional status. For a meniscectomy to be successful, the meniscal tear must be the source of the pain. Meniscal tears are also very common in asymptomatic older adults, being found in as many as 65% of asymptomatic individuals evaluated by MRI.

Bone marrow edema detected by MRI is a potent risk factor for structural deterioration in the affected site and the pain associated in knee OA. Its relation to progression is explained in part by its association with limb alignment. Bone scan studies in persons with OA have reported late-phase uptake of tracer in subchondral bone, signifying accelerated bone turnover. This increase in tracer has been associated with joint pain and a markedly increased risk of radiographic progression in OA of the knee.

Musculoskeletal aging factors include the described changes in chondrocytes and tissue function, sarcopenia (age-associated muscle loss), loss of proprioception (conscious and unconscious perception of joint position and movement that is more pronounced in sedentary elderly) and balance, and increased joint laxity (prone to develop varus [knock knee] or valgus [bow leg] deformity that is more significant in women). The described changes of aging within the musculoskeletal tissues do not cause OA directly but rather predispose older adults to its development. Nonaging factors include musculoskeletal underuse or misuse due to lack of exercise or abnormal joint loading. Both cause musculoskeletal dysfunction with or without pain. OA risk factors include obesity, previous or recent joint injury/instability, genetics (accounting for at least 50% of cases of OA in the hands and hips and a smaller percentage in the knees), and abnormal anatomy (knee alignment is knee position in reference to the hip and ankle, and malalignment predicts worse surgical outcomes).

An important risk factor for development of OA includes previous or recent injuries such as fractures of articular surfaces and tears of menisci and ligaments that increase joint instability. Job-related activities in which workers do repetitive tasks, overworking the joints and fatiguing muscles that protect the joints, increase the risk of OA in those joints. Moderate regular running has low risk (if any) of leading to OA. Participation in high-demand, high-intensity, acute, direct joint impact increases the risk of OA. It is well recognized that quadriceps muscle weakness is common in patients with OA, and whether it precedes or is a consequence of disuse due to pain remains to be elucidated.

Knee and hip OA accounts for its high risk of disability in the elderly, mostly with climbing stairs and walking. OA is the most common cause of knee and hip replacement. Factors associated with disability include pain and stiffness. OA has been considered to be a disease whose characteristic pathological feature is loss of hyaline cartilage, but that tissue contains no pain fibers. Pain fibers are present in several other surrounding structures. Depression, muscle weakness, poor aerobic capacity, and radiographic disease severity are other factors associated with disability. It is known that radiographic findings relate poorly to pain and function. However, in some individuals, aging-related changes in the musculoskeletal system might be as important in determining pain and function as are changes related to the development of OA.

Knee OA is the most common site for OA where weight loss is strongly correlated with improvement in symptoms and signs of disease. The relationship of increased body weight with hip OA is weaker than its association with disease of the knee. Unilateral disease of the hip is not clearly associated with being overweight, whereas bilateral disease is. For each 1-pound increase in weight, the overall force across the knee in a single-leg instance increases 2 to 3 pounds.

Management of OA includes a multidisciplinary approach for prevention and treatment. Objectives include relief of symptoms, maintenance and improvement of joint function, reduced disability and handicap, and limited progression (or even facilitation of joint healing). Nonpharmacological and nonsurgical measures include patient education; physical therapy; use of a cane, brace, or special footwear; and weight management programs for overweight patients. Three categories of exercise therapy are used for OA: range of motion and flexibility exercise, muscle conditioning, and aerobic cardiovascular exercise. Two thirds of elderly with arthritis do not meet public health physical activity recommendations; that is, 30 minutes of moderate-intensity physical activity on 5 or more days per week or at least 20 minutes of vigorous-intensity physical activity on 3 or more days per week. Well-conditioned muscle and muscular balance are needed to attenuate impact loads, provide joint stability, and support function and independence.

Drug therapy includes analgesics (e.g., acetaminophen, tramadol, topical analgesics), nonsteroidal anti-inflammatory drugs (NSAIDs), and intra-articular injections of corticosteroids or hyaluronan. There is a lack of agents that may prevent, retard, or reverse disease progression (disease-modifying osteoarthritis drugs [DMOADs]). Candidates include glucosamine, a nutraceutical now used extensively by patients with OA, often in combination with chondroitin sulfate.

Nonbiological surgical approaches for OA include osteotomy, debridement and lavage, arthrodesis, and arthroplasty. Osteotomy is performed in persons with early OA and may relieve symptoms and slow the rate of progression. Arthroscopic debridement and lavage can also successfully alleviate symptoms, particularly in the presence of meniscal tears associated with mechanical symptoms. Arthrodesis or joint fusion successfully alleviates pain and is commonly performed in the spine and in small joints of the carpus, hand, and foot. Arthrodesis of the major proximal joints of the upper and lower extremities is not well tolerated because of the major functional deficits

associated with loss of motion. Total joint arthroplasty is the mainstay of surgical treatment of the hip, knee, and glenohumeral (shoulder) joint OA. For most persons, especially elderly ones, total joint replacement is a highly successful procedure that will probably last for the duration of their lives. Total joint replacement has limited durability in persons with life expectancies exceeding 20 years and those who wish to participate in high-demand activities. Biological surgical approaches for OA are promising and include biological restoration of articular cartilage loss either by stimulating the resident hyaline cartilage to repair defects or by transplanting cartilage.

—*Yuri R. Nakasato and Bruce A. Carnes*

See also Arthritis and Other Rheumatic Diseases; Fractures in Older Adults; Injury Prevention; Normal Physical Aging; Osteoporosis

Further Readings and References

Felson DT, conference chair. Osteoarthritis—New insights: I. The disease and its risk factors. *Ann Intern Med.* 2000; 133:637–639.

Felson DT, conference chair. Osteoarthritis—New insights: II. Treatment approaches. *Ann Intern Med.* 2000; 133:726–729.

Loeser RF, Shakoor N. Aging or osteoarthritis? *Rheum Dis Clin N Am.* 2003;29:653–673.

Minor, M, Stenstrom CH, Klepper SE, Hurley M, Ettinger WH. Work group recommendations: 2002 Exercise and Physical Activity Conference, St. Louis, Missouri. *Arthr Rheum. (Arthr Care Res.)* 2003;49:453–454.

NATIONAL HEALTH INTERVIEW SURVEY

The National Health Interview Survey (NHIS) is one of a family of health surveys conducted by the National Center for Health Statistics (NCHS), the U.S. government's health statistics agency. The NHIS was authorized in 1956 by an act of Congress, the National Health Survey Act, which stipulated that the NCHS was to supply continuing survey and special studies for protected, precise, and current statistics on illness and disability in the United States. The NCHS is now part of the Centers for Disease Control and Prevention (CDC), which is part of the U.S. Department of Health and Human Services.

The NHIS is an annual national household survey of the civilian noninstitutionalized population of the United States conducted throughout the year. The annual NHIS sample now consists of approximately 100,000 persons of all ages who reside in approximately 40,000 households. Trained interviewers from the U.S. Census Bureau conduct in-person interviews using computer-assisted personal interviewing.

Since its inception in 1957, the NHIS has covered a wide range of health topics, including general health status, acute and chronic conditions, use of health care services, health insurance coverage, and disability and its consequences, as well as basic demographic and socioeconomic information. The NHIS questionnaire was revised substantially in 1997, and its stable "core" now contains three major submodules that cover the entire family (about whom a knowledgeable adult responds), a randomly sampled child (about whom a knowledgeable adult responds), and a randomly sampled adult (who responds for himself or herself).

The Family Core questionnaire covers everyone in the family, asking about demographics, general health, and health-related topics. It includes a set of age-appropriate questions on activities of daily living (ADLs) and instrumental activities of daily living (IADLs) as well as questions on cognitive functioning. Health conditions causing these limitations are identified. Other questions deal with use of medical services, medically attended injuries and poisonings, and disability days. Detailed information on health insurance coverage for each family member is obtained.

The Sample Adult Core covers persons age 18 years and older. Topics include functional limitations and selected conditions such as heart disease, respiratory conditions, diabetes, arthritis and joint problems, and hearing and visual impairments. Other questions cover mental health status and impact, smoking, drinking, and leisure time physical activity. Questions are asked about use of health care services, including having a usual place of health care, hospitalizations, and use of doctor and dentist services.

The Sample Child Core roughly parallels the adult questionnaire; in both, the health conditions covered are age appropriate. In the child questionnaire, there are additional questions on developmental problems, school-related difficulties, and mental health.

Each year, supplements (additional questions that go into more detail and/or cover new topics) are sponsored by other government agencies and added to the NHIS. For example, several supplements on disability, including longitudinal ones, were fielded during the 1980s and 1990s. Recent supplement subjects have included health promotion, diabetes, cancer, children's mental health, and complementary and alternative medicine. For example, the 2005 Cancer Control Supplement, which included topics on diet and nutrition, physical activity, tobacco use, cancer screening, genetic testing, and family history, was sponsored by the National Cancer Institute at the National Institutes of Health (NIH) and by the National Center for Chronic Disease Prevention and Health Promotion at the CDC. Another example is the 2004 Children's Mental Health Supplement that contained the Strengths and Difficulties Questionnaire, 32 questions asked of parents/guardians about their children, sponsored by the National Institute of Mental Health at NIH. NHIS supplements, or variations of them, are often repeated during different years.

The NCHS publicly releases NHIS microdata annually from both the core and supplements. Microdata collected during 2004 were released less than 7 months after the end of the data collection year. Currently, all public use files and supporting documentation for data years 1997 through the year of the most recent release are available without charge from the NHIS website. Previous years of public use files back through 1969 are available on data tapes or CD–ROMs and will soon be available for downloading from the NCHS website as well.

Since data year 2000, the NCHS has been releasing quarterly estimates for 15 key health indicators through its Early Release (ER) program. After each new quarter of data collection, these estimates are updated and then released on the NCHS website 6 months after the data collection quarter. The 15 measures covered by ER are lack of health insurance coverage and type of coverage, usual place to go for medical care, obtaining needed medical care, receipt of an influenza vaccination, receipt of a pneumococcal vaccination, obesity, leisure time physical activity, current smoking, alcohol consumption, human immunodeficiency virus (HIV) testing, general

health status, personal care needs, serious psychological distress, diagnosed diabetes, and asthma episodes and current asthma. For each of these health measures, a graph of the trend since 1997 is presented, followed by figures and tables showing age-specific, sex-specific, and race/ethnicity–specific estimates for the new data quarter. Key findings are highlighted. A separate in-depth report on health insurance is also updated and released every 3 months as part of the ER program. Both quarterly ER reports are released only electronically on the NCHS website.

In addition to releasing NHIS microdata to the public, NCHS staff members publish their own analyses of the data. Series 10 reports provide results of analyses of NHIS data in substantial detail. Among those series reports are three volumes of descriptive statistics and highlights published annually based on data from the NHIS Family Core, Sample Child Core, and Sample Adult Core. The NCHS's series Advance Data From Vital and Health Statistics publishes single articles from the various NCHS programs. *Health United States,* the NCHS's annual report on the health status of the United States, contains numerous tables and other analytic results based on NHIS data.

Multiple years of NHIS microdata are periodically linked to other databases such as the National Death Index (NDI) and Medicare records. The NDI is an NCHS-maintained central computerized index of state death record information. Linkage to the NDI ultimately provides outcome information about underlying and contributing causes of death.

The NHIS also serves as a sampling frame for the Medical Expenditure Panel Survey (MEPS), which was designed to provide policymakers, health care administrators, businesses, and others with information about health care use and costs as well as to improve the accuracy of their economic projections. The MEPS surveys families and individuals, their medical providers, and their employers across the United States. The MEPS families are a subset of those interviewed within the previous year for the NHIS.

When analysis of NHIS data requires access to confidential microdata that are not released publicly, the NCHS Research Data Center allows researchers meeting certain qualifications to access such data under strict supervision. Researchers must submit a proposal for review and approval. Access may be on-site at the NCHS or remotely.

—*Jane F. Gentleman and Susan S. Jack*

See also Activities of Daily Living and Instrumental Activities of Daily Living

Further Readings and References

Agency for Healthcare Research and Quality. MEPS: Medical Expenditure Panel Survey. Available at: www.meps.ahrq.gov. Accessed September 24, 2006.

Bloom B, Dey A. Summary health statistics for U.S. children: National Health Interview Survey, 2004. *Vital Health Stat.* 2006;10(227). Available at: www.cdc.gov/nchs/data/series/sr_10/sr10_227.pdf. Accessed September 24, 2006.

Cohen RA, Martinez ME. Health insurance coverage: Estimates from the National Health Interview Survey, January-June 2005. Available at: www.cdc.gov/nchs/nhis.htm. Accessed September 24, 2006.

Lethbridge-Cejku M, Rose D. Vickerie J. Summary health statistics for U.S. adults: National Health Interview Survey, 2004. *Vital Health Stat.* 2006;10(228). Available at: www.cdc.gov/nchs/data/series/sr_10/sr10_228.pdf. Accessed September 24, 2006.

Schiller JS, Adams PF, Coriaty Nelson Z. Summary health statistics for the U.S. population: National Health Interview Survey, 2003. *Vital Health Stat.* 2005;10(224). Available at: www.cdc.gov/nchs/data/series/sr_10/sr10_224.pdf. Accessed September 24, 2006.

National Institute on Aging

The National Institute on Aging (NIA), one of the National Institutes of Health (NIH), works to increase understanding of the nature and implications of aging and to extend the healthy active years of life. The NIA was established in 1974 after the White House Conference on Aging recommended its creation and Congress authorized, through Public Law 93-296, formation of NIA to provide leadership in aging research, training, health information dissemination, and other programs relevant to aging and older adults.

Subsequent amendments to the legislation designated the NIA as the primary federal government agency for Alzheimer's disease research.

The NIA's mission is to improve the health and well-being of older Americans through research and specifically to do the following:

- Support and conduct high-quality research on aging processes, age-related diseases, and special problems and needs of the aged
- Train and develop highly skilled research scientists from all population groups
- Develop and maintain state-of-the-art resources to accelerate research progress
- Disseminate information and communicate with the public and interested groups on health and research advances and on new directions for research

NIA Research Programs

The NIA sponsors aging-related research through its extramural and intramural programs. The extramural program funds research and training at universities and other research centers throughout the United States and abroad. The intramural program conducts laboratory and clinical research at facilities in Baltimore and Bethesda, Maryland. Within these programs, NIA scientists and those supported by NIA grants and contracts are exploring everything from cell function to social interaction, with major focuses on the biology of aging, reducing disease and disability, Alzheimer's disease and cognitive changes, and the behavioral and social aspects of aging. During recent years, the NIA also has increasingly promoted the study of sex and racial/ethnic disparities in health, developed strategies to include more minorities in research, and encouraged the training of more minority scientists.

Extramural Research

Approximately 80% of the NIA's funding is disbursed through extramural awards made to universities, medical centers, and other public and private research organizations. The NIA's extramural program encompasses four major areas of emphasis: the biology of aging, behavioral and social research, neuroscience and neuropsychology of aging, and geriatrics and clinical gerontology.

The Biology of Aging Program supports research to enhance and extend the health of older people through studies of the basic biological processes associated with aging. Research within this program examines many of the fundamental mechanisms of aging—in genes, in the biochemistry of cells, and in critical organs of the body. This work includes studying the gradual or biologically programmed alterations of structure and function that characterize normal aging as well as changes that are risk factors for, or accompany, age-related disease states. For example, NIA-funded scientists are using animal models and organisms such as fruit flies and yeast to learn about the genetics of longevity and disease.

The Behavioral and Social Research Program looks at how people change during the adult life span, the interrelationships between older people and social institutions, and the societal impact of the aging population. Research within this program examines diverse concerns such as health disparities; psychological development; cognitive functioning; reducing disability; behavior change interventions; genetics, behavior, and the social environment; and the burden of illness and the efficiency of health systems. A major program initiative, the Health and Retirement Study (HRS), is one of the most extensive surveys on health and retirement ever conducted in the United States. Every 2 years since 1992, HRS researchers have surveyed 22,000 people over 50 years of age to paint a comprehensive picture of older Americans' health and disability status, work and retirement circumstances, income and wealth, and other aspects of aging.

The Neuroscience and Neuropsychology of Aging Program fosters research and training to better understand the neural and behavioral processes associated with the aging brain. This program focuses on the neurobiology, neuropsychology, and dementias of aging, with the overall goal of elucidating how normal and pathological aging affect the central nervous system and behavior. Alzheimer's disease (AD) research is a priority within the Neuroscience and Neuropsychology of Aging Program. In this arena,

the NIA supports and coordinates more than 30 Alzheimer's Disease Centers (ADCs) at major medical institutions nationwide. Within these centers, investigators clinically evaluate people with AD, conduct systematic research with that population, and offer patient education. The NIA also supports the Alzheimer's Disease Cooperative Study, through which academic medical centers conduct collaborative clinical trials studying drugs to manage, treat, and prevent AD symptoms. In addition, NIA funding encourages drug discovery initiatives and supports a national repository of blood samples from people with AD and their families that are used to study genetic defects associated with the disease.

The Geriatrics and Clinical Gerontology Program supports research on both health and disease in older adults and research on aging during the life span. Research within this program focuses on topics such as falls and frailty, the effects of physical activity on disease and disability, aging-related pathological changes, and clinical issues during the life span. The program also plans and administers clinical studies testing interventions designed to address problems associated with disability, concurrent use of multiple drugs, menopause, and other concerns.

Within the extramural program, the Office of Extramural Affairs organizes the work of the National Advisory Council on Aging (NACA), which was created by Congress in 1975 to advise on programmatic and policy matters related to the NIA's mission. The 18-member NACA also keeps NIA staff apprised of the research community's opinions and scientific concerns and informs the scientific community, Congress, and the public about the NIA's activities.

In addition, the Office of Extramural Affairs manages peer review of all extramural applications—a process ensuring that NIA-funded research is of the highest quality and serves the health needs of the nation—and coordinates the NIA's research training and career development activities. Grant applications are first reviewed by either an NIH Center for Scientific Review group or an NIA review committee, and then they are reviewed by panels of scientific experts, including NIH grantees. The review panels assess the quality and originality of the proposed science, the investigators' qualifications, the quality of the proposed research facilities, the treatment of any animals to be used, and (for research involving humans) proposed plans for recruiting women and minorities into the studies. Qualified applications for amounts exceeding $50,000 must then receive NACA approval to be eligible for funding.

Intramural Research

The NIA's intramural program seeks to uncover new knowledge about age-related pathological changes and people's ability to adapt to environmental stress. This knowledge helps scientists to understand changes associated with healthy aging and age-related diseases, to define criteria for evaluating when a change is linked to disease, and to explore the development of new treatment strategies. Through both laboratory and clinical research, the NIA's multidisciplinary intramural scientists study age-related diseases, including AD, Parkinson's disease, stroke, atherosclerosis, osteoarthritis, diabetes, and cancer.

The NIA intramural research program is composed of 11 scientific laboratories, 2 scientific sections, a Clinical Research Branch, and a Research Resources Branch. The research team includes experts in scientific disciplines such as biochemistry, cell and molecular biology, structural biology, genetics, behavioral sciences, epidemiology, statistics, and clinical research as well as in medical disciplines such as neurobiology, immunology, endocrinology, cardiology, rheumatology, hematology, oncology, and geriatrics. The program also offers scientists laboratory and clinical medicine training opportunities within these disciplines.

The intramural program's state-of-the-art laboratories are located at the Gerontology Research Center in Baltimore and on the NIH campus or offsite in Bethesda. Researchers working within these labs investigate a wide range of topics such as the biological processes of aging, cardiac function, interventions to slow aging processes, genetic determinants of aging, immune function, the epidemiology of aging, and personality and cognition. Many of the intramural studies involve collaborations with other scientists within the NIA and NIH or at other research centers.

The intramural program's Clinical Research Branch conducts longitudinal studies of aging and interventional clinical trials, with a focus on cardiology, neurology, endocrinology, and oncology. Ongoing projects include two major studies: the Baltimore Longitudinal Study of Aging (BLSA) and the Healthy Aging in Neighborhoods of Diversity Across the Life Span (HANDLS) study.

Also within the intramural program, the Research Resources Branch offers the NIA's intramural scientists specialized laboratory and instrumentation expertise, animals for use in research, and other biomedical research resources and support.

Information Dissemination and Public Outreach

Complementing its scientific programs, the NIA disseminates information about aging-related topics and research to the public and professionals. This mission is accomplished through two clearinghouses: the Alzheimer's Disease Education and Referral (ADEAR) Center and the NIA Information Center (NIAIC).

The ADEAR Center answers questions, disseminates materials about AD, offers referrals to local supportive services and ADCs, and provides clinical trial information and literature searches. The NIAIC disseminates NIA publications and other materials and also participates in a variety of outreach programs. Both centers offer services and materials in English and Spanish through their websites and toll-free information lines as well as by e-mail, snail mail, and fax. All materials developed by these centers are researched carefully and reviewed thoroughly by NIA scientists and health communicators to ensure scientific accuracy and audience appropriateness.

In addition, the NIA disseminates health information to consumers through NIHSeniorHealth.gov, a "senior-friendly" website developed and maintained by the NIA and the National Library of Medicine, also part of the NIH. This award-winning resource offers reliable information on dozens of aging-related topics, ranging from AD and arthritis to shingles and sleep.

—Jack M. Guralnik

See also Government Health Surveys; Health and
Retirement Study

Further Readings and References

National Institute on Aging. About NIA. Available
at: www.nia.nih.gov/AboutNIA. Accessed
September 24, 2006.

National Institute on Aging. *Aging Under the Microscope:
A Biological Quest.* Bethesda, Md: NIA; 2002.
NIH Publication No. 02–2756. Available at:
www.niapublications.org/pubs/microscope/index.asp.
Accessed September 24, 2006.

National Institute on Aging. *NIA's Portfolio for Progress.*
Bethesda, Md: NIA; 2001. NIA Publication No. 02–4995.
Available at: www.niapublications.org/pubs/portfolio/
html/index.asp. Accessed September 24, 2006.

National Institutes of Health. National Institute on
Aging. Available at: www.nih.gov/about/almanac/
organization/NIA.htm. Accessed September 24, 2006.

NATIONAL LONG TERM
CARE SURVEY

The National Long Term Care Survey (NLTCS) is a
longitudinal study of the health and functioning of the
U.S. elderly population and its use of acute and long-
term care (LTC) health services. The NLTCS was conducted in 1982, 1984, 1989, 1994, 1999, and 2004. Its
sample is drawn from Medicare enrollment lists. In
1982, a procedure using 101 reduction sets of 500
individuals was used to determine the prevalence of
chronic disability and institutionalization in a
Medicare list sample of enrollees age 65 years and
older. In the 1982 NLTCS, 35,000 individuals were
interviewed to identify 6,000 chronically disabled
community residents (the number of detailed interviews that the budget permitted).

NLTCS interviewing is done in two stages. The first
stage involves screening all persons for activity of
daily living (ADL) impairment or instrumental activity
of daily living (IADL) impairment lasting at least
90 days. After chronically disabled persons are identified, they are given a face-to-face interview lasting

60 minutes and covering medical conditions, ADL and
IADL disabilities, the health and social services
received to help the persons manage with disabilities,
demographic and housing traits, and socioeconomic
factors.

In 1984, it was determined that a sample of 6,000
disabled community residents could be generated by
reinterviewing surviving disabled persons from the
1982 NLTCS and roughly half of the 25,000 persons
found not to be disabled in 1982. In 1984, the deaths
of 1982 respondents were included in the sample so
that the next of kin could be interviewed about health
trajectories prior to death (e.g., nursing home entry).
An institutional interview was developed and
was administered to institutional residents in 1984.
Only the fact of institutional residence was recorded
in 1982.

The 1982 and 1984 NLTCSs were conducted by
Health Care Financing Administration (HCFA) with
support from the Assistant Secretary for Planning and
Evaluation (ASPE). The 1989 NLTCS was conducted
under a National Institute on Aging (NIA) grant with
funds and design input provided by the ASPE. In
1989, both community-dwelling disabled residents
and institutionalized persons were interviewed. As in
1984, all persons identified as chronically impaired in
a prior NLTCS were given a detailed interview so that
improvements and declines in functional status could
be monitored. In 1989, there was evidence of a decline
in disability prevalence. As in 1982, an informal caregiver survey was administered. As for the 1982 and
1984 NLTCSs, all NLTCS sample persons in 1989
were linked to Medicare Part A records. The 1982 and
1984 NLTCSs bridged the period of introduction of
Medicare hospital prospective payment. The 1989
NLTCS was administered after the Catastrophic Care
Act of 1988 was passed—and repealed shortly thereafter—although it had significant consequences for
LTC in the United States.

In 1994, the same two-stage interviewing process
was used. As in 1984 and 1989, a replenishment sample of roughly 5,000 persons was drawn from lists of
Medicare enrollees 65 to 69 years of age (i.e., persons
who were under 65 years of age in the prior survey but
who passed the age of eligibility between the 1989

and 1994 NLTCSs). This replenishment sample ensures that all NLTCSs are nationally representative longitudinally (once a chronically disabled person is identified, he or she receives a detailed interview up to the time of his or her death) and cross-sectionally (because of the 65- to 69-year-old replenishment sample). In 1994, three innovations were made. First, an oversample ($n = 540$) of very elderly persons (age 95 years and older) was drawn and screened. Second, nutrition questions were added to the community interview. Third, a sample of persons who did not report disability in the screen were given a detailed interview to improve the precision of estimates of the prevalence of traits of nondisabled persons. In 1990, the Medicare administrative record system was changed to include all types of Medicare services, including Part B outpatient services.

In 1999, the same sample design was used with a 65- to 69-year-old replenishment sample of 5,500 persons, an oversample ($n = 600$) of very elderly persons (age 95 years and older), and replenishment of the 1994 healthy oversample. An informal caregiving survey was added in 1999. A major innovation was the conduct of a pilot study of the ability to collect blood samples or buccal wash samples. Roughly 640 blood samples and 2,000 buccal wash samples were completed with biospecimens archived at the University of Washington. Apolipoprotein E (APOE) and other genetic assessments were conducted, as was a pilot study ($n = 168$) of 17 cytokines potentially associated with inflammation and other physiological aging changes from blood serum.

In 1999, the continuation of a decline in chronic disability and institutionalization found from 1982 to 1994 was confirmed, with the rate of decline accelerating from 1994 to 1999. These declines and the acceleration from 1994 to 1999 were confirmed in independent studies by Eric Stallard and colleagues. Significant declines were found in the prevalence of both serious disability (chronic ADL impairment) and less serious disability (chronic IADL impairment). Significant declines in institutional use were noted along with increased use of assisted-living residences.

In addition, it was confirmed that severe cognitive impairment declines observed from 1982 to 1999 could be linked to declines in dementia associated with stroke and circulatory disease using *International Classification of Diseases, Ninth Revision* (ICD-9) diagnoses found in Medicare records. It was found that Medicare costs of nondisabled persons rose less rapidly than did those of chronically disabled persons and that national estimates of the age-specific incidence of major chronic diseases could be made from linked Medicare records.

The 2004 NLTCS had the same structure in 1999, with healthy oversamples and a larger ($n = 1,584$) oversample of very elderly persons (age 95 years and older). An informal caregiver survey, with an expanded definition of caregivers, was conducted in 2004. A helper file for 1989, 1994, and 1999 was also produced. On the screener in 2004 was added a question identifying veterans. This identified roughly 4,000 elderly veterans who were linked to Department of Veterans Affairs (VA) administrative records. A total of 9,187 veterans were identified in all waves. Medicaid records are now available for all 50 states (for 1999–2000), and the feasibility of linking respondents to Medicaid records is being assessed. Given that medical costs in the oldest old tend to involve LTC and institutional care, often funded by Medicaid, the linkage of Medicare, Medicaid, and VA administrative records provides a powerful tool for the analysis of health services use by the elderly and oldest-old populations.

—*Kenneth G. Manton*

See also Government Health Surveys; Institutional Care; Long-Term Care; Long-Term Care Insurance

Further Readings and References

Manton KG, Gu X. Disability declines and trends in Medicare expenditures. *Ageing Horizons.* 2005;2: 25–34.

Manton KG, Gu X, Ukraintseva SV. Declining prevalence of dementia in the U.S. elderly population. *Adv Gerontol.* 2005;16:30–37.

Stallard E, Wolf RM, Weltz SA. Morbidity improvement and its impact on LTC insurance pricing and valuation. *Record Soc Actuaries.* 2004;30(1).

Native Americans and Alaska Natives

Because of their unique relationship with the federal government, American Indians and Alaska Natives, members of more than 500 federally recognized tribes who live on or near reservations, are entitled to free health services provided by the federal government. However, the federal government considers Indian health care to be a discretionary program rather than an entitlement program, and it determines the level of funding based on political considerations.

There is consistent evidence that health care expenditures for American Indians are substantially less than what is spent on the general population. Federally funded Indian health care is frequently characterized as an "I/T/U" system composed of the Indian Health Service (IHS), Tribal, and Urban components. However, urban Indians, who constitute more than half of the population, are provided with few or no IHS benefits. In fact, both urban and rural American Indians experience health care rationing. Older Indians who are provided "comprehensive" federally funded health services experience rationing through inadequate funding and shortages of personnel, training, facilities, and services, whereas urban Indians over 65 years of age are subject to rationing based on ability to pay.

In general, systematic health status information has been available for only the approximately 60% of the Indian population for which the IHS has responsibility, but the quantity and quality of this information have deteriorated during the past decade.

Mortality

Mortality data for American Indians are subject to three primary sources of error: misclassifications of cause of death, misidentifications of race of decedent, and inaccurate population estimates. Studies have documented that mortality is underestimated by 10% to 21%, especially for those age 65 years and older, urban residents, and those with lower Indian blood quantum.

A number of studies have noted the recent shift in mortality and morbidity from acute and infectious diseases to chronic and degenerative diseases. Despite this trend, far fewer American Indians than Whites live to old age, with 86% of all deaths among Whites, compared with only 59% of all deaths among Indians, occurring among individuals age 55 years and older. Much of this difference is attributable to premature mortality among Indian males from accidents, suicides, chronic liver disease and cirrhosis, and homicides. Between 1994 and 1996, only 39% of American Indian male deaths were among those age 65 years and older, compared with 53% of American Indian female deaths.

Based on age-specific mortality rates, a "mortality crossover" occurs during advanced old age, although the precise age has not been established. After 55 years of age, differences in life expectancy between Whites and American Indians are greatest in the younger age groups and for women. Overall, elderly Indian female life expectancy is 20% to 25% longer than that of Indian males.

Slightly more than half of all deaths among American Indians age 65 years and older are attributed to heart disease or cancer, and approximately three quarters of all deaths were the result of the top two causes plus diabetes, cerebrovascular disease, pneumonia, and chronic obstructive pulmonary disease (COPD). Indians in this age group have 20% to 30% lower death rates than do Whites of the same age group from heart disease, cancer, cerebrovascular disease, and COPD. In contrast, older Indians experience higher mortality rates for diabetes mellitus (2.9 times), chronic liver disease and cirrhosis (2.4 times), and nephritis, nephritic syndrome, and nephrosis (1.6 times).

Morbidity

There is a large specialized Indian health research literature on type 2 diabetes, heart disease and hypertension, rheumatoid arthritis, and cancer. Compared with their peers age 65 years and older in the general population, older Indian males experience substantially higher rate of diabetes (1.5 times), gallbladder disease (1.4 times), and rheumatism (1.3 times).

However, Indian females age 65 years and older appear to have an advantage over females in the general population, with the exception of diabetes (2.4 times higher).

Substantial gender differences in chronic health conditions among older Indians have been documented. Compared with older females, the proportion of Indian males age 65 years and older with emphysema is nearly three times higher, the proportion of older Indian males with cancer is double, and the rates of older Indian males are substantially higher for cardiovascular disease (1.5 times) and rheumatism (1.4 times). In contrast, among older Indian females, the rates are higher for gallbladder disease (1.6 times) and diabetes (1.4 times).

Older adults commonly experience two or more chronic health problems. This "multimorbidity" predicts a range of adverse health outcomes. Based on self-reports, approximately one quarter of a sample of community-dwelling older Indians did not experience multiple problems, 17% reported simple comorbidity, but 57% reported three or more chronic conditions. Multimorbidity was consistently the most important predictor of four measures of health-related quality of life: activity of daily living (ADL) impairments, self-assessed physical health, self-assessed mental health, and the degree to which health troubles impede other activities.

Mental Health

A number of studies have documented that American Indians tend to somatize mental health problems and present them as physical health complaints. Based on the current state of knowledge, depression has been, and remains, the most prevalent mental health problem among older American Indians. A number of scholars have suggested that depression may be related to stressful life events, including bereavement, the bicultural experience, functional impairments, and external factors such as chronic unemployment and poverty-level income.

Although a lower prevalence of Alzheimer's disease has been reported, the only detailed community study found that the prevalence of all dementias was similar to the non-Indian comparison group (4% for each). This study found that Alzheimer's disease was markedly lower but that multi-infarct and alcohol-related dementias were more common. Suicide is another indicator of mental health status. In comparison with Whites of the same age and sex, older American Indians have much lower suicide rates, although the suicide rate among older Indian males remains significantly higher than among older females.

Disability

Research suggests that American Indians experience accelerated aging and that disability is a bigger problem than it is among non-Hispanic Whites. Regardless of the measure, evidence suggests that there is no "disability crossover." Compared with Whites, more American Indians at all adult ages have problems that limit mobility, self-care, use of public transportation, and work. Older American Indian females experience higher levels of disability than do males.

Longer life for American Indians means more years of disability. In other words, American Indians have experienced an expansion, rather than a compression, of morbidity with a length of inactive life that is the highest among all ethnic groups. For older Indians, comparatively low mortality means longer life, but approximately half of those years are spent with disabilities.

Self-Rated Health

Self-rated physical health among older Indians is relatively poor. Among those age 65 years and older, the proportions of Indian men (32.6%) and Indian women (34.0%) with fair or poor health are approximately 1.2 times higher than those of their White age peers. Self-appraisals of recent physical health, mental health, and activity limitations reveal that American Indians age 65 years and older perceive themselves to be less impaired than do Indians 55 to 64 years of age. Comparisons among men 55 to 64 years of age from five ethnic groups revealed that American Indians reported the highest mean number of impairment days for each health indicator studied.

Use of Medical Services

Healthy People 2010 documents that American Indians are less likely than other groups to receive timely routine screenings and other preventive measures. Although little research has been conducted on health risk behaviors, one study documented that Indian women 50 to 64 years of age have the highest prevalence (49.3%) of three or more of the following risk factors: obesity; being physically inactive; smoking; heavy alcohol consumption; diabetes; and inadequate seatbelt use, Pap smear screening, mammography screening, colorectal screening, and immunization.

Most research suggests that older American Indians have high levels of need for health care services but have lower rates of hospitalization and ambulatory care. Among Indians age 65 years and older in the IHS service population, approximately two thirds of hospitalizations during fiscal year 1997 were for diseases of the respiratory system, circulatory system, digestive system, symptoms, signs and ill-defined conditions, and endocrine, nutritional, and metabolic disorders.

According to IHS figures for fiscal year 1997, although pronounced gender differences were evident, half of all ambulatory visits among Indians age 65 years and older were for circulatory system diseases, preventive health services, nervous system and sensory organ diseases, respiratory system diseases, and endocrine, nutritional, and metabolic disorders. Public health nurses and community-based health care paraprofessionals are important sources of health care services to older Indians.

Lower service use rates probably indicate barriers that restrict Indian elders' receipt of needed health care services. Potential barriers include problems with availability, awareness, accessibility, acceptability, and affordability of health care services.

Long-Term Care

Older American Indians lack long-term institutional care provided by the IHS or any other federal agency. The IHS continues to define its mission as acute care and does not consider custodial long-term care to be its responsibility. Currently, there are a limited number of American Indian nursing homes and too few in-home

and community-based services available to relieve families of long-term caregiving responsibilities. This means that American Indian families, especially in rural settings, are the primary, if not sole, providers of long-term care to functionally dependent older Indians.

For older Indians, problems exist with access, use, and quality of health care, and there is some evidence of discrimination or unequal treatment. Individual beliefs and behaviors also contribute to poor health outcomes. Clearly, older Indians experience deficits in both health care process and outcomes. Moreover, older American Indians do not use services to the same extent or in the same way as do more privileged older adults, as seen in less use of preventive health care services, lower rates of hospitalization, and less use of ambulatory care, including dental care. In addition, health care quality is not comparable, and health care is rationed by available institutional and individual resources.

Older American Indians need to have better access to preventive health services, especially routine health checkups, health education, screenings, and early access to better diagnostic procedures. Improving Indian health will also require better funding for community and public health services. Health improvement depends most on improvement of the social context of the communities in which these elders live, including fundamental changes that effectively address adequate nutrition, economic security, educational opportunities, quality housing, protection of the natural environment, and comprehensive community-based health efforts.

—*Robert John*

See also African Americans; Asian and Pacific Islander Americans; Ethnicity and Race; Hispanics

Further Readings and References

Hahn RA, Teutsch SM, Franks AL, Chang M-H, Lloyd EE. The prevalence of risk factors among women in the United States by race and age, 1992–1994: Opportunities for primary and secondary prevention. *J Am Med Women's Assoc.* 1998;53:96–107.

Hayward MD, Heron M. Racial inequality in active life among adult Americans. *Demography.* 1999;36:77–91.

Indian Health Service. *Trends in Indian Health: 1998–1999.* Rockville, Md: IHS; 1999.

John R. Aging and mortality among American Indians: Concerns about the reliability of a crucial indicator of health status. In: Markides KS, Miranda M, eds. *Minorities, Aging, and Health.* Thousand Oaks, Calif: Sage; 1997:79–105.

John R. Health status and health disparities among American Indian elders. In: Whitfield KE, ed. *Closing the Gap: Improving the Health of Minority Elders in the New Millennium.* Washington, DC: Gerontological Society of America; 2004:27–44.

John R, Kerby DS, Hennessy CH. Patterns and impact of comorbidity and multimorbidity among community-resident American Indian elders. *Gerontologist.* 2003; 43:649–660.

Johnson A, Taylor A. *Prevalence of Chronic Diseases: A Summary of Data From the Survey of American Indians and Alaska Natives.* Rockville, Md: Public Health Service, Agency for Health Care Policy and Research; 1991. AHCPR Publication No. 91–0031.

U.S. Department of Health and Human Services. *Healthy People 2010.* 2nd ed. Washington, DC: Government Printing Office; 2000.

NEGATIVE INTERACTION AND HEALTH

Negative social interactions, variously termed negative social exchanges, negative or harmful support, social strain, or interpersonal conflict, appear to have potent effects on mental health, but their effects on physical health have been less widely studied. Because humans have a great need for affiliation, disruptions in social relationships are an important source of stress. Given the widely recognized role of stress in relation to health, negative social interactions are likely to be an important psychosocial determinant of health as well.

Whereas past research has focused primarily on the social support's beneficial effects on health, recent literature has begun to explore the consequences of negative social interactions. These negative interactions consist of contacts with others that are hurtful or harmful. Research has revealed that negative interactions are far more distressing than positive interactions are

uplifting in spite of the fact that negative interactions occur relatively rarely in comparison with positive interactions. Support, which is often categorized into domains according to their function, includes instrumental or tangible support (providing actual physical help), emotional support (giving encouragement or other reassurances), informational support (offering helpful advice or information), and (more rarely) companionship (being included in events and activities with friends or family). Negative interactions may transpire in parallel domains of social functioning such as inadequate, unwanted, or unsuccessful attempts at help; criticisms or expressions of dislike; invasions of privacy or unsolicited advice; and exclusion from social activities. It should also be emphasized that negative interactions can range in severity from major transgressions, such as physical or financial abuse, to minor annoyances, such as thoughtless actions by acquaintances.

Although they are sometimes measured in parallel ways, negative interactions can be distinguished from positive interactions and social support. It is easy to imagine that the more social support an individual has, the less conflict he or she will experience; however, this is not necessarily the case. The absence of support does not automatically mean there is social conflict, especially if support is not expected in the first place. For example, if an older adult is not in need of assistance with work around the home, a lack of help from others is not problematic. Similarly, the presence of conflict is not necessarily indicative of less support. Disputes over one matter with a daughter, for example, does not necessarily mean that the same daughter will be unsupportive on other matters. Furthermore, difficulties with one individual often provide the impetus for a person to seek out others for support. Research findings appear to mirror these complex associations between negative interactions and support. Although some studies report that less negative interaction is associated with more support, others find the reverse. Still others find no relationship at all. There are a number of reasons why negative interactions might not imply less support, including that the two occur simultaneously in different life domains or with different individuals.

Negative interactions have been measured in a variety of ways. Most commonly, researchers measure the frequency with which certain types of negative interactions (e.g., criticisms) occur over a period of weeks or months. This approach parallels the measurement of received support. Unlike measures of social support, which commonly focus on instrumental and emotional domains, the domains of negative interactions that have been assessed by researchers have not been as consistent across studies. A less common approach to measuring negative interaction is to count the number of family members or friends in the social network who are sources of disagreement or conflict. This approach is parallel to social network measurement of positive or supportive ties. Although researchers have measured perceptions of social interactions less often, there is good reason to do so more often. Some supportive attempts can be interpreted as interference, meddling, or otherwise unwelcome. A number of studies have found that support can cause more distress, rather than less distress, under some circumstances, although the exact reasons for this type of failed support and the circumstances under which it occurs are not yet fully understood by researchers. Similarly, negative interactions may vary in the degrees to which they cause distress.

The link between positive aspects of social relationships and health appears to be well established, but the health consequences of negative social interactions have received much less attention. Most of the existing evidence that has identified a connection between negative social interactions and health comes from studies of marital conflict. Marital conflict has been associated with poorer self-reported health, higher cardiovascular disease incidence, and increased rates of mortality due to coronary heart disease. Much less work has investigated the health effects of nonmarital conflict, although negative exchanges in other relationships have been found to be associated with rheumatoid arthritis flair-ups, slower recovery from knee surgery, lower self-reported health, increased cardiovascular reactivity, and greater cognitive impairment. Investigations of negative interactions and health have rarely been experimental and have most often assessed both negative interaction and health at one point in time. Therefore, it is difficult to conclude with certainty that negative interactions are causal.

There are several pathways by which negative interactions may affect health. Negative interactions may impair the immune system, increase arousal, lead to depression, and interfere with healthy behaviors, all of which play an important role in acute and chronic health conditions. Specific immune system functions that may be affected include elevated cortisol levels, increased inflammation, and interference with the immune protein interleukin 6 (IL-6). IL-6 is important in T-cell and B-cell production, and it may affect viral and cancer response, cardiovascular inflammation, and tissue inflammation and repair. Stressful interactions with others may also lead to autonomic arousal, such as high blood pressure, which eventually will have effects on heart disease if experienced repeatedly or persistently. Furthermore, stress is known to cause vascular lesions that attract cholesterol deposits in the process of atherosclerosis. Another pathway by which negative interactions may affect health is through their effects on depression. A number of studies suggest that depression is an independent risk factor for heart disease and mortality.

An additional route by which negative interactions may affect health is through their impact on health behaviors. Lifestyle choices, such as diet, smoking, and exercise, may be affected because interpersonal problems take time and energy away from engaging in more positive health behaviors. The stress of interpersonal problems may also reduce the motivation to engage in healthier behavior by affecting depression, self-esteem, and/or anxiety. Studies reveal some initial evidence that negative interactions and other types of stressors may affect health behaviors, but more work is needed in this area. Few studies have examined the impact of negative interactions on preventive care or chronic disease maintenance, such as adherence to medical regimens and dietary management, but evidence that interpersonal conflict is associated with poorer health behaviors suggests that this is yet another way in which negative interactions may affect the health of older adults. Conversely, negative interactions can also be seen as a potentially positive force on health. *Social control* refers to well-intentioned actions that are intended to improve another person's health behavior. Social control appears to have beneficial effects on health behaviors while simultaneously creating negative affect. Consider the situation of a husband who nags his wife to take her blood pressure medicine. Although the nagging may be emotionally aversive for the wife, it also may increase the regularity with which she takes her medication, thereby having a positive impact on her physical health.

Although studies indicate that negative interactions have physical health consequences, other evidence suggests that illness can lead to interpersonal problems as well. A growing number of studies suggest that older adults who receive assistance from a spouse or an adult child do not always respond favorably to the help they receive. These studies reveal that up to 40% of older adults who receive help with daily tasks from an informal caregiver find some of the help they receive to be unpleasant. Negative reactions to caregiving assistance may occur for several reasons, and researchers are just beginning probe more deeply into the nature of these kinds of responses. Individuals who receive help with physical functioning (e.g., crossing the street, going up stairs) may view the help as indicating an inadequacy or as a reminder of increasing frailty. In some studies, care recipients have reported feelings of incapability or negative self-attributions in response to help they receive. One study that linked lower overall self-esteem with a greater likelihood of distress in response to help from a caregiver is consistent with this notion. Alternatively, help might be provided at the wrong time, in the wrong way, or in inappropriate amounts by a caregiver. Another study reports that insufficient amounts of help overall were related to unpleasant reactions when help was provided. Further research also shows that conflict may arise when the caregiver is critical, overprotective, or insensitive in some situations.

Several studies indicate that, even over a matter of several years, the frequency with which individuals report negative interactions is highly stable during later life. Such stability may be a sign that older adults who report more negative social interactions are, at least in part, responsible for creating their own interpersonal problems. Consistent with this hypothesis, older adults who report negative interactions with one individual within their social circle are perhaps more likely to report such interactions with other members of their social circle. Alternatively, stability over time, or negative interactions with multiple network members, may simply indicate that older adults who experience more conflicts are members of dysfunctional families or networks. The question of whether those reporting more conflict are the victims or the perpetrators of negative interactions will require further inquiry, but one recent study found a high correlation between older adults' reports of giving and receiving negative interactions, suggesting that distinguishing between the victims and the perpetrators may be difficult.

—*Jason T. Newsom and Ann E. McQueen*

See also Psychosocial Theories; Social Networks and Social Support

Further Readings and References

Kiecolt-Glaser JK, Loving TJ, Stowell JR, et al. Hostile marital interactions, proinflammatory cytokine production, and wound healing. *Arch Gen Psychiatry.* 2005;62:1377–1384.

McEwen BS, Lasley EN. *The end of stress as we know it.* Washington, DC: Joseph Henry Press; 2002.

Newsom JT. Another side to caregiving: Negative reactions to being helped. *Curr Direct Psychol Sci.* 1999;8:183–187.

Rook KS, Pietromonaco PR. Close relationships: Ties that heal or ties that bind? In: Jones WH, Perlman D, eds. *Advances in Personal Relationships.* Vol. 1. Greenwich, Conn: JAI; 1987:1–35.

Uchino BN. *Social Support and Physical Health: Understanding the Health Consequences of Relationships.* New Haven, Conn: Yale University Press; 2004.

NEUROBIOLOGY OF AGING

The 1990s were designated the "decade of the brain," and we have in fact learned much about this most mysterious of the human bodily organs over the past few years. As we have gained knowledge about the brain, we have also learned much about the dynamics of the brain as it develops over time—changes that have a profound impact on the aging process overall.

The brain shrinks (the term used is *atrophy,* designating both the shrinking of brain tissue and the widening of spaces or sulci between the lobes of the brain) for both men and women at about the same rate. For example, the average brain weight for a healthy man at 65 years of age is approximately 1,360 grams, and this decreases to approximately 1,290 grams by 90 years of age. The frontal and temporal cortex gradually atrophies in 30% to 50% of normally aging individuals, but the parietal and occipital cortices do not atrophy. In addition, the cerebral ventricles enlarge in size roughly threefold (i.e., the pockets of fluid at the base of the cortex). These changes are usually exaggerated in dementing disorders. Individuals vary significantly, and these individual differences rarely reflect cognitive capacity, although there is a loose association between brain size and cognitive function. Older adults with brains that appear to be markedly reduced in size at autopsy may perform perfectly normally up until the times of their deaths.

The adult brain contains approximately 20 billion neurons. Neurons are the key cells for transmitting information through the brain. A number of small protrusions from the main body of the neuron collect information from neighboring cells. A long single projection transmits this information to other cells. There is debate as to the extent of neuronal loss in the cortex with aging. Most agree, however, that neurons do not usually reproduce during late life (as compared with, e.g., liver cells) and that the numbers of neurons gradually decrease throughout life. Neurons may decrease in size with aging, yet this varies from one part of the brain to another (e.g., less decrease in the brain stem nuclei, much greater decrease in the hippocampus). Although the neuron is generally no longer able to divide after formation, it is continually changing its synaptic connections. This action permits the brain to recover from destruction of some parts such as from a stroke. Such neuroplasticity has been recognized to be a most important characteristic of the aging brain. As nerve cells die off, there is a compensatory lengthening and an increasing number of dendrites in the remaining nerve cells.

Neurons cluster together in networks or nuclei, such as the dentate nucleus located in the cerebellum, and project their axons often to distant portions of the brain. The brain is not like most other organs such as the kidney and heart; in the brain, precise anatomical connections are extremely important. Therefore, the axons of a particular nucleus will project to specific regions of the brain to provide networks for complex signal transduction.

In addition, there are numerous supportive cells, such as astrocytes and glial cells (an abnormal proliferation of which can lead to a cancers such as an astrocytoma or a glioblastoma). These cells may actually increase in number with aging in areas where neurons decrease in size and number.

With aging, deposits of materials increase in the brain, and these deposits are frequently associated with brain diseases. Senile plaques composed of amyloid (they are immunoreactive for β-amyloid) first begin to appear in the cortex with normal aging. If diffuse, they are generally considered to have no pathological significance. When they mature, pieces of neurons filled with β-amyloid and crosslinked protein begin to accumulate around a central amyloid core, forming the plaque that is considered to be the primary pathology of Alzheimer's disease. Neurofibrillary tangles are normally limited to the entorhinal cortex and the inferior temporal lobe. By the time when neurofibrillary tangles spread to the cortex, cognitive impairment is usually apparent—another pathological sign of Alzheimer's disease. Lipofuscin, a brown "wear-and-tear" pigment, begins to accumulate in neuronal bodies with aging but is not associated with any specific disease process. Lewy bodies are composed of ubiquitin or α-synuclein cytoplasmic inclusions that are the defining histological lesions in the substantia nigra in Parkinson's disease. Lewy bodies outside the substantia nigra are present in people with late-onset dementia who do not have typical Parkinson's disease. They are found in the limbic and neocortical areas of the brain.

Chemical messengers or neurotransmitters are the key connections between neurons. These chemicals, produced in the neuron, are exuded from the axon of one neuron and attach to receptors in another neuron.

They are released into the synaptic cleft (the space between neurons), and once they attach to receptors, they create a physiological response (e.g., increasing the flow of sodium across the cell membrane). Some neurotransmitters, such as norepinephrine and serotonin, are produced by nerve cells predominantly in the midbrain. The axons from these cells extend to the forebrain in pathways that are specific to one another. In other words, neurons that produce different neurotransmitters are selective as to the areas of the brain to which they project. Acetylcholine, in contrast, is produced in many areas of the brain, although the long projection neurons that use acetylcholine as a neurotransmitter are found only in a few discrete places in the midbrain.

Different neurotransmitters have been associated with different disease processes. Dopamine depletion is associated with many of the functions that decrease with aging, such as locomotion and cognitive function, which involve dopamine and dopamine receptors. There is a loss of receptor binding in the frontal, temporal, and cingulated cortices associated with age. Overall cholinergic function declines with normal aging (but this is not necessarily directly associated with memory loss and aging). Acetylcholine regulation is severely and adversely affected in Alzheimer's disease. γ-Aminobutyric acid (GABA) is a widespread neurotransmitter that is thought to be associated with the inhibition of neuron excitability. The antianxiety drugs, such as the benzodiazepines, interact with GABA to enhance this inhibition.

There may be a 10% to 20% loss of serotonin receptors with aging (but only to middle age); however, the significance of these findings is not known. Serotonin is thought to be associated with both sleep and depression; many of the new-generation antidepressant drugs are selective serotonin reuptake inhibitors, meaning that they increase the concentration of serotonin in the synaptic cleft by reducing the reuptake of the neurotransmitter into the cell of origin. Norepinephrine is another neurotransmitter thought to be associated with mood because blockage of neurotransmission can lead to severe depressive episodes. Age-related changes in norepinephrine circuits, such as those of serotonin, are not as clear as those in dopamine circuits.

In addition to neurotransmitters, the brain contains many hormones such as cortisol, opioids, estrogen, and thyroid-releasing hormone. Much of the neuroendocrine activity in the brain takes place in the hypothalamus as it releases both stimulating and inhibiting factors that reach the pituitary gland, which in turn releases a variety of hormones that target different organs throughout the body. For example, adrenocorticotropin hormone (ACTH) is released from the pituitary gland and targets the adrenal gland, which in turn produces cortisol. Cortisol concentrations in the blood subsequently feed back information to the brain on the concentrations of these hormones via the hypothalamus; therefore, they control the secretion of hormones by modulating the secretion of corticotropin-releasing hormone from the hypothalamus.

Hormones can affect the brain in a number of ways. For example, chronic elevated levels of cortisol, which may result from chronic stressors in the environment, can lead to permanent dysfunction of some brain regions such as the hippocampus. Some have speculated that people who have experienced considerable stress throughout their lives may be at risk not only for late-life depression but also for atrophy of the hypothalamus and memory loss.

Vascular changes in the brain, such as small strokes (microinfarcts) and stroke, increase in frequency with aging. These small infarctions can lead to cognitive dysfunction and depression. There is emerging evidence that these vascular changes are associated with inflammatory mechanisms. Vascular occlusion derives from the development of vascular plaques and thrombosis (blood clots). Brain amyloid plaques show many indications of inflammatory processes, as evidenced by increased activation of microglia. This is associated with increased production of inflammatory markers such as IL-6. The interest in nonsteroidal anti-inflammatory agents (e.g., aspirin) as a preventive for Alzheimer's disease derives from the possibility of lowering risk by reducing the potential for inflammation.

The brain has many compensatory mechanisms to counteract these brain changes with aging. When speech centers in the dominant hemisphere are damaged, the nondominant hemisphere may compensate and speech function may return gradually. Areas of the cerebellum may be destroyed by a stroke, and other motor systems will take over. Compensation is greater in the higher cortical centers and decreases in the peripheral nervous system. Therefore, it is much more difficult to recover from a spinal cord injury than from a brain injury.

We are now only at the threshold of understanding the mechanisms by which the brain works and how these mechanisms change with age. However, these mechanisms do not inevitably determine what humans think and how they feel. Cognitive psychology adds an additional and necessary dimension to our understanding of mood and behavior.

—Dan G. Blazer

See also Alzheimer's Disease; Anxiety Disorders; Apolipoprotein E; Behavioral Disorders in Dementia; Calcium Disorders of Aging; Delirium and Confusional States; Depression and Other Mood Disorders; Imaging of the Brain; Lewy Body Dementia; Memory; Mild Cognitive Impairment; Neurological Disorders; Pseudodementia; Schizophrenia, Paranoia, and Delusional Disorders; Stroke; Vascular Dementia; Vascular Depression

Further Readings and References

Burns RA, Abou-Saleh MT. Neuroendocrinology of ageing. In: Copeland JRM, Abou-Saleh MT, Blazer DG, eds. *Principles and Practice of Geriatric Psychiatry.* London: Wiley; 2002:51–55.

Byrum CE, Moore SD, Hulette CM. Neuroanatomy, neurophysiology, and neuropathology of aging. In: Blazer DG, Steffens DC, Busse EW, eds. *American Psychiatric Press Textbook of Geriatric Psychiatry.* Washington, DC: American Psychiatric Press; 2004:53–81.

Powers RE. Neurobiology of aging. In: Coffey CE, Cummings JL, eds. *Textbook of Geriatric Neuropsychiatry.* Washington, DC: American Psychiatric Press; 1994:35–70.

NEUROLOGICAL DISORDERS

A number of disorders affect primarily the peripheral neurological system of older adults. These include Parkinson's disease (PD), tardive dyskinesia (TD), spinocerebellar ataxias (SA), amyotropic lateral sclerosis (ALS), and progressive supranuclear palsy (PSP).

The major clinical features Parkinson's disease are bradykinesia (a slowness of movement), rigidity, and tremor at rest (experienced primarily in the hands). These symptoms emerge gradually. Older adults with PD also may have trouble with their balance, and so falls can become a concern. Depression is a frequent comorbid condition with PD. During the late stages of PD, memory impairment emerges as a prominent symptom, and the neuropathological correlates of this memory impairment are nearly identical to those of Alzheimer's disease. Onset before 30 years of age is rare, with the average age of onset being around 60 years. Nearly 1 person in 1,000 people develops PD during a given year among those 70 to 79 years of age. The lifetime risk is approximately 2.5%. Once the disease begins, people with the disease live approximately 15 years, but the life expectancy decreases with increased age of onset.

Classic PD is caused by degeneration of nerve cells in the base of the brain (the substantia nigra). These pigmented neurons produce dopamine and project this neurotransmitter to other parts of the brain, especially the striatum. Therefore, the main biochemical abnormality in PD is a marked deficiency of dopamine in the base of the brain. This leads to an imbalance between acetylcholine and dopamine in the striatum of the brain. Bradykinesia is the symptom of PD that is associated most closely with the loss of dopamine. Most cases of PD are sporadic, but PD has been linked to a mutation on chromosome 4. A number of medications can also cause Parkinson's-like symptoms. These especially include antipsychotic medications such as haloperidol. The frequency of PD-like symptoms is much lower with the new-generation antipsychotic drugs such as olanzapine and risperidone.

The primary treatment of PD is with medications. Anticholinergic drugs, such as trihexyphenidyl and benztropine, can be prescribed to correct the imbalance between acetylcholine and dopamine. The dopamine precursor levodopa is often prescribed in combination with carbidopa (Sinemet), which makes dopamine available to brain tissues. Bromocriptine and other drugs enhance the effectiveness of dopamine (they are dopamine agonists). Amantadine's mode of action is unknown, but it also enhances the effectiveness of dopamine. Selegiline is frequently used as an adjunct to Sinemet.

Tardive dyskinesia is one of the most serious side effects when using antipsychotic drugs, especially the older drugs such as thioridazine and haloperidol. The disorder manifests itself primarily with abnormal involuntary movements that typically involve the face initially (e.g., involuntary movements of the tongue) and then move to include the limbs and trunk. TD is much more common in the elderly taking these medications than in younger people. There is no known treatment. Withdrawal of the antipsychotic drug may increase the symptoms, but with time off the drug the symptoms can decrease. Switching to an atypical (new-generation) antipsychotic drug may improve symptoms, and beginning patients on these drugs, rather than the older drugs, reduces the risk.

Spinocerebellar ataxias constitute a collection of disorders related by a prominent ataxia (unsteadiness of gait). Most of these disorders are sporadic and the cause is not known, but roughly one third are inherited and are usually autosomal dominant. Clinical features include disturbed gait, limb incoordination and tremor, and dysarthria (difficulty with speech). The onset of the sporadic forms of SA usually occurs after 55 years of age. The condition progresses slowly, with loss of ability to walk occurring 5 to 20 years after onset. Drug treatment of these disorders is generally unsuccessful.

Amyotropic lateral sclerosis is the most common motor neuron disease, although it is relatively rare (prevalence of approximately .005%). The average age of onset is 60 years. The condition progresses rapidly, and 50% of patients die within 3 years of onset. Long-term survivors of ALS do occur, however, with the progression ceasing after symptoms have become moderate to severe. The primary symptoms include paralysis of the arms and legs, muscle cramps, difficulty in speaking, and (eventually) difficulty in breathing. There is typically no loss of sensory function. The underlying pathology is the dramatic loss of nerve cells in the spinal cord that eventually reaches the brainstem.

Progressive supranuclear palsy is a relatively rare disease that afflicts older men more than it does older women. The onset is between 50 and 70 years of age. The survival after onset is usually approximately 6 years. Symptoms resemble those of PD, but with some clear differences. For example, PSP patients lose their ability to voluntarily gaze downward, followed by loss of the ability to move the eyes in all directions. The eyes, however, will move involuntarily in response to turning the head. The underlying cause is atrophy of the midbrain with preservation of the cerebellum. There is no known treatment.

—*Dan G. Blazer*

See also Alzheimer's Disease; Behavioral Disorders in Dementia; Creutzfeldt–Jakob Disease; Neurobiology of Aging; Stroke

Further Readings and References

Burke JR. Other neurodegenerative disorders. In: Hazzard WR, Blass JP, Ettinger WH, Halter JB, Ouslander JG, eds. *Principles of Geriatric Medicine and Gerontology*. 4th ed. New York: McGraw-Hill; 1999:1283–1294.

Jeste DV, Wetherell JL, Dolder CR. Schizophrenia and paranoid disorders. In: Blazer DG, Steffens DC, Busse EW, eds. *Textbook of Geriatric Psychiatry*. 3rd ed. Washington, DC: American Psychiatric Press; 2004:269–282.

Rajput AH. Parkinson's disease and related disorders. In: Hazzard WR, Blass JP, Ettinger WH, Halter JB, Ouslander JG, eds. *Principles of Geriatric Medicine and Gerontology*. 4th ed. New York: McGraw-Hill; 1999:1271–1281.

NEW ZEALAND

See AUSTRALIA AND NEW ZEALAND

NORMAL PHYSICAL AGING

Normal physical aging refers to the physiological changes that occur with age and that are distinct from the disorders that increase in prevalence as people grow older. For example, age-related structural and functional changes in the arterial blood vessels lead to increasing systolic blood pressure. However, hypertension, which is much more common among the elderly, is not a normal consequence of aging.

Much of what we know about normal aging comes from long-term follow-up (longitudinal) studies of "normal" individuals such as the Baltimore Longitudinal Study of Aging, the Established Populations for Epidemiologic Studies of the Elderly (EPESE), the MacArthur Study of Successful Aging, the Women's Health and Aging Study, and the Health, Aging, and Body Composition Study. These longitudinal studies have revealed that there are tremendous differences in normal aging among individuals. Such differences demonstrate the importance of both genes and environment in the aging process. Despite this variability, however, the studies have demonstrated several important changes that occur with age such as the following:

- Decreased muscle mass, power, and strength
- Decreased bone mass
- Increased stiffness and decreased elasticity in the cardiovascular system
- Decreased metabolic rate
- Decreased hormone secretion
- A decline in the regulation of the neuroendocrine system
- Decreased maximum breathing capacity

In every organ system in the human body, there are physical manifestations of aging that are characterized by a progressive loss in reserve capacity to maintain homeostasis. The adaptive response of the body to maintain homeostasis in the setting of stress—acute or chronic, physical or psychological—is also referred to by gerontologists as *allostasis*. This term can also be defined more simply as the ability to achieve stability through change. The mediators of allostasis are the neuroendocrine system, the autonomic nervous system, and the immune system. It has been hypothesized that individual differences in aging may be associated with the total amount of "wear and tear" of major stressors, which gerontologists call *allostatic load*. Because allostatic load accumulates with age, it is an important component of the normal aging process.

In the individual sections that follow, normal physical aging in different organ systems is described. In addition, examples of differences in the physiological adaptations to stress associated with older age are described for each organ system.

Cardiovascular System

Arterial walls thicken and dilate with age due to an increase in matrix deposition and cellular accumulation. The walls of the arteries also stiffen with age because of a loss of elasticity and an increase in collagen deposition. These changes make the arteries more susceptible to atherosclerosis. The functional implication of the loss of vascular compliance associated with arterial stiffness is an increase in blood pressure. Systolic pressure rises more precipitously than does diastolic pressure, so the pulse pressure (systolic blood pressure–diastolic blood pressure) also increases with age.

The Heart

The size of the left ventricular wall appears to increase with age due to a decrease in the number of heart muscle cells (myocytes) and an increase in myocyte size. Accompanied by focal collagen deposition, this increase in size leads to a slight increase in early diastolic cardiac filling pressure. Studies of cardiovascular aging have shown minimal or no change in resting heart rate, cardiac output, and stroke volume. There are also no known normal changes with age in ejection fraction.

The effects of aging on cardiovascular activity are more pronounced during exercise. Maximum cardiac output, peak aerobic capacity, and maximum heart rate decrease with age, but tremendous individual variation exists. However, the effect of exercise on cardiovascular function, even at older ages, is quite dramatic. Physical conditioning can lessen vascular stiffening and also increase aerobic capacity by increasing cardiac output and oxygen use.

Respiratory System

Normal aging of the respiratory system is characterized by the following:

- Lung stiffness due to loss of elasticity
- Chest wall and upper airway rigidity due to calcification of cartilage
- Loss of alveoli (air wall sacs), resulting in decreased surface area by 20%

The consequences of these changes include a reduction in forced vital capacity (the volume of air forcibly expired in a normal breath) and maximum oxygen uptake. Over time, these changes lead to decreased exercise capacity that can be exacerbated by inactivity.

Gastrointestinal System

There are minimal gastrointestinal changes with aging. Most examples of gastrointestinal dysfunction are related to the interaction of these minor changes with disease and lifestyle factors. For example, although large intestine transit time lengthens with age, constipation becomes a significant problem with aging mostly in the presence of other risk factors such as a low-fiber diet and dehydration.

The gastrointestinal functional changes include the following:

- Reduced saliva production
- Increased esophageal dysmotility
- Decreased lower esophageal pressure
- Decreased stomach contractions
- Reduced peristalsis (wall muscle contraction) of the of the large intestine
- Decreased liver metabolism

Renal Function

Kidney function decreases with age. Many of the clinically meaningful changes in function of the kidney are due to reduction of the renal vasculature with age. It has been estimated that blood flow to the kidney decreases by as much as 10% per decade. In addition, kidneys can lose 30% to 40% of glomeruli by 60 years of age, leading to a decreased rate of kidney filtration. These changes are also accompanied by dysregulation of the hormone vasopressin, increasing the risk of dehydration.

Musculoskeletal System

Muscle

Age-related changes in muscle include decreased strength, endurance, size, and weight. Increased body fat and decreased lean body mass contribute to these associated changes. Although the degree to which these changes occur is also influenced by inactivity, nutrition, and disease, the effects can be minimized by exercise.

Bone

Peak bone mass is reached by 30 years of age. After that, bone mass declines with age, resulting in a more porous bone matrix. Osteopenia and osteoporosis are manifestations of the increased thinning of the bone matrix.

Skin

Much of the skin changes we normally associate with age, such as wrinkles, heavily reflect cumulative exposure to the sun. Skin changes that do occur with age are exacerbated by damage due to the sun's ultraviolet radiation. The skin changes with age include the following:

- Thinning of the area between the dermis and the epidermis
- Decreased elastin and collagen, reducing the skin's ability to retain moisture and causing the dry cracked appearance of skin
- Cell size reduction
- Decreased subcutaneous layers of fatty deposits beneath the dermis, possibly causing an "emaciated appearance"

Sensory System

The sensory system loses its acuity with age. Some normal changes in the eye that affect vision are the following:

- Corneal flattening, reducing transmitted light
- Diminished lens transparency, causing difficulty with vision of "cool colors"
- Diminished retinal function due to the cumulative effects of decreased blood flow and radiation exposure, causing a reduction in spatial and contrast discrimination
- Reduced lens elasticity that affects the focusing power of the eye, leading to the common form of visual changes with age known as presbyopia

Presbycusis, which is the most common type of hearing loss associated with aging, is characterized by a decrease in perception of high-frequency tones. This is manifested by a decline in speech discrimination, especially when there are competing sounds such as background noise. The degree of presbycusis varies widely among individuals and may also be exacerbated by environmental factors such as cumulative noise exposure, chronic disease, and ear wax accumulation.

The sensations of smell, taste, and touch also diminish with age. The numbers of receptors in all three of these sensory systems decrease with age, requiring a higher threshold of stimulus for the sensations. This can cause impairment in responding to noxious stimuli such as natural gas (smell) and heat (touch).

Neuroendocrine System

The neuroendocrine system, through the release of hormones to target organs and regulated by the central nervous system, controls important functions such as energy metabolism, reproduction, and stress response Aging of the neuroendocrine system is characterized by changes in the regulation and response of hormone and neurotransmitter release. However, although there may be declines in the secretion of some hormones, concomitant decreases in renal clearance lead to the maintenance of some hormone levels. Specific neuroendocrine changes are described in the remainder of this entry.

Metabolism

Slowed metabolism with aging results in increased fat deposition and reduced muscle mass. In addition, normal aging is associated with a decreased appetite and energy intake, also called the "anorexia of aging." Fasting glucose levels have not been shown to be related to aging, but insulin resistance, reflected in a prolonged response to a glucose tolerance test, does increase with age. Metabolism is controlled by several endocrine systems, including the growth hormone axis.

Growth Hormone Axis

Insulin-like growth factor I (IGF-I) mediates the peripheral actions of growth hormone (GH). The plasma levels of both GH and IGF-I decline with age. (The body composition changes previously discussed

areas associated with these alterations in GH and IGF-I.) The GH–IGF axis also plays a major role in metabolism efficiency and in antagonizing the adverse effects of chronic stress on the immune system. GH and IGF-I also have neuroprotective effects; therefore, reduction of these levels also has been shown to be associated with poor cognitive functioning.

Hypothalamic–Pituitary–Adrenal Axis

Although basal levels of cortisol are unchanged with age, peak cortisol levels and increased duration of a cortisol response to stress, such as after surgery, remain higher in older persons. This is due to a decline in sensitivity to the negative feedback inhibition of cortisol on the hypothalamus. Chronic stimulation of the hypothalamic–pituitary–adrenal (HPA) axis can lead to hypersecretion of glucocorticoids, in turn leading to deleterious affects on multiple organ systems.

Thyroid

There appears to be a decrease in thyroid hormone (serum T4 and serum T3) with age; however, this decrease in thyroid hormone correlates with the decrease in metabolically active tissue (lean body mass) with age. The thyroid gland also atrophies with age. However, it appears that when the thyroid gland is stimulated, it can normally produce thyroid hormone.

There is tremendous individual variability in these neuroendocrine changes. Exercise has been shown in several experimental studies to increase both GH secretion and insulin sensitivity.

—*Marjorie Marenberg*

See also Body Composition; Exercise and Physical Activity; Neurobiology of Aging

Further Readings and References

Izaks GJ. Ill or just old? Toward a conceptual framework of the relation between aging and disease. *BMC Geriatr.* 2003;3:1–6.

Lakatta EG. Cardiovascular aging. In: Rich MW, ed. *Clinics in Geriatric Medicine.* Philadelphia: W. B. Saunders; 2000:419–444.

Lambert CP, Evans WJ. Adaptations to aerobic and resistance exercise in the elderly. *Rev Endocr Metab Disorders.* 2005;6:137–143.

McEwen BS. Sex, stress, and the hippocampus: Allostasis, allostatic load, and the aging process. *Neurobiol Aging.* 2002;23:921–939.

Smith RG. Molecular endocrinology and physiology of the aging central nervous system. *Endocr Rev.* 2005;26:203–250.

NORMATIVE AGING STUDY

The Normative Aging Study (NAS) is a longitudinal study of aging in men initiated by the Department of Veterans Affairs (VA) in 1963. Its aims are to (a) characterize the biomedical and psychosocial parameters of normal aging as distinct from the development of disease, (b) define the incidence and precursors of the diseases accompanying aging, and (c) examine the influence of lifestyle and major life events on aging. This entry briefly describes the study design and current status of the cohort and also summarizes some recent research.

Study Design

Originally, men reported every 3 to 5 years for a clinical exam (every 5 years if < 52 years of age, otherwise every 3 years); since 1984, all are seen every 3 years. The exam includes a medical history, a standardized physical and medical exam, clinical chemistry, anthropometric measurements, and a medication and smoking history. Periodically, surveys are mailed to assess various psychosocial topics such as health behaviors, work and retirement, and personality and well-being. Although most men participate in both the exam and the survey sequences, approximately 200 to 400 men participate only in the surveys.

NAS Cohort

As of December 2005, 1,114 (49%) of the original 2,280 men are continuing participants. A total of 1,045 (> 45%) have died, 117 (5%) have dropped out, and 4 (< 1%) have been lost to follow-up. Among current participants, the mean age is 77 years ($SD = 7$,

range = 60 to 100); half are 72 to 82 years of age. The Dental Longitudinal Study (DLS), which began in 1968, recruited 1,231 NAS men for a longitudinal study of dental health and aging. Approximately 30% of these men are still actively participating in this study, now conducting its 12th cycle of triennial examinations.

Research Activities

This section briefly describes research activities in several domains. (For further information on the study, available data, and a list of publications, see www .maveric.org/route/maveric/news/readnew.asp?id=27.)

Personality

Personality has been studied in its own right as well as in relation to health and health behaviors. Longitudinal changes within-person in personality, well-being, and affect have been examined, and between-person predictors of changes, including health and life events, have been identified. Using data from the Minnesota Multiphasic Personality Inventory-2 (MMPI-2) administered in 1991, positive (e.g., optimism) and negative (e.g., hostility, depression, anxiety) emotions have been studied in relation to health outcomes such as incidence of coronary heart disease (CHD) and pulmonary function. In general, positive emotions were associated with lower risk of CHD and with slower decline in pulmonary function, whereas negative emotions were associated with greater risk of CHD incidence.

Cognition

The impact of vascular disease on cognition, as well as modifying effects of environmental and dietary exposures, has been examined. Christopher Brady and colleagues studied the cognitive effects of hypertension and found that men with uncontrolled hypertension performed worse on several tasks than did normotensives who did not differ from controls or from untreated hypertensives. Marc Weisskopf and colleagues found that higher bone lead concentrations were associated with faster decline on the Mini-Mental State Examination (MMSE), with a one-interquartile higher lead concentration being equal to roughly

5 years of aging. Examining the effects of B vitamins on cognition, Katherine Tucker and colleagues found that men with lower plasma B vitamin levels and higher homocysteine had greater declines in constructional praxis, as assessed by a spatial copying task.

Posttraumatic Stress Disorder

Although many NAS men served in World War II or in the Korea conflict, and approximately 25% experienced combat, the prevalence of posttraumatic stress disorder (PTSD) by self-report is low, as noted by Avron Spiro III and colleagues in 1994. However, men with current or lifetime PTSD (by clinical exam) experienced greater increases in mental and physical health symptoms during and after retirement than did men with trauma only or with no exposure. E. H. Davison and colleagues examined three samples of older veterans, including NAS men, to describe the construct of late-onset stress symptomatology (LOSS), a late–late sequel to early-life traumatic exposure such as combat.

Oral Health

Judith Jones and colleagues examined oral health-related quality of life (OQOL) measures in NAS men and in a sample of VA patients and found that OQOL scales were reliable and valid in both. However, oral clinical assessments were associated with OQOL measures in the latter sample but not in the NAS men.

Biomedical Research

S. W. Tsaih and colleagues found that renal function, especially among men with hypertension or diabetes, was negatively affected by both stored and circulating lead levels. Joel Schwartz and colleagues found an interaction among the presence of the glutathione-S-transferase M1 (GSTM1) allele, statin use, and fine particulate exposure on heart rate variability (HRV), such that men without the GSTM1 allele had greater decreases in the high-frequency component of HRV than did men with the allele; the use of statins eliminated the particulate effect.

—*Avron Spiro, III and*
Pantel S. Vokonas

See also Economics of Aging; Health and Retirement Study

Further Readings and References

Bossé R, Ekerdt D, Silbert J. The Veterans Administration Normative Aging Study. In: Mednick SA, Harway M, Finello KM, eds. *Handbook of Longitudinal Research,* Vol. 2: *Teenage and Adult Cohorts.* New York: Praeger; 1984:273–289.

Brady CB, Spiro A III, Gaziano JM. Effects of age and hypertension status on cognition: The VA Normative Aging Study. *Neuropsychology.* 2005;19:770–777.

Davison EH, Gugliucci MR, King LA, et al. Late-life emergence of early life trauma: The phenomenon of late-onset stress symptomatology among aging combat veterans. *Res Aging.* 2006;28:84–114.

Jones JA, Kressina NR, Spiro A III, et al. Self-reported and clinical oral health in users of VA health care. *J Gerontol A Biol Sci Med Sci.* 2001;56:M55–M62.

Schwartz J, Park SK, O'Neill MS, et al. Glutathione-S-transferase M1, obesity, statins, and autonomic effects of particles: Gene-by-drug-by-environment interaction. *Am J Resp Crit Care Med.* 2005;172:1529–1533.

Spiro A III, Schnurr PP, Aldwin CM. Combat-related posttraumatic stress disorder symptoms in older men. *Psychol Aging.* 1994;9(1):17–26.

Tsaih SW, Korrick S, Schwartz J, et al. Lead, diabetes, hypertension, and renal function: The Normative Aging Study. *Environ Health Perspect.* 2004;112:1178–1182.

Tucker KL, Qiao N, Scott T, Rosenberg I, Spiro A. High homocysteine and low B vitamins predict cognitive decline in aging men: The Veterans Affairs Normative Aging Study. *Am J Clin Nutr.* 2005;82:627–635.

Weisskopf MG, Proctor S, Wright RO, Schwartz J, Spiro A III, Sparrow D, Aro A, Hu H. Prospective study of cumulative lead exposure and cognitive test scores among elderly men: The VA Normative Aging Study. *Epidemiology.* 2007;18:59–66.

NURSING ROLES IN HEALTH CARE AND LONG-TERM CARE

Nurses comprise the largest proportion of employees in long-term care (LTC). Residents require nursing care more than any other service provided by institutions of LTC. The majority of residents in LTC require custodial care, which consists of assistance with bathing, dressing, feeding, and mobility. Other residents may require a higher level of care called skilled nursing care, which includes treatments to management disease such as tube feedings, ostomy care, and rehabilitation services. This wide variation of resident needs serves as the basis for the multiple levels of nurses working in LTC. Registered nurses (RNs) in the United States care for more than 1.4 million older adults in the nation's 16,000 nursing homes. The role of the RN can vary depending on the size of the LTC facility but is primarily a role of management and leadership. An advanced practice nurse, such as a geriatric nurse practitioner (GNP), holds a master's degree in nursing and provides residents with primary care that includes health promotion, maintenance of care, and case management. Licensed practical nurses or licensed vocational nurses (LPNs/LVNs) are the largest providers of skilled nursing care in LTC and represent the largest number of licensed nurses in LTC. The role of the LPN/LVN often entails entry-level management as charge nurses of units within the LTC facility. Certified nursing assistants (CNAs) are not nurses but provide the bulk of custodial nursing care for residents. The American Nurses Association defines a CNA as an unlicensed individual who is trained to function in an assistive role to the licensed nurse in the provision of patient care. To gain the title of CNA, each nursing assistant must complete a course of study and be certified by a national examination that has both a written and clinical component.

The role of the RN is the most versatile nursing role in any LTC facility. RNs are directors of nursing (DONs), assistant directors of nursing (ADONs), infection control officers, risk managers, and quality improvement and compliance coordinators. Depending on the size of the LTC facility, these roles may be separate positions or combined into one or more positions. All LTC facilities are required to have an RN who is accountable for the nursing care delivered to residents. The title of this RN is usually the director of nursing, and the areas of responsibility include the coordination and management of the day-to-day operations of the nursing department. Other responsibilities include administrating the budget, hiring and supervising the nursing staff, conducting employee performance appraisals, retaining employees, and coordinating interdisciplinary resident care teams. DONs have direct responsible for the clinical activities of preventing and controlling infections in the LTC facility, promoting client safety, and keeping

the facility in compliance with federal and state regulatory agencies. In light of the current nursing shortage, qualifications to be a DON are often based on experience in geriatric nursing and LTC rather than on the college degree held. However, there is a growing trend to employ nurses with a baccalaureate or master's degree whenever possible. The National Association of Directors of Nursing Administration in Long-Term Care offers a certification examination for RNs in DON positions.

Advanced practice nurses (APNs) are RNs who have received additional education, especially in diagnosis and treatment of disease. APNs generally hold a master's degree and must have a national certification in a specialty area. Most APNs working in LTC are nurse practitioners with education in gerontology. Gerontological nurse practitioners are particularly suited to care for older adult residents in LTC. APN roles and skills include conducting health assessments, conducting history and physical examinations, ordering and interpreting diagnostic and laboratory tests, prescribing medications, and providing teaching and counseling. APNs have been shown to significantly improve the health and care of older adults in LTC facilities by providing timely urgent/sick resident visits, preventive care, and disease management. APNs influence the quality of care in LTC facilities by participating in staff development and new program initiatives to improve care and resident/family satisfaction. As a result of APN practice in LTC; residents experience fewer hospital admissions and emergency room visits.

RNs or LPNs/LVNs can fill the role of charge nurses in LTC facilities. In most cases, this role is assumed by LPNs/LVNs. Charge nurses report to the ADON or DON. Primary responsibilities of the charge nurse are staff assignments, work schedules, delegation of care, and supervision of staff during a shift. In addition, charge nurses may have direct care responsibilities such as medication administration, treatments, and documentation. Charge nurses assume a leadership role by assisting the DON or ADON with team building and conflict resolution that can affect staff morale. Charge nurses are most often used on weekends, evenings, and night shifts.

The staff nurse role can be assumed by either RNs or LPNs/LVNs, but it is usually assumed by

LPNs/LVNs in LTC facilities. The responsibilities of the staff nurse depend on the type of nursing care delivery system that is in place at the facility. Two common approaches to nursing care delivery in LTC are functional nursing and team nursing. Functional nursing assigns the staff nurse to a specific aspect of care. For example, one nurse may be assigned to administer all of the medications, whereas another nurse will do all of the treatments on a unit. Team nursing requires an RN to lead the team and uses a mix of RNs, LPNs/LVNs, and CNAs to provide care for a group of residents. It is the sole responsibility of the RN staff nurse or team leader to assess and formulate a holistic plan of care for each resident and to coordinate the care that the resident is to receive from the interdisciplinary team. RNs may also provide direct care to the resident. LPN/LVN staff nurses provide direct care, such as administering medications and treatments, and carries out the resident's plan of care under the supervision of the RN. Traditionally, the care of older adults in LTC would include management of multiple chronic illnesses such as diabetes mellitus, hypertension, and arthritis; rehabilitation of acute illnesses such as stroke, hip fractures, and joint replacements; and prevention and management of common geriatric syndromes such as falls and polypharmacy. The American Nurses Credentialing Center offers a certification in gerontological nursing for RNs. The American Nurses Association has developed and published the second edition of the *Scope and Standards of Gerontological Nursing Practice.*

CNAs represent 60% to 70% of nursing staff in LTC and provide as much as 70% of the direct care to the residents. The licensed nurse, usually in the role of charge nurse, is responsible for the care provided to residents by CNAs. Responsibilities of the CNA include bathing, feeding, maintaining the residents' environment, and helping the residents with mobility needs. As primary caregivers, CNAs often develop close relationships with the residents, and this can be a source of resident satisfaction. Residents depend on CNAs for meeting personal care, social, safety, and environmental needs on a 24-hour basis. These caregivers play a key role in the delivery of nursing care in all LTC facilities.

Nurses have myriad roles and responsibilities in caring for older adults in LTC. Various levels of nursing are used to provide care from a core set of roles. In their daily activities working with older adults, nurses are healers, caregivers, educators, coordinators of care, and advocates, as noted by Charlotte Eliopoulos in 2001. As healers, nurses help older adults to overcome and cope with illness, assist in restoring function, and support quality of life. The caregiver role ensures that the personal care needs of older adults are met. Nurses are educators both formally and informally as they share knowledge and skills with older adults about their health. Nurses use a holistic approach to resident care, making nurses ideal for the role of coordinators of care. Coordinating the services that the residents require from the interdisciplinary team ensures that resident needs will be met in a timely, cost-effective, and efficient manner. As advocates, nurses help older adults to assert their rights and obtain services to meet their needs in an ethical and dignified manner. The Department of Health and Human Services estimates that the population of older Americans will double by 2030. The fastest-growing segment of this older population is those age 85 years and older. More than 18% of people in this age group will reside in LTC facilities, making nurses a valuable resource for the future.

—*Gloria Brandburg*

See also Geriatric Team Care; Gerontological Nursing; Long-Term Care

Further Readings and References

American Nurses Association. *The Scope and Standards of Gerontological Nursing Practice.* 2nd ed. Washington, DC: ANA; 2001.

Eliopoulos C. *Gerontological Nursing.* 5th ed. Philadelphia: J. B. Lippincott; 2001.

Fitzpatrick JJ, Fulmer T, eds. *Geriatric Nursing Research Digest.* New York: Springer; 2000.

Ignatavicius DD. Introduction to Long Term Care Nursing: Principles and Practice. Philadelphia: F. A. Davis; 1998.

Nutrition and Public Health

The maintenance of good nutritional health is essential to healthy aging. Healthy aging can be described as the maintenance of physical and cognitive functioning, the prevention or delay of chronic disease and disease-related complications, and the fostering of overall quality of life. The older population is rapidly growing in absolute numbers and as a proportion of the total population, especially in rural areas, where more than 20% of the population is age 60 years and older. Length of life is also increasing, and the increased longevity is often accompanied by a greater presence of single and multiple chronic illnesses for a longer period of time. An expanding body of literature suggests that health conditions or illnesses may drive a progressive process that includes impairment, functional decline (both cognitive and physical), disability (difficulty and dependence in daily activities), and adverse health outcomes such as more frequent and longer hospitalizations, institutionalization, and premature death. Considering that nutrition has been shown to be associated with 4 of 10 leading causes of death (coronary heart disease, some types of cancer, stroke, and type 2 diabetes), as well as with hypertension and osteoporosis, healthy eating is a modifiable factor that influences the prevention and management of chronic illness and promotes overall health and function. Thus, the critical role of nutrition in aging makes nutritional health a public health issue. Nutritional health is determined to a large extent by the intake of the appropriate type, amount, variety, and quality of foods that are necessary to provide the needed calories, protein, carbohydrates, lipids, vitamins, and minerals to achieve and maintain optimal health and function.

The achievement and maintenance of good nutritional health and a longer and healthier life require public health efforts at the level of individuals, families, organizations, communities, and policy. Public health linkages with nutrition in older adults have taken many forms. These include articulating a national agenda, developing and disseminating nutritional recommendations, and providing nutrition assistance programs. There is a history of public health recognition of an association between nutrition and healthy aging. The Older Americans Act has a national aim to promote better health through improved nutrition and at the same time to help older adults remain independent and functioning in their own homes. In 1992, an Institute of Medicine (IOM) report highlighted the importance of nutrition in the maintenance of health, quality of life, and physical independence in older persons. In 2000, with the IOM report on *The Role of Nutrition in Maintaining Health in the Nation's Elderly,* a need was cited for improved coverage of nutrition services in the older population. Older adults were identified as being at high risk for malnutrition, with malnutrition generally considered as poor nutritional health status. Malnutrition may result from an inadequate or excessive intake and from reduced absorption of overall calories, protein, carbohydrates, lipids, vitamins, and minerals. Building on more than two decades of prior work, the national priorities of *Healthy People 2000,* a U.S. government publication detailing disease prevention and health promotion objectives, identified nutrition as 1 of 22 priority areas. This was followed by *Healthy People 2010,* which provided a comprehensive set of objectives that focused on disease prevention and health promotion to increase quality and years of healthy life and to eliminate disparities. These objectives are spelled out in several *Healthy People 2010* objectives that address nutrition-related topics such as osteoporosis, diabetes, cancer, heart disease and stroke, mental health, oral health, food safety, weight status, food and nutrient consumption, and food security.

There are two different sets of nutritional recommendations that have become part of national policy; one addresses individual nutrients, and the other addresses foods and food groups. Historically, recommended dietary allowances (RDAs), which were introduced to characterize age and gender group levels of adequate intake of individual nutrients, were designed to address the needs of healthy people. Prior to 1997, all persons age 50 years and older were given the same recommendation. In 1997, the Food and Nutrition Board extended prior reports by introducing dietary reference intakes (DRIs), which were based on the most current scientific information to provide age and gender group reference values for dietary intake of protein, fiber, vitamins, and minerals. In an effort to recognize different requirements for older adults, the DRIs categorized two groups of older adults: 51 to 70 years of age and over 70 years of age. There is much disagreement in the literature as to the adequacy of individual nutrient recommendations for older adults who are less healthy, have multiple chronic illnesses, take prescription medications from a variety of therapeutic classes, and/or live in different settings (community dwelling, hospitalized, postacute hospital, assisted living, adult day care, long-term residence care, or hospice). Because scientific inquiry is a dynamic process and current scientific information is expanding, it is not clear how the recommendations themselves will continue to evolve. Several questions of particular interest to older adults have been raised. What will trigger a new review, especially of nutrients such as calcium and Vitamin D? Is there an ongoing process for reviewing and revising recommendations? Even with concerns that current nutrient recommendations may underestimate actual needs of older adults, numerous studies have shown that substantial proportions of various subgroups of older adults usually consume individual and multiple nutrients at less than the recommended levels. This underconsumption is problematic for older adults, especially women, minorities, and rural residents, when considering the demonstrated importance of some vitamins and minerals to older adults in several cross-sectional studies. For example, a large proportion of older adults consume low levels of calcium and even lower levels of Vitamin D. These are two critical nutrients that are known to influence muscle metabolism and bone health; deficiency in these areas may lead to low bone mineral density, increased risk of fracture, falls, poor lower extremity physical performance (e.g., balance, walking, lower leg strength), and disability. Three additional vitamins—B12, B6, and folate—are needed for the nervous system, to protect against cognitive decline, and to regulate levels of homocysteine.

Other vitamins and minerals serve as antioxidants in normal immune function, vision function, and so on. The importance of these nutrients is increased for older adults due primarily to physiological changes and increased use of prescribed and over-the-counter (OTC) medications that affect the efficiency of synthesis, absorption, and/or use of nutrients.

Whereas DRIs described nutritional recommendations at the level of individual nutrients, another set of recommendations, Dietary Guidelines for Americans (DGA), stressed an overall healthy pattern of eating. As illustrated with the Food Guide Pyramid, the emphasis is on a daily diet that includes whole grains; dark-colored vegetables; deeply colored fruits; low-fat or fat-free milk or milk alternatives; lean or low-fat meats, poultry, fish, beans, eggs, and nuts; and foods low in fat, saturated fat, trans fat, cholesterol, salt (sodium), and added sugars. Older adults who eat this way will be more likely to achieve higher levels of vitamins, minerals, and fiber. The recommendations also stress the importance of food safety practices (hand and surface washing, cross-contamination avoidance, cooking temperatures, and refrigeration) that can prevent foodborne disease. Foodborne disease is an increased problem for older adults who may be compromised by smaller doses of foodborne disease and be more likely than others to suffer more severe consequences.

There are several federal programs that provide food assistance to older adults. The most commonly used programs are the U.S. Department of Agriculture's (USDA) Food Stamp Program and the Older Americans Act Nutrition Program's (OAANP) congregate and home-delivered meals. Although many older adults are eligible for food stamps, a small percentage of eligible older adults choose to participate in this program. The literature suggests a variety of reasons for lack of participation such as stigma attached to receiving benefits, difficult or demeaning application process, and minimal benefits. The congregate meals program was initiated to provide both nutrition and socialization to older adults, whereas the home-delivered meals program provides nutritious meals to homebound older adults. In both meals programs, each meal must provide at least one third of

RDAs and use the framework of the DGA. In addition, the providers of OAANP regularly screen their participants for nutritional risk based on a 10-item instrument that focuses on food group intake, adequacy of resources, eating in isolation, medication use, weight change, and physical limitations. Despite participation in food assistance programs, the literature shows that many older adults still have less than adequate diets.

What makes nutrition in older adults a critical public health issue is the complex nature of nutritional health. First, there are many different indicators of deficiency, excess, or both in nutritional health. Overall nutritional deficiency or excess can be shown through anthropometric (body mass index [BMI] or waist circumference), clinical (unintended weight change, bone density, or muscle strength), biochemical (serum levels of specific markers), or dietary measures (usual self-reported dietary intake). Individually, these measures describe deficiency or excess; in combination, they may describe both deficiency and excess. For example, studies reported in the literature suggest that an older adult may be obese and still have deficiencies on key nutrients because of the consumption of less nutrient-dense (empty calorie) foods that are high in fat and deficient in key nutrients. Second, nutritional health, independent of dietary intake, may be influenced by altered absorption, use, or excretion as a result of underlying health conditions, physiological changes, and/or medication use. All three are highly prevalent in older adults. For example, physiological changes result in reduced synthesis in the body of Vitamin D, low levels of Vitamin D reduce the absorption of calcium, and use of diuretics increases the excretion of fluids and water-soluble vitamins such as Vitamins C and B.

Food intake is influenced directly by the number of meal occasions, meal size, and food choice. Studies have shown that nearly 20% of older adults do not usually eat a breakfast meal. The breakfast meal is a nutrient-dense meal; for older adults who do not regularly consume a breakfast meal, their usual nutrient intake in total calories, vitamins and minerals, and fiber is significantly lower than that of older adults who usually have a breakfast meal. In addition, many older adults face the risk of not having enough food; they may adopt strategies such as limiting the size of meals or portions to stretch the available food. The literature suggests that this may be the result of having competing demands for limited resources; that is, choosing among medications, bills, and food when spending money. In this case, older adults may choose cheaper or smaller meals, thereby limiting the quality and quantity of food and increasing the risk for low nutrient intake.

Healthy eating relies on food choice. The process of food choice is influenced by personal factors, adequacy of individual and community resources, social context, and food environment, and it involves decisions made on convenience and quality. Individual and community resources might not be enough for older adults to be able to choose the types of foods for optimal nutritional health. Food assistance programs may be inadequate in light of expected and unexpected out-of-pocket expenses. Other community programs, such as meals programs, might not be available due to lack of money or volunteer resources. The most recent evaluation of these programs reported that many programs maintained large waiting lists for program participation. Other community factors, such as neighborhood safety, lack of business community involvement, geographic isolation, and minimal or lack of transportation, challenge the ability of older adults to access food stores for healthy choices. This is exacerbated by the overall lack of supermarkets or grocery stores in certain areas, especially rural and impoverished urban areas, and by challenges of the home environment, such as inadequate refrigeration. This means that some older adults must shop more frequently for fresh groceries or make other choices. Furthermore, the type of stores that may be available, such as convenience stores, provide food options that restrict the quality of the diet and improved eating patterns by selling few fresh fruits and vegetables (or none at all), processed meats (or no meat at all), canned vegetables high in sodium, and limited low-fat or fat-free dairy products. Closer proximity to supermarkets is associated with increased fruit and vegetable intake. Furthermore, differences in access to food stores can significantly affect the prices that older adults face, older adults' average food costs, and their overall food purchasing power. Reports indicate that comparable foods are more expensive in convenience stores than in supermarkets or grocery stores. For older adults without access to transportation, transportation costs for grocery shopping further reduce the amount of money available for food purchases. Despite published research showing that the local food environment is associated with diet quality and that poor and minority communities have less access to supermarkets and face higher prices for food, this knowledge has not translated into improved access to healthy food choices, especially among older adults.

In addition to having access to suitable healthful foods that are affordable, there are psychosocial and physiological factors that also influence the choice of foods such as culture, ethnic background, food texture and appearance, perceived intolerance, cognitive function, depression, and life stressors. Physiological factors that particularly influence older adults include burden of individual and multiple diseases, alterations of sense of taste or smell, dental status, long-term effects of earlier periods, and medications. Having few or new teeth poses a nutrition problem for older adults. Endentulousness is more of a problem for minorities and results in a diet that is lower in good nutrients and higher in sweets and desserts. The literature reports that non-Hispanic White older adults who are edentate eat more fats, cholesterol, saturated fat, and meats and also consume less Vitamin A than do those who are dendate. The type of foods that older adults choose to eat is also determined by challenges they face in meal preparation such as difficulty with mobility or balance, reduced manual dexterity or hand grip, diminished vision, and memory loss. These affect whether individuals can prepare foods in the home on their own or whether they need to choose foods that are already prepared or that require minimal preparation.

In sum, a new paradigm of nutrition and aging recognizes a number of key nutritional issues. Diet is a critical component of healthy aging; good nutritional health plays a role in maintaining physical and cognitive function. The focus of nutrition and public health is shifting from alleviating nutrient deficiencies as an outcome to stressing meal patterns and chronic disease prevention and management. The maintenance of good nutritional health for a growing older population requires approaches that recognize multiple levels of influence on the individual from social networks, organizations, communities, and policy. More attention needs to be given to the nutritional needs and challenges of healthy eating of various subgroups of older adults such as individuals with chronic conditions, those from different racial/ethnic minorities, and those who reside in rural settings. Research also needs to consider the challenges to older adults from the food environment—accessibility, availability, affordability, and acceptability of healthful food.

—*Joseph R. Sharkey*

See also Dietary Variety; Nutrition, Malnutrition, and Feeding Issues; Obesity; Vitamins, Minerals, and Dietary Supplements

Further Readings and References

Jensen GL. Obesity and functional decline: Epidemiology and geriatric consequences. *Clin Geriatr Med.* 2005; 21:677–687.

Lee JS, Weyant RJ, Corby P, et al. Edentulism and nutritional status in a biracial sample of well-functioning, community-dwelling elderly: The Health, Aging, and Body Composition Study. *Am J Clin Nutr.* 2004;79:295–302.

Sharkey JR, Branch LG, Zohoori N, Guiliani C, Busby-Whitehead J, Haines PS. Inadequate nutrient intake among homebound older persons in the community and its correlation with individual characteristics and health-related factors. *Am J Clin Nutr.* 2002;76:1435–1445.

Singh MAF, Rosenberg IH. Nutrition and aging. In: Hazzard WR, Blass JP, Ettinger WH, Halter JB, Ouslander JG, eds. *Principles of Geriatric Medicine and Gerontology.* 4th ed. New York: McGraw-Hill; 1999:81–96.

Nutrition, Malnutrition, and Feeding Issues

Nutrition is a fundamental necessity with special considerations in the older adult. Maintaining adequate nutrition is essential to healthy aging, yet this population is at high risk for malnutrition and undernutrition, primarily because of physiological and social changes that transpire over the course of their lives. Malnutrition exists in community-dwelling, hospitalized, and institutionalized older adults and is associated with increased morbidity and mortality. Macronutrient (protein energy) and micronutrient (vitamins and minerals) deficiencies are common. Age-related changes in physiology, metabolism, and functional status alter nutritional requirements. For example, there is redistribution of muscle mass and fat content that changes energy requirements as well as immunological changes that increase susceptibility to infection. Gradual reduction in alimentation is also common and is recognized as anorexia of aging. Other contributors to the propensity for malnutrition include underlying medical conditions, medication use, an unsupportive social environment, and dentition or feeding issues. The consequences of malnutrition can affect cognitive and functional abilities and, if severe, can be detrimental to the older adult. Osteoporosis, for example, results from inadequate calcium and Vitamin D intake and is associated with a higher risk of hip fracture. Hip fractures consequently have a high mortality rate. Nutritional assessments should identify those at risk and allow for developing a plan that focuses on nutrient replacement and preserving functional independence while maintaining quality of life.

Physiological Changes of Aging

Reduced Metabolic Rate

The most dramatic physiological change that affects nutrition occurs in body composition. Lean body (muscle) mass decreases and fat content increases naturally over the decades of life. This situation is preventable with nutritional balance and exercise. Muscle mass is slowly lost because there is a reduction in protein synthesis and an inability for the body to retain by-products for efficient muscle production as the body ages. Loss of muscle mass (or sarcopenia) begins after 25 years of age and accelerates after 45 years of age. The development of sarcopenia is multifactorial in origin and is due to a reduction of motor neurons, a decrease in anabolic hormonal influences, and disuse atrophy. Sarcopenia influences muscle strength, gait, and balance and also contributes to the increased risk of falls and frailty. The biggest impact of sarcopenia on nutrition is reduced energy requirements and metabolism. This reduction in metabolic rate can be countered by increasing exercise and protein intake to maintain healthy muscle mass. Particular attention must be given to the increase in protein requirements of the older adult because proteins are not produced or used as efficiently by the aging body. In general, 1 milligram per kilogram (mg/kg) of body weight per day of protein consumption is considered to be adequate.

The composition of body fat also changes in quantity and location. Body fat increases over time and is associated with metabolic consequences such as insulin resistance, elevation of triglycerides, and an increased risk of diabetes or hypertension. There is a linear increase of total body fat mass between 40 and 80 years of age. The distribution seems to favor a truncal, abdominal, and visceral distribution. This centripetal distribution is associated with an increased risk of those conditions noted previously and cardiovascular disease. Despite the natural propensity for these changes, lifestyle interventions of diet and exercise can delay the process by preserving muscle mass, in turn reducing fat production. Resistance exercises focus on strengthening and rebuilding larger muscle groups not only to increase metabolic rate but also to improve functional status.

Immunological Changes

The immune system serves to protect the body from being compromised by infection. This duty is carried out primarily by lymphocytes. The basal dysregulation present in the aging immune system directly involves reduction in lymphocyte numbers as well as impaired function. Chronic changes include lymphocyte (T-cell) depletion, senescence, membrane rigidity that impairs T-cell signaling, and reduced T-cell reactivity. The main function of the T-cell is to destroy intracellular bacteria, viruses, fungi, parasites, and mycobacteria.

This reduction in T-cell number and function explains the increased susceptibility to upper respiratory infections, shingles, tuberculosis, and other infections commonly seen in older adults. B-lymphocytes assist in the antibody response and are less affected by the aging process. The presence of protein energy malnutrition (PEM) leads to reduced lymphoid proliferation, further compromising immune function and prolonging the recovery phase after illness.

Anorexia of Aging

The reduced metabolic rate and physical activity seen with aging lead to a decline in food intake throughout life that predisposes the older adult to PEM. Changes in hormone levels and digestive tract function also contribute to this anorexia of aging. Cholecystokinin, the hormone responsible for making a person feel full, increases with age. Delayed stomach emptying also occurs. Solid foods stay in the stomach longer, thereby maintaining elevated levels of cholecystokinin. The passage of liquids through the stomach is unchanged and has little effect on cholecystokinin levels. Therefore, liquid supplements given between meals do not tend to decrease the amount of food intake at meals. This allows for meaningful supplementation in ill or malnourished older adults. Sex hormones also influence hunger. Testosterone increases and estrogen decreases appetite in men and women, respectively. As testosterone levels decrease with aging, there may be an association with reduced oral intake and sarcopenia. Estrogen reduction in menopause may explain why the level of oral intake in women does not decline in parallel with that in men. Older adults should make an effort to maintain proper protein energy intake and exercise regularly. Supplements consumed between meals can enhance a suboptimal diet.

Malnutrition

The presence of malnutrition is associated with increased complications and adverse health outcomes. Although micronutrient deficiencies are common, moderate to severe macronutrient deficiencies or PEM has the greatest clinical impact. There is altered immunity, impaired wound healing, increased health care use, increased incidence of delirium, and increased mortality. Identifying those at risk can be challenging because older adults are at high risk for malnutrition independent of their living situation. In increasing order, community-dwelling, hospitalized, and institutionalized individuals are at risk for malnutrition. Homebound older adults are at higher risk than are more independent community-dwelling individuals. Health care providers may detect those at risk by monitoring for weight loss, screening diet, obtaining a medical history, identifying prescription and over-the-counter drug use that may affect appetite, and evaluating the social support available to the older adult.

Weight loss may be an early indicator for those at risk for malnutrition. The presence of unexplained weight loss should raise suspicion of possible underlying nutrition problems. A loss of 10% of body weight during a 6-month period or a loss of 5% of body weight during a 1-month period is widely accepted as posing a significant risk of malnutrition. Various anthropometrical measures and screening methods are available, but no single measure seems reliable enough to support a diagnosis of malnutrition alone. These tools used in combination with a detailed medical history, weight history, and diet screen seem to better reflect the older adult's nutritional status. Markers associated with malnutrition in older adults include a low body mass index and a low serum albumin level. In more severe cases, a low serum total cholesterol level can be seen.

Feeding Issues

The list of medical illnesses associated with micronutrient or macronutrient malnutrition is extensive and involves essentially all body organ systems. Cognitive disorders, such as dementia, have been associated with Vitamin B deficiencies. Medical conditions associated with weight loss and malnutrition include congestive heart failure, emphysema, cancer, and chronic kidney and liver disease. Micronutrient and nutritional support given in the form of vitamins and oral supplements is instrumental in establishing the best possible physical condition. A gastrostomy tube should be considered for those who cannot meet their nutritional requirements.

The use of gastrostomy tubes or intravenous nutritional replacement should be considered in situations where this will have a positive impact on the older adult's quality of life. These artificial means of alimentation might not be useful in severely ill or debilitated individuals or in those with advanced dementia.

In addition, social, functional, and financial issues affect access to food and should be addressed with health care providers and social services. Poor dentition, mouth pain, lack of dentures, and swallowing difficulties all contribute to poor alimentation. These issues should be evaluated and corrected whenever possible.

—*Anita C. Mercado*

See also Anabolic Therapies; Gastrointestinal Aging; Normal Physical Aging; Nutrition and Public Health; Obesity; Oral Health; Vitamins, Minerals, and Dietary Supplements

Further Readings and References

Adolfsson O, Meydani SN. Nutrition and the aging immune response. In: Rosenberg IH, Sastre A, eds. *Nutrition and Aging: Nestle Nutrition Workshop Series Clinical and Performance Program,* Vol. 6. Basel, Switzerland: S. Karger; 2002:207–221.

Fiatarone Singh MA, Rosenberg IH. Nutrition and aging. In: Hazzard WR, Blass JP, Ettinger WH, Halter JB, Ouslander JG, eds. *Principles of Geriatric Medicine and Gerontology.* 4th ed. New York: McGraw-Hill; 1999:81–96.

Morely JE. Anorexia of aging: Physiologic and pathologic. *Am J Clin Nutr.* 1997;66:760–763.

Reuben DB, Greendale GA, Harrison GG. Nutrition screening in older persons. *J Am Geriatr Soc.* 1995;43:415–425.

Wicks G, Grubeck-Loebenstein B. Primary and secondary alterations of immune reactivity in the elderly: Impact of dietary factors and disease. *Immunol Rev.* 1997;160:171–184.

OBESITY

The national epidemic of obesity has now extended to older persons. Substantial evidence links overweight and obesity to an increased risk of serious comorbidities that include hypertension, dyslipidemia, heart disease, insulin resistance and diabetes, metabolic syndrome, cholelithiasis, respiratory impairment, gout, and osteoarthritis. Obesity among older persons has also been linked with increased likelihood of self-reported functional limitations, a decline in measured physical performance, and an elevated risk of functional decline. An obese Medicare beneficiary costs $1,486 more in health care expenses per year than does an individual of healthy weight. This entry focuses on obesity in the elderly to include recent trends, etiologies, impact on health and function, and potential interventions.

Defining Overweight and Obesity

Body mass index (BMI) has become a widely used formula to assess body fat indirectly. BMI is calculated as body weight in kilograms (kg) / height in meters squared (m^2). In 1998, the National Institutes of Health set criteria to define overweight and obesity as BMI $\geq$ 25 and BMI $\geq$ 30, respectively, but standards have not been adopted specifically for older persons. Although BMI suffers from limitations as a proxy of measure of adiposity, it is nonetheless useful for screening applications and for guiding interventions.

Prevalence and Trends of Obesity

The prevalence of overweight and obesity in older Americans has increased dramatically (Table 1). Obesity is more prevalent among older women than among older men, and it is appreciably greater among young-older persons than among old-older persons. The prevalence of obesity declines precipitously after 80 years of age.

The Causes of Obesity

Obesity is a multifactorial chronic disease. Selected key risk factors include genetic predisposition, certain medications, lifestyle, and behavior. Studies with twins reveal marked concordance in obesity. Pairs of twins exposed to periods of positive and negative energy balance experienced greater similarities for rate of weight gain, proportion of weight gain, and body site of excessive fat deposition than did non-twin pairs. A number of gene polymorphisms have also been linked to increased risk of obesity.

Weight gain is frequently experienced during middle age. The onset of menopause in women can be associated with additional weight gain. Body fat tends to peak later in women than in men and may occur as late as 50 to 60 years of age. A decrease in lean body mass (sarcopenia) and an associated decline in resting energy expenditure also occur with aging. Most obese older persons were overweight or obese as middle-aged adults and have suffered weight excess for many years.

Table 1 Prevalence of Obesity (Percentages): National Health and Nutrition Examination Survey, 1988–1994 Versus 1999–2000

Age (years)	Men (1988–1994)	Men (1999–2000)	Women (1988–1994)	Women (1999–2000)
60 to 69	24.8	38.1	29.8	42.5
70 to 79	20.0	28.9	25.0	31.9
≥ 80	8.0	9.6	15.1	19.5

Source: Adapted from Flegal KM, Carroll MD, Ogden CL, Johnson CL. Prevalence and trends in obesity among U.S. adults, 1999–2000. *JAMA.* 2002;288:1723–1727.

Polypharmacy is common among older persons, and selected medications may also contribute to weight gain. Antidepressants (e.g., fluoxetine, mirtazapine, phenelzine sulfate), antipsychotics (e.g., piperazine phenothiazine, risperidone, olanzapine), anticonvulsants (e.g., carbamazepine, valproic acid), and corticosteroids (e.g., cortisone, prednisone) are associated with increased caloric intake and increased body fat.

Ultimately, weight gain results from positive energy balance and excessive energy intake from food in combination with decreased energy expenditure from reduced physical activity. Food choices have a substantial influence on diet quality. Older people with higher intakes of foods with low-nutrient density (e.g., breads, sweet breads, desserts, processed meats, eggs, fats, oils) are twice as likely to be obese, twice as likely to have low serum Vitamin B12 levels, and 3 to 17 times more likely to have low nutrient intakes. Those who consume foods with high-nutrient density, such as cereal, vegetables, fruits, milk, poultry, fish, and beans, benefit from lower energy intake overall; higher energy-adjusted intakes of fiber, iron, zinc, folate, and Vitamins B6, B12, and D; higher plasma Vitamin B12; and smaller waist circumferences. Sedentary living is common for older persons and contributes to reduced energy expenditure. Television watching and functional mobility limitations are important contributing factors. Recent studies have suggested that obesity is increasingly common among homebound elders. Unfortunately, many older adults accept inactivity and weight gain as a natural part of the aging process and exert minimal effort toward prevention.

The Impact of Obesity

Obesity-associated comorbidities include hypertension, dyslipidemia, heart disease, insulin resistance and diabetes, metabolic syndrome, cholelithiasis, respiratory impairment, gout, and osteoarthritis of the knee. Hypertension, affecting more than 50 million Americans, is one of the most common chronic diseases in the United States. Hypertension is associated with increased risk of cardiovascular disease, stroke, and renal failure. The strongest predictors of blood pressure in humans are BMI and weight. Weight loss, even in modest amounts, has been shown to reduce both blood pressure and the need for blood pressure medications. The risk of older people developing type 2 diabetes also increases with obesity. Findings from the second National Health and Nutrition Examination Survey (NHANES II, 1976 to 1980) showed that the risk of developing diabetes was 3.8 times greater for obese individuals 45 to 75 years of age. Diet and exercise can improve glycemic control in those with diabetes; moreover, diet and exercise alone can sometimes curtail the need for pharmacological treatment. Together, dyslipidemia, hypertension, and diabetes comprise metabolic syndrome, which is both prevalent among obese older persons and strongly associated with risk of cardiovascular disease.

Many older adults suffer from arthritis, most commonly osteoarthritis. Obese adults are particularly vulnerable to the development of destructive joint disease of the knees secondary to mass-related shear forces and inflammation. Knee osteoarthritis can lead to poor balance, decreased mobility, and muscle atrophy, ultimately leading to physical disability.

Not only is obesity associated with increased risk of developing chronic diseases, it also is associated with increased prevalence of functional impairments, especially mobility. High current or past BMI is associated with increased risk of reporting functional limitations. These findings have been confirmed with objective physical performance testing. Obesity also places a person at risk for functional decline, as supported by observations in longitudinal outcome studies. Increasingly, many homebound older persons are found to be obese.

Intervention and Treatment

The 1998 National Institutes of Health guidelines suggest that individual determinations should be made as to the appropriateness of weight reduction interventions for older persons. Nonvolitional weight loss in older persons often portends an ominous outcome because it is a proxy indicator of underlying inflammatory condition or disease. Another concern is that weight loss in postmenopausal women may be associated with a modest reduction in bone mineral density. Nevertheless, the longitudinal Nurses Health Study found that weight loss among overweight/obese women was associated with improvements in self-reported physical function and lower levels of bodily pain.

A tailored intervention for older persons might include large-font instructional materials, supplementation of calcium and Vitamin D, and realistic moderate weight loss and physical activity goals. Weight loss medications and bariatric surgery have not been tested adequately in older adults to warrant recommendations for their use.

Few weight reduction intervention studies have been conducted in older persons. The Trial of Nonpharmacologic Interventions in the Elderly (TONE) was a randomized controlled study that compared the efficacies of reduced sodium intake, weight loss, both reduced sodium intake and weight loss, and usual care in the treatment of hypertension in older people. The results indicated that a decrease in both sodium intake and body weight reduced the amount of antihypertensive medication needed. Messier and colleagues studied obese older persons with knee osteoarthritis. After the participants completed a 6-month intervention program consisting of diet and/or aerobic/strength exercises, it was observed that the combination of both weight loss and exercise, rather than weight loss alone, contributed to improvements in physical performance, pain, and disability. Gordon Jensen and colleagues enrolled community-dwelling obese women 60 to 75 years of age in a 3-month weight-reduction program with diet modification and exercise. Self-selected obese older women who achieved moderate weight loss and

physical activity goals were found to have improved laboratory, physical performance, self-reported function, vitality, and quality of life outcomes. For many frail older persons, emphasis should perhaps be placed on the prevention of further weight gain with the promotion of strength and flexibility.

Conclusion

It is evident that the prevalence of obesity is increasing among older persons. A serious burden of chronic disease and functional decline may result. Age alone should not dictate restricted access to treatment for obese older people. Reasonable intervention goals should be considered based on patient's wishes and individual opportunity for health improvement.

—Allison R. Thompson and Gordon L. Jensen

See also Body Composition; Body Mass Index; Diabetes; Health Promotion and Disease Prevention; Metabolic Syndrome; Midlife; Multiple Morbidity and Comorbidity; Nutrition and Public Health; Nutrition, Malnutrition, and Feeding Issues

Further Readings and References

Flegal KM, Caroll MD, Ogden CL, Johnson CL. Prevalence and trends in obesity among U.S. adults, 1999–2000. *JAMA.* 2002;228:1723–1727.

Galanos AN, Pieper CF, Cornoni-Huntley JC, et al. Nutrition and function: Is there a relationship between body mass index and the functional capabilities of community-dwelling elderly? *J Am Geriatr Soc.* 1994;42:368–373.

Jensen GL, Roy MA, Buchanan AE, Berg M. Weight loss intervention for obese older women: Improvements in performance and function. *Obesity Res.* 2004; 12:1814–1820.

Ledikwe JH, Wright HS, Mitchell DC, Jensen GL, Friedmann JM, Still CD. Nutrition risk assessment and obesity in rural older adults: A gender difference. *Am J Clin Nutr.* 2003;77:551–558.

Messier SP, Loeser RF, Mitchell MN, et al. Exercise and weight loss in obese older adults with knee osteoarthritis: A preliminary study. *J Am Geriatr Soc.* 2000;48:1062–1072.

Morley JE. Anorexia of aging: Physiologic and pathologic. *Am J Clin Nutr.* 1997;66:760–773.

Van Itallie T. Health implications of overweight and obesity in the United States. *Ann Intern Med.* 1985;103:983–988.

OLDEST OLD

The population over 85 years of age has represented the fastest-growing age group for the past four decades, primarily because of the increase in life expectancy at 65 years of age. Beginning in 2025, this age group will experience an additional increase in the United States due to the aging of baby boomers. The data on this population can be misleading, however, because approximately one quarter of persons in this age group live in institutions, mainly nursing homes. Therefore, surveys of the community-dwelling population over 85 years of age exclude those who have the poorest health status. A large majority of those over 85 years of age are female, a result of the more rapid increase in life expectancy among women than among men. To discuss the oldest old is to talk about a world that is predominantly female. To speak in gender-neutral terms produces a misunderstanding of the problems facing the oldest old and contributes to misinformed policy choices; this has been the case with suicide, which is an issue primarily for oldest-old men. Another source of confusion is that this population is a small minority of the population over 65 years of age, so that data that refer to all elderly persons will hide the situation of this group. For example, the oldest old are much more likely to be poor than are members of the general population over 65 years of age, and the poverty in this age group is related to its majority female population living alone.

The most critical health factor is disability, with mortality being less of a concern because both men and women at these ages are living beyond their cohort's life expectancy. They are the survivors; there is no "excess" mortality. There is, however, widespread concern over issues related to disability, both from the perspective of the individuals and their families and from the perspective of the medical and social costs to society. The medical and social costs for this population are more closely related to disability and disabling diseases than to acute medical care. It is important to remember, however, that more than one quarter of the oldest old are not disabled in any way.

The most prevalent chronic diseases in this age group, musculoskeletal conditions and Alzheimer's disease, are not usually causes of mortality. The oldest-old person is likely to die of another cause, most commonly a cardiovascular condition. Even cancer, although it may be present, is not likely to be a cause of death because some other disease or disorder is likely to kill the person first. Although a history of high blood pressure or cancer is very prevalent among this population, these factors are not significant causes of disability. Neither is the presence or absence of a disease significant; disability depends on the degree of severity of the disease in combination with other conditions. At this age, disability is most likely the result of two or more diseases or disorders. In the case of oldest-old persons who have both macular degeneration and musculoskeletal conditions, the disabling effect is the result of poor vision together with limited mobility. If only one of these conditions were present, the disability could be much less.

Discussions of health and well-being of the oldest old are often marred by the use of gender-neutral terms. The oldest old must be disaggregated into men and women. Disability is much more prevalent among women than among men, yet it is the men who are more likely to be married and to have help at home. The discussion of married oldest old is really a discussion of men, the majority of whom are married even at these advanced ages. For oldest-old women in the community, the most likely situation is living alone, even with their higher rates of disability. These factors indicate the need for a gender analysis in program planning. For example, housing issues for the oldest old need to be separated into older women's housing issues (e.g., the need for safe and affordable apartments for single women) versus older men's issues (e.g., the need for housing for older married couples that eases the caregiving burden).

The most important cause of severe disability among the oldest old—inability to perform the activities of daily living (ADLs)—is Alzheimer's disease. Although this disease is less prevalent than musculoskeletal problems, it is progressive and soon requires custodial care. It is the disease that most often results in placement in a nursing home as care needs overwhelm the ability of friends and family. It is a disease that can cause death, although the person can live with the disease for many years and generally dies of something else. Although research offers hope to slow its progression, no clear protocol has emerged to either treat or prevent Alzheimer's disease.

Issues associated with Alzheimer's disease are indicative of the difficulty faced in understanding the health of this population. Women are more likely to be victims of this disease because they live longer and Alzheimer's is strongly correlated with age. Even in Alzheimer's, which dominates care issues, the general level of disability (in this case cognitive impairment) is key. Cognitive impairment is a disability that can have multiple causes. Of course, Alzheimer's is a predominant cause, but as with other diseases of the oldest old, another disease likely aggravates the cognitive impairment of Alzheimer's, especially during the early stages. Thus, often comorbidity is the most important cause of disability due to cognitive impairment. Other causes of cognitive impairment, such as Parkinson's disease, are also linked to age. Comorbidity may explain why oldest-old women in the community do better on measures of cognitive function than do oldest-old men in the community. Items used in measures of cognitive impairment, however, need to be examined for a gender effect.

The most prevalent conditions causing at least mild disability among the oldest old are related to musculoskeletal problems. It is often these problems, more common among women, that cause difficulties in the instrumental activities of daily living (IADLs). The two most common diseases causing these problems are osteoporosis and osteoarthritis, both of which are more prevalent among women than among men. In fact, there appears to be a special interaction effect of the presence of these diseases and being female. Furthermore, although musculoskeletal conditions are critical, the disability itself is often the result of comorbidity that can lead to further disability; for example, when poor vision combined with osteoporosis results in a fall.

For the oldest old, it is important to examine carefully the measure of disability used. The Asset and Health Dynamics Among the Oldest Old (AHEAD) survey uses a measure of disability asking "having difficulty with" such as having difficulty with any of the ADLs (e.g., bathing, dressing, eating, transferring). But for the oldest old, "having difficulty with" often means needing the help of another person. If that help is not available, there can be a high risk of falls (e.g., from bathing). The young old can often manage the ADLs with difficulty or with the assistance of a device. For the oldest old, it is important to measure the degree of difficulty as well as the need for personal assistance. This is especially true for oldest-old women who are most likely to be living alone.

Discussions of health for the oldest old are necessarily broad ones of population health. The multiple determinants of health include a long personal medical history as well as the physical and social environment. Socioeconomic status and housing are critical in providing resources that can counterbalance the progression of disability. Furthermore, a gender analysis is necessary because the minority of oldest old—men—are in a marital and/or economic situation very different from that of the vast majority of this population, which is female. Women outlive men and are likely to need to deal with issues of low income and disability while living alone. For society, the immediate policy issue is finding a way to provide assistance to the oldest old who need help with their daily activities. In the long run, more effort should be devoted to preventing disability among coming generations of oldest old.

—*Sally Bould*

See also Centenarians; Compression of Morbidity; Demography of Aging; Disability and the Disablement Process; Longevity

Further Readings and References

Bould S, Smith MH, Longino CF Jr. Ability, disability, and the oldest old. *J Aging Soc Policy.* 1997;9(1):13–31.
Finlayson M. Changes predicting long-term care use among the oldest old. *Gerontologist.* 2002;42:443–454.
Smith J, Borchelt M, Jopp D. Health and well-being in the young old and the oldest old. *J Social Issues.* 2002; 58:715–733.

Tomassini C. The demographic characteristics of the oldest old in the United Kingdom. *Pop Trends*. 2005;120:15–22.

Van Exel E, Gussekloo J, DeCraen AJM, et al. Cognitive function in the oldest old: Women perform better than men. *J Neurol Neurosurg Psychiatry*. 2001;71:29–32.

Von Strauss E, Fratiglioni L, Viitanen M, Forsell Y, Winblad B. Morbidity and comorbidity in relation to functional status: A community-based study of the oldest old (90+ years). *J Am Geriatr Soc*. 2000;48:1462–1470.

ORAL HEALTH

Increasing numbers of people are becoming older adults. The "graying" of America has often been described in the media and is well documented by U.S. census. Baby boomers approaching retirement age are expected to make this trend even more pronounced. The age considered to be geriatric usually (and arbitrarily) begins at 65 years. This is entirely an artificial construct; many so-called geriatric processes are well evident in people years younger, and many do not manifest themselves in others until much later. That caveat aside, the transition from "elderly" to "frail elderly," or between "young old" and "old old," is characterized by physiological and functional change. This entry discusses these changes, their effects on oral health, and the relationship between oral health and systemic health.

Plaque Diseases

The most common of the oral diseases are the plaque diseases, namely caries and periodontal disease. Plaque is an adherent, gelatinous-like material consisting of salivary components, food residues, and bacteria. Caries is the dental term for tooth decay, and periodontal disease affects the tissues surrounding the teeth. These bacterial diseases are both chronic and progressive in nature. Progressive demineralization of the teeth by bacterial acid causes enamel breakdown (cavities), which can develop into abscess and tooth loss.

Periodontal disease causes destruction of the fibers attaching teeth to bone. Advanced periodontal disease results first in tooth mobility and then in tooth loss. During this process, recession of gum tissues exposes the root surfaces of teeth. Because these root surfaces are not protected by enamel, they are more susceptible to caries. The resulting decay is difficult to treat, and recurrence is common. More than 95% of people age 65 years and older have periodontal damage.

Other Oral Diseases

Like all conditions discussed in this entry, the following pathologies are not exclusive to an aging population, but older adults have particular susceptibility.

Fungus

Fungal infections, such as candidiasis and angular cheilitis, are common among older people. They are usually associated with other medical conditions. People with diabetes who also wear dentures are at particular increased risk, as are those who have suppressed immune systems. Oral candidiasis is especially serious for people who are HIV positive and for those taking immunosuppressive medications. It can spread to the esophagus or lungs, creating an immediate threat to life.

Angular cheilitis is a fungal condition of the lips, causing dry and cracked tissues at the corners of the mouth. If untreated, the lesions can persist indefinitely, with periodic bleeding and occasional secondary infection. It afflicts immunocompromised people, and those who wear dentures have reduced salivary flow. This seemingly minor lesion causes significant misery and decreased quality of life.

Neoplasm

Neoplasms range from epulis fissuratim, a benign growth of tissue caused by an ill-fitting denture, to life-threatening malignancies. An epulis can cause irritation, inflammation, and secondary infections. The malignancy most threatening to life is squamous cell carcinoma. It is frequently found on the side of the tongue in the back of the mouth, although it is also found on the lip, palate, cheek, and floor of the mouth. It has a poor prognosis, and successful treatment requires early diagnosis. The survival rate for people with lip cancer is high because these lesions are quite visible, and early diagnosis is typical. Lesions on the floor of the mouth or the side of the tongue have a significantly higher mortality rate. These more posterior lesions tend to be more aggressive, and diagnosis is often delayed because they are hidden from view.

Xerostomia

Fully 70% of elderly people suffer from xerostomia (reduced salivary flow). The primary cause is prescribed medications, including blood pressure medications, antidepressants, antihistamines, diuretics, narcotics, and antianxiety medications. Other causes include radiation therapy and substance use/abuse.

Xerostomia is a major contributor to tooth decay and periodontal disease. It impairs chewing, swallowing, and speech. It causes tissues of the lips, tongue, and oral mucosa to become dry and cracked. Loss of intraoral lubrication causes recurrent abrasions and ulcerations. Fungal infections, aphthous ulcers (canker sores), and herpetic lesions all occur more readily in the dry mouth. Xerostomia plus acid reflux produces burning sensations in soft tissue and acid erosion of tooth structure.

Xerostomic people should sip water continuously. Artificial saliva and salivary stimulants such as sugar-free gum help. Gum with xylitol, a noncaloric sweetener, also helps to protect against tooth decay. Topical medications provide some relief. Aggressive disease prevention efforts are an absolute necessity for xerostomic patients.

Prostheses

Fixed prostheses are used to replace missing teeth. They include bridges, which anchor artificial teeth to the remaining natural teeth, and implants, which surgically anchor replacement teeth in bone. Their function is similar to that of natural teeth, and people adapt to them readily. Fixed prostheses require meticulous care, however, and their success depends on the good health of the surrounding tissues.

Partial and full dentures are removable prostheses. Full dentures replace all of the teeth in the arch. They restore some, but not all, function. Denture stability requires a snug fit and maximum contact with broad areas of tissue. People wearing dentures experience loss of taste, reduced proprioception, and impaired chewing ability. A common, but incorrect, perception is that when all of one's teeth are gone, there is no longer a need to visit the dentist. However, tissues under dentures change rapidly, and resulting pathologies require care. Dentures are implicated in many conditions, including denture stomatitis, traumatic ulceration, fungal infection, and the previously mentioned epulis fissuratim. When dentures no longer fit well because of changes to the underlying tissues, their function is impaired and the risk of oral lesions rises.

Changes Associated With Aging

Many of the processes of aging affect oral health, including changes in anatomy, cell physiology, gastrointestinal activity, immune function, and sensory integration. Loss of teeth causes reduced appetite, chewing capacity, and taste. Eating habits change, and nutritional capacity is reduced. Tooth loss also contributes to social isolation and depression. Gastrointestinal changes impair digestion and absorption processes, and maintaining adequate nutrition levels becomes more difficult.

Physiological changes affect the metabolism of therapeutic drugs. Altered protein levels in plasma change the transport efficiency and half-life of some drugs. This profoundly affects function and optimal dose, and it increases the risk of overdose. Periodic reassessment of the effectiveness and safety of medications is an essential part of health care for aging adults.

Aging is associated with dysregulation of the immune response even in healthy elderly people. These changes in the immune system may predispose older persons to infectious, neoplastic, autoimmune, and inflammatory diseases, all of which find fertile ground in the oral environment.

Chronic Disease and Oral Health

Incidence of chronic disease among older people has increased dramatically. Oral health and systemic health are indistinguishable; each affects the other with remarkable consistency. Chronic disease has significant impact on oral health, and oral disease certainly affects systemic health adversely. Existing cardiovascular disease correlates highly with periodontal disease, and oral infections can cause cardiac infections. The valves of the heart are especially susceptible to oral bacteria transported through the vascular system. The resulting infection, called endocarditis, is life threatening and can require surgical replacement of the heart valves.

Diabetes is a prime example of the interrelationship of systemic and oral health. The effects of diabetes on oral health include an increase in oral bacterial infections, periodontal disease, and fungal infections. Conversely, poor oral health creates problems with glycemic control, increasing the difficulty of managing the diabetic condition.

Today, more individuals have multiple chronic diseases, and medication use has risen accordingly. The typical nursing home resident's pharmacological regimen is eight medications daily. Many of these drugs have profound effects on oral health. Reduction in salivary flow was discussed previously. Calcium channel blockers and antiseizure medications cause gingival overgrowth and increased plaque levels, resulting in bleeding gums, tooth decay, and periodontal disease.

A variety of neurological, musculoskeletal, and inflammatory conditions reduce motor function. Of these, arthritis is certainly one of the most widespread. Reduced mobility from arthritis can deprive people of full independence, reducing their quality of life. Of critical importance is the arthritic's reduced capacity for self-care. Arthritic hands might not be able to use dental floss or manipulate a toothbrush effectively. The risk of oral disease increases profoundly.

Functional Dependence and Cognitive Impairment

More than 1.75 million people currently live in convalescent care centers. Three quarters of these people have poor oral hygiene. Most need help with activities of daily living (ADLs), and 70% have some level of cognitive impairment. Assisted-living facilities are enrolling increasing numbers of people, many of whom have reduced functional and cognitive capacity. The unmet oral health need of this population is staggering, and the problem is expected to get worse.

Untreated oral disease increases demands on the immune system and can lead to systemic infection, with very serious consequences for frail seniors.

Oral health is particularly poor among people with dementia. Oral hygiene is difficult, and the need for dental care is extremely high. Most of these needs are never addressed satisfactorily, and dental disease is largely untreated. Communication difficulties often cause oral pain not to be reported. Diagnosis of oral problems from behavioral anomalies is difficult, and most often the real oral difficulty remains unaddressed. Even when care is accessed, it is often limited to emergency care rather than the ongoing comprehensive care needed to maintain good oral health.

Oral problems such as pain and reduced salivary flow affect nutrition, weight, hydration, speech, behavior, and social interactions. Loss of function is evidenced by impaired speech, impaired digestion, and reduced chewing capacity. Effects of acid reflux can be devastating. Loss of muscle tonicity makes dentures less functional and more uncomfortable. Sleep apnea is common. In short, reduced functional capacity and cognition can diminish oral health profoundly, exacerbate systemic health problems, and reduce quality of life substantially.

Nutritional Factors

The oral condition can enhance or impair the capacity for nutrition. Oral factors that reduce nutritional capacity include tooth loss, pain, denture use, oral pathosis, and xerostomia. Infection and inflammation reduce appetite. Tooth loss restricts types of food that can be eaten. Meat, fresh fruits, and fresh vegetables are difficult to eat if diseased teeth are loose or painful.

In an aging population, chewing, swallowing, and digestion are often impaired. Dietary restrictions are common, collagen metabolism can be dysfunctional, underlying medical conditions abound, osteoporosis is common, and substance dependency is rising and is largely untreated. The supplements used to maintain nutrient supply lack necessary dietary texture and fiber for normal gastrointestinal function. For all of these reasons, adequate nutrition and good eating habits are critical for geriatric health.

Nutrients

Micronutrient depletion is directly associated with oral pathology. Mucosal lesions are linked with iron deficiency, and reduced calcium absorption contributes to osteoporosis. Reduced vitamin absorption impairs mucosal cell metabolism, collagen metabolism, and the healing response. Vitamin D facilitates intestinal absorption of calcium, and it is instrumental in bone remodeling. Aging people experience a fourfold decrease in the ability of the skin to produce Vitamin D. Even healthy older people have been found to have low dietary intakes of iron, folate, calcium, magnesium, and zinc.

Vitamin C is the nutrient most associated with oral health. It has antioxidant properties preventing cell damage. It acts as a cofactor in collagen synthesis, essential for connective tissues, blood vessels, and bone. Vitamin C is involved in DNA/RNA synthesis, essential for new cell growth. Given that mucosal cells replace themselves every 3 to 7 days, this is of particular importance. People at risk for an insufficiency of Vitamin C include those who eat few fruits and vegetables, those with restricted diets, those with chronic illnesses, and those who are substance dependent. This description fits far too many aging people far too well.

Nutritional Impact of Dentures

The nutritional effects of losing teeth are often underestimated. Even excellent dentures do not work as well as natural teeth. Over time, denture wearers experience alveolar bone loss, making the dentures unstable or unwearable. Chewing becomes painful, and people eat mostly soft foods. Seniors are second only to persons 15 to 24 years of age in the amount of processed foods and refined sugars they eat. Such a diet increases risk of obesity and dental disease.

Psychosocial and Behavioral Issues

Psychosocial changes in an aging population lead to lifestyle changes. Many people can make adjustments to accommodate mental, emotional, and physical changes. Adaptive change that maintains independence also maintains quality of life. Loss of independence reduces the ability to engage in everyday activities such as shopping and preparing meals. Lack of exercise, reduced social interaction, and inadequate nutrition adversely affect wellness. Depression and isolation further reduce functional capacity and quality of life.

New onset substance dependency is developing at alarming rates among aging adults. The substance of choice is usually alcohol or prescribed medication. Substance dependency has a profound effect on both oral and systemic health. Alcohol use, particularly in conjunction with tobacco use, increases the risk of oral cancer. Other oral effects include xerostomia, attrition of the teeth, dental hypersensitivity, and poor oral hygiene. Alcoholics may suffer from gastrointestinal bleeding and impaired absorption. People with active substance dependencies do not take good care of themselves, and oral health deteriorates rapidly.

Access to Care Issues

Reduced mobility and physical incapacity limit access to oral care, even for those with sufficient financial assets. One third (33%) of men and nearly half (45%) of women are expected to spend parts of their lives in nursing homes. Unfortunately, regular and consistent oral health care is in very short supply in assisted-living situations. Residents must depend on others for even the most rudimentary oral hygiene. Reduced personal oral hygiene inevitably leads to poor oral health. Access to services of dental professionals is limited by transportation difficulties and the scarcity of professionals willing to make house calls. The result is reduced access for people just as their need for care is escalating.

Cultural Expectations

Many people approaching their "golden years" have an image of senior life as people in good health enjoying a plethora of recreational activities as a reward for well-lived lives. For many, this picture will be accurate. Many others, however, will experience the personal dissonance of the cultural promise not matching the reality. The sheer number of people entering their senior years will substantially increase oral health needs. Medicare does not cover oral health costs, and many older people with fixed incomes are unable to pay for care themselves. The challenge for policymakers and health care providers will be to develop effective ways of addressing these needs.

Proactive Prevention and Wellness

Anticipating the physiological changes associated with aging can enhance quality of life. Knowing what to expect and how to prepare for the changes of aging will do much to help people enjoy life during their later years. Regular care and personal measures of prevention will promote oral and systemic health and, therefore, a better life. Health care oriented toward wellness will enhance the quality of that life. Health begets health, and at no time is this more evident than during the senior years.

—*Robert Johnson, Gary Chiodo,*
and David Rosenstein

See also Health Promotion and Disease Prevention; Nutrition, Malnutrition, and Feeding Issues; Smoking

Further Readings and References

Carlos JP, Wolfe MD. Methodological and nutritional issues in assessing the oral health of aged subjects. *Am J Clin Nutr.* 1989;50:1210–1218.

Chávez E, Ship J. Sensory and motor deficits in the elderly: Impact on oral health. *J Public Health Dent.* 2000;50: 297–303.

Gabre S. Experience and assessment of pain in individuals with cognitive impairments. *Spec Care Dent.* 2002;22: 174–180.

Jablonsky RA, Munro CL, Grap MJ, Elsnick RK. The role of biobehavioral, environmental, and social forces on oral health disparities in frail and functionally dependent nursing home elders. *Biol Res Nurs.* 2005;7:75–82.

Meydani SN, Wu D, Santos MS, Hayek MG. Antioxidants and immune response in aged persons: Overview of present evidence. *Am J Clin Nutr.* 1995;62(Suppl.): 1462S–1486S.

Papas AS, Joshi A, Belanger AJ, Kent RL, Palmer CA, DePaola PF. Dietary models for root caries. *Am J Clin Nutr.* 1995;61(Suppl.):417S–422S.

Payette H, Gray-Donald K. Dietary intake and biochemical indices of nutritional status in an elderly population. *Am J Clin Nutr.* 1991;54:478–488.

Smith BJ, Shay K. What predicts oral health stability in a long-term care population? *Spec Care Dent.* 2005;25: 150–157.

Soini H, Routasaio P, Lauri S, Ainamo A. Oral and nutritional status in frail elderly. *Spec Care Dent.* 2003; 23:209–215.

Stoller EP, Pyle M. Priorities for oral health goals in a sample of older adults. *Spec Care Dent.* 2004;24:220–228

Sweeney MP, Bagg J, Fell GS, Yip B. The relationship between micronutrient depletion and oral health in geriatrics. *J Oral Pathol Med.* 1994;23:168–171.

Taylor G, Loesche W, Terpenning M. Impact of oral diseases on systemic health in the elderly: Diabetes mellitus and aspiration pneumonia. *J Public Health Dent.* 2000; 60:313–320.

OSTEOPOROSIS

Osteoporosis is defined as a decrease in bone mass, disruption of bone architecture, and resultant increased risk of fracture. It is common and has significant population impact; osteoporosis leads to more than 1.4 million fractures in the United States each year. Approximately 800,000 of these fractures occur in the spine and result in pain and immobility. Only 20% to 30% of individuals with fragility fractures (nontraumatic and due to very thin bone) receive appropriate evaluation and treatment. This lack of appropriate detection was the subject of a public health initiative in the 2004 *Bone Health and Osteoporosis: A Report of the Surgeon General.*

As with many disease processes, osteoporosis is best managed by prevention. Prevention not only is cost-effective in this disease but also reduces the incidence of pain and suffering due to fracture. Approximately 20% of men and women die within 1 year after a hip fracture. The Surgeon General's 2004 report outlined four specific components to guide individuals to better bone health: good nutrition with vitamin supplementation, physical activity, safe environment, and appropriate medical evaluation.

Risk factors for osteoporosis include female gender, older age, loss of female hormones (e.g., menopause), Caucasian or Asian race, personal history of fracture, and current smoking. Other contributions to a higher risk of osteoporosis include maternal history of fracture, low body weight (< 127 pounds), and a calcium-deficient diet.

Calcium and Vitamin D play an important role in bone health. Calcium helps bones to maintain strength, and the average American consumes an insufficient amount of calcium. Three 8-ounce glasses of low-fat milk are recommended daily with a well-balanced diet. High-protein diets might not provide enough calcium to reach a goal of 1,200 milligrams (mg) per day for the average adult over 50 years of age. There has been no evidence that coral calcium (derived from coral reefs) provides easier absorption than other forms of calcium supplements. Most experts in the field recommend brand-name over-the-counter supplements that can be easily found in most pharmacies. Vitamin D not only is present in the diet but also must be metabolized in the skin into an active form. With age, the ability of skin to synthesize active Vitamin D decreases. Adequate sunlight is necessary for Vitamin D metabolism in the skin. Older persons in long-term care facilities are at increased risk for Vitamin D deficiency, in part due to low sunlight exposure combined with aging effects on the skin. For most patients, 400 international units (IU) per day of Vitamin D supplement can be used for prevention. Patients with established osteoporosis should take 800 IU/day.

Physical activity has a clear role in fracture prevention. Exercise preserves bone mass and also reduces the risk of falling, helping to prevent fractures. Exercise should focus on muscle strengthening and balance. Evaluation and treatment of balance problems, including therapeutic exercise, is an important component of fracture prevention.

Screening for osteoporosis helps detect disease before serious problems develop. The diagnosis of osteoporosis is often overlooked in clinical practice. Only a quarter of patients receive bone mineral density tests after hip fractures, and less than a quarter receive any type of treatment. Bone density tests should be performed in women over 65 years of age, women who have lost ovarian function due to surgery or medical conditions, people who take medications that increase the risk of osteoporosis (e.g., corticosteroids, some seizure prevention medications), and anyone who has had a previous fracture not due to trauma.

Bone density can be tested using several methods, but the most common approach in practice today is dual energy X-ray absorptiometry (DEXA), which measures bone mass at several important sites, including the spine, wrist, and hip. DEXA is used both for initial detection and for follow-up testing of the effect of treatment. Because DEXA machines vary, it is important to use the same type of machine for follow-up so as to assess changes in bone density accurately.

Osteoporosis can also be seen in men. Men who have a history of fracture, have a history of hypogonadism (low testosterone), or are taking steroids are at increased risk for future fracture.

Although many cases of osteoporosis are due to late-life hormone changes, there are certain medical conditions—including primary hyperparathyroidism, Vitamin D deficiency, and multiple myeloma—that affect bone and require specific testing and treatment. Currently, there are many safe and effective options for medical therapy. Because of their cost and efficacy, calcium and Vitamin D together should be considered as first-line therapy. This combination has been shown not only to improve bone mineral density but also to prevent vertebral fracture. The most common class of prescription medications, antiresorptive agents, includes bisphosphonates, selective estrogen receptor modulators, estrogen and progesterone, and calcitonin. Currently, there is one anabolic (bone-building) agent, namely parathyroid hormone.

Bisphosphonates, such as alendronate, risedronate, and ibandronate, are the most commonly used agents to prevent fractures related to osteoporosis. These drugs increase bone strength and reduce fracture by 50%. Both risedronate and alendronate have been shown to reduce fractures in the spine, in the hip, and in other sites. They are available in a once-a-week formulation. Ibandronate is a newer medication in the same class and has been Food and Drug Administration (FDA) approved for preventing and treating postmenopausal osteoporosis. Studies have shown that ibandronate decreases fractures in the spine and prevents fractures in the hip in severely osteoporotic women. This medication is available in a once-a-month formulation.

Selective estrogen receptor modulators such as raloxifene have been used for the treatment and prevention of osteoporosis. They have been shown to increase the bone strength in the spine and to prevent fractures in the spine only. These medications have been associated with hot flashes and increased number of clots in the leg.

Calcitonin, a medication that has been given in nasal form, may provide convenience, but only one major clinical trial has shown its benefit. Calcitonin has been approved for the treatment of osteoporosis, but due to the lack of potency, most health care providers do not use this agent as a first-line medication.

Synthetic parathyroid hormone (teriparatide) is a relatively new injectable medication used for the treatment of osteoporosis. This medication has been shown to build bone and prevent fracture in women with osteoporosis. A black box warning in the package insert states that teriparatide, Forteo's active ingredient, was given to rats and that some rats subsequently developed osteosarcoma, a bone cancer; and that it is not known whether humans treated with Forteo likewise have a higher risk. This medication may provide benefit to patients with severe osteoporosis or individuals who fail on bisphosphonates. Its cost, as well as and the fact that it must be injected daily, limits its use.

—*Rajib K. Bhattacharya*

See also Calcium Disorders of Aging; Complementary and Alternative Medicine; Fractures in Older Adults; Gait Disorders

Further Readings and References

Office of the Surgeon General. *Bone Health and Osteoporosis: A Report of the Surgeon General.* Washington, DC: Government Printing Office; 2004.

Rosen CJ. Postmenopausal osteoporosis. *N Engl J Med.* 2005;353:595–603.

Outcome and Assessment Information Set (OASIS)

The Outcome and Assessment Information Set (OASIS) is a set of data items designed to enable the systematic rigorous measurement of home health care patient outcomes. The data set was developed during the 1990s by a University of Colorado research team funded by the Centers for Medicare and Medicaid Services (CMS), the New York State Department of Health, and the Robert Wood Johnson Foundation. National panels of clinicians, administrators, and researchers participated in item selection, and extensive empirical testing was conducted. In 1999, the CMS mandated the collection of OASIS data by all Medicare-certified home health agencies for adult (age 18 years and older) nonmaternity Medicare and Medicaid patients. Selected items from the OASIS were incorporated into the home health resource groups (HHRGs) for the prospective payment system for home care in October 2000.

OASIS data are collected at the start of each home health episode, at every 60 days thereafter, and at the end of the episode (defined as discharge or admission to an inpatient facility). The OASIS items were designed to be integrated into an agency's routine patient assessment. The start-of-care OASIS contains 71 items covering demographics and patient history (13 items), living arrangements (2 items), supportive assistance (4 items), sensory status (5 items), integumentary status (13 items), respiratory status (2 items), elimination status (5 items), neurological/emotional/behavioral status (7 items), functional status (activities of daily living [ADLs] and instrumental activities of daily living [IADLs], 14 items), medication (3 items), equipment management (2 items), and therapy need (1 item).

The primary purpose of OASIS data collection is to measure patient outcomes, which are central to home health agency efforts to improve quality. An outcome is defined as a change in a patient attribute (e.g., ambulation/locomotion) between two points in time, specifically the beginning and the end of a patient's episode. OASIS data currently are used to derive three types of outcome measures: improvement outcomes, stabilization outcomes, and utilization outcomes. A patient improves when the scale value for the OASIS item shows that the patient is less dependent at discharge than at start of care (i.e., the scale value at discharge is lower). If the patient is at the most independent or "healthiest" extreme of the scale at the start of care (e.g., a value of 0 for the ambulation/locomotion item), it is impossible to improve and therefore the measure is not defined for the patient. When aggregated to the agency level, "improved in ambulation/locomotion" is the percentage of a home health care agency's patients who improve in ambulation/locomotion based on the start of care and discharge OASIS data.

Stabilization outcomes are similar to improvement outcomes but measure "nonworsening"; that is, the patient's condition either improves or stays the same. Stabilization occurs when the patient's discharge OASIS item is at the same scale value as, or at a lower scale value than, the scale value at the start of care. (Because stabilization measures nonworsening, patients at the most dependent scale value at the start of care cannot worsen and therefore are excluded.) Utilization outcomes are measures that serve as proxy indicators of a patient's health status. The three utilization outcomes currently obtained from OASIS data are acute care hospitalization, discharge from home health care to the community, and emergent care.

These outcome measures are used for outcome-based quality improvement (OBQI), which starts with periodic outcome reports for each Medicare-certified home health agency generated by the CMS. The outcome reports consist of 41 outcomes: 26 improvement, 12 stabilization, and 3 utilization. Currently, 30 outcomes are adjusted for differences in patient characteristics (i.e., risk factors) that have been shown to affect outcomes independently of the care provided. For example, urinary incontinence, obesity, and orthopedic conditions are risk factors for improvement in ambulation/locomotion. In the reports, an agency's risk-adjusted outcome rates are compared with the national rates (adjusting for the agency's case mix so that the agency is treated fairly in the comparison). For the 11 outcomes that are not risk adjusted—termed *descriptive outcomes*—the reference values are national means. The outcome reports also provide each agency with a comparison of its current and prior year's outcomes, adjusting for changes in patient risk factors for the agency between the two periods. Under the OBQI approach, agencies use the outcome reports to select target outcomes for focused improvement efforts. An agency's report for the next year indicates the results of its efforts. National and New York State demonstrations during the late 1990s showed that home health agencies successfully improved outcomes under the OBQI approach. Quality improvement organizations (QIOs) now assist agencies seeking to improve performance. To enable consumers and others (e.g., hospital discharge planners) to compare the outcome performances of home health agencies, 10 of the 41 outcomes are available to the general public on the Home Health Compare website as part of the CMS Home Health Quality Initiative (www.cms.hhs.gov/quality/hhqi).

—*Robert E. Schlenker and Andrew M. Kramer*

See also Activities of Daily Living and Instrumental Activities of Daily Living; Assisted Living; Home Care; Institutional Care; Long-Term Care

Further Readings and References

Hittle DF, Shaughnessy PW, Crisler KS, et al. A study of reliability and burden of home health assessment using OASIS. *Home Health Care Serv Q.* 2003;22(4):43–63.

Shaughnessy PW, Hittle DF, Crisler KS, et al. Improving patient outcomes of home health care: Findings from two demonstration trials of outcome-based quality improvement. *J Am Geriatr Soc.* 2002;50:1354–1364.

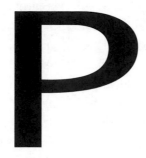

PACIFIC ISLANDER AMERICANS

See ASIAN AND PACIFIC ISLANDER AMERICANS

PAIN

Pain is an unpleasant sensory and emotional experience that is among the most complex of human experiences. It affects an estimated 65 million Americans and has varied psychological, physical, and social consequences such as sleep disturbance, physical disability, anxiety, and depression. The American Pain Society reports that pain costs approximately $100 billion annually in medical expenses and lost workdays.

Pain has traditionally been defined as a physiological response to disease and tissue damage, and it is often classified into different categories based on its origin: nociceptive (tissue damage or inflammation), neuropathic (nerve damage), and mixed or unspecified (unknown causes or a combination of nociceptive and neuropathic). Yet these categorizations do not encompass the social, environmental, and cultural factors that influence the pain experience. Myriad psychological factors affect pain perception regardless of the extent of tissue or nerve damage. For example, depression, anxiety, and personality can significantly affect the perception and experience of pain. This clearly demonstrates that pain can be biological in origin yet influenced by psychological factors.

Pain can also be categorized as acute (shorter in duration, often resulting from an identifiable disease or injury) or chronic (persistent and extending beyond the usual recovery period for an illness or injury). Muscle and lower back pain are the most common causes of acute pain and are the primary reasons why individuals seek medical care. Lower back problems, arthritis, repetitive stress injuries, phantom limb sensation, and diabetic neuropathy are common causes of chronic pain. The pain experience is subjective and contingent on several factors, including history of current illness, duration of medical condition, type of pain (acute or chronic), location, number of painful days, variability of daily pain, physiological changes, cultural background, and sociodemographic factors (e.g., gender, age).

With advancing age, individuals are more likely to suffer from painful medical conditions. Approximately 20% to 58% of community-dwelling adults over 65 years of age and 49% to 83% of nursing home residents report some degree of pain. Osteoarthritis, rheumatoid arthritis (and other bone and joint disorders), osteoporosis, back problems, cancer, diabetes, and herpes zoster are common painful syndromes affecting adults over 50 years of age. The presence of these chronic conditions in older adults is widespread and can result in depression, anxiety, poor quality of life, decreased socialization, sleep disturbance, immobility, increased health care costs and use, cognitive dysfunction, and malnutrition.

The physical and psychological outcomes of pain require a multidimensional approach to assessment and treatment. This comprehensive plan should include a medical history, a physical examination, a review of all laboratory and diagnostic tests, and an assessment using a standard pain scale. Specific approaches have been identified as effective methods to assess pain in older adults: self-report psychometric measures, behavioral–observational methods, and third-party proxy ratings. *Self-report psychometric measures,* such as single-item scales (numeric rating and pictorial pain faces scales), demonstrate good reliability when used in older adults whose cognitive functioning ranges from intact to mildly or moderately impaired. Pain assessment questionnaires are also effective in that they provide clinicians with invaluable information about individuals' pain experience that can be useful in determining the most appropriate means of pain management. Difficulties with verbal communication, multiple chronic medical illnesses, physical impairments, vision or hearing loss, and cognitive impairment can interfere with standard pain assessment. Thus, the *behavioral–observation* approach can be particularly useful when attempting to assess the pain experience in older adults with these conditions. The standardized procedure in this type of assessment has been to observe the frequency of pain-related behaviors such as sighing, rubbing, and grimacing. *Third-party proxy rating* is another approach in which pain is assessed by medical staff, caregivers, and others who can provide information about the pain experience of older adults. Other mechanisms of assessing pain in older adults include examining how pain limits physical functioning and patterns of health care use. Despite the utility of these methods, it has been suggested that untreated pain results in unnecessary suffering, increased health care expenditures, unproductive and lost workdays, and longer hospital stays.

Older adults are at an increased risk for undertreatment of pain. This disparate treatment can be traced to several myths and beliefs that have plagued the general population's knowledge regarding older adults and pain. This may explain why the majority of pain treatments have been tested primarily in younger individuals. Despite this finding, there is a wide range of treatment options, such as pharmacological, surgical, behavioral, and physical therapies, that are just as effective in older adults. Specifically, the treatment or control of acute pain depends on the treatment of the disease itself along with short-term administration of analgesic drugs. Treatment of chronic pain, however, usually requires a multidimensional approach of nonpharmacological strategies (e.g., biofeedback, physical therapy, prayer, meditation) and analgesic drug treatment. Multidisciplinary pain management facilities may also be beneficial in treating more complex chronic pain problems, particularly when more conventional methods of treatment prove to be ineffective. When treating chronic pain patients, it may be necessary to modify standard treatment program procedures to accommodate the needs of older adults. Such modifications include setting age-relevant treatment goals, acknowledging comorbidities and their influence on treatment decisions, allowing more time for assessment and treatment instructions, and providing an adequate social environment for older adults. Overall, older adults who experience pain should be observed regularly for improvement, deterioration, or complications related to treatment.

Pain is a serious public health concern, and the assessment, treatment, and management of pain in the geriatric population should be a priority. Future work should be directed at developing models that assess how social, behavioral, cultural, and environmental factors influence the experience of pain in varied populations. More important, clinical treatment needs to focus more on means to prevent and treat pain and to ameliorate its potential impact on physical health, psychological functioning, and quality of life in older adults, particularly those from special populations such as the frail, those from diverse racial/ethnic groups, and the cognitively impaired.

—*Tamara A. Baker*

See also Arthritis and Other Rheumatic Diseases; Ethnicity and Race; Osteoporosis; Quality of Life

Further Readings and References

Farrell MM, Gibson SJ. Psychosocial aspects of pain in older people. In: Dworkin RH, Breitbart WS, eds. *Psychosocial*

Aspects of Pain: A Handbook for Health Care Providers. Seattle, Wash: IASP Press; 2004:495–518. Progress in Pain Research and Management, Vol. 27.

Ferrell BA, Ferrell BR. Principles of pain management in older people. *Compr Ther.* 1991;17(8):53–58.

Green CR, Anderson KO, Baker TA, et al. The unequal burden of pain: Confronting racial and ethnic disparities in pain. *Pain Med.* 2003;4:277–294.

Green CR, Baker TA, Smith EM, Sato Y. The effect of race in older adults presenting for chronic pain management: A comparative study of Black and White Americans. *J Pain.* 2003;4(2):82–90.

Tait RC. Assessment of pain and response to treatment in older adults. In: Lichtenberg PA, ed. *Handbook on Assessment in Clinical Gerontology.* New York: John Wiley; 1999:555–584.

Turk DC, Akiko O. Psychological factors in chronic pain: Evolution and revolution. *J Consult Clin Psychol.* 2002; 70:678–690.

PALLIATIVE CARE AND THE END OF LIFE

The term *palliative care* was coined by Canadian urological surgeon Balfour Mount in 1974. Mount visited St. Christopher's Hospice in England before opening one of the first hospice programs in Canada, and he found the word *hospice* to be objectionable to some Canadians. To members of the French Canadian culture, the word implies a place of last resort for the poor and other disenfranchised members of society rather than a place that provides care and comfort for dying patients and their families. Mount came up with *palliative care,* a term considered as acceptable to both English-speaking and French-speaking Canadians.

The World Health Organization defines palliative care as improving the quality of life of patients with life-threatening illnesses and their families. Pain has been a major contributor to the low quality of life for some patients facing imminent death, and proponents of the palliative care approach developed expertise over the years in how to manage pain.

Managing pain at the end of life can include administering traditional analgesics such as aspirin, ibuprofen, codeine, and morphine. In addition, counseling, psychological and spiritual support, relaxation techniques, music, and imagery all are components of palliative care.

The experience of pain is subjective and to some degree defies description. Using pain assessment tools, especially with children and nonverbal adults, has been helpful in quantifying individuals' pain and, in turn, in finding more optimal pain management. Such tools include the Abbey Pain Scale and the Face, Legs, Activity, Cry, Consolability pain assessment tool.

Pain might not be treated effectively because physicians do not prescribe adequate doses of opioids and nurses do not give patients all of the doses that physicians prescribe. Physician and nurse reluctance to prescribe and give sufficient opioids to relieve patients' pain is attributed to their fear of contributing to patients' physical and psychological dependence, increased physical tolerance, and ultimate addiction to the prescribed analgesic medications. Their reluctance also stems from knowledge of the side effects that some medications can cause, including the unintended hastening of the patient's death—the most dreaded fear of physicians and nurses. However, controlling pain, in spite of the serious side effects, is ethically justified through the "rule of double effect."

The rule of double effect distinguishes between intended effects and expected effects. This important distinction allows practitioners to prescribe needed palliative care medications to alleviate pain and suffering without carrying the moral burden of having caused the death of the patient. The key question in such a situation is as follows: What is the *intent* of prescribing the dose of medicine that may prove fatal to the patient? If the intent is to kill the patient, thereby alleviating the pain, then prescribing the medication cannot be ethically justifiable. However, if the intent is to relieve the patient's pain and suffering, and death is hastened as a result of administering the medication, then the action is justifiable. Although death may be expected, it is not intended. Some physicians who oppose euthanasia and physician-assisted suicide (PAS) may hesitate to use an opioid analgesic such as morphine to control the pain and suffering of dying patients because of its potential to hasten death. Double effect is an important and effective tool to justify its use in the care of dying patients.

Palliative care is distinguished from euthanasia and PAS. *Euthanasia* is a term that originated from the Greek (*eu* [good] + *thanatos* [death]). It is the active termination of someone else's life to end his or her suffering. Euthanasia is not legal in the United States, but it became legal under certain circumstances in 2001 in the Netherlands and in 2002 in Belgium. In 1992, Edmund Pellegrino described PAS and euthanasia as violent acts that disguise themselves as good acts committed to achieve a result that is in the patient's best interest.

The end of life literature is replete with justification for PAS when the suffering is intolerable and death is inevitable. In a landmark 1991 article describing a case of PAS, Timothy Quill narrated his involvement in the death of his patient Diane by prescribing the medication she needed to commit suicide. PAS is now a legal medical intervention in the state of Oregon.

Although opponents of PAS fear that legalizing this practice would result in abuses and premature deaths of healthy individuals, the Oregon experience has not supported this fear. During the 8 years following 1997, when PAS became legal in Oregon, a total of 208 patients died after ingesting medications prescribed by their physicians. A total of 64,706 died during the same 7 years of the same underlying diseases. Oregon has stringent age, residency, decisional capacity, medical and psychological assessment, diagnosis, and reporting requirements before a patient is eligible for PAS. Quill did not advocate PAS for all patients who request it, but he recommended listening to the patient, being compassionate, promising to be there until the end, being honest, and approaching end of life suffering with an open heart and an open mind. The Oregon experience supports the research that people request PAS to maintain control over their lives. Oregon physicians report that 87% of their patients cite losing their autonomy and right to self-determination at the end of life as a concern.

One means of maintaining control over health care decision making at the end of life is through advance health care planning. This approach includes completing advance directives. This general term refers to giving family and health care providers one's directives in advance before decisional capacity is impaired. The two main types of directives are the living will and the designation of a health care decision maker. The living will is an instructional document that specifies which treatments the patient is willing to endure and which treatments would not be tolerated. The appointment of a decision maker merely designates an entrusted individual—a family member or a friend—to take over the decision-making authority when the patient's decisional capacity is no longer intact. These directives, when written in clear language specifying what is considered as intolerable to the patient, can maintain the person's control over end of life interventions. The living will can include written wishes addressing cardiopulmonary resuscitation, mechanical ventilation, dialysis, administration of artificial hydration and nutrition through tube feeding, use of antibiotics, chemotherapy and radiation therapy, surgery, or any other medical intervention. The responsibility of the designated health care decision maker is to advocate for the patient and ensure that physicians write "do not resuscitate" (DNR) orders when appropriate and that unwanted interventions are withheld or withdrawn when they are no longer consistent with the patient's previously expressed wishes. Following patients' end of life care wishes is legal in all 50 states, and applying advance directives is not considered to constitute either euthanasia or PAS.

—*Hana Osman*

See also Advocacy Organizations; Death, Dying, and Hospice Care; Drug Underuse; Ethical Issues and Aging; Pain; Suicide and the Elderly

Further Readings and References

Abbey J, Piller N, De Bellis A, et al. The Abbey Pain Scale: A 1-minute numerical indicator for people with end-stage dementia. *Intl J Palliat Nurs.* 2004;10(1):6–13.

Beauchamp TL, Childress JF. *Principles of Biomedical Ethics.* 5th ed. New York: Oxford University Press; 2001.

Materstvedt LJ, Clark D, Ellershaw J, et al. Euthanasia and physician-assisted suicide: A view from an EAPC ethics task force. *Palliat Med.* 2003;17:97–101.

Pellegrino ED. Doctors must not kill. *J Clin Ethics.* 1992; 8:95–102.

Quill T. Death and dignity: A case of individualized decision making. *N Engl J Med.* 1991;324:691–694.

Voepel-Lewis T, Merke S, Tait AR, Trzcinka A, Malviya S. The reliability and validity of the Face, Legs, Activity, Cry, Consolability observational tool as a measure of pain in children with cognitive impairment. *Anesth Analg.* 2002;95:1224–1229.

PARANOIA

See SCHIZOPHRENIA, PARANOIA, AND DELUSIONAL DISORDERS

PATIENT SAFETY

Patient safety is defined by the Institute of Medicine as freedom from injury associated with accidents or medical errors that can occur across the life span. Joshua A. Perper wrote in 1994 that the most vulnerable patients, who are likely to experience the most frequent and severe injuries, include (a) elderly in poor health; (b) persons with chronic disabling conditions or disabilities, and (c) persons hospitalized for long periods of time. Often, a frail elderly patient "fits" into each of these three high-risk categories, increasing risk exponentially. The purpose of this entry is to elucidate the challenge of promoting patient safety for vulnerable elderly populations, depicting unique hazard conditions, and suggesting safety defenses to prevent adverse outcomes.

Challenge of Promoting Patient Safety in Elderly

Patient safety emerged as a national health care priority in 2000, when the Institute of Medicine report, *To Err Is Human,* was published. Prior to this, errors and adverse events were common but fairly invisible to the public. The Institute of Medicine emphasized that patient safety was a serious problem crossing all health care facilities and that medical errors occurred even in good hospitals with conscientious care providers. A key finding was that medical errors or adverse events were not the fault of individual practitioners but rather a result of the process of health care. The goal of patient safety involves the redesign of patient care processes to make them more resistant to error occurrence (error reduction) and more accommodating to its consequences (error containment), as noted by Patrice L. Splath in 2000.

Although not all medical errors cause injuries, accidental injuries are common in elderly and can be associated with medical errors. The Institute of Medicine states that a medical error is the failure of a planned action (e.g., diagnosis, treatment) to be completed as intended and/or the selection of a wrong treatment plan. Medical errors can contribute to the occurrence of adverse events. An adverse event is an unintentional error that results in negative consequences for the patient such as a drug reaction, a hip fracture, or a pressure ulcer. Studies of adverse events in health care reveal that approximately 70% of all adverse events are preventable. Of the remaining 30% of adverse events, 24% are typically unavoidable and the remaining 6% are viewed as "potentially" preventable, as noted by Lucian Leape in 1994. Regardless of the etiology of the adverse events, associated injuries result in significant cost, including morbidity, mortality, loss of function, and diminished quality of life.

Risk Factors/Hazard Conditions

Patient risk factors are the most obvious contributor to medical errors and accidents, especially in geriatric patients. These risk factors include diminished reserves due to normal aging changes as well as type and severity of illness or disability, medications (changes in pharmacokinetics and pharmacodynamics in older individuals), multiple morbidities, and psychosocial factors (e.g., lack of compliance, depression). Patient risk factors can facilitate or impede safety barriers and have a direct effect on situational risk factors. Understanding the epidemiology related to adverse events in subpopulations is critical for identifying patients at high risk, designing models for predicting adverse events, designing screening tools, and designing primary and secondary prevention strategies. For example, we know from research that the risk of a person falling increases dramatically as the number of risk factors increases, ranging from a probability of .27 for those with no risk factors or one risk factor to .78 for those with four or more risk factors. In a 1996 study by T. V. Nguyen and colleagues, the probability of fractures ranged from 0 for those with no identified predictors to 0.129 for those with all six predictors present. The injury susceptibility in older adults stems from a high prevalence of comorbid diseases (e.g., osteoporosis, neurological problems), increased likelihood of medication side effects, and age-related decline (e.g., slowed reflexes), all of which can make even a relatively mild fall dangerous. Risk factors can also be categorized as nonmodifiable (e.g., age, gender) or modifiable (e.g., deconditioning), allowing the identification of clinical interventions to decrease risk such as review and modification of risky medication regimens, exercise regimens, smoking cessation, weight loss, and environmental interventions. They also can be categorized as intrinsic (related to normal aging changes, functional status, and comorbidities) or extrinsic (outside of the patient; i.e., related to the environment and medication use).

In addition to the unique risk factors for each patient, we cannot exclude risks inherent in the health care delivery system. Normal accident theory posits that accidents are inevitable and that the likelihood of accidents increases based on complexity in health care organizations combined with the necessary interdependency among providers to provide health care services, as noted by Charles Perrow and John Langton in 1994. In any given health care encounter (inpatient, outpatient, home based, or nursing home), many different sources of potential error interact with patient risk factors to produce injury to the patient.

Health care providers commit errors. The characteristics of providers, such as years of experience, expertise in geriatrics, type of training, and familiarity with patients, can make a difference in the risk to a patient. Other factors, including fatigue and memory lapse, contribute to provider error. Cognitive scientists provide a way to identify and understand provider risk factors for adverse events. These sciences (based on a variety of disciplines such as artificial intelligence, neuroscience, philosophy, and psychology) focus on perception, learning, memory, language, concept formation, problem solving, and thinking as factors that contribute to errors and adverse events.

Although not unique to geriatric health care settings, medical errors are often blamed on the health care provider (also known as "active failures"), but in fact many of these errors are the result of delayed consequences of administrative decisions about the design, maintenance, operation, or organization (known as "latent failures"). This means that managers and administrators, who have no direct contact with patients, can create stressful working conditions for direct care providers that ultimately compromise patient safety. Latent failures include hazards in the built environment, training and selection of staff, staff scheduling, information management, and resource allocation. Health care administrators can make bad decisions that create risk for patients. For example, chaotic implementation of a change in practice, patient scheduling, or another key process can make the patient vulnerable to errors. W. A. Wagenaar and colleagues wrote in 1990 that equipment in poor repair, inadequate staff coverage, and excessive workload demands are other examples of latent failures that set providers up to fail no matter how dedicated they are or how hard they try to provide safe care. These latent failures may lie dormant for a long time until activated by more apparent actions in the system, when suddenly a medical error will occur. James T. Reason wrote in 1990 that the number of latent factors embedded in organizational systems can align at random intervals, causing injuries. Moreover, the link between latent risk factors and an error is more difficult to prove than is the more obvious link between direct patient care provided by a health care professional.

Safety Barriers

Efforts to promote patient safety must necessarily focus on modifying patient risk factors and limiting the effects of latent system failures. These actions are supported by high reliability theory, which states that errors and adverse events can be prevented through organizational design and management decisions and actions, as noted by Karlene H. Roberts and Denise M. Rousseau in 1989.

Safety barriers are forces that intervene to minimize the impact of latent errors and to prevent errors from progressing to errors with bad outcomes. Also, safety barriers can be planned interventions that target identified risk factors, thereby reducing the likelihood of adverse events. Flaws in the system safety barriers can almost always be demonstrated; however, interventions to prevent adverse events involve designs to create or strengthen safety defense barriers. Safety barriers can be weak or strong and multidimensional or focused, and they involve the ability to absorb the effect of, or prevent, active failures.

Patient safety defenses protect patients by changing modifiable patient risk factors through psycho-educational efforts ultimately to reduce the occurrence and severity of adverse events. Examples include health promotion programs targeting health-related behaviors such as exercise, smoking cessation, and weight loss. Patient-focused strategies are supported by a range of social–psychological theories such as social learning theory, the transtheoretical model of change, and the theory of planned behavior.

Humans are error prone. Provider safety defenses protect patients by overcoming human limitations imposed by memory, fatigue, practice variations, complex processes, and provider–patient communication. Examples of patient safety defenses include clinical tools such as standardized protocols, clinical practice guidelines, and simplification of complex processes through using algorithms or decision trees and limiting call duty hours. Provider safety defenses are supported by diffusion theory that addresses the spread of new knowledge or innovation to a defined population, over time, and through specific channels as well as by multidimensional models for implementing evidence-based practice.

Technology safety defenses protect patients by overcoming technology limitations imposed by equipment or lack of proper equipment. Technology is often designed to be protective of patients (e.g., use of hip protectors to prevent hip fractures), but it also can impose risk. New technology introduced in a chaotic fashion often results in unintentional errors and injuries. Staff members often look for shortcuts in using technology (i.e., "work-arounds"), and these can increase risk. Individuals must have the knowledge and skills to use technology safely; otherwise, it could pose additional safety risks.

Organizational safety defenses protect patients by reshaping organizational structures and processes most likely to contribute to medical errors or patient accidents. One of the most researched organizational safety defenses is nurse staffing levels. Other common organizational safety defenses include error reporting systems and workload.

Conclusions

Efforts to create health care environments that promote patient safety include one of five proactive approaches in the ways patient care delivery systems are designed. Optimally, systems of care should be designed to (a) eliminate errors, (b) reduce the numbers of errors, (c) catch errors before harm occurs and thereby eliminate injuries, (d) contain errors to mitigate adverse outcomes associated with them, and (e) review errors and learn from them. We can learn a lot about how to make health care safer by learning from other high-risk industries such as aviation. Aviation has several decades of experience in designing approaches to create high-reliability solutions. Furthermore, human factors engineering and cognitive–social psychology are two disciplines that hold great promise for addressing patient safety issues.

Creating a culture of safety is a necessary step toward patient safety. There is no universally agreed-on definition of a safety culture, yet many have written on the topic and described attributes of a positive culture of safety. These attributes include leadership that allocates resources for improving safety, public leadership support for reducing errors and improving patient safety, reporting systems that are nonpunitive and that create an atmosphere where one learns from one's mistakes, accountability at all levels of an organization, and open communications about errors. Culture of safety is learned and therefore can be changed. Culture is multifaceted and includes behaviors, attitudes, values, artifacts (e.g., health care technology and equipment), language, social interaction (e.g., communication), social organization (e.g., structures of hospitals and health care workforce, policies, roles of individuals in the organization), and material life (e.g., how resources and funding are allocated to safety initiatives).

There is a national call for action to change the culture of health care addressing the following key points: (a) recognition that health care is a high-risk industry, (b) support for a "blame-free" environment that encourages providers at all levels to report unintended errors and identify root causes of errors, (c) leaders that value safety with the same level of enthusiasm as they value productivity/efficiency, and (d) support for actively redesigning safety hazards. More research related to patient safety in health care is needed, especially targeting vulnerable patient populations, particularly the frail elderly given the current demographic shifts of individuals over 85 years of age being the fastest-growing segment of the U.S. population.

—*Audrey Nelson and Tatjana Bulat*

See also Advocacy Organizations; Caregiving; Ethical Issues and Aging; Mobility Assessment

Further Readings and References

Institute of Medicine. *To Err Is Human.* Kohn LT, Corrigan JM, Donaldson MS, eds. Washington, DC: National Academy Press; 2000.

Leape LL. The preventability of medical injury. In: Bogner MS, ed. *Human Error in Medicine.* Hillsdale, NJ: Lawrence Erlbaum; 1994:13–26.

Nguyen TV, Eisman JA, Kelly PJ, Sambrook PN. Risk factors for osteoporotic fractures in elderly men. *Am J Epidemiol.* 1996;144:255–263.

Perper JA. Life-threatening and fatal therapeutic misadventures. In: Bogner MS, ed. *Human Error in Medicine.* Hillsdale, NJ: Lawrence Erlbaum; 1994:27–52.

Perrow C, Langton J. The limits of safety: The enhancement of a theory of accidents. *J Conting Mgmt.* 1994;2:212–220.

Reason JT. *Human Error.* New York: Cambridge University Press; 1990.

Reason J. *Managing the Risks of Organizational Accidents.* Brookfield, VT: Ashgate; 1990.

Roberts KH, Rousseau DM. Research in nearly failure-free, high reliability systems: Having the bubble. *IEEE Trans.* 1989;36:132–139.

Spath PL, ed. *Error Reduction in Health Care.* San Francisco: Jossey–Bass; 2000.

Wagenaar WA, Hudson PT, Reason JY. Cognitive failures and accidents. *Appl Cogn Psychol.* 1990;4:273–294.

Performance Measures of Physical Function

During recent years, performance measures of physical functioning have been used increasingly for the assessment of older adults in both clinical and epidemiological settings. One of the main reasons for their increasing popularity among clinicians and gerontological researchers is that they provide an objective and standardized method of assessment in an area that has traditionally relied nearly exclusively on self- and proxy-reported measures. Furthermore, the evaluation of other functional domains, such as cognitive function, vision, and hearing, has long required the use of both self-report or proxy-report of functional difficulty and standardized testing for the objective assessment of decrements in functional status.

Physical performance measures can be defined as assessment tools that objectively evaluate a particular aspect of physical function by asking an individual to perform a standardized task that is evaluated using objective predetermined criteria. For most of these tests, performance level is assessed by timing the task alone, timing the task performed over a predetermined distance, or counting repetitions. A growing number of clinical and epidemiological studies conducted during recent years demonstrate that physical performance measures represent a valuable source of information for the comprehensive evaluation of older persons in the research setting and may be an important addition to the health care of older people. Performance measures can provide information about functional problems not reported accurately by older adults or their families. They have been shown to provide objective information across a broad spectrum of physical function, including the upper end of the spectrum, thereby assessing the full range of performance better than self-report measures. There is evidence that performance measures predict several relevant health outcomes such as institutionalization, health services use, hospitalization, falls, incident disability, and mortality. Finally, they show improvement in response to lifestyle interventions such as exercise and show decline in response to events such as hospitalization and new health problems and conditions.

The theoretical pathway leading from disease to disability proposed by Saad Z. Nagi and the Institute of Medicine, and later expanded by Lois Verbrugge and Allan Jette, provides a useful framework to identify the different functional domains that can be assessed using objective performance measures. According to Nagi, the disablement process can be viewed as a sequence of steps in which disease leads to impairments (defined as dysfunctions or structural abnormalities in specific body systems), which in turn lead to functional limitations (defined as an individual's limitations at performing basic physical and cognitive tasks), which then lead to further restrictions or inability to perform socially defined roles within a determined social and cultural environment (disability). Objective measures of physical performance may be used for the assessment of impairments, functional limitations, or disability, but most are indicators of functional limitations. Because they were originally developed without being specifically linked to the steps along the Nagi disablement pathway, several of the physical performance tools currently used combine elements that assess not only functional limitations but also physical impairments and disability. Functional limitations and disability represent different behaviors rather than different ways of measuring a behavior, and both can be measured using either performance measures or self-report tools. When selecting a measurement tool, it is the content and purpose of the assessment rather than the measurement technique that determines which one of the steps along the Nagi pathway is being evaluated.

The Nagi pathway also provides a framework for the selection of assessment instruments. When assessing functional limitations, if only one single physical performance measure can be included, the best choice would be a gait speed test. When a more comprehensive assessment is needed, it must be decided whether a tool that provides a multidimensional approach targeting not only functional limitations but also impairments and disability is required. A more focused battery, such as one targeting upper or lower body extremities, should be selected when the factor(s) under study or the intervention being evaluated has a hypothesized impact on any of these specific areas. A large number of individual tests and batteries of physical performance measures have been developed over the past 40 years. Selected physical performance tools currently used for the assessment of physical function among older adults are described briefly in what follows.

Selected Physical Performance Tests

Purdue Pegboard Test

The Purdue Pegboard Test is a performance test that measures two kinds of upper body activities: (1) gross movements of hands, fingers, and arms and (2) "fingertip" dexterity assessed with an assembly task. This test, which was originally developed for the selection of employees for industrial jobs, has been used extensively in clinical geriatrics and rehabilitation centers.

Gait Assessment Tests

The ability to walk is a critical element of daily life and an important component of most basic activities of daily living (ADLs) and instrumental activities of daily living (IADLs). Mobility functioning can be assessed using tests that evaluate an individual's ability to walk under different conditions and different distances. Several standardized walk tests have been developed and used widely in aging research for the assessment of mobility disability, walking endurance, effect of exercise training, and cardiopulmonary functional capacity. These physical performance measurement tools can be classified based on the specific distance (short-distance walks [4 to 10 meters] vs. long-distance walks [400 meters]), the pace at which the test is performed (usual vs. fast), or whether there are specific time limits for completion of the test (6-minute walk test). Mobility function can also be assessed with the use of complex walking tests in which a challenge task is added to a basic standard walk test with the purpose of evaluating an individual's ability to adapt gait to environmental challenges similar to those that are encountered routinely during daily activities. Examples of complex walk tests include walking over obstacles, walking while talking, walking while picking up a small object, and walking while carrying a large, light, or heavy package. Walk tests have been shown to be predictors of incident disability, morbidity, institutionalization, and mortality.

Short Physical Performance Battery

The Short Physical Performance Battery (SPPB), originally developed for the Established Populations for Epidemiologic Studies of the Elderly (EPESE) project, is a comprehensive functional measure that provides a physical performance score (range = 0 to 12) by aggregating an individual's performance in a short timed walking test conducted at usual speed (4 meters), five repeated chair stands, and a set of standing balance tests. Each individual performance test is timed and scored on a scale from 0 to 4. A summary performance score is created by summing the individual categorical scores for the walking, balance, and chair stand tests. The cutoff points for the SPPB are based on normative data developed from observations on more than 5,000 older persons in the EPESE project. This battery has been administered in several population studies and has been found to predict mortality, institutionalization, and health care use in older populations. In addition, among older nondisabled persons, SPPB scores were found to consistently identify those individuals at risk for the development of ADL and mobility disability. The battery is now being used in clinical trials to identify candidates who have functional limitations and as an outcome for clinical trials.

Timed Up and Go

The timed Up and Go is a short test of basic mobility skills commonly used for the assessment of older adults in both clinical and community settings. This performance test measures the time taken by a person to stand up from a standard chair, walk a distance of 3 meters at a usual pace, turn, walk back to the chair, and sit down again. The person is allowed to use walking aids, but no physical assistance is provided. It has been shown that time to complete this test is correlated with self-report of mobility function. Older adults who are able to complete the timed Up and Go test in less than 20 seconds have been shown to be independently mobile, have higher scores on the Berg Balance Scale, and have a gait speed adequate for community mobility (0.5 meters per second). In contrast, older adults requiring at least 30 seconds to complete this test tend to need assistance for the performance of ADLs, require assistive devices for ambulation, and have lower scores on the Berg Balance Test.

Physical Performance Test

The Physical Performance Test (PPT) is designed to measure older adults' ability to use upper and lower extremities in everyday activities and was developed as both a short (7-item) and long (9-item) test. Test items in the short form are timed and scored from 0 (lowest) to 4 (highest): writing a sentence, simulated eating, lifting a book and putting it on a shelf, picking up a small object from the floor, putting on and removing a jacket, turning 360 degrees, and walking 15.2 meters. The long form includes 2 additional items: climbing one flight of stairs and counting the number of flights of stairs an individual is able to ascend. The overall PPT score is obtained by adding the individual item scores. It has been shown that the PPT score predicts institutionalization, risk of falls, and mortality.

Physical performance measures have provided important information in the assessment of older individuals, and their use should continue to expand in both research and clinical applications.

—*Antonia K. Coppin and Jack M. Guralnik*

See also Activities of Daily Living and Instrumental Activities of Daily Living; Disability and the Disablement Process; Geriatric Assessment; Mobility Assessment

Further Readings and References

Guralnik JM, Ferrucci L. Assessing the building blocks of function: Utilizing measures of functional limitation. *Am J Prev Med.* 2003;25:112–121.

Guralnik JM, Simonsick EM, Ferrucci L, et al. A short physical performance battery assessing lower extremity function: Association with self-reported disability and prediction of mortality and nursing home admission. *J Gerontol A Biol Sci Med Sci.* 1994;49:M85–M94.

Nagi SZ. An epidemiology of disability among adults in the United States. *Millbank Mem Fund Qual Health Soc.* 1976;54:439–467.

Podsiadlo D, Richardson S. The timed "Up and Go": A test of basic functional mobility for frail elderly persons. *J Am Geriatr Soc.* 1991;39:142–148.

Reuben DB, Siu AL. An objective measure of physical function of elderly outpatients. The Physical Performance Test. *J Am Geriatr Soc.* 1990;38:1105–1112.

Verbrugge LM, Jette AM. The disablement process. *Soc Sci Med.* 1994, Jan;38(1):1–14.

Periodontal Disease

See Oral Health

Perioperative Issues

Some 50 years ago, surgery was considered to be too risky for elderly patients. Today, centenarians undergo a wide variety of surgical procedures. The development of information regarding the perioperative care of elderly surgical patients is in its infancy; however, there is some information that suggests pathways caring for these patients. Ther word *perioperative* refers to the complete experience surrounding an operative procedure—deciding to have an operation, preparing for surgery, undergoing anesthesia, recovering from the surgery, and getting back to the expected level of function (which may include active rehabilitation).

The principal risk to patients undergoing surgery is not chronological age but rather a combination of physiological age and disease load. A robust 90-year-old may have a relatively low risk from undergoing many surgical procedures, whereas a 65-year-old with disease in one or more systems may be at high risk.

When making a decision to undergo surgery, patients should understand that techniques have evolved rapidly. An impressive example is the treatment of abdominal aortic aneurysms. In the past, this disease, in which the largest artery of the body becomes enlarged and distorted and can burst, thereby causing rapid death, was treated with a very involved open abdomen surgical operation that required days in an intensive care unit (ICU). Currently, the same disease frequently can be treated by passing a replacement tube into the ballooned vessel by passing a very sophisticated device by way of an artery in the groin. The development of such endovascular (operating from inside the blood vessels) techniques require very short recovery times with very little pain, and the patient frequently goes home the following morning. Many procedures in the abdomen are accomplished using laparoscopes; that is, instruments that allow surgeons to operate through three or four small (quarter-inch) holes rather than a long incision in the middle of the belly. These "minimally invasive" techniques appear to have significant benefit for elderly surgical candidates when they can be used safely.

Because getting old and developing illness tend to occur simultaneously, coordinated perioperative care includes paying attention to general medical conditions with the perspective of both assessing function and, where possible, improving or maximizing the function of a particular body system. A general preoperative history and physical examination should indicate whether any additional testing is required. For example, if the patient has congestive heart failure, a circumstance in which the pumping function of the heart is limited, special tests are frequently requested to assess that function. Occasionally, doctors find other medical problems that should be fixed before surgery.

Some sort of anesthesia is required for all surgical procedures. Some procedures, such as removal of lesions of the skin and removal of cataracts (i.e., when the lens of the eye becomes white and the patient cannot see through it), can be performed by using medications called local anesthetics to numb the affected area. The risk of these procedures is very limited. For some procedures, local anesthesia is supplemented with additional drugs to diminish pain and provide sedation. Major procedures require either general anesthesia or a major regional technique. General anesthesia involves the administration of drugs either by direct injection into the blood or by inhalation. From the patient's perspective, the principal feature of general anesthesia is loss of consciousness. Regional anesthesia blocks nerve transmission at different levels. For operations on the lower body, techniques that block the nerves of the spinal cord can be used. Spinal or subarachnoid anesthesia administers local anesthetic agents directly around the lower spinal cord and nerves. It is accomplished by placing a small needle in the back. Spinal anesthesia produces complete numbness and lack of motor control (i.e., the patient cannot move his or her legs) but does not change the patient's level of consciousness. The anesthesia can last from 1 to 6 hours depending on the drugs used. Additional sedation can be administered if necessary. An epidural is a similar technique in which the local anesthetic is administered to the nerves at the space where they leave the spine. This technique is generally done with a small catheter that is left in the epidural space. This allows continuous administration of local anesthetic drugs so that the anesthesia can last as long as needed. Epidural catheters can also be used to provide pain relief after surgery. Although there are very strong advocates for regional anesthetic techniques, multiple studies have failed to demonstrate a significant difference in morbidity or mortality between regional and general anesthesia. Particularly for orthopedic procedures such as hip and knee replacements, the choice between regional and general anesthesia is based on local practice. The risks of anesthesia have decrease markedly over the past few decades. During general anesthesia, the anesthesiologist is responsible for maintaining respirations for the patient because the drugs typically impair breathing. In this regard, local anesthesia with sedation is frequently described as limited and safe because it is not general anesthesia. However, elderly patients are extremely sensitive to anesthetic drugs, so the line between sedation and general anesthesia is difficult to determine. Undertaking a procedure under deep sedation without airway control is not safer than doing so with a planned general anesthetic. There is also a group of regional anesthesia techniques that block nerves in an arm or a leg and can be very effective in providing anesthesia in the operating room and pain relief after surgery.

Following a surgical procedure, the patient goes to a postanesthesia care unit (PACU, still sometimes called the recovery room) or to an ICU. Some procedures are done on an ambulatory basis, meaning that the patient will go home the same day. Advanced age by itself is not a reason to keep a patient in the hospital. Ambulatory PACUs tend to have the patient sit in a chair and frequently invite family members to stay with the patient. More acute PACUs have varying policies. Patients recovering from sedation or general anesthesia may be sleepy. Some may appear to be aware but frequently do not remember things said at this time. Pain control should be a major focus of the recovery room experience.

Pain in the elderly is not substantially different from pain in any other human. Although there are physiological changes associated with age that alter pain perception, they cannot be invoked to explain why a patient should experience substantial pain. There is a general tendency to undertreat pain, particularly in the United States. Elderly patients are particularly prone to receive inadequate pain management. This is partly because all pain regimens are associated with significant side effects. The mainstay of all pain regimens is narcotics—either morphine or its synthetic derivatives. These drugs will come close to eliminating pain if given in sufficient doses. They also cause respiratory depression that can make a person stop breathing completely and die. Most narcotics cause itching and constipation. Many are associated with euphoria and/or delirium. Thus, it is important to give just the right amount of medication at just the right time. Computerized pumps, called patient-controlled analgesia (PCA) pumps, allow individuals to receive pain medication on demand without requiring a nurse to administer the drug. These pumps can be used by most elderly patients so long as they can understand the instructions, which should be explained before the surgery. Family members should never assist a patient by pushing the button for him or her because this can result in a narcotic overdose. On the other hand, more than moderate pain should be unacceptable.

A number of problems commonly occur in elderly patients following major surgery. The amount of fluid administered to elderly patients remains controversial. Intravenous fluids, the bags of water and electrolytes that are administered by intravenous infusion, are severely limited in Europe; however, this practice is not yet popular in the United States. When fluids are administered generously, it is important to be sure that excess fluid does not accumulate in the body. When limited fluid is administered, it is important to be sure that sufficient fluid is present to support proper circulation. Pneumonia is probably the most common complication following surgery in the elderly. The cause of pneumonia is not completely clear, and whether current attempts to get the patient out of bed early and to encourage deep breathing actually decrease the amount of pneumonia is still under consideration.

A particularly distressing complication that appears to be primarily a disease of the elderly is postoperative delirium. Occurring typically 24 to 48 hours after a major operation and following a lucid interval after emergence from anesthesia, delirium is a fluctuating alteration of consciousness. There is a prominent disturbance of attention and reduced clarity of awareness of the environment. Delirium can develop within hours to days and tends to fluctuate during the course of the day such that not all individuals visiting the patient will necessarily observe the same symptoms. Patients may also be disoriented and suffer from perceptual disturbances such as misinterpretations, illusions, and/or even hallucinations. The cause of delirium is unknown; however, coordinated care programs organized by experienced geriatricians have been effective in preventing delirium. The family of a delirious patient may be asked to actively provide orientation points for the patient, including family photos and calendars. Pharmacological treatment is available for agitation associated with delirium. A distinct but possibly related problem has been called postoperative cognitive dysfunction (POCD). POCD refers to certain individuals who show marked deterioration on specific cognitive tests when tested both before and after surgery. The not uncommon complaint that someone is never the same after surgery may be related to POCD. POCD has been noted in high numbers of individuals undergoing cardiac surgery and in lower numbers following noncardiac surgery. The status of POCD as a diagnostic and clinical entity has yet to be established.

Skin breakdown and the development of decubitus ulcers (bed sores) should be a completely preventable complication of hospitalization in elderly surgical patients. Observation for skin breakdown and aggressive treatment of wounds are important to avoid serious prolongation of hospitalization.

Full recovery—a return to a preoperative level of function or better—can take more time that one might expect. For abdominal surgery patients, it is not uncommon to require 3 to 6 months to return to the level of function the patients had before they needed surgery. Patients and family should be patient, but active, in pursuing recovery following surgery.

—*Jeff Silverstein*

See also Surgery

Further Readings and References

Deiner S, Silverstein JH, Abrams KJ. Management of trauma in the geriatric patient: Resuscitation and trauma anesthesia. *Curr Opin Anaesthesiol.* 2004;17:165–170.

Lawrence VA, Silverstein JH, Cornell JE, et al. Higher Hb level is associated with better early functional recovery after hip fracture repair. *Transfusion.* 2003;43:1717–1722.

Liu LL, Leung JM. Predicting adverse postoperative outcomes in patients aged 80 years or older. *J Am Geriatr Soc.* 2000;48:405–412.

Meiler S. *Influence of Perioperative Care on Outcomes: An Issue of Anesthesiology Clinics.* San Diego, Calif: Elsevier; 2006.

Silverstein J. Perioperative anesthetic management of geriatric trauma. *Anesthesiol Clin N Am.* 1999; 17:263–275.

Silverstein J, Tagliente TM, Auerbach AD, Goldman L. When should perioperative β-blockers be discontinued? *JAMA.* 2002;287:3079–3080.

Thomas DR, Ritchie CS. Perioperative assessment of older adults. *J Am Geriatr Soc.* 1995;43:811–821.

PERSONALITY DISORDERS

Personality disorders (PDs) are defined as chronic psychiatric disorders that involve a pervasive pattern of inflexible and maladaptive inner experiences and behaviors in several spheres of function: perception and interpretation of experiences, emotional expression, interpersonal relations, and impulse control. These disorders are typically present since young adulthood and often persist, in one form or another, into later life. Individuals with PDs often create conflicts in social and clinical settings and end up being labeled as difficult, hateful, unpleasant, or strange, depending on the disorder subtype. There are 12 subtypes of PDs, with each one having 8 to 10 diagnostic criteria, and individuals must meet a specified number of them in any combination to qualify for a diagnosis. Individuals may demonstrate a single disorder or a combination of maladaptive traits from several disorders. Brief descriptions of each PD appear in Table 1.

Table 1   Descriptions of Personality Disorder Subtypes

Antisocial	Lack of conscience, reckless, criminal behaviors
Avoidant	Fearful of rejection, timid, inhibited, isolative
Borderline	Unstable relationships, impulsive, with self-injurious behaviors
Dependent	Excessively reliant on others for decisions and support
Depressive	Gloomy, pessimistic, critical, guilt prone
Histrionic	Extraverted, seductive, provocative, but with shallow emotions
Narcissistic	Self-entitled, arrogant, grandiose, demanding
Obsessive–compulsive	Preoccupation with orderliness and cleanliness, rigid, controlling
Paranoid	Suspicious and distrustful, prone to hostility
Passive–aggressive	Passive resistance to authority, critical, resentful, with procrastination
Schizoid	Lack of desire for social relations, isolative, odd
Schizotypal	Odd or inappropriate beliefs and behaviors

An estimated 10% to 22% of adults in the community suffer from PDs, with significantly higher rates seen in psychiatric settings and in individuals with other psychiatric disorders such as depression. This rate declines to a range of 5% to 10% in the elderly, although this decrease might not reflect a true change in the prevalence of PDs as much as it reflects the challenges in making an accurate diagnosis during late life. It is not clear which PDs are more common because prevalence rates vary widely by setting; several PDs are more likely to be seen in clinical settings (e.g., borderline, dependent, obsessive–compulsive), whereas others may tend to avoid treatment (e.g., antisocial, avoidant, schizoid). Epidemiological data suggest that the most common PDs in adults in the community are obsessive–compulsive, paranoid, and antisocial.

In general, diagnosis of PDs is challenging because it requires a longitudinal view of the person across many different settings. Such information is not always available and requires reliable informants, especially with older adults. Without sufficient longitudinal information, it can be difficult to distinguish long-standing personality traits from more recent disruptions in mood and behavior. In addition, clinicians are not always familiar with the large number of diagnostic criteria, especially for less well-established categories such as depressive and passive–aggressive PDs. As a result, PD diagnoses are often deferred or replaced with Axis I diagnoses that seem to encompass the more salient presenting symptoms such as depression, anxiety, and mood instability.

Not all individuals with seemingly troublesome or maladaptive personality traits have PDs. The diagnosis of an adjustment disorder might best account for acute changes in personality due to severe stressors such as the loss of a loved one, a severe or chronic medical illness, and psychological trauma due to war or natural disaster. For example, physical pain and disability can lead to dependent or avoidant behaviors that resemble those seen in PDs. Similarly, the emotional lability seen in bipolar disorder can mimic behaviors of borderline and histrionic diagnoses. Dementing illnesses can also lead to marked changes in personality such as increased egocentricity seen in Alzheimer's disease and impulsivity seen in frontotemporal dementia. In each of these cases, the delineation of an actual PD will depend on identifying a pervasive and consistent pattern of maladaptive traits that have existed for many years and that have predated in some form any more recent life stressors or diagnoses. This process is particularly difficult in older adults given the limited timeline of available history and the presence of so many confounding stressors and comorbid medical and psychiatric disorders.

PDs are, by definition, chronic conditions, although this does not rule out the possibility of change. Longitudinal data are quite limited but indicate that a substantial percentage of individuals with borderline and antisocial PDs improve into middle age, with less impulsivity and recklessness. Individuals with more rigid traits, such as those found in obsessive–compulsive, paranoid, schizoid, and schizotypal PDs, tend to have persistent clinical presentations. Regardless of their course over time, individuals with PDs remain at high risk for comorbid psychiatric disorders, such as depression, anxiety, and substance abuse, and are less responsive to treatment. Even when there is improvement, older individuals with PDs may demonstrate reemergent symptoms during late life, often triggered by stressors such as the loss of key social or psychological supports. These symptoms may resemble earlier symptoms or may be shaped by age-associated losses in physical and cognitive capabilities.

Treatment of PDs focuses on management of symptoms and prevention of crises rather than on cure. To the extent possible, treatment should always be based on a consistent therapeutic relationship with one or more clinicians and on a clear understanding of the underlying dynamics. A team approach, in which a multidisciplinary group has coordinated a plan and identified appropriate target symptoms, is often the best approach. Many individuals with PDs will evade or resist treatment or will disrupt the treatment setting. Others will need treatment for comorbid depression, substance abuse, eating disorders, anxiety, and/or other conditions that are more acute and that serve to exacerbate maladaptive personality traits.

Individual psychotherapy can be helpful for certain subtypes of disorders in which the individual has motivation for treatment, but it depends on a consistent and long-term therapeutic relationship. Dialectical behavioral therapy (DBT) is a specialized form of psychotherapy that focuses on teaching the individual to recognize and manage disruptive symptoms. DBT initially was developed for borderline PD and later was adapted for other PDs and for older adults.

Psychotropic medications can also play a role in treatment targeted at the PD itself, specific salient personality traits or behaviors, or comorbid conditions. Again, the goal is not to cure the PD but rather to reduce the intensity and frequency of maladaptive behaviors. Prior to selecting an appropriate medication, it is important for the clinician to have an understanding of how the dynamics of the PD may influence the use of medications. For example, borderline and antisocial individuals may be at greater risk for using medications in hazardous or abusive ways. Paranoid and passive–aggressive individuals may have poor adherence to medications. Obsessive–compulsive and dependent individuals may seek an excessive or unnecessary focus on medication use as a means of avoiding important therapeutic tasks. In each situation, it may be best to defer or minimize the use of medications. With every PD, however, it is critical to obtain and document informed consent prior to prescribing any agent.

Research into the pharmacological treatment of PDs has been limited largely to borderline and schizotypal diagnoses. Numerous studies have found a variety of medications to be useful, but for any PD there is no single medication of choice and there is little research to support the long-term efficacy of any agent. A variety of antidepressants have demonstrated efficacy in treating impulsive, aggressive, self-injurious, and depressive behaviors, including monoamine oxidase (MAO) inhibitors, tricyclics, and serotonin selective reuptake inhibitors (SSRIs). Both antidepressants and anxiolytics may reduce the intensity of PD symptoms characterized by depression and anxiety, including avoidant and obsessive–compulsive behaviors.

Antipsychotic medications may be helpful for transient paranoia, impulsive aggression, agitation, and self-injurious behaviors. Atypical antipsychotic agents that have demonstrated efficacy with these symptoms include clozapine, risperidone, olanzapine, and quetiapine. In one representative study, olanzapine and fluoxetine alone, as well as in combination, substantially reduced symptoms of chronic dysphoria and impulsive aggression in a sample of women with borderline PD.

Other studies have shown that mood stabilizers such as divalproex sodium, carbamazepine, and lithium carbonate have reduced symptoms of anxiety, aggression, and agitation in both antisocial and borderline PDs.

—*Marc E. Agronin*

See also Psychiatric Rating Scales; Schizophrenia, Paranoia, and Delusional Disorders

Further Readings and References

Agronin ME, Maletta GJ. Personality disorders in late life: Understanding and overcoming the gap in research. *Am J Geriatr Psychiatry.* 2000;8:4–18.

American Psychiatric Association. *Diagnostic and Statistical Manual of Mental Disorders.* 4th ed., text rev. Washington, DC: American Psychiatric Press; 2000.

Grant BF, Hasin DS, Stinson FS, et al. Prevalence, correlates, and disability of personality disorders in the United States: Results from the National Epidemiologic Survey on Alcohol and Related Conditions. *J Clin Psychiatry.* 2004;65:948–958.

Hirose S. Effective treatment of aggression and impulsivity in antisocial personality disorder with risperidone. *Psychiatry Clin Neurosci.* 2001;55:161–162.

Markovitz PJ. Recent trends in the pharmacotherapy of personality disorders. *J Personal Disord.* 2004;18:90–101.

Rinne T, Van den Brink W, Wouters I, van Dyck R. SSRI treatment of borderline personality disorder: A randomized, placebo-controlled clinical trial for female patients with borderline personality disorder. *Am J Psychiatry.* 2002;159:2048–2054.

Zanarini M, Frankenberg F, Parachini EA. A preliminary, randomized trial of fluoxetine, olanazapine, and the olanazapine–fluoxetine combination in women with borderline personality disorder. *J Clin Psychiatry.* 2004;65:903–907.

Zweig RA, Agronin ME. Personality disorders in late life. In: Agronin ME, Maletta GJ, eds. *Principles and Practice of Geriatric Psychiatry.* Philadelphia: Lippincott Williams & Wilkins; 2006:451–469.

PETS IN HEALTH CARE SETTINGS

Recognition of the strong bond between older adults and pet animals has led to the proliferation of programs in health care settings designed to improve the health and well-being of residents through the use of animals. Pets have long been considered sources of unconditional love and acceptance, so it is not surprising that the medical field is exploring the benefits of incorporating animals as treatment tools for physical and emotional therapy.

Some health care settings have included pets as an integral part of their environment. On entering one of these settings, it is not unusual to be greeted at the door by the resident dog, to find a jar of pet treats on the program administrator's desk, or to encounter a cat sleeping on a resident's bed. The Eden Alternative, a popular model used by residential care facilities, uses companion animals, as well as children and gardens, to create more enlivened environments for older adults. Promising research on the effects of pet animal contact on older adults has also resulted in pet-assisted therapy programs that take dogs, cats, and other small animals into hospitals, nursing homes, and other health-related settings to visit residents.

Introducing animals to health care settings may help improve the well-being of older adults by creating a home-like environment. Several studies conducted in health care environments have used an experimental design to examine the effects of introducing an animal on the social behavior of older adults. Animal-visiting programs in residential care facilities have produced improvements in social interaction and competence, psychosocial function, life satisfaction, mental function, and psychological well-being in residents. For older adults with low social functioning and involvement, companion animals themselves can be an accessible source of social and tactile contact. Facilitating contact between older adults and animals in health settings has also been found to have a positive impact on humans' physical health. Researchers have found that regularly stroking an animal lowers blood levels of the stress hormone cortisol while releasing other hormones with physiological benefits. Other studies have demonstrated that pain and anxiety are reduced in older adults who spend time with pets. Most programs where animals have been used in an attempt to benefit older adults have not identified the characteristics of the individuals who showed improvement. Those studies that did include information about participants' past experiences with pet animals showed that individuals with strong positive experiences demonstrated more significant improvement than did those individuals with less positive experiences.

There is increasing evidence that pets improve the quality of life for many older adults. Although not a substitute for human contact and a positive environment, the therapeutic use of pet animals has been shown to promote quality of life and positive health benefits for older adults in health care settings.

—*Mary Kaplan*

See also Depression and Other Mood Disorders; Health Promotion and Disease Prevention; Institutional Care; Long-Term Care; Quality of Life

Further Readings and References

Banks MR, Banks WA. The effects of animal-assisted therapy on loneliness in an elderly population in long-term care facilities. *J Gerontol A Biol Sci Med Sci.* 2002;57: M428–M432.

Likourezos A, Burack OR, Lantz MS. The therapeutic use of companion animals: AAGF Psychiatry Rounds. *Clin Geriatr.* 2002;10(4):31–33.

Saylor K. Pet visitation program. *J Gerontol Nurs.* 1998; 24(6):36–38.

PHYSICAL ACTIVITY

See EXERCISE AND PHYSICAL ACTIVITY

PHYSICAL FUNCTION

See ACTIVITIES OF DAILY LIVING AND INSTRUMENTAL ACTIVITIES OF DAILY LIVING; DISABILITY AND THE DISABLEMENT PROCESS; FRAILTY; MOBILITY

PHYSIOLOGICAL DECLINE

See ACTIVITIES OF DAILY LIVING AND INSTRUMENTAL ACTIVITIES OF DAILY LIVING; DISABILITY AND THE DISABLEMENT PROCESS; FRAILTY

PICK'S DISEASE

Pick's disease is a subtype of frontotemporal dementia (FTD), and FTD accounts for approximately 5% to 10% of dementia cases. Historically considered a rather rare degenerative illness, it was first described in 1892 by Arnold Pick. The disorder is characterized by a progressive deterioration of social skills coupled with alterations in personality and language, eventually involving intellect and memory. The disease generally affects individuals from 40 to 60 years of age but has been reported to occur in individuals as early as the 20s and as late as the 80s.

History

The initial criteria developed to recognize FTD was the Lund and Manchester Groups (Lund–Manchester) criteria published in 1994 that required the presence of at least two of the following features: loss of personal awareness, strange eating habits, perseveration, and mood change. In addition, patients needed to have at least one of the following: frontal executive dysfunction, reduced speech, and preserved visuospatial ability. Supportive features included onset before 65 years of age, a family history of FTD, early urinary incontinence, motor neuron disease, and (during the late stages) akinesia, rigidity, and tremor.

David Neary and colleagues in 1998 developed the second set of consensus guidelines for diagnosing FTD, retaining the general framework of the Lund–Manchester criteria but subdividing the patients into three distinct clinical presentations: frontotemporal dementia (personality change and social conduct disturbance), progressive nonfluent aphasia, and semantic aphasia. Frontotemporal lobar degeneration was the term used to refer to any of the three symptoms.

The diagnostic framework was further refined in 2001 by the Work Group on Frontotemporal Dementia and Pick's Disease, which eliminated the three subdivisions in favor of calling all of them frontotemporal dementia but noted that patients would experience either a behavioral presentation or a language presentation to their illness. Specific criteria included the development of behavioral or cognitive deficits manifested by either (a) early and progressive change in personality, characterized by difficulty in modulating behavior, often resulting in inappropriate responses or activities, or (b) early and progressive change in language, characterized by problems with expression of language or severe naming difficulty and problems with word meaning. These deficits must cause significant impairment in social or occupational functioning and represent a decline from a previous level of functioning and must not be better accounted for by another medical condition, delirium, or psychiatric condition.

Clinical Presentation

Pick's disease differs from Alzheimer's disease in several ways, and the two diseases are distinct in their neuropathology. Pick's disease is identified by the presence of Pick bodies; that is, rounded structures identified within affected neurons that give them a balloon-like appearance. The characteristic plaques and tangles found in Alzheimer's disease are not typically present in Pick's disease, and the two types of dementia affect primarily different cerebral structures. Pick's disease is characterized by significant and marked frontal atrophy, whereas Alzheimer's disease appears to involve temporal structures early and then progresses to involve parietal areas and frontal areas later in the course of the disease. This differing neuropathological distribution corresponds to the clinical course of the two diseases, as the early signs of Pick's disease commonly involve personality changes, whereas the early signs of Alzheimer's disease involve anterograde memory.

The personality changes identified during the early stages of Pick's disease are diffuse and vary across affected individuals. Apathy may be an early sign of the disease, as can social indifference, inappropriate social behavior, and disregard for social norms and the feelings of others. Attentional deficits are prominent and frequently occur early in the course of the illness. Severe presentations of the disease may involve grossly inappropriate behavior or physical or sexual aggression. Alternatively, a syndrome of inappropriate laughter and comedy may present reminiscent of a pseudobulbar affect or *Witzelsucht*. Executive function declines early in the course of the illness, and patients often have severe difficulty in planning and executing specific behaviors. This leads to a "randomness" and unpredictable nature in the initiation of behavior, but patients can potentially maintain the ability to follow commands.

Patients with Pick's disease invariably develop language difficulties as the disease progresses, and at least two recognized variants of FTD affect language predominantly. Patients may become quiet or increasingly frustrated in the inability to produce speech, and this may further increase the apathy and isolation experienced during the course of the illness as well as contribute to the emergence of affective syndromes, including severe depression. Patients have been reported to develop a Kluver–Bucy-type syndrome involving hyperorality with gluttony, sexual aggression, and severe apathy. Patients eventually become moribund and succumb to secondary complication of the disease, as occurs in advanced Alzheimer's dementia.

Pick's disease is an illness of middle life and occurs earlier than typical Alzheimer's dementia. The disease has a variable course, and average life expectancy after diagnosis is 5 years but ranges between 2 and 15 years.

Diagnosing Pick's disease is difficult, and it is likely underestimated as a cause of dementia. Neuropsychological testing may reveal prominent frontal deficits with relatively preserved memory; this would support the diagnosis, but it is not diagnostic of the condition. Computed tomography (CT) and magnetic resonance imaging (MRI) may demonstrate circumscribed frontal atrophy, and this would again be supportive of a diagnosis of Pick's disease in the appropriate clinical scenario. The presence of highly circumscribed atrophy would be helpful in differentiating the illness from dementia of the Alzheimer's type (DAT) in that DAT generally produces more global or nonspecific atrophy. Ultimate diagnosis of Pick's disease rests with a postmortem microscopic examination of the patient's brain; this can often reliably differentiate this condition from other dementing illnesses such as DAT.

Neuropathology and Genetics

Neuropathological abnormalities include involvement of the second and third cortical layers, spongiosis, swollen neurons, and the variable presence of argyrophilic round inclusions called Pick bodies. Other more recent data support the hypothesis that Pick's disease (FTD) involves abnormalities in both ubiquitin and tau proteins, and some evidence suggests a potential link to other degenerative illnesses such as corticobasal degeneration and progressive supranuclear palsy. Few definite genetic linkages in FTD have been identified, but various abnormalities on chromosome 17q21–22, which contains the microtubule-associated protein tau gene, have been described. Most cases of FTD appear to be spontaneous and without an obvious genetic basis, but rare familial cases involving an autosomal-dominant pattern have been reported in the literature.

Treatment of FTD is primarily supportive given that no current medications have proven to be effective in double-blind, randomized, placebo-controlled trials. Patients with FTD do not have primary cholinergic abnormalities, so the cholinesterase inhibitors used to treat DAT have not appeared to be especially effective. No trials have examined the potential role of memantine in this patient population.

Treatment

Weak evidence supports the potential use of amantadine or bromocriptine in patients with expressive language deficits, but tolerability can be difficult to achieve with these agents. Methylphenidate has been reported as a potential modifier for the attentional deficits frequently observed in this condition, but its evidence is limited to a single case report in the literature.

Depressive syndromes can be especially prominent and severe in frontotemporal dementia, especially among those patients who retain some degree of insight while experiencing greater language difficulties. No antidepressant agent has been evaluated satisfactorily in these patients, but preference should be given to agents that are more tolerable with fewer side effects such as the newer generation of antidepressants, including selective serotonin reuptake inhibitors (SSRIs) and serotonin/norepinephrine reuptake inhibitors (SNRIs). Tricyclic antidepressants can burden patients with a profound anticholinergic load that could potentially worsen remaining cognition, making them less desirable in treating affective syndromes associated with dementing illnesses. Electroconvulsive therapy (ECT) can be used in refractory depressive cases, although evidence for its direct use in frontotemporal dementia is scant and limited to one case report.

Patients demonstrating obsessive–compulsive-type behavior may benefit from SSRI therapy, but there are few well-studied options to treat the behavioral symptoms of disinhibition, sexual aggression, and anxiety. Atypical antipsychotics have long played an important role in treating refractory aggression, agitation, and psychosis in DAT patients, but recent concerns regarding cardiovascular and cerebrovascular safety have prompted a reevaluation of using these agents as first-line options, although they can remain very useful in severe cases. Other options include trazodone and mood stabilizers, but only trazodone has the benefit of a small, double-blind, randomized, placebo-controlled trial. Benzodiazepines should typically be avoided in these patients because the risks of further cognitive impairment and falls have been well documented in the elderly patient population. Behavioral interventions offer alternative options early in the course of the disease, but benefit is likely to be reduced as the disease progresses.

Pick's disease, although an unusual type of dementia, may be a relatively common cause of presenile-type dementias given its propensity to arise during the fifth and sixth decades of life. Most cases are nonhereditary, but rare familial cases are inherited in an autosomal-dominant pattern. Treatment is generally supportive and nonspecific, but mild benefit may be obtained by cautious trials of psychotropic agents in appropriate patients.

—*Harold W. Goforth*

See also Alzheimer's Disease; Lewy Body Dementia; Vascular Dementia

Further Readings and References

Chow TW, Miller BL, Boone K, Mishkin F, Cummings JL. Frontotemporal dementia classification and neuropsychiatry. *Neurologist.* 2002;8:263–269.

Lund and Manchester Groups. Clinical and neuropathological criteria for frontotemporal dementia. *J Neurol Neurosurg Psychiatry.* 1994;57:416–418.

McKhann GM, Albert MS, Grossman M, Miller B, Dickson D, Trojanowski JQ. Clinical and pathological diagnosis of frontotemporal dementia: Report of the Work Group on Frontotemporal Dementia and Pick's Disease. *Arch Neurol.* 2001;58:1803–1809.

Neary D, Snowden JS, Gustafson L, et al. Frontotemporal lobar degeneration: A consensus on clinical diagnostic criteria. *Neurology.* 1998;51:1546–1554.

PNEUMONIA AND TUBERCULOSIS

Pneumonia is a common illness that causes significant morbidity and mortality in older adults. Older adults with pneumonia are more likely to require hospitalization and are at an increased risk for death compared with younger adults with pneumonia. In fact, pneumonia is the fifth leading cause of death in persons age 65 years and older in the United States. Prompt antimicrobial therapy, supportive care, and risk factor modification are paramount in treating this illness.

Several factors contribute to older adults' increased risk of pneumonia, including comorbid illnesses (e.g., diabetes mellitus, chronic obstructive pulmonary disease, malignancy) and nursing home residence. In addition, feeding tube placement, poor dental hygiene, and neurological impairment from cerebrovascular

accidents or Alzheimer's disease place older adults at an increased risk for aspiration pneumonia. Furthermore, symptoms of pneumonia might not be recognized in older adults as quickly as they are in their younger counterparts because older adults with pneumonia often complain of fewer symptoms, often presenting with merely a change in functional status. This may contribute to a delay in prompt antimicrobial therapy and thus place patients at higher risk for poor outcomes.

When a diagnosis of pneumonia is made, prompt antimicrobial therapy should be instituted and targeted toward the most likely infecting organisms. *Streptococcus pneumoniae* is the most common cause of community-acquired pneumonia, followed by *Staphylococcus aureus* and aerobic gram-negative bacilli. Atypical bacteria, such as *Legionella pneumophilia, Chlamydia pneumoniae, and Mycoplasma pneumoniae,* commonly cause community-acquired pneumonia as well. The Infectious Diseases Society of America has published guidelines for the treatment of community-acquired pneumonia in adults. In short, it states that patients who will be treated on an outpatient basis and who have not received recent antibiotic therapy may be treated with doxycycline or a macrolide. If patients have recently received antibiotics, a respiratory fluoroquinolone or an advanced macrolide plus high-dose amoxicillin (or amoxicillin–clavulanate) may be used. In hospitalized patients, a respiratory fluoroquinolone alone or an advanced macrolide plus a β-lactam antibiotic is appropriate. In patients who are severely ill, have necrotizing pneumonia, or are at risk for methicillin-resistant *S. aureus* infection, vancomycin should be added to the empiric antibiotic regimen.

In hospitalized patients, an attempt to isolate the causative agent should be made. Thus, blood cultures and sputum for gram stain and culture should be obtained. Additional tests should be considered for selected patients (e.g., urine legionella for pneumococcal antigen, sputum for acid-fast bacilli (AFB) smear and culture, serum testing for HIV infection, nasopharyngeal swab for Influenza A and B virus antigens).

Supportive care with supplemental oxygen and intravenous fluid rehydration should be provided as needed in addition to antimicrobial therapy. Patients' response to therapy can be monitored by physical examination and pulse oximetry. In patients who fail to improve on appropriate therapy, a computed tomography (CT) scan of the chest or a bronchoscopy may be necessary. A follow-up chest X-ray should be performed at 12 weeks to evaluate for resolution of the pneumonia.

The risk of pneumonia can be reduced in some instances. For example, vaccines can help prevent some types of pneumonia. The pneumococcal vaccine, recommended for patients age 65 years and older as well as patients under 65 years of age with comorbid conditions, reduces the risk of severe (i.e., bacteremic) disease. The influenza vaccine, recommended annually for all patients over 50 years of age or with underlying medical illnesses, reduces hospitalization, pneumonia, and death in those over 65 years of age.

The increased incidence of *Mycobacterium tuberculosis* (TB) infection in older adults is most often caused by reactivation of a primary infection. This may be caused partly by cell-mediated immune senescence, but other comorbid illnesses such as diabetes, malignancy, renal insufficiency, and poor nutrition also place older adults at increased risk. In addition, persons in this age group are more likely to have been exposed to *M. tuberculosis* during childhood due to the much higher prevalence at that time. Clinicians should have a high index of suspicion for pulmonary tuberculosis in older patients because the elderly might not exhibit classic features of TB infection such as hemoptysis, fever, and night sweats. Instead, TB infection in the elderly may present insidiously with cognitive impairment, weight loss, prolonged low-grade fever, and/or fatigue. The chest X-ray findings in older adults might not reveal the characteristic cavitary lesion in the apex. Infection in the middle lobes, lower lobes, or pleura may occur. Also, infiltrates may present bilaterally, as interstitial infiltrates, or as patchy infiltrates.

A two-step tuberculin skin test is suggested for the workup of TB in older adults because there is an increase in anergy to cutaneous antigens in this population. However, false-negative results may occur with waning delayed-type hypersensitivity, corticosteroids, and disseminated TB. Thus, a negative tuberculin skin test cannot be used to rule out TB. Sputum samples for AFB smear and culture should be obtained from all patients in whom pulmonary tuberculosis is suspected. In patients who are unable to give sputum samples, bronchoscopies should be performed.

Once TB infection is confirmed, antituberculous chemotherapy should be initiated. In the United States, most cases of TB in the elderly will be susceptible to isoniazid and rifampin, but many areas of the world have isoniazid resistance and most tuberculosis in the United States now occurs in immigrants. In any event, initial therapy should almost always consist of four drugs: isoniazid (300 milligrams [mg]/day), rifampin (600 mg/day), ethambutol (25 mg/kilogram [kg]/day), and pyrazinamide (25 mg/kg/day up to 2.5 grams [g]/day). Pyridoxine (50 mg/day) should also be added to the regimen to reduce the risk of peripheral neuropathy from isoniazid therapy. Specific drug choices and duration must be selected after susceptibility testing is performed on the isolate. Sputum should be examined monthly to document clearing of the mycobacterium. If sputum cultures are still positive after 3 months of therapy, drug resistance should be suspected. Liver function tests should be obtained at baseline and monitored monthly because the elderly are at an increased risk for hepatitis from antituberculous chemotherapy. A follow-up chest X-ray should be obtained 2 to 3 months after initiation of therapy as well.

—*Vera Luther and Kevin P. High*

See also Infectious Diseases; Pulmonary Aging

Further Readings and References

American Thoracic Society. Diagnostic standards and classification of tuberculosis in adults and children. *Am J Respir Crit Care Med.* 2000;161:1376–1395.

Centers for Disease Control and Prevention. Division of Tuberculosis Elimination website. Available at: www.cdc.gov/nchstp/tb. Accessed September 27, 2006.

Conte HA, Chen YT, Mehal W, et al. A prognostic rule for elderly patients admitted with community-acquired pneumonia. *Am J Med.* 1999;106:20–28.

Mandell LA, Bartlett JG, Dowell SF, et al. Update of practice guidelines for the management of community-acquired pneumonia in immunocompetent adults. *Clin Infect Dis.* 2003;37:1405–1433.

Marrie TJ. Pneumonia. In: Hazzard WR, Blass JP, Halter JB, et al., eds. *Principles of Geriatric Medicine and Gerontology.* 5th ed. New York: McGraw-Hill; 2003: 1083–1096.

Rajagopalan S, Yoshikawa TT. Tuberculosis. In: Hazzard WR, Blass JP, Halter JB, et al., eds. *Principles of Geriatric Medicine and Gerontology.* 5th ed. New York: McGraw-Hill; 2003:1099–1105.

Polypharmacy

Polypharmacy simply means using too many drugs. By convention, it refers to a patient being on more than three drugs. The risk of dangerous drug events in elderly patients rises exponentially with the increasing number of prescribed and nonprescribed drugs. These adverse drug events, according to a 1999 Institute of Medicine report, are major contributors to emergency room visits and hospitalizations in the elderly. The adverse events, in part, reflect harmful drug–drug, drug–disease, and drug–diet interactions. These interactions are more likely to occur with multiple medications in elderly patients with multiple comorbidities and age-related decline in drug-metabolizing capacity. In most cases, the additional drugs are potentially inappropriate because they are unnecessary, ineffective, or even counteractive to other drugs. However, polypharmacy, in specific clinical conditions, can also be appropriate and beneficial to patient care. Therefore, it is important for clinicians to recognize when polypharmacy is harmful and when it is appropriate.

The two types of polypharmacy are harmful polypharmacy and appropriate polypharmacy

Harmful Polypharmacy

The causes of harmful polypharmacy are (a) prescribing cascade, (b) failure to consider nondrug approaches, (c) failure to stop a drug when the initial indication no longer exists, and (d) polydoctors and polypharmacists.

Prescribing Cascade

Prescribing cascade is a common clinical scenario whereby the clinician prescribes a second drug to treat the side effects of the first drug for which indication is often unclear. This is followed by a third drug to treat the side effects of the second drug, and so the cascade of incremental prescribing continues. To illustrate this point, consider the case of "Mr. A," a healthy and functional 79-year-old man visiting his doctor for an annual checkup:

1. Mr. A has a blood pressure of 140/85. "I feel great," he says.

2. He receives amlodipine (5 milligrams [mg], once daily) for high blood pressure.

3. He then develops swollen feet, a common side effect of amlodipine.

4. He then receives furosemide and potassium for the swelling.

5. The potassium pills then aggravate his heartburn.

6. He then receives omeprazole to relieve the heartburn.

7. He develops diarrhea.

8. Now he receives lomotil (atropine/diphenoxylate) for diarrhea.

9. He feels dizzy and delirious, causing him to fall and sustain a hip fracture.

Although this is hypothetical, it is a common outcome of polypharmacy resulting from a prescribing cascade. This outcome is potentially avoidable if the clinician (a) considers a nondrug approach, such as diet and exercise, as the initial treatment for this borderline hypertension and (b) considers that any new symptoms in an elderly person could be drug related.

Failure to Consider Nondrug Approaches

Failure to consider nondrug approaches is another factor contributing to harmful polypharmacy. The case of Mr. A aptly illustrates this point. Prescribers might not consider nondrug approaches, in part, because of time pressure to see patients quickly. This pressure, in turn, can lead to "reflexive prescribing" with little time to consider alternative but safer approaches such as dietary changes, exercise, and smoking cessation for mildly elevated blood pressure and cholesterol.

Failure to Stop a Drug When the Initial Indication No Longer Exists

A common reason for continued use of a nonindicated drug is poor communication between health care providers during transitions of care. For example, a patient with transient hospital-related volume overload and pulmonary edema from intravenous fluids may continue to receive diuretics and potassium for years after the pulmonary edema has resolved. As another example, anti-insomnia pills for transient hospital-related insomnia may continue to be used by a patient when the initial cause, such as an unfamiliar and noisy hospital setting, no longer exists.

Polydoctors and Polypharmacists

This term refers to a patient who is seeing multiple doctors and using multiple pharmacists. Many seniors receive care from several specialists who prescribe different drug regimens. Because of cost and insurance rules, the prescriptions are frequently filled at multiple pharmacy stores where patients also buy additional nonprescription herbal and nonherbal drugs. This practice commonly leads to a patient being on multiple drugs, some with no indication and others with potentially dangerous interactions. To illustrate this point, consider the case of "Ms. D," a functional 79-year-old woman with a history of irregular heartbeat (atrial fibrillation) and depression:

1. Ms. D sees a cardiologist and is prescribed metoprolol and Coumadin for atrial fibrillation.

2. She sees a psychiatrist and is prescribed paroxetine for depression.

3. She then goes to the drugstore to pick up her prescriptions.

4. She buys *Ginkgo biloba* for memory problems.

5. Two weeks later, she collapses.

6. On examination, she has bradycardia, hypotension, and bloody stools.

The adverse outcome directly reflects drug–drug interaction between *G. biloba* and Coumadin, a drug that can cause bleeding, as well as an interaction between paroxetine and metoprolol, potentially causing hypotension and bradycardia. Paroxetine inhibits the breakdown of metoprolol, whereas *G. biloba* increases the blood-thinning action of Coumadin. Preventing this type of outcome requires open communication among patients, doctors, and pharmacists.

How to Stop Harmful Polypharmacy

The clinician should always ask the following:

- Is a drug the best approach for this symptom?
- Does this drug indication still exist?

The patients should always ask his or her doctor and pharmacist the following:

- Do I still need this drug?
- Is this drug interacting with other drugs I am using?
- Can my illness be due to, or worsened by, this drug?

Clinicians should consider using one drug to treat multiple symptoms, as with the following examples:

- *Mirtazapine:* depression, weight loss, insomnia, anxiety, and nausea
- *Duloxetine:* diabetic neuropathic pain, depression, anxiety, and incontinence

Clinicians should always do the following:

- Review all medications, including nonprescription and herbal preparations.
- Check for adverse interactions between drugs and drugs, between drugs and food, and between drugs and disease.
- Avoid "as needed" drugs in patients who have acute or chronic cognitive impairment.
- Consider any new disease or symptom in the elderly as potentially related to drugs.

Appropriate Polypharmacy

With aging comes increased prevalence of multiple comorbidities requiring multiple drugs. Because of advances in treating cardiovascular and other diseases, we now have several drugs from different classes that are combined effectively to treat elderly patients. For example, to improve patient health-related quality of life and survival, congestive heart failure patients are prescribed an angiotensin-converting enzyme inhibitor, a β-adrenergic receptor blocker, a diuretic, and (in some cases) digoxin, spironolactone, and other drugs for hypertension and atrial fibrillation. Not only is this combination of drugs effective, it also is appropriate and considered to be the "standard of care."

—*Mukaila A. Raji*

See also Adverse Drug Reactions; Age-Related Changes in Pharmacokinetics and Pharmacodynamics; Drug–Disease Interactions; Drug–Drug Interactions; Inappropriate Prescribing

Further Readings and References

Fick DM, Cooper JW, Wade WE, Waller JL, MacLean JR, Beers MH. Updating the Beers criteria for potentially inappropriate medication use in older adults: Results of a U.S. consensus panel of experts. *Arch Intern Med.* 2003;163:2716–2724.

Institute of Medicine. *To Err Is Human: Building a Safer Health System.* Kohn LT, Corrigan JM, Donaldson MS, eds. Washington, DC: National Academy Press; 2000.

Raji MA. Management of chemotherapy-induced side-effects. *Lancet Oncol.* 2005;6:357.

Raji MA, Brady SR. Mirtazapine for treatment of depression and co-morbidities in Alzheimer disease. *Ann Pharmacother.* 2001;35:1024–1027.

Rochon PA, Gurwitz JH. Optimizing drug treatment for elderly people: The prescribing cascade. *Br Med J.* 1997;315:1096–1099.

POSITIVE ATTITUDES AND HEALTH

"Is the glass half full or half empty?" Many people use this question as a litmus test of whether a person is an optimist or a pessimist; that is, whether they tend to have positive attitudes or negative attitudes. There are many other tests of positive attitudes, happiness, life satisfaction, and subjective well-being, and most studies using these tests find that positive attitudes are associated with good health. Indeed, the association of health and happiness is so obvious that all of the studies establishing this association need not be reviewed here. It is common sense that good health contributes to happiness. Somewhat less obvious is the idea that happiness or "positive thinking" can contribute to good health.

However, there are two major problems with most of these studies. First, they are unable to untangle the problem of causality; does the positive attitude cause the good health, or does the good health cause the positive attitude? Second, even if there is evidence that the positive attitude causes the good health, what are the explanations or mechanisms by which such a mental state can affect the physical state of health?

This entry reviews some of the major studies of this relationship among older people in an attempt to answer these problems.

Causality

One way to solve the problem of causality is to use longitudinal studies in which one can establish which comes first—the good health or the happiness. In the Duke Longitudinal Studies, for example, it was found that each predicts the other; good health was one of the strongest predictors of happiness at later rounds of examination, and happiness was one of the strongest predictors of good health at later rounds. This indicates a kind of "chicken and egg" relationship, good health causes happiness, and happiness causes good health.

Another way to solve the problem of causality is to use longevity as the outcome variable to see whether happiness predicts greater longevity. By definition in this type of analysis, the happiness comes before the longevity and therefore must be the cause of the longevity rather than vice versa. Again in the Duke Longitudinal Studies, in multiple regression analysis in which other variables (e.g., age, sex) were held constant, it was found that the happiness rating was the second strongest predictor of greater than expected longevity. Happiness was even more important for women, among whom it was the single strongest predictor of longevity.

Similarly, Morton Lieberman did extensive psychological testing of 180 aged men and women and correlated these tests with longevity (intact survival over 2 years). He found that three of the strongest predictors of longevity were self-esteem and the absence of anxiety and depression. A more recent study of the life trajectories of a group of nuns indicated that those who had expressed the most positive emotions during early adulthood lived up to 10 years longer than did those who expressed the least positive emotions.

Another recent study found that people with more positive attitudes toward their aging lived an average of 7.5 years longer than did those with less positive attitudes. This advantage remained after age, gender, socioeconomic status, loneliness, and functional health were statistically controlled. The study was based on 660 individuals age 50 years and older who participated in a community-based survey in Ohio.

Explanations

How can this strong association of happiness and health be explained? There are three major types of explanations.

1. Both happiness and health are caused by other variables such as socioeconomic status (SES), social support, intelligence, and personality. People with higher SES (more education and/or higher income) tend to be both happier and healthier. People with more social support also tend to be both happier and healthier. Also, more intelligent people tend to be both happier and healthier. Finally, people who are less neurotic, but more conscientious and extraverted, tend to be happier and healthier.

2. Happiness or positive attitudes cause more effective coping styles, optimization of resources, and healthier lifestyles, and these in turn cause better health and longevity. Much of this type of research is called the "broaden-and-build theory," which posits that positive emotions have expanding consequences that are beneficial to people. Positive emotions, whether joyful or merely contented, are likely to color the ways in which people respond to others and to

their environments. For example, positive emotions can broaden the scope of people's visual attention, expand their repertoires for action, and increase their capacities to cope in a crisis. This theory also suggests that positive emotions produce patterns of thought that are flexible, creative, integrative, and open to information. Such patterns in turn may contribute to better health and longevity.

3. Positive attitudes tend to cause the release of healthier hormones and other chemicals in the body, as well as to reduce the release of stress hormones, in turn causing better health and longevity.

Happy Marriages and Good Health

A 20-year longitudinal study of 90 married couples recently concluded that the couples who reported low levels of stress were less prone to illness than were those who had conflict-ridden marriages. Janice Kiecolt-Glaser and her colleagues at the Institute for Behavioral Medicine suggested that positive marital relations help people avoid stress and stress-related hormones such as cortisol. Earlier studies by this group demonstrated that lower cortisol levels correlated with lower risks of infectious diseases and cancer. On the other hand, extramarital sex may be life threatening. A 2002 British study indicated that the risk of heart attack during sex was substantially higher for those having extramarital sex than for those having within-marriage sex.

Positive Attitudes Toward Aging

If positive attitudes are so beneficial, what can people do to develop them? The answer will depend on the type of positive attitude desired. The following are some ways in which to develop positive attitudes toward aging:

- *Think about admired older people (e.g., Albert Einstein).* Two studies have found that focusing attention on such positive images produced more positive attitudes toward older people in general.
- *Think about the many advantages of old age.* These include leisure time to travel, do voluntary activities, take up a hobby, visit friends and relatives, or do whatever one wants; economic security because of pensions and Social Security; having grandchildren;

freedom from pregnancy and child rearing; fewer accidents in the home and on the highway; less criminal victimization; and discounts in stores, on movies, on travel, and so on.

- *Think about positive slogans about old age.* These include "Aging is living"; "The best is yet to be"; "It's not how old you are, but how you are old"; "Better over the hill than under it"; "Old age is the consummation of life"; and "Things of quality have no fear of time."
- *Develop an active sense of humor.* "Laughter is the best medicine" is the slogan for this approach. However, avoid ageist and cynical humor that is likely to have negative effects rather than positive ones.
- *Become a model of "successful aging."* Maintain health by good nutrition, exercise, and regular medical care. Maintain cognitive function with mental stimulation and activities. Maintain social support and voluntary activities.

The bottom line is this: Not only are positive attitudes good for people's health and longevity, but also there are many ways in which people can increase their positive attitudes.

—*Erdman B. Palmore*

See also Bereavement and Grief; Depression and Other Mood Disorders; Duke Longitudinal Studies; Emotions and Emotional Stability; MacArthur Study of Successful Aging; Quality of Life; Self-Rated Health; Subjective Well-Being; Successful Aging

Further Readings and References

Cohen H. Why a good marriage is good for heart and health. *Philadelphia Inquirer.* 2005;(February 27):M2.

Palmore E. *Social Patterns in Normal Aging.* Durham, NC: Duke University Press; 1981.

Palmore E. *Ageism.* 2nd ed. New York: Springer; 1999.

Palmore E, Jeffers F, eds. *Prediction of Life Span.* Lexington, Mass: Heath Lexington Books; 1971.

Posttraumatic Stress Disorder

Posttraumatic stress disorder (PTSD) was first introduced as a diagnosis in 1980 in the *Diagnostic and Statistical Manual of Mental Disorders* (DSM), the most commonly used diagnostic reference for mental health professionals in the United States. PTSD is an anxiety disorder that presents as a worldwide problem, particularly prevalent in communities after mass trauma and in countries torn by violent turmoil. It is chronic in nature and is associated with significant and persistent disability and comorbidity. Effective available treatments include both pharmacotherapy and psychosocial treatment and can produce a meaningful reduction in distress and improvement in overall functioning in people who suffer from PTSD.

Epidemiology

PTSD is an anxiety disorder that affects approximately 7% to 9% of Americans at some points in their lifetimes. Its prevalence rate is even higher among individuals who have been exposed to mass trauma such as U.S. citizens 2 months after the 9/11 terrorist attacks (17%) and survivors of the Oklahoma City bombing (34%). In other parts of the world, the prevalence of PTSD varies widely (range = 1% to 37%), with higher rates found in countries where civilians are exposed to ongoing violence and unrest. Women are twice as likely to develop PTSD than are men. Among treatment-seeking populations, such as in psychiatric and primary care clinics and in certain specialty settings (including gastrointestinal, gynecological, neurological, pain, and eating disorder clinics), PTSD also appears to be more prevalent than in the general population.

Trauma and Risk Factors

PTSD develops following exposure to traumatic events, but not everyone exposed to trauma develops PTSD. An event is considered to be "traumatic" if it poses a threat of death or serious injury or a threat to the physical integrity of self or others. Common examples include war, terrorism, physical or sexual assault, natural disaster, childhood neglect and abuse, sudden and unexpected death of a loved one, and other catastrophic events. It has been estimated that the majority of the population will experience at least one extremely traumatic event during the course of their lives and that approximately 25% of trauma survivors will develop PTSD. For men, combat exposure and witnessing someone being injured or killed are the most common traumatic experiences associated with PTSD; for women, rape, sexual molestation, and childhood physical abuse are among the most frequent causes of PTSD.

Although trauma is probably the strongest risk factor for developing PTSD, with more severe and early-onset traumatic events being more predictive of PTSD, other factors also confer a higher risk than do others. Female gender, family history of psychiatric disorder, past history of behavior or psychological problems, substance abuse disorder, and neurotic or antisocial personality all are associated with increased risk of PTSD.

Neurobiological Mechanisms

Many studies suggest that PTSD may represent a state of sustained fear and arousal following trauma, influenced by neurochemical and neuroanatomical abnormalities as well as by genetic vulnerabilities. Some neurobiological abnormalities are well established, including adrenergic hyperactivity and enhanced negative feedback of the hypothalamic–pituitary–adrenocortical (HPA) axis, the body's stress response system that controls levels of cortisol and other important stress-related hormones. Dysregulations in other neurochemical pathways, including those for corticotropin-releasing factor (CRF), serotonin, dopamine, γ-aminobutyric acid (GABA), glutamate, and opioids, have also been indicated. Neuroanatomically, volumetric reductions in certain brain structures, such as the hippocampus, have been shown using neuroimaging studies. Furthermore, data from family and twin studies also implicate a genetic contribution to the development of PTSD.

Typical Symptoms and Disease Course

Typical PTSD symptoms encompass three major domains of symptoms: (1) persistent reexperiencing of the traumatic event such as nightmares or flashbacks, recurrent unwanted memories, and/or extreme reactions to reminders; (2) avoidance and numbing such as avoidance of any reminders of the trauma, inability to experience emotions, reduced interest, and distancing oneself from others; and (3) hyperarousal symptoms such as irritability, disturbed sleep, poor concentration, hypervigilance, and exaggerated startle response.

PTSD is a chronic and debilitating illness. A person with PTSD typically experiences more than three episodes—periods during which the individual has active symptoms that meet criteria for the diagnosis of PTSD—during their lifetimes. The average episode lasts approximately 7 years, suggesting that a person with PTSD often suffers from active symptoms for more than 20 years overall.

Comorbidity and Health Cost

PTSD patients are at considerable risk for developing other psychiatric and medical conditions. According to the National Comorbidity Survey (NCS), a nationally representative face-to-face survey of persons 15 to 54 years of age carried out in 49 states, 88% of the men and 79% of the women with lifetime PTSD had at least one other lifetime psychiatric disorder, most commonly major depression, alcohol dependence, or phobic disorder. Suicide risk is significantly higher among individuals with PTSD, with lifetime suicide attempts occurring as much as six to eight times more often than in the general population, even after controlling for comorbid lifetime depression.

Adverse health effects in PTSD are also demonstrated by increased rates of hypertension, bronchial asthma, peptic ulcer, and other abnormalities in the cardiovascular, respiratory, digestive, musculoskeletal, endocrine, and nervous systems as well as increased rates of infectious disease for up to 20 years following exposure to major trauma and after controlling for other variables.

The health service use and cost for PTSD are tremendous. It is estimated that the average work impairment for a person with PTSD is very similar to that associated with major depression, with approximately 3.6 days' work loss per month, translating into an annual productivity loss of more than $3 billion in the United States.

Pharmacological Treatment

Evidence of effective treatment is strongest for the following antidepressant drugs: sertraline, paroxetine, venlafaxine, mirtazapine, and fluoxetine. Older drugs, especially amitriptyline, imipramine, and phenelzine, are also more effective than placebo in male U.S. combat veterans with PTSD. When one of these agents alone does not produce an adequate response, other psychotropic drugs, including atypical antipsychotics (e.g., risperidone, olanzapine, quetiapine) and mood stabilizers (e.g., lamotrigine) can be added as augmentation agents or (sometimes) used alone as monotherapies. Other drugs, such as prazosin and clonidine, have been found to help relieve nightmares associated with PTSD.

Psychosocial Treatment

In addition to pharmacotherapy, psychosocial treatment produces significant improvement and appears to persist over time after completion of treatment. Psychological treatments proven to be effective include anxiety management (stress inoculation training), cognitive therapy, exposure therapy, play therapy, and psychoeducation. Anxiety management includes relaxation and breathing training, positive thinking and self-talk, assertiveness training, and thought stopping. Cognitive therapy helps to change unrealistic assumptions, beliefs, and automatic thoughts that lead to disturbing emotions. Exposure therapy, and particularly prolonged exposure, is most effective in helping people to confront any situations or objects that remind them of the trauma by recounting and recording their traumatic experiences, listening to their accounts, and being exposed to objects or situations they may otherwise avoid because of fear. For children, play therapy employs games to introduce the topic and facilitates healing of the traumatic memories. Finally, psychoeducation informs patients and their families about the symptoms and available treatments for PTSD and normalizes any emotions or feelings that may otherwise be experienced with guilt and shame.

Prevention and Management in the Immediate Aftermath of Trauma

It is highly recommended that people seek help after exposure to traumatic events. Early treatment helps to relieve psychological distress and may prevent development of chronic PTSD. Health care professionals should talk with trauma survivors and their families about normal reactions to trauma and identify more severe symptoms such as persistent depression, thoughts of hurting self or others, and disruptive or violent behaviors that warrant timely intervention. Although definitive evidence is lacking, short-term use of sleep-enhancing medication such as trazodone may help people to cope better with stress and resume functioning. Caution should be exercised in the use of benzodiazepines, which may interfere with the cognitive reprocessing and learning behavior that are so important in trauma recovery. In addition, maintaining general physical and psychological well-being prior to the occurrence of trauma is critical in predicting a person's resilience and in facilitating successful adaptation to extreme stress, thereby preventing stress-related psychopathology.

—*Wei Zhang and Jonathan R. T. Davidson*

See also Anxiety Disorders; Control; Disasters and Terrorism; Stress

Further Readings and References

Davidson JR, Connor KM. Management of posttraumatic stress disorder: Diagnostic and therapeutic issues. *J Clin Psychiatry.* 1999;18:33–38.

Davidson JRT, Hughes D, Blazer DG, George LK. Post-traumatic stress disorder in the community: An epidemiological study. *Psychol Med.* 1991;21:713–721.

Friedman MJ. What might the psychobiology of posttraumatic stress disorder teach us about future approaches to pharmacotherapy? *J Clin Psychiatry.* 2000;7:44–51.

Kessler RC. Posttraumatic stress disorder: The burden to the individual and to society. *J Clin Psychiatry.* 2000; 61:4–14.

Kessler RC, Sonnega A, Bromet E, Hughes M, Nelson CB. Posttraumatic stress disorder in the National Comorbidity Survey. *Arch Gen Psychiatry.* 1995;52:1048–1060.

Nutt DJ, Malizia AL. Structural and functional brain changes in posttraumatic stress disorder. *J Clin Psychiatry.* 2004; 1:11–17.

Silver RC, Holman EA, McIntosh DN, Poulin M, Gil-Rivas V. Nationwide longitudinal study of psychological responses to September 11. *JAMA.* 2002;288:1235–1244.

POVERTY

See SOCIOECONOMIC STATUS

PRESSURE ULCERS

Pressure ulcers are areas of local skin and tissue injury, usually developing over bony prominences such as the sacrum and heels. Pressure ulcers are also known as pressure sores, decubitus ulcers, and bed sores. Although friction, shearing forces, and moisture have also been implicated in the development of skin injury, *pressure ulcer* reflects the primary cause and is the preferred term for the problem.

Pressure ulcers are classified by the depth of visible damage. Fat, muscle, and blood vessel cells are sensitive to pressure and shearing forces and can be injured or die after exposure to 2 hours of persistent pressure. A sign of early tissue damage is unblanchable erythema, a reddened area of intact skin that does not lose its color when an examiner presses on the area. In darkly pigmented skin, erythema presents as a purple, blue, or darkened area. These types of pressure ulcers are classified as Stage 1 ulcers. Shallow ulcers, involving loss of only the epidermis and dermis, are classified as Stage 2 ulcers. Stage 3 ulcers involve deep tissue injury extending into subcutaneous tissue or fat. Ulcers extending into muscle or bone are classified as Stage 4 ulcers. Ulcers covered with necrotic tissue cannot be staged accurately.

Frequency of Pressure Ulcers

Most pressure ulcers develop during acute care hospitalizations. Among persons whose activity is limited to a bed or chair, as many as 30% may develop at least Stage 2 pressure ulcers during hospitalization. Nearly a quarter of persons in nursing homes have pressure ulcers, most of which are Stage 1 or Stage 2.

Besides decreased mobility and activity levels, incontinence, nutritional factors, and altered level of consciousness have been consistently documented to increase the risk of pressure ulcers. More than 50% of pressure ulcers occur in persons over 70 years of age.

Appropriate Management of Pressure Ulcers

Less than half of Stage 2 ulcers heal after 1 month. Even after 6 months, up to 40% of Stage 3 and Stage 4 ulcers do not heal. Therefore, prevention should be the priority of every pressure ulcer management program.

Persons with impaired ability to reposition in a bed or chair should be assessed for additional risk factors on admission to any health care facility. Assessments should be repeated on a regular basis and when a change in activity or mobility is noted. Interventions targeting identified risk factors reduce pressure ulcer occurrence.

Repositioning every 2 hours has been the primary method used for preventing pressure ulcers. If a person with limited ability to change position needs to sit in a chair, he or she should not remain in the chair for more than 1 hour at a time. When possible, individuals should be taught to shift their weight every 15 minutes while seated. The head of the bed should be maintained at the lowest degree of elevation and for the shortest periods of time possible.

Pressure-reducing mattresses have been shown to reduce the risk of developing pressure ulcers, and specialized beds may reduce the frequency of repositioning required and improve pressure ulcer outcomes. The use of foam-padded chairs, stretchers, and wheelchairs also may be helpful. Donut cushions and massage should not be used because they decrease blood flow to the skin.

Optimizing dietary intake and correcting nutritional deficiencies consistent with overall goals of care are also important. A daily high-potency vitamin and mineral supplement is recommended for persons suspected of vitamin deficiencies, but available evidence does not support the use of high-dose zinc, Vitamin C, supplemental Vitamin E, or arginine.

The location, stage, size, and wound characteristics of each pressure ulcer should be recorded. Follow-up assessments should be repeated at least weekly to determine ulcer progress. Within 2 to 4 weeks, a pressure ulcer should show improvement. If there is no evidence of ulcer improvement after 2 weeks of treatment, changes in management strategy should be considered.

Necrotic tissue needs to be removed before an ulcer will heal, but dry heel eschar may be left in place if there is no evidence of underlying infection. Removal of necrotic tissue can be accomplished using sharp debridement, mechanical approaches (e.g., hydrotherapy, irrigation), enzymatic approaches (e.g., collagenase, papain–urea), or autolytic techniques with moisture-retentive dressings (e.g., occlusive transparent films, hydrocolloid dressings). Autolytic approaches are contraindicated in infected ulcers. A 19-gauge, 35-ml syringe is recommended when wound irrigation is used.

Bacteria can temporarily be found in the blood of up to 50% of patients after debridement of pressure ulcers, but bloodstream infections due to pressure ulcers are relatively uncommon. However, when pressure ulcers are the source of bloodstream infections, the in-hospital mortality is nearly 60%. Broad-spectrum systemic antibiotics are indicated for patients with cellulitis, osteomyelitis, or sepsis.

Because all Stage 2, Stage 3, and Stage 4 ulcers are colonized with bacteria, routine swab cultures have no diagnostic value and should not be used. A 2-week trial of a topical antibiotic, such as silver sulfadiazine, can be considered for clean pressure ulcers that are not healing or are continuing to produce wound drainage after 2 to 4 weeks of optimal management. Topical antiseptics, such as povidone–iodine, iodophor, sodium hypochlorite, hydrogen peroxide, and acetic acid, impair wound healing and should not be used.

Once an ulcer is clean, healing is optimized with moisture-retentive dressings or gauze dressings kept moistened with normal saline to maintain a moist wound environment. Transparent films and hydrocolloids have been shown to improve healing of Stage 2 ulcers and to reduce nursing care time.

Adequate analgesia should be provided for ulcer pain. Electrotherapy for clean Stage 3 and Stage 4 ulcers, or negative pressure wound therapy for large draining ulcers, may be considered when no improvement is noted after 4 weeks of otherwise optimal therapy. Surgery can be used to close deep pressure ulcers; however, recurrence rates may be as high as 80%. Mortality in older patients can be as high as 50% during the year after surgery. There is no evidence for the effectiveness of hyperbaric oxygen use in pressure ulcers.

—*Barbara M. Bates-Jensen and Richard M. Allman*

See also Cellulitis; Foot Problems; Long-Term Care; Surgery; Wound Healing

Further Readings and References

Allman RM. Pressure ulcers. In: Hazzard WR, Blass JP, Halter JB, Ouslander JG, Tinetti ME, eds. *Principles of Geriatric Medicine and Gerontology.* 5th ed. New York: McGraw-Hill; 2003:1563–1569.

Bates-Jensen BM. Pressure ulcers: Pathophysiology and prevention. In: Sussman C, Bates-Jensen BM, eds. *Wound Care: A Collaborative Practice Manual for Physical Therapists and Nurses.* 2nd ed. Gaithersburg, Md: Aspen; 2001:235–270.

Cullum N, McInnes E, Bell-Syer SE, Legood R. Support surfaces for pressure ulcer prevention. *Cochrane Database Syst Rev.* 2004;(3):CD001735.

Langer G, Schloemer G, Knerr A, Kuss O, Behrens J. Nutritional interventions for preventing and treating pressure ulcers. *Cochrane Database Syst Rev.* 2003;(4):CD003216.

National Pressure Ulcer Advisory Panel. *Pressure Ulcers in America: Prevalence, Incidence, and Implications for the Future.* Cuddigan J, Ayello E, Sussman C, eds. Reston, Va: NPUAP; 2001. Available at: www.npuap.org. Accessed September 27, 2006.

Thomas DR. Issues and dilemmas in the prevention and treatment of pressure ulcers: A review. *J Gerontol A Biol Sci Med Sci.* 2001;56:M328–M340.

PROGERIA

See ACCELERATED AGING SYNDROMES

PSEUDODEMENTIA

Pseudodementia, as the term implies, is a condition that resembles and can be mistaken for dementia. Historically, the term was used to describe reversible deterioration of cognitive function secondary to many conditions, including medical and psychiatric diagnoses. Currently, the term refers primarily to the cognitive impairment seen in patients who have depressive disorders. Recently, it has been replaced by a more descriptive term, namely depression-related cognitive dysfunction. This entry provides an understanding of the term, describes how it differs from dementia, and describes its course and outcome.

Depressive symptoms are quite common in older adults. Population-based studies suggest that nearly 30% of people over 65 years of age show some depressive symptoms. The symptoms of depression in this age group include feelings of sadness; lack of interest in usually enjoyable activities; changes in sleep and appetite; poor energy, motivation, and/or concentration; feelings of hopelessness, worthlessness, and/or excessive guilt; and suicidal thoughts that may be mild (e.g., feeling that life is not worth living) to severe (e.g., intent, plan, and means to end one's life). Many older adults who become depressed can exhibit problems with their cognitive functioning, including memory. C. E. Wells in 1979 distinguished cognitive difficulties associated with depression, termed *pseudodementia,* from true dementia. Today in doctors' offices, when a patient presents with a new-onset memory complaint, depression is one of the main conditions that needs to be considered in the diagnostic evaluation.

There are several differences between pseudodementia and mild dementia as described by Wells, and some of these differences can be readily elicited in the doctor's office by asking about the patient's medical and psychiatric history. In general, cognitive changes of depression tend to have an abrupt onset and a short course, as opposed to dementia where the cognitive deterioration is gradual. Those patients who primarily have depression often have personal or family histories of depressive symptoms, and these are not common in patients with dementia. Another important difference is in the presentation. Depressed patients are acutely aware of their cognitive dysfunction, may even highlight or exaggerate it, and are distressed by it. On the other hand, demented patients are often unaware of their memory deficits and are often unconcerned about them; if they are somewhat aware, will try to conceal the disability. Typically, demented patients do not seek help from doctors for memory complaints but rather are brought in by family members who have noticed the decline. It is important to note that not all patients with a comparable severity of depression will have cognitive dysfunction; this is a heterogeneous group.

Formal neuropsychological testing carried out by trained psychologists is a more specific way to differentiate between pseudodementia of depression and dementia. Depressed patients are likely to abandon efforts on difficult tests, whereas demented patients will make adequate effort. Depressed patients tend to have inconsistency in test results over time and across a variety of tasks of similar difficulty, whereas demented patients have consistently poor performances. Although both conditions can affect memory, depressed patients are more likely to respond to cueing and do better on memory testing with coaching and feedback, whereas demented patients are not likely to make such gains.

The distinction between pseudodementia and dementia has become increasingly important with the availability of very effective treatment modalities for depression. These include a variety of antidepressant medications that can be well tolerated by the elderly and other biological treatments such as electroconvulsive therapy, which is usually reserved for treatment-resistant depression or the most severe forms of depression. Treatments for dementia are evolving at a slower pace. The most promising so far involve a class of drugs called cholinesterase inhibitors that slow down cognitive decline and may even improve cognitive function, albeit modestly and temporarily. A variety of other treatments are being studied to expand the armamentarium of physicians in fighting dementias.

With effective and adequate treatment of depressive symptoms, cognitive dysfunction can be ameliorated in many, but not all, patients. These ongoing cognitive impairments may be early signs of co-occurring Alzheimer's disease or vascular dementia. In fact, even in depressed patients whose cognitive symptoms go away altogether after treatment, there is a high rate of subsequent dementia. In a study done by G. S. Alexopoulos and colleagues in 1993, when depressed patients with or without cognitive symptoms were followed for an average of nearly 3 years after recovery, 43% of those with cognitive symptoms of depression went on to be diagnosed with dementia, compared with only 12% of those without cognitive symptoms. This finding has led to the suggestion that depression with cognitive changes, or pseudodementia, may be a harbinger of later dementia. Even so, it is important to recognize the difference and to treat the depression to improve patients' quality of life for possibly several years.

In fact, even in Alzheimer's disease patients, there can be co-occurring depression. Studies in such patients have shown that depression and cognitive status both independently affect the ability to perform day-to-day activities. It then becomes important to treat the depressive component in these patients because doing so may improve functioning, decrease health care costs, and reduce caregiver burden. Thus, regardless of whether all cognitive impairment is reversible, management of the depression is critical.

In conclusion, both depression and dementia can cause memory and cognitive impairment in the elderly. Current research aims at refining the understanding of reversible and irreversible cognitive impairment using neuropsychological and neuroimaging techniques. In the meantime, it is very important to use all available resources to differentiate between the two conditions and to treat each one appropriately.

—Mugdha Ekanath Thakur

See also Behavioral Disorders in Dementia; Lewy Body Dementia; Vascular Dementia

Further Readings and References

Alexopoulos GS, Meyers BS, Young RC, Mattis S, Kakuma T. The course of geriatric depression with "reversible dementia": A controlled study. *Am J Psychiatry.* 1993; 150:1693–1699.

Breitner JCS, Welsh KA. An approach to diagnosis and management of memory loss and other cognitive syndromes of aging. *Psychiatric Serv.* 1995;46:29–35.

Wells CE. Pseudodementia. *Am J Psychiatry.* 1979;136: 895–900.

PSYCHIATRIC RATING SCALES

With the exception of cognitive impairment, the prevalence of psychiatric disorders in older adults is lower than that observed in other age groups. Researchers have suggested that this may be due in part to selective survival or to a cohort effect. Although the prevalence of disorders may be low, older adults often report many clinically significant symptoms. These symptoms have been linked to adverse outcomes such as impairments in social and physical functioning, increased health care use, and decreased overall quality of life. Numerous scales have been used successfully in older populations to assess overall mental health status. Some of these are clinician rated, whereas others are self-administered or symptom checklists. The psychiatric rating scales discussed in this entry have been used successfully in research studies of older adults and are intended to identify psychiatric symptoms rather than disorders.

One instrument used frequently is the Global Assessment Scale (GAS), a clinician-rated scale to assess overall functioning during a specified time period, generally within the past week. The scale covers a wide range of severity, with a value of 1 indicating the hypothetically sickest and a value of 100 representing the hypothetically healthiest. Scores of 71 to 80, for example, represent individuals with only minimal psychopathology, if any, but not "positive mental health." Individuals receiving outpatient treatment would likely have scores of 31 to 70, and inpatients would likely have scores of 1 to 40. Rather than focusing on symptoms, the scale assesses the overall severity of psychiatric disturbance and therefore can be used across a variety of populations, from those with no psychiatric symptoms to those with severe illness. The clinician, using any information available from interviews and records, assigns the rating based on social and psychological functioning. The rating is time specific and not dependent on prior diagnosis or information. The scale is sensitive to changes over time, can be used in longitudinal studies, and has been translated into multiple languages.

The General Health Questionnaire (GHQ) is used to screen for the presence of psychiatric symptoms in the context of general medical illness. The GHQ is self-administered, and there are four versions available, each with a specific number of items: 12, 28, 30, and 60. Each symptom is scored as either present or absent, and symptoms present are summed. The GHQ covers various dimensions, including depression, anxiety, somatic symptoms, feelings of incompetence, difficulty in coping, and sleep disturbance, and has been translated into many languages.

The SF-36 Health Survey (SF-36) is a self- or interviewer-administered assessment of psychological status. Respondents provide self-reported indicators of behavioral functioning and psychological well-being. The 36 items in the scale are grouped into eight domains—physical functioning, physical role functioning, bodily pain, general health perceptions, vitality, social functioning, social role functioning, and mental health—and each domain has a range of scores. For example, a low score for general mental health would correspond to feelings of nervousness and depression all of the time, whereas a high score would correspond to feeling peaceful, happy, and calm all of the time, during the previous month. Scale scores range from 0 to 100, with higher scores indicating better health.

The Symptom Checklist-90–Revised (SCL-90-R) is a self-administered checklist of 90 items to measure the outcome or status of psychopathology across nine domains: somatization, obsessive–compulsive symptoms, interpersonal sensitivity, depression, anxiety, hostility, phobic–anxiety, paranoid ideation, and psychoticism. For each item, respondents mark the degree to which each symptom caused them discomfort during the previous week using a 5-point Likert scale. Each symptom is preceded by "How much were you distressed by . . . ," with a value of 0 = *not at all* and 4 = *extremely.* The SCL-90-R is available in multiple languages.

Some of the most widely used scales in community and clinical research studies of older adults are brief self-rating scales or symptom checklists for depressive symptoms. The Center for Epidemiologic Studies–Depression Scale (CES-D) contains 20 items assessing symptoms such as depressed mood, loss of appetite, sleep disturbance, feelings of worthlessness and hopelessness, fatigue, and loneliness. The scale can be self- or interviewer-administered. For each symptom (e.g., "I was bothered by things that usually don't bother me"), respondents are asked to rate on a scale from 0 to 3 how often they felt that way during the preceding week, with 0 = *less than 1 day* and 3 = *most or all of the time.* Positive symptoms are reverse coded to obtain the summary score. Total scores range from 0 to 60, with higher scores indicating more depressive symptoms. Scores higher than 16 are traditionally considered to be clinically significant for screening purposes. Factor analyses have shown the CES-D items to load on four factors: positive affect, negative affect, somatic symptoms, and interpersonal relationships. The CES-D has been translated into several languages, and shortened versions are available.

Other scales to screen for depressive symptoms include the Geriatric Depression Scale (GDS), the Beck Depression Inventory (BDI), and the Hamilton Rating Scale for Depression (HAM-D). The GDS is a self-rating scale developed specifically to measure depressive symptoms in older adults. It contains 30 items such as low mood, poor self-esteem, decreased motivation, obsessive traits, agitation, life satisfaction, and hopefulness, with questions such as "Are you basically satisfied with your life?" There is less focus on somatic symptoms of depression, such as sleep difficulties, decreased libido, and decreased energy, that are common during late life in the absence of depression. Because this scale has been validated in samples of older adults, it is particularly useful in research studies of this population. Rather than rating on a continuum, respondents indicate *yes* or *no* to indicate whether the symptom was present during the past week. Positive items are reverse coded, and scores are summed, with higher scores indicating more depressive symptoms. Abbreviated forms are also available. The GDS has been used successfully in nursing home patients and medically ill older adults. The BDI was developed to identify behavioral manifestations of depression. A total of 21 symptoms are listed, including mood, crying spells, irritability, and social withdrawal, and respondents indicate the severity of the symptom experienced at the time of the assessment (e.g., for mood, 0 = "I do not feel sad" and 3 = "I am so sad or unhappy that I can't stand it"). The scale can be self- or interviewer-administered. The scale has been modified since its original version to extend the time frame to 1 or 2 weeks and to include fewer items. The BDI is useful in following patients with depressive symptoms over time to monitor changes in severity. The HAM-D is used in clinical samples of patients to monitor changes in severity of depression over time and in general populations to measure level of depressive symptomatology. In its original form, the scale contained 21 items, but a modified 17-item scale is now the usual choice. Each symptom in the checklist is rated on a scale of either 0 to 2 or 0 to 4, with the higher score indicating greater severity (e.g., for depressed mood, 0 = *absent* and 4 = *severe*). The scale is interviewer administered by individuals with and without clinical training.

Screening instruments to identify clinically significant anxiety symptoms include the Beck Anxiety Inventory (BAI), the Hamilton Anxiety Rating Scale (HARS), and the Spielberger State–Trait Anxiety Inventory (STAI). The BAI is a 21-item self-report questionnaire focusing on somatic symptoms such as dizziness, nervousness, and difficulty in breathing. It is useful for identifying overall anxiety and distinguishing anxiety from depression, but it is not a useful screening tool for specific types of anxiety such as phobias and panic. Similarly, the HARS is a clinician-administered scale containing 14 items with a focus on somatic and psychic symptoms. The HARS measures symptoms of overall anxiety and includes symptoms such as mood, tension, fear, insomnia, depressed mood, cognitive and somatic symptoms, and cardiovascular, respiratory, and gastrointestinal symptoms. Like the BAI, the HARS may be less effective as a screening tool. The range of scores on the HARS is 0 to 56, with a score of at least 14 indicative of clinically significant anxiety. The STAI has been used successfully to measure the prevalence of anxiety symptoms in hospitalized geriatric patients.

The Comprehensive Psychopathological Rating Scale (CPRS) has been used in a community sample of older adults to measure the prevalence of paranoid symptoms. The CAGE instrument has been used to identify alcohol problems in older adults. The scale is made up of four items: whether the older adult has felt that he or she needed to *cut down* (C) on drinking, whether people had *annoyed* (A) the respondent by criticizing his or her drinking, whether the respondent felt *guilty* (G) about his or her drinking, and whether the respondent ever had a drink to wake up in the morning; that is, an *eye opener* (E). Each question is answered *yes* or *no* for a range of 0 to 4 points, with a score of at least 2 suggesting clinical significance. The CAGE instrument is administered quickly and has been translated into many languages. The Michigan Alcoholism Screening Test (MAST) has a geriatric version available (MAST-G). The MAST-G is interviewer administered and contains 24 items. Responses are weighted, with a score of at least 5 indicating possible alcoholism. No time period is associated with the symptoms listed, resulting in somewhat less utility as a screening tool for current problems.

—*Celia F. Hybels*

See also Agitation; Anxiety Disorders; Depression and Other Mood Disorders; Emotions and Emotional Stability; Geriatric Assessment; Vascular Depression

Further Readings and References

American Psychiatric Association. *Handbook of Psychiatric Measures.* Washington, DC: APA; 2000.

Endicott J, Spitzer RL, Fleiss JL, Cohen J. The Global Assessment Scale. *Arch Gen Psychiatry.* 1976; 33:766–771.

Radloff LS. The CES-D Scale: A self-report depression scale for research in the general population. *Appl Psychol Measure.* 1977;1:385–401.

Yesavage JA, Brink TL, Rose TL, et al. Development and validation of a geriatric depression screening scale. *J Psychiatric Res.* 1983;17:37–49.

PSYCHOSOCIAL THEORIES

Human development is a multifaceted phenomenon. But to recognize that development has many facets is merely to begin to understand the phenomenon. Just what are the facets? How do they emerge in culture and in individuals? What are their adaptive functions? Decades of longitudinal research have made it clear that relatively few people follow the same path of individual development or ontogenesis. Although ontogenetic development is a lifelong process that extends from conception onward, it is believed to take on new meaning and significance during old age because of normative reductions in biological, cognitive, and social reserve capacities. The allocation of available resources, the maintenance of individual functioning, and the regulation of loss all constitute major adaptive tasks during later life. Understanding how older adults adapt successfully in the face of finite capacities and limited resources is a primary concern of psychosocial theories of aging.

Two psychosocial theories in particular—selection, optimization, and compensation (SOC) and socioemotional selectivity theory (SST)—have guided many studies of successful development. Derived from life span psychology, both theories represent descriptive–interpretive accounts of evidence obtained primarily from two types of research: (a) developmental research, or studies designed to indicate the ways in which individuals develop with age and particularly during adulthood, and (b) intervention research, or studies directed at identifying features of individual development that can be changed, refined, and maintained throughout adulthood.

Central to SOC theory is the assumption that, throughout life, individuals encounter both opportunities and constraints. According to the theory, the quintessence of successful individual development is found in the adaptive expression of gains and losses through the coordinated regulation of three central developmental processes: selection, optimization, and compensation. The first process, s*election,* gives direction to successful development by allocating finite resources to specific goal-directed behavior. Selection can occur in response to new demands and challenges (i.e., elective selection) or in response to actual or anticipated losses (i.e., loss-based selection). The second process, *optimization,* denotes the process of acquiring and refining relevant resources to attain desired outcomes in selective life domains. Finally,

compensation concerns efforts to maintain normative functioning (e.g., crystallized or pragmatic abilities, motivation, positive health behaviors, sensorimotor functioning). Thus, a primary focus of the SOC model is to understand how older adults adapt successfully to the risks and vulnerabilities of advancing age through the orchestration of selection, optimization, and compensation strategies.

Although considered to be a metamodel of life span development, the SOC model has provided a general framework for understanding the nature and limits of what is referred to as *successful aging.* Supportive evidence for the key proposition that successful aging entails selective optimization with compensation comes from empirical research demonstrating the social–environmental foundation and adaptational significance of behavioral dependence and wisdom-related knowledge during adulthood and old age. Of particular interest to the study of dependency in old age has been the model of learned dependency. In this theory, the dependency of old age is not considered to be an inevitable consequence of decline; rather, it is attributed in large part to the differential contingencies present in the social environment. Unlike the model of learned helplessness, which views dependent behaviors as instantiations of dysfunctionality, the model of learned dependency highlights the dynamic and adaptive interplay between losses and gains during later adulthood. The basic premise of the model is that although dependency may lead to a loss of autonomy, dependent behaviors can be highly functional when they are enacted to maintain or gain control over social contacts. Intervention studies with older adults have further established that the social behavior of partners can be modified to be more responsive to needs of the elderly for both autonomy and dependence.

Another area in which the SOC model has been applied is the study of wisdom-related knowledge during later adulthood. Theoretical writings suggest that wisdom involves deep insight into the meaning and purpose of life. Accumulating empirical evidence indicates that wisdom represents an extremely broad and diverse range of knowledge—the knowledge of a culture (shared societal beliefs, values, attitudes, customs, and behaviors). Foundational support for the adaptive function of wisdom during later life comes from studies demonstrating that pragmatic knowledge of one's own good and the good of others can be implemented successfully through the life management strategies of selective optimization with compensation.

That wisdom appears to be more prevalent in older cohorts is also demonstrated by studies suggesting that older adults are more likely to select engagements that preserve emotional well-being and to withdraw from those that are sullied by negative emotions. How socioemotional functioning develops and is maintained throughout adulthood is a key concern of SST, a theory initially conceived to provide an explanation of the well-established reduction in social contacts observed during old age. SST is a descriptive alternative to two previously influential, but conflicting, sociological explanations of the reliable age-related decrease in social interaction. Activity theory considered inactivity to be an environmentally induced problem emanating from social norms, whereas the alternative, disengagement theory, suggested that impending death motivates a mutual psychological withdrawal between the older individual and society. In contrast, SST holds that the reduction in older persons' social networks and social involvement represents a motivated redistribution of resources by older adults.

According to SST, individuals are guided by certain fundamental socioemotional goals throughout life, including seeking autonomy, feeling needed, and building efficacy and competency. The relative priority of different sets of goals, however, changes as a function of perceived time left in life. When the future is perceived as expansive, individuals prioritize goals that optimize the future; when the future is perceived as limited, current goals that maximize emotional meaning become more important. Thus, time perspective is seen as being integrally involved in human goal-directed behavior. Future time perspective is inherently associated with chronological age; as people age, they perceive their futures as more limited. This general observation is supported by developmental research indicating that, across the life span, older adults foresee a relatively less expansive future

than do younger adults. SST further postulates that the age-related motivational shift in time perspective leads to alterations in the dynamic interplay between individuals and their environments such that people place greater importance on emotionally meaningful goals as they age and devote more social resources to attaining them.

In sum, the general observation that age is accompanied by both gains and losses in selective life domains leads to a series of questions about the adaptive functions of SOC- and SST-related processes that hold promise for illuminating important questions about how some older adults manage to adapt successfully in the face of declining resources and how they may experience both harm and benefit as a result of their experience. For example, how people sustain positive health and functional capacities as life challenges multiply is a question of considerable import during old age. Research directed at understanding how negative life events and persistent life strains can accumulate to compromise health during later adulthood is needed. In addition, a focus on the untapped reserve capacity of older adults may have important implications for interventions designed to enhance the potential for continued adaptive development throughout adulthood. Elevating the side of human strengths and resilience, more attention also needs to be given to ethnic minority research. Scientific investigations of ethnic minorities during later life have focused disproportionately on pathology and deficits and have given relatively little attention to the unique resources and cultural strengths within minority populations. Together, such research has much promise for advancing knowledge of how successful adaptation is forged in the face of adversity.

—*Anthony D. Ong and C. S. Bergeman*

See also Expectations Regarding Aging; Motivation; Self-Rated Health; Social Networks and Social Support

Further Readings and References

Baltes MM. *The Many Faces of Dependency in Old Age.* New York: Cambridge University Press; 1996.

Baltes PB, Baltes MM, eds. *Successful Aging: Perspectives From the Behavioral Sciences.* New York: Cambridge University Press; 1990.

Carstensen LL, Isaacowitz DM, Charles ST. Taking time seriously: A theory of socioemotional selectivity. *Am Psychol.* 1999;54:165–181.

Rowe JW, Kahn RL. Human aging: Usual and successful. *Science.* 1987;237:143–149.

Pulmonary Aging

Acute respiratory symptoms are among the most common reasons why older persons seek medical attention. In addition, clinical manifestations of the more chronic respiratory diseases play a major role in reduced function, acute hospitalizations, and increased mortality seen in older persons. Despite decades of research in respiratory physiology and lung biology, there is still difficulty in isolating age-related changes in lung structure and function from the many other confounding risk factors encountered by most individuals during 70 or more years of living. These "cohort effect" uncertainties should perhaps not be surprising. The current generation of persons over 65 years of age was born and raised in the preantibiotic era, when the devastating effects on lung development of formerly common childhood respiratory viral infections, such as pertussis and measles, were rampant. Tuberculosis was the most common cause of death during the teens and early adulthood of this cohort, and exposure as measured by the common tuberculosis skin test was nearly 100%. As a whole, there has probably been a higher prevalence of cigarette smoking in the generation born between 1910 and 1930 than at any time in the history of the human race. As adults during the post–World War II era, they have had the longest potential exposure to high levels of particulate air pollution ever experienced to date.

The health impact of chronic obstructive pulmonary disease (COPD) in elderly patients is enormous. The fourth leading cause of death among persons age 65 years and older, COPD in its various clinical forms is relatively common in older adults and probably underdiagnosed. For example, chronic bronchitis, defined as production of phlegm for at least 3 months of the year for at least 2 consecutive years, is present in 15% of community-dwelling persons age 65 years and older. The presence of chronic bronchitis is associated with more acute respiratory infections and hospitalizations. In addition to being very common in older adults, chronic bronchitis has strong prognostic implications. In fact, this symptom complex of cough and phlegm production is associated with a 30% excess mortality over a 10-year period. For at least the past 25 years, there has been a steady increase in age-adjusted office visits, hospitalizations, and mortality for COPD in both men and women. There is a particularly high symptom burden in community-dwelling older adults with advanced COPD. Individuals with COPD have 71% more moderate or severe symptoms than do participants with advanced congestive heart failure. As is often the case in geriatric care, the frequency and range of symptoms associated with COPD may be distinct from those experienced by younger patients. For example, predominating presenting symptoms, such as limited activity, fatigue, and physical discomfort, are nearly as prevalent as shortness of breath. Compared with the general population, older patients with COPD are twice as likely to rate their health as fair or poor, are nearly twice as likely to report limitations in their usual activities, and visit physicians for medical care more frequently.

Asthma is a relatively common and potentially serious disease in older persons. Moreover, asthma is frequently underdiagnosed in older age groups. Various studies cite an asthma prevalence rate of 7% to 9% in persons over 65 years of age compared with prevalence rates of 6% to 7% in the general population. Rates of hospitalization for asthma are highest in the age groups over 65 years. Asthma death rates also rise dramatically with advancing age. Although many older patients with asthma have clear lifelong clinical histories of symptomatic bronchospasm, there is growing appreciation that asthma may commonly become manifest after 65 years of age. In some surveys of older asthmatics attending a pulmonary referral clinic, 48% had developed asthma after 65 years of age.

Lung cancer is responsible for 18% of all cases of cancer in men and 12% in women. Of all deaths related to cancer, approximately 34% in men and 22% in women are attributable to lung cancer. Half of all cases of lung cancer occur in patients age 65 years and older, with the peak incidence occurring at around 75 years of age. The increased importance of this neoplasm with age in both sexes is attributable mainly to cigarette smoking and possibly to an age-related diminution in immunological surveillance.

Pulmonary embolization (blood clot in a lung artery) is a major cause of morbidity in older persons, especially among the more sedentary and bedbound elderly. A number of factors predispose older persons to deep venous thrombosis (blood clot in the leg), which can travel to the lung to cause pulmonary embolus. There is a higher frequency of factors contributing to venous stasis (slowed blood flow in veins) such as congestive heart failure and general immobility. There is also increasing evidence that older persons frequently have a hypercoagulable state in which blood tends to clot more easily than normal.

Interstitial pulmonary fibrosis (IPF) encompasses an extremely heterogeneous group of disorders. Several points bear emphasis. These are not predominantly diseases of the young; in fact, in carefully performed studies of the clinical course of IPF, the most common age group experiencing onset of symptoms attributable to IPF is the 60- to 65-year-old group. Fully a third of IPF patients have no clinical manifestations before 65 years of age.

When Sir William Osler called pneumonia old age's enemy, he could scarcely have anticipated the status of lower respiratory tract infection among the elderly in the current age. Community-acquired pneumonia remains the leading cause of death from infectious disease in the United States. Pneumonia and influenza currently rank as the fifth most common cause of death in those over 65 years of age in the United States. Influenza virus infection is perhaps the most dramatic example of the importance of respiratory infection in these age groups. Despite the enormous clinical importance of influenza infection among older persons and the availability of safe inexpensive immunizations, annual rates of vaccine administration among persons over 65 years of age in most American communities is approximately 40% to 60%. It is well known that influenza immunization is associated with reductions in rates of hospitalization by 50% and reductions in mortality of 40% to 55%. Increasing the frequency of annual immunization in persons over 65 years of age is perhaps the most cost-effective practice that primary care physicians can bring to their older patients.

Sleep-related problems among older persons are extremely common. In most instances, these complaints lead to an evaluation focused predominantly on the respiratory system. Three types of sleep-disordered breathing abnormalities bear mentioning: sleep apnea, periodic leg movements of sleep (PLMS) in the elderly, and rapid eye movement (REM) sleep behavior disorders. Snoring is very common in the elderly. *Sleep apnea* in older men is also common and seems to increase with advancing age. Prevalence figures of 10% to 75% have been cited. Studies have suggested an adverse impact on cognitive functioning and possibly an increase in cardiovascular mortality. However, the great majority of older persons with sleep apnea experience no adverse consequences of these episodes. *PLMS* is a geriatric syndrome characterized by periodic episodes of repetitive limb movements and wakefulness. Most patients have an uncontrollable urge to move their legs as they are falling asleep. Prevalence figures suggest that 25% to 60% of older persons may have manifestations of PLMS. Patients are often brought to medical attention by their spouses or well-meaning caregivers who mistake the movements for seizure activity. Therapy consists of initial discontinuation of some drug classes, especially certain antidepressants. In *REM sleep behavior disorders,* the usual sharply reduced motor tone characteristic of REM sleep is replaced by a tendency to act out dreams, sometimes in very dramatic fashion. As opposed to sleepwalking, which occurs during the third and fourth stages of sleep when individuals are very hard to arouse, patients with REM disorders remember the dream content, which is often very frightening. Not surprisingly, these episodes can be mistaken for manfestations of dementia.

—William J. Hall

See also Cancer, Common Types of; Cardiovascular System; Immune Function; Infectious Diseases; Pneumonia and Tuberculosis; Sleep; Stroke

Further Readings and References

Hey JC. Lung cancer in elderly patients. *Clin Geriatr Med.* 2003;19:139–155.

Lange P, Parner J, Prescott E, Vestbo J. Chronic bronchitis in an elderly population. *Age Ageing.* 2003;32:636–642.

Steinman MA, Sauaia A, Maselli JH, Houck PM, Gonzales R. Office evaluation and treatment of elderly patients with acute bronchitis. *J Am Geriatr Soc.* 2004;52:875–879.

Torres OH, Munoz J, Ruiz D, et al. Outcome predictors of pneumonia in elderly patients: Importance of functional assessment. *J Am Geriatr Soc.* 2004;52:1603–1609.

Walke LM, Gallo WT, Tinetti ME, Fried TR. The burden of symptoms among community-dwelling older persons with advanced chronic disease. *Arch Intern Med.* 2004;164: 2321–2324.

Zeleznik J. Normative aging of the respiratory system. *Clin Geriatr Med.* 2003;19(1):1–18.

QUALITATIVE RESEARCH ON AGING

The complexity and wealth of lived experiences that exemplify the health and lives of older adults call for research approaches that fully capture their richness and breadth. Qualitative researchers believe that the intricacies of the human experience cannot be understood adequately by depending only on the "objective" measurements of positivist researchers, nor do they believe that objective reality can be known even if it exists. Rather, they believe that there are multiple realities that are equally viable, realities that can be uncovered by asking participants how they interpret and construct their social worlds. In place of statistics, the words, meanings, contexts, and conceptualizations of persons form the fundamentals of this approach.

Qualitative Research as a Method

Qualitative research is an umbrella term often used interchangeably with *interpretive/constructivist research* or *naturalistic inquiry* and is used in at least two ways. Sometimes, the term refers to a diverse set of methods or procedures for conducting research, and numerous discipline-specific qualitative research traditions have developed. For example, sociology lays claim to symbolic interactionism, grounded theory, and ethnomethodology; psychology to hermeneutics and ecological psychology; anthropology to ethnography; philosophy to phenomenology; and sociolinguistics to discourse analysis. Other disciplines, such as health services research, nursing, education, and marketing, have developed their own styles by borrowing liberally from other traditions. The quest for an organizational map of qualitative methods has been likened to the search for the Holy Grail as the methods derive from 30 or more traditions and multiple disciplines characterized by a proliferation of conceptual jargon.

Most of the research on health-related issues of older adults appears to draw on four preferred methods. The first is *grounded theory,* the intent of which is to generate new theory or to add to, or revise, existing theory. The second, *ethnography,* describes and interprets the meaning of behavior in a cultural context and is both a process and an outcome. The third is *phenomenology,* which seeks to capture the lived experience of a person as it relates to a specific concept or phenomenon. The last preferred method is *discourse analysis,* in which the participant's words are analyzed for verbal interaction and dialogue.

Qualitative Research as a Philosophy

In contrast to the understanding of qualitative research as method, the term also denotes a philosophy or worldview in competition with quantitative research and based in positivism. Beginning in the late 1970s, adherents to the philosophical position of postpositivism challenged the tenets of positivist inquiry, arguing that there could be multiple interpretations of reality and that researchers' own feelings and values influence the research process and findings. Thus, although qualitative inquiry breaks down the complexity of the real world, at the same time it is deeply embedded in the socialization of its adherents and practitioners. It is not unusual, however, for authors to vacillate between these methodological and philosophical traditions without stating clearly which of the two forms the basis for their approach.

Qualitative Research in Health and Aging

Whether as a method or a philosophy, qualitative research has greatly enriched the study of health and aging. Observational fieldwork, in-depth interviews, and analyses of text—separately or in combination—interpret the meanings of what people say, do, and think in topics encompassing both structure and process. For example, health researchers have explored social isolation in nursing home residents, the organization of work in health care settings, the experience of stroke recovery, and resilience in the face of chronic illness.

A common thread among all of these studies is that researchers place themselves in direct contact with, or in the immediate proximity of, those being studied. This enables them to appreciate the processes of the social world and to incorporate the realm of subjective experience (including their own) in the production of data. Researchers and participants become mutually interactive and influence each other simultaneously.

Evaluation of Qualitative Health Research

Qualitative researchers resist the view that their investigations of the subjective aspect of experience lack scientific rigor, spawning a growing body of literature for evaluating qualitative studies. A broad evaluation can be made by asking two questions. First, was the method of data collection comprehensive enough to support robust and rich descriptions of the event under study? Second, were the analyses appropriate and the findings corroborated? Alternatively, one may use

four criteria—credibility, transferability, dependability, and confirmability—that mirror the positivist paradigm: internal validity, external validity, reliability, and objectivity. At the policy level, the U.K. government has devised a list of 18 appraisal questions to evaluate qualitative evidence.

The criteria used to evaluate grant applications and manuscripts in health research have been based traditionally on quantitative principles. However, the increasing ability to guide the evaluation of qualitative studies bodes well for the success of qualitative research applications. The growing maturity and acceptance of qualitative inquiries guarantee that the intricacies of human experience will be recognized as a stand-alone valued avenue of health and aging research and not only as an "add-on" to quantitative investigations.

—*Barbara J. Payne*

See also Demography of Aging; Epidemiology of Aging; Longitudinal Research; Social Networks and Social Support

Further Readings and References

Cobb A, Forbes S. Qualitative research: What does it have to offer the gerontologist? *J Gerontol A Biol Sci Med Sci.* 2002;57:M197–M202.

Denzin N, Lincoln Y, eds. *Handbook of Qualitative Research.* 3rd ed. Thousand Oaks, Calif: Sage; 2005.

Devers K. How will we know "good" qualitative research when we see it? Beginning the dialogue in health services research. *Health Serv Res.* 1999;34:1153–1188.

Giacomi M, Cook D. Users' guide to the medical literature: XXIII. Qualitative research in health care: Are the results of the study valid? *JAMA.* 2000;284:357–362.

Glaser B, Strauss A. *The Discovery of Grounded Theory.* Chicago: Aldine; 1967.

Gubrium J. *Living and Dying at Murray Manor.* New York: St. Martin's; 1975.

QUALITY OF LIFE

Medical advances during the past century have dramatically increased average life span and changed the course of illness during older age. Many illnesses previously considered to be terminal are now treated as chronic conditions. As people live longer with chronic illnesses, quality of life has become an increasingly important issue to older adults and researchers alike. The current emphasis on quality of life during later life has shifted the focus of geriatric health care from increasing the quantity of years to increasing the quality of years. Despite increased knowledge of disease causes, healthy lifestyle changes, and successful treatment options, there is scant evidence that rapid advances in science and medicine have resulted in improved quality of life for elder adults. This entry reviews the emergence of quality of life as a concept and major goal of health and social policy, explores its meaning and measurement, details a new approach to assessment, and suggests possible directions for future research.

Historically, quality of life has been a concern of the humanities, religion, philosophy, sociology, medical science, and social gerontology. Although the concept existed earlier, quality of life did not receive significant attention until after World War II. In 1948, the World Health Organization (WHO) expanded its definition of health to include "health as a state of complete physical, mental, and social well-being." Simultaneously, dramatic social inequities and health disparities across Western societies captured the attention of researchers. Concerns about quality of life and poverty during older age gave rise to reform movements, Social Security, and the policy initiatives of the 1960s' "War on Poverty" in the United States.

Although not defined, quality of life was identified as a goal during the mid-1960s in the *Report of the President's Commission on National Goals in the United States.* The term was used primarily in reference to objective social indicators such as number of households with telephones, material wealth, divorce rates, and crime statistics. Following the political and social upheavals of the 1960s, emphasis shifted from objective indicators to subjective dimensions of quality of life such as personal freedom, enjoyment, and caring. It was argued that quality of life is a state of mind rather than a state of health or wealth. Because people respond to subjective impressions, their feelings and perceptions need to be considered when assessing quality of life.

The increasing use of the term *quality of life* in the popular press of the 1960s was followed by its use in medical research. The term first appeared in academic literature in the *International Encyclopedia of Social Sciences* in 1968 and in *Index Medicus* during the mid-1970s. As interest in this topic grew over the subsequent 30 years, numerous health-related instruments were developed as medical research shifted its focus from mortality and morbidity to the broader impact of chronic disease on quality of life.

Although there is a burgeoning research literature devoted to the measurement of quality of life, a precise definition remains elusive. Despite this limitation, a consensus has emerged that quality of life is multidimensional in nature and must include both objective and subjective dimensions. Current researchers often cite the WHO's definition of quality of life as an individual's self-perception of his or her position in life in the context of that individual's own culture and value systems. Quality of life measures are increasingly used to evaluate the value of medical and social services, assess life course changes, and distinguish disadvantaged population groups. Consequently, our understanding of the relationship between specific therapeutic interventions and quality of life across the life span has increased.

Research suggests that what constitutes quality of life changes with age. When older adults are asked about their primary values and concerns, their own health and the health of significant others are cited most often as vital to a good quality of life. However, a host of other issues—physical, social, and psychological—are also regarded as important. As a result of the expanding definitions of quality of life in today's geriatric population, medical professionals are beginning to focus on treating the whole person while also appreciating that for some patients a long life is not necessarily a good life.

Not surprisingly, the process of defining quality of life across different cultures, geographic areas, age groups, and socioeconomic conditions is a complex task. In reviewing the global research literature, one finds that the definitions used are as numerous and diverse as the methods of assessment. Despite increased research and public policy attention, few instruments exist specifically to measure quality of life in older adults. Definitions for quality of life among this group range from broad socioeconomic measures to narrow health-related measures.

As indicated previously, health alone does not determine most older people's perception of their quality of life. Someone in good health can claim a poor quality of life, whereas someone in poor health can claim a good quality of life. Some critics argue that if quality of life is defined primarily, or even partly, as a state of mind, it becomes impossible to develop an objective measure for quality of life. Be that as it may, most researchers embrace a broad approach to this important topic.

When measuring quality of life in older adults, a valid multidimensional approach—one allowing for individual values and both objective assessments and subjective perceptions—is most useful. A comprehensive measure should evaluate a variety of dimensions deemed to be important by older adults. In particular, because chronic illness can exert a wide range of effects, quality of life measures must encompass at least three overarching dimensions. Building on prior research, the Wisconsin Quality of Life Index (WQLI) was developed as a multidimensional instrument for older adults encompassing both objective and subjective criteria and spanning multiple dimensions of individuals' lives (Figure 1).

The WQLI allows information to be collected from multiple points of view and over extended periods of time. It is organized to evaluate the following dimensions: (a) objective quality of life indicators such as housing and environment, (b) meaningful activities, (c) psychological well-being, (d) physical health, (e) social relations, (f) economics, (g) activities of daily living (ADLs), (h) physical symptoms, and (i) achievement of personal goals. The WQLI is designed to be self-administered, easy to use, and appropriate for a variety of research and clinical settings. If an older adult is unable to read or write, someone can

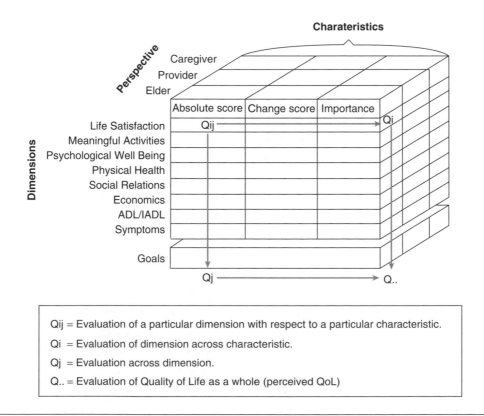

Qij = Evaluation of a particular dimension with respect to a particular characteristic.

Qi = Evaluation of dimension across characteristic.

Qj = Evaluation across dimension.

$Q..$ = Evaluation of Quality of Life as a whole (perceived QoL)

Figure 1   Conceptual Model for Evaluating Quality of Life in Older Adults

Note: ADL/IADL = activities of daily living/instrumental activities of daily living.

assist him or her with filling out the questionnaire. A caregiver can complete the WQLI on behalf of an incapacitated older adult. Quality of life assessments can then be used to monitor the course of chronic illness and the impact of medical treatment and other services. By examining separate domains of quality of life with a multidimensional instrument such as this, the interrelationship among physical, psychological, and social dimensions can be explored and better understood. Future research should focus on the complex interrelationships among quality of life, illness severity, and health outcomes in older adults

—*Marion A. Becker and Ezra Ochshorn*

See also Expectations Regarding Aging; Positive Attitudes and Health; Social Networks and Social Support; Successful Aging

Further Readings and References

Becker M, Diamond R, Douglas J. *Wisconsin Quality of Life Assessment Manual.* Madison: University of Wisconsin Press; 1996.

Bond J, Corner L. *Quality of Life and Older People.* Berkshire, England: Open University Press; 2004.

Farquhar M. Elderly people's definitions of quality of life. *Social Sci Med.* 1995;41:1439–1446.

Feinstein A. Problems in defining quality of life. In: Levy J, Jasmin C, Bez G, eds. *Cancer, AIDS, and Quality of Life.* New York: Plenum; 1997:11–15.

World Health Organization. Preamble to the Constitution of the World Health Organization as adopted by the International Health Conference, New York, June 19–22, 1946; signed on July 22, 1946, by the representatives of 61 states (official records of the World Health Organization, No. 2, p. 100) and entered into force on April 7, 1948.

RACE

See ETHNICITY AND RACE

REHABILITATION THERAPIES

Rehabilitation constitutes the act or process of therapeutic intervention that restores or redevelops the sensory, physical, and/or cognitive capacities of the individual. Alternatively, in cases where full recovery is not possible, rehabilitation involves maximizing functional outcomes within the limits of the individual's physical disability. Those individuals who perform therapeutic intervention are a part of the rehabilitation team that typically is composed of physicians; nurses; physical, occupational, and speech therapists; nutritionists; care managers; and supportive staff. As a result of increasing need, specialties in each of these disciplines have evolved to improve the management and care of older adults and to facilitate their return to independence. Physical and occupational therapy are the disciplines that are primarily responsible for the act of providing the therapeutic rehabilitation. They are involved in the preventive, acute, rehabilitative, and chronic stages of rehabilitation, and their focus is on restoring health, alleviating pain, preventing the onset of permanent dysfunction, and addressing and reversing functional limitations,

impairments, and disabilities as well as general declines in health status.

The overall goal of the rehabilitation team is to successfully identify and address the four major components of the disabling process defined by the Institute of Medicine in 1990 as pathology, impairment, functional limitation, and disability. *Pathology* reflects the changes at the tissue level caused by disease, infection, trauma, and/or other factors affecting molecules and cells of the body. *Impairment* results from the functional loss of biochemical, physiological, or mental control at the organ or organ system level. The inability to accomplish tasks that require the coordinated use of the organ system lead to *functional limitations* such as rising from a chair and getting out of bed. *Disability* is the culmination of the preceding three components and reduces the individual's ability to function fully within society or at the level of expected performance. In the geriatric setting, disability has a narrower range of expectations because society has a diminished expectation of older people's ability or capacity to function as individuals within society.

Rehabilitation starts with a thorough evaluation. This involves gathering pertinent patient history such as past medical (e.g., hypertension, chronic obstructive pulmonary disease) and surgical (e.g., total knee arthroplasty, coronary bypass surgery) histories and current living status (e.g., living alone in a home, living in an assisted-living facility). During the interaction with the older adult, the therapist will develop a sense of overall arousal level and mentation as well as the older adult's ability to process information. A physical examination will reveal the general status of the musculoskeletal, cardiopulmonary, neurological, and integumentary systems, and specific tests will determine motor function, coordination, balance, muscle strength and power, joint integrity, mobility and range of motion, aerobic capacity and endurance, and ambulation status. The assimilated information, along with a clinical diagnosis provided by the geriatrician, will allow the development of a plan of care that will then outline a course of action in terms of therapeutic intervention. Short-term goals, which will specify time points for meeting certain levels of progress critical for the overall attainment of long-term goals, will be established. Long-term goals are those levels of performance that are to be accomplished by the end of rehabilitation. Once the goals have been established, a treatment plan specifying the frequency of treatment, duration of treatment, and intensity and type of exercises prescribed will be organized. With older adults, the primary focus is on maintaining, regaining, or maximizing physical function at the independent level in activities of daily living (ADLs).

Physical function refers to those sensory, motor, and cognitive tasks that work in a coordinated manner and are necessary for performing ADLs. ADLs are those tasks involving daily self-care such as feeding, dressing, personal hygiene, and physical mobility. The tasks that an individual needs to perform to function independently within his or her community are referred to as instrumental activities of daily living (IADLs) and involve driving, shopping, cooking, and managing the home environment. The main function of rehabilitation is to return as much physical function as is possible. The therapist's role is to identify needs and facilitate the return of the individual's function through strengthening affected limbs, enhancing endurance for functional needs, and reestablishing motor control. In the geriatric setting, this is often a prolonged process because older adults typically enter the rehabilitation setting with muscle loss and declines in strength that are exacerbated by imposed bed rest incurred while receiving care.

Restoration of function requires the integration of several therapies. Nearly all conditions in the geriatric setting involve restoring or increasing strength. Strength gains in the acute care setting typically involve progressive resistive exercises, isometric contractions, and/or proprioceptive neuromuscular facilitation. *Progressive resistive exercises* involve serial increases in resistance to accommodate gains in strength achieved during therapy. Typically, resistance must be greater then 65% of a one repetition maximum (the maximal amount of weight that can be lifted through full range of motion with proper form) and requires periodic reevaluation to adjust for acute gains in maximal strength. *Isometric contractions* involve contraction of the muscle without overt joint motion. Both forms of strengthening are used routinely in the hospital setting as exercises performed while the therapist is not present. *Proprioceptive neuromuscular facilitation* is often employed when overt or suspected upper motor neuron dysfunction or spasticity is present. Range of motion exercises involve restoring the range through which a target limb or appendage moves. This is particularly pertinent in patients after orthopedic surgery (e.g., total knee arthroplasty, total hip replacement) but is determined on a case-by-case basis. Active range of motion seeks to restore the ability of the individual to move the affected limb or appendage through the range of motion without the assistance of the therapist. Functional range of motion is similar to active range of motion but is subject to the ability of the individual to function within the attained functional range (e.g., whether the older adult can put on a shirt or climb stairs) but might not be full range of motion as measured with a goniometer. Any number of techniques may be applied to gain range of motion, including heat, cold, contract relax, sustained stretch, oscillations, and manual techniques of joint play. Bed mobility and transfer training are necessary and early components of therapy with the ultimate goal of ambulation. Bed mobility involves the ability to transition from a horizontal position to a vertical alignment at the edge of the bed. Transfers involve transitioning from the seated position to a chair, a bedside commode, or a standing position. Both bed mobility and transfers involve motor planning, balance (static and dynamic) training, strengthening exercises, and repetition of task. Assistive devices can be, and often are, employed to aid the older adult with transfers as well as with ambulation or locomotion such as lifts, wheelchairs, sliding boards, walkers, hemi-walkers, and single-point canes. The transition from the bedbound horizontal position to the upright or vertical position may be a prolonged process (e.g., in the case of severe stroke) but is critical to improving the chances of gaining independence as well as to minimizing the chances of opportunistic infection (e.g., pneumonia) from setting in while the patient is in the acute care setting. In addition, in the geriatric setting, this progression constitutes the bulk of regaining physical independence.

Currently, we have three levels of preventive medicine: *primary prevention,* which focuses on preventing disease in persons who are, or who may become, susceptible through health promotion, inoculations, and regular physician visitation; *secondary prevention,* which initiates rehabilitation to minimize the duration and degree of illness as well as to address the comorbidities through early diagnostic evaluation and intervention; and *tertiary prevention,* which is long-term or permanent rehabilitation that attempts to limit the severity of disability and promote function in persons with chronic conditions. Traditionally, older adults have entered the rehabilitative setting at the secondary level for postsurgical recovery or because of injury, an acute change in status, and so on. Invariably, regardless of the clinical diagnosis, the recovery phase involves rehabilitating in the form of strengthening exercises. This is because, as a consequence of the normal aging process, there is a progressive decline in muscle mass and strength that is not necessarily the result of disease but is present in all aging mammals and is referred to as *sarcopenia.*

Sarcopenia is the involuntary decline in lean muscle mass, strength, and function that occurs in older adults. Maximal skeletal muscle mass and strength are generally realized between 20 and 35 years of age and thereafter decline progressively at a rate approximating 3% to 8% per decade. The resulting condition of sarcopenia increases the risk of functional decline and disability and also constitutes a major hurdle for the

physical therapist in the acute care setting. Estimates suggest that 14% of persons 65 to 75 years of age require assistance with ADLs, and the percentage increases to 45% for those 85 years of age and older. Thus, at a time when older adults are suffering from an increased occurrence of chronic illness, such as diabetes, cancer, osteoporosis, and cardiovascular disease, they are also experiencing a progressive loss of strength. A component of the decline in muscle mass and strength in older adults is reduced physical activity. However, the loss of muscle mass in the elderly is also highly associated with a poorer prognosis following an illness, surgery, trauma, or hospitalization. Interestingly, malnutrition may exacerbate the loss of muscle mass in older adults as they increase the proportions of their diets consisting of carbohydrates and fats and reduce the proportions of protein, the latter of which is necessary for maintaining adequate muscle mass. Therefore, the therapeutic use of anabolic nutritional interventions in combination with physical therapy may be very useful for counteracting sarcopenia.

—*Hans C. Dreyer and Blake B. Rasmussen*

See also Assistive Devices; Disability and the Disablement Process; Mobility; Motivation; Sarcopenia

Further Readings and References

Dreyer HC, Volpi E. Role of protein and amino acids in the pathophysiology and treatment of sarcopenia. *Am Col Nutr.* 2005;24:140S–145S.

Evans WJ. What is sarcopenia? *J Gerontol A Biol Sci Med Sci.* 1995;50:5–8.

Lamberts SW, van den Beld AW, van der Lely AJ. The endocrinology of aging. *Science.* 1997;278:419–424.

Melzer K, Kayser B, Pichard C. Physical activity: The health benefits outweigh the risks. *Curr Opin Clin Nutr Metab Care.* 2004;7:641–647.

Roubenoff R, Casteneda C. Sarcopenia: Understanding the dynamics of aging muscle. *JAMA.* 2001;286:1230–1231.

RESPIRATORY AGING

See PULMONARY AGING

RHEUMATIC DISEASES

See ARTHRITIS AND OTHER RHEUMATIC DISEASES

RURAL HEALTH AND AGING VERSUS URBAN HEALTH AND AGING

There is no unitary designation or single definition of a rural place in the United States, as compared with urban or suburban places. However, rural America is distinct from its counterparts in a number of significant ways. Despite the lack of a simple definition, researchers have identified a number of indicators that serve to represent how a rural place is unique. These indicators include population size and density, commuting patterns, and various measures of isolation. The strength of these indicators varies in the ability to explain how rural America is distinct from other parts of the country.

One such distinction that begs explanation is the finding that rural areas differ significantly from other areas in the domains of health and aging. Significant health disparities persist between metropolitan and nonmetropolitan groups, and the health needs of rural Americans are unique and challenging. Socioeconomic conditions, geographic isolation, and cultural factors often have a negative impact on the access, quality, cost, and use of health services. Furthermore, relatively little is known about rural health and aging overall as compared with metropolitan places.

It has been established that rural residents self-report significantly poorer health status throughout the aging process than do other groups. Adults in rural areas are 36% more likely to report their health status to be fair or poor than are adults in urban areas. Rural adults during later life report more chronic illness, physical impairment, and functional limitations than do older adults in metropolitan areas. These additional functional limitations include activities of daily living (ADLs), such as eating, dressing, and bathing, as well as instrumental activities of daily living (IADLs), such as shopping, transportation, and paying bills.

Furthermore, in the United States, nonmetropolitan adults report higher rates of cardiovascular disease, ischemic heart disease, diabetes, and hypertension than do others nationwide, particularly in the South. Older rural adults also appear to experience poor emotional health, including depression, when compared with urban and suburban groups. In addition, the increased level of loneliness and depression experienced by older rural adults is particularly acute for women, roughly half of whom live alone. Rural communities are at higher risk for motor vehicle fatalities, deaths from serious injuries, and suicides than are individuals in other areas. Finally, mortality from chronic health conditions and accidents increase as counties become less urban. Clearly, many health outcomes are worse for rural people throughout life, creating many challenges for healthy aging.

There are several possible explanations for the inferior health of rural inhabitants in general. Rural populations display increased health risk behaviors throughout the life course, including higher rates of cigarette smoking, obesity, and alcohol use as well as lower rates of seatbelt use, preventive care, and physical exercise. Each of these factors likely contributes to the observed higher rates of chronic illness and injuries in rural communities. Related to these negative health behaviors and increased rural morbidity and mortality is the frequent and persistent experience of poverty in rural America.

Poor rural families tend to stay poor for longer periods of time than do other families, and this has harmful implications for health. For instance, in nearly 25% of all rural counties, one in five people has been below the poverty level for at least four decades. One factor explaining this persistent poverty is that education levels for older rural adults are lower than those for their metropolitan and suburban counterparts. It is well established that educational attainment has significant influences not only on income, retirement benefits, and health maintenance behaviors but also on all aspects of mental and physical health.

Rural individuals on average have lower socioeconomic status over time than do their more urban counterparts. Poverty and unemployment rates are higher and earnings are lower in rural locations. Among all older persons in 2003, 28.2% of nonmetropolitan residents were poor or near poor, as compared with 23.5% of metropolitan elders. Poverty rates for older people increase with both age and rurality, as reported by the U.S. Census Bureau. The risk of rural poverty is also greater for older women than for older men. Among the older (age 65 years and older) rural population in 2003, 8.3% of men and 13.1% of women were poor. For the oldest old (age 85 years and older), 9.9% of men and 16.9% of women were poor. The possibility of living in poverty for older rural women is increased for those who live alone and those who have been widowed. The impacts of individual-level poverty on health during later life likely occur through a variety of mechanisms, including chronic exposure to stress, less insurance coverage and use of health care, poorer nutritional status, and inability to pay for prescription medications.

The increased morbidity and mortality of rural adults is also linked to concentrated and enduring area-level poverty, paired with the jeopardy of geographic isolation that defines rural places. Rural places in the United States bear a disproportionate share of the nation's poverty. The vast majority (82%) of persistently poor counties between 1970 and 2000 were nonmetropolitan, with the greatest number of these counties being located in the South. These factors together create significant problems for healthy aging, primarily a lack of available and quality health care systems on which metropolitan areas depend.

In short, living in a poor rural community is itself a health risk for many older individuals due to numerous factors. Rural towns frequently have fewer community-based resources, such as health promotion programs, to benefit the health of aging populations. When possible, rural residents depend regularly on informal networks of family and friends to meet health needs. There is often limited access to physical, mental, and dental care, with more than half of rural older adults leaving their counties of residence to receive health services. Moreover, there is a shortage of rural transportation services, affordable housing, home health care services, skilled care, emergency services, nutritional and meal programs, and community centers as compared with other places. All of these shortcomings are correlated with greater health risks for older rural persons and may lead to rural adults needing to enter nursing home facilities earlier than their urban counterparts.

Furthermore, due to economic declines that many rural counties have experienced during recent decades, financial resources for health care from employment, retirement benefits, and/or pension funds are scarce. The decline in natural resource-based industries, such as agriculture, timber, and mining, has resulted in a higher number of older dislocated workers proportionate to the population, making access to affordable health care even more difficult. Accordingly, the most critical health needs of older rural adults are believed to be affordability of medical care, access to health insurance, and less expensive prescription drugs.

Perhaps most at risk for poor health in rural communities are older minorities. These groups report higher rates of cerebrovascular disease, hypertension, diabetes, and disability than do White older adults living in rural localities. Older African Americans, Latinos, and Native Americans face a double burden in terms of health risk, facing the previously mentioned health risks associated with rurality in addition to the well-documented health disadvantages related to minority race/ethnicity status. For example, risk factors previously linked to minority status include lower levels of income and wealth as well as distinct cultural beliefs and behaviors, which may combine to result in lower health care use, increased levels of work in dangerous or hazardous occupations, and less insurance coverage as compared with White and Asian older adults. The increasing racial/ethnic diversity in rural places complicates meeting the health needs of rural senior citizens. Recognizing and addressing the unique health needs of older minorities is necessary to ensure that specific health problems are prevented and treated adequately.

To increase the quality and years of life among rural individuals during later adulthood, more data on the experiences of aging and health are needed for this population. This can be accomplished through an oversampling of rural sites in ongoing data collection efforts and making better use of existing smaller rural samples by adding data such as descriptive and demographic information. Much of the existing research on rural health addresses circumstances in specific locations, and these findings are not generalizable to all other rural areas. As many more rural individuals age, more research is needed to understand their distinctive needs. Policymakers and service providers are often unfamiliar with the specific requirements of this growing and changing population.

Researchers and policymakers have identified programs aimed at bolstering the health of older rural individuals. Such programs include investing in more assisted-living facilities, developing more comprehensive rural systems of care, and increasing "telehealth" opportunities to overcome travel distances for medical care. These options may be accomplished via collaboration with rural governmental, local, civic, and religious organizations. The oldest portion of the rural populace will need increased health care as baby boomers age but will also need economic and social support due to the disadvantages associated with rural poverty.

Finally, understanding the specialized needs of rural adults during later life is particularly important in that rural areas generally have higher proportions of older persons in the total population than do urban areas. In 2003, older persons in nonmetropolitan areas accounted for 14.6% of the population, whereas older persons in metropolitan areas accounted for 11.9% of the population. Rural areas are also aging rapidly as a result of several factors. The majority of older rural adults do not relocate from their counties of residence as they reach later adulthood, there is significant out-migration of younger groups in many rural places, and there is in-migration of older persons from metropolitan areas in a rising number of rural places. Thus, the greater percentages of older persons in rural areas will require proportionally more medical, rehabilitative, and social services over time to address the already greater risks of chronic health conditions and disability.

—*Jessica Ziembroski*

See also Activities of Daily Living and Instrumental Activities of Daily Living; Environmental Health; Living Arrangements; Quality of Life; Socioeconomic Status

Further Readings and References

Beverly CJ, McAtee R, Chernoff R, Casteel J. Needs assessment of rural communities: A focus on older adults. *J Community Health.* 2005;30:197–212.

Jensen L, McLaughlin D, Sachs C, eds. *Challenges for Rural America in the 21st Century.* University Park: Pennsylvania State University Press; 2004.

Moore R. *The Hidden America: Social Problems in Rural America for the Twenty-First Century.* Selinsgrove, Pa: Susquehanna University Press; 2001.

S

SARCOPENIA

Sarcopenia, which means "loss of flesh," is the age-related involuntary loss of muscle mass, strength, and function in skeletal muscles that develops progressively over decades and becomes a significant contributor to disability in the older population.

Aging is associated with a number of changes in muscle mass and function that may be caused by age-related endocrine changes and, conversely, may also be responsible for changes in the effects of some hormones. The most sticking effect of age is the involuntary loss of muscle mass, strength, and function. Sarcopenia increases the risk of falls and vulnerability to injury and, consequently, can lead to functional dependence and disability. A decrease in muscle mass is also accompanied by changes in body composition and bone density and is associated with an increased incidence of insulin resistance in the elderly. Reductions in endocrine function, physical activity, and appropriate nutrition all play important roles in regulating muscle mass during aging.

Muscle is affected profoundly by age. Muscle mass decreases approximately 3% to 8% per decade after 30 years of age, and this rate of decline is even higher after 60 years of age. The involuntary loss of muscle mass, strength, and function is a fundamental cause of, and contributor to, disability in older people. Sarcopenia may lead to a reduction in physical activity, which in turn may have possible metabolic effects, including decreased bone density, obesity, and impaired glucose tolerance.

The etiology of sarcopenia is not clearly understood, but several mechanisms have been proposed, including (a) irreversible fiber damage or permanent denervation resulting in a loss of contact between the nerve and muscle; (b) mitochondrial DNA deletion mutations subsequent to oxidative damage; (c) changes in satellite cell recruitment; (d) altered endocrine function, such as changes in hormone, growth factor, or cytokine release, and/or impaired muscle responsiveness to the hormonal stimuli; (e) changes in muscle response to nutrients and/or malnutrition; and (f) disuse (e.g., sedentary lifestyle). Sarcopenia is caused by a multifactorial problem. This entry examines three possibilities that are directly or indirectly related to the endocrine system: endocrine dysfunction, nutrition, and disuse.

Age-Related Endocrine Changes Relevant to Muscle

A variety of hormonal changes are seen during the aging process. Here, the most important ones in relation to their effect on skeletal muscle are discussed.

Insulin Resistance

The ability of muscle tissue to respond to insulin is an important aspect of overall insulin sensitivity. The incidence of insulin resistance and type 2 diabetes increases with aging, and sarcopenia may play an important role. It is still unclear whether the increase in insulin resistance observed with aging is due to age per se or whether it is secondarily due to the reduction in metabolically active lean body mass. Although insulin is usually considered in the context of its ability to increase glucose uptake into cells, there is emerging evidence that insulin resistance of muscle protein metabolism in the elderly may be an important contributor to sarcopenia. For example, when glucose is ingested with a regular meal, the subsequent increase in insulin concentrations has a negative effect on muscle protein synthesis. This implies that, with normal aging, the ability of muscle cells to respond properly to circulating insulin (by increasing muscle protein synthesis) is impaired.

Somatopause

Somatopause is the gradual decrease in circulating growth hormone (GH) and insulin-like growth factor I (IGF-I) that normally occurs with aging. The GH/IGF-I axis also exhibits a gradual decline during normal aging. Although providing GH replacement therapy to GH-deficient adults results in an increase in muscle mass and strength, more recent studies in which GH replacement therapy was given to aged individuals have shown no effect on muscle strength. Therefore, GH replacement therapy in the elderly may be beneficial for lowering fat mass, improving blood lipid profiles, and increasing lean body mass, but these changes do not lead to an increase in muscle strength and function. In fact, studies show that muscle strength increases only when GH is given to elderly men undergoing a weight training program as compared with GH replacement therapy alone. It is also important to underscore that the methodologies used to measure body composition may be affected by water retention. Thus, an increase in muscle mass with a reduction in fat mass and no change in strength following GH therapy should be interpreted with caution because GH notoriously increases water retention, which can be misinterpreted as an increase in lean body mass. As for testosterone, GH replacement also is not currently recommended for the treatment of sarcopenia due to both the results of the published studies and the potentially serious side effects such as arthralgia, edema, insulin resistance, and cardiovascular risk.

Menopause

Menopause is the physiological cessation of menstruation secondary to termination of ovulation, resulting in an abrupt decrease in circulating estrogens. Estradiol levels decrease abruptly during menopause. Very little information is available regarding the role of menopause in sarcopenia. It appears that muscle mass is not affected by the decrease in estrogens. Cross-sectional studies evaluating the effects of age on lean body mass and appendicular muscle mass have shown that the rate of decline of muscle mass in women does not increase after menopause, suggesting a marginal role, if any, for this event in the development of sarcopenia in women. On the other hand, hormone replacement therapy can increase serum steroid hormone-binding globulin significantly, leading to a significant decrease in serum-free testosterone levels in women. Low serum-free testosterone levels in women are associated with lower muscle mass. Therefore, hormone replacement therapy may play a role in further reducing, rather than increasing, muscle mass in older women.

Andropause

Andropause is the decrease in androgens (primarily testosterone) that occurs gradually during the normal aging process. The primary and most potent androgen is testosterone. In approximately 60% of men over 65 years of age, testosterone levels decrease to below the normal values of younger men. Testosterone values decrease gradually throughout the aging process, unlike the immediate decrease in estradiol seen with menopause. It has been proposed that the decrease in testosterone may cause a decrease in muscle protein synthesis and result in a loss of muscle mass. With this in mind, several studies have examined the effect of testosterone replacement therapy in men with overt hypogonadism or testosterone concentrations at the lower normal range. Testosterone was administered via injection, transdermal patch, or dermal gel. From these studies, it was shown that testosterone replacement to mid-normal levels resulted in a significant increase in muscle mass, muscle strength, muscle protein synthesis, and bone density. The results are positive and may lead to a reversal or attenuation of sarcopenia. However, testosterone is currently not recommended for the treatment of sarcopenia, and a careful evaluation of the potential benefits against the potential risks (e.g., increased prostrate-specific antigen, cardiovascular risk) should be performed before initiating testosterone replacement therapy for sarcopenia.

Adrenopause

Adrenopause is the gradual decrease in dehydroepiandrosterone (DHEA) that occurs normally with aging. The concentrations of DHEA in the blood also decrease gradually with normal aging. In fact, levels may be up to five times lower in older men than in younger men. Oral supplementation of DHEA to older persons restores DHEA levels to younger men's values, increases IGF-I levels in men and women, increases estrogens in men, and increases testosterone in women. Unfortunately, no changes in lean body mass may be detected, and high-density lipoprotein (HDL) cholesterol levels may be significantly decreased. However, in one study, muscle strength was increased in older men (but not in older women) undergoing DHEA supplementation. Recently, a very large study in older persons showed that DHEA replacement therapy has no effect on muscle size, strength, or function.

Aging and Muscle Plasticity

Muscle plasticity is an inherent property of skeletal muscle that allows muscle cells to adapt to external and internal stimuli. Human skeletal muscle is one of the most adaptable tissues in the body. The ability of muscle cells to respond to external and internal stimuli is often termed muscle plasticity. Exercise and nutrition, two common anabolic stimuli of skeletal muscle anabolism, are involved in the development of

sarcopenia and may be used to counteract muscle loss with aging.

Exercise

Inactivity reduces muscle mass, even over a short period. Typical examples are the reduction of muscle mass observed in bedridden patients, following immobilization for fractures, and in weightlessness (e.g., space flight). Resistance exercise and aerobic exercise have a significant influence on skeletal muscle mass, strength, plasticity, and metabolism. Resistance exercise training results in hypertrophy of muscle cells and large increases in strength. Aerobic exercise training does not alter muscle cell size but has significant effects on the aerobic capacity of muscle cells (i.e., increases in oxidative enzymes and mitochondrial volume) with minimal effects on muscle strength. Both resistance exercise and aerobic exercise stimulate muscle protein synthesis acutely in young people and older people alike. Both types of exercise also reduce insulin resistance and increase glucose and fat oxidation. The elderly respond very well to resistance exercise training by increasing muscle mass and strength, and they increase their aerobic capacity following aerobic exercise training. Recent data also suggest that aerobic exercise increases muscle protein synthesis acutely in older people. Thus, both types of exercise can be very useful to counteract sarcopenia and the associated metabolic alterations of the muscle.

Nutrition

Malnutrition leads to muscle wasting. Several studies have shown that the caloric intake of many elderly individuals is too low and may be an important factor in the development of sarcopenia. Recent data also suggest that the recommended daily intake of protein for the elderly (0.8 grams per kilogram [g/kg] per day) might be insufficient to maintain a neutral nitrogen balance. In addition, older people may voluntarily reduce their protein intake to comply with reduced fat and cholesterol diets. Amino acids from ingested protein stimulate muscle protein synthesis directly. Interestingly, healthy elderly people respond to an amino acid stimulus with an increase in muscle protein synthesis that is not significantly different from the effect observed in their younger counterparts. Unfortunately, high-protein diets given to older people have not been shown to be effective on muscle size or strength. This may be explained by the fact that in these trials the additional protein was given in combination with carbohydrates, which stimulated insulin secretion. Recent data indicate that when carbohydrates are included in a protein meal for the elderly, the positive effect of amino acids on muscle protein synthesis is blunted, possibly due to the negative effect that insulin exerts on muscle proteins in the elderly. There have been no long-term studies in which older people were given only amino acids or proteins with no carbohydrates to stimulate muscle protein synthesis and provide additional energy.

Muscle Changes With Aging

A variety of morphological and biochemical changes are detected in the aged human body and in skeletal muscle. Here, the alterations in body composition, skeletal muscle tissue, and muscle metabolism are highlighted.

Body Composition

There is a progressive decrease in fat-free mass and a progressive increase in fat mass as a person ages. Furthermore, bone density decreases, joint stiffness increases, and there is a small reduction in stature (kyphosis). These changes in body composition have probable implications for several conditions, including type 2 diabetes, obesity, heart disease, and osteoporosis.

Muscle Tissue

The primary alteration is a reduction in total skeletal muscle mass. After 30 years of age, the average person will lose approximately 3% to 8% of his or her muscle mass with each passing decade of life. Specific cellular alterations include reductions in muscle cell number, muscle twitch time and twitch

force, sarcoplasmic reticulum volume, and calcium pumping capacity. Sarcomere spacing becomes disorganized, muscle nuclei become centralized along the muscle fiber, the plasma membrane of muscle becomes less excitable, and there is a significant increase in fat accumulation within and around the muscle cells. Neuromuscular alterations include a decrease in the nervous firing rate to muscle, the number of motor neurons, and the regenerative abilities of the nervous tissue. Motor unit size also increases.

Muscle Metabolism

Biochemical changes are also associated with the aging process. These include reductions in glycolytic and oxidative enzyme activities, creatine phosphate and adenosine triphosphate (ATP) stores within the muscle cell, and mitochondrial volume as well as a slight reduction in overall metabolic rate (approximately 10%). These metabolic changes in muscle contribute to the overall physical fitness capacity of the elderly and are an important component of the approximately 30% reduction in ability to use oxygen during exercise. Initial studies on a small number of elderly individuals had also suggested that aging is associated with a reduction in the basal muscle protein synthesis, which might have been responsible for the progressive reduction in muscle mass. However, more recent data obtained in the largest cohort of healthy older men did not confirm the earlier reports and concluded that differences in basal muscle protein turnover between elderly and young men cannot explain muscle loss with age, suggesting that future research should focus on responses to specific stimuli such as nutrition, exercise, and disease.

Conclusion

Sarcopenia is a multifactorial process. Reductions in endocrine function, physical activity, and inadequate nutrition all play an important role in the reduction of muscle mass with normal aging. Testosterone replacement therapy could be a useful intervention in hypogonadal older men for increasing muscle mass and strength, although it is not currently recommended.

Hormone replacement therapy for menopause, adrenopause, or somatopause appears to have marginal or no positive effect on muscle mass and strength.

Exercise training and proper nutrition can have dramatic effects on muscle mass and strength. An optimal intervention program may include an exercise training schedule that incorporates both resistance and aerobic exercise with adequate intake of total calories and protein. This not only would improve muscle mass and strength but also would reduce insulin resistance, which is more prevalent in the elderly. Providing a nutritional supplement of only amino acids or protein might also be beneficial to promote muscle growth by stimulating muscle protein synthesis and increasing the total daily caloric intake, but further investigations are needed.

Fortunately, aged muscle is still very plastic and can respond to anabolic stimuli by increasing its mass and strength. This knowledge is vital for designing interventions to reverse and/or attenuate the loss of muscle mass with aging and to improve functional abilities in the elderly.

—*Jerson Cadenas and Elena Volpi*

See also Body Composition; Gait Disorders; Mobility; Stroke

Further Readings and References

Baumgartner RN, Waters DL, Gallagher D, Morley JE, Garry PJ. Predictors of skeletal muscle mass in elderly men and women. *Mech Ageing Dev.* 1999;107:123–136.

Bhasin S, Buckwalter JG. Testosterone supplementation in older men: A rational idea whose time has not yet come. *J Androl.* 2001;22:718–731.

Lamberts SWJ, van den Beld AW, van der Lely A-J. The endocrinology of aging. *Science.* 1997;278:419–424.

Morley JE, Baumgartner RN, Roubenoff R, Mayer J, Nair KS. Sarcopenia. *J Lab Clin Med.* 2001;137:231–243.

Roubenoff R, Castenada C. Sarcopenia: Understanding the dynamics of aging muscle. *JAMA.* 2001;286:1230–1231.

Volpi E, Rasmussen BB. Nutrition and muscle protein metabolism in the elderly. *Diab Nutr Metab.* 2000; 13:99–107.

Yarasheski KE. Managing sarcopenia with progressive resistance exercise training. *J Nutr Health Aging.* 2002;6:349–356.

SCHIZOPHRENIA, PARANOIA, AND DELUSIONAL DISORDERS

Psychosis, a serious mental illness characterized by problems with interpreting reality and associated with delusions or hallucinations, occurs in a variety of conditions among older adults, including "primary" syndromes (e.g., schizophrenia, delusional disorder) and "secondary" syndromes (e.g., psychosis of Alzheimer's disease). The prototypical example of a chronic primary psychotic disorder is schizophrenia. The great majority of descriptive and treatment-related research about schizophrenia has been conducted among younger patients. However, the absolute number of older adults with severe psychiatric illnesses, including schizophrenia, will increase dramatically as the baby boom population ages. Available data suggest that older persons with schizophrenia have differing symptom presentations, distinct treatment needs, and some surprising advantages over their younger counterparts.

Epidemiological studies provide an estimated prevalence of schizophrenia of 0.5% to 1% of the population among community-dwelling adults. Some surveys, including the Epidemiologic Catchment Area Study, indicate that the prevalence of schizophrenia declines with age, although these studies did not use age-related diagnostic criteria. The prevalence of psychotic symptoms is approximately 4% to 10% among older adults, with dementia accounting for a majority of these individuals. The ratio of women to men with schizophrenia during late life is roughly 3 to 2. In contrast to the stereotypical notion that older adults with schizophrenia typically reside in long-stay locked psychiatric facilities, it is estimated that 85% reside in the community. Those who do reside in institutions are typically placed in nursing homes. A majority of older persons with schizophrenia have few economic or social resources available to them.

In terms of its symptoms, schizophrenia is a heterogeneous syndrome that consists of a group of related illnesses and presentations. The hallmark symptoms of schizophrenia are positive symptoms (e.g., delusions and hallucinations, disorganized thoughts and behavior), negative symptoms (e.g., emotional flattening, reduced motivation, anhedonia, poverty of speech, social withdrawal), and cognitive deficits (e.g., impairment of learning and executive functioning). To meet the criteria for a diagnosis of schizophrenia according to the *Diagnostic and Statistical Manual of Mental Disorders, Fourth Edition* (DSM-IV), symptoms must be present for at least 1 month, causing significant impairment in occupational or social functioning. Continuous signs of this disturbance, which may include prodromal or residual symptoms, must be present for 6 months. Available data indicate that the positive symptoms appear to become less severe with age among both community-dwelling and institutionalized patients. The negative symptoms do not appear to change significantly in severity with age.

People who experience delusions that are not bizarre, without accompanying prominent auditory or visual hallucinations and without overall personality deterioration, are classified as having *delusional disorder*. Delusional disorder is somewhat less common than schizophrenia and has received little study. Common delusions among elderly people include those of being spied on or followed, suspecting infidelity of the spouse, and having a physical disease (e.g., tumor) without evidence. Depression and anxiety are frequent among older adults with schizophrenia, and each contributes significantly to reduced quality of life. *Schizoaffective disorder* encompasses persons who have a major depressive or manic episode superimposed on symptoms of schizophrenia but who experience schizophrenic symptoms in the absence of mood problems for at least 2 weeks. As with delusional disorder, little is known about schizoaffective disorder in elderly people.

Among older patients, age-related cognitive impairments in memory and in ability to plan and coordinate activities are often present and contribute to disability and difficulty in daily functioning. However, these cognitive deficits do not appear to be "progressive" in schizophrenia, as are those associated with Alzheimer's disease. Another major factor in the clinical picture of older adults with schizophrenia is medical comorbidity. Chronic physical illnesses increase disability and complicate treatment yet often go unrecognized (and are consequently more severe when finally recognized). Cardiovascular and pulmonary diseases are particularly common among older people with schizophrenia, at least partly related to poor health habits such as smoking, poor diet or limited access to healthy foods, and lack of exercise. On the other hand, older adults are less likely to abuse alcohol or illicit substances than are younger adults with schizophrenia.

Although a majority of persons with schizophrenia develop the disorder in their late teens or early 20s, a subset of persons manifest late-onset schizophrenia after 40 years of age. A review of studies of late-onset schizophrenia found that approximately 23% of people with schizophrenia experience onset of this disorder after 40 years of age, 13% after 50 years of age, and 7% after 60 years of age. Late-onset schizophrenia may be a neurobiologically distinct syndrome from early-onset schizophrenia. In general, late-onset patients have similar symptom characteristics and response to treatment as do early-onset patients. However, late-onset patients are more likely to be women than are those with an earlier onset of the disease. Also, negative symptoms and cognitive deficits tend to be less severe among late-onset patients.

Regardless of when it manifests first, schizophrenia typically follows a chronic course, with most sufferers continuing to experience its disabling effects into old age and not attaining full recovery. However, there appears to be a subset of older adults who attain full and sustained remission of symptoms, and research is under way to understand how these older adults differ from those who continue to experience active symptoms. Persons with schizophrenia experience excess mortality compared with older adults without psychiatric illnesses, and rates of completed suicide are high among those with schizophrenia, occurring in approximately 10% of persons diagnosed. The highest risk of suicide is within the first 5 to 10 years of onset of illness. It has been argued that persons who manage to reach old age with schizophrenia are a "survivor cohort," and this may explain why they tend to have less severe symptoms than their younger counterparts.

Despite considerable research, the etiology of schizophrenia remains unclear. Genetic contributions are certain but relatively small. The identified brain changes associated with this disorder are subtle. There is fairly good evidence that neurotransmitters, particularly dopamine and serotonin, are implicated in the expression of psychosis. Many of the medications used to treat schizophrenia modulate these chemicals. However, the negative symptoms, such as emotional flattening and the cognitive deficits of schizophrenia, appear to arise from some other unknown biological mechanism, and consequently medications are less effective in treating these symptoms. It is now believed that schizophrenia involves problems in the development of connections between neurons, and future research with neuroimaging and other techniques may help discover the cause(s) of this illness.

The diagnosis of schizophrenia and related disorders begins with a clinical interview, including history gathering from medical records and family members or others who are aware of the patient's situation. Psychosis may arise from many medical causes, including medication-related or substance use-related psychotic reactions and psychoses due to neurological disorders (e.g., Alzheimer's disease). Research has shown that risk factors for psychosis in elderly people can include sensory impairment and social isolation. Particularly in the case of new-onset psychosis in an older patient, a detailed physical examination and laboratory workup, such as blood tests and brain imaging, are often conducted to rule out medical causes before a diagnosis of schizophrenia can be made.

Once nonpsychiatric causes of psychosis are ruled out, treatment for schizophrenia usually begins with the administration of antipsychotic medications. Although much of the research on the effectiveness of these drugs has been conducted with younger adults, existing evidence suggests that they are likely as effective among older adults. However, several important modifications are necessary. Older adults require lower doses due to age-related changes in the brain, liver, and kidneys. Moreover, the risk of side effects increases with age. The older "conventional" or "typical" neuroleptic or antipsychotic medications carry a high risk of motor side effects, in particular extrapyramidal symptoms such as parkinsonism and tardive dyskinesia, the latter of which involves abnormal movements of the tongue, facial muscles, limbs, and (occasionally)

trunk. The longer an individual receives antipsychotic medications, the more likely tardive dyskinesia is to occur, and old age is an independent risk factor for the development of this potentially persistent and disabling side effect. The newer "atypical" antipsychotic medications carry a significantly lower risk of tardive dyskinesia. However, they do produce other side effects, including metabolic changes that may induce weight gain and type 2 diabetes mellitus. Nonetheless, most patients with schizophrenia need antipsychotics for many years to avoid relapses that are common following discontinuation of these medications. Therefore, drug treatment of schizophrenia in older adults is often a balance between reducing symptoms and limiting the emergence of side effects.

Given that schizophrenia affects the whole person, including social relationships, ability to participate in work and leisure activities, and other life domains, medication is typically not sufficient as a stand-alone treatment. *Psychosocial rehabilitation* refers to treatments intended to improve daily functioning. Treatments empirically tested in younger adults include cognitive behavior therapy, social skills training, family therapy, and vocational rehabilitation, and appropriate modifications can make these treatments suitable for older adults. Other emerging psychosocial treatments that may be helpful for older adults include direct teaching of skills required for daily life (e.g., taking medications, reading maps) and cognitive rehabilitation (e.g., memory training). Older patients may use case managers to help manage medical appointments and gain access to social services. The costs associated with the treatment of schizophrenia across the life span are considerable; this disease affects 1% of the population yet accounts for 2.5% of the nation's health care costs. Thus, it is a public health imperative that clinical and basic research on aging and schizophrenia be conducted, in addition to the development of age-adapted treatments, in light of the growing number of people with schizophrenia who are reaching older age.

—Colin Depp and Dilip V. Jeste

See also Behavioral Disorders in Dementia; Delirium and Confusional States; Depression and Other Mood Disorders; Mental Assessment; Psychiatric Rating Scales

Further Readings and References

Cohen C, ed. *Schizophrenia Into Later Life*. Arlington, Va: American Psychiatric Press; 2003.

Harris MJ, Jeste DV. Late onset schizophrenia: An overview. *Schizophrenia Bull*. 1988;14:39–55.

Howard R, Rabins PV, Castle DJ, eds. *Late Onset Schizophrenia*. Petersfield, England: Wrightson Biomedical; 1999.

Jeste DV, Alexopoulos GS, Bartels SJ, et al. Consensus statement on the upcoming crisis in geriatric mental health: Research agenda for the next two decades. *Arch Gen Psychiatry*. 1999;56:848–853.

Jeste DV, Symonds LL, Harris MJ, Paulsen JS, Palmer BW, Heaton RK. Non-dementia non-praecox dementia praecox? Late-onset schizophrenia. *Am J Geriatr Psychiatry*. 1997;5:302–317.

Jeste DV, Twamley EW, Eyler Zorrilla LT, Golshan S, Patterson TL, Palmer BW. Aging and outcome in schizophrenia. *Acta Psychiatr Scand*. 2003;107:336–343.

Miller NE, Cohen GD, eds. *Schizophrenia and Aging: Schizophrenia, Paranoia, and Schizophreniform Disorders in Later Life*. New York: Guilford; 1987.

Palmer BW, McClure FS, Jeste DV. Schizophrenia in late-life: Findings challenge traditional concepts. *Harvard Rev Psychiatry*. 2001;9:51–58.

SELECTIVE OPTIMIZATION WITH COMPENSATION

Most older adults achieve and sustain a quality of life that is considered to be successful both personally and socially. Survey research has consistently supported the optimistic view that aging well is a reasonable expectation for most older adults in the United States. Limited comparative study of many societies worldwide during recent decades also suggests the same conclusion. The social survey research of Angus Campbell and Hadley Cantril provides classic illustrations of both theory and evidence documenting positive views of aging as the rule, rather than the exception, during late adulthood. Their research also documents the variability of criteria used to gauge successful aging within and between societies. A 2004 Harris Interactive Poll confirmed the persistence of an optimistic view of aging in the United States among adults of all ages. Among professionals, such findings have also sustained a widely shared sense of realistic optimism about aging successfully.

Paul Baltes and Margret Baltes and their colleagues have made a significant contribution over several decades to understanding how success in aging is achieved and sustained through a developmental theory of selective optimization with compensation (SOC). As physical, cognitive, and social resources diminish with age, choices need to be made and increased dependency on compensatory personal adaptation and social support need to be considered. SOC, initially developed systematically in an introductory chapter of a book on successful aging in 1990, has been developed continuously and extensively as a construct for explaining successful adaptation during later life. Through early 2005, the psychology program of the Max Planck Institute in Berlin recorded 36 publications exploring the concept: 10 overview articles and 26 research articles exploring its possible applications. SOC is accurately described as an account of how adaptive functioning is achieved and maintained successfully as age-related capacities diminish and external expectations, demands, and resources change. SOC forecasts that adaptive choices are selected with attention to established personal preferences (a sense of ego integrity) even as personal capacity and external opportunities and resources diminish. The evidence for understanding the transactions implicit in individuals' adaptive choices is necessarily multidisciplinary (biological, psychological, social, and institutional). And because successful aging involves transactions between persons and social contexts, SOC provides a conceptual platform for relating developmental theory to issues of policies and practices that affect successful aging.

Recognizing that success in aging has multiple connotations, Baltes and Baltes (in a systematic discussion of how SOC evolved as a developmental theory of successful aging) specified a range of subjective and objective criteria that can, in some combination, serve as criteria for valuing a successful life (e.g., survival, quality of life, physical and mental health, competence, productivity, control, satisfaction). Then they summarized seven key evidence-based generalizations (from behavioral, social, and biological research on human development and aging) on which the concept of SOC builds:

1. There are major differences among normal, optimal, and sick aging.

2. Heterogeneity of social, behavioral, and biological characteristics among older adults is the rule.

3. Latent reserves of underused energy and creativity of older adults are large.

4. Reserves of energy and creativity, however, are limited and tend to decrease with age—and particularly during very late life.

5. Knowledge-based pragmatics (e.g., wisdom) can, to some degree, compensate for diminished cognitive mechanics during late adulthood.

6. During very late life, however, compensation of knowledge-based pragmatics for decline of cognitive mechanics diminishes.

7. Resilience of the self tends to persist.

This succinct summary of multidisciplinary gerontological evidence relevant for understanding SOC expectedly leads to an important conclusion, namely that various combinations of adaptive transformative transactions can produce effective successful old age. The options chosen by individuals in pursuit of successful aging are constrained differently by factors such as levels of available energy, cognitive competence, personal preference, and available social resources. Consequently, one would not anticipate either a single successful strategy or strategies totally independent of age or social context for achieving success during later life. SOC assumes transactions between individuals with developmental histories who adapt in various ecological settings with different social expectations, resources, opportunities, and social supports.

This transactional view of multiple adaptive strategies for successful aging is quite different from the reductionistic theory of disengagement that was widely debated and largely abandoned during the 1970s. Disengagement theory forecast biologically driven, and hence inevitable, emotional and social detachment during late adulthood. SOC, in contrast, stresses behavioral options during later life chosen for selective continued engagement.

The role of wisdom in successful aging was noted in the initial presentation of SOC and illustrated later in the Berlin Aging Study that documented the interplay of knowledge-based and cognitive pragmatics observed in older adults. Wisdom refers to evidence of good judgment and advice regarding important but uncertain matters of life, to factual and strategic knowledge of options and consequences of choices, and to consideration of uncertainty and relativism of one's choices. Wisdom, therefore, potentially informs the assessment and the behavioral choices perceived to be successfully adaptive during later life. Successful adaptive choices during late life would be expected to reflect both a sense of ego integrity and an age-related tendency to value perceived achievement of personal goals more than fleeting emotional satisfaction (happiness).

Human aging, in sum, ensures changing and eventually declining physical and intellectual capacities. Social expectations and resources also change, particularly as roles related to work and family are modified. The good news is that older adults typically adapt successfully to these changes by choosing from a variety of culturally available and personally acceptable strategies observed to produce successful outcomes. Individual adaptations developed in response to challenges during late adulthood are varied because personal preferences developed over a lifetime must be negotiated with available resources and opportunities in mind. Disability, widowhood, and retirement from work illustrate significant challenges to which most adults adapt successfully.

This optimistic view of successful aging is challenged, however, by some not so good news from very late life (i.e., age 85 years and older). Evidence relevant for evaluating SOC as a developmental strategy anticipates, particularly during very late life, that waning personal and social resources limit adaptive choices, even choices for which compensatory assistance is available. Popular distinctions in gerontology among young, old, and very old elders have typically noted increasing limitations of very late life, limitations documented in detail in the Berlin Aging Study among elders over 85 years of age. Such age-related challenges to successful aging were in fact forecast in the initial review of evidence by Baltes and Baltes. During very late life, physical capacity and resilience decline significantly; the ability to learn is compromised, frailty and multimorbidity increase, the incidence of dementia elevates significantly, and death with dignity becomes increasingly problematic. The necessity of compensatory strategies and social support of individual functioning increases significantly during very late life. The level of demand for compensatory support of very old individuals raises practical questions of public policy and practice, not about the capacity of communities to provide necessary compensatory support but rather about the equitable distribution of social costs over the life course.

The usefulness of SOC as a platform for gerontological practice can be illustrated briefly. For example, Margret Baltes, in her research on the adaptive strategies of older adults in long-term care settings, documented that dependency can be a resident's adaptive strategy—a cry for help in achieving some sense of autonomy. And research on assisted-living housing, which during recent decades has become a very popular type of housing for elders in the United States, documents how the perceived needs of frail older adults both for autonomy and for reliably available compensatory care in response to anticipated dependency can be accommodated in a designed living environment.

The usefulness of SOC as a theory of successful aging continues to be explored. Most older adults continue to age successfully using adaptive transactions that are increasingly well documented. A challenge of future research on SOC will be to identify various compensatory strategies of individuals and communities that will also increase the probability of aging successfully during very late life.

—*George L. Maddox*

See also Emotions and Emotional Stability; MacArthur Study of Successful Aging; Positive Attitudes and Health; Psychosocial Theories; Self-Efficacy; Successful Aging

Further Readings and References

Baltes M. *The Many Faces of Dependency in Old Age.* New York: Cambridge University Press; 1996.

Baltes P, Baltes M. Psychological perspectives on successful aging. In: Baltes P, Baltes M, eds. *Successful Aging: Perspectives From the Behavioral Sciences.* New York: Cambridge University Press; 1990;1–34.

Baltes P, Mayer KU, eds. *The Berlin Aging Study: Aging From 70 to 100.* New York: Cambridge University Press; 1999.

Cantril H. *The Pattern of Human Concerns.* New Brunswick, NJ: Rutgers University Press; 1965.

Maddox G. Housing and living arrangements: A transactional perspective. In: Binstock R, George L, eds. *Handbook of Aging and the Social Sciences.* 5th ed. San Diego, Calif: Academic Press; 2001:426–443.

SELF-CARE

Self-care is a term that describes a variety of behaviors that can be performed to help treat disease and promote health. Research has established that self-care of chronic disease has a meaningful and positive influence on symptomatology, length of illness episodes, and psychosocial coping. Due to clear links with health, many studies have focused on exercise, diet, smoking, and alcohol use. By choosing to exercise regularly, eat healthy food, avoid tobacco products, and limit alcohol intake to enhance health or prevent disease, older adults can increase the number of healthy vital years and decrease the number of disabled years.

In addition to the major lifestyle variables, researchers have examined many other behaviors that can aid treatment of chronic illness and promote health. Some examples include reading about one's condition, meditating or praying, consulting friends or relatives, joining a self-help group, and trying alternative remedies. Although these behaviors are not as clearly linked to improved treatment and health as are lifestyle variables, many older adults report performing such behaviors to reduce stress and cope with illness.

Although self-care is a term often reserved to describe lay or informal responses to chronic illness, it is important to note that much of formal (e.g., physician-related) care is initiated by the individual or a family member. Therefore, self-care should also include the interaction between informal and formal care. Some self-care behaviors that reflect this interaction include scheduling physical exams, taking medication according to the prescribed regimen, and checking one's blood pressure to assess treatment and disease progression.

Research varies quite considerably in the number and types of self-care behaviors that are measured. Much research has focused on performance of specific behaviors that are deemed to be most important in the treatment of a particular illness. This approach requires recruitment of individuals with a particular chronic illness and a priori identification of the most important self-care behaviors to be performed. Lifestyle variables have been a favorite choice because of the self-care benefits for so many different illness conditions. Results from such studies can be quite effective for the development of self-care intervention programs that target specific illness groups (e.g., arthritis, heart disease). However, because many older adults suffer from more than one chronic illness, studying one illness group in isolation and a priori identification of self-care behaviors can be too simplistic. Another research approach, then, involves recruitment of individuals with several chronic illnesses and descriptive identification of self-care behaviors they perform. This approach is certainly more general and thus less useful for targeting particular behaviors for interventions, but it might represent a more realistic picture of the complex nature of self-care for multiple chronic illnesses. Add to this complexity the issue of disease progression and changes in ability to participate in self-care over time (e.g., with disability and frailty), and the picture becomes very difficult to clarify. However, some general findings have emerged across different studies.

Demographic variables, such as age, sex, and socioeconomic status, have been hypothesized to influence self-care indirectly. Many studies have found that, on average, older adults perform more self-care behaviors than do younger adults and that women perform more favorable self-care activities than do men. Not surprisingly, individuals with higher socioeconomic status (e.g., education, income) tend to be in better health with greater access to formal health care. It has been suggested that such demographic variables are useful for understanding the self-care

process, but these variables are not primary explanatory variables because most of the effects are hypothesized to be indirect. For example, older adults might perceive illness as more serious than do younger adults and therefore might perform self-care differently. Thus, it is hypothesized that such demographic variables represent important developmental, social, and cultural influences that may shape health-related behaviors and attitudes directly.

One way to understand why older adults do or do not participate in self-care is to distinguish between the objective and subjective health contexts. The objective health context reflects the role that health status plays in self-care participation. For example, the number of chronic conditions or the seriousness of one's conditions is predicted to play a role in the amount of self-care participation. Individuals who are in poorer health make decisions to, or are asked to, perform more self-care, take more medications, and become more involved with the formal health care system. Participation in self-care can be a direct reaction to health problems or deteriorating health, such that the effect of age on self-care is an indirect result of changing health conditions.

The subjective health context reflects the role that patient beliefs play in self-care participation. Indeed, the bulk of research conducted on self-care has focused on belief-laden variables that influence behavior. From this body of research, there is little doubt that beliefs play central roles in health-related behavior. Psychological variables, such as one's illness representation, perceived ability to care for one's condition, general self-efficacy in the health context, perceived benefits and barriers to self-care, and emotional reactions to illness, all are potentially important predictors of self-care participation. Some models, such as the health belief model, the theory of reasoned action, protection motivation theory, and subjective expected utility theory, have been used to identify a large number of health beliefs that potentially influence health-protective and self-care activities. Drawing from this body of knowledge, one can conclude that individuals must manage multiple health perceptions when making health-related decisions (e.g., to participate in a self-care activity). However, it has been difficult to specify the individual variables that are most influential in predicting behavior, especially over time and across illness types. This makes somewhat difficult the creation of effective self-care interventions that can be generalized across different conditions.

There are three primary ways in which self-care education programs can assist older adults. First, educational programs can be used to empower patients to be more involved in their own health care. Older adults are increasingly being encouraged to practice healthy lifestyle behaviors to aid treatment, stem disease progression, and improve well-being. Older adults are also being encouraged to educate themselves about health practices (e.g., the connection between diet and certain types of cancer, healthy food preparation) and how to interact more effectively with their physicians (e.g., accurately recording health history). The goal of these programs is to increase patients' sense of control over their treatment and health to promote self-care behavior. Without a sense of empowerment or control, it is unlikely that self-care behaviors will be performed or that they will aid treatment effectively. Some organizations, such as the American Association of Retired Persons and the Gerontological Association of America, are important vehicles for this type of self-care education.

Self-care education programs can also be very helpful for teaching older adults about normal and pathological aging. This requires a person to distinguish between normal physical and psychological changes that occur with aging and changes associated with a disease process. This information can, in turn, aid older adults' decisions about when and when not to seek formal care. Because this distinction between normal and pathological aging is often very difficult to make, many older adults struggle with assessing the need for formal care accurately.

The use of self-care education programs also addresses societal concerns about the cost of older adults' health and the effect on the economy. Another goal, then, is the reduction of unnecessary or avoidable health care costs. As 78 million baby boomers enter their 50s, it is increasingly important to our society that older adults make healthy lifestyle choices to fend off frailty and diseases associated with aging. Much of the future impact we will see on formal health care services will depend on older adults' lifestyle choices and adequate performance of self-care.

In summary, self-care can involve a number of behaviors that an individual performs to help treat chronic illness and promote health. Older adults perform many types of self-care behaviors that have been shown to reduce symptomatology and enhance well-being. Self-care education programs can be used to empower older adults to participate in self-care, provide information about the distinctions between normal and pathological aging, and reduce unnecessary use of costly health services.

—*Leslie McDonald-Miszczak*

See also Education and Health; Health Promotion and Disease Prevention; Positive Attitudes and Health; Self-Efficacy

Further Readings and References

McDonald-Miszczak L, Wister AV. Predicting self-care behaviors among older adults coping with arthritis: A cross-sectional and 1-year longitudinal comparative analysis. *J Aging Health.* 2005;17:836–857.

Newsom JT, Kaplan MS, Huguet N, McFarland BH. Health behaviors in a representative sample of older Canadians: Prevalences, reported change, motivation to change, and perceived barriers. *Gerontologist.* 2004;44:193–205.

Ory MG, Ables RP, Lipman PD. *Aging, Health, and Behavior.* Newbury Park, Calif: Sage; 1992.

Weinstein NK. Testing four competing theories of health-protective behavior. In: Salovey P, Rothman AJ, eds. *Social Psychology of Health: Key Readings.* New York: Psychology Press; 2003:33–46.

SELF-EFFICACY

Albert Bandura defined *self-efficacy* as a person's belief in his or her capability to perform a particular task successfully. Together with the goals that people set, self-efficacy is one of the most powerful motivational predictors of how well a person will perform at nearly any endeavor. A person's self-efficacy is a strong determinant of his or her effort, persistence, and strategizing as well as that person's subsequent training and job performance. Besides its being highly predictive, much is also known about how self-efficacy can be developed to harness its performance-enhancing benefits. This entry, after outlining the nature of self-efficacy and how it leads to performance and other work-related outcomes, discusses the measurement and sources of self-efficacy. It concludes by briefly considering whether it is possible to have too much self-efficacy.

Nature of Self-Efficacy

Because self-efficacy pertains to specific tasks, people may have high self-efficacy for some tasks and low self-efficacy for others simultaneously. For instance, a manager may have high self-efficacy for the technical aspects of his or her role, such as management accounting, but low self-efficacy for other aspects, such as dealing with employees' performance problems.

Because self-efficacy is more specific and circumscribed than either self-confidence (a general personality trait that relates to how confident people feel in most situations) or self-esteem (the extent to which people like themselves), it is generally also more readily developed than self-confidence or self-esteem. Self-efficacy is also a much stronger predictor of how effectively people will perform a given task than is either their self-confidence or their self-esteem.

How Self-Efficacy Affects Performance and Well-Being

A high degree of self-efficacy leads people to work hard and persist in the face of setbacks, as illustrated by many great innovators and politicians who were undeterred by repeated obstacles, much ridicule, and minimal encouragement. Thomas Edison, believing that he could eventually succeed, reputedly tested at least 3,000 different unsuccessful prototypes before eventually developing the first incandescent light bulb. Finally, high self-efficacy was exhibited by Abraham Lincoln in response to the numerous and repeated public rebukes and failures he incurred prior

to his eventual political triumphs. Research has found that self-efficacy is important for sustaining the considerable effort required to master skills involved in public speaking, losing weight, becoming an effective manager, and so on.

When learning complex tasks, high self-efficacy causes people to strive to improve their assumptions and strategies rather than to look for excuses such as not being interested in the task. High self-efficacy improves employees' capacity to collect relevant information, make sound decisions, and then take appropriate action, particularly when they are under time pressure. Such capabilities are invaluable in jobs that involve, for instance, dealing with irate customers when working in a call center and overcoming complex technical challenges in minimal time when working on a project team. In contrast, low self-efficacy can lead to erratic analytic thinking, which undermines the quality of problem-solving competency in an increasingly knowledge-based society.

In a dynamic work context, where ongoing learning and performance improvement are needed, high self-efficacy helps individuals to react less defensively when they receive negative feedback. In areas where their self-efficacy is low, people often see a negative outcome as confirming the incompetence they perceive in themselves. This can set up a vicious cycle, whereby ambiguous results are considered as evidence of perceived inability, thereby further decreasing individuals' self-efficacy, effort, and subsequent performance. When people have low self-efficacy, they also tend to blame either the situation or other people when things go wrong. Denial of any responsibility for poor performance inhibits the chance that individuals will learn how to perform more effectively in the future.

People are inclined to become anxious and/or depressed when they perceive themselves as unable to manage aversive events or to gain what they value highly. Thus, self-efficacy is also related to the experience of stress and occupational burnout. Specifically, low self-efficacy can readily lead to a sense of helplessness and hopelessness that people are incapable of learning how to cope more effectively with the challenges and demands of their work. When this occurs, low self-efficacy can be distressing and depressing, thereby preventing even highly talented individuals from performing effectively.

Measurement of Self-Efficacy

Because self-efficacy is task specific, there is no single standardized measure of self-efficacy. Rather, there is a need to develop measures that gauge an individual's self-assessed capacity to either (a) achieve a certain outcome on a particular task (outcome self-efficacy) or (b) engage in the processes likely to lead to a certain desired outcome (process self-efficacy). For instance, an *outcome* self-efficacy scale in the domain of job search may include items such as "I believe that I can get a new job within 4 weeks" and "I believe I can get a new job with a starting salary of at least $65,000," with response anchors ranging from *not at all confident* to *extremely confident.* Alternatively, a *process* self-efficacy scale may focus on items such as "I believe I can network effectively to at least six people during the next 4 weeks" and "I believe I can send out 15 résumés during the next 4 weeks," with response anchors similar to those for the outcome self-efficacy scale. The key point here is that measures of self-efficacy will be most informative, predictive, and useful for addressing areas where self-efficacy is lacking if they are highly specific.

Sources of Self-Efficacy

There are three key sources of self-efficacy. The most powerful determinant of self-efficacy is enactive self-mastery, followed by role-modeling and then verbal persuasion.

Enactive self-mastery is achieved when people experience success at performing at least portions of a task. It serves to convince them that they have what it takes to achieve increasingly difficult accomplishments of a similar kind. Self-mastery is best achieved through progressive mastery, attained by breaking down difficult tasks into small steps that are relatively easy so as to ensure a high level of initial success. Individuals should then be given progressively more difficult tasks, where constructive feedback is provided and accomplishments are celebrated, before increasingly challenging tasks are attempted. Building self-efficacy through enactive self-mastery essentially entails structuring situations that bring rewarding successes and avoid the experience of repeated failures. An example of enactive self-mastery is when people learning to pilot an aircraft are given many hours to develop their skill and confidence at the separate component skills before they ever attempt to combine them by actually flying solo. Initial flying lessons are designed so that trainee pilots are challenged but also experience efficacy-building successes during each session. For individuals to develop self-efficacy through enactive self-mastery, managers similarly need to provide challenges where individuals regularly encounter and celebrate successes as they develop proficiency at their work tasks.

Role-modeling occurs when people observe others perform a task that they are attempting to learn or vividly visualize themselves performing successfully. Role-modeling can provide people with ideas about how they could perform certain tasks and can inspire their confidence that they could act in a similarly successful manner. Effective role models approach challenging activities as an opportunity to learn and develop their knowledge, skills, and effectiveness rather than as a test of how talented they are. They also respond to setbacks by exploring what can be done differently in the future. In short, good role models demonstrate the development of skill, persistence, and learning rather than the defensiveness and blaming that cause mistakes to recur and subsequent performance to decline. Role models are most effective at raising self-efficacy when they are liked personally and are seen as having attributes (e.g., age, gender, ethnicity) similar to those of the individuals who observe them. One implication is that managers should think carefully before assigning mentors, especially without the input of those being mentored. Individuals may also learn and become more confident from observing both the successes and failures of others so long as they feel confident that they can avoid repeating the errors they observe.

Verbal persuasion builds self-efficacy when respected managers encourage and praise individuals for their competence and ability to improve their effectiveness. Positive self-talk can also raise self-efficacy. Regardless of its source, verbal persuasion is most likely to increase self-efficacy when it is perceived as credible and emphasizes how success results from devoting sufficient effort to mastering acquirable skills rather than depending on inherent talent. Efficacy-raising feedback highlights how consistent efforts have enabled substantial improvements, as well as the progress made, rather than involving peer comparisons or making reference to how far individuals need to go before their ultimate objectives are achieved. Effective verbal persuasion is reinforced with corresponding actions. For instance, telling individuals that they are capable but not assigning them any challenging tasks tends to erode both employees' self-efficacy and managers' credibility. Having individuals draw up a progress chart before complimenting them on their genuine progress, where applicable, is another potent way of raising employees' sense of what they can achieve.

Underminers of Self-Efficacy

These approaches contrast with the subtle but common messages that individuals have low ability, serving to erode their self-efficacy beliefs. Such signals include consistently being assigned to unchallenging tasks, receiving praise for mediocre performances, being treated indifferently for faulty performance, and being offered unsolicited help repeatedly. Fault finding and personal criticisms are particularly destructive because these actions undermine motivation to explore and experiment, whereby individuals discover what they are actually able to achieve. Although encouraging messages can raise self-efficacy, attempts at building self-efficacy through verbal persuasion may easily degenerate into empty sermons unless they are soon supported by efficacy-affirming experiences; that is, enactive self-mastery.

Too Much of a Good Thing?

Extremely high self-efficacy can lead to excessive risk taking, hubris, and dysfunctional persistence, although in most cases the resultant failures that people experience soon recalibrate their self-efficacy to a more realistic level. In general, the many benefits of high self-efficacy make it a worthwhile attribute to cultivate. This is best done though the simultaneous and systematic application of the enactive self-mastery, role-modeling, and verbal persuasion principles just outlined.

—*Steven H. Zarit and*
Suzanne Robertson

See also Control; Positive Attitudes and Health; Selective Optimization With Compensation; Self-Care

Further Readings and References

Bandura A. *Self-Efficacy: The Exercise of Control.* New York: Freeman; 1997.
Bandura A. *Social Foundations of Thought and Action.* Englewood Cliffs, NJ: Prentice Hall; 1986.
Wood R, Bandura A. Social cognitive theory of organizational management. *Acad Mgmt Rev.* 1989; 14:361–384.

SELF-RATED HEALTH

The way people self-assess their health can have a significant influence on their health behaviors and health outcomes. In the research literature, the most frequent method by which people have demonstrated their self-rated health is through the simple question, "How do you rate your health?" The responses from the Duke University (Piedmont Health Survey) Established Populations for Epidemiologic Studies of the Elderly (EPESE) sample of community-dwelling elders were as follows: excellent (15%), good (39%), fair (32%), and poor (14%). More specific questions might include assessment of overall health beliefs, perceived susceptibility to illness, perceived seriousness of an illness, expected benefits of treatment, expected barriers to treatment, and beliefs about carrying out health-related tasks.

There is little evidence that older adults perceive their health to be worse than it actually is. In fact, older adults who actually have significant health problems are just as likely to rate their health as excellent or good as older adults who actually are in excellent health are to rate their health as fair or poor. Yet some older adults do greatly exaggerate their health problems, even to the point of being hypochondriacal. An essential feature of hypochondriasis in older persons is a belief that they have one or more several serious illnesses. Older adults do not imagine physical symptoms or signs; rather, they exaggerate the interpretation of these signs and sensations. It is not uncommon for a medical workup to reveal some physical abnormality but not support a medical diagnosis that explains the severity and breadth of symptoms experienced.

Self-rated health is of importance to the actual health of older adults for at least two reasons. First, these beliefs may influence the decision-making process that leads to many health-related behaviors. On the one hand, the belief that one has a serious illness may lead an older adult to "doctor shop"—that is, to see many professionals—often without these professionals knowing of the consultations with other professionals. Receiving care from multiple professionals, in turn, may lead to multiple medications being taken simultaneously, even to the point where the older adult is taking medications that adversely interact with one another. On the other hand, fear of a chronic illness may lead some elders to not seek the necessary preventive and early intervening care that they require to avoid the development of a more serious condition over time.

Perhaps of more interest among investigators of health outcomes in older adults is the strong association between poor self-rated health and poor health outcomes, even when actual health status and health habits are controlled. In a study of the Duke EPESE sample (Piedmont Health Survey), the impact of self-rated health on mortality was greatest among those elders who were among the most healthy. To date, no good explanations have emerged to explain this strong association. Yet one might theorize that a latent factor, perhaps a biologically driven one, may contribute to more robust physical health while at the same time contributing to a sense of psychological well-being. The question often predicts mortality more strongly

than most physical and behavioral indicators. The increased association of depression and self-rated health with aging in studies would substantiate this view in part.

Given the interest in self-rated health, at least one question on the topic is usually included in most large surveys, including the National Health Interview Survey, the EPESE project, the Medical Outcomes Study, and the RAND Health Insurance Experiment.

—*Dan G. Blazer*

See also Expectations Regarding Aging; Positive Attitudes and Health; Self-Care; Self-Efficacy

Further Readings and References

Blazer D, Houpt J. Perception of poor health in the healthy older adult. *J Am Geriatr Soc.* 1979;27:330–334.

Cornoni-Huntley J, Blazer D, Lafferty M, Everett D, Brock D, Farmer M, eds. *Established Populations for Epidemiologic Studies of the Elderly: Resource Data Book.* Vol. 2. Bethesda, Md: National Institute on Aging; 1990.

Schnitker J. When mental health becomes health: Age and the shifting meaning of self-evaluations of general health. *Milbank Memor Q.* 2005;83:397–423.

SENIOR NUTRITION PROGRAMS

See CONTINUUM OF CARE

SEXUALITY

Sexuality is most often regarded as the province of younger adults. Older adults, especially women, are rarely regarded as sex symbols or even as sexually active persons. But many older adults do indeed have healthy sex lives that contribute to their overall physical and psychological well-being.

Stating that sexual expression persists into later life is different from stating that sexual expression remains the same across adulthood. Indeed, although there are no longitudinal studies of sexuality that are representative of the population, the several large-scale, representative, cross-sectional studies of sexuality that exist suggest that sexuality changes with age. Sexual desire is greater in younger people than in older people. Younger people have more frequent partnered sex and engage in more frequent masturbation than do older people.

The lack of longitudinal evidence leaves researchers in the realm of speculation about the reasons for the differences observed across age groups. Some differences are probably due to cohort effects. For example, norms about the behaviors that constitute healthy sexuality (e.g., masturbation) have likely changed with the generations. But most differences are probably due to age effects.

The natural course of aging can present challenges to sexual expression. For women, the hormonal changes of the climacteric (the transition period surrounding and including a woman's menopause; i.e., last menstrual bleeding) represent the largest influence of physical aging on sexual function. Postmenopausal women experience atrophy of reproductive tissues, including those in and around the vagina. During sex, older women experience less blood flow to and lubrication of the vagina than do premenopausal women. These changes may produce reduced sensitivity to stimulation and/or dyspareunia (pain during sex), especially for women who have sex infrequently. For aging men, hormonal changes are not as dramatic as they are for women, but they do occur. Older men produce less testosterone than do younger men, resulting in decreased sensitivity to stimulation. During sex, older men may take longer, and may need more physical stimulation, to attain an erection. Both men and women retain the capacity for orgasm into old age, but orgasms may be less intense.

In addition to normal aging, age-related illnesses can produce changes in sexual functioning. Some chronic illnesses, such as cardiovascular disease, diabetes, arthritis, and benign prostate conditions, are commonly associated with sexual problems in older people. For example, insofar as cardiovascular disease causes problems in the circulatory system, it will adversely affect blood flow to genitalia. An enlarged prostate leads to difficulty with urination and painful urinary tract infections—symptoms that obviously reduce men's eagerness for sex.

The negative effects of an illness can be compounded by its treatment. Although it would seem that treatment should reverse the negative effects of illness, medications often have effects above and beyond those that are intended (side effects). Antihypertensive (blood pressure–reducing) and psychiatric drugs are most often implicated in the development of sexual problems, including difficulty in attaining orgasm for both women and men. The specific causes of these sexual side effects are unknown but appear to be related to the effects of the drugs on the nervous system. Sex hormone-related cancers (e.g., prostate cancer, breast cancer) may be treated with drugs that stop or slow sex hormone production, resulting in atrophy of sex organs as well as the cancer.

An individual's social world also changes with increasing age. Importantly, the average woman outlives the average man. In 2003, among persons 55 to 64 years of age, there were 92 living men for every 100 living women. That ratio was 83/100 among persons 65 to 74 years of age and was 67/100 among persons 75 to 84 years of age. Thus, single men have many romantic prospects, whereas single women have few. Single people with few opportunities for sexual relations often stop seeking them so as to prevent frustration and depression.

Older adults who have romantic partners are more likely to have satisfactory sex lives than are single older adults, especially if other aspects of their relationships are good. Partnered older adults have usually been in the same relationship for many years. The love such a pair experiences may be more companionate than passionate, and the couple may desire relatively infrequent sex as a result. Alternatively, sex in a long-term relationship may become monotonous, and boredom might drive a lack of desire.

Sex researchers rely on individuals' self-reports, which are always of uncertain validity because of the sensitive and private nature of the topic. As noted previously, the sexuality of older persons is a particularly taboo subject. Older people may misreport, or fail to report, on sexual questions because they perceive this societal censure. The more the individual internalizes these norms—that is, the more the individual believes that older people are physically unattractive and/or that sexual expression at older ages is inappropriate or unhealthy—the more pronounced the effects will be.

Socially speaking, later life may be a good time for homosexual individuals. Sexual expression in older adults is not sanctioned, but it is also often not expected. A pair of young women holding hands or hugging in public may attract a great deal of attention, but a similar pair of older women is not likely to be regarded through a sexual lens. Also, the natural and pathological physical changes of later life affect penile–vaginal intercourse most severely. Whereas that form of sexual expression is the "main event" for many heterosexual couples, homosexual couples have wider repertoires of acceptable sexual behaviors, including oral sex that is largely unhampered by physical aging (and may also decrease the probability of sexual boredom in long-term relationships).

Indeed, interactions between the biological and the social are perhaps the most interesting aspect of sexuality during later life. The instances are numerous. Consider the case of Viagra and other drugs that treat erectile dysfunction. Some couples had ceased intercourse because of a male's impotence and had not engaged in it for many years. The dynamics of these relationships changed when medications made sex physically possible again. Some couples enjoyed the second honeymoon portrayed in commercials, whereas other relationships became strained when the status quo was interrupted.

A second interaction concerns older adults' use of contraceptives. Obviously, postmenopausal women do not need to prevent pregnancies, and many sexual encounters between older people do not involve any type of protection. But older adults remain fully capable of contracting sexually transmitted infections (STIs). In fact, weak vaginal tissues may tear and bleed in older women, increasing the risk of transmission (relative to younger women) of STIs such as HIV/AIDS. Because educational programs have targeted young adults, many older adults know little about STIs. As early as the late 1980s, 10% of Americans

diagnosed with HIV/AIDS were age 50 years and older. Many STIs are misdiagnosed or remain undiagnosed because of misinformation on the part of older people, reluctance and/or neglect of doctors and older people to discuss sex, and other causes.

A third, and especially intriguing, biosocial interaction concerns the climacteric. Physical symptoms appear to vary systematically across social contexts. Low socioeconomic status is associated with high symptomatology in the United States and Europe but with low symptomatology in Asia. Fully 80% of Dutch women report having "hot flashes," whereas no Mayan women do. Some languages have no words for symptoms generally considered to be common (e.g., there is no term for *hot flash* in Japanese). Women in these cultures might not experience the symptom for some reason, or they might consider it of little importance. In cultures where age confers power and authority on women relative to men or to younger women (e.g., Thailand, Peru), women look forward to menopause. Where women have negative attitudes about menopause, they experience more symptoms.

In summary, although further research is needed, increasing age is associated cross-sectionally with decreasing desire for and participation in sexual activity. Normal aging and age-related illness and its treatments are biological correlates of sexual expression, and relationships, relationship quality, and social norms are among it social correlates. Biological and social variables interact to produce interesting and important outcomes for older persons.

—Sara M. Moorman
and John DeLamater

See also Menopause and Hormone Therapy; Men's Health; Women's Health

Further Readings and References

Dennerstein L. Well-being, symptoms, and the menopausal transition. *Maturitas.* 1996;23:147–157.

Lindau S, Laumann EO, Levinson W, Waite L. Synthesis of scientific disciplines in pursuit of health: The interactive biopsychosocial model. *Perspect Biol Med.* 2003;46(3): S74–S86.

Masters W, Johnson V, Kolodny R. *Heterosexuality.* New York: HarperCollins; 1994.

Rossi AS, ed. *Sexuality Across the Life Course.* Chicago: University of Chicago Press; 1994.

Schiavi R. *Aging and Male Sexuality.* Cambridge, England: Cambridge University Press; 1999.

Trudel G, Turgeon L, Piche L. Marital and sexual aspects of old age. *Sex Relationship Ther.* 2000;15:381–406.

SHINGLES

Shingles (herpes zoster) is a disabling disease of sensory nerves and skin caused by the reactivation of a virus, varicella zoster virus (VZV). VZV infects persons during childhood or adolescence and causes chickenpox (varicella). VZV is fascinating because it is not cleared from the body after the chickenpox resolves. Instead, it has the ability to establish a dormant infection of sensory nerves for the lifetime of the host and retains the capacity, after many decades, to emerge at unpredictable times to cause shingles.

Although shingles can occur in anyone who has been infected with VZV, it is much more common in older adults and in persons who have diseases that impair the immune system such as leukemia, Hodgkin's disease, and HIV infection. Shingles is more likely to occur in older persons because of a decline in immunity to VZV with aging. The incidence of shingles increases sharply at around 50 to 60 years of age. The incidence in persons over 65 years of age is as high as 11 per 1,000 persons per year.

The first symptom of shingles is usually a prodrome of pain or discomfort in a localized area. This worrisome prologue bewilders patients, caregivers, and physicians, and it masquerades as many other painful conditions in the elderly. Eventually, the virus infects cells in the skin and produces a characteristic rash. The rash is on one side of the body and in the area of skin innervated by the sensory nerve bundle in which VZV is reactivating (called a dermatome). It begins as a red bumpy eruption and then usually develops blisters. Along with the rash, most patients experience pain in the involved area. The characteristic rash and pain make shingles easy to diagnose.

The rash heals in 2 to 4 weeks, but the pain continues after the rash has healed in as many as 60% to 70% of persons over 60 years of age and develops into a chronic pain condition known as postherpetic neuralgia. Postherpetic neuralgia is much more common in older adults than in younger adults and can have a devastating impact on elders' quality of life. Some patients suffer from severe pain after the lightest touch of the affected skin by things as trivial as a cold wind or a piece of clothing.

The main goal of the treatment of shingles in older adults is the reduction of pain. Antiviral therapy with a drug such as acyclovir, famciclovir, or valacyclovir can reduce the acute pain and the duration of postherpetic neuralgia, especially if given early in the shingles episode. Corticosteroid drugs such as prednisone do not affect postherpetic neuralgia. Pain control with analgesics is also important during shingles. Sometimes, anesthetic nerve blocks reduce severe pain in persons not responding to antiviral and analgesic drugs. Once postherpetic neuralgia is established, it can be very difficult to treat. However, drugs such as gabapentin, pregabalin, opioids, and tricyclic antidepressants, as well as a 5% lidocaine patch, may reduce postherpetic neuralgia pain in some older adults.

The incidence of chickenpox has declined dramatically in the United States recently because of the widespread use of the varicella (chickenpox) vaccine in children. The vaccine is very effective in preventing chickenpox. As the cohorts of children now receiving the vaccine age into older adulthood, it is likely that shingles and postherpetic neuralgia will also decline markedly. However, there are still billions of people who harbor VZV and are at risk for shingles. Recently, investigators reported that a zoster (shingles) vaccine reduced the incidence of shingles by 51% and the incidence of postherpetic neuralgia by 66% in adults over 60 years of age. Experts are hopeful that both shingles and chickenpox can be reduced markedly with the widespread use of the two vaccines.

—*Kenneth E. Schmader*

See also Pain; Skin Changes

Further Readings and References

Gnann JW Jr, Whitley RJ. Herpes zoster. *N Engl J Med.* 2002;347:340–346.

Oxman MN, Levin MJ, Johnson GR, et al. A vaccine to prevent herpes zoster and postherpetic neuralgia in older adults. *N Engl J Med.* 2005;352:2271–2284.

Schmader KE. Herpes zoster in older adults. *Clin Infect Dis.* 2001;32:481–486.

Skin Changes

Skin changes with aging occur due to physiological, structural, and environmental factors. They are more prominent in the older population and become more marked throughout the aging process. These changes are due to both intrinsic and extrinsic factors. Intrinsic factors, part of the natural aging process that is determined genetically, involve the three layers of skin and result in changes such as graying of the hair and thinning of the skin. Extrinsic factors are a result of environmental conditions such as exposure to the sun's rays. Both factors are important in the changes that occur with aging.

The skin consists primarily of three layers: the epidermis, dermis, and subcutaneous fatty tissue (or hypodermis). The epidermis, which contains pigment and skin cells, thins with aging. The number of pigment-containing cells, the melanocytes, decreases, and the largest population of epidermal cells that contain the protein keratin, the keratinocytes, change in shape and size. There is also a decrease in the number of Langerhans cells; that is, highly specialized cells involved in immunological reactions in the body. These changes result in the skin appearing pale, thin, and translucent.

The dermis contains dense fibrous tissue, numerous blood vessels, nerve endings, and sebaceous glands. The dermis nourishes the epidermis. With aging, degenerative changes in the connective tissue (or elastosis) decrease the skin's elasticity and strength. The blood vessels of the dermis become more fragile, leading to bruising. Sebaceous glands tend to produce less oil, resulting in less moisture, and this can lead to dry itchy skin.

The purpose of the subcutaneous fatty layer is to provide insulation by attaching the skin to underlying bone and muscle. This layer thins with age and decreases the body's ability to regulate temperature, and this can lead to hypothermia in cold temperatures. Sweat glands, also located in this layer, decrease in number and distort in structure as one ages. These sweat glands produce less sweat, and this can lead to increased risk of overheating in older patients.

The main extrinsic factor affecting the aging of the skin is the sun. Photoaging is aging caused by exposure to the sun's rays. The amount of damage depends on a person's skin color and the history of sun exposure. Those with fair skin are more affected than those with darker skin. Photoaging develops over years and is thought to be caused by free radical damage. The repeated ultraviolet exposure breaks down collagen and elastin, and the skin loses its ability to repair itself. This damage results in loose, wrinkled, leathery skin. The best way to prevent sun damage is to always use sunscreen. Smoking is another factor that causes premature skin aging. It results in wrinkled leathery skin, often with a yellow hue. This is thought to be due primarily to decreased circulation secondary to nicotine. The skin tone and wrinkles improve with cessation of smoking. Other extrinsic factors that contribute to skin aging are include poor diet, stress, alcohol consumption, sleep deprivation, and environmental toxins.

—*Geetha Rao*

See also Biological Theories of Aging; Cancer, Common Types of; Normal Physical Aging; Shingles; Skin Neoplasms, Benign and Malignant

Further Readings and References

Abrams WB, Berkow R, Fletcher AJ, Beers MH, eds. *Merck Manual of Geriatrics.* Whitehouse Station, NJ: Merck Research Laboratories; 1995.

Harding J. *Medical Encyclopedia: Aging Changes in Skin.* Bethesda, Md: National Institutes of Health, National Library of Medicine; 2004.

SKIN NEOPLASMS, BENIGN AND MALIGNANT

Skin neoplasms are very common in the elderly and can be categorized into benign, premalignant, and malignant tumors. Malignant melanoma is the leading cause of death due to skin disease. The incidence of melanoma and other skin cancers is rising. Older patients, particularly men, have disproportionately greater mortality and morbidity from melanoma. Therefore, it is important that the older population be aware of risk factors, preventive measures, clinical presentation, and treatments associated with skin cancers.

Ultraviolet light exposure is a major risk factor and increases the risk of skin cancer among people with all skin types, but especially those who are fair-skinned. Those with red or blond hair and fair skin that burns easily are most vulnerable. The incidence of melanoma among Whites is 20 times higher than the incidence among Blacks and is 4 times higher than that among Hispanics. Using sunscreen has been shown to prevent skin cancers. Sunscreens that block both Ultraviolet A and Ultraviolet B light may be the most optimal. Other preventive measures include wearing protective clothing, limiting the amount of time exposed to sunlight (especially during midday), and avoiding tanning salons. Physicians should educate patients early because damage can occur years before skin cancer develops. Other risk factors are a personal or family history of melanoma, older age, and atypical moles. Suspicious moles should be evaluated by a health care professional as soon as possible. For those at increased risk, an annual skin exam is recommended.

Benign Tumors

Seborrheic keratoses are benign, waxy raised plaques that characteristically appear to be stuck or pasted onto skin. They are extremely common in the elderly. Although no treatment is necessary, they can be treated with cryotherapy (repeated freezing and thawing of tumor cells to cause cell death, usually with liquid nitrogen) or curettage and light cautery. *Acrochordons* are skin tags, commonly found in middle-aged and elderly people on the neck, axillae, and trunk. They can be flesh-colored or pigmented, and they can be removed with a scalpel. *Verruca vulgaris,* commonly called warts, are benign lesions characterized by flesh-colored plaques and papules with a verrucous surface. Their causative agent is the human papillomavirus. Although they are often resistant to treatment, common treatment modalities include cryotherapy and salicylic acid solutions. *Keratoacanthomas* are rapidly enlarging nodules with a smooth outline and central keratin plug. They are generally benign, but because they can be difficult to differentiate from squamous cell carcinoma, they are often treated aggressively with curettage, cautery, or excision.

Premalignant Tumors

Actinic keratoses are a precursor to squamous cell carcinoma that are more common in Whites and are related to cumulative lifetime sun exposure. They are characteristically scaly, sandpaper-like patches on sun-exposed areas with an erythematous base. Prevention is geared toward using sunscreen and avoiding the sun. The risk of transformation to squamous cell cancer is estimated to be less than 1% to 20% for an individual over a year. Patients with multiples lesions should be screened at least once per year for the presence of cancer. For early lesions, avoidance of sun may be sufficient for regression of tumor. For lesions further along, treatment is usually cryotherapy with liquid nitrogen or topical 5-fluorouracil (5-FU) cream. *Bowen's disease,* or squamous cell carcinoma in situ, can present as scaly plaques with well-defined margins on both sun-exposed and protected skin. These lesions are usually small (1 to 3 centimeters), but over time they may progress to invasive squamous cell carcinoma. Treatments vary but include excision, cryotherapy, curettage and cautery, and topical 5-FU cream.

Malignant Tumors

Basal cell carcinoma is the most common skin cancer and is related to chronic ultraviolet light exposure. The typical lesion is a papule or nodule with a pearly appearance and telangiectasias on its surface. Most lesions are on the neck and head (especially the nose) and are often nonhealing. If untreated, the carcinoma may invade deep tissues. A biopsy is required to confirm diagnosis. Treatment is determined by the patient's medical history, the size of the lesion, and the depth of tumor invasion. In general, small lesions can be treated by curettage and cauterization or cryotherapy. Mohs surgery, a surgical technique that allows complete effective tumor removal, is used for large or high-risk tumors and has a high cure rate. Radiotherapy can be used when surgery is not an option or for recurrent cases. Topical 5-FU is occasionally used for superficial lesions, but recurrence is high. Patients with histories of basal cell carcinoma should be followed carefully for at least 5 years. There is approximately a 45% chance of recurrence of disease over 3 years.

Squamous cell carcinomas account for approximately 20% of all skin cancers. Unlike basal cell, squamous cell carcinoma is more likely to metastasize. If suspected, nearby lymph nodes should also be palpated. The lesions are usually papules or nodules with secondary changes of ulcerations and scaling. These lesions are often nonhealing and appear on sun-damaged skin or areas of prior radiation or burns. A biopsy is required to confirm the diagnosis. In general, smaller tumors can be treated with surgery (Mohs) or cryotherapy. Radiotherapy is reserved for poorly differentiated or recurrent tumors. There is approximately a 20% chance of recurrence of disease over 3 years.

Melanoma, derived from the melanocytes of the skin, is the most lethal of all skin cancers and has the greatest potential for metastasis. The incidence of melanoma is rising faster than that of any other cancer. In the United States, 50% of deaths from melanoma are in men over 50 years of age. The primary lesion can be a macule, papule, plaque, or nodule and is usually deeply pigmented. The face and neck are more likely to be affected in the older population. Melanomas are usually characterized by asymmetry, irregular border, varied color, and/or increase in diameter. Bleeding, pain, and ulcerations are usually late signs. The diagnosis is made by biopsy. The most important prognostic factor is tumor thickness. Treatment is surgical excision with a margin of normal skin. Adjuvant therapy, such as with interferon, often complements surgery to improve cure rates. Regional node dissection may be beneficial in some cases. Once melanoma metastasizes, survival is less than 1 year and treatment is palliative. Common sites of metastasis are brain, liver, and bone. The 5-year survival rate for early disease (in situ and into the papillary dermis) is 82% to 100% but drops to 49% once the disease penetrates into the subcutaneous fat.

—Geetha Rao

See also Cancer; Cancer, Common Types of; Normal Physical Aging; Skin Changes

Further Readings and References

Abrams WB, Berkow R, Fletcher AJ, Beers MH, eds. *Merck Manual of Geriatrics.* Whitehouse Station, NJ: Merck Research Laboratories; 1995.

Sober AJ, Koh H, Tran N, Washington C. Melanoma and other skin cancers. In: Fauci AS, Braunwald E, Isselbacher KJ, Martin JB, eds. *Harrison's Principles of Internal Medicine.* New York: McGraw-Hill; 1998:543–549.

Loo AS, Gilchrest BA. Common skin disorders. In: Landefeld CS, Palmer R, Johnson MA, Johnston CB, Lyons W, eds. *Current Geriatric Diagnosis and Treatment.* New York: McGraw-Hill; 2004:289–304.

Rager EL, Bridgeford EP, Ollila DW. Cutaneous melanoma update on prevention, screening, diagnosis, and treatment. *Am Fam Physician.* 2005;71:269–276.

Sleep

Sleep difficulties are highly prevalent in the elderly population, but sleep problems are not an inevitable consequence of aging. They are reported by approximately half of those over 65 years of age. As a result, when a problem with sleep is identified in this age group, instead of assuming that it is just "old age," a thorough evaluation for a pathological basis should be carried out. Increasing the identification and effective treatment for sleep disorders in the elderly promises to decrease their adverse consequences, which include diminished quality of life, increased risk of falls and accidents, and long-term care placement.

Aging and Sleep Functions

Although it has long been believed that sleep naturally deteriorates with age, the more carefully individuals with associated medical, psychiatric, and sleep disorders are excluded from studies, the less sleep pathology is found. The most consistent findings in the normal elderly are a decrease in slow wave sleep, an increase in arousals and awakenings during the night, and a tendency to sleep during the day. The last of these represents a loss of strength of the circadian rhythm, which represents the day versus night changes in a host of biological functions. Among these is the tendency to sleep versus be awake, temperature, and cortisol, all of which manifest less day versus night difference with aging. Psychosocial factors may influence sleep disturbances in the elderly as well; for example, the elimination of time markers for the circadian system related to loss of usual daily routines. Individuals with age-related changes in the sleep–wake system often do not complain of sleep difficulties or experience impairment in function or quality of life. This is in contrast to the many elderly persons with sleep disorders that occur due to a wide range of causes, including primary sleep disorders and medical and psychiatric conditions.

Sleep Disorders in the Elderly

Sleep apnea is a condition characterized by multiple episodes during sleep where breathing ceases for periods of 10 seconds or more either because no effort is being made to breathe (central apnea) or because an obstruction in the upper airway prevents airflow during attempts to breathe (obstructive). Obstructive sleep apnea is more common in elderly patients, and its incidence increases with age. Associated symptoms include excessive sleepiness, morning headaches, morning dry mouth, hypertension, and impotence. Diagnosis and treatment require referral to a sleep center for an overnight sleep study; that is, polysomnography (PSG). The most common current treatment is continuous positive airway pressure (CPAP), which involves blowing air through the nose at night to increase upper airway pressure and prevent upper airway obstruction. Other treatments include upper airway surgery and oral appliances that resemble mouth guards and generally change the position of the tongue or the mandible.

Periodic limb movement disorder (PLMD) is characterized by repetitive muscular contractions occurring during sleep and most commonly involves the legs that cause sleep disturbance. PLMD is more prevalent in the elderly population, and some studies indicate that it is seen in 30% to 45% of adults age 60 years and older as compared with 5% to 6% of all adults. The disorder is measured in terms of the number of movements associated with arousals that occur per hour of sleep. Although adults tend to report symptoms with more than 10 events per hour, symptoms tend not to develop in the elderly until the severity exceeds roughly 15 events per hour. Complaints by those with PLMD include insomnia and daytime fatigue and sleepiness, and bed partners may observe repetitive jerking during sleep. The condition is difficult to diagnose based on history alone. PSG is indicated to diagnose this condition definitively prior to initiation of medical therapy. Obtaining PSG before instituting treatment is recommended because all current therapies have side effects.

Restless legs syndrome (RLS) is often associated with PLMD and is defined as an uncomfortable, creeping, or crawling feeling in the lower extremities that is associated with an irresistible urge to move. RLS is also more prevalent in the elderly population and has been noted to occur in approximately 28% of patients over 65 years of age as compared with 6% of the total adult population. RLS can be diagnosed reliably based on a careful history; as a result, PSG is not required for the diagnosis.

RLS is twice as prevalent in elderly women as in elderly men, and both RLS and PLMD have been associated with anemia with serum ferritin levels less than 45 micrograms per liter. When low ferritin levels are found, the administration of oral supplemental iron can often be an effective treatment. Other comorbid conditions associated with PLMD and RLS include diabetes mellitus, pregnancy, iron deficiency anemia, and use of medications, including many antidepressants and antipsychotics.

Treatment of both RLS and PLMD is most commonly carried out with the same medications, which appear to have equal efficacy for both conditions. The first-line treatment is with dopaminergic agonists. Benzodiazepines (most commonly clonazepam), anticonvulsants (most commonly gabapentin), and opiates are also sometimes effective. Opiates are typically reserved for patients who are refractory to treatment with other agents. Effective treatment of RLS and PLMD often significantly improves the quality of life of afflicted individuals.

Bereavement can commonly affect sleep in elderly patients even though bereavement is considered a normal psychological process. Difficulties with sleep maintenance, the most common type of sleep disruption reported by the elderly, is also the most common sleep problem experienced during bereavement. A short course of a sedative–hypnotic medication may prove to be helpful but should be tapered as the symptoms of bereavement diminish. Behavioral treatment of the patient's related insomnia is another option that may provide substantial relief with minimal or no adverse events. Some individuals with bereavement may develop major depression, which is diagnosed when the symptoms have persisted for more than 2 months after a loss or when symptoms become severe such as psychosis, severe neurovegetative symptoms, or suicidality. In such instances, antidepressant medication is indicated.

Major depression is a frequent cause of sleep disruption in the elderly. Approximately 15% of individuals over 65 years of age experience clinically significant depression. Treatment of these patients should always include an antidepressant medication. Using sedating antidepressants in this setting may alleviate the insomnia as well as treat the depression. The main limiting factor of this approach is that many individuals cannot tolerate the side effects of sedating antidepressants. In this case, a sedative–hypnotic medication may be used along with antidepressant therapy. In adults, adding a hypnotic to escitalopram for the first 8 weeks of treatment not only improves sleep but also leads to a greater degree of improvement in symptoms of depression other than sleep difficulties and a greater overall rate of depression response and remission. No such studies in the elderly have been carried out.

Alzheimer's disease and other dementias have been associated with increased numbers of awakenings and arousals, an increase in daytime napping, and a reduction of slow wave and rapid eye movement (REM) sleep. Nocturnal agitation and confusion are also common and are a leading reason for institutionalization. Risk of "sundowning" (the appearance or exacerbation of behavioral disturbances associated with the evening hours or darkness) increases with dementia severity, pain, fecal impaction, malnutrition, number of concomitant medications, infections, PLMD, and environmental factors. Treatment of these sleep disruptions should begin with an evaluation of the preceding factors; however, if none is felt to be significantly present, treatment options include behavioral regimens, light therapy, and medication management. Benzodiazepines tend to be viewed as ineffective, although there is little prospective research on their use in this setting. Antipsychotics have the most evidence of efficacy, and newer atypical agents are recommended over older agents due to an improved side effect profile. These agents have recently appeared to increase the cerebrovascular adverse event rate in treatment of patients with dementia, so they should be used in the lowest possible dose and with appropriate caution.

Sleep-related complaints occur in 60% to 90% of Parkinson's disease patients. Common sleep difficulties in this population include difficulty in initiating and maintaining sleep, daytime fatigue, RLS, and discomfort related to being unable to turn over in bed. REM behavior sleep disorder is a condition in which the usual paralysis that occurs during REM sleep is absent, leading affected individuals to literally act out their dreams. This can lead to injuries for both these individuals and their bed partners and is seen in Parkinson's disease more frequently than in the general population. Dopaminergic medications used to treat Parkinson's disease may contribute substantially to these sleep disturbances. Few studies are available to guide practitioners in the management of these sleep disorders.

Medical conditions are frequently identified in the elderly, and many of them can affect sleep directly. Pain is a common feature of geriatric illness, and disruption of sleep is frequently identified in patients with inadequate pain control. Combined behavioral and psychopharmacological treatment designed to address both pain and secondary sleep disturbance can have a significant effect on quality of life.

Chronic obstructive pulmonary disease (COPD) can cause both subjective and objective evidence of disturbed sleep, and the degree of sleep disruption is not related to hypoxia. COPD is also different from apnea in that daytime sleepiness does not appear as a prominent feature, and PSG is not routinely indicated in COPD patients with sleep complaints. Nocturnal hypoxemia appears to be closely correlated with daytime hypoxemia, and patients may benefit from nocturnal oxygen administration. Oral theophyllines used in the treatment of COPD often have a sleep-disruptive effect. Benzodiazepines should be used with great caution because they may decrease ventilatory drive and worsen hypoxemia.

Cerebrovascular disease has been associated with myriad sleep disorders, and the presenting symptom appears to depend on the area of the brain affected by the condition. Hypersomnia has been associated with the lesions of the cephalad portions of the ascending reticular-activating system, including the midbrain and portions of the thalamus. Hemispheric lesions and lesions of the caudate and striatum are associated with hypersomnia less frequently. Insomnia directly related to damage of specific areas of the brain is much less common, and treatment should be directed toward associated conditions.

Nocturia is a frequently underdiagnosed cause of nocturnal awakenings in the elderly and has been offered as the most common explanation given by elderly patients for difficulty in maintaining sleep (reported by up to 72%). Common causes of nocturia are benign prostatic hypertrophy in men and decreased urethral resistance due to decreased estrogen levels coupled with stress urinary incontinence in women. Treating the primary cause of nocturia can improve symptoms effectively.

Sleep Disorders Evaluation

An evaluation of sleep disorders should begin with a comprehensive history and physical examination. Specific attention to address medical, psychiatric, and environmental conditions should be a priority. In cases where sleep apnea or PLMD is suspected based on the results of the history and physical examination, PSG should be considered. Sleep logs, sleep scales, and actigraphy can also be useful, depending on the complaint.

Special Issues in the Elderly

Two major types of treatment for sleep-related disorders in the elderly exist: cognitive behavioral therapy and pharmacotherapy. A range of behavioral interventions exists for patients with insomnia. The most effective interventions address the consequences of spending too much time in bed awake. Individuals with insomnia often repeatedly experience long periods in bed awake. This can lead to the bed becoming associated with the frustration, anxiety, anger, and so on via conditioning. Furthermore, there is evidence that spending more time in bed than an individual is able to sleep on a regular basis tends to promote greater fragmentation of sleep in terms of more periods of wakefulness in the middle of the night and diminished quality of sleep. These difficulties can be addressed most effectively by shortening the time spent in bed to roughly the usual amount of sleep attained and by getting out of bed and doing something nonarousing if individuals find themselves in bed for more than 20 minutes awake, worrying, or getting frustrated, angry, anxious, and so on. Because elderly persons have the tendency to nap during the day and have their day/night cycles disrupted, another important behavioral intervention in this group is to eliminate naps and to wake up at the same time every day.

Pharmacological approaches to the treatment of insomnia can also be very effective in the elderly. Lower doses are recommended because of the changes in metabolism and distribution of these medications that tend to occur with age. Elderly persons are also more sensitive to some side effects that can be seen with a number of pharmacological agents used for the treatment of insomnia, including memory difficulties, risk of falls, confusion, urinary obstruction, constipation, and sleeping during the day. All treatment decisions should involve a risk–benefit analysis of available options.

The most commonly administered pharmacological options include benzodiazepines, nonbenzodiazepines (not chemically related to the benzodiazepines but achieving their effects by binding to the same sites as benzodiazepines, although appearing to bind preferentially to sites affecting sleep), sedating antidepressants (primarily trazodone, mirtazapine, and tricyclic antidepressants), and antihistamines. The attributes of these medications differ substantially within and between the classes listed and as a function of dose level. Key attributes to consider include evidence for insomnia efficacy (greatest for the benzodiazepines and nonbenzodiazepines), expected duration of action (combination of half-life and dosing issues), risks of memory impairment (associated with benzodiazepines, nonbenzodiazepines, antihistamines, and anticholinergic or antihistaminergic antidepressants), risks of ataxia (associated with benzodiazepines, nonbenzodiazepines), risks of dizziness (can be seen with all), risks of orthostatic hypotension (particularly associated with antidepressants), risks of cardiac complications (greatest with some of the antidepressants and antihistamines), urinary retention (associated with antidepressants and antihistamines), constipation (associated with antidepressants and antihistamines), and interactions with other medications taken by the patient.

—*Andrew D. Krystal and Harold W. Goforth*

See also Bereavement and Grief; Depression and Other Mood Disorders; Neurobiology of Aging; Normal Physical Aging

Further Readings and References

Ancoli-Israel S, Cooke JR. Prevalence and comorbidity of insomnia and effect on functioning in elderly populations. *J Am Geriatr Soc.* 2005;53:264–272.

Blazer DG, Steffens DC, Busse EW. *Textbook of Geriatric Psychiatry.* 3rd ed. Washington, DC: American Psychiatric Press; 2004.

McCall WV. Diagnosis and management of insomnia in older adults. *J Am Geriatr Soc.* 2005;53:S272–S278.

SMOKING

Roughly one in four American adults smokes cigarettes, and many more are former smokers, with differences in smoking rates by age, sex, race/ethnicity, marital status, and social status. According to 2003 data from the National Health Interview Study of community-dwelling Americans, nearly 45 million adults were current smokers. The percentages of adults who were current smokers varied across age groups: 29% of those 18 to 24 years of age, 26% of those 25 to 44 years of age, 23% of those 45 to 64 years of age, and 9% of those age 65 years and older. Smoking rates may be higher in long-term care facilities than in the community. In addition, Health and Retirement Study (HRS) data show that 44% of older Americans are former smokers. The much lower proportion of older adults who are current smokers is largely due to the much higher rates of premature mortality in smokers, half of whom die during midlife.

Older men are more likely to be current smokers, and much more likely to be former smokers, than are women. African American and American Indian men are more likely to be smokers than are Hispanic, Asian, and European American men. Among older women, American Indians are more likely to be current smokers, and European Americans least likely to be current smokers, compared with older women in other racial/ethnic groups. Smoking status also differs between adults who are married and unmarried; adults who are married are less likely to be smokers than are those who are unmarried, smokers tend to marry other smokers, and nonsmokers tend to marry other nonsmokers.

In general, higher social status (measured as greater education and/or economic advantage) is associated with never smoking or being a past smoker (vs. being a current smoker) during older age. Interestingly, older adults who had better-educated parents are more likely to be current smokers. This may be due to the fact that during the first half of the 20th century, smoking was considered to be a luxury afforded most easily by those with higher social status—and a luxury not easily quit. Compared with younger smokers, older smokers may be longer term and more heavily addicted smokers who have successfully resisted decades of widely available information on the health dangers of smoking. Their unique characteristics may contribute to their resisting public health programs targeted to the wider smoking community or to younger smokers.

Links Between Smoking and Health

The landmark Surgeon General's report on smoking and health in 1964, as well as subsequent reports from the Surgeon General's office, provided increasing evidence that cigarette smoking is the foremost preventable cause of death in the United States. Half of all long-term smokers eventually die from smoking-related diseases. Studies since 1964 show clear links between cigarette smoking and the three leading causes of death in older U.S. adults: heart disease, cancer, and stroke. According to the American Cancer Society, nearly 1 in 3 cancer deaths and 9 in 10 lung cancer deaths are due to smoking. Women may be particularly susceptible to lung cancer. That these conditions often take years to develop may explain why most smoking-related deaths occur in older adults. In fact, of the approximately 438,000 smoking-related deaths per year in the United States, more than 94% are of persons age 50 years and older and more than 70% are of persons age 65 years and older. The mortality rate for chronic lung disease, the fourth leading

cause of death in older adults, has increased since 1980 as a result of the higher past smoking rates in older adults. Long-term exposure to secondhand smoking extends the negative health effects of smoking to nonsmokers. Approximately 50,000 premature deaths per year are due to environmental tobacco smoke in the United States, with approximately 3,000 of these being from lung cancer and 35,000 from cardiovascular disease, the majority in older adults and young children.

In addition, smoking is associated with the onset and complications of many other acute and chronic conditions—pneumonia, postsurgical wound infections, type 2 diabetes, sensory impairments, osteoporosis and hip fractures, impotence, and dementia (including Alzheimer's disease)—that affect the longevity and quality of life of older adults who are already at higher risk for health problems compared with younger adults. Smoking is also the primary cause of accidental fires that kill older adults. Finally, nicotine in smoking products may cause commonly prescribed medications used by older adults to work less effectively.

Smoking has other social and economic consequences. Smoking causes significant indirect costs from the increased workplace absenteeism and lower productivity of smokers of any age compared with former or never smokers. Smokers and nonsmokers alike may be bothered by environmental tobacco smoke, further reducing productivity. In addition to premature deaths, each year smoking costs the nation approximately $76 billion in excess health care, accounts for 5.5 million years of potential life lost, and is responsible for one third of all Medicare costs, according to the Centers for Disease Control and Prevention (CDC).

Smoking Cessation

Older smokers benefit from quitting smoking in ways similar to those in younger smokers—improved cardiovascular functioning, reduced risk of lung disease and smoking-related cancers, and decreased complications from a wide range of other health problems—although their improvements may be somewhat slower than those in younger smokers. Despite the slower improvements, an older adult's risk of a smoking-related death can be reduced by 50% simply by quitting, according to the Surgeon General's report on the health consequences of smoking in 2004.

The proportion of older adults who smoke has fallen from approximately 29% to 9% since the 1964 Surgeon General's report, with the majority of the decrease resulting from higher quit rates and premature deaths in men across all racial/ethnic groups. The reasons why some people quit and others continue to smoke are not entirely clear. Understanding the reasons may help interventionists to meet the government's health objective of reducing the rates of cigarette smoking by half, as outlined in *Healthy People 2010.* Although few cessation studies focus specifically on older adults, what is known suggests that social status, health beliefs, recent health events, and physician encouragement are among the factors that may play important roles in the smoking cessation of older adults (as well as younger adults).

Social status clearly plays a role: The rates of quitting smoking since 1964 have increased consistently (and have increased even more rapidly over time) for people with more education and/or economic advantage. For example, college graduates have quit at significantly higher rates than have high school graduates, suggesting that people with higher education may have better understood the risks of cigarette smoking and acted on the Surgeon General's recommendations. Other factors related to social status may also influence smoking behavior. For example, according to HRS data, smoker cessation is lowest among workers employed (or previously employed) in manufacturing or day labor jobs as well as people who are depressed or heavy alcohol users, have poorer self-assessed health, have lower confidence in their ability to quit, are more heavily addicted smokers, and are unmarried.

Smoking cessation clearly increases the quality of life for older adults, and 8 in 10 older smokers would rather not be smoking. Although older smokers are also more likely than younger smokers to be successful in quitting, older smokers quit at roughly the same rates as do younger smokers, perhaps due to

their health beliefs. The American Association of Retired Persons found that only half of older smokers believe smoking has negative health consequences or cessation potential health benefits for them and that even though smokers in general perceive their health risks for cardiovascular diseases and cancer to be greater than those of nonsmokers, they underestimate their health risks. Nevertheless, results of HRS data show that that older smokers are more likely to quit smoking following the experience of a serious health event, particularly one that is more immediately life threatening such as a heart attack. In addition, results show that the experience of a heart attack interacts with higher levels of smokers' education to dramatically increase rates of quitting in older smokers.

Studies showing that more than one third of older smokers with access to regular physician care report never having been advised by their physicians to quit point to another area of important influence, namely physician encouragement. Yet other studies indicate that older smokers are more likely than nonsmokers to be without a regular physician as well as to have fewer physician or dental visits, lower social support, and psychological distress. In addition, older Hispanic, Asian, and African American adults are less likely than European American adults to have regular access to health care and may face language or cultural barriers in that care. Issues of access to regular, appropriate, and culturally competent health care represent challenges for providers and interventionists who seek to decrease smoking rates in older adults.

Finally, the vast majority of older smokers want to quit, and older adults are important targets for national smoking cessation programs. Identifying the most effective ways to promote quitting in all smokers—both older and younger—is critical for reducing disease, extending life expectancy, and increasing years lived without disability in older adults. The CDC recommends using a combination of educational, economic, clinical, and regulatory strategies to reduce smoking in all adults. The unique characteristics of older smokers may require specially designed smoking cessation programs that address their particular barriers to quitting. In 2002, the U.S. government began a pilot program in seven states through

Medicare and Medicaid to identify the best clinical strategies to help Medicare beneficiaries who smoke to quit—certainly a hopeful start.

—Linda Ann Wray

See also Cancer; Cancer, Common Types of; Cancer Prevention and Screening; Health Promotion and Disease Prevention; Oral Health; Pulmonary Aging

Further Readings and References

Burns DM. Cigarette smoking among the elderly: Disease consequences and the benefits of cessation. *Am J Health Promot.* 1999;14:357–361.

Franks MH, Pienta AM, Wray LA. It takes two: Marriage and smoking cessation in the middle years. *J Aging Health.* 2002;14:336–354.

U.S. Department of Health and Human Services. *The Health Consequences of Smoking: A Report of the Surgeon General.* Rockville, Md: U.S. Department of Health and Human Services, Centers for Disease Control and Prevention; 2004.

Wray LA, Herzog AR, Willis RJ, Wallace RB. The impact of education and heart attack on smoking cessation among middle-aged adults. *J Health Social Behav.* 1998;39: 271–294.

SOCIAL NETWORKS AND SOCIAL SUPPORT

Social support is an essential element of late-life well-being but has defied easy definition. Social support generally involves the quantity and quality of three types of support one receives from other persons: emotional support, instrumental (or material) support, and informational support. Social support also involves the individual's appraisal of whether such support is adequate. The social support network—that set of persons with whom one interacts, to whom one feels attached, and from whom one might receive support—is variably viewed as either a fifth dimension or an antecedent of social support. An individual's network of support includes those with whom he or she has a formal or institution-based relationship such as health care providers and clergy. Social networks also include numerous informal relationships such as those with family members, friends, and neighbors.

Background and Significance

Two theorists are generally credited with early attention that focused on the concept and phenomenon of social support. Sociologist Émile Durkheim (1859–1917) was the first to observe the relationship between lack of social support and suicidal behavior. John Bowlby (1907–1990), a British psychiatrist, closely observed the developing relationship of support between mothers and young children, and he proposed a theory of attachment that has been influential to explain social attachments beyond the mother–child dyad. More recent theories suggest that structural and functional dimensions of social support among humans is influenced by factors operating in the broad social environment as well as in the individual's psychobiological makeup.

Understanding the role of social support during late life has taken on renewed urgency because of demographic trends. These include the increasingly disproportionate ratio of older adults to younger adults in the population, trends toward smaller family sizes, higher rates of divorced and never-married older persons, and the prevalence of chronic debilitating conditions for which social support is required. These concerns have spawned a vast body of research, much of which has focused intensely on the antecedents and consequences of social support during late life.

Nature and Experience of Social Support

Social support has been studied in a variety of population groups. Studies based in local, regional, and U.S. locations, as well as in numerous international communities, have yielded important demographic differences. Compared with younger adults, older adults appear to require a smaller and less diverse network of supportive individuals to enjoy the benefits of social support. Older women are more likely than older men to receive emotional support from a confidante, but men receive more instrumental assistance from others than do women; both older women and older men receive increasing amounts of social support from their grown children over time. Racial differences in social support vary somewhat during late life. The social networks of African Americans include disproportionately more kin than do those of European Americans, and African Americans report somewhat less frequent interaction with their networks. However, both races report similar trends toward more emotionally close social partners, and fewer peripheral social partners, in their networks as they age.

Family structure provides opportunity advantages for social support. Older persons with siblings and married older persons are at a social support advantage. Frailty during late life exacerbates the impact of family structure on social support. Among frail elders, material and instrumental social support is particularly dependent on larger kinship networks, more female kin, and more geographically proximal kin.

Role choices during late life (e.g., retirement decisions, membership in religious or community organizations) also affect availability of social support. Remaining employed during late life significantly increases the number of coworker friends and the amount of material support received. However, retirees and older workers tend not to differ in their appraisal of the quality of their overall social support. Participation in religious organizations has been the focus of extensive research. The evidence is overwhelming that both informal and formal social support are associated with religious involvement, with such associations being particularly evident in African American communities. Social support is sensitive to unbidden changes during late life as well. Physically disabling conditions expand the network of supportive persons, whereas cognitive disability shrinks such networks.

Social support has generally been observed to have a positive influence on late-life outcomes. Of major interest are how social support functions in general to protect late-life well-being and whether it has a particularly ameliorative function in the presence of stress, experienced either as stressful life events or as more chronic stressful conditions. These effects appear to be quite specific to the type of stressor experienced. For example, patients with osteoarthritis derive more benefit from social support than do patients with rheumatoid arthritis. Such preliminary effects require much more study.

Social Support and Physical Health

One of the most robust and consistent findings regarding the consequences of lack of social support is its deleterious effect on survival. Social isolation is associated with premature death from all causes as well as from specific causes such as coronary heart disease, cancer, hip fractures and other accidents, and suicide. This finding has been replicated in regionally and racially diverse studies and in national samples from the United States, Australia, Denmark, Great Britain, Japan, and Norway.

The dimensions of social support implicated in research on mortality are diverse. Structural characteristics of the social network can place older persons at risk. These include being unmarried and having few or no children, having no connections to community organizations, being a newcomer to the neighborhood, and generally having a limited network of family, friends, and acquaintances. However, even smaller social network structures can protect against early mortality if the frequency of interactions with their members is great enough. Visiting and talking with friends and relatives is a powerful inhibitor of mortality, although efficacious interactions differ across cultures. Interaction with friends and confidants appears to be the most helpful as a safeguard against early mortality among Australian older persons, whereas interaction with relatives has the strongest effect among Japanese older persons. Gender differences in mortality are also marked. Older men appear to be particularly susceptible to lack of social support. A dearth of emotional and instrumental social support places older men at greater risk for early mortality compared with older women.

The disease-specific mechanisms by which social support protects against early mortality have been the focus of numerous clinical studies. Heart disease is managed more successfully when patients feel loved and receive assistance from their social networks. Among cancer patients, being able to talk freely about their disease among friends and relatives leads to improved outcomes of the disease. Diabetes patients, especially African Americans, depend heavily on their social support networks to help manage their disease.

Lack of social support is also found among older persons with disabling conditions, including those related to pain. Diverse social relations, frequent participation, and emotional support tend to protect older persons from developing physical limitations and help them recover from acute disabling states. Social relationships may also protect older persons from developing physical disability by keeping feelings of depression at bay. Older persons who report high levels of social support, especially older persons who are depressed, are also less likely to develop cognitive limitations.

When older persons report that their overall physical health is very good, they often give simultaneous reports that some element of their social support is particularly strong and salient. The belief that help will be available if one becomes sick is key to ratings of good health. Among those reporting significantly high levels of overall good health were (a) Israeli elders highly satisfied with support of friends and relatives, (b) U.S. elders with strong spiritual and emotional support from religious congregations, and (c) Japanese elders receiving strong support from members of their neighborhoods.

Social Support and Mental Health

Lack of social support undermines mental health and contributes to feelings of depression, demoralization, and psychological distress. This phenomenon has been described in the general population of older persons as well as in groups of clinically depressed patients. In the general population of older people, all dimensions of social support have been shown to be protective against feelings of sadness and lack of interest in life. Particularly helpful are having a partner, having many and diverse close ties, visiting in each other's homes, feeling satisfied with support, and receiving and providing instrumental aid. Among older persons who are undergoing special challenges such as relocation to retirement communities, the recent loss of a spouse, and encroaching disability,

the mediating effects of social support are especially salient. Social support appears to buffer against the expected consequences of such losses.

Certain kinds of social support can be harmful to the psychological well-being of older persons. Ambivalent and negative social interactions increase feelings of psychological distress. Particularly vulnerable are men and European Americans, who report significantly more distress following negative interactions with others than do women and African Americans, respectively.

Among older depressed patients, symptoms of depression are more severe when satisfaction with the amount and quality of social support is low. Social support also is a factor in recovery from a major depressive episode. Patients with more social interaction and instrumental assistance are more likely to see their depressive symptoms diminish over time and to report shorter time spans until remission of symptoms.

Social Support and Quality of Life

When older persons assess the overall quality of their lives, social support is a key ingredient to a positive assessment. Large networks of close family and friends and frequent visits in each other's homes contribute to a good quality of life, especially among rural dwellers. Reciprocity of social support (i.e., both giving and receiving emotional and instrumental aid), especially between generations, is important to older persons, even in cultures such as Korea, where the expression of filial piety is of high value. Studies of populations in Great Britain, Scandinavia, central and southern Europe, and Israel demonstrate strong relationships between social support and overall well-being.

—*Judith C. Hays*

See also Depression and Other Mood Disorders; Quality of Life; Self-Rated Health; Work, Health, and Retirement

Further Readings and References

Berkman LF, Glass T, Brissett I, Seeman TE. From social integration to health: Durkheim in the new millennium. *Social Sci Med.* 2000;51:843–857.

Hays JC, Steffens DC, Flint EP, Bosworth HB, George LK. Does social support buffer functional decline in elderly patients with unipolar depression? *Am J Psychiatry.* 2001;158:1850–1855.

Langford CP, Bowsher J, Maloney JP, Lillis PP. Social support: A conceptual analysis. *J Adv Nursing.* 1997; 25:95–100.

Seeman TE, Lusignolo TM, Albert M, Berkman L. Social relationships, social support, and patterns of cognitive aging in healthy, high-functioning older adults: MacArthur Studies of Successful Aging. *Health Psychol.* 2001;20:243–255.

Winemiller DR, Mitchell ME, Sutleff J, Clinc KJ. Measurement strategies in social support: A description review of the literature. *J Clin Psychol.* 1993;49:638–648.

SOCIAL SECURITY

See ECONOMICS OF AGING

SOCIAL WORK ROLES IN HEALTH AND LONG-TERM CARE

Gerontological social workers provide clinical services to older adults and their families, develop programs to serve older adults and reshape current programs where consumers are aging, administer health and long-term care organizations, and help develop health and social policies. Gerontological social workers provide these services in health and long-term care settings, including health care clinics, hospitals, extended care and rehabilitation units, assisted-living facilities, and nursing homes. They also serve older adults in private homes through home health, hospice, and other community-based care agencies (both public and private). Social workers work with other allied health professionals in these settings, often as part of interdisciplinary teams. They are distinguished from other professionals by their knowledge of community resources and the range of options available to meet the biopsychosocial needs of clients, their psychosocial perspective and multidimensional assessment skills, and their skills in engaging elderly persons, their families, and the community in aspects of problem solving.

Social work interventions in health and long-term care often begin with a referral from another provider, such as a doctor or an administrator, or from routine screening or outreach protocols. Referrals are generally made in response to complicated psychosocial situations, the need to transition between settings, or the need for service arrangements. The social worker often completes a multidimensional assessment covering physical functioning, mental status, emotional health, social resources, living arrangements, physical environment, informal and formal service use, and financial resources. Social work values also call for assessing values and preferences of older adults and their families to enhance care planning.

Social workers implement a variety of interventions in health and long-term care settings. Clinical case management is often needed in these settings. Case management is an intervention aimed at organizing an effective and efficient package of services to meet client needs. Primary tasks include assessing service needs, planning with older clients and their families, care arrangement and coordination, follow-up, and monitoring. The term *clinical case management* is used because counseling is important in this process; it is more than just information and referral. Family dynamics are complex, clients refuse services, clients and personal care workers clash, and service needs change for clients who have degenerative conditions. Family care and assistance from formal sources must be balanced. Also, the development of service arrangements depends on client resources and entitlements, which the social worker must understand accurately. This can be challenging because even though numerous federal, state, and local programs provide health and social services and income to older adults, financing care packages is usually difficult. Social workers must know the programs that affect their clients, assist clients in obtaining coverage, and maximize the use of these financial supports while helping clients and their families to budget costs that must be borne privately.

Social workers provide discharge-planning services to patients in nursing homes, day treatment programs, and hospitals. They are also called on to help with other transitions such as home to day care center and home to nursing home. Social workers strive to ensure continuity of care, to ease adjustment, and to maximize client self-determination and choice. Within health care facilities, and in conjunction with community-based organizations, they organize and lead therapeutic groups that address various challenges such as widowhood, caregiving, and recovering from or adjusting to stroke or Parkinson's disease. Critical to the counseling function offered by social workers is psychoeducation to clients and families about disease and disease management (e.g., depression, Alzheimer's, diabetes, sensory impairment). Social workers are also members of hospice teams that provide planning for end of life care as well as counseling for dying patients and their families.

—*Nancy Morrow-Howell*

See also Assisted Living; Caregiving; Continuum of Care; Geriatric Team Care; Institutional Care; Long-Term Care

Further Readings and References

U.S. Department of Health and Human Services/ Administration on Aging. Elders and families: More resources. Available at: www.aoa.gov/eldfam/more/ More.asp. Accessed October 3, 2006.

SOCIOECONOMIC STATUS

Socioeconomic status (SES) has been a central concept in gerontological research on health and health care. A large body of literature has documented a positive association between health and wealth, with higher SES correlating with better health outcomes. This health–wealth connection has been demonstrated consistently in all age groups, across societies, over time, and for multiple measures of both SES and health. Furthermore, the SES–health relationship is observed throughout the SES hierarchy and not simply above and below a certain economic threshold (e.g., poverty status).

The way in which SES concepts and measures are used in health research has changed over time. Earlier studies of health and aging typically used SES indicators to describe the study participants or respondents and treated SES as a potential confounding variable in analyses of more proximate causes of health outcomes. More recently, greater attention has been paid to the causal role of SES itself in producing variations in mortality, morbidity, and disability patterns. SES has been termed a *fundamental social cause* of health outcomes, meaning that SES influences multiple health outcomes because it operates through multiple pathways (i.e., through more proximate causes such as health behaviors, psychosocial stressors, and access to quality health care). Evidence increasingly links various causal mechanisms to health outcomes.

Measuring SES in Older Populations

In general, SES refers to an individual's access to, or possession of, economic and social resources; that is, the individual's property, power, and prestige in his or her social setting. The most commonly used measures of adult SES are the individual's education, income, and occupation, but researchers have also examined alternative measures such as wealth (total assets), poverty status, neighborhood-level SES, and childhood SES.

Education is measured numerically as number of years of schooling completed or categorically in terms of specific educational credentials (e.g., high school degree, college degree). Annual *income* may be assessed for the individual or household and typically includes all sources, including wages, investments, and pensions. *Occupations* are usually grouped into broad classes such as professional/managerial, clerical, skilled labor, and unskilled labor. Alternatively, occupations may be assigned prestige scores based on social opinion surveys regarding the relative amounts of prestige associated with specific jobs. *Wealth* measures place a total value on all assets or all liquid assets or, alternatively, may indicate ownership or value of specific assets (e.g., home, cars, savings, investments). *Poverty status* is a dichotomous indicator of whether the individual's annual family income exceeds federal poverty standards (based on number and ages of family members). *Neighborhood SES* is assessed by aggregate measures such as median household income and percentage of household heads with college degrees. Measures of *childhood SES* include information on parents' education levels and occupations or the individual's subjective assessment of his or her family's relative social standing.

Education is the most widely used SES indicator in health studies of older populations, in part because it is relatively simple to obtain. Education has an additional advantage in that it typically does not change past young adulthood and thus causally exists prior to the development of most health problems. Income and occupation measures are more problematic to use in older populations because postretirement conditions might not adequately reflect the economic resources available to seniors. Furthermore, current status measures of income and occupation do not assess conditions in younger and middle adulthood when chronic diseases are beginning to develop. Measures of wealth have been used more frequently in recent studies of health and aging. Wealth indicators give a broader assessment of the material and financial resources owned by older, especially retired individuals, and they incorporate information on economic status during the preretirement years.

SES and Health Outcomes in Older Populations

The number of studies examining SES differences in health status and outcomes in older populations is voluminous and growing. Although not every study has found significant effects of SES on health, the research picture is remarkably consistent. Compared with higher SES individuals, persons of lower SES have higher mortality risks, higher prevalence and incidence of chronic diseases, more rapid disease progression, higher rates of functional limitations and disability, worse cognitive functioning, and greater likelihood of depressive symptoms.

Evidence of an association between SES and health outcomes in cross-sectional studies does not necessarily mean that SES is a fundamental cause of health outcomes. Some researchers have suggested that the health–wealth connection is observed because persons in ill health cannot work and thus have reduced incomes and assets (the *health selection hypothesis*). Longitudinal research has examined this hypothesis, however, and found that although there is some causal influence of health on SES, the causal effects of SES on health (the *social causation hypothesis*) dominate the association.

Explanations offered for the SES effect on health outcomes are of three types: material, behavioral, and psychosocial. The explanations described in what follows are not competing hypotheses; rather, they likely represent the multiple causal pathways through which SES may influence health. In fact, evidence can be found for each of these potential pathways between SES and health. Of particular relevance to health studies of older adults is the *cumulative disadvantage hypothesis*. This hypothesis suggests that the effects of multiple forms of disadvantage experienced throughout adulthood (and childhood) accumulate to elevate health risks in lower SES individuals. Thus, the health effects of any single type of disadvantage may be limited, but their additive effects hold greater explanatory power.

Material explanations suggest that lower SES individuals have more limited access to tangible resources that can be used to ensure health. Lower SES persons have less income and fewer assets with which to purchase health resources such as healthy foods, safe housing in safe neighborhoods, gym memberships, medications, and access to quality health care. *Behavioral explanations* argue that persons with higher SES have greater knowledge and better attitudes about various health-related behaviors (e.g., diet, physical activity, smoking, alcohol consumption, illicit drug use, sexual risk taking, health care seeking) than do lower SES individuals. These differences in knowledge and attitudes are thought to result primarily from educational inequalities and are posited to translate into differences in health risk taking, thereby leading to differential health outcomes. *Psychosocial explanations* for SES differences in health focus on the stressors that people face and their coping resources. Lower SES persons are thought to experience more daily and chronic stressors and to have fewer social resources (e.g., less social support) with which to cope. The greater exposure to stressors may stem from multiple sources, including a lack of financial resources, limited autonomy or control in the workplace, unsafe neighborhoods, and a sense of relative deprivation.

Studies of older adult mortality, morbidity, and disability have linked education, income, occupational group, occupational prestige, assets, home ownership, and neighborhood SES to health outcomes. Many of these studies use multiple indicators of SES and find independent effects for these indicators. In other words, although these measures of SES are intercorrelated, they appear to exert unique effects on health outcomes through distinct causal pathways. Furthermore, SES effects on health outcomes are not eliminated by including individual risk factors into explanatory models. For example, accounting for SES differences in risky health behaviors (e.g., smoking) or health resources (e.g., having health insurance) does not fully explain SES differences in health outcomes. Taken together, these results support the fundamental cause perspective on the SES–health association by providing evidence that SES affects multiple health outcomes through multiple causal pathways.

Some studies of health and mortality during adulthood have demonstrated a weakening effect of SES on health outcomes from middle to older ages. The *convergence hypothesis* suggests that although SES differentials in health outcomes may be observed throughout adulthood, the relative health risks for low-SES versus high-SES individuals are lower in the older age groups. This convergence is posited to be a result of selective survival to older ages in the lower SES groups. In other words, the low-SES individuals who survive to old age are healthier and hardier. Many studies of the SES–health association cannot examine the convergence hypothesis because the study samples have restricted age ranges. In studies with wide age ranges, however, SES effects on both mortality and onset of disability appear to be stronger among middle-aged and young-old adults (i.e., between 40 and 70 years of age) than among younger and old-old adults. These findings are consistent with

the convergence hypothesis but do not clarify why the weakening of SES effects on health are observed. A limited number of studies have specifically examined the selective survival explanation and found some empirical support; however, the convergence of health risks during older ages is not explained completely.

—*Laura Rudkin*

See also Demography of Aging; Education and Health; Ethnicity and Race; Longitudinal Research; Selective Optimization With Compensation; Successful Aging

Further Readings and References

Crimmins EM, Hayward MD, Seeman TE. Race, socioeconomic status, and health. In: Anderson NB, Bulatao RA, Cohen B, eds. *Critical Perspectives on Racial and Ethnic Differences in Health in Late Life.* Washington, DC: National Academy Press; 2004: 310–352.

House JS, Lantz PM, Herd P. Continuity and change in the social stratification of aging and health over the life course: Evidence from a nationally representative longitudinal study from 1986 to 2001/2002 (Americans' Changing Lives Study). *J Gerontol B Psychol Sci Social Sci.* 2005;60(Spec. No. 2):15–26.

Phelan JC, Link BG. Controlling disease and creating disparities: A fundamental cause perspective. *J Gerontol B Psychol Sci Social Sci.* 2005;60(Spec. No. 2):27–33.

Rudkin L, Markides KS. Measuring the socioeconomic status of elderly people in health studies with special focus on minority elderly. *J Mental Health Aging.* 2001;7:53–66.

Seeman TE, Crimmins E, Huang M-H, et al. Cumulative biological risk and socio-economic differences in mortality: MacArthur Studies of Successful Aging. *Social Sci Med.* 2004;58:1985–1997.

SPINAL STENOSIS

Low back pain is the third most common reason for physician visits among older adults. Spinal stenosis is one of several common causes of low back pain and is a common cause of back surgery in older adults. Degenerative spinal stenosis (narrowing) occurs when the structures of the spinal canal, or the openings where individual nerves exit the spine, narrow gradually with age. Such degenerative changes may include loss of intervertebral disc height and osteophyte (new bone) formation due to osteoarthritis, which can encroach on the central spinal canal and nerves. Bulging vertebral discs also may compress nerve structures. Spinal stenosis in older adults most commonly affects the lower lumbar spine. Resulting compression on these nerve structures causes pain and, in more severe cases, weakness.

Classically, patients complain of diffuse low back pain and pain in the legs exacerbated by standing or walking. Other activities that extend the spine, such as standing and lying prone, may also worsen symptoms. Positions that flex the spine, such as sitting and leaning forward while walking, may improve symptoms. Neurological abnormalities on physical examination may be lacking, but when they are present they may occur after a period of activity that evokes changes in reflexes, sensation, and increased pain. Other conditions that can cause similar back pain include peripheral arterial disease, in which leg pain occurs after a period of physical exertion (known as claudication), tumor, disc herniation, and mechanical back pain due to muscle strain.

Diagnosis is often made based on a description of pain and a physical examination. Radiographic studies are often reserved for those with more urgent symptoms or those not responding to a trial of conservative therapy. There may be a poor correlation between the severity of symptoms and the severity of X-ray changes. Most adults develop disc degeneration and arthritis of the spine, but not symptoms of spinal stenosis, as they age. In one study, up to 21% of older adults with stenotic changes on magnetic resonance imaging (MRI) were symptom-free. On the other hand, some patients have significant pain and functional disability despite minimal radiographic changes. For patients with atypical or continued pain or muscle weakness, or for those contemplating injections or surgical interventions, MRI is often done. A computed tomography (CT) scan with myelography may be used instead in selected circumstances.

Conservative management is frequently successful using anti-inflammatory or other analgesic medications to control pain and physical therapy to strengthen abdominal muscles. Walking, water therapy, and/or other exercise to maintain mobility is important. If these modalities do not bring relief over time, lumbar steroid injections may provide relief for many patients. Those who remain symptomatic may be candidates for surgical intervention to relieve pressure on the affected nerves. A majority of surgically treated patients reported good to excellent outcomes in one study. Ongoing work in this area continues to develop newer, less invasive decompressive procedures.

—*Lynne Kallenbach*

See also Arthritis and Other Rheumatic Diseases; Fractures in Older Adults; Musculoskeletal Aging: Osteoarthritis

Further Readings and References

Gunzberg R, Szpalski M. The conservative surgical treatment of lumbar spinal stenosis in the elderly. *Eur Spine J.* 2003;12(Suppl. 2):S176–S180.

Hu SS, et al. Lumbar disc herniation section of disorders, diseases, and injuries of the spine. In: Skinner HB, ed. *Current Diagnosis and Treatment in Orthopedics.* 3rd ed. New York: McGraw-Hill; 2003:231–239.

Szpalski M, Gunzberg R. Lumbar stenosis in the elderly: An overview. *Eur Spine J.* 2003;12(Suppl. 2):S170–S175.

STRESS

Stress is part of life, and throughout their lives all people are exposed to stressful events. It is clear that across their lifetimes, older people accrue more stressful experiences than do younger people, and these experiences and the coping strategies used to deal with them may play a role during later life. In addition, older people experience more losses such as bereavement and declining health. The impact that stressful events have on people's lives depends on several factors related to both the stressful events and the persons involved.

Definitions

Stress is a commonly encountered concept, and it is difficult to give a precise definition of its meaning. Stress seems to relate to three components: environmental demands, people's psychological appraisal of these demands, and people's emotional response to them. Experiences such as bereavement and moving home are commonly called *life events* and have been used to study the impact of environmental stressors on people's physical and mental health. In addition to discrete life events, stress can develop from more minor but long-term irritating, frustrating, or distressing events such as a difficult relationship with a neighbor and financial problems; these are known as *chronic hassles*. When stressful events occur, they place a *strain* on people's equilibrium and can trigger psychological distress and even illness due to the physiological and emotional response. People all respond to stress individually, and the mechanisms they put in place to deal with stressful events are called *coping mechanisms*.

Factors Influencing the Stress Response

The timing of a stressful event in a person's life is significant in determining its impact and is related to the socially expected "norm" for that particular event. During later life, certain events are more socially normal than they would be earlier in life, including retiring, a spouse dying, and children leaving home. These would be considered "on-time" events for an older person's stage of development; in contrast, the death of a child or grandchild would be considered an "off-time" event. The distinction between on-time and off-time events is important in that on-time events may be less stressful because they are expected to some extent, and therefore adaptation may be more straightforward. Retirement, for example, may be viewed less negatively by older people than by younger people. Less expected events, such as being mugged and experiencing a natural disaster, may well have a greater impact on an older individual's psychological well-being. Important factors related to the event also include considerations such as the degree of threat (or negative impact) caused by the event and the amount of time that has elapsed since the event occurred.

Characteristics of the person experiencing the stressful event are also important when studying the impact of stress. Factors such as the individual's natural resilience and coping strategies, having a predisposing vulnerability to developing a certain illness, having additional problems contributing to raised adversity, and the presence of social support all are important. Older people often have reduced physical reserves, potentially making them more vulnerable to the consequences of stress. However, many older people have survived demanding and stressful events in the past and may have developed a resilience and capacity to adapt in response to stress. Events may also have a greater impact where they affect the most salient roles that the older person has. There is strong evidence that older people with good networks of social support will live longer and experience better health. For example, in one study, older people with depression who self-harmed were more likely to have poor social support than were older people with depression who had not self-harmed. In particular, having a key confidant may help buffer the effects of stressful events. Moreover, positive events, such as a recent marriage, have been linked to positive mood.

Measuring Stressful Events

Research into the effects of life events and chronic hassles on the elderly population requires the use of specific measurement tools. One of the first developed was a checklist derived from Thomas Holmes and Richard Rahe's research looking at life events and chronic hassles and known as the Social Readjustment Rating Scale (SRRS). Life events, in order of decreasing severity (by a sample of the U.S. adult population), include the following:

- Death of spouse
- Divorce
- Marital separation

- Jail term
- Death of close family member
- Personal injury or illness

Daily hassles (by the same criteria) include the following:

- Not enough time
- Too many things to do
- Troubling thoughts about the future
- Too many interruptions
- Misplacing or losing things
- Health of a family member
- Population

Many SRRS items are skewed toward younger people (e.g., jail term, pregnancy, trouble with in-laws), and the scale has been adapted as the Geriatric Social Readjustment Scale, which consists of events thought to be particularly relevant to the elderly. Another way of eliciting events is by a standardized interview such as the Life Events and Difficulties Schedule (LEDS). This more accurate method of eliciting and rating life events uses a panel of independent raters to assess the events elicited by the interview. The raters use contextual information to rate the degree of "threat" to the person without knowledge of the person's emotional response to the event. This gives a reliable objective rating and has been found to have good reliability when used with older people. Finally, some scales that have been developed look at stress caused by specific circumstances, such as the Zarit Burden Interview, which measures the stress caused by caregiving and is therefore particularly useful in the elderly because many older people are carers.

Stress and Illness

Research into the links between stress and illness has inherent difficulties and is often open to interpretation. Many studies rely on retrospective reporting of stressful life events that may be subject to recall bias. Also, increased smoking and alcohol consumption, poor sleep, and reduced exercise are associated with stress and act as confounding factors that have their own detrimental effect on health. Because older people are more at risk for physical illness and are more likely to be physically frail, any link between physical ill health and stress will be particularly relevant for them.

Much research into the association between specific illnesses and stress has found links to cardio-vascular disease, wound healing, diabetes, gastrointestinal disease, musculoskeletal disorders, and even death. Bereavement is a common life event for older adults, and evidence suggests that the recently bereaved have a lower level of immune response than do control groups. Also, during the 6 months following bereavement, widowers over 55 years of age have been found to have a 40% increased risk of mortality, with the most common cause of death being complications of atherosclerosis such as myocardial infarction.

Accumulating evidence suggests that a person's psychological state can affect the body's immune system, leading to a possible impact on infection, the development of cancer, and autoimmune diseases. Exposure to chronic hassles and stress over a long period of time consistently has been found to appear to lead to down-regulation of the immune system. Conversely, having a positive attitude seems to correlate with an increased ability of the immune system to fight diseases. However, the immune system is complex, and it is difficult to identify whether changes caused by stress have a clinical impact.

A number of large studies have been conducted looking at stress as a risk factor for coronary heart disease (CHD). Strong and consistent evidence suggests that depression and social isolation increase the risk of coronary artery disease, although the risk from life events is less conclusive. Dysregulation of the autonomic nervous system (ANS), including elevated heart rate, exaggerated heart rate responses to physical stressors, and high variability in ventricular repolarization, is one explanation for why patients who experience stress are at increased risk. A large case–control study using the LEDS showed that stroke patients were significantly more likely to have experienced a severely threatening life event during the past year than were age/sex-matched controls.

Mental Illness and Stress

Stressful life events and chronic hassles are linked to depression in older adults in studies using both the LEDS and checklists. One study using the LEDS found that older people with depression had more severely threatening life events and major social difficulties. The lack of a confiding relationship seemed to act as a "vulnerability factor," making those exposed to life events more susceptible to depression. A study using the SRRS found that depressed people had more arguments with friends and more deaths of friends. Another study using the Geriatric Schedule of Recent Life Events indicated that life events that the participant felt helpless to control were significant in the onset of depression. Spousal bereavement is probably the most studied of all life events in the elderly and would normally be classified as a severely threatening event. It has been shown that 17% to 26% of widows and widowers are still depressed 1 year after the bereavement.

People with dementia have fewer resources to adapt to stressful situations, and several studies have looked at the effects of relocation and life events in people with dementia. Relocation can lead to depressive symptoms, disturbed behavior, and disorientation that can persist for several months. Life events have also been linked with depression in people with dementia.

Future Considerations

Stressful life events and chronic hassles are a risk factor for psychiatric disorders (e.g., depression), physical disorders (e.g., heart disease), and death in the elderly. Social support consistently has been found to be a protective factor. There have been a number of scales developed to study this relationship, and larger studies using well-validated scales such as the LEDS will help further clarify the impact of stress on older people's health.

—*Martin Orrell and Amber Selwood*

See also Anxiety Disorders; Bereavement and Grief; Control; Disasters and Terrorism; Multiple Morbidity and Comorbidity

Further Readings and References

Davies ADM. Life events in the normal elderly. In: Copeland JRM, Abou-Saleh MT, Blazer D, eds. *Principles and Practice of Geriatric Psychiatry.* Chichester, England: Wiley; 1994:106–114.

Dennis M. Self-harm in older people with depression: Comparison of social factors, life events, and symptoms. *Br J Psychiatry.* 2005;186:538–539.

Holmes TH, Rahe RH. The Social Readjustment Rating Scale. *J Psychosom Res.* 1967;11:213–218.

Krause N. Stressors arising in highly valued roles, meaning in life, and the physical health status of older adults. *J Gerontol B Psychol Sci Social Sci.* 2004;59:S287–S291.

Orrell M, Davies ADM. Life events in the elderly. *Intl Rev Psychiatry.* 1994;6:59–71.

STROKE

Stroke is a disorder that results in sudden loss of brain functions resulting from occlusion of blood supply to the brain. Stroke is a common disabling and deadly disease. Stroke is the third major cause of death in the United States. Approximately one third of patients afflicted with stroke die within a year of the event. More than 70% of those who survive are permanently disabled. The annual health care costs that result from stroke are believed to be in the range of $40 billion per year, and that is in addition to the morbidity and suffering imposed on patients and their families. More than one half of Americans consider major stroke to be a fate worse than death. Stroke is a common clinical disorder, and a new case is diagnosed every 45 seconds. There are more than 4.5 million stroke survivors in the United States, and the number appears to be increasing each year. Stroke is believed to be the leading cause of disability among older adults.

Description of Stroke

Stroke or cerebrovascular accident is the death (infarction) of brain tissue secondary to a compromise in the blood supply to the brain. It is the brain equivalent of a heart attack (which is caused by compromise to the blood supply to the heart) and is caused by blockage of blood vessels that supply the brain. So far, all attempts to salvage the infarcted brain tissue through treatment have met with only modest success. Consequently, most focus has been on reducing the risk of developing a stroke, reducing the loss of brain tissue through early diagnosis, and treating the underlying conditions causing the stroke. In addition, medical attention has focused on minimizing the disability resulting from stroke and enhancing the quality of life of stroke victims.

Development and Recognition of Stroke

The human body depends on an intricate network of blood vessels to circulate important nutrients and oxygen to different organs. Blockage of those vessels that supply the brain (known as cerebral arteries) results in stroke. The brain receives its blood supply through two sets of blood vessels called the carotid and vertebral arteries. The two carotid arteries supply the frontal areas (front) of the brain, whereas the two vertebral arteries supply the back of the brain. Each of these arteries supplies the right and left halves of the brain (known as right and left hemispheres). The right hemisphere of the brain controls the functions of the left half of the body, whereas the left hemisphere controls the right half of the body.

Stroke results when blood supply to the brain is compromised, thereby depriving the brain of oxygen and glucose, both of which are vital to cell survival. This blockage can be caused by clots formed in the blood vessels themselves (thrombosis) or by clots that travel to the brain from other parts of the body such as the heart (embolism). Less frequently, the loss of blood supply results from the rupture of blood vessels of the brain and resulting hemorrhage into the brain tissue. Deprived of oxygen and nutrients, the part of brain supplied by these arteries develops infarction. Each brain area is functionally specialized in performing one highly specialized function; for example, language skills and limb movements are associated with frontal lobes of the brain supplied by carotid arteries, whereas visual function is located on the back part (occipital lobes) supplied by the vertebral arteries. Thus, blockage of one artery often leads to loss of functions served by that area of the brain, resulting in signs such as paralysis, blindness, and inability to speak. This is often referred to as a *focal brain deficit*. Understanding the pattern of these deficits allows not only an early diagnosis of stroke but also identification of the blocked blood vessels so that medications can be administered to dissolve the clots.

However, in the case of a hemorrhage, medications that dissolve clots may increase bleeding and cause the patient's clinical status to deteriorate. Consequently, a computed tomography (CT) or magnetic resonance imaging (MRI) scan that can identify these conditions is performed before these medications are administered. If it is determined that these clots might come from other parts of the body, such as heart or other blood vessels, these sources will need to be identified and the underlying condition will need to be treated.

Risk Factors and Their Prevention

Risk factors for stroke have been broadly divided into nonmodifiable and modifiable. Leading *nonmodifiable risk factors* include age, sex, ethnicity, and heredity. Older males appear to be at a higher risk for developing stroke. African Americans appear to have twice as great a risk of developing stroke as do Caucasians even after adjusting for age, sex, and place of residence. Heredity confers a modest influence on stroke risk. The occurrence of stroke in a close family member (first-degree relative; i.e., parent or sibling) is believed to result in a twofold increase in risk of stroke. Thus, although most of the risk factors are not modifiable and confer a moderate risk of stroke, they help identify a group of patients in whom aggressive control of modifiable risk factors should be pursued.

Important *modifiable risk factors* are divided into predisposing conditions, predisposing behaviors, and heralding events. *Predisposing conditions* include diseases such as hypertension (elevated blood pressure), diabetes (elevated blood sugar), elevated levels of cholesterol, and certain heart conditions—all of which can be managed effectively by regular visits to a family doctor. *Predisposing behaviors* include tobacco and alcohol use and physical inactivity. Therefore, stopping tobacco and alcohol use and getting adequate physical exercise are strongly recommended for individuals at increased risk for developing stroke. *Heralding events* include previous occurrence of strokes or "mini-strokes." Mini-strokes, or transient ischemic attacks (TIAs), are characterized by stroke-like symptoms that last for an hour or less and lead to a full stroke in 24% to 29% of patients. Previous attacks of stroke result in a recurrent stroke in 25% to 40% of patients. Thus, aggressive identification and treatment of conditions such as elevated blood pressure, cessation of behaviors such as tobacco use, and early diagnosis and treatment of strokes and mini-strokes may be of great help in preventing the occurrence of stroke disorders.

Treatment of Acute Stroke

A rapid identification of stroke is imperative to minimize the extent of damage to brain tissue and to save the patient's life. The key to accomplishing this objective is controlling blood pressure (preventing the patient's blood pressure from falling too low or rising too high), maintaining an adequate concentration of oxygen and glucose in the patient's blood, and ensuring stability of heart functioning, all of which are critical for the preservation of life. Most recent studies have focused on therapies aimed at dissolving the blood clots that block the blood vessels. This is accomplished by the rapid administration of anticoagulant medications (blood-thinning medications such as heparin and aspirin) and clot-dissolving medications. Medications that dissolve clots are effective but can be administered only by trained emergency/medical personnel and often need to be given within the first 3 hours of the onset of signs or symptoms for optimal benefit. Medications to repair and/or prevent brain damage are also being developed.

How to Help a Stroke Victim

Sudden onsets of symptoms, such as loss of muscle power in one or more limbs, loss of vision, and loss of speech or memory, are important signals for immediate intervention. Another important step would be to check the patient's breathing and pulse; if needed, cardiopulmonary resuscitation (CPR) should be administered by an appropriately trained individual(s) while awaiting arrival of emergency services.

Symptoms of stroke include the following:

- Sudden numbness or weakness of the face, arm, or leg (especially on one side of the body)
- Sudden confusion and difficulty in speaking or understanding speech
- Sudden difficulty in seeing in one eye or both eyes
- Sudden difficulty in walking, dizziness, and loss of balance or coordination
- Sudden severe headache with no known cause

Recovery and Rehabilitation From Stroke

Although the immediate threat to life diminishes rapidly over the first few days, functional recovery from stroke usually takes 3 to 6 months, with lesser degrees of improvement occurring up to 18 months longer after the initial event. It is believed that for recovery to occur, newer nerve cells leading to alternative pathways need to be recruited into performing the functions of the dead cells. Training exercises, such as physical, occupational, and speech therapies, facilitate the learning process. It is also important to identify and treat mental conditions and disorders that can interfere with this learning process. Thus, treatment of memory disorders (e.g., delirium, dementia) and mood disorders (e.g., depression) are of paramount importance at this stage. Transplantation of cell lines derived from precursor or progenitor cells that can develop the capacity to develop into mature neural cells is being studied in regeneration of dead tissue in stroke patients.

—*Ebrahim Haroon and Anand Kumar*

See also Aneurysms; Imaging of the Brain; Vascular Dementia; Vascular Depression

Further Readings and References

Caplan LR. *Caplan's Stroke: A Clinical Approach.* 3rd ed. Boston: Butterworth-Heinemann; 2000.

National Institute of Neurological Disorders and Stroke. (2006). Know stroke: Know the signs—Act in time. Available at: www.ninds.nih.gov/disorders/ stroke/knowstroke.htm. Accessed October 3, 2006.

Zvin JA. Approach to patients with cerebrovascular diseases. In: Goldman L, ed. *Cecil's Textbook of Medicine.* Philadelphia: W. B. Saunders; 2004:2281–2287.

SUBJECTIVE WELL-BEING

Quality of life during late life is a key focus of much research on aging. How satisfied people are with their lives—especially as they compare their own lives with those of people around them—is of great importance to older individuals themselves and to different stakeholders in the society at large. Subjective well-being—how individuals evaluate their overall existence—has been studied by gerontologists over the past six decades. However, defining *subjective well-being* (or its synonyms *quality of life, life satisfaction,* and *health-related quality of life*) has remained an elusive task for those doing research in this area.

By estimating their subjective well-being, older adults provide a measure of how completely they feel they are integrated into society. Although the early research in this area tried to evaluate subjective well-being objectively, researchers soon became convinced that it was not effective to generalize to an individual, or a group of individuals, from a single answer. They came to subdivide subjective well-being into four discrete dimensions: physical, financial, social, and psychological. Although it is probably easier to evaluate older people on these four separate dimensions, the measure of overall well-being or quality of life remains a challenge. Both objective and subjective assessments must be used. For example, finances can be measured as assets or income, both of which are objective measures. But the question "Do you have sufficient funds to allow you to live in your accustomed style?" is a subjective and critical part of the overall answer.

Social interaction can also be measured objectively by counting the number of contacts individuals have with others; for example, a subjective measure might ask, "Would you say that you would like to see friends and relatives *more, less,* or *at about the rate* as you see them now?" This same bifurcation exists in physical health and psychological well-being. A count of chronic conditions can provide an objective measure of physical health, but it is critical to measure the subjective consequences of these conditions as well. And although psychological well-being can be determined by counting the number of mental health symptoms, it is important to measure the overall psychological gestalt as well. Operationalizing the four dimensions in this way supplies an objective measure of certain key aspects of well-being. However, these scores provide the presence or absence of these characteristics without any assessment of their impact on individuals. Subjectively, however, characteristics such as self-rated health, financial security, and impact of chronic conditions may play an even greater role in assessment of overall life conditions during late life. In fact, research has shown that the subjective indicators are more strongly related to outcomes than are the objective measures. In all, subjective self-assessments contribute a great deal to well-being, especially during late life.

Terms such as *overall well-being, quality of life, life satisfaction,* and *subjective well-being* seem to be used interchangeably in the literature on late life. In looking at the substantial literature that discusses these issues, there appear to be trends in terminology that cannot be overlooked. *Subjective well-being* appears to be the term used in social and social–psychological research, whereas *health-related quality of life* is used more frequently in journals that include research on chronic illness and functional capacity. For our purposes here, *subjective well-being* is used as the overall term, and *health-related quality of life* is used in discussions associated with chronic diseases that influence well-being.

Importance

Why should we focus on subjective well-being as we examine the human condition during later life? Clearly, an individual's perception of the good (and not so good) aspects of her or his current life play an important role in how life is lived out. Some researchers point out that subjective well-being is also important during earlier life stages (e.g., young adulthood), but it appears to be central to a real understanding of the challenges and rewards of old age. Because old age is associated with losses in nearly every dimension of life (e.g., health, family and friends, mobility), we might expect that subjective well-being would begin a downward trajectory that continued until the end of life. Interestingly, research on well-being during late life seems to reject that assumption. Several studies have shown that, despite a downward trend in positive affect that seems to be associated with age, negative affect and life satisfaction have no parallel downward trends.

Furthermore, subjective well-being is multidimensional, the result of which is to make definition and measurement of the term increasingly difficult. Broadly defined, subjective well-being is a composite of at least four (and sometimes six) dimensions: physical, social, financial, and psychological/emotional. This multidimensionality contributes to the difficulty of measuring subjective well-being.

Measurement

Measurement of any subjective entity is challenging. Reliability can be demonstrated (i.e., the same person can have the same evaluation over time), but establishing validity of an instrument is a much greater challenge. Another part of that challenge comes from the fact that subjective well-being is a multidimensional construct in which different domains have stronger or weaker influences on different individuals. Remember that people, when responding to questions about subjective well-being, are evaluating their own lives against their own standards. Unless those standards can be articulated and compared, measurement of subjective well-being will always be indistinct. Subjective well-being is truly a personal perception that is unique.

For the most part, measurement of subjective well-being occurs in the context of self-report surveys. Despite potential problems with self-report of

any information (e.g., social desirability, bias, faulty memory), who but an individual can really evaluate her or his personal experiences and position in the social environment? Perhaps not surprisingly, the various measures of quality of life are typically highly correlated. Researchers are challenged to identify specific instruments that accurately capture subjective perceptions in a variety of realms. When the goal has been to capture the overall life satisfaction, researchers have used single-item questions such as "How would you rate the quality of your life?" Although single-item measures have virtually no respondent burden, they also provide only one-dimensional access to a multidimensional construct.

Literally dozens of measures of quality of life exist currently, each with its unique twist. Some focus more on general perceptions of well-being, whereas others look at single dimensions of quality of life (e.g., health). Probably the most widely used measure that captures multiple dimensions of quality of life and that focuses on health-related issues is the short-form (SF-36) of the Medical Outcomes Study (MOS) questionnaire. It has been used in multiple research projects, especially with older adults suffering from physical illness or limitation.

Health-Related Quality of Life

As we began to better understand the impact of health status on quality of life, a more focused concept emerged. Health-related quality of life (HRQOL) is defined as those aspects of general subjective quality of life affecting a person's health or health perceptions. The Centers for Disease Control and Prevention (CDC) and other public health organizations use this as a measure of the way in which disease has an impact on the individual's (or group's) everyday life.

The principal research focus in HRQOL has been on chronic illness. Given the preponderance of chronic conditions during late life, one might expect older adults to have the worst HRQOL of any age group. Yet several researchers suggest that older adults (those age 65 years and older) report being mentally healthier than younger adults (those 18 to 64 years of age). These findings refer, of course, to community-dwelling older adults. Institutionalized older adults would be less likely to report high levels of mental health or satisfaction. The message of this finding is that stereotypes of older adults as frail and demented should not be perpetuated and that very good or excellent HRQOL is not an unknown phenomenon during late life.

Perhaps the biggest controversy in HRQOL research centers around the choice of generic versus disease-specific HRQOL measures. The generic measures are desirable when comparisons across chronic diseases are desired, whereas the disease-specific measures do a better job of highlighting the unique challenges presented by a given chronic illness. Both outcomes are valuable, and despite several studies that have tried to compare the utility and efficacy of generic versus disease-specific measures, there is no clear evidence that one is better than the other. In truth, measuring both (if possible) is probably ideal.

Conclusions

Subjective well-being, regardless of what it is named or how it is measured, is a critical expression of how an individual rates her or his quality of life overall. This construct is especially important during late life as people strive to understand better what factors contribute to positive subjective well-being and successful aging. We also need to explore how we can improve subjective well-being for older adults at all ages and with all levels of disability. Measurement challenges abound despite the availability of many generic measures and disease-specific scales for individuals with virtually every chronic disease experienced by older adults.

—*Deborah T. Gold*

See also Positive Attitudes and Health; Quality of Life; Self-Rated Health

Further Readings and References

Cheng S. Age and subjective well-being: A discrepancy perspective. *Psychol Aging.* 2004;19:409–415.

Diener E, Suh E. Subjective well-being and age: An international analysis. *Annu Rev Gerontol Geriatr.* 1997;17:304–324.

George LK. Perceived quality of life. In: Binstock RH, George LK, eds. *Handbook of Aging and the Social Sciences.* 6th ed. San Diego, Calif: Academic Press; 2006: 320–336.

Warr P, Butcher V, Robertson J. Activity and psychological well-being in older people. *Aging Mental Health.* 2004;8: 172–183.

SUCCESSFUL AGING

Compared with illness, functional decline, and death, successful aging is a relatively unexplored area for gerontologists, although pondering it is not new. For early Greek philosophers, a successful life meant a virtuous character, political community, friendship, and family. In 44 B.C., the Roman philosopher Cicero distinguished between "normal" and "sick" aging, warning that old age should not be confused with illness and that positive growth and change could be achieved through physical activity and social connection. The German philosopher Immanuel Kant, writing at the end of the 18th century, viewed successful aging as the ability to experience life in positive ways that, in turn, could influence physical health and well-being. During recent decades, the study of successful aging (also called healthy or productive aging) has intensified, in part because of an influx of older adults living to advanced ages. Also, our view of old age has shifted from treatment of illness to promotion of well-being. That is, some researchers, clinicians, and policymakers believe that a past overemphasis on negative aspects of aging should now be balanced by analyzing what it means to age successfully. The following perspectives of various disciplines on what it means to age successfully provide an incomplete, and sometimes overlapping, list of characteristics or indicators of successful aging.

Theories of Successful Aging

Medically, aging well means having good physical and functional health. Research has sought to identify the health measures of successful aging, particularly by examining the physiological profiles of older individuals. Researchers noted that, given the increased variance with age of nearly any physiological measure (e.g., bone density, cardiac output, cognition), some older individuals functionally still fall within the normal range for younger adults. This type of classification showed the enormous variance within the "non-pathological" aging group and opened the possibility that physiological changes of normal aging could be modified by avoiding risky behaviors (e.g., smoking, alcohol abuse) and adopting healthy behaviors (e.g., education, physical activity). If the human life span is fixed and life expectancy is increasing, substituting healthy behaviors for risky behaviors leads to compression of morbidity and a rectangularization of the survival curve, wherein most individuals maintain good health into advanced older age and then sicken and die over a relatively brief period.

To classify a few older individuals as aging successfully, based only on biomedical criteria, raises questions about whether those living with disease or disability can also age successfully or consider themselves to be aging successfully. Many older individuals, at one time or another, will have experienced illness, loss, or other health-related problems. The term *resilience* has been used to define older individuals who have experienced major life events and yet managed to adapt effectively. Resilient individuals appear to be able to form lasting relationships, are good problem solvers, have strong personal identities, and are motivated to continue to develop and grow. Resilient individuals also typically display optimistic attitudes about their future well-being. Emerging studies document the importance of remaining optimistic in the face of a health challenge, indicating that a positive attitude may affect health directly by keeping the body in balance via chemical and neural responses and may also affect health indirectly by increasing one's intellectual, physical, and social resources.

To answer the question "What is successful aging?" we need only define *successful aging* and then measure the degree to which older persons fit this definition. This task has not proved to be easy, however, because successful aging is an elusive concept on which few agree given that *success* characterizes achievement, gain, or the attainment of a desired outcome, whereas *aging* is a process that often implies decline, loss, and death. However, aging can also be expressed in positive terms such as growth, development, maturity, and wisdom. Psychologists Erik Erikson and Abraham Maslow described successful aging as a series of stages or met needs. Erikson, for example, described eight developmental stages from infancy to old age through which all successful individuals pass. After successfully negotiating the crisis of maturity (25 to 65 years of age), in which the adult moves from self-absorption to giving and nurturing life, the task of old age is to achieve integrity (actualization needs, the highest described in Maslow's pyramid of needs), avoid despair, and attain wisdom through this process.

Economists, especially in the West, have equated a successful life with accumulation of resources. Economic theory would suggest that those with more wealth should be happy and report high life satisfaction, but evidence suggests that once basic needs have been met, wealth is a poor predictor of who will age successfully. This holds true at both the individual and societal levels. Similarly, although genetics is important, it may predict less of the successful aging variance than was originally believed, especially at advanced age. Findings from twin studies, for example, suggest the importance of potentially modifiable factors (e.g., diet and nutrition, exercise, lifestyle choices) in aging well.

Social resources have been widely cited as crucial to aging successfully. Much research shows social relationships associated with physical health, mental health, and speedy recovery. Isolation, or a lack of social connection, increases the risk of poor health outcomes as much as does high blood pressure, obesity, sedentary lifestyles, or smoking. Conversely, the ability to maintain strong social connections with family and friends has been linked with beneficial effects on the cardiovascular, endocrine, and immune systems (e.g., lower heart rate and systolic blood pressure, lower serum cholesterol, lower uric acid).

Examining social connection on the community level emphasizes the matrix of political, cultural, and economic settings in which aging takes place. Variation in the local community setting, for example, may affect health through the quality of the physical and built environment (e.g., housing, public infrastructure, sanitation services, exposure to environmental toxins, availability of medical care) or the social environment (e.g., peers' healthful or unhealthful behaviors, civility and safety of public space, prevalence of crime, discrimination, income disparity, integration into supportive social networks and institutions).

Two Basic Models: Biomedical and Sociological

Two basic models, then, are used to describe what it means to age successfully. In one, successful aging is a biomedical process, emphasizing illness and functional health outcomes. Implicit in this model, which stresses the ability to perform daily tasks and fulfill occupational and societal roles, is a threshold that defines whether or not one is aging successfully. One concern with this classification is that normal aging is seen as a disease—a failure to age successfully. Although few older individuals will report no disease or functional limitation, many of those currently classified as aging successfully would "fail" if exposed to a full medical examination to exclude all of those older individuals with subclinical disease, disability, or physiological loss. Then, too, if clinicians, policymakers, and researchers transform successful aging from a philosophical pursuit of the good life to a prescription or algorithm, this algorithm may more likely reflect the priorities or standards of health professionals rather than those of older individuals.

The second psychological model views successful aging as a process whereby the individual learns to adapt to and cope with changing life events. Implicit in this model, which stresses autonomy, subjective evaluation in achieving goals, and a continued purpose in life, is that individuals constrained by physical or functional limitations are not necessarily aging unsuccessfully. Reports show strong associations between an individual's subjective evaluation of his or her well-being and physical or functional health.

Qualitative research also suggests that older individuals rate their physical functioning as no more important than subjective characteristics. However, the psychological model sometimes fails to recognize the importance of other factors (e.g., genetics, environment, behavior). Because the mind has a remarkable ability to adapt, other more objective health indicators are needed to fully characterize successful aging. In addition, little information currently exists about causal pathways or the role of protective factors when assessing successful aging psychologically.

The Value of Knowing What Successful Aging Is

What does the study of successful aging offer to older individuals, their families, or society in general? First, knowledge from studies of successful aging may help us to better extend health throughout life. Building on studies of successful older individuals can help us to understand optimal human flourishing and well-being. Longitudinal studies in particular have been valuable in identifying individuals engaged in positive behaviors or possessing positive traits. These studies indicate that, in addition to living longer, older individuals are physically healthier and more active than ever before. Second, successful aging studies offer new perspectives on how the mind and body are linked to promote health and well-being. Third, to counterpoint the long-standing focus on disease and functional impairment during later life, studies of successful aging show that many older populations can be characterized as aging well. During the 20th century, life expectancy at birth in the United States increased from less than 50 years to more than 77 years. The challenge for the 21st century is to make these added years as healthy and productive as possible. While medical, psychological, and social perspectives of successful aging are being integrated, future work will need to include the views of older individuals themselves.

—Glenn V. Ostir

See also Bereavement and Grief; Compression of Morbidity; Disability and the Disablement Process; Exercise and

Physical Activity; MacArthur Study of Successful Aging; Quality of Life; Self-Efficacy; Self-Rated Health; Subjective Well-Being

Further Readings and References

Baltes PB, Baltes MM, eds. *Successful Aging: Perspectives for the Behavioral Sciences.* New York: Cambridge University Press; 1993.

Bowling A. The concepts of successful and positive aging. *Fam Pract.* 1993;10:449–453.

Fries JF. The compression of morbidity. *Millbank Mem Fund Q.* 1983;61:130–136.

Rowe JW, Kahn RL. Human aging: Usual and successful. *Science.* 1987;237:143–149.

Von Faber M, van der Wiel AB, van Exel E, et al. Successful aging in the oldest old: Who can be characterized as successful aged? *Arch Intern Med.* 2001;161:2694–2700.

Vaillant GE, Mukamal K. Successful aging. *Am J Psychiatry.* 2001;158:839–847.

SUICIDE AND THE ELDERLY

Suicide in older adults is a salient concern for geriatric public mental health care in the United States and around the world. The U.S. population age 65 years and older has the highest suicide rates of any age group despite clinical advances in risk factor assessment and intervention strategies targeting older adults at high risk. In 2002, the suicide rate for older adults was 15.6 per 100,000 compared with 11.0 per 100,000 for the entire population, and although older adults comprised only 12.3 % of the population, they accounted for 17.5% (5,548 persons) of all completed suicides (31,635 persons).

A greater degree of premeditation and lethality are observed in the population age 65 years and older. The high mortality in large part reflects access to firearms; more than 70% of elder suicides involve firearms, compared with 57% for the general population. Older adults average 4 attempts for every completed suicide, in contrast to 100 to 200 attempts for every completed suicide in younger age groups. Careful planning, increased vulnerability, decreased reserve capacity to recover, and relative social isolation also contribute to increased lethality in the aged. Older persons are less likely to be discovered after a suicide attempt, and they are less communicative about their suicidal ideation than are younger persons.

Suicide rates in the United States increase dramatically after 65 years of age, due largely to a sharp rise in rates for older men, particularly older White men, who commit more than 80% of all suicides. The rates for older White men are more than five times higher than those for younger and middle-aged adults, and the rates increase every 5 years after 65 years of age. Suicide rates also vary by gender, race, and ethnicity. In 2002, the age-adjusted suicide rate for men age 65 years and older (32.8 per 100,000) was nearly three times higher than the national rate, whereas the rate for older women (4.1 per 100,000) was less than half the national rate. White persons age 65 years and older had a higher suicide rate (16.7 per 100,000) than did Black older adults (5.3 per 100,000). The rate for Asian or Pacific Islander older adults (10.4 per 100,000) were higher than that for Native American Indian or Alaska Natives (4.5 per 100,000), and non-Hispanic or Latino older adults had a higher rate (15.8 per 100,000) than did Hispanics or Latinos (8.8 per 100,000).

Elder suicide is also a global geriatric mental health challenge. Extrapolating from 2002 data, the World Health Organization estimated that approximately 1.53 million people will die by suicide in 2020 and that the rates will be higher for the older population than for other age groups. An analysis of elder (age 65 years and older) suicide rates in 2003 among the 30 countries in the Organization for Economic Co-operation and Development (OECD) revealed that Korea had the highest rate (71 per 100,000) and that Luxemburg ranked second highest (53 per 100,000). Proportionally more Asian countries experienced an increase in elder suicide rates compared with countries in Europe, and the rates are predicted to continue to increase.

Risk Factors and Protective Factors

The biopsychosocial and environmental risk factors for suicide among older adults are different than those among younger age groups. Major risk factors include depression coupled with real or perceived medical illnesses, male gender, Caucasian race, advanced age, guns in the home or easy access to other methods such as poison, and disconnectedness from meaningful social supports. Cognitive impairment is a modest risk factor for suicide attempts and completed suicide, perhaps affecting up to 3% of patients with dementia. Other psychological risk factors include difficulty in coping with negative life events and financial distress, hopelessness and pessimism about the future following a visit to a physician, and personality vulnerabilities (e.g., low scores on the personality trait of openness to experience).

Affective disorders or substance abuse problems occur in more than 90% of older adults who commit suicide. Compared with younger persons who commit suicide, older persons are more likely to have been experiencing their first episode of a major depressive disorder and less likely to have made a prior suicide attempt. Personality disorders appear to occur more frequently among persons age 60 years and older who commit suicide than among age-matched controls, with the risk of dying by suicide being four times higher for the former group.

Social, political, and economic changes within countries and cultures also have a significant impact on suicide rates. Major risk factors include economic recession, higher rates of unemployment, family disorganization, and inadequate social welfare systems to support retirement income and health benefits. These sociopolitical and environmental forces, alone or in combination, can have a potent negative impact on psychological functioning and quality of life, leading to hopelessness, depression, and substance abuse.

Little is known about protective factors against elder suicide, but several research hypotheses are promising. Because suicide rates of older women are low compared with those of older men in most countries, investigations of gender differences might elucidate factors associated with women's resilience and decreased suicide risk such as adaptive coping with change and loss, willingness to seek help, and capacity to form caring interpersonal relationships. The low suicide rates of other racial groups suggest that studies of racial/ethnic differences would also be useful to understand how various factors, such as religiosity, cultural expectations, and family patterns, contribute to decreased risks. Finally, the rapidly rising suicide rates of the older populations in Asian countries, compared with those of other countries, suggest the importance of country-specific studies of risk factors such as changes in traditional family support for older relatives, family and cultural stigma associated with mental disorders and suicide, and inadequate government funding for pensions and health care benefits.

Evaluation and Intervention

Suicide prevention among older adults depends on a comprehensive assessment of suicide potential and imminent risk because the first suicide attempt is more likely to be successful—and therefore the last. Not all suicides can be prevented, but a careful and thorough assessment of risk factors is essential, especially in primary care settings, because most older adults in the United States who commit suicide have long-standing relationships with primary care physicians and see their doctors shortly before their suicides. Fully 70% visit their physicians within 1 month before killing themselves, with 40% seeing their physicians within 1 week before they commit suicide and 20% seeing their physicians on the day they commit suicide.

Clinical practice guidelines addressing detection and intervention, such as those of the American Psychological Association and the American Psychiatric Association, emphasize the diagnosis of mental health problems and frequent monitoring of risk and protective factors. Thus, a determination of the risk of suicide is based on the clinician's ability to get a thorough medical and personal history, including collecting and organizing information from collateral informants; to recognize, assess, and document risk factors to determine lethality; to address high risk factors and situations; and to develop and implement a care plan that includes precautions against completed suicide. Psychiatric hospitalization is the strategy of choice when individuals manifest significant suicidal ideation and intent and when clinical judgment indicates that suicide is imminent.

Medications, psychotherapies, and electroconvulsive therapy are effective for the treatment of depression in older adults, but little is known about the effectiveness of these clinical interventions to prevent suicide during later life. However, several clinical models linking older patients in primary care with psychiatric specialists are effective in treating depression and reducing suicidal ideation. These include the Prevention of Suicide in Primary Care Elderly–Collaborative Trial (PROSPECT), Improving Mood-Promoting Access to Collaborative Treatment (IMPACT), Primary Care Research in Substance Abuse and Mental Health for the Elderly (PRISM-E), and Reengineering Systems for Primary Care Treatment of Depression (RESPECT-D). However, it remains to be determined whether these health care programs actually reduce suicide risk.

Health and Social Policies and Prevention of Suicide

Public awareness of, and education about, depression and suicide in the older population is a salient consideration in the development of suicide prevention strategies. Ageism and beliefs that depression and suicide are normal aspects of aging are significant barriers to older persons and family members recognizing the need for care as well as to clinicians recognizing and intervening appropriately. These forces create even greater obstacles in Asian countries where long-standing cultural traditions, such as Confucianism, influence personal and family behaviors and interactions when an older relative has mental health problems.

Health and social policies affecting the physical, social, and economic well-being of the older population influence suicide rates. The dramatic reduction in suicide rates of the U.S. population age 65 years and older from 1930 to 1980 was attributed largely to improvements in economic security, whereas the increasing suicide rates from 1980 to 1993 were attributed to diminishing economic, health, and social support. Elder suicide rates have been dropping slowly, from 19.0 per 100,000 in 1993 to 15.6 per 100,000 in 2002, but it is possible that negative economic repercussions of changes in Social Security and Medicare may contribute to increasing suicide rates in the future.

Firearm control advocates have argued that gun control will reduce lethal violence, and suicide rates across all age groups in the United States are lower in states with the strictest firearm control laws. In nations such as Great Britain, where gun access is significantly limited, suicide rates in older adults are half those observed in the United States. However, firearms are prohibited in Korea, the country with the highest suicide rates for older people in the OECD countries. Ingestion of poison and hanging are the most common methods of suicide in that country, where agricultural toxins and rope are easily available and accessible.

Death by suicide and death by assisted suicide have provoked emotionally charged debates where personal experiences, religious background, and other factors often interfere with understanding the vulnerabilities of people who seek a hastened death. Unfortunately, these debates frequently ignore the fact that suicides in the older population are manifestations of psychopathology, and this has the untoward effect of endorsing the acceptability of suicide for depressed older adults as part of the "right to die" argument. There may be limited circumstances where a suicide is a rational act, but nearly all suicides occur in the context of psychopathology and other circumstances such as health problems, alcohol use, disrupted relationships, helplessness, hopelessness, and anomie. Assisted-suicide decisions may occur in the context of unrecognized depression, lack of geriatric care or appropriate palliative care, unwillingness to adhere to medical regimens, and lack of confidants. The salient issue is not the right to die but rather the right to have access to trained, compassionate health care professionals.

Urgency of Suicide Prevention

The urgency of preventing suicide is underscored by a number of recent national reports. In 1999, then Surgeon General David Satcher issued a groundbreaking report, *The Surgeon General's Call to Action to Prevent Suicide,* and in 2001, the Office of the Surgeon General followed up with the *National Strategy for Suicide Prevention,* which specified goals and recommendations for action, including the importance of reducing suicide mortality in the aged. In 2002, two reports were issued: The Centers for Disease Control and Prevention published *Suicide Prevention Now: Linking Research to Practice,* and the Institute of Medicine published *Reducing Suicide: A National Imperative.*

These documents are critical road maps for a challenging future where older people, at the highest risk for suicide, are the fastest-growing segment of the population. Suicide rates in the United States are also projected to increase in the older population because of increasing rates of depression in successive birth cohorts. Suicide rates in the baby boom generation, those 76 million persons born between 1946 and 1959, are higher than suicide rates in previous generations. If this sequential birth cohort effect continues, suicide prevention will be even more urgent. The challenge to geriatric mental health professionals is truly a matter of life and death.

—Donna Cohen and Hyoung Soo Kim

See also Bereavement and Grief; Depression and Other Mood Disorders; Emotions and Emotional Stability

Further Readings and References

American Association of Suicidology. AAS website [U.S. suicide statistics]. Available at: www.suicidology.org. Accessed October 4, 2006.

American Psychological Association. Guidelines for psychological practice with older adults. *Am Psychol.* 2004;59:236–260.

Bruce ML, Ten Have TR, Reynolds CF III, et al. Reducing suicidal ideation and depressive symptoms in depressed older primary care patients: A randomized controlled trial. *JAMA.* 2004;291:1081–1091.

Centers for Disease Control and Prevention. *Suicide Prevention Now: Linking Research to Practice.* Washington, DC: U.S. Department of Health and Human Services; 2002.

Cohen D, Eisdorfer C. Violent deaths: Suicide, homicide, and homicide–suicide. In: Cohen D, Eisdorfer C, eds. *An Integrated Textbook of Geriatric Mental Health Care.* Baltimore, Md: Johns Hopkins University Press; in press.

Conwell Y, Pearson J. Editorial theme issue: Suicidal behaviors in older adults. *Am J Geriatr Psychiatry.* 2002;10:359–361.

Heisel MJ, Duberstein PR. Suicide prevention in older adults. *Clin Psychol Sci Pract.* 2005;12:242–259.

Institute of Medicine. *Reducing Suicide: A National Imperative.* Washington, DC: National Academy of Sciences Press; 2002.

World Health Organization. Suicide [world suicide statistics]. Available at: www.who.int/health_topics/suicide/en. Accessed October 4, 2006.

Sun Exposure

See Skin Neoplasms, Benign and Malignant

Surgery

Surgery is an essential part of treatment for many conditions, such as hip fracture, cancer, osteoarthritis, coronary artery disease, and cataracts, that is more common with advanced age. Surgery in those over 65 years of age was once considered to be too risky, but as the population has aged we have acquired additional knowledge and new technology, making surgery in older adults more common and less dangerous. In the United States, nearly a quarter of all surgeries are performed in older adults, with the annual rate of surgery nearly double the rate for younger adults.

Traditionally, the risk of surgical procedures focused more on age than on physiological function. Patients of advanced age were generally considered to be at higher risk for complications and death. As a result, cardiac, vascular, and oncologic procedures were frequently not performed on patients of advanced age. A better understanding of surgical care in geriatric patients and continuous technological advances (especially in minimally invasive procedures) have permitted surgeries once considered to be too risky. A physician's understanding of the benefits of certain surgical procedures such as open heart surgeries, vascular procedures, and joint replacements—even during very old age—has increased the number of these procedures performed in the United States. As a result of our enhanced knowledge, refined technology, and changing demographics, the number of surgical procedures performed in the older adult population is expected to increase.

Types of Surgery

Surgeries are usually classified as elective or emergency. In general, elective surgery in healthy older adults carries a lower risk than does emergency surgery and has a risk of complications similar to that in younger people. However, emergency surgery carries a higher risk of complications and death, especially in older adults. A review by S. M. Keller and colleagues found postoperative mortality rates to be significantly higher for emergency surgeries (20%) than for elective surgeries (1.9%) in older adults. To reduce the number of complications and deaths that after emergency surgery, it is essential to identify those at risk for emergency surgery before it is required. For example, an older adult with an abdominal aneurysm will need frequent evaluation to determine when an elective surgery will be beneficial. These frequent evaluations may prevent the need for an emergency abdominal aneurysm repair.

The incidence of emergency surgery increases with advancing age. Close to half of the emergency surgical procedures and a third of the postoperative deaths after emergency surgery occur in older people. The most common emergency procedure in older people involves the large bowel, abdominal wall, stomach, biliary tract, and small bowel.

Complications

Several factors increase the likelihood of complications after surgery. First, the type of surgical procedure significantly influences the risk of complications. The vast majority of surgeries in older adults—noncardiac elective surgeries—are divided into three surgery-specific risk groups: high surgery-specific risk, intermediate surgery-specific risk, and low surgery-specific risk. *High surgery-specific risk* procedures include emergency surgeries, aortic and other major vascular surgeries, surgical procedures with anticipated prolonged duration, and surgical procedures associated with large fluid shifts or blood loss. These types of surgeries have the highest risk of complications and mortality. *Intermediate surgery-specific risk* procedures include carotid endarterectomy, head and neck surgery, orthopedic surgeries, and prostate surgery. The *low surgery-specific risk* procedures include endoscopic and superficial procedures, cataract surgery, and breast surgery. For these types of surgeries, geriatric patients may return home after the procedures with a low likelihood of serious complications.

In addition to the type of surgical procedure, other factors associated with postoperative complications in older adults include the skill of the surgeon performing the surgery and individual specific factors such as coexisting medical conditions and functional status prior to surgery. Coexisting conditions, such as recent myocardial infarction, diabetes mellitus, recent stroke, uncontrolled high blood pressure, anemia, and malnutrition, all increase the risk of postoperative complications.

Preoperative Assessment

Functional status or capacity before surgery is also an important clinical predictor of future outcome after surgery. In general, functional status is considered to be good to moderate if the person can climb one flight of stairs, mow the lawn, or work in the garden. This level of functional status is adequate for surgery, and older adults with this capacity have a lower risk of postoperative complications than do those with poor functional status.

It is critical to establish appropriate care before and after surgery by using the surgery-specific risk and the patient's clinical factors and functional capacity. These factors are vital to understand the risk of surgery and to prevent complications. Ordinarily, an older adult with well-controlled medical conditions, good functional status, and a low or intermediate surgery-specific risk can undergo most surgical procedures with a low risk of complications and death. On the other hand, if the older adult has multiple active medical problems and poor functional status, the physician will need to control or stabilize the coexisting medical conditions (e.g., electrolyte imbalance, infection, severe anemia, dehydration, hypoglycemia) when possible before the surgery to minimize the risk of complications.

Before surgery, the physician commonly reviews the geriatric patient's history and performs a physical examination to assess for potential problems. Depending on the type of surgery and the patient's health, the patient may need additional testing such as a stress test to assess cardiovascular risk. In complex situations where the risk of complications is high, the primary care physician, surgeon, anesthesiologist, and cardiologist may work together to minimize the surgical risk.

The main goals of this preoperative assessment are to decrease the probability of complications, especially cardiac complications, during and after surgery. Routine parts of preoperative care, in addition to the preoperative evaluation of risk, include discussion of the possible risks and benefits of the proposed operation and the patient's desire for rehabilitation during postoperative care. The potential benefit must then be weighed against the potential risk. The risk versus benefit ratio for the surgery should be discussed, taking into consideration individual wishes, life expectancy, risk of performing or not performing the surgery, life benefits with or without the surgery, other possible therapy, duration of rehabilitation, and possible changes in quality of life. The risk versus benefit ratio of surgery varies and is specific to each individual.

Decisions about having surgery, especially in those over 85 years of age, is complicated due to the heterogeneity of this age group and the limited information available on the group. Also, very old adults have a higher risk of complications and mortality from surgery that can be attributed to a decreasing physiological reserve and an increase of coexisting conditions. Factors associated with postoperative complications after surgery in very old adults are decreasing pulmonary, cardiac, renal, and cognitive functions. The risk of postoperative complications will depend mainly on the patient's overall state of health rather than on age. Chronological age is still important, however, because factors associated with postoperative complications are more prevalent in those over 85 years of age.

Postoperative Care

After surgery, the geriatric patient may go home with minimal instructions or stay in the hospital for observation and care. In general, postoperative care will include surgery-specific postoperative care and symptom management such as pain, nausea, and constipation. Pain is extremely common and should be assessed daily and treated to minimize the chances of delirium, depression, and other conditions associated with poor pain control.

Postoperative care also includes preventing complications such as deep venous thrombosis, surgical wound infection, delirium, and physical deconditions. Common postoperative complications and problems include the following:

- Congestive heart failure or myocardial infarction
- Delirium or cognitive dysfunction
- Dysrhythmias
- Thromboembolic event (deep venous thrombosis)
- Respiratory problems or atelectasis
- Urinary retention or urinary incontinence
- Infections (pneumonia, urinary tract infection)
- Adverse drug event
- Fall or immobility
- Pressure sores or pressure ulcers
- Dehydration or undernutrition
- Depression
- Functional decline
- Hypertension or hypotension
- Stress-induced gastrointestinal ulceration
- Constipation or diarrhea

Conversely, interventions to prevent postoperative complications include the following:

- Support and educate the patient and family.
- Avoid dehydration and overhydration.
- Encourage nutrition.
- Treat pain.
- Avoid unnecessary medications, especially those with high anticholinergic activity.

- Follow for signs of infection (i.e., perform daily surgical wound check).
- Avoid or discontinue bladder catheter or any unnecessary tube or line.
- Encourage early rehabilitation such as getting out of bed and sitting in a chair.
- Avoid excessive stimulation, especially at night.
- Encourage incentive spirometry and deep breathing exercise, especially for those with pulmonary conditions.
- Use β-blocker medications in those with increased risk of myocardial infarction.
- Give special attention to thromboembolic prophylaxis, bacterial endocarditis prophylaxis, pressure sore precaution, fall precaution, and aspiration precaution when indicated.

Postoperative Delirium

One of the most frequent and feared postoperative complications is postoperative delirium, an acute disorder characterized by fluctuating disturbances in cognition, attention, perception, and arousal, either with or without prior intellectual impairment. Incidence of postoperative delirium varies widely, depending on surgical intervention or procedure. For example, postoperative delirium is estimated in 40% of older adults after hip fracture surgery, as compared with less than 5% after cataract surgery.

Postoperative delirium is probably the result of the dysfunction of multiple interacting neurotransmitter systems in the central nervous system. Age-associated decline in brain physiological reserve makes older adults more susceptible to it, as does an increased number of coexisting diseases and numerous medications. Other associated risk factors include a preexisting cognitive deficit, an emergency operation, use of a bladder (Foley) catheter, physical restraint, a history of alcohol abuse, medications, and untreated pain.

Postoperative delirium can be caused by an event(s) that happened before, during, or after the surgery. Clinical features of postoperative delirium include an acute onset of marked fluctuations in consciousness, behavior, and cognition after surgery. The older adult may appear to be sedated or hyperactive, to have difficulty in maintaining attention, to be disoriented, to be unable to recall events, and to have hallucinations. These symptoms are distressing for the individual, the patient's family, and the primary care team.

Postoperative delirium can often be prevented by reducing risk factors such as pain, medication with high anticholinergic activity, anemia, dehydration, and sensory overload or deprivation. Managing postoperative delirium requires prompt detection and management of the cause(s). A key to management is to provide supportive care to minimize complications and improve comfort. For example, older adults with postoperative delirium will benefit from having adequate space with necessary objects (e.g., eyeglasses, hearing aids, lamp) close by, a comfortable room temperature, adequate lighting, no excessive noise or interruptions, and appropriate nutrition and hydration. Finally, geriatric patients with postoperative delirium may have behavioral changes (e.g., aggression, agitation) that require appropriate treatment. These behaviors can put patients and/or staff in danger but can usually be managed with medication.

Postoperative delirium typically improves within a few days of treatment, although patients may experience cognitive deficits that last for several weeks or even months. Older adults who suffer from postoperative delirium have worse health outcomes that do those who do not. Outcomes include an increased risk of nursing home placement, increased disabilities, increased length of hospital stay, and mortality.

Other Postsurgical Complications

Another common complication after surgery in older hospitalized adults is the risk of losing the ability to perform activities of daily living (ADLs). Early rehabilitation after surgery is required to decrease the decline of functional loss and independence. Rehabilitation is frequently needed before patients have become deconditioned secondary to prolonged bed rest. It can be tailored for specific issues such as those encountered after open heart surgery, hip fracture surgery, and leg amputation.

Many barriers common with aging present when older adults receive rehabilitation, including cognitive impairment, dizziness, uncontrolled pain, sarcopenia, and an increased number of medical conditions. Also, older adults may recover more slowly than younger adults and may require a longer and slower rehabilitation process. These challenges, however, can be managed by a geriatric multidisciplinary team.

—*Luis Felipe Amador*

See also Geriatric Assessment; Geriatric Team Care; Oldest Old; Perioperative Issues

Further Readings and References

Amador LF, Goodwin JS. Postoperative delirium in the older patient. *J Am Coll Surg.* 2005;200:767–773.

Ergina PL, Gold SL, Meakins JL. Perioperative care of the elderly patient. *World J Surg.* 1993;17:192–198.

Hamel MB, Henderson WG, Khuri SF, Daley J. Surgical outcomes for patients aged 80 and older: Morbidity and mortality from major noncardiac surgery. *J Am Geriatr Soc.* 2005;53:424–429.

Keller SM, Markovits LJ, Wildewr JR, Aufses AH. Emergency and elective surgery in patients aged over 70. *Am Surg.* 1987;53:636–640.

Pofahl WE, Pories WJ. Current status and future directions of geriatric general surgery. *J Am Geriatr Soc.* 2003;51: S351–S354.

SYNCOPE

Syncope is defined as a sudden loss of consciousness and postural tone followed by spontaneous recovery. The incidence is approximately 6 per 1,000 adults per year; however, it becomes increasingly more common with age, particularly after 70 years. In addition to age, cerebrovascular disease, cardiac disease, use of cardiac medication, and a diagnosis of hypertension are risk factors for syncope. The underlying mechanism is inadequate oxygenation of the cerebral cortex and reticular-activating system of the brain due to either inadequate blood flow or inadequate oxygen content in the blood.

There are several categories of causes of syncope. Neurally mediated (reflex) syncope is the most

common; it involves either reflex venous pooling in the legs or bradycardia; common precipitants include emotional stress (the "common faint"), urination, carotid sinus stimulation, and gastrointestinal stimulation. Syncope resulting from orthostatic hypotension involves a drop in arterial pressure due to hypovolemia or impaired vascular tone; common causes include medications, viral illness, blood loss, dehydration, and autonomic insufficiency (e.g., from Parkinson's disease). Cardiac syncope occurs when reduced heart function, due to arrhythmia, myocardial damage, or outflow obstruction, leads to impaired cerebral blood flow. Psychiatric syncope is a syndrome in which syncope occurs in the setting of psychiatric disease, a detailed examination is normal, and syncope is documented without any change in blood pressure or pulse. Many patients with syncope have more than one cause or contributing factor.

Because there are many possible causes of syncope, and often multiple risk factors contribute or lead to loss of consciousness, medical evaluation is often complex. The basic evaluation involves a history, an examination, and an electrocardiogram; additional tests and procedures are then ordered based on this initial evaluation. Persons with known or suspected cardiac disease, severe chronic illness, advanced age, or a life-threatening medical condition (e.g., pulmonary embolism) should generally be hospitalized for observation and further evaluation; others can often be managed as outpatients, especially if a cause has been identified and treated.

The treatment of syncope depends on its cause. Often, reductions in medication, treatment of underlying conditions (e.g., anemia), maintenance of adequate hydration, and avoidance of triggers (e.g., learning to stand up slowly) will prevent recurrences. If these measures do not alleviate symptoms, persons with orthostatic hypotension or neurally mediated syncope may be treated with compression stockings or pharmacological therapy (e.g., sympathomimetics, fludrocortisone). For persons with bradycardia-related syncope, a permanent cardiac pacemaker is often curative. For persons with ventricular tachycardia and unexplained syncope in the face of severe cardiac disease, an implantable defibrillator may be considered.

—*Philip D. Sloane*
and Lorraine M. Stone

See also Arrhythmias; Cardiovascular System; Neurobiology of Aging

Further Readings and References

Brignole M, Alboni P, Benditt DG, et al. Guidelines on management (diagnosis and treatment) of syncope: Update 2004, executive summary. *Eur Heart J.* 2004;25:2054–2072.

Morillo CA, Baranchuk A. Current management of syncope: Treatment alternatives. *Curr Treat Options Cardiovasc Med.* 2004;6:371–383.

Pires LA, Ganji JR, Jarandila R, et al. Diagnostic patterns and temporal trends in the evaluation of adult patients hospitalized with syncope. *Arch Intern Med.* 2001; 161:1889–1895.

SYSTEMIC INFECTIONS

The literature on bacteremia and sepsis is filled with jargon, and so the terms used in this entry are defined first. *Bacteremia* is the presence of viable bacteria in the blood, whereas *infection* is the inflammatory response to invasion of sterile tissues by microorganisms. The *systemic inflammatory response syndrome* (SIRS) is a physiological response to inflammation and/or infection along with two or more of the following conditions: temperature > 38 degrees Celcius or < 36 degrees Celcius; heart rate > 90 beats per minute; respiratory rate > 20 per minute; partial pressure of carbon dioxide (P_aCO_2) < 32 millimeters of mercury (mm Hg); and white blood cells (WBC) > 12,000 cells per millimeter cubed (mm^3), < 4,000 cells/mm^3, or > 10% band forms. *Sepsis* is defined as SIRS plus microbiologically confirmed infection—usually a positive blood culture.

Risk factors for severe infection in elderly patients include dementia, delirium, excess injury, aspiration, decreased gag and cough reflex, endocrine deficiency, poor nutrition, immunosenescence of T- and B-cells, immobility, and skin breakdown. The risk factors for severe sepsis and mortality include those factors plus concomitant medical illness, diminished cardiopulmonary reserve, and age-related decrease in organ function, particularly renal function.

The genitourinary tract is the most common source of bacteremia in elderly patients, with gram-negative bacteria being the most commonly isolated causative agents. *Escherichia coli* is the leading isolate, accounting for the majority of urinary tract infections, followed by *Klebsiella, Providencia,* and *Proteus.* Other frequent sources of bacteremia include the respiratory tract, the gastrointestinal tract, and endovascular devices. Among the gram-positive organisms causing sepsis, *Staphylococcus aureus* is the most common, followed by *Enterococcus* spp. and viridans group streptococci.

Diagnosing sepsis in elderly patients can be challenging. Fever may be blunted or absent in many elderly patients, and others may be hypothermic—a poor prognostic sign. Presenting symptoms in elderly patients may include delirium, weakness, anorexia, malaise, urinary incontinence, and falls. Awareness of these manifestations may increase the recognition of sepsis in older patients.

Prompt source control and early administration of antibiotics are the keys to successful management of sepsis. Broad-spectrum antibiotic therapy should be initiated as soon as possible and no later than 1 hour after the recognition of sepsis. Blood cultures and other cultures from suspected sites should be collected before antibiotic administration (if possible). Aggressive initial resuscitation with fluid is almost always required, and vasopressors (agents that increase blood pressure) may be needed to maintain adequate tissue perfusion. Treatment with recombinant human-activated protein C should be considered in patients with a high risk of death due to severe sepsis unless there is the presence of active bleeding or platelet counts of less than 30,000/mm^3, and older adults have been shown to benefit as much as younger adults. Steroids are reserved for patients with documented relative adrenal insufficiency. Packed red blood cell transfusions should be considered in patients with hemoglobin less than 7 milligrams per deciliter (mg/dl), except for older patients with histories of coronary artery disease, in whom the hemoglobin level should be kept above 10 mg/dl.

Physicians taking care of elderly patients with severe sepsis must be prepared to discuss end of life issues early in the patients' illness. Prolonging life may be futile in some cases, and withholding or withdrawing care may be in the best interest of the patients. Advanced directives, if available, should always be followed.

Infective Endocarditis

Infective endocarditis results from infection of the heart valves or endothelium of the heart with any of a variety of bacteria, fungi, rickettsiae, or other agents. The majority of native valve infective endocarditis cases are caused by α-hemolytic viridans group streptococci. The other important pathogens are *S. aureus* and *Staphylococcus epidermidis*. Blood cultures are positive in 95% of the cases in the absence of prior antibiotic therapy. In cases of culture-negative endocarditis, the following organisms should be considered: *Legionella* spp., *Chlamydia psittaci* and *pneumoniae*, *Coxiella burnetti*, *Bartonella* spp., fungi, the HACEK group (*Haemophilus* spp., *Actinobacillus actinomycetemcomitans*, *Cardiobacterium hominis*, *Eikenella* spp., and *Kingella kingae*), and *Tropheryma whipplei*. Polymerase chain reaction (PCR) assays are available for some of these agents, others require that the blood cultures be kept for up to 3 weeks, and in still others serological studies will support the diagnosis.

Skin invasion, intravenous drug abuse, and many medical procedures that are a part of hospitalization can cause infective endocarditis with gram-positive cocci. Urinary tract and gastrointestinal procedures can cause infective endocarditis with gram-negative bacilli and enterococci. With a high prevalence of

prosthetic valve replacement surgery in older adults, prosthetic valve infective endocarditis (PVE) is an important entity to consider. Early PVE (< 60 days after replacement) is almost always caused by *S. epidermidis* or *S. aureus* with occasional isolates due to enterococci or gram-negative bacilli usually due to a nosocomial bacteremia. Late PVE is still characterized by *S. epidermidis* and *S. aureus* as the most likely causes, but the spectrum of organisms shifts more toward that of native valve endocarditis with viridans streptococci and other mouth organisms comprising a significant minority.

Patients with infective endocarditis may present with or without fever; nonspecific symptoms such as lethargy, nausea, and vertigo are most common in subacute presentations. Vascular phenomenon, Roth spots in the eyes, new or changing murmur, and embolic events are the most common signs. The diagnosis of infective endocarditis can be made with transthoracic echocardiogram (TTE), but unlike young adults in whom the sensitivity of TTE approximates 80%, the sensitivity of TTE in older adults is only 40% to 50% due to poor visualization of smaller vegetations secondary to increased echogenicity of the valves consequent to calcium deposition. Transesophageal echocardiogram (TEE) increases sensitivity to 80% to 90% in older adults.

Treatment of infective endocarditis consists of antibiotic treatment directed at the identified pathogen or the most likely causative microorganism if blood cultures are negative. Duration of therapy depends on the organism and antibiotic regimen used, but it ranges from 2 to 6 weeks and requires intravenous administration almost universally. Indications for surgical therapy include marked congestive heart failure, severe valvular dysfunction, recurrent emboli, myocardial abscess formation, fungal endocarditis, and failure of appropriate antibiotics to sterilize blood cultures.

Antibiotic prophylaxis is available and is effective for bacterial endocarditis in at-risk patients undergoing dental, upper respiratory tract, gastrointestinal, or genitourinary procedures. Recommendations for endocarditis prophylaxis have been published in the literature and are widely available.

—Vipul Ganatra and Kevin P. High

See also Advance Directives; Surgery; Valvular Heart Disease

Further Readings and References

Gavazzi G, Mallaret MR, Couturier P, Iffenecker A, Franco A. Bloodstream infection: Differences between young–old, old, and old–old patients. *J Am Geriatr Soc.* 2000;50:1667–1673.

Girard TD, Opal SM, Ely EW. Insights into severe sepsis in older patients: From epidemiology to evidence-based management. *Clin Infect Dis.* 2005;40:719–727.

Yoshikawa TT, Norman DC. *Infectious Disease in the Aging: A Clinical Handbook.* Totowa, NJ: Humana; 2001.

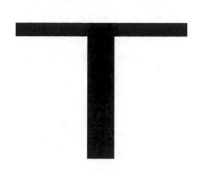

TELEMEDICINE

The strict dictionary definition of the word *telemedicine* is distance or remote medicine, and therefore it encompasses a wide variety of approaches. The simple act of providing medical advice to patients by a plain old telephone system (the abbreviation POTS is actually used to refer to this) is perhaps the oldest and most rudimentary approach. POTS-based transmission of radiological images began during the late 1940s, whereas the late 1960s saw an early version of interactive video linkage established between Boston's Logan International Airport and Massachusetts General Hospital.

In medical settings, the traditional approach to telemedicine uses integrated services data networking (ISDN), a variant of the standard phone line that permits high-speed, but expensive, audio–video transmission. Usually, this involves a remote and proximal site, with a patient and a trained assistant (often a nurse or physician's assistant) at one end and a medical consultant at the other end. The assistant is an invaluable resource for physical examination because the provider at the proximal site is unable to touch the patient and relies on the expertise of the assistant when peripheral devices are used. For psychological or psychiatric consultation, a document camera is provided in addition to the basic camcorder and television monitor hookup. The document camera allows cross-site viewing of documents as well as written communication and drawing. The capability of writing is an asset for psychological

test taking. For medical consultations, a number of peripheral devices may be connected, with the most common being otoscopes, dermatology scopes, and stethoscopes. Occasionally, the transmission may extend from point to point (e.g., two sites) to multipoint (three or more sites). For example, a geriatrician might be brought in from a third site to actively participate with the primary provider and client. Although the majority are live interactive transmissions, video and images such as X-rays may be transmitted at a later date—a procedure often referred to as *store/forward*. The latter are generally reimbursed at a rate lower than that for live transmissions.

In the public sector, the Department of Defense (DoD) is the world's heaviest user of telemedicine in all of its formats and is the source of many innovations that are readily transferable to civilian health care. In addition to innovations in peripherals and portable, battlefield-ready units, the DoD has for years been developing telesurgical approaches. To date, pigs and similar animals have been the primary beneficiaries of telesurgery, but this is expected to change rapidly. Ongoing research by the U.S. Defense Advanced Research Projects Agency (DARPA) on unmanned vehicles and robotic "mules" may provide support for cognitively and mobility-impaired elders.

With the advent of cable and digital subscriber line (DSL), medical-quality transmission is increasingly possible in private dwellings. One barrier to home use has been the quality of transmission, which is affected by bandwidth capacity. Full-motion video at 29.97

frames per second is considered the standard for medical transmission. This standard is available over systems using integrated services digital network (ISDN), an approach that is compliant with Health Insurance Portability and Accountability Act (HIPAA) guidelines. For the Internet, the Moving Picture Experts Group (MPEG) has established standards for the bandwidth requirements necessary to support various video transmission qualities. MPEG1, for example, requires a bandwidth of up to 1.5 megabits (Mbits) per second and can render medical-quality video. To compensate for lower bandwidth connections, manufacturers of videoconferencing equipment have resorted to the use of codecs (compressor/decompressor software) to preprocess the video signal.

The most frequent use of telemedicine outside the standard clinical setting has been Internet chat sessions between patients or between patients and providers as well as e-mails between patients and providers. New technologies that allow other applications of telemedicine are increasingly available. The following are some examples:

• *Home Uses.* Telemedicine technologies are being used by consumers as an adjunct to medical care and as a stand-alone way of monitoring health. For years, POTS-based video systems have allowed health teams to visit newly discharged patients and the chronically ill with considerable success. These virtual visits permitted the medical teams to listen to heart and lung sounds, view pill containers, check progress of wound healing, and so on. Overall, technologies associated with telemedicine have the potential to support personal wellness strategies for aging in place. In some scenarios, robotics will serve as a virtual assistant to the practitioner—or to the client. Robotic assistants have been tested in assisted-living facilities. They can be tasked with reminding patients of upcoming doctor visits, escorting them to physicians' offices, and providing a stable platform to support slow-moving patients as they walk. These robots can use speech recognition software to respond to patient requests in multiple languages.

• *The "Smart House."* Researchers are developing elder-friendly homes that will monitor inside and outside activities and also adjust lighting, adjust temperature, prompt activities of daily living (ADLs), and detect behavioral abnormalities that might be symptomatic of a deteriorating medical condition.

• *Satellites and Wireless.* Researchers are currently working on mobile health care toolkits that rely on wireless connections between a cellular telephone and peripheral medical devices (e.g., blood pressure cuff, electrocardiograms [EKGs], respirometers). These devices can interact with devices such as pill monitors to detect patient medication noncompliance. Similarly, the DoD is experimenting with vests that transmit vital signs and wound status of troops in combat as well as portable handhelds to transmit and download medical information, robot patient extractors (to remove injured soldiers in the heat of combat), and numerous other approaches and devices that may ultimately facilitate the care of elders. Global positioning systems (GPSs), including those available in devices such as cellular phones, not only allow tracking of individuals but also detect movement outside of preset zones such as a room or yard or deviations from a familiar route to a local store. Such technologies are being evaluated for their efficacy in tracking and managing wandering in persons with dementia.

A number of legal and policy issues currently affect users of telemedicine applications. Legal issues arise when the provider is not licensed to practice in the state or country in which the patient resides. Consider the complication in the circumstance of an airline passenger from Boston being treated while flying over Ohio by a physician in Florida. When the Internet is used, privacy concerns become significant because e-mail and many Internet applications are not secure. HyperText Transfer Protocol Secure (HTTPS) is currently used to encrypt and restrict access to online medical records or to protect financial transactions. Video encryption is more processor intensive because bidirectional streams must be compressed and encrypted during the transmission. Processing load increases significantly with larger images.

Reimbursement policies have historically been a major barrier to telemedicine, but Medicare and Medicaid and many health insurers provide coverage for many of the associated costs. Coverage also varies from state to state. Users of telemedicine should determine which health care providers are covered by insurers and determine the extent to which remote site costs are covered.

Looking to the future, we find the paradox that although telemedicine-based approaches would seem to be the antithesis of the "high-touch, low-tech" approach to health care that has long defined the health care of older clients, these older patients, for the most part, readily accept telemedicine programs. As expertise and technology advances, the practice of telemedicine—and the closely aligned fields of robotics and computer science in general—may provide cost-effective approaches to health care. Although telemedicine has traditionally been regarded as an approach best suited to clients at substantial distances from providers, especially clients in rural settings, the rapid growth of broadband connectivity suggests that telemedicine may in the future provide a vehicle for what might be called a "virtual" day hospital or clinic. In the case of mobility-impaired elders, the possibility of visiting multiple health professionals from one site makes perfect sense. That one site might be a clinic or physician's office or even the client's home.

Ultimately, telemedicine is a concept and approach that should be considered apart from any particular technology. Many strategies indeed can be packaged together under its rubric. Currently, more than 35 hospitals have some version of a mobile robotic device that allows health professionals to "visit" patients without leaving their offices. The possibilities for future applications are nearly endless.

—David Chiriboga
and William Kearns

See also Health Care System for Older Adults; Rural Health and Aging Versus Urban Health and Aging

Further Readings and References

Chiriboga DA, Ottenbacher KJ, Rahr RR. Geriatrics. In: Viegas SF, Dunn K, eds. *Telemedicine: Practicing in the Information Age.* Philadelphia: Lippincott–Raven; 1998:275–278.

Flynn E. Telesurgery in the United States. *Homeland Defense J.* 2005;(June):24–27. Available at: www.tatrc.org/news/1HDJJunTelesurgery.pdf?.v=14. Accessed October 5, 2006.

Maheu M, Pulier ML, Wilhelm FH, McMenamin JP, Brown-Connolly NE. *The Mental Health Professional and the New Technologies: A Handbook for Practice Today.* Mahwah, NJ: Lawrence Erlbaum; 2004.

National Institutes of Health/National Library of Medicine. Fact sheet: Telemedicine related programs. Available at: www.nlm.nih.gov/pubs/factsheets/telemedicine.html. Accessed October 5, 2006.

Pineau J, Montemerlo M, Pollack M, Roy N, Thrun S. Toward robotic assistants in nursing homes: Challenges and results. *Robot Auton Syst.* 2003;42:271–281.

Telemedicine and Advanced Technology Research Center. TATRC website. Available at: www.tatrc.org. Accessed October 5, 2006.

Wade SL, Wolfe CR. Telehealth interventions in rehabilitation psychology: Postcards from the edge. *Rehab Psychol.* 2005;50:323–324.

TEMPERATURE REGULATION

Temperature regulation is a complicated process that is altered by aging. Temperature is controlled primarily by the hypothalamus in the brain, but the body relies on a complex mechanism of neurological, circulatory, metabolic, and cardiac pathways to respond appropriately to heat and cold. Body temperature is maintained by balanced abilities to generate/maintain heat and to lose heat. These abilities are influenced by the body's basal metabolic rate, muscle activity, and effects of stress and thyroid hormones. In addition, many older adults have a diminished ability to recognize changes in the ambient temperature that necessitate changes needed to maintain body heat (e.g., changing location, changing amount/type of clothing). Cognitive impairment can further reduce the likelihood that older adults can initiate appropriate compensatory behaviors in hot or cold environments.

Hypothermia is the presence of a core temperature less than 35 degrees Celsius (95 degrees Fahrenheit). In older adults, it can be due to exposure to air just 15 degrees cooler than body temperature and can be complicated by physiological changes with aging or disease. Shivering, which serves to generate heat, can be less effective in older adults. In addition to a reduced basal metabolic rate, older adults might not be able to mediate thermogenesis via the β-adrenergic system. Disease processes can cause hypothermia (e.g., profound hypothyroidism, sepsis), but much more common risk factors are living alone, dementia, and use of alcohol and certain medications such as benzodiazepines, barbiturates, and phenothiazines. Social circumstances, including lack of adequate heating, are frequent contributors to hypothermia. Outdoor exposure to extreme cold is not necessary for hypothermia to develop in older persons; older persons trying to conserve on use of heating may become hypothermic in their own homes.

Clinically, hypothermic symptoms can be nonspecific and include weakness, confusion, fatigue, and cool skin. As core temperature decreases, consciousness is frequently lost and cyanosis, bradycardia, and hypotension can occur. The most significant complications are cardiac arrhythmias. Ventricular fibrillation is a common cause of death in hypothermic patients, and it can be refractory to treatment until the core temperature has been raised above 28 degrees Celcius. The most specific electrocardiogram (EKG) finding is a J wave (Osborne wave) following the QRS complex. Treatment includes rewarming and intensive care monitoring for multiorgan system dysfunction. Rewarming techniques include passive techniques for those with mild hypothermia (> 32 degrees Celcius) and core rewarming for those with more severe hypothermia. Passive maneuvers include removal from the cold environment and insulation with blankets and dry clothing. Active treatments include warmed intravenous fluids and peritoneal dialysis with warmed dialysate. More rapid warming is required in cases of more severe hypothermia and cardiac irritability.

Hyperthermia is the presence of a core temperature higher than 40.6 degrees Celcius. Older adults generally present with nonexertional heat stroke due to impaired homeostatic mechanisms. Older adults may have a decreased ability to sense an environment as too warm due to impaired function of thermoregulatory centers. With age, decreased or absent sweating may occur due in part to atrophy of skin and associated sweat glands, and a higher threshold is required for sweating to be initiated. Age-related increases in peripheral vascular resistance may impede cutaneous vasodilatation as a compensatory cooling mechanism. Physiological or medication-induced inability to increase cardiac output may also impair the ability to dissipate heat through the skin. Medications associated with reduced sweating include anticholinergics and phenothiazines. Persons with cognitive impairment or mental health problems might also not recognize the need to take steps to compensate for hot environments.

Clinically, heat stroke is a hyperthermic state associated with a systemic inflammatory response and central nervous system malfunction ranging from impaired judgment to frank delirium or coma. Patients experience tachycardia and hyperventilation, and a quarter experience hypotension. Patients also present with dry hot skin and may have nausea, vomiting, and shortness of breath. The most seriously ill patients experience multiorgan system dysfunction. Treatment is based on rapid cooling to 39 degrees Celcius within the first hour. This can be accomplished by external cooling via immersion in cold water; a fan can be added to aid in convective cooling but is not as effective. It is recommended that the patient be massaged vigorously during active cooling to prevent cutaneous vasoconstriction and shivering.

Steps can be taken to prevent hypothermia and heat stroke. Periodic medication reviews should be undergone to eliminate medication that might put patients at risk during extremes of temperature. During warm weather, older adults should be encouraged to drink plenty of cool liquids and to increase their salt intake (if possible). Older adults should also wear loose-fitting, light-colored cotton clothing during heat waves. Studies of heat-related deaths during prolonged summer heat waves have found mortality to be higher for older persons, urban dwellers, persons living alone, persons using psychoactive medications that impair sweating, and persons living without air-conditioning in at least one room in their home. Persons receiving home health services—a marker of poor health and physiology vulnerability—are also at high risk for heat-related illness and death. Vulnerable persons should be targeted for special assistance during heat waves. Community programs deploying air-conditioners to medically and socioeconomically vulnerable persons can be of benefit, as can the use of cooling centers for even a few hours a day during extreme heat. Given the important interactions among age, health status, and social environment in compensating for heat- and cold-related stressors, patients and the public should be better educated regarding the risks that extremes of temperature present to older adults.

—Lynne Kallenbach

See also Injury Prevention; Normal Physical Aging; Skin Changes; Socioeconomic Status

Further Readings and References

Abrass I. Disorders of temperature regulation. In: Hazzard W, Blass J, Halter J, Ouslander J, Tinetti M, eds. *Principles of Geriatric Medicine and Gerontology.* New York: McGraw-Hill; 2003:1587–1591.

Ballester J, Harchelroad F. Hyperthermia: How to recognize and prevent heat related illnesses. *Geriatrics.* 1999;54: 20–24.

Ballester J, Harchelroad F. Hypothermia: An easy-to-miss, dangerous disorder in winter weather. *Geriatrics.* 1999; 54:51–57.

Bouchama A, Knochel J. Heat stroke. *N Engl J Med.* 2002; 346:1978–1988.

TERRORISM

See DISASTERS AND TERRORISM

THERAPEUTIC FAILURE

Therapeutic failure has been defined as a failure to accomplish the goals of treatment resulting from inadequate or inappropriate drug therapy and not related to the natural progression of disease. A lack of therapeutic effect from inadequate drug therapy may include noncompliance, recent dose reduction or discontinuation, drug–drug interaction, too low a dose of drug prescribed, and inadequate therapeutic drug monitoring.

Therapeutic failure is an important problem because of its clinical significance and its impact on the use of health care resources. As a group, older adults consume more prescription and nonprescription medications than does the rest of the population. The risks associated with high levels of medication use include therapeutic failure, medical noncompliance, and adverse drug reactions. Elderly patients on inadequate drug therapy may suffer from serious morbidity or mortality. These adverse clinical events may result in emergency department visits and hospitalization. Therapeutic failure is a costly problem estimated at billions of dollars.

Investigators have reported that the prevalence of therapeutic failure in consecutive hospitalizations for any reason ranged from 2.7% to 11.4%, whereas the prevalence of therapeutic failure in hospital admissions due only to drug-related problems ranged from 42% to 55%. Among drug-related hospital admissions of patients presenting to emergency rooms, therapeutic failure has been reported to be as high as 55.6%.

Few studies have systematically explored the effectiveness of interventions designed to reduce therapeutic failure. One study analyzed the effect of an educational intervention in a department of internal medicine on drug-related hospital admissions and found a nonsignificant decrease in admissions. Investigators have suggested implementing more intensive monitoring of patients, promoting appropriate prescribing through education and quality improvement efforts, and improving patient understanding of prescription drugs and their use. No randomized clinical trials have addressed the efficacy of any of those proposed intervention strategies, either alone or in combination.

Standardizing the definition of therapeutic failure and adopting a valid reliable instrument of measurement would be desirable and helpful in determining the incidence and risk factors of therapeutic failure and in designing effective interventions. One group of investigators recently designed and tested a new instrument for therapeutic failure. Large prospective studies could be useful in clarifying epidemiological issues, and multicenter randomized clinical trials could also identify which interventions would be most effective in reducing therapeutic failure and its associated costs.

—*Robert M. Kaiser and Kenneth E. Schmader*

See also Adverse Drug Reactions; Age-Related Changes in Pharmacokinetics and Pharmacodynamics; Drug Underuse; Inappropriate Prescribing; Medication Adherence; Medication Errors; Polypharmacy

Further Readings and References

Franceschi A, Tuccori M, Bocci G, et al. Drug therapeutic failures in emergency department patients: A university hospital experience. *Pharmacol Res.* 2001;49:85–91.

Hanlon JT, Schmader KE, Ruby CM, Weinberger M. Suboptimal prescribing in older inpatients and outpatients. *J Am Geriatr Soc.* 2001;49:200–209.

Kaiser R, Schmader K, Lindblad C, Ruby C, Pieper C, Hanlon J. Therapeutic failure and hospitalization in the frail elderly. Poster presented at the annual meeting of the American Geriatrics Society, Baltimore, Md, May.

THYROID DISEASE

Thyroid disease is seen quite often in mature adults, especially hypothyroidism (sluggish thyroid disease), which may occur in 10% of the population. Typical symptoms include fatigue, weakness, weight gain, constipation, and feeling colder than other people. In the elderly, many of these symptoms are subtle or nonexistent. The most common causes of hypothyroid disease include autoimmune disease (when the body attacks the thyroid), neck irradiation, and previous thyroid surgery. Many medicines can interfere with the function of the thyroid (e.g., amiodarone) or mimic the symptoms of hypothyroidism (e.g., metoprolol).

Hypothyroidism can cause individuals to have heart failure, depression, dementia, cholesterol problems, and many other difficulties. It is important to have a simple blood test to evaluate for thyroid dysfunction.

The reassuring fact about hypothyroidism is that it can be easily treated with medication (thyroid hormone). The most common thyroid hormone is levothyroxine (or T4). T4 should be started very slowly in older adults, and regular laboratory tests are needed. Placing a patient on too high of a dose can lead to complications such as chest pain, irregular heart rhythm, and worsening of osteoporosis.

Taking T4 is simple, and in the majority of individuals there are no significant side effects. Many patients are not fully educated in the administration of this drug. It must be taken on an empty stomach with water only, and no food should be eaten for 1 to 2 hours after the dose. T4 should not be taken with any other medication or else it will not be absorbed adequately. Sometimes with age, it may be difficult to remember to take T4; in these situations, a spouse or family member may be needed to assist in adherence. In general, patients should take only brand-name medications such as Synthroid and Levoxyl. The brand-name medications are not significantly more costly, and are more reliable, than the generics.

Hyperthyroidism (hyperactive thyroid) is seen less often in elderly individuals and can manifest in many ways such as atrial fibrillation (irregular heartbeat), heart failure, heat intolerance, and weight loss. Long-term hyperthyroidism can lead to osteoporosis. Many elderly individuals may present "apathetic" symptoms such as depression, muscle wasting, and confusion.

The most common causes of hyperactive thyroid are Graves' disease (when the body stimulates the thyroid excessively) and toxic multinodular goiter (when an area in the thyroid produces excess thyroid hormone autonomously). Further testing is usually needed to arrive at a clear diagnosis.

Treatment usually consists of two strategies. Medication is often tried first. Although medications can be effective, they are not optimal management. Individuals who take medication to suppress an overactive gland usually need multiple blood tests, adding cost and time. Finally, individuals may become too ill to take the oral medications they need, and this becomes a serious challenge because antithyroid medications cannot be given by intravenous (IV) administration in the United States. The second strategy is to use radioactive iodine to destroy the thyroid gland—a safe and effective therapeutic choice offered by most medical centers. After the thyroid is destroyed, resultant hypothyroidism must be treated with T4 as described previously.

—*Rajib K. Bhattacharya*

See also Normal Physical Aging; Men's Health; Women's Health

Further Readings and References

Rehman SU, Cope DW, Senseney AD, Brzezinski W. Thyroid disorders in elderly patients. *South Med J.* 2005;98: 543–549.

Transient Ischemic Attacks

See Stroke

Tuberculosis

See Pneumonia and Tuberculosis

Twin Studies

Unlike in animal research, researchers cannot conduct prospective experiments to identify specific factors for human aging by assigning individuals with similar genetic makeup to a variety of environments to "see what happens" over the life course. As a surrogate design, researchers study siblings born as a result of a twin gestation. The basic logic behind twin studies capitalizes on the following biological concept: Members of identical (monozygotic) twin pairs share 100% of their genes, whereas fraternal (dizygotic) twin pairs share 50% of their genes. The greater resemblance of monozygotic twins than of dizygotic twins is consistent with genetic influence.

Simplistically speaking, persons with identical genes *and* an identical intrauterine environment will have differences in the course of aging that can be attributed to factors or exposures unique to one member of the pair. On the other hand, if both members of the pair manifest an aging-related disease, this is interpreted to mean that the appearance of the disease is influenced significantly by genetic factors common to each member of the pair. Additional nuanced interpretations of results from twin studies can be gained by including fraternal or nonidentical twins and opposite sex pairs in the study sample. Longitudinal studies of variation in psychological traits among twins have been a staple of aging research. Historical cohorts of twin studies include the Swedish Twin Registry with its Swedish Adoption Twin Studies of Aging and the Octogenarian Twin Study. The twin study design is now being replicated among populations not represented in Scandinavian and European twin cohorts, including regional twin samples of Whites in the United States, mainland Chinese, Sri Lankans, and African Americans. These ethnically diverse samples of twins add depth to our understanding of the aging process by allowing researchers to estimate the proportions of genetics and environment to disease and then to compare the population-specific proportions. In the case of some diseases, genetics makes a major contribution (> 80%) in all populations. This does not, however, mean that the same genes are operational in all groups. When there are observed population differences in the relative proportions of genetic and environmental influences, the interpretation is less clear.

Historically, interpretation of results from twin studies has been controversial. One major objection has been inherent bias in the twin sample due to small size and biases in ascertainment. This objection has been largely overcome by the creation of population-based twin registries where researchers can estimate the number of twins born during a given year. In many registries, pairs available for statistical analysis range from a few hundred to more than a thousand, providing sufficient statistical power for statistical genetics methods to model complex traits. A second major objection to twin studies is the potential for heightened disease risk among twins when compared with singletons. This increased risk is thought to be attributable to the stress of a twin pregnancy. However, one study focused specifically on early childhood (0 to 6 years of age) did not show excess mortality risk for twins. To completely assess the potential effect of a twin gestation on disease across this life course, more work needs to be done. To illustrate the problem, consider the association between maternal starvation and risk of adult-onset schizophrenia. This association has been demonstrated using a Chinese cohort and a Dutch cohort among adults who were born during the period immediately after a famine. In each cohort, rates of the disease were two to three times greater than the worldwide average of 1 per 100 persons. The interpretation of these data is that risk of schizophrenia is influenced largely by nutritional deficiencies regardless of population genetic makeup. Twin studies provide a unique opportunity to weigh the effect of changing environments or historical events on disease risk in populations with homogeneous genetics.

During the past 20 years, conceptual, technological, and statistical advances have led to improvements in the construction of twin samples, the collection of genetic markers, and the analysis data obtained from these studies. A systematic review of reports published between 2000 and 2004 using the search term "twin studies and aging" resulted in 103 English-language citations. In addition to long-standing registries in Sweden, Finland, Denmark, and Norway, there are other registries in Australia, China, Sri Lanka, and regional areas of the United States. This list of registries is not comprehensive and is intended to provide the reader with a starting point for more extensive searches. Statistical advances include improved computational technology as well as the application of matrix algebra and latent trait analysis techniques to increase the ability of researchers to capture sources of trait variation. Collection methods and improved definition of genetic markers have benefited from the availability of data from the Human Genome Project as well as from an explosion of population-based molecular epidemiological studies documenting the presence of critical genes and the strength of their association with the common disorders of aging such as cancer, heart disease, osteoporosis, Alzheimer's disease, and other mental disorders. There is widespread evidence from quantitative genetics studies revealing the importance of environmental effects for nearly every phenotype studied. The new frontier in twin and family studies seeks to identify specific features of the environment to measure. It is also important to understand when during the developmental timeline these assessments should be conducted. The significance of measurement timing can be best understood with the disease osteoporosis. Bone that has increased risk of fracture is usually measured during late middle age and old age to identify persons who might benefit from medication and exercise-based therapies. Childhood—between 8 and 18 years of age—represents a critical period in bone development when genetic and dietary factors have their greatest impact on the variation in age of onset of disease. For prevention purposes, these genetic and dietary factors are best measured during childhood. With the goal of understanding why there is so much individual variation in aging, current research with twins and families is now incorporating key development-specific environmental measures to bear on genetic inquiry. This line of research should yield clinically useful information in pharmacogenetics, age-related disease onset, and (ultimately) the development of frailty during old age.

—*Toni D. Miles*

See also Age–Period–Cohort Distinctions; Biomarkers of Aging; Epidemiology of Aging

Further Readings and References

Kaprio J, Koskenvuo M. Genetic and environmental factors in complex diseases: The older Finnish Twin Cohort. *Twin Res.* 2002;5:358–365.

McClearn GE. Nature and nurture: Interaction and coaction. *Am J Med Genet B Neuropsychiatric Genet.* 2004;124:124–130.

Tennant C. Life events, stress, and depression: A review of recent findings. *Austral N Zeal J Psychiatry.* 2002;36:173–182.

Visscher PM. Power of the classical twin design revisited. Twin Res. 2004;7:505–512.

URBAN HEALTH AND AGING

See RURAL HEALTH AND AGING VERSUS URBAN
HEALTH AND AGING

URINARY INCONTINENCE

See INCONTINENCE

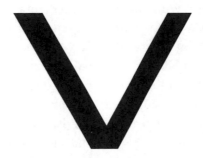

VALVULAR HEART DISEASE

The heart has four valves that regulate the blood flow through the upper (atria) and lower (ventricles) chambers of the heart, keeping the flow in one direction. Valvular heart disease occurs when one or more of these valves functions incorrectly, disrupting normal flow through the heart. Common symptoms associated with valvular heart disease include shortness of breath, leg swelling, and fatigue.

Normal Heart Valve Function

The four valves of the heart are the tricuspid valve (connecting the right atrium to the right ventricle), pulmonic valve (between the right ventricle and pulmonary arteries), mitral valve (connecting the left atrium to the left ventricle), and aortic valve (connecting the left atrium to the aorta). The valves are composed of a ring of tissue, the annulus, with two or three leaflets or flaps of tissue attached that open and close like a swinging door. These leaflets open to allow blood flow through the valve and then close to prevent backward flow of blood into the previous chamber.

Heart Valve Malfunction

Heart valves can malfunction in two ways: by becoming stenotic or by becoming regurgitant. Stenotic valves have a narrowed opening, due to stiffening of the leaflets, that can partially block blood flow across the valve. Regurgitant or "leaky" valves do not close properly, resulting in backward blood flow with contraction of the heart. Valves can be both stenotic and regurgitant. Both conditions can result in decreased forward flow of blood through the heart (and therefore to the rest of the body). The heart needs to work harder to compensate for the decreased forward flow so as to ensure adequate perfusion of the body. When the heart is unable to meet these demands, symptoms of valvular disease occur. Mitral valve prolapse (MVP) is a specific heart valve malfunction that occurs when the mitral leaflets flap backward with contraction of the heart. This may result in a leaky valve. It occurs in 1% of the population and infrequently becomes severe enough to warrant treatment.

Causes

Valvular heart disease can be congenital (a developmental abnormality) or acquired. Bicuspid aortic valve disease, the most common congenital valve disease, is characterized by having only two leaflets, rather than the usual three, resulting in a regurgitant or stenotic aortic valve. Acquired valvular heart disease can be caused by infection or changes in the structure of the valve. Endocarditis and rheumatic fever are the two most common infectious etiologies. Endocarditis is a potentially life-threatening infection in which bacteria in the bloodstream attaches to one or more of the heart valves. The infection causes growths, or "vegetations," on the valve and also causes degradation and scarring of the valve tissue. With these changes, the valve can become either stenotic or regurgitant. Rheumatic fever results from untreated streptococcal infection, especially in children. It causes rheumatic heart disease; that is, an inflammation of the leaflets that makes them scarred, rigid, and sticky. It typically affects the mitral valve and can also result in a stenotic or regurgitant mitral valve.

Acquired changes in valve structure can be caused by a heart attack or by trauma. The resulting disruption to the underlying papillary muscles, which contract to pull on the chordae tendineae that connect to the valve leaflets, can impair adequate opening and closing of the valve. If the chordae are stretched, the leaflets can flap backward, resulting in a regurgitant valve. Acquired changes can also be caused by fibrocalcified degeneration, which typically affects aortic valves in older adults. It causes thickening of the leaflets, resulting in aortic stenosis. The annulus of the heart valve can also be damaged by a heart attack, heart failure, high blood pressure, and syphilis. Widening of the annulus of the valve prevents the leaflets from closing properly, resulting in a regurgitant valve. Other causes of valvular heart disease include coronary artery disease, cardiomyopathy, hypertension, syphilis, radiation, and aortic aneurysms.

Symptoms

The most common symptoms of valvular heart disease are shortness of breath; palpitations; swelling (edema) in the feet, ankles, legs, and abdomen; weakness or lightheadedness; and chest pain or discomfort. Symptoms can present suddenly or progress slowly over time, reflecting the progression of the underlying valve disease. However, symptoms do not always correlate with the degree of stenosis or regurgitation detected on diagnostic studies.

Diagnosis

The initial presumption of valvular heart disease is typically made by history and physical exam. Symptoms of shortness of breath, leg edema, and fatigue with evidence of fluid in the lungs (pulmonary edema), an enlarged heart (cardiomegaly), and/or the presence of a heart murmur on physical exam suggest valvular heart disease. A heart murmur indicates turbulent blood flow across a leaky or stenotic valve. The most commonly used diagnostic test to confirm the presence of valvular disease is the echocardiogram, that is, a Doppler ultrasound of the heart's movement and blood flow across the valves. Cardiac catheterization, radionuclide scans, and magnetic resonance imaging (MRI) may also be used to assess the presence and severity of valve disease.

Treatment

In individuals with underlying valve disease, prophylaxis with antibiotics prior to dental procedures (which can introduce bacteria into the bloodstream) may be indicated to prevent endocarditis and further damage to the valves. Medications are used primarily to control blood pressure and to decrease the work demands of the heart. Weight gain and leg edema are treated with diuretics. When valve disease progresses to the extent that symptoms persist despite these therapies, both surgical and nonsurgical procedures are available. Balloon valvotomy can be used to open a stenotic mitral or aortic valve. Surgery procedures include both repair and replacement of the damaged valve. New valves can be biological or mechanical. Although mechanical valves tend to function longer, lifelong blood thinners are required.

—Laurie Lavery

See also Arrhythmias; Cardiovascular Disease; Congestive Heart Failure

Further Readings and References

Bonow RO, Carabello B, de Leon AC, et al. Guidelines for the management of patients with valvular heart disease: Executive summary—A report of the American College of Cardiology/American Heart Association Task Force on Practice Guidelines (Committee on Management of Patients With Valvular Heart Disease). *Circulation.* 1998;98:1949–1984.

Boon NA, Bloomfield P. The medical management of valvular heart disease. *Heart.* 2002;87:395–400.

Carabello BA, Crawford FA. Valvular heart disease. *N Engl J Med.* 1997;337:32–41.

Schoen FJ. Cardiac valves and valvular pathology: Update on function, disease, repair, and replacement. *Cardiovasc Pathol.* 2005;14:189–194.

Tighe DA, Meyer TE, Aurigemma GP. *Dx/Rx: Valvular Heart Disease.* Sudbury, Mass: Jones & Bartlett; 2004.

VASCULAR DEMENTIA

Dementia is a clinical syndrome characterized by an acquired progressive impairment of memory accompanied by persistent decline in abstract thinking, judgment, and/or language. This decline affects quality of life and interferes with work, social activities, and interpersonal relationships. Dementia may be caused by degenerative disorders of the brain (e.g., Alzheimer's disease) or by a number of other medical conditions. Dementia caused by cerebrovascular disease (strokes or infarctions) is called vascular dementia.

After Alzheimer's disease, vascular dementia is the second most common cause of dementia, affecting 12% to 20% of patients with dementia. Compared with Alzheimer's disease, vascular dementia tends to occur at a younger age, affects men more often than it affects women, and is associated with a shorter length of survival after onset. Vascular dementia may begin at any time during late life but becomes less common after 75 years of age, while the incidence of Alzheimer's disease continues to rise. Patients with vascular dementia commonly survive for 6 to 8 years after the illness begins, and death usually results from cardiovascular disease or stroke.

The risk factors for vascular dementia are essentially those for vascular disease and stroke. Common vascular risk factors include advanced age, high cholesterol, hypertension, obesity, cigarette smoking, arteriosclerosis, diabetes, elevated homocysteine levels, and the presence of apolipoprotein E (a protein component essential to lipid metabolism). Alone or together, these risk factors produce inflammation and damage to the vessel wall, resulting in narrowing of vessels and loss of blood flow to the region supplied by that vessel. Elevated homocysteine levels cause damage to arteries and brain cells by producing endothelial damage through oxidative stress. Apolipoprotein E, often found in patients with Alzheimer's disease, can increase the risk of dementia in stroke patients through its effect on lipid metabolism and atherosclerosis. Stroke may also occur as a result of vessel occlusion from an embolus originating in the heart or in larger vessels. Those who are older, have less education, and have experienced multiple strokes are more likely to develop dementia.

There are several types of vascular dementia based on whether the dementia results from strategically placed single infarctions, occlusion of small vessels, decreased blood flow (or "hypoperfusion") to brain regions on the borders of the brain's main vessels, or multiple brain infarctions. The clinical characteristics of vascular dementia correspond to the location of the ischemic brain changes, the volume of ischemic tissue, and the etiology of the vascular disease. The clinical hallmark of vascular dementia is the presence of focal neurological deficits such as localized weakness and numbness.

A single brain infarct can cause dementia if it occurs in a brain region critical to intellectual function. Well-recognized dementia syndromes may result from strategically placed strokes in the distributions of the carotid, anterior, middle, or posterior cerebral arteries. These strokes cause syndromes specific to the site of the lesion. Involvement in the frontal lobe results in aphasia, apraxia, disinhibition, and apathy. A stroke in the hippocampus may result in amnesia, a stroke in the gyrus angularis may result in constructional problems, and a stroke in the parietal lobe may result in alexia and agraphia. Strokes in the left hemisphere of the brain tend to increase the risk of vascular dementia fivefold, especially if the infarctions involve the posterior cerebral artery or anterior cerebral artery territories. Single large vessel strokes are due primarily to atherosclerosis. The course of this condition is fluctuating, with episodes of major impairment interspersed with prolonged lucid periods. However, not all strokes—even those that occur in functionally critical areas of the brain—result in dementia. The risk of developing dementia following a stroke can be up to nine times greater than in patients who have never had a stroke. One year after a stroke, 25% of patients develop new-onset dementia.

Occlusion of small vessels (e.g., lenticulostriate arteries, subcortical arterioles) may also cause dementia. Such occlusion is typically caused by damage to the vessel wall from long-standing hypertension and atherosclerosis. Subcortical structures, such as the thalamus, basal ganglia, and frontal white matter, are commonly affected, leading to disruptions of their connections to the cerebral cortex (particularly the frontal lobes). This disconnect between subcortical and cortical structures may result in mental deterioration as well as localized weakness, exaggeration of deep tendon reflexes, loss of memory, urinary dysfunction, and parkinsonism. Apathy, depression, pseudobulbar palsy, psychosis, and gait disturbance are also often present. The absence of cortical findings typically denotes the presence of subcortical dementia.

Decreased blood flow to brain regions on the borders between the brain's main vessels can result in intellectual decline. These strokes typically occur in the border zone region between the territories of the middle and posterior cerebral arteries and are due primarily to severe hypotension such as that which may occur during cardiac arrest or loss of blood volume.

Multi-infarct dementia results from the cumulative effect of multiple large vessel cortical strokes. Infarctions are typically due to atherosclerotic disease and can affect both cortical and subcortical areas of the brain. The clinical picture is often variable and includes memory impairment in conjunction with patchy deficits across several areas of cognitive function. The observed neurological symptoms coincide with the affected regions of the brain. Multi-infarct dementia typically has an abrupt onset with stepwise deterioration.

A diagnosis of vascular dementia is made in patients with both dementia and cerebrovascular disease, where the latter is believed to be causing the former. Causality is suggested by the dementia occurring close in time with the vascular event and either an abrupt or stepwise deterioration in cognitive function. Although these criteria sound straightforward, the diagnosis of vascular dementia can actually be complex because of the overlap in symptoms with Alzheimer's disease. Many patients may actually have elements of both disease processes, a condition known as *mixed dementia.* A variety of scales (e.g., the Hachinski Ischemia Scale) have been developed to help distinguish vascular dementia from dementia caused by Alzheimer's disease.

All patients with dementia should receive a full general medical and neuropsychiatric history and examination. Certain laboratory studies should also be obtained, including blood tests for hypothyroidism and Vitamin B12 as well as imaging of brain structure with either magnetic resonance imaging (MRI) or computed tomography (CT) scans. A patient with vascular dementia should undergo a full evaluation of the heart and arteriole system, including an electrocardiogram and other laboratory tests as indicated. Neuropsychological testing may be helpful in establishing a formal baseline of cognitive functioning, which can then be followed over time to assess the effects of illness and treatment. All patients with dementia should also be screened for depression, which is common in patients with dementia and which is associated with significant comorbidity.

The treatment of vascular dementia is aimed at prevention of further stroke and control of dementia symptoms. Primary prevention of stroke focuses on the control of vascular risk factors such as hypertension, hypercholesterolemia, diabetes, overweight, and smoking. Secondary prevention concentrates on the prevention of stroke in patients with existing cerebrovascular disease and includes use of antiplatelet (e.g., aspirin), anticoagulant, and vasodilating medications as well as surgery (e.g., carotid endarterectomy). Although these preventive measures may reduce the risk of stroke and death, it has not been shown whether they do so in patients with vascular dementia. Although no current biological treatment can reverse the effects of a completed stroke, rehabilitative efforts—including physical, occupational, and speech therapy)—may help the patient to recover lost function.

Treatment of the cognitive and behavioral disturbances in vascular dementia generally employs the same measures used in patients with Alzheimer's disease. The ultimate goal of treatment is to maximize the patient's level of function and to ensure safety for patients and their families. Patients with vascular dementia may have deficits in brain cholinergic function (as seen in patients with Alzheimer's disease) and may show mild improvement in cognition, behavior, and activities of daily living (ADLs) with cholinesterase inhibitors (e.g., Aricept). Patients who experience comorbid depression, agitation, anxiety, and emotional lability may benefit from the use of antidepressant or atypical antipsychotic medications and psychological therapies. Caring for patients with dementia is extraordinarily stressful, and caretakers should be evaluated for depression.

—*Lisa MacLean and C. Edward Coffey*

See also Alzheimer's Disease; Cardiovascular System; Lewy Body Dementia; Memory; Mental Status Assessment; Mild Cognitive Impairment; Neurobiology of Aging; Neurological Disorders; Pick's Disease; Pseudodementia; Stroke; Vascular Depression

Further Readings and References

Knopman DS, DeKosky ST, Cummings JL, et al. Practice parameter: Diagnosis of dementia (an evidence-based review). *Neurology.* 2001;56:1143–1153.

Practice guidelines for the treatment of patients with Alzheimer's disease and other dementias of late life. *Am J Psychiatry.* 1997;154(5):1–39.

Reichman WE. Nondegenerative dementing disorders. In: Coffey CE, Cummings JL, eds. *Textbook of Geriatric Neuropsychiatry.* Washington, DC: American Psychiatric Press; 2000:491–509.

Yudofsky SC, Hales RE. *Neuropsychiatry and Clinical Neurosciences.* 4th ed. Washington, DC: American Psychiatric Press; 2002.

VASCULAR DEPRESSION

The link between depressive disorders and cerebrovascular disease has been recognized since the mid-19th century. Depression following brain vascular injury or vascular depression is now a well-recognized clinical entity. The most studied subtype of vascular depression, poststroke depression, occurs in 20% to 50% of cases within 12 to 24 months following cerebrovascular accident. The *Diagnostic and Statistical Manual of Mental Disorders, Fourth Edition* (DSM-IV) categorizes poststroke depression as a mood disorder caused by a general medical condition with depressive features, major depressive-like episodes, or mixed features.

The location of the stroke lesion is an important predictor of depression and its duration. Major depression is significantly more frequent among patients with left anterior lesions than among those with any other lesion locations. However, there is some disagreement on the role of laterality in the development of depression.

Vascular risk factors contribute to late-life major depression. This thesis is supported by data from computed tomography (CT) and magnetic resonance imaging (MRI) studies that have identified signal hyperintensities (HIs) or "silent cerebral infarctions" in such patients, the association of HIs with age and cerebrovascular risk factors, and the pathophysiological evidence indicating that HIs are associated with widespread diminution in cerebral perfusion. The neuropathological correlates of HIs are diverse and represent ischemic changes together with demyelination, edema, and gliosis.

Abnormalities on CT or MRI scans can be classified into three types. First, periventricular hyperintensities (PVHs), halos or rims adjacent to ventricles, in severe forms, invade surrounding deep white matter. Second, single, patchy, or confluent foci may be observed in subcortical white matter or deep white matter hyperintensities (DWMHs). Third, HIs may be also found in deep gray structures, particularly the basal ganglia, thalamus, and pons. Collectively, these three types of abnormalities have been referred to as leukoareosis or encephalomalacia. The rate of these findings is higher in persons with geriatric depression than in normal controls and may be comparable to that in persons with multi-infarct dementia. Smaller brain volumes and HIs may provide complementary or autonomous pathways to late-life major depressive disorder.

Vascular depression has been named only since 1997, when G. S. Alexopoulos and colleagues and

K. R. Krishnan and colleagues separately proposed the concept on the premise that cerebrovascular disease may be etiologically related to geriatric depressive syndromes. Patients with clinically defined vascular depression experienced more cognitive dysfunction, disability, and retardation, but less agitation and guilt feelings, than did patients with nonvascular depression. Patients with MRI-defined vascular depression were older and had a later age of onset, more apathy, and a lower incident of family history of depression compared with those with nonvascular depression.

On the other hand, growing evidence indicates that depression may also affect brain vasculature and increase cerebrovascular risk. In a large cohort of elderly patients with diagnosed hypertension, those with high depressive symptoms were 2.7 times more likely to suffer from stroke than were nondepressed hypertensive patients, thereby supporting the increased risk of stroke with depression.

Provided that cerebrovascular disease and depression are two interdependent processes, prompt treatment and prevention of either process is very important for improving outcomes of these chronic debilitating illnesses.

—Helen Lavretsky

See also Depression and Other Mood Disorders; Imaging of the Brain

Further Readings and References

Alexopoulos GS, Meyers BS, Young RC, Campbell S, Silbersweig D, Charlson M. "Vascular depression" hypothesis. *Arch Gen Psychiatry.* 1997;54:915–922.

Krishnan KR, Hays JC, Blazer DG. MRI-defined vascular depression. *Am J Psychiatry.* 1997;154:497–501.

Post F. The Significance of Affective Symptoms in Old Age: A Follow-up Study of One Hundred Patients. London: Oxford University Press; 1962.

VENOUS STASIS ULCERS

Ulcers of the lower extremity are very common in the older population and require specific treatment based on the etiology of the lesions. Venous stasis ulcers are the most common (60% of all lower extremity ulcers), followed by neuropathic ulcers (secondary to diabetes mellitus and other conditions that cause nerve damage and decreased sensation), ischemic ulcers (secondary to arterial insufficiency), and then miscellaneous causes (e.g., trauma, autoimmune).

Venous stasis ulcers occur secondary to pedal edema (swelling) from venous hypertension. The most common cause of venous hypertension is stenosis of the deep veins of the leg or abdomen from deep vein thrombosis (DVT). A postphlebitic syndrome, consisting of pain, swelling, and/or ulcerations in the extremity, may develop following venous thrombosis. In long-term follow-up studies of individuals with histories of DVT, up to 80% of patients had some symptoms of postphlebitic syndrome over a 20-year follow-up period.

The pathophysiology of ulcer formation is that venous return from the leg to the heart is impeded by a fixed obstruction or stenosis. For venous drainage to occur, the peripheral venous pressure in the leg must increase to overcome this gradient. If the venous pressure exceeds the oncotic (fluid absorption) pressure in the capillary bed, fluid will extravasate (leak) into the interstitial tissues. Compared with other types of ulcer development, venous stasis ulcers have a relatively higher pressure of venous hypertension in the skin and soft tissues. Therefore, a state of ischemia occurs, especially where the skin is thinnest such as over bony protuberances. This is why venous stasis ulcers typically occur over the medial and lateral malleolus of the ankle. It is also common for degradation products of hemoglobin to extravasate into the interstitial tissues and impart a brown woody appearance to the leg.

Treatment of a venous stasis ulcer is aimed at healing of the current ulcer and prevention of further ulcers. Treatment consists of four main parts:

1. Treatment of sepsis and debridement (removal) of devitalized tissues

2. Ensuring an adequate blood supply (i.e., checking for arterial insufficiency)

3. Keeping the wound in a clean, moist healing environment with appropriate dressings (Although the wound is infected, this usually consists of frequent

saline dressings. As the wound heals and the sepsis is controlled, weekly dressings with bacteriostatic properties such as an Unna boot can be used.)

4. Decreasing venous hypertension (The legs should be elevated above the level of the heart while sitting or laying flat. Compression stockings should be used after the wounds have healed to prevent recurrence.)

There are a number of invasive procedures of varying efficacy that may ameliorate the underlying venous obstruction (which causes venous hypertension) and that may be used in patients with severe symptoms not amenable to conservative therapy. These include catheter-directed thrombolysis for acute and subacute proximal iliofemoral DVT with or without balloon venoplasty and stenting. More invasive procedures include superficial vein stripping, ligation of perforating veins, and more complex venous bypass and venous reconstruction procedures. All of these more aggressive therapies should be carried out only after thorough evaluation of deep vein physiology (aeroplethysmography) and anatomy (proximal and distal venography) under the direction of a vascular surgeon with experience in taking care of this problem.

—Geetha Rao

See also Congestive Heart Failure; Foot Problems; Hypertension; Pressure Ulcers

Further Readings and References

Cameron JL. The diagnosis of venous insufficiency. In: Ascher E, ed. *Current Surgical Therapy*. 8th ed. Philadelphia: Elsevier Mosby; 2004:860–863.

Trent JT, Falabella A, Eaglstein WH, Kirsner RS. Venous ulcers: Pathophysiology and treatment options. *Ostomy Wound Mgmt.* 2005;51(5):38–54.

VISION AND LOW VISION

Older adults constitute the most vulnerable age group for vision impairment. Prevalence estimates based solely on vision acuity criteria of worse than 20/40 indicate that as many as 10% of older adults (65 to 84 years of age) have vision impairment. At the same time, national health surveys of adults report that between 13% and 20% of those age 65 years and older, and 25% of those age 75 years and older, self-report problems with their vision even when wearing corrective glasses or lenses. These self-report figures include vision impairments due to eye disorders as well as those resulting from inappropriate refraction and lack of access to available medical or surgical treatments. Given the consequences of vision impairment for functional ability and psychological well-being among older adults, vision impairment during later life represents a significant public health issue.

There are both normal changes to vision with age and pathological changes due to eye disorders that may occur. It is important to know the difference and to provide appropriate interventions for both to maximize functional independence for older persons with age-related vision loss.

Normal Age-Related Vision Changes

Presbyopia is the most common, normal age-related vision change. The cornea (outer layer of the eye) tends to become denser and less elastic and yellows, making it hard to focus on near-vision tasks, typically resulting in the need for reading glasses. Furthermore, the pupil reduces in size, meaning that less light is processed and it is slower to accommodate changing light conditions. Thus, older adults increasingly need more light to accomplish the same tasks with each passing decade. Older adults also tend to have diminished contrast sensitivity, and colors appear to be less vivid. All of these normal changes can be accommodated by wearing eyeglasses or contact lenses, using additional lighting, and/or taking more time to allow the eyes to adjust to changing light conditions.

Common Age-Related Eye Disorders

An individual's visual function is affected differently by various eye disorders, specifically causing overall blur, central vision loss, and/or peripheral field loss. Low vision refers to situations in which the impairments caused by eye disorders cannot be corrected by refraction, medical, or surgical interventions.

Cataract, the most common age-related eye disorder, causes overall blur. Cataract causes a clouding of the lens, and as the lens darkens it makes visual tasks difficult to perform. Fortunately, cataract extraction with an intraocular lens implant is a highly successful procedure that restores visual function for those who are able to have the surgical procedure.

Diabetic retinopathy, one of the potential complications of long-term diabetes, creates overall hazy, splotchy, or distorted vision. It is caused by leaking blood vessels in the eye that can be sealed by laser treatment. However, scar tissue forms at the point of the laser intervention and blocks vision in that part of the retina. Persons with diabetes may report fluctuating vision at various times of the day due to unstable blood sugar levels.

Age-related macular degeneration (AMD) affects one's central vision and is the leading cause of vision impairment in older adults in the United States. A scotoma (blind spot) blocks the central field of view, making reading, writing, recognizing faces, or any other near-distance task very difficult. There are two types of AMD, "wet" and "dry," with the latter accounting for 90% of the cases. The dry form has a gradual onset and course, and although it may start in one eye, both eyes will be affected. The wet form is due to leaking blood vessels beneath the retina and may be sudden and severe. There is no cure for either type of AMD, but there are recent treatments that are becoming available for both types.

Glaucoma is the most common age-related vision disorder causing peripheral field loss. Glaucoma gradually destroys the cells of the optic nerve. Although the cause remains unknown, medications, laser treatments, and/or surgery can be used to slow or arrest the progression of the disease. This type of field loss affects safe mobility in the home and community, but it leaves the near tasks of reading and writing intact.

A stroke or head trauma can result in hemianopia, which is vision loss in half of the visual field. It could be the right, left, upper, or lower half of the visual field. Regardless of location, half of the visual field in both eyes is blocked, making all visual tasks difficult and making rehabilitation essential to accommodate the loss.

Consequences of Age-Related Vision Impairment

Recent research has underscored that age-related vision impairment can have profound consequences for older adults that span functional, psychological, and health-related domains of everyday life. The relationship between vision loss and functional disability during later life has been well established. Vision impairment is independently associated with concurrent disability in activities of daily living (ADLs) and also is a significant predictor of future functional decline. These relationships have been documented both in community-based populations and among older adults in nursing homes. Vision impairment also places older adults at greater risk for depression, with as many as one third found to experience significant depressive symptomatology, a proportion that is greater than that among the general population of older people in the community and that is equal to or greater than the prevalence of depression among other groups of medically ill older adults. Similar to other medical conditions, the experience and severity of depression are generally not related to objective indicators of the severity of the disease (e.g., poorer visual acuity and/or fields); rather, they are related to the subjective assessment of the vision loss and its perceived functional consequences.

At the same time, personal resources (e.g., coping strategies) and social resources (e.g., perceived availability and adequacy of informal support) have been found to mediate the relationship between vision impairment severity and depression. There is also recent research suggesting that rates of anxiety symptoms and disorders are similarly high, affecting between one quarter and one third of older adults with vision impairments.

There is emerging evidence pointing to significant consequences of vision impairment in terms of health services use, secondary health conditions, and mortality. Specifically, vision impairment, as measured by both clinical indicators and self-report, has been found to place older adults at greater risk for falls and hip fractures. Vision impairment has been associated with increased length of hospital stays, higher number of physician visits, and greater use of emergency room services. Finally, several studies have found that vision impairment is associated with increased risk of mortality among older adults.

Vision Rehabilitation

Specially trained professionals provide vision rehabilitation services in settings that include hospitals, vision rehabilitation organizations, private optometric and ophthalmologic practices, and university facilities. Low vision specialists are optometrists or ophthalmologists who have specialized training in the assessment of remaining functional vision. They prescribe optical devices such as magnifiers, telescopic lenses, and other adaptive aids including computer technology to maximize usual residual vision. Learning compensatory methods to accomplish ADLs, function in the workplace, participate in social activities, and travel safely both inside and outside the home is an important component of vision rehabilitation. These skills are taught by vision rehabilitation therapists, orientation and mobility instructors, and occupational therapists with specialized training in vision rehabilitation. Counseling and/or psychotherapy are often important components to aid in the emotional adjustment to vision loss. The goal of any vision rehabilitation intervention is to maximize functional independence and prevent excess disability for the individual experiencing vision impairment. Although there is currently only a limited research literature on the effects of vision rehabilitation for older adults, recent studies point to the efficacy of these services in maximizing functional ability and slowing functional decline. Unfortunately, knowledge about vision rehabilitation is limited in the general community as well as among aging and vision care professionals, and so many older adults do not access these services. A resource for locating "Help Near You" vision rehabilitation services can be found on a relatively recent website (www.visionconnection.org) created by Lighthouse International.

—*Amy Horowitz and Cynthia Stuen*

See also Eye Diseases

Further Readings and References

Burmedi D, Becker S, Heyl V, Wahl H-W, Himmelsbach I. Behavioral consequences of age-related low vision: A narrative review. *Vision Impair Res.* 2002;4(1):15–45.

Burmedi D, Becker S, Heyl V, Wahl H-W, Himmelsbach I. Emotional and social consequences of age-related low vision. *Visual Impair Res.* 2002;4(1):47–71.

Horowitz A, Brennan M, Reinhardt JP. Prevalence and risk factors for self-reported vision impairment among middle-age and older adults. *Res Aging.* 2005;27:307–326.

Horowitz A, Reinhardt JP. Mental health issues in visual impairment: Research in depression, disability, and rehabilitation. In: Silverstone BM, Lang M, Rosenthal R, Faye E, eds. *The Lighthouse Handbook on Vision Impairment and Vision Rehabilitation,* Vol. 2: *Vision Rehabilitation.* New York: Oxford University Press; 2000:1089–1109.

Horowitz A, Stuen C, eds. Aging and the senses. *Generations.* 2003;27(1).

Prevent Blindness America. Vision problems in the U.S. Available at: www.preventblindness.org/vpus/vp.html. Accessed October 5, 2006.

Reuben DB, Silbey M, Damesyn M, Moore AA. The prognostic value of sensory impairment in older persons. *J Am Geriatr Soc.* 1999;47:930–935.

VITAMINS, MINERALS, AND DIETARY SUPPLEMENTS

Vitamin, mineral, and non-nutrient dietary supplements are widely used but vary in their safety and efficacy. Issues include the high requirements for calcium and Vitamin D, the need for crystalline Vitamin B12, the possible health benefits of Vitamin E and fish oils, and drug nutrient interactions with Vitamin K. Older people should discuss their need for, and use of, supplements with their physicians rather than self-prescribe.

Multivitamin/Minerals

A multivitamin/mineral supplement does not have direct health benefits, but it will increase the likelihood of meeting the requirements for most vitamins and minerals. Supplements marketed to older adults are preferred because they are usually higher in Vitamin B12, and lower in Vitamin K and iron, than are other supplements. No more than one tablet should be taken daily.

Calcium and Vitamin D

Calcium and Vitamin D are required for bone health and possibly for prevention and management of many age-related disorders. Older people need 1,200 milligrams (mg) of calcium and 1,000 international units (IU) of Vitamin D daily. Vitamin D-fortified milk is the richest food source, with 300 mg of calcium and 100 IU of Vitamin D per cup. In the United States, milk intake is one to two cups daily (or less for some ethnic groups). Thus, most older people need supplements of these nutrients but should not exceed the upper levels (2,500 mg for calcium and 2,000 IU for Vitamin D).

Vitamin B12

Vitamin B12 is necessary for the brain, other nervous tissue, and red cell development. Approximately 5% to 15% of older people are Vitamin B12 deficient. Digestion of protein-bound Vitamin B12, but not crystalline Vitamin B12, is impaired by atrophic gastritis (affecting up to 30% of older people) and antacids. So, older people should consume crystalline Vitamin B12 from fortified foods or supplements. Although the recommended dietary allowance (RDA) is 2.4 micrograms (mcg), several studies show that at least 12 mcg of crystalline Vitamin B12 daily helps to prevent Vitamin B12 deficiency. Supplements marketed to older adults often contain 12 to 50 mcg—levels considered to be safe. Those diagnosed with Vitamin B12 deficiency need high amounts provided orally (500 to 2,000 mcg per day) or intramuscularly (1,000 mcg per month).

Vitamin E

Vitamin E is an antioxidant with many other cellular functions. The health benefits of the different chemical forms in foods are not entirely known, so consumption of Vitamin E–rich foods such as vegetable oils is recommended. The preferred chemical form in supplements is "d-alpha," which has the highest affinity for Vitamin E transporters in the body. Average consumption from foods is only approximately half of the RDA. There may be health benefits to consuming 200 to 400 IU, which is far above the RDA and well below the upper level of 1,000 IU. These intakes of Vitamin E maximize blood concentrations and have been associated with improved immune function in some studies. A few studies also have suggested that high intakes may slow the progression of dementia. Physician supervision of high intakes of Vitamin E is prudent because of concerns about increased risk of bleeding.

Fish Oils

Fish and fish oil supplements contain omega-3 fatty acids, show strong evidence for lowering the risk of cardiovascular disease, and show emerging evidence of benefits for brain and joint health. A weekly intake of 8 ounces of fatty fish, such as salmon, trout, and herring, is recommended. Those who do not eat fish should consider taking 1 to 3 grams of fish oil daily. It is not yet clear whether plant sources of omega-3 fats have the same health benefits as do those from fish.

Vitamin K

Vitamin K is found mainly in green vegetables and vegetable oils, is well known for its role in blood clotting, and is needed for skeletal and cardiovascular health. The RDAs are 120 mcg for men and 90 mcg for women, and there is no upper level. High and/or variable intakes of Vitamin K may interfere with blood-thinning medications (e.g., warfarin [Coumadin]). One serving of green vegetables (½ cup cooked vegetables or 1 cup raw leafy greens) daily is recommended to help meet Vitamin K requirements. Those taking blood thinners should eat the same amount of green vegetables each day but should not completely avoid Vitamin K because doing so may cause Vitamin K deficiency and/or a high sensitivity to Vitamin K-containing foods and supplements.

Non-Nutrient Supplements

Few non-nutrient, or "herbal," supplements have been reviewed systematically for safety and efficacy, for example, by the Agency for Healthcare Research and

Quality or the Cochrane Review System. Such reviews show that glucosamine is both effective and safe for relieving some symptoms of osteoarthritis, St. John's wort may be effective for short-term treatment of mild to moderately severe depressive disorders, *Ginkgo biloba* may modestly improve cognition and function in those with cognitive impairment or dementia, and garlic modestly improves blood lipid profiles but has little effect on other indexes of cardiovascular health or cancer. Non-nutrient supplements may interact with medications. For example, garlic, *G. biloba,* echinacea, ginseng, St. John's wort, and kava are of concern, especially regarding interactions with anticancer drugs and blood thinners.

Recommendations

Individuals should discuss their use of, and need for, supplements with their physicians; consider interactions with prescribed medications; avoid self-prescribing; buy name brands or store bands from a trusted source such as a local pharmacy or grocery store; and avoid buying on the Internet. Those choosing to take nutrient supplements should take close to 100% of the daily value for most nutrients. Multivitamin/mineral supplements generally do not provide adequate calcium and Vitamin D, so additional supplements of these nutrients are needed for most people. Assuming a typical intake of 1 cup of Vitamin D–fortified milk daily, the following supplements may offer health benefits: one multivitamin/mineral formulated for older adults with 400 IU of Vitamin D and at least 12 mcg of Vitamin B12, additional calcium supplements to provide 500 to 600 mg of calcium, additional Vitamin D supplements to provide approximately 800 IU of Vitamin D (e.g., two 400-IU tablets, one 1,000-IU tablet), between 200 and 400 IU of Vitamin E in the d-alpha form, and (for those who do not eat fish) additional supplements of 1 to 3 grams of fish oil. High-dose antioxidant supplements are not warranted at this time for prevention of cancer or heart disease. Caution should be used with non-nutrient herbal supplements, and they should be discontinued before surgery because several may promote bleeding and interfere with other aspects of surgery and recovery.

—Mary Ann Johnson

See also Nutrition and Public Health; Nutrition, Malnutrition, and Feeding Issues

Further Readings and References

Johnson MA. Hype and hope about foods and supplements for healthy aging. *Generations.* 2004;8(3):45–53.

Johnson MA. Nutrition and aging: Practical advice for healthy eating. *J Am Med Women's Assoc.* 2004;59: 262–269.

Johnson MA. Influence of Vitamin K on anticoagulant therapy depends on Vitamin K status and the source and chemical forms of Vitamin K. *Nutr Rev.* 2005; 63(3):91–97.

National Institutes of Health/Office of Dietary Supplements. ODS website. Available at: http://ods.od.nih.gov. Accessed October 5, 2006.

U.S. Food and Drug Administration/Center for Food Safety and Applied Nutrition. Are there any risks, especially to older consumers? Available at: www.cfsan.fda.gov/~dms/ds-savv2.html#risks. Accessed October 5, 2006.

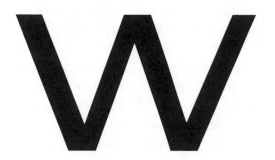

WANDERING

See BEHAVIORAL DISORDERS IN DEMENTIA

WIDOWHOOD

See BEREAVEMENT AND GRIEF; MARITAL STATUS

WOMEN'S HEALTH

Women outnumber men in the U.S. geriatric population. Currently, approximately 40 million Americans are postmenopausal women, with a projected increase to 60 million by 2030, when one in four women will be over 65 years of age. Fully 66% of all 85-year-olds are women, and women make up 85% of all nursing home residents. Of the approximately 32 million elderly Medicare beneficiaries, 19 million are women. Therefore, by default, geriatric medicine is a specialty concerned predominantly with the health of older women. A thorough understanding of this topic is important for all who care for older adults.

Appreciating principal causes of mortality is the first step to better understanding. Coronary heart disease is the leading cause of death for American women; one in five women is affected by some form of the disease. In 2001, 498,900 women died from heart attacks and other coronary events, comprising 53.6% of all coronary deaths that year. Unfortunately, many women remain unaware of their heart disease risk, considering it a primarily "male" disease. Public awareness campaigns are under way to help change this misconception. Cancer is the second leading cause of death, and stroke is the third, in women over 65 years of age.

Screening and preventive medicine remain important components of comprehensive health care as a woman ages. The U.S. Preventive Services Task Force (USPSTF) recommends annual mammography and clinical breast exams to at least 70 years of age and potentially thereafter if a woman has a reasonable life expectancy at that point in her life. Pap smear testing can be stopped in most women by 65 years of age if they have a single established sexual partner (or are abstinent), have had regular screening throughout their lifetime, and have no history of an abnormal Pap smear. Pelvic exams, however, should be continued annually as a screening measure for intrapelvic or vaginal abnormalities. Finally, the USPSTF recommends bone densitometry at least once for all women age 65 years and older.

Women undergo predictable physiological changes as they age. On average, menopause begins at 51 years, after which estrogen levels drop precipitously. Estrogen target organs, such as the vagina, uterus, cervix, and oviducts, undergo atrophy in the low-estrogen environment. Vaginal atrophy results in decreased vaginal secretions, wall thinning, and greater susceptibility to infection. Resultant vaginal dryness can lead to painful sexual intercourse and decreased libido. Menopause-related skin changes in collagen synthesis and hair distribution cause decreased skin elasticity and increased prominence of coarse facial hair. Loss of estrogen receptor stimulation in the bladder wall leads to decreased bladder muscle tone, which can exacerbate urinary frequency and incontinence. Following menopause, levels of total and low-density lipoprotein cholesterol and triglycerides increase, whereas levels of high-density lipoprotein decrease. This results in a lipid profile of increased risk, and rates of myocardial infarction and stroke amplify. The relationship between the loss of estrogen and cognitive dysfunction remains unclear.

Hormone replacement therapy has been used to help mitigate some of these physiological changes, but its role in menopause has changed dramatically over the past 10 years. In 2002, the Women's Health Initiative (WHI), a large nationwide randomized controlled trial of conjugated estrogen and medroxyprogesterone versus placebo therapy, stopped prematurely after an average of 5.2 years of follow-up due to increased risks of coronary heart disease, stroke, venous thromboembolism, and breast cancer in the population receiving hormonal therapy. However, the absolute risk of an adverse event in a woman on hormonal therapy remained very low (19 additional events per year per 10,000 women). Fracture and colon cancer rates were reduced in the treated group, but those who did develop colon cancer had more aggressive tumors. As a result of the WHI findings, hormone replacement therapy's primary indication is now one of perimenopausal symptom control, with therapy used for the shortest duration possible. Because systemic absorption is negligible at appropriate doses, local vaginal estrogen therapy remains an acceptable long-term therapeutic option for many women with atrophic vaginitis or other postmenopausal genitourinary conditions.

With normal aging comes a markedly increased risk of urinary incontinence. Prevalence of urinary incontinence in elderly women ranges from 35% to 45%. Women with histories of vaginal delivery are 2.5 times more likely to report incontinence than are nulliparous women. Estrogen loss at menopause leads to changes in urogenital tissues, significantly increasing the risk of urge, stress, and mixed incontinence. In some women, medical treatments, including vaginal estrogen, can be effective as the sole therapy. However, because the etiology of urinary incontinence is usually multifactorial, lone medical therapy might not be enough to control symptoms adequately. Constipation, poor mobility, dementia, medications, and many other factors can contribute to urinary incontinence, especially in the frail elderly. As such, a multipronged therapeutic approach (e.g., Kegel exercises, pessaries, medication review, bladder retraining, scheduled toileting, constipation therapies, mobility enhancement, [sometimes] surgery) is usually the most effective.

Osteoporosis is also a common consequence of the physiological changes of aging in women. Women's peak bone mass is maintained until their mid-30s, when gradual loss of bone density begins. This loss accelerates rapidly at menopause. Estrogen is critical in the bone remodeling process. Loss of estrogen, either via premenopausal oophorectomy (surgical removal of the ovaries) or at menopause, leads to an imbalance in bone remodeling with resultant decreases in bone mineral density. Other risk factors for osteoporosis are known, but in women estrogen loss is likely the most significant. Estrogen replacement therapy is effective in increasing bone density. However, given the known risks of hormonal therapy and the availability of other effective agents, specifically bisphosphonates, estrogen is no longer the first-line agent for osteoporosis treatment.

Dementia risk also increases as women age. Approximately 5% of American women over 60 years of age have dementia. This figure rises to 12% after 75 years and to 28% after 85 years. The risk of dementia is higher and the average life span is longer in women than in men. As such, considerable study of female-specific dementia therapies has been undertaken. Estrogen receptors are found throughout the brain. The memory-critical cholinergic system is enhanced by estrogen. Cohort studies examining estrogen therapy and dementia risk initially raised hopes that estrogen therapy would be beneficial in preventing dementia. However, more recent data from the cognitive dysfunction arm of the WHI, the WHI Memory Study, showed that combination estrogen–progesterone therapy in women over 65 years of age increased the risk of developing dementia. Another group in this study treated with estrogen alone showed neither protective benefit nor increased risk. As a result, hormonal therapy is no longer recommended for dementia prevention. Cholinesterase inhibitors remain first-line dementia treatment in both women and men.

Depression is a common, but underrecognized, condition of older women. Women are twice as likely as men to experience major depression. Decreased estrogen levels may be associated with depressed mood. In some women, social factors and transitions may exacerbate depression. It is common for social supports to change or fall away as women age. Fully 70% of women over 75 years of age are widows. Depression symptoms are associated directly with increased mortality, especially cardiovascular deaths. Unfortunately, depression is not the only underrecognized issue in older women's health.

Older women experience many unrecognized social and systematic inequities. Despite the fact that women comprise the overwhelming majority of the geriatric population and make up the most common population in geriatric practice, most studies of geriatric diseases have been conducted in predominantly male populations. For example, even though women experience congestive heart failure (CHF) at rates surpassing those of men, most CHF studies not only have been done in predominantly male populations but also have focused on a type of CHF found more often in men than in women. Efforts are under way to increase the number of women in clinical trials. Financial discrepancies exist as well. In 1993, the median annual income of an older man living alone was $14,983, whereas it was $8,499 for a single older woman. The discrepancies are even more pronounced for minority elderly women. In 1998, 54% of nonmarried Black women over 65 years of age and 61% of elderly Hispanic women had incomes below the poverty line. In Medicare patients, three of the four most common illnesses with the highest out-of-pocket costs (e.g., arthritis) are more common in women than in men. In addition, studies in 1996 and 1997 found that, on average, Medicare reimbursed male-specific procedures at

rates 44% higher than those for comparable female-specific procedures.

In summary, older women's health is an important topic encompassing multiple epidemiological, biological, and social aspects of medical care. It is the major focus of geriatric practice. Older women not only experience diseases specific to females but also experience common diseases in unique ways. Increased attention to gender-specific research is needed to help further knowledge in this area. Disparities in income and financial structures continue to abound. Improved awareness of these disparities may help spark efforts to improve both the quality of life and the quality of medical care for elderly women in America.

—*Amy Jo Haavisto Kind and Molly Carnes*

See also Alzheimer's Disease; Depression and Other Mood Disorders; Economics of Aging; Incontinence; Menopause and Hormone Therapy; Osteoporosis

Further Readings and References

Butler RN. On behalf of older women: Another reason to protect Medicare and Medicaid. *N Engl J Med.* 1996;334:794–796.

Craig MC, Maki PM, Murphy DG. The Women's Health Initiative Memory Study: Findings and implications for treatment. *Lancet Neurol.* 2005;4:190–194.

U.S. Department of Health and Human Services/Office on Women's Health. Office on Women's Health website. Available at: www.4woman.gov/owh/older.htm. Accessed October 5, 2006.

Wise PM. The female reproductive system. In: Timiras PS, ed. *Physiological Basis of Aging and Geriatrics.* 3rd ed. Boca Raton, Fla: CRC Press; 2003:189–211.

Writing Group for the Women's Health Initiative Investigators. Risks and benefits of estrogen plus progestin in healthy postmenopausal women: Principal results from the Women's Health Initiative randomized controlled trial. *JAMA.* 2002;288:321–333.

WORK, HEALTH, AND RETIREMENT

The relationships among work, health, and retirement are instances of the more general association between individual capacity and role performance. Occupational and economic roles, including leisure consumption, want healthy capable occupants. Individuals, for their part, favor roles that conserve physical and emotional well-being. Health, therefore, figures significantly in the allocation processes that operate to convert cohorts of older workers into retirees.

The two major empirical questions in this area are, first, how health affects the decision to work or retire and, second, how retirement affects health. Research findings about these matters might not always be consistent because the definition of the two main constructs—health and retirement—can vary considerably across research designs. Health can be measured by objective or subjective indicators and as physical or mental status. Retirement can be a full or partial withdrawal from work (paid employment) and occasionally plays out as a series of transitions. To further complicate matters, the nature of jobs and the labor market changes over time, as does the composition of the older worker cohort, and thus the question of work, health, and retirement merits periodic reappraisal.

Before Retirement

Retirement as it is now understood—as pensioned leisure—is not widely available to workers until national governments can organize social security programs and tax incentives that marshal replacement income as an inducement to leave the labor force. In the United States, this had occurred by the mid-20th century. Prior to this time, people who could not self-finance their retirements were prone to work until their health no longer permitted such activity. In the modern welfare state, workers can now exit the labor force voluntarily at ages far in advance of likely disability or death.

Yet health still limits the productive careers of some workers when they find themselves unable to perform on the job. Approximately 20% to 30% of retirements involve ill health or disability as the primary reason for retirement. Moreover, health is probably implicated in an even greater share of job exits; for example, when employers discourage older workers who are believed to lack productive capacity. Laws against age discrimination have largely eliminated mandatory retirement on the basis of age, yet some workers still face age limits on employment because certain occupations are legally deemed to be too strenuous or cognitively demanding past a certain age (e.g., commercial airline pilots, police officers, firefighters).

Health and the means to maintain it figure into retirement in other ways. Some workers are motivated to retire out of a desire to preserve their health or enjoy retirement "while they can." The timing of retirement can also hinge on the continued availability of employer-sponsored health insurance prior to the Medicare eligibility age of 65 years. Because working couples collaborate in timing their exits, the health issues of one spouse can influence the retirement decision of the other spouse.

Even as impaired health—actual or anticipated—can limit work careers, sustained good health can extend working life in a labor market that includes more service, retail, and part-time jobs. Although the average American worker retires prior to 65 years of age, substantial numbers still work into later life. At 70 to 74 years of age, nearly 20% of men and more than 10% of women are still in the labor force on a part-time or full-time basis.

After Retirement

Because disability and impairments can prompt retirement, when groups of workers and retired age peers are compared with each other, the retirees will, on average, appear to be less healthy. This observation may have given rise to a common idea that retirement puts workers at risk for declining health. In addition, if working is believed to be crucial to one's identity and self-fulfillment, retirement would seem to be a perilous step.

However, epidemiological studies have shown reliably that occupational retirement does not generally raise the risk of mortality or decline in physical and mental health. In fact, there are suggestions that, if anything, retirement benefits health somewhat. Such studies are more conclusive when they follow continuing workers and new retirees over time while taking into account ill health as a reason for having retired in the first place. The absence of an average adverse effect of retirement on health nevertheless admits the possibility of circumstances (e.g., involuntary retirement, income loss) that are distressing to the point of dysphoria and illness, but such outcomes are not common. Whereas a minority of exiting workers may be vulnerable to emotional upset, contemporary surveys show that a large percentage of men and women alike express satisfaction with retirement. Because retirement is now a normative transition of the life course, workers can anticipate and prepare for it while drawing on the experience of earlier retirees, easing its potential as a stressful life event.

Would the health of individuals be better served by working or being retired? This question is not answered easily. Advocates can tout the tonic qualities of work or the salutary features of retirement leisure, yet so long as retirement is a voluntary step, it is well to remember that people tend to elect the work or retirement status that is congenial to them.

Finally, if retirement is viewed as a stage of life, health also shapes people's views about when that stage ends. Some regard retirement as a "third age" of life—free from work and devoted to personal fulfillment—that presumes a capacity to function independently. When debility curtails one's accustomed leisure pursuits, the retirement stage makes way for a "fourth age" of dependence, frailty, and death. Thus, health enables the retirement lifestyle, just as it enables work careers.

—David J. Ekerdt

See also Disability and the Disablement Process; Positive Attitudes and Health; Social Networks and Social Support

Further Readings and References

Charles KK. Is retirement depressing? Labor force inactivity and psychological well-being in later life. *Res Labor Econ.* 2004;23:269–299.

Costa DL. *The Evolution of Retirement: An Economic History.* Chicago: University of Chicago Press; 1998.

Kasl SV, Jones BA. The impact of job loss and retirement on health. In: Berkman LF, Kawachi I, eds. *Social Epidemiology.* New York: Oxford University Press; 2000:118–136.

Weiss RS. *The Experience of Retirement.* Ithaca, NY: Cornell University Press; 2005.

WOUND HEALING

Older adults may experience negative changes in several aspects of the wound-healing process, including changes in the structure of the skin, in inflammatory responses, and in immunological regulation. Age-related changes in the structure of the skin contribute to delayed wound healing. Although the overall thickness of the epidermis changes little with age, there is increased unevenness due to more variability in the size, shape, and structure of keratinocytes—cells that produce keratin, which forms the outer layer of the epidermis. The rate of keratinocyte production and its migration to the skin surface—a critical feature of healing—decreases with age. Other age-related changes include decreases in soluble collagen and decreases in elasticity. These changes in skin structure contribute to inefficiency of wound healing with age and lead to increased risk of infection.

Aging is also related to changes in the inflammatory responses of healing, including delayed permeation of macrophages and lymphocytes into wounds and a decreased proliferative response by lymphocytes. Age-related changes in neuroendocrine function, including decreased production and secretion of human growth hormone (hGH) as well as decreased insulin-like growth factor 1 (IGF-1), may also contribute to slowing of the wound-healing process. However, aspects of wound healing may be enhanced by age-related changes, including increased secretion of leukocytes and a heightened inflammatory response.

Wound healing among older adult caregivers of persons with dementia is significantly slower than wound healing among age-matched controls due to immunological dysregulation associated with the chronic psychological stress of caregiving. In the absence of stress or immune dysregulation, production of cytokines increases early during the process of wound healing and then diminishes over time. Stress-induced elevations in glucocorticoids may inhibit fibroblast growth and cytokine production, and this then contributes to delayed wound healing. Stress-related elevations in cortisol are associated with suppressed cytokine production. In turn, suppressed cytokine production among stressed older adults has been associated with significant delays in wound healing, and lower levels of proinflammatory cytokines have been found at the wound sites of middle-aged and older women with higher levels of self-reported stress. Thus, psychological stress appears to interact with age to promote immune down-regulation, and this may contribute to delayed wound healing.

Behavioral factors that are more common among older adults, such as sedentary behavior and poor nutrient intake, may impair wound healing by delaying the inflammatory response. Recent research suggests that increased physical exercise may have a positive effect on wound healing among healthy older adults. Behavioral interventions that improve nutritional status or reduce stress (e.g., relaxation, stress management) may have future applications for enhancing wound healing among older adults.

—Charles F. Emery
and Jamie L. Jackson

See also Immune Function; Infectious Diseases; Skin Changes; Stress; Venous Stasis Ulcers

Further Readings and References

Gosain A, DiPietro LA. Aging and wound healing. *World J Surg.* 2004;28:321–326.

Kiecolt-Glaser JK, Glaser R. Psychological stress and wound healing: Kiecolt–Glaser et al. (1995). *Adv Mind–Body Med.* 2001;17:15–16.

Thomas DR. Age-related changes in wound healing. *Drugs Aging.* 2001;18:607–620.

Appendix

Online Resources and Health and Aging Organizations

Agency for Healthcare Research and Quality
www.ahcpr.gov

The Agency for Healthcare Research and Quality (AHRQ) supports health services research that will improve the quality of health care and promote evidence-based medicine and decision making. The AHRQ is one of 12 agencies within the Department of Health and Human Services. It is the lead agency charged with improving the quality, safety, efficiency, and effectiveness of health care for all Americans.

Alzheimer's Association
www.alz.org

The Alzheimer's Association is the first and largest voluntary health organization dedicated to finding prevention methods, treatments, and (eventually) a cure for Alzheimer's disease. It is the world leader in Alzheimer's research and support.

Alzheimer's Disease Education and Referral Center
www.nia.nih.gov/alzheimers

The Alzheimer's Disease Education and Referral (ADEAR) Center website is designed to provide current, comprehensive Alzheimer's disease information and resources from the National Institute on Aging.

American Academy of Nursing
www.nursingworld.org/aan

The American Academy of Nursing (AAN) is dedicated to serving both the public and the nursing profession by advancing health policy and practice through the generation, synthesis, and dissemination of nursing knowledge.

American Association for Geriatric Psychiatry
www.aagpgpa.org

The American Association for Geriatric Psychiatry (AAGP) is a nationwide association representing and serving its members and the field of geriatric psychiatry. The AAGP is committed to promoting the mental health and well-being of older people and improving the care of those with late-life mental disorders. The AAGP's mission is to further the knowledge base and standard of practice in geriatric psychiatry through education and research and to advocate for meeting the mental health needs of older Americans.

American Association of Colleges of Nursing
www.aacn.nche.edu

The American Association of Colleges of Nursing's (AACN) educational, research, data collection, governmental advocacy, publications, and other programs work to establish quality standards for bachelor's and graduate degree nursing education. The AACN assists deans and directors with implementing those standards, influences the nursing profession to improve health care, and promotes public support of baccalaureate and graduate education, research, and practice in nursing.

American Association of Retired Persons
www.aarp.org

The American Association of Retired Persons (AARP) is the leading nonprofit, nonpartisan membership organization for people age 50 years and older in the United States. The AARP has more than 35 million members. The group is known for providing a host of services to this ever-growing segment of the population.

American Association of Retired Persons International Section

www.aarp.org/international

The International Section of the American Association of Retired Persons (AARP) website addresses global aging issues through the Global Aging Program. The program aims to help people live longer, healthier, more financially secure, and productive lives by identifying the best ideas and practices on key policy issues. The section convenes international opinion leaders and policymakers to share their expertise and develops research on health and long-term care, livable communities, older workers, and retirement income.

American Cancer Society

www.cancer.org

The American Cancer Society (ACS) is a nationwide community-based volunteer health organization dedicated to eliminating cancer as a major health problem by saving lives, preventing cancer, and diminishing suffering from cancer through education, research, advocacy, and service.

American College of Preventive Medicine

www.acpm.org

The American College of Preventive Medicine (ACPM) is the national professional organization for physicians committed to preventing disease and promoting good health. The ACPM has approximately 2,000 members who are engaged in preventive medicine practice, teaching, and research. It was established in 1954.

American Counseling Association

www.counseling.org

The American Counseling Association (ACA) is a nonprofit professional and educational organization that is dedicated to the growth and enhancement of the counseling profession. The ACA is the world's largest association, exclusively representing professional counselors in various practice settings.

American Diabetes Association

www.diabetes.org

Founded in 1940, the American Diabetes Association (ADA) is the nation's leading nonprofit health organization, providing diabetes research, information, and advocacy. The ADA conducts programs in all 50 states, reaching hundreds of communities. Its goal is to prevent and cure diabetes as well as to improve the lives of all people affected by diabetes.

American Geriatrics Society

www.americangeriatrics.org

The American Geriatrics Society (AGS) is a not-for-profit national organization composed of geriatric health care professionals, researchers, and other concerned individuals. The AGS's mission is to improve the health, independence, and quality of life for all older people.

American Heart Association

www.americanheart.org

The American Heart Association is a national voluntary health organization whose mission is to reduce disability and death from cardiovascular diseases and stroke.

American Medical Association

www.ama-assn.org

On issues ranging from tobacco to adolescent health, and from AIDS to Medicare, the American Medical Association speaks out on issues important to patients and the nation's health.

American Psychiatric Association

www.psych.org

The American Psychiatric Association is a medical specialty society that is recognized throughout the world. With more than 35,000 U.S. and international member physicians, the association works to ensure humane care and effective treatment for all persons with mental disorder. It is the voice and conscience of modern psychiatry. Its vision is a society that has available, accessible, quality psychiatric diagnosis and treatment.

American Psychological Association

www.apa.org

The American Psychological Association (APA) is a scientific and professional organization that represents psychology in the United States. The APA is the largest association of psychologists worldwide, with more than 150,000 members.

American Society on Aging

www.asaging.org

The American Society on Aging (ASA) is the largest organization of professionals in the field of aging. The ASA's resources, publications, and educational opportunities are geared toward increasing the knowledge and skills of people working with older adults and their families.

Arthritis Foundation

www.arthritis.org

The Arthritis Foundation is a national not-for-profit organization that provides advocacy, programs, services, and research for the more than 100 types of arthritis and related conditions.

Centers for Disease Control and Prevention

www.cdc.gov

The Centers for Disease Control and Prevention (CDC) is one of the 13 major operating components of the Department of Health and Human Services. Since it was founded in 1946 to help control malaria, the CDC has remained at the forefront of public health efforts to prevent and control infectious and chronic diseases, injuries, workplace hazards, disabilities, and environmental health threats.

Centers for Medicare and Medicaid Services

www.cms.hhs.gov

The Centers for Medicare and Medicaid Services' (CMS) mission is to ensure health care security for beneficiaries. The CMS's vision is to serve beneficiaries by opening its programs to full partnership with the entire health community so as to improve quality and efficiency in an evolving health care system.

Centro Latinoamericano y Caribeno de Demografia/Envejecimiento y Desarrollo

www.eclac.cl/celade/envejecimiento

The Centro Latinoamericano y Caribeno de Demografia/ Envejecimiento y Desarrollo (CELADE) is the population section of the United Nations Economic Commission for Latin American and the Caribbean (CEPAL). The CELADE includes a section on regional information on aging. This website provides access to full-text documents, statistical data, and events. Site and texts are in Spanish.

Gerontological Society of America

www.geron.org

The mission of the Gerontological Society of America (GSA) is to provide researchers, educators, practitioners, and policymakers with opportunities to understand, advance, integrate, and use research on aging to improve the quality of life for aging persons. The GSA is a nonprofit association with more than 5,000 members in the field of aging.

Global Aging Initiative Program

www.csis.org/gai

The Center for Strategic and International Studies (CSIS) established the Global Aging Initiative (GAI) in 1999 to raise awareness of the scope and magnitude of the challenges of an aging world and to encourage timely reform. Since its inception, the GAI has pursued an ambitious educational agenda by organizing a half dozen major international conferences—in Beijing, Berlin, Brussels, Paris, Tokyo, Zurich, and Washington, D.C.—that have brought together world leaders to discuss common problems and explore common solutions.

HelpAge International

www.helpage.org

HelpAge International is a worldwide network of nonprofit organizations with a mission to work with, and for, disadvantaged older people worldwide to achieve a lasting improvement in the quality of their lives.

Hospice Foundation of America

www.hospicefoundation.org

The Hospice Foundation of America provides guidance in the development and relevance of hospice and its philosophy of care with the goal of enhancing the American health care system and the role of hospice within it.

International Association of Gerontology and Geriatrics

www.iagg.com.br

The International Association of Gerontology and Geriatrics (IAGG) is dedicated to promoting the highest levels of achievement of gerontological research and training worldwide and to interacting with other international, intergovernmental, and nongovernmental organizations in the promotion of gerontological interests globally. The IAGG promotes the highest quality of life and well-being of all people as they experience aging at individual and societal levels.

International Federation on Ageing

www.ifa-fiv.org/en/accueil.aspx

The International Federation on Ageing seeks to inform, educate, and promote policies and practice to improve the quality of life of older persons around the world.

International Psychogeriatric Association

www.ipa-online.net

The International Psychogeriatric Association (IPA) is a unique and diverse professional health care society promoting better geriatric mental health across disciplines, borders, and geriatric issues. The IPA was founded in 1982.

Meals on Wheels

www.mowaa.org

The Meals on Wheels Association of America (MOWAA) is the largest and oldest organization in the United States representing those who provide meal services to people in need.

National Alliance on Mental Illness

www.nami.org

The National Alliance on Mental Illness (NAMI) is the nation's largest grassroots mental health association dedicated to improving the lives of persons living with serious mental illness and their families. Started in 1979, the NAMI has become the nation's voice on mental illness and includes NAMI organizations in every state and in more than 1,100 local communities across the country whose members join together to meet the NAMI mission through advocacy, research, support, and education.

National Association of Computerized Data on Aging

www.icpsr.umich.edu/nacda

The National Association of Computerized Data on Aging's (NACDA) mission is to advance research on aging by helping researchers to profit from the underexploited potential of a broad range of data sets. The NACDA acquires and preserves data relevant to gerontological research, processes them as needed to support effective research use, disseminates them to researchers, and facilitates their use.

National Center for Complementary and Alternative Medicine

http://nccam.nih.gov

The National Center for Complementary and Alternative Medicine (NCCAM) is 1 of 27 institutes and centers that make up the National Institutes of Health. The NCCAM is committed to exploring complementary and alternative healing practices in the context of meticulous science, training complementary and alternative medicine researchers, and disseminating reliable information to the public and professionals.

National Center for Health Statistics

www.cdc.gov/nchs/default.htm

The National Center for Health Statistics (NCHS) website is a rich source of information about America's health. As the United States' principal health statistics agency, the NCHS gathers statistical information to guide actions and policies to improve the health of the nation's people. It is a unique public resource for health information and a critical element of public health and health policy.

National Council on Aging

www.ncoa.org

The National Council on Aging (NCOA) is dedicated to improving the health and independence of older persons and increasing their continuing contributions to communities, society, and future generations. The

NCOA was founded in 1950 and is a 501(c)3 organization located in Washington, D.C.

National Institute on Aging

www.nia.nih.gov

The National Institute on Aging (NIA) leads a broad scientific effort to understand the nature of aging and to extend the healthy active years of life. The NIA is one of the 27 institutes and centers of the National Institutes of Health. In 1974, Congress granted authority to form the NIA to provide leadership in aging research, training, health information dissemination, and other programs relevant to aging and older people. The NIA is now the primary federal agency designated to conduct Alzheimer's disease research.

National Library of Medicine

www.nlm.nih.gov

The National Library of Medicine (NLM) is the world's largest medical library. The NLM collects materials and provides information and research services in all areas of biomedicine and health care.

National Science Foundation

www.nsf.gov

An independent federal agency, the National Science Foundation (NSF) was created by Congress in 1950 "to promote the progress of science; to advance the national health, prosperity, and welfare; [and] to secure the national defense." The NSF is the funding source for approximately 20% of all federally supported basic research conducted by America's colleges and universities with an annual budget of roughly $5.5 billion.

NIHSeniorHealth.gov

http://nihseniorhealth.gov

NIHSeniorHealth.gov features authoritative and up-to-date health information from centers and institutes of the National Institutes of Health. In addition, the American Geriatrics Society provides independent reviews of some of the material found on this website. Each health topic includes general background information, open-captioned videos, quizzes, and frequently asked questions. New topics are added to the site on a regular basis.

Parkinson's Disease Foundation

www.pdf.org

The Parkinson's Disease Foundation (PDF) is a leading national presence in Parkinson's disease research, public advocacy, and patient education. The PDF works for the nearly 1 million people in the United States living with Parkinson's disease by funding hopeful scientific research and supporting people with Parkinson's, their families, and their caregivers through educational programs and support services.

Red de Investigación del Envejecimiento en América Latina y el Caribe

www.realce.org

The Red de Investigación del Envejecimiento en América Latina y el Caribe (REALCE) was formed by a group of researchers seeking to enhance all aspects of research about the social, economic, health, well-being, and quality of life aspects of the process of population aging in Latin America and the Caribbean region. The REALCE seeks to maximize the research capacity in the region through dissemination of research news such as research findings, ongoing studies, available data and how to obtain them, upcoming conferences and similar professional events, study findings, and training opportunities.

United Nations Program on Ageing

www.un.org/esa/socdev/ageing

The objective of the United Nations is to contribute to the creation of an international community that enables the building of secure, just, free, and harmonious societies offering opportunities and higher standards of living for all. The United Nations Program on Ageing website contains the United Nations programs and policies pertinent to global aging.

U.S. Census Bureau

www.census.gov

First gathered in 1790 on horseback, the U.S. Census is one of the oldest regular activities in the United States. The sole purpose of the census and is to collect general statistical information from individuals and establishments so as to compile statistics.

U.S. Social Security Administration

www.ssa.gov

The U.S. Social Security Administration (SSA) pays retirement, disability, and survivors benefits to workers and their families and also administers the Supplemental Security Income program. The SSA also issues Social Security numbers.

World Health Organization

www.who.int/en

The World Health Organization (WHO) was established in 1948 and is the United Nations specialized agency for health. The WHO's objective is the attainment by all peoples of the highest possible level of health. Health is defined in WHO's constitution as a state of complete physical, mental, and social well-being and not merely the absence of disease or infirmity.

Index

Dynamic equilibrium theory, 114
Dyslipidemia, 148, 151, 434
Dyspnea, 44, 116

Ear diseases, 173–176
   age-related changes and, 173–174
   air conduction measures and, 175
   arthritis and, 174
   bone conduction measures and, 175
   central nervous system, neuronal degeneration and, 174
   cerumen production and, 173, 175
   cochler presbycusis and, 174
   communication losses and, 173
   drug history and, 175
   functional assessment of, 175
   hearing devices and, 176
   hearing loss management, 175–176
   inner ear hearing loss, 174
   middle ear aging changes, 173–174
   neural presbycusis and, 174
   nutritional intake and, 174
   otoscopic examination and, 175
   outer ear carcinomas, 173
   physical examination and, 175
   presbycusis, diagnosis of, 174–175
   presbycusis, types of, 174
   prevalence of, 173
   Rinne and Weber tests, 175
   risk factors for, 173, 174
   sensory presbycusis and, 174
   speech discrimination and, 174
   strial presbycusis and, 174
   See also Hearing; Quality of life
Early adversity and late-life health, 176–178
   adverse social environments and, 178
   ascribed adverse social status and, 177
   diminished psychological resources and, 178
   disadvantaged communities and, 177, 178
   discriminatory practices and, 177
   family structural difficulties and, 177
   historical adverse circumstances and, 177
   inadequate health care/proper nutrition and, 177–178
   intergenerational transmission of health risk
      behaviors/lifestyles and, 178
   life course compounding of early adversities, 176
   mental/physical health status and, 176
   negative emotions and, 178
   parental educational attainment and, 177
   parenting adequacy levels and, 177, 178
   physical-mental health relationship and, 178
   social adversity, mental illness and, 178
   social adversity, physical illness and, 177–178
   socioeconomic status, early adversity and, 176–177
   stressful daily experiences and, 178
   See also Demography of aging; Life course perspective on adult
      development; Successful aging
East Baltimore Mental Health Survey, 138
East Boston Senior Health Project, 198, 199
Eating disorders. *See* **Nutrition, malnutrition,
      and feeding issues**
Echinacea, 577
Echocardiography, 116
Economics of aging, 179–185

   baby boomers and, 182–183
   cost-of-living adjustments, 180
   current elderly populations, economic status of, 180–182
   Disability Insurance program, 180
   disaggregated data on, 181, 182, 182 (figure)
   future prospects for economic security, 182–185
   health care costs and, 184–185
   long-term care expenditures, 184–185, 184 (table)
   Medicaid/Medicare and, 180, 184, 184 (table)
   nursing facilities and, 307–308
   poverty thresholds and, 180–181, 183
   private pension programs, 179, 180, 183–184
   reform of Social Security provision, 180
   replacement rate for retirement income, 183
   retirement income support system and, 179–180
   social insurance, 180
   Social Security income and, 179–180, 181 (table), 182, 183
   sources of income, relative importance
      of, 181–182, 181 (table)
   spending down for Medicaid, 26, 308, 345, 350
   Supplemental Security Income and, 180, 349
   welfare, 179, 180
   See also Critical perspectives in gerontology;
      Health and public policy; Homelessness and health
      in the United States; Long-term care (LTC); Long-term care
      (LTC) insurance; Managed care; Medicaid; Medicare;
      Socioeconomic status (SES); Work, health, and retirement
Edema, 106
   bone marrow edema, 398
   congestive heart failure and, 116
   diuretics and, 224
   peripheral edema, 116
   pulmonary edema, 116
   valvular heart disease and, 568
   venous stasis ulcers and, 572
   volume overload, older patients and, 221
Eden Alternative nursing home model, 462
Education and health, 185–187
   active life expectancy and, 186
   age-associated medical conditions/disability and, 186
   allostatic load and, 34
   arthritis incidence, 52
   centenarians and, 108
   credential approach to analysis, 186–187
   early adversity, health effects and, 177
   economic returns on education, non-uniformity of, 187
   employment opportunities/earnings and, 185
   exercise/physical activity and, 213
   frailty and, 230
   higher education levels, human capital development and, 186
   life course perspective and, 185
   mortality patterns and, 185–186
   quality/selectivity aspects of education, 187
   quantity of education, 186
   research on, 185–186
   social stratification system and, 185
   socioeconomic status and, 185
   See also Demography of aging; Economics of aging; Ethnicity
      and race; Self-care; Socioeconomic status
Eikenella, 554
Elastin, 42, 98
Elastosis, 518
Elder abuse and neglect, 188–190, 239

demographic/health-related factors and, 382
environmental factors, mobility limitations and, 383
immobility, 138, 301, 381
independent living/functioning and, 383
instrumental activities of daily living and, 381–382
interventions to reduce limitations, 383
limitations in, 381, 382–383
loneliness and, 329
overweight/obesity and, 382
prediction of future mobility limitations, 383
prevalence of impairments, 382
successful mobility, factors in, 383
See also Arthritis and other rheumatic diseases; Disability
    and the disablement process; Exercise and physical activity;
    Gait disorders; Obesity; Sarcopenia
Mobility aids, 60
exercise and mobility, 213
independent mobility and, 390–391
Mobility assessment, 384–391
ambulatory populations and, 384
balance testing, 389–390
bend over/pick up object test, 389
chair stand test, 388, 388 (table)
epidemiology of mobility problems, 384–385
four square test, 389
functional mobility problems and, 384
gait speed test, 386–388, 387 (table)
independence, home/community mobility and, 384
methods of assessment, 385–386
mobility problems, primary causes of, 385
person-environment assessment, biopsychosocial
    process and, 390–391
primary care physicians and, 385
simple tests for mobility problems, 386–390
360 degree turn test, 389
up and go test, 388, 389 (table)
See also Geriatric assessment; Mobility; Performance measures of
    physical function
Moffitt Cancer Center study, 89
Monoamine oxidase (MAO) inhibitors, 461
Mood disorders. *See* **Depression and other
    mood disorders; Emotions and emotional stability**
Mood stabilizers, 70, 462, 465, 474
Morale, 87
Morbidity. *See* Compression of morbidity; Multiple
    morbidity and comorbidity; Summary measure of population
    health (SMPH)
Morphine, 449, 458
Mortality:
air pollution and, 193
allostatic load and, 34
anemia and, 39–40
apolipoprotein E gene effects, 48
body mass index and, 82–83
cancers and, 89
educational attainment and, 185–186
excessive heat events and, 193
mortality data, 250
See also Death, dying, and hospice care; Demography of aging;
    Palliative care and the end of life; Summary measure of
    population health (SMPH)
Motivation, 391–393
alcohol abuse treatment and, 31–32

empirical studies of, 392, 393
exercise adherence and, 214
health behaviors, definition of, 391
healthy behaviors, good physical/mental health and, 391
individualized intervention strategies and, 392–393
motivation to perform health behaviors, 391–392
negative interactions/health behaviors and, 412–413
self-efficacy and, 392
self-regulation models and, 391–392
social-cognitive theories of, 392
transtheoretical model of change and, 392–393
utility models and, 391
See also Exercise and physical activity; Health promotion and
    disease prevention; Quality of life; Self-care; Smoking
Motivational interviewing approach, 31–32
Motor function:
Creutzfeldt-Jakob disease and, 128
See also Gait disorders; Immobility; Mobility; Performance
    measures of physical function
Motor vehicle safety, 268, 304
See also Driving
Mouth cancer, 89, 95
Mouth health. *See* Oral health
Moving Picture Experts Group (MPEG), 558
Multiple-domain mild cognitive impairment, 377
Multiple morbidity and comorbidity, 393–395
aging populations and, 393
comorbidity research results, 394–395
definition of, 393
future of research on, 395
measures of multiple health conditions, 394
multiple morbidity research results, 393–394
sources of information, 394–395
See also Activities of daily living and instrumental
    activities of daily living; Arthritis and other rheumatic
    diseases; Depression and other mood disorders;
    Diabetes; Hypertension; Obesity
Multistate life table method, 3
Muscle cramps, 36, 85, 417
Muscle loss, 42, 230, 233, 419
Muscle relaxants, 165, 166
Muscruinic antagonist medication, 297
Musculoskeletal aging: inflammation, 395–397
C-reactive protein and, 395
aging processes and, 395
autoimmune diseases and, 396
degrees of inflammation and, 395–396
erythrocyte sedimentation rate and, 395, 396
immunosenescence and, 396
inflammation, definition of, 395
management of inflammatory conditions, 396–397
vaccinations and, 396
See also Arthritis and other rheumatic diseases; Biological
    theories of aging; Infectious diseases; Musculoskeletal
    aging: osteoarthritis
Musculoskeletal aging: osteoarthritis, 50–51, 397–399
C-reactive protein and, 397
aging processes and, 397
Australian/New Zealand elders and, 61, 62
bone marrow edema and, 398
cartilage, deformability of, 397
chondrocytes and, 397
diagnosis of, 397

integrated services data networking and, 557, 558
Internet chat sessions, 558
legal/policy issues with, 558
medical-quality transmission and, 557–558
mobile health care toolkits, satellites/wireless
technology and, 558
plain old telephone system and, 557
reimbursement policies and, 558–559
robotics and, 557, 559
smart house technology and, 558
telesurgical approaches and, 557
videoconferencing, 558
See also Health care system for older adults; Rural health
and aging versus urban health and aging
Telomerase, 88
Temperature regulation, 559–561
age-related difficulties with, 559, 560, 561
community programs/cooling centers and, 561
core temperature drop, 560
disease processes and, 560
environmental heat and, 560–561
heat stroke, 560
hyperthermia, 560–561
hypothermia, 559–560
medication reviews and, 560
See also Injury prevention; Normal physical aging;
Skin changes; Socioeconomic status (SES)
Terazosin, 298
Terbinafine, 225
Teriparatide, 444
Terrorism. *See* **Disasters and terrorism**
Testosterone levels, 37–38, 81, 362, 364, 368,
430, 443, 500–501, 515
Tetrahydrocannabinol (THC), 38, 39
Theophylline, 23
Therabands, 214
Therapeutic failure, 561–562
adverse clinical events, 561
clinical significance/impact of, 561
definition of, 561
health resource depletion and, 561
intervention effectiveness and, 561
medication overuse, risks of, 561
prevalence of, 561
reliable measurement instruments for, 561
See also Adverse drug reactions; Age-related changes in
pharmacokinetics and pharmacodynamics; Drug underuse;
Inappropriate prescribing; Medication adherence; Medication
errors; Polypharmacy
Therapeutic touch, 113
Thiazide diuretics, 151, 166, 224, 286
Thiazolidinediones, 151, 153 (table), 369
Thioridazine, 417
Third National Health and Nutrition Examination
Survey (NHANES III), 148
Thirst reflex, 89
Thoracic aortic aneurysms, 41
3-hydroxy-3-methy-glutaryl-coenzyme A reductase
(HMG-CoA reductase) inhibitors, 169, 314
360 degree turn test, 389
Thymus-derived lymphocytes (T-), 294
Thyroid cancer, 89, 94
Thyroid disease, 562–563

hyperthyroidism, 45, 46, 146, 562–563
hypothyroidism, 36, 560, 562
radioactive iodine therapy and, 563
secondary hypertension and, 284
thyroid cancer, 89, 94
thyroid hormone treatments, 562
treatments for, 562–563
See also Men's health; Normal physical aging; Thyroid cancer;
Women's health
Thyroid gland aging, 420
Timed Up and Go test, 230
Tinea pedis, 106
Tinetti gait and balance test, 238
Tingling in hands/feet, 44, 85
Title 18, 351
Title XXL, 350
Toe deformities, 224, 226
Tolterodine, 297
Tooth loss, 438, 439, 440
Total joint replacements, 51
Trait affect, 87
Transesophageal echocardiogram (TEE), 554
Transforming growth factor-beta (TGF-B), 313, 314
Transient ischemic attacks (TIAs), 96, 165, 539
See also Stroke
Transmissible spongiform encephalopathies (TSEs), 126
Transplantation, 117
corneal transplants, 127
dura mater grafts, 127
kidney transplantation, 315
liver transplants, patient age and, 237
Transthoracic echocardiogram (TTE), 554
Transthyretin-based anyloids, 99
Trazodone, 38, 465, 524
Treatment Improvement Protocol (TIP), 30, 32
Tremors, 44
Trial on Nonpharmacologic Interventions in the
Elderly (TONE), 435
Tricyclic antidepressant (TCA), 23, 38, 166, 297,
461, 465, 517, 524
Trihexyphenidyl, 416
Trisomy 21, 35
Trpheryma whipplei, 554
Tuberculosis. *See* **Pneumonia and tuberculosis**
Tubulointerstitial fibrosis, 313
Twin Studies, 563–564
development-specific environmental measures and, 564
disease etiology and, 563
environment/historic context, effects of, 564
ethnically diverse sample of twins and, 563
genetic/dietary factors, age at onset of disease and, 564
heightened disease risk among twins and, 563–564
Human Genome Project data and, 564
identical genes/identical intrauterine environment and, 563
interpretation of results from, 563–564
longitudinal studies of variation and, 563
maternal starvation, adult-onset schizophrenia and, 564
measurement timing and, 564
population-based twin registries and, 563
surrogate research design of, 563
technological/statistical advances and, 564
See also Age-period-cohort (APC) distinctions; Biomarkers of
Aging; Epidemiology of aging